International Encyclopedia of Adolescence

International Encyclopedia of Adolescence

VOLUME 1
A–J
INDEX

Jeffrey Jensen Arnett

EDITOR

Routledge
Taylor & Francis Group
New York   London

Routledge is an imprint of the
Taylor & Francis Group, an informa business

Routledge
Taylor & Francis Group
270 Madison Avenue
New York, NY 10016

Routledge
Taylor & Francis Group
2 Park Square
Milton Park, Abingdon
Oxon OX14 4RN

Printed in the United States of America on acid-free paper
10 9 8 7 6 5 4 3 2 1

International Standard Book Number-10: 0-415-96667-1 (Hardcover)
International Standard Book Number-13: 978-0-415-96667-2 (Hardcover)

Visit the Taylor & Francis Web site at
http://www.taylorandfrancis.com

and the Routledge Web site at
http://www.routledge-ny.com

CONTENTS

INTRODUCTION

Adolescence as a field of scholarship is widely viewed as having originated about a century ago with the publication of G. Stanley Hall's two-volume *Adolescence* in 1904. Hall was an American, and he drew primarily from American and European sources in his description of adolescence. A century later, the study of adolescence remains a predominantly American enterprise. The Society for Research on Adolescence (SRA) is, to a large extent, a society for research on American adolescents. At SRA's biennial conferences, over 90% of the presentations are written by American scholars on topics relating to American adolescents, and SRA's *Journal of Research on Adolescence* publishes papers that are written almost entirely by American scholars, with an occasional European author represented. The other major adolescent journals are similarly dominated by American and European scholarship.

The dominance of Western scholarship in the field of adolescence studies is not surprising, given the abundant research resources in Western countries and their relatively long scholarly traditions. However, this dominance is oddly incongruent with the realities of life as experienced by adolescents around the world. Of the world's 6.5 billion people, fewer than 10% live in the West. Furthermore, that proportion is shrinking daily. By the year 2050, the world's population is projected to surpass nine billion, and virtually all of the growth will come from non-Western countries.

The global scope of the *International Encyclopedia of Adolescence* is unprecedented. Previous encyclopedias of adolescence have focused on adolescents in the West, mainly the United States, with either cursory attention to the other 90+ % of the world's adolescents or no mention of them at all. This encyclopedia covers adolescents throughout the world. It contains 88 articles in all, with 28 from Africa (including North Africa and the Middle East), 18 from Asia, 27 from Europe, and 15 from the Americas. The countries covered range in size from Belize (population 250,000) to China (population 1.3 billion).

Some articles in the encyclopedia discuss countries that rarely appear on the world's stage, such as Kyrgyzstan, Guinea, and Oman. The lives of adolescents in these countries provide an especially sharp contrast to the lives of adolescents in the West. For example, although in industrialized countries adolescence is typically associated with attending secondary school, the reader of this encyclopedia may read about several countries where attending school beyond the early teens is the exception rather than the rule, especially for girls. By that age many adolescents in developing countries have left school to assist their parents on the family farm or to go to work in a factory in order to contribute to their family's income.

Nevertheless, not all regions are equally represented. Finding authors for the Islamic countries of North Africa and the Middle East proved to be the most difficult challenge. Many of these countries have a limited tradition of social science research. Despite the limited research traditions, we were able to include ten articles from countries in this region, including Egypt, Iran, Morocco, and Sudan.

The more familiar countries are included as well, of course, but the information in those articles may be unfamiliar. For example, readers may be surprised to learn that 65 to 70% of Canadian adolescents reported gambling within the past year, or that in Japan until recently adolescents attended school six days a week.

Defining Adolescence

"Adolescence" is widely recognized by scholars as a socially- and culturally-constructed period of the life course, so it is important in an international encyclopedia of adolescence to be clear about how we define it and why. In view of the vast range of cultures to be included in the encyclopedia, we wanted to be as inclusive as possible in how we defined adolescence, to accommodate the entire range of perspectives likely to exist across cultures. Consequently, we asked authors to cover development during the age range from 10 to 25. Scholars view adolescence as beginning with puberty, and age 10 is when the first outward signs of puberty occur for most girls in industrialized countries (boys usually begin about 2 years later). In recent decades this age has become typical in developing countries as well, as nutrition and access to medical care in these countries has improved.

Setting the upper age boundary of adolescence is more difficult and more subject to cultural variability. Scholars generally view adolescence as ending when adulthood begins, which sounds simple enough—until one tries to answer the question of when adulthood begins. If we use marriage as the quintessential marker as anthropologists and sociologists have in the past, then the end of adolescence varies worldwide from the early teens for girls in places such as rural India and northern Africa, to the early 30s for young people in northern Europe. Furthermore, it is highly questionable that marriage remains the quintessential marker of adulthood around the world, given research showing that young people in industrialized countries no longer regard it as such, preferring psychological markers such as accepting personal responsibility and making independent decisions.

Age 25 was chosen as the upper boundary partly for practical reasons. Many international organizations such as the United Nations and the World Health Organization use age ranges up to 24 or 25 years old for the information they collect on "youth" around the world.

The question of the age boundaries of adolescence is explicitly addressed in the encyclopedia. Each article contains a Period of Adolescence section in which the authors indicate whether adolescence is recognized as a distinct life stage in their country and, if so, when it is considered to begin and end.

Organization

Each country article in the *International Encyclopedia of Adolescence* is a composite made up of several smaller essays and followed by references. This organization allows the reader easily to find specific information on a given topic within the article, while also encouraging the comparison of data among different countries.

Each composite country article includes the following sections:

Background Information: provides basic, general information on the country's geography, history, demographics, economics, and political system.

Period of Adolescence: discusses whether, and how, adolescence exists as a separate life stage in the country. If so, the ages at which adolescence is generally considered to begin and end are presented, while any adolescent rites of passage or initiation are also discussed.

Beliefs: explores the primary religions practiced in the country, how those religions are transmitted to and practiced by adolescents, whether the culture of the country as a whole tends toward individualism or collectivism, and how this shapes the development of the adolescent.

Gender: examines gender-specific adult roles for which adolescents are prepared. Physical ideals as expressed by both male and female adolescents are presented, as are gender role expectations.

The Self: provides an overview of the development of personal and cultural identity by adolescents. Special attention is paid to the formation of ethnic identity among immigrants and minority groups.

Family Relationships: examines the nature of relationships between parents and adolescents, common parenting practices, sources of parental–adolescent conflict, and the amount of time adolescents spend with various family members.

Friends and Peers/Youth Culture: examines the amount of time adolescents spend with their peers compared to the time spent alone or with family. Youth culture, cliques, youth organizations, and popular activities are also discussed, as they exist in the country in question. The impact of Western and American culture, as well as globalization in general, is also discussed, if applicable.

Love and Sexuality: explores dating, cohabitation, marriage, sexual experimentation, birth control, pregnancy, sexually transmitted diseases, parental attitudes toward adolescent sexuality, sex education, and homosexuality.

Health Risk Behavior: provides an overview of adolescent drug and alcohol use, crime activity, gang involvement, and rates of suicide and depression. Any other factors that pose a threat to overall adolescent health are also discussed.

Education: examines literacy rates, characteristics of secondary schools, participation rates in secondary schools, gender differences in access to education, performance on international tests of achievement, and programs, if any, for gifted or disabled adolescents.

Work: presents an overview of what work, if any, adolescents perform, and their incentives for working (extra pocket money, contributing to the overall family income, etc.). Apprenticeships and other job training programs are discussed, if they exist in the country. Working conditions (for example, sweatshops, sexual exploitation, slavery) are also examined as applicable.

Media: discusses rates of media use by adolescents, including television, recorded music, computer games, the Internet, magazines, and movies. Authors also consider such questions as to what extent are media indigenous or imported, to what extent are media viewed as a positive or negative influence on adolescents, and to what extent are adolescents targeted by media advertisers.

Politics and Military: explores whether adolescents are involved in politics and how they are involved in politics (voting age, Anti-WTO rallies), as well as the extent to which they participate in military activities (compulsory service, armed combat, military training programs, para-military organizations).

Unique Issues: examines issues pertaining to adolescents that are especially important in the country, but are not addressed in the other sections of the composite article.

Countries differ greatly in terms of how much information is available on each of these general topics. In general, more information is available on demographic topics than on psychological and social topics. For example, nearly all countries record information on rates of parental divorce, but not all publish information on how adolescents respond to it. Nevertheless, the authors did an admirable job of providing useful and relevant information. Nearly all authors of articles are indigenous to the country on which they wrote, thus enabling them to write as informed observers and interpreters of the research evidence available.

How to Use This Book

The *International Encyclopedia of Adolescence* is a two-volume work containing information about 10 to 25 year olds in every region of the world. The composite articles range in length from 4,000 words to over 15,000, but most are 6,000 to 11,000 words in length. All composite articles include each of the sections described above. Together the composite articles provide a global portrait of what life is like today for young people aged 10 to 25.

The composite articles are organized in an A to Z format across the two volumes, rather than geographically by region, which will allow the reader to find an article of special interest quickly without having to determine the region first. Each composite article is followed by a References and Further Reading section, which includes sources used by

the author as well as additional sources that may be of interest to the reader. A thorough, analytical index that covers both volumes is provided at the end of each volume to assist the reader. Each volume also contains a list of country articles organized by geographical region.

A total of 144 authors and co-authors contributed to the encyclopedia. As noted, nearly all of them are indigenous to the country on which they wrote. Most of the authors are psychologists, but contributors also include sociologists, educators, economists, and demographers.

The five Regional Editors—Ramadan Ahmed (North Africa/Middle East), Nancy Galambos (the Americas), Bame Nsamenang (Africa), T.S. Saraswathi (Asia), and Rainer Silbereisen (Europe) —are all psychologists, and all are indigenous to their region. They are recognized in their regions and around the world as outstanding scholars on adolescence. Together, the Regional Editors and the authors have provided an extraordinary panorama of adolescent life that is compelling and engaging in its diversity.

Acknowledgments

I have many people to thank for their contributions. Marie-Claire Antoine, Senior Editor at Routledge Reference, first invited me to serve as editor of the encyclopedia, and advised me on the format and structure of the encyclopedia as I developed it. Kristen Holt, Developmental Editor for the encyclopedia, did a wonderful job in the administration of it, which included helping to find authors, mediating communication between authors and editors, and keeping the whole project on track to completion.

The five Regional Editors were crucial to the success of the project. Each did an admirable job of finding authors for the countries within their region and providing the first review of the composite articles. Their stature as scholars within their regions surely enhanced the appeal of the project for the authors who were invited to participate. Finally, I would like to thank each of the authors who contributed to the encyclopedia. Most of them I have never met and perhaps never will, but I admire the work they have done here. I thank them for what they have taught me about adolescence in their countries, and I am delighted for the opportunity to share their work with other readers who are eager to learn more about how adolescents around the world experience this dramatic, fascinating, rapidly changing time of life.

JEFFREY JENSEN ARNETT

ASSOCIATE EDITORS

Ramadan A. Ahmed
Kuwait University, Kaifan (North Africa and the Middle East)

Nancy Galambos
University of Alberta, Canada (The Americas)

Bame Nsamenang
University of Yaoundé, Cameroon (Africa)

Tharakad S. Saraswathi
M.S. University of Baroda, India (Asia and Oceania)

Rainer Silbereisen
University of Jena, Germany (Europe)

CONTRIBUTORS

Maher M. Abu Hilal United Arab Emirates University, United Arab Emirates

Sigrún Adalbjarnardottir University of Iceland, Iceland

Maria Adamek University of Vienna, Austria

Abdelbagi Dafalla Ahmed University of Khartoum, Sudan

Ramadan A. Ahmed Kuwait University, Kuwait

Samir Al-Adawi Sultan Qaboos University, Sultanate of Oman

Jasem M. A. Al-Khawajah Kuwait University, Kuwait

Eileen P. Anderson-Fye Semel Institute for Neuroscience and Human Behavior, University of California, United States

Berhane B. Araia University of North Carolina–Chapel Hill, United States

Huda Ayyash-Abdo Lebanese American University, Lebanon

Delali Badasu Institute of African Studies, University of Ghana, Ghana

Joséphine Bangurambona Ministère de L'Education Nationale, Burundi

Maan A. Barry University of Aden, Yemen

Karla Berdichevsky Population Council, United States

Silvia Bonino University of Torino, Italy

Margaret Zoller Booth Bowling Green State University, United States

Luba Botcheva Children's Health Council, United States

Andreja Brajša-Žganec Ivo Pilar Institute of Social Sciences, Croatia

Leonid Burlachuk Kiev Shevchenko National University, Ukraine

CONTRIBUTORS

Christine Bieri Buschor Zurich University of Applied Sciences, Switzerland

Jennifer Catino Population Council, Latin America and Caribbean Regional Office, Mexico

Elena Cattelino University of Aosta, Italy

Nermin Celen Maltepe University, Turkey

Florence Chamvu University of Zambia, Zambia

Agnes Chang Nanyang Technological University, Singapore

Lei Chang Chinese University of Hong Kong, Hong Kong

Nandita Chaudhary Lady Irwin College, University of Delhi, India

Xinyin Chen University of Western Ontario, Canada

Regis Chireshe Masvingo State University, Zimbabwe

Silvia Ciairano University of Torino, Italy

Figen Cok Ankara University, Turkey

John Coleman Trust for the Study of Adolescence, United Kingdom

Patricio Cumsille Pontificia Universidad Católica de Chile, Chile

Andrea Dalton University of Alberta, Canada

Douglas A. Davis Haverford College, United States

Susan Schaefer Davis Development Anthropologist, United States

Aporn Deenan Burapha University, Thailand

Cristina del Barrio Universidad Autónoma de Madrid, Spain

Dirus Dialé Dore Direction Nationale de la Protection de l'Enfance, Guinea

Eva Dreher Ludwig-Maximilians-Unversität, Germany

Ingrid Dries-Daffner Pharmacy Access Partnership, United States

Anastasia Efklides Aristotle University of Thessaloniki, Greece

Iris Erazo National Pedagogical University, Honduras

Alicia Facio National University of Entre Ríos, Argentina

Yvette G. Flores University of California–Davis, United States

António Castro Fonseca University of Coimbra, Portugal

Maria das Dores Formosinho University of Coimbra, Portugal

Erica Frydenberg University of Melbourne, Australia

Márta Fülöp Institute for Psychology, Hungarian Academy of Sciences, Hungary

Nancy L. Galambos University of Alberta, Canada

Luc Goossens Catholic University of Leuven, Belgium

Sheila Greene Children's Research Centre, Trinity College, Ireland

Pesanayi Gwirai Seke Teacher's College, Zimbabwe

Kelly Hallman Population Council, United States

Fredrik Hansen Research Centre for Health Promotion, University of Bergen, Norway

Muhammad Nazmul Haq Institute of Education and Research, University of Dhaka, Bangladesh

Helena Helve University of Helsinki, Finland

Gilbert Herdt San Francisco State University, United States

Eduardo A. Lugo Hernández University of Puerto Rico, Río Piedras Campus, Puerto Rico

Nigmet Ibadildin Kazakhstan Institute of Management, Economics, and Strategic Research, Kazakhstan

Peace N. Ibeagha University of Ibadan, Nigeria

Rosnah Ismail Universiti Malaysia Sabah, Malaysia

Baktygul Ismailova Queen's University, Canada

Adel Jendli Zayed University, United Arab Emirates

Jacqueline P. Jere University of Zambia, Zambia

Samvel Jeshmaridian Yerevan Acharian University, Armenia, and Fordham University, United States

Fumiko Kakihara University of Nebraska at Omaha, United States

Anie Kalayjian Association for Trauma Outreach and Prevention, and Fordham University, United States

CONTRIBUTORS

Plamen Kalchev Sofia University, Bulgaria

Maher Khelifa Zayed University, United Arab Emirates

Angeline Khoo National Institute of Education, Nanyang Technological University, Singapore

Woldekidan Kifle Freelance Researcher and Consultant, Ethiopia

Narasappa Kumaraswamy Clinical Psychology Unit, RIPAS Hospital, Brunei Darussalam

Lyda Lannegrand-Willems University Victor Segalen Bordeaux 2, France

P. Herbert Leiderman Stanford University, United States

Melita Puklek Levpušček University of Ljubljana, Slovenia

José Luis Linaza Universidad Autónoma de Madrid, Spain

Jodie Lodge University of Melbourne, Australia

Koen Luyckx Catholic University of Leuven, Belgium

Petr Macek Masaryk University Brno, Czech Republic

Brad A. MacNeil University of New Brunswick, Canada

M. Loreto Martínez Pontificia Universidad Católica de Chile, Chile

Paula Mayock Children's Research Centre, Trinity College, Dublin, Ireland

Eva Mayr University of Tübingen, Germany

Wim Meeus Utrecht University, Netherlands

Rebeca Mejia-Arauz ITESO University, Mexico

Hera Lestari Mikarsa University of Indonesia, Indonesia

Tijana Mirović University of Belgrade, Serbia and Montenegro

Benedict Missani

Despina Moraitou Aristotle University of Thessaloniki, Greece

Sven Mørch University of Copenhagen, Denmark

Amparo Moreno Universidad Autónoma de Madrid, Spain

Elias Mpofu Pennsylvania State University, United States

Tuntufye S. Mwamwenda University of KwaZulu-Natal, South Africa

Yuka Maya Nakamura Zurich University of Applied Sciences, Switzerland

Nde Ndifonka International Organization for Migration, Regional Office for Southern Africa, South Africa

Agapit Manzanza Musula Ntotila University of Kinshasa, Democratic Republic of the Congo

Mary Phiri Chirunga Early Childhood Education Center, Malawi

Juana Pinzás Pontifical Catholic University of Peru, Peru

Andrei Podolskij Moscow State University, Russia

Eva Polášková Masaryk University Brno, Czech Republic

Nosheen K. Rahman University of Punjab, Pakistan

Murari Prasad Regmi Tribhuvan University, Nepal

Santiago Resett National University of Entre Ríos, Argentina

Debi Roker Trust for the Study of Adolescence, United Kingdom

Alan Russell Zayed University, United Arab Emirates

Colette Sabatier Université Victor Segalen Bordeaux 2, France

Katariina Salmela-Aro University of Helsinki, Finland

Heather A. Sears University of New Brunswick, Canada

Iva Sedlak University of Zurich, Switzerland

Elizabeth Gabaswediwe Seeco University of Botswana, Botswana

Rachel Seginer University of Haifa, Israel

Neerja Sharma Lady Irwin College, University of Delhi, India

Ruby Sheets Instituto Tecnológico y de Estudios Superiores de Occidente, Mexico

Shirli Shoyer University of Haifa, Israel

Almon Shumba University of KwaZulu–Natal, South Africa

Mary G. Simmering University of New Brunswick, Canada

Jolanta Sondaite Mykolas Romeris University, Lithuania

CONTRIBUTORS

Madelene Sta.Maria De La Salle University-Manila, Philippines

Birgitta Stolpe University of Chicago, United States

Chandraseagran Suppiah Sultan Hassanal Bolkiah Institute of Education, Brunei Darussalam

Erica Swenson Westmont College, United States

Maria da Conceição Taborda-Simões University of Coimbra, Portugal

Getnet Tadele Addis Ababa University, Ethiopia

Keiko Takahashi University of the Sacred Heart, Japan

Kiyoshi Takeuchi Sophia University, Japan

Therese Mungah Tchombe International Society for the Study of Behavioural Development, University of Yaoundé, Cameroon

Carlota Tello Instituto Tecnológico y de Estudios Superiores de Occidente, Mexico

Carolina Thibaut Pontificia Universidad Católica de Chile, Chile

Lauree C. Tilton-Weaver University of Nebraska at Omaha, United States

Kari Trost Stockholm University, Sweden

Maria da Luz Vale-Dias University of Coimbra, Portugal

Martha Villasenor Instituto Mexicano del Seguro Social, Mexico

Sami Wadi United Arab Emirates Ministry of Health, United Arab Emirates

Rowan E. Wagner The International Business School "Kelajak Ilmi," Uzbekistan

Rebecca Williams University of Alberta, Canada

Bente Wold Research Centre for Health Promotion, University of Bergen, Norway

Jacqueline Woodfork Loyola University, New Orleans, United States

Rita Zukauskiene Law University of Lithuania, Lithuania

Horst Zumkley Universitaet des Saarlandes, Germany

Maja Zupančič University of Ljubljana, Slovenia

ALPHABETICAL LIST OF ENTRIES

REGIONAL LIST OF ENTRIES

Africa

Botswana
Burundi
Cameroon
Democratic Republic of the Congo
Eritrea
Ethiopia
Ghana
Guinea
Malawi
Nigeria
Senegal
Somalia
South Africa
Sudan
Swaziland
Tanzania
Zambia
Zimbabwe

Asia and Oceania

Armenia
Australia
Bangladesh
Brunei Darussalam
China, People's Republic of
India
Indonesia
Japan
Kazakhstan
Kyrgyzstan
Malaysia
Nepal
Pakistan
Papua New Guinea
Philippines
Singapore
Tajikistan
Thailand

The Americas

Argentina
Belize
Canada
Central America: Costa Rica, El Salvador,
    Nicaragua
Chile
Ecuador
Guatemala
Honduras
Mexico
Panama
Paraguay
Peru
Puerto Rico
United States of America
Uruguay

Europe

Austria
Belgium
Bulgaria
Croatia
Czech Republic
Denmark
Finland
France
Germany
Greece
Hungary
Iceland
Ireland
Italy
Lithuania
Netherlands

A

ARGENTINA

Background Information

Argentina, a vast nation located in the south of the American continent, had a population of about 36 million people (52% female) in 2001, with one-third living in the capital city, Buenos Aires, and its surrounding area. It is a developed country ranked 34th among the 173 nations of the world, according to the Human Development Index. This index is estimated by the United Nations Development Program taking into account life expectancy at birth (72 years of age in Argentina), educational level (adult literacy is 97%), and average standard of living according to real gross domestic product per capita adjusted by purchase power ($12,013 USD per year). Argentina is the best-positioned nation in Latin America, and it is closely followed by Chile and Uruguay, which also belong to the high human development group. Further national data include a 90% rate of urbanization and an economic structure in which the gross domestic product is composed of 6% primary activities (mainly agriculture and livestock), 28% industry, and 66% services.

According to age, 22.7% of the Argentinean population is made up of children younger than 12 years; 12.6% is 12- to 18-year-old adolescents;

55% are adults; and 10% are elderly people 65 years of age or older.

During the period between 1870 and 1930, millions of immigrants—mainly Italians and Spaniards—arrived in Argentina. This enormous immigratory flow turned Argentina into the most Europeanized country in Latin America, with less than 3% of the population claiming pure Native American or non-European status. Immigrants compose only 4% of the population, with 2.4% coming from bordering countries and 1.6% from other countries. Approximately 89% of Argentineans are Catholic.

Argentina, a representative, federal, and republican democracy, is characterized by political instability and repeated economic crises that began around 1930. Since then, a series of military administrations that seized power through coups d'état have ruled, only to be replaced by constitutional governments elected by the people. In the 1970s, the last years of prosperity were witnessed. The 1970s marked the end of the welfare state that, although never reaching the level of European countries, granted free education until leaving university, free health service, housing plans, and fair pensions.

In 1976, when the military forces seized power, state terrorism was installed. Thousands of "missing" citizens were abducted, tortured, and murdered. The national economy was destroyed with the indiscriminate opening of importation, and a large debt was contracted with international banks.

Between 1982 and 1985, after the Malvinas war, the military dictatorship underwent such a crisis that it had to allow the return of democracy. After the initial euphoria, the Argentinean people discovered with great disappointment that this did not ensure the recovery of either the earlier living standard or the smooth functioning of institutions. The chronically high Argentinean inflationary rate reached an annual increase of almost 5,000% in 1989.

In 1992, the implementation of neoconservative policies generated, on the one hand, the reduction of the inflationary rate to normal levels; but, on the other hand, a severe impoverishment of the country also resulted: a high unemployment rate; job precariousness; the transformation of ample sectors of middle-class and retired people into "the new poor," who were added to the structural poor; and the government's desertion of its leading role in securing social justice.

In December 2001, the political and institutional crisis intensified to such an extent that Argentina was first-page news in the world mass media. The federal administration took possession of all the savings that citizens had deposited in the banks. Popular riots forced the president to resign. Five successive presidents took office over the course of a fortnight. The Argentinean peso was devalued from 1 peso equaling 1 U.S. dollar to a third of its rate. In 2002, Argentina was amidst its worst crisis in the last 100 years. For example, the already high annual rate of unemployment rose to 22%, one of the highest in the world.

Although the new government, elected in 2003, has generated hope, the upward mobility dream has been severely menaced. Forty-six percent of the population still lives below the poverty line, and 17% is extremely poor. Polls indicate that crime, unemployment, poverty, and corruption are the greatest concerns of the population. Most Argentineans have lost faith in the executive branch of their government, the legislature, and the judiciary as well as in politicians and the police.

In spite of the serious difficulties that Argentina has undergone, their adolescents have been as optimistic about their personal futures as those in more prosperous and foreseeable countries. Compared to 1992, the percentage of optimists was higher instead of lower in 2002, when the economic and institutional context worsened.

Period of Adolescence

There is scarce research on normal adolescents in Argentina. Psychology is characterized by a strong predominance of psychoanalytic theory, little interest in quantitative research, and a bias toward psychopathological clinical cases.

Adolescence has been recognized as a life stage for a long time in Argentina. As early as 1918, Víctor Mercante, an outstanding educator, authored the book *The pubertal crisis and its educational consequences,* where G. Stanley Hall was quoted and where adolescence was the stage ranging from 14 to 17 and 17 to 20 years after puberty. Other historical literary milestones are *Adolescent Ambition and Anguish* and *Intimate Diary of an Adolescent Girl,* which were written by the medical doctor Aníbal Ponce during the 1930s.

People in Argentina consider this stage as beginning with the visible pubertal changes: breast and hip development in girls; facial hair and voice change in boys; and growth spurts in height and changes in complexion, such as oily skin and pimples, in both sexes. Between the ages of 12 and 13 years, menarche is present in more than 50% of females, and, before 14 years of age, in 85% to 90% girls; at 13 to 14 years, 95% boys reported having pubic hair, and 60% reported having undergone voice change.

Although the full legal adult status is acquired at 21, at 18, the complete labor capacity and—if parents grant emancipation—the complete civil capacity are attained. Marriage is permitted at 16 for females and 18 years of age for males, although parental authorization is required up to age 21. Driving licenses may be acquired at age 18. Among those attending secondary school, graduating and moving on to work is seen by many people as an important marker of the end of adolescence.

No rites of passage exist showing that puberty or adult status has been reached. Habits like the 15-year-old birthday indicating a girl has become a *señorita* (a young lady), able to attend dances, wear makeup, or receive her boyfriend's visit at home and the sexual debut of the 14- to 15-year-old boy taken to the brothel by friends or family members became outdated several decades ago.

Emerging adulthood is a distinct period in the life course of many Argentinean people during their mid twenties. The percentage of those going through these years of exploration of a variety of life directions in love, work, and worldviews is similar to that of the United States, at least in the upper two-thirds of Argentineans who had received some high school education. Moreover, an overwhelming majority agreed with American young people in considering the individualistic criteria "accepting responsibility for one's self," "making independent decisions," and "becoming financially independent" as very important in defining adult status. That these facts take place in a Latin American country is a good example of the spread of American culture throughout the world.

Beliefs

As regards individualistic or collectivistic values, Argentina belongs to the Latin and Catholic cultural tradition that has a high regard for the collectivistic values, especially family ones. Family is seen as much more important than country, religion, or political ideas. Greater closeness to parents (especially mothers), siblings, and even members of the extended family over friends, as compared to North Americans and Northern Europeans, has been found once and again in Argentinean adolescents. At 15 to 17 years old, when asked about the ten people they loved most, 87% ranked their mothers first or second; only 4% did not include their mothers. A lower percentage of 64% ranked their fathers first or second; 13% did not mention their fathers. Although both genders preferred mothers to fathers, the gap was wider among girls. Siblings were in the third place, but 21% put them first or second, a position usually occupied by parents; only 5% not being an only child did not incorporate them. Friends were ranked fourth to seventh in 54%; a small group of 6% put them first or second, and a substantial 20% did not include any. Among those having a boyfriend or girlfriend, just 16% mentioned them first or second, and 32% did not list a romantic partner among the most beloved ones.

Notwithstanding the increase in individualistic values, family values do not diminish; more than half of 17- to 18-year-old adolescents agreed that "family responsibilities should be more important than my career plans in the future" or that "despite opportunities in other areas of the country or outside the country, I should try to live near my parents in the future."

Even though research work on this subject is scarce, it seems that family, school, church, and mass media together convey the message of family preeminence. In addition, the majority of adolescents have witnessed a close relationship between their parents and their grandparents, especially between their mothers and their maternal grandmothers.

Argentina is a primarily secular society. Although only a small percentage do not believe in God, the majority of adolescents reported being alienated from church activities or not belonging to church anymore. In Paraná, one out of five or less attended services monthly or more frequently. In Greater Buenos Aires, few young people reported being faithful followers of the beliefs and moral norms sanctioned by their church (Deutsche Bank 1993). Those belonging to minority religions—mostly Protestants—were more committed practitioners than the Catholic majority.

In the Catholic Church in Argentina, adolescents do not receive obligatory catechism instruction as children do for their first communion. A small percentage voluntarily participate in church organizations, such as Argentinean Catholic Action, Caritas, missionary groups, Catholic movements, and youth groups, which are available in each parish. Evangelism and charity are usually the main activities.

Gender

In Argentina, the *macho* attitude has steadily decreased, and the gap between the genders in work, education, and political activity has been narrowing over the decades. Forty-five percent of 15- to 65-year-old women have a job (INDEC 2001). Although no sex discrimination exists regarding access to different work activities (including the military) as in many Western countries, some jobs are seen as more "feminine" (teachers, nurses and other paramedical professionals, psychologists, secretaries) or more "masculine" (building industry workers, public transportation drivers, engineers) than others. Traditionally masculine professions (medicine, law, chemistry, architecture) have similar percentages from both sexes today. As in other countries, fewer women than men reach the top management positions in private or public organizations; females earn lower salaries on average; and the female unemployment rate was higher until 2001 (INDEC 2001).

Where political involvement is concerned, due to a quota law passed in 1991, 34% of parliamentarians are female in both houses at both the national and provincial levels. There are women presiding over ministries and, as of 2004, there are female members of the Supreme Court of Justice; however, almost no female governors or big city mayors have been elected.

No gender differences are made in the preparation for adult work roles in formal education; both genders attend the same schools, with the vast majority being coeducational. Moreover, girls were more academically successful, according to different indexes (for example school attainment), and their academic motivation was higher than that of boys. In spite of these facts, Argentinean girls evaluated their scholastic competence as being lower than that of boys.

Although women are highly regarded for their maternal role, young people of both genders considered "being capable of caring for children" as important for defining an adult man as it is for defining an adult woman. In addition, although females attached more importance to women being capable of supporting a family financially and of keeping it physically safe than men did, the majority of males also adhered to these statements. In spite of the fact that adolescent girls were more involved in domestic chores and less involved in jobs than boys, the majority of the latter (55%) had "sometimes" or "always" done housework during the last year.

Gender differences in several internalized problems were greater in Argentina than in North America. Girls scored lower than boys in global self-esteem throughout adolescence. In the Harter Self-Perception Profile for Adolescents, for example, the gap was mainly made up of higher scores among Argentinean boys compared to American teenagers rather than of Argentinean girls scoring lower than their American counterparts. Other times—for example, with Kovac's Child Depression Inventory—the average of Argentinean boys was markedly better and the mean of Argentinean girls markedly worse than that of American teenagers. With regard to externalizing problems, boys scored higher than girls for antisocial behavior, but no gender difference was found for substance use.

When judging other-sex attractiveness, the criteria used by Argentinean adolescents were very similar to those endorsed by other Western youth. Regarding an adolescent boy's heterosexual appeal, boys equally underscored physical attractiveness, seduction, and kindness-maturity; girls, instead, ranked kindness-maturity, reliability, fidelity, tenderness, gentleness, and not being arrogant above physical appearance and seduction. Both genders shared the criteria for judging a girl's heterosexual allure: beauty tied with seduction and kindness, especially at the end of adolescence; virginity or affluence did not turn out to be requirements. Boys and girls mentioned females' physical attractiveness to a greater extent than males' (75% versus 50%).

Argentinean girls were markedly less satisfied with their physical appearance than boys, whose contentment in this area was higher than that of their American counterparts. Throughout adolescence, the average boy felt he was "good-looking," whereas the average girl thought the same only at age 13 and 14; afterward, she judged herself just as "fair." In boys, the most valued physical feature was strength, fitness, or musculature at ages 13 and 14 years, and height at 17 and 18. In girls, face and weight were the most frequently mentioned sources of contentment and discontent, respectively, throughout adolescence.

In different samples, 30% to 60% of females desired being slimmer despite only one out of seven being truly overweight according to body mass index. Girls struggled to get an under-than-normal weight and the lower their weight, the more satisfied they felt, regardless of the risks involved (Vega 2004).

No epidemiological studies of eating disorders as defined by the American Psychiatric Association's *Diagnostic and Statistical Manual IV* exist in Argentina. The population at risk, according to David Garner's Eating Attitudes Test, was 0.5% of boys in secondary school and 20% of girls. Twenty-three percent of girls and 5% of boys were involved in pathological diets, and 6% of females and 2% of males reported bulimic behaviors. In Argentina, girls' risk for eating disorders, according to Garner's screening procedure, was higher than it was in Spain or Canada but similar to Chile and Brazil (Vega 2004).

The Self

Research work on Argentinean adolescent identity development is almost nonexistent. In a cross-sectional study (Piccini Vega 2004) about Jane Loevinger's ego development stages, at ages 12 to 14 years, 87% of boys versus 44% of girls were in the Conformist stage, in which the ability to identify one's own welfare with that of family—and, later, with peers—develops. At age 15 to 18, 48% of both genders were in the Self-awareness level, in which realization of individual differences and differentiation between one's real from one's ideal self begin to emerge.

When those entering college were requested to write a short essay about "I" (Wasser Diuk 1997), most narratives included relationships with significant others, mainly family members, suggesting that they defined themselves mostly through their family relations. They focused their aspirations on carrying out present tasks rather than considering them as steps within a life project. Only a small percentage referred to future goals or to their plans after graduating from college, and only 15% mentioned expecting to achieve a sense of personal gratification through studying or, later on, practicing their profession. Just a few considered knowledge being valuable and pleasurable by itself.

When 14- to 24-year-olds from Greater Buenos Aires reported about their most important life goals (Deutsche Bank 1993, 1999), "to be happy" ranked first, at 86%, followed by "raising a family," "being a good parent," and "having a rich emotional life" (71%, 63%, and 59%, respectively). Only in fifth place (54%) did a goal referring to work appeared: "developing a professional career." "Studying to be a scholar" was endorsed by 34% and "being a hard worker" by 31%. Almost half included "to care and protect my parents," and 31% adhered to humanitarian values, which were defined as "helping those in need." Patriotism—"contributing to the country welfare"—was espoused by 13%, and being an influential, prestigious person was only chosen by 7%. Small percentages adhered to "following the beliefs and moral standards enforced by my religious affiliation" (12%) and to "devoting an important part of my life to spirituality" (5%). Throughout the 1992 to 1998 period the surveys detected some changes consisting in an increase in family values, work values, and social sensitivity.

Family Relationships

The average Argentinean adolescent has parents with lower school attainment, lives within a biparental family with a higher number of children, and shares the household with non-nuclear relatives to a greater extent than the average adolescent studied by North American and Northern European researchers. In addition, the percentage of working mothers is lower: 58% in the 25 to 49 age range.

Family relationship satisfaction was high among Argentinean adolescents. Only 6% reported the relationship with their mothers to be "fair" or worse, and only 8% felt misunderstood "almost always" or "always." The relationships with their fathers were less satisfactory; 17% of boys and 26% of girls rated it as "fair" or worse, whereas 13% of boys and 25% of girls felt misunderstood "almost always" or "always."

Approximately one out of four regarded the relationships with their siblings—excluding half and step siblings—"fair" or worse, and "frequent" or "very frequent" quarrels with them were nonnormative (22%).

Although no research work on parenting practices reported by parents is available, there is information about the degree of warmth and of control exerted by parents as viewed by adolescents. With regard to support, which is one aspect of warmth, whether adolescents would resort to parents or friends depended on the kinds of problems involved. Parents were overwhelmingly preferred when health, unwanted pregnancy, alcohol or drug addiction was at issue, although the difference as to academic difficulties was narrow. Conversely, friends markedly overcame parents as favorite confidants. Regarding problems with sexuality, romantic relationships, and friendship, parents tied with friends during early adolescence, and friends prevailed during the middle and late teenage years. A vast majority preferred mothers to fathers as help providers. Siblings were the main support for a minority, and an even smaller group preferred romantic partners in this respect.

Concerning the degree of control parents exert, during early and middle adolescence 10% and 22% perceived their fathers and mothers, respectively, as overcontrolling, and one out of five reported that one or the other "sets too much norms." At the other end of the continuum, throughout adolescence, only 8% stated that parents were not interested in knowing their whereabouts, and around 10% stated that neither parent set any norms to be obeyed. At ages 17 and 18, the majority were satisfied with the degree of autonomy that both parents granted them: parents allowed their children to choose their own friends (78%), their own dating partners (83%), their own career goals (79%), and so on, "without interfering too much." Girls considered themselves as autonomous as boys did with respect to their relationships with their mothers and fathers.

Concerning violence, throughout adolescence, almost half stated that one or both parents yelled at them or insulted them when they did something wrong. At ages 13 to 15, 9% said that they were currently beaten by one or both progenitors, a percentage that decreased to 4% when the adolescents were 15 to 17. Almost half reported having been beaten at a younger age but not currently. Additional information about the degree of violence within Argentinean families was that around 5% of adolescents asserted that their parents argued "almost always" or "always, and" 17% stated that physical violence—beating, shoving, throwing things at each other, and other hostile acts—had occurred "sometimes" and, for 3%, "many times" between their parents.

As was found in Anglo-Saxon countries, during middle adolescence, school matters were the most recurrent area of conflict between children and their parents (more than one in four cases), followed by curfew of outings and little responsibility. Almost 20% affirmed that they were not criticized by their parents, and the same percentage also said that there were no arguments with them. Although school has retained its importance as a conflict area, during the last decade, a notable decrease in parental disapproval of some friends of the same or the other gender has been detected, from more than 20% in 1986 to 8% in 2000, thus showing some decline in the caution Argentinean parents used to feel regarding the influence of peers. In the same period, clothing and hairstyle as conflict topics decreased, too, from 32% to 12%. Consistent with the traditional gender role socialization, both in 1990 and in 2000, the percentage of girls reporting being criticized with respect to other—but not same-sex—friends was higher than that of boys; in addition, girls stated that they experienced closer parental monitoring of their whereabouts than boys did.

At ages 17 and 18, the highest degree of negative interchanges happened with siblings; mother and father held second place, romantic partners the third, and best friends the last rank. However, in none of these five relationships did the average level of conflict and antagonism exceed the category "somewhat."

In a comparison with Anglo-Saxon and Nordic adolescents, it seems as if a higher proportion of Argentinean parents—almost half, according to their adolescents' report—did not set norms explicitly, did not monitor their children's behavior, or, if doing so, did not consistently punish their breaking of the rules. Some clues suggest that many Argentinean parents have moved from a propensity for authoritarianism, in use until the 1970s, toward an indulgent or permissive parental style. As an example, from age 15 on a lot of adolescents attend discos where they stay until 8 a.m. drinking alcohol abundantly, despite prohibition against minors' consumption.

No national data are available about the divorce or separation rate in parents of adolescent children. In 1999, 16% of conjugal homes were monoparental, and three out of four were led by a woman. In Paraná, at ages 13 to 15, 3.5% of students were born to single mothers, 12.5% of parents had divorced, and 4% of parents—mostly fathers—had died; when they were two years older, divorce had increased to 14% and deceased parents to 5%. Among those whose parents were divorced or never married (cohabiting), more than half lived with their single mothers, and almost one-third lived with mothers and stepfathers. These percentages changed remarkably when the adolescents were two years older: two-thirds were living with their single mothers and only 20% with their mothers and stepfathers, suggesting some fragility of remarried couples. Having a romantic partner was more common among divorced fathers (almost 68%) than divorced mothers. Although half of mothers had a partner, this person was not living at the household in one out of two cases.

Despite the fact that the divorce rate is much lower than in the United States, the effects of divorce on children's personality, well-being, conduct, and self-concept were as small as those shown by American studies. Father relationship—but neither mother nor romantic partner relationships—was jeopardized by divorce; however, 50% thought they were on good or very good terms with their father.

Twenty-one percent of Argentinean conjugal homes included a non-nuclear relative (INDEC 2001). In Paraná, 16% of adolescents lived with one or more non-nuclear relatives in the household, such as grandparents, uncles, cousins, siblings-in-law, nephews, or nieces. Grandparents, who were present in 12% of the homes, were ranked fifth among the people adolescents loved most, whereas an uncle or an aunt occupied the sixth and a cousin the eighth place.

Friends and Peers/Youth Culture

There is a lack of research regarding how much time adolescents spend either alone or with peers or family. In Paraná, when asked about the two leisure activities they preferred most, at ages 13 and 14, 57% chose being at home or going out with family, and 73% chose sharing time with friends, especially outings and going dancing. Almost 60% of those having a romantic partner preferred spending their leisure time with her or him. Four years later, 81% of these adolescents chose an activity shared with peers, and 38% preferred to spend leisure time with family, mainly at home. Among those having a romantic partner, 71% preferred spending leisure time with her or him. Only 11% mentioned solitary activities like "watching TV" or "resting." In short, although the preference for being with friends and/or romantic partners increased throughout adolescence, spending time with family retained part of its attraction.

Social cliques do not seem to exist in Argentina as they do in some other countries. There are no groups that could be labeled as jocks, brains, druggies, or populars. The degree of social acceptance peers feel toward the adolescent is more relevant than, for example, being a successful sports person or attaining high academic achievement.

No barriers against different-gender friendships are prevalent in Argentina. In Paraná, throughout adolescence, over 80% of teenagers belonged to a group of friends who know each other well; in around two-thirds of the cases, these groups were mixed-sex. At 13 to 14 years old, among 76% of boys having a best friend, almost a third of them were girls; however, among 85% of females having a best friend, only 8% of them were males. At ages 17 and 18, 89% of both genders reported having a best friend; for 16% of males and 10% of females, a cross-gender friendship was at issue.

The vast majority of Argentinean teenagers do not suffer from restrictions to friendship caused by religious beliefs or ethnicity. Although all forms of discrimination—due to race, sex, religion, social class, or physical appearance—are illegal in Argentina, some degree of subtle discrimination due to social class is evident in everyday life. Adolescents prefer not socializing with either the *chetos,* as they call those belonging to a socioeconomic level higher than their own, who are viewed as arrogant, or with the *negros* or *grasas,* as the slang denominates those who have a lower status and who are ill mannered according to stereotypical conventions.

Public, free, secular schooling used to be the institution par excellence amalgamating different social classes in Argentina. However, as the secondary school enrollment expansion jointly with the miserable educational budget deteriorated public education, increasing numbers of parents began sending their children to religious or nonreligious private schools. At age 13 to 14, almost 80% of adolescents reported that they had met their best friend in their neighborhood or at school, which are both two fairly homogeneous contexts with regard to social class. Although the big public secondary schools—where the janitor's and the judge's children were seated together—still exist, during the last decades (reflecting the increment in the gap between the rich and the poor undergone by Argentinean society), adolescents have developed within environments that are more highly differentiated with respect to socioeconomic strata than in previous generations.

The most frequently attended institutions, second place to schools, were sports and health clubs that were not specifically aimed at adolescents. In 1992, around 40% of secondary school students were members of a sports club in Paraná, and 35% of 14- to 17-year-olds in Greater Buenos Aires were as well (Deutsche Bank 1993). At ages 13 and 14, 84% practiced a sport, whether at a club or at a more informal place; this percentage descended to 64% when the adolescents were four years older. Between the end of the 1980s and the beginning of the 1990s, a high increment in girls' participation in sports—mainly aerobic gym—was detected; however, when competitive sports were at issue, the gap between boys (42%) and girls (11%) widened. Small percentages of teenagers belonged to youth organizations, whether religious, charitable, or political.

There is a distinct youth culture in Argentina that is marked off from adult culture by image (dress, hairstyle, tattooing/piercing), demeanor, argot, and mass-media consumption. It is so much influenced by American culture that vast sectors of Argentinean youth look very similar to their American counterparts. This happens to a lesser extent in rural and lower-socioeconomic-status urban environments; in the latter, a youth subculture prevails in which the hallmark is attending dancing places called *bailantas* in which the *cumbia villera,* an underground version of a kind of popular music that originated in Columbia, is preferred.

Love and Sexuality

In Paraná, the percentage of those having a romantic partner increased from 18% to 32% in boys and from 17% to 45% in girls across adolescence. Small percentages of both genders (never higher than 10%) reported they were "just dating." The modal category, except in girls aged 17 to 18, was "I'm interested in someone but we are not dating."

At ages 15 to 19, only 2.8% of adolescents were cohabiting, and 1% were married; 2% of adolescents in this age range were heads of household, with 58% of them being female (INDEC 2001). In Paraná, cohabitation and marriage showed up just at ages 17 and 18 (.5% of boys, 3% of girls).

With regard to sexual experimentation, despite Argentina being a Latin and Catholic country where restrictive attitudes toward female premarital sex were held until the 1980s, men's average age of sexual debut was 16 and women's was 18, similar to 16 and 17, respectively, seen in the United States. As it is observed in diverse countries, in Argentina, females initiated coitus at later age than males. The proportion of adolescent boys with sexual experience was equal to that of girls two years older. Although cross-cultural research indicates a historic trend—more pronounced among girls than boys—toward progressively earlier initiation of coitus, this did not apply to Argentina, where the historic trend was made up of an earlier initiation of coitus in girls and a postponement of coitus in boys, who now rarely resort to prostitutes as boys used to do.

The National Program for Sexual Health and Responsible Procreation, passed in 2002, provides, among other objectives, preventing unwanted pregnancy and promoting adolescent sexual health. Authorizing the prescription and free supply of condoms and oral contraception in public hospitals even to minors has allowed the access of lower-economic-status adolescents to birth control. As laws change according to jurisdiction, in some places, parents must authorize this type of medical consultation. The so-called morning-after pill and the intrauterine device are not usually permitted in public health institutions due to the pressure exerted by Catholic groups that consider them abortive.

Abortion, a controversial issue, although illegal except when endangering the mother's life, is frequently practiced in Argentina, especially in lower economic status (Torrado 2003). Those who can pay for it are operated on by a gynecologist in a private clinic, whereas the poor turn to practitioners with insufficient or null training, which poses serious health risks. In Argentina, abortion is the main cause of maternal mortality: it causes 23 deaths per 100,000 living newborns in females younger than 20 years.

Fifteen percent of living newborns had mothers who were less than 20 years old (INDEC 2001). Adolescent pregnancy frequently leads to marriage or cohabitation, and the adolescent girl who becomes a single mother by choice or because of a lack of money for an illegal abortion, although not socially condemned as during previous decades, is not fully accepted, either. In the Paraná sample, at ages 17 and 18 1% of boys and 7% of girls had at least one child; 75% of the latter were single mothers, living mostly in their parents' home.

Adolescent pregnancy is much higher among those who do not even enter secondary school. In a study of teenage mothers (Gogna et al. 2004), only 41% lived with their partners; almost half had dropped out of school before getting pregnant, and, among the remainder, only four out of ten continued their education up to childbirth. Feeling ashamed of being pregnant or the fear of being discriminated against were the reasons for dropping out adduced by one-third of them.

In 1982, the AIDS epidemic began in Argentina. Mortality due to this cause was not high (0.29% in 2002), and it has been decreasing since 1996. Eleven per 100,000 15- to 18-year-old adolescents suffered this disease, and an even lower rate was infected with HIV. AIDS prevention has been incorporated to the curricula at all levels of education. In Greater Buenos Aires in 1992 (Deutsche Bank 1993), young people were fairly conscious of the risk AIDS entailed for their health, and they knew very well how the infection could be caught; nevertheless, although they reported their intention to take protective measures, the real application of them was relatively low: only 22% of all adolescents used condoms.

In Paraná, fewer than one out of five adolescents were dissatisfied with the sex education that they had received during their lives, but those who were sexually experienced considered it somewhat less adequate. In more than 50% of cases, family members—mostly parents—had been the most important sex educators. Although this percentage did not decrease throughout adolescence, friends incremented their influence to more than 20% at ages 15 to 18. School and media were reported by one-third, and one out of ten asserted having received sex education from nobody. Whereas those acknowledging the influence of friends accepted both sexual intercourse and masturbation to a greater extent, those acknowledging the influence of parents experienced a higher level of psychological well-being. Almost all adolescents agreed that sex education should be part of the school curriculum, but many of them criticized the instruction received there for being late, incomplete, tinged by teachers' ideological views, and for not training practically in contraception.

At ages 13 and 14, parents were the favorite confidants regarding sexual concerns (41%). Two years later, friends and romantic partners held the first place (44%) and parent the second (34%); four years later, the preeminence of peers had increased even more (58%) versus parents (22%).

No research work exploring parents' attitudes toward their adolescent children's sexuality is available, but facts such as adolescents considering parents to be their principal sex educators and their main support providers if problems regarding sexuality or unwanted pregnancy arise suggest a parental attitude that is more understanding than punitive in this respect. Another sign of acceptance is that the vast majority of teenagers were satisfied with the relationship between their progenitors and their romantic partners, which was increasingly rated as good or very good throughout adolescence (60% at ages 13 and 14, 81% at ages 15 and 16, 88% at ages 17 and 18). Simultaneously, the percentage of parents and romantic partners not knowing each other decreased from 32% to 4% during those years.

Based on nonscientific observation, parents seem much more preoccupied about sexual aggression, sexually transmitted diseases, pregnancy, and female promiscuity, in decreasing order of importance, than about their adolescents having sexual intercourse. Accepting or not of sexual relationships at that age, the majority of parents consider them as an almost inevitable fact that will happen sooner or later.

Argentinean society's tolerance toward homosexuality has been increasing over the last decades. In some jurisdictions, laws conceding some rights to the homosexual cohabiting partner have been passed. In 1992 in Paraná, in a random sample of 17- and 18-year-old adolescents, 43% considered homosexuality a sexual choice rather than an illness (a belief espoused by 37%). In Greater Buenos Aires (Deutsche Bank 1999), only 40% of young people would rent a room in their homes to a homosexual without any hesitation; the refusal was even higher when a union leader, a politician, a policeman, or a military person, among others, was under consideration. No research work is available on Argentinean gay and lesbian adolescents.

Health Risk Behavior

The use of licit drugs was widespread among Argentinean adolescents (SEDRONAR 2001). Smoking tobacco cigarettes increased with age, from 22% having smoked at least once during the last year at ages 13 and 14 to 42% at ages 15 and 16 and to 53% at ages 17 and 18. In the oldest group, 31% had smoked six or seven days during the last week, and 20% had smoked five or more cigarettes daily. Only 15%, however, considered their tobacco use problematic. Girls were heavier consumers of cigarettes than boys.

Drinking alcohol increased with age as well, from 52% having drunk at least once during the last year at ages 13 to 14 to 77% at ages 15 to 16 and to 85% at ages 17 to 18. When reporting about the last week, the figures decreased to 23%, 42%, and 49% in the three successive age groups, respectively. One or more episodes of binge drinking during the last month were reported by 7% at ages 13 to 14, by 21% at ages 15 to 16, and by 36% at ages 17 to 18. Beer was adolescents' favorite beverage, followed by wine, and, in lower percentages, whisky, vodka, and others.

Only 1% of adolescents admitted to using marijuana at least once during the last year at ages 13 to 14, although that rose to 4% at ages 15 to 16 and to

8% at ages 17 to 18. With regard to cocaine, the figures were 1%, 3%, and 4%, respectively, in the three successive age groups. Glue consumption descended from 5% at 13 to 14 to 2% at 17 to 18. The use of tranquilizers without a medical prescription at least once during the last year was reported by 1% at ages 12 through 14, 3% at ages 15 to 16, and 4% at ages 17 to 18; the use of stimulants was admitted by 1%, 2%, and 2% in the three successive age groups, respectively (SEDRONAR 2001).

In Paraná, at ages 17 to 18, only 7% acknowledged having significant problems with alcohol and/or drugs. The access to illicit drugs is easy in Argentina, where the prohibition of selling tobacco and alcohol to minors is laxly enforced. In Greater Buenos Aires (Deutsche Bank 1999), drugs were made available to almost one-third of adolescents at the disco, to 29% in the street, to 21% at parties, and to 12% at the football ground. Girls were offered drugs to a lesser extent than boys were.

According to the National System of Criminal Information (Ministerio de Justicia 2003), 5.8 per 10,000 Argentinean adolescents between the ages of 15 and 19 died yearly of homicide, accidents, or suicide. The gender difference was wide: almost three boys for each girl. More than 50% of deaths among males between the ages of 15 and 24 years were the result of accidents: 18% were motor vehicle accidents, and 36% were other types of misfortune. Argentina had a high rate of traffic casualties in relation to the total number of cars: 1,164 per 1 million vehicles, which was well above countries like Sweden, Holland, the United States, and Spain. Victims 18 years old or younger amounted to 12% of the total (60% of them were boys), which is a percentage very similar to the 18- to 24-year-old period. An important proportion of casualties were caused by driving motorcycles, which are widely used by adolescents. Among the defendants of traffic accidents, adolescents younger than 18 years constituted only 2%. Although in most jurisdictions a driving license can be acquired at age 18, driving motorcycles at age 15 to 16 is permitted. In Paraná, 12% at ages 13 to 14 and 28% at ages 15 to 16 admitted having driven cars one or more times without a license and without being accompanied by an adult. Criminal homicides were seen at a rate of eight per 100,000 inhabitants yearly. Among the victims, 9% were younger than 18 years, and 24% were 18 to 24 years old; boys made up the overwhelming majority. Among the defendants, 11% were younger than 18, and 29% were 18 to 24 years old.

According to Argentinean laws, those aged 16 to 17 can be partially imputed of their crimes; this

9

means that, although they are prosecuted, the penalty is suspended, and the minors are placed in juvenile detention facilities instead of adult jails. At age 18, the young are fully imputable; however, until age 21, they will serve their sentences in pavilions for people their age located inside the adult prison.

Statistics provided by the Argentinean Ministry of Health indicated that approximately six per 100,000 people ages 15 to 24 years committed suicide in 1996. The rate, although much lower than that of Scandinavian countries and slightly inferior to that of industrialized countries like Germany and Japan, was one of the highest in Latin America. In recent years, two trends have been observed: first, the sex ratio became increasingly uneven (three boys for each girl), and, second, an increment of suicide rate in adolescents but not in adults.

When depressive syndrome was assessed in Paraná in more than 600 adolescent students, Argentinean boys scored lower and girls higher than Americans aged 13 to 17 years. Depressive syndrome decreased between ages 15 and 17. With respect to suicidal ideation, 28% at 13 to 14 years, 23% at 15 to 16 years, and 13% at 17 to 18 years agreed that "I think about killing myself but I would not do it" or "I want to kill myself."

No epidemiological research is available on the prevalence and incidence of different mental disorders in Argentinean adolescents based on randomly selected community samples completing diagnostic instruments of well-known validity and reliability. When over 1,000 students from three schools were examined with a list of symptoms extracted from the *Diagnostic and Statistical Manual of Mental Disorders, Version III,* and a structured diagnostic interview, an 18% prevalence of major depressive episodes was found throughout adolescence (Casullo 1998).

With respect to vandalism, in Paraná, 3% of boys at ages 13 to 14, 3% boys and 2% girls at ages 15 to 16, and 3% of boys at ages 17 to 18 reported having destroyed school furniture, trash baskets, street posters, public bathrooms, bus seats, and so on "many times."

The influence of parents and the parental relationship is a main source of adolescents' problems. Having a less-than-satisfactory relationship with the mother or father matched increased levels of either emotional or behavioral problems, including low self-esteem, depression, anxiety, antisocial behavior, substance use, and early sexual activity among both male and female adolescents. Although a problematic relationship with either the mother

or the father was equally damaging, the impact of mothers was greater on girls, and the impact of fathers was greater on boys. Research findings are lacking with regard to the interplay among family, peers, school, and neighborhood influences on adolescent risk problems. Lay people attribute adolescent problems to mostly environmental causes: poverty, unemployment, the bad models presented in the media, lack of family support (due to divorce, marital distress, paternal alcoholism), and excessive demands—especially achievement demands—placed on youth.

Education

The Argentinean educational system includes four levels: initial, primary (first to seventh grades), secondary (eighth to twelfth grades), and higher education (university and non-university institutions). Since 1884, public education had been free, secular, and compulsory from the first to the seventh grade, but, in 1993, mandatory schooling was extended from kindergarten (for 5-year-old children) through the ninth grade. Now elementary school ranges from first grade to ninth grade, and secondary school has been reduced to tenth through twelfth grades. Because the transformation has been slow as a result of bureaucracy and the severe economic crisis the country has been undergoing, the reference to eighth to twelfth grade secondary school is maintained here. In Argentina, adolescents go to school because they and their families consider it to be important rather than because authorities enforce attendance.

There are three types of secondary schools: (1) the schools originally conceived to prepare for higher education; (2) the commercial schools, which train for clerical jobs; and (3) the technological schools from which students graduate, generally in the thirteenth grade, as "technicians" with building, mechanics, electricity, electronics, or computing skills.

The illiteracy rate was 1% in the age groups of 10 to 14 and 15 to 19; 61% of those found to be illiterate were boys. Ninety-nine percent of boys and 99% of girls were attending primary school, 82% (79% boys and 85% girls) were in secondary school, and 39% (36% males and 41% females) were attending higher-education institutions. At age 13, 96% were enrolled in some kind of school, whereas at 17 and 18 the percentages diminished to 72% and 58%, respectively. These figures (INDEC 2001) indicate that, regarding gender differences in access to education, a small bias favoring women exists in Argentina. Moreover, girls scored higher in reading, mathematics, and scientific literacy in international achievement tests.

Significant problems relating to school performance afflict Argentinean secondary school. Sixteen percent of students entered this level of education belatedly, 31% repeated one or more grades, and 16% dropped out. These are the reasons why, at ages 18 to 24, only 43% have completed twelve years of schooling. Nevertheless, unlike other countries, nearly all who finish twelve-year schooling go into postsecondary education.

Since the last decades of the twentieth century, the access of lower-economic-level adolescents to secondary school increased significantly. In 1980, 53% boys and 62% girls were enrolled as compared with 73% and 81%, respectively, in 2000. Another sign of this expansion of enrollment is that 81% of those 20 to 29 years old exceeded their parents' educational attainment. In a random sample of secondary-school students in Paraná, only 56% had at least one parent who had graduated from high school.

In Argentina, secondary schools can be public or private, large or small, for the poor or for the rich; they are of different types and administered by more than twenty different provincial governments. In spite of their diversity, the vast majority of them suffer from low budget, poor building, insufficient teaching resources, and meager salaries paid to their teachers, who divide their working hours among several secondary schools. In 2002, only 2% of schools were equipped with computers with Internet access (Telefónica 2004).

The teacher-to-student ratio is one to nine. Educators' pay is lower in Argentina than in Chile or Brazil.

The majority of students attend classes 4.5 to 5 hours daily. Teachers' absenteeism, turnover, and professional illnesses in addition to the numerous days they go on strike for better salaries bring about a lot of "vacant hours" during which students just socialize or are sent to their homes. Adolescents have 180 school days yearly in the United States and 220 in the United Kingdom; in Argentina, they attended 179 days in 1998 and 175 in 2000.

Numerous differences are observed between the Argentinean and the American secondary schools. In Argentina, optional subjects are almost nonexistent. As the training in foreign languages, the use of computers, and music and the arts is insufficient in most schools, middle-class parents send their children to private institutes devoted to these activities. Sports are mostly practiced at private clubs, and neither dances nor other social meetings are held at schools.

For the majority of students, starting eighth grade means moving to a bigger school with 400 to 1,000 students, where they have thirteen teachers instead of two, as they had during the last years of elementary school.

In the opinion of many, the whole educational system in Argentina has been undergoing a deep crisis, and the secondary level is described as the worst for its failure to meet desired goals. The public is concerned with school performance and academic achievement. In 2003, on the Program for International Student Assessment tests (Organisation for Economic Co-operation and Development 2003), which evaluate the competencies of 15-year-old children in forty-one countries, Argentina ranked thirty-third in reading literacy, above Thailand, Mexico, Chile, Brazil, Macedonia, Albania, Indonesia, and Perú. In 2001, it ranked thirty-fourth in mathematics literacy, tied with Mexico and above Chile, Brazil, and Perú, and thirty-sixth in scientific literacy, surpassing Brazil and Perú.

Argentinean public universities, where the greater proportion of young people who decided to continue their postsecondary education enroll, are free, and, in the majority of them, no entrance examinations are required.

It is said that motivation to learn is minimum in most adolescents and that an anti-intellectual attitude is increasing. In the media and in everyday conversations, it is stated that adolescents are negatively biased toward school and that it only interests them as a place for socializing with peers. Nevertheless, in Paraná, only 19% of 13- to 15-year-old students adhered to that statement, and an overwhelming majority thought that secondary school did provide them with useful knowledge for their future. They were more critical regarding their teachers: two-thirds felt they demanded too much (in spite of educators' acknowledgment that they are requiring increasingly less and less), one-fourth felt that teachers explained things poorly, and 15% felt that teachers did not treat students well.

Argentina is a rather difficult place for the 3% of the 15- to 19-year-old population with disabilities. Notwithstanding the vast legislation, most of the regulations concerning this sector of the population are ignored. Regarding education, although special schools exist for children with different types of disabilities, less resources are available at the secondary-school level. Many adolescents with sensory and motor impairments attend common secondary schools, and, frequently, they simultaneously receive especial education to overcome their difficulties at other institutions. Teenagers with mental retardation attend especial schools, where capacitation to perform some kinds of jobs is included. Although there are a few secondary schools where highly intelligent youth is overrepresented, no programs for gifted adolescents exist in Argentina.

Work

Working is not a widespread activity among Argentinean adolescents. Among youth under the age of 18, parents' authorization before a family court, later authenticated by the Ministry of Labor, is required. Adolescent work is protected by special restrictions, like working only part-time, which are efficiently enforced. Parental authority permits demanding that children help with family work without being paid and that work can be computed as length of service for retirement purposes.

Situating adolescent work within the Argentinean labor context, it has to be remembered that the unemployment rate was 19% in September 2004 (15% unemployed plus 4% receiving a modest monthly benefit from the federal government because they are jobless). Among those with jobs, 49% hold a post within the informal economy, with the resulting decrease in salary and lack of social security.

According to the 1991 National Census, at ages 14 to 19, 36% of males and 21% of females had a job, and 7% and 5% of males and females, respectively, were searching for a job without finding one. Four percent of economically active boys were employed in the public sector, and 58% were in the private one; 15% worked for a family member (without a salary), and 20%, on their own account. In the case of girls, the figures were 3% in the public sector, 35% in the private one, 38% in domestic service, and 12% for a family member (without a salary); 10% were on their own account. At the ages of 15 to 19 years, 14% were socially excluded: they neither studied nor worked.

In Paraná, 12% of those ages 13 to 14, 16% of those ages 15 to 16, and 29% of 17- and 18-year olds had worked "always or almost always" during the last year, whether helping family members or neighbors in their jobs or being employed in a workshop, an office, a shop, or as a teacher, among other occupations. Using this definition of work, no gender difference in the proportion of working youth was found, although boys were employed to a greater extent.

In this sample, at ages 17 to 18, 61% were only studying, 22% were both studying and working, 7% were only working, and 8% were neither working nor studying; 3% of females were homemakers.

Among those not working, 31% reported looking for a job without finding one; this occurred more frequently among girls than boys. Two-thirds of those who neither studied nor worked, 71% of housewives, and a quarter of those who just studied were searching for a job. In short, at ages 17 and 18, the worker role had become either a reality or an aspiration for more than half of Argentinean adolescents.

Secondary-school students usually found a job through family members or friends. Generally, they were low-paying jobs in the informal economy that were carried out on school vacations or part-time during the school year, requiring minimum qualification. The majority of them lasted shortly, on average less than six months. Despite the precarious conditions, job satisfaction was high (80%). Asked about their projects upon graduating from secondary school, 79% chose "studying and working," whether for paying their personal expenditures or for increasing family income. Concerning the personal capital they counted on for getting a job, they mentioned "the desire to work" in the first place and "the high school certificate" in the second. The obstacles they anticipated were "lack of experience," "the scarcity of posts," and "lack of training," in order of importance (Aisenson et al. 2002).

For Argentinean adolescents, work seemed to have a value between moderate and high. When assessing the absolute and relative centrality of work among twelfth-grade students in Buenos Aires surrounding area, work, although important, held the third position, after family and leisure. The most valued aspect of work was the income it provided; in second place—but at a great distance—was how interesting and satisfactory it was, followed by the social contacts it made possible, the service to community made through it, and, lastly, as a means of keeping oneself busy (Aisenson et al. 2002). Considering these meanings, it was easier to understand why 38% of 14- to 17-year-old adolescents in Greater Buenos Aires asserted that they would enjoy a life without working; this percentage decreases only to 30% in adults (Deutsche Bank 1993).

In Argentina, secondary school and work are not tightly connected, as it happens in some European countries (Germany for example). Although the institution of apprenticeship exists and is legally regulated, the training for technical or clerical jobs provided by secondary schools takes place, in the majority of cases, within school (generally with insufficient equipment and time devoted to this purpose), with no apprenticeships carried out in the workplace.

There are some schools providing two-year work training for 15- to 18-year-old adolescents who have dropped out of secondary school. The Ministry of Labor carries out training in trades as well; the most important program, called Youth Project, which prepared 100,000 people 16 years old or older between 1995 and 2000, included apprenticeships in different enterprises. However, these initiatives usually result in being insufficient for or unsatisfactory to the youth who drop out from secondary school.

Media

Nine out of every ten homes in Argentina own at least one TV. The country has the most developed TV cable market in Latin America, with approximately 40% connected homes (and almost one in five of them, illegally connected) (Telefónica 2004).

TV viewing has increased in 14- to 17-year-old adolescents; in Greater Buenos Aires, the median category was "2–3 hours" of daily watching on working days in 1992 and "3–4 hours" in 1998; the segment of heavy users (more than 4 hours daily) increased from 21% to 31%. The types of programs they preferred most were comedies (48%), sports (41%), popular music (41%), and youth programs (36%). TV was used to a lesser extent for informative purposes: 11% preference for newscasts, 7% for politics-economics-religion, 13% science and technology, 26% animals and environment, and 15% for arts and literature (Deutsche Bank 1993, 1999). Programs are 75% Argentinean and 25% foreign; serials and movies by and large come from America.

The vast majority of adolescents go to the cinema. In 1999, they watched 52% American versus 15% Argentinean movies. Boys' favorite genre was action and adventure films, and girls preferred romantic stories; both genders enjoyed terror and science fiction.

In 2002, 27% of Argentinean homes owned a personal computer, but only half had an Internet connection. Despite this fact, 28% of those under 20 years old (41% in the biggest cities) were Internet users. Notwithstanding the economic hardship, this percentage has strongly increased in recent years due to the increasing popularity of public access among youngsters. In cybercafés and other places for Internet renting, available even in small villages in isolated areas, they chat and play computer games by paying a minimum charge. Unfortunately, with regard to the quality of educational programs about communication and information technologies, Argentina ranks fifty-fourth in a list of eighty-two countries, below Costa Rica, Chile, Uruguay, and Brazil (Telefónica 2004).

The radio, especially FM radio, is very popular among adolescents. In Greater Buenos Aires, 90% of 14- to 17-year-old adolescents listened to it during working days, and almost 50% listened for more than 2 hours daily. Heavy users (more than 4 hours daily) made up 20% of this group. Music was their major interest for radio listening (Deutsche Bank 1999).

Regarding recorded music, 48% of adolescents, much like the adult population, bought compact discs by Argentinean soloists or groups; 18% bought albums by other Spanish-speaking musicians, and 31% by performers who spoke other languages (mostly English).

In Argentina, people read half a book per inhabitant per year, as compared with four per year in France. Adolescents were not the exception. Whereas, in the United States, teenagers in eighth grade read an average of six books yearly, in Argentina, most secondary-school students did not study from textbooks but rather from photocopies or from class notes. In 1986, in Paraná, only 42% of 15- to 19-year-old students could name the titles and authors of three books that they had read; the majority mentioned literature in Spanish which was compulsory reading assignment; this was followed by fiction best sellers by Argentinean or foreign authors. This picture has been worsening over the subsequent years.

In regards to newspapers, in Greater Buenos Aires, 42% of 14- to 17-year-olds read them "almost never," and only 13% read them "regularly." Boys were more interested in newspapers than girls, mainly for the sports section (Deutsche Bank 1999).

Whereas reading is viewed as positive, adults in general think that modern media exert a negative influence on adolescents. So much so that many tried to explain the October 2004, first Argentinean school shooting—when three students were murdered and another three seriously wounded—because of the adolescent killer's admiration for a Gothic singer. Adolescents as well as children are intensely targeted by the media and by advertisers, especially by beverage, candy, beer, and jeans campaigns.

Politics and Military

Argentinean adolescents are not involved in military activities. Compulsory service was established in 1901 for all healthy males of 20 years of age and, later on, of 18 years of age, aiming at "public moralization" and the speeding up of the fusion of the diverse ethnic groups recently settled in the country. The practice was abolished in 1994 due to the active repulsion generated by the death of a conscript caused by the physical abuse inflicted by his superiors. As from 1995, conscripts were replaced by both gender volunteers aged 18 to 24. The Malvinas War, fought against the United Kingdom in 1982, was the only occasion from the nineteenth century onward in which 18-year-old Argentinean boys participated in an armed combat.

Most Argentinean adolescents' political involvement is circumscribed to voting. As of 18 years of age, they are legally required to participate in the elections. Although the payment of the fine for failing to do so is rarely demanded, the vast majority actually vote.

Although age 18 years is required to become a member, political parties have a department for 15- to 17-year-olds. Nevertheless, only a small percentage of teenagers are active participants. In 1992, in Paraná, 3% of 17- to 18-year-old students reported being active members, 2% being affiliates, and 21% being sympathizers without affiliation; the remainder included "no preferred party," "not interested in politics," and "rejecting politics." In Greater Buenos Aires, only 4% of 14- to 24-year-olds participated in political rallies or parties (Deutsche Bank 1999).

Adolescents' political involvement has been decreasing since the 1960s and the 1970s, when it reached its peak. The most dramatic consequence of teenagers' association with politics was the almost 250 13- to 18-year-old "missing" boys and girls, who were abducted from their homes, from the streets, or when leaving their schools during the terrorism of state established by the military dictatorship, which ruled the country between 1976 and 1983. A paradigmatic case was "The Night of the Pencils." In La Plata city on September 16, 1976, seven secondary-school students who were fighting for a cheaper student bus fare were abducted from their homes while sleeping and tortured by the military; only one of them reappeared alive. "Missing" adolescents due to the repression exerted against their parents must be added to the victims involved in politics.

Student associations, which exist in almost every public secondary school, play a role of some importance in adolescent political socialization. In them, the steering committee and the representatives of each grade are elected through the vote of students. In addition to discussing social problems, these associations devote themselves to other affairs, such as organizing parties and sports events, publishing the school magazine,

collaborating in the maintenance of the school building, and so on.

Youngsters between the ages of 14 and 24 did not differ from the adult population with regard to their trust in different state institutions. In Greater Buenos Aires, 11% trusted the executive and the legislature, 27% trusted the judiciary, 18% trusted the police, 26% trusted the military, and 23% trusted the public administration. Only 68% considered democracy was the best form of government for Argentina (Deutsche Bank 1999).

Volunteer work is not common among Argentinean adolescents. The vast majority of those involved do it through church organizations where social help is intertwined with evangelism. Nonreligious service associations like Rotary Club or Lions Club include a very small percentage of adolescents.

All of the information provided in this chapter, unless otherwise indicated, has been derived from the published and unpublished work of Facio and colleagues carried out in Paraná, a city with a population of 250,000. Two longitudinal random samples were studied: one of 175 students surveyed for the first time in 1988, when they were 13 or 14, and again at ages 15 to 16, 17 to 18 and 25 to 26, and the other one of 698 students surveyed in 1998, when they were 13 to 16 years old, and again at ages 15 to 18 and 17 to 21.

Alicia Facio and Santiago Resett

References and Further Reading

Aisenson, D., and Research Team on Guidance Psychology. 2002. *Después de la escuela (After leaving school)*. Buenos Aires: Eudeba.

Casullo, M. 1998. *Adolescentes en riesgo (At-risk adolescents)*. Buenos Aires: Paidós.

Deutsche Bank. 1993. *La juventud argentina (Argentinean Youth)*. Buenos Aires: Planeta.

Deutsche Bank. 1999. *Jóvenes hoy (Youth today)*. Buenos Aires: Planeta.

Facio, A., and M. Batistuta. 1997. *Los adolescentes y sus padres. Una investigación argentina (Adolescents and their parents. An Argentinean research)*. Paraná: National University of Entre Ríos Press.

Facio, A., and M. Batistuta. 1998. Latins, Catholics and from the far south: Argentinean adolescents and their parents. *Journal of Adolescence* 21:49–67.

Facio, A., and M. Batistuta. 2000. *La sexualidad de los adolescentes. Una investigación argentina (Sexuality in adolescents. An Argentinean research)*. Paraná: National University of Entre Ríos Press.

Facio, A., and M. Batistuta. 2001. What makes Argentinean girls unhappy? A cross-cultural contribution to understanding gender differences in depressed mood during adolescence. *Journal of Adolescence* 24:671–80.

Facio, A., and M. Batistuta. 2004. El inventario de depresión para niños de Kovacs en una muestra comunitaria de adolescentes argentinos (Kovacs Children Depression

Inventory in a commnunity sample of Argentinian adolescents). *Investigación en Psicología* 2:77–91.

Facio, A., M. Batistuta, F. Micocci, and C. Vivas. 2003. Intimidad con padres y hermanos en adolescentes de 13 a 15 años (Intimacy with parents and siblings in 13- to 15-year-old adolescents). *Ciencia, docencia y tecnología.* 27:43–60.

Facio, A., and F. Micocci. 2003. Emerging adulthood in Argentina. *New Directions for Child and Adolescent Development* 100:21–31.

Gogna, M., A. Adaszko, V. Alonso, et al. 2004. "El embarazo en la adolescencia Pregnancy in adolescence" Ministerio de Salud y Ambiente de la Nación, http://www.msal.gov.ar/htm/site/pdf/Resumen%20ejecutivo%20embarazo%20CEDES.pdf.

INDEC. 2001. *Censo nacional* (*National Census*) Buenos Aires: Ministerio de Economía.

Ministerio de Justicia de la Nación. 2003. "Sistema nacional de información criminal National system of criminal information." http://wwwpolcrim.jus.gov.ar/SNIC.htm.

Organization for Economic Cooperation and Development. 2003. *Literacy skills for the world of tomorrow. Further results from PISA 2000.* Paris: UNESCO.

Piccini Vega, M. 2004. Estudio comparado de la evolución de las lógicas del yo en la adolescencia por medio del test de completamiento de frases de Jane Loevinger Study of ego development in adolescence thorough Jane Loevinger's Sentence Completion Test *Anuario de Investigaciones* 11:529–38.

Schufer, M., A. Mendes Diz, A. Teisaire, M. Estrugamou, and A. Climent. 1988. *Así piensan nuestros adolescentes.* (*The way our adolescents think.*) Buenos Aires: Nueva Visión.

SEDRONAR. 2001. "Encuesta nacional a estudiantes de enseñanza media" ("National survey of secondary school students"). http://www.sedronar.gov.ar/encuestas%20nacionales/ense%F1anza%20media%202001/encuesta.pdf.

Telefónica. 2004. "La sociedad de la información en la Argentina" ("The information society in Argentina"). http://www.telefonica.com.ar/sociedaddelainformacion/.

Torrado, S. 2003. *Historia de la familia en la Argentina moderna* (*History of the family in modern Argentina*). Buenos Aires: Ediciones de la Flor.

Vega, V. 2004. Epidemiología de los trastornos de la conducta alimentaria en población escolar adolescente (Epidemiology of eating disorders in adolescent students). In *Memorias de las 11° jornadas de investigación*, In Facultad de Psicología de la Universidad de Buenos Aires (ed.). Facultad de Psicología de la Universidad de Buenos Aires Press.

Wasser Diuk, L. 1997. "La evaluación del self mediante relatos escritos Self-assessment through written essays" In *Evaluación psicológica en el campo socioeducativo*, M. Casullo (ed.). Paidós.

ARMENIA

Background Information

The Republic of Armenia occupies one tenth of the territory between the Caucasus and Asia Minor. It is bordered by the countries of Georgia, Azerbaijan, Turkey, and Iran. As a landlocked country, Armenia does not have direct maritime routes for use in transportation or for importing or exporting goods via oceanic trade routes. Although Armenia is on maps from the fifth century B.C., the Republic of Armenia (RA) emerged as a result of the Soviet Union's (USSR) dissolution in December 1991. The RA became one of the 15 newly independent nations of the former USSR, and gained admission into the United Nations soon thereafter. With a territory of 11,306 square miles (29,800 square kilometers) and a population of 3.5 million inhabitants (National Statistical Service of the Republic of Armenia 2004), Armenia is the smallest in area and the thirteenth in population among the post-Soviet Republics. Yerevan, the capital of Armenia, has 1,100,000 inhabitants. This 2,790-year-old city has survived a steady succession of wars, natural disasters, foreign and aggressive rulers, and holocausts.

In 1828, Armenia was integrated into Russia. Almost a century later (1920), Armenia became part of the USSR. From 1895 to 1923, the nation was brought to the brink of annihilation as almost two million Armenians—more than half of the total population—were massacred by the Ottoman Turkish rulers. As an example of the drastic effect this had upon the country, the village of Parchanj, with an original Armenian population of 2,000, only had 269 residents (mostly elderly and disabled) after the massacre (Dzeron 1938/1984). Turkish soldiers and military men killed Armenians in their homes and villages by brutal means, such as dismembering, shooting, burying or burning alive, and impaling. To this day, the Ottoman Turkish genocide of the Armenians is denied, even by the Turkish government. In July 2005, the Turkish Prime Minister's adviser stated that the accusations of genocide are no more than "biased and one-sided allegations" (Bagis 2005). He contends that it was a civil war triggered by Armenian rebellion. This denial causes tremendous feelings of anger and resentment in Armenians (Kalayjian et al. 1996). During the following 70 years under Communism, Armenians experienced more pain and suffering. The government relied on oppression of individual needs for the sake of the Communist Party of the Soviet Union. As elsewhere in the USSR, any rebellious gesture could lead to a person's disappearance.

The Republic of Artsakh (Nagorno Karabakh), with a territory of 4,400 square kilometers just east of Armenia, has a population of 200,000, which is 100% ethnic Armenian. Artsakh, formerly a part of Armenia, declared its independence in 1992. During the late 1920s, Moscow assigned Nagorno Karabakh—a primarily Armenian-populated enclave—to Soviet Azerbaijan, which has a mainly Muslim population. This caused conflicts between Armenia and Azerbaijan. By 1988, the tension over the enclave escalated to the point of violence. The struggle worsened after both countries attained independence from the Soviet Union in 1991. More than 7,400 young Armenians were killed in the war over which country would keep the desirable region. At the time of a ceasefire in May 1994, Armenian forces held on to Nagorno Karabakh, as well as a significant portion of Azerbaijan proper. The economies of both sides have suffered high costs because of their inability to reach a peaceful resolution.

Period of Adolescence

According to the Armenian educational system, the adolescence period begins at 12 to 13 years old and lasts until 19 to 21 years old. In actuality, families consider adolescence as starting when youths demonstrate the ability to take responsibility and to make decisions more independently. Puberty is another key aspect signifying the start and end of adolescence. However, different classes and levels of socioeconomic status consider adolescence as beginning at different ages. For example, in villages, adolescence begins earlier than in towns due to greater responsibilities demanded at a younger age. Often the male adolescent years are perceived to occur slightly later and to last longer than the female adolescent years. For men, adolescence

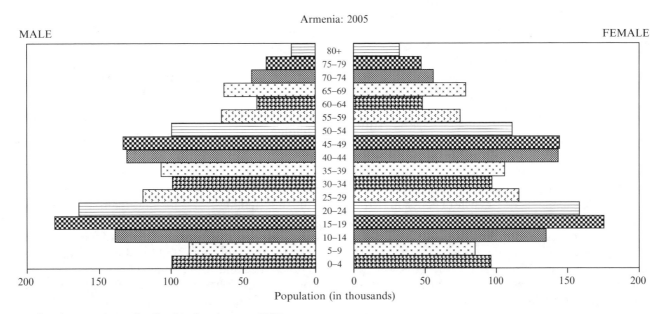

Armenia: 2005

MALE   FEMALE

Population (in thousands)

Predicted age and sex distribution for the year 2005.
Source: U.S. Census Bureau, International Data Base.

often starts around 14 to 18 years of age and goes on to 21 to 24 years of age.

The number of people in Armenia between the ages of 15 and 24 is estimated at 675,000, making this age group 20% of the total population. They represent one of the largest age groups in Armenia. The frequency distribution of people of different ages for the Armenian population appears in the following bar graph.

One rite of passage for males entering young adulthood is to serve in the army. According to the Article 46 of the Constitution of the Republic of Armenia (adopted in July 1995), all 18-year-old male citizens must join the army for two years. The Legislative Acts excuse some citizens from military duty, such as those with mental or physical disabilities and those in jail. Young men attending state-certificated universities may defer their military participation until after they receive their bachelors or masters degree. Serving in the army is optional for those male citizens who earn their PhD. With few exceptions, the army only enlists men under 27 years old. A great deal of separation anxiety and heavy responsibility are faced during service in the military; this is a step in their preparation for adulthood. Other rites of passage include citizenship, which comes at age 16, and reaching the juridical age to be convicted for crimes, at age 14 (age 16 must be attained for full responsibility).

Following adolescence is a period of emerging adulthood called 'early adulthood.' According to the perceptions of Armenians, early adulthood starts at age 18 to 21 and extends until age 33 to 35, when middle adulthood starts. Early adulthood is understood as a period of spiritual maturation, whereas adolescence is considered primarily a time of physical maturation. This approach to age division is used by most Armenian psychologists and social workers. Traditionally, early adults are formally considered adults when they are married.

Beliefs

The Armenian population in the Trans-Caucasus has long been, like the people of Israel, an outpost of Western beliefs and values in the Middle East (Jeshmaridian 1999, 2000; Jeshmaridian and Takooshian 1994). The history of the Armenian people, or 'the Anglo-Saxons of the Near East,' as former U.S. President Woodrow Wilson described them, is a history of escaping annihilation, such as the genocide by the Turks. Following the genocide, many citizens of Armenia permanently migrated to other countries. Collectively, they are referred to as 'the Diaspora.' The number of Armenians living in the Diaspora exceeds the Armenian population living in the country itself; there are over 4.5 million people of Armenian ancestry in the United States, the Middle East, Russia, France, Iran, Turkey, Argentina, Australia, and smaller numbers elsewhere.

Ninety-eight percent of the population of Armenia belongs to the same cultural heritage, sharing the same written language and religious tradition.

The remaining 2% of the population includes Russians, Ukrainians, Molokans, Kurds, Yezidis, Jews, Greeks, and others (UN 2005). Sixty-four percent of the population lives in urban areas, whereas 36% lives in rural areas (NationMaster 2005). Female life expectancy is 77.3 years, and male life expectancy is 70.3 years.

The RA's main and official language is Armenian, which is an old Indo-European language that has some similarities with Greek in grammatical structure and with Persian in etymology. More than 80% of Armenian families speak a second language, which tends to be English or Russian. Most Armenian families are bearers and representatives of two cultures, as connoted by two languages. They embody these different cultures seamlessly and simultaneously. First-generation Armenians who reside in the Diaspora usually speak both Armenian and the language of their resident state. Overall, there are 8 million Armenian-speaking people throughout the world (Jeshmaridian 1997, 1999a).

Armenian religious beliefs are Christian. Religion has always been a major component of Armenian selfhood. Officially adopting Christianity in the year 301, Armenia was the first Christian nation in the world. All the Armenians in the RA, its close neighbor Artsakh, and those scattered elsewhere in the Diaspora have shared the same religious tradition for seventeen centuries. Since the ancient times of Noah's Ark and Mount Ararat (The Bible, Genesis, 8:4), having independent nationhood (statehood) has been a main goal for Armenians. Armenia is located precisely where the Bible describes Noah's Ark alighting atop Mount Ararat. According to Armenian mythology and legends, Noah's descendant Hayk, who fought against enemies for freedom, is the founder of the Armenian people. With this as an example, Armenia became the first country to fight for its Christian religion against Zoroastrian Persians in 451.

During the 1990s, the Armenians of the Republic of Artsakh fought for their freedom against the Muslim Azeris. Although both groups officially declared that the conflict was territorial, the undercurrent of religious differences was palpable. Even the Armenian genocide of 1915 presumably occurred because of religious rather than economic or political reasons (Rubenstein 1983).

The Christianity of Armenians is represented by several branches: apostolic-illuminatory (orthodox), which is the most common and widespread (almost 90%), as well as Catholic, Protestant, and Evangelical. After a major earthquake in 1988, many different religious confessions and conversions, especially Protestant Christian, came to the RA, thus increasing its spiritual diversity. In Armenia, Catholics are few in number, but they tend to be financially influential. Jehovah's Witnesses became numerous after the earthquake (officially, 20,000), but are not recognized by the government and are not well accepted by the population.

Gender

Armenian clan structure and kinship have always been patriarchal. Less than a century ago, Armenian family trees only listed sons' proper names, omitting females or labeling them as a certain number of daughters (Dzeron 1938/1984). Interestingly, gender roles during the Soviet regime were not traditional for Middle Eastern countries. Women became more educated and held higher positions during this period. In 1921, women gained suffrage, making Armenia one of the first countries to allow women to vote (Takooshian et al. 1993).

Now women have full social and professional equality and prospects for financial independence. The policy of gender equality is widely publicized by international organizations and grants. Although on the surface women are respected by men, in reality they are often still "confined to the kitchen." Many men still see females as responsible for domestic tasks and for tending to their husbands' or fathers' needs. Research on attributes of feminism in Armenia found that Armenian men stated that they respected women and that women enjoyed equality and equity, just as long as they "knew their place" (Kalayjian 1993). Ironically, women and men do not agree about where that place is. When females do not conform to traditional views, they may face few prospects for getting married. If they do marry, non-subservient wives may encounter serious problems in their new family, where traditional gender roles and expectations prevail.

Despite the nation's history, gender roles are changing significantly among adolescents, especially in urban areas. The young population has much less rigid views of the women's "place." As women gain liberties to speak, work, and dress how they like, they are beginning to wear more revealing Western-inspired clothing. In young marriages and families, traditional patriarchal relations are increasingly becoming partnership relations.

The Self

Armenian society today can be described as being in a transitional state with regard to modernization.

Although the industrialization process has begun, the majority of the population is not tangibly affected by it. As a result, most young Armenians are under economic stress. Moreover, as a post-socialist and post-genocidal society, adolescents' inner conflicts arc apt to grow into interethnic and intra-ethnic conflicts. Because of the difficulties adjusting to the new changes, today's adolescents are sometimes referred to as a distressed youth in a modernizing society.

As the RA shifts from a traditional society to a modern, industrialized society, the identities of adolescents are shaped by historical, family, and Western influences. Adolescent minds are still pliable, so these influences are particularly important during the teenage years. These various factors have a significant impact on the development of an adolescent's identity.

Situated between the Caucasus and the Middle East, Armenia has been an outpost of Western values in an often unfriendly neighborhood (Jeshmaridian 1999a, 1999b, 2000; Jeshmaridian and Takooshian 1994). This geographical-political position has been a major factor in the acquisition and development of the modern Armenian selfhood. The Soviet legacy taught Armenians that knowing how to survive is more important and useful than having honor and piety; this has had enduring implications on the character and values of modern Armenians. Armenians want to show the world that they can survive as an independent nation. Every person is expected to struggle for national independence and to do his or her share to keep public order.

During the Soviet years, the reigning forces (including the satellite Armenian government) tried to control all aspects of society, especially striving to influence the younger generations. Political, religious, and social ideologies were relentlessly presented to Armenia and to other Soviet states via schools and media. Despite strong efforts to shape the identity of young Soviet-Armenians, Communist ideology could never outweigh the powerful values and traditions that were transmitted to them through Armenian families.

Family Relationships

The traditional Armenian family consists of several nuclear families built around parents and grandparents. During the nineteenth century, Armenian families usually had five to ten children; now they typically have one or two. During the past century, the number of extended families dwelling in the same residence decreased. Nuclear families now tend to live in separate homes. However, kinship relations among Armenians remain very close.

Among all types of influences, the family has always had the greatest impact on young Armenians' developing identity. For Armenians, family is not simply a social group or a social institution: it is an all-encompassing structure. Armenians take pride in their family cohesiveness, discipline, and strict moral standards. Family and clan honor is very important. Cultural, social, and political values are transmitted to young people via parents and family. Through the examples they set and their didactic statements, the family teaches young people to stand up for Armenian nationality. Most families want to show the world that Armenians are able to survive as an independent nation.

Above all, the mother plays a crucial role in shaping her children. The mother is the symbol of security and identity for the whole society. Family influences remain strong during the adolescent years. Even as teenagers develop the ability to make choices independently, they are expected to discuss their decisions with family members and to take their parents' advice into account. The strong family influence continues into early adulthood. Married couples remain close to their families, and the husband's mother still has authority in the family (Jeshmaridian 1995, 1999b).

From an early age, Armenians are taught the importance of taking care of their younger siblings and their grandparents. The stability of the Armenian family structure compensates for the lack of governmental stability. Whereas the state largely neglects and overlooks the population's well-being, the family tends to every need of their relatives. Otherwise homeless citizens and destitute elderly persons reside in the homes of family members. Armenian families play the role of a governmental social security system, a retirement pension, and welfare for relatives in need. The families of Artsakh (Nagorno Karabagh) and those of the Diaspora are very similar to those in Armenia with regard to their structure, family values, and methods of child rearing (Jeshmaridian 2000).

Historically, Armenian marriages were arranged by the couple's parents (Dzeron 1938/1984). Following World War II, marriage partners began to select one another. Although the choice of a spouse is ultimately their own, many young men and women still listen to advice from their parents and respected elders. During the early 1990s, the average age of marriage was 21.7 years for women and 25.8 years for men; now the estimated age of marriage is 25 years for women and 30 years for men (Geneva Foundation for Medical Education and

ARMENIA

Research 2005; HyeEtch 2005). This age increases among individuals who pursue higher education.

Armenians' decision to delay marriage is largely due to poor economic conditions. Males are expected to have employment and a house to live in before marriage. Armenian culture considers husbands to be financially responsible for their family. In a time of economic uncertainty, high unemployment, and widespread poverty, young men do not have the resources necessary to provide for a wife and family's material well-being. The family often plays a large role in the lives of newlyweds by offering help during economic hardships.

Marriage and divorce registration and processing, conducted according to the laws of Armenia's Family Code, are similar to the Western version. The divorce process is simple: couples must file a written application in the court system and go through a two-month waiting period. Both spouses must give their agreement to the divorce. Divorce in Armenia tends to occur in couples without children. For those with children, the mother gains custody. Fathers have weekly visitation rights to see their children. When parents separate or divorce, the surrounding relatives provide those children with extra love, often treating them like their own. The average divorce rate is 185 per 1,000 marriages (Karatnycky et al. 2001), and it is increasing. This may be due to the necessity of men migrating to other countries for jobs, leaving their families behind. Also, extramarital sexual relations are relatively widespread among Armenians (11% among women and 65% among men).

Armenians are deciding to have fewer children. In 1955, women of childbearing age had 4.5 children. In 2005, the number of children per woman of childbearing age was 1.3 (Worldfacts 2005). Over 60% of married women use contraception (NationMaster 2005). Out-of-wedlock births are uncommon, although they are no longer shameful as they were prior to the 1960s. The lower birth rate may also be due to the proportion of the population in their childbearing years. Infant mortality has also decreased greatly since the 1980s; now there are fewer than 11 infant deaths in 1,000 births (Karatnycky et al. 2001). Over 97% of births are attended by trained medical staff (NationMaster 2005).

Friends and Peers/Youth Culture

Since independence in 1991, Armenian youth have adopted Western fads in music, attire, food, and activities. Although the RA is not yet a modern society, it is no longer a traditional society. Middle-class adolescents in large cities are paving the way toward a more liberal, Westernized Armenian culture. For example, the European fad of bare midriffs caught on in the attire of adolescent Armenian girls. Although tattoos and body piercing are not widespread in the RA, these practices are gaining prevalence as well.

Adolescents are spending more time in school and peer activities than ever before. In large cities, such as Yerevan, adolescents frequently visit Internet clubs, disco clubs, night clubs, and cafés. Rural towns and villages lack most of these popular urban attractions, so young people gather in groups on street corners. Youth organizations have burgeoned, giving young Armenians access to new activities. Sports teams and clubs, particularly soccer and karate, have become popular. Most of the youth nongovernmental organizations try to adhere to some political party. Since the Soviet days, adolescents have watched TV and listened to the radio. There is only one TV program especially designed for adolescents; it is called "16." Young people currently are active users of computer games and the Internet. The Internet reinforces teens' existing social ties and helps foster new, more diverse ties. Being proficient with computers opens many possibilities for jobs as well. Adolescents' increased involvement with friends, in its various forms, provides them with a strong source of emotional support, in addition to their family of origin.

Love and Sexuality

Armenian girls have always been expected to preserve their virginity until marriage. Women who do not maintain their virginity are considered shameful to their families and are often avoided by suitors. However, somewhat of a double standard has arisen, because it is generally tolerable and even expected for men to engage in sexual intercourse before marriage.

Romantic relationships are an important expanding domain of the adolescent interpersonal experience in Armenia. Dating was not customary for many decades, but it is now common. Love and sexuality are acceptable thanks to the media's portrayal of adolescent relationships. As the age at which people marry becomes older, increasing numbers of adolescents and young adults are in dating relationships and engaging in sexual intercourse.

Until late 2004, Armenian schools did not offer sexual education. This is mainly due to the widespread belief that it would entice adolescents into having premarital sex (Ghukasyan 2002). However, the government decided to introduce the subject of "healthy lifestyles," which includes sex education, into their curricula (UNFPA in the News 2004). This was a large step that demonstrated the official recognition of adolescents' sexuality.

Armenian society has always had an unfavorable attitude toward homosexuality and prostitution. Because some Armenians openly identify themselves as homosexual or bisexual, it is clear that adolescents are less concerned about public opinion or judgment than ever before.

The occurrence of sexually transmitted diseases in Armenians remains fairly low, although it is predicted to increase. The number of officially registered HIV-positive persons in 2004 in Armenia was 374, with over 300 between the ages of 21 and 45. A realistic estimate of all people (both adults and children) with HIV/AIDS is over 2,600, which is 0.86 per 1,000 people. Among adults between the ages of 15 and 49, about 0.1% is estimated to have HIV (NationMaster 2005). The primary sources of HIV transmission are injection drug use and heterosexual intercourse; HIV infection via homosexual intercourse is less than 3%. Contaminated blood and blood products account for less than 2% of HIV cases, and prenatal transmission also accounts for less than 2% of cases (UNAIDS, UNICEF, World Health Organization 2004).

Health Risk Behavior

Armenia has a low crime rate. Out of sixty-one nations, only four countries had a lower crime rate overall. A total of 12,048 crimes were committed in 2000 (4.02 crimes per 1,000 people). Armenia ranks especially low on burglaries and rape: it is thirty-eighth out of thirty-nine countries for burglaries (0.03 per 1,000 people) and forty-fourth out of forty-seven countries for rape (0.00 per 1,000 people). The RA's rates of embezzlements and frauds are slightly higher, ranking twentieth out of thirty-three nations for embezzlement (0.07 per 1,000 people) and thirty-second out of forty-four for frauds (0.25 per 1,000 people). Armenia has a moderately high murder rate (0.04 per 1,000 people), making it sixteenth highest out of forty-six nations (NationMaster 2005).

Armenia is not a major drug-producing country, and its domestic abuse of drugs is relatively small. However, its location makes it vulnerable for becoming a route for international drug trafficking. As a transit point between Southwest Asia and Russia, opium and hashish could fairly easily be transported through Armenia (NationMaster 2005). In 2002, the Armenian Parliament passed a bill aimed at strengthening the police mandate to combat drug sales and trafficking. Armenia participates in the UN-sponsored Southern Caucasus Anti-Drug Program, which was launched in 2001 (Embassy of the United States 2005).

Most of the minimal drug use among Armenian youth involves cannabis, which is grown for personal consumption (NationMaster 2005). Some hashish or heroin is consumed by upper-class groups of teens. Recently, a minimal number of adolescents have been observed using toxic inhalants and glues. Smoking tobacco is popular among men; 64% of the male population smoke, but only 3% of women smoke. The average number of cigarettes smoked per adult each year is 1,095 cigarettes (NationMaster 2005).

Armenian adolescents are sometimes called "distressed youth," and they reveal some anxiety and unhappiness. During the late 1990s, the Heck & Hess 40-Scale Questionnaire was used to investigate psychological distress among Armenians. The surveys were administered to 242 subjects ages 15 through 35. The study found that 49% of young, healthy inhabitants of Armenia experienced a state of psychological stress, frustration, and mild anxiety, with 25% experiencing high levels of psychological distress (Jeshmaridian and Jeshmaridian 2001; Jeshmaridian 2003).

According to the World Database of Happiness (2004), which studied ninety nations to evaluate how much citizens differ in their overall enjoyment of life (cited in Health 2005), Armenians rate their life satisfaction fairly low. Their life satisfaction ranks sixty-fifth out of sixty-nine nations surveyed. Only 6% of the Armenian population reports that they are "very happy." A large 43% say that they are "not very or not at all happy," making them one of the unhappiest of fifty nations (seven countries are unhappier) (World Database of Happiness 2004; cited in Health 2005). The dramatic changes Armenian adolescents are facing have taken a toll on their psychological well-being.

Suicide rates in Eastern Europe differ among countries, ranging from low (fewer than 5 per 100,000 people) to high (15 to 30 per 100,000 people) to very high (more than 30 per 100,000 people). In 1992, Armenia had the lowest overall suicide rate of Eastern European nations, at 2.8 per 100,000 people (Research Machines 2005). However, males between the ages of 15 and 24 have the highest suicide rate in Armenia, at 64.3 per 100,000; young females' rate is 2.1 per 100,000 (NationMaster 2005).

Education

Armenia's compulsory education lasts ten years. The primary grades comprise four years, and secondary school lasts six years. The ratio of students to teachers is 22:1 (NationMaster 2005). Very few children attend private schools. Literacy, which is defined as people over the age of 15 years being able to read and write, is 98% for females and 99.4% for males. Adolescents often study with the goal of attending a university. Attending graduate school is still relatively rare; only 5,000 Armenians hold PhDs. According to the State Commission of Statistics of Republic of Armenia (2004), the following data describe the level of education in Armenia:

- 42% of the population has college, university, or higher education (14 or more years of schooling)
- 53% of the population has only secondary education
- 4% of the population has only full primary or presecondary education (more than 4 but less than 10 years of schooling)
- 1% of the population over the age of 21 years has preprimary education (less than 4 years of schooling)

Armenian public schools teach some orthodox Christian religious beliefs. The mandatory course "History of Armenian Church" was introduced in 2003 for fourth and fifth grades (ages 10 to 12 years). However, some schools do not adhere to this government rule. Children and adolescents also learn about the Christian Armenian church through a TV program called "Shoghakat."

Although most public schools still adhere to the traditional Soviet educational style of the rote memorization of words and numbers, some revolutionary schools are moving toward a system that promotes art, self-expression, imagination, and freedom. On the pedagogic level, students are encouraged to go as fast as they want, and they are also encouraged to integrate literature, art, and self-expression. For example, in one elementary level class, students read a poem and then take a brush and palate to put their thoughts into a painting. In these schools, older students help with the preparation of some of the workbooks used by children in the lower grades.

Work

Officially, about 41% of the population makes up the national workforce (Karatnycky et al. 2001). However, official data tend to exaggerate the actual number and fail to take into account the high rates of unemployment or underemployment. This percentage also includes people nominally listed as employees of dormant or idle state agencies. The official unemployment rate is around 12%, but a more accurate estimate is 25% to 28% (Karatnycky et al. 2001).

In 1999, the official average monthly wage was 17,000 drams ($33 USD). Again, this is probably an underestimate, because many people report making less than they really earn to pay less income and social security taxes. Minimum wage is around 5,000 drams ($10 USD) (Karatnycky et al. 2001). Armenians often make ends meet thanks to money transfers from relatives living outside the cities and in the Diaspora.

The Armenian economy was seriously ineffective throughout the Soviet reign, particularly during the final years. Officially, Soviet Armenia was an industrial republic with developed agriculture. Officially, its economy collapsed due to broken ties following the disintegration of the USSR. However, neither of these statements is true. In actuality, the economy failed because of Azerbaijan's and Turkey's transport blockades of Armenia; the war in neighboring Artsakh; civil wars in Russia, Georgia, and Azerbaijan; and, above all, the widespread economic corruption.

After the dissolution of the USSR in 1991, the national economy of Armenia worsened as an era of a "casino economy" started. Technically, Armenia has a free market and capitalistic economy. Despite currently receiving the most (after Israel) U.S. financial assistance per capita, the Armenian economy continues to decline each year. The disastrous condition of today's Armenian economy is due to massive, unchecked corruption. Although the majority of Armenians remain powerless and uninformed about the specifics of corruption, a small circle of people holding strategic positions in economics and politics make influential decisions. Corruption in the RA ranges from the dishonest use of employee surplus funds to aggressive bribing. Often, citizens must pay bribes for the services of governmental agencies, such as fixing the phone cables. From the Soviet years to present, people have paid bribes for acceptance to prestigious state universities (Karatnycky et al. 2001). Many top government officials covertly own private businesses, which are registered in the names of friends. Those who do not actually own companies often have deals in which the government official gives a private enterprise special treatment in exchange for a share of their profits (Karatnycky et al. 2001). Sadly, political and economic dishonesty and manipulation continue to grow. The nation's wealth is sucked into this vast and bottomless black hole (Jeshmaridian 2005), which undermines and degenerates any wealth-creating mechanisms in Armenia's newly established free market.

Armenia has progressed further than many other newly independent states in creating a favorable climate for business. However, the investments made in Armenia often take on debt for the country. In 1997, the debt of the RA government was $503.3 million USD, and, in 1998, it increased to $546.9 million USD. In 2004, it exceeded $1 billion USD. The debt of the Central Bank of RA in 1997 was $137.1 million USD, and, in 1998, it increased to $191.9 million USD. The Armenian government and the Central Bank also have an internal debt of more than $1 billion USD to the population of Armenia. In 2004, the Central Bank of Armenia was sold to Russia.

Like other aspects of their society, Armenian economics have a great need for improvement. The Armenian economy lacks a global strategy (e.g., for expanding participation in foreign markets). The RA has no technological and competitive forces for worldwide innovation. Growing pressures for localization are present, because Armenians have a tendency to use more local-level—as opposed to wide, corporate-level—economic strategies. An international economy that includes multinational flexibility, global efficiency, and worldwide learning is still a far-off dream for Armenia (Fukuyama 1995; Yip 1995). During the 1990s, the only key factor was the activities of the International Monetary Fund for multinational corporations. Even this multinational model—which greatly differs from the global model—is in question.

Poverty is widespread in Armenia. The poverty level in Armenia is 55% in 2004, which is a significant decrease from 1997, when it was 70% (Karatnycky et al. 2001). From a social and economic point of view, the lifestyle in the RA can be characterized as a "culture of poverty." Around the time the economy hit rock-bottom, 100,000 homeless families resided in Armenia after the devastating earthquake (1988). Now, around 10,000 families are homeless, showing some improvement in the economic conditions. In addition, these homeless people do not live primarily on the streets but rather in temporary cabins and huts.

Natural disasters have added to impoverishment in Armenia. The earthquake in December 1988 killed over 55,000 people and left several cities and towns in ruins (The World Almanac 1992). The number of families with single parents rapidly increased, and over 29,000 people became disabled. In Armenia, there are currently 110,000 disabled citizens, and essentially all are poverty-stricken. Twenty-four percent of them are between 14 and

30 years old. Although the number of orphans is large in Armenia, there are less than 2,000 orphans in the Armenian orphanages. Because of close Armenian kinship ties, the relatives of orphans often take them into their own households and have the right to adopt them. Despite some small improvements, the economic situation in Armenia remains very bleak.

Politicians and business leaders take a parochial view of sovereignty and jobs. Because of spreading corruption, the inhabitants of Armenia perform poorly with regard to strategic partnering behaviors and activities; this is especially true for the young population of Armenia. Insecurity about the future of any private business has led investors and entrepreneurs to be individualistic. Observing the very limited success of collectivist endeavors (e.g., community development policies) has made Armenians resistant to collectivistic thinking. They see this approach as a way for people to get rid of responsibility by projecting it onto others. Because of these factors, globalization and networking are not likely in Armenia's near future.

Many young Armenians are forced to abandon their native country in search of jobs and more opportunities. During the last 15 years, one in four young Armenians restarted their lives in another country. This indicates that enduring the marginal conditions they face as new immigrants outweighs the plight of poverty in their native country (Jeshmaridian 2000a). Each year, almost one million of these predominantly young men become temporary emigrants working in Russia and other nearby nations to earn their families' living; families depend heavily on the money that these workers send home. Another cause of migration and immigration involves the unsettled, dangerous conditions in Armenia and the surrounding areas. Citizens from bordering countries may enter Armenia to escape the situation in their homeland. For example, from 1988 to 1990, over 360,000 people flew to Artsakh and Armenia from Azerbaijan due to pogroms and massacres conducted by Azeris.

Politics and Military

The adolescents of Armenia no longer believe Soviet ideas. The youth of present-day Armenian society increasingly recognize that many of the propagandized teachings of the former Soviet era are false. Jeshmaridian (2000b, 2005) identifies five fallacies of this sort:

1. The world is divided into "we" and "they" (insiders and outsiders).
2. There is one philosophy of life that is the best.

3. Democracy in post-Soviet nations can be attained only via authoritarian power.
4. There are no tensions between the executive and legislative branches of government.
5. There is a magic wand (or a wise leader) to solve all of society's problems.

New light has been shed on these Communist ideas since Armenia achieved independence, particularly in the eyes of adolescents. It is evidence of the youth's changing ideologies that they can recognize these as fallacies.

Although adolescents now have a more realistic conception of government, they tend to be apathetic toward the RA's current democracy. They tend not to be involved with or concerned about politics. After years of government lies and unreliability, many young people believe it is useless to care about politics, because things will remain the same. Officially, Armenia is a presidential democratic republic (NationMaster 2005). However, the unwritten Soviet motto "people for government" seems to have become "a government for itself and people for democratic process."

Although Armenia has more faith in the present government than their former Soviet government, they still distrust basic social programs and institutions. The Armenian Sociological Association, supported by the United States Agency of International Development, found that almost 70% of people think that authorities fail to pay attention to the problems of ordinary people (Pogosian 1999). Many people between the ages of 18 and 30 years old do not expect or anticipate fair treatment from social assistance programs (64%), hospitals (59%), police (60%), and law enforcement (61%). Only 0.5% of respondents believe that they can get help in their workplace. This pattern is documented by the proportion of youth who say they trust various societal institutions (with the percent saying yes in parentheses): church (35.5%), army (27.5%), local authorities (6.9%), justice institutions (3.7%), police (3.5%), trade unions (2.6%), newspapers (2.1%), political parties (1.6%), parliament (1.2%), and place of work (1.2%). The level of trust toward various institutions among young people is very low. Armenia was among the first of the former Soviet republics to secede and gain democracy. Any citizen over the age of 18 years has the right to vote, and their first democratic election was held in 1990 (Karatnycky et al. 2001). Current elections face some problems. For example, tens of thousands of citizens trying to vote in the 1999 Parliamentary elections were turned away because their names were not on the voter list (Karatnycky et al. 2001).

In spite of the atmosphere of distrust of government and voting problems, the young Armenian generation realizes that compared to Communist times, they have more freedom and liberty: 73.5% of respondents believe that people today have more freedom of liberal actions (freedom of speech, freedom of religion, freedom to join political groups). Adolescents use this freedom to discuss topics such as their views on homosexuality.

ANIE KALAYJIAN, SAMVEL JESHMARIDIAN, and ERICA SWENSON

The authors wish to thank Aram Jeshmaridian, Abigail Ortega, Jane Lipnisky, Fiorella Paradisi, Meline Karakashian, Karen Harutyunian, and Ray Paloutzian for their help with this chapter. This chapter is dedicated to the 160th anniversary of the Armenian alphabet.

References and Further Reading

Armenia: Epidemiological fact sheet on HIV/AIDS and sexually transmitted infections. 2002. UNAIDS/WHO Epidemiological Fact Sheet 2002 Update. Retrieved July 14, 2004, from http://www.childinfo.org/eddb/hiv_aids/factsheets/pdfs/Armenia_en.pdf.

Bagis, E. 2005. Turkish letter to U.S. legislators to stop Armenian Genocide Recognition. *Turkish Press*, July 17th.

CIA World Factbook. Armenia: Total fertility rate of all nations. Retrieved November 20, 2005 from http://globalis.gvu.unu.edu/indicator_detail.cfm?IndicatorID=138&Country=AM.

Dzeron, M. B. 1938/1984. *Village of Parchanj: General history (1600–1937)*. A. S. Avakian (trans.). Fresno, Calif. Panorama West Books.

Embassy of the United States. 2005. Yerevan, Armenia, Retrieved July 22, 2005, from Embassy of the United States, http://www.usa.am/doc/drugcontrol.html.

Fukuyama, F. 1995. *Trust: The social virtues and the creation of prosperity*. New York: Free Press.

Geneva Foundation for Medical Education and Research. 2005. Reproductive health in Armenia, 2005. http://www.gfmer.ch/Endo/Reprod_health/Reprod_Health_Eastern_Europe/armenia/Armenia_Martirosyan.html.

Ghukasyan, G. 2002. Integrating HIV/AIDS/STI education program in the school curriculum: Research proposal, Retrieved July 21, 2005, from International Policy Fellowships, http://www.policy.hu/ghukasyan/2002Proposal.html.

HyeEtch (Armenian History, Culture, Art, Religion & Genocide). 2005. "The Armenian family (a brief snapshot)," HyeEtch, http://www.hyeetch.nareg.com.au/armenians/family.html.

Jernazian, L., and A. Kalayjian. 2001. Armenia: Aftershocks. In *Beyond invisible walls: The psychological legacy of Soviet trauma*. New York: Brunner-Routledge.

Jeshmaridian, A. S., and S. S. Jeshmaridian. 2001. Post-Soviet trends in psychology or in search of a magic wand, in *Christianity and mental health*, S. Sukiasyan and S. Jeshmaridian (eds.). pp. 111–18. Yerevan, Armenia: Asoghik.

Jeshmaridian, A. S., A. S. Sargsian, and S. S. Jeshmaridian. 2001. The relations of generations in cross-cultural perspective. In *Contemporary issues in psychology*. Yerevan, Armenia: Yerevan State University, pp. 160–67.

Jeshmaridian, S. S. 1995. The Armenian family, In *The worldwide state of family*. G. L. Anderson (ed.). pp. 5, 18–19, 97. St. Paul, Minn.: A PWPA Book.

Jeshmaridian, S. S. 1997. The understanding of identity in Armenia, In *Identity and character: A worldwide survey*. G. L. Anderson (ed.). pp. 9–12. Washington, D.C.

Jeshmaridian, S. 1999a. National identity, society, and human rights: The perception of human rights in Armenia (in English and Armenia). In *Democracy Building in Armenia* (seminar proceedings), 22–25, 98–101, 156–57.

Jeshmaridian, S. 1999b. Youth and education in transition society of Armenia, In *The education in Armenia in transition period*. A. Avetisyan (ed.). pp. 89–97. Yerevan, Armenia: Yerevan State University.

Jeshmaridian, S. S. 2000a. The economy and society in Armenia, In *The global economy and society: A world survey*, St. Paul, Minn.: A PWPA Book.

Jeshmaridian, S. 2000b. *Armenia and peace*. Yerevan, Armenia: BECA.

Jeshmaridian, S. A. O. 2002. *September 11, 2001 tragic events' echoes in Armenia*. Singapore: ICAP.

Jeshmaridian, S. 2003. Social psychological dimensions of mental health situation in Armenia. *European Journal of Public Health* 11:71.

Jeshmaridian S. 2005. The consequences of democracy limitation in Armenia. In *Democracy Building in Armenia: New Challenges* (seminar proceedings). Yerevan, Armenia. pp. 30–37.

Jeshmaridian, S. S. and H. Takooshian. 1994. Country profile: Armenia. *Psychologist International* 5:8–9.

Kalayjian, A. S. 1995. *Disaster and mass trauma: Global perspectives on post disaster mental health management*. Long Branch, N.J.: Vista Publishing.

Kalayjian, A. 1999. Forgiveness and transcendence. *Clio's Psyche* 6:116–119.

Kalayjian, A. S. 2000. Coping through meaning: The community response to the earthquake in Armenia, in *When a community weeps: Case studies in group survivorship*, M. B. Williams and E. S. Zinner (eds.). New York: Taylor & Francis.

Kalayjian, A. 2002. Biopsychosocial and spiritual impact of trauma. In *Comprehensive handbook of psychotherapy*, Vol. 3, *interpersonal, humanistic existential approaches to Psychotherapy*, R. F. Massey and S. D. Massey (eds.). pp. 615–634. New York: Wiley & Sons.

Kalayjian, A., and S. P. Shahinian. 1998. Recollections of aged Armenian survivors of the Ottoman Turkish genocide: Resilience through endurance, coping, and life accomplishments. *Psychoanalytic Review*, 84:490–503.

Kalayjian, A. S., S. P. Shahinian, E. L. Gergerian, and L. Saraydarian. 1996. Coping with Ottoman Turkish genocide: An exploration of the experience of Armenian survivors. *Journal of Traumatic Stress* 9:87–97.

Karatnycky, A., A. Motyl, and A. Piano (eds.). 2001. Armenia. In *Nations in transit 1999–2000: Civil society, democracy, and markets in East Central Europe*. pp. 68–91. Freedom House.

NationMaster. 2005. "Armenia profile: Background." NationMaster. http://www.nationmaster.com/country/am/Background.

Pogosian, G. 1999. "Citizen participation survey: General public opinion survey report," United States Agency of International Development, Armenian Sociological Association. http://www.asa.am/surveys/part.pdf.

Research Machines. 2005. "Suicide," Helicon Publishing. http://www.tiscali.co.uk/reference/encyclopaedia/hutchinson/.

Rubenstein, R. L. 1983. *The age of triage: Fear and hope in an overcrowded world*. Boston, Mass.: Beacon Press.

State Commission of Statistics of Republic of Armenia (SCRSA). 2004. *Facts for education in Armenia*.

Takooshian, H., A. S. Kalayjian, and E. Melkonian. 1993. Life in the Soviet and post-Soviet era. In *International handbook on gender roles*. L. Alder (ed.). Greenwood Publishing Group, Inc.

The World Almanac and Book of Facts. 1992. New York, 730.

UNAIDS, UNICEF, World Health Organization. 2004. "Armenia: Epidemiological fact sheet on HIV/AIDS and sexually transmitted infections. UNAIDS/WHO Epidemiological Fact Sheet 2004 Update," UNICEF. http://www.childinfo.org/eddb/hiv_aids/factsheets/pdfs/Armenia_en.pdf.

UNFPA in the News. 2004. "Armenia: Government ready to introduce sex education in schools." http://www.unfpa.org/news/coverage/august21-10-2004.htm.

U.S. Census Bureau, International Data Base. 2005. Armenia population pyramid for 2005. Cited in NationMaster. 2005. "Armenia profile: Background." NationMaster, http://www.nationmaster.com/country/am/Background.

Woman Suffrage Timeline International—Winning the Vote Around the World. 2005. http://www.womenshistory.about.com/od/suffrage/a/intl_timeline.htm.

World Database of Happiness. 2004a. Rank report: Average happiness in 90 nations: 1990–2000. Cited in NationMaster. 2005. "Armenia profile: Background." NationMaster. http://www.nationmaster.com/country/am/Background.

World Database of Happiness. 2004. Rank report: Equality of happiness in 90 nations: 1990-2000. Cited in NationMaster. 2005. "Armenia Profile: Background," NationMaster, http://www.nationmaster.com/country/am/Background.

Worldfacts. 2005. "Fertility rate in Armenia 2000–2005." http://www.airninja.com/worldfacts/countries/Armenia/fertilityrate.htm.

Yip, G. S. 1995. *Total global strategy: Managing for worldwide competitive advantage*. Englewood Cliffs, N.J.: Prentice Hall.

AUSTRALIA

Background Information

Australia is a Western democratic industrialized country with a population of 20 million indigenous inhabitants that dates back at least 50,000 years; the population was increased by British colonists who arrived after 1788, when Sydney was established as a penal settlement. Since 1945, over six million people from 232 countries have come to Australia as new settlers (Thomas 2004). People born overseas make up almost one quarter of the total population. Although English is Australia's national language, due to cultural diversity, 200 languages are spoken in the community: Aboriginal and Torres Strait Islanders speak more than 60 languages. Around 88% of all people less than 25 years old speak English well or very well. Although the dominant culture is Anglo-Celtic and Christianity is the most widely reported religion (74%), the country cannot be described as a religious one. A keen interest and pursuit of sports is evident in the leisure activities of the community and in the sporting representations in international meetings, such as the Olympics.

In land area, Australia is the sixth largest nation after Russia, Canada, China, the United States, and Brazil. It is the largest island and the smallest and driest inhabited continent on earth. The bulk of the Australian land mass lies between the latitudes of $10°$ $41'$ south (Cape York, Queensland) and $43°$ $38'$ south (South East Cape, Tasmania) and between the longitudes of $113°$ $09'$ east (Steep Point, Western Australia) and $153°$ $38'$ east (Cape Byron, New South Wales). Australia comprises a land area of almost 7.7 million square kilometers. Australia includes six states (New South Wales, Victoria, Queensland, South Australia, Western Australia, and Tasmania) and two territories (the Northern Territory and the Australian Capital Territory).

Politically, Australia is a stable parliamentary democracy. Each state has its own governing body with particular areas of responsibility, and there is a federal parliamentary system, which is elected every three years. There are two major political parties who are elected to two houses of parliament. In addition to the two major parties, there are several minor parties that represent 11% of the electoral vote. Australia is one of only two countries that have a compulsory voting system from the age of 18 years. All Australian citizens over the age of 18 years must enroll to vote. About 15% of young people eligible to vote are not enrolled (Saha and Edwards 2004). It is compulsory by law to enroll, and it is also compulsory by law to attend a polling place at election time. National participation by eligible young electors in the 18- to 25-year-old age group is approximately 76% (Australian Electoral Commission 2005). A recent study found that a major disincentive for young people to participate in Australia's voting is the lack of trust in political leaders (Saha and Edwards 2004). The law that addresses compulsory voting works mainly by voluntary compliance rather than fear of the penalties. If a person does not vote and is unable to provide a "valid and sufficient" reason, a small penalty is imposed (e.g., $20 Australian dollars) (Australian Electoral Commission 2005). There is no compulsory military system in Australia.

Period of Adolescence

Adolescence is deemed to encompass both physiological and psychological changes. Psychological changes generally include a questioning of identity and movement toward personal independence. It is a time when peer-group relations gain importance. For many young people, it is also a period of rebellion against adult authority figures, often parents or school officials, in the search for personal identity. Both extensions in the social network and growing sexual maturation (see Section on Love and Sexuality) bring opportunities for growth and risk during adolescence (see Section on Health Risk Behavior).

As Wyn and White (1997) point out, adolescence as a transition to adulthood has meaning only if the specific circumstances of social, political, and economic circumstances are taken into account. Although the exact period of adolescence varies from person to person, in Australia, it is typically considered to fall between the ages of 12 and 20 years.

However, common practice in survey and census data is generally to use 15 years as a lower cutoff age for youth. Some researchers suggest that the range encompassing the period of adolescence has also expanded (Sercombe et al. 2002). A trend for Australian youth statistics is to now encompass those aged up to 24 years. This is consistent with trends in Western communities, where there is now a period of emerging adulthood that follows adolescence due to extended periods of study and consequent dependence on parents as well as the postponement of marriage to later years (Arnett 2004). In Australia, 97% of school students, 78% of full-time tertiary students aged 15 to 19 years, and 52% of tertiary students aged 20 to 24 live at home (ABS 2002).

Given that historical, geographical, and cultural contexts contribute to different meanings and life experiences of those categorized as adolescents, it is often difficult for researchers to make data comparable across these contexts. This struggle is also evident in Australia, particularly in relation to the indigenous population that has a younger age structure than that of the broader population. Aboriginal and Torres Strait Islander young people make up 26% of the total estimated indigenous population of 458,520 whereas the proportion of non-indigenous young people is approximately 18% (AIHW 2003). Moreover, in all states and territories (except the Northern Territory), indigenous young people constitute less than 6% of the total youth population. In the Northern Territory, more than a third of young people are indigenous Australians (AIHW 2003). To facilitate comparison between indigenous and other groups, the Australian Bureau of Statistics now employs age standardization techniques to data.

Beliefs

Many young Australians are highly socially conscious as a group, and their opinions about political and social issues tend to be more socially progressive than those of older age groups. For example, in two youth surveys, well over half of young people supported Republicanism, which is a system of government that has no hereditary monarch; they were opposed to the mandatory detention of asylum seekers; and they supported reconciliation or a treaty with indigenous Australians (Australian Democrats 2002; Beresford and Phillips 1997). The national youth survey (Mission Australia 2004) found that issues relating to alcohol and drugs (43.5%), bullying and emotional abuse (36.5%), and coping with stress (35.1%)

were the three most common concerns among young Australians between the ages of 11 and 24 years. An annual youth poll that contains the views of young people between the ages of 15 and 20 years (Australian Democrats 2002) identified issues relating to health, family, employment, education, environment, and relationships being the most important, with money, social justice, and racism the next most important areas of concern for young Australians. This is not too different from the hierarchy of concerns found in the 1980s and reported by Frydenberg and Lewis (1996a). Young people then were found to be concerned about getting on in the world, relationships, and social issues such as world poverty or the threat of nuclear war.

Although religious values in Australia are predominately Christian (68%), studies reveal that most young people have very little or no involvement in religion (78%) (Abbott-Chapman and Denholm 2001). Figures for church attendance indicate that active participation in religious life is lowest among young Australians between the ages of 15 and 30 years, with only 6% of parishioners aged between 15 and 19 years and a further 8% aged between 20 and 29 years (Bellamy and Kaldor 2001). The National Church Life Survey found that young people have a preference for less-traditional worship (Youth Monitor 2002).

In Australia, the number of adherents to the other main world religions of Buddhism, Hinduism, Islam, and Judaism is relatively small, representing just 4.9% of the total population. However, the proportion of 15- to 24-year-old adherents to Buddhism (43.7%) make up the largest group of all young people affiliated with one of the other four main world religions, followed by Islam (37.5%), Hinduism (11.6%), and Judaism (7.3%) (ABS 2001a).

Gender

For young Australians, the influence of gender varies in different aspects of their lives. Coping research is promising in its capacity to provide data to help understand what is happening in our communities with respect to gender-related adaptation. The notion of how boys and girls differ in their behavior has formed the basis of much psychoeducational research. In the Australian context, boys tend to focus more on sports, and girls tend to use more interpersonal support (Frydenberg and Lewis 1993). There is also evidence that, by the age of 18 years (in the final year of schooling), boys and girls use different coping strategies, with boys more successfully reducing both fear and anxiety (Byrne 2000). Longitudinal studies have shown that there are complex age and gender-related changes in coping across the adolescent years. For example, both boys and girls remain relatively stable in their declared inability to cope between the ages of 12 and 14. However, although boys report much the same low level during later years, girls report significantly higher levels of an inability to cope by the time they are 16 years old (Frydenberg and Lewis 2000).

The consistent patterns of gender differences in coping that have been reported by researchers may reflect the different adaptation patterns of boys and girls and the different issues with which they have to cope.

Gender differences seem to be particularly complex for indigenous Australians. The United Nations Committee on the Elimination of Discrimination Against Women has recognized this, expressing concern at the "continuing adverse situation of Aboriginal and Torres Strait Islander women," including a higher incidence of maternal mortality, a lower life expectancy, reduced access to the full range of health services, a high incidence of violence (including domestic violence), and high unemployment rates (United Nations 1997).

Young Australian males are more at risk of dying intentionally or by accident. Three-quarters of the young people 15 to 24 years old who die prematurely in Australia are males. Road traffic accidents are the leading contributor to their burden of disease and injury, followed by suicide and self-inflicted injuries. The national suicide rate for young people between the ages of 15 and 24 years is 20.3 per 100,000 for males as compared with 4.8 per 100,000 for females (ABS 2001b). Rates of suicide for young males are consistently higher in small country towns than they are in metropolitan areas, where some young people describe overwhelming loneliness (Bourke 2003).

Although young Australian females between the ages of 10 and 24 years account for 58% of hospitalizations after attempted suicide (ABS 2001b), in general, health risk behaviors for young females tend to cluster around sex and reproduction, particularly teenage pregnancy and sexually transmitted infections (see Section on Love and Sexuality).

Research over the last 20 years has revealed that most young women in Western societies want to be thinner (WHQW 2003). In Australia, the incidence of eating disorders is relatively low, estimated at between 1% and 3% of the population (CDHAC 2000). However, Australian research has found that more than 85% of girls between the ages of 14 and 16 years have been on a diet of some form,

whereas 7% have been found to be extreme dieters (Patton et al. 1997). Body dissatisfaction has been found to be a predictor of restrictive eating in Australian adolescent girls, and having been teased about weight predicts later increases in bulimic behaviors, such as binge eating (Wertheim et al. 2001). Although females make the vast majority of contacts to the national Kids Help Line (2004), body dissatisfaction and dieting are increasingly being recognized as concerns for young Australian males. For example, it has been found that some 27% of 12- to 15-year-old boys want to weigh less, and more than 60% of 14- to 16-year-old boys have engaged in some form of dieting (Nowak 1998; Patton et al. 1997). Nevertheless, the pressures for boys and girls remain somewhat different. This is demonstrated by a study comparing indigenous and nonindigenous young people with regard to issues relating to body image. Both the indigenous and the nonindigenous boys were found to perceive less pressure than girls to lose weight (Ricciardelli et al. 2004). However, the indigenous young people, overall, reported receiving fewer messages to lose weight than the nonindigenous young people.

In Australia, the recent focus on gender differences has been on education. There is now evidence to suggest that young Australian males are now performing more poorly than young Australian females. For example, in a study of the reading, mathematical, and scientific literacy skills of young people aged 15 years, Australian females were found, on average, to perform better in reading literacy than were males (ABS 2004b). On the whole, school retention rates are lower for young Australian males, and they are less likely to attend university. However, once in the workforce, young Australian males are more likely to earn a higher salary (ABS 2004b).

The Self

Adolescence is a crucial period for the development of self, which is described as being primarily a cognitive appraiser, an identity, a sense of knowing where one is going (Erikson 1968; Hattie 1992). During adolescence, self-concept becomes increasingly differentiated, with self-descriptions varying across different social roles or contexts. The increasing numbers of these categories of self-description have been documented in multidimensional measures of self. Marsh's (1990a) Self-Description Questionnaire II measures eleven specific areas of self-concept in adolescents between the ages of 13 and 17 years: (1) physical ability; (2) physical appearance;

(3) opposite-sex relationships; (4) same-sex relationships; (5) honesty/trustworthiness; (6) parent relationships; (7) emotional stability; (8) self-esteem; (9) verbal; (10) math; and (11) academic. Instruments based on the SDQs have been developed with a narrower focus. For example, the Academic Self-Description Questionnaire II (ASDQII) (Marsh 1990b) measures 14 school subjects (English, foreign languages, history, geography, commerce, computer studies, science, mathematics, physical education, health, music, art, industrial arts, religion) and school self-concept.

Drawing on Marsh's conceptualizations, Australian adolescent boys report consistently higher self-concepts than girls with regard to math, physical abilities, and physical appearance (Marsh 1989). Self-concept has been associated with a range of personal achievements and outlooks. In particular, self-concept of academic ability has been found to have an effect on engagement with school (Fullarton 2002) and to have an impact on academic performance (Marsh and Yeung 1997) and on tertiary school entrance performance scores among Australian adolescents (Marks et al. 2001).

Australian indigenous students tend to have lower self-concepts as compared with their non-indigenous peers. However, indigenous students score higher with regard to art and physical self-concepts as well as general and appearance self-concept as compared with non-indigenous students. Indigenous students' scores for academic self-concept (math, school, verbal), peer relations (opposite-sex and same-sex relations), honesty, and emotional self-concept are lower as compared with those of non-indigenous students (Craven and Marsh 2004).

At the individual level, identity formation involves the development of both personal identity and group identity. Cultural experiences are becoming increasingly important in identity formation as a large number of young people are exposed to cultures other than their own. In Australia, this is most likely to occur either through direct contact (e.g., migration, travel) or indirect contact (e.g., the media).

For many young Australians, backpacking overseas has become something of a rite of passage. Young Australians between the ages of 20 and 24 years account for 70.4% of all overseas travelers, with almost half returning within a year (ABS 2001c). For other young people, moving to major cities can provide opportunities for exploration as well as new experiences, including educational, employment, and social opportunities. Major cities in Australia have the highest percentage of young people between the ages of 15 and 24 years.

Between 1996 and 2001, the net migration of young people to major Australian cities was at a rate of 51.5 per 1,000 (Trewin 2003).

Identity is also achieved during later adolescence in terms of careers and career aspirations. However, in recent times, there has been a changing pattern of young people's expectations of achieving a lifelong career, because young people today are expected to have as many as five different careers during their adult lives (Wyn 2005).

Cultural identity has been defined as a process involving cognitive appraisal, which results from self-awareness achieved either through collective experience within a membership group or individual perception as a person compares him- or herself with a reference group (Germain 2004). This is particularly relevant to young people in Australia. Australia has one of the most culturally diverse populations in the world. It is one of only nine countries in the world that operates a dedicated offshore resettlement program.

Young people arriving to live in Australia make up 14.9% of all young Australians between the ages of 15 and 24 years (ABS 2001c). The largest groups of young people living in Australia who were born overseas come from countries in Southeast Asia (i.e., Singapore, Malaysia, and Indonesia), with the largest single group coming from Vietnam (5.6%). Hong Kong (4.9%) and China (4.5%) make up the two main groups in the Northeast Asia category. In the European category, the largest group of overseas-born youth are from the United Kingdom (10.4%), whereas young people born in New Zealand make up the largest group (11.8%) in the Oceania category (ABS 2001c).

Australia also allocates visas for refugees. Overall, there are an estimated 16,000 to 20,000 young people with refugee experience currently in Australia who arrived under Australia's Humanitarian Program. In 2000 and 2001, 59% of refugee young people entering under this program were between the ages of 12 and 25 years. A further 38% entered Australia as unauthorized arrivals and were granted temporary protection visas. Young asylum seekers made up 31% of all unauthorized arrivals, with around a fifth aged between 15 and 17 years. It is estimated that almost a third have experienced family persecution, whereas some 70% come from countries experiencing high levels of violence (Coventry et al. 2002).

In research on coping, there are consistent differences among ethnically different young people in the same community. In other words, both their identity and adaptation are different. For example, in one study of Australian adolescents,

European-Australian young people used more spiritual support than other young people (Frydenberg and Lewis 1993), and cultural variations are also supported by cross-cultural studies (Frydenberg et al. 2003).

Group identity is of particular importance among members of minority groups within a multicultural society (Phinney 1990). In a study by Germain (2004), which examined the issue of cultural identity among minority culture adolescents living in rural and remote regions of North Queensland, visible ethnicity was found to be a major factor in shaping cultural identification. In other words, young people who reported "looking" white were more likely to identify with the Anglo-Australian identity and to describe themselves as Australian. By contrast, young people who reported being visibly ethnic were likely to report biculturality rather than original culture identification.

Family Relationships

The family is regarded as an intricate arrangement of interconnecting relationships (Heaven 1994). In contrast with the myth that migrant groups do not merge, 75% of children of migrants in Australia marry people of different ethnic backgrounds, and 17% of marriages occur between people born overseas and people born in Australia (Penny and Khoo 1996). In Australia, a two-parent family continues to be the predominant family type; however, family relationships and experiences are becoming more diverse. There has been a decline in the number of couple families with children. In 2001, couple families with children accounted for 47% of all families, whereas single-parent families made up 15% (Australian Institute of Family Studies 2001). On the whole, family relationships are becoming more complex, with changing patterns of partnering and repartnering. Although a third of all marriages involve the remarriage of one or both partners, increasingly the repartnering of parents is involving cohabitation rather than remarriage. Partners are cohabiting in 44% of step-parent families and 26% of blended families. Polls also estimate that one in five same-sex couples in Australia have children (Wise 2003).

Although the divorce rate has been decreasing in Australia over the last 20 years, it is estimated that one in three marriages will end in divorce, with half of all divorces involving children. Based on this estimate, around 18% of young people will be affected by divorce by the time they are 18 years old (Wise 2003). Adolescents show marked individual differences when coping with their parents'

separation (Hetherington 2003). Some show resilience, whereas others show developmental delays (Hetherington 2003; Peris and Emery 2004). Long-term effects have been found to be more related to the young person's developmental status, sex and temperament, qualities of the home and parenting environment, and the resources and support systems available than to the divorce or separation per se (Farber et al. 1983; Rutter 1985).

When questioned, one in three young people are concerned about issues related to the family, whether the family is intact or separated. Family-related concerns of young people include fights with parents (27%) and happiness (20%). For young people in separated households, a major concern is the lack of access to the non-residential parent (30%). Interestingly, girls are almost twice as distressed as boys in both separated and intact families, or, alternatively, boys are more likely than girls to deny their concerns. For example, in intact families, it appears that fighting with parents was a more common concern for females (36%) than it was for males (20%). In separated families, girls professed more concern about their lack of access to the non-residential parent (35%) than did boys (22%) (Frydenberg and Lewis 1996b).

Central to the discussion of family relationships is the extent to which parenting practices influence adolescent development. There is evidence that suggests that parenting behaviors influence adolescents' emotional adjustment and behaviors. For example, parenting practices were found to indirectly affect engagement in risk behaviors (e.g., alcohol consumption) among Australian adolescents through attitudes, subjective norms, and perceived behavioral control (Williams and Hine 2002).

Others have found that parental qualities such as emotional support and the type of discipline style used are important influences on the psychological adjustment of adolescents. In their study of Australian high school students, Heaven, Newbury, and Mak (2004) found that it was the fathers' parenting style that was particularly important to the adjustment outcomes of adolescents. A physical parenting style increased the risk of delinquency among young males, whereas low warmth from fathers appeared to relate to depression, especially among young females. Studies across cultures in Australia have also highlighted the importance of parenting practices on youth outcomes. In a study of Vietnamese-Australian and Anglo-Australian adolescents, parenting characterized by high levels of overprotection and low levels of acceptance were found to predict low levels of self-esteem in both cultural groups (Herz and Gullone 1999).

Survey results suggest that family conflict is an important issue for 32% of Australian adolescents (Mission Australia 2004). Although many family units comprise harmonious relationships, some experience mild to severe levels of conflict. It was found that both the structure of the family and the relationship of members within the family determined the amount of time family members spent together (Fallon and Bowles 1997).

Conflict with parents, experience of abuse, parental incapacity, and substance abuse issues are among the complex reasons for youth homelessness in Australia. It is estimated that 40,000 young people experience homelessness each year in Australia (Rossiter et al. 2003). Domestic violence in Australian families also continues to be of great concern. It is reported that one in four adolescents in Australia have witnessed physical violence toward their mother. The experience of domestic violence is also reported to be significantly higher among indigenous Australian households than other sections of the community (Crime Research Centre 2001).

Conflict within families has been found to be a significant predictor of the use of tension-reduction strategies such as eating, drinking, smoking, or sleeping too much (Fallon and Bowles 2001; Frydenberg et al. 2000). By contrast, Australian adolescents who rated their families as high on cohesion reported making less use of emotion-related and nonproductive coping strategies. These young people were less likely to declare that they could not cope, to use self-blame, and to ignore their problems or concerns. At the same time, they were inclined to work hard and achieve and to make good use of physical recreation (Fallon and Bowles 2001; Frydenberg et al. 2000).

Families that are cohesive and that have warm, open lines of communication foster both individuation and connectedness in relationships and more positive outcomes among young people. For example, close, secure, and trustworthy relationships with parents contribute to adolescents evaluating their own attributes and worth more highly. Wilkinson (2004) found that quality parental attachment contributed to Australian adolescents' self-judgements; this in turn contributed to the psychological adjustment of the adolescent. More cohesive families are also important to the academic performance of young people. In particular, fathers' conscientiousness and milder parenting practices have both been found to predict self-rated academic performance among Australian adolescents. For boys, the effect of a warm parenting style from mothers is more prominent, whereas, for girls, higher levels of conscientiousness among mothers has been found to have a greater impact on self-rated academic performance (Heaven and Newbury 2004).

However, close, secure, and trustworthy relationships appear to decline with adolescent development. Almost three-quarters of young Australians between the ages of 11 and 14 years feel comfortable to seek support and advice from parents as compared with 68.8% of those 15 to 19 years old and 62.2% of those 20 to 24 years old (Mission Australia 2004).

Friends and Peers/Youth Culture

The notion of leisure is subjective and may differ widely among Australians; however, it is generally considered to be free time. This free time can be seen as the amount of time remaining after time spent on such things as personal care, family responsibilities, and work/education responsibilities.

In Australia, young people between the ages of 15 and 24 years have a greater amount of free time than Australians between the ages of 25 and 54 years. For those in school, their school day is generally 6.5 hours long, and those who are employed full-time work a 37-hour week. Although these are the formal working hours, there are many young people in high-powered positions, such as medicine, law, and commerce, who work 10 to 12 hours or more each day. On average, young males spend 10 hours and 12 minutes and females spend 10 hours and 6 minutes each day on all free-time activities (ABS 1997).

Regardless of age group, Australians prefer sedentary leisure pursuits such as talking, socializing, listening to the radio or compact discs, and reading. On an average day, young Australians between the ages of 15 and 24 years spend 70.1% of their passive leisure time watching TV (ABS 1997). Young people are also the highest proportion of computer users among all adult age groups (89%) (ABS 2000). Younger adolescents between the ages of 12 and 14 years are also most likely to engage in sedentary pursuits, such as watching TV or videos, using the Internet, or playing computer or electronic games (ABS 2001d). Nevertheless, 20% of those aged 12 to 14 years do participate in more active leisure pursuits, such as dancing, drama, singing, and playing a musical instrument, with girls twice as likely as boys to participate in these activities (ABS 2004a).

Australia is regarded as a sporting nation. A recent national youth survey (Mission Australia 2004) clearly indicates that the majority of young people (61.3%) are actively involved in sports, either as participants or spectators. Young males (68.8%) had higher rates of involvement than young females (55.4%). Research investigating the coping strategies of Australian adolescents confirms this gender difference and has highlighted the idea that "boys play sport and girls turn to each other" in a paper by that title (Frydenberg and Lewis 1993).

At the onset of adolescence, physical activity among females generally declines, and, by the age of 18 and 19 years, most young females undertake no regular physical activity except that required at school (Kimm et al. 2002). In Australia, school-aged boys most commonly participate in soccer, swimming, Australian rules football, and outdoor cricket, whereas girls most commonly participate in netball, swimming, tennis, and basketball. Equal numbers of boys and girls participate in athletics (ABS 2004a).

During adolescence, an increasing amount of time is spent with peers. Spending time with friends is a normal part of growing up and is considered by many to be an important developmental task of adolescence (Heaven 1994).

Although there is debate over the prevalence of youth gangs in Australia, informal groups of young people tend to come together mainly through shared interests and preferences in fashion and music (White et al. 2001).

There are numerous youth organizations within Australia that adolescents can access for recreational purposes (e.g., sports clubs, bands, choirs), travel and exchange (e.g., the Australia Youth Hostel Association), religious interests (e.g., the Tertiary Catholic Federation of Australia), or political pursuits (e.g., the Young National Party and the Young Liberal Movement) (United Nations 2002). The National Union of Students of Australia represents all Australian tertiary students and has more than forty affiliated campus student organizations (United Nations 2002).

Through the Internet, adolescents can also access a variety of youth services easily and anonymously. Web sites such as *Beyondblue, Reach Out!,* and *Kids Help Line* provide information and support for issues pertaining to youth employment, education, health, and drug abuse, among others. Further, adolescents can locate services within their communities through the Web sites' databases. For instance, there are more than 7,000 different services listed in the Kids Help Line database, which are searchable by postcode or keyword (Kids Help Line).

Music is very important to many young people in Australia, with a significant amount of their leisure time spent on music-related activities. Interests are varied and range from rock to rap and heavy metal to dance. Some 18% of young people in Australia name rock as their favorite type of music, followed by dance techno and trance (11%), pop (9%), heavy metal and thrash (8%), and alternative music (8%). Taste in music for most young Australians (85%) is influenced by friends. Eighty percent of young people have participated in music at some stage, and 35% participate in music on a regular basis, with playing a musical instrument the most frequently mentioned activity (Australian Broadcasting Authority 1999).

Love and Sexuality

The development of sexual identity and associated sexual behaviors have the potential to be powerful influences on well-being. In Australia, the age of consent for engaging in sexual intercourse is 16 years. Young females can be prescribed the contraceptive pill at age 16 without their parents' consent, and young people may purchase condoms at any age. In 2002, the Australian Research Centre in Sex, Health, and Society surveyed 2,388 Year 10 (ages 15 and 16 years) and Year 12 (ages 17 and 18 years) students about their levels of sexual activity (Smith et al. 2003). As reported in Table 1, most students said that they had experienced sexual activity, including kissing and sexual touching, and a smaller proportion had engaged in sexual intercourse. Most students surveyed reported being sexually attracted to the opposite sex. Some 4.6% of

Table 1. Sexual Activity Reported by Australian Adolescents Aged 15–18 Years

Sexual Experience	Percentage
Sexually active	66.9%
Intercourse	34.7%
Unwanted sex	25.9%
Contraception	
Always used condoms	52.1%
Thought other people always used condoms	64.9%
Perceptions	
Reported feeling "happy" after their last sexual encounter	50.1%
Felt confident saying no to unwanted sex	72.9%
Source of information about sex and contraception	
School program	63.1%
Mother	40.9%
Media	34.5%

Compiled using data from Smith et al. 2003.

males and 8.8% of females reported same-sex attraction.

As illustrated in Table 1, young Australians obtain their knowledge of sex and contraception from a number of different sources.

Young Australians are often reluctant to engage their parents in discussions about sex. However, although still rare, one study found that it was more common between mothers and daughters than between either parent and sons. Despite the lack of covert communication, sons were far more likely than daughters to perceive liberal parental attitudes toward sex (Moore and Rosenthal 1991).

Moore and colleagues (1986) investigated the assertion that parental communication and monitoring would discourage premarital sexual activity and revealed that this assertion was not so, with one exception. Parents who held traditional attitudes toward sex and who had communicated these beliefs to their daughters were the only group whose attitudes had influenced their children's sexual behavior. Daughters of these parents were less likely to have intercourse. However, in general, adult behavior has more influence on teenage sexual practice than adult talk (Moore and Rosenthal 1993).

Rosenthal and colleagues (1992) indicated that, in comparison to non-homeless 16-year-old youths, who had a maximum of five sexual partners, homeless 16-year-old boys reported an average of twelve and homeless 16-year-old girls an average of seven sexual partners during the preceding 6 months, with the maximum for both being one hundred partners.

For young women, research suggests that sexual relationships are interpreted as a quest for love rather than a consideration for personal safety. Explanations for being sexually active often provided by young women included the need to accommodate the male sex drive as part of the expectations of romance (Kirkman et al. 1998).

Like their American peers, Australian youth appear to be well informed about HIV/AIDS. Adolescents have shown reasonably high levels of knowledge about HIV transmission and AIDS, although there is uneven knowledge in some groups. For instance, ethnicity plays a part, with less knowledge found among non-English-speaking groups (Rosenthal et al. 1990). Not only do many feel invulnerable to the threat of AIDS, but also concerns about HIV infection rarely figure in their decision making about whether or not to have intercourse (Moore and Rosenthal 1991; Rosenthal et al. 1992). There are also a high proportion of young people who continue to take risks by not using condoms at all times. For example, in 1997,

only 37% of sexually active males in Year 12 were using condoms *sometimes,* and 9% *never* used them (AIHW 2003). In a study of condom use among young apprentices, a higher incidence of use was found when there was planning for the first occasion of intercourse (Grunseit 2004).

The adolescent fertility rate, which is defined as the annual number of live births per 1,000 females between the ages of 15 and 19 years, is estimated at 50 per 1,000 worldwide for the period from 2000 to 2005 (UNICEF 2005). A comparison of teenage birth rates among twenty-eight countries ranked the Australian birth rate as the eleventh highest, with a rate of 18.4 births per 1,000 females between the ages of 15 and 19 years. Korea had the lowest rate of teenage births, with a rate of 2.9 per 1,000 females, and the United States had the highest rate, with 52.1 births per 1,000 females (UNICEF 2001).

It is believed that the rate of teenage pregnancy in Australia is underestimated (AIHW 2003). In 2001, there were 246,393 births in Australia. Of these, 11,704 were live births to females aged 19 years old or younger, and 37,208 were live births to females between the ages of 20 and 24 years, which respectively accounted for 5% and 15% of all live births. Female indigenous Australians are more likely to have babies at a young age, with indigenous teenage females accounting for 23% of all births to Aboriginal and Torres Strait Islander women (AIHW 2003).

For young Australian women under the age of 20 years, induced abortions or "terminations of pregnancy" are among the highest in the Organisation for Economic Co-operation and Development countries (Skinner and Hickey 2003). In 2003 and 2004, some 5,891 abortions were performed for young females 24 years old or younger in the state of Victoria, Australia (Health Insurance Commission 2004). However, one study estimates that at least 15% of all induced abortions in the state of New South Wales were not recorded in Health Insurance Commission data (Adelson et al. 1995), and similar figures are likely in other states of Australia. In general, family planning organizations cater to sexual and reproductive health needs in Australia, with an average of 150,000 clients visiting family planning clinics and more than 85,000 attending community education programs each year (Sexual Health and Family Planning Australia 2002).

Health Risk Behavior

Obesity is considered to be a current health-related concern in the Australian context. It is linked to adolescent concerns about body image and a more general concern about the health risks associated with it. Obesity is estimated to cause 4% of the total burden of disease in Australia, with cardiovascular disease and diabetes being the major contributors (Mathers et al. 1999). During 1989 and 1990, the health costs of obesity and its resulting disease were estimated to be around $840 million in Australia (NHMRC 1997b). According to the 2001 Household Income and Labour Dynamics in Australia survey, approximately 8% of males and 11% of females between the ages of 15 and 17 years old were classified as overweight or obese using self-reported height and weight data. Of those between the ages of 18 and 24, 16% of males and 25% of females were classified as overweight or obese (AIHW 2004).

Population-based strategies to increase activity, decrease sedentary behavior, and improve dietary intake are being called for to decrease the prevalence of overweight and obesity in our youth and the subsequent development of type 2 diabetes (McMahon et al. 2004). A high proportion of young Australians between the ages of 12 and 24 years consume lower than the recommended daily amounts of five servings of vegetables (77%) and two servings of fruit (44%) as set by the National Health and Medical Research Council (2003).

Australia is among the top ten global markets for weekly fast-food consumption, with 30% of the population eating at take-away restaurants at least once a week (AC Nielsen 2004). An audit of junk-food advertising by the Australian Divisions of General Practice (2003) found that more than 99% of food advertisements broadcast during children's TV programming were for junk food. The main categories were, in descending order, fast food (hamburgers, 30%; pizza, 25%; and fried chicken, 7%); soft drinks (22%); ice cream (7%); chocolate confectionery (5%); and miscellaneous (4%).

It is illegal for young people under the age of 18 years to be sold alcohol or cigarettes; however, many young people find ways to obtain these substances and to engage in experimentation. A report prepared by the National Drug Research Institute and the Centre for Adolescent Health (2004) indicated that one in ten teenagers drink to harmful levels in Australia. According to the report, 72% of males between the ages of 14 and 17 years old drink alcohol, and 29% engage in high-risk behaviors, including drunk driving, at least once a month after binge drinking. About 74% of females between the ages of 14 and 17 drink alcohol, and 33% participate in risky behavior. The most common cause of death as a result of high-risk drinking is non-pedestrian road injury (i.e., the passenger or driver of a vehicle). Suicide is the second most common cause of death in this age group, particularly for females (Chikritzhs et al. 2004).

In a recent study of 983 Australian adolescents, young people who reported eating and drinking problems also reported a high negative and low positive sense of self-control coupled with self-identification. Problem drinking was mainly related to traits of negative masculinity (e.g., being bossy, noisy, aggressive), whereas binge eating was mainly related to negative femininity (e.g., being shy, needing approval) (Williams and Ricciardelli 2003).

Although alcohol and other drugs continue to be a concern for young Australians as compared with other age groups, young people are more likely to identify smoking as problematic and less likely to identify excessive alcohol consumption as a concern (Mission Australia 2004). Tobacco use usually starts during early adolescence, with a considerable proportion of young people between the ages of 15 and 17 years (14.5%) identifying themselves as occasional smokers (AIHW 2003).

Illicit drugs include cannabis, heroin, and cocaine, which are not legal to obtain. The most common illicit drug in Australia is cannabis. In a longitudinal study of 2,032 young Australians between the ages of 14 and 15 years, it was found that most cannabis use remained occasional during adolescence but escalated to potentially harmful daily use during the late school years. Cigarette smoking was an important predictor of both initial and persisting cannabis use (Coffey et al. 2000).

In another study, one in four adolescents between the ages of 13 and 17 years reported using cannabis. Young people in single-parent households as well as those young people who have conduct disorders or depression are more likely to be cannabis users (Rey et al. 2002). The most commonly reported reasons for trying illicit drugs were curiosity (69%), followed by a friend using or offering a drug (38%). Of those respondents who had not tried any illicit drugs, the most commonly reported reason for not trying was worry about health problems (39%), followed by not being interested (37%) (Premier's Drug Prevention Council 2004).

Juveniles between the ages of 10 and 16 years of age accounted for about one-quarter of the offender population. In 2001, the incarceration rate for male juveniles was almost eight times higher than that of female juveniles; however, a decline in the male overrepresentation has been recorded since 1995 (Australian Institute of Criminology 2002).

Patterns for risky behaviors come from a range of sources. Australian research with high school students (mean age, 15 years) and their biological parents reveals that there is link between depression and self-reported delinquency. Personality characteristics such as conscientiousness, agreeableness, extroversion, neuroticism, and psychoticism were the strongest predictors of the outcome measures, although fathers' personality and parenting styles (e.g., physical parenting) were also associated with adolescent adjustment. In particular, physical parenting by fathers increased the likelihood of delinquency for boys, whereas low fatherly warmth increased the likelihood of depression more markedly for girls than for boys (Heaven et al. 2004).

According to the Australian temperament project, which followed 2,443 infants through to young adulthood, rates of antisocial behavior were highest during mid adolescence and then declined with age. Males were involved in physical fights, property damage, driving offenses, computer-related antisocial acts, buying and selling stolen goods, selling illegal drugs, and carrying weapons. Females tended to report police contact for driving offenses and physical fights, shoplifting, buying or selling stolen goods, and damaging property (Prior et al. 2000).

Risk factors for adolescent antisocial behavior have also been found to include prior problem behavior (i.e., aggression and attention/restlessness problems at the age of 5 years) and marital instability, which doubled or tripled the odds of antisocial behavior in a longitudinal study of 8,000 women and children (Bor et al. 2004). Strong sibling resemblance, particularly for boys, has also been reported as predictive of adolescent delinquency (Fagan and Najman 2003).

One way of conceptualizing the daily hassles experienced by young people is according to where they primarily occur, namely the self (e.g., stammering, shape of nose); school, including peers (e.g., teasing by others, in canteen queues); and family (e.g., bedtime arguments, teasing by siblings) (Moulds 2003). Hassles such as these range from being moderately concerning to highly stressful. The experiences of stress and depression are closely linked.

There is a continuum of severity that can be considered as moving from sadness to depression to unendurable despair, which sometimes leads to suicide. Suicide is characterized by a total sense of despair and a feeling of extreme futility. Adolescent suicide is of concern in many communities. The incidence has grown through the 1970s and 1980s and was continuing to grow during the 1990s, but it has been considered to plateau during recent years. Although there is a gradation of severity for the diagnosis of depression and there are varying criteria used for establishing the prevalence, it is generally acknowledged that approximately one in five adolescents experience depression at some time. This is manifested in a range of behaviors that are generally associated with self-harm and risk.

Depression and anxiety are the most common mental health problems among young people. At any point in time, between 2% and 5% of young people will experience depression that is of sufficient severity to warrant treatment, and around 20% of young people will have experienced depression by the time they reach adulthood (NHMRC 1997a). Each month in Australia, 20,000 prescriptions for antidepressant drugs are issued to people who are less than 19 years old (Hickie 2004).

Self-harming behaviors among Australian adolescents are a growing concern. Some 12% of young people between the ages of 15 and 16 years reported a lifetime history of self-harm in a recent study of 3,757 Australian adolescents (De Leo and Heller 2004). Deliberate self-harm was more pronounced among young females than among young males; this is consistent with prior research that indicates that males are more likely to use more lethal means, such as a noose or a firearm, when attempting suicide (ABS 2001b). However, self-harm is not always a suicide attempt. More commonly, adolescents who engage in self-harming behavior feel isolated, and they perceive their futures to be bleak. For them, self-harming becomes a way of relieving extreme anxiety. It is an expression of inner psychological turmoil and a signal that adaptive coping strategies are not working (Kerbaj 2004).

The majority of young people do not seek help for health-related matters, and, when they do, it is from someone whom they know and trust (Booth et al. 2003). Adolescents that are most likely to reattempt suicide within the 12 months after their first attempt are those that have substance abuse problems, nonaffective psychotic disorders, chronic medical conditions, or a history of sexual abuse (Vajda and Steinbeck 1999).

In Australia, young, novice drivers represent only a minor proportion of the licensed driving population (e.g., 14% in Victoria in 2002), yet they are substantially more likely to be involved in fatal and injury accidents than older, more-experienced drivers. The differential between younger drivers and older drivers has remained, despite a 42% reduction in the road fatality rate across all ages in Australia over the last 20 years. There is clear evidence from accident statistics that young Australian drivers between the ages of 17 and 25 years have double the risk of all-age drivers for being involved in a fatal road accident (Injury Research Centre 2003). Hospitalization rates for road traffic accidents are higher among Australian females between the ages of 17 and 25 years than they are among males (Lam 2003; Attewell 1998). Research findings report that inexperienced Australian drivers show a greater tendency to take risks (i.e., speeding), whereas experienced drivers are more susceptible to perceptual distortion (Leung et al. 2003). Young drivers also tend to drive in conditions of greater risk (e.g., on weekends, at night, with peers in recreational circumstances) more often than experienced drivers (Lam 2003).

The single most-common traffic violation committed by young drivers is speeding, with young Australian males incurring their first speeding infringement substantially earlier than females. For 17- to 19-year-old adolescents, committing an "excessive" speeding offense significantly increases the risk of being involved in a road accident. Being male, having a high disposition for risk-taking, high self-rated confidence, and adventurousness as a driver are factors that significantly and consistently predict speeding among young Australian drivers (Injury Research Centre 2003). Fatigue is also a factor that doubles the risk of a road accident for all young drivers (Lam 2003).

Education

School education in Australia is compulsory between the ages of 6 and 15 years (16 years in Tasmania and recently South Australia, which equates to Year 10), and it can then be followed by two senior years of schooling (Years 11 and 12), which are necessary for those students wishing to proceed to higher education (Federal Department of Education 2001). Generally, schools in Australia have a considerable degree of autonomy. Regional administrations in most states and territories are responsible for matters such as planning school buildings and deploying staff. Typically, individual schools determine teaching and learning approaches within the given guidelines of a central curriculum unit and offer various course options.

Education is important for employment opportunities and future financial independence, and it affects the overall well-being of young people. Australian research suggests that, when adolescents have a high sense of efficacy to be self-regulated in their learning, they are likely to be more prosocial and popular than adolescents who believe that they lack these forms of academic efficacy (Purdie et al. 2004).

In May 2004, 84.5% of Australian teenagers 15 to 19 years old were in full-time study or full-time work, whereas 15.5% (214,800) were not. The proportion of teenagers not performing full-time study or full-time work has declined only slightly since the recession of the early 1990s, and it was higher in May 2004 than at any other time during the last six years (ABS 2004b).

Focusing on getting a job or an apprenticeship and earning some money are among the main reasons for school noncompletion in Australia. Negative experiences at school also figured among top reasons for noncompletion, with 18% of males and 24% of females reporting that they left Year 12 because they were doing poorly, they did not like school, or teachers advised them to leave (Marks and Fleming 1999).

Prospects of work and further education for early school leavers have changed very little in recent years, despite the improving economic conditions; 43% of early leavers and 19% of school completers are less likely to make a successful transition to full-time employment (Long 2004). The evidence suggests that obtaining suitable educational qualifications is an important element for assisting young people in the transition to full-time employment. However, female school leavers are more likely to experience a troubled transition from school than male school leavers, despite a higher rate of females completing Year 12 and a higher participation rate in post-secondary education (Long 2004).

The two main types of post-secondary education in Australia are vocational education and training and tertiary (higher) education. Young Australians identifying their family ethnicity as Asian, European, and Middle Eastern are more likely to attend university than young Australians from Anglo-Australian and English families. The odds are also higher for young women than young men (Majoribanks 2004). In a multicultural context in which there are minority students, the expectations of Asian girls in the Australian context to be smart, for example, has been identified as a concern (Mathews 2002).

There were 9,607 schools operating in Australia at the time of the 2003 schools census, of which 72% were government schools, 17.7% were Catholic schools, and 10.2% were independent schools (ABS 2004b). Most young people in Australia attend coeducational government schools. However, there has been widespread concern about whether coeducational settings are appropriate for girls (Cuttance 1995) and, more recently, for boys (West 2001).

The merits of single-sex versus coeducational school settings have been extensively debated, with concerns stemming from perceptions that coeducational schools are potentially risky environments. A 10-year longitudinal study of school settings in Australia found that coeducational environments create possible social/interaction disadvantages for girls but that their academic self-concept is not adversely affected by transferring from single-sex environments into mixed-sex ones (Jackson and Smith 2000).

However, there is evidence to suggest that young people from government schools and in rural areas are overrepresented among students who do not complete Year 12. Boys and those from a lower socioeconomic background are also less likely to complete school in Australia (Marks and Fleming 1999).

In Australia, there are national benchmarks for reading, writing, and mathematics for schooling in Years 3, 5, and 7. These benchmarks are nationally agreed minimum standards without which a student has difficulty with progressing at school. Since 2000, Australia has also participated in the Organisation for Economic Co-operation and Development's Programme for International Student Assessment (PISA), with 6,200 students from 2,000 schools being studied. In the most recent report, which assessed the skills of 15-year-old students in more than thirty countries with regard to reading literacy, mathematics, and science, Australia was among the highest-performing nations in all three areas, with only Finland outperforming in reading literacy and Japan in mathematics. In scientific literacy, Australian students were ranked third, behind Japan and Korea. Although, on average, Australian students performed well in the program, indigenous Australians performed poorly in all three areas of literacy, and boys as compared with girls achieved low results in reading literacy (AIHW 2003). Both are areas of concern for educational authorities.

In Australia, school bullying is a prominent issue on the agenda of educational authorities, with the incidence of bullying at a relatively high level by world standards. It is estimated that one in six school-aged young people are bullied on a weekly basis. Overall, boys report being bullied more frequently, especially in secondary schools (Rigby 1997). For most young people, bullying consists largely of offensive verbal behavior, with insults about one's social qualities and persona reported as common forms of attack (Lodge 2004). There is evidence from Australian studies that victimization has a significant impact on young people's ability to learn as well as their school attendance. About 20% of frequently victimized young people stay away from school and almost 50% consider this option to avoid continuous bullying from peers (Rigby 1998).

A recent focus of research has been on peers who are witness to bullying episodes at school. Through their behavior in these situations, peers can affect the outcome of the episodes. Peer bystanders can encourage and prolong the bullying by providing attention or actually joining in with the harassment (Craig and Pepler 1997). In a self-report Australian study of young adolescents between the ages of 10 and 13 years, peers expressed feelings of disgust and anger at witnessing the verbal harassment of others. Although they endorsed support for the victim, they were also inclined to "not get involved" (i.e., to passively watch) (Lodge and Frydenberg 2005).

Over the years, educational authorities in Australia have put in place policies and programs to tackle this problem. In 2003, the first national approach was formulated in the form of The National Safe Schools Framework, which represents a collaborative effort by the commonwealth, state, and territory governments and nongovernment school authorities to assist school communities with minimizing bullying, harassment, and violence.

Work

Over the last three decades, the trend in the youth labor market in Australia has seen a deferral of entry into full-time employment as young people increase their participation in education. However, between 1982 and 2002, the proportion of young people employed in part-time work has increased from 12% to 32% for 15- to 19-year-old adolescents and from 8% to 23% for 20- to 24-year-old individuals (AIHW 2003).

For many young Australians, combining school and work is common. Participation tends to peak during Year 11 and to decline slightly during Year 12 (ABS 2002). In a recent survey, a higher proportion of adolescent males (43.1%) than females (25.2%) valued getting a job (Mission Australia 2004). Although parents remain the main source of income for most young people, by the time young people have reached early adulthood, there is a fourfold increase in the proportion who are employed and a corresponding increase in those receiving a government allowance (Mission Australia 2004).

The pathways to full-time work vary between young Australian males and females and between school non-completers and completers. Undertaking an apprenticeship or a traineeship is a common pathway for male school non-completers (30%) as compared with young males who complete secondary schooling (16%). Postcompulsory pathways for training or study commonly incorporate participation in further education, such as the Institutes of Technical and Further Education and university. Young males (14.8%) are more likely than young females (9.1%) to start an apprenticeship or to commence studies at the Institutes of Technical and Further Education. Conversely, young females (20.9%) are more likely than young males (17.3%) to attend university (ABS 1998).

Between 1997 and 2002, the demand for postcompulsory schooling increased. In May 2002, 2.6 million people between the ages of 15 and 64 years applied to enroll in a course of study. Although participation in education may occur at any age, some 77% of young people between the ages of 15 and 19 years and 35% of young people between the ages of 20 and 24 years attend a tertiary (postsecondary) institution. During the first half of 2003, there were 371,263 young people enrolled in an undergraduate university course and 20,471 in a postgraduate program (AIHW 2003).

Occupations of young people vary considerably depending on their employment status (part-time or full-time) and their education and training. For young people between the ages of 15 and 19 years, most work in elementary clerical, sales, and service areas (41%), followed by laboring (18.4%). For 20- to 24-year-old individuals, there is a greater proportion working in intermediate clerical, sales, and service areas (23.8%). For those 25 years old and older, professional occupations account for 21.6% of the labor market (AIHW 2003).

In recent years, Australia has enjoyed relatively low unemployment rates (5% to 6%). However, the proportion of young people who are unemployed and not pursuing full-time education is consistently higher for those between the ages of 20 and 24 years than for those aged 15 to 19 years. Young people who are unemployed for the long term are the most disadvantaged in the Australian labor market. Although the figures fluctuate, between 1.5% and 4.7% of 20- to 24-year-old individuals are unemployed for more than 52 weeks (AIHW 2003).

Media

Computers and the Internet are increasingly becoming standard household equipment, with more than half of all Australian households (3.8 million) having at least one computer in their home (ABS 2003). Young people up to 17 years old are the most likely to use a computer at home (52% as compared with 44% for all age groups), whereas people between the ages of 18 and 34 years are the most likely to have accessed the Internet at home (38% as compared with 29% for people of all ages). Reasons for computer use vary with age. Young people, many of whom are studying, are most likely to use their computer for learning or study activities (63%). Young people between the ages of 18 and 24 years were also the most likely to have played computer games (55%) (ABS 2003). A recent Australia-wide telephone survey found that 84% of males and 60% of females between the ages of 16 and 17 years have accidentally been exposed to sex sites on the Internet. Perhaps more disturbing was the trend that nearly two in five young males had searched the Internet for sex sites (Flood and Hamilton 2003).

Mobile phones are also experiencing rapid growth in use by young people in Australia, particularly when used for short message service text messaging. The majority (83%) of Australian adolescents are mobile phone users, and the average age for owning a mobile phone is 13 years. Young people report making phone calls or sending text messages fewer than three times a day. The main reason given for mobile phone ownership was for reasons of safety and keeping in touch with their family. For a small number of young people, it was an important tool for promoting better friendships and inclusion in the peer group (Mathew 2004).

On average, young Australians buy six compact discs per year. The biggest influences on young people's taste in music are friends (85%), followed closely by radio (75%) and less so by TV (51%). Although compact discs remain a popular medium for music media among young Australians, radio remains the most common source of information about new or latest-release music. Young people spend much of their leisure time listening to music, watching TV, and using the computer and the Internet (Australian Broadcasting Authority 1999).

Politics and Military

A majority (60%) of young people between the ages of 18 and 24 years have a high level of interest in politics. The most trusted sources of political information for 687 young people in a recent survey were teachers (75%) and family (73%), whereas the least trustworthy were media (36%) and politicians (33%) (Mission Australia 2004).

In a survey of twenty-eight democratic countries, Year 9 (ages 15 and 16 years) Australian students were considered average with regard to their levels of "civic knowledge" (Mellor et al. 2001). Nevertheless, only half of Australian Year 9 students had a grasp of the essential preconditions for a properly working democracy. Only half of Australian students in that age group considered it important to participate in a peaceful protest against a law they believe to be unjust; this response was significantly below the international mean. In a state survey in Victoria, it was found that 84% of Victorian students 15 and 16 years of age rarely or never became involved in political activities such as writing letters or attending protests (Mellor 1998).

The youth vote in Australia, which is made up of voters between the ages of 18 and 24 years, accounts for 13% of the electorate: around 1.5 million voters. In recent federal elections, the major political parties have increasingly targeted young Australians. However, for many young Australians, allegiance to one party over their voting lifetime is unlikely. As one small-scale study revealed, young people want to exercise choice and swap between political parties (Beresford and Phillips 1997).

In 1999, in an effort to give young people the opportunity to speak directly with the government about issues that are important to them, the Australian government established the National Youth Roundtable. The Roundtable brings together fifty young people between the ages of 15 and 24 to meet with the government to discuss issues that affect their generation. Roundtable members undertake a series of consultations with their peers across Australia to develop a comprehensive picture of the views and attitudes of young people, which are then reported back to the government. For example, in 2004, the Youth Roundtable investigated topics related to communities, cultural diversity, environment/rural matters, health, leadership and enterprise development, and youth participation in society.

In a study investigating civic responsibility among 500 adolescents, it was found that one in five adolescents engaged in behaviors reflecting community and civic responsibility and that less than one in ten participated in the political arena. However, positive levels of social awareness among young people were identified (Silva et al. 2004). Flanagen and colleagues (1999) found that 19% of the Australian population who were more than 16 years old undertook some type of volunteer work; they also found that Australian adolescents found politics to be the least important of civic activities.

These findings are somewhat different from students' interest in politics (Rosenthal et al. 1998). Adolescents were more likely to volunteer if they had higher cognitive abilities. Group-related empathy and sympathy were strongly related to altruism and civic commitment (Prior et al. 2000).

When it comes to political participation or representation, young people are able to hold office. For example, a 26-year-old female is a South Australian representative in the national parliament, and, at the local government level, a 23-year-old woman became Australia's youngest female mayor on March 17, 2004, representing 124,000 residents in the City of Greater Dandenong, a suburb of Melbourne, which is the major city in the state of Victoria.

Unique Issues

The issue of reconciliation, which is often represented as an expectation of a formal apology by the government of the day for wrongs done in the past to indigenous young people, appeared to be foremost in indigenous young people's minds as a concern. For example, 98.5% of indigenous Australians identified Aboriginal reconciliation as "very important" or "important" in a survey conducted in 2003. This was followed by equal level of concern for education (97.1%), family relations (94.1%), crime and personal safety (86.8%), and youth suicide (83.6%) (Manning and Ryan 2004).

It is clear that, despite the recent gains in legal rights, land rights, self-government, and access to services, many Aboriginal communities face issues that are unique to indigenous Australians. Domestic violence, child abuse, child neglect, substance abuse, and youth suicide are among these issues. Of particular concern are the disproportionately high rates of suicide among young indigenous Australians. The limited statistics available suggest that the indigenous youth suicide rate overall is about 1.4 times that of nonindigenous young people. Suicides by indigenous Australians are much more likely to be by hanging (for males, 67% of indigenous cases, 31% of nonindigenous cases) and much less likely to be by poisoning, including poisoning by motor vehicle exhaust gas (Steenkamp and Harrison 2000).

The rate of detention among indigenous juveniles in Australia was 256.7 per 100,000, whereas the rate for nonindigenous juveniles was 13.6 per 100,000. This means that, as of June 2002, indigenous juveniles were approximately 19 times more likely to be detained in Australian detention facilities than nonindigenous juveniles. However, there are some promising signs: since 1994, the indigenous juvenile detention rate has decreased by 35%, whereas the nonindigenous rate has remained stable (Bareja and Charlton 2003).

Deaths in custody among indigenous Australians has been a matter of public concern. Between 1990 and 1999, two thirds (67%) of the deaths of indigenous people in Australia that occurred during police operations involved young people under the age of 20 years. Death during police operations refers to a death that occurs during the process of police or prison officers attempting to detain a person. Fourteen percent of indigenous deaths in custody, prison, or other place of detention during that period were of young people under the age of 20 (Williams 2001). Although suicide is the most common form of death in these cases, there is no clear understanding of why this occurs so frequently. There are suggestions that a sense of shame, hopelessness, and, now, of a cultural phenomenon play a part.

Young indigenous Australians are at a three times greater risk for disengagement from learning and work than nonindigenous young people. In 2001, a high proportion (45%) of indigenous young people between the ages of 15 and 19 years were not participating in full-time learning or work. This figure rose to 70% (52% unemployed or not in labor force) in the 20- to 24-year-old age group. It is estimated that up to 45% of indigenous young people between the ages of 15 and 24 years are likely to receive government income support (Curtain 2003).

Educational attainment levels of Aboriginal and Torres Strait Islander young people are substantially lower than those of other Australian young people. For young males, 29% of Aboriginal and Torres Strait Islanders were still in school at age 19 or had completed Year 12 as compared with 68% of other Australian males. For females, 38% of Aboriginal and Torres Strait Islander females were still at school at age 19 or had completed year 12 as compared with 78% of other Australian females (AIHW 2003). Overall, educational participation, educational attainment, and mean literacy and numeracy scores are lower for indigenous Australians than for other Australian young people (AIHW 2003). However, there are hopeful signs that the retention rates for indigenous secondary students during the postcompulsory years of schooling are steadily rising. For example, overall Year 12 retention rates for indigenous students increased from 29.2% in 1996 to 38% in 2002 (ABS 2004b).

ERICA FRYDENBERG and JODIE LODGE

References and Further Reading

Abbott-Chapman, J., and C. Denholm. 2001. Adolescents' risk activities, risk hierarchies and influences of religiosity. *Journal of Youth Studies* 4:279–97.
Australian Bureau of Statistics (ABS). 1997. *National health survey: Summary of results.* ABS Cat. No. 4364.0. Canberra: ABS.
ABS. 1998. *Australian social trends.* Canberra: ABS.
ABS. 2000. *Household use of information technology.* ABS Cat. No. 8146. Canberra: ABS.
ABS. 2001a. *Australian social trends.* Canberra: ABS.
ABS. 2001b. *National health survey.* Canberra: ABS.
ABS. 2001c. *Migration.* Canberra: ABS.
ABS. 2001d. *Children's participation in cultural and leisure activities.* Cat. No. 4901. Canberra: ABS.
ABS. 2002. *Australian social trends.* Canberra: ABS.
ABS. 2004a. *Year book Australia 2004.* Cat. No. 1301.0. Canberra: ABS.
ABS. 2004b. *Schools.* Canberra: ABS.
A. C. Nielsen. 2004. *Consumers in Asia Pacific—our fast food/take away. Consumer report, 2nd half.* A. C. Nielsen Australia.
Australian Government Department of Education, Science and Training (AGDEST). 2003. *National safe schools framework.* Commonwealth of Australia.
Australian Institute of Health and Welfare (AIHW). 2004. *Australia's health 2004.* Cat. No. 44. Canberra: AIHW.
AIHW. (2003). *Australia's young people: Their health and wellbeing 2003.* Cat. No. PHE 50. Canberra: AIHW.
Arnett, J. J. 2004. *Emerging adulthood: The winding road from the late teens through the twenties.* New York: Oxford University Press.
Attewell, R. 1998. *A statistical overview of road crash involvement.* Women Behind the Wheel Series, CR 178, Federal Office of Road Safety.
Australian Broadcasting Authority. 1999. *Head banging or dancing? Youth and music in Australia.* Monograph No. 8, Pt. 2. Australian Broadcasting Authority. http://www.aba.gov.au/radio/research/projects/head.htm.
Australian Democrats. 2002. *Youth poll. Australian Democrats press release.* Australian Democrats. http://www.democrats.org.au.
Australian Divisions of General Practice (ADGP). 2003. *What are we feeding our children? A junk food advertising audit.* ACT: ADGP.
Australian Electoral Commission. 2005. *Information centre.* Australian Electoral Commission. http://www.aec.gov.au.
Australian Institute of Criminology (AIC). 2002. *Australian crime: Facts and figures 2002.* Canberra: AIC.
Australian Institute of Family Studies. 2001. *Family Matters.* 60(Spring/Summer):16
Bareja, M., and K. Charlton. 2003. *Statistics on juvenile detention in Australia: 1981–2002.* Technical and Background Paper Series, no. 5. Canberra: Australian Institute of Criminology.
Barrett, P. M., R. Sonderegger, and N. L. Sonderegger. 2002. Assessment of child and adolescent migrants to Australia: A crosscultural comparison. *Behaviour Change* 19:220–35.
Bellamy, J., and P. Kaldor. 2001. *National church life survey initial impressions.* Adelaide: Openbook Publishers.
Beresford, Q., and H. Phillips. 1997. Spectators in Australian politics? Young voters' interest in politics and political issues. *Youth Studies Australia* 16:11–16.

Booth, M. L., D. Bernard, S. Quine, et al. 2003. Access to health care among Australian adolescents: Young people's perspectives and their sociodemographic distribution. *Journal of Adolescent Health* 34:97–103.

Bor, W., T. R. McGee, and A. A. Fagan. 2004. Early risk behaviors for adolescent antisocial behavior: An Australian longitudinal study. *Australian and New Zealand Journal of Psychiatry* 38:365–72.

Bourke, L. 2002. How can you deal with that? Coping strategies among young residents of a rural community in New South Wales. *Journal of Family Studies* 8:197–212.

Bourke, L. 2003. Toward understanding youth suicide in an Australian rural community. *Social Science & Medicine* 57:2355–65.

Byrne, B. 2000. Relationships between anxiety, fear, self-esteem, and coping strategies in adolescence. *Adolescence* 35:201.

Catanzaro, S. J., and J. Laurent. 2004. Perceived family support, negative mood regulation expectancies, coping, and adolescent alcohol use: Evidence of mediation and moderation effects. *Addictive Behaviors* 29:1779–97.

Centers for Disease Control and Prevention (CDC), National Center for Chronic Disease Prevention and Health Promotion. 1999. *Adolescents and young adults fact sheet.* CDC, http://www.cdc.gov/nccdphp/sgr/adoles.htm.

Chikritzhs, T., R. Pascal, and P. Jones. 2004. *Under-aged drinking among 14-17 year olds and related harms in Australia.* Bulletin 7, National Drug Research Institute. Curtin University, WA.

Coffey, C., M. Lynskey, R. Wolfe, and G. C. Patton. 2000. Initiation and progression of cannabis use in a population-based Australian adolescent longitudinal study. *Addiction* 95:1679–90.

Commonwealth Department of Health and Aged Care (CDHAC). 2000. *What is an eating disorder?* No. 2616. Canberra: CDHAC, Mental Health and Special Programs Branch.

Coventry, L., C. Guerra, D. Mackenzie, and S. Pinkney. 2002. *Wealth of all nations. Identification of strategies to assist refugee young people into transition and independence.* National Youth Affairs Research Scheme. Hobart: Australian Clearinghouse for Youth Studies.

Craig W. M., and D. J. Pepler. 1997. Observations of bullying and victimization in the school yard. *Canadian Journal of School Psychology* 13:41–59.

Craven, R. G., and H. W. Marsh. 2004. The challenge for counsellors: Understanding and addressing indigenous secondary students' aspirations, self-concepts and barriers to achieving their aspirations. *Australian Journal of Guidance and Counselling* 14:34–47.

Crime Research Centre. 2001. *Young people and domestic violence: National research on young people's attitude and experiences of domestic violence.* Perth: University of Western Australia and Donovan Research.

Curtain, R. 2003. *How young people are faring: Key indicators 2003.* Sydney: Dusseldorp Skills Forum.

Cuttance, P. 1995. Educational outcomes for girls: A review of NSW government secondary schools. *Unicorn* 21:28–38.

De Leo, D., and T. S. Heller. 2004. Who are the kids who self-harm? An Australian self-report school survey. *Medical Journal of Australia* 181:140–4.

Erikson, E. H. 1968. *Identity: Youth and crisis.* Oxford, England: Norton & Co.

Fagan, A. A., and J. M. Najman. 2003. Sibling influences on adolescent delinquent behaviour: An Australian longitudinal study. *Journal of Adolescence* 26:546–58.

Fallon, B. J., and T. V. Bowles. 1997. The effect of family structure and family functioning on adolescents' perceptions of intimate time spent with parents, siblings, and peers. *Journal of Youth and Adolescence* 26:25–43.

Fallon, B. J., and T. V. Bowles. 2001. Family functioning and adolescent help-seeking behavior. *Family Relations* 50:239–45.

Farber, S. S., J. Primavera, and R. D. Felner. 1983. Older adolescents and parental divorce: Adjustment problems and mediators of coping. *Journal of Divorce* 7:59–75.

Federal Department of Education. 2001. *The development of education: National report of Australia.* Training and Youth Affairs and the South Australia Department of Education, Training and Employment. Adult Learning Australia, Inc.

Flanagan, C., B. Jonsson, L. Botcheva, et al. 1999. Adolescents and the 'social contract': Developmental roots of citizenship in seven countries. In *Roots of civic identity: International perspectives on community service and activism in youth.* M. Yates and J. Youniss (eds.). pp. 135–55. New York: Cambridge University Press.

Flood, M., and C. Hamilton. 2003. Youth and pornography in Australia: Evidence on the extent of exposure and likely effects. Discussion Paper Number 52, February 2003. The Australia Institute.

Frydenberg, E., and R. Lewis. 1993. Boys play sport and girls turn to others: Age, gender and ethnicity as determinants of coping. *Journal of Adolescence* 16:253–66.

Frydenberg, E., and R. Lewis. 1996a. Measuring the concerns of Australian adolescents: Developing a concise classificatory system. *Australian Educational Research* 23:47–64.

Frydenberg, E., and R. Lewis. 1996b. The coping strategies used by adolescents in intact and separated families. *Australian Journal of Guidance Counselling* 6:87–99.

Frydenberg, E., and R. Lewis. 2000. Coping with stresses and concerns during adolescence: A longitudinal study. *American Educational Research Journal* 37:727–45.

Frydenberg, E., L. Lade, and C. Poole. 2000. Do adolescents adopt their parents coping style? Health perspectives. *Research Policy & Practice* 1:25–30

Frydenberg, E., R. Lewis, G. Kennedy, et al. 2003. Coping with concerns: An exploratory comparison of Australian, Colombian, German and Palestinian adolescents. *Journal of Youth and Adolescence* 32:59–66.

Fullarton, S. 2002. Student engagement with school: Individual and school-level influences. *Longitudinal Surveys of Australian Youth (LSAY) Research Report, 27.* Camberwell, Victoria: ACER.

Germain, E. R. 2004. Culture or race? Phenotype and cultural identity development in minority Australian adolescents. *Australian Psychologist* 39:134–42.

Grunseit, A. C. 2004. Precautionary tales: Condom and contraceptive use among young Australian apprentices. *Culture, Health and Sexuality* 6:517–35.

Hattie, J. 1992. *Self-concept.* Hillsdale, NJ, and England: Lawrence Erlbaum Associates, Inc.

Health Insurance Commission. 2004. Medicare-funded abortion in Victoria by age group, 2003–2004. *The Age* 30/08/04, p. 5.

Healy, K. 2001. *Choices and pathways for young women who are pregnant and parenting: Supporting health relationships, education and training.* Canberra: Commonwealth of Australia.

Heaven, P. C. L. 1994. *Contemporary adolescence: A social psychological approach.* Melbourne: MacMillian Education Australia Pty Ltd.

Heaven, P. C. L., and K. Newbury. 2004. Relationships between adolescent and parental characteristics and adolescents' attitudes to school and self-rated academic performance. *Australian Journal of Psychology* 56:173–80.

Heaven, P. C. L., K. Newbury, and A. Mak. 2004. The impact of adolescent and parental characteristics on adolescent levels of delinquency and depression. *Personality and Individual Differences* 36:173–85.

Herz, L., and E. Gullone. 1999. The relationship between self-esteem and parenting style: A cross-cultural comparison of Australian and Vietnamese Australian adolescents. *Journal of Cross Cultural Psychology* 30:742–61.

Hetherington, E. M. 2003. Social support and the adjustment of children in divorced and remarried families. *Childhood: A Global Journal of Child Research* 10:217–36.

Hickie, I. 2004. Beyondblue. *The Age,* Apr. 10, 1

Injury Research Centre, University of Western Australia. 2003. *A longitudinal investigation of psychosocial risk factors for speeding offences among young motor car drivers.* Criminology Research Council, Griffith, ACT.

Jackson, C., and I. D. Smith. 2000. Poles apart? An exploration of single-sex and mixed-sex educational environments in Australia and England. *Educational Studies* 26:409–22.

Kerbaj, R. 2004. Deepest cuts, self-inflicted. *The Australian,* Aug. 21, C4.

Kids Help Line. 2004. *State reports.* Kids Help Line. http://www.kidshelp.com.au.

Kids Help Line. n.d. *Get help.* Kids Help Line. http://www.kidshelp.com.au.

Kimm S. Y., N. W. Glynn, A. M. Kriska, et al. 2002. Decline in physical activity in black girls and white girls during adolescence. *New England Journal of Medicine* 347:709–15.

Kirkman, M., D. Rosenthal, and A. M. A. Smith. 1998. Adolescent sex and the romantic narrative: Why some young heterosexuals use condoms to prevent pregnancy but not disease. *Psychology, Health and Medicine* 3:355–70.

Lam, L. T. 2003. Factors associated with young drivers' car crash injury: Comparisons among learner, provisional and full licensees. *Accident: Analysis and Prevention* 35:913–20.

Leung, S., S. Godley, and G. Starmer. 2003. *Gap acceptance and risk-taking by young and mature drivers, both sober and under the influence of alcohol, in a simulated driving task. A report prepared for the motor accidents authority of New South Wales.* Sydney: University of Sydney.

Lodge, J. 2004. Coping with school bullying among young Australian adolescents. Paper presented at the 25th Stress and Anxiety Research Society conference. Amsterdam, Netherlands.

Lodge, J., and E. Frydenberg. 2005. The role of peer bystanders in school bullying: Positive steps towards promoting peaceful schools. *Theory Into Practice* 44:329–36.

Long, M. 2004. *How young people are faring: Key indicators 2004: An update about the learning and work situation of young Australians.* Dusseldorp Skills Forum.

Majoribanks, K. 2004. Environmental and individual influences on Australian young adults' likelihood of attending university: A follow-up study. *Journal of Genetic Psychology* 165:134–9.

Manning, B., and R. Ryan. 2004. *Youth and citizenship: A report for NYARS.* Canberra: National Youth Affairs Research Scheme.

Marks, G., and N. Fleming. 1999. *Early school leaving in Australia: Findings from the 1995 Year 9 LSAY cohort. Longitudinal Surveys of Australian Youth (LSAY). Research Report 11.* Camberwell, Victoria: ACER.

Marks, G., J. McMillan, and K. Hillman. 2001. *Tertiary entrance performance: The role of student background and school factors. Longitudinal surveys of Australian youth (LSAY). Research Report 22.* Camberwell, Victoria: ACER.

Marsh, H. W. 1990a. *Self-description questionnaire II: Manual.* Sydney: University of Western Sydney.

Marsh, H. W. 1990b. The structure of academic self-concept: The Marsh/Shavelson model. *Journal of Educational Psychology* 82:623–36.

Marsh, H. W., and A. S. Yeung. 1997. Causal effects of academic self-concept on academic achievement: Structural equation models of longitudinal data. *Journal of Educational Psychology* 89:41–54.

Mathers, C., T. Vos, and C. Stevenson. 1999. *The burden of disease and injury in Australia.* Cat. No. PHE17. Australian Institute of Health and Welfare. Canberra: AIHW.

Mathews, R. 2004. Psychosocial impact of mobile phone use amongst adolescents. *Inpsych APS Bulletin* 26:16–19.

Matthews, J. 2002. Racialised schooling, ethnic success and Asian-Australian students. *British Journal of Sociology of Education* 23:193–207.

McMahon, S. K., A. Haynes, N. Ratnam, et al. 2004. Increase in type 2 diabetes in children and adolescents in Western Australia. *Medical Journal of Australia* 180:459–61.

Mellor, S. 1998. *What's the point? Political attitudes of Year 11 students.* Melbourne: Australian Council for Educational Research.

Mellor, S., K. Kennedy, and L. Greenwood. 2001. *Citizenship and democracy: Students' knowledge and beliefs—Australian fourteen year olds and the IEA Civic Education Study.* Canberra: Department of Education, Science and Training.

Mission Australia. 2004. *National youth survey. Media release.* Mission Australia. http://www.mission.com.au.

Moore, K., J. Peterson, and F. Furstenberg Jr. 1986. Parental attitudes and the occurrence of early sexual activity. *Journal of Marriage and the Family* 48:777–82.

Moore, S., and D. A. Rosenthal. 1991. Adolescents' perceptions of friends' and parents' attitudes to sex and sexual risk-taking. *Journal of Community and Applied Social Psychology* 1:189–200.

Moore, S., and D. A. Rosenthal. 1993. *Sexuality in adolescence.* London: Routledge.

Moore, S., and D. A. Rosenthal. 1996. Young people assess their risk of sexual transmissible diseases. *Psychology and Health* 11:345–55.

Moulds, J. D. 2003. Stress manifestation in high school students: An Australian sample. *Psychology in the Schools* 40:391–402.

National Health and Medical Research Council (NHMRC). 1997a. *Depression in young people: Clinical practice guidelines.* Canberra: Australian Government Publishing Service.

NHMRC. 1997b. *Acting on Australia's weight. The Report of the NHMRC.* Working Party on the prevention of overweight and obesity. Canberra: NHMRC.

NHMRC. 2003. *Dietary guidelines for children and adolescents in Australia: Incorporating the infant feeding guidelines for health workers.* Canberra: NHMRC.

Nowak, M. 1998. The weight-conscious adolescent. *Journal of Adolescent Health* 23:389–98.

Ollendick, T. H., B. Yang, N. King, and Q. Dong. 1996. Fears in American, Australian, Chinese, and Nigerian children and adolescents: A cross-cultural study. *Journal of Child Psychology and Psychiatry, and Allied Disciplines* 37:213–20.

Organisation for Economic Co-operation and Development. 2005. *Programme for International Student Assessment home page.* http://www.pisa.oecd.org.

Patton, G. C., J. B. Carlin, Q. Shao, et al. 1997. Adolescent dieting: Healthy weight control or borderline eating disorder? *Journal of Child Psychology and Psychiatry, and Allied Disciplines* 38:299–306.

Penny, J., and S. E. Khoo. 1996. *Intermarriage: A study of migration and integration in Australia.* Canberra: Bureau of Immigration.

Peris, T. S., and R. E. Emery. 2004. A prospective study of the consequences of marital disruption for adolescents: Predisruption family dynamics and postdisruption adolescent adjustment. *Journal of Clinical Child and Adolescent Psychology* 33:694–704.

Phinney, J. S. 1990. Ethnic identity in adolescents and adults: Review of research. *Psychological Bulletin* 108:499–514.

Premier's Drug Prevention Council. 2004. *Annual Report 2003–2004.* Melbourne, Victoria: Rural and Regional Health and Aged Care Services Division, Victorian Government Department of Human Services.

Prior, M., A. Sanson, D. Smart, and F. Oberklaid. 2000. *Pathways from infancy to adolescence: Australian temperament project 1983–2000.* Melbourne: Australian Institute of Family Studies.

Purdie, N., A. Carroll, and L. Roche. 2004. Parenting and adolescent self-regulation. *Journal of Adolescence* 27:663–76.

Rey, J. M., M. G. Sawyer, B. Raphael, G. C. Patton, and M. Lynskey. 2002. Mental health of teenagers who use cannabis. *British Journal of Psychiatry* 180:216–21.

Ricciardelli, L. A., M. P. McCabe, K. Ball, and D. Mellor. 2004. Sociocultural influences on body image concerns and body change strategies among indigenous and non-indigenous Australian adolescent girls and boys. *Sex Roles* 51:731–41.

Rigby, K. 1997. What children tell us about bullying in schools. *Children Australia* 22:28–34.

Rigby, K. 1998. The relationship between reported health and involvement in bully/victim problems among male and female secondary school students. *Journal of Health Psychology* 3:465–76.

Rosenthal, D. A., C. Hall, and S. Moore. 1992. AIDS, adolescents, and sexual risk taking: A test of the Health Belief Model. *Australian Psychologist* 27:166–71.

Rosenthal, D. A., S. Moore, and I. Brumen. 1990. Ethnic group differences in adolescents' responses to AIDS. *Australian Journal of Social Issues* 25:220–39.

Rosenthal, S., C. Feiring, and M. Lewis. 1998. Political volunteering from late adolescence to young adulthood: Patterns and predictors. *Journal of Social Issues* 54:477–93.

Rossiter, B., S. Mallett, P. Myers, and D. Rosenthal. 2003. *Living well? Homeless young people in Melbourne.* Melbourne: Australian Research Centre in Sex, Health and Society, La Trobe University.

Saha, L., and K. Edwards. 2004. *Youth electoral study—Report 1: Enrollment and voting.* Australian Electoral Commission. http://www.aec.gov.au.

Sercombe, H., P. Omaji, N. Drew, T. Cooper, and T. Love. 2002. *Youth and the future: Effective youth services for the year 2015: A report to the National Youth Affairs Research Scheme.* Hobart: Australian Clearinghouse for Youth Studies.

Sexual Health and Family Planning Australia. 2002. *Who do family planning organisations service in the Australian community? Fact Sheet 2.* Sexual Health and Family Planning Australia. http://www.fpa.net.au.

Silva, L., A. Sanson, D. Smart, and J. Toumbourou. 2004. Civic responsibility among Australian adolescents: Testing two competing models. *Journal of Community Psychology* 32:229–55.

Skinner, R., and M. Hickey. 2003. Current priorities for adolescent sexual and reproductive health in Australia. *Medical Journal of Australia* 179:158–61.

Smith, A., P. Agius, S. Dyson, A. Mitchell, and M. Pitts. 2002. *Secondary students and sexual health 2002.* Melbourne: Australian Research Centre in Sex, Health and Society, La Trobe University.

Smith, A., C. Russel, J. Richters, A. Grulich, and R. De Visser. 2003. Australian study of health and relationships. *Australian and New Zealand Journal of Public Health* 27:138–46.

Steenkamp, M., and J. Harrison. 2000. Suicide and hospitalised self-harm in Australia. AIHW Cat. No. INJCAT 30. Canberra: Australian Institute of Health and Welfare.

Thomas, T. 2004. Psychology in a culturally diverse society. *Australian Psychologist* 39:103–6.

Trewin, D. 2003. *Australian social trends 2003.* Cat. No. 4102. Canberra: Australian Bureau of Statistics.

UNICEF. 2001. *A league table of teenage births in rich nations.* Innocenti Report Card, 3. http://www.unicef-icdc.org/publications/indexFullCat.html.

UNICEF. 2005. *Fertility and family planning report.* UNICEF. http://www.unicef.org/specialsession/about/sgreport-pdf.

United Nations. 1997. *UN committee on the elimination of discrimination against women. Concluding comment: Australia.* United Nations. http://www.un.org.

United Nations. 2002. *Australia: National youth and student coordinating bodies.* United Nations. http://www.esa.un.org.

Vajda, J., and K. Steinbeck. 2000. Factors associated with repeat suicide attempts among adolescents. *Australian and New Zealand Journal of Psychiatry* 34:437–45.

Wertheim, E. H., J. Koerner, and S. Paxton. 2001. Longitudinal predictors of restrictive eating and bulimic tendencies in three different age groups of adolescent girls. *Journal of Youth and Adolescence* 30:69–81.

West, P. 2001. *Report on best practice in boy's education.* Sydney: University of Western Sydney.

White, R., S. Perrone, C. Guerra, and R. Lampugnani. 2001. Ethnic youth gangs in Australia: Do they exist?

Paper presented at the Policing Partnerships in a Multicultural Australia: Achievements and Challenges Conference convened by the Australian Institute of Criminology in conjunction with The National Police Ethnic Advisory Bureau and The Australian Multicultural Foundation. Brisbane.

Wilkinson, R. B. 2004. The role of parental and peer attachment in the psychological health and self-esteem of adolescents. *Journal of Youth and Adolescence* 33:479–93.

Williams, P. 2001. *Deaths in custody: 10 years on from the Royal Commission*. Canberra: Australian Institute of Criminology.

Williams, P. S., and D. W. Hine. 2002. Parental behaviour and alcohol misuse among adolescents: A path analysis of mediating influences. *Australian Journal of Psychology* 54:17–24.

Williams, R. J., and L. A. Ricciardelli. 2003. Negative perceptions about self-control and identification with gender-role stereotypes related to binge eating, problem drinking, and to co-morbidity among adolescents. *Journal of Adolescent Health* 32:66–72.

Wise, S. 2003. *Family structure, child outcomes and environmental mediators: an overview of the development in diverse families study. Research Paper No. 30*. Melbourne: Australian Institute of Family Studies.

Women's Health Queensland Wide (WHQW). 2003. *Health information fact sheet*. WHQW. http://www.womhealth.org.au/index.html.

Wyn, J. 2005. *Occasional address, faculty of education*. Melbourne: The University of Melbourne.

Wyn, J., and R. White. 1997. *Rethinking youth*. New South Wales, Australia: Allen & Unwin.

Youth Monitor. 2002. *Youth Studies Australia* 21:9.

AUSTRIA

Background Information

Austria is a small country in Central Europe with slightly more than 8 million inhabitants. Geographically, it is characterized by the Alps in the west and south and the mostly flat or gently sloping area along the Danube in the north and around the Neusiedler Lake in the east (CIA 2005).

As in most European countries, the proportion of adolescents in the population is declining (Spannring 2003). Twelve percent of the Austrian population were between 10 and 19 years old in 2001, 17% were in this age group in 1981, and 15% were in 1961 (Statistik Austria 2005). The population consists mainly of Austrians (91%; CIA 2005), but also of people from the former Yugoslavia (4%), Turkey (2%), Germany (1%), and other countries (2%). The official language is German, but the languages of three minority groups are also official in Carinthia (Slovenes) and Burgenland (Croatians, Hungarians).

Economically, the country is relatively prosperous and stable: the per capita gross domestic product is higher than the European Union (EU) average (Statistik Austria 2005). The general public debt is high, but it is similar to that of other European countries. Inflation is near the EU average, and unemployment rates are somewhat below the EU average (Beham-Rabanser et al. 2004).

The political system changed significantly during the twentieth century. In 1918, when the Habsburg Empire collapsed, the democratic federal republic of Austria was established. From 1938 to 1945, Austria was part of the Nazi empire, and it was occupied by the Allied forces after the war until 1955, when it became a republic again and political neutrality was declared. In 1995, Austria entered the European Union (CIA 2005).

Period of Adolescence

Austrian law distinguishes between children (up to 7 years), non-legally liable minors (7 to 14 years), and legally liable minors (14 to 19 years). The main legal changes during adolescence are listed in Table 1. The age limits diverge through the nine regions of Austria, but they are similar to the one described here. Legally, children and adolescents up to age 19 have the right of maintenance from their parents. This right can be prolonged until the age of 27 years if the young adults are studying or are not able to support themselves (Spannring 2003). During childhood, adolescence, and education (until the age 27 maximum), the Austrian republic pays family allowances to families with children to meet the maintenance costs (Richter and Kytir 2005).

When asking the young people themselves if they consider themselves to be adolescents, young adults, or adults, 90% of those in the 14- to 15-year-old age group call themselves adolescents. In a more recent study by Adamek, Mayr, and Dreher (2005), only 22% of the teenagers (mean age, 16.9 years) thought that they were not adult in any way, 58% said that they were adult in some ways, and 20% regarded themselves as fully adult.

Because children enter puberty earlier today than they did some decades ago (e.g. first menstruation at the age of 11 years [Perner et al. 2004]), they come to be regarded as adolescents earlier than before. Alternatively, they do not take over full adult roles and responsibilities until their mid twenties (e.g., marriage, first child [Pfeiffer and Nowak 2001]). Perhaps it is for these reasons that only 44% of 25-year-old individuals regard themselves as adults (Nemetz et al. 2003), with many young adults feeling not or only partly adult (65%; Adamek et al. 2005).

The transitions to adolescence and adulthood are no longer marked by cultural rites. Confirmation is a religious rite of transition to adulthood among Catholics, in which many adolescents take part. In addition, in some rural areas, there are different traditional rites (e.g., in some villages, the youth is responsible for erecting a tree on the main square on May 1), but they are not widely practiced in Austria.

As was described in the United States by Arnett (2000), the transition to adulthood was prolonged during the last decades in Austria, too, resulting in what has been termed *emerging adulthood*. For example, there was a shift in the age of founding one's own family: adolescents still start to work and leave home at a similar age than some decades ago, but marriage and first childbirth are now taking place later (Pfeiffer and Nowak 2001).

Table 1. Legal Status During Childhood and Adolescence in Austria

Age	Legal Status	Rights/Responsibilities
0–7 years	Children	
7–14 years	Non-legally liable minors	
14–19 years	Legally liable minors ("youth")	Allowed to enter contracts, to some extent
		Responsible for one's own actions by youth criminal law
		14 years: Allowed to have heterosexual sex
		15 years: Allowed to work full-time
		16 years: Allowed to smoke, drink, visit pubs, and obtain driving licenses for small motor bikes
		17 years: Allowed to obtain driving licenses for cars
		18 years: Allowed to have homosexual sex, vote, and marry
19+ years	Adults	Allowed to enter contracts
		Responsible for one's own actions by criminal law
		35 years: Eligible for presidential elections

Beliefs

Like most middle European countries, Austria tends toward individualistic values. When Austrian adolescents are asked to define what makes one an adult, many individualistic criteria are chosen (Mayr et al. 2005). Friesl (2001) reports that adolescents also act in individualistic ways: they assume responsibility for themselves and do not think that society or the government will assist them. Despite these individualistic attitudes, the family is still very important to as many adolescents (69%; Friesl 2001) as it was 10 years before.

Values are most often transmitted within the family; for example, gender roles are adopted as gender practices are experienced in the family (Friesl 2001). During the last 10 years, the importance of family (67% to 69%) and of work and spare time (59% to 61%) was constantly high for adolescents. Constantly low were their interests in politics (4% to 7%) and religion (6% to 8%). The importance of friends increased from 54% to 73% (Friesl 2001).

Roman Catholicism is the majority religion in Austria (74%). Minor religious beliefs are Protestant (5%) and Muslim (4%). Twelve percent profess no religion (CIA 2005), and there has been an upward trend in this category in recent years. The participation in religious confessions is also declining for adolescents, as it is in the whole Austrian population. Nevertheless, 83% are members of a religion, but only 50% really believe in God, and most adolescents are not practicing their religion (e.g., only 9% attend mass weekly [Friesl 2001]). Religious values are transmitted in school, where all children and adolescents are taught their own religion as long as they do not sign themselves off.

The presence of cults in Austria is quite low, because most members of the population belong to the major religions. Nevertheless, about one third of adolescents are interested in esoteric beliefs and occultism (Rollett and Felinger 2004). Most young people do not actively take part in such practices on a regular base, but two-thirds have tried them at least once.

Gender

Since the 1960s, there has been a trend toward gender equality (Perner et al. 2004). Women and men are getting more and more equal by law, but, in many areas, equality has not yet taken over in real life: the caretaking of children, possibilities and wages in the labor market, and the running of the household are just some examples in which gender differences are still apparent. Adolescents' attitudes towards gender equality are very positive: most want to share the responsibilities in the household for both childrearing and other family issues (Friesl 2001). However, when asked about specific household routines, most adolescents think that the man should be responsible for repairs, whereas the woman should do the ironing and take parental leave after the birth of a child. Also, most adolescents—females to an even greater extent than males—think that men do a better job than women.

Friesl (2001) thinks that parents' gender practices are transmitted to adolescents. Heineck (2004) explains these attitudes toward more traditional gender roles as being transmitted by religion, because they are similar in the Italian population.

Since 1920, both Austrian men and Austrian women have been allowed to attend university (Pfeiffer and Nowak 2001), but they tend to choose different subjects to study as they attend different secondary schools (BMSG 2005). Looking at the jobs that require vocational training, girls, in contrast with boys, choose those that are seen as traditional female ones: retail saleswomen (25%), office clerks (14%), and hairdressers (13%). Three out of four girls in vocational training are educated in one of the top ten jobs; for boys, this percentage is only 49%. Boys are most often trained for being a motor mechanic (9%), a plumber (7%), or a joiner (6%).

Many girls try to attain extreme slimness (Nemetz et al. 2003), which is still seen as the physical ideal in Austria. About 13% of girls do not like their bodies, and this increases to 16% for young women. On the boys' side, 12% do not like their bodies, and this percentage also increases with young adulthood. In contrast with girls' behavior with regard to their body image, only a minority of boys spend much time with styling and beauty, and for only 32% is their body image of importance. However, 59% take an interest in their clothes, and 57% participate in sports.

The percentage of girls that believe they need to diet (age 11 years, 36%; age 13 years, 49%; age 15 years, 53%) or that are on a diet (1 out of 5; Nemetz et al. 2003) is increasing with age and is a lot higher than the percentage in boys (age 11 years, 29%; age 13 years, 30%; age 15 years, 18%; percentage on a diet, 9%). This is a quite high percentage compared with other countries according to a World Health Organization study by Currie and colleagues (2000).

The Self

Because Austrian society offers the possibility of choosing differing—even inconsistent—values, the period of adolescence is often used for "value sampling": values are chosen, changed, and combined in new ways according to a specific situation. It is important to adolescents to be authentic and original (Nemetz et al. 2003).

In 1956, after the Allies left Austria, 47% of the Austrian population did not believe that Austria was a nation of its own right. In 2005, 76% thought that there was an Austrian identity, whereas 16% felt the country was in a developing phase. The end of monarchy, the repression by the Nazis, and the pervasive idea that Austria was merely a miniature replica of Germany made it difficult for Austria to develop a national identity of its own right (Der Standard 12.5.2005). The generation of the new republic, which adolescents are born into today, did not experience these historical difficulties. However, only 59% of 15- to 18-year-old adolescents feel like Austria is a nation of its own right. Patriotism and national consciousness are only

important for 21% of this age group, whereas 40% of 24- to 29-year-old individuals regard patriotism as being important. This could be due to changes in generations, or due to the fact that national identity is not developed during adolescence but rather later during emerging adulthood.

Xenophobia is not a big problem among Austrian adolescents, but right-wing extremists are rejected by two-thirds of them with an increasing tendency (by 35% in 1990; Friesl 2001). Young people in Austria are also quite tolerant toward foreigners (89%; Friesl 2001). However, there are some negative attitudes toward guest workers and their families, who are expected by most of the population to assimilate (Spannring 2003).

Apart from meeting friends, it is important for Austrian adolescents to relax (42% to 44%) or to listen to music (72% to 73%; Nemetz et al. 2003).

Family Relationships

Eight out of ten girls and two out of three boys regard their families as important parts of their lives (Nemetz et al. 2003).

In 1991, 24% of children were only children; this was up from 17% being only children in 1971. During the 1970s, it was quite common to have three or more siblings in families that lived out of the cities; now, however, the two-child family dominates in both the rural and urban areas of Austria (Spannring 2003). It can also be said that the number of one-parent families is increasing: 15% of the population younger than 15 years of age live with a single parent only, and 93% of this group live with the mother (Richter and Kytir 2005).

In Austria, family life is restricted to the nuclear family (parents and their children). Other relatives are seen only occasionally, depending on vicinity and relationship quality, but they are not generally important for adolescents. Nevertheless, the relationship between grandchildren and their grandparents is described as quite good by the adolescents (Richter and Kytir 2005).

Generally, education in an Austrian family is marked by tolerance and cooperation by children and their parents. Parents want to raise their children to be responsible, independent, tolerant, and well-behaved (Richter and Kytir 2005). In the adolescents' view, only 50% report their parents to be very liberal (meaning that they are very open but also authoritative; Nemetz et al. 2003). Ten percent to 15% report that their parents use a "laissez-faire" style, and 40% see their parents as not liberal. Most adolescents report that their opinions are important in their families; only three out of ten think that they are not taken seriously by their parents (Nemetz et al. 2003). Fewer conflicts with parents are reported than there were some decades earlier, as parents now tend to be more open.

Fifteen percent of adolescent girls and 25% of adolescent boys were beaten by their own parents. As compared with the 25% of young women and the 32% of young men who were beaten, the percentage in the adolescent group is low, which could mean that parents are getting away from corporal punishment (Nemetz et al. 2003).

Adolescents experience their siblings in a positive way: for having fun, emotional support, quarreling, or help during difficult situations, siblings are regarded as important (Nemetz et al. 2003).

Divorce rates increase with the age of the children: only two-thirds of the adolescents are living with both biological parents. The parents' divorce took place during toddlerhood for 10% of the adolescents, during childhood for another 10%, and during adolescence for the last 10% (Nemetz et al. 2003). Many of the divorced parents remarry, which results in step- and patchwork families for about 6% of the Austrian population (Richter and Kytir 2005).

In Austria, as in several other countries, women leave their parents' homes earlier than men do (average age of 20.2 years versus 22.5 years, respectively; Pfeiffer and Nowak 2001). About 23% of men have still not moved out by the end of their twenties (Richter and Kytir 2005), and some later return to their parents' home due to financial problems or separation.

Friends and Peers/Youth Culture

Seventy-two percent of Austrian adolescents find their friends to be a very important part of their lives, and 25% find them to be an important part (Nemetz et al. 2003). Most Austrian adolescents have about four to five closer friends; however, these bonds are not too strong, and there are no cliques.

For Austrians (as it can be said for other countries, too), the family loses importance during puberty: only 10% of the 14- to 19-year-old boys and 19% of the girls in this age group talk with their parents about their problems, whereas 23% and 42%, respectively, talk with their friends. They are also spending more spare time with their friends (58% and 61%, respectively) than with their parents (9% and 4%, respectively; Nemetz et al. 2003). However, this is true only for everyday problems. When they are confronted with severe problems, they tend towards asking their parents for "trouble shooting" instead of their friends.

Most adolescents are part of loose groups of friends, and only 34% are part of bigger peer crowds (mean size, 13 persons). Important commonalities of these peer crowds are having fun together and liking each other (83% each), common interests in music (65%), common meeting points (50%), vicinity (53%), and common lifestyles (40%). Clubs, common values or political interests, and Internet communities are not important for the building of peer crowds (Nemetz et al. 2003).

Youth organizations lessened in attraction during the last decades (Beham-Rabanser et al. 2004): at the beginning of the 1990s, two out of three children and adolescents (9 to 17 years) took part in a youth organization, whereas currently only 28% are in such an organization. Boys, through sports activities, and adolescents in rural areas are more likely to spend their spare time in a youth organization.

More common than being part of youth organizations is being part of a youth culture: about 75% of young people are part of at least one youth scene (Grossegger et al. 2001), and boys are again more likely than girls to do so. These scenes are characterized by special clothes, special music, and common leisure activities. In many scenes, there are male and female members, but the most popular scenes for boys and girls differ: boys most often regard themselves as soccer fans (40%), computer-game players (28%), computer freaks (23%), and fans of a particular band (23%), whereas girls are most often animal-welfare supporters (26%), fans of particular bands (21%), inline skaters (18%), and snowboarders (14%).

Love and Sexuality

Ninety-one percent of Austrian 14-year-old adolescents have already had a date (Perner et al. 2004), and 89% have received their first kiss (average age, 13 years). At age 14, on average, the first romantic relationship is started, with 72% already having a steady partner (mean duration, 11 months). Petting was practiced by 62% of the 15-year-old adolescents.

By law, women are allowed to marry at age 16 and men at age 19 (Perner et al. 2004). The actual age of marriage has increased during the last decades, being later for men (28.5 years) than for women (26.4 years) (Pfeiffer and Nowak 2001; Richter and Kytir 2005). There can be noted a trend toward unmarried cohabitation (about 20% of 25- to 30-year-old individuals; Nemetz et al. 2003).

Friesl (2001) explains this delay as being a result of changes in values: it is important for adolescents to have a partner, but they do not want to have children or marry early in their life course. The values seen as important for a relationship are fidelity (81%), tolerance (85%), and sexuality (67%). Children (27%; 1990, 49%) and financial situation (21%) are not viewed as important for a relationship any more.

The partner is chosen most frequently during education rather than in discos, cafés, or youth groups, which are losing importance generally (Richter and Kytir 2005). The new facilities on the Internet are used for pairing up only by older adults (30 to 40 years), but they may be used for fun and experimentation by younger adults and adolescents. Most women are searching for a partner with a similar or higher education level as themselves, but many marry below their educational level (due to higher participation rates of women in tertiary education).

Women and men are legally seen as sexually mature by the age of 14, but men are not allowed to take part in homosexual intercourse until age 18 (Perner et al. 2004). The first sexual experiences of most children are autoerotic: masturbation was practiced by 60% of 13-year-old and 100% of 16-year-old boys but only by 25% of 13-year-old and 50% of 17-year-old girls. The first sexual intercourse takes place at age 15.5 years, on average. Most adolescents (40%) have a steady partner when they have sexual intercourse frequently.

Weidinger and colleagues (2001) studied the use of contraception at the first sexual intercourse. Nearly all adolescents in Austria know condoms and birth-control pills are possibilities for contraception. Alternatively, four out of five adolescents do not know when a girl can get pregnant. Because the usage of contraception is quite high and Austrian adolescents are not very sexually promiscuous, sexually transmitted diseases are not a problem.

The birth of the first child in Austrian families takes place later than it did a few decades ago, but it is still earlier for women (24.0 years) than for men (28.4 years; Pfeiffer and Nowak 2001). The fertility rate is only 1.5 children per woman (Perner et al. 2004); Richter and Kytir (2005) report even lower rates. The amount of teenage births (age, under 20 years) is 3.28%, which is much lower than the rate seen, for example, in the United States (UNICEF 2001). However, about one-third of these Austrian teenage mothers are unemployed, and another third has a low income. Only a low percentage (12%) of these women are without partners.

In Austria, sex education is an interdisciplinary (e.g., biology, religion) principle of instruction in school, but it is not often taught to the extent needed (Perner et al. 2005). There are more informal sources of sex education that are often used, such as magazines like *Bravo* and radio shows. According to Weidinger and colleagues (2001), the main sources of adolescents' knowledge about sexuality and contraception are friends; teachers and parents are not regarded as important.

Health Risk Behavior

The World Health Organization studied the health status and behavior of 11- to 15-year-old adolescents in a cross-national study (Currie et al. 2000). Austrian adolescents generally report very positive feelings in their lives (92.8%) and that they feel healthy. Nevertheless, symptoms like headache (girls, 23%; boys, 16% to 19%), stomachache (girls, 17% to 18%; boys, 6% to 10%), and backache (girls, 9% to 22%; boys, 7% to 19%; increasing with age) are reported by some adolescents. Also, the use of medication is moderately high, ranging from 10% for nervousness to 30% for headache.

Many Austrian adolescents (70% to 86%) are exercising 2 hours a week or more, which makes them top in the World Health Organization study (Currie et al. 2000). This high rate may be because there are sports in school, which are taught about 2 to 3 hours per week.

In Austria, a fairly high rate of adolescents have already tried smoking cigarettes and drinking alcohol: 14% of 13-year-old girls and 26% of 13-year-old boys have already smoked, and 52% of girls and 63% of boys in this age group had drunk alcohol at least once (Currie et al. 2000). Alcohol and cigarettes are often regarded as transition markers (Nemetz et al. 2003): those who drank alcohol or smoked a cigarette regarded themselves not as a child anymore but rather as an adolescent. When looking at the 15-year-old adolescents, the rate of having tried cigarettes increased to 75% for girls and 69% for boys; nearly all of them had tried alcohol (96% of girls and 94% of boys), and slightly less than half of them (36% of girls and 49% of boys) had been drunk at least once (Currie et al. 2000), which supports the argument of Nemetz and colleagues that these behaviors mark the transition to adolescence.

The problem of juvenile delinquency is less important in Austria than in other countries (e.g. Germany, Netherlands; Tebbich 2000). However, there can be noted an increase in official offenses during the last decades. However the actual number cannot be derived from the number of trials for delinquency, because, in Austria, there is the possibility of compensation for delinquent acts without trial (e.g., community service). Criminal prevention is part of youth social work, but there is also individual prevention provided for adolescents of high risk.

The death rates among Austrian adolescents are on international average in the 15- to 24-year old age group, 29.4 females and 116.3 males per 100,000 adolescents die every year (Kolip and Schmidt 1999). Important causes of death are traffic accidents (girls, 10; boys, 47.3), malignant neoplasm (girls, 3.4; boys, 4.8) and suicide (girls, 3.5; boys, 25.8). One-quarter of the 15-year-old adolescents reports a severe injury during the last year, about half of them as a result of sports.

The percentage of adolescents feeling depressed is very low as compared with other countries (girls, 10% to 15%; boys, 5% to 6%) (Currie et al. 2000).

In Austria, the most widely used addictive drug among adolescents is tobacco. The rate of 15-year-old adolescents smoking weekly is ranked second highest in the World Health Organization's cross-cultural comparison (36% of girls, 30% of boys; Currie et al. 2000). Although, legally, smoking is not allowed until the age of 16 years, it is quite common among Austrian adolescents.

Education

In 1774, Marie Therese introduced six years of compulsory education for all Austrian children. Today, every Austrian child has to attend school from age 6 to age 15. Therefore, literacy rates are quite high (98%; CIA 1995).

The attitudes toward school in Austria are quite positive (Organisation for Economic Co-operation and Development 2004), but they decrease with age (Currie et al. 2000). Adolescents generally perceive only low achievement pressure from their teachers and parents.

School-leaving age in Austria is 15 years (ninth grade). About 5% of 15-year-old students are leaving school without reaching ninth grade (e.g., due to retaking classes), and they are at risk because of their lack of education (Spannring 2003). However, most adolescents take part in further education: 76% of 15- to 19-year-old students go on to secondary education, and 17% of the 20- to 29-year-old individuals are still in school.

Men and women both have the same access to education. However, females are leaving school earlier than males (average age, 18.2 years versus 18.8 years), and they start to work before men do (average age, 18.7 years versus 18.9 years). When comparing different cohorts, it can be seen that the end of education and entry into the labor market were postponed during the last decades (Pfeiffer and Nowak 2001). In particular, more women are now entering secondary or tertiary education.

The Organisation for Economic Co-operation and Development's Programme for International Student Assessment study (2004) revealed large differences within Austria: because the selection of school takes place early (10 years old) during the course of education, there is a high variance among different school types. The performance on the achievement tests was on average according to the Organisation for Economic Co-operation and Development, although it decreased from 2000 to 2003. Subjectively, only one out of five 11-year-old adolescents thinks his or her academic achievement is good, and this decreases with age.

In Austria, there are different achievement-oriented school types at the lower secondary school stage, the main school stage ("hauptschule"), and the general higher school stage ("gymnasium"). For disabled children, there are special-needs schools as well as the possibility of being integrated into a regular school with extra teaching resources.

Work

Adolescents do work in their family households (mainly doing dishes, shopping, washing the car, and performing repairs), but less than after they left home (Mikula et al. 1997). A great amount of household work is done by the mothers only (especially cooking and ironing), but the other family members also have individual housework responsibilities, and about 20% of the household work is done with the cooperation of the whole family.

About 60% of 15- to 25-year-old individuals participate in the labor force (Lassnigg 1999). In rural areas, this percentage increases to 74% (Jentsch and Shucksmith 2004). Twenty-six percent of 15- to 19-year-old adolescents are students in addition to being employed. Many adolescents in this group take part in an apprenticeship training program or attend a vocational school (Spannring 2003).

Many adolescents take a job during holiday seasons, take part in an apprenticeship, or have part-time or marginal jobs (less than 20 hours per week, with no insurance). Therefore, financial support by their parents is very important (Spannring and Reinprecht 2004). In Austria, adolescents can take part in the "dual education system": for 3 years, they are trained on the job, in addition to being educated in a vocational school 2 days a week (Pfeiffer and Nowak 2001).

Adolescents often do not have the option of being trained for their first-choice job or to work in the job in which they were trained because of a shortage in the youth labor market (Spannring and Reinprecht 2004). This could be part of the reason that 69% of unemployed adolescents and 50% of employed adolescents are worried about their occupational future.

The youth unemployment rates are quite low in Austria as compared with other countries: 2.6% for the 15- to 19-year-old age group and 6.3% for the 19- to 25-year-old age group in 2000. However, 15.8% of all unemployed persons were between 15 and 25 years old (Spannring 2003). When looking at the working population between the ages of 19 and 25 years, only 7.3% were unemployed in 1997 (Lassnigg 1997). Also, there are many programs offered by the state-run Austrian job service, AMS, for unemployed adolescents to help them to find a new job or to offer further training.

Media

Listening to music (58% to 73%) or radio (51% to 63%) is important for many adolescents (Nemetz et al. 2003). Playing computer games is more popular for boys than for girls: 23% of 11-year-old and 42% of 15-year-old boys are playing games for 4 hours a week or more (Currie et al. 2000). Access to the Internet is possible for 92% of the 12- to 19-year-old adolescents and for 79% of 20- to 24-year old young adults (OIF 2004). Watching TV is quite popular for both boys and girls (about 75%; Nemetz et al. 2003), but frequent watching (more than 4 hours a day) is quite low as compared with other countries (Currie et al. 2004).

Girls between the ages of 14 and 24 years speak on the phone frequently (55% to 56%), and sending text messages is especially popular for them (41% to 51%; Nemetz et al. 2003). Boys are using communication media to a smaller extent (phone, 36% to 44%; text messages, 37%).

Politics and Military

Austrian adolescents are allowed to vote when they are 18 years old. However, interest and faith in politics and also political activity are losing importance for young people. Nevertheless, they are still interested in society and want to participate in the community, whether through outside political parties, on their job, in their neighborhoods, or via some form of community service (Nemetz et al. 2003).

There is compulsory military service in Austria for males: 18-year-old adolescents must either serve in the military for 8 months or work in community service for 12 months; however, both services' durations are going to be reduced during the next few years (CIA, 2005). After compulsory military service, men can stay in the military as professional soldiers.

For girls, military service is on a voluntary base for those who want to become professional soldiers. They can also do volunteer work in the community service, or they may perform ecological work.

About half of adolescents would be interested in doing volunteer work in the areas of children and adolescents (55%), sports (47%), environment/nature (45%), animal care or social work (44% each), and emergency aid (35%) (Zuba and Milovanovic 2004). Political work is not an area of interest for most adolescents (13%). However, 42% of this age group think that volunteer work helps with personality development. Taking part in community service is motivated by the urge to have new experiences (74%) or do something that makes sense (70%). Forty-five percent want to do volunteer work if they are unemployed.

EVA MAYR and MARIA ADAMEK

References and Further Reading

Adamek, M., E. Mayr, and E. Dreher. 2005. *Criteria for emerging adulthood—fact or fiction?* Paper presented at the Second Conference on Emerging Adulthood, Miami.

Arnett, J. 2000. Emerging adulthood: A theory of development from the late teens through the twenties. *American Psychologist* 55:469–80.

Beham-Rabanser, M., H. Wintersberger, K. Wörister, and U. Zartler. 2004. Childhood in Austria: Costs and care, time and space, children's needs, and public policies. In *Children's welfare in ageing Europe, Vol. I.* A. -M. Jensen, A. Ben-Arieh, C. Conti, D. Kutsar, M. N. G. Phádraig, and H. W. Nielson (eds.). Trondheim: Norwegian Center for Child Research.

BMSG. 2005. *Girls go business.* Wien: BMSG.

Central Intelligence Agency (CIA). 2005. *The world factbook. Austria.* CIA. http://www.cia.gov/cia/publications/factbook/geos/au.html.

Currie, C., K. Hurrelmann, W. Settertobulte, R. Smith, and J. Todd. 2000. *Health and health behaviour among young people.* Copenhagen: World Health Organization.

Friesl, C. 2001. *Experiment jung-sein (Experiment: Being young).* Wien: Czernin.

Großegger, B., G. Heinzlmaier, and M. Zentner. 2001. Youth scenes in Austria. In *Transitions of youth citizenship in Europe: Culture, subculture and identity.* A. Furlong and I. Guidikova (eds.). Strasbourg: Council of Europe Publishing.

Heineck, G. 2004. *Religion, attitudes toward working mothers and wives' full-time employment.* Wien: OIF.

Jentsch, B., and M. Shucksmith. 2004. *Young people in rural areas in Europe*. Hants: Ashgate.

Kolip, P., and B. Schmidt. 1999. *Gender and health in adolescence. WHO Policy Series "Health policy for children and adolescents" Issue 2*. Copenhagen: World Health Organization.

Lassnigg, L. 1999. *Youth labour market policy in Austria 1980–1997. Sociological Series No 58*. Vienna: Institut for Advanced Studies.

Mayr, E., M. Adamek, and E. Dreher. 2005. *Being adult—is it reaching an age or just a feeling?* Paper presented at the Second Conference on Emerging Adulthood, Miami.

Mikula, G., H. H. Freudenthaler, S. Brennacher-Kröll, and B. Brunschko. 1997. Division of labor in student-households: Gender inequality, perceived justice, and satisfaction. *Basic and Applied Social Psychology* 17:189–208.

Nemetz, K., P. Michl, B. Großegger and M. Zentner. 2003. *4. Bericht zur lage der jugend in Österreich*. Wien: BMSG.

Organisation for Economic Co-operation and Development (OECD). 2004. *Learning for tomorrow's world. First results from PISA 2003*. OECD.

Perner, R. A., L. Kneucker, R. Kneucker, and M. Voracek. 2004. Austria. In *International encyclopedia of sexuality*. R. T. Francoeur and R. J. Noonan (eds.). New York: Continuum.

Pfeiffer, C., and V. Nowak. 2001. Transition to adulthood in Austria. In *Transitions to adulthood in Europe*. M. Corijn and E. Klijzing (eds.). Ort: Kluwer Academic Press.

Richter, R., and S. Kytir. 2005. Families in Austria. In *Handbook of world families*. B. N. Adams and J. Trost (eds.). Thousand Oaks, CA: Sage.

Rollett, B., and M. Felinger. 2004. *Sekten- und kultgefährdung bei kindern und jugendlichen in Niederösterreich (Interference of sects and cults in Lower Austrian children and adolescents)*. St. Pölten: Niederösterreichische Landesregierung.

Spannring, R. 2003. *State of the art and socio-demographic background: Austria*. http://www.sociology.ed.ac.uk/youth/docs/Austria_Sociodem.pdf.

Spannring, R., and C. Reinprecht. 2002. Integration and marginalisation—young people in the Austrian labour market. *Nordic Journal of Youth Research* 10:5–13.

Statistik Austria. 2005. *Statistical yearbook 2005*. Wien: Statistik Austria.

Tebbich, H. 2000. Youth at risk—juvenile delinquency and criminal prevention in Austria. In *Child and juvenile delinquency*. R. Bendit, W. Erler, S. Nieborg, and H. Schaefer (eds.). Utrecht: Verwey-Jonker Instituut.

UNICEF. 2001. *Teenage births in rich nations*. Innocenti Report Card, 3. Florence: UNICEF Research Center.

Weidinger, B., W. Kostenwein, and G. Drunecky. 2001. *Das erste mal (First sexual intercourse)*. Wien: ÖGF.

Zuba, R., and S. Milovanovic. 2004. *Einstellung von burschen und mädchen zur freiwilligenarbeit in Österreich (Attitudes of boys and girls towards volunteer work in Austria)*. Wien: ÖIJ.

B

BANGLADESH

Background Information

Bangladesh is situated to the eastern side of India and is surrounded by that country to the west, north, and east. It is situated between 20° 34′ and 26° 38′ north latitude and between 88° 01′ and 92° 41′ east longitude. It has an area of 147,570 square kilometers and a population of 140 million by the year of 2005. It has the highest population density in the world.

Bangladesh is a tropical country washed by many rivers, largely covered with paddy fields and green vegetation. Due to the monsoon rainfall and the silt carried by the three great rivers, the Ganges, the Brahmaputra, and the Meghna, Bangladesh became a fertile land.

The country has a history of Mongoloid, Austro-Mongoloid, and Austro-Dravidian settlers. Previously, the country was a part of Pakistan. After nine months of war in 1971 with the former military government of Pakistan, the people have, however, come to be known as Bangladeshis.

With the highest density of population in the world, a low level of literacy, and slow economic progress, the people of this country are trapped in a sort of vicious cycle of poverty and malnutrition. About 50% of the people who live below the poverty line are not able to provide for their basic needs and amenities. Despite many odds Bangladesh has shown a steady progress in national income, world trade, and manpower supply in the external world.

With a population of 123 million (as per 2001 census) Bangladesh is the eighth largest country in the world. The average population density is 834 people per square kilometer (Bangladesh Bureau of Statistics 2003). Age-wise distribution of adolescents is shown in Table 1. The population of younger adolescents is significantly larger than that of older adolescents.

About 22% of the total population of Bangladesh falls into the adolescent category (ages 10 to 19). Since the 1970s, Bangladesh has made progress in reducing fertility levels; the average family now has four children. The fertility rate for adolescents (ages 15 to 19) is not negligible; it is 47 per 1,000 women. The fertility rate of the older adolescents in the next cohort (ages 20 to 24) is 174 per 1,000 women (BBS 2004).

Period of Adolescence

Like most other countries in the world, in Bangladesh puberty occurs from ages 11 to 14 in girls, and

Table 1. Distribution of Adolescents by Their Age and Sex as per 2001 Census Survey of Bangladesh (Population in Millions)

Age group	Both Sexes	Male	Female
10–14	15.85 (12.80)	8.42 (13.18)	7.43 (12.39)
15–19	11.96 (9.66)	6.29 (9.84)	5.67 (9.46)
20–24	10.91 (8.81)	4.86 (7.61)	6.06 (10.11)
Total population	123.85	63.89	59.96

Note: Figures in parentheses indicate percentage.
Source: BBS 2004.

from ages 12 to 15 in boys, or later where nutrition and living conditions are deficient. In Bangladeshi society these years may apply with little modification. Bangladeshi children are socialized to take up their respective male and female roles well before puberty sets in (Aziz and Maloney 1985). This happens mostly due to their lifestyle of living in extended families. For this reason, they face fewer problems during their puberty. A girl is expected to begin learning proper decorum for a female before the end of childhood so she can play the part well once puberty sets in. A Bangladeshi girl is in this stage from about age 9, 10, 11, or whenever her growth spurt begins, and until she attains menarche. In comparison to girls, boys are less concerned about the preparation for adult life in this stage. On the other hand, girls expect to start family life much earlier than boys. In this respect boys slowly prepare themselves for the future by learning the tasks of their father's occupations.

The beginning of puberty marks an important transition in life for the people of Bangladesh. A pre-pubertal boy is known as *nabalak*, meaning immature boy, but one who has entered puberty is called *sabalak*, meaning mature boy. A pre-menarchal girl is termed a *nabalika*, meaning immature girl, but one who has had her first menstruation is called *sabalika*, mature girl. However, these terms have equivalent Bangla names in Hindu communities. Getting the exact age of menarche for Bangladeshi girls is difficult, but different studies with small samples indicate it to be 12.6 years to 15.8 years. Among a selected group of school-going girls, Haq (1984) observed it to be 12.6 years, while in his different study among illiterate rural women it was found to be 13.4 years (Haq 1986a). Another significant study conducted in a controlled research field in Matlab, Bangladesh, found the age of menarche to be 15.8 years (Chowdhury

et al. 1977). The higher age was due to famine in the area. From these studies it is safely stated that most of the girls in Bangladesh achieve menarche between their twelfth and thirteenth birthdays. Like in other countries, information regarding adolescent boys is very much scarce in Bangladesh. This stage is the time for growth spurt and production of semen, which may occur two or more years later in Bangladesh than in well-nourished Western populations (Aziz and Maloney 1985).

There is no public ceremony in Bangladesh for a girl on her attainment of menarche, nor does she receive any formal education from any source regarding the problems of menarche. In Bangladesh menarche is a private matter; only mothers or elder sisters help the girl to manage menstruation in more informal and crude ways. In rural areas there are some rituals associated with the menarche, like special washing afterwards, but in urban areas there is no such ritual.

After the pubertal stage, boys and girls gradually attain the age of early and late adolescence, between 14 and 16 respectively. This period is more important to girls than boys, because most of the girls marry in their middle or late teens. At this age the secondary sex characteristics become prominent in both boys and girls, and they start to attain their adult roles in society.

Scientific studies on adolescence, particularly on its psychosocial aspects, are less common in Bangladesh than in many other nations, but in novels and literature it has been a long-studied subject. Many writers have highlighted the life and style of adolescents in this culture. The great Bangli poet Rabindra Nath Tagore, in one of his short stories depicted the adolescent life in a beautiful manner. He indicated that adolescents are not understood by the adults, and they are forced to follow the decisions of the adults in the society. For biological reasons they look awkward (particularly boys), and psychologically they feel restless. Adults try to avoid them, ignore their interests and desires, and push them to observe adult norms. Muslim culture also, to some extent, holds authoritarian views for adolescents; it is stricter for girls than boys.

In modern societies of Bangladesh adolescence appears as a great concern for parents. The media, modern culture, and age all have respective influences on the adolescents. When children are grown up, particularly girls, parents begin to watch them continuously and resist most of their actions, like dressing, roaming and other interests.

Beliefs

Bangladeshi adolescents are socialized to take up their respective male and female roles, which are derived from the beliefs and rituals of the people. Girls, from the beginning of their late childhood, start facing the restrictions in their manners and movements. During their early adolescence, girls are not allowed to roam alone in the evening, must wear long dresses, and cover their bodies with additional pieces of cloth. If the girl belongs to a conservative Muslim family, then the restrictions become stronger. The girls are asked to speak softly and not too much, behave politely, and in most families to perform compulsory prayers and fasting. She may be expected to work in the kitchen and at other domestic chores for hours.

It is believed in rural communities that a menstruating girl should not walk over a bridge, eat fish, or take betel leaf. If she eats fish then a bad odor comes out of her body; if she eats betel leaf then a spot of menstrual blood cannot be removed from her clothes (Aziz and Maloney 1985). Contrary to such beliefs, boys do not have to face any such restrictions. At this stage a girl is not expected to be caressed by her father, and a boy approaching adolescence is not expected to be caressed by his mother. A child older than nine is no longer considered suitable to share a bed with either parent. During this stage children learn whatever they know of sex from their peers, older children, or by observation.

In late adolescence girls tend to worry about their conjugal life with an as-yet-unknown male. The common belief among the mature girls is that if they remain virtuous they will find a good husband. On the other hand, adolescent boys remain less concerned about their marriage and do not have such beliefs regarding their conjugal life. Both the boys and girls have fantasies about the opposite sex and dream of each others' face, body, and genitalia but it is considered sinful among them so they hardly discuss the matter publicly. Masturbation is frequently practiced by males and females, but it is more common in males than females. Masturbation is thought of as a fault or bad habit and marriage as the best way to get rid of it. It is also thought to induce physical weakness.

There are differences in beliefs among urban and rural adolescents. Urban educated adolescents have fewer problems with such beliefs and practices. They have opportunities to learn about their lifestyle from different sources of mass media and knowledgeable senior friends. Schools also sometime disseminate about malpractices and wrong beliefs about sex and adolescence. However, girls who take home economics in their course of study receive some knowledge on adolescence, but it is also delivered in a very conservative way.

Gender

Gender roles among adolescent boys and girls are distinctly separate in Bangladesh. These roles are set by culture, customs, and religion. Masculinity and femininity are determined by physical attributes; a muscular build, facial hair, and a deep voice are perceived as attributes of masculinity, while long hair, developed breasts, and a high voice are perceived as feminine. A girl is expected to learn her proper gender role before the end of childhood so she can play the part well once puberty sets in. A girl in the pre-adolescent period wears pants and a blouse, or a skirt, but as she grows up she must change to wearing long dresses. There is no such restriction for the boys regarding short or long dresses. A boy in a rural setting or poor community may play naked while swimming in a pond or canal up to the pre-adolescent stage, but after that he becomes ashamed to do so. He is expected to learn farming tasks such as plowing, or other work of the family occupation. Such behavior and expectations are not evident in urban societies.

Gender role expectations are more prominent in rural communities. Girls are likely to remain engaged in domestic chores; they should help their mothers at home with household work or keep themselves busy with sewing, knitting, and other tasks. Once a girl is grown up she must wear *sari,* or a gown-like dress, to keep her body and head covered. Girls are not supposed to loiter around in the roadside or be involved in outdoor activities, and they should not dress like boys or engage in fights in public places. She is not allowed to go outside her dwelling alone during the night, but if it is necessary for her to go, she should be accompanied by an elderly woman or an adult male relative. Girls in conservative families are expected to perform *parda,* or seclusion, with veil in front of unknown men. It should not be assumed that *parda* is just imposed by males onto females, rather it is observed by cultures and religious faiths in significant numbers of middle-income families. The observance of *parda* is not at all prominent among the hard core poor people who live either in rural or urban areas.

A boy will help his father in the field or do what are perceived as masculine jobs either at home or outside. During adolescence, a boy from a lower-class family has to work outside the home and often contributes more to the family income than he consumes, unless he is a student. In middle- and upper-middle-class families, boys focus more on school than work. But it is considered disgraceful if an adolescent girl has to work outside the home; even poor families will rarely permit it unless it is a dire necessity. People think that if a girl works in the field or outside the home, sexual mishaps are bound to occur. Adolescent girls are not permitted to mix with boys or men to whom they are not connected by blood relationship in secluded places.

Smoking is very much associated with males rather than females. Adolescent boys are expected not to smoke before any respected persons or elderly relatives. Girls are not at all permitted to smoke before anyone in the society. Smoking by girls is seen as an indication of her bad character. However, among the upper classes, smoking by boys and girls is not taken as a serious offense. Drinking alcohol in average Bangladeshi culture is always forbidden for adolescents, irrespective of gender.

The gender of adolescents also plays a very important role in education and sports in both rural and urban areas. There are separate schools for boys and girls at the secondary level, although girls can attend to some boys' schools and colleges, but boys cannot attend to any girls' schools or colleges. Even in schools where boys and girls study together they sit apart in the same room. Curricula also differ according to gender differentials. Boys can take agriculture, carpentry, or some other income-generating activities, while girls can take home economics, cutting, and knitting, which are perceived as their discipline. In sports boys and girls have different events, provided it is not a unisex school. Even in jobs girls prefer teaching, office work, or nursing, but for boys there is no limit of choice.

Though gender roles are not strictly followed in urban settings, the majority of girls in adolescence try to abide by the rules. Parents take more care of their adolescent girls to protect them from any societal evils than boys. Loitering in public places, such as shopping malls or cinemas, is more common among boys than girls. Unless there are many girls in a group, they would not stay outside home in the evening. Mixing among boys and girls is a common sight on urban college and university campuses, but not at rural colleges. The free mixing of younger adolescents at school is frowned upon by society in general.

The Self

The beginning of puberty marks an important transition for Bengali adolescents. From around the age eleven the boys are known as *kishor* and the girls are called *kishori* (terms synonymous with *shabalak* and *shabalika*); these identifications greatly influence the construction of a sense of self among adolescents. These identified stages are defined by their own set roles; as one becomes *kishor* or *kishori*, one tends to abide by those roles. Their selves start to develop from the interaction with the family and the society, but adolescents in Bangladesh have a limited scope of such interaction. Research shows that parents rarely recognize the needs and desires of their adolescent children (Haq et al. 2003). The opinions of adolescents are not valued in the family. School-going adolescents have a greater opportunity to develop their selves than unschooled adolescents. Boys are more extroverted than girls, and the rate of extroversion is higher in school-goers than out-of-school adolescents (Haq et al. 2003). Most girls' social activities, apart from visiting in the neighborhood, take place within the home, allowing them negligible interaction with the outside world, and again this interaction also decreases with age. While girls have restrictions on their mobility, boys have a more active social life than girls in Bangladesh.

The psychological development of adolescents receives little to no attention from parents, teachers, or social workers in Bangladesh. Sporadic studies on the topic of adolescents' self have been done by psychologists, who indicated the adolescents are normal, confident, happy, and self-sustained. Psychologically, the teenagers are quite sound, they have good control over their impulses and emotions, and they are satisfied with their body and self-image (Haq 1986b). An international cross-country study on adolescent self-image among 12 nations is given in Offer et al. 1988 (present author is one of the collaborators of this study). This study shows that Bangladeshi adolescents are rather low in expressing their psychological and social selves compared to other countries. Bangladeshi adolescents also have good control over their adjustments in relation to other national youths.

Family Relationships

Boys and girls in their teens develop a looser bond with their family. Parents see their offspring first as children and then as adults, effectively ignoring their adolescence (Haq et al. 2003). This creates conflicting views of their relationship among parents and adolescents. Adolescents receive very little time from their parents for socializing and discussing personal issues compared to their younger siblings. This is common in both rural and urban communities. Adolescents of working parents are the worst sufferers. In general, girls in poor families do not have as much access to basic human needs like food, clothing, and medical treatment as do boys in a family. This disparity is seen the most in rural families. Many parents have a mentality that there is no benefit to educating girls as girls will go away to their husbands' homes after marriage. So parents look after their sons and educate them in the hope that when they will be grown they will earn and take care of their old parents. Thus, parents deprive their daughters of various services in the families (Zaman 1998).

The economic status of the family and the earning capacity of the head of the family in particular contribute to the formation of family. The men's role is very crucial for family development as most of the families in Bangladeshi society financially depend on men's income. The majority of adolescents do not have any income, and thus they remain dependent on their families. Other than providing food, clothing, and shelter, few demands of the adolescents are fulfilled by the family. In this regard boys receive greater attention from their families than girls. As soon as the teenage girl gets married, she leaves the family home and is no longer dependent on her father's family. On the other hand, marriage of an adolescent boy increases the dependence on family provided he is not earning. So marriage is the turning point of a family, as it begins to change in its dependence on the father's family. In the case of a boy, his dependence on his own family increases, because the boy brings his wife to his father's house. On the other hand, due to her marriage, a girl becomes dependent on her husband's house.

Despite negligence from different quarters, adolescents possess good feelings about their parents, siblings, and other relatives (Haq 1986b). In the absence of social security, poor parents want to be free of responsibility for their young daughters by subjecting them to an early marriage. Dowry is still a factor in marriage. Poor parents view education as a burden on her dowry—the higher a girl's level of education, the higher a dowry she requires.

Within the family, adolescents—particularly girls—take care of their older parents. It is commonly understood that boys in the future will take care of their older parents; that is, they will bear the financial burden of the elderly. The situation arises when older parents live with the boy and his wife in the same house after the boy marries. On the other hand, although girls do not take on the financial responsibility, they shoulder the burden of the physical well-being of the elderly. Adolescent girls look after their elderly parents or grandparents.

Parents' dependency on their adolescents is more common in rural families but in urban settings the incidences are far less common. Here, in affluent societies adolescents still remain busy with study and have less time to devote to their older parents or grandparents.

Friends and Peers/Youth Culture

Like many other nations, Bangladesh is a male-dominated country, where boys enjoy more opportunities in the society than the girls. Boys can socialize and thus enhance their knowledge and skills, while girls are kept confined at home. As a result many girls become indifferent or remain ignorant about their rights and dignity and confused about many actions. Most adolescents have friends of their own sex, and friendship with the opposite sex at this age is not very much appreciated by the society. Adolescents prefer to trust their friends more than parents. They like to make friendships with like-minded peers of similar age.

Adolescents achieve friendship through school, outdoor activities, gossiping centers like the tea stall, cinema hall, and neighborhood. Boys have access to these places while girls mostly remain isolated in someone's house or to a solitary place in the neighborhood. In rural areas, girls also meet in the public washing spots at a pond, river, or tube well sites. Most girls' social activities, apart from visiting the above places, take place within the home, allowing them negligible interaction with the outside world. This interaction also decreases with age. One baseline survey conducted on rural adolescents in Bangladesh indicated that 6% of girls, compared to 64% of boys, reported visiting a tea stall in the past one week. Similarly, 3% of girls, compared to 23% of boys, reported going to the cinema. Girls' main outdoor activity is visiting friends and neighbors. Nearly one in three girls reported having done so in the past week. Boys were more than twice as likely to report this activity. Girls of any age are rarely reported to be involved in outdoor games as the boys are (Department of Women's Affairs 2002).

Watching television has now become a major indoor entertainment for rural adolescents of both sexes, as has listening to the radio. Thirty-seven percent of girls, compared with 67% of boys, reported that they watch television, and 33% of girls compared with 58% of boys reported that they listen to the radio. A low proportion of adolescents play indoor games and read newspapers, probably because few households subscribe to a newspaper in rural areas or have amenities available for indoor games (Department of Women's Affair 2002).

Unlike rural adolescents, boys and girls living in urban areas—particularly in bigger cities—have a much limited scope of making friendships with boys and girls other than their schoolmates or neighbors. Due to unsecured life in the city, parents do not allow their adolescents to move freely without their notice. However, in late adolescence such restrictions gradually start to disappear, but only boys enjoy more freedom than the girls in the same household.

Adolescents actively engage with many media products, such as cultural programs, educational activities, games and sports, and television. There are no statistics available on Bangladeshi adolescents and their use of media.

There are national competitions for music, dance, and debate for adolescents. These programs are very popular, and a large number of boys and girls take part in these competitions. There is a Shishu Academy (Children's Academy) in every district of the country. This is a government department under the Ministry of Women's and Children's Affairs. This academy holds various programs and national competitions for the development of both children and adolescents.

Numerous social organizations geared toward children and adolescents present various developmental and cultural activities. Kachi Kachar Mela and Mukul Fauz are the renowned ones, engaging adolescents in preparing for their future development. The young people active in these groups take part in rallies and perform in parades on festival grounds during the celebration of national holidays. Nationwide, various organizations hold art competitions for children and adolescents.

Most of the events on national holidays involve urban children and adolescents; few similar opportunities are extended to rural children. The observance of national holidays and the children's competition by the Shishu Academy are mostly limited to families who are financially solvent; children and adolescents from poor families largely remain deprived of these activities. Recently, a few private commercial enterprises have come forward to organize beauty competitions and music and art competitions for children and adolescents but these events are also seriously limited to a select class of children and adolescents.

Love and Sexuality

The terms "love" and "sexuality" both are considered taboo during the period of adolescence. Parents always want to keep their young adolescents away from these two acts in different ways, sometimes through advice and sometimes through punishment. More adolescent girls than boys are concerned about their physical developments, manners, and movements, which makes them shy and isolated. Girls' interest in love and sex is more restricted in the society; they cannot freely mix with boys openly in front of elderly persons. Though the situation is now gradually decreasing among some educated and affluent societies. Minor sex offenses or expression of unapproved love in pre-adolescence or early adolescence is not considered serious, but during late adolescence such behavior goes with reprimand or heavy punishment. Societal approval in this matter goes in favor of boys over girls. Studies show that it is not considered shameful for a male to look at the body of a female with sensuous eyes, on the contrary, if a girl expresses pleasure at seeing a male's physical features, her girlfriends will criticize her for being shameless (Aziz and Maloney 1985).

The sexual life of adolescents is greatly influenced by religion. They are taught to remain virtuous despite temptation, for the creator will give them the best reward for this. However, besides all these social and religious bindings, a good number of boys and girls fall in love or express their likings about members of the opposite sex in their early and late adolescence. But very few of these relationships are finally sustained and transformed into marriage.

Information about adolescents' health and sexuality is very limited. Scattered reports exist about sexuality (Aziz and Maloney 1985). It is generally recognized that other issues like smoking, substance abuse, and violence are also problems of Bangladeshi young people. It is also perceived that these problems are far more prevalent in the male section of this population (Talukder 1999).

A recent study (Haider et al. 1997) on adolescents in Bangladesh observed high rates of premarital sex among male unmarried adolescents, while husbands of adolescent women also reported high levels of both pre- and extramarital sex. Of those men who had sex with partners outside marriage, 71% mentioned commercial sex workers. Another study reports that in rural Bangladesh incidence of abortion is 35 times higher in unmarried adolescents who are less than 18 years of age than married adolescents (Ahmed et al. 2005). The incidence is more common in educated (up to primary-level education) girls than in the illiterate girls. No statistics are available about the incidence of abortion among urban and rural girls for comparison.

Family planning among married adolescents has been mentioned in the demographic health survey (2004). It indicates that about 29% of 10- to 14-year-old married adolescents and 42.2% of 15- to 19-year-old married adolescent girls are currently users of some family planning methods. This figure is little higher among 20- to 24-year-olds (52.9%). The low rate of family planning methods is probably due to the absence of sex education in school.

There are no statistics available on the prevalence of masturbation and homosexuality in this culture, but it is believed to be evident in a larger number of boys than girls. To the adults as well as adolescents, homosexuality is considered highly immoral and an unusual practice among the boys. Adolescents' knowledge about sexually transmitted diseases, including AIDS, is minimal. In a local UNICEF publication, it was noted that about 60% of boys and 57% of girls had heard of HIV/AIDS. Over half of these adolescents (55% of boys and 52% of girls) know that having sex with an infected person may cause them to become infected as well (UNICEF and BBS 2004). Large numbers of people, including adolescents, consider that HIV/AIDS is a disease given by God to sinful persons.

According to WHO statistics approximately 1,300 people in Bangladesh are HIV-positive, and HIV prevalence in the adult population is 0.01%. National HIV surveillance indicates that the rate of HIV infection among street-based sex workers in central Bangladesh is high compared to sex workers in other parts of South Asia. HIV among injecting drug users is 4% (WHO Internet source 2005).

Selection of mates for marriage is mostly done by the parents, though a trend is gradually increasing among the middle- to high-income groups to select one's own partner. However, in the case selecting life partners, boys enjoy greater freedom than girls. Though a few adolescent boys choose their life partner independently, the marriage is arranged by the parents. On the other hand, very few of girls independently choose their life partners. Even so, a significant number of adolescents continue to marry young. The exchange of dowry is still evident in Bangladesh among the rural poor (Government of Bangladesh 2002). The incidence of dowry is also evident among the affluent urban sector. Other than in a few cases, the dowry is not transacted in cash; instead, the parents of the bridegroom demand furniture, electronic goods (refrigerator, television), jewelry, a motorbike or bicycle, or land.

As per the Bangladesh marriage law, the marital age for a girl is 18 and for boys it is 21. Marriage before this age limit is regarded as early marriage and is treated as a punishable offense. The punishment for early marriage is a monetary fine or one month imprisonment or both. Guardians, matchmakers and other concerned persons involved in an early marriage will receive this punishment. Nevertheless, marriage among adolescents is quite high. The marriage rate of both males and females between the ages of 10 and 19 is about 53% (NIPORT 2001).

Health Risk Behavior

A great deal of health risks emerge from substance misuse and some excessive smoking and drinking behavior. There are no national level data on substance misuse in young people, but there is increasing concern about the use of indigenous cigarettes (*Biri*) that are made of locally produced, poor-quality tobacco. These cigarettes are very cheap and widely available in rural and urban slum areas.

Alcohol is not publicly sold, but it is available from unauthorized hidden retailers. However, these alcohols are indigenous substances and of poor quality. Large numbers of black marketers keep the cough syrup Fensidel, which contains 10 to 15% alcohol as an ingredient. Young people, particularly the older adolescents and youths who are habituated to alcohol, drink large quantities of this syrup for satisfaction. A large number of Fensidel bottles are dispatched illegally from the neighboring countries.

Substances like hashish, marijuana, and even heroin are also used by some young people in urban areas. Many of these substance users also take Pathedin and other injectable drugs. However, there are no authentic statistics available in the country regarding the use of this substance. Substance misuse has been increasing in the country, and large numbers of parents are concerned about their children's drug addiction. In this respect a few clinics and rectification centers for drug addicts have been established in the bigger cities of the country.

There are incidences of violence and suicide among young people, but there are no systematic data on these events. There are frequent reports of rape, acid-throwing, and violence against girls in the press. Such incidences occur as revenge as a result of denial in love or marriage. Political violence has become more prominent among young men, especially in institutions of higher education such as colleges and universities. A fundamentalist militant group of students became violent and simultaneously blasted explosives in over 500 spots in 60 districts on August 17, 2005. Many young men associated with political parties get involved in gun violence and entangled in substance abuse. Some of these young men may have come from a poor family background and hence need the support of political parties as an alternative to the ever-growing competition of the job market in the country.

Education

In the early twenty-first century there were 27 million adolescents (13 million girls) in Bangladesh. Their literacy rate was 53% for girls and 54% for boys, compared to the adult literacy rate of 56% for men and 35% for women. In 2001 the total enrollment of adolescents in secondary school was 7.3 million; 35.5% of adolescents were enrolled in secondary level school and 14% were enrolled in higher secondary level school (Education Watch 2001). According to another nationwide sample-based survey (Education Watch 2005) the gross enrollment rate of adolescents in secondary level (grades 6 to 10) was 64.5% and the net enrollment rate was 45.1%. Gross enrollment consisted of adolescents between 11 and 15 years and beyond, while the net enrollment rate was composed of adolescents of 11 to 15 years only. The study also indicated that 71.7% of the 11 to 15 years age group of adolescents were currently enrolled in both primary and secondary level institutions. The gross and net enrollment rate of girls at secondary level was 69% and 50.6% respectively. The corresponding figures for boys were 60.2% and 39.6% respectively (Education Watch 2005). Still another survey (DHS 2004) provided age-wise breakdowns of school enrollment of adolescents that has some consistency with the 2005 Education Watch report. The survey indicated that the school attendance rate of adolescents 11 to 15 years old was 68.2%; 16 to 20 years was 27%, and 21 to 24 years was 11% (NIPORT 2005). The attendance rate among younger adolescent girls was higher than the boys.

Girls are largely deprived of education in poor families. In some families, education for a girl-child is thought to be useless and unproductive. So girls remain illiterate, which results in their lower status. Male children are treated by their parents as their old age shelter. This traditional outlook leads parents to provide education for the male adolescents. However, such attitudes are not evident in the educated families and in the higher income groups.

Religious education is known as *madrasa*, which includes all the three levels of primary, secondary, and tertiary levels, but with different names. Large numbers of adolescents are enrolled in the secondary level, which is known as *alim*. There are approximately 6,500 *madrasas* for children and adolescents in the country, of which about 760 are exclusively for girls.

There are differences in the curricula between schools and *madrasas*. The *madrasa* curriculum largely includes Arabic, theology, Koranic education, Hadith (sayings of the Prophet Mohammad), and other religious rituals. However, the *madrasa* students also study some secular subjects like Bangla, English, science, mathematics, and social studies to a limited extent. But in schools all subjects are secular.

Considering the educational situation of the adolescents—particularly of the lower income groups and working adolescents—a large number of NGOs and government agencies came forward to provide them with some education. So nonformal education programs for out-of-school adolescents and adolescents who are hard to reach due to their involvement in the working force were considered. Nonformal education for children and adolescents is famous for its magnitude and quality. Many NGOs bring the illiterate adolescents to a learning center for about two hours a day and teach them functional literacy and life skills. This education not only provides the adolescents literacy skills, it also allows them a second opportunity to learn and continue their education in the mainstream schools up to whatever level they can go.

The government is keen to provide education to the girls in secondary schools. In order to encourage a large number of girls to continue their education, all the rural girls in Bangladesh (outside metropolitan or municipal areas) receive some stipend (which is less than half a dollar a month) from the government and study in school without any tuition. Other than the monthly stipend, girls also get some money at times for purchasing clothes and

Table 2. School Attendance of Adolescents in Bangladesh (2004)

Age	Boys	Girls	Both
11–15	66.1%	70.1%	68.2%
16–20	30.2%	24.4%	27.0%
21–24	17.6%	6.7%	11.1%

Source: Demographic Health Survey of Bangladesh 2004.

other necessary educational materials. Large numbers of girls are attracted to this scheme and enroll themselves in secondary schools after completing their education in primary schools. Boys, however, do not receive any support from government for their education.

Work

Working adolescents remain one of the main groups who are excluded from formal education. There are approximately five million children in Bangladesh, most of whom are poor and working in the informal sector. While there are more working children in rural areas, there are also 1.1 million boys and 400,000 working girls living in urban areas (UNICEF 2004). Among these workers the large majority are adolescents. Although these young workers earn for their families, their wages are not sufficient to support their families. Some statistics regarding the working status of adolescents are shown in Tables 3 and 4.

The tables indicate that a larger number of adolescent boys are involved in various work than girls. But the figure is higher among rural adolescents than urban adolescents.

A great amount of adolescents' work takes place in hazardous conditions, and there is a potential threat to their health, as well as a threat of accidental death. Adolescents' typical jobs include brick breaker, welder, bus and other motor vehicle helper, and domestic worker. While doing these jobs, many adolescents have accidents frequently, but the employer does not take responsibility for

Table 3. Work Participation Rates among Male and Female Adolescents

Age	Male	Female
10–14	43.3%	33.8%
15–19	64.9%	46.8%
20–24	81.0%	57.8%

Table 4. Work Participation Rates among Urban and Rural Adolescents

Age	Urban		Rural	
	Male	Female	Male	Female
10–14	34.7%	27.3%	45.6%	36.0%
15–19	54.3%	30.4%	67.3%	51.8%
20–234	74.2%	37.1%	83.4%	64.3%

such occurrences and does not bear the cost of treatment.

Adolescents are easily exploited through work. Most of the motor garages are filled with young adolescents, and many of them work there for five to ten years but do not get any wage. It is mentioned that these workers work there for the whole day, and in the absence of any salary they survive on their own expenses. However, this free work does not make any workers unhappy, because they feel that it is their learning time; if they can learn motor mechanics at their own cost, then in future they will be benefited.

There are a group of street children and adolescents who are popularly known as *tokai* ("waste pickers"). They are the rootless adolescents who loiter in the street and collect saleable garbage. There are a group of small traders who purchase this garbage and recycles it into various utility products like paper board, plastic, glass, and polythene bags. There is no exact figure of this *tokai* population but the estimate is about 380,000 in six major cities in the country. Many of the girls among the *tokais* work as floating sex workers and are at risk for becoming carriers of HIV. These are the abandoned children of poor parents who migrated to cities for work. There are some NGOs in the city that provide them with a little education, food, and shelter for their development.

Media

Adolescents in Bangladesh are rarely the subject of media scrutiny. Most cultural organizations allow adolescents to participate in various events and allow them to organize programs. Every television channel has programs intended for adolescents. One of these channels has a group of adolescent employees who produce adolescent-oriented programs themselves. TV channels have adolescent journalists, camera crews, producers, and directors. Adolescent media workers were first introduced by one of the TV channel, ETV, which was disbanded for political reasons. On another channel a group of adolescents produced a drama which won an international Emmy Award.

Bangladesh is well-covered by radio and TV channels. Almost all parts of the country have access to these media. There are around 400 newspapers, five TV channels including one four privately owned and a national radio network in the country. Besides these windows in media, a large number of satellite channels are working that are also accessible to a limited number of children and adolescents. Families who can pay for these channels have access. Every channel has programs for children and adolescents. How much time the adolescents give to these media is not known. We do not have any study on the effect of these channels on the life of adolescents. Though satellite channels have limited coverage, they have a tremendous effect on the adolescents and youth particularly in the matters of lifestyle and culture. This "sky culture" has now molded our TV programs, fashions, and even language patterns. For example, youths and adolescents who have access to these media sometimes follow amalgamated language and styles instead of using their own native mother tongue and style.

Large numbers of video game centers and cyber-cafés have been growing up in bigger cities, and similar shops are also found in smaller towns as well but to a limited extent. There is no authentic figure of these shops, but according to various newspaper sources there are over one thousand in the country. Most of those cybercafés remain crowded with young people. There have been news stories about the misuse of such cybercafés by the adolescents. The government is quite concerned about the bad effects of the mushroom-growth of these cafés. Large numbers of young people (mostly from affluent societies) have access to computers and video games in their homes. These people are also fond of music as well. The country has a supply of audio and video compact discs, but mostly they are pirated, though there are some legal import channels. Any movie released in neighboring countries or overseas appears in the market in just a couple of days.

Unique Issues

Bangladesh is a country where a significant number of adolescents lead vulnerable lives in the community. Their rights are not protected, they do not receive an appropriate wage for their work, and they are prone to disease and malnutrition. Statistics shows that about 59% of adolescent boys and 47% of adolescent girls are engaged in various income-generating work outside the home in various unhealthy working conditions. Over 41% of working children between the ages of 5 and 15 work over eight hours a day outside the home.

In 1996 the Institute of Child and Mother Health (ICMH) in Dhaka, in collaboration with the Centre for International Child Health (CICH) in London, carried out a nutrition survey on adolescents (10–17 years old) in four villages in Rupganj thana, Bangladesh. This study observed that 67% of these adolescents were thin, 48% were stunted, and 75% had hemoglobin deficiencies. Though these findings cannot be generalized for the whole country, the health conditions of Bangladeshi adolescents overall can be gleaned from this survey.

A large number of adolescents in religious educational institutes such as *madrasas* are deprived of many human rights; like many of them are confined in the *madrasa* house in subnormal accommodations, and in some occasions it was reported in newspapers and on TV media that they are not even allowed to read newspapers, watch TV, and talk to outsiders. The upsurge of suicide bombers in the country in the early twenty-first century was also found to be associated with the *madrasa*-educated adolescents. Some deranged religious leaders mislead the young adolescents towards this path.

MUHAMMAD NAZMUL HAQ

References and Further Reading

Ahmed, M. K., J. Van Ginneken, and A. Razzaque. 2005. Factors associated with adolescent abortion in rural area of Bangladesh. *Tropical Medicine and Internal Health* 2:189–205.

Aziz, K. M. Ashraful, and C. Maloney. 1985. *Life stages, gender and fertility in Bangladesh*. Dhaka, Bangladesh: International Centre for Diarrhoeal Disease Research.

Bangladesh Bureau of Statistics. 2003. *Statistical pocketbook*. Dhaka.

Bangladesh Bureau of Statistics. 2004. *Statistical yearbook—2002*. Dhaka.

Chowdhury, A. K. M. Alauddin, S. L. Huffman, and G. T. Curlin. 1977. Malnutrition, menarche, and marriage in rural Bangladesh. *Social Biology* 24:316–25.

Department of Women's Affairs, Ministry of Women and Children Affairs, Government of Bangladesh. 2002. Kishori Abhijan: Baseline survey report on rural adolescents in Bangladesh. Dhaka.

Education Watch. 2001. Renewed Hope Daunting Challenges. Dhaka: Campaign for Popular Education and University Press.

Government of Bangladesh. 2002. *Statistical yearbook of Bangladesh*. Dhaka: Bangladesh Bureau of Statistics.

Haider, S. J., S. N. Saleh, N. Kamal, and A. Gray. 1997. *Study of adolescents: Dynamics of perception, attitude, knowledge and use of reproductive health care*. Dhaka: Population Council.

Haq, M. N. 1984. Age at menarche and the related issues: A pilot study on urban school girls. *Journal of Youth and Adolescents*, Vol. 13, No. 6.

Haq, M. N. 1986a. Adolescent mothers in Bangladesh. *Journal of Institute of Economic Research*. Vol. 21, No. 1.

Haq, M. N. 1986b. Pattern of adolescent self-image in Bangladesh. *Bangladesh Journal of Psychology*, Vol. 9, No. 1.

Haq, M. N. et al. 2003. *Situation of out-of-school adolescents in Bangladesh*. Bangladesh: UNESCO.

National Institute of Population Research and Training (NIPORT). 2001. *Bangladesh demographic and health survey 1999– 2000*. Dhaka.

National Institute of Population Research and Training. 2005. *Bangladesh demographic health survey 2004*. Dhaka.

Offer, D., E. Ostrov, K. I. Howard, and R. Atkinson. 1988. *The teenage world*. New York: Plenum Medical Book Co.

Talukder, K. 1999. Child health and nutrition: National perspective. In *Institute of Child and Mother Health Inauguration Souvenir*. Dhaka.

Talukder K., et al. 1998. Adolescent nutrition in a rural community in Bangladesh. In Programme and abstracts of the 7th Annual Scientific Conference (ASCON) of the International Centre for Diarrhoeal Disease Research, Bangladesh (ICDDR,B). Khan and M. A. Rahim (eds.).14–15 February. Dhaka.

UNESCO. 2002. *EFA Global monitoring report, 2002*. Paris: UNESCO.

UNICEF and Bangladesh Bureau of Statistics. 2004. *Progotir Pathey 2003*. Dhaka: UNICEF.

Zaman, M. A. 1998. *A concept on adolescent development*. Dhaka: USC Canada Bangladesh.

BELGIUM

Background Information

Belgium is a small country in northwest Europe. The country takes up about 0.31% of the European mainland and slopes gently from the Ardennes (rising to 694 meters or 2,200 feet) to the North Sea. In 2003, Belgium had 10,355,844 inhabitants. Because the country is relatively small (30,527 square kilometers or 11,779 square miles), it has a very high population density (339 inhabitants per square kilometer).

The country comprises three economic regions. About 57.9% of the inhabitants live in the Flemish region, 32.5% in the Walloon region, and 9.6% in the region of Brussels, the capital of Belgium (NIS 2003). The population of the Walloon region comprises a small German minority (about 2% of the inhabitants of that region) in the east. Belgium is a multilingual country. People in Flanders speak Dutch, those in the Walloon region speak French, and the inhabitants of the East Cantons speak German. All three languages are official in their respective regions. Brussels is officially bilingual (Dutch and French).

A constitutional monarchy since 1831, Belgium was initially governed as a unitary state. Through successive revisions of the Constitution, the organization of the state has increasingly come to reflect its linguistic and regional diversity. Important powers (such as foreign affairs and defense) still reside with the federal government, whereas responsibilities that touch directly upon people's lives (such as education) have been transferred to both regional governments (of the Flemish, Walloon, and Brussels regions) and community governments (of the French- and German-speaking communities).

The population of Belgium is aging. In 2003, 23.3% of the population were children or adolescents (0 to 19 years of age), 59.6% were adults from 20 to 64 years of age, and 17.1% were adults older than 65 years. In 2001, the mean age of the population was 39.8 years with women being slightly older than men (41.2 and 38.3 years of age, respectively). The average life expectancy at birth was 78.3 years in general. This figure was 81.5 years for women and 75.1 years for men (NIS 2003).

In terms of nationality, Belgium is a rather homogeneous country. About 8.2% of the inhabitants of Belgium are not native Belgian citizens. More than 50% of these are citizens of other member states of the European Union (EU) and about 25 to 30% come from Maghreb countries (Morocco, Algeria, or Tunisia) or Turkey. These foreigners, many of whom initially immigrated to Belgium in the 1960s and 1970s, are unequally distributed across the country (Goossens 1994). They make up 4.7% of the population in Flanders, 9.2% of the Walloon region, and 26.2% of the Brussels region.

Period of Adolescence

This entry intends to represent the most recent and representative information on adolescence in Belgium as of the first decade of the twenty-first century. The linguistic and regional diversity of the country is a complicating factor in this regard. General information on adolescents can readily be obtained from census data and official reports. In many cases, however, more specific information has to be gleaned from surveys on samples on adolescents from, say, a single linguistic community or region. To alert the reader to this complication, it will be indicated explicitly if the figures described in this chapter refer to Belgian, Flemish, or Walloon adolescents.

There are indications that the boundaries of adolescence are changing in Belgium, as they are in other regions of the globe. On the one hand, children seem to reach puberty at an earlier age than they once did. No reliable data on the extent of this phenomenon in Belgium is available as of yet, but the Flemish minister of public health has commissioned a new anthropometric study on a large sample of young people to update the existing norms for physical development. On the other hand, young people seem to postpone the transition to adulthood. Leaving the parental home, marriage, and giving birth to a first child (among women) are no longer strictly tied to a particular age and do not necessarily occur in that neat order any longer.

By age 25, almost all young adults in Flanders have completed their education and started their first job, whereas by age 30 almost all young adults have married or are cohabiting, and most young women have had their first child. Only among men is there a considerable postponement of marriage and parenthood beyond age 30. Among young males born in 1961–1965, 14% were still living at home at the age of 30 (Corijn 2001). As a result of these demographic changes, many young people in Belgium go through a period of "emerging adulthood" during which they are more independent of their parents, but are not yet committed to adult roles such as marriage and parenthood.

Beliefs

On the whole, Belgium tends toward individualism rather than collectivistic values. The country ranked eighth in a sample of 53 countries on Hofstede's (2001) Individualism Index (IV), preceded only by a number of English-speaking countries (such as the United States, Australia, Great Britain, and Canada) and the Netherlands. These individualistic values are transmitted through the family and various other institutions. Children live in nuclear families and are taught to define themselves in terms of personal characteristics rather than group membership. There are no indications that this individualistic tendency, which is characteristic of many Western nations, is currently changing.

The most important religion in Belgium is Roman Catholicism, with small Protestant and Jewish minorities and a sizeable Islamic minority (among the immigrant population). The 1999 European Values Survey (Dobbelaere et al. 2000) revealed that 63% of the Belgian population identified with a religious group; 96% of these with the Catholic Church. An increasing number of the population claims to be non-religious. At the end of the 1990s, approximately 80% of children and adolescents were baptized and 70% of 12-year-olds were administered the rite of confirmation (by which they were recognized as full adult members of the Catholic Church). However, a clear decline in formal admission to the Roman Catholic Church has taken place over the years. Whereas in 1967, 93.6% of all newborns were baptized, only 64.7% of them were baptized in 1998.

Religious affiliation among adolescents reflects the situation in the population at large. A survey conducted on 5,000 high school students in Flanders (De Witte, Hooge, and Walgrave 2000) indicated that 52% identified themselves to a certain degree with the Catholic Church (they described themselves as being religious, Catholic, or Christian). About 40% described themselves as non-religious or freethinkers, 2% as atheists, and 6% as professing another religion (Islam or some Eastern religion). Girls were found more frequently than boys among the self-acknowledged Catholics, whereas boys were overrepresented among the non-believers, freethinkers, and atheists. At the age of 12, about 71% described themselves as being religious, while at the age of 18 years, this proportion dropped to only 44%.

Religious beliefs are not firm among Flemish adolescents. About 13% were absolutely convinced of the existence of God or a supernatural reality, 17% did not believe in its existence, and 59% had doubts about whether or not God exists. Again, the proportion of believers decreased with advancing age throughout adolescence.

Religious practices are not widespread among adolescents. Only 18% reported going to church once a month and 11% went to the church on a weekly basis. These figures contrast sharply with the percentage of adolescents who are formal members of the Catholic Church. With regard to the percentage of churchgoers, however, adolescents do not differ much from adults. Again, the proportion of church-attendees dropped significantly with age: about one-third of the 12-year-olds attended church at least once a month, in contrast to only 8% of the 18-year-olds. About 36% of the adolescents in the survey—again, more girls than boys—prayed occasionally or on a regular basis. Some 54% did so at 12 years and only 24% at 18 years. These results clearly indicated that the decline over time in religious beliefs and practices observed in the 1970s and 1980s (Hutsebaut and Verhoeven 1991) continued throughout the 1990s.

Traditionally, Catholics are strongly opposed to abortion and euthanasia. However, the legal situation has changed dramatically in recent years as the Belgian Parliament passed an Abortion Act (in 1990) and a Euthanasia Act (May 16, 2002). Belgium was the second country in the world, preceded only by the Netherlands, where euthanasia is declared legal under particular circumstances. A large survey conducted in 1999–2000 on 13,000 high school students in Flanders (Siongers 2002) indicated that 68% of the adolescents approved of euthanasia if, and only if, the patient him- or herself asked to perform euthanasia (which is the main condition stipulated in the Euthanasia Act). If the family but not the patient asked to perform euthanasia, only 35% of the adolescents in the survey could approve of it. Adolescent opinions were also divided on the topic of abortion. About 31% objected to abortion under all circumstances, whereas 28% found abortion to be justified in most cases.

BELGIUM

Gender

Compared to other countries, Belgium as a nation tends to be a masculine culture. The country ranked twenty-eighth in a sample of 53 countries on Hofstede's (2001) Masculinity Index (MAS). A masculine culture in this conceptualization implies that socially prescribed gender roles are clearly distinct. Men are supposed to be assertive, whereas women are expected to be nurturing.

Gender role expectations among adolescents tend toward gender equality, but classical gender distinctions still loom large. The survey on Flemish adolescents conducted by De Witte et al. (2000) indicated that 85.4% of all adolescents found that child care was both a male and female responsibility. However, the proportion of adolescents who stated that household chores had to be divided equally among both partners was much smaller (64.6%). On a summary index of gender-related opinions, only 1.4% of adolescents were found to be very traditional, and 23.5% rather traditional. About 52% could be described as nontraditional, and 23% were strongly in favor of a more equal division of household and caregiving tasks between both genders. This distribution was affected by several demographic variables: girls, older adolescents, and nonbelievers were less traditional. More than 70% of the boys wished to continue working full-time if they were to have children, whereas only 34% of the girls expressed this wish. Conversely, more than 55% of the girls preferred part-time work, as opposed to 22% of the boys. Again, this proportion decreased significantly with increasing age, with only 30% of the 18-year-old girls wanting to work part-time when they would have children. The intention to quit working upon having children was low for both boys and girls (1.6% and 5.5%, respectively).

Preparation for adult work roles continues to be gender-specific and strongly inspired by the male and female gender roles. A national survey conducted with more than 18,000 adolescents (DREAM 2002) indicated that adolescent girls were more interested in a future job in fields such as education, health care, and law, thus with a strong emphasis on interpersonal and relational dimensions. Boys, by contrast, were more interested in fields such as multimedia, sports, and economics, thus with a strong emphasis on knowledge and competition. Striking differences between both genders were found for the fields of education (40% of the girls and 14% of the boys expressed a preference for this sector) and multimedia (6% of the girls and 31% of the boys expressed a preference for this sector).

Gender-specific physical ideals continue to exert their influence on adolescents and adults alike. Weight issues are the most common topic of concern among girls and young women. A large-scale interview and survey study with over 10,000 people—adults and adolescents—indicated that in the general population, 34% worried about their weight and 24% wanted to lose weight (Scientific Institute for Public Health, Epidemiology Unit 2004). Women were overrepresented in the latter category. The Health Behavior in School-Aged Children Study (HBSC; Maes and Vereecken 2002) revealed that the proportion of adolescents who wanted to change some aspect of their body or physical appearance increased with age, and was significantly greater in adolescent girls than boys. Losing weight was reported most frequently as the desired change by both boys and girls. At the age of 11 to 12 years, 28% of the boys and 46% of the girls expressed this wish, and, at the age of 17 to 18 years, 38% of the boys and 69% of the girls did so. Satisfaction with one's weight was lower in girls than in boys. About 52% of the adolescent boys and 35% of the girls were satisfied with their weight, while 25% of the boys and 54% of the girls found themselves too fat. During the last year, 43% of adolescent girls reported trying losing weight during at least one week, while only 17% of the boys reported doing so. These results are all the more surprising when one bears in mind that less than 5% of the 15- to 24-year-olds are considered obese, defined as having a body mass index of 30 or more (Scientific Institute for Public Health, Epidemiology Unit 2004).

Body image is important in adolescence, particularly among girls. As the adolescent body changes dramatically, a growing sense of insecurity and confusion may set in. Combined with other risk factors that have to be present (such as the societal ideal of being slim, which prevails in Western countries such as Belgium), this vulnerability can lead to a disturbed eating pattern and, in some cases, to a full-blown eating disorder. In Belgium, no reliable data on the prevalence of eating disorders are available. Based on research conducted in the Netherlands, it was estimated that each year 1,800 out of 100,000 girls develop an eating disorder such as anorexia or bulimia nervosa. Only one fifth of them is diagnosed as such by their general practitioner and only 200 patients effectively get a treatment for these diseases. These numbers are alarming, when one realizes that 5 to 18% of all known anorexia cases die from lack of nutrition. When the diagnostic criteria are defined less strictly, it is estimated that 1% of adolescent girls between 12 and 20 years develops anorexia nervosa, and approximately 3 to 5% develop bulimia nervosa (Vandereycken et al. 2002). These eating disorders are much rarer in adolescent boys, but exact numbers are not known. Some 90 to 95% of all known cases of anorexia nervosa are estimated to occur in females, whereas the corresponding figure for bulimia nervosa is estimated at 80%.

The Self

In an individualistic country such as Belgium, young people learn to define themselves in terms of their personal characteristics and to derive their general sense of well-being, in large part, from their success at doing so. Important information on the adolescent self in such a culture can therefore be obtained through research on identity, self-esteem, and well-being.

Using a broad measure of adolescent identity, a large-scale survey in Flanders indicated that almost 90% of the adolescents had a stable sense of identity (they scored at the positive end of the scale; De Witte et al. 2000). Boys and girls had equally strong identities, thus defined. About 80% of the adolescents evidenced average to high self-esteem. Conversely, 20% did not have a positive self-image. Boys' self-esteem was substantially higher than that of girls. The lowest self-esteem was found in the age category of 16- to 17-year-olds. On average, Flemish adolescents scored high on well-being, and 60% of them scored higher than 8 out of 10 on the Cantrill scale. Boys and younger adolescents, on average, scored higher on general well-being. Taken together, these findings on adolescent identity, self-esteem, and well-being do not confirm the negative "storm and stress" stereotype about adolescence. Nearly 80% of the adolescents did not correspond to the popular stereotype of the emotionally disturbed adolescent, and only a minority had to deal with a pronounced identity crisis.

The situation may be different for adolescents who belong to cultural minorities. Collectivistic values within their culture may prompt them to define themselves in terms of the membership of their cultural group, and they have to define themselves in relation to the dominant culture. Research on ethnic identity formation among immigrants and ethnic groups is rather limited in Belgium. Two important studies, however, converged in their conclusions (Phalet, Derycke, and Swyngedouw 1999; Snauwaert et al. 2003). Snauwaert et al. (2003) examined the acculturation orientations among high school students from two cultural groups residing in Belgium (Turks and

Moroccans) using two scientific frameworks (the contact theory and the adoption and identification theory). Integration was the most popular orientation according to the first framework, but separation was the most popular one according to the second one. Apparently, most people who belong to ethnic minorities wanted to have good and regular contacts with Belgians. Their own ethnic identity, however, remained important because they were far less inclined to identify with Belgians or to adopt large parts of the Belgian culture. This pattern reveals that a desire to have good contacts with Belgians does not imply identification with them, and a lack of identification with Belgians does not imply a rejection of intercultural contacts.

Time spent on one's own is highly valued in individualistic cultures and may contribute to identity formation. De Witte et al. (2000) reported that 8.9% of adolescents were alone most of the time when they had leisure time. When forced to spend time alone or during social contacts, adolescents may experience a discrepancy between the desired quality of their social relationships and the actual quality of those relationships. If such a discrepancy emerges, adolescents will feel lonely. Several studies indicate that a non-negligible proportion of Flemish adolescents are lonely and that girls are at greater risk of feeling lonely. In one study, about 8% of the 12- to 18-year-olds reported feeling lonely (De Witte et al. 2000). The HBSC study found that 11% of the 11- to 18-year-old adolescents reported feeling lonely often to very often, and only 36% never felt lonely. In both studies, girls felt significantly more lonely than did boys.

Family Relationships

In Belgium the marriage rate is decreasing and the divorce rate is going up. In 2002, there were 40,434 marriages (that is, a rate of 3.92 per 1,000 inhabitants) and 30,628 divorces (that is, a rate of 2.97 per 1,000 inhabitants) in Belgium (NIS 2003). The median age of marriage was 30 years and 4 months for men, and 27 years and 9 months for women. The median age at divorce was 40 years and 8 months, and 38 years and 4 months, for men and women respectively, and divorces, on average, took place after a median marriage duration of 12 years and 5 months. On average, 33.5% of the marriages contracted in 2002 involved divorced people, with the most frequent ones being two divorced people marrying each other.

These changes in living arrangements have an impact on the family structure that adolescents find themselves in. The HBSC study indicated that 82% of the 11- to 18-year-olds lived with both parents, 10% primarily lived with their mother (with 50% of them having a stepfather), and 2% primarily lived with their father (with again about 50% having a stepmother). Adolescents from the vocational level in high school were overrepresented in the category of families who had gone through a divorce.

Belgian families with adolescents tend to share a number of activities. Having meals together and watching television together (reported by 73 and 70% of the adolescents, respectively) were the most important daily family activities. However, less than 50% of the families talked about things that are important to adolescents on a regular basis. A weekly visit to family or friends with the nuclear family was reported by 58% of the adolescents. The Flemish Regional Indicators (VRIND 2003), for instance, revealed for 2000 that in the broad age category of people younger than 25, 44.9% of children, adolescents, and young adults visited members of their extended family at least once a month. Many adolescents (32.5%) spend a significant amount of their leisure time with their parents, brothers, or sisters, thus with members of the nuclear family (De Witte et al. 2000). Finally, the HBSC study indicated that up to 65% of all young people did sports or played a game with the family. These figures were of course higher for children than for adolescents. On the whole, adolescents were satisfied with their home situation, and even at 17 to 18 years of age 89% reported that they enjoyed being at home.

Parenting practices, as perceived by adolescents, seem to approximate the Western ideal of authoritative parenting. In one large-scale study of Flemish adolescents, both mothers and fathers received high scores on average on two constituent dimensions of this particular parenting style, that is, responsiveness and monitoring. They received lower scores, however, on the third constituent dimension, that is, autonomy granting (De Witte et al. 2000). So the majority of Flemish adolescents felt that their parents were responsive to their needs and knew well about their friends, activities, and whereabouts, but somewhat failed to encourage them to try out things on their own.

Interesting differences emerged between mothers and fathers. Mothers were seen as more responsive to adolescents' needs and as more knowledgeable about their lives. These findings may reflect the greater involvement of mothers in daily interactions with their adolescent children. Mothers and fathers did not differ in the degree of autonomy they granted to their adolescents. Adolescents'

experiences of the parenting process also differed as a function of their age, gender, and the type of family they lived in. These effects can be illustrated for the third parenting dimension, that is, encouragement of autonomy. The older the adolescents, the more encouragement of autonomy they experienced. Boys were encouraged more strongly to try out things on their own than were girls, in line with Western role expectations where boys are expected to be more autonomous and independent. Finally, adolescents from divorced families reported greater encouragement to act autonomously than did their age-mates from intact families.

Friends and Peers/Youth Culture

Several studies reveal that Belgian adolescents, in general, have many friends, spend a lot of time with them, and feel satisfied about their relationships with their friends. A large-scale research survey conducted on over 13,000 Belgian high school adolescents (Elchardus and Glorieux 2002) indicated that 1.1% have no best friends, 8.3% have one best friend, 47.8% have 2 to 4 best friends, and 42.8% have five or more. In the broad age category of people younger than 25 who live in Flanders, 55.6% meet several times a month with their friends. About 10% meet with their friends only a couple of times a year or even less frequently (VRIND 2003). Another study reported that approximately 65% of Flemish high school students meet with their friends on a daily basis. About 5% of them meet their friends only during the weekends, whereas less than 5% meet their friends only a couple of times a month (De Witte et al. 2000). Finally, a large survey conducted on Belgian adolescents in the age category of 15 to 24 years (Scientific Institute for Public Health, Epidemiology Unit 2004) indicated that only 2% had infrequent social contacts, 4% were dissatisfied with their social contacts, 8% had a limited social network, and 8% experienced weak social support. Compared to the older age groups examined in that study, the percentages in this age group were the lowest. These findings suggest that the social life of adolescents in Belgium is satisfactory on the whole.

As expected, the classroom and the school are the most important meeting places for adolescents (Elchardus and Glorieux 2002). Other important meeting places are, in descending order of importance, at home or with friends (41%), in a sports club or youth organization (29%), at the pub or a party (20%), and on the street or in a park (18%; De Witte et al. 2000). As adolescents grow older, the school becomes less important as a meeting ground. The 15- to 16-year-olds in particular meet with their friends on the street or in a park. For adolescents of non-Belgian origin, regardless of their age, these places are also the most important venues to meet their friends.

Formal organizations (organizations led by adults) are popular among Belgian adolescents. In 2001, a total of 875,223 Flemish people were members of a registered sports federation, that is approximately 15% of the total Flemish population in that year. In the age category of 0 to 19 years, this percentage reached 25%. Moreover, 53.7% of those younger than 25 indicated that they did sports or exercised at least a couple of times a month. However, almost 15% of them never did sports or only once a year. In 2001, a total of 469,216 youngsters (that is, approximately 30%) were members of an organized youth movement (such as the Boy Scouts or Girl Guides). Almost 49% of these children and adolescents were between 6 and 12 years, 23% between 13 and 16 years, and 13% between 17 and 20 years of age (VRIND 2003).

Many adolescents are members of several organizations. Counting across all types of organizations, 64.3% of the youngsters in Flanders are members of a certain club or organization, 22% are members of two organizations, and 5.3% are even members of three organizations (De Witte et al. 2000). Boys are slightly overrepresented in organizations in comparison to girls, and with increasing age, the number of adolescents who are member of an organization decreases. The sports club and the youth movement—in that order—are the two most popular organizations. However, being in a sports club or in a youth movement were not the most popular pastimes for adolescents in general. (These activities could be found at the fourth and seventh place in the ranking, respectively). Watching television and listening to music were the most popular ones, and visiting friends ranked third. However, important differences between boys and girls have to be mentioned. Being in a sports club was the most important pastime for boys, whereas it was only the fifth most important pastime for girls. Conversely, visiting friends was a more important pastime for girls (where it ranked third) than for boys (where it occupied the fifth place in the popularity ranking).

Like many Western countries, Belgium has a distinct youth culture, or, put more precisely, a whole range of youth cultures. Most of these cultures are influenced by other cultures and by musical trends from English-speaking countries such as the United States in particular. Most youth cultures in Belgium are characterized, first and foremost, by their interest in a particular type of music, such as house/techno, hardcore/metal, straight edge, hip hop/rap, punk, and new wave. Several youth cultures are also characterized by distinctive hair and dress styles, and different ideas, values, and habits. Striking examples in terms of clothing and ideals, for instance, are the punks, the hip hoppers, and the straight edgers.

Actual numbers on how many youngsters are members of these distinct youth cultures are hard to obtain in Belgium. But youth cultures are hugely popular. In one study in Flanders, 70% of the adolescents reported that they felt attracted to a specific youth culture, and to house/techno and hardcore/metal in particular (De Witte et al. 2000). Almost 95% of them named the specific type of music associated with that youth culture as the main reason for this attraction. Far fewer adolescents mentioned clothing and hairstyle (17.5%) or the ideals and values associated with these youth cultures (15.6%) as reasons underlying their cultural affiliation or preference.

Love and Sexuality

Many adolescents in Belgium are involved in romantic relationships. One study found that approximately 40% of Belgian high school students had a relationship (Elchardus and Glorieux 2002). At the time of assessment, these relationships had lasted already for about six months in half of the cases. Approximately 30% reported already having a relationship that lasted longer than one year. More 18-year-olds than 16-year-olds had relationships, and these relationships lasted longer with increasing age. Another study found that approximately 35% of Flemish high school students had a relationship, and that the odds of having a relationship increased with increasing age (De Witte et al. 2000). Finally, a study of 629 university students revealed that 44% of them had a relationship, with the majority of them being satisfied about their relationship (Centrum voor Relatie en Zwangerschapsproblemen 2002).

Many adolescents become sexually active at an early age. In one study, 20% of Flemish adolescents aged 12 to 18 reported that they already had sex, and this proportion increased with increasing age, as expected (De Witte et al. 2000). The HBSC study reported that, at the age of 13 to 14, twice as many boys than girls reported that they already had sex with a person of the opposite sex (10% and 5%, respectively). At the age of 15 to 16 years, boys and girls were equally experienced (20% and 18%, respectively), and at 17 to 18 years, slightly more girls than boys reported that they already had sexual intercourse (51% and 45%, respectively). Furthermore, age at first intercourse was reported as being younger than 11 years in 7% of the cases, younger than 12 years in another 7% of the cases, younger than 13 years for 9% of the cases, and younger than 14 in 15% of the cases. In general, boys reported having sex for the first time at a younger age than girls did. Caution is warranted when interpreting these and subsequent gender-specific results due to potential response biases. In sum, at the age of 17 years, approximately half of the adolescents already had sexual intercourse, and at the age of 19 years almost 90% had (Sensoa 2003). Young people in the academic track in school or in higher education and adolescents with a Catholic background reported having their first sexual experience later in life.

Adolescent boys reported having had more sexual partners than girls. The HBSC study indicated that 58% of the girls who reported that they ever had sex had done so with only one partner, whereas 5% reported to have had sex with more than five partners already. Among sexually experienced boys, 37% reporting having had sex with only one partner, whereas 22% reported that they had sex with more than five partners already. The initiative to have sex for the first time mostly came from both sides. However, girls appeared to be the more assertive partners. In 52% of the cases, they consistently said "no" when they did not feel like having sex, whereas only 35% of the boys did so.

Adolescents in Belgium readily have access to contraceptives. In general 80% of the adolescents reported that they protected themselves against unwanted pregnancies by using a condom or oral contraceptives. At the same time, however, only 66% protected themselves against sexually transmitted diseases such as AIDS by using a condom (Sensoa 2003). Only 20% of the youngsters reported using both a condom and oral contraceptives. Girls seem somewhat reluctant to ask their male partners to use a condom. The HBSC study indicated that approximately 66% of 15 to 18-year-old boys used a condom the last time they had sexual intercourse, whereas only 50% of 15 to 18-year-old girls reported doing so. These figures are alarming because in 24% of the cases, adolescents reported having no or just partial information about the past sexual experiences of the partner when they were not using a condom.

Exact figures on homosexuality are hard to come by. The HBSC study indicated that at the age of 17 to 18 years, 3% of the adolescents had been intimate with someone of the same gender, and 2% already had had sex with someone of the same gender. At university, almost 2% reported having a relationship with a partner of the same sex (Centrum voor Relatie en Zwangerschapsproblemen 2002). In a large-scale survey on more than 41,000 youngsters, 2.2% of the high school students reported being homosexual or bisexual (Pelleriaux 2004). In general gay adolescents do not feel well-accepted by the society at large. Despite the fact that 56% of adolescents found homosexuality to be acceptable, almost 23% of homosexual children and adolescents were verbally or physically threatened or assaulted at school (Peeters 2001). Another study found that only a minority of gay youth would tell their friends or even parents that they were homosexual (Pelleriaux 2004).

Sex education is not implemented systematically at the school level in Belgium. In fact, Belgium is one of the few European countries, together with Greece and Finland, in which systematic sex education is not part of the standard curriculum (Sensoa 2003). Several programs do exist but they are rather limited efforts and are not evaluated systematically. In approximately 75% of the Flemish high schools, some sort of relationship and sex education is offered (Van Oost and Buysse 1994). Despite the fact that they were quite diverse, those programs focused mainly on promoting social skills and knowledge about contraceptives and sexually transmitted diseases. Systematically organized relationship and sex education at the school level, however, is badly needed because adolescents rarely talk with their parents about these topics.

Teenage pregnancies are not seen as an important social issue in Belgium, partly because most adolescent girls protect themselves adequately against unwanted pregnancies (but not STDs) by means of oral contraceptives. Teenage mothers are relatively rare. In the age category from 15 to 19 years, Belgium counted only 9.1 mothers per thousand girls in 1995. With this figure, the country formed part of the middle group of Western European countries, with Great Britain scoring the highest and the Netherlands scoring the lowest in terms of the proportion of teenage mothers. In 1999, there were 5,038 teenage pregnancies in Belgium in girls younger than 20 years, of which 2,022 were ended through abortion. These numbers were 1,433 and 895, respectively, in girls younger than 18 years. Put differently, 1.7% of the girls younger than 20 years have to deal with a pregnancy (Sensoa 2003), willingly or not. This proportion was significantly higher in the French-speaking part of the country, and Turkish and Moroccan girls were overrepresented in this group. Finally, research indicated that teenage pregnancies were associated with much greater health risks for the child than pregnancies at a later age. Moreover, the younger the pregnant teenager, the longer she waited to consult a gynecologist or general practitioner for the first time (with only 43% of the 17-year-olds and 55% of the 19-year-olds doing so during the first three months of the pregnancy).

Health Risk Behavior

Alcohol, which can be sold freely to anyone over the age of 16, is a frequently used substance among Belgian adolescents. Approximately 81% of them reported having drunk alcohol during the past 12 months, with more boys than girls doing so (85% and 78%, respectively). More than 22% of the 15 to 24-year-olds reported having drunk at least six glasses of alcohol on one day during the past six months, with a ratio of boys to girls of 3 to 1. Furthermore, 1.5% reported using alcohol every day. Approximately 63% reported using alcohol during the weekend, whereas 20% of the boys and 10% of the girls did so during the week. About 4.6% of adolescents between 15 and 24 years of age—approximately 6% of boys and 3% of girls—can be labeled as problematic drinkers (Scientific Institute for Public Health, Epidemiology Unit 2004). The HBSC study indicated that the lifetime prevalence of alcohol use at the age of 11 to 12 years is 72% for boys and 57% for girls. At 17 to 18 years, almost everyone (96%) had had a drink at least once in their life. During the last week, 25% of the 13 to 14-years-olds, 50% of the 15 to 16-year-olds, and 66% of the 17 to 18-year-olds reported having drunk alcohol. Boys who attended the vocational track in high school were the heaviest drinkers: 17% reported having drunk 20 alcoholic drinks the last week, and 24% reported being drunk for at least ten times.

Cannabis is the most popular illicit drug among Belgian adolescents. The Association for Alcohol and Other Drug-Related Problems (2003) surveyed, from 1999 on, about 260,000 youngsters in secondary schools about their cannabis use. About 25% of them had ever used cannabis. Some 15% did so during the last year (1% of the 12-year-olds and 30% of the 18-year-olds), with 5% using the drug at least on a weekly basis. Significantly more boys than girls use cannabis. The Belgian National Report on Drugs 2002 (Sleiman and Sartor 2002) reported that XTC was the second most frequently used illegal drug. XTC has a lifetime prevalence of approximately 5% in 15 to 16-year-olds, and about 10% in 17 to 18-year-olds. Other illegal drugs used

by Belgian adolescents were sniff or volatile inhalants, amphetamines, LSD, cocaine, and heroin, with the latter two having a last-month prevalence, in the age category of 15-18 years, of less than 1%.

Official police records show that youth delinquency is a substantial problem, particularly in the five largest cities of Belgium which have a combined youth population of 260,000 (with approximately 25% having a foreign nationality). One study counted 13,549 registered delinquent acts perpetrated by 14 to 24-year-olds in those cities for the period 1997–1999 (Van San and Leerkes 2001). The most frequent types of delinquent acts were theft (66.1%), drug trafficking (20.5%), and vandalism (8.1%). In most cases, these crimes were committed by boys (Goris and Walgrave 2002). In 2000, approximately 1,450 youngsters were sent to an institution (VRIND 2003) and 14,487 youngsters were referred to child protection committees because of their delinquent record.

According to self-report surveys, the number of young people who commit delinquent acts is much higher. About half of the respondents in a representative sample of Flemish high school students claimed to have committed some sort of crime (such as theft, drug use, or vandalism) during the last year (De Witte et al. 2000). Almost 70% of them reported having committed only a single offense. Fifty-five percent of all cases of physical violence never came to the attention of the authorities, and 70 to 90% of other crimes were never discovered. In general, the rate of delinquency drops with increasing age throughout adolescence. Violent behavior also decreases significantly from 16 to 17 years on (Van Welzenis 2001).

Traffic accidents occur very often in Belgium and take a heavy toll among adolescents in particular. Across all age categories about 50,000 traffic accidents that involve injuries take place every year, with almost 70,000 victims, including 1,500 deaths. In 1998, the probability of having a deadly accident (relative to the number of kilometers traveled in a motor vehicle) was almost 35% higher in Belgium than the European average. Recent statistics for Flanders indicated that 42% of the victims of traffic accidents were between 15 and 29 years of age, whereas this age category accounts only for one-fifth of the total population. In this age category, traffic accidents account for 44% of deaths in men and 30% of deaths in women.

Internalizing problems are also common in adolescence. About 21% of male adolescents and 32% of female adolescents in the age category of 15 to 24 years in Belgium reported some sort of minor psychological problems, whereas 11% and 15%, respectively, reported having serious psychological problems (Scientific Institute for Public Health, Epidemiology Unit 2004). Approximately 5% of boys and 9% of girls reported suffering from depressive symptoms; 5% and 7%, respectively, from anxiety problems; and 8% and 14%, respectively, from some sort of sleeping disorder. Comorbidity was quite common: of the adolescents who reported having one type of psychological problem, about 34% reported at least one additional type of problem. About 3.2% in the age category of 15 to 24 years reported having had a depressive disorder during the last year, with 29.7% of these consulting a general practitioner, 42.4% a specialist, and 37.6% taking psychotropic medication. In all, 2.7% of adolescents reported having used psychotropic medication of any sort during the last two weeks. Another large-scale survey revealed that 9% of all adolescents reported feeling depressive to a certain degree during the last week. Furthermore, about 15% of adolescents stated that they have thought several times during the past 12 months about committing suicide, and between 20 and 30% stated that they had thought at least once about suicide (De Witte et al. 2000).

Actual suicide rates in Belgium are relatively high. In 1995, the general incidence of suicide was 19.8 per 100,000, with an incidence rate of 13.8 per 100,000 in the age category of 15 to 24 years (WHO 2003). Suicide is the second most frequent cause of death in the age category of 15 to 25 years in Belgium (Portzky and Van Heeringen 2001). Between 1991 and 1996, the number of suicides in Flemish men between 15 and 19 years of age tripled. About 8% of all adolescents stated that they already attempted once to end their lives, with significantly more girls than boys having attempted to do so (Van Heeringen, Meerschaert, and Berckmoes 1999). However, because of the different means adopted, boys actually commit suicide four times more often than do girls. Most girls take large doses of sleeping pills, whereas boys use firearms or hang themselves. In comparison with adults, adolescents undertake twice as many suicide attempts, but adults succeed in their attempts four times more often than do adolescents. Suicide recidivism is extremely high in adolescence. One out of three attempts is performed by young people who have already tried to take their lives at least once before.

Education

Compulsory education in Belgium extends to the age of 18 years. However, young people are obliged to receive full-time education between age 6 and age 15 only. Therefore, from the age of 15 years on, a limited number of young people opt for part-time work combined with part-time education to comply with compulsory education. Compulsory education finishes at the end of the school year in which the pupil reaches the age of 18 or when he or she obtains the certificate of secondary education (irrespective of age). However, compulsory education does not mean compulsory schooling. Children do not have to attend school; they can also be educated at home by their parents.

Educational attainment is high and has increased in recent years, as younger cohorts stay longer in school than older ones (VRIND 2003). In 1990, about 61% of the Flemish population between 25 and 64 years had attended school until they were 15 years or younger, 22% until they were 18, and 17% had a degree of higher education. In 2000, these figures reached 40%, 33%, and 26%, respectively. Current rates of participation are high at all levels of schooling. Virtually all of the 5- to 14-year-olds (99.1%) participated in the educational system, which is comparable to the Netherlands and Germany, both countries with educational laws similar to the Belgian one. Likewise, 90.5% of the 15 to 19-year-olds participated in the educational system, which is a very high percentage in comparison to the European average. Only Sweden does better.

Participation in higher education is also high. In 2001, all Flemish colleges of higher education combined counted 99,258 students, and 56,118 students were enrolled in the Flemish universities. Young women comprised 59% of total enrollment in the first type of institutions and 41% in the second. Females are overrepresented in areas such as social healthcare (83%), psychology and educational science (79%), and pharmacological science (77%). Conversely, the female participation degree is the lowest in areas such as applied science (21%) and philosophy (37%). The international orientation of the Flemish student, however, is rather low; only 1.8% of the Flemish students participated in the SOCRATES/ERASMUS program in 2001. This program was launched in 1987 by the European Commission to give students a chance to study abroad (VRIND 2003).

Special education, both at the primary and secondary level, is aimed at children and adolescents who need special help, temporarily or permanently. Divided into eight types, this type of education caters to the educational and developmental needs of particular groups of pupils. Types one and two offer special education for youngsters with a mental disability (slight or serious), type three does so for youngsters with serious emotional or behavioral disorders, and type four is designed for youngsters with a physical disability. Type five offers special education to youngsters admitted to a hospital or put into quarantine for medical reasons, types six and seven do so for youngsters with visual and auditory impairment, respectively, and type eight is for children with serious learning difficulties. More boys than girls attend special education schools. In the Flemish educational system, the proportions of young people enrolled in this type of education were the highest in the age category of 11 to 12 years (6.6% of the boys and 4.2% of the girls; Ministerie van de Vlaamse Gemeenschap, cel Publicaties Onderwijs 2003).

No specific education for the gifted is provided or funded by the government, but there are some private schools and special organizations for talented young people (Freeman 2002). In addition, there are limited initiatives for the gifted within normal secondary schools, such as the "kangaroo-classes" (Ministerie van de Vlaamse Gemeenschap, cel Publicaties Onderwijs 2003). In those classes gifted students come together during a couple of hours a week to work on special enrichment projects or to take more difficult courses. However, exact figures on how many schools organize such classes or how many students are enrolled in such programs are not available.

Flemish high school students generally perform well on international tests of achievement. On example is the Program for International Student Assessment (PISA), conducted since 2000, which compares more than 30 countries on indicators such as reading skills, mathematical skills, and scientific literacy rates in 15-year-olds. In this program, Flemish students, together with those from Great Britain and Finland, scored the highest on mathematical competencies, the second highest, after Finland, on reading skills, and the fourth highest on scientific competencies.

On the whole, Flemish high school students feel satisfied about their life at school. Belgian schools are typically small. In 2002, primary schools in Flanders counted 274 pupils on average, and secondary schools 451 pupils. Students perceive their relationships with their teachers as rather satisfactory. About 60% of Flemish high school students do not report having any specific problems at school, whereas 16% report having behavioral problems, 15% having negative feelings about school, and 8% having both (De Witte et al. 2000). Absenteeism in school is generally low. In 2001–2002, problematic absenteeism occurred in 2.8% of the cases in general secondary education (academic

track), in 8.6% of the cases in technical secondary education (vocational track), and in 27.9% of the cases in trade schools (VRIND 2003).

Work

In Belgium it is prohibited by law to employ children younger than 15 years of age. Therefore, systematic child labor or slavery does not exist in Belgium. Employment rates among adolescents and emerging adults are relatively low. About 60% of the inhabitants of Belgium between 15 and 64 years of age had a job in 2001, with significantly more men than women being in that position (VRIND 2003). This percentage was the highest in Flanders (63.4%) and the lowest in the Walloon and Brussels region (55.4% and 53.9%, respectively). In the age category of 15 to 24 years, 29.7% had a job in Belgium, with again significantly more men than women being in that position (33.2% and 26.0%, respectively). This proportion was as high as the one observed in France, but much lower than in Germany, the Netherlands (70.4%), or the average in the European Union (40.3%).

With regard to unemployment, young people can be regarded a high-risk group. The general unemployment rate in Belgium in 2001, determined in accordance with the International Labour Organisation (ILO) criteria, was comparable to the average rate in the European Union. However, in the age category of 15 to 24 years, this rate (16.9%) was slightly higher in Belgium and much higher than those found in Germany and the Netherlands. Furthermore, 49.2% of these unemployed youngsters were unemployed less than six months, 20.7% between six and 11 months, and 30.1% for 12 months or more. In general, the unemployment rate in people of non-Belgian origin was much higher, particularly among those stemming from non-EU countries (Steunpunt WAV 2002). When interpreting these figures, one has to bear in mind that the total proportion of the Belgian population that is inactive (housewives, students, and older unemployed people who do not meet the rather stringent ILO criteria) reached 34.9% in 2000, which again is higher than in the surrounding countries and higher than the average in the European Union (Steunpunt WAV 2002).

To increase the employment rate in the age category of 15 to 24, the Flemish government, in collaboration with the Flemish Service for Employment and Vocational Training (VDAB), launched the Rosetta Plan (since 1999) to provide jobs for those younger than 26 years. All firms and organizations with more than 50 employees were obliged to employ a number of adolescents of that age group under special contractual specifications and received extra funding if they did so. In addition, the VDAB provides numerous educational and training programs, both at the individual and group level, to help unemployed people find their way into the labor market. The VDAB also provides support for people on an individual basis in the organization in which they work, with 7,755 people receiving this type of help in 2002. In total, 170,976 unemployed people were supported in some way by the VDAB, with 41% of them being younger than 25 years (VDAB 2002).

Most adolescents have a positive attitude toward their future work. About 73% of Flemish school students found a steady job to be an important part of their future life and only 3% indicated that this was not important at all (De Witte et al. 2000). About 80% of the 16- to 18-year-olds feel well prepared for their future profession (DREAM 2002). Furthermore, 67% of them feel confident about their professional future but one out of five youngsters really worries about it (they fear being unemployed, not being able to realize one's dream, or not being able to meet the demands of the workplace). About 44% of this age category viewed a job as a way to earn money, another 44% as a way to be financially independent, and 39% as a way to support the family. About half of the youngsters in this age category indicated that their choice of profession was, to a large extent, influenced by meeting people who actually performed these jobs. Parents, friends, counselors employed at pupil guidance centers, and teachers had much less influence on their vocational choice or preference.

Media

Belgian adolescents make extensive use of the media and all figures obtained are comparable to what is found in the United States. In a sample of Flemish high school students, the mean overall TV viewing volume was 74 hours and 15 minutes per month, whereas the mean overall video game playing volume was 18 hours and 29 minutes per month (Van Mierlo and Van den Bulck 2004). Ninth graders watched more TV and played more video games than did twelfth graders. Another study (De Witte et al. 2000) found that 15- to 16-year-olds watched TV the most and 11- to 12-year-olds the least. On average, only 3.1% of adolescents do not watch TV during the week; during the weekend this percentage is somewhat higher. About 60% reported watching less than two hours a day,

but 7% watched more than four hours a day. The HBSC study also indicated that playing computer games was very popular among adolescents. Only 11% of the 11- to 18-year-old boys and 30% of the 11- to 18-year-old girls never play computer games. In 2000, only a minority of those younger than 24 years reported never going to the movies. The majority, however, (about 41%) went several times a year, whereas 22% went several times a month (VRIND 2003).

In Belgium, like in many other European countries, most of the TV programs, and fiction programs in particular, are imported from the United States. North America is the leading export country for movies and television series in Western Europe, with 62% and 51%, respectively, being imported from the United States. Depending on the different channels, programs imported from the United States accounted for 34.5% up to 84.7% of the television series, and for 58.3% up to 100% of the movies shown in Flanders in 1996. Exactly these two types of programs (TV series and films) are the most popular ones among adolescents (De Witte et al. 2000), which implies that Belgian youth are subjected to visual media imported from North America and much less to indigenous visual media.

Music is also a very important pastime for adolescents. Music ranks first in the list of items that adolescents spend money on, with 37.7% of adolescents doing so. Movies, computers, books, and magazines were less important, with 18.3%, 14.2%, and 9.1%, respectively, of all adolescents spending money on them (De Witte et al. 2000). The Youth On-Line Survey (2000) indicated that 35% of the 12 to 17-year-olds regularly surfed on the Internet, whereas 43% of the 18- to 24-year-olds could be called frequent surfers. Almost 45% of youngsters in Flanders practically never read a newspaper, 15% do so on a weekly basis, and another 15% on a daily basis, with boys being represented more in the latter category than girls (De Witte et al. 2000). In 2002, 21.5% of Flemish youth (that is, all people under the age of 25) reported that they visited a library several times a month and 29.5% of them indicated that they never did so. Almost 31% reported that they did so several times a year (VRIND 2003).

TV viewing has been shown to have negative influences both on adolescent attitudes and on their health-related behaviors that are similar to those found in research in the United States. One study found important cultivation effects. As adolescents viewed TV more often, they came to see violence as more common and crime as more likely to occur, and they experienced greater fear of crime and greater anomie (Van Mierlo and Van den Bulck 2004). Another study on 1,035 Flemish 17- and 18-year-olds demonstrated that TV viewing coincided with a high consumption of snacks, soft drinks, and alcohol (Van den Bulck 2000). Among heavy viewers, these behaviors accompany viewing more regularly. A rather high percentage of adolescents also reported lack of sleep or sleeping problems as a result of watching TV. No link was found between TV viewing and obesity, but the amount of TV viewing was significantly related to various aspects of people's self-assessments regarding their weight, their ideal weight, and their looks. Finally, Eggermont (in press) demonstrated that television viewing was related to the idea that a romantic partner needed to be attractive and to have a pleasant personality, both among romantically experienced and inexperienced adolescents.

Politics and Military

Adolescents' actual participation in the political process is high, but their interest in politics is generally low. Voting is mandatory in Belgium with the voting age being 18 years. Therefore, the overwhelming majority of emerging adults take part in public elections. In 1995, only 1.3% of emerging adults between 18 and 24 years of age did not vote, and 3.5% of them cast an invalid vote (Siongers 2002). However, when asked what they would do if voting were not mandatory in Belgium, 25.5% of young people in that age category reported in 1998 that they would not vote. Only 11.5% of adolescents between 18 and 24 years of age indicated that they were strongly interested in politics. About 20% indicated that they were not at all interested in politics. Political apathy was even stronger in the younger age groups: almost 80% of the 14- to 18-year-olds had little or no interest in politics, whereas 6% indicated that they were moderately to strongly interested in politics (De Witte et al. 2000).

Political involvement is limited and adolescents' knowledge about politics leaves much to be desired. Almost 40% of the 15- to 16-year-olds reported that they did not have a preference for a particular political party, whereas 29% of the 17- to 18-year-olds did so. The latter figure was very similar to the percentage found among Belgian adults. In 1998, about 22% of adolescents expressed a preference for right-wing parties, whereas 23% did so for left-wing parties (De Witte et al. 2000). In that same year, about 73% of all high school students stated that they were familiar with the names of the six major political parties at that time in Flanders. Only

3.5% stated that they knew none of these parties. Older adolescents and boys were more knowledgeable about politics.

Finally, political involvement, both active and passive, is very low among Belgian adolescents and emerging adults. In a representative sample of Flemish adolescents, only 2.6% were members of a political party (with 39% being active members, being defined as participating in at least one activity during the last year; Elchardus and Glorieux 2002). Slightly higher figures were found for young people's reported membership of other social organizations. About 15% were members of an environmental organization (with 20.1% being actively involved), 8.7% of a third world organization (with 32.2% being actively involved), and 8.6% reportedly did volunteer work. Furthermore, 4.0% were members of a peace organization (with 34.6% being actively involved), and 3.6% of an anti-racist organization (with 39% of them being active members).

The military no longer occupies an important place in the lives of Belgian adolescents. Compulsory military service was abolished in Belgium in 1992. Today, the Belgian army comprises approximately 40,000 troops (7% of whom are females), stationed in different barracks across the country. Belgian soldiers currently have a mean age of 38 years, so that adolescents and emerging adults no longer are the dominant age group in the military. The Belgian army was not involved in any armed conflict at the time of this writing. However, Belgian soldiers do participate in logistic and support missions mandated by the United Nations (UN) and operated under the auspices of the North Atlantic Treaty Organization (NATO). One such mission is the International Security Assistance Force (ISAF) in Afghanistan.

Luc Goossens and Koen Luyckx

References and Further Reading

Association for Alcohol and Other Drug-Related Problems. 2003. "Cannabisgebruik bij Vlaamse jongeren" ("Cannabis use in Flemish youth"). http://www.gezondheid. be/index.cfm?fuseaction=art&art_id=1686.

Centrum voor Relatie en Zwangerschapsproblemen. (2002). "Relaties en seksualiteit bij eerstejaarsstudenten van de KU Leuven" ("Relationships and sexuality in freshman students at the Catholic University of Leuven"). http://www.crz.be.

Corijn, M. Transition to adulthood in Flanders (Belgium). 2001. In Transitions to Adulthood in Europe, ed. M. Corijn and E. Klijzing. Dordrecht, the Netherlands: Kluwer.

De Witte, H., J. Hooge, and L. Walgrave, eds. 2000. *Jongeren in Vlaanderen: Gemeten en geteld. 12- tot 18-jarigen over hun leefwereld en toekomst* (*Youth in Flanders: 12- to 18-year-olds report about their life-world and future expectations*). Leuven: Universitaire Pers.

Dobbelaere, K., M. Elchardus, J. Kerkhofs, L. Voyé, and B. Bawin-Legros. 2000. *Verloren zekerheid: De Belgen en hun waarden, overtuigingen en houdingen* (Certainty lost: *The Belgians and their values, convictions, and attitudes*). Tielt: Lannoo.

DREAM. 2002. "Jongeren en hun professionele toekomst: Tussen droom en realisme" ("Young people and their professional future: Between dream and reality"). www.dream-it.be/dreamsite/binfiles/actiondream/Rapport_enquete_DREAM_site_NL.pdf.

Eggermont, S. (in press). Television viewing, perceived similarity and adolescents' expectations of a romantic partner. *Journal of Broadcasting and Electronic Media.*

Elchardus, M., and I. Glorieux. 2002. *De symbolische samenleving. Een exploratie van de nieuwe sociale en culturele ruimtes* (*The symbolic society: An exploration of new social and cultural spaces*). Tielt: Lannoo.

Freeman, J. 2002. "Out-of-School Educational Provision for the Gifted and Talented Around the World." http://www.warwick.ac.uk/gifted/professional-academy/downloadable-materials/documents/out-of-school-provision-research.pdf.

Goossens, L. 1994. Belgium. In *International Handbook of Adolescence*, ed. K. Hurrelmann. Westport, Conn.: Greenwood Press.

Goris, P., and L. Walgrave. 2002. *Van kattenkwaad en erger: Actuele thema's uit de jeugdcriminologie* (*Current themes in youth delinquency*). Leuven: Garant.

Hofstede, G. 2001. *Culture's Consequences: Comparing Values, Behaviors, Institutions, and Organizations Across Nations.* 2nd ed. Thousand Oaks, Calif.: Sage.

Hutsebaut, D., and D. Verhoeven. 1991. The adolescent's representation of God from age 12 to 18: Changes or evolution? *Journal of Empirical Theology.* 4: 59–72.

Maes, L., and C. Vereecken. 2002. "HBSC Study: Health Behavior in School-Aged Children (Flemish Community)." http://www.iph.fgov.be/epidemio/morbidat/nl/Bases:ACCN01.htm.

Ministerie van de Vlaamse Gemeenschap, cel Publicaties Onderwijs. 2003. "Vlaamse onderwijsindicatoren in internationaal perspectief" ("Flemish educational indicators: An international perspective"). http://www.ond.vlaanderen.be/berichten/2003pers/onderwijsindicatoren_synthese.htm.

NIS. 2003. "Statistics Belgium." http://www.statbel.fgov.be/.

Peeters, B. 2001. "Graag zien. Een brochure voor ouders van homo's, lesbiennes en bi's" ("Information flier for parents of gay, lesbian, and bisexual youth"). http://www.holebifederatie.be/downloads/d_graagzien.pdf.

Pelleriaux, K. 2004. "Resultaten van de Scholierenenquête 2003" ("Results of the 2003 school student survey"). http://www.holebifabriek.be/.

Phalet, K., L. Derycke, and M. Swyngedouw. 1999. Culturele waarden en acculturatievormen bij Turken en Marokkanen in Brussel (Cultural values and types of acculturation among Turks and Moroccans in Brussels). In *Minderheden in Brussel: Sociopolitieke houdingen en gedragingen.* M. Swyngedouw, K. Phalet, and K. Deschouwer (eds.). Brussels: VUB Press.

Portzky, G., and K. Van Heeringen. 2001. *Het stillen van de pijn. Over preventie van suicide* (*Alleviating the pain: On suicide prevention*). Diegem: Kluwer.

Scientific Institute for Public Health, Epidemiology Unit. 2004. "Health Interview Survey 2001." http://www.iph.fgov.be/epidemio/epien/index4.htm.

Sensoa. 2003. Feiten (Facts on Sexually Transmitted Diseases). http://www.cgso.be.

Siongers, J. 2002. "Jongeren en politiek: Voices from Brussels" ("Youth and politics: Voices from Brussels"). http://www.bocobrussel.be:VoicesSiongers.htm.

Sleiman, S., and F. Sartor. 2002. "Belgian National Report on Drugs 2002." http://www.iph.fgov.be/epidemio/epien/birn/BelgianNr2002.pdf.

Snauwaert, B., B. Soenens, N. Vanbeselaere, and F. Boen. 2003. When integration does not necessarily imply integration: Different conceptualizations of acculturation orientations lead to different classifications. *Journal of Cross-Cultural Psychology* 34:231–39.

Steunpunt WAV. 2002. "Vlaamse Kerncijfers" ("Basic figures on employment in Flanders"). http://www.steunpuntwav.be/stat/2000/Vlamsgewest2000/kerncijfers_februari2002.xls.

Van den Bulck, J. 2000. Is television bad for your health? Behavior and body image of the adolescent "couch potato." *Journal of Youth and Adolescence* 29:273–88.

Vandereycken, W., A. Vandeputte, C. Braet, Y. Goris, H. Lakiere, B. Paerewijck, and R. Van den Broeck. 2002. "Professionalisering van preventie en behandeling van jongeren met eetstoornissen" ("Professionalization of prevention and treatment of young people with eating disorders"). http://www.alexianentienen.be/terberken/Problemen/INDEX.htm.

Van Heeringen, K., T. Meerschaert, and A. Berckmoes. 1999. Epidemiology of attempted suicide in Ghent: Results from the WHO/EURO multicentre study on parasuicide in 1996. *Archives of Public Health* 57:171–84.

Van Mierlo, J., and J. Van den Bulck. 2004. Benchmarking the cultivation approach to video game effects: A comparison of the correlates of TV viewing and game play. *Journal of Adolescence* 27:97–111.

Van Oost, P., and A. Buysse. 1994. *Je zou er AIDS van krijgen. Onderzoek van het CGSO multidimensioneel aidspreventieprogramma* (*Evaluation of the CGSO multidimensional AIDS prevention program*). Belgium: CGSO.

Van San, M., and A. Leerkes. 2001. *Criminaliteit en criminalisering. Allochtone jongeren in België. Rapportage ten behoeve van de minister van Justitie* (*Criminality and migrant youth in Belgium*). Brussels: Ministerie van Justitie.

Van Welzenis, I. 2001. Jongeren en geweld in diverse contexten: Dedramatisering en ernstig nemen (Youth and violence in various contexts: Dedramatizing and taking seriously). In *Veiligheid, een illusie? Theorie, onderzoek en praktijk*, ed. L. Walgrave. Brussels: Politeia.

VDAB. 2002. "De VDAB-dienstverlening in 2002" ("Flemish service for employment and vocational training: Services rendered in 2002"). http://vdab.be/trends/jaarverslag.html.

VRIND. 2003. "Vlaamse regionale indicatoren" ("Flemish regional indicators"). http://aps.vlaanderen.be/statistiek/publicaties/stat_Publicaties_vrind.htm.

WHO. 2003. "Suicide in Belgium." http://www.who.int.

Youth On-Line Survey. 2000. "An expanding Belgian web generation." http://www.insites.be/freeff/press/yol2_eng_051200.asp.

BELIZE

Background Information

Belize, a nation of 250,000 people, is both Central American and Caribbean in its location, population, language practices, and cultural makeup. Located on the eastern edge of Central America and the western edge of the Caribbean Sea, Belize occupies approximately the land size of Massachusetts with a diverse geography spanning rain forest to offshore cay areas. There has been a longstanding land dispute with Guatemala over the western border of the nation, though that border has remained relatively stable.

In addition to geographic diversity, Belize boasts ethnic diversity with a wide range of people, and with most of its inhabitants being of multi-ethnic descent. About 50% of the population is Mestizo or "Spanish" (mixed Mayan and European heritage); about 25% is Creole (African and Afro-European heritage); 10% is Mayan, 7% is Garifuna (mixed African and Native Carib heritage); and the remainder is from other backgrounds (Mennonite, Chinese, European, Middle Eastern, and North American). Historically, these various peoples settled in the different regions of the nation, creating some separation among groups (Sutherland 1998). However, through internal migration due to searching for jobs and cheaper land on which to build homes, more diverse communities have been forming. Interethnic relations in Belize are thought to be among the best in the world. English is the national language, though Spanish and Creole are almost ubiquitous. Most adolescents speak at least these three languages, and many also speak Mayan and Garifuna. Forty-one percent of the population is under 15 years of age, and 52% is under 20. Because of the substantial diversity, it is challenging to characterize adolescence for all Belizeans, though common themes do emerge.

Belize, previously British Honduras, peaceably gained independence from Britain in 1981 and became a parliamentary democracy with two major parties. Its main areas of commerce have been forestry and agriculture, though tourism is rapidly becoming the primary industry with an emphasis on service jobs.

Period of Adolescence

Adolescence as a separate life stage is a relatively recent concept in Belize, though it is a salient one. Adolescence is generally thought to begin around the time puberty begins, and when mandatory schooling—primary school—is completed. These events often coincide around 12 or 13 years of age. Adolescence is thought to consist of a time of experimentation, learning, and taking increased responsibility ending with marriage, childbearing, or graduation from high school. Such events take place anywhere from the mid to late teens. Thus, many refer to adolescence as the teenage years. However, the effective period of adolescence varies by region and by educational status. In rural and sparsely populated areas, where there is less opportunity for formal schooling, adolescence may be a short period following puberty. In Belize's eight towns and in Belize City (the only city in the country), adolescence tends to last longer until high school graduation, between ages 16 and 19. In predominantly Spanish areas and among the Spanish population elsewhere, *quinceaños* (fifteenth birthday) has been an important coming of age ritual for girls, though this tradition is now more of a symbolic celebration rather than a marker for being ready to marry. No comparable formal rituals are practiced for boys. For both genders, educational markers are eclipsing religious and subcultural rituals regarding movement from childhood to adulthood.

The period of adolescence, particularly for girls, has extended with the demographic shift. That is, as childbearing is delayed, girls as well as boys are offered an increased period without assuming a full range of adult responsibilities. Improved educational opportunities throughout the past 30 years have offered respectable alternatives to marriage, childbearing, and immediately entering the workforce. Particularly in the last 15 years, girls of many class backgrounds have made impressive strides in completion of secondary schooling. Book and uniform scholarships are available in some areas, and public schooling is widespread, providing relatively democratic access to secondary schooling.

The new service industry jobs require high school diplomas and therefore create a job market that furthers the trend toward increased schooling. Most adolescents today are educated at least four to six years longer than their parents were.

For a small percentage of Belizeans, adolescence extends beyond high school into sixth form (junior college) or a four-year college. Most of the youths who attend this post-graduate schooling come from wealthier families, though there are opportunities for students from poorer families to attend. Scholarships and simultaneous jobs with advanced schooling are not unusual. Recently, there has been movement toward opening night schools offering sixth form classes for high school graduates who work full-time, have families, or both, further broadening access to education.

As the numbers of educated young Belizeans have increased and childbearing has been delayed, a period that could be called emerging adulthood has materialized that tends to follow one of several trends. Youths who have finished their educations but are not yet married nor parents may still live at home while working full-time. Most of these youths are not considered full adults until they are married, in common-law marriages, or are parents. For those who do not go on to secondary schooling but rather enter the work force, they may also live at home in a period of what could be considered emergent adulthood until they have families of their own. Teenage single mothers who live with their parents may also be considered part of emerging adulthood until they are providing for themselves economically, or they enter another relationship with someone who will support them. The line between adolescence and full adulthood continues to evolve as young people delay building families for educational or work reasons.

Beliefs

Adolescents in Belize tend to report feeling a strong sense of an individual self, though that self is intimately connected with family, friends, community, and nation. Personal boundaries, thoughts, feelings, and experiences are reported, though important others are referenced often in reflections upon the self. In this way, Belizean adolescents exhibit a tension between individualism and collectivism. Elder Belizeans report that the youth of today exhibit more individualism than in the past, though most think this direction is generally a positive one. Significant differences on this axis are not reported among the three major ethnic groups in the nation but vary more by other factors.

Some variation in these values exists depending on level of education and exposure to media, both of which are related to level of development of a particular area. In general, more education is associated with a more individualistic sense of self whereas less formal schooling is associated with a more collectivistic sense of self that is intensely embedded in family and community. Formal schooling, and particularly high school, allows in another set of models and standards where students are judged as individuals among a peer group. International literature and teaching materials also introduce non-Belizean models of social organization and decision-making.

Western media, and particularly television, are perhaps some of the greatest influences upon today's adolescents in Belize. Television is almost ubiquitous, even in remote areas where generators facilitate the introduction of dozens of channels of U.S. and Mexican programming. Adolescents voraciously consume talk shows, *telenovelas* (soap operas), sitcoms, dramas, and a host of feature-length movies. These media strongly influence the beliefs and even the reported experiences of the youth. For example, in one study, many young women turned to U.S.-based talk shows to learn vocabulary and even emotional patterning to deal with difficult issues in their lives (Anderson-Fye 2003). In this study, the talk show-watching young women reported spending more time on individualistic introspection than did their peers who did not watch talk shows. Such findings indicate a movement over time toward more individualism.

Religion is playing a decreasing role in many adolescents' lives. Catholicism is the most widespread religion, and the public schools are corun by the Catholic diocese. Rituals such as first communion and confirmation continue to be important, though they tend to share the stage with secular rituals and concerns. Religious teachings enter adolescents' decision-making processes, though they have moved from being the central factor to one of many. Adolescents who practice Protestant evangelical religions such as Seventh Day Adventism are more likely to report religion as central to their decision-making. Both Catholic and Protestant religions in Belize are likely to integrate some practices and beliefs with Mayan and Garifuna religions. In particular, traditional knowledge about healing and illness persists and is practiced by adolescents in tandem with religious teachings. Biomedicine is also practiced, though traditional healing systems are not generally thought to conflict with biomedical means of alleviating suffering.

Gender

Appropriate gender role behavior for Belizean adolescents is extremely important and also changing. Among most ethnic groups, women have traditionally been in charge of private home life, while men have been providers in the public sphere (Sutherland 1998). Some women did gain public access through their roles in religion or beauty pageants, or through economic necessity, but these roles were severely limited. Some men played a larger role in the domestic sphere either through loving participation or dominance (McClaurin 1996). Adolescents today are growing up with a wider range of acceptable gender roles, particularly in the face of economic and symbolic globalization. Girls appear to be the first to embrace the new roles as they are presented with more opportunities. The increasingly tourism-based economy requires female service workers. This market provides high school graduates with jobs that allow them to independently support themselves and any children. Concurrently, changing attitudes about appropriate roles for women have allowed them to make inroads into other careers such as commercial banking and politics. The young women of today no longer necessarily expect to be economically dependent on a man, and many plan careers, though those in rural areas have fewer opportunities. This potential economic independence, coupled with both local and transnational awareness of gender equity, has placed young women in a position of increasing power in relationships with men compared with prior generations. The change appears in educated girls' expectations of dating and intimate relationships with men, in which they expect more equitable treatment as well. One study found a general emphasis on self-care and self-protection among Belizean adolescent girls from diverse backgrounds (Anderson-Fye 2003).

Boys also have a wider array of job opportunities related to the tourism economy, however, they do not have as much to gain as girls. Boys can procure a respectable job without a high school diploma, and now face more competition in service-industry jobs due to girls' increasing participation. Boys also express more gender-role confusion in relationships with girls. Particularly in regions that have a history of machismo among men, adolescent boys today are finding this role rejected by their female peers.

Similarly, the role of provider may be shared by a female partner, eroding a traditional sense of masculinity. Some boys are demonstrating resilience with the changing roles, enjoying more time with traditionally feminine tasks such as cooking and childcare, while others are exhibiting considerable distress. However, despite wider gender roles for ordinary Belizeans, the elite positions in business and politics remain overwhelmingly filled by men.

Beauty for girls and women is an important Belizean characteristic. Beauty pageants are ubiquitous and span age groups (Wilk 1996), though they are most heavily concentrated in adolescence. Pageants provide significant prizes for girls such as travel, money, and scholarships. Pageant winners also command communal respect and gain a public voice that can lead to improved job progression and dating opportunities. The pageants persist despite other gains made by women, and in fact have become a common public arena where appropriate gender roles for women are publicly debated. Pageant winners today are usually accomplished *and* beautiful. Despite this focus on beauty, body image and eating disorders are thought to be rare among young women. While some girls express distressed attitudes about their bodies, very few follow through with self-harming behaviors (Anderson-Fye 2004). A curvaceous body *shape* is much more important than body *size*. Boys do not have the same focus on the body, though some express concern about being muscular enough through working out.

The Self

Personal identity is tightly tied to national identity for most Belizean adolescents. Great pride is taken in being Belizean. This sense of appreciating one's national identity, which connotes peacefulness, friendliness, well-being, multiculturalism, and good character, has also been found among Belizean adolescent immigrants to the U.S. Many Belizeans also carry a sense of belonging to their region of origin. This is especially true in the more diverse areas of Belize where people come from many places. Similarly, Central American immigrant adolescents simultaneously hold onto the identity of their country of origin while also embracing their new country. Connections are made back to the nation of origin through visits, language, food, and ritual, though a Belizean identity is also expansive enough to hold the diversity of many immigrants. Though some underlying tensions exist between native born and immigrant Belizeans—especially when there is competition for jobs—the history of the nation as comprised of immigrant groups helps to smooth relations.

Ethnic identity is also important for adolescents. Ethnic festivals, pageants, holidays, and rituals are public displays important to adolescents. Most adolescents not only are of mixed ethnic heritage, but they also regularly interact with people from other ethnic groups. In some ways, this diversity aids ethnic identity formation when differences are observed, though there is fluidity of ethnic practices in this multicultural nation. For example, it is possible for a Creole, Garifuna, or Anglo girl to experience a *quinceaños,* or for Spanish youth to dance the traditional Garifuna Punta. Ethnic identity becomes more salient during adolescence than childhood due to dating and mating relationships.

Family Relationships

Family organization in Belize may follow Mexican (patriarchal) or Caribbean (matriarchal) patterns. In some regions, the patterns coexist. Parental relationships are very important to Belizean adolescents of all backgrounds. The majority of births in the nation are to single mothers, however this accounting includes women in common-law marriages. It is not uncommon for parents to have multiple common-law or legal spouses throughout their lives, though the children tend to stay with their mothers. While some fathers are centrally involved in childrearing, others are absent. Because of the high rates of re-partnering, many Belizean adolescents have step-fathers with whom they live. These relationships vary in quality from loving and enriching to abusive (Cameron 1997). Early adolescents in particular report that these relationships with parents and stepparents are extremely important whether in the positive or negative. A longitudinal study showed that parental relationships grow more complex during adolescence, with early adolescents reporting their parents as all "good" or all "bad," and later adolescents parsing out subtle behaviors perceived as more ambiguous (Anderson-Fye 2002). Parental relationships were generally regarded as supportive, encouraging, and valuable, with most older adolescents planning to remain living close to one or both parents in their adulthood.

Conflict with parents occurs for a variety of reasons and tends to peak in adolescence. Due to rapid socio-cultural changes in Belize, most families experience some sort of intergenerational conflict over varying standards of comportment. For example, adolescents' quests for independence, including later curfews, more time with peers, and wider exploration of the social world, can engender disagreement over appropriateness. Perhaps an even more volatile realm of conflict is interpretive disagreement related to the rapid change and introduction of Western media and migration (Wilk 1993). For example, contemporary adolescents are likely to see disciplinary measures such as hitting and yelling as abusive whereas such behaviors were normative less than a generation ago. Similarly, adolescents are likely to view spousal maltreatment between their parents as abusive rather than normative, which creates intergenerational conflict particularly between girls and their mothers. Arguments over gender-role appropriateness more generally are common.

Belizean children tend to contribute to family life through sibling care, food preparation, and household maintenance. Some work in family businesses or work outside the home for extra income. During adolescence, the amount of time spent with parents is reduced as peers become increasingly important, though adolescents living at home are expected to contribute to the family's well-being.

Social networks are generally dense, particularly in the smaller towns. Grandparents, aunts, uncles, cousins, and other family members are plentiful and participate in both daily life and milestones such as birthday celebrations. Internal migration and transnational immigration interrupt these networks to some extent, though improving communications help them to continue from afar. In the towns that are rapidly growing, changing composition, or both, adults comment that whereas a generation ago anyone would discipline a child out of order in the street, now such public corrections are off limits. Such a change is due to a greater diversity of judgment of appropriate or inappropriate behavior and because everyone in the town does not necessarily know one another anymore.

Relationships such as *madrina* (godmother) and *padrino* (godfather), chosen by the parents at baptism and again by the adolescents themselves at confirmation or *quinceaños,* remain important in adolescents' lives. *Padrinos* may be a favorite uncle or older cousin, or they may be nonrelatives one either favors or wants to form an alliance with. Most *padrinos* feel a sense of responsibility toward the adolescent and maintain a sort of advisor role in their lives.

Friends and Peers/Youth Culture

Belizean social life tends to be cross-generational. At the many community festivals, people of all ages attend. Similarly, at other social events such as private parties or dance clubs, people of multiple ages are usually found. However, because of the increase in high school attendance, adolescents of this generation spend more time with peers than in previous generations. Schooling has also provided opportunity for expanded peer networks. In addition to the school day, many schools also offer after-hours programming such as sports, music, and art classes, further expanding time with peers. Because of this exposure, friendships are increasingly being made based on mutual interests rather than family background. Whereas previously friendships centered around family relations (such as cousins) and close family friends, adolescents now have the opportunity to spend time with peers outside of the family network in various activities. Adolescents who do not complete high school tend to spend time with fewer same-aged friends than those who do. Most adolescents are also allowed weekend social time with friends once family obligations are completed.

Non-school–based, same-aged peer groups exist for adolescents, though they vary by region. Adolescents who live in the city or larger towns tend to have more opportunities such as scouting or other international youth organizations. Gender-segregated peer groups exist formally and informally. Girls may participate in pageantry or dance troupes, whereas boys may participate in community-based sports leagues. In recent years, gangs have also become more common in multiple areas of the country, particularly among boys. These gangs tend to mimic Los Angeles gangs and sometimes have loose affiliations through immigrants.

Many friendships cross lines of ethnicity, social class, immigration status, and gender, though students reporting a best friend in one town matched on most of these factors (Anderson-Fye 2002). Belizeans tend to pride themselves on viewing the individual and not his or her status or background, a personality trait that contributes to the relative openness in friendships. Still, some deep divisions remain that are more likely to surface in dating relationships than in friendships. Some Spanish families do not condone dating relationships with Creole or Garifuna partners, and vice versa.

The quality of friendships may vary substantially. In one study of adolescent girls in a mid-sized island community, participants rarely reported telling their best friends everything (a main characteristic of U.S. girls' intimate friendships) due to fears of gossip (Anderson-Fye 2002). On the other hand, friendliness was the single most valued character trait reported among these same girls. Most youths have a wide social circle. Small groups of friends often appear to be a preferred social structure among both genders for "hanging out." Friendly companionship is thought to enhance most experiences for both genders.

Because adolescents are still relatively integrated into the larger social fabric of communities, youth culture is not as salient as it is elsewhere. Still, preferences in music, clothing styles, and slang language—heavily influenced by both U.S. and Mexican media accessed through television, magazines, and the Internet—can set youths apart even within the community setting.

Love and Sexuality

Standards regarding adolescent dating vary by region, ethnic group, gender, education, and also by family and individual preferences. In the Spanish population, celebrating the age of 15 usually formally marks the beginning of dating. While the *quinceaños* celebration is focused around female coming of age, boys of this age are also allowed to date. Many adolescents of both genders covertly date before this time, something that parents usually discover due to community gossip. Girls are sanctioned more severely than boys for dating too early and they also are more likely to attempt early dating. While other ethnic groups do not have such a clear marker of acceptable dating age, a similar range of 14 to 16 years of age for dating is common.

Technically, it is against most high schools' rules for students to date. In practice, many high school students date though some do wait until they have graduated. The concern about dating during schooling centers around females because of the possibility of pregnancy. In most high schools, pregnant girls are expelled. If the fathers are in high school, they are usually allowed to complete their studies without interruption. This double standard is beginning to change in some schools as they allow young women to reenroll after birth. Belize has one of the highest rates of teenage pregnancy in the region (23% of all births are to women under 19), and therefore much to gain through the changed rule. Some schools are trying to implement more chaperoned social events such as dances so that covert dating is unnecessary.

Sex education classes are rare, though many high schools offer a course in Christian marriage. The Christian marriage curriculum teaches abstinence as the only sexual option before marriage. Some adolescents report learning the rhythm method of birth control from this class, a method that is taught to be saved until after marriage. Other types of birth control are taught informally by pharmacists, doctors, and older sympathetic family members. Still, many girls report shock at not knowing what was happening during their first experience of menstruation and also at becoming pregnant during their first sexual encounter, when they report being "swept away" in the moment. The onus for controlling sexuality and for birth control falls upon girls, since boys often suffer much less severe consequences for early pregnancy, and in fact, are often congratulated on their manhood by other men (Cameron 1997).

Cohabitation in common-law marriage is widespread among couples and may begin in the teenage years. Many couples live this way for long periods of time while others get formally married. Separation and divorce are not uncommon, with many Belizeans having serial relationships. Infidelity in marriages and common-law marriages is also reported regularly (Sutherland 1998), something the adolescents of today comment upon, with many aiming for lifelong fidelity.

Discrimination against gay and lesbian Belizeans remains high, though individuals may be accepted within their local community.

Sexually transmitted diseases (STDs) appear to be increasing in frequency according to health care providers. Rates of HIV infection in Belize have been reported as the highest in Central America (2.4%; UNICEF 2004), with many of the affected being older adolescents and young adults. Prostitution is widespread, creating more concern about disease transmission. Many of the newer prostitutes are adolescent women from neighboring Central American countries who are misled into the jobs and then cannot get out of them. Their experiences of adolescent sexuality vary greatly from the majority. In the areas of the country frequented by tourists, sex between adolescents and North American tourists is reported, as is the transnational spread of STDs. Often, promises of continued relationships are made to both young women and young men, with many of them broken.

Health Risk Behavior

In general, Belizean adolescents are remarkably physically and mentally healthy. Reports of stress-related illness are low, and very few students miss school for illness. When they do, they are likely to be home with nothing more severe than a flu. However, there are several threats to good health and also some indications that mental health problems may be rising.

Drug and alcohol abuse is one of the largest problems among adolescents. Access to both drugs and alcohol is plentiful and easy in many parts of Belize, with most students reporting their first exposure in primary school. Messages about alcohol are mixed. Schools teach the moral and physical problems with underage drinking. Students can be expelled if they are caught drinking when school is in session. On the other hand, no sanctions are necessarily taken during school break times. Alcohol use is normalized and even glamorized in many places. Respected adults freely consume alcohol in multi-age community settings, particularly during celebrations and on Sundays, many people's day off from work. In tourist areas, students may literally walk through bars on their way to school. Moreover, children and adolescents in these areas also witness heavily drinking tourists daily. Instead of seeing this as vacation behavior, it appears regular and corresponds with many television images of American life. Alcohol is then associated with wealth, relaxation, and fun.

Alcohol use and abuse among adolescents serves many functions. It may be condoned at family celebrations such as weddings. Some adolescents report experimentation with alcohol as a way to combat boredom. Yet others report peer pressure as a catalyst for drinking in order to appear older and more attractive. Alcohol is implicated in risky sexual behaviors among adolescents as well. Regardless of the reasons, this underage drinking is of concern given high rates of alcoholism and alcohol-related crime among adults. Alcohol abuse among men has also been associated with maltreatment of children and women (Cameron 1997; Henderson and Houghton 1993; McCluskey 2001).

While drug use is substantially lower than alcohol use among adolescents, it is not uncommon. In particular, marijuana is abundant and easy to obtain in most locations though it remains illegal. Newspaper police reports frequently include possession of marijuana among adults in their early twenties. However, adolescents also report experimentation with the drug. While exact use rates are not known, boys are more likely to try marijuana than girls. Harder drugs such as cocaine also appear among adolescents. Belize is a stop for drug trafficking between South America and the United States. While the police continue to battle this route, some of the drugs find their way into the country and into the hands of older adolescents. Violent crimes and murder in Belize are usually linked with drug consumption. A small number of older adolescents die every year due to homicide, and their deaths are often related to drugs, alcohol, and gang activity.

A serious adolescent health risk that other nations face—automobile accidents—is rare in Belize. Most adolescents do not drive automobiles, so reports of injury and death due to car accidents seldom occur.

Mental health among Belizean adolescents is generally robust, though significant problems do exist. Depression appears to be increasing among adolescents of both genders. It is unclear whether depression was unreported in previous generations, or if the rates are rising. Depression is often thought to be related to family stress such as fighting or divorcing parents, abuse, or significant hardship such as illness or job loss. Occasionally, severe depression among adolescents is thought to lead to suicide. However, overall suicide rates are low in Belize (12.1 per 100,000 for males, .9 per 100,000 for females), with few of these being adolescents.

Other mental health problems that are reported among adolescents in Belize include posttraumatic stress symptoms, self-mutilation, anxiety disorders, and obsessive-compulsive disorder. Posttraumatic stress symptoms have been found among adolescent girls who have experienced physical or sexual abuse. It appears that the expression of symptoms has been affected to some extent by U.S. media such as television talk shows in which experiences and emotional responses to those experiences are discussed and modeled (Anderson-Fye 2003). While some girls show no posttraumatic response to abuse, others—many of whom have high levels of exposure to U.S.-based media and culture—do report an array of symptoms such as night terrors, intrusive thoughts, and hyperstartle. Self-mutilation occurs on a continuum of severity and is more common among boys. Case reports of anxiety disorders and obsessive-compulsive disorder indicate onset in adolescence, with boys being more affected in both cases. As mentioned above, eating disorders are currently rare, though there is some indication that they may be increasing. In general, it is difficult to gain accurate reports of adolescent mental health since mental health care is limited outside of the city. In rural areas, high schools are generally not equipped to assess or treat mental health disorders per se. While community-based mental health treatment is increasing, many areas remain without professional mental health resources.

Education

The literacy rate in Belize is officially listed as 93 percent, one of the highest in the region. However, that number has been questioned, with some estimates of functional literacy as low as 40%.

Schooling in Belize is based on the British Caribbean system. Formal schooling begins at age 4 and is mandatory through age 14, or the completion of primary school (the U.S. equivalent of eighth grade). Approximately 30 secondary schools run by both the church and state are found throughout the country, with an increasing number of students from all socio-economic backgrounds attending them. Belize City has the most developed schooling system and also boasts the most prestigious secondary schools. The most selective private, single sex, Catholic schools draw students from all over the country. National attrition rates remain highest in the first two years, and the repetition rate averages 8% across the four years. All instruction is conducted in English, though Spanish is also taught formally and other languages are heard within school walls.

Rates of secondary school attendance have increased dramatically in the last two decades, particularly among girls. Consistent with other findings from the Caribbean and Central America, females now make up slightly more than half of all students and graduates of secondary schools and are among the highest achievers. Historically, boys within a family had priority for resources for schooling. Increasingly, girls are fighting for these resources, particularly in areas benefiting from tourism dollars. Girls have a stronger pull toward a diploma since the types of service jobs young women tend to enter require a high school diploma, while young men may find high-paying jobs in such areas as construction or tour guiding without having graduated. While secondary school success remains correlated with socio-economic status, scholarships for school fees, uniforms, and books have provided opportunities for students from poorer families. Still, students from poorer backgrounds and those in rural areas are less likely to attend and complete secondary schooling than other students.

Two major tracks of classes are available for secondary students in their final two years—commercial and academic. Commercial classes include accounting, typing, and office procedures. Most students who choose commercial classes do not attend tertiary schooling. The commercial track prepares students well for the nation's many service jobs and sometimes provides job placement internships. The academic track includes a focus in science, mathematics, and the arts. Students who plan to attend tertiary schooling usually have the academic training, as do some who do not go on to further schooling. A third secretarial track is taught in some areas, though the commercial track has absorbed these classes elsewhere.

At the end of secondary schooling, many students take the Caribbean Examination Council (CXC) tests in a variety of subjects. Those tests are used for entrance into Sixth Form and other post-secondary schooling as well as for employment. Over 1,500 students took the test in various areas in 2002, with results placing Belize at about the median relative to other CXC nations.

Work

Most adolescents have substantial work responsibilities in addition to school responsibilities. Some of these are in the home, and some are at jobs outside the home. Girls tend to shoulder more responsibilities in the home than boys do in both the rural areas and towns, and they work outside the home in rates roughly equivalent to the larger towns. Housework is generally gender segregated in the usual way. Girls are likely to have responsibilities for sibling childcare, shopping, cooking, and cleaning. If a girl's mother works outside the home, it is more likely that the girl will shoulder a larger portion of these responsibilities. Attitudes toward these responsibilities vary, though most girls expect some amount of home responsibilities.

Many adolescents also work in family businesses or in other external jobs. Adolescents who are not in high school are likely to work full time. Those in high school are likely to work after school, on weekends, over holiday breaks, or all of the above. Boys work in agriculture, construction, or in one of the many service jobs. Service jobs for boys may include working as a waiter, cook, or assistant to a tour operator or hotel manager. Girls work as maids, nannies, and also at a variety of jobs considered desirable such as receptionist, cashier, secretary, or bank teller. Many of these adolescents contribute a substantial portion of their earnings to their family. Those who go to school while working buy their own books and pay their own school fees and sometimes those of younger siblings. Many adolescents use their jobs as stepping stones to an adult career in a similar line of work. Of course, some adolescents from wealthier families are expected to contribute neither to household nor external work.

In contrast to many in their mothers' generation, girls of today often expect to have a job or career while they are raising children. If they do not have a continuous job, many report desiring a high school diploma and skills for a future job, should they want or need one. In the past, women have been dependent on their husbands for subsistence (though the level of dependency has varied by ethnic group, with Spanish women being the most dependent and Garifuna women the least in general). Even if a husband maltreated them, many women felt they had no choice but to endure the maltreatment due to economic necessity (Henderson and Houghton 1993). For women whose husbands left or passed away, job options were limited and undesirable for most. This situation was observed by the young women of today from all ethnic groups who express the desire to have economic independence if they want or need it. Because of a combination of increasing jobs available to women in addition to changing gender roles, adolescent girls today see more options for their futures than did their mothers.

For a few adolescents, work conditions are unsafe and exploitative. As mentioned above, some recent immigrants from neighboring Central American nations end up being coerced into prostitution under the false promise of Belizean citizenship and a good job. Other girls report experiencing considerable sexual harassment from employers whether performing home-based or office-based work. Boys who work in construction or agriculture may face dangerous working conditions with heavy machinery, precarious positions, or other risks.

Media

Several types of media are increasingly important to Belizean adolescents' lives. Television is ubiquitous, with most programming originating in the United States. Mexican programming, such as soap operas (*telenovelas*) is also popular. Very little programming originates in Belize. As mentioned above, adolescents regularly watch a variety of television programs such as talk shows, sitcoms, reality shows, dramas, music videos, and feature-length movies. Television exposure has been shown to have important effects on adolescents. Adolescents have been found to turn to the shows for skills to solve the problems in their own lives (Cameron 1997). Similarly, magazine articles from U.S.-produced magazines introduce concepts to adolescents. However, Belizean adolescents do not passively absorb messages from the media. They have been found to interact with and filter media messages through their own psychological constructs (Anderson-Fye 2003). For example, while television exposure to images of thin Western women has been linked to eating disorders in other parts of the world, Belizean adolescent girls have been found to question and reject these images in favor of local standards of beauty and well-being (Anderson-Fye 2004). On the other hand, transnational media messages of gender equity and individual rights have been embraced by young women (Anderson-Fye 2003).

The Internet is playing an increasingly important role in many adolescents' lives. Adolescents have access to the Internet at home, at school, or at relatively inexpensive Internet cafés (in increasing order of access). Adolescents in sparsely populated rural areas have much less access than those in towns or the city. Girls appear to have slightly more usage than boys, though both "surf the net" regularly for a variety of purposes. One of the most popular reasons adolescents use the Internet is for chat rooms, joining others from Belize, the United States, England, or elsewhere. Some of the virtual relationships from these rooms end up in physical visits, and occasionally in marriage or other long-term relationships. This global space to "hang out" impacts language usage, music tastes, and other topics adolescents report thinking and talking about. The time spent on the Internet varies considerably due to differential access. Very little monitoring of adolescents' Internet usage occurs, except at school. Many parents are unfamiliar with computers, and some do not feel comfortable enough with literacy skills to check on adolescents. Adolescents who use it consider the Internet an excellent resource for learning, entertainment, and expanding social networks.

Other types of media that play important roles in adolescents' lives are recorded music and video games. Music created in Belize, other Caribbean nations, Mexico, the United States, and England is most popular and is accessed via the radio, personal compact discs, or cassette tapes. Adolescents enjoy a range of music types from Belizean Punta Rock to hip hop. Video games are much less widely accessed than recorded music. Only wealthier Belizeans can afford the imported game consoles. However, the games become very important for those who do have them, particularly among early and mid-adolescent boys who are likely to spend all their free time with the games.

Transnational media consumption has risen considerably in the past two decades in Belize. There is little popular critique of adolescents' media use, though individual parents or educators may evaluate and limit access.

Politics and Military

The Belizean military, the Belize Defense Force (BDF), is a voluntary force comprised of Belizeans aged 18 to 25. Since Belize has few disputes or threats to its peace, the military aids internal affairs such as policing drug trafficking and participating in infrastructure projects. The BDF also maintains the border with Guatemala and controls other border crossings. Approximately 1,200 Belizeans are part of the BDF, about 50 of whom are women. The BDF works closely with the police, and members sometimes move from one organization to the other. Only a small percentage of eligible youth enter the military each year.

A number of Belizeans with dual U.S. citizenship and those who immigrate to the United States join the U.S. military. The U.S. military is seen as a very desirable career path, as it provides training, education, benefits, and a stable salary. Members of the U.S. military who come home to Belize are admired by adolescents. Among Belizean immigrants in the United States, military service is seen as at least as advantageous as going to college, and sometimes even more so due to the possibility of simultaneous earning and learning.

Belizean youth are not particularly active in political life as a cohort group. While some young adults run for local offices, they usually do so as individuals. Most youth have a preference for one of Belize's two political parties, and may even feel very strongly about them, though they do not necessarily organize around political issues. Political involvement by youth is usually done in the context of multiage groups and is often tied to family preferences.

Unique Issues

Themes of globalization, immigration, and transnationalism are prevalent in the lives of many Belizean adolescents today. Partially due to the increasing importance of the global ecotourism industry, transnational contact is a part of adolescents' lives in multiple ways. Transnational dollars fuel many of the available jobs for Belizean youth. In order to succeed at their jobs, adolescents working in the tourism industry become aware of tourist preferences, tastes, and beliefs that may then influence their own. As mentioned above, transnational media such as television, the Internet, and magazines also are a part of the daily lives of many Belizean adolescents.

Many adolescents are part of transnational families. The majority of immigrants are from other Central American countries coming in pursuit of jobs and relative political stability, but many are also families emigrating from the Middle East, East Asia, North America, and Europe. Belizeans also immigrate to the United States and other nations in pursuit of higher education and better job prospects. Although exact figures are unknown, many of these immigrants return to Belize or continue to move back and forth between the two countries. Transnational networks of family and friends remain strong between Belize and the United States, England, and other Central American nations. If the adolescents themselves do not have an immigration history, others close to them such as a family member or friend are likely to. These experiences and relationships can profoundly affect how adolescents understand themselves and the world around them. For example, one study of African-descended Belizean adolescent immigrants in Los Angeles found that racial categorization and discrimination became salient issues in students' lives, whereas racism and racial and ethnic identity were perceived differently in the home communities in Belize (Lemmel 2002).

EILEEN P. ANDERSON-FYE

References and Further Reading

Anderson-Fye, E. P. 2002. Never leave yourself: Belizean schoolgirls' psychological development in cultural context. Unpublished PhD diss., Harvard University.

Anderson-Fye, E. P. 2003. Never leave yourself: Ethnopsychology as mediator of psychological globalization among Belizean schoolgirls. *Ethos* 31(1):59–94.

Anderson-Fye, E. P. 2004. A "Coca-Cola" shape: Cultural change, body image, and eating disorders in San Andres, Belize. *Culture, Medicine, and Psychiatry* 28:561–95.

Cameron, S. 1997. *From girls to women: Growing up healthy in Belize.* Belize City: Government of Belize.

Henderson, P., and A. Houghton (eds.) 1993. *Rising up: Life stories of Belizean women.* Toronto: Sister Vision.

Lemmel, D. 2001. Racial socialization and Black identity formation in the initial postsecondary school pathways choices in three African-descended groups. Unpublished PhD diss., University of California Los Angeles.

McClaurin, I. 1996. *Women of Belize: Gender and change in Central America.* New Brunswick, N.J.: Rutgers University Press.

McCluskey, L. 2001. *Here, our culture is hard: Stories of domestic violence from a Mayan community in Belize.* Austin, Tex.: University of Texas.

Sutherland, A. 1998. *The making of Belize: Globalization in the margins.* Westport, Conn.: Bergin & Garvey.

UNICEF. 2004. "Belize: Statistics." http://www.unicef.org/infobycountry/belize_statistics.html (accessed date December 28, 2004).

Wilk, R. 1993. "It's destroying a whole generation": Television and moral discourse in Belize. *Visual Anthropology* 5:229–44.

Wilk, R. 1996. Connections and contradictions: From the Crooked Tree Cashew Queen to Miss World Belize. In *Beauty queens on the global stage: Gender, contests, and power.* C. Cohen, R. Wilk, and B. Stoeltje (eds.). pp. 217–32. New York: Routledge.

BOTSWANA

Background Information

Botswana is a landlocked country situated south of the Sahara in southern Africa. It shares its borders with Angola, Namibia, South Africa, Zambia, and Zimbabwe. Botswana is a semidesert region with a flourishing and successful beef industry. The country also enjoys a diamond-dominated economy that also enjoys a fair amount of tourism, with small-scale manufacturing and agricultural sectors that are struggling to survive. Economically, Botswana is ranked as a middle income and stable country with a GDP of U.S. \$3,200 (UNICEF, 2000 and 2002).

Botswana is a sparsely populated country of 1.6 million people. It is dominated by youth under 18 years of age, who constitute 50% of the total population (UNICEF 2000 and 2002). Like most regional nations, Botswana is occupied by various Bantu-speaking ethnic groups including the Bakalaka (the Kalanga), Bambukushi, Basubiya, Bakgatla, Bakgalagadi, Babirwa, Batswapong, and Wayeyi (UNICEF 2000 and 2002). These ethnic groups make up the main Setswana-speaking people of Botswana. Besides these main ethnic groups, there are also some other minority ethnic groups that are not Bantu-speaking nations, such as the Khoisan (the Bushmen), including the Baherero and Damara (UNICEF 2002).

Period of Adolescence

In Botswana, when a girl reaches puberty this is referred to in Setswana as *go itlhalefa,* which literally means to discover oneself in life. Referring to this stage in this manner emphasizes the psychological significance of the adolescent's establishment of her female identity. One may argue that it is as a result of this self-discovery that girls who reach adolescence in the San tradition (as will be discussed in more detail in a later section) go into hiding and end their association with girls who have not yet experienced menstruation. From a psychological perspective it can also be argued that the anxiety shown by the girl-child as she impatiently awaits puberty (as again discussed in a later section) could be attributable to this notion

that the girl-child discovers who she is and what she is capable of (reproduction) at puberty. This seems to suggest that there is an implicit knowledge that "there is more to who I can be," which unconsciously drives the girl-child and results in the anxiety she shows. This kind of anxiety continues into the next important stage of development, adolescence.

Adolescence is regarded as a "fascinating, interesting and challenging period of human growth and development in which rapid physical change, social, emotional, physiological and psychological change occurs" (Mwamwenda 2004, 60). During this period, the adolescent is neither a child nor an adult, but is in transition or being culturally socialized from childhood to adulthood. This period exists in Botswana because it is a period in which the youths are initiated and socialized into adult roles within the various societies and cultures. In this regard, both boys and girls are socialized differently into specific adult roles as defined within the African context.

In Botswana, adolescence is generally understood as a period of development starting from puberty, around 11 years of age (*Mmegi* 2005) to adulthood (Gage and Berliner 1988; Mwamwenda 2004; Santrock 1994; Woolfolk 2003). This stage is accompanied by several physical, emotional, and psychological changes. In Botswana most children are in the last standard (the equivalent of grade seven in a British school) of their primary schooling. In accordance with the centrality of age in Setswana cultures, education on sexuality was according to age groups and was administered to young people to mark their transition from childhood to adulthood when they reached puberty in what is known as *bogwera* (for boys) and *bojale* (for girls) rites of passage (Cox 1998; Dineo 2000; Phiri 1998; Schapera 1938). To the traditional Batswana of Botswana, adolescence is a period of initiation characterized by circumcision for boys and cultural initiation schools for girls (referred to as *bogwera* and *bojale* rites of passage, respectively). According to Schapera (1938), *bogwera* rites marked the transition from boyhood into manhood, accompanied by privileges and responsibilities. A man who has not passed through this kind of cultural initiation rite is always regarded as a boy no matter how old he is. Such a man might not sit or eat with other men at the *kgotla* (community court) or take part in tribal discussions and is not allowed to marry (Chakanza 1998; Mpassou 1998; Schapera 1938). While some of these cultural rites have been largely abandoned, they still remain significant because they represent space in which education on sexuality and gender roles was memorably impressed upon the young as they stood ready to cross the boundary from childhood to adulthood (UNICEF 2002; Schapera 1938). Specifically, boys are led into the know-how of hunting as the "real man's" role was to be able to hunt in order that he may provide for his family. The girl-child is initiated into the subservient role of looking after her husband. The ideas that are inculcated are that she should give priority to bearing children for her husband and be up early in order to make fire to ensure that her husband is in time to leave for the *kgotla* meetings, which were then conducted first thing in the morning. The husband should then find breakfast ready when he returns from such meetings. Some ethnic groups or tribes within Botswana society continue to practice initiation rites for girls and boys. Such initiation "schools" confer on the particular youth special status and recognition within their communities and societies. For example, community members tend to shun or look down upon those who have not undergone these kinds of initiation cultural practices. It must also be pointed out that the initiation ritual process for boys is private and is carried out by well-trained and respected male elders within the community in secret places, normally during the cold season (that is, in winter). The initiation ritual for boys is culturally believed to prepare boys for sexuality and make them strong, brave, and healthy men after the ordeal (Chakanza 1998; Cox 1998; Dineo 2000; Mpassou 1998; Phiri 1998; Schapera 1938).

Corresponding to men's regiments are the regiments of women, known as *bojale* (Chakanza 1998; Mpassou 1998; Schapera 1938). Traditionally girls' ceremonies, known as *bojale*, were elaborate and held in the village in certain selected homesteads carefully screened off from the public view. The initiates were first subjected to some form of operation, which among the Kgatla consisted of branding the inner part of the right thigh close to the vulva. After their wounds were healed, the girls spent the greater part of each day out in the veld where they were instructed by women in matters concerning womanhood, domestic and agricultural activities, sex, and behavior towards men. In the evenings, they sang and danced at home in

semipublic masquerades in honor of various deities. Like boys, the girls were subjected to severe punishments and other hardships. They wore distinctive dresses woven from cornstalks and painted with white lines. Their work was generally lighter than that of boys. They were to do such tasks as putting up the walls and thatching the roof of the hut at the *Kgotla,* drawing water for any tribal or royal work, getting wood for the chief's wife, putting up huts in the chief's homestead, cleaning the village, fetching earth and smearing the walls of the chief's homestead, and weeding his wife's fields (Chakanza 1998; Mpassou 1998; Schapera 1938; UNICEF 2000 and 2002).

For girls in Botswana, the stage of adolescence is only noticeably recognized at the onset of menstruation. Traditionally in Botswana the beginning of menstruation for girls was perceived with abomination (Phiri 1998; UNICEF 2002; Schapera 1938). It conveyed as meaning that the suspected girl-child had been exposed to sexual intercourse, and that such a girl was suspected to have done something that was expected only of older women and should therefore be regarded as a woman. Younger girls were cautioned against interacting with her, and they would discuss the issue among themselves, defining the newly menstruating girl as a woman. At the same time the context was one filled with awe and disgust, since it implied that the girl in question indulged in sexual relationships, and this was unacceptable. The girl-child would even be removed from school in some cases.

Girls, therefore, used to become embarrassed and upset when experiencing menstruation for the first time, since the implication was that one had had sexual intercourse. It was as such frustrating for the girl who knew that this was not the case, and yet it would be concluded thus once she began her menstruation. The manner in which the girl-child was treated could also be interpreted to suggest that the girl should now be given respect as the child is now "grown up" and a "woman." For some of the societies, the girl experiencing menstruation for the first time would be surrounded by older women and told about the do's and don'ts of that stage. Some of the rules that went with the onset of menstruation were that the girl should not take a bath when having her menstruation periods and that she should be as confined to the house as much as possible. In the traditional Tswana societies (the words "Tswana" and "Batswana" are used interchangeably to refer to the people of Botswana), where the practice was wearing a kilt, which exposed a large portion of the body, the girl now outgrows this stage; boys too stop wearing *khiba,* which was a piece of cloth covering only the front lower part of the body but exposing the buttocks and leaving the rest of the body uncovered (Chakanza 1998; Dineo 1998; Phiri 1998; Schapera 1938). In Setswana (the word "Setswana" is used to refer to the national language of the people of Botswana as well as to mean the lifestyle and culture of the people), it is very important that a girl should share her experience with someone who is older. When a girl reaches the stage, early in the morning an old woman takes different kinds of utensils and teases the girl by having her try to hold them; this is done in order to encourage the girl to tell her parents when she experiences menarche. It is the belief that if a girl does not inform anyone, she will break utensils very easily, and so this would give away the fact that the girl has already reached puberty. The underlying philosophy being that the girl will break the items as she will be anxious, afraid and not being sure whether or not that people realize that she is experiencing her menstruation.

Some traditional medicine men do not allow girls to enter their shrines during menstruation, although this extends to even when they are adults. It is held that menstruation will weaken the powers of the bones that the doctors use as charms.

The adolescent is often conscious of her or his body, and this is often influenced partly by seeing others around them. The girl tries very hard to make her breasts look bigger; however, when the breasts do become enlarged the adolescent develops shyness and attempts to hide the breasts by crouching when walking; this happens more particularly when they see boys. The shyness concerning their breasts also leads girls to dress in big sweaters that are thought to help make the breasts less obvious. The girls do strongly object to anyone who attempts to hold them by the breasts (a tendency by men to tease girls, which was less regarded as abuse previously in the Tswana culture, unlike as is the case nowadays). The girls at the early stage of development are taught by their mothers, grandmothers, and sisters that if they wake up early enough and rub ash over the budding breasts, the breasts will disappear. The breasts at that stage are given the name *dikolamelora* (literally meaning "that which is taken away by ash from the fire"), suggesting that they are not fully developed breasts. Girls can be seen doing this desperately. The other belief is that the breasts can be swept away using a traditional broom. Girls are also impatient for their first period to come, but once they experience it they hate having their periods (*Mmegi* 2005). What may be said in short is that

once the reality of adolescence, which they were anxious to experience, sets in girls no longer want to be grown ups with breasts; hence girls do not receive the onset of adolescence with joy. Of course, with time they forget about the frustration caused by the development of their breasts. They accept it as more and more of their age mates experience similar bodily changes, and they share their experiences about some of the changes. Adolescents feel more comfortable if they do not perceive themselves as different from others. Girls' shy behavior also spreads to other aspects. They would, for example, not eat or even carry certain types of food such as fat cakes in the presence of the opposite sex, or even get a second helping of food—especially if they are at boarding school.

Evidence from research suggests that teachers are also the ones who reinforce the culture in which boys are expected to take initiative and girls to be subordinate (sexually and in other ways; Pattman and Chege 2003). Observation of mixed-sex groups in a life skills lesson in a school in Botswana shows that girls mostly do secretarial work while boys chair the group discussions (Pattman and Chege 2003). Girls just sat waiting for the boys to tell them what to write. Teachers are challenged to reflect upon the gender dynamics in class, particularly when teaching HIV/AIDS and life skills. It is the researchers' opinion that this may result in girls having difficulty in negotiating relationships with boys. The danger envisaged is that it will increase the chance of boys and girls engaging in relationships with little communication and perhaps little respect and empathy for each other, which may lead to a greater risk of unprotected sex and HIV/AIDS infection (Pattman and Chege 2003).

Beliefs

This section seeks to show how adolescence in modern Tswana society is different from that in traditional Tswana culture. However, some of the beliefs and practices of traditional Tswana culture continue to exist despite certain changes for children in modern Tswana society (Mwamwenda 2004; Schapera 1938). This is because of the prevalent increase in exposure to sex education than was the case before. Children, for example, learn about the physical development and changes that should accompany this developmental stage as early as grade seven. This is a new concept in Tswana culture, since sex-related issues were usually issues that could not be discussed openly with children (Chakanza 1998; Mpassou 1998; Phiri 1998;

Schapera 1938). The girl experiencing her menstrual period for the first time was only told that it means that she should not mix with boys or else she will get a child, and that this is something that she would experience every month (there was no elaboration on the meaning of the word "mix"). The adolescent experiencing menarche would be nursed or treated as if she were a sick person.

However, in the twenty-first century, young mothers tell their children what to expect, although still not explicitly enough for the young mind to comprehend clearly. Children also discuss their experiences with peers at school (*Mmegi* 2005). Newspaper inserts such as *BOKAMOSO* (literally meaning "the future") in *Mmegi* may also be regarded as evidence of changes in tradition, because these are enlightening to the youth.

For some children it is particularly different since their experience of menstruation comes when they are at boarding school, where children discuss such issues in a different light. Up to around the late 1970s, there was common observation that girls bandaged their left knee when they were having their menstruation. Menstruation came with some feeling of weakness or numbness in the left leg. Bandaging one's leg resulted in the adolescent being teased by those around her, especially boys. This bandaging of the leg no longer occurs.

At the onset of puberty, body odor becomes stronger and most children demand deodorants as they become conscious of the odor. In traditional Tswana culture, deodorants were not commonly available. Using deodorants was a prestigious sign of being an adult. Boys also begin to show concern if their development seems to be slow compared to what they believe should be the changes taking place in their bodies; they become anxious and ask when they will start growing hair under their armpits. It can be said that in this respect both boys and girls look forward to adolescence. The boy feels proud, although also partly shy, when people remark about the change in his voice. Another noticeable physical change is the appearance of acne during adolescence (Child 1993; Woolfolk 2003). This kind of development usually causes a lot of concern and anxiety because adolescents tend to become overly conscious about their appearance. Boys, for example, get very worried when they look fat and feel they have to trim down their weight (Gage and Berliner 1988; Santrock 1994; Woolfolk 2003).

Socially, girls prefer to keep the company of girls and likewise for boys; however, it is apparent that this is a sort of defense mechanism as it is noticeable that each sex group usually gangs up against the opposite sex and teases them, the motive often being to draw their attention. They do not want to lose sight of the opposite sex, and yet do not want to openly admit that they are interested in them. It is still apparent that adolescents are conscious about their bodily development. While girls and boys no longer wear kilts and the traditional *khiba*, one finds that boys detest wearing school shorts or short pants in general. School authorities, too, comply. It is no longer seen as normal in Botswana to see a man wearing short pants, except for three-quarter long ones.

There is also noticeable concern about privacy. The girl-child never leaves her body exposed; she always ties a towel around her or a gown if she has one so that the breast and bottom part of the body are not exposed, not even to the mother. Boys, too, often make sure that the bedroom and bathroom doors are securely locked. Interestingly, each sex is aware of the other's attempt to conceal their bodies, and more often than not they tease each other by wanting to force the door open if one or even a group of the same sex lock themselves in a room.

One could say that there is a lot of pretense about shyness, especially when it comes to performing acts like dancing and singing in front of others, because they really want to show off such ability, but they also want to be begged to act by the opposite sex. That is to say, qualities which one excels at have to be bargained for if others want to see them. Adolescents' play is characterized by teasing the opposite sex. Members of one sex can even lock themselves in a room just to induce those of the other sex to want to force their way in. Adolescents also yearn to have more access to the telephone. Adolescents receive more calls than everyone in most households. This may happen to an extent where adults even tend to ignore phone calls because it is always assumed that it is for the adolescent member of the house.

Adolescence is a stage of rebelliousness. Some parents notice a greater degree of difficulty or fussiness in their child, especially a female child. She does not do house chores all that willingly, although this sometimes fluctuates, meaning that there are days when she is okay. She tends to be a little moody. The adolescent is very secretive about her diary if she keeps one and about her movements. This is the time when some parents develop anxiety because they do not understand what the girl might be up to if she is not at home. For some of the girls it becomes suspicious that they may be involved in love relationships with people who are a little older, because they even become secretive about where they get money if it is realized that they have spending money.

It ought to be realized, however, that while they want to be treated as mature and responsible, the money adolescents receive is often spent on trivial items like sweets. This is a contradiction of maturity, since it is not a wise way of spending money. On the other hand, it may be that the adolescent fears that she will have to account if they spend it on reasonable items like clothing because the parents may notice it.

Adolescent individuals like to feel that they can make independent decisions. They like to dress the way they like and wear hairstyles that they like. It becomes obvious that there is a lot of influence from peers and magazines as well as films and so on. They want to identify with certain people who are celebrities. To the parents, some of the styles their children prefer are roguish. Some want to have a very gentlemanly image; it is a question of the source of influence, for instance, it might be the church that influences one's behavior.

Changes in adolescents' behavior may be perceived as intimidating to some elders, including teachers, since such elders tend to be defensive and always blame children's behavior on the stage, blackmailing them in the processes. Statements such as "*ke bona gore o a nkgolela*" (translated to mean "I think you are becoming too big for your boots," or, "if you think you are a man or woman because you are beginning to behave in such and such a manner") are not uncommon. It may be argued that this suppresses the opinions of adolescents and might be what leads them to do things in secret or become more rebellious as perceived from the point of view of the older person.

In some cases, as adolescents become more responsible they look forward to showing that they can do things for or by themselves. They feel proud if they can do their own washing, do some cooking, and are generally given some responsible tasks. This is, however, short lived, as reality shows that they gradually become lazy or realize that they are not old enough to handle certain tasks. Adolescents, however, want to be given a chance to prove their worth. Hence, in most times it is being the same as others that pushes them to make certain life decisions.

Gender

Gender is a culture-specific construct that "refers to the widely shared expectations and norms within

the society about appropriate male and female behavior, characteristics and roles" (Gupta 2000, 1). In traditional Setswana cultures, age is a major category that defines the borders of social relations between different generations, between age-mates, and between parents and siblings in the home and public space (UNICEF 2002). In such cultures, age sometimes overrides female gender categories of inferiority, because an elderly woman or man (grandmother or grandfather) will have power over some female and male family members on the basis of age (UNICEF 2002). As such, adolescents are expected to respect all elderly people regardless of whether they are their relatives or not (Mwamwenda 2004; Schapera 1938). It is however the girl-child in Botswana who is expected to do household chores when she returns from school. Furthermore, when parents die from HIV/AIDS, the girl-child left behind is expected to care for the other siblings, and often this means having to compromise her education (*Mmegi* 2005).

Construction of the self among adolescents begins from birth, since some names of children communicate the roles expected by society on boys and girls, men and women (UNICEF 2002). Within Setswana cultures, typical names for girls include Seamokeng/Segametsi ("one who fetches water"), Mosidinyana ("one who grinds corn"), Bontle ("beauty"), Dikeledi ("tears"), Lorato/Ludo ("love"), and Boithumelo/Kushatha ("joy"), all of which define the expected roles of girls (UNICEF 2002). Similarly, boys could be named Modisaotsile ("the shepherd has come"), Kgosietsile ("the leader has come"), or Mogale ("the brave one") as a way to define their roles within the society. It is clear from the above names that girls' names are associated with domestic roles and particular values or emotions, while gendered names of boys associate them with leadership, property ownership, bravery, and intelligence (Chilisa, Tabulawa and Maundeni 2002). Names such as Bogadi (meaning *lobola*) and Khumo (meaning "riches") given to girls have the connotation that parents immediately anticipate that the girl will grow up to be married and that they will get rich from the bride price (*lobola*), as is the tradition in Setswana culture. The gender identity of children was also constructed through folktales and sayings taught to children within the family (Chilisa et al. 2002). Some of these cultural practices are still being practiced in the twenty-first century by some Setswana cultures as a way to maintain their values and identity.

The Self

As already mentioned in the gender section, construction of the self among adolescents begins from birth since some names of children communicate the roles expected by society on boys and girls, men and women (Schapera 1938; UNICEF 2002). It must be pointed out that within the Tswana culture most families are farmers who own cattle, goats, donkeys, and sheep. This signifies a symbol of wealth within the Tswana culture. As such, most Batswana families have cattle posts where they keep their cattle, normally these are long distances from their villages. Cattle posts are areas where cattle and other domestic animals are kept for survival since Botswana is mainly covered by the Kalahari and Namibian deserts. These cattle posts are normally situated in grazing areas where there is water and grass so that their animals can feed throughout the year. As such, most Batswana adults tend to be nomadic and have another "home" at the cattle posts where their wealth is kept. It is against this background that most adolescents do not stay with their parents in the villages for most of the time, because some of the parents will be looking after their cattle at their cattle posts. Such a scenario makes adolescents in Botswana tend to mature early in their lives and become dependent on the self or other siblings (or even the mother if she is not working in town or has not left for the cattle post). It is clear from such a scenario that adolescents who grow up under these circumstances tend to develop an independent or interdependent self as expected from the African culture. In other words, such adolescents tend to be self-reliant and resilient during hard times, especially in situations where parents are not available to nurture them during this critical period of development (Mwamwenda 2004; Schapera 1938).

Family Relationships

Adolescence is a stage where family relations are sometimes strengthened. This is the time where fathers bond more with their sons because they now do more things together. The sons are let into the family secrets, which usually involves knowing the property share of the father—his cattle—which is the most cherished symbol of wealth. The son is gradually prepared for the responsibility that he may have to assume in the event that the father dies. This makes the adolescent feel very proud and responsible. Fathers can now discuss issues as man-to-man, as when the father wants to know whether or not the son may have established a

sexual partnership. In the process the father transmits knowledge to the son about how to treat women.

The relationship between mothers and their daughters also becomes stronger as they become closer and share secrets about the girl's love life. The mother knows much more about the girl than her father does. In the event that the girl falls pregnant, the mother is blamed by the father for being too permissive.

There is, however, tension between parents and their adolescent children if the adolescent thinks that the parenting style is too authoritarian. There is also a lot of tension if the parents are not happy about their daughter's partner, as the girl often feels that she has the right to make her own choice.

As much as it is expected that the adolescent has intimate relationships, she is treated like a child until she is married. She is expected to stay at home with the parents. Where the girl stays away from home because of circumstances such as her workplace being away from home, she still cannot bring a boyfriend home openly if the parents are there.

The relationship between the adolescent and her siblings is also at times mutual when the adolescent can trust the younger sister or brother to keep her secrets about her private life and who she is seeing.

Friends and Peers/Youth Culture

At the beginning of adolescence male and female children establish friendships. They share ideas and information mostly about developments in the music world. They talk about their experiences at school especially if they attend different schools.

Schools encourage adolescents to seek advice from one another through movements such as Peer Approach Counseling by Teens (PACT) at secondary schools. This is necessary as most adolescents experience a lot of peer pressure, which in turn adversely affects their school performance and their relationships with their parents if they behave in a manner considered to be unacceptable by parents, or when they become unrealistically demanding to their parents.

The government, too, encourages youths' capacity for building and sharing of culture through the Department of Youth and Culture. Formation of YOHO (Youth Health Organization) through BOTUSA (Botswana United States of America) and Pathfinder, just to mention a few, train youth in such life skills as peer education and peer counseling (*Mmegi* June).

Christian churches, too, play a role in the lives of adolescents in Botswana. They have *mekgatho ya basha* (youth groups) that target children from 14 years upwards. The youths are encouraged to initiate projects and to address issues that are related to youth in general. One month, September, is regarded as the month of the youth. Churches, in most cases, give opportunities to members of the youth movements to lead sermons. It becomes apparent that adolescents have a lot of insight about problems that face the youth in general. Such issues include HIV/AIDS, not attending church, and not finding employment, to mention a few.

Love and Sexuality

In Botswana, the stage of adolescence is the beginning of developing sexual desires and establishing love relationships (Mwamwenda 2004; Schapera 1938; UNICEF 2000). However, it is apparent that girls start having love relationships earlier than their male counterparts. This is so because they may be approached by older boys. Girls subsequently become victims of "sugar daddies" or relationships with older men (Shumba 2001, 2002, and 2003; Shumba and Moorad 2000). Peer pressure is sometimes responsible for the irresponsible love relationships that girls find themselves in. It is sometimes because the girls are tempted by the fact that sugar daddies will afford them what they cannot get (clothes and cell phones) on their own, and therefore they will look like other girls.

Boys before 15 years of age do not feel confident about themselves and do not approach girls because they feel that their proposals might be rejected or that they will be mocked by the girls. Boys at this age are also still strongly influenced by school rules and are also afraid of their parents. Around this age, boys are attracted to girls but they spend more energy in just talking about them. Boys also spend more time discussing and showing off to one another about their muscles.

Traditionally, it was held that adolescents are sexually active (Mwamwenda 2004; Shumba 2001). For example, adolescent girls were not allowed to enter a room in which a nursing mother was still in confinement, as it was believed that she would make the child sick. Even for some religions, girls at that stage are not allowed to hold things such as the scepter used by the priest; the girls are deemed to have unholy ways (which specifically means interacting with boys in sexual relationships) that will weaken the power of the scepter.

In fact it is evident that girls in Botswana regard dating to be boys' responsibility in boyfriend-girlfriend relationships. Boys make the main decisions like where and when to have fun, have sex, or do anything (Mwamwenda 2004; Schapera 1938).

In some cultures, adolescence is treasured as it is regarded as a prime stage during which a girl should be married (Cox 1998; Mwamwenda 2004; Phiri 1998; Schapera 1938). A girl who is married whilst she is still an adolescent is perceived as being of more worth and value (Mwamwenda 2004; Schapera 1938). This is shown through the customary practice of paying *lobola* in Botswana. *Lobola* is the bride price (paid in cattle) that a man gives to the woman's parents as a sign of appreciation when he marries their daughter. If the bride is still an adolescent and has no child, the man is asked to pay more cattle (like eight herds of cattle, or even more depending on whether the girl is still a virgin) than if the bride is past the stage of adolescence or has had a child outside marriage. Even where money substitutes for cattle, as is sometimes the case nowadays because of modernization, the bride price is more if the girl is still an adolescent and a virgin. This is a sign of appreciation and respect within the African traditional customs. Such adolescent girls are viewed by the Botswana society as setting acceptable standards among the youth.

Research shows that sub-Saharan Africa (Botswana included) has been more devastated by the HIV/AIDS epidemic than any other region of the world (Bankole et al. 2004; Chipeta Mazile and Shumba 2000). About 2.3 million people had died of AIDS-related illness and almost 27 million people were estimated to be living with HIV/AIDS in this region by the end of 2003. The epidemic is taking an enormous toll on the region's youth, resulting in nearly 10 million women and men between the ages of 15 and 24 (roughly 1 in 14 young adults) living with HIV/AIDS (UNICEF 2003). Behavioral, physiological, and socio-cultural factors make young people more vulnerable than adults to HIV infection. It is during the adolescence period that young people naturally explore and take risks in many aspects of their lives, including sexual relationships (Bankole et al. 2004; Chipeta et al. 2000; Mwamwenda 2004). Those with more than one partner might engage in unprotected sex, increasing the risk of young people contracting HIV (Anderson 1991; UNAIDS 2000). Such a scenario has made young women in sub-Saharan Africa to be at a greater risk of contracting HIV than young men, because adolescent women are married to men who are considerably older. Against this background, it is clear that marriage in sub-Saharan Africa actually increases the number of adolescent women contracting HIV. Compounding young people's greater vulnerability to HIV from behavioral and physiological factors, especially in sub-Saharan Africa and the developing world, is that young people's reproductive health care needs receive little attention (Chipeta et al. 2000; Kiragu 2001). There is no doubt for the need by sub-Saharan African governments (including Botswana) to introduce policies, educational programs, and reproductive health services that could change the course of the HIV/AIDS epidemic (Anderson 1991; Bankole et al. 2004; UNAIDS 2000). There is no doubt that such efforts are likely to yield positive results and rescue adolescents in the HIV/AIDS epidemic high-prevalence countries.

Current research shows that the HIV/AIDS pandemic in Botswana has led to the introduction of sex education in the school curriculum (*Mmegi* 2005). This implies that by the time children reach adolescence, they are largely aware of the physical, emotional, and psychological changes that they are likely to experience as they develop. Hence, this prepares girls in particular to cope with the onset of menstruation with less stress and anxiety.

Introducing sex education into the curriculum has also made it easier for children to discuss sex-related issues with their parents. For older parents it is, however, still difficult to discuss such issues with children since this is not part of the Tswana culture in which they grew up.

As mentioned earlier, movements such as PACT help adolescents to develop more insight about their stages and gives them a better opportunity to cope with problems they may encounter, as such movements create forums for youths to open up to one another.

Adolescents in Botswana may, however, be disadvantaged by the perceived drawbacks in effectively integrating HIV/AIDS in the school curriculum. Research shows that most teachers feel embarrassed, vulnerable, and express discomfort when discussing explicit sexual and HIV/AIDS issues with children in schools (Pattman and Chege 2003). As such, this inhibits adolescent learners and does not give them the opportunity to learn or find out more about HIV/AIDS.

In Botswana, warnings about the HIV/AIDS pandemic are conveyed through the media, churches, and schools (Pattman and Chege 2003). There are, however, some problems reported in teaching HIV/AIDS education. Some pupils are said to have come to suffer from HIV/AIDS fatigue. The feeling is that too much is being said about the

"horror of HIV/AIDS and images of death and suffering that they do not want to hear anything more about it" (Pattman and Chege 2003, 67).

Health Risk Behavior

In modern Tswana society, nightlife and socializing are based around partying and night clubs (*ECHO* 2005). This kind of lifestyle occurs mainly in the urban areas of Botswana. Many adolescents who indulge in this kind of social activity end up being highly exposed to health risk behavior. There is the temptation to drink, smoke, and abuse drugs. As a result, Botswana has large numbers of teenage pregnancies, which subsequently lead to school dropouts. Some young pregnant women dump their newborn babies in unsafe locations, or undergo dangerous "back alley" abortions.

Incidents that suggest the prevalence of health risk behavior among adolescents in Botswana are not uncommon. For instance, *ECHO* (2005), a local Botswana newspaper, cited an incident in which a 19-year-old form five student alleged that she was drugged and raped by a former parastatal executive. The student alleged that her assailant spiked her drink at a party she had been invited to, and upon regaining consciousness the following day she discovered that she had been sexually violated. Such incidents hitherto suggest the inevitability of the spread of HIV/AIDS among youth (Chipeta et al. 2000).

The problem of dropping out of school due to pregnancy (*Mmegi Monitor* 2005) would also suggest that adolescents still engage in health-risk behavior. However there is positive development relating to teenage pregnancy in the education policy. In order to redress equity and access to education for boys and girls, students who dropped out of school due to pregnancy are allowed to re-enter school. In the past adolescent girls who became pregnant were not allowed to continue with their schooling, and similarly boys who were responsible for impregnating a schoolgirl were forced to leave school for one year to help raise the child (Molefe, Pansiri, and Weeks 2005). This policy reform can, however, be said to have been received with mixed feelings by teachers and students who still viewed the returnees as "bad" adolescents who could be a bad influence on younger pupils. As a corollary, before the 1990s re-entrants were only allowed to go to another school and not return to the one from which they dropped out (Chipeta et al. 2000; Molefe et al. 2005).

It is, however, evident that the government is highly concerned about the spread of HIV/AIDS among adolescents. The establishment of a Girl's Education Movement (GEM) in line with the birth of the movement in Kampala, Uganda, in Botswana has as one of its objectives to teach life skills in regards to HIV/AIDS (*Mmegi* 2005).

Education

The projected adult illiteracy rate in Botswana for the year 2000 stands at 22.8% for males and 20.2% for females (Thomson Gale 2005). As of 1999, public expenditure on education was estimated at 9.1% of GDP. The government of Botswana aims to achieve universal education. Education at the primary level lasts for seven years and is not compulsory. Subsequent to that is five years of secondary education (two years of lower secondary followed by three years of upper secondary education). Schooling is conducted in Setswana for the first four years and in English for the remaining years.

In 1996, Botswana had 318,629 students and 12,785 teachers at the primary level and 109,843 students enrolled in general secondary education, with 6,214 teachers. The pupil-teacher ratio at primary school level was 27 to 1 in 1999. Until 1961, primary schooling was completely financed by tribal treasuries, with some tribes spending up to 70% of their budgets on education. Between 1985 and 1994, the government of Botswana launched a major program of secondary school construction. As of 1999, 84% of primary-school-age children were enrolled in school, while 59% of those eligible attended secondary school. The University of Botswana, established on July 1, 1982 by an act of parliament, has faculties of social sciences, education, sciences, agriculture, and humanities. Universities and equivalent institutions had 8,850 pupils and 765 teaching staff in 1997 (Thomson Gale 2005).

Education at both primary and secondary levels is highly subsidized by the Botswana government. This has made it easier and cheaper for most adolescents to attend school. A move to reintroduce school fees in Botswana schools caused controversy, with politicians and education experts warning that it may be a step backwards. Opposition parties called on parents to defy the government decision to reintroduce fees when the 2006 term started. In October 2005, Botswana's parliament approved legislation reintroducing school fees for pupils at junior secondary and senior secondary schools in 2006. Fees were abolished in 1987 in a bid to get more children into schools, and enrollment rates soared. However, the government has said it would have to cut high annual expenditures on basic education (IRIN Report 2005). Although the Botswana government is still committed to the principle of equal access to education, it has said that it cannot no longer economically continue with a wholly subsidized education system (IRIN Report 2005).

According to the new law, pupils at junior secondary school are to pay 300 pula ($54 USD) per year, while the fees for those at senior secondary school will be P450 ($81 USD) per year. The president of the opposition party, the Botswana National Front (BNF), was reported to have said that most people are struggling below the poverty line and cannot afford to pay such fees. It is a wait and see attitude, because as of this writing the situation is still not very clear about whether the new fee structure will be implemented or not in 2006 (IRIN Report 2005).

Most adolescents attend school, because all adolescents have access to school and most parents can afford to pay their children's education fees, especially those with children who receive their secondary education in neighboring countries such as Zimbabwe and South Africa. Population-wise, there are more females than males in Botswana, and this kind of trend is typical of Botswana secondary schools. It is very difficult to distinguish the participation rate in secondary schools, because both girls and boys appear to participate fully in their school work (Chipeta, Mazile, and Shumba 2000). Unlike in the past, the attitude of adolescents towards school has changed because most people now seem to be familiar with the value of education in their lives (Mwamwenda 2004). A limited number of students in selected Botswana schools sit for the British Ordinary and Advanced Level examinations (International British Cambridge Examinations), because there are very few such schools available in the country. Besides, all students with "O"- or "A"-level qualifications compete for entry into the only local university, the University of Botswana (UB) located in the capital city, Gaborone.

Adolescence raises concerns about the safety of the adolescent as a learner. It is during this stage that teachers find learners, both boys and girls, to be uncooperative and troublesome. Adolescents' preoccupation with love relationships, cell phones, and their appearance can distract them in learning and, hence, result in poor performance.

The safety of adolescents is a concern also as it becomes apparent that not only are girls sexually harassed by boys at school but also by teachers, some of whom are "constructed as sugar daddy figures, offering various inducements accruing from their power as teachers in exchange for sex" (Pattman and Chege 2003, 110). What is more worrying is the fact that some girls confess that they fear retribution by such boys and teachers. As such, they rarely report such cases of sexual harassment from these boys, partly because they fear being beaten or even being rebuked (Pattman and Chege 2003). There is no doubt that there is a likelihood of unreported child abuse and sexual harassment in Botswana schools (Shumba 2001, 2002, and 2003; Shumba and Moorad 2000). This also implies that such adolescent girls are vulnerable to child abuse. Therefore, the Botswana government needs to intervene and address such issues that make the girl-child vulnerable to such forms of child abuse in schools.

Work

Until they finish their secondary schooling, most children in Botswana are still at the stage of adolescence (Child 1993; Gage and Berliner 1988; Mwamwenda 2004; Woolfolk 2003). Those who do not go for further education have to find employment. Even when they do go to the University of Botswana or abroad, they now think in terms of being in a position to take charge of their own lives. This is a change in the thinking by adolescents in Botswana. In the early 1980s, university students studying at the University of Botswana did not show any interest in part-time employment or vacation jobs. They saw themselves as children who did not need to work. It can be said, however, that the trend in the economy of the country has contributed to the way adolescents think about survival. It has been an eye-opener to the Botswana adolescent because life can be difficult without a source of income. As such, the spirit of relaxation that was prevalent among Botswana adolescents up to the 1980s is gradually disappearing. During that time period, there was a lot of reliance on parents' economic status, particularly wealth as symbolized by cattle. Hence, such adolescents saw no need to work since everything was provided for by their parents. It must also be pointed out that with the impending drought that has affected the southern African region, most cattle died, leaving some parents poor.

Private sectors and the government encourage adolescents to think more seriously about being self-reliant (self-reliance being one of the philosophies of the country). There are grant schemes such as Kick-Start by Botswana Breweries Company that help to finance youth-initiated projects.

Besides beef and minerals, the economy of Botswana rests on tourism. The advent of tourism has had both a positive and negative impact on the life of the youth. The youth are challenged and they begin to reason more maturely as entrepreneurs in business ventures that promote tourism are increasing. Botswana youth are embarking on projects such as hotel management and catering. Encouraging adolescents to participate in tourism activities also helps them develop pride in their country. They begin to have more appreciation of some cultural practices, such as dancing and traditional food. On the other hand, the adverse impact of tourism is that it leads to health-risk behavior among the youth, particularly those living around areas that attract tourists. To such groups, commercial sex is seen as a means of earning a living. Tourism also encourages crime as tourists often have valuable items such as cameras, which tempt some individuals to steal.

Media

The media in Botswana also plays a big role in helping adolescents, as do those who play a part in the lives of adolescents, such as parents and teachers. One of the newspapers, the *ECHO* in Botswana, for instance, has a column titled "Students' Column" that allows students to air their views by writing articles on issues related to their lives. This, like the youth movements in churches and movements such as PACT, suggests that adolescents in Botswana are enlightened about problems that face them and are also in a position to contribute to their solutions.

The Botswana television program "Talk Back" has won an award for being educational. This program provides a forum for adolescents to air their views about sex-related issues, HIV/AIDS issues, and so on. Another related program, *Remmogo* (literally translated to mean "we are together"— presumably implying that people should work together in the struggle against HIV/AIDS) creates more HIV/AIDS awareness in Botswana.

Politics and Military

The political arena in Botswana recognizes adolescence as a stage where the individual is at a prime time to take responsibility. The voting age in Botswana is 18 years, and this implies that adolescents can now exercise their right to vote. Incidentally, all children are also required by law to have *Omang* (the Botswana national identity card) at the age of 16 years.

The military sector also recruits males of ages 18 and older. There has, however, been gender discrimination in the recruitment of women in the military force, as women are still not recruited to be soldiers and this is a highly contentious issue (*Mmegi* 2005).

Unique Issues

Adolescents' behavior and values are highly affected by general changes in the developing world. For instance, the manner of dressing is expected to change with the onset of adolescence. Girls are expected to wear dresses that extend below their knees in length, but this is not the case as girls do what they consider fashionable. Adolescents are prepared for certain roles but because nowadays people hire maids and workers, it is not always that children have such responsibilities. Schools also expect children to spend more hours at school; therefore they cannot get the chance to help around as was the case traditionally. One finds girls sleeping out and individuals below the age of 21 cohabiting with their lovers, and this seems to be generally accepted especially where the couple have a child and where the girl-child is not employed. Such freedom can be said to have its repercussions, as there has been a lot of passion killing in Botswana since 2002, and some of the individuals involved in such killings have been adolescents.

The San (known as the Basarwa in Setswana) are a primitive and nomadic tribe known to have lived in the Kalahari Desert throughout the history of mankind as hunters, and who are also referred to as the Bushmen (Schapera 1938). With regards to people of San origin, there is nothing notable that is done concerning the boy who reaches that stage. Boys, like their fathers, are normally engaged in animal hunting and looking for water in the desert. They are trained by their male adults to be vigilant and aggressive as men. Besides, they are trained how to make bows and arrows that they use in hunting animals for feeding their families. The other unique skill that boys acquire is the making of fire using firewood. This requires a special talent and traditional skill in order for one to be able to make such a fire in a desert. All in all, the San boy is expected to gather fruits, water, and meat for the family in their search for survival.

However, for girls, it becomes obvious as they gradually begin to stop wearing *makhabe* (the traditional San skin dresses). When the girl first realizes the onset of menstruation, she keeps it to herself and then she runs away from the homestead and goes into hiding. This becomes a sign within the San tradition that the girl has experienced the symptoms of menstruation. Young girls are not informed about what has happened to the other girl during this period. What the younger girls know is just that the particular girl has gone missing and they were not made to understand why that was the case. This is kept as a traditional secret to the young girls still yet to go through such an experience themselves. Where she hides would not be in such an obscure bushy area, but would, however, be a place concealed enough to necessitate a search. The girl can remain in this place of hiding even if it means spending nights out there. Only women go out in search of her.

Once she is found the girl is taken back to the settlement or village, and she is confined to the hut. Her age-mates are not allowed to go near her; she remains in the company of older women. If the girl has to go outside for reasons such as having to answer the call of nature, she is completely covered with a blanket and is escorted by some older women; people are not supposed to see her face. While she is in the house her body is covered with special red make-up powder (*letsoku*) and she does not wash her body until her days of menstruation elapse. During the period that she is in the house, the girl is given lessons pertaining to womanhood, especially in regard to being a wife and mother in order to prepare her for that stage in her life. During the course of her being in the house, women sing songs around a fire every night as a sign of appreciation and honor.

When the girl reaches her last day of menstruation, a goat is killed and there is intense feasting, but only the women eat the meat. The women form a horse-shoe circle around the fire in front of the house and they sing throughout the night while the girl who has reached puberty remains inside the house. The singers use a metal piece of a hoe as an instrument to produce sound and add tune to the music. The girl's age-mates now join in the celebration, and the following morning they are given *moretlwa* (wild berry tree) sticks to beat her up. She has to run while they give chase beating her. The belief associated with this act is that it prepares the girl entering adulthood and womanhood to be able to endure the hardships that accompany the new life.

The behavior of a girl who reaches puberty in the San tribe changes because she no longer mixes with younger girls. The girl also appears to be very depressed, reserved, and withdrawn. She behaves strangely, as she just keeps to herself and does nothing in terms of work. She is no longer free to play with her friends. The dramatic turn of events is when the girl suddenly shows mature behavior. She does not appear to receive it with joy and shows a lot of anxiety. The experience of entering adolescence causes embarrassment to the San girl. (The San do not share their experiences much, so it becomes difficult to know about their seemingly strange behavior). Note that it is only strange to the outsider.) It can, however, be assumed that this is a result of anxiety and fear, which the adolescent presumably experiences as she is soon to be married off. It is observed that as soon as a girl reaches adolescence it does not take long for her to be married off. The intent to abolish such cultural practices as early marriages by GEM (*Mmegi* 2005) might provide relief for such feelings in the future.

However, the Basarwa, like all other people of Botswana, are not left out of the HIV/AIDS awareness campaigns and youth capacity building programs in the country. The formation of youth groups and activities of organizations such as BOTUSA, Pathfinder, and YOHO have encouraged youth development through a variety of means, such as training in theater development and putting up plays about alcohol abuse, promiscuity, abstinence, HIV testing, youth delinquency and government support programs. It reaches out to remote area dwellers, such as the training in Darkar, a settlement for the Naro-speaking Basarwa (*Mmegi* 2005). They also improve youth skills in peer education and peer counseling (*Mmegi* 2003).

Adolescence for San girls takes away the joy of childhood completely, because the transition to adulthood is not gradual. There is a high expectation for an immediate transition to maturity by the girl. However, on the whole there is minimal health-risk behavior as there is less promiscuity among women. An eminent problem, however, is that the San are very reluctant to use condoms (*Mmegi* 2005). Immigration by Botswana youth into South Africa is minimal and very rare. This is perhaps because Batswana perceive South Africans as leading a lifestyle that is completely different from theirs and has a different culture. Such immigration was much more common in the 1960s and seems to have affected the male-to-female ratio in Botswana, because most of the Batswana men who left to work in South African mines never came back. It is alleged that some of them got married to South African women and are now South African nationals.

However, an increase in the number of students placed to study in South African universities by the government has enlightened the youth about better employment opportunities in South Africa. This has subsequently tempted some of the youths studying in South Africa to remain there upon completion of their studies. One foresees gradual migrations also as student love relationships established whilst studying in South Africa become potential marital relationships. This again might further compound the male-to-female ratio in Botswana.

ALMON SHUMBA and ELIZABETH
GABASWEDIWE SEECO

References and Further Reading

Anderson, R. M. 1991. The transmission dynamics of sexually transmitted diseases: The behavioral components. In *research issues in human behavior and sexually transmitted diseases in the AIDS era*. ed. J. N. Wasserheit, S. O. Aral, and K. K. Holmes (eds.). p. 41. Washington, D.C.: American Society for Microbiology.

Bankole, A., S. Singh, V. Wong, and D. Wulf. 2004. *Risk and protection: Youth and HIV/AIDS in sub-Saharan Africa*. New York: Alan Guttmacher Institute.

Chakanza, J. 1998. Unfinished agenda: Puberty rites and the response of the Roman Catholic Church in southern Malawi 1901–1994. In *Rites of passage in contemporary Africa*. James Cox (ed.). Cardiff: Cardiff Academic Press.

Child, D. 1993. *Psychology and the teacher*, 5th ed. London: Cassell.

Chilisa, B., R. Tabulawa, and T. Maundeni. 2002. *Gendered school experiences: Effects on achievement and retention*. London: DFID.

Chipeta, D. P., B. M. Mazile, and A. Shumba. 2000. *Curriculum development: Contemporary issues and instructional materials development techniques*. Mogoditshane, Botswana: Tasalls Publishing and Books.

Cox, J. 1998. *Rites of passage in contemporary Africa*. Cardiff: Cardiff Academic Press.

Dineo, L. 2000. *Expression of concepts of personhood among Tswapong puberty rites*. Gaborone: University Botswana.

ECHO. 2005. September 8. 8th September 2005 Issue No. 8 (Botswana local Newspaper).

ECHO. 2005. September 15. 15th September 2005 Issue No. 8 (Botswana local Newspaper).

Gage, N. L., and D. C. Berliner. 1988. *Educational psychology*, 4th ed. Boston: Houghton Mifflin.

IRIN Report. 2005. Botswana: Access to education may be limited by new fees policy. http://www.irinnews.org/report.asp?ReportID=50496&SelectRegion=Southern_Africa (accessed January 1, 2006).

Kiragu, K. 2001. Youth and HIV/AIDS: Can we avoid catastrophe? *Population Reports* 12:7.

Mmegi. 2003. 20 –26th June 20–26.

Mmegi. 2005. March 15. 15th March 2005, Vol.22, No.40.

Mmegi. 2005. June 15. 15th June 2005, Vol.22, No.90.

Mmegi. 2005. June 16. 16th June, 2005, Vol. 22 No 91.

Mmegi Monitor. 2002. September. 2004, Vol.4 No. 38.

Mmegi Monitor. March 2005. Vol. 5 No. 9.

Mmegi. March 7. Molefe, D., O. Pansiri, and S. Weeks. 2005. Pregnancy and dropping out.

Mpassou, D. M. 1998. The continuing tension between Christianity and the rites of passage in Swaziland. In *Rites of passage in contemporary africa*. James Cox (ed.). Cardiff: Cardiff Academic Press.

Mwamwenda, T. S. 2004. *Educational psychology: An African perspective*. 3rd ed. Sandton, South Africa: Heinemann.

Pattman, R. and F. Chege. 2003. *Finding our voices: Gendered and sexual identities and HIV/AIDS in education*. Botswana: UNICEF.

Phiri, I. 1998. The initiation of Chewa women of Malawi. In *Rites of passage in contemporary Africa*. James Cox (ed.). Cardiff: Cardiff Academic Press.

Santrock, J. W. 1994. *Child development*, 6th ed. Madison: Brown & Benchmark.

Schapera, I. 1938. *A handbook of Tswana law and custom*. London: Frank Cass.

Shumba, A. 2001. "Who guards the guards in schools?" A study of reported cases of child abuse by teachers in Zimbabwean secondary schools. *Sex Education* 1:77–86.

Shumba, A. 2002. Teacher conceptualization of child abuse in schools in the new millennium. *Journal of Interpersonal Violence* 17:403–15.

Shumba, A. 2003. Children's rights in schools: What do teachers know in the new millennium? *Child Abuse Review* 12:251–60.

Shumba, A., and F. Moorad. 2000. A note on the laws against child abuse in Botswana. *PULA: Botswana Journal of African Studies* 15:253–58.

Thomson Gale. 2005. Botswana Education. http://www.nationencyclopedia.com/Africa/Botswana_Education.html (accessed January 11, 2006).

UNAIDS. 2000. *Report on the global HIV/AIDS epidemic 2000*. Geneva: UNAIDS.

UNICEF. 2001. *Botswana's children: Leading the battle against HIV/AIDS*. Gaborone, Botswana: UNICEF.

UNICEF. 2002. *Breaking the silence with subject centered research methods: Young people, gender, sexuality and HIV/AIDS in Botswana*. Gaborone, Botswana: UNICEF.

UNICEF. 2003. *Africa's orphaned generations*. New York: UNICEF.

Woolfolk, A. 2003. *Educational psychology*, 9th ed. New York: Allyn & Bacon.

BRUNEI DARUSSALAM

Background Information

Negara Brunei Darussalam, meaning "the abode of peace," is situated on the northwest coast of the island of Borneo with a land area of 5,765 square kilometers. Brunei benefits from extensive petroleum and natural gas fields, the source of one of the highest per capita GDPs in the developing world.

The sultanate of Brunei's influence peaked between the fifteenth and seventeenth centuries, when its control extended over coastal areas of northwest Borneo and the southern Philippines. Brunei subsequently entered a period of decline brought on by internal strife over royal successions, colonial expansion of European powers, and piracy. In 1888, Brunei became a British protectorate; independence was achieved in 1984. The same family has ruled Brunei for over six centuries. His Majesty Sultan Haji Hassanal Bolkiah Mu'izzaddin Waddaulah, the Sultan, and Yang Di-Pertuan of Brunei Darussalam, is the twenty-ninth of his line, which dates back to the fourteenth century. Being the eldest son, he became crown prince in 1961 and ascended to the throne in 1967 following the voluntary abdication of his father, Al-Marhum Sultan Haji Omar Ali Saifuddien Sa'adul Khairi Waddien.

Brunei is an independent sovereign sultanate that is governed on the basis of a written constitution. His Majesty is the supreme executive authority in Brunei Darussalam. His Majesty has occupied the position of prime minister since resumption of independence in 1984. Besides being the sultan and the ruler, His Majesty Sultan Haji Hassanal Bolkiah is concurrently the prime minister, defense minister, finance minister, and head of the religion of Brunei Darussalam. Being a working monarch, he is involved in the conduct of the state affairs internally and internationally. His Majesty officially proclaimed the institutionalization of the philosophy of the Malay Islamic Monarchy (MIB) on January 1, 1984, when Brunei Darussalam assumed its independent and sovereign status. It has become the nation's formal ideology and guiding light as a way of life for Brunei Darussalam. It is a blend of Malay language, culture, and customs; the teaching of Islamic laws and values; and the monarchy system, which must be esteemed and practiced by all.

It is estimated that the population of Brunei is 372,361 and that 29% (52,243 males and 52,013 females) is below 14 years old (*World Factbook* 2005). Population density is 53 persons per square kilometer, with an average growth at 3.1% per year. The annual birth and death rates are 19.01 per 1000 and 3.42 per 1000, respectively. Life expectancy for men is 72.36 and 77.36 years for women. Males account for about 52.9% of the population and females 47.1%. In terms of racial groups, Malays account for 67% of the population, whereas Chinese form 15%, indigenous populations account for 6%, and others for 12%. Although the Malays form the largest ethnic group in Brunei, followed by Chinese and various indigenous groups, Malay, or *Bahasa Melayu,* is the national and official language of the country. English is also widely spoken and understood. Chinese groups speak Mandarin, Hokkien, and Cantonese.

Period of Adolescence

In traditional Brunei culture, there is no clear evidence of a stage in life called adolescence. In the early 1950s, adolescence was a period in which young people would start to become independent from their parents. They would look for a job, a life partner, start a family, and move on to full adulthood, committing to adult roles of marriage and parenthood. Girls would get married as early as 15 years old and males around the age of 18 or 19. Therefore, in traditional Brunei culture the child became a young adult without going through a transitional period. This pattern continued up until the early 1980s. A drastic change in the education system and lifestyles took place after Brunei gained independence in 1984. The government stressed the importance of education and the need to have trained locals in the professional areas. Scholarships and opportunities for further studies became available to the locals. Parents are now aware of the importance of education, and adolescents are encouraged to concentrate on studies. Marriage normally comes later, around the age of 24 or 25.

In modern Brunei the adolescent stage is comparable to adolescence in other advanced countries. In the Malay language there are many terms that are used to refer to adolescents such as *anak muda* (young child), *remaja* (adolescent), and *belia* (youth). In the Bruneian context, students in the secondary school system between the ages of 11 and 18 can all be considered to be in the adolescent stage. However, between the ages of 11 and 14, one is usually still considered to be in late childhood; therefore, 11- to 14-year-olds are not considered adolescents by society. In terms of common understanding among Bruneians, the period of adolescent proper can be between the ages of 15 and 20. Those who are between the ages of 20 and 24 are usually considered as *belia*, or youth. This again is due to tradition and culture. Those between the ages of 20 and 24 are still considered youth, not adults. Twenty- to 24-year-olds have few responsibilities. Youth or young adult status is closely associated with individuals who are not married, still living with the parents, and most likely unemployed or have just begun employment. However, those who are married and have children, even if they are below 24, are accepted as adults. Currently, in Brunei Darussalam adolescents account for about 10–20% of the population and play an important role in the development of the country.

Beliefs

Islam is the official religion of the country. Muslims account for 67% of the population, Buddhists 13%, Christians 10%, and indigenous beliefs and other religions 10%. As most of the population are Muslims, their lifestyle and code of behaviors are based on Islamic values and laws. Bruneians are also known for their strong adherence to traditional culture and beliefs. These have shaped the identity of the Bruneian, who is known to be well-mannered, soft spoken, highly religious, and loyal. As mentioned earlier, Brunei Darussalam adheres to its own unique philosophy of *Melayu Islam Beraja*, or Malay Islamic Monarchy. The philosophy is deeply entrenched throughout the population and the government. It is widely implemented in a more systematic way in the hope of molding the identity of the people of Brunei Darussalam. The ideology of Malay Islam Monarchy is taught in schools, colleges, and in the local university. Here the main emphasis is on the tradition of monarchy and the respect accorded to the highest authority (the sultan). This is strictly followed by the people of the sultanate.

Since Bruneians are strongly rooted in their traditions and culture, the country as a whole pays attention to collectivism based on Malay culture and Islamic values. These values are practiced at all levels of life, such as government functions and cultural and religious celebrations. Caring for others, sharing and participating in prayers, and all activities from weddings to death are done collectively, and they are strongly reinforced by the society and the government. Collectivism and group values are so deeply entrenched that independence and individualism are not emphasized. For example, teachers and lecturers often find that students are more comfortable and less threatened when assignments are given as group projects. The majority of adolescents adhere to the societal, moral, and social code of behavior embedded in Malay culture and religion. They adhere to the Muslim religious obligation of attending prayers on Fridays. In terms of dressing they do follow a certain restrain, especially the girls. The adolescent male dresses more like any Asian or Western counterpart; however, they are uniquely guided by cultural and Islamic values in their behavior. Therefore, in terms of fashion in dressing, social activities, and conduct, the Brunei adolescents mix modern day trends with respect for traditions, religious values and beliefs.

Gender

The learning of sex-appropriate behavior and gender roles, or gender typing, is given an important emphasis in Bruneian culture. In Brunei, very early in life children begin to learn about appropriate gender role behavior. Gender stereotypes are firmly established, based on unquestioned beliefs about male-female differences. The female is expected to be appropriately attired, show respect to men, and show obedience and restraint in their public behavior. The men are expected to be leaders, providers, and the main decision makers in the family. The traditional roles of females based on Islamic values and cultural norms are still prevalent among Brunei adolescents. However, these norms are going through a challenging phase; as women are rapidly moving up the ladder of academic success, they are being liberated. Some of the gender differences may no longer seem as apparent in the early twenty-first century as they did 50 years ago. The general pattern of academic performance in Brunei indicates that the adolescent girls are performing far better in academic achievement at the school and tertiary levels in most disciplines compared to adolescent boys. Even in government administration women have moved significantly to senior positions. In the private sector women are playing a very active role. As such, the stage is set for Brunei adolescents to play equitable roles in many aspects of the economy, administration, family and social life. Like other Asian countries, Brunei is experiencing the combined effects of rapid technological advances and economic and social globalization, which is now impacting strongly the way of life especially for adolescents, including gender equality.

The Self

Development of self-identity is mostly based on the societal values (Malay customs and traditions and Islamic beliefs). Children grow up strongly guided by religious values and traditions. All Malay Muslim children attend *Ugama* (Religious) school in the afternoon where they study Islam. In addition in regular school, the religious teaching is a part of the curriculum 30 minutes per week, which is compulsory for the Malay Muslim student.

Family Relationships

Family structure in Brunei is still very much based on the traditional extended family concept. Due to cultural beliefs and the emphasis on collectivism, the Bruneian society cherishes family values and unity among friend and neighbors. Celebrations and religious activities are strongly emphasized and given high priority. The society believes in uniting with one another, and certain occasions such as weddings and religious activities provide the opportunity for all to mingle and establish rapport among the family members, relatives, and friends. For example, in a typical Bruneian wedding it is common for neighbors and friends to play an active role, and normally all age groups are involved in different roles. The men will be busy with setting up the tents and cleaning the area, while the women will be busy in the kitchen preparing the food, and some will be busy with the bride and the groom. Wedding ceremonies for the Malay society consists of many stages, for a certain period of time and for each occasion, all the family members are expected to take part. This provides the opportunity for relatives and friends to spend time together. Children are happy as this is the time they get to play around. Adolescents as well are encouraged to participate in most of the activities by helping the elderly in the hope that they will learn the culture and pass it to the next generation.

Bruneians are very strongly family oriented, with an emphasis on extended family values and community collective involvement for the common good. As such, the adolescent is very much closely involved in all family and social activities, and their peer relationships are within this parameter. In line with Asian values, all adolescents are expected to live with their parents until they are married. It is not uncommon for people in Brunei to live with their parents with their spouse and children as an extended family even after marriage.

There has been a gradual increase in drug abuse and alcohol use among adolescents. The most commonly used drug is *syabu* or "ice," which are amphetamines. Reports from the media often indicate that adolescents in Brunei, like others in this region, are exposed to rapid changes, declining job opportunities, new demands, and more stressful challenges in life than their predecessors. Generally, Brunei adolescents are responsible and well-behaved citizens. Problem behaviors include gang membership, drug abuse, alcohol abuse, and teenage pregnancy.

Sometimes this causes concern to parents, leading to conflict. Most of the conflicts that occur between adolescents and parents center on adolescents' unruly behavior, impulsiveness, and time spent on the Internet (a popular means of chatting with friends). Even in the twenty-first century, in rural areas the family often lives with the grandparents, and often working parents leave their children to be cared for by the children's grandparents. But when those children grow up as adolescents with conflicting role models (strict parents versus affectionate grandparents), problems may arise between adolescents and their parents.

Dating is not totally prohibited, and it is usually carried out under parental supervision and guidance. Generally, the parents of a girl will approve of the boy she wishes to date if he has earned a good education and a stable job. If a young man and woman choose to marry, parental approval (especially that of the father) is necessary; otherwise, the marriage will not be considered valid.

Friends and Peers/Youth Culture

Due to modernization and rapid economic development, adolescents in Brunei are spending more time with peers and social groups or being alone compared to being with the family. This is particularly true for children who have both their parents working. There are several reasons why people join social groups. Most people join social groups because there are many benefits for belonging to a group. People like to feel connected and feel that they can relate to others. Socialization is the process by which one learns to adapt the behavior patterns of the surrounding culture. When kids get so interested in what other people are wearing that they do not care what they want to wear—they just want to look like everyone else to fit in—this is called conformity. After a few people start wearing what is trendy, not too long after everyone will be wearing it because they want to feel "cool" and that they are "fitting in." In Brunei there are different groups of adolescents marked by their dress, hairstyle, slang, tattoos, and body piercing, which is influenced by other cultures and countries.

Love and Sexuality

Dating is unacceptable in Brunei due to the influence of Islam, and premarital sex is strongly discouraged. Contraception is not legal in Brunei, and sexual education is not taught in schools. According to the Islamic religion, sex before marriage is forbidden. A couple discovered to be indulging in premarital sexual relations will be fined and forced to wed. In Brunei, the national religion of Islam influences sexual mores. A man is allowed to get married four times because the Prophet Mohammad married four times. However, the Prophet married to help the women, who were divorced and unable to have children. Contemporary Brunei society abuses what the prophet was teaching.

Islam considers homosexuality a sin. However, the homosexual population is gradually, increasingly visible in the capital.

Health Risk Behavior

In a rapidly changing society, the adolescent is faced with many developmental tasks and decisions. Although serious behavioral disturbances are evident in only a minority of adolescents, few individuals pass through adolescence without experiencing problems in at least some areas of their behavior (Harper and Marshall 1991).

Bruneians adhere to strict Islamic moral conduct in behavior, especially the adolescent female. Dating and partying are not common, as they are against their religious values. However, there are sufficient opportunities for adolescents to interact in the schools as most of the secondary schools in Brunei are coeducational. Another common source of healthy interactions is during social functions such as weddings, family gatherings, and sociocultural events.

Adolescents in Brunei are exposed to current events in the world through media such as television, newspapers, and the Internet. A sizable proportion of them are well-traveled and exposed to other cultures. Since there is a large expatriate community in Brunei, they are also used to interacting with people from different cultures. Their lifestyle involves movies and peer activities; adolescents in Brunei do not socialize in cybercafés, malls, or parks.

Since Brunei is a rich country, the general health level of Brunei adolescents is similar to that of developed countries. Like their counterparts in other parts of the world, adolescents in Brunei are not completely free from problematic health risk behaviors. Media reports indicate that the rate of car accidents is high. Drug abuse has been identified as one of the major problems faced by adolescents in Brunei. However, in terms of numbers, they are statistically insignificant. The government of Brunei has set up narcotics bureaus and has organized effective prevention laws and rehabilitation programs. Adolescent involvement in alcohol is minimal because alcohol use is banned for the Muslims in Brunei. Even among the non-Muslim adolescents there are no known reports linking them to alcohol use. This is probably due to the strong efforts of the government: alcohol sales and drinking in public are strictly prohibited by the law. Adolescent involvement in other crimes such as vandalism, petty thefts, and gang activity is minimal. Suicide amongst adolescents is very rare, and this is probably due to strong adherence and influence of Islamic faith.

In Brunei Darussalam there is very limited data derived from reliable and valid research regarding adolescents and specifically what they regard as their major problems and concerns. Suppiah and Burns (2004) measured the concerns and problems that adolescents in Brunei believed to be most pressing by applying a modified Malay version of the Mooney Problem Check List, which had been trialed in a pilot study (Suppiah and Burns 1998). It was found that 746 respondents, 234 male and 512 female students aged 11 to 18 years, ranked adjustment to schoolwork, personal psychological relations, future vocational issues, and morals and religion as their main categories of problems. While there was considerable similarity between genders in the ratings of the ranking of the category problems, one noticeable difference was in the area of courtship and marriage, which appears to be a more important issue for females (ranked seventh) than males (ranked eleventh). However, significant differences were found in six categories of problems between boys and girls. Overall, females tend to report greater number of problems. Age differences also generated significant variations in the relative saliency of problems. Younger students reported personal psychological relations and adjustment to schoolwork as main concerns, while older students were more concerned with future vocational issues, which were results similar to those raised in studies of adolescents in other parts of the world (Langulung 1977; Harper and Marshall 1991). Overall, younger students generally possess significantly fewer concerns than older students across all categories of problems.

Suppiah et al. (2001) reported a study of coping behavior among Bruneian adolescents with a sample of 383 secondary students (221 girls and 162 boys). The results indicate that Bruneian adolescents seem to engage in both positive and negative coping behaviors (Table 1 summarizes the most common and the least common coping strategies of Bruneian adolescents). However, in terms of ranking, the first four coping strategies, "work hard and achieve," "focus on solving the problem," "seeking spiritual support," and "seeking to belong" can be considered as positive coping behaviors. These findings are similar to findings reported by Frydenberg and Lewis (1993) in Australia, and D'Rozario (1998) in Singapore, but with one major exception. In this study, seeking relaxing diversions is only ranked number 11, while in other studies mentioned, seeking relaxing diversions was ranked first. This difference could be attributed to the fact that in Brunei seeking relaxing diversions may not be a typical way of coping due to strong cultural and contextual differences compared to countries like Singapore and Australia. In Brunei, there is much emphasis on religious and cultural activities as an important aspect of social life. Bruneians are expected to strictly adhere to the philosophy of Malay Islamic Monarchy as the guiding principle in their conduct. As such, seeking relaxing diversions are not strongly encouraged, especially for adolescent girls, and this may explain why this was not chosen as the main coping behavior. Similarly, strong emphasis on Islamic values can also explain the reason why seeking spiritual support seems to be a strong coping behavior. Furthermore, within Bruneian culture, seeking spiritual support will be reinforced as a very positive way of coping.

The coping strategies that are seldom used are "not coping," "seeking professional help," "social action," and "tension reduction." The data also indicates that adolescents' nonproductive coping behaviors, such as worry and wishful thinking, are also common among Bruneians. The most common coping strategies and the least common strategies used by Bruneian adolescents are not surprising. For example, tension-reduction behaviors such as alcohol and drug use are not a serious problem in Brunei. As the majority of the citizens are Muslim, they are prohibited from the consumption of alcohol. Another coping behavior that is seldom common is "social action." This is understandable as the socio-political and administrative structure of Brunei is such that individuals or even groups do not get involved in social action or controversies and it is not encouraged. Overall, it can be concluded that adolescents in Brunei are managing themselves well in terms of health risk behaviors, coping with stress, and the normal problems of development.

Education

The government provides free education to all its citizens from preschool onward. Malay is the national language and is promoted as a medium of instruction in nontechnical subjects. English remains the language of business and education in Brunei Darussalam.

Education consists of six years of primary education and five years of secondary school (form one to form five). Form five is equivalent to the British GCE O level and form six (two years) is equivalent to the A level. Brunei has two established international schools. The exam for entrance into an institute of higher learning is conducted as per the syllabus stipulated by the British government. The students who earn straight A's in all subjects at O levels and A levels are eligible for government scholarships to study abroad (mostly in the United Kingdom and Australia). This is applicable to students who are citizens of Brunei.

Many Brunei students at O and A levels participate in international competition events in science and mathematics. Degrees taught in English can be obtained from the University of Brunei Darussalam (UBD) in the following areas: education, mathematics and computer science, electronics and electrical engineering, geography/economics, management studies, and public policy and administration. Degrees taught in Malay offered by UBD are in education, Brunei studies, Malay literature, and Islamic studies.

The literacy rates for males and females are 93.7% and 84.7% respectively. Brunei's bilingual policy has been beneficial to the country, as it produces a pool of educated people able to communicate in both English and Malay. A small number of selected students who excel academically are sent abroad for further studies. Usually they are sent to the United Kingdom, Australia, Malaysia, or New Zealand. Students who do well in Islamic education are sent abroad to become Islamic scholars. Technical education is also provided at the certificate and diploma levels by local colleges. Students who are interested in the paramedical field are sent to a local nursing college.

Work

There have been frequent media reports concerning the high level of unemployment, especially among school leavers, in Brunei. The Asian financial crisis of 1997 further aggravated the unemployment problem in this region. In the year 2000, it was estimated that about 5,000 to 6,000 were unemployed in Brunei (*Borneo Bulletin,* March 15, 2000). As of June 2003, according to the Brunei Labour Department, 7,600 job seekers have registered with them. Out of this figure, some 3,554 are form five school leavers who hold GCE O levels while another 3,110 are form three school leavers holding the *Penilaian Menengah Bawah* (PMB) certificate (*Borneo Bulletin,* August 13, 2003). The government is concerned and has embarked on various measures to overcome the problem. As a long-term measure, effective implementation of a school career guidance program will be one way of overcoming the problem.

Studies on adolescent problems in Brunei Darussalam have clearly indicated that adolescents in Brunei are very concerned and often worried about their future career prospects. In a pilot study on adolescent problems in Brunei Darussalam (Suppiah and Burns 1997), among 11 categories of adolescent problems (based on an adapted version of Mooney Problem Checklists), problems related to their future and vocation were ranked the highest. In another study, Aryati, Amir, and Suppiah (1998) compared problems faced by academically low-achieving students with those of high achieving students using the Mooney instrument. Among the 11 categories of problems in the Mooney Problem Checklists, problems related to future vocation and career were ranked number one for high-achieving students. Low-achieving students reported future vocation and career as second in importance after the personal psychological relations category. In a study consisting of 746 secondary school students from form one to six, adolescents ranked future career and vocational concerns as their third major problem. There was a progression in the ranking of the concern in relation to age. The older students were more concerned with their future in relation to

a career than the younger students. For example, 11-year-olds ranked concern for future vocation as number six compared to 18-year-olds, who placed it as number three. There were no significant differences in perception among male and female subjects (Suppiah and Burns 2000).

In another study of career awareness and preferences among 625 secondary school Brunei students, Suppiah and Lourdusamy (2004) reported that the students in Brunei Darussalam are not in a hurry to enter into the job market after completing their secondary education. More than 80% of the respondents indicated that they would like to continue with their education at the post-secondary level. Although a majority of the school leavers did indicate that they have a clear career ambition, 37% of the respondents have no clear idea of what they were going to do at the end of their secondary schooling. Parents, family members, and friends seem to play a major role in directing the respondents towards their preferred future career and they are also the ones with whom the respondents discuss the career ambitions. Factors that are considered important in the selection of a career and that attract students in Brunei Darussalam towards a career are: jobs that pay well, offer tenure or pensions, and are interesting and challenging. Science students and high academic ability students prefer jobs that are interesting and challenging. Whereas the arts and Arabic stream students and students with low academic ability prefer jobs that are easy and provide short working hours. Male students prefer jobs that are easy and give them power, while female students prefer jobs that pay well, have tenure of service, are valued by society, and are interesting. In terms of ethnicity Malays like jobs that offer tenure more than the others. Another glaring trend observed in the study was the desire of young Bruneians to gain employment in the government sector. There is a need to wean them from overdependence on the government for their employment. The government is in the process of diversifying the economic base, and school leavers ought to be made aware of the opportunities in the developing private sector and also the scope for self-employment. Adolescents who drop out of the school system between the ages of 15 and 18 may get employed in the army, government sectors, or private sectors but not well paid. Students who did well academically proceed to university, religious college, technical colleges, nursing college, and other government institutions of higher learning. They are given full scholarships and monthly allowances to study. However, these students are not allowed to be employed while studying, and they are usually bonded by contract to work for the government.

Media

Bruneian adolescents are exposed to satellite television and have the resources and technology of modern media. They are exposed to the events, entertainments, and fads of adolescents throughout the world. There are strong inclinations to indicate that Bruneian adolescents are influenced by what is portrayed in the media. However, a majority of the adolescents still maintain the values of the society.

The Brunei government runs a television station, Radio Television Brunei (RTB), which broadcasts on two channels. One is the international channel, on which all the programs focus on developments in science, the economy, agriculture, education, and politics. The second channel is a local channel, which shows locally made shows on artistic and cultural topics. However, most affluent people have a satellite connection and can thus watch television from around the world. In addition to this there is a private pay channel, supplying programs from National Geographic, Discovery News (BBC, CNN, and SKY news) MTV, HBO, STAR, and sports channels. Most popular among adolescents are music and movie channels. Adolescents tend to watch more Western programming, although Malaysian programming, including local dramas and films, is also available. The government passed a law stating that all films shown on television must carry Malay subtitles and must be approved by a censoring committee before they are shown.

Cell phones are common and popular in Brunei. Most adolescents have the latest phone styles and use them frequently for talking and sending text messages. Internet access is available in many cybercafés. The Internet is popular among adolescents as a tool for communication. Frequent Internet use is a cause of concern to some parents.

Politics and Military

The political system in Brunei is governed by the constitution and the tradition of the Malay Islamic Monarchy, the *Melayu Islam Beraja.* His Majesty, Sultan Haji Hassanal Bolkiah is provided with supreme executive authority and is also the prime minister, finance minister, and defense minister. Several councils advise His Majesty on national policies covering religion, privy, the cabinet, succession, and legislature. The country is a member of the United Nations and ASEAN. In past years,

Brunei has actively participated in the Asia Pacific Economic Conference (APEC), World Trade Organization (WTO), ASEAN Regional Forum (ARF), ASEAN Free Trade Area (AFTA), and East Asean Growth Area (EAGA).

Brunei successfully hosted the twentieth South East Asian (SEA) Games. The Brunei government has been instrumental in planning and developing its economy. The country is geared towards economic diversification with a budget of B$7.3 billion. Brunei also hosted APEC 2000 in November 2000, playing host to world leaders, leading business personalities, and international media. The year 2001 was declared Visit Brunei Year.

Brunei has its own military force. Most of the adolescents who join the military have to undergo training. They begin as soldiers and can advance to the level of Major General. In order to enter the armed forces, one must be a citizen of Brunei. The minimum educational qualification required for entry level is form three. The army, air force, and naval force each have their own training centers. Military service is not mandatory.

Unique Issues

There a number of interesting issues that are unique among Brunei adolescents, including how affluence and rapid development and change have affected their views and lifestyle. Another interesting issue is how youth cope with the conflicting demands of collectivism, tradition, and religion with that of modernism, and Western values of individualism, equality, and liberation. The strong commitment to family values within society, the high standard of living, and government funding for children's welfare provides most children with a healthy and nurturing environment. Education is free, compulsory, and universal for the first nine years, after which it is still free but no longer compulsory. With a few exceptions involving small villages in extremely remote areas, nutritional standards are high and poverty is almost unknown. Medical care for all citizens, including children, is subsidized heavily and widely available.

Since adolescents and the younger generation form a sizable and ever-increasing chunk of the demographic population, the government of Brunei Darussalam is very concerned about the role of the adolescents in a future in which declining job opportunities and massive shifts in local regional and global economies are predicted, and in which social structures will be disrupted in an unpredictable context of change. The Bruneian adolescent is at a crossroads, facing the challenges of development in a context of change within a traditional Islamic Malay setting. He or she faces both global and traditional economic and social pressures that bear clashing messages about values, attitudes, and behaviors.

NARASAPPA KUMARASWAMY and
CHANDRASEAGRAN SUPPIAH

The authors kindly acknowledge Ms. Hani Haji Maiden and Mr. Yusri Hj.Kifli, Psychologist, Clinical Psychology Unit, Ripas Hospital, for their kind assistance in collecting data.

References and Further Reading

Aryati Binti Mohd Daud, Amir bin Awang, C. Suppiah. 1998. Problems of students—A case study of form I and form IV students in a secondary school in Brunei. *Research Monograph*, Number 3. University Brunei Darussalam.

Borneo Bulletin. 2003. August 13.

Borneo Bulletin. 2000. March 15.

Chiam, H. K. 1984. A profile of rural adolescents in Malaysia. Proceedings of 3rd Asian Workshop on Child and Adolescent Development. Kuala Lumpur, 323–37.

Clements, H. M., and M. C. Oelke. 1967. *The adolescent girl: An Australian analysis*. Sydney: Cassel.

Compas, B. E., J. K. Connor, H. Saltzman, A. H. Thomsen, and M. E. Wadsorth. 2001. Coping with stress during childhood and adolescence: Problems, progress, and potential in theory and research. *Psychological Bulletin* 127:87–127.

D'Rozario, V., and G. Michael. 1998. How adolescents cope with their concerns: A review and study of Singaporean students. *REACT* 13–20.

D'Rozario, V., et al. 2001. National Institute of Education, Nanyang Technological University, Singapore. Unpublished data.

Fanshawe, J. P. 1994. Adolescent problems and coping strategies: An investigation of stress, problems, coping and self esteem among Queensland secondary students preceding and following of a new tertiary entry system. School of learning and development. Unpublished PhD diss., Queensland University of Technology.

Frydenberg, E., and R. Lewis. 1991. Adolescent coping: the different ways in which boys and girls cope. *Journal of Adolescence* 14:119–33.

Frydenberg, E., and R. Lewis. 1993. *Adolescent Coping Scale—Administrators Manual*, research edition, Melbourne: Australian Council for Research Education (ACER).

Harper, J. F., and E. Marshall. 1991. Adolescents' problems and their relationship to self-esteem. *Adolescence*. Vol. 26. Issue 104.

Harper, J. F., and J. K. Collins. 1975. A differential study of the problems of privileged and underprivileged adolescents. *Journal of Youth and Adolescence* 4:349–57.

Hess, R. S., and M. L. Richards. 1999. Developmental and gender influences on coping: Implications for skills training. *Psychology in the Schools* 36(2). John Wiley & Sons.

Langulung, H. 1977. *Psikologi dan Kesihatan Mental di Sekolah-sekolah, terbitan*. Malaysia: Universiti Kebangsaan.

Mooney, R. L. 1942. Surveying high school students' problems by means of problems checklist. *Educational Research Bulletin* 22:101–08.

New York Times, 2000. April 3.

Nicholson, S. I., and J. K. Antill. 1981. Personal problems of adolescents and their relationship to peer acceptance and sex-role identity. *Journal of Youth and Adolescence* 10:309–25.

Puskar, K., and J. Lamb. 1991. Life events, problems, stresses and coping methods of adolescents. *Issues in Mental Health Nursing* 12:267–81.

Ross, B. W., W. A. Walford, and G. A. Espnes. 2000. Coping styles and psychological health in adolescents and young adults: A comparison of moderator and main effects models. *Australian Journal of Psychology* 52:155–62.

Suppiah, C., and R. Burns. 1997. Adolescent problems—A profile of adolescents in Brunei Darussalam. In *Preparing Children and Adolescents for the Next Millennium*. R. Burns.(ed.). Brunei: Universiti Brunei Darussalam.

Suppiah, C., and R. B. Burns. 1998. A pilot study of adolescents in Brunei Darussalam. In *Collaborative Agenda Research in Education Review 1998*. pp. 30–38. Bandar Seri Begawan: Universiti Brunei Darussalam, Centre for Applied Research in Education.

Suppiah, C., and R. B. Burns. 2004. Counselling for Peace and Harmony. Asia-Pacific Educational Counsellors Association (APECA) 15th Biennial Conference, Johor Bahru, Malaysia.

Suppiah, C., and A. Lourdusamy. 2004. Career awareness and preferences among secondary school leavers in Brunei Darussalam. In *Review 2004, Colloborative Agenda for Research in Education (CARE)*. S. Upex (ed.). pp. 7–26. Brunei: Centre for Applied Research in Education, Sultan Hassanal Bolkiah Insstitute of Education, Universiti Brunei Darussalam.

Suppiah, C., Rohani Haji Awg Matzin, Jamilah Pg Awg Othman, Ummi Kalthum, Vilma D'Rozario, and Angela Wong. Adolescent ways of coping: A study of Bruneian secondary school students. Accepted for publication in *Studies in Education*, Universiti Brunei Darussalam.

World Factbook. 2005. Brunei.

BULGARIA

Background Information

The description of adolescence in any country cannot take place without delineating the sociocultural context of the particular society and the particular historical period under exploration. Since a complete and comprehensive analysis of Bulgarian adolescence is beyond the scope of this brief essay, we alert the reader that the adolescents being described here are those residing in a South Balkan country with a relatively homogeneous population, who have experienced the transition from authoritarian socialism to a democratic free market system. Most of the studies used in the essay refer to adolescents living in the larger urban areas. The cultural norms of the society, which are slow to change, reflect the background of a South Slavic society with strong family ties that have continued to be intact throughout political and social transformations.

Because of the relative paucity of empirical data, our presentation will be partly narrative and partly empirical in form. Where empirical data is not available, the narrative approach will depend on quasi-systematic observations and ethnographic impressions.

Bulgaria, situated in the heart of the Balkan Peninsula, is one of the most ancient states on the European continent. It occupies 111,000 square kilometers and has a relatively homogeneous population of 7.8 million, of whom 83.9% are Bulgarian, 9.4% are Turk, 4.7% are Roma, and 2% are others, including Armenian, Tatar, Circassian, Macedonian (National Statistics Institute 2000). The median age of the country is 38.5 years. Youth (age 15 to 24) represent 13.9% of the total population (Ministry of Labor and Social Services 2004).

During its thirteen-century-long history, Bulgaria had a relatively short 500-year period of independence until the 1200s. This was followed by 500-years under Turkish occupation until 1878 when Bulgaria became an independent state. The period from 1878 to 1912 was marked by wars of negative outcomes with other Balkan countries. Bulgaria participated in the two World Wars, in which Bulgaria turned out to be on the wrong side and had to give up territories. From 1944, Bulgaria was part of the Eastern bloc under the strong influence of the Soviet Union until the dissolution of the USSR in 1989.

Since 1989, the country has embarked on a course of political democratization and economic liberalization. During the last 15 years positive steps have been taken to establish a working democratic society, such as rebuilding dominant political institutions, establishing mechanisms for a market economy, and fostering conditions to ensure basic human and religious rights. Nonetheless, prolonged political instability (ten governments from 1989 to 2005) and economic suffering (13.9% unemployment for the adult population, 28% for the young population; Ministry of Labor and Social Services 2004), and decreased standards of living has ensued. The economy has not yet reached the economic levels of 1989, creating obstacles for the establishment of a civil society. The Communist social safety net was broken, particularly affecting marginal groups such as the aged and other vulnerable groups. Privatization of public industry benefited the wealthy and did little for the lower classes.

Recent governments began steps for the improvement of the economy and the ending of a prolonged period of kleptocratic economic turmoil. Economic and social programs were put in place to enable Bulgaria's inclusion in the European Union. Since the 1996–1997 crisis, the country has achieved macroeconomic stability and has a stable currency, low basic interest rate, and substantial foreign-exchange reserves. Real economic growth significantly accelerated from 2.4% in 1999 to 4.2% in 2003 (Ministry of Labor and Social Services 2004).

There are high hopes for further improvement of the country's economy following the integration with the European Union. Still, high rates of potential emigration among youth to Western Europe and the United States (14.4% among 15- to 19-year-olds and 14% among 20- to 29-year-olds; Ministry of Labor and Social Services 2004) indicates that perception of constructive possibilities within Bulgarian youth remains bleak.

Period of Adolescence

Adolescence is a recognized life stage. Its recognition can be traced to the establishment of the modern schooling system at the end of the nineteenth century, when separate schools for boys and girls were founded with appropriate curriculum preparing them for gender-defined adult roles.

Biosocial development indicative of puberty is first evident at the age of 11 to 12. No formal special rites of passages recognizing that puberty exist, although both school and health professionals prepare young people for the physiological and psychological changes associated with puberty. Full adult status is achieved at the age of 18 when young people are expected to assume legal adult responsibilities and obligations, such as the right to vote, to join the military, and become fully employed.

Legislation mandates compulsory education until the age of 16. Sixteen is also the age at which adolescents can first be employed, although certain restrictions exist regarding the jobs that they can take. For example, the law forbids heavy jobs that are potentially harmful for the health of youth. Rural youth undoubtedly participate in work at an earlier age, helping the family in their farm responsibilities.

As in many modern countries a special stage of emerging adulthood (Arnett 2004) exists. This is a stage in which young people are more independent from their parents but are yet not committed to adult roles, which are defined by such as events or developments as marriage and parenthood. During this period, 24% of young people attend college (Bekhradnia 2004), 21% obtain work, 10% help with family business or indulge in petty trade, and the remaining group is part of the drifting unemployed (Ministry of Labor and Social Services 2004). Older adolescents and young adults maintain close physical and social ties with their natal families. A delay of the age of first marriage has been observed especially in the last years (for men, from 24.7 years in 1991 to 27.1 years in 1999; for women, from 21.7 in 1991 to 23.8 years in 1999; National Statistical Institute 2000). Due to the economic conditions and family and paternalistic values, most of the young people continue to live with their parents after they graduate from high school and even after they marry. Extended families in Bulgaria make up to 17% of all households. This tradition is significantly more prevalent in the rural regions (Botcheva and Feldman 2004).

Beliefs

Bulgarian culture has been historically described as a collectivist culture with an emphasis on interdependence of people, especially that of family members upon each other (Botcheva and Feldman 2004). Family life has always been one of the most important values in Bulgarian society (Teneva 1995); respect for the elderly is very high, and family ties are very strong whether parents live with their grown offspring or live alone. Individualism in the form of choice of job or profession appears to be growing, as indicated by employment in the private sector where nonfamily members are in charge, or migration to other areas of Bulgaria or to the West where jobs are more plentiful. Individual entrepreneurships are relatively new and will take time to learn, if this is to become the preferred mode of employment in a free market society.

During the Communist era there was much emphasis on the ideological content of the school curriculum, which enforced Marxist Communist values. After the fall of communism the ideologicalization of the curriculum was revoked. With the increased Western influence a shift in the values towards more individualistic ones can be expected, although it likely will take several generations to change the predominant values and earlier collectivist orientations. Botcheva (1998) in a longitudinal study with 217 16- to 18-year-old adolescents from Smolyan, a rural city in Bulgaria, studied changes in adolescents' social values before and after the fall of the Communism in Bulgaria. She showed that over a period of three years (1989–1991) an increase in youths' appreciation of active and entrepreneurial behavior was noted. However, at the same time youth defined themselves as less active and independent in their social life, which might reflect the slower rate of psychosocial change for exercise of independence and autonomy when contrasted with the change in economic orientation. Situational external opportunities may play a large role in the determination of the specific beliefs and behaviors under the new social conditions (such as the availability of jobs, housing, and provision of more community resources for mobility).

Almost 83% of Bulgarians are Christian Orthodox, 12.2% are Sunni Muslim, 0.6% are Roman Catholic, 0.1% are Jewish, and 3.4% are other religions such as Protestant, Gregorian-Armenian Orthodox, etc. (National Statistics Institute 2000). The Bulgarian Orthodox Church, which played a crucial role in preserving the Bulgarian culture during the Ottoman occupation, remained central to the sense of Bulgarian nationhood even under the anti-religion Communist regime. The Bulgarian Orthodox Church is an independent national church like the Russian Orthodox and the other national branches of Eastern Orthodoxy. Because of its national character and its status as the national church in the Bulgarian State Religion until the advent of Communism, the church became and was considered an inseparable element of Bulgarian national consciousness. Although Communist regime could not eliminate all its influence, it did undermine Church authority significantly through propaganda and financial constraints. After the fall of Communism, the Orthodox Church and other religions, including Islam, experienced revival.

Islam is the second most predominant religion. The Muslim population of Bulgaria, including Turks, Pomaks, Gypsies, and Tatars, live mainly in Northeastern Bulgaria and in the Southern Rhodope mountains. Bulgarian Muslims (Pomaks) were subject to particular prosecution in the later years of the Communist regime. This was partly because the Orthodox Church traditionally considered them foreigners, despite the fact that they were ethnically Bulgarians. The Bulgarian Communist regime declared traditional Muslim beliefs to be diametrically opposed to Communist and Bulgarian beliefs. This justified repression of Muslim beliefs and consolidation of Muslims into the larger society as part of ideological struggle. Like the practitioners of the other faiths, Muslims in Bulgaria enjoyed greater freedom after the fall of the Communist regime. New mosques were built in many cities and villages; one village built a new church and a new mosque side by side.

After the fall of Communism, there was an increase in young people's interest in other religions. The Adventist Church gained popularity along with "Eastern" religions avowing New Age orientations.

Gender

Gender role expectations toward Bulgarian adolescents are shaped both by the traditional family-oriented culture and the changing context of the society's transition from socialism to a market-oriented society.

Traditionally, women are expected to take care of the home and to raise the children. Family policy during the Communist period assumed that all adults should work, and most of the structural barriers to women's employment were addressed, such as equal educational opportunities, paid maternity leave, and low cost childcare. Women made major advances in education, skilled work, and the professions. They moved rapidly into positions of authority in education, politics, science, as well as commerce, especially in urban areas. Having a profession was considered an important aspect of self-fulfillment for women. Still there was not parallel change either in interpersonal relations or in gender responsibilities. Women were assumed to have equality, but in reality bore the burden of having to maintain the home while working full time (Bollobas 1993).

Under communism women continued to be socialized into conservative gender roles while supposedly enjoying gender equality (Toth 1993). Gender equality remained elusive after communism. A study by Dimova (2002) with a national representative sample of 1,160 adults showed that while women and men were equal within the family and in terms of household budget management and decision-making responsibilities, household work is mainly a female duty.

Since 1989 the decline in social welfare services and the transition to a market economy has placed even a greater burden on women (Macek et al. 1998). Women are still more likely than men to balance the responsibilities of home with paid employment. However, now they face increased competition for employment without the support of responsibilities for parenthood. Nonetheless, women are very much interested in full employment, not only because they want to support the family, but because they see employment as a way of self-fulfillment and independence. According to one study, 63.6% of working women would continue working even if they had enough money to live without deprivation (Dimova 2002). The main reason is the popular understanding that having a job is the best way for women to become independent persons, to have social contacts, and to fulfill themselves outside of the home.

In a study of 184 adolescents from a convenient sample of high school students from Sofia, with the Bem Sex Role Inventory, Kalchev (2000) showed that boys and girls have similar mean scores on the scale of masculinity but are significantly different on the scale of femininity, with girls exceeding boys. These data reflect the prevailing contradictory cultural norms and expectations regarding women—women and men are expected to perform well in masculine roles, females are expected to perform better in feminine roles.

This study also is supported by the work of Dimitrov (2005) about the personal qualities that describe the ideal adolescent. Using the list of personal qualities of Torrance (1967) he asked 220 ninth- to eleventh-grade high school students to assess the desirability of different personal qualities. The sample was drawn from two types of high schools (gymnasium and vocational) in two Bulgarian big urban cities. Both boys and girls reported being healthy and physically strong, remembering well, and being well organized as among the most desired personal qualities. There were gender differences in the assessment of the qualities related to feminine stereotype—girls scored higher on qualities related to the feminine stereotypes, such as being emotionally sensitive, neat and orderly, and having a greater sense of beauty than boys.

The continuing pervasiveness of feminine stereotypes in society is also suggested by the work of Silgigan (1998). Using Offer and Howard's (1977) self-image questionnaire, she studied body image among 304 13- to 15-year-old adolescents and 114 16- to 18-year-old adolescents from five urban cities in Bulgaria. Bulgarian girls scored significantly lower than the boys in regard to their body image. Sixty percent of studied girls were not satisfied with the way they looked at the present time, and 40% were concerned about how they will look like in the future. This can be contributed to the pressures the society puts on girls in regard to their appearance.

The Self

The formulation of self-concept derives chiefly from empirical studies done in the United States. There are relatively few studies available from Bulgaria. As a dynamic process the self-concept appears to be completed by mid- to late adolescence, remaining stable in variety of contexts, though modified by changing social and cultural contexts. Therefore we would expect the self-concept of Bulgarian youth to be fairly stable based on the support of family, school, friends, and church. We would also expect to find some uncertainty in self-concept due to shifts in the collectivist-individualistic orientation of the larger society based upon recent political and economic changes.

Using the objective Measure of Ego Identity Statuses of Psychosocial Identity, Stefanova (2003) studied adolescent identity development with a convenience sample of 555 high school students aged 16 to 18 years from five gymnasiums in Sofia and 168 undergraduate students aged 19 to 20 from two universities in Sofia. Results showed that more than half of the students (56%) were in moratorium status, 20% in diffusion, 13% foreclosure and only 11% had achieved identity status. Thus, more than two-thirds of Bulgarian adolescents have not committed to an identity, which might be due to the changing social context in which they live. When compared with similar samples from the United States (Adams, Bennion, and Huh 1989) there are a higher percentage of Bulgarian adolescents in the moratorium status, while among the American adolescents the prevailing statuses are diffusion and foreclosure. Moratorium is the most frequently

observed status both in early and late adolescence in Bulgaria, which is different from the results reported elsewhere (Adams et al. 1989; Kroger 1995; Streitmatter 1993), where for late adolescence the number of adolescents in moratorium status is significantly less than those in early adolescence. However, as in studies from other countries Bulgarian adolescents with more defined identity statuses report higher satisfaction with life and subjective well-being.

These data support the hypothesis that Bulgarian youth have a different developmental age pattern in their self-identity compared to Western youth, with greater numbers reported to be in the moratorium status. Whether this can be attributed to the social, economic, and political flux of the Bulgarian transition from collectivist to individualistic orientation, or to the particularities of Bulgarian culture remains to be clarified.

Using the Offer Self-Image Questionnaire with a convenience sample of 301 early adolescents and 214 late adolescents from five urban cities in Bulgaria, Silgigan (1998) showed that late adolescents have a more negative self-image than younger adolescents in terms of their vocational attitudes, family functioning, and emotional tone. The only aspect of self-image on which late adolescents score higher than young adolescents was their sexuality. Late adolescents feel more confident about their relations with opposite gender partners and feel better about their attractiveness.

During recent years Bulgaria, like many Eastern European countries, witnessed the increasing need of minority ethnic groups to find their roots and strengthen the ties to their own subgroup as well as to establish legitimate commitment to the larger social, economic, and political entity where they reside. It might be expected that ethnic identity becomes more salient during times of social changes, one result being an increase of attendance of religious holidays. This is especially evident among the Turk and Roma minority groups. Yet, a study of Dimitrov (1997) with a representative sample of 1,016 fifth- to eleventh-grade adolescents from nine cities in Bulgaria has shown that less than 5% of all students refer to their ethnicity when asked to describe themselves with the question: "Who am I?" Despite the paucity of ethnic self-identification, the students who do refer to their ethnicity in their self-identification have a higher perceived status in the classroom than those who do not refer to their ethnicity. A tendency was observed by students of Bulgarian origin to more often point out their ethnicity when they were a majority in class, while the students of

Turkish origin pointed out their ethnicity when they were the minority group of the class. Students who perceive that their personal status is higher than the others in the class refer to their ethnicity as part of their "who am I?" description, and those of lower status are less likely to refer to their ethnicity. Results about students' peer relations in school showed that ethnic self-identification did not negatively affect peer relations with students from other ethnic groups in terms of reported misunderstandings, communications, and lowered peer status.

Family Relationships

Members of Bulgarian families (both immediate and extended) are generally very close. Usually both parents work, and they are both involved in handling important family issues. The role of grandparents as caretakers is very important. Although this role diminishes as children get older, grandparents continue to be a source of important instrumental and emotional support in the life of adolescents. This is especially true for adolescents living in rural areas where familism is very strong.

Balev (2001) studied parenting styles for both the mother and the father based on Baumrind's typology with a convenience sample of 800 13- to19-year-old adolescents from four gymnasiums in three urban cities. He showed that among investigated youth the permissive style of parenting for both the mother and the father was most common, followed by the authoritarian style of parenting for both parents, and the combination of indifferent father and authoritarian mother. There were differences in the prevailing types of parenting according to the gender of the adolescents. While for the girls the prevailing type of parenting style was permissive parenting for both the mother and the father, followed by combination of unengaged father and authoritative mother, for the boys the prevailing parenting styles were authoritarian parenting for both the mother and father, followed by permissive mother and father.

Family relations have been affected by changes in the economy in recent years, especially by the general impoverishment and increased economic hardship. In a survey with a national representative sample of 1,160 adults, Dimova (2002) showed that life in deprivation due to the economic hardships has affected family life in the following way: increased discord, quarrels, and insults (reported by 64.1% females, and 65.1% of males respondents); drawing into oneself, lack of desire for social contacts (57.1% female; 60.6% males); and loss of self-esteem (53.3% females, 60.4% males).

Similarly, in a study with 62 extended families with 16-year-old adolescents from a rural town in South Bulgaria, Botcheva and Feldman (2004) showed that the experience of economic stress negatively affected family relations and parenting, which led to an increase of adolescent depression and problem behaviors. However, the existence of supportive grandparents in the family buffers these negative effects of economic pressure. When grandparents' support was available in such families, parents reported less harsh parenting despite economic stresses, and adolescents reported less depression despite harsh parenting. Also, a longitudinal study of the protective factors for adolescent development during social changes (Botcheva, Feldman, and Leiderman 2002) with a convenience sample of 104 high school students with a mean age of 14.3 from five secondary schools in Sofia showed that perceived parental warmth is very high for both young and old adolescents and has a tendency to increase during major social transformations. Thus, the supportive relations in the Bulgarian family moderate the negative effects of major social transformations.

The divorce trends in Bulgaria show that not only is the number of divorces increasing steadily, but also the average age at the time of divorce is increasing. Geographic differences in the divorce rate have also been noted, with higher rates in the more urbanized areas. Divorce has negative effects on adolescents' well-being. For example, Cristopoulis (2001) in a study with 50 college students showed that adolescents whose parents were divorced reported more somatic complaints and depression than adolescents who were not from divorced families.

Polnareva and Mihova (1995) studied a sample of 150 adolescents and their parents who have sought psychological counseling in the Outpatient Clinic of Child Psychiatry, at the Medical Academy in Sofia between 1991 and 1993. They revealed three main groups of problems for which clients seek help: (1) problems related to the readjustment of the family to the developmental changes of the adolescent; (2) problems related to power struggles between the adolescent and the parents, and (3) problems related to the alienation of the parents towards their adolescent child.

Friends and Peers/Youth Culture

Friends and peers play an important role in the life of Bulgarian adolescents. Most close friendships develop in school contexts, or through extracurricular activities and within the neighborhood community. A study of time used by adolescents in

Europe and the United States (Flammer and Alsaker 1999) showed that eleventh-grade Bulgarian adolescents from Sofia gymnasiums, along with adolescents from Finland and Norway, spend significantly more time per day hanging out with friends (2.2 hours) than late adolescents from the other countries (who spend on average 0.5 hours). This could be due to the fact that late adolescents in Bulgaria are granted more freedom by parents. Also, adolescents in this age group spend time with friends while engaging in different activities related to their interests (music, computers, etc.). The cross-national difference might be due to the fact that the sample consisted of adolescents in their senior year, who may be more relaxed in terms of their free time than adolescents from other grades in high school (ninth through eleventh). Younger Bulgarian adolescents (less than 14 years old) from this study spend significantly less time hanging out with friends, similar to the early adolescents from other countries. No gender differences were found in time spent with friends.

Kalchev (1996) studied peer group acceptance and trust communication with a representative sample of 973 eighth- to twelfth-grade adolescents from three main urban cities in Bulgaria. Using a 56-item, self-description questionnaire, he found that trust communication was significantly higher among older adolescents. The highest scores of peer acceptance were found among seventh and tenth graders, which might be related to the fact that these are the years in the middle and high school experience when adolescents feel more comfortable with their peers. Similarly, in another study with a convenience sample of 600 eighth to twelfth-grade students from Sofia (Botcheva et al. 2002) found that eleventh-grade adolescents report significantly higher levels of friends' warmth than ninth graders. Girls report higher scores of friends' warmth than boys. These results suggest that the developmental process should be considered along with gender differences.

Peer relations of Bulgarian adolescents are important factors in their subjective well-being and psychosocial adaptation. Kalchev (1996) in the study with a representative sample of eighth- to twelfth-grade adolescents from three urban cities in Bulgaria studied three dimensions of adolescents' subjective well-being following the Flammer et al. (1989) model of subjective well-being: self-esteem, positive outlook on life, and depressive mood. Structural equation model analyses showed that both peer acceptance and closeness with parents determine adolescents' self-esteem, positive outlook on life, and lower level of depressive

mood. While in early adolescence both peer acceptance and closeness with parents determine adolescent well-being, in late adolescence the dominant role for adolescent well-being is peer acceptance, although closeness with parents is still a factor, but not as strongly as in early adolescence. Unexpectedly, trust communication with peers did not determine adolescent self-esteem and depressive mood.

As part of the study of protective factors for adolescents during social changes, Botcheva et al. (2002) studied friends' warmth among 600 eighth- to twelfth-grade students from different types of high schools in Sofia. Friends' warmth was positively correlated with adolescents' psychosocial maturity and optimism.

Results suggested that the quality of peer relations is not affected by major social transformations in Bulgaria. Data about ninth- and eleventh-grade cohorts studied at two points of time (prior to and after an intense period of social and economic dislocation) revealed no significant differences in peer relations.

While close relations with peers were not expected to be affected by social change, the type of youth organizations in which adolescents participate have changed considerably during and after the 1990s. During the Communist period adolescents were part of the major Youth Organization (*Komsomol*), which was related to the Communist Party and was political in nature. Immediately after the overthrow of the Communist regime, alternative youth groups and organizations began to form, with diverse characters and purposes, such as political, religious, cultural, and social.

Most youth social, extracurricular, sports, and arts activities take place in regional youth centers, which are still supported by the state and are free of charge. New forms of extracurricular activities have started to emerge, such as Scouts organizations, Red Cross organizations, and youth clubs for building leadership and social skills.

There is a distinct youth culture in the country, very much influenced by Western Europe and the United States. Bulgarian adolescents are very open to foreign cultures, study foreign languages, and express interest in travel to meet people from other countries. As part of the Euronet Study, Flannagan and Botcheva (1999) studied adolescents' preferences for other countries. Bulgarian adolescents were more interested in meeting adolescents from other countries than from their own. Just as adolescents from other Eastern and Central European countries, they were especially interested in meeting adolescents from United States and Western Europe, which might be a result of the historical changes taking place in these countries. After several decades of censure, opportunities for travel and free exchange of information began to open up. Under these circumstances the importance that young people assign to meeting foreigners may reflect the novelty of the opportunity. Our prediction is that until standards of living increase in Bulgaria, the desire to know more about styles and mores from the West and elsewhere will not diminish.

Love and Sexuality

Bulgarian adolescents do not differ significantly from adolescents in other European countries in terms of time spent in dating. Results from the Euronet study showed that Bulgarian adolescents 13 to 18 years of age spent on average .39 hours for dating, which is similar to the time spent by adolescents in Hungary (.35 hours), Poland (.41 hours) and Russia (.44 hours), (Flammer, Alsaker, and Noack 1999).

The median age for first sexual intercourse for both girls and boys is 16 years (Koceva and Kostova 2003). Although contraceptives are available in the country, they are expensive. Contraceptive knowledge and attitudes are in the process of evolution.

A study with a representative national sample of youth between the ages of 15 and 19 years showed that among adolescents who were sexually active, 37% use contraceptives regularly, 23% from time to time, and 40% do not use contraceptives (Ministry of Youth and Sports 2003).

Contraceptives are not included in the health insurance package, but the Bulgarian Family Planning and Sexual Health Association (BFPSHA) provides free of charge or subsidized contraceptives—oral, IUDs, and condoms—in its outlets and national family planning programs in university hospitals. Condoms are distributed as well through a network of health and youth-oriented NGOs, a regional unit of hygiene inspectorate. BFPSHA introduced the concept for youth friendly services in the mid-1990s. The concern for anonymity and confidentiality is relevant, especially for young people looking for counseling in smaller towns. This is the reason why the majority of them prefer to travel to the nearest larger urban area. In Bulgaria there are no legal limitations on the access to contraception. There is no need for parental consent for provision of any contraception for persons under 18. All types of contraception are available in the pharmacies under prescription (officially) and also for purchase without such authorization in the majority of "points of sale pharmacies," a pragmatic reality.

Abortion is legal in the country (in officially registered, adequate to the service hospitals and outlets) up to the twelfth week of gestation and under hospital conditions until the twentieth week of gestation. It is paid for through insurance, with some social exceptions. Young women up to the age of 18 can obtain an abortion with the written consent of one of their parents. Bulgaria has one of the highest rates of abortion in Europe, similar to other Eastern European countries. Eastern Europe has the highest proportion of pregnancies ended by abortion worldwide (65%; Henshew, Singh, and Haas 1999).

There has been an increase in the rates of sexually transmitted diseases in the early twenty-first century. For example, the number of persons infected by syphilis in 1990 was 378, while in 2000 it increased to 1,615. The number of those registered HIV positive was 350 for 2001 (although the number of unregistered could be much higher). Forty-one percent of the registered cases were between the age of 20 and 29 (Ministry of Youth and Sports 2003).

Sex education is not part of the school curriculum in Bulgaria. Partially it is included in the health education lectures in the secondary schools. The Ministry of Health and the Ministry of Youth and Sports, and nongovernmental agencies (National Anti-AIDS Coalition, BFPSHA) started the process of creating a comprehensive educational package for 12- to 18-year-old students. By 2005, the package was under testing. It included a manual for teachers, students' notebook, and a special edition for parents. The main topic is combined health and sexuality education and life skills.

Cohabitation before marriage is increasingly popular, especially in the larger cities. A survey with a representative national sample of 1,160 adults (Dimova 2002) showed that 50% of respondents believe that it is normal to have family without marriage.

Health Risk Behavior

In societies undergoing political, economic, and social change with only the family, school, and church as sources of stabilization, it should be expected that adolescents will reveal the effects of these changes in their behavior, attitudes, and feelings, as well as in their interactions with peers. We will now consider aggressive behavior towards peers, alcohol, smoking and drug use, criminal activity, depression, anxiety, fears and depression, which should be on the increase. Baseline data are difficult to obtain, that is why we will present data from recent studies and official statistics, supported by narrative reports.

Using a version of the Olweus Bully/Victim Questionnaire (1978), Kalchev (2003) studied bullying in school with a random sample of 882 fourth through tenth-grade young and late adolescents drawn from three big urban cities. Data showed that 10.7% of children described themselves as victims, 4.1% as bullies, and 1.7% as bully/victims, which is comparable to the other South European countries (Italy, Spain, and Portugal), but are higher than England and the Scandinavian countries (Smith, Junger-Tas, Olweus, Catalano, and Slee 1999). Boys are more often in the role of bullies and bully/victims than girls. The most frequent forms of bullying are verbal bullying followed by physical bullying. Indirect bullying (gossip, inciting group pressure) is less frequent. Bullying takes place in school corridors, the schoolyard, and places where the teachers are not present, and less frequently in the classrooms. Bullying also exists outside of school, although it is not so frequent. While one-to-one bullying (individual bullying) is more typical for the boys, girls are more often victims of group bullying. With an increase of age the relative amount of bullying by individuals decreases, while the amount of group bullying increases.

In another study with a random sample of 3,303 fourth- to twelfth-grade students drawn from three types of public schools (elementary, gymnasium, and vocational) in seven urban cities, Kalchev (2003) researched four forms of victimization (physical, verbal, indirect, and power related) and three forms of aggression (physical, verbal, and indirect) among adolescents using the Peer Victimization-Aggression Questionnaire. This self-reported measure, developed by exploratory and confirmatory factor analyses, consists of 29 "victimization/social support" items and 12 "aggressive items." He showed that boys report more frequently being subjects of physical victimization, while girls report indirect victimization. There are no gender differences in verbal victimization. Not surprisingly, boys also display a higher level of direct physical and verbal aggression, but no gender differences exist with respect to the indirect aggression. Cross-sectional analyses showed that with the increase of age the level of all forms of victimization decreases, with the biggest decrease of physical victimization among girls.

Both boys and girls in early adolescence reported most frequently being subjects of verbal victimization, followed by physical victimization, indirect victimization, and power-related victimization. Older adolescents (tenth-grade) continued to report most frequently verbal forms of victimization followed by indirect victimization.

Problem and risk behaviors of Bulgarian adolescents will be discussed within the context of increasing criminal activity and drug use from 1995 to 2005, which is typical for most transitional societies. There is a relatively high rate of smoking among Bulgarian youth, especially among young adolescents. According to a national survey in 2000 (Tencheva 2004) 51% of the girls and 48% of boys smoke. Every third adolescent has smoked his/her first cigarette before the age of 13. As for alcohol, a recent study with a national representative sample of 1,400 ninth- through twelfth-grade students (Ministry of Youth and Sports 2003) asked students to report whether they had drunk alcohol three or more times during the last 30 days: 43% of the students reported drinking beer; 25% reported drinking hard alcohol (vodka, brandy, gin), and 12% reported drinking wine three times or more in the last 30 days. Bulgaria ranks seventeenth among the other European countries in consumption of hard alcohol. The rate of alcoholism also has been increasing recently among ninth- through twelfth-grade teenagers, many of whom require special help for their alcoholism. Most of the Bulgarian youth have their first drink, usually beer, at a very early age (12 years for the urban youth and 10 years for rural youth).

Data from a survey about drug abuse with a representative national sample of high school students (Ministry of Youth and Sports 2003) showed that the most popular drug used by the students is marijuana. Twenty-six percent of the respondents had tried it, and 4.4% were frequent users (more than 40 times). The average age for drug use is 18.3 years (Ministry of Youth and Sports 2003).

Data regarding criminal activity in Bulgaria in 2002 shows that 17.6% of all committed crimes were by youths under the age of 17 (Central Committee for Antisocial Behavior of Adolescents 2003). A total of 1.74% of the population between ages 8 and 17 years was registered by the police for antisocial behavior in 2003 (burglary, running away from home, prostitution, begging). A total of 4.63% of punished crimes were committed by youths under the age of 16 and 12.98% by youths between ages 16 and 18 years. The most common crimes committed by youth are burglary and thefts (86.7% of all committed crimes under the age of 16 and 76.9% of all committed crimes for youths between the ages of 16 and 18). The rate of armed robbery is much lower (1.6% for adolescents under the age of 16, and 4.9% among adolescents 16 to 18 years of age). There was a peak in the overall criminal activity in 2002 (103.7 % in comparison with 1998). The percentage of crimes committed by youths under the age of 16 (2.10% in 1998 to 4.63% in 2002) and for youths between the ages of 16 and 18 (7.6% in 1998 to 13% in 2002) has also increased. The main reasons attributed for this change in youth criminal activity are low living standards, bad family environment, and low education (two-thirds of youths involved in criminal activity are school drop-outs).

Data about adolescent anxiety were obtained by Kalchev (2005) in a study with representative sample of 1,272 sixth- to tenth-grade adolescents, stratified for sex, age, and types of school from Sofia. Data was collected using the Multidimensional Adolescent Anxiety Scale, an 88-item self-report questionnaire constructed according to definitions provided in DSM-IV (1994) on diagnostic criteria for anxiety disorders by exploratory and confirmatory factor analyses. The response format used was: (1) never or almost never; (2) sometimes; (3) often; (4) always or almost always. The criterion used to define an arbitrary cut off point for a "clinical significant" score was a mean of scale item >2.5. Following this criterion, the percent of students with "clinically significant" scores on the generalized anxiety scale was 8.6%; for panic attacks 1.8%; for social anxiety 11.7%; for separation anxiety 5.9%; for obsessions and compulsions 3.8%; for fears of physical injury 3.8%. These results suggest that problem areas for studied adolescents were related to social phobias, generalized anxiety, and—unexpectedly—separation anxiety.

Several gender differences were revealed. Following other studies (March, Parker, Sullivan, Stallings, and Conners 1997; Muris, Meesters, Merckelbach, and Schouten 2002), results showed that girls report higher levels of general anxiety, panic attacks, and physical injury fears than boys. No gender differences were observed in regard to reported obsession and compulsions and social anxiety.

Cross-sectional analyses showed that in comparison to early adolescence, late adolescent girls reported higher levels of generalized anxiety and panic attacks and lower levels of separation anxiety. No significant age differences for girls were found in regard to their social anxiety, physical injury fears, and obsessions and compulsions. Late adolescent boys reported lower levels of social anxiety, separation anxiety, and obsession and compulsions than younger adolescent boys with no differences on the other anxiety scales.

Similarly, in another study using the Revised Children's Manifest Anxiety Scale (Reynolds and Richmond 1978), Kalchev (2005), with a random sample of fifth- through eleventh-grade students from different types of schools of the main urban cities in Bulgaria, conducted cross-sectional comparisons of early and late adolescents' generalized anxiety. While girls reported higher levels of anxiety in late adolescence in comparison with early adolescence, there were no significant differences in boys' levels of anxiety in early and late adolescence.

In a study with 849 fourth- through seventh-grade students (a random sample from different types of schools in several cities in Bulgaria), Kalchev (2000) using the Revised Fear Survey Schedule for Children FSSC-R (Ollendick 1983), showed that in early adolescence students report fears related more frequently to danger and death, and less so fears related to the unknown, failure and criticism, medical fears and minor injuries, and small animals. No significant age differences between students in this early adolescent group were found, which suggest that early adolescence is not an age period in which a decrease in reported fears is observed.

Using the Center for Epidemiologic Studies–Depression Scale (Radloff 1977) with a random sample of 1,019 13- to 19-year-old students (443 boys and 576 girls), Kalchev (2002) showed that girls have higher levels of depressions. Cross-sectional data showed a decrease in depression among late adolescent girls and no significant differences between early and late adolescent boys. according to the study, 7.9% of boys and 13.5% of girls were within the clinical range of depression. These data are rather similar to reported data for Swedish adolescents where 4.1% of boys and 15.7% of girls were in the clinical range (Olson and Knorring 1997). Cross-sectional analyses of the Bulgarian data showed that the percentage of girls in the clinical range decreased in the late adolescent group (16.3% vs. 11.5%), while the percentage of boys in the clinical range was relatively stable (7.8% vs. 8.1%).

Overall, data from self-reported measures of the two main aspects of internalizing problems of Bulgarian adolescents (anxiety and depression) showed that while there is an increase of anxiety in late adolescence, especially among the girls, there is a decrease or stabilization of depression for both boys and girls in late adolescence.

Education

Education in Bulgaria is free at all levels and is supported by the state through the Ministry of Education and Science. It is compulsory for children between the ages of 7 and 16. Complete literacy in Bulgaria was claimed in 1990. There was an extensive growth in the education system in the post-World War II era, with a rigidly Marxist ideological curriculum; complete restructuring, modernization, and depoliticization of the school program begun in 1990 after the fall of Communism.

The Bulgarian educational system falls within the continental European tradition. Students study in elementary schools until seventh or eighth grade and then continue in secondary schools, which includes grades nine through twelfth. The main types of secondary schools in the country are general educational, vocational, language schools, and foreign schools. Private schools are also being established, and they are beginning to compete with the state schools. There are over fifty higher education institutions in Bulgaria offering degrees at the undergraduate and graduate levels.

In 1999 and 2000, only 69% of 17 year-olds and 46% of the 18-year-olds were enrolled in secondary schools full-time. Only 75% of the 22-year-olds had certificates for completing high school, which gave them the opportunity to continue with a college education (Behradnia 2004). The main reasons given for dropping out were unwillingness to study, family reasons, or going abroad.

The average teacher-student ratio is 1:21. Data from the Euronet study (Alsaker, Flammer, and Noack 1999) showed that Bulgarian adolescents spent on average 1.94 hours for homework, slightly behind Poland and Romania and other European countries where the average is more than two hours. Bulgarian students perform above average in the international achievement tests in math and science, which may be attributed to their diligence in homework study for these subjects.

Overall, adolescents' attitudes were very positive towards schooling following the Bulgarian tradition, in which education is seen as a tool for success. In a study of 1,016 with a representative sample of fifth- through eleventh-grade adolescents from nine cities encompassing different ethnic groups, Dimitrov (1997) showed that attitudes towards schools were very positive—students perceived their teachers as concerned with them and rated their schools as democratic institutions. Students were more emotionally involved, rather than task-involved, with the school. Emotional involvement with school is influenced by communication with peers, which in adolescence is very important. Older adolescents report lower emotional involvement in attending classes and a decline in the acceptance of educational tasks and requirements than younger adolescents. Older adolescents also are less convinced than younger adolescents that

teachers are really concerned about them as individuals, about their needs and problems, and that the teachers are more engaged with resolution of conflicts between students in the classroom and elsewhere. No differences were observed in the perceptions of teachers' democratic control (that is, perceptions of teachers' ability to encourage autonomy and personal choices) between younger and older adolescents.

School plays an important role for a student's well-being. Especially during times of major social transformations such as the transition from socialism to democracy. The longitudinal study of Botcheva et al. (2002) with 104 eighth- and ninth-grade students from Sofia showed that perceptions of stability in school diminish the negative effects of a deteriorating family and peer environments on youths' adaptation during major social changes.

Work

Bulgarian adolescents are involved in household tasks; the Euronet study showed that studied Bulgarian adolescents spend approximately 50 minutes per day in household chores (Alsaker and Flammer 1999). The work contributed to the family is even higher in rural areas. There are no hourly rate jobs for adolescents, although it can be expected that with the development of market economy that number will increase. Most adolescents help with family businesses. There are special vocational secondary schools that prepare adolescents for jobs that can be taken after high school.

Twenty-nine point three percent of the 15- to 24-year olds were employed in 2003 (Ministry of Labor and Social Services 2004). A relatively low percentage (0.7%) of these youth own a business or are employers who hire other people. Also, the percentage of youth that are independent contractors is relatively low—4.4%—and predominantly male. Four point nine percent of the working youth work for their relatives without a salary. Most of the working youth (83.1%) work in the private sector, and a smaller percentage in the public sector (15.9%). According to the UNDP report in 2003, the unemployment rate among youth aged 16 to 24 is 28%. Special programs have been launched by the government to train young people and secure jobs, which will decrease considerably the number of unemployed youth.

Media

Study of use of leisure activities as part of the Euronet study (Alsaker et al. 1999) showed that

Bulgarian adolescents spent on average 2.37 hours watching television, making them leaders among European and U.S. adolescents in time spent in this activity. Bulgarians watch cable television, which includes European and U.S. programs. Bulgarian adolescents use the Internet either through their home computers or through Internet clubs, which have increased in number since 2000. With the increase of Western commercials in Bulgarian media, youth have increasingly become a target of advertisements.

Politics and Military

The voting age in Bulgaria is 18 years. This is the age when Bulgarian boys also can join the military. The law requires all men at the age of 18 to serve nine months, except those with a university degree who serve six months. During the Communist era the Communist Party and its youth branch, The Dimitrov's Comsomol, governed most political activities. After the fall of Communism, several youth political organizations were established, some of them related to major parties or political entities. Bulgarian students were very politically active after the fall of Communism and played an important role in the country's movement towards democracy. In the early twenty-first century, there has been a decrease in the participation rates of youth in political life, likely due to personal concerns and an emphasis on individual and economic endeavors.

Tzakova (1997) studied adolescents' civic culture in the post-totalitarian society of Bulgaria with a high school sample from the main urban cities of Bulgaria. Results showed that although adolescents had relatively good knowledge of democratic principles and institutions, they also expressed some authoritarian attitudes (such as low tolerance for other ethnic groups, approval of an authoritarian power, the so-called "strong hand" and acceptance of party bans). They also showed signs of political passivity and indifference, reflected by their low interest in voting, low participation in youth organizations, and poor participation in group activities, such as holiday celebrations, competitions, and balls. On the other hand, adolescents demonstrated some readiness for assuming civic responsibilities, as shown by their negative attitudes toward the corruption of civil servants and other violations of the public order, their respect for the law, and their readiness to pay taxes in good faith.

Supportive of these findings was the study of adolescents' psychosocial maturity (Botcheva et al.

1998) among 546 eighth- through eleventh-grade students from two urban and one rural city of Bulgaria. It showed that adolescents expressed relatively high levels of social responsibility, which was positively influenced by such aspects of their social environment as family cohesion, parental warmth, and cohesive neighborhood climate.

Youth participate in various voluntary and community activities. A study by Flannagan et al. (1999) with a convenience school sample showed that 42.2% of investigated 13- to 18-year-old Bulgarian adolescents reported being involved in voluntary work. Schools, youth clubs, and nonprofit organizations mostly organize the voluntary work. The biggest nonprofit organization for voluntarism is the Red Cross, which has around 400 clubs with around 6,000 participants. Volunteer activities include helping the elderly, the homeless, and socially deprived groups; ecological activities (cleaning up parks and rivers and restoration of public lands); and public health education.

Unique Issues

Contemporary Bulgarian adolescents live in a country on the geographical crossroads of the Muslim and Orthodox Christian worlds and the historical crossroads of democratization and globalization. Several forces shape the life of Bulgarian adolescents. On one hand, the traditional culture with strong family values and the relatively homogeneous community offers familiarity with the norms and values throughout the society, which along with the previous quasi-egalitarian value system emphasizes conformity to the group and places less emphasis on individual achievement and recognition. On the other hand, the tides of change related to the forces of globalization and democratization provide a powerful pull, especially on urban youth, to take on new attitudes and values of individualism, opportunism, and to give less respect to tradition. This transition will be easy for some, for others a disruptive shock with related personal and social costs. The optimism comes from the fact that these are just the growing pains of the new generation that will join Europe and the modern world.

Luba Botcheva, Plamen Kalchev, and
P. Herbert Leiderman

References and Further Reading

Adams, G. R., L. B. Bennion, and K. Huh. 1989. *Objective measure of ego development status. A reference manual.* Canada: University of Guelph.

Alsaker, F., A. Flammer, and P. Noack. 1999. Time use by adolescents in an international perspective. I. The case of leisure activities. In *The adolescent experience: European and American adolescents in the 1990s*. F. Alsaker and A. Flammer (eds.). pp. 33–61. Mahwah, New Jersey: Lawrence Elbaum Associates.

Alsaker, F., and A. Flammer, A. 1999. Time use by adolescents in an international perspective. II. The case of necessary activities. In *The Adolescent Experience: European and American Adolescents in the 1990s*. F. Alsaker and A. Flammer (eds.). pp. 33–61. Mahwah, New Jersey: Lawrence Elbaum Associates.

American Psychiatric Association. 1994. *Diagnostic and statistical manual of mental disorders* 4th ed. Washington, DC: American Psychiatric Association.

Arnett, J. J. 2004. *Emerging adulthood: The winding road from the late teens through the twenties*. New York: Oxford University Press.

Balev, G. 2001. *Roditelski modeli na povedenie i dezaptivno psihosocialno funcionirane v junosheska vuzrast*. (Parent styles and desadaptive psychological functioning in adolescence). Unpublished PhD diss., Sofia University.

Bekhradnia, Bahram. 2004. Higher education in Bulgaria: A review for the Ministry of Education and Science. Paper presented at a seminar for higher education in Bulgaria, Sofia.

Bollobas, E. 1993. "Totalitarian lib." The legacy of communism for Hungarian women. In *Gender politics and post-communism*. N. Funk and M. Mueller (eds.). pp. 201–6. New York: Routledge.

Botcheva L. 1998. The gains and losses of Bulgarian youth. In *Adolescents, cultures, and conflicts: Growing up in contemporary Europe*. J. Nurmi (ed.). pp. 109–28. New York: Garland.

Botcheva, L., and S. S. Feldman. 2004. Grandparents as family stabilizers during economic hardship in Bulgaria. *International Journal of Psychology* 39:157–68.

Botcheva, L., S. S. Feldman, and P. H. Leiderman. 2002. Can stability in school processes offset the negative effects of socio-political upheaval on adolescents' adaptation. *Youth and Society* 34:55–88.

Botcheva, L., P. H. Leiderman, and A. Inkeles. 1998. The transition to adulthood in society undergoing social change: Final report to the Johann Jacobs Foundation. Sofia: Center for Interdisciplinary Studies.

Central Committee for Antisocial Behavior of Adolescents. 2003. Sustoyanie i tendencii na prestipnostta i protovoobshtestvenite proyavi na maloletnite i nepulnoletnite (Trends of crimes and antisocial behavior among youth in 2002). *Obshtestveno vuzpitanie* 4:56–78.

Cristopoulos, A. 2001. Relationships between parents' marital status and university students' mental health: A study in Bulgaria. *Journal of Divorce and Remarriage* 34:179–90.

Dimitrov, I. 1997. Attitude to school and personal well-being of adolescent pupils from different ethno-cultural groups. In *Interaction between the school and the cultural environment for pupils*. I. Dimitrov (ed.). pp. 35–57. Sofia: UNESCO.

Dimitrov, I. 2005. Etnoculturalna sreda i razvitie v junosheska vuzrast (Ethnocultural context and adolescent development). *Journal of Psychological Investigations* 2, in press.

Dimova, L. 2002. *Bulgaria: Gender aspects of poverty and inequality in the family and labor market research and policy recommendations*. Sofia: Agency for Social Analyses.

Flammer, A., and F. Alsaker. 1999. Time use by adolescents in an international perspective. II. The case of necessary activities. In *The adolescent experience: European and American adolescents in the 1990s*. F. Alsaker and A. Flammer (eds.). pp. 61–85. Mahwah, New Jersey: Lawrence Elbaum Associates.

Flammer, A., R. Grob, and F. Kaiser. 1989. *Kontrollattributionen und Wohlbefinden von Schweizer Jugendlichen. Forschungsberichte aus dem psychologischen*. Bern: Institut der Universitaet Bern.

Flannagan, C., and L. Botcheva. 1999. Adolescents' preferences for their homeland and other countries. In *The adolescent experience: European and American adolescents in the 1990s*. F. Alsaker and A. Flammer (eds.). pp. 131–45. Mahwah, New Jersey: Lawrence Elbaum Associates.

Flannagan, C., B. Johnsson, L. Botcheva, B. Csapo, J. Bowes, P. Macek, I. Averina, and E. Sheblanova. 1999. Adolescents and the "social contract": Developmental roots of citizenship in seven countries. In *Roots of civic identity: International perspectives on community service and activism in youth*. M. Yates and J. Youniss (eds.). pp.135–54. Cambridge: Cambridge University Press.

Henshew, S., S. Singh, and T. Haas. 1999. The incidence of abortion worldwide. *Family planning and perspectives* 25: supplement.

Kalchev, P. 1996. Subektivno blagopoluchie i vzaimootnosheniya s roditelite i vrustnicite prez prehodnata vuzrast (Subjective well-being and relationships with peers and parents in adolescence). *Bulgarian Journal of Psychology* 3.

Kalchev, P. 2000. Balgarska versiya na skalata na Olendik za ocenka na strahovete v detska vasrast (Bulgarian version of the revised fear survey schedule for children). *Bulgarian Journal of Pedagogy* 2.

Kalchev, P. 2000. Adolescence sex roles: Unpublished data.

Kalchev, P. 2002. Ocenka na depresiyata v yunosheska vasrast s CES-D. (Depression among Bulgarian adolescents measured by CES-D) Unpublished data.

Kalchev, P. 2003. Tormoz i viktimizaciya na vrustnicite (Bullying and peer victimization). Sofia: Paradigma.

Kalchev, P. 2005. Trevojnost v yunosheska vasrast. Konstruirane i izpolzvane na mnogomerna scala za ocenka. (Adolescent anxiety. Constructing and using the Multidimensional Adolescent Anxiety Scale). Sofia: Paradigma.

Koceva, T., and D. Kostova. 2003. Faktori i tendencii v seksualniya debjut na mladite hora v Bulgaria (Factors and trends in the sexual debut of Bulgarian youth). *Naselenie*, 69–85.

Kroger, J. 1995. The differentiation between "firm" and "developmental foreclosure" identity statuses: A longitudinal study. *Journal of Adolescent Research* 10:317–37.

Macek, P., C. Flanagan, L. Gallay, L. Kostron, L. Botcheva, and B. Csapo. 1998. Postcommunist societies in times of transition: Perceptions of change among adolescents in Central and Eastern Europe. *Journal of Social Issues* 54:547–61.

March, J., D. Parker, K. Sullivan, P. Stallings, and K. Conners. 1997. The Multidimensional Anxiety Scale for Children (MASC): Factor structure, reliability and validity. *Journal of the American Academy of Child and Adolescent Psychiatry* 36:554–65.

Ministry of Labor and Social Services. 2004. *Nacionalen doklad za trudova zaetost na mladegta v Republika Bulgaria* (National report on Bulgarian youth employment). Sofia.

Ministry of Youth and Sports. 2003. *Godishen doklad za mladegta* (Annual report about youth). Sofia.

Muris, P., C. Meesters, H. Merckelbach, and E. Schouten. 2002. A brief questionnaire of DSM-IV defined anxiety and depression symptoms among children. *Clinical Psychology and Psychotherapy* 9:430–42.

National Statistics Institute. 2000. *Annual report.* Sofia.

Offer, D., E. Ostrov, and I. Howard. 1977. *The Offer Self-image Questionnaire for Adolescents: A Manual.* Chicago: Michael Reese Hospital.

Ollendick, T. 1983. Reliability and validity of the Revised Fear Survey Schedule for Children (FSSC-R). *Behavior Research and Therapy* 21:685–92.

Olson, G., and A. L.V. Knorring. 1997. Depression among Swedish adolescents measured by the self-rating scale center for Epidemiology Studies—Depression Child (CESD-DC). *European Child and Adolescent Psychiatry* 6:81–87.

Olweus, D. 1978. *Aggression in the schools: Bullies and whipping boys.* Washington, DC: Hemisphere (Wiley).

Polnareva, N., and Z. Mihova. 1995. Adolescent crisis as an indicator of family dysfunction. *Bulgarian Journal of Psychology* 2:13–19.

Radloff, L. S. 1977. The CES-D Scale: A self-report depression scale for research in the general population. *Applied Psychological Measurement* 1:385–401.

Reynolds, C. R., and B. O. Richmond. 1978. What I think and feel: A revised measure of children's manifest anxiety. *Journal of Abnormal Child Psychology* 6:271–80.

Silgidgan-Georgieva, H. 1998. Az-koncepciya i psihosocialna identichnost: Gisneniyat prehod kum zrelostta (Self-concept and psychosocial identity: Life transition to maturity). Sofia: University Publishers.

Smith, P. K., Y. Morita, J. Junger-Tas, D. Olweus, R. Catalano, and P. Slee (eds.). 1999. *The nature of school bullying. A cross-national perspective.* London: Routledge.

Spence, S. 1997. Structure of anxiety symptoms among children: A confirmatory factor-analytic study. *Journal of Abnormal Psychology* 106:280–97.

Stefanova, M. 2003. Statusi na psihosocialnata identichnost pri junishite (Psychosocial identity statuses in adolescence). Unpublished PhD diss., Sofia: Bulgarian Academy of Sciences.

Streitmatter, J. 1993. Gender differences in identity development: An examination of longitudinal data. *Adolescence*, 28:55–66.

Tencheva, D. 2004. Vuv vseki klas po edin piyanica (In every classroom one drunk). *Trud* 5–6.

Teneva, N. 1995. *The world of Bulgarian woman.* Sofia: Katerini.

Toth, O. 1993. No envy, no pity. In *Gender politics and post-Communism.* N. Funk and M. Mueller (eds.). pp. 213–23. New York: Routledge.

Tzakova, I. 1997. Civic culture of the Bulgarian adolescents: Results from an empirical survey. Sofia.

BURUNDI

Background Information

Burundi is a land-locked country of Central Africa. It is bordered to the north by Rwanda, to the west by the Democratic Republic of the Congo, and to the south and to the east by Tanzania. It had a population of 7.2 million inhabitants in 2004 in a surface area of 27,834 square kilometers. More than 90% of the population lives in rural areas. The population growth rate is 3%. Just over half of the population (51%) is female.

The country includes three ethnic groups: the Hutus (85%), who are farmers; the Tutsis (14%), who are stockbreeders, and the Twas (1%), who are hunters and potters living scattered in the country's hills. The main religions are Catholic (65.05%), Protestant (13.78%), and Muslim (1.58%). The rest of the population practices either traditional religion or professes atheism.

In historical and political terms, the cohabitation among the three ethnic groups has not been easy since the country's independence in 1962, as the interethnic conflicts of 1965, 1969, 1972, 1988, 1991, and 1993 testify. These situations condemned many Burundians to inland displacement and exile or refugee status abroad.

This situation of economic recession conjugated with the devastating effects of HIV/AIDS has only increased the number of vulnerable populations (women, orphans, not-accompanied children—children who have neither parents nor guardians nor families. They are homeless or live in houses left by their parents).

With the peace agreements signed in 2000 and 2002 between belligerent parties and succeeding Burundian governments, the security situation has sharply improved. The municipal, legislative, senatorial, presidential, and hills elections that took place testify as much.

Period of Adolescence

As all around the world, in Burundi adolescence is one of the most fascinating stages of life and one of the most complex ones. It is difficult to fix a precise age for the beginning of adolescence, as puberty itself is of variable age according to the child in question: from 10 to 20, 12 to 18, or 13 to 19, for example. There are also several types of majority during this period, in particular the civil and legal majority (21 years), the partial penal coming-of-age (13 years), full penal coming-of-age (18 years), the matrimonial coming-of-age (18 years) for girls and (21 years) for boys, and the minimum age for admittance to employment (16 years). Adolescence is the last of the age groups of children being confronted with various problems: school abandonment, begging, unemployment, crime, drug addiction, or military recruitment. At this time, the girl becomes freer and more autonomous. Her parents consider her grown-up enough to discern what is or is not appropriate for her behavior. The mother trusts her in many fields, including meal preparation and the education of the young ones. The father has almost nothing to do in the education of his daughter. He respects her more than he does his wife. The girl also shows a lot of respect towards her father.

Prohibitions exist around girls during the adolescence, including prohibitions related to periods (menses). When a girl is menstruating, she must not put a newborn child on her knees (as the child will develop eczema), or pass in a field of gourds (as they will rot), or drink milk.

In Burundi there are no rites of initiation, which in other parts of Africa may integrate the young people into the sphere of the adults. The connections between the mother and the girl become tighter. The mother hides nothing from her daughter and will speak to her openly about domestic difficulties. The mother teaches her daughter to behave like an adult.

Beliefs

In traditional Burundi culture, teamwork and aid to the less fortunate were encouraged. These positive values were taught to children and young people by the adults.

With the introduction of foreign values, however, the situation changed. Furthermore, with the growing poverty and excessive urbanization, the family framework has lost more of its reason for being. Thus, collectivist tendencies are being gradually replaced by more individualist ones, as are evident in Western societies.

Besides parents and school, religion plays a key role in educating the population. Although the state is officially secular, the religions contribute to the moral and socio-cultural development of the populations. We count in 2005 more than 100 sects, the Catholic religion being the most widespread (65% of the population). Generally, the values of love, solidarity, and mutual aid are being taught, but the ascertainment is that individualism dominates collectivism. Also, occult popular beliefs persist in spite of the multiplicity of sects (obscurantism, witchcraft, rainmakers, people who fly in the air).

Generally, there is no choice of religion or sect. Most individuals adhere to the religion of their parents. This habit is decreasing, however, as more adolescents and adults currently practice a different religion from that of their childhood.

Gender

Responsibilities, behaviors, values, and standards are assigned by the society to one sex or the other. Some examples suggest that the education of children and young people was and still is being made according to gender. Concerning the distribution of tasks, the adolescent girl assists the mother as the individual responsible for household and domestic work. If the father is absent, the boy takes on the role of primary authority. According to tradition, a man does not sweep or make the bed. A woman cannot fix the roof of the house or build the house itself.

Several restrictions face women. They must not appear at the entrance of the house in the evening nor walk outside during the night. A woman must never squat nor sit with her legs apart. Reserve and modesty are the first points on which a young girl is judged. Work and obedience are very important. Misbehavior and laziness are major flaws.

Boys are expected to know how to behave like a man, as it is construed by traditional culture. This means he is expected to be diligent and to know how to give commands. He is expected to obey his parents and to be social.

Some of these customs have a negative impact on girls' life and condemn them to conformism and restriction. As culture is not static, initiatives aiming to improve gender relations are being explored and put into practice. Some current actions are focused on the educational needs of girls, special programs for girls' schooling, the revision of laws related to inheritance, and the elimination of stereotypes related to sexes and the obstacles of any kind preventing the girl-woman from reaching the resources and the power in the same way as boys.

The Self

In everyday life, any person, male or female, should be able to set personal objectives, thus giving him or her a sense of a more planned and better-structured organization. However, setting personal objectives is not recognized by traditional Burundi culture.

Young Burundians have potentialities in terms of personality development. They have gifts, talents, and capacities. It is to the responsibility of the society, community, parents, and educators to help young people to develop capacities of a personal and social nature.

It is necessary to lead them in: (1) knowing each other; (2) having self-confidence; (3) having a positive insight of themselves; (4) wielding themselves autonomously; (5) having socially responsible behavior; (6) knowing how to resolve problems; (7) communicating with others in an appropriate manner.

Such behavior acquired from an early age enables a harmonious development of the adults.

Family Relationships

The notion of family covers a number of concepts and traditions in various African traditional societies. In Burundi there are three types of family: the extended family, the household family, and the ménage family. The extended family regroups several families united by their belonging to the same clan, or to the same lineage, around a common ancestor. The household regroups the father, his spouse or spouses, his children, his married sons and their children. The ménage family includes the father, the mother, and the young children who are not married yet. Thus, the family relationships regulate life among the community members. The rights and obligations of each member (young or old) are regulated by the head(s).

At different life stages, adults become involved in the child's education, according to the gender of the parent and the child. Such education was better provided in case of harmony and understanding among the family members, particularly of the ménage family.

The causes for the lack of familial harmony are varied and include polygamy, divorce, conflicts among family members, and conflicts among the familial generations. Such situations are detrimental to the education and future of children. Generally, grandparents interfere in their grandchildren's lives or affairs in the parents' absence. Grandparents may provide food, clothes, or educational opportunities if parents are unable to do so.

Polygamy is a primary source of family conflicts. As Christianity became the majority religion in Burundi, polygamy became less widespread. However, it is still practiced among the Muslim population. The consequences of polygamy are multiple. It leads to conflicts and disagreements concerning inheritance, rivalry between wives, tension between children, and the overtaxing of household resources. Therefore, polygamy is officially prohibited in Burundi.

Friends and Peers/Youth Culture

In Burundi, as elsewhere in the world, the parents are the first party responsible for the education of their children. Parents must ensure the complete and harmonious development of their children. Cultural beliefs, and appropriate attitudes, behavior, and knowledge are transmitted to young people by adults.

The school system constitutes a better framework for the acquisition of new knowledge and techniques leading to the complete development of the young person. Moreover, in terms of culture, the young people, whether schooled or not, somehow participate in activities for absorbing the national culture. For that purpose there are various frameworks where young people can practice cultural traditions and activities, such as national councils of young people, associations of young people, and cultural clubs.

Generally speaking, young people do not have their own distinct culture in Burundi. They adapt themselves to the culture of their father, given that the system is patriarchal and passed from generation to generation through a common language. Adolescents spend a significant amount of time in school. In their time outside of school, adolescents meet with their peers in the street or take part in leisure activities, such as sports, music, surfing the Internet, or reading. Social outings and leisure activities are influenced by social rank. Young people from poor families do not regularly socialize with wealthier peers. Ethnic problems lead young people to organize their leisure activities according to their ethnic group. At school there are regularly organized sporting events, theatrical activities, and singing, drawing, and literary composition competitions. Outside of school the adolescent generally stays in his or her own neighborhood and interacts with his or her own ethnic group.

Love and Sexuality

In Burundi, sexuality is a taboo subject among family members. Sex education was traditionally transmitted only from the paternal aunt or the paternal grandmother to the female adolescent. However, with the increased influence of Western values, there has been an erosion of traditional cultural values. Young people have become more exposed to sexuality and to the use of drugs. This has led to an increase in exposure to sexually transmitted diseases (STDs) such as gonorrhea, syphilis, and HIV/AIDS.

The rate of adult seroprevalence in terms of HIV/AIDS was 11.3% in 1999. That makes Burundi among the countries most affected by AIDS in Africa. The situation worsened because of the catastrophic interrelations between the effects of the conflicts (wars and regrouping of the populations) and the situation of poverty and the spreading of HIV/AIDS. Consequently, we can especially quote the increase in populations at risks (refugees, displaced, orphans, prostitutes), the falling schooling rates, and the degradation of health conditions.

With the war the situation worsened. Nevertheless prohibited by the legislation, sexual relations before the age of majority are frequent. Thus, the rape of minors, pregnancies of minors (less than 18 years old), and sexual harassment are frequent. This situation is most frequent in urban environments or in displacement and refugee camps.

Facing the dangers threatening the population, the government introduced plans and programs for fighting HIV/AIDS. The Code of Persons and Family sets the minimum age for marriage at 18 years for the girl and at 21 years for the boy. Theoretically, sexual relations before the age of maturity are prohibited. The prohibition against premarital sex is officially supported by the majority Catholic religion. However, reality does not always reflect the official idea. Although statistics are lacking, sexual relations are frequent before, and especially during, the period of adolescence.

Children of the street, demobilized soldiers, rebels, and military personnel all rape women and minors. Homosexuality is a reality, mostly in urban environments. Both rape and homosexuality are punishable under the Burundian penal code.

Health Risk Behavior

Traditionally, the child in Burundi was educated by society as a whole. With the introduction of a formal school system, the traditional education based on values and workmanship gave way to the foreign values imposed by the colonizing forces. The parents then relaxed in their role of educating the children instead of helping the teacher. There was then an opposition between the two educational types instead of complementarity. That situation provoked an internal crisis in adolescents, resulting in their discouragement with school or even the decision to drop out of school.

School dropouts, faced with uncertain futures, may turn to alcohol or drugs. They may also start associating with gangs of criminals, committing various felonies such as robberies, rapes, and murders, ignoring or disregarding the laws and regulations in force.

This phenomenon of juvenile delinquency is much more frequent in the cities than in the countryside. The breakup of the domestic unit, poverty, and war underlie this phenomenon. Toward the numerous problems of the adolescents and their consequences on the life of young people, various strategies are to be implemented in order to improve their social, cultural, physical, and health environment.

Education

Within the framework of parental orientation in the Burundian tradition, the custom recognizes the dominant role played by the extended family in the orientation, education, and advice imparted to the child, as well as in the transmission of the culture. It is the family framework, centered on the parents, which dictates to the youth moral rules, techniques, and knowledge, the assimilation of which will allow him or her to become a man or woman playing his or her appropriate role in society.

The breakup of the traditional family and the introduction of the basic educational structure in the African environment has led to a lesser role for family members in the shaping and influence of young people and children. Parents expect the school to answer to all the developmental needs of their children; however, the school environment is incapable of shouldering such responsibility by itself. Most of the time the school focuses more on the acquisition of academic knowledge and skills required by the work environment, to the detriment of other needs of the learners. The result of this situation is that neither parents nor teachers are really prepared to help young people, especially girls, face the challenges of a society in constant mutation. In order to face this situation, the Burundian Ministry of National Education and Culture introduced into the educational system two special programs: the Program of Orientation and Guidance and the Development of the Youth with a particular accent on Girls, and the Initiative Program of the United Nations for Education of Girls (AGEI/UNGEI). We also note the introduction in the curricula of English for favoring regional integration, education in peace and in the reconstruction of the country; and human rights. Two studies were made in order to serve as a draft for the policy of education of girls, one on the obstacles for the schooling of girls and the other one on the stereotypes existing in the school environment.

Work

Traditionally, the work of children has been considered as a preparation for adult life. This education in the working world was based on the gender of the child. Household work was incumbent upon the girl, and workmanship upon the boy. At the level of the law, the labor code of 1993 settles the age of admittance to employment at 16 years. Nevertheless, there is a derogation for specific work provided that the work "should not be of nature to make damage to the faculty of benefiting from instruction, may impair the prescriptions in school matter, should not be harmful to their health or their development." Despite that, the work of children remains a reality in Burundi. A study supported by UNICEF in 2000 reveals that 25% of the children under 14 years old are being used in various sectors (agriculture, breeding, commerce, building, restoration, mechanics).

With the poverty, which does not stop increasing, the work of the children took on another dimension. Parents send children to paid work (babysitting, cooking, commerce) apart from the domestic dwelling. The problem is that we do not take into account the age and physical abilities of the child, given that it is almost about exploitation. This injures the complete development of the child. Graver yet, children are used in armed conflicts. Others are delivered to sexual exploitation by adults. There are other adults looking for children of the street, for orphans, or for poor children in order to sell them abroad for various lucrative activities. The child, the future of the country, must be protected against hard work, which risks damaging his complete development.

In the formal sector we apply the provisions of the statutes of public service and the labor code. Given that the official age to begin the school is 7, it is very uncommon to find agents beginning the work at the age of 16. Indeed, in order to be employed, it is necessary to have completed at least four years post-primary school. On the other hand, the primary school lasts six years.

Media

The media (radio, television, newspapers, cinema) represent training and educational channels for adolescents. Through various subjects, adolescents select messages for their moral, cultural, scientific, and technical growth. It is only necessary to watch that the given messages are framing well the educational objectives.

In Burundi there are bodies allowing the public and the adolescents to reach information. At present, eight broadcasting stations and a dozen newspapers and magazines deliver messages to adolescents. Various subjects are approached, notably HIV/AIDS, peace, and development.

Certain radio shows are especially popular with adolescents, including "Champion 2000," a general knowledge program; "Deux stars en vedette" (Two stars), in which young people express themselves in famous songs; "Mercredi tempo" (Wednesday tempo), translations of the songs of an artist from English into French; "Au delà du son" (Beyond the sound), broadcasts of various songs; and "C'est pas sorcier" (It's no sorcery), a scientific broadcast.

Computers are used by young adolescents for games mostly. Adolescents also enjoy visiting sports-related websites. In terms of magazines, sports magazines and comic books are especially popular. Serial television programs aimed toward young people include "Umuco" (The light), "Ninde" (Who am I), "Ishaka" (Devotion), and "Sida yarateye" (AIDS is there).

Politics and Military

The minimum voting age is 18. However, demographic registry services are quasi-nonexistent, and thus the official age restriction is not generally enforced. Given that Burundi has been shaken by 12 years of crises and war, almost all administrative structures have been destroyed.

When elections are impending, politicians look to recruit political workers and activists. They may take advantage of the ignorance of young people, promising them money, goods, scholarships, or jobs if they volunteer to work for the campaigning politicians. Adolescents may even abandon their schooling if they are enticed by such offers. After the elections, the promises are rarely honored, leading to disillusionment in quite a lot of young people. Given this disillusionment, there is little loyalty to a single political party among the populace.

Adolescents enroll willingly in the military or they may be forced to do so. Not knowing the conflict cause, they are poisoned and given drugs before being enrolled in the army. They are then used in slaughters, especially of civilians, or in thefts. Once demobilized, most of them integrate with difficulty back into the society. In these conditions, we do not take into account the age required to be enrolled in the army, which is 18 years.

Unique Issues

Burundi and Rwanda are home to the same ethnic groups (Hutu, Tutsi, and Twa) in roughly the same numbers. The languages spoken (Kirundi and Kinyarwanda) are almost identical. Ethnic problems are entwined in Burundi and in Rwanda. Some believe that the social revolution of 1959 in Rwanda, which led the Rwandan Tutsi to exile in Burundi, influenced the bloody events of 1965, 1969, 1972, 1988, 1991, and 1993 in Burundi.

JOSÉPHINE BANGURAMBONA

References and Further Reading

Accord d'Arusha pour la paix et la réconciliation au Burundi, Arusha, 28 Août 2000. (Arusha agreement for peace and reconciliation in Burundi, Arusha, August 28th, 2000).

Anonyme, Burundi traditionnel, Aperçu sur les relations familiales (Anonymous traditional Burundi, survey on the family relationships). 1974.

Bangurambona, J. 1994. Le rôle de la tente paternelle à travers quelques épithalames et rondes populaires (The role of the paternal aunt across a few popular epithalamia and rounds). Diss., Burundi University.

Ben Yahmed, D. 2001. La Santé de A à Z pour la femme et l'enfant (Health from A to Z for woman and child). Paris: Jaguar Publishing House.

Convention relative aux Droits de l'Enfant. 1997. Rapport Initial de mise en application, BURUNDI CRC/Additif Burundi, 17 décembre 1997 (Convention related to the rights of the child. Enforcement initial report. BURUNDI CRC/Burundi Additive, December 17, 1997. Bujumbura).

Décret-loi n° 1/024 du 28 avril 1993 portant modification du Code des personnes et de la famille (Law-decree No. 1/024 of April 28th, 1993 modifying the Code of Persons and Family).

Furuguta, O. 1997. Impact du VIH/SIDA sur la gestion publique en Afrique des Grands Lacs, Analyse Socio-économique, Memoire de 3ème cycle (Impact of HIV/AIDS on the public administration in Great Lakes' Africa, Socio-economic Analysis, Dissertation of the 3rd cycle). Paris: University of Paris.

Ntahokaja, J. 1978. Imigenzo y'i kirundi. Bujumbura: University of Burundi.

Officiers burundais, l'armée burundaise et les institutions démocratiques. 1994. (Burundian officers, the Burundian army and the democratic institution). Brussels.

Programme des Nations Unies pour le Développement (PNUD), Atelier sur le VIH et le Développement, Manuel du Facilitateur, Pretoria, 1999. (United Nations Program for Development (PNUD), Workshop on HIV and Development, Facilitator's Manual, Pretoria).

Rapport final du premier Séminaire Régional de Formation des Formateurs en Orientation et Conseil pour l'Afrique Francophone, Côte d'Ivoire, 22 Novembre—11 Décembre 1999, p. 69. (Final report of the first regional training seminary of trainers in orientation and guidance for the Francophone Africa, Ivory Coast, November 22–December 11, 1999, p. 69).

Rapport périodique Initial sur Convention relative aux Droits de l'Enfant. (Initial periodic report on the convention concerning the rights of the child).

République du Burundi. 1983. Ministère de la Jeunesse, des Sports et de la Culture, Revue Culture et Société (Ministry of Youth, Sports and Culture, Culture and Society Magazine) 4:66–104.

République du Burundi. 1992. Récensement général de la population et de l'Habitation (General Census Report of Population and Dwelling, Bujumbura). Bujumbura.

République du Burundi. 1997. Convention relative aux droits de l'enfant (Convention concerning the rights of the child). Bujumbura.

République du Burundi. 2002a. *Burundi consultation thématique, plan national de lutte contre le VBIH/SIDA 2002–2006* (Burundi thematic consultation, national plan for fighting HIV/AIDS 2002–2006). Bujumbura.

République du Burundi. 2002b. Politique Sectorielle du Ministère de l'Education Nationale (Sectorial policy of the Ministry of National Education). Bujumbura.

République du Burundi. 2002c. Ministère de l'Education et de la Culture, Module Organisation Personnelle de la vie, revu et adapté (Ministry of Education and Culture, Personal organization module of life, revised and adapted). Bujumbura.

République du Burundi. 2004a. Enquête socio-démographique et de la santé de la reproduction (ESD/SR-Burundi 2002) (Socio-demographic enquiry and on reproduction health (ESD/SR-Burundi 2002)). Bujumbura.

République du Burundi. 2004b. Evaluation de la prise en compte des questions de population et de l'approche genre dans les politiques sectorielles (Evaluation of the recognition of the population issues and of the type approach in sectorial policies). Bujumbura.

République du Burundi. 2004c. Population burundaise en 2003, Bujumbura, Septembre 2004 (Burundian population in 2003, Bujumbura, September 2004). 53. Bujumbura.

Rodegem, F. M. 1961. *Sagesse kirundi, proverbes, dictons, locations usités au Burundi* (Kirundi wisdom, proverbs, dictions, idioms in use in Burundi). Tervuren.

Rodegem, F. M. 1973. *Anthologie rundi, Classiques Africains* (Rundi Anthology, African Classics). 417p.

C

CAMEROON

Background Information

Cameroon has been marked by varied colonial and contemporary sociopolitical and linguistic experiences. Accordingly, family life and socialization processes are influenced by both indigenous practices and foreign values.

Cameroon's population of 16 million is 71% Francophone and 29% Anglophone. The age structure is 0 to 14 years: 42.1% (male 3,44,505; female 3,367,571); 15 to 64 years: 54.5% (male 4,4431,524; female 4,392,155); and above 65 years 3.4% (male 253,242; female 296,751). The annual growth rate is 2.36% (2002).

Cameroon has about 279 ethnic groups. Examples of the Bantus are the Doualas, Bamilekes, Tikars, Bassas, and the Bamauns in the south; the Euondos and the Fulbes in the west; the Fulanis and Sudanese in the north; and the Baka Pygmies in the southeast (Country Guide 2001). There are about 230 African languages spoken in Cameroon, classified in three main groups: Bantus, Semi-Bantus, and Sudanic.

Cameroon has one of the best-endowed primary commodity economies in sub-Saharan Africa because of its oil resources and favorable agricultural conditions. The main exports are cocoa, coffee, rubber, cotton, banana, petrol, timber, and aluminium. The political system of Cameroon is multi-party, with a democratically elected government.

Cameroon comprises 475,442 square kilometers, with a coastline bordered to the west by the Gulf of Guinea with access to the Atlantic Ocean. Cameroon's land boundaries are Nigeria to the west, the plains of the Lake Tchad basin northward, the Republic of Tchad and Central Africa to the east, and Equatorial Guinea, Gabon, and Congo Brazzaville to the south (Country Guide 2001).

The geography of Cameroon is characterized by plateaus and mountain chains, with the highest being the volcanic Mount Cameroon (4,070 square meters). Four types of vegetations are savannah, humid grassland, rich volcanic soil, and equatorial forest. Climatic features are equatorial, tropical, and Sahelien types with two major seasons, dry and wet.

Major historical events include the granting of the independence of French Cameroon on January 1, 1960, and the reunification of the British and French colonies on February 12, 1961 (Country Guide 2001). A referendum held on May 20, 1972 resulted in a 99% "yes" vote for the new unitary constitution. The unitary system, it was hoped, would help eradicate partisan mentality and behavior. But unity and integration were problematic as people identified more with regions than with the nation. The United Republic was officially recognized on June 2, 1972.

The bicultural nature of the country enriched the potential of the people, increasing their access to the outside world. Yet the two foreign cultures had differential effects on the personality and philosophy of the people, leading to the proliferation of differing outlooks. The colonial policies of "association and assimilation" (French) and "paternalist" (British) addressed different developmental goals. Enforcing bilingualism as a major unifying mechanism was compounded by a defined sense of identity as a Cameroonian.

Period of Adolescence

To indicate the beginning and end of adolescence from a chronological perspective would overlook maturational and other indigenous differences. Adolescence has a long history, marked by the young person leaving behind the phase of protective childhood and becoming independent and capable of fending for him- or herself. Accordingly, adolescence constitutes a special developmental phase in African ontogeny, with respect to sociocultural interpretations (Barthelemy 1998). Local and global elements combine in different and changing ways, shaping pathways that are both secured and precarious (Larson, Brown, and Mortimer 2002). The role of biology in shaping the adolescent experience remains important, but current research identifies it more as a contributor to individual differences than as a template for universal pathways (Larson, Brown, and Mortimer 2002).

Biologically, pubertal changes are generally first evident between the ages of 10 and 14. Puberty is a period marked by sensitization to appropriate gender identity and roles. Among many ethnic groups in Cameroon, adolescence is ushered in by puberty rites of initiation. Different ethnic groups understand and handle the period with sensitivity, characterizing the period in different ways and with special activities and labels. Information from oral traditions of different tribes and from students of education provided the following information here reported. The Bamileke ethnic group of the western province for example, terms the 6 to 12 years *mooh-goh* "girl child" and *mooh seup* "boy child." The developmental activities are circumcision, socialization into practical life, and participation in community activities. The 12- to 15-year-olds are known as *tchieu-goh*, "young girl" and *tchieu-seup,* "young boy." Their common problems

are related to identity. They can participate in ceremonies and rituals. The period is marked by retreat and isolation. The 15- to 20-year-olds are known as *Goh* "girl" and *Seup* "boy." They are at the age of marriage, with total submission to parents, elders, social laws, and regulations. These activities and approach (apprenticeship) give the adolescents more natural outlets for their interests and powers, allowing them to grow up freely into full responsibility in the community. The social internship that precedes the rites of passage is designed to cultivate virtuous character and instill values of cooperation and generosity.

Typically, the initiation of adolescent boys includes circumcision, a collective affair. For adolescent girls initiation is subtler and less public as it focuses on training for proficiency in housekeeping and reproduction, accompanied by rites concerned with fertility. Puberty rites mark the point at which adolescent boys and girls begin to take their place in cultural affairs of society, first as their parents' representatives (Nsamenang 2002) and later in their own right, particularly for boys. Adolescence is also a time for social integration into cultural life and economic activities.

The socialization of the Cameroonian youth is changing, being affected by prolonged schooling and the exigencies of urbanization and commercialization (Nsamenang 2002). The duration of adolescence spans from about 10 to 20 years, with the duration being shorter for girls than for boys. Changes in length of adolescence is more for individuals going on to tertiary education and lacking in financial autonomy (Durkin 1995). Cameroonian adolescents do not automatically attain adult status. Full adulthood status requires being married with one's own property (Nsamenang 1992). The period of 20 years onward is marked as adulthood. During this period, there is perfect social integration and full participation in management of community's affairs and ownership of a house and business. Adulthood is from 19 to 50.

Beliefs

African values of individuality and autonomy are essentially relational and interdependent, not individualistic and independent (Turnbull 1978). Ties between individuals are collective and not loose because each person is expected to work for the common good of society. From birth children are educated and initiated into strong cohesive ingroups where a strong notion of interdependence is felt and practiced throughout life. Collectivism for Cameroonians consists of precepts in the value system that has been a great source of stability, security, cohesiveness, and unity inculcated through socialization. Collectivist cultures, however, foster group needs, and their members see themselves as fundamentally connected with others (Markus and Kitayama 1991). In Africa people find both physical and psychological security not in individual achievement but in terms of the group and the community (Turnbull 1978). Turnbull addressed the existence of a complex network of interconnecting, crosscutting human relationships. As he further pointed out, it is toward the maintenance and strengthening of this network that all effort is directed, not toward individual advancement. Age groups are a vital organizational mechanism for the allocation of various tasks according to age. Acting together increases sentiments and loyalties providing a healthy channel for resolving conflicts and controlling one another as well as working for the growth of all. Collectivism encourages a spirit of solidarity, team spirit, collaboration, and cooperation. The view of the human being here is embedded in social context and related to others by which interdependence has an element of control from others.

The adolescence period is more complicated today in terms of values because of the conflicting values from other cultures. But the various strands of Cameroon's rich cultural values determine the very fabric of adolescents' personality. The values concerned are those that the culture strongly addresses through enabling the development of a sense of responsibility to care for others. Through such a communal sense of responsibility for one another, some adolescents do easily find support when confronted with developmental crises.

These values are taught through modeling by parents and family members, ensuring the basis for learning and for continuity. Sharing socialization among family members means that a child can be reared in any extended family household. It also means that a child can share in this responsibility by caring for younger siblings. This demonstrates family solidarity and communality in socialization.

Such initial social support systems and family networking highlight the sustainability of collectivism. This mechanism exists for children at all levels, and when they are unmarried or unemployed, they remain economically, socially, and emotionally dependent on parents and family members. Cameroonian adolescents and youths studying out of the country continue with the spirit of working for the common good. This is evident in the institution of the spirit of supporting group members when problems occur. Collectivism is not changing, but

there is no doubt that with globalization some values of individualism can be incorporated.

The sociocultural dimension of adolescence is marked by a set of cultural norms and practices that govern the transition from childhood to adulthood. Some examples are initiation rites, marriage, participation in certain traditional or cultural activities, and changed ways of dressing.

Religious beliefs are central in the lives of Africans, as they are central in the social organization. Religious life in Africa centers on belief in spirit. Acknowledging the existence of a supreme being, they think He is remote and unknowable, and some believe that His intermediates are the ancestors. So they believe in God and in life after death. Religion, therefore, is a source of external control through religious norms as religious values become internalized. There is no doubt that about half (40%) of the Cameroonian population practice traditional African cult worship (World Guide 1997–1998). Christians are a majority in the south (40%), while Islam (20%) predominates in the north (Country Guide 2001). These traditional religious practices vary in expressions among different ethnic groups. For example, with the Kom religious beliefs are manifested through the *Kwifon,* "sacred societies," believed to govern the whole land. As the adolescent boy approaches adulthood, he is expected to offer a goat sacrifice for a maternal aunt or uncle and also for his father. Girls also perform corn flour sacrifice. The adolescents have been conditioned to believe that they have to perform these sacrifices if they are to succeed. The adolescents from the Bakweri ethnic group are aware of such religious beliefs through rituals and rites performed to appease the *Epasa moto* the "god of the mountain." Adolescents are taught through tales, fables, dance, songs, and participation in these activities.

There are few age differentials in religious activities since parents insist on religious engagement as common family practice. Nevertheless, many youths join various cults and some end up being mad or depressed, which may lead to suicide.

Gender

Gender role expectations are embedded in the socialization process to the extent that parents clearly accept the existence of gender differential practices (Tchombe 1998), with a focus on the reproductive role functions of females and the productive role functions of males. Understanding such gender-typing, parental childrearing practices leading to different childhood activities can only be explained better by indigenous psychology. Beliefs about achievements and other favored developmental constituents for boys and girls point to the role of sociocultural factors, highlighting the importance of everyday activities and sociocultural practices. The social context consists of determinants of expected gendered ways of behavior that direct adolescents' learning process.

Orientation to specific gender roles is necessary in order to prepare adolescents for the gendered work they will take on as adults. This orientation is led by the parent of the same sex as the adolescent, older siblings, and extended family members living with the family. They model appropriate gender roles for adolescents. Observation and participation in the apprenticeship models prevail. At the age of seven, gender differential preparations begin in earnest. Mothers in Cameroon inculcate good working habits in the girl child, including how to care for children, how to cook, basic hygiene, and female ethics concerning values and norms of good morals and habits. In some tribes, skills for attracting the attention of potential husbands are taught. Girls are restricted from extensive explorations of their immediate environment for fear of their inability to have children. Boys are oriented more toward activities that encourage explorations of the wider community, whereby more knowledge of the environment is acquired, given their future roles in the family and society as a whole.

In a longitudinal study on the psychological value of education in preparing the adolescent for living in Cameroon, parents engaged more adolescent boys than girls in family businesses to ensure continuity (Tchombe and Nsamenang 1999). There is a prevalent belief that employing boys ensures continuity, as girls will eventually belong to another family through marriage. In rural more than urban settings, boys hunt and fish with their parents. In agricultural settings, adolescents (both males and females) work on farms. Parents insist on these orientations to build self-reliant skills in their adolescents and to encourage them to appreciate manual work and nature. In a country whose main economic activity is agricultural, parents help their adolescents to build up a gender schema through gender-linked activities consistent not only with defined gender roles but also with respect of the nature of the country.

Both boys and girls copy adolescent modes of other cultures in terms of weight-watching and hair styles. They also pierce their ears and noses and wear rings or earrings. Body tattoos are done to beautify the body and as a group membership symbol. These are done mainly around the arms and palms of the hands.

Male and female circumcision is prevalent in Cameroon. Adolescence is marked by initiation rites, with male circumcisions taking place in traditional settings, although today most families would circumcise their male child immediately after birth. Ninety-three percent of males are circumcised according to 2004 statistics. Lower rates of male circumcision are prevalent among males in the far north (62%), the rural areas (87%), and the nonreligious (77%).

Female circumcision, also known as female genital mutilation (FGM), is a traditional practice that is usually performed primarily on children and adolescents and also on some adult women. Circumcision is undertaken during a special ceremony after which the circumcised are taught how to dance. In effect 1.4% of women are circumcised (L'EDSC-III 2004). It is more common for women between the ages of 20 and 24 to be circumcised among rural populations (2.1%) and populations living in the far north (5.4%), the north (2.2%), and the southwest (2.4%). Uneducated women (4.7%) and Muslim women (5.8%) also engage more in this practice. While some women (including Princess Euphrasia Etta Ojong) think FGM violates the physical and mental rights of the girl and woman, others say it protects the integrity of the woman and is a valuable cultural heritage. It is also seen as having aesthetic, medicinal, and socioeconomic benefits while maintaining the sexual purity of the woman before marriage. The practice is prevalent among the Ejagam people of Mamfe in the southwest province and among the Muslim population in northern province of Cameroon (O. Songe, BBC 2002; Cameroon Princess, BBC 2002).

The Self

Formation of identity in the Cameroonian context is nurtured in shared roles. Developmental tasks impact identity formation and perception of self. Accordingly, a balanced sense of self and one's emerging identity is circumscribed by a sense of place within an extended family that is perceived as part of the community. The values implied in social processes override personal identity, thus reducing crises of self-identity among Cameroonian adolescents. Since the interdependent self is a prevailing construct in non-Western cultures, this construal is characterized by a fundamental connectedness of persons to each other (Oerter, Oerter, Agostiani, Kim, and Wibowo 1996). This principle prevails in the Cameroonian setting, where the interdependent self is viewed not as separated from the social context but as more connected and less differentiated from others. Accordingly, personal identity can be defined within a social group structure. For example, among the Fulanis cultural identity is characterized by dress code and praying models; for Bakwerians, it is excellence in the activities such as hunting, fishing, preparation of traditional food, and the enhancement of physical beauty; among the Kom identity can be measured by the ability to speak the traditional language and age group membership. The identity of adolescents becomes salient because the implicit cultural scripts prescribe that adolescents work on interpersonal relationships within a broader cultural perspective. Defining identity or self through relationships with others makes the individual become aware of the self as determined by obligations and duties toward others and the society. On this account individuals have a responsibility towards each other.

Of necessity, adolescents construct and modify their social identities through successive interpersonal encounters and experiences making up their ontogenetic history. In response to societal expectations, adolescents construct gender and ethnic identities consistent with cultural scripts and gender demands of their worldviews and economic obligations (Nsamenang 2002). Girls are socialized to see marriage, good wifehood, and raising children as self-defining and self-esteeming. Getting married becomes the ultimate ambition for most female adolescents. Boys already begin to see themselves as future family heads.

Adolescents have little time to be alone. Most often adolescents are either with parents at home or in the farms, in the family compound with other siblings and extended family members, with peers at schools and universities, or in the neighborhood. The main activities they engage in outside of school are playing sports such as football and basketball, playing video and computer games, studying with friends, working in cybercafés, singing in choirs, or joining youth organizations focused on activities such as drama or support for illnesses such as HIV/AIDS.

Family Relationships

Adolescents are socialized to consider the family as a unit comprised of people beyond the nuclear family unit. Parenting practices influenced by family type, size, and resource allocation constitute processes of gradual adaptation with parents requiring obedience, yet with much care and love. Many children are not brought up by their biological parents. Such children live and are brought up by either their uncles, aunts, cousins, grandparents, or elder siblings. They take care of these children as they would their own biological children. On this account all children living in such a household share available family resources equally. This communal spirit is a hallmark of family solidarity in children's upbringings, which occurs for various reasons such as poverty, death, problem children, and distance from schools. Parents and all those involved with childrearing inculcate early in children the required ethical values and skills. Skills and behaviors inherent in parental expectations are to ensure cultural continuity (Tchombe and Nsamenang 1999).

Adolescents are expected to immerse themselves in the practical demands of community activities, where they learn through participation rather than preparation. Parents vary patterns of interaction for each child according to their psychological make-up. With gender differentials in chaperonage associated with awareness of girls' sexual vulnerability, their modesty impedes them from educating their children about sexuality.

Adolescents remain close to their parents and warmly engage with family members as much as possible. The amount of time spent with the different family members is a function of the types of family economic engagements and schooling programs. Adolescents, like others, engage in family chores, devotions, and family social events.

Incidence of contentious exchanges between parents and adolescents is visibly connected with problems of participation in family chores, appropriate dress code, and personal hygiene. Related more to late adolescents are conflicts about dating, cohabiting, late nights, alcohol use, and smoking. More intense conflict with girls is about matters related to sex and choice of friends. Adolescents' economic dependence on their families delays physical separation. A major source of conflict is not only the amount of financial allowance allocated but the demand for accountability by parents on how the money has been used. In all of these the demand for autonomy and acceptance without condition becomes another source of conflict.

Siblings constitute the basis for establishing relationships and practicing social values. Usually, adolescents are left with the responsibility for directing and caring for younger siblings. These inter-sibling activities are characterized by helping with homework, bathing, and preparing evening dinners. An emerging sense of interdependence among siblings develops skills for interpersonal relationships and understanding.

In most households there are what we call "house help" or "fictive kin." Some of these would have been with the family from the time most adolescents were born. The house help sees to the hygiene and welfare of the adolescents and is very caring. They are protective of the adolescents with strong bonds. Other members found in the household would be extended family members (such as cousins, grandparents, uncles or aunts, and friends' children). Each one of these persons significantly influences the lives of the adolescents as sources of information and counselling.

The divorce rate, especially among adolescents in the Muslim community, is high and remarriage is very common, though not approved by society. Marriage is a family affair and there are three stages that are usually followed. The first step is the traditional marriage with two levels, beginning with the introductory phase to establish family contact. At this phase the girl's family gives orientations on the conduct of the traditional marriage process. After the fulfillment of all traditional rites, such as payment of dowry for those who request it and giving presents, the girl now becomes the wife of the said family. The second step is the civil marriage in court. The third is the religious marriage for those who respect this tradition. At each stage there are celebrations financed by both families.

Friends and Peers/Youth Culture

Since adolescents spend more time in institutional settings, they are bound to interact more with peers than family as they offer the opportunity to participate in the development of youth culture. This provides the arena for involvement in romantic and sexual relationships (Larson, Wilson, Brown, Furstenberg, and Verma 2002). Time spent with peers (compared to time spent with family or alone) increases adolescents' life experiences through interactions that permit the development of skills for cooperative horizontal relations important to adulthood (Larson, Wilson, and Mortimer 2002). Friends and peer groups are constituted on the basis of age, gender, or neighborhood. Friends are very important in adolescents' lives because they share common goals, ideology, and feelings, and are supportive. Many of the groups are becoming very effective because of the existence of a self-regulatory mechanism within the peer culture. For example there are the "peer group educators" who help educate and control adolescents' sexual behavior in the domain of HIV/AIDS. Others such as "age groups" organize activities that permit the monitoring and control of each other's psychological behavior and when necessary approach elders for effective mentoring to help with group management. Where peer group activities are not positive and too much emotional energy is spent to sustain relationships in such situations, some families address control mechanisms.

Cameroon is greatly known for its sporting activities, especially football (soccer). Group affiliation is seen as a function of love for the same football team. Other sporting activities with peer crowds are basketball and table tennis. The many different great musicians lead to groups with common interests. Older adolescents may sneak into nightclubs when these have shows. Peer crowds are also defined by an involvement in songs and dance, as is the case with those who can dance the *fumban* (female dance) and the *nelng* (male dance) of Kom, also known as ballet. Kom ballet dance is not the conventional Western style of ballet. Rather, Kom ballet is characterized by graceful and very dignified body movements performed during very special traditional celebrations. Females dress differently from males and dance using a rhythm that is soft, gentle, and elegant. The females dance apart from the males. The dressing and rituals that accompany the dance are very rich and colorful.

Other groups are bound by their interest in academic excellence. Their main activities center more on educational activities such as study groups; they search for information and continue discussions on school assignments. Another common interest group is made up of adolescents interested in projecting cultural values through songs, drama, and dance. So peer crowds are formed on the basis of sports and cultural involvement.

Groups that meet and hang out in the streets also exist; they are formed based on common interests. Some focus on business, others on crime. These street children by virtue of their activities can be classified as living "in," "on," or "of" the street. Aptekar (1994) mentioned two categories of street children: those that live at home and work to earn money for their families, and those who live in the streets and support themselves. The existence of these two categories found support with Musoke (1996), who, drawing conclusions from other studies, identified three categories (Peralta 1994):

1. Those children on the streets with their parents, who are handicapped or blind.
2. Those who come to cities, beg, and go home at night.
3. Those who have no relatives and nowhere to sleep.

In summary, Peralta's three categories can be applied to Cameroon as follows: (1) Independent street workers; some of these attend school. They work to help their families and to earn enough money to be able to continue their education. (2) The family street worker; the children in this group work with other family members selling food and other things. These children are part of a family unit working in the street. (3) The most troubled group of children as pointed out by Peralta are the children who are homeless. This group were more likely to admit involvement in illegal work, gang membership, drug abuse, and serving time in institutions.

We observed here that the concept "street children" is used in a more general context to address children and adolescents of schoolgoing age roaming the streets, engaged in income-generating activities including crime.

Even though the choice of friends is made by adolescents themselves, some parents most often would want to have a say, particularly if they suspect the comportment of the friends or groups of friends. Accordingly, parents restrict different-sex friendship during early adolescence but will tolerate this for older adolescents. Restrictions on friendship may occur in situations where two families have land disputes or where certain families and ethnic groups are noted for witchcraft and magical practices. Social class does exist with each class maintaining its psychological distance. However, there is free friendship across linguistic groups and social class.

Many youth organizations exist, based around sports, religious, social, or political activities. Through these activities the role of adolescents in the development of Cameroon is well-defined, and what is most significant are the collective efforts to ensure individual development.

There is a distinct youth culture that is marked off from adult culture by dress, hairstyle, tattooing/piercing, music, and slang. Adolescents are interested in new modes of style and self-expression. Their dress code, music, sports, and other ideals are all the latest fashion of the Euro-American cultures, though they will always return to their own cultural modes, especially during traditional festivals. Tattooing and piercing seem to be coming back in fashion. It is as much an African cultural practice as well as a practice of Euro-American culture. Larson, Wilson, and Mortimer (2002) concluded that cultures in developing countries typically blend elements of the traditional and modern worlds and adolescents attempt to negotiate these worlds.

Love and Sexuality

Larson, Wilson, Brown, Furstenberg, and Verma (2002) pointed out that within the domain of peer interaction, romantic relationships are an important expanding sub-domain of adolescent interpersonal experience. With sex being a taboo subject in most family contexts, the apparent lack of information about it is evident in adolescents' lack of knowledge in understanding of sexuality and its expressions (Tchombe 1994). Yet in Cameroonian society, psychological teachings are gradually taking the place of the taboo. This is more in the rationalization of old attitudes than in dissemination of accurate knowledge. Increasing incidence of adolescent sexuality today can be attributed to lack of knowledge, earlier sexual maturity, increasing mobility (Tchombe 1998), and globalizing sexual values and practices (Nsamenang 2002).

Although physical attraction is the main reason for most cases of romantic relationships among adolescents, the desire for material and/or financial gain closely follows as a motivation for sexual relationships (Temin et al. 1999). By the age of 15 years some adolescents are already having intercourse. A report from the Ministry of Health (1998–2001) illustrated that more girls (26%) than boys (18%) have had sexual intercourse before the age of 15. About 41.1% of adolescents attending school are sexually active (Leke 1998). Leke (1998) postulated that 28% of pregnancies recorded at the Yaounde maternity hospital are among adolescent girls, and adolescent girls are responsible for 20% of all births annually in Cameroon. In a study carried out by Awasum (1991), it was estimated that about 50% of teenage pregnancies occur within the first six months of sexual intercourse, whereas 6.4% of the adolescent girls wish to get pregnant. On this account abortion is widespread among adolescent girls. Leke's study of abortion statistics (1989) in Cameroon showed that adolescents represent half (49.6%) of such cases. Enculturation restricts sexuality to procreate, with both boys and girls encouraged to delay sexuality until they can assume more productive responsibilities (Nsamenang 2002), become emotionally mature, and develop positive attitudes.

Dating is a common practice; even cohabitation is. But cohabitation, though limited, is seriously discouraged because most adolescents are still living at home or in boarding schools. Only adolescents living in hostels may cohabit, even though it is discouraged.

Marriage is a family issue because in the African traditional context you marry into a family not to an individual. Early marriage during adolescence is encouraged only by some ethnic groups (such as Muslim families and girls in rural areas). Early marriages ensure girls' virginity, attract a dowry, allow early insertion in the roles as wife and mother, and avoid the fear of the HIV/AIDS scourge that results from engaging in multiple partnerships and increasing sexual experimentations.

Like adolescents the world over, sexual experimentation starts very early during childhood. In one study, adolescents who had experienced early sex thought it was not real sexual intercourse because they had it standing up and the excitement was too brief (Tchombe 1994). The desire for experimentation is highly provoked because of exposure to sexual stimuli in magazines, television, and movies. Adolescents are least prepared to handle sexual stimulation, and many of the casualties of unwanted pregnancies are the result.

Birth control is not an open topic for discussion as parents see this as encouraging adolescents' promiscuity, though some adolescents are already using condoms and pills. For some condom usage is problematic because it signifies lack of trust and undermines emotional relations. However, a variety of folk remedies (quinine tablets, whisky, and traditional herbs) to prevent pregnancy or induce menstrual flow abound among adolescents (Tchombe 1998; Njikam 1998). The dependency of adolescents and youths on their parents and the desire to pursue their education are the factors leading to increased abortions. However, a certain proportion of boys (18%) and girls (31%) in the age range of 15 to 19 have no knowledge of any birth control measures to protect against HIV/AIDS (Demographiques et Sanitaires 1994–1999). A central communication strategy is used to train adolescent peer educators of both sexes in communication skills with regard to STDs, HIV, and family planning. They work to inform their peers and advocate behavioral changes using educational talks, interpersonal discussions, and youth-produced information.

Precocious sexuality is linked with sexually transmitted diseases (STDs) and HIV, and a majority of Cameroonian adolescents are very aware of this. Various studies with adolescents have shown that in a sample of 200 adolescents, 18% have already contracted an STD (Kaptue 1998). Among them 25% are girls and 75% boys (Kaptue 1998). In Cameroon the total HIV/AIDS adult population of 15 to 49 years was estimated at 12% from 1994 to 1999. During this period the prevalence among youths of 15 to 19 years was estimated at 11.5%, while 20- to 24-year-olds represented 12.2%, well above the national average at the time. A more recent report from Cameroon Demographic and Health Study (2004) revealed that at the national level the prevalence is 5.5% with the following presentations: 15 to 19 years, 1.4%; 20 to 24 years, 5.5%; 25 to 29 years, 7.8%; 30 to 34 years, 8.9%; 35 to 39 years, 8.2%; 40 to 44 years, 5.8%; and 45 to 49 years, 4.7%. From these results it was found out that there are more women (6.8%) with HIV/AIDS than men (4.1%). The prevalence is higher among women of ages 25 to 29 years (10.3%) and men of ages 35 to 39 years (8.6%). Focusing on the statistics related to gender in the age ranges of 15 to 19 (females, 2.2% and males, 0.6%) and 20 to 24 (females, 7.8% and males, 2.5%), it is also evident that there are more female adolescents and youths infested with HIV/AIDS.

Parental attitudes towards adolescents' sexuality are closed since sex is sacred and a taboo subject that must not be handled outside marriage. A source to check in traditional settings to see if an adolescent girl has had intercourse is through the use of an egg (Njikam and Savage 1992). What happens is that when a daughter is suspected for being promiscuous, the mother takes an egg with the rounded end facing her and places the pointed end in the opening of the vagina with the girl laying on her back. Passage will be difficult if the girl has never had intercourse, but the reverse would be the case if she has. What the mother is trying to do is measure the width of the vaginal passage using an egg to find out if it is still intact.

Sex education was and is in some cases handled through initiation rites, chaperones, folklore, and the orientation of adolescents to acceptable sexual behaviors by grandparents through oral tradition (Tchombe 1998). In schools sex education is taught as an integrated topic through other disciplines.

Homosexuality is more common among adults than adolescents. On the whole some adolescents are ignorant of homosexuality, while others are aware of the concept and its practices.

Health Risk Behavior

Though the changing cultural trend has had some positive effects on family life and its functioning, it has led to a breakdown in parental authority, increased urbanization, and abject poverty. This scenario has led more children and adolescents to engage in activities leading to health risk behaviors. Much attention is not usually paid to adolescents' health related issues because it is a period with less mortality and morbidity. In Cameroon teenage pregnancy is the second highest risk factor (22.4%) as around 6% of all pregnancies occur in adolescents aged 16 years or under (Leke 1998). But today with the increasing spread of HIV/AIDS, the percentage of adolescents at risk and dying youth are alarming. Like adolescents everywhere they engage in new discoveries and exploratory behaviors, patterned within adolescence culture.

The abuse of substances is a major contributing factor to mental health. It is normal to observe adolescents in secondary schools in urban towns like Yaounde in groups smoking or drinking alcohol during school hours. Drinking is a highly social activity during adolescence and is expected in a peer context as their social life is organized around drinking sites. With economic constraints in Cameroon, it is quite common to find adolescents hawking and trading along major streets. In addition to inadequate protection by family or society, they lose the opportunity of being formally educated, and while in the streets they are at risk to various forms of health and sociobehavioral problems including drug abuse. More seriously are those taking marijuana and other such drugs that permit them to engage in serious crime activities, such as vandalism, hold-ups, and killing in some cases. Under such conditions they are hired as instruments for destruction.

Adolescents may engage in delinquent acts such as robbery, fights, and use of guns and knives. If they are caught for these infractions, they are taken to the courts as minors. Some are sent to reformatory schools. Statistics drawn from 10 to 18-year-old delinquent adolescents in Yaounde show an increasing trend. In 1999 there were 19 such adolescent cases in courts. In 2000 the number increased to 35 and in 2001 104. In 2002 and 2003, the numbers have moved up to 166 and 185 respectively. With increasing use of drugs and alcohol, the absence of employment and breakdown in family authority, the number of adolescents engaged in crime has increased in recent years.

Car accidents increase to the extent that parents adopt the strategy of registering their adolescents to a formal driving school, as the adolescents with no driving skills steal their parent's car and drive out with friends. The percentage may not be known as parents always manage these incidents at their level to avoid police intervention, except of course in cases of death. Only a few adolescents have died as a result of car accidents in more recent times since they rarely have access to a car. Legally in Cameroon, children can drive, smoke, and drink alcohol from the age of 18 years, but this usually is not respected.

A discussion was held with 96 adolescents for basic information about adolescent suicide; only 1.04% knew of any such incident. But they manifested fear, worry, and pity. Suicide is not common among Cameroonian adolescents, though suicidal behavior is more common at adolescence. Suicide is more a developing world phenomenon because of the sociocultural settings and family relationship mechanisms.

Little to no empirical and theoretical data is available on the topic of depression among adolescents in Cameroon. Yet adolescence as a stage in development is prone to provoking depressed incidences. Depression is associated today with anxiety about the future and the fear of contracting HIV/AIDS or rejection in the professional realm. These are compounded by worries that life goals are not achievable in the face of increasing poverty.

The desire to be slim is a phenomenon of almost all adolescents and can lead to anxiety, eating disorders, and depression. But in traditional African settings, an aspect of initiation rites for girls is to fatten them up. Experiences of acculturation to Western lifestyles tend to increase the prevalence of depression. Pursuing further studies in America or Europe is a phenomenon among adolescents. Some of these adolescents pressure their parents to send them abroad to study, particularly when the courses they are interested in are not offered by state universities.

The main sources of problems related to health risk behaviors are family background and adjustment difficulties that may lead some adolescents to run away from home. There are also school-related problems such as truancy, leading to missing classes and poor performance. Other sources are the engagement in self-destructive behavior like breaking into homes.

Education

Education in Cameroon is generally Eurocentric in its content and approach; consequently, it has not adequately responded to the African thought system and its processes. Traditional education expects that through engagement in everyday activities, the child by the period of adolescence would have completed his or her education, addressing physical, social, intellectual, and practical skills. It ensures adolescents' engagement in activities that would nurture different potentials for sound development. The literacy rate in Cameroon is increasing. The adult literacy rate is 63.4%, with about 70% of adolescents literate and 80% of children in Cameroon attending school.

Cameroon's educational system has two subsystems (English and French), each with its own programs and examination practices and responding to its colonial heritage. English and French are both languages for transmission of knowledge as well as curriculum content materials. Secondary education is offered by the government, lay, private, and religious groups. It is offered in both grammar and technical education structures offering two cycles, including post-primary vocational institutions. Each stage ends with submission to public examinations specific to the subsystem. Secondary education, which is not compulsory, is a seven-year program for first and second cycles, with five years for the first cycle. The schools are coeducational as well as single-sexed, with boarding and day facilities offered at varying degrees.

About 50% of adolescents attend secondary education and 20% attend higher education. At the secondary technical level, there were a total of 146,469 students enrolled with boys (90,493) outnumbering girls (55,976). The success rate showed that girls were leading (38.12%) over boys (32.4%). For the year 2003–2004, there were 1,230 secondary schools, 924 in the Francophone zone and 306 in the Anglophone zone. Secondary school enrolment at this period in both subsystems was 762,053 (406,401 boys and 355,652 girls). Of these figures, 519,259 students were in public school, while 242,794 were in private schools. However, some adolescents are enrolled in primary and postprimary institutions. In effect 35.30% of adolescents (38.8% of boys and 32% of girls) were at first cycle, while 19.8% (22.8% of boys and 17% of girls) were in second cycle. In 2002 and 2003 the pass rates were 23% and 30% respectively. Failure rate remains high at 70%. The pass rate for these levels in the year 2003–2004 was as follows: General Certificate of Education at 58.27% and its French equivalent (BEPC) was 34.90%. The rate for the Probatoire was 37.33%, Bacc 40.26% and GCE advanced level 59.21%. Not many adolescents continue to university, but more students are entering university at adolescence and the participation rate in 2001–2002, in the six state universities indicated an enrollment figure of 71,091 (43,519 boys and 27,572 girls) (source for school statistics: Carte Scolaire du Cameroun Annuaire Statistique 2003–2004).

The closing of the gender gap in terms of access to education is visible, particularly with the increasing awareness of the importance given to girls' education on the international scene. This new trend has had a trickling positive effect on the attitudes of Cameroonian parents towards the education of their daughters.

As concerns performance in international tests of achievement, many Cameroonian adolescents are required to take achievement tests to enable them to have access to foreign universities. A considerable percentage does succeed.

Though Cameroon has many gifted and disabled adolescents, there are no specific programs for gifted adolescents, but there are some institutional structures for the disabled provided more by private venture than by government. However, the Ministry of Social Affairs with help from nongovernmental organizations (NGOs), provides institutional support both for material and human resources.

Work

The family expects the adolescent to participate in household chores and other family engagements as their contribution to the family. Adolescent boys and girls from the Fulani tribes take cattle to the field for grazing as early as 8 a.m. until 2 p.m. daily. This contribution enables them to own their herds of cattle by the age of 17 years. Even though girls stay at home and take care of younger siblings, clean the compound, and wash dishes, they are expected to milk the cows and sell the milk. Equally, in the absence of male siblings and fathers, girls are also expected to take the cattle for grazing. Even adolescent street workers such as park boys, hockers, and porters share the proceeds by paying their fees and those of younger siblings for buying food and medications. Although this may be the case for working-class adolescents in rural towns, in middle-class families other types of engagements are insisted upon. Of course these homes have paid house helps, but parents insist that their adolescents should not leave all the house chores to the house help. They should also clean and wash. So, in the Cameroonian family traditions, each family member, according to his or her ability, contributes to the welfare of the family to a varying degree. Yet striking a balance between academic demands and domestic work puts a lot of stresses on the adolescents.

Many more adolescents are engaged in school than in work because of the value attached to schooling. Work is very scarce for full-time as well as part-time workers. The school enrollment in relation to the youth population in Cameroon highlights the access rate. But these adolescents, given the situation and their upbringing, combine work and school effectively and succeed.

Adolescents are engaged in all types of income generating activities through self-help projects, driving, mechanics, park loaders, car washers, hair dressers, and clerical work. They also work as domestic servants and gardeners.

Working conditions cannot be generalized for these adolescents, because the conditions of work are usually not well determined in some cases as they are usually temporary. There are elements of exploitation, which adolescents tolerate because they need money. In some cases the conditions are good in terms of payment, working hours, and even access to resources for health problems.

Apprenticeships and training within the family are ingrained in the socialization process. Each Cameroonian child by adolescence is well equipped with at least knowledge of a basic skill. On this account at varying degrees, there exists various forms of nonformal education and vocational training for out-of-school youths, school dropouts, and disabled persons in different types of institutions. It takes more than economic growth to underwrite exclusion, unemployment, and poverty (Nsamenang 2002).

Unemployment is a source of social ills, leading to increasing numbers of delinquent adolescents. At present in Cameroon, the employment rate is 79.9% with more adults being employed than adolescents. On this account the employment rate is very low for adolescents; consequently, many adolescents and youths are unemployed. With increasing school enrollment and more youths making the effort to qualify, the urgent challenge facing the Cameroonian government is to create job opportunities.

Media

Cameroon's indigenous culture is threatened by the culture of other countries as television and the computer revolution bring in foreign cultures. Endangered aspects include music, manners of dressing and expression, arts and crafts, as well as cinema. For example, music from Congo or America eclipses Cameroonian music. Also, film from Nigeria stifles all initiative at creating a genuine Cameroon film industry. On this account great effort has to be made to create pure Cameroon culture. The rate of media use by adolescents is higher in urban towns in Cameroon than in rural areas because practically all homes in urban towns do have TV. With TV in public places more adolescents with no home TVs stay out late to watch TV, particularly during various World Cup football games.

From observation, adolescents' leisure time is spent on watching TV for entertainment, playing computer games, and participating in video clubs. Playing video games is restricted because of the cost. They do spend much time at cybercafés, exploring the Internet through chatting, and watching pornographic films. Some do research. Since the reading culture is low, only 1% of adolescents read newspapers, but they read magazines that have love and beauty information. In the case of music, they tune to both foreign and national music channels and are seen carrying radios around. Major acculturation influences from these stimuli encourage behavioral shifts leading to the coexistence of the endogenous and the exogenous influences. To an extent the acculturative and globalizing forces have wrought changes on value foundations and perceptions of Cameroonian adolescents (Nsamenang 2002).

Adolescents are well targeted by media. The different advertisements in terms of different fashions, models and others provide stimulating stimuli that take up much of adolescents' interests. Most adolescents spend valuable hours and money on the Internet searching for all kind of information and watch different types of activities of interest. Vigilant parents control adolescents' access and use of media, and schools with Internet facilities are strict on the programs available for students' use. This control is limited to homes and schools. The cybercafés have no control, given their commercial nature.

Politics and Military

Adolescents in Cameroon are involved in politics, serving more as pressure groups than as political mechanisms. They have served different political parties from early days. Even in the twenty-first century the ruling Cameroon Peoples' Democratic Movement (CPDM) has a youth wing known as YCPDM. They participate greatly in party political activities and rallies when they are organized. Since the voting age is 18 many of the youths do fulfill this civic duty. During the early years of the introduction of multiparty politics, youths were on the forefront of most rallies and were used for reactionary engagements, which were termed as autodefense.

The period from 1990 to 1992 and afterward was turbulent for adolescents because it was the period when multiparty politics was being instituted and there was resistance. Students became involved either through their own will or they were forced to do so. At the university different student groups were created depending on their political interests. Some students supported the government while others the opposition. Different pressure groups were mounted and these youths were caught in a political game they knew nothing about. Growing up became a nightmare because of the exploitations by different political groups. Although these experiences may be behind them, the lessons learned were enormous and some would be more cautious if these occasions were posed in the future. In the first decade of the twenty-first century, more adolescents were being recruited into the army and other such services with a brief training period. Compulsory military service existed for civil servants newly recruited in the public service, but not necessarily for adolescents. This no longer exists for political and economic reasons. More youth are recruited into army through competitive examinations and interviews. Civic Service for Participation in Development encourages and engages youths to be involved in development programs at all levels. Accordingly, community spirit is developed.

Adolescents do engage in volunteer work, community services, and with NGOs helping HIV/AIDS patients, orphanages, and the poor. They offer services by working in areas like the botanical gardens and in research activities with development objectives. The significant outcomes of these free community services have created openings for employment and scholarships for further studies for some youths.

Unique Issues

In the new millennium, Cameroonian adolescents are growing up in rather difficult times, marked by a lack of resources. Many of them go to school or university but do not have the required basic textbooks to ease and facilitate learning. Because of increased poverty of some families, scholarships or book schemes are necessary to enhance schooling opportunities for adolescents. Book schemes can take different models: (1) Schools can be equipped with textbooks that students can borrow, perhaps with a fee, (2) Books can be subsidized so that students can afford to buy and own their books, and (3) The number of books required can be reduced to the very essential.

A legitimate concern for Cameroonian adolescents has been that of job opportunities after schooling. Many youths obtain educational credentials with no idea where to go or what to do. Schooling increases the population of emerging discontented adolescents moving towards delinquency because of frustration. Increased rural-to-urban migration in search of jobs with no assurance of improved life conditions only increases adolescents'

problems. The reverse is sometimes also the case, with urban-to-rural migration due to recession in urban settings. The problems encountered by adolescents in both rural and urban settings are enormous, such as problems related to poor nutrition, negative peer pressure, and health. These youths are the potential adults of the Cameroonian society on whom the burden of socioeconomic and political development of the nation depend. In the absence of sustained psychological balance, there is no way these adolescents can be able to share in the transmission of the treasured cultural values.

To continue to ensure stability among adolescents, parents and the society as a whole should address the once-strong adult authority in maintaining order in children's lives. Among Cameroonian families, power structures are changing, with fathers in particular losing their authority over the family. Many more mothers are working outside the home, and the effect on family life and mothers' own psychological well-being has been enormous. But breakdowns in family authority structures lead to breakdowns in society, and a weakening of the power of values that have continuously provided psychological balance for Cameroonian adolescents. These values are being eroded with foreign influence, creating confusion in the minds of the emerging youth on what constitutes acceptable norms of behavior. These growing youths need more preparation to face challenges of a new environment, the absence of which is contributing to an increased proportion of adolescents being translated into high health risk behaviors and other social ills. Sex education has to be removed from its taboo domain and be addressed by all responsible persons.

The absence of visible structures to provide for Cameroonian gifted adolescents poses a problem. There is need for new orientations and attitudes change, whereby new perceptions about adolescents with unique needs, capabilities, or goals—such as gifted adolescents or disabled adolescents—would permit the institution of modern programs for better growth and development.

THERESE MUNGAH TCHOMBE

References and Further Reading

Aptekar, L. 1994. Research on street children: Some conceptual and methodological issues. *ISSBD Newsletter* 1(25).

Barthelemy, K. D. 1998. Emerging patterns in adolescent sexuality, fertility and reproductive health in Africa. In *Sexuality and reproductive health during adolescence in Africa*. K. D. Barthelemy (ed.). pp. 15–35. Ottawa: University of Ottawa Press.

Carte Scolaire du Cameroun Annuaire Statistique. 2003–2004.

Central Bureau of Census and Population Studies. 2004. Statistics of Employment in Cameroon.

Country Guide. 2001. Dominique Auzias and Associese.

Durkin, K. 1995. *Developmental social psychology: From infancy to old age*, Cambridge, Mass.: Blackwell.

Enquete Demographiques et Sanitaires. 1994–1999.

Enquete Demographique et de Sante. 2004. Rapport Preliminaire, National Commission for the fight against HIV/AIDS and the Ministry of Health. Institute National de la Statistique Yaounde, Cameroun.

Kaptue, L. 1998. Adolescents and HIV/AIDS. In *Sexuality and reproductive health during adolescence in Africa*. K. D. Barthelemy (ed.). pp. 261–69. Ottawa: University of Ottawa Press.

Larson, R. W., S. Wilson, B. B. Brown, F. F. Furstenberg, Jr., and S. Verma (eds.). 2002. Changes in adolescents' interpersonal experiences: Are they being prepared for adult relationships in the twenty-first century? In *Adolescents' preparation for the future: Perils and promise. A report of study group on adolescence in the twenty-first century*. R. W. Larson, B. B. Brown, and J. T. Mortimer (eds.). Society for Research on Adolescence.

Larson, R. W., S. Wilson, J. T. Mortimer. 2002. Conclusion: Adolescents' preparation for the future. In *Adolescents' preparation for the future: Perils and promise. A report of study group on adolescence in the twenty-first century*. R. W. Larson, B. B. Brown, and J. T. Mortimer (eds.). Society for Research on Adolescence.

Leke, R. J. I. 1989. Commentary on unwanted pregnancy and abortion complications in Cameroon. *International Journal of Gynaecology and Obstetrics* 3:supplement.

Leke, R. J. I. 1998. Reproductive health of adolescents in sub-Saharan. In *Sexuality and reproductive health during adolescence in Africa*. K. D. Barthelemy (ed.). pp. 255–60. Ottawa: University of Ottawa Press.

Ministry of Health. 1998–2001. Enquete sur la population et la sante.

Ministry of Higher Education. 2002. *Statistical year book of higher education*.

Njikam, O. M. 1998. Adolescents' beliefs and perceptions toward sexuality in urban Cameroon. In *Sexuality and reproductive health during adolescence in Africa*. K. D. Barthelemy (ed.). pp. 77–90. Ottawa: University of Ottawa Press.

Nsamenang, A. Bame. 1992. *Human development in cultural context: A Third World perspective*. London: Sage.

Nsamenang, A. B. 2002. Adolescence in sub-Saharan Africa. An image constructed from Africa's triple inheritance. In *The world's youth adolescence in eight regions of the globe*. B. Bradford Brown, W. Reed, W. Larson, and T. S. Saraswathi (eds.). pp. 261–304. Cambridge: Cambridge University Press.

Oerter, R., A. H. O. Kim, and S. Wibowo. 1996. The concept of human nature in East Asia: Etic and emic characteristics. *Journal of Culture & Psychology* 2:9–51.

Omer Songe. 2002. Africa. Drama changes attitudes towards genital mutilation. Cameroon Princess fights female genital mutilation Africa. BBC.

Peralta, F. 1994. Street children of Mexico. *ISSBD Newsletter*.

Tchombe, T. M. 1998. School-based approach to adolescent sexuality and reproductive health. In *Sexuality and reproductive health during adolescence in Africa*. K. D. Barthelemy (ed.). pp. 301–19. Ottawa: University of Ottawa Press.

Tchombe, T. M., and Nsamenang, A. B. 1999. The psychological value of education in preparing the adolescent for living in Cameroon: A longitudinal study financed by Jacobs Foundation.

Temin, M. J., F. E. Okonofua, F. O. Omorodion, et al. 1999. Perceptions of sexual behaviour and knowledge about sexually transmitted diseases among adolescents in Benin City Nigeria. *International Family Planning Perspectives* 25:186–190, 195.

Turnbull, C. 1978. *Man in Africa*. London: Penguin.

UNAIDS. 2002. HIV/AIDS in Cameroon. In *Report on the global HIV/AIDS epidemic*. San Francisco: University of California San Francisco School of Medicine.

UNAIDS/WHO. 2002. A fact sheet for HIV/AIDS in Cameroon.

World Guide. 1997–1998. Courtesy of Internationalist.

CANADA

Background Information

Canada is located in North America north of the United States, and borders the North Atlantic, North Pacific, and Arctic Oceans. It is the second largest country in the world, with an area of 9,984,670 square kilometers, and consists of ten provinces and three territories (*World Factbook* 2004). The capital city is Ottawa. Canada's population exceeds 31.5 million and is 50% male and 50% female. About 12% of individuals are 0 to 9 years of age, 20% are 10 to 24 years, 55% are 25 to 64 years, and 13% are 65 years or older (Statistics Canada 2004a). In the 2001 census, 39% of people identified their ethnic origin as Canadian, with the majority of others reporting that they were of British Isles, French, other European, or aboriginal (North American Indian, Metis, Inuit) origin. Immigrants make up over 18% of the total population (Statistics Canada 2004e). Canada's two official languages are English and French. Christianity is the dominant religion, with 44% of people identifying as Roman Catholic and 29% as Protestant (Statistics Canada 2004e). Canada has a parliamentary democratic government system. It obtained independence from the United Kingdom on July 1, 1867, but remains connected to the British Crown. Canadians celebrate Canada Day on July 1. Economically, Canada is a highly technological country that became mostly industrial and urban following growth in manufacturing, mining, and service sectors after World War II (*World Factbook* 2004).

Period of Adolescence

There are over six million youths in Canada between the ages of 10 and 24 years (49% girls, 51% boys). They are equally distributed among three age groups: 10 to 14 years, 15 to 19 years, and 20 to 24 years (Statistics Canada 2004a). Within the population of 15- to 24-year-olds, about 4% identify their ethnic origin as Aboriginal and about 12% are immigrants (Statistics Canada 2003, 2004c). Approximately 64% of young people list their mother tongue as English, 21% list French, and 9% list one of Canada's official languages (either English or French) and one nonofficial language (Statistics Canada 2002a). The period of adolescence is recognized as a unique developmental stage in Canada, as is indicated by various national studies of youths (Canadian Youth, Sexual Health and HIV/AIDS Study, Youth in Transition Survey). The onset of adolescence may be marked by one's chronological age (typically 12 or 13 years) or physical and social changes, such as pubertal development (typically between 11 and 13 years), or the transition from elementary school to secondary school (often after grade five). Markers of the end of adolescence are less well defined, and may include a school-to-work transition, the attainment of legal adult status (age 18), or specific characteristics, such as accepting responsibility for one's actions (Cheah and Nelson 2004; Tilton-Weaver, Vitunski, and Galambos 2001). While the length of this developmental period is difficult to estimate, as it may be short for some (ages 12 to 18) or considerably longer for others (ages 10 to 24), a lengthier adolescent period for many of today's youths is related to larger demographic trends, including a longer period living with parents, and a later age at completion of education, first marriage, and parenthood (Beaujot 2004).

What do Canadian adolescents view as salient markers of adulthood? In a study of 12-year-olds and 15-year-olds, the majority of adolescents described one of two images of being "grown up." The first image, labeled genuine maturity (49%), depicted majority cultural standards of both behavioral and psychosocial maturity (being independent and responsible); and the second image, labeled a focus on privileges (25%), involved engaging in adult behaviors (such as smoking or drinking) without the psychological maturity of adults (Tilton-Weaver et al. 2001). Older adolescents were more likely to describe genuine maturity, whereas girls were more likely to describe a focus on privileges (Tilton-Weaver et al. 2001).

Youths' ideas of adulthood are also linked to identification with their culture. In a university sample, aboriginal students defined adulthood using criteria that reflect their own culture as well as criteria that are used in other cultures, and they were more likely than European Canadian students to believe that they had reached adulthood (Cheah and Nelson 2004). Further, aboriginal students' higher level of identification with aboriginal traditions was related to higher importance of specific criteria for adulthood, such as less alcohol use, earlier achievement of specific criteria for adulthood such as having a family, and higher importance of religious beliefs and future obligations to parents (Cheah and Nelson 2004).

Beliefs

Overall, youths in Canada are more individualist than collectivist in their values and views. They highly value having freedom and choices, and they believe that they have a key role in determining the course of their future (Bibby 2001). Nevertheless, they also value connections to others, specifically friendship and being loved. These latter values are particularly important to girls, and perceptions of mattering to others are related to youths' sense of purpose in life and relatedness to family and friends (Bibby 2001; Marshall 2001). In addition, adolescents value honesty and humor, although more girls than boys view honesty as very important (Bibby 2001). In terms of religious beliefs, the majority of adolescents (76%) report a religious affiliation, although substantially fewer (22%) attend a religious organization weekly. However, many youths (43%) are open to greater involvement with religious groups, and the majority (85% to 90%) anticipate turning to religious groups for ceremonies when they encounter specific rites of passage (such as marriage). In addition, 75% of teens believe in God, 78% believe in life after death, and 55% of girls and 40% of boys report having spiritual needs (Bibby 2001). Having religious doubts or commitments has been associated with various aspects of youths' development. For example, at age 17 or 18, adolescents, on average, report mild but stable religious doubts, and religious doubting is related to less personal religiousness, an inclination to consult antireligious information sources, moratorium and diffuse identity statuses, less family cohesion, and less parental warmth (Hunsberger, Pratt, and Pancer 2001, 2002). There is mixed evidence for a link between religious doubts and poorer personal adjustment. However, a study of teenagers attending grades nine through twelve in Catholic high schools found that religious commitment is related to prosocial values which promote social adjustment and, in turn, personal adjustment. This pattern of relationships was stronger for boys than girls (Schludermann, Schludermann, and Huynh 2000).

The meaning and importance of spirituality for youths' mental health has also been considered. A focus group study with adolescents 14 to 18 years old found that adolescent ideas about spirituality are diverse and contrast with adult definitions. Specifically, the teenagers indicated that spirituality and religion are not synonymous or mutually exclusive, and that spirituality is more fluid and universal than religion (Sveidqvist, Joubert, Greene, and Manion 2003). In addition, they perceive spirituality as an individual's personal philosophy or approach to life and a part of one's identity. While spirituality is usually a positive aspect of one's self, it is negative when it is dictated, manipulated, or taken to extremes. Related to this view, spirituality is positive and potentially beneficial to mental health to the extent that it provides an individual with a sense of purpose, support, or security and peace. In contrast, a lack of spirituality may be a risk to one's mental health. Finally, the teenagers stated that spiritual experiences are essentially private and individual, and that fear of judgment is the main barrier to youths' spiritual exploration and expression (Sveidqvist et al. 2003).

The Self

Canadian youths' identity and moral development during adolescence and how these aspects of self are related to teenagers' behavior and adjustment have been evaluated. For example, a study of identity styles and markers of maladjustment in youths 12 to 19 years found that a diffuse-avoidance identity style, characterized by procrastination and an avoidance of decision-making, was linked to adolescents' reports of higher levels of conduct problems and hyperactivity (Adams et al. 2001). In contrast, a normative identity style, characterized by conforming to the expectations of significant others, or an informational identity style, characterized by actively seeking out and selectively using relevant information, appeared to reduce the risk for behavioral difficulties. The authors reported few age or gender differences in these patterns (Adams et al. 2001).

The cultural context in which identity development occurs is also important when assessing links to adolescents' sense of self and their behavior and adjustment. A program of research on identity development has documented that aboriginal and non-aboriginal youths (12 to 20 years) prefer to use different strategies to think about personal persistence (that is, a need to change *and* a need to stay the same within one's sense of self, and to tie together the past, present, and future) (Chandler,

Lalonde, Sokol, and Hallett 2003). Aboriginal youths' choice of narrative strategies, which focus on changes across time and connections linking these changes, and non-aboriginal youths' choice of essentialist strategies, which marginalize change and keep a part of one's self separate from change over time, are strongly related to their culture of origin, and not to their age, gender, linguistic ability, or ethnic identification. Further, adolescents who are not able to develop and sustain a sense of personal persistence, and therefore do not see themselves as continuous in time, appear to be at increased risk for suicide. In addition to personal continuity, cultural continuity is also important. While youth suicide rates are very high in aboriginal communities that have not met various standards of self-determination, substantially lower rates and even no cases are found in aboriginal communities that are preserving and promoting their culture (Chandler et al. 2003).

Acculturation experiences also contribute to immigrant youths' identity development and adjustment. For young adolescents in immigrant Chinese-Canadian families, affiliations with the Canadian and the Chinese cultures develop independently rather than in a linear fashion (Costigan and Su 2004). Among foreign-born youths, greater involvement in Canadian culture does not interfere with maintaining their ethnic identity and traditional values, and among Canadian-born youths, this involvement appears to encourage acceptance of ethnic identity and traditional values. While most immigrant teenagers show a remarkable ability to adapt to their new country, many do find it difficult to feel totally accepted as Canadians, especially at school (Canadian Council on Social Development 2000).

One key challenge for these youths is learning the English language. In an adolescent sample of Chinese Canadians (12 to 19 years), poorer English reading ability and a lower social class status predicted acculturative stress whereas younger age at arrival in Canada, longer length of stay, higher social class status, and better English reading ability predicted acculturation (Kuo and Roysircar 2004).

Moral development during adolescence has also received empirical attention. Research with Canadian youths suggests that interaction styles with parents and same-sex friends are related to the rate of moral reasoning over four years, across early adolescence and mid-adolescence, but influence development in different ways (Walker, Hennig, and Krettenauer 2000). Parents and friends both promote higher rates of moral reasoning

development by engaging in representational interactions (such as eliciting opinions and checking for understanding), and lower rates through highly informative interactions. In contrast, interfering interactions by parents are linked to minimal moral development, but to moral growth when enacted by friends. In addition, supportive interactions by friends predicted moral growth when combined with representational interactions, but not when combined with informative interactions (Walker et al. 2000). Canadian high school students' endorsement of explicit moral values as ideals for self at age 17 and again two years later has been related to their concurrent involvement in community activities.

However, it is adolescents' community involvement, especially participation in helping activities, that appears to foster their subsequent endorsement of positive moral values, especially those of kindness and caring, rather than the reverse (Pratt, Hunsberger, Pancer, and Alisat 2003). While emerging adults who demonstrate exemplary moral commitments towards social organizations are more advanced in their moral reasoning, it is their more advanced faith and identity development and their agreeableness that distinguishes them from comparison individuals (Matsuba and Walker 2004).

Family Relationships

Based on the 2001 census, over 90% of youths 10 to 19 years are living with one or both parents. Over 70% of these adolescents reside in a two-parent family (12% of which are remarried families), and about 20% are in a single-parent family (80% of which are headed by mothers). In contrast, 56% of 20- to 24-year-olds live with one or both parents (Statistics Canada 2004b). Aboriginal and immigrant youths are more likely than other youths to live with members of their extended family (Statistics Canada 2002b). A recent study of 11-13-, and 15-year-olds indicated that most adolescents have a happy home life. They report that their parents trust them, and that they value what their parents think of them (Boyce 2004). However, some youths (more boys than girls) also feel that their parents expect too much of them, especially with respect to school. In addition adolescents view multiple extended family members as significant in their lives, more often their maternal than paternal grandparents. Although they see these family members infrequently (on average every two months), they look to them for affection and companionship (Claes, Lacourse, Bouchard, and Luckow 2001).

As in many other countries, several studies of Canadian adolescents and their families have focused on two topics: parenting style and parent-adolescent conflict. Consistent with previous research linking authoritative parenting and healthy adolescent development, youths' perceptions of an authoritative parenting style are associated with their openness and responsiveness to parental influence on decisions, higher parent-adolescent congruence on moral and nonmoral values (both warmth and strictness components of authoritativeness contributed), and identity achievement and foreclosure (Mackey, Arnold, and Pratt 2001; Pratt et al. 2003). Further, teenagers' reports of authoritative parenting are linked to various aspects of their development as emerging adults, such as higher levels of care reasoning, higher self-esteem, fewer depressive symptoms, and more years of postsecondary education (Jackson, Pratt, Hunsberger, and Pancer, in press; Pratt, Skoe, and Arnold 2004).

In addition, processes linking authoritative parenting and youth development are emerging. For example, a relationship between parental strictness, but not parental responsiveness, and boys' moral self-ideals was mediated over time by perceived parental moral ideals and perceived peer moral ideals (Pratt et al. 2003). Similarly, the above-mentioned associations between authoritative parenting and higher self-esteem and fewer depressive symptoms, respectively, were mediated over time by youths' level of optimism (Jackson et al., in press).

Turning to parent-adolescent conflict, one study with high school students (grades nine through twelve) found that 40% of adolescents reported arguments with parents at least once per week, and 15% reported arguments with parents every day. The most common areas of conflict between teens and parents were chores at home, school, parents' reactions to the way youths talk to them, concerns about safety (such as driving), and teens questioning parents' authority (Bibby 2001). However, assessing parent-adolescent conflict from both participants' perspectives is critical, since parents' and youths' views on these interactions may differ. Research with young adolescents shows that parents and their children may disagree on what occurred during conflicts, with parents reporting more use of reasoning than their children perceive, and adolescents reporting parents' use of more verbal aggression than parents report (Rinaldi and Howe 2003). Parent-adolescent differences in conversational style may contribute to these diverse perspectives. Adolescents (12 to 15 years) use a high involvement conversational style with their parents, involving more frequent interruptions and overlaps between turns and more simultaneous speech, whereas parents use a high considerateness style, characterized by fewer interruptions and overlaps and less simultaneous speech. These differences in conversational styles and parents' rates of disgust expressions are related to adolescents' rates of disgust expressions, which, in turn, predict adolescents', but not parents', perceptions of parent-adolescent conflict (Beaumont and Wagner 2004).

Conflicts between parents and adolescents in immigrant families have also been evaluated. Overall, there are frequent, but low intensity, disagreements between parents and young adolescents in immigrant Chinese families. Fathers report more intense conflicts with daughters, mothers report more intense conflicts with sons, and youths report similar levels of conflict intensity for their mothers and fathers (Dokis, Costigan, and Chia 2002). Greater discrepancies between parents and youths on traditional cultural values are linked to more areas of conflict with fathers and more intense conflicts with mothers. However, parent-adolescent differences in behavior, such as an adolescent not speaking his/her parents' native language, do not negatively affect the relationship (Costigan and Dokis 2004; Dokis et al. 2002). During midadolescence, disagreements between parents and their children in Asian families in Canada often occur over decision-making roles in the family (such as parental authority, children's rights), yet the families are cohesive and parents and teenagers share similar views about family obligations (Kwak and Berry 2001).

In addition to parent-adolescent interactions, sibling relationships have also received empirical attention. This research indicates that during early adolescence, youths disclose more frequently to their closest-in-age siblings than to friends or parents, and they are equally likely to discuss family, friendship, and academic issues (Howe, Aquan-Assee, Bukowski, Rinaldi, and Lehoux 2000). In addition, disclosure to siblings is more likely when adolescents perceive their sibling relationships as warm, and less likely when they do not trust their siblings or expect to receive emotional support from them. However, disclosure is not related to emotional understanding, frequency of conflict, or interaction styles (reciprocal or complementary) between siblings (Howe, Aquan-Assee, Bukowski, Lehoux, and Rinaldi 2001; Howe et al. 2000).

How are sibling relationships affected by family transitions, such as parental divorce? One study of young adolescents suggests that as negative emotional responses to their parents' divorce increase so do negative issues of status and power between the siblings. Further, youths' perceptions of which parent is to blame for the divorce are also related to their sibling relationships, with maternal blame being linked to increased conflict between siblings and paternal blame being linked to sibling rivalry (Jennings and Howe 2001). However, the majority of older adolescents and emerging adults (17 to 24 years) who experienced their parents' divorce before age 15 report that the divorce brought them closer to their sibling (Bush and Ehrenberg 2003). This closeness may develop as a result of various situations, including being alone in the house with their sibling because of the custodial parent's need to work, the siblings' need to transition between two homes, a new understanding between siblings, or their perception of their sibling as the only person to whom they could turn. While some youths may experience increased conflict with siblings related to feelings of insecurity and confusion during the divorce crisis, this conflict appears to have no lasting impact on their relationship. Only a small number (10%) indicate that the divorce has had a lasting negative impact on their sibling relationship (Bush and Ehrenberg 2003).

Friends and Peers/Youth Culture

Friends play a central role in the lives of Canadian adolescents. Friendship tops the list of things that teenagers value, time with friends is a common source of enjoyment among youths, and it is their friends to whom many adolescents turn when they have problems (Bibby 2001). Boys and girls have at least two or three close same-sex friends across adolescence (Bibby 2001; Boyce 2004; Rotenberg et al. 2004). In contrast, the proportion of boys who have three or more close opposite-sex friends varies by grade level (ranging from 55% in grade six to 70% in grade nine), whereas the proportion of girls is relatively stable (62% to 66%) (Boyce 2004).

Research has explored how adolescents' individual characteristics are associated with various aspects of their friendships. For example, among young adolescents, trustworthiness, as reported by peers, has been related to the number of friendships they have concurrently and across time and to peer preferences (Rotenberg et al. 2004). Personality characteristics, such as communion (closeness) and agency (individuation), have also been linked to young adolescents' friendship needs (Zarbatany, Conley, and Pepper 2004). In addition, an allocentric (collectivist) value orientation has

been associated with more social support from peers and with greater intimacy and companionship in significant relationships (Dayan, Doyle, and Markiewicz 2001).

Friends' behavior toward each other is also important to the quality of adolescent friendships. Teenagers who are more responsive and express more positive affect toward a friend report a more positive friendship quality, and those who are more critical and express negative affect verbally and nonverbally report a more negative friendship quality. A friend's negative behavior toward an adolescent (initiated conflict) is also related to the adolescent's perceptions of a more negative friendship quality. There were no gender differences in these relationships, although girls rated their friendship quality more positively and less negatively than boys, and showed more positive and less negative behavior with friends than boys (Brendgen, Markiewicz, Doyle, and Bukowski 2001).

Youths' association with deviant friends is another aspect of peer relations that has been evaluated. Young adolescents' friendships with deviant peers are related to their behavioral and emotional adjustment, specifically, their involvement in delinquency and more depressive symptoms (Brendgen, Vitaro, and Bukowski 2000a). Longitudinal research indicates that youths' individual characteristics may set the stage for these links, in that their attitudes toward delinquent behavior predict stability/change in their affiliations with delinquent and nondelinquent friends across time, which, in turn, predict subsequent delinquent behavior. Adolescents who consistently affiliate with deviant peers over time and those who change from nondelinquent to delinquent friends show the highest levels of delinquency one year later (Brendgen, Vitaro, and Bukowski 2000b). However, parental behaviors when youths associate with deviant peers may alter the course of this trajectory. Parents' use of monitoring and behavioral control reduces their teenagers' involvement with deviant peers and delinquency, respectively (Brendgen et al. 2000b; Galambos, Barker, and Almeida 2003).

Another important dimension of teenagers' peer relationships is dating. About 20% of young adolescents in Canada report that they are currently in a romantic relationship (Connolly, Craig, Goldberg, and Pepler 2004; Doyle, Brendgen, Markiewicz, and Kamkar 2003). The transition to dating occurs as a sequential progression from same-sex friendships to mixed-sex friendships to romantic involvement with a partner (Connolly et al. 2004; Connolly, Furman, and Konarski 2000). Boys and girls are similar in their romantic activities and in the sequencing of these activities. Asian-Canadian adolescents report less mixed-sex affiliation and less interest and involvement in romantic activities than European-Canadian and Caribbean-Canadian adolescents (Connolly et al. 2004). The characteristics of youths' romantic relationships and their impact on adjustment are also linked to peer and family relationships. For example, young adolescents' involvement in dating is related to lower self-esteem and higher antisocial behavior among those with low social acceptance among same-sex peers (Brendgen, Vitaro, Doyle, Markiewicz, and Bukowski 2002). Similarly, dating is associated with lower self-esteem among young girls who report higher marital conflict at home, and with more depressive symptoms among those who report authoritarian parenting. Girls who are not dating steadily and have secure attachments to their mothers have higher grades (Doyle et al. 2003). Given that young adolescents' dating relationships typically last from two to six months (Connolly et al. 2004; Doyle et al. 2003), romantic break-ups are a common experience. Although they are usually distressed immediately following this event, most youths ultimately attribute the break-up to their own unmet needs and view it as a learning experience (Connolly and McIsaac 2004; Drolet, Lafleur, and Trottier 2000).

Peer experiences during adolescence may also involve aggressive behavior, including bullying and sexual harassment. About 24% of boys and 19% of girls in grades six to ten report that they have bullied others but have not been victimized (Boyce 2004). Very similar proportions of boys and girls have been victimized but have not bullied others, or have been both bullies and victims. These experiences peak for girls in grade eight and for boys in grade ten. More girls are teased or have rumors spread about them whereas more boys are physically victimized (Boyce 2004). Sexual harassment is also common during adolescence. Although more boys than girls report perpetrating unwanted sexual attention (36% vs. 21%, respectively), similar proportions of boys and girls report being victimized (42% and 38%, respectively) (Boyce 2004; McMaster, Connolly, Pepler, and Craig 2002). It also appears that cross-sex harassment, which is perpetrated and experienced by more girls, is distinct from same-sex harassment, which is perpetrated and experienced by more boys. Specifically, cross-sex harassment increases in frequency across grades six to eight, and is linked to pubertal development and participation in mixed-sex peer groups, whereas same-sex harassment is not (McMaster et al. 2002).

Aggression may also occur in adolescents' dating relationships. Psychological, physical, and sexual violence have all been reported in this context. Among boys, 41% report having used psychologically abusive behaviors in their dating relationships, 24% report having used physical violence, and 18% report having used both psychologically and physically abusive behaviors (Brendgen, Vitaro, Tremblay, and Wanner 2002; Lavoie et al. 2002). In comparison, 22% of girls and 12% of boys report having had an upsetting psychologically and/or physically abusive experience, and 19% of girls and 4% of boys report having had an upsetting sexually coercive experience (Price et al. 2000). Although girls view physical and sexual aggression as more serious than boys, many girls do not leave violent relationships because of their desire for a dating partner, the social status that dating brings, and the risk to their reputations if they go (Artz 2000; Banister et al. 2003; Hilton, Harris, and Rice 2002). Youths attribute dating violence to individual and contextual factors, such as jealousy, boys' need for power, alcohol and drug abuse, communication problems between the partners, and violent peers (Banister, Jakubec, and Stein 2003; Lavoie, Robitaille, and Hébert 2000). Longitudinal research suggests that harsh parenting practices, parent-to-child aggression, low parental warmth and caregiving, and affiliation with aggressive friends is linked to boys' subsequent use of physical violence in dating relationships (Brendgen, Vitaro, Tremblay, and Lavoie 2001; Brendgen, Vitaro, Tremblay, and Wanner 2002; Lavoie et al. 2002). The impact of these earlier negative experiences on boys' attitudes toward violence and sensitivity to rejection are two pathways to this behavior (Brendgen et al. 2002). Adolescents have indicated that they want specific skills to help them develop healthy relationships (Price et al. 2000), and teacher- and youth-led programs have been developed to address this need (several are Making Waves (www.mwaves.org); STOP (www.meq.gouv.qc.ca/condfem/publications.htm); The Fourth R (www.thefourthr.ca)).

Love and Sexuality

Significant proportions of youths (and similar proportions of boys and girls) have engaged in preliminary sexual activities at least once. According to a national study of adolescents in grades seven, nine, and eleven, 66% of grade nine students and over 80% of grade eleven students have participated in deep kissing, and 55% of grade nine students and 75% of grade eleven students have engaged in touching below the waist (Boyce, Doherty, MacKinnon, and Fortin 2003). Although fewer grade seven students report these behaviors, more boys than girls are having these experiences. About 30% of grade nine students and over 50% of grade eleven students have had oral sex. Finally, about 20% of grade nine students and 43% of grade eleven students have had vaginal sexual intercourse (Boyce et al. 2003). Rates of 32% and 53% for sexual intercourse have been reported elsewhere by grade ten and grade twelve students, respectively (Hampton, Jeffery, Smith, and McWatters 2001). While grade seven students in the national study were not asked about sexual intercourse, other studies indicate that about 10% of young adolescents have had intercourse (Byers et al. 2001; Doyle et al. 2003).

As the data above suggest, the median age of first intercourse for both girls and boys is 17 years (Hampton et al. 2001; Maticka-Tyndale 2001). Teenagers' reasons for having sexual intercourse most frequently include "love for the person," which was chosen by more girls, and "curiosity/experimentation," which was chosen by more boys (Boyce et al. 2003). Adolescent girls have identified several factors that are related to first intercourse at or before age 15, including self-reported delinquency, higher family adversity, not living with both parents, more liberal attitudes about sex, younger age at first menstruation, and perceiving contraceptive methods as complicated (Langille and Curtis 2002; Tremblay and Frigon 2004). Girls who attend church more frequently and have fathers with more education are less likely to have had intercourse by this age (Langille and Curtis 2002).

More sexually active adolescents are using contraceptive methods. About 65% of these teenagers report using a condom the last time they had sexual intercourse (Boyce 2004; Byers et al. 2001; McCreary Centre Society 2004). While condoms are used more frequently at younger ages, as adolescents get older, the birth control pill becomes a preferred contraceptive method (Boyce et al. 2003; Hampton et al. 2001; McCreary Centre Society 2004). Although this practice places girls at increased risk for health problems as a result of sexually transmitted infections (STIs), Canadian youths are more concerned about pregnancy as an undesired consequence of sexual intercourse than they are about contracting HIV or other STIs. However, neither of these potentially negative health outcomes are major reasons for abstaining from sex (the most common reasons are "not ready" for girls and "have not had the opportunity" for boys) (Boyce et al. 2003). Inconsistent or no

condom use has been related to adolescents not expecting to have sex, their belief that they have a faithful partner, self-reported delinquency, and they or their partner not feeling comfortable using condoms (Boyce et al. 2003; Tremblay and Frigon 2004).

Given that approximately 25% of sexually active adolescents use either withdrawal or no birth control (Boyce 2004; McCreary Centre Society 2004), and that other teens do not use contraceptive methods consistently, it is not surprising that youths, especially girls, are at high risk for contracting STIs. Girls 15 to 19 years have the highest rates of STIs of any age group in Canada, accounting for 40% of all cases of chlamydia and 41% of all cases of gonorrhea reported in 2000 (Public Health Agency of Canada 2004). These rates are significantly higher than those for boys (six times higher for chlamydia and two times higher for gonorrhea). As of June 2003, there were 649 cases of AIDS among adolescents and young adults aged 10 to 24 years in Canada, accounting for 3.4% of all AIDS cases (Public Health Agency of Canada 2004). Sixty-one percent of the 93 cases in 10- to 19-year-olds were attributed to being recipients of blood/blood products, whereas 51% of the 556 cases among 20- to 24-year-olds were attributed to men having sex with men, and another 20% to heterosexual contact. The major source of HIV infection in young people is involvement in risk behaviors, such as unprotected intercourse and sex with multiple partners (Public Health Agency of Canada 2004). While most adolescents are knowledgeable about how HIV/AIDS is transmitted, they are less sure about how to protect themselves, and 64% of grade nine students and 43% of grade eleven students believe there is a vaccine to prevent HIV/AIDS (Boyce et al. 2003).

Pregnancy is another potential consequence of inconsistent or no use of contraception during intercourse. Approximately 6% of adolescents in school (grades seven through twelve) have ever been pregnant or caused a pregnancy (Boyce et al. 2003; McCreary Centre Society 2004). The likelihood of a pregnancy increases substantially among youths who have intercourse with multiple partners (Boyce et al. 2003). According to Statistics Canada (2004e), in 2001, there were 541 pregnancies among 14-year-olds (2.7 per 1,000) 12,383 pregnancies among 15- to 17-year-olds (20 per 1,000), and 24,666 pregnancies among 18- to 19-year-olds (60 per 1,000). The vast majority of these pregnancies lead to either an abortion (16.5 per 1,000) or to a live birth (13.5 per 1,000) (Statistics Canada 2004). In addition to individual factors, community level factors are also associated with teenage pregnancy. In one study, the probability of pregnancy between ages 15 and 20 was higher in communities where there was a higher proportion of single-parent families, a larger black or native population, and a higher rate of female labor force participation, and lower in communities with higher levels of education and a high proportion of individuals with a religious affiliation (Langille, Flowerdew, and Andreou, in press).

Because of the various negative consequences that can result from sexual intercourse, it is important for sexually active youths to have knowledge and skills to protect themselves and their partners. It is also important that they be aware of ways in which they can promote their sexual health (Health Canada 2003). School serves as an important source of sexual health information (Boyce et al. 2003). Although all Canadian provinces and territories mandate that schools provide sexual health education (SHE), the implementation of this directive is variable. Research with adolescents (grades six through twelve) about their attitudes toward and experiences with SHE at school and at home has indicated that most students are in favor of SHE at school, and the majority agree that parents and schools should share this responsibility (Byers et al. 2003a, 2003b). They also think that SHE should cover a wide range of topics and that most topics should be covered by the end of grade eight. Many students report that the sexual health topics in which they are most interested are not covered, and that they need more factual information and practical skills. While many students feel positive about their most recent SHE teacher, about 35% of students report that their parents are doing a fair or poor job providing SHE at home (Byers et al. 2003a, 2003b). Similar studies with parents and teachers of adolescents have shown that they also agree that SHE should be provided in the schools, parents and schools should share responsibility for providing SHE, SHE should cover a wide range of topics, and most topics should be covered by the end of grade eight (Cohen, Byers, Sears, and Weaver 2004; Weaver, Byers, Sears, Cohen, and Randall 2002).

Health Risk Behavior

Most young people in Canada have good physical and emotional health (Boyce 2004; McCreary Centre Society 2004). Nevertheless, a substantial proportion of youths engage in risk behaviors that have the potential to compromise their health. While both boys and girls take risks, boys more frequently engage in behaviors that result in injuries or death. Many adolescents report that they have sustained injuries requiring medical attention. These injuries are caused primarily by sports and recreational activities, although cycling, roller-blading, and skateboarding also contribute (Boyce 2004; McCreary Centre Society 2004). Accidents, the majority of which are motor vehicle, account for almost half of all deaths among Canadian youths, followed by suicide. The death rate among young men is more than twice the rate for young women (Statistics Canada 2002b). More frequent risk behaviors during adolescence are linked to several factors, such as impulsivity, academic status, peer conformity, deviant peer affiliations, and low parental monitoring (Ma and Zhang 2002; Santor, Messervey, and Kusumakar 2000; Vitaro, Brendgen, Ladouceur, and Tremblay 2001). Less frequent risk behaviors are seen among youths who feel strongly connected to family or school, have a positive circle of friends, get higher grades, have postsecondary educational aspirations, and participate in extracurricular activities (Ma and Zhang 2002; McCreary Centre Society 2004).

Tobacco, alcohol, and marijuana are the three substances most commonly used by Canadian adolescents. Across grades seven to twelve, about 25% of youths have smoked and about 15% are regular smokers by grade eleven, both of which represent marked decreases in smoking over the past four to five years (Liu, Jones, Grobe, Balram, and Poulin 2002; McCreary Centre Society 2004; Willoughby, Chalmers, Busseri, and YLC-CURA 2004). In comparison, about 55% of youths have tried alcohol, about 32% report binge drinking, and about 35% report using marijuana (Liu et al. 2002; McCreary Centre Society 2004; Willoughby et al. 2004). Looking at gender differences, smoking rates for girls exceed those for boys whereas similar proportions of girls and boys use alcohol and have engaged in binge drinking in the last month (Liu et al. 2002; McCreary Centre Society 2004). Although girls and boys also use marijuana at similar rates, among those who have ever used almost twice as many boys are frequent users as girls (31% versus 17%). Use of tobacco, alcohol, and marijuana shows a linear increase across age (Liu et al. 2002; McCreary Centre Society 2004). A substantial majority of youths have never used harder drugs (McCreary Centre Society 2004; Willoughby et al. 2004).

Turning to delinquency, one study found that about 30% of adolescents participated in minor delinquency in the previous year (such as shoplifting, joyriding). In contrast, only 8% of youths had been involved in major delinquency over this time (such as carrying a gun or knife as a weapon) (Willoughby et al. 2004). More boys than girls participate in delinquent behaviors, and, within types of offenses, boys and girls commit minor acts at similar rates whereas boys commit more serious acts than girls (Fitzgerald 2003; Reitsma-Street and Artz 2005). This gender difference may be explained at least in part by similarities and differences between boys and girls who act aggressively. While these boys and girls do share perceptions and experiences, such as acceptance of use of violence, affiliation with a deviant peer group, participation in substance use and other antisocial behaviors, and families that are low in support and high in conflict, the girls differ from the boys in their lower quality relationships with mothers, increased fear of and experiences with physical and sexual abuse, and endorsement of prosocial values (Artz 2004). Youths 12 to 17 years in Canada who commit illegal acts are adjudicated by the Youth Criminal Justice Act (http://canada.justice.gc.ca/en/ps/yj/repository/index.html). Currently, boys represent about 80% of convictions in youth court, and the most common sentence or disposition for girls and boys is probation (Reitsma-Street and Artz 2005).

Studies of adolescents' risk behaviors suggest that gambling is common among youths. Between 65% and 70% of teens report participating in gambling over the past year (Hardoon, Gupta, and Derevensky 2004; Poulin 2000). Typical activities include betting on cards or board games or on games of skills, such as pool or darts. However, youths also purchase lottery tickets and instant win games, despite a legal age restriction of 18 years in most provinces (Marshall and Wynne 2004). Between 5% and 10% of teenagers are involved in at-risk or problem gambling, with higher rates among boys than girls but stable rates across grades seven through twelve (Hardoon et al. 2004; Poulin 2000; Willoughby et al. 2004). Serious gambling-related problems are linked to individual, peer, and family characteristics (impulsivity, substance use, conduct problems, deviant peers, family problems, and parental involvement in gambling and substance use) (Hardoon et al. 2004; Vitaro et al. 2001).

Adolescents' emotional well-being may also increase their risk of health problems. A significant minority of youths experience serious emotional distress during the teenage years, and 4% to 10% have an episode of clinical depression. Girls report higher rates of depressive symptoms and depressive disorders than boys (Boyce 2004; Galambos, Leadbeater, and Barker 2004; McCreary Centre Society 2004; Statistics Canada 2002b). Disconnection from others appears to be especially salient for girls' understanding and experience of depression (Galambos et al. 2004; Hetherington and Stoppard 2002). Although the suicide rate among young people in Canada is lower than that of older age groups, suicide is the second leading cause of death among youths (Statistics Canada 2002). In one study 16% of students (grades seven through twelve) reported thinking seriously about suicide in the past year, 11% had planned a suicide, and 7% had attempted suicide (McCreary Centre Society 2004). While suicidal ideation and attempts are two to three times higher among girls, boys are almost three times as likely to commit suicide. Suicide also increases across the course of adolescence. However, even among young adolescents, suicide is a concern, with 5% of 12-year-old girls, 11% of 13-year-old girls, and 13% of 14-year-old girls reporting suicidal ideation over a six-month period (Breton, Tousignant, Bergeron, and Berthiaume 2002). Suicide also occurs at a higher rate among aboriginal youths, although cases are not randomly distributed across this population. Instead, youth suicide is more common in aboriginal communities that have not been able to preserve their culture (Chandler et al. 2003).

During adolescence, many teenagers express dissatisfaction with their appearance, especially body weight. Research indicates that at least 40% of girls are dissatisfied with their weight, that more girls than boys are dissatisfied, and that girls' dissatisfaction increases with age (Barker and Galambos 2003; Jones et al. 2001; McCreary Centre Society 2004; McVey, Pepler, Davis, Flett, and Abdolell 2002). Risk factors associated with girls' body dissatisfaction include weight (higher body mass index), greater figure management, and being teased about their appearance. Being teased about their appearance is also a risk factor for boys' dissatisfaction (Barker and Galambos 2003). Many youths act on their dissatisfaction and place their health at risk by dieting, binge eating, and purging, and these behaviors increase across age (Boyce 2004; Jones et al. 2001; McCreary Centre Society 2004). Among young adolescents, higher levels of disordered eating are related to lower competence in physical appearance, higher importance of social acceptance, higher self-oriented perfectionism, and lower paternal support (McVey et al. 2002). Although about 75% of adolescents actually have a healthy weight for their age and gender, a subset of youths are overweight or obese. More boys than girls are found in these two groups, and this pattern is consistent across adolescence (Boyce 2004; McCreary Centre Society 2004).

Education

The vast majority of Canadian children and adolescents attend public school full-time for approximately 13 years (kindergarten to grade twelve; about 5 years to 17 years old). School attendance is compulsory in most jurisdictions until age 16. As a result, enrollment exceeds 90% until this age, and then drops to 75%–80% in the final years of high school. Because each province and territory establishes its own curriculum and general education structure, the availability of second-language immersion and alternative education programs varies across the country (Boyce 2004). Public education is generally nondenominational. Currently, the effectiveness of Canadian schools is being evaluated using national and international assessments. Results from the Student Achievement Indicators Program (SAIP), sponsored by the Council of Ministers of Education, Canada (CMEC), indicate that over 68% of 13-year-olds and less than 50% of 16-year-olds have attained expected performance for their age in mathematics, and about 75% of 13- and 16-year-olds have attained expected performance for their age in science (Canadian Education Statistics Council 2003). According to the 1999 International Math Report from the Trends in Mathematics and Science Study (TIMSS) for 14-year-olds, Canada placed tenth among 40 countries on mathematical achievement; and on the TIMSS 1999 International Science Report, Canada placed fourteenth on science achievement (Martin et al. 1999; Mullis et al. 1999). On the 2000 Programme for International Student Assessment (PISA) for 15-year-olds, in comparison to 31 other countries, Canada ranked sixth in mathematics, fifth in science, and second in reading (Human Resources Development Canada 2002). While there were no gender differences in the mathematics and science results from the SAIP, TIMSS, or PISA, on the 2000 PISA girls outperformed boys in reading (Canadian Education Statistics Council 2003). Canada's literacy rate is 97% (*World Factbook* 2004).

Most provinces and the territories require two school transitions, one from elementary to middle school or junior high school (after grade five or grade six) and one from middle/junior high school to high school (after grade eight or grade nine). The majority of adolescents experience these transitions as positive (resulting in less loneliness, higher self-esteem), especially when they have more same-sex reciprocal friendships at the end of one grade, and more same-sex and other-sex reciprocal friendships at the end of the subsequent grade (McDougall and Vaillancourt 2003). Other research suggests that even though peer acceptance may fluctuate during a school transition, with girls experiencing greater instability in their reciprocated friendships than boys, shortly after the transition many students form new friendships with previously unfamiliar peers (Hardy, Bukowski, and Sippola 2002). Given that about 50% of young people continue their education after graduating from high school by attending technical school, college, or university (more girls [52%] than boys [43%]) (Statistics Canada 2002), many teenagers make another school transition during late adolescence. In Canada students usually attend college for one to two years and graduate with a diploma or certificate, whereas they attend university for a minimum of three to four years and graduate with a degree. Research on factors that facilitate the adjustment of youths who transition to university suggests that specific personality features (extraversion, optimism), prepared expectations about university, and parent-adolescent relationships characterized by mutual reciprocity and discussions may each play a role, and that at least some of these effects vary across mothers and fathers and daughters and sons (Jackson, Pancer, Pratt, and Hunsberger 2000; Jackson et al., in press; Wintre and Sugar 2000; Wintre and Yaffe 2000).

Turning to school climate, a majority of adolescents report that they enjoy school, participate in extracurricular and volunteer activities, and feel comfortable asking school staff for help. However, many teenagers also feel pressure to do well at school and are concerned about what they will do when they finish school (Bibby 2001; Boyce 2004; McCreary Centre Society 2004). School experiences also vary by one's gender and one's ethnicity. For example, in a study that compared girls in an elective grade eleven all-female computer science class to girls and boys in mixed-sex computer science classes over three consecutive years, the girls in all-female classes reported higher levels of perceived support from teachers, computer-related confidence, and future academic and occupational intentions to pursue computer science than the girls in mixed-sex computer science classes (Crombie, Abarbanel, and Trinneer 2002). Racial and ethnic minority high school students, especially black students, are more likely than white students to perceive discrimination with respect to teacher treatment, school suspension, use of police by school authorities, and police treatment at school. This pattern is more likely for boys than girls and for youths born in Canada or who immigrated at a young age, and is linked to students' views of school climate (such as racial segregation among peer groups and perceptions of personal safety and violence, especially for blacks and South Asian students) (Ruck and Wortley 2002).

Although a large majority of grade nine and grade eleven students, particularly girls, plan to complete high school and go on to college or university (Bibby 2001; Boyce et al. 2003), a substantial minority of youths leave high school without a diploma. While the proportion of Canadian adolescents who drop out of school has decreased significantly, in 1999 12% of 20-year-olds had not completed high school. Boys and aboriginal youths are more likely to leave school than girls and non-aboriginal peers, respectively (Statistics Canada 2002). Given that most immigrant youths experience ostracism, bullying, and difficulties with school work and school staff (Canadian Council on Social Development 2000), it is not surprising that 20% of refugee youths do not expect to finish high school, and an additional 30% expect to have difficulty finishing school (Wilkinson 2002). Their educational success is linked to their individual characteristics (ethnicity, more months spent in Canada, appropriate grade placement on arrival) and family influences (urban residence, parents' health) (Wilkinson 2002). Leaving school is also related to family adversity, early disruptiveness and early academic performance, less involvement in school and less time on homework, working 30 or more hours per week, affiliation with deviant friends, and for at least 25% of girls, having at least one child (Canadian Education Statistics Council 2003; Vitaro, Larocque, Janosz, and Tremblay 2001). About 14% of youths who leave high school return to school by ages 20 to 22 (Statistics Canada 2004g).

Work

More youths than ever before are participating in the labor force, either full- or part-time. In 2001, 44% of teenagers 15 to 19 years were employed, representing 6% of all workers in Canada. Over 70% of these teens were working part-time. In comparison, 69% of 20- to 24-year-olds were employed, and 27% worked part-time (Statistics Canada 2002). The majority of adolescents and emerging adults work in sales, service, or clerical occupations. Their jobs generally do not require extensive education or experience and provide little opportunity for advancement. In addition tasks are often simple and repetitive and the pay is low.

While similar proportions of girls and boys are employed, they tend to have different jobs: boys are more likely to work as gardeners, janitors, and laborers, and girls are more likely to work as food servers, babysitters, and house cleaners. Boys often work more hours a week than girls and they are paid more per hour (about 15% higher) (Statistics Canada 2002).

Most young people work part-time because they are also going to school. While only 23% of 15-year-olds are combining school and work, by age 18 35% are juggling these commitments (Canadian Education Statistics Council 2003). The combination of working and going to school has different effects on girls and boys. Overall, girls report feeling rushed, are less satisfied with their free time, and worry about not spending enough time with family and friends, whereas boys are more likely to be happy and satisfied with their life, their finances, and their studies (Franke 2003). However, the number of hours teenagers are employed also plays a role in the impact work has on them. Typically, adolescents work between 15 and 20 hours a week, although about 10% of youths work 30 hours per week or more. While jobs of less than 15 hours per week do not dramatically change the time that adolescents spend on their schoolwork, teens with these jobs do sleep about one hour less per day, and boys also reduce their leisure time by over an hour. When they have more demanding jobs, both girls and boys reduce their leisure activities (such as watching television) by at least an hour, and girls reduce their sleep by an hour and eliminate nearly all sports (Franke 2003).

An aspect of youth employment that has received relatively little consideration is the extent to which adolescents and emerging adults sustain injuries in the workplace. In 2003, 50 young Canadians died as a result of a workplace accident and approximately 110,000 others were seriously injured (Workplace Health, Safety and Compensation Commission (WHSCC) of New Brunswick 2004). According to the Occupational Health and Safety Act, all employees have three rights regarding safety on the job: the right to know about workplace hazards and to receive training on how to do the job safely, the right to participate in solving health and safety problems, and the right to refuse dangerous work (WHSCC of New Brunswick 2004). Although a workplace is legally responsible for providing all workers with the training necessary to perform their job safely, there are gaps between what is legislatively required, what is desired, and what actually exists in terms of new employee safety training. This is a critical issue for youths because even though the provision of job safety training is a key factor in decreasing accidents among young workers in particular, young people do not necessarily make job safety a priority and many of them are not clear about their rights with respect to job safety (Association of the Workers' Compensation Boards of Canada 2003; Workers' Compensation Board of British Columbia 2003). In the early twenty-first century, young workers in Canada were being recruited to increase their knowledge of rights and practices concerning workplace health and safety by participating in "Passport to Safety," a national injury-prevention initiative open to youths 14 to 24 years (http://www.passporttosafety.com).

A full school-to-work transition can take up to about eight years to complete and may include working and studying at the same time or alternating periods of attending school and working at a paid job (Franke 2003). Studies of high school students indicate that over 60% of them expect to graduate from university, and over 85% expect not only to be able to find work, but also to get the job that they want. According to teenagers, desirable jobs involve interesting work, provide a feeling of accomplishment, have opportunities for advancement, and pay well (Bibby 2001). Interestingly, a large majority of adolescents expect to be more financially comfortable than their parents, although less than half of them think that they will have to work overtime to do it. These expectations are very similar for boys and girls and for immigrant and Canadian-born youths (Bibby 2001). These aspirations are noteworthy since youths have the highest unemployment rate of any age group in Canada. In 2003, 16% of men 15 to 24 years and 12% of women 15 to 24 years were unemployed (Statistics Canada 2004). As is indicated, unemployment rates are slightly higher among young men, and they are particularly high among aboriginal and immigrant youths (Statistics Canada 2002).

What are the employment prospects for young people who complete postsecondary education? A national study of 1997 and 2000 labor market outcomes for young college and university graduates who entered their programs directly from high school and were starting their transition to the work force in 1995 showed that college and university graduates were more likely to have a job two years and five years after graduation than individuals with a high school diploma. Gender differences in employment were also more pronounced among emerging adults with a high school education only (77% for men, 68% for women) than among college graduates (95% men, 92% women) and university graduates (91% men, 89% women) (Allen, Harris, and Butlin 2003). While college graduates made the transition to employment more quickly than university graduates, by 2000 university graduates were more likely to have a job requiring their level of education and were being paid better (over 20% higher) (Allen et al. 2003).

Media

As is indicated in a position statement by the Canadian Paediatric Society (2003), the potential impact of media on the health of children and youths is vast, and based on what is known, involves both beneficial and harmful effects. Canadian youths have access to and make extensive use of various forms of media (television, video games, music, the Internet). Almost all households in Canada have television sets, and 92% of adolescents watch television daily (Bibby 2001). Television viewing appears to peak in early adolescence and then declines, likely in response to competing media and the demands of school and social activities. Although television can be a powerful teacher and offers opportunities to learn and be entertained, many programs communicate messages about risk behaviors in which youths engage (substance use, violence, sexual behavior) (Canadian Paediatric Society 2003). While many adults have also expressed concern about the negative effects of exposure to video games, little is known about how these games, which range considerably in their content, affect various aspects of adolescents' development.

Music is another form of media that contributes to the lives of adolescents. Teenagers list music as an important source of enjoyment, and the vast majority of them listen to music every day, favoring pop, alternative, and rap/hip-hop genres (Bibby 2001). Adolescents' music preference may reflect specific personality features. For example, youths who prefer heavy metal music are more likely to be overly assertive, indifferent to others' feelings, and more discontented and disrespectful. In comparison, teens who prefer light music are overly responsible and conforming, and more concerned about peer acceptance and their developing sexuality (Schwartz and Fouts 2003). A preference for rap music is related to youths' involvement in deviant behaviors, with French rap related to more deviant behaviors (violence, street gangs) and hip hop/soul linked to less deviant behaviors (theft, drug use) (Miranda and Claes 2004).

Turning to computer use, the majority of adolescents now have a home computer and Internet access, both of which are more likely when they live in two-parent families, immigrant families, or with parents who have more prestigious occupations and higher levels of education (Boyce 2004; Willms and Corbett 2003). Over 85% of 15- to 24-year-olds have used the Internet in the last month, with the majority spending one to seven hours online in the previous week. In terms of activities, while boys and girls use the Internet for e-mail and participate in online chats, boys are more likely than girls to play games and to access information on goods and services (Rotermann 2001; Willms and Corbett 2003). However, not all online experiences are positive. Among youths who use the Internet, about 60% have found websites that contain pornography, 24% have encountered websites that promote hate or violence, and 10% have received a threatening or harassing e-mail (Rotermann 2001).

Politics and Military

Youths in Canada are eligible to vote at age 18. However, about 75% of high school students have little interest in politics (Bibby 2001). It is not surprising then that relatively few young people typically participate in the political process by voting. In response to this situation, Elections Canada has implemented a variety of initiatives for youth, including a new Young Voters Web site, and a Canada Road Trip contest. They also have partnered with nongovernmental organizations, such as Rush the Vote, to enhance political awareness (Kingsley 2004). Based on results from the June 2004 federal election, the proportion of eligible first-time voters who registered for the election increased to 77%. In addition, the voter turnout rate was 39% for 18- to 21-year-olds and 35% for 22- to 24-year-olds, also an increase from the 2000 election. While young people are also less cynical about the political process than adults, they still appear to be uninterested in electoral participation. Specifically, youths were more likely than adults to feel that their vote really mattered, but only 11% of 18- to 24-year-olds reported that they followed the election very closely, and only 5% felt very knowledgeable about the policies of the parties who ran candidates in the election (Kingley 2004).

Military service is not compulsory in Canada. Adolescents who are 17 years or older can enlist in one of three branches of the Canadian Forces, the army, the navy, or the air force (minors are required to have parental consent) (Department of National Defence 2004). Currently, there are 5,074 men and 533 women between the ages of 17 and 24 in the army; 1,318 men and 252 women in

this age range in the navy; and 1,464 men and 378 women in this age range in the air force (D. Martin 2004). Alternatively, youths can join the Reserve Force and pursue a part-time career in the naval, army, air, or communication reserves. These individuals (10,755 men and 2,089 women 16 to 24 years of age) support Canada's Regular Forces while obtaining a variety of new skills and earning extra income. Through partnerships between the Canadian Forces and the Army Cadet League of Canada (http://www.armycadetleague.ca), the Navy League of Canada (http://www.navyleague.ca), and the Air Cadet League of Canada (http://www.aircadet.com), respectively, teenagers participate in local programs designed to develop the resourcefulness and leadership potential of young people through discipline and team building. Although these programs are based on a military structure and are staffed by members of the Canadian Forces Reserves and regular or reserve force volunteers, the youths are civilians and have no commitment to serve in the military. These programs appeal to many young people, with over 15,000 youths enrolled in sea cadets, over 21,000 youths attending army cadets, and over 24,000 youths participating in air cadets.

HEATHER A. SEARS, MARY G. SIMMERING, and BRAD A. MACNEIL

References and Further Reading

Adams, G., B. Munro, M. Doherty-Poirer, G. Munro, A. Peterson, and J. Edwards. 2001. Diffuse-avoidance, normative, and informational identity styles: Using identity theory to predict maladjustment. *Identity* 1:307–20.

Allen, M., S. Harris, and G. Butlin. 2003. Finding their way: A profile of young Canadian graduates. *Statistics Canada Catalogue No. 81-595-MIE2003003.* Ottawa, ON: Statistics Canada.

Artz, S. 2000. The guys here degrade you: Youth perspectives on sex. *Journal of Child and Youth Care* 14:29–46.

Artz, S. 2004. To die for: Violent adolescent girls' search for male attention. In *Development and treatment of girlhood aggression.* D. Pepler, K. Madsen, C. Webster, and K. Levene (eds.). pp. 137–59. Hillsdale, NJ: Lawrence Erlbaum.

Association of Workers' Compensation Boards of Canada (AWCBC). 2003. *Workplace health and safety: It's time to act!* http://www.awcbc.org (accessed November 18, 2004).

Banister, E., S. Jakubec, and J. Stein. 2003. "Like, what am I supposed to do?": Adolescent girls' health concerns in their dating relationships. *Canadian Journal of Nursing Research* 35:16–33.

Barker, E., and N. Galambos. 2003. Body dissatisfaction of adolescent girls and boys: Risk and resource factors. *Journal of Early Adolescence* 23:141–65.

Beaujot, R. 2004. *Delayed life transitions: Trends and implications.* Vanier Institute of the Family.

http://www.vifamily.ca/library/cft/delayed_life.html (accessed November 21, 2004).

Beaumont, S., and S. Wagner. 2004. Adolescent-parent verbal conflict: The roles of conversational styles and disgust emotions. *Journal of Language and Social Psychology* 23:338–68.

Bibby, R. 2001. *Canada's teens: Today, yesterday, and tomorrow.* Toronto, ON: Stoddart.

Boyce, W. 2004. *Young people in Canada: Their health and well-being.* Ottawa, ON: Health Canada.

Boyce, W., M. Doherty, D. MacKinnon, and C. Fortin. 2003. *Canadian youth, sexual health and HIV/AIDS study: Factors influencing knowledge, attitudes and behaviours.* Council of Ministers of Education, Canada. http://www.cmec.ca/publications/aids (accessed September 26, 2003).

Brendgen, M., D. Markiewicz, A. B. Doyle, and W. Bukowski, 2001. The relations between friendship quality, ranked-friendship preference, and adolescents' behavior with their friends. *Merrill-Palmer Quarterly* 47:395–415.

Brendgen, M., F. Vitaro, and W. Bukowski. 2000a. Deviant friends and early adolescents' emotional and behavioral adjustment. *Journal of Research on Adolescence* 10:173–89.

Brendgen, M., F. Vitaro, and W. Bukowski. 2000b. Stability and variability of adolescents' affiliation with delinquent friends: Predictors and consequences. *Social Development* 9205–25.

Brendgen, M., F. Vitaro, A. B. Doyle, D. Markiewicz, and W. Bukowski. 2002. Same-sex peer relations and romantic relationships during early adolescence: Interactive links to emotional, behavioral, and academic adjustment. *Merrill-Palmer Quarterly* 48:77–83.

Brendgen, M., F. Vitaro, R. Tremblay, and F. Lavoie. 2001. Reactive and proactive aggression: Predictions to physical violence in different contexts and moderating effects of parental monitoring and caregiving behavior. *Journal of Abnormal Child Psychology* 29:293–304.

Brendgen, M., F. Vitaro, R. Tremblay, and B. Wanner. 2002. Parent and peer effects on delinquency-related violence and dating violence: A test of two mediational models. *Social Development* 11:225–44.

Breton, J., M. Tousignant, L. Bergeron, and C. Berthiaume. 2002. Informant-specific correlates of suicidal behavior in a community survey of 12- to 14-year-olds. *Journal of the American Academy of Child & Adolescent Psychiatry* 41:723–30.

Bush, J., and M. Ehrenberg. 2003. Young persons' perspectives on the influence of family transitions on sibling relationships: A qualitative exploration. *Journal of Divorce & Remarriage* 39:1–35.

Byers, E. S., H. Sears, S. Voyer, J. Thurlow, J. Cohen, and A. Weaver. 2001. New Brunswick students' ideas about sexual health education. Final report submitted to the New Brunswick Department of Education, Fredericton, NB. http://www.gnb.ca/0000/publications/ss/studentsexeducation.pdf.

Byers, E. S., H. Sears, S. Voyer, J. Thurlow, J. Cohen, and A. Weaver. 2003a. An adolescent perspective on sexual health education at school and at home: I. High school students. *Canadian Journal of Human Sexuality* 12:1–17.

Byers, E. S., H. Sears, S. Voyer, J. Thurlow, J. Cohen, and A. Weaver. 2003b. An adolescent perspective on sexual health education at school and at home: II. Middle school students. *Canadian Journal of Human Sexuality* 12:19–33.

Canadian Council on Social Development. 2000. *Immigrant youth in Canada.* http://www.ccsd.ca/pubs/2000/iy/hl.htm (accessed July 28, 2004).

Canadian Education Statistics Council. 2003. Education indicators in Canada: Report of the Pan-Canadian education indicators program 2003. *Statistics Canada Catalogue No. 81-582-XPE.* Toronto, ON: Author & Council of Ministers of Education, Canada.

Canadian Paediatric Society. 2003. Impact of media use on children and youth. *Paediatric Child Health* 8:301–6.

Chandler, M., C. Lalonde, B. Sokol, and D. Hallett. 2003. Personal persistence, identity development, and suicide: A study of native and non-native North American adolescents. *Monographs of the Society for Research in Child Development* 68.

Cheah, C., and L. Nelson. 2004. The role of acculturation in the emerging adulthood of Aboriginal college students. *International Journal of Behavioral Development* 28:495–507.

Claes, M., E. Lacourse, C. Bouchard, and D. Luckow. 2001. Adolescents' relationships with members of the extended family and non-related adults in four countries: Canada, France, Belgium, and Italy. *International Journal of Adolescence and Youth* 9:207–25.

Cohen, J., E. S. Byers, H. Sears, and A. Weaver. 2004. Sexual health education: Attitudes, knowledge, and comfort of teachers in New Brunswick schools. *Canadian Journal of Human Sexuality* 13:1–15.

Connolly, J., W. Craig, A. Goldberg, and D. Pepler. 2004. Mixed-gender groups, dating, and romantic relationships in early adolescence. *Journal of Research on Adolescence* 14:185–207.

Connolly, J., W. Furman, and R. Konarski. 2000. The role of peers in the emergence of heterosexual romantic relationships in adolescence. *Child Development* 71: 1395–1408.

Connolly, J., and C. McIsaac. 2004, March. Romantic dissolutions in adolescence: Negative affect, attributions, and romantic confidence. In J. Connolly and C. Feiring (chairs) *Positive and negative processes within romantic relationships.* Poster symposium presented at the Biennial Meeting of the Society for Research on Adolescence, Baltimore, Md.

Costigan, C., and D. Dokis. 2004. *Parenting adolescents after immigration: The impact of within-family acculturation differences.* Paper presented at the FRC IV Summer Institute, San Juan, Puerto Rico.

Costigan, C., and T. Su. 2004. Orthogonal versus linear models of acculturation among immigrant Chinese Canadians: A comparison of mothers, fathers, and children. *International Journal of Behavioral Development* 28:518–27.

Crombie, G., T. Abarbanel, and A. Trinneer. 2002. All-female classes in high school computer science: Positive effects in three years of data. *Journal of Educational Computing Research* 27:383–407.

Dayan, J., A. B. Doyle, and D. Markiewicz. 2001. Social support networks and self-esteem of idiocentric and allocentric children and adolescents. *Journal of Social and Personal Relationships* 18:767–84.

Department of National Defense 2004. Canadian forces recruiting. http://www.recruiting.dnd.ca (accessed November 16, 2004).

153

Dokis, D., C. Costigan, and A. Chia. 2002, June. *Parent-adolescent conflict in immigrant Chinese families*. Poster presented at the Annual Meeting of the Canadian Psychological Association, Vancouver, BC, Canada.

Doyle, A. B., M. Brendgen, D. Markiewicz, and K. Kamkar. 2003. Family relationships as moderators of the association between romantic relationships and adjustment in early adolescence. *Journal of Early Adolescence* 23:316–40.

Drolet, M., I. Lafleur, and G. Trottier. 2000. Differential analysis of adolescent heartbreak: Do males and females react differently? *Canadian Social Work* 2:30–40.

Fitzgerald, R. 2003. An examination of sex differences in delinquency. *Crime and Justice Research Paper Series, Catalogue No. 85-561-MIE2003001*. Ottawa, ON: Canadian Centre for Justice Statistics.

Franke, S. 2003. Studying and working: The busy lives of students with paid employment. *Canadian Social Trends* (Statistics Canada Catalogue No. 11-008), 22–25.

Galambos, N., E. Barker, and D. Almeida. 2003. Parents *do* matter: Trajectories of change in externalizing and internalizing problems in early adolescence. *Child Development* 74:578–94.

Galambos, N., B. Leadbeater, and E. Barker. 2004. Gender differences in and risk factors for depression in adolescence: A 4-year longitudinal study. *International Journal of Behavioral Development* 28:16–25.

Hampton, M., B. Jeffery, P. Smith, and B. McWatters. 2001. Sexual experience, contraception, and STI prevention among high school students: Results from a Canadian urban centre. *Canadian Journal of Human Sexuality* 10:111–26.

Hardoon, K., R. Gupta, and J. Derevensky. 2004. Psychosocial variables associated with adolescent gambling. *Psychology of Addictive Behaviors* 18:170–79.

Hardy, C., W. Bukowski, and L. Sippola. 2002. Stability and change in peer relationships during the transition to middle-level school. *Journal of Early Adolescence* 22:117–42.

Health Canada 2003. *Canadian guidelines for sexual health education*. Ottawa, ON.

Hetherington, J., and J. Stoppard. 2002. The theme of disconnection in adolescent girls' understanding of depression. *Journal of Adolescence* 25:619–29.

Hilton, N., G. Harris, and M. Rice. 2003. Adolescents' perceptions of the seriousness of sexual aggression: Influence of gender, traditional attitudes, and self-reported experience. *Sexual Abuse: A Journal of Research and Treatment* 15:201–14.

Howe, N., J. Aquan-Assee, W. Bukowski, P. Lehoux, and C. Rinaldi. 2001. Siblings as confidants: Emotional understanding, relationship warmth, and sibling self-disclosure. *Social Development* 10:439–54.

Howe, N., J. Aquan-Assee, W. Bukowski, C. Rinaldi, and P. Lehoux. 2000. Sibling self-disclosure in early adolescence. *Merrill-Palmer Quarterly* 46:653–71.

Human Resources Development Canada 2002. Measuring up: The performance of Canada's youth in reading, mathematics and science. http://www.pisa.gc.ca/pisa/brochure_e.pdf (accessed November 18, 2004).

Hunsberger, B., M. Pratt, and S. M. Pancer. 2001. Adolescent identity formation: Religious exploration and commitment. *Identity* 1:365–86.

Hunsberger, B., M. Pratt, and S. M. Pancer. 2002. A longitudinal study of religious doubts in high school and beyond: Relationships, stability, and searching for answers. *Journal for the Scientific Study of Religion* 41:255–66.

Jackson, L., S. M. Pancer, M. Pratt, and B. Hunsberger. 2000. Great expectations: The relation between expectancies and adjustment during the transition to university. *Journal of Applied Social Psychology* 30:2100–2125.

Jackson, L., M. Pratt, B. Hunsberger, and S. M. Pancer. In press. Optimism as a mediator of the relation between perceived parental authoritativeness and adjustment among adolescents: Finding the sunny side of the street. *Social Development*.

Jennings, M., and N. Howe. 2001. Siblings' perceptions of their parents' divorce. *Journal of Divorce & Remarriage* 35:91–106.

Jones, J., S. Bennett, M. Olmsted, M. Lawson, and G. Rodin. 2001. Disordered eating attitudes and behaviours in teenaged girls: A school-based study. *Canadian Medical Association Journal* 165:547–52.

Kingsley, J. P. 2004. *Chief electoral officer's keynote speech to the Centre for Research and Information on Canada research seminar on the political engagement of Canadian youth*. http://www.elections.ca (accessed November 19, 2004).

Kuo, B., and G. Roysircar. 2004. Predictors of acculturation for Chinese adolescents in Canada: Age of arrival, length of stay, social class, and English reading ability. *Journal of Multicultural Counseling and Development* 32:143–54.

Kwak, K., and J. Berry. 2001. Generational differences in acculturation among Asian families in Canada: A comparison of Vietnamese, Korean, and East-Indian groups. *International Journal of Psychology* 36:152–62.

Langille, D., and L. Curtis. 2002. Factors associated with sexual intercourse before age 15 among female adolescents in Nova Scotia. *Canadian Journal of Human Sexuality* 11:91–99.

Langille, D., G. Flowerdew, and P. Andreou. In press. Teenage pregnancy in Nova Scotia communities: Associations with contextual factors. *Canadian Journal of Human Sexuality*.

Lavoie, F., M. Hebert, R. Tremblay, F. Vitaro, L. Vezina, and P. McDuff. 2002. History of family dysfunction and perpetration of dating violence by adolescent boys: A longitudinal study. *Journal of Adolescent Health* 30:375–83.

Lavoie, F., L. Robitaille, and M. Hébert. 2000. Teen dating relationships and aggression: An exploratory study. *Violence Against Women* 6:6–36.

Liu, J., B. Jones, C. Grobe, C. Balram, and C. Poulin. 2002. New Brunswick student drug use survey 2002: Highlights report. http://www.gnb.ca/0378/pdf/studentdrugusesurvey2002eng.pdf.

Ma, X., and Y. Zhang. 2002. *A national assessment of effects of school experiences on health outcomes and behaviours of children: Technical report*. Ottawa, ON: Health Canada, Division of Childhood and Adolescence.

Mackey, K., M. Arnold, and M. Pratt. 2001. Adolescents' stories of decision making in more and less authoritative families. *Journal of Adolescent Research* 16:243–68.

Marshall, K., and H. Wynne. 2004, Summer. Against the odds: A profile of at-risk and problem gamblers.

Canadian Social Trends (Statistics Canada, Catalogue No. 11-008), 25–29.

Marshall, S. 2001. Do I matter? Construct validation of adolescents' perceived mattering to parents and friends. *Journal of Adolescence* 24:473–90.

Martin, M., I. Mullis, E. Gonzalez, K. Gregory, T. Smith, S. Chrostowski, R. Garden, and K. O'Connor. 1999. TIMSS 1999 International Science Report. http://timss.bc.edu/timss1999i/publications.html.

Maticka-Tyndale, E. 2001. Sexual health and Canadian youth: How do we measure up? *Canadian Journal of Human Sexuality* 10:1–17.

Matsuba, M., and L. Walker. 2004. Extraordinary moral commitment: Young adults involved in social organizations. *Journal of Personality* 72:413–36.

McCreary Centre Society 2004. Health youth development: Highlights from the 2003 Adolescent Health Survey III. http://www.mcs.bc.ca (accessed November 22, 2004).

McDougall, P., and T. Vaillancourt. 2003. *The high school transition: Still getting by with a little help from my friends*. Poster presented at the Biennial Meeting of the Society for Research on Child Development, Tampa, FL.

McMaster, L., J. Connolly, D. Pepler, and W. Craig. 2002. Peer to peer sexual harassment in early adolescence: A developmental perspective. *Development and Psychopathology* 14:91–105.

McVey, G., D. Pepler, R. Davis, G. Flett, and M. Abdolell. 2002. Risk and protective factors associated with disordered eating during early adolescence. *Journal of Early Adolescence* 22:75–95.

Miranda, D., and M. Claes. 2004. Rap music genres and deviant behaviors in French-Canadian adolescents. *Journal of Youth and Adolescence* 33:113–22.

Mullis, I., M. Martin, E. Gonzalez, K. Gregory, R. Garden, K. O'Connor, S. Chrostowski, and T. Smith. 1999. TIMSS 1999 International Mathematics Report. http://timss.bc.edu/timss1999i/publications.html.

Poulin, C. 2000. Problem gambling among adolescent students in the Atlantic Provinces of Canada. *Journal of Gambling Studies* 16:53–78.

Pratt, M., B. Hunsberger, S. M. Pancer, and S. Alisat. 2003. A longitudinal analysis of personal values socialization: Correlates of a moral self-ideal in late adolescence. *Social Development* 12:563–85.

Pratt, M., E. Skoe, and M. Arnold. 2004. Care reasoning development and family socialization patterns in later adolescence: A longitudinal analysis. *International Journal of Behavioral Development* 28:139–47.

Price, E. L., E. S. Byers, H. Sears, J. Whelan, M. Saint-Pierre, and the Dating Violence Research Team. 2000. *Dating violence among New Brunswick adolescents: A summary of two studies*. Muriel McQueen Fergusson Centre for Family Violence Research Paper Series, Vol. 2. Fredericton, NB: University of New Brunswick.

Public Health Agency of Canada. 2004. HIV and AIDS among youth in Canada: HIV/AIDS Epi Update. http://www.phac-aspc.gc.ca/publicat/epiu-aepi/epi_update_may_04/4_e.html (accessed November 27, 2004).

Reitsma-Street, M., and S. Artz. 2005. Girls and crime. In *Issues and perspectives on young offenders*, J. Winterdyk (ed.). 3rd ed. pp. 57–82. Toronto, ON: Thomson Nelson.

Rinaldi, C., and N. Howe. 2003. Perceptions of constructive and destructive conflict within and across family subsystems. *Infant and Child Development* 12:441–59.

Rotenberg, K., P. McDougall, M. Boulton, T. Vaillancourt, C. Fox, and S. Hymel. 2004. Cross-sectional and longitudinal relations among peer-reported trustworthiness, social relationships, and psychological adjustment in children and early adolescents from the United Kingdom and Canada. *Journal of Experimental Child Psychology* 88:46–67.

Rotermann, M. 2001. Wired young Canadians. *Canadian Social Trends* (Catalogue No. 11-008), 4–8.

Ruck, M., and S. Wortley. 2002. Racial and ethnic minority high school students' perceptions of school disciplinary practices: A look at some Canadian findings. *Journal of Youth and Adolescence* 31:185–95.

Santor, D., D. Messervey, and V. Kusumakar. 2000. Measuring peer pressure, popularity, and conformity in adolescent boys and girls: Predicting school performance, sexual attitudes, and substance abuse. *Journal of Youth and Adolescence* 29:163–82.

Schludermann, E. H., S. M. Schludermann, and C. Huynh. 2000. Religiosity, prosocial values, and adjustment among students in Catholic high schools in Canada. *Journal of Beliefs & Values* 21:99–115.

Schwartz, K., and G. Fouts. 2003. Music preferences, personality style, and developmental issues of adolescents. *Journal of Youth and Adolescence* 32:205–13.

Statistics Canada. 2002a. Language composition of Canada (Table 97F0007XCB01001). http://www12.statcan.ca/english/census01/products/standard/themes (accessed November 24, 2004).

Statistics Canada. 2002b. *Youth in Canada*, 3rd ed. (Catalogue No. 89-511-XPE). Ottawa, ON.

Statistics Canada. 2003. Aboriginal peoples of Canada (Table 97F0011XCB01002). http://www12.statcan.ca/english/census01/products/standard/themes (accessed November 24, 2004).

Statistics Canada. 2004a. Annual demographic statistics 2003 (Catalogue No. 91-213-XPB). Ottawa, ON.

Statistics Canada. 2004b. Families and household living arrangements (Table 95F0313XCB01009). http://www12.statcan.ca/english/census01/products/standard/themes (accessed November 24, 2004).

Statistics Canada. 2004c. Immigration and citizenship (Table 95F0357XCB01003. http://www12.statcan.ca/english/census01/products/standard/themes (accessed November 15, 2004).

Statistics Canada. 2004d. Pregnancy outcomes by age group. http://www.statcan.ca/english/Pgdb/hlth65a.htm (accessed November 16, 2004).

Statistics Canada. 2004e. Profile of census divisions and subdivisions in New Brunswick (Catalogue No. 95-218-XPB). Ottawa, ON.

Statistics Canada. 2004f. Social indicators. *Canadian Social Trends* (Catalogue No. 11-008), 31.

Statistics Canada. 2004g. Youth in transition survey. *The Daily*, April 5.

Sveidqvist, V., N. Joubert, J. Greene, and I. Manion. 2003. Who am I, and why am I here? Young people's perspectives on the role of spirituality in the promotion of their mental health. *International Journal of Mental Health Promotion* 5:36–44.

Tilton-Weaver, L., E. Vitunski, and N. Galambos. 2001. Five images of maturity in adolescence: What does "grown up" mean? *Journal of Adolescence* 24:143–58.

Tremblay, L., and J. Frigon. 2004. Biobehavioural and cognitive determinants of adolescent girls' involvement in sexual risk behaviours: A test of three theoretical models. *Canadian Journal of Human Sexuality* 13:29–43.

Vitaro, F., M. Brendgen, R. Ladouceur, and R. Tremblay. 2001. Gambling, delinquency, and drug use during adolescence: Mutual influences and common risk factors. *Journal of Gambling Studies* 17:171–90.

Vitaro, F., D. Larocque, M. Janosz, and R. Tremblay. 2001. Negative social experiences and dropping out of school. *Educational Psychology* 21:401–15.

Walker, L., K. Hennig, and T. Krettenauer. 2000. Parent and peer contexts for children's moral reasoning development. *Child Development* 71:1033–48.

Weaver, A., E. S. Byers, H. Sears, J. Cohen, and H. Randall. 2002. Sexual health education at school and at home: Attitudes and experiences of New Brunswick parents. *Canadian Journal of Human Sexuality* 1:19–31.

Wilkinson, L. 2002. Factors influencing the academic success of refugee youth in Canada. *Journal of Youth Studies* 5:173–93.

Willms, J. D., and B. Corbett. 2003. Tech and teens: Access and use. *Canadian Social Trends* (Catalogue No. 11-008), 15–20.

Willoughby, T., H. Chalmers, M. Busseri, and YLC-CURA. 2004. Where is the syndrome? Examining co-occurrence among multiple problem behaviors in adolescence. *Journal of Consulting and Clinical Psychology* 72:1022–37.

Wintre, M., and L. Sugar. 2000. Relationships with parents, personality, and the university transition. *Journal of College Student Development* 41:202–14.

Wintre, M., and M. Yaffe. 2000. First-year students' adjustment to university life as a function of relationships with parents. *Journal of Adolescent Research* 15:9–37.

Workers' Compensation Board of British Columbia. 2003. Young worker officer blitz survey - Young workers: Abbreviated survey results. http://www.worksafebc.com/publications.

Workplace Health, Safety and Compensation Commission (WHSCC) of New Brunswick. 2004. *Work smart, work safe*. Saint John, NB. CD-ROM.

World Factbook. 2004. Canada. http://www.cia.gov/cia/publications/factbook/geos/ca.html (accessed November 19, 2004).

Zarbatany, L., R. Conley, and S. Pepper. 2004. Personality and gender differences in friendship needs and experiences in preadolescence and young adulthood. *International Journal of Behavioral Development* 28:299–310.

CENTRAL AMERICA: COSTA RICA, EL SALVADOR, NICARAGUA

Background Information

Central America consists of seven nations, including Belize, Costa Rica, El Salvador, Guatemala, Honduras, Nicaragua, and Panama. In this chapter, adolescence is discussed in three countries not covered by other entries: Costa Rica, El Salvador, and Nicaragua. Nicaragua shares its southern border with Costa Rica; both countries have coasts on the North Pacific Ocean to the west and the Caribbean Sea on the east. El Salvador also has a coast on the North Pacific Ocean and is located between Guatemala and Honduras. At 129,494 square kilometers, Nicaragua is the largest, followed by Costa Rica (51,100 square kilometers) and El Salvador (21,040 square kilometers). The climate in these areas is generally tropical, but with cooler temperatures in the highlands. All three countries have volcanic mountainous regions with coastal plains or belts, and all are subject to earthquakes, volcanoes, and hurricanes (CIA 2005). Indeed, two earthquakes in El Salvador in 2001 had a devastating impact on the population, reversing some improvements in economic conditions that had occurred by 2000 (World Bank 2005).

Costa Rica (population: 4,016,173) is a democratic republic and maintains a relatively stable economy with a generally good standard of living. Eighteen percent of the population lives below the poverty line. Costa Rica enjoys political stability, with little political violence in the last century. It is attractive to foreign investors, and as such, it is a model for other Central American countries. El Salvador has a population of 6,704,932. It is a republic and has widespread poverty (36% live below the poverty line) with a very unequal income distribution. Between 1980 and 1992, a civil war cost 75,000 lives. The current government is attempting to attract foreign investments and to stimulate the economy. Nicaragua (population 5,465,100) is a republic, and is the poorest of the three countries, with 50% below the poverty line. Income distribution is one of the world's most unequal. A civil war in 1978–1979 rose to oppose government corruption, and Marxist Sandinistas were brought to power. The Sandinistas have since been defeated in free elections that have taken place in the last 15 years. Some economic improvement occurred in the 1990s, but in 1998 Hurricane Mitch stalled progress. Costa Rica, El Salvador, and Nicaragua all serve as transshipment points for cocaine from South America. All three countries established independence from Spain in 1821 (CIA 2005).

With respect to age distribution, Costa Rica, El Salvador, and Nicaragua have young populations. The relative youth of these nations is attributable to the fact that birth rates exceed death rates (18.6 versus 4.3; 27. versus 5.9; and 24.9 versus 4.5 per 1,000 in Costa Rica, El Salvador, and Nicaragua, respectively). In Costa Rica, the median age of the population is 26 years, with 29% 14 years old or younger. Two-thirds are between 15 and 64 years, while only 6% are 65 and older. The ethnic distribution is 94% white (including mestizo), 3% black, and 3% other (including Amerindian and Chinese). Spanish is the official language.

The populations of El Salvador and Nicaragua are younger than that of Costa Rica. The median age in El Salvador is 22 years, with 37% age 14 and under. Fifty-eight percent are between 15 and 64, and 5% are over 64. Ninety percent of the population is mestizo, 9% is white, and 1% is Amerindian. The language is Spanish, with some Amerindians speaking Nahua. The median age of Nicaragua is 21 years. Thirty-seven percent are 0 to 14 years, 60% are between 15 and 64, and 3% are 65 and older. Sixty-nine percent are mestizo (mixed Amerindian and white), 17% white, 9% black, and 5% Amerindian. Spanish is the official language. English and indigenous languages are spoken in some areas of Nicaragua (CIA 2005).

Period of Adolescence

Age at first marriage is one indicator of when the period of adolescence has come to an end. The average age at first marriage among women is 22, 19, and 18, in Costa Rica, El Salvador, and Nicaragua, respectively. Respective percentages of women ages 15 to 19 who are currently married are 15%, 22%, and 26% (PRB 2005). These figures suggest a shorter period of adolescence in El Salvador and Nicaragua compared to Costa Rica, and a lower likelihood in these two countries of an exploratory period of emerging adulthood. These statistics mirror educational trends, as educational attainment is higher in Costa Rica than in El Salvador and Nicaragua (UNICEF 2005). Moreover, in El Salvador during the period 1986–2003, 38% of children under the age of 18 were married. Child marriage was higher in rural (46%) than in urban (32%) areas. In Nicaragua, during the same period, 43% of children under the age of 18 were married; 36% in urban and 55% in rural areas (UNICEF 2005). These statistics suggest that when a period of adolescence exists, it is more likely to be found in urban areas. With the higher standard of living and higher rates of educational attainment in Costa Rica, there may be a larger proportion of individuals experiencing longer periods of adolescence and emerging adulthood, although even here, the average age at first marriage among women is considerably lower than in developed countries like Canada and Australia, where the average age of first marriage among women is 26 (PRB 2005).

Insights into periods of adolescence and emerging adulthood can be gleaned from examining the age at which young people leave their parents' home. Based on data gathered in the 1970s in Latin America, De Vos (1989) noted a steady decline in the 20s in the percentage of young people living in their parents' home. In Costa Rica, for example, half of young people moved out by age 24. The strongest predictor of leaving home was marriage. In addition, children with lower levels of education left home earlier than did children with higher levels. De Vos (1989) speculated that those who achieved a high school education or entered postsecondary studies were more likely to require help from their parents. At the same time, young people who pursued higher education were probably in middle-class families who shared the belief in adolescence as a life stage and who could afford to support their children living at home. These data also showed that daughters left home earlier than did sons; sons may be expected to contribute to the household economy whereas daughters marry. Thus, females likely have a shorter period of adolescence compared to males (De Vos 1989).

Welti (2002) points out that adolescence may not be a meaningful concept for some Latin Americans. In indigenous groups, among those who marry early, and in those who take over head of household duties at puberty, childhood moves directly into adulthood, thereby eliminating adolescence as a life stage. The percentage of women giving birth by age 20 in El Salvador and Nicaragua is 46% and 52%, respectively (comparable figure not available for Costa Rica) (PRB 2005). These figures indicate that adolescence has ended for a substantial proportion of 20-year-olds in these countries.

Beliefs

Hispanic cultures tend to have collectivistic values; they are characterized as high on interdependence, cooperation, and conformity and low on competition. There are strong family ties and less extrafamilial contact than seen in individualistic cultures (deRosier and Kupersmidt 1991; Schneider, Woodburn, del Pilar Soteras del Toro, and Udvari 2005). Indeed, children in Costa Rica report more positive relationships with family members, including mothers, fathers, siblings, and grandparents than do children in the United States (DeRosier and Kupersmidt 1991). These values, however, may differ somewhat depending on socioeconomic status and urbanicity. Middle-class urban families in Costa Rica, for example, foster harmony and relatedness in their children in accordance with traditional collectivistic values, but also engage in parenting behaviors that enable the child to develop autonomy (Keller et al. 2004). Other research in Costa Rica shows that young adults leave home later in rural areas than they do in urban areas, presumably because rural families need the help that children can provide at this age (De Vos 1989).

With respect to religious affiliation, Costa Rica, El Salvador, and Nicaragua are largely Roman Catholic (76%, 83%, and 73%, respectively), with Protestant religions making up most of the rest. In El Salvador, Protestant evangelicals are very active (CIA 2005). Catholicism, however, has been a part of the religious practice and beliefs of many people in these countries. As a consequence, virginity in girls is highly valued, and loss of virginity prior to marriage is associated with loss of respect by others. Furthermore, contraception and abortion are seen as sinful, and they are forbidden. It is very difficult for sexually active young women to protect themselves from unwanted pregnancies (Budowski and Bixby 2003). Although religions in Latin America forbid premarital sex and living together outside of marriage, and youth have increasingly conservative views on the acceptability of premarital sex, significant proportions of youth still choose to cohabitate (Welti 2002).

Little research exists on the religious activities of adolescents in Central America. One study found, however, that in a sample of 12- to 20-year-olds from schools in seven Central American countries, older adolescents spent less time in religious activity (attending church, praying, or reading the Bible) than did younger ones. Moreover, girls were significantly more likely than boys to report engaging in religious activity. Furthermore, adolescents in private schools were less involved in such activity than public school enrollees (Chen et al. 2004b).

Gender

On some indicators for Costa Rica, El Salvador, and Nicaragua, there is equality of the sexes in adolescence. School enrollment rates at any level, for instance, show that just as many girls are enrolled as boys; in Nicaragua, a slightly larger percentage of girls attend school. Literacy rates are also comparable for females and males in Costa Rica, El Salvador, and Nicaragua (UNICEF 2005). One way to capture how gender impacts the lives of adolescent girls and boys is to examine their roles as adults. Where political and economic conditions are relatively good (as in Costa Rica), women have made important inroads. Roughly half as many women as men ages 15 to 64 are in the labor force in Costa Rica (84% of men; 45% of women), an increase of 12% for women since 1990 (a decrease of 1% for men). In El Salvador, 80% of men and 47% of women ages 15 to 64 are in the labor force, a decrease of 7% for women and 3% for men since 1990. Amid poverty and economic crisis in Nicaragua, 22% of women and 51% of men ages 15 to 64 are in the labor force, a decrease of 20% for women and 38% for men since 1990. As in many countries, including developed nations, Central American women have a lower share of the political power than do men, although the inequity differs dramatically by country. United Nations data show, for example, that the percentage of seats in Parliament held by women is 35% for Costa Rica, 10% for El Salvador, and 21% for Nicaragua. The numbers of women in managerial or technical positions almost tripled in Costa Rica and more than tripled in El Salvador since 1990, showing considerable progress (UNFPA 2005b).

As is true almost everywhere, women in Central America engage in work (domestic labor) that contributes to the economy but is unpaid. This unrewarded labor begins in girlhood. In Costa Rica, for example, of the total amount of unpaid housework performed by children and adolescents, 30% is done by boys and 70% is done by girls; the distribution is reversed for paid labor (Trejos and Pisoni 2003).

Violence against women when they are children, when they are partners, and when they are wives, is reported to be high in Central America. Furthermore, domestic violence and sexual abuse are not taken as serious crimes. In Nicaragua, for example, the criminal justice system is weak on convictions against sex offenders (Olsson et al. 2000).

As noted earlier, many girls are already married by the time that they are legally permitted to marry (age 18 in most Central American countries). The United Nations Population Fund (UNFPA 2005a) warns against the assumption that early marriage aids girls in achieving a successful transition to adulthood. Rather, particularly when adolescent girls are married to older men, they are likely to experience social isolation and restricted freedom, limited educational attainment and work skills, pressure to conceive, early pregnancy, higher risk of maternal mortality, increased exposure to HIV and other sexually transmitted infections, limited access to the media, and spousal abuse. In Latin America and the Caribbean, the average age gap between teen girls and their husbands is between six and eight years (UNFPA 2005a).

The Self

Research on the development of self in adolescents in Costa Rica, El Salvador, and Nicaragua is scarce. Some cross-national research on self-efficacy (perceived competence to handle or cope with difficult and demanding tasks and situations), however, indicated that university students in Costa Rica felt at least as efficacious as students in Turkey, Poland, Germany, and the United States. Costa Rican students who were higher on self-efficacy were also more optimistic, and less depressed and anxious (Luszczynska, Gutiérrez-Doña, and Schwarzer 2005).

In examining gang membership in Nicaragua, Maclure and Sotelo (2004) noted that opportunities for identity and social development in urban youth in poverty are extremely restricted. In fact, rather than developing their own identities, the social structural system places an undesirable identity on them. Thus, these adolescents seek out other youth in similar circumstances as an alternative (gangs). These gang associations, even if they lead to the violation of norms, enhance the adolescent's well-being, personal control, and social status, at least in the short term.

The establishment of basic rights for as well as the implementation of laws and policies devoted to the protection of children and youth in Costa Rica, El Salvador, and Nicaragua will go a long way in affording adolescents healthy opportunities to explore who they are and where they belong. Some progress has been made. Costa Rica, for example, has instituted a legal framework that meets standards of the United Nations Convention on the Rights of the Child, and has appointed a Minister for Children and Adolescents. UNICEF programs in Costa Rica aim to develop a centralized system that works to increase the quality of education, eliminate sexual exploitation of children, prevent child labor and protect the rights of teen workers, and promote fair judicial processes for adolescents. El Salvador's major accomplishment in this regard is the approval of a National Code for Children. The code is based on the Convention on the Rights of the Child, which seeks to protect children's economic, political, civil, cultural, and social human rights. UNICEF is working in the country to create programs that reduce the devastating impacts of natural disasters, such as earthquakes, on children and adolescents—impacts that lead to the abuse of their rights. Promotion of policies and laws that foster child rights is occurring at the local level. Nicaragua's major challenge is to reduce widespread poverty and inequity. Malnutrition and the lack of safe water are among the many social problems. UNICEF programs in Nicaragua are aimed at mobilizing coalitions that can work to promote children's rights, improve health, and provide access to education for everyone (UNICEF 2005).

Family Relationships

In Costa Rica, El Salvador, and Nicaragua, family life is largely characterized by the traditional Hispanic pattern of close extended kinship ties. A survey of a random sample of Central American adolescents, including those in the three nations discussed here, indicated that spending time with family was one of the most frequent activities in which they engaged (Chen et al. 2004b). Nuclear families often have relatives (grandparents) living with them, particularly when economic circumstances are difficult. Family connections are so strong that they play an important part in establishing social status, political orientations, and job and other opportunities. Godparents play a central role in helping to raise children as well. *Compadrazgo*, which is a system in which there are strong ties between children and their godparents, is an important source of social and economic support. Children may rely on godparents for help when

they need it; godparents feel a responsibility to provide children with assistance in finding jobs or dealing with other difficult circumstances. The extended kinship system, including godparents, is especially critical when the social structure does not function to provide support to families, due to economic or political instability, or natural disasters (El Salvador 2005; Nicaragua 2005; Schneider et al. 2005).

Latin American countries have long had high percentages of mothers who are parenting on their own, although they would typically live with their own parents rather than heading their own household. Despite decreasing fertility in Costa Rica, there were increases from the 1980s through the 1990s in teen pregnancies (especially among girls under age 15), births to unmarried mothers, births without a named father, and divorces. Births with an unacknowledged father were significantly higher in Nicaraguan immigrants in Costa Rica than in native Costa Ricans. About one in five children under age 15 in Costa Rica do not live with a father or stepfather. Unestablished paternity has been an important barrier to child support, as unacknowledged fathers are not bound to provide financial resources (Budowski and Bixby 2003). A landmark Responsible Paternity Law was passed in Costa Rica in 2001 that grants children the right to know who their fathers are, and requires fathers to provide financial support (UNFPA 2005b).

In Nicaragua 25% of households are headed by women, and more than a third of children are not legally registered (UNICEF 2005). Undoubtedly, the severe poverty in Nicaragua contributes to deterioration in families. In addition, the civil war in which so many men were killed meant that many children grew up in the 1980s and 1990s in father-absent households. Typically, the mothers and children who were left behind lived with other family members (Nicaragua 2005).

Friends and Peers/Youth Culture

Friendships and peers are important to adolescents in Latin America (Welti 2002). Peers may not attain the same level of importance, however, as family. Children in Costa Rica, for instance, perceived relationships with their mothers and fathers to be more companionate, intimate, satisfying, and affectionate than relationships with their best friends. Children in the United States, however, reported equally positive relationships with their best friends as with their parents (DeRosier and Kupersmidt 1991). One study of adolescents (ages 12 to 17) in four nations, including Costa Rica, found that when it comes to adolescents' views about their future lifestyles and goals, what it means to be an adult, and whether they would like to be an adult already, adolescents reported that their friends had similar perspectives as they did on these issues. The authors interpreted these results as indicating that alliances with peers are important to adolescents in diverse nations and that the perception of shared views on the transition to adulthood might make that transition easier (Seltzer and Waterman 1996).

In a study that compared the friendships of Costa Rican and Canadian seventh graders, cultural differences were found in the effects of excessive competition (competing to establish superiority over one's friend) on friendship stability. That is, in the Costa Rican subsample, when one friend was high (versus low) on excessive competition the friendship was more likely to be terminated within six months. In Canada, however, friendships were more likely to be terminated when one friend scored very high or very low on the measure of excessive competition; a moderate level of competition seemed to be important for the continuation of friendship. The authors speculated that strong competitiveness is not valued in collectivist cultures like Costa Rica, where cooperation is important. Canada is more individualistic, however, which may be reflected in the result that low scores on excessive competition seemed to be as detrimental to friendship maintenance as high scores (Schneider et al. 2005).

Little research is available on peer influences on health and risk behaviors in adolescents in Central America. In a study of the predictors of healthful eating among high school students in Costa Rica, however, girls and boys indicated that nutritious eating is considered by adolescents to be an effeminate behavior. Moreover, boys in groups may make it a practice to eat unhealthful foods, almost as a way to exhibit masculinity. This study found that many adolescents feel peer pressure not to bring snacks and lunch to school, but it is more acceptable for girls than boys to do so (Monge-Rojas, Garita, Sanchez, and Muñoz 2005).

Love and Sexuality

There is very little research on dating and love in Central American countries. One study found, however, that like the pattern of adolescents elsewhere, older Central American adolescents (in their later teens) report more socializing activities such as going on dates, dancing, and going to bars than do younger adolescents (in their early teens). Teens

with more educated fathers were also more likely to report engaging in socializing activities, compared to teens with less educated fathers (Chen et al. 2004b).

Data on the sexual activities and reproductive behaviors of young people in Central America are spotty, so it is difficult to obtain a complete picture. Welti (2002) claimed that the onset of sexual relations in Latin Americans begins earlier than in previous generations, thus increasing the risk of sexually transmitted diseases and unwanted pregnancies. PRB (2005) indicates that 11% of single women ages 15 to 19 in El Salvador are sexually active (meaning they have had intercourse). Comparable figures are not available for Costa Rica and Nicaragua. Ali and Cleland (2005) reported, however, that 10% of Nicaraguan single women ages 15 to 24 were sexually active. Moreover, they found that in Central American countries with higher virginity rates (Nicaragua as compared to Colombia, for example), the small percentage of sexually active women were least likely to use contraception. In Costa Rica, approximately 38% of sexually active single women ages 15 to 19 use modern methods of contraception. Abortion is outlawed in El Salvador and Nicaragua except to save the mother's life; in Costa Rica, abortion may be permitted for physical and mental health reasons (PRB 2005). Given the relatively low usage of contraception among sexually active single women and the prohibition of abortion, it is not surprising that most conceptions in single women in Latin America end in a live birth. Indeed, conception rates are increasing along with the decline in virginity. Although contraceptive use (particularly condoms) may be increasing as well, it is not high enough to offset the increase in premarital sexual intercourse (Ali and Cleland 2005).

Protection against sexually transmitted diseases in Latin America is of concern. The percentage of the population ages 15 to 24 with HIV/AIDS in 2001 was .4 in Costa Rica, .6 in El Salvador, and .2 in Nicaragua. Figures available for Nicaragua indicate that only 16% of the poorest fifth of women have knowledge about the sexual transmission of HIV/AIDS, whereas 49% of the richest fifth have this information (PRB 2005).

With respect to homosexuality, Welti (2002) indicates that Latin American society is essentially "macho" and homophobic. Historically, the church forbids homosexuality, and homosexual behavior is not supposed to be seen in public. Homosexuals experience discrimination in their families, communities, and work settings. Interestingly, the first sexual experience among males in rural areas may be with a member of the same sex, but this is not seen as homosexual.

Health Risk Behavior

Statistics on health risk behaviors like alcohol and drug use, involvement in crime, and suicide attempts and completions in young people in Costa Rica, El Salvador, and Nicaragua are difficult to locate. Welti (2002), however, concluded that in Latin America, alcohol use and drug consumption are increasing, while rates of smoking among adolescents remain high. Data on accidental deaths and the prevalence of various mental health problems are not collected in a standardized manner. We know that life expectancy at birth is higher in Costa Rica, at 77 years (74 and 80, in males and females, respectively), than in El Salvador (71 years overall; 68 for males and 75 for females) and Nicaragua (70 years overall; 68 for males and 72 for females). Similarly, infant mortality is considerably lower in Costa Rica (10 deaths per 1,000 live births) than in El Salvador (25 deaths per 1,000 live births) and Nicaragua (29 deaths 1,000 live births) (UNICEF 2005). The extent to which health risk behaviors play a role in these differing life expectancy and infant mortality rates is unknown.

In Nicaragua, suicide rates increased from 2.80 (per 100,000) in 1992 to 6.74 in 2002, with more men than women completing suicides (by a ratio of 2.5 to 1). In 2001, suicide was the chief cause of death in 15- to 34-year-olds. Fifty percent of suicide attempts occurred in individuals under the age of 25, with more than 75% of these acts carried out by females (primarily through the use of drugs) (WHO 2005). In general, depression and suicide have been said to be high in Latin America, with suicide rates increasing (Welti 2002).

Alcohol and drug use of adolescents in rural Costa Rica was assessed in 1995 through a random sample of adolescents in grades seven through eleven (average age being 14 years) completing an anonymous survey (Sandi, Diaz, and Uglade 2002). The results revealed that alcohol use was the most common licit substance; lifetime prevalence for alcohol was 67%, with no gender difference. Past-year use was also high, at 57% for males and 47% for females. Furthermore, adolescents reported that their first use of alcohol occurred at 11 years for both genders. Tobacco was second highest in prevalence, with 11% of males and 5% of females indicating that they had used tobacco in the past year. The lifetime and past-year use of other licit substances was under 3%. With respect to illicit

substances, lifetime and past-year prevalence was also under 3%. Males were more likely to use cocaine and marijuana, with an average age at first use of 17 and 16 years, respectively. Females did not report using cocaine and marijuana, but did use amphetamines, with the mean age of first use at 13 years (Sandi et al. 2002). Higher involvement in religious practices protects against exposure to and first use of tobacco and marijuana in Central American adolescents. Furthermore, young people who are more devoted to their religion are less likely to be exposed to alcohol and to try it (Chen, Dormitzer, Bejarano, and Anthony 2004a).

Extreme poverty in Nicaragua seemed to lead to increased crime (including kidnapping) and the rise of youth gangs in Nicaragua through the 1990s (Maclure and Sotelo 2004; Nicaragua 2005). Estimates of gang membership in Nicaragua's capital city of Managua indicate that at least 5,000 youth are actively involved. Economic conditions are so bad that many Managuan youth are not in school, have little hope of obtaining paid employment that will ensure them adequate living conditions, have poor health, and do not have ready access to potable water, electricity, and sewage. There are few facilities available for recreation, almost no planned sporting or social events, little access to social assistance, and no real prospect for obtaining an education. These conditions generally have created many distressed and broken families, with few emotional and economic resources available to the adolescent. As a result, youth turn to other youth for support, forming gangs. The criminal activities of youth gangs (such as robbery) provide a means for them to access the material goods that they cannot obtain in a legitimate manner. The violent activities of these gangs, primarily against youth in other gangs, serve to cement a sense of community that is otherwise lacking (Maclure and Sotelo 2004).

Education

Costa Rica has a high literacy rate, with 96% of the total population age 15 and over able to read and write. The literacy rate is lower in El Salvador; 80% of those ages ten and over can read and write (83% and 78% for males and females, respectively). Sixty-eight percent of the population age 15 and over in Nicaragua are literate, with similar proportions of females and males. Literacy rates likely reflect trends in educational enrollment and achievement. Costa Rica meets most educational goals set by the World Summit for Children, whereas in El Salvador, advances have been made but further effort is required to improve access and quality of education. Severe poverty affects educational access and quality in Nicaragua (CIA 2005; UNICEF 2005).

In Costa Rica, school attendance for children ages 6 to 15 years is compulsory; primary and secondary schools are free. Costa Rica has several public and private universities (Costa Rica 2005). El Salvador has made public schools compulsory through grade nine, and attendance is free. Students can continue through grade twelve and receive a high school diploma. In fact, compulsory education is not consistently enforced, particularly in some urban slum and rural areas. There are several public and private universities; some universities were closed through the civil war of the 1980s (El Salvador 2005). In Nicaragua, prior to 1980, access to education was limited, and even unavailable in some remote areas. Through the 1980s, however, the Sandinista government doubled primary education spending, making it free and compulsory. Schools were established in rural areas. The economic and political problems in the late 1980s, however, disrupted this agenda, resulting in poor school attendance. Nicaragua has several public and private universities, but the majority of students do not attend full-time, and many do not graduate (Nicaragua 2005).

In Costa Rica, 91% of children attend primary school. Administrative data suggest that 94% reach grade five. Two-thirds of Costa Rican youth are enrolled in secondary school. Thirty percent drop out, however, before completing their basic education. By comparison, in El Salvador, primary school enrollment stands at 89%, and 67% of primary school entrants reach grade five. Only 56% of youth are enrolled in secondary school. There are no discernible gender differences in enrollment rates in Costa Rica and El Salvador. In Nicaragua 75% of male and 80% of female children attend primary school. Fifty-four percent reach grade five. Statistics indicate that 52% of male and 61% of female adolescents are enrolled in secondary school (UNICEF 2005).

Work

Sexual exploitation of minors for commercial gain (sex tourism, trafficking) and child labor are significant problems in Costa Rica, El Salvador, and Nicaragua (U.S. Department of Labor 2003). Naturally, children who work are more likely to live in households characterized by poverty. In 2002, 10% of children (ages 5 to 17 years) were involved in child labor in Costa Rica, with a larger percentage of boys (73%) than girls (27%) in the work force

(Trejos and Pisoni 2003). Twelve percent of children ages 5 to 17 work in El Salvador (U.S. Department of Labor 2003) whereas 14% of children ages 5 to 17 are engaged in labor in Nicaragua (74% male, 26% female); serious efforts are being made by the government of Nicaragua to eliminate child labour (Silva 2003). A report by Human Rights Watch (2004) documented a high prevalence of child labor in El Salvador's sugarcane industry. Up to a third of sugarcane workers were children under age 18; many began working in the period from ages 8 to 13. Such work is dangerous, and medical care and food are not made available by employers. Furthermore, children working on plantations may miss weeks or months of school and eventually drop out.

Although more boys than girls work in these countries, more girls than boys participate in unpaid family work. As noted earlier, in Costa Rica, 70% of minors performing unpaid housework are girls. Participation in household chores increases with age, with 5- to 9-year-olds working 14 hours per week, 10- to 14-year-olds working 16 hours per week, and 15- to 17-year-olds working 23 hours per week. Children and adolescents engaged in unpaid housework in Costa Rica are more likely to be poor, living in rural areas, and to drop out of school (Trejos and Pisoni 2003).

Among youth of working age, much employment takes place in the informal (unregulated, illegal, and/or small business) rather than formal economies. These jobs are underpaid, offer no contracts, and have no benefits. Overall unemployment rates are 6.6% in Costa Rica, 6.3% in El Salvador, and 7.8% in Nicaragua, and there is severe underemployment in El Salvador and Nicaragua. Unemployment rates in Latin American youth (ages 15 to 24) who are not in school are twice as high as for older adults. Moreover, unemployment is more prevalent in rural than urban inhabitants and among females compared to males. Many youth in these countries flock to the cities, searching for employment. Impoverishment in some urban communities, with its attendant joblessness, sets up a context in which youth may become involved in gangs, violence, and criminal activity (CIA 2005; Maclure and Sotelo 2004; Welti 2002).

Media

Even in the smallest towns in Latin America, adolescents will learn about world events through radio and TV. Furthermore, it is common for middle- and upper-class adolescents living in urban areas in Latin America to have access to e-mail (Welti 2002).

A study of adolescents ages 12 to 20 in seven Central American nations, including Costa Rica, El Salvador, and Nicaragua, indicated that watching TV and listening to music or radio were two of the most highly endorsed items on a measure of involvement in various activities (Chen et al. 2004b). General statistics on telephone, TV, radio, and Internet use are helpful in assessing access to media. For example, in Costa Rica in 2002, there were 36 telephone sets per every 100 people and a total of 528,047 cell phones. In 1997, there were 980,000 radios and 525,000 TVs, showing that substantial portions of the population had access to radio and TV shows. Data for 2002 show that there were 19 Internet users for every 100 people in Costa Rica.

Access is somewhat more limited in El Salvador. For example, in 2002, the number of phone sets per 100 people was 24. There were over 1,000,000 cell phones in use in 2003. There were 2.75 million radios in 1997 and 600,000 TVs in 1990. The number of Internet users in 2002 was only 5 out of 100.

Compared to Costa Rica and El Salvador, Nicaragua's access to communications and media is lower. In 2002, there were only seven phone sets for every 100 people; there were 202,800 cell phones. In 1997, 1.24 million radios and 320,000 TVs were counted. Only 2 out of 100 people were Internet users. Although Costa Rica shows the highest levels of access to telephone and the Internet, it is interesting to note that comparable figures for the United States are 113 telephones per 100 people, and 55 Internet users per 100 (CIA 2005; UNICEF 2005).

Politics and Military

In Costa Rica and El Salvador the right to vote is granted at age 18. Adolescents in Nicaragua, though, are given the right to vote at age 16 (CIA 2005). According to Welti (2002), adolescents in Latin America are woefully uninvolved in political parties and action. Women's groups are active politically in Nicaragua, lobbying in support of the many serious social issues. In addition, Nicaragua was the first Central American nation to elect a woman president, in 1990. The political involvement of women in Nicaragua is stronger than in most Central American countries due to the earlier efforts of the Sandinista government (Nicaragua 2005).

These three countries differ in their approach to the military. In Costa Rica, there are no regular military forces, but there is a Ministry of Public Security, Government, and Police, with a minimum enrollment age of 18. El Salvador has an army, navy, and air force. At age 18, young people are required to join the service for 12 months. At age 16, youth can volunteer for military service. Nicaragua has an army, as well as a navy and air force. Military service is voluntary, and the minimum enlistment age is 17 years. Recent figures indicate that military expenditures were $64 million USD for Costa Rica, $157 million USD for El Salvador, and $33 million USD for Nicaragua (CIA 2005).

During the 12-year civil war in El Salvador ending in 1992, many children were exposed to violence, personally experiencing physical trauma and suffering, losing relatives to the war, living through persecution, threats, and capture, and having parents who were put in prison. The mental health of these children fifteen or so years later varied depending on family socioeconomic status, perceived competence, and of course, their personal experience with war. Those with the highest war experience showed more mental health problems, including posttraumatic stress and difficulty in envisioning a future (Walton, Nuttall, and Nuttall 1997). The negative effects of warfare in Nicaragua linger, not only in continuing poverty, lack of services, poor health care, and high crime rates, but 76,000 landmines are left, threatening the lives of children and adolescents (UNICEF 2005).

Unique Issues

In general, adolescents in Latin America cite violence and insecurity as frequent sources of concern (Welti 2002). Sexual abuse and violence are two issues that seem to run through some descriptions of life in El Salvador and Nicaragua. For example, an anonymous survey of adults ages 25 to 44 conducted in Nicaragua's largest city, indicated that 20% of men and 26% of women reported having experienced sexual abuse as a child or adolescent, with the majority having been victims prior to age 12. Most respondents knew their abusers, and for many girls, a family member was the perpetrator. These figures are likely underestimates, as improbably few participants reported spouse or partner sexual abuse. Public awareness campaigns and services directed toward sexual abuse have begun to break down barriers to discussing the taboo topic of sexual abuse in Nicaragua (Olsson et al. 2000). UNFPA (2005b) reported that domestic violence is rampant, with a third of Nicaraguan women in partnerships experiencing abuse. It is not uncommon for the abuse to take place in children's presence and to occur during pregnancy. Women's organizations have raised the visibility of this problem.

As is typical of postconflict countries, violence never really ended after the civil war in El Salvador (World Bank 2005). UNICEF (2005) reports that adolescent violence is growing in El Salvador, and student violence is particularly rampant in the capital city of San Salvador, home to extensive slums as well as very wealthy areas. Few effective solutions are in place, but the results of a pilot project organizing students to prevent violence were encouraging, and the program will be expanded. This intervention involves engaging the youths in cultural and artistic works as well as teaching them mediation and conflict resolution skills. As noted earlier, Nicaragua has a significant and increasing problem with youth gangs. Humanitarian agencies, child and youth rights organizations, and the Nicaraguan government understand the importance of intervening into this situation, and of developing positive alternatives for youth. The challenge, however, is formidable and will require coalitions of organizations as well as the active involvement of youth in the design of policies and interventions (Maclure and Sotelo 2004).

NANCY L. GALAMBOS

References and Further Reading

Ali, M. M., and J. Cleland. 2005. Sexual and reproductive behaviour among single women aged 15–24 in eight Latin American countries: A comparative analysis. *Social Science & Medicine* 60:1175–85.

Budowski, M., and L. R. Bixby. 2003. Fatherless Costa Rica: Child acknowledgement and support among lone mothers. *Journal of Comparative Family Studies* 34:229–54.

Central Intelligence Agency (CIA). 2005. *World Factbook.* http://www.odci.gov/cia/publications/factbook/index.html (accessed October 4, 2005).

Chen, C-Y., C. M. Dormitzer, J. Bejarano, and J. C. Anthony. 2004a. Religiosity and the earliest stages of adolescent drug involvement in seven countries of Latin America. *American Journal of Epidemiology* 159:1180–89.

Chen, C-Y., C. M. Dormitzer, J. Bejarano, L. H. Caris, J. B. Diaz, M. Sanchez, K. Vittetoe, and J. C. Anthony. 2004b. The adolescent behavioral repertoire: Its latent structure in the PACARDO region of Latin America. *Behavioral Medicine* 30:101–11.

DeRosier, M. E., and J. B. Kupersmidt. 1991. Costa Rican children's perceptions of their social networks. *Developmental Psychology* 27:656–62.

De Vos, S. 1989. Leaving the parental home: Patterns in six Latin American countries. *Journal of Marriage and the Family* 51:615–26.

Human Rights Watch. 2004. El Salvador: Child labor on sugar plantations. http://hrw.org/english/docs/2004/06/10/elsalv8772_txt.htm (accessed October 6, 2005).

Keller, H., R. Yovsi, J. Borke, J. Kärtner, H. Jensen, and Z. Papaligoura. 2004. Developmental consequences of early parenting experiences: Self-recognition and self-regulation in three cultural communities. *Child Development* 75:1745–60.

Luszczynska, A., B. Gutiérrez-Doña, and R. Schwarzer. 2005. General self-efficacy in various domains of human functioning: Evidence from five countries. *International Journal of Psychology* 40:80–89.

Maclure, R., and M. Sotelo. 2004. Youth gangs in Nicaragua: Gang membership as structured individualization. *Journal of Youth Studies* 7:417–32.

Microsoft Encarta Online Encyclopedia. 2005a. Costa Rica. http://encarta.msn.com/encyclopedia_761572479/Costa_Rica.html (accessed July 19, 2005).

Microsoft Encarta Online Encyclopedia. 2005b. El Salvador. http://encarta.msn.com/encyclopedia_761557648_8/Salvador_El.html (accessed July 19, 2005).

Microsoft Encarta Online Encyclopedia. 2005c. Nicaragua. http://encarta.msn.com/encyclopedia_761577584/Nicaragua.html#s1 (accessed July 19, 2005).

Monge-Rojas, R., C. Garita, M. Sanchez, and L. Muñoz. 2005. Barriers to and motivators for healthful eating as perceived by rural and urban Costa Rican adolescents. *Journal of Nutrition Education and Behavior* 37:33–40.

Olsson, A., M. Ellsberg, S. Berglund, A. Herrera, E. Zelaya, R. Peña, et al. 2000. Sexual abuse during childhood and adolescence among Nicaraguan men and women: A population-based anonymous survey. *Child Abuse & Neglect* 24:1579–89.

Population Reference Bureau (PRB). 2005. Search population and health data. http://www.prb.org/datafind/datafinder6.htm (accessed October 20, 2005).

Sandi, L., A. Diaz, and F. Uglade. 2002. Drug use and associated factors among rural adolescents in Costa Rica. *Substance Use & Misuse* 37:599–611.

Schneider, B. H., S. Woodburn, M. del Pilar Soteras del Toro, and S. J. Udvari. 2005. Cultural and gender differences in the implications of competition for early adolescent friendship. *Merrill-Palmer Quarterly* 51:163–91.

Seltzer, V. C. and R. P. Waterman. 1996. A cross-national study of adolescent peer concordance on issues of the future. *Journal of Adolescent Research* 11:461–82.

Silva, M. C. 2003. National report on the results of the child and adolescent labour survey in Nicaragua. http://www.ilo.org/public/english/standards/ipec/simpoc/nicaragua/index.htm (accessed October 20, 2005).

Trejos, C. D., and R. Pisoni. 2003. *National report on the results of the child and adolescent labour survey in Costa Rica.* http://www.ilo.org/public/english/standards/ipec/simpoc/costarica/index.htm (accessed October 20, 2005).

United Nations Children's Fund (UNICEF). 2005. Information by country. http://www.unicef.org/infobycountry/index.html (accessed October 5, 2005).

United Nations Population Fund (UNFPA). 2005a. Child marriage fact sheet. http://www.unfpa.org/swp/2005/presskit/factsheets/facts_child_marriage.htm (accessed October 12, 2005).

United Nations Population Fund (UNFPA). 2005b. Country profiles. http://www.unfpa.org/profile/ (accessed October 12, 2005).

U.S. Department of Labor. 2003. *The Department of Labor's 2003 findings on the worst forms of child labor.* http://www.dol.gov/ILAB/media/reports/iclp/tda2003/ (accessed October 6, 2005).

Walton, J. R., R. L. Nuttall, and E. V. Nuttall. 1997. The impact of war on the mental health of children: A Salvadoran study. *Child Abuse & Neglect* 21:737–49.

Welti, C. 2002. Adolescents in Latin America. In *The world's youth: Adolescence in eight regions of the globe*. B. B. Brown, R. W. Larson, and T. S. Saraswathi (eds.). pp. 276–306. Cambridge: Cambridge University Press.

World Bank. 2005. El Salvador country brief. http://web. worldbank.org/WBSITE/EXTERNAL/COUNTRIES/ LACEXT/ELSALVADOREXTN/0,,menuPK:295253 ~pagePK:141132~piPK:141107~theSitePK:295244,00. html (accessed October 5, 2005).

World Health Organization (WHO). 2005. Mental health atlas 2005. http://www.who.int/mental_health/evidence/ atlas/ (accessed October 29, 2005).

CHILE

Background Information

Chile is located in the southwest of South America, was colonized by Spain, and proclaimed its independence in 1810. Its long democratic tradition was interrupted by seventeen years of military rule after the military coup in 1973. Democracy was restored in 1990 and brought about social and political changes. Rapid economic growth, the modernization of the state, educational and health care reforms, and changes in the job market starting in the early 1980s, have changed Chilean society's norms, values, cultural products, and symbols (PNUD 2003).

The country's population is about 15 million (Instituto Nacional de Estadísticas, INE 2004). Development in Chile has been characterized by high rates of growth in urban areas, where over 85% of the population lives. Life-expectancy rates have increased and fertility rates have decreased, thus changing the age distribution of the population. Chilean adolescents and emerging adults (15 to 29 years of age) represent approximately 25% of the country's population (3,674,239) (INJUV 2004), but their numbers are decreasing more sharply than in other Latin American countries. Similarly, the percentage of youth 18 years or under has decreased from 34.5% in 1990 to 31% in 2003 (MIDEPLAN 2003). The adolescent group (13 to 17 years) represents 9.4% of the total population (MIDEPLAN 2003).

The youth population concentrates in urban areas (86.4% in 2003), and exhibits the highest migration rates from rural to urban areas. Almost 19% of the adolescent population lives in poverty, and 6.6% lives in extreme poverty (MIDEPLAN 2003). Ethnically, the majority of Chileans are *mestizo* (an ethnic blend of Spanish and natives). Consequently, 92.3% of adolescents do not identify with any ethnic minorities. Only 6.2% considers themselves *mapuche* (natives of the south of Chile and Argentina) (INJUV 2004).

As a target for research and social policy, the adolescent group has been neglected. Four nationally representative surveys of the population (15 to 29 years) have been conducted since 1994 to characterize the social and economic status of youth.

The National Youth Institute was created in 1991 with a two-fold goal, namely to plan and coordinate initiatives aimed at youth across different government sectors (such as education, health, justice) and to collaborate in the design, planning, and coordination of youth policies. Main topics underlying current policy initiatives are to improve youth quality of life and to promote citizenship. Policy efforts have focused on promoting youth social integration, social participation, and strengthening youth identity and culture.

Period of Adolescence

The identification of adolescence as a distinctive developmental phase is linked to the field of adolescent medicine in Chile. The first studies focused on physical growth and development (Muzzo and Burrows 1986) and the provision of health services tailored to adolescents' needs (Florenzano, Maddaleno, Bobadilla, Alvarez et al. 1988; Molina 1988). Subsequent studies examined adolescents' behaviors that pose risks to their health (Florenzano, Pino, and Marchandón 1993; Molina 1994).

Definitions of adolescence reflect society's expectations and demands on adolescents. The social and political movements of the late 1960s and mid-1970s in Latin America motivated youth engagement in social movements and political revolutions. Consequently, youth's endorsement of social and political causes was seen as a marker of their quest for identity.

Mattelart and Mattelart (1970) characterized the aspirations and future prospects, as well as the social involvement and political engagement of 400 males and females (18 to 24 years) stratified by occupation (college students, employees, and unskilled workers). Back then, youth from rural and urban backgrounds perceived that their issues were deeply intertwined with social inequity and segregation. Over 90% of them acknowledged social inequality. Urban respondents depicted a society divided into three social classes (low, middle, and high), whereas rural youth held a two-class conception (the rich and the poor). Across occupations females were less involved in social organizations and movements than males, and this difference was greater among working-class youth.

Later findings (INJUV 2003) indicated that social inequality was still an issue for adolescents 15 to 18 years of age. Forty-seven percent of them believe there was unequal access to opportunities, 35% believed social class differences and social inequity should be reduced, and 29% demanded social justice. These figures increased for older youth.

Mattelart and Mattelart's (1970) findings suggested that transition to work occurred at younger ages in the 1970s, and therefore, work status was a meaningful descriptor of youth identity. Greater access to education and higher expectations for youth attainment later extended the duration of adolescence. By the beginning of the twenty-first century, the majority of Chilean adolescents were students.

Adolescence is recognized as a transitional developmental phase. Though publications provide different age ranges for the adolescent period, most concur that adolescence covers the second decade of life (Florenzano 1997). For health policy and programs, adolescence extends from 10 to 19 years. Other publications use the term "youth" to include the early twenties and to characterize diverse groups of young people (INJUV 1999). However, empirical studies of adolescence are still scarce in Chile.

In adolescents' views, adolescence is a transitional phase in which youth assume more responsibility for their personal attainment and well-being (Soto, Matute and Peña 2003). In youths' conceptions, adolescence is a time to decide what to do with one's personal life. Forty percent of adolescents think that during adolescence one should make important decisions about one's personal future, and over 20% state that adolescence is a period to learn how to make a living (INJUV 1994, 1997). Support for the view that adolescence is a period to endorse great ideals decreased from 22.5% in 1994 to 17.2% in 1997. At the same time, support for the view that adolescence is a period to have fun in life increased from 12% in 1994 to 23.1% in 1997. Significant differences by socioeconomic status (SES) are observed in that high-SES youth report stronger support for the view that adolescence is a time for fun, whereas low-SES youth report stronger support for the view that adolescence is a time to figure out how to make a living.

During the 1990s, efforts to address youth issues were targeted through intervention programs, oftentimes lacking a comprehensive perspective on the reality of diverse groups of youth (Asún, Alfaro, and Morales 1994). Policy efforts at the turn of the century focused on the promotion of healthy lifestyles in adolescents.

Globalization and modernization have changed the transition to adulthood in Chile. Demographic trends suggest that the tasks and role transitions traditionally associated with adulthood (such as completing a career, getting a job, getting married, and having children) are no longer acknowledged by emerging adults as the single path to adulthood. Alternatively, diverse paths that place value on self-development are seen as markers of adulthood (Programa de Naciones Unidas para el Desarrollo 2003). As the educational level and expectations for educational attainment have increased, economic independence and leaving home have been postponed. Similar trends are observed in expected ages for marriage and parenthood, particularly among high-SES groups (INJUV 2004).

Beliefs

Like in other Latin American countries, the Spanish colonization brought together a strong imprint of the Catholic Church in Chile's religious and cultural beliefs. Catholicism strongly influenced the organization of social life and values of Chilean society, and separation between the Catholic Church and the government occurred relatively late in Chilean history, in 1925. Chile's constitution proclaims freedom of religious beliefs; however, most of the population continues to identify with the Catholic creed.

Starting in the 1990s the landscape of beliefs changed, with Catholics decreasing and Protestants increasing in numbers (Instituto Nacional de Estadísticas 2004). Seventy percent of the general population 15 years and older reported to be Catholic and 15% Protestant (Instituto Nacional de Estadísticas 2004). Though most of the population identifies with the Catholic Church, large numbers of people are not involved in church or religious activities.

For the young population 15 to 29 years old, identification with the Catholic Church is reported to be around 50%, and identification with Protestant churches to be around 17% (INJUV 2004). Interestingly, the percentage of adolescents and emerging adults 15 to 29 years who do not identify with any religious denomination went down from 31% in 2000 to 23% in 2003 (INJUV 2004). At the same time 29% of adolescents believe that "faith in God" is an important asset for personal success (INJUV 2004), and the Catholic Church is one of the most trusted public institutions. While 95.6% of 16- to 18-year-old adolescents report believing in

God, only 32% of them attend church on a weekly basis (INJUV 2004).

Profound political and social changes in Chile over the last three decades have influenced culture, values, and beliefs (Programa de Naciones Unidas para el Desarrollo 2002). The uniform view of society promoted by the military during the 1970s and 1980s has evolved into a more diverse society with democracy. At the same time, economic development and the liberal market system have promoted individualistic value orientations in Chilean society (Programa de Naciones Unidas para el Desarrollo 2002). Further, the orientation toward individualistic values is more prevalent in Chilean youth (18 to 21 years) than in older groups (Programa de Naciones Unidas para el Desarrollo 2003). The same difference is true for middle and upper-middle class as compared to low-SES youth. In the same way, a higher percentage of males than females endorse individualistic values. Saiz and Gempp (2001) similarly concluded that individualistic values are more characteristic of Chilean youth than older adults in Chile.

Interestingly, other findings depict Chilean society as oriented toward values uncharacteristic of individualistic societies. For example, in a study that maps value orientation across different countries, orientation toward mastery and independence were low in Chileans. Instead, Chilean society stood close to what Schwartz names "harmony" values. These are characterized by "... emphasis in fitting into the world as it is, trying to understand and appreciate rather than change, direct, or to exploit" (Schwartz 2004, 5). According to Schwartz, values characteristic of cultures in this pole, as opposed to the mastery pole, are peace, unity with nature, and protection of the environment.

Gender

Gender roles have been influenced by values associated with women's rights and status in Chile. Historically, the role of women in Chilean society has been contradictory. Though women gained important rights ahead of their counterparts in Latin America (they graduated their first medical doctor in 1886, gained voting rights in municipal elections in 1934, and in national elections in 1949), gender inequality remains as a major issue in Chilean society, especially in regard to women's access to power and decision-making positions (Schkolnik 2004). Women's participation in the labor force in Chile (39%) is one of the lowest in South America (SERNAM 2004). Chilean females have on average lower social status, less power, and fewer resources than males.

Only 13% of the parliament lower-level chamber seats and government positions are held by women (SERNAM 2003). During the years of the military regime, a conservative image of women's roles (Mattelart 1976) was promoted. Consistent with the latter, gender-equality issues were almost completely absent from official discourse, and women were minimally represented in government positions.

As a consequence of the active participation of women in the transition to democracy, recent democratic governments have made concerted efforts to increase women's participation in the labor force and power positions (PNUD 2002). An indicator of change is the fact that women were named as the Secretary of State and the Secretary of Defense.

In Chile prevalent cultural standards of women as caretakers and men as providers operate early in the primary socialization contexts of families and schools (Schkolnik 2004). Gender roles conform to the traditional pattern with fathers perceived as strong authority figures who set rules at home. Alternately, mothers are perceived as more caring and involved with the family but are granted less authority (SERNAM 2002a). Traditional family roles are also observed in that women take responsibility for larger proportions of household chores, such as cleaning, grocery shopping, and caring for children (PNUD 2002). A similar division of labor is observed in the population 15 to 19 years of age, where girls' involvement in household chores is almost three times that of boys (SERNAM 2004). Interestingly, boys and girls perceive mothers as responsible for socializing children into traditional role expectations and values (SERNAM 2002b).

Clear gender differences are observed in beliefs and attitudes regarding women's roles. For example, 26% of men ages 18 to 24 consider that women should be most responsible for household chores, compared with only 13% of women in that age range (SERNAM 2002a). In the same way, higher percentages of young men, as compared to young women, consider that married women should not be involved in politics (26% versus 10%, respectively), and that a woman should not insist her point of view is correct over a man's view (26% versus 9%, respectively) (SERNAM 2002a). These views and attitudes are highly influenced by SES, with low-SES respondents endorsing more traditional views of family roles. For example, 53% of men with elementary education or less believe women are mainly responsible for house chores, compared to only 10% of college educated men (SERNAM 2002a).

Differences in attitudes toward family roles by SES are also observed for adolescents. Interestingly, low- and high-SES adolescents expect more traditional roles for women, whereas middle-SES adolescents expect more egalitarian relationships between men and women. While both boys and girls consider that both groups are equally talented, there is a tendency in males to consider themselves more talented in traditional areas such as math and sports (SERNAM 2002b).

Consistent with their attitudes and beliefs, a higher percentage of males aspire to professions requiring math as compared to females (43.1% versus 12.2%) (SERNAM 2002b). Further, a higher percentage of females than males (47% versus 28%) believes math to be the most difficult subject in high school. On the other hand, higher percentages of women aspire to careers in the social sciences (33.3% versus 19.5%) and education (14.2% versus 1.6%). In terms of vocational expectations, women manifest a wider variety of professional preferences, while men concentrate in careers strong in math.

In terms of future work preparation, a higher percentage of girls (65.9%) aspire to pursue a college degree compared to boys (56.9%), and both groups feel supported by their parents to study what they want. The latter signals a change in expectations compared with past generations (SERNAM 2002b). Another interesting difference emerges in the value assigned to work. Men tend to value work as a means to be successful and gain economic status, whereas women value work as a means for personal and professional advancement.

The Self

Adolescents' personal identities have been shaped by changes in values and beliefs systems in Chile (INJUV 2004). During the 1980s and in the midst of fast social and economic change that excluded part of the population, youth identity was depicted as antagonistic to adult mainstream values (Espinoza 1999). This view was disconfirmed in the 1990s by findings that Chilean youth shared mainstream orientations, valuing education and hard work as the means for social integration (INJUV 2001, 2003). Findings from different surveys (INJUV 1994, 1997) indicate that the majority of Chilean youth (85%) think of themselves as different from the adult generation in terms of thinking and acting. At the same time they recognize ample diversity within their group (INJUV 1994).

Physical appearance is highly valued by Chilean adolescents. In their views adolescents should take care of their physical bodies (Soto, Matute, and Peña 2003). Because of prevalent beauty standards, weight is a common referent in adolescents' assessments of their physical identities. According to their body size, 58.8% of adolescents 12 to 18 years consider themselves as "normal," 15.2% thin, and 18.8% overweight. Seventy percent are satisfied with their physical appearance.

Building one's own personal identity is seen as an important means to accomplishing life goals. Chilean adolescents 15 to 18 years have positive self-concepts and high self-esteem. They describe themselves with positive attributes such as solidarity (36.9%), sociability (34%), reality-oriented (28.7%), easygoing (28.6%), and optimistic (25.4%) (INJUV 2003). Negative attributes are not frequently selected in adolescents' or young adults' self-descriptions.

Work accomplishments and building one's own personal identity are considered markers of competence. Thirty-eight percent of adolescents 15 to 18 years consider that having a good job or building one's career are the most important accomplishments for future well-being. Similarly, 35.1% consider that investing in their development as a person is conducive to happiness in life (INJUV 2003). Over 60% of adolescents believe persistence and hard work are key to their future accomplishment, and 31% believe that having clear goals in life is most important (INJUV 2003).

Chilean adolescents report high future-oriented aspirations and expectations (INJUV 2001; PNUD 2003). However, Martínez, Cumsille, and Rivera (2004) found that adolescents' future-oriented aspirations and expectations decrease as adolescents grow older, a finding reflecting their enhanced capacity for self-evaluation. Changes in postsecondary educational aspirations have been more dramatic for girls (Martínez, Cumsille, and Rivera 2004; Ministerio de Educación 2001), a finding related to changes in social-role expectations for women (PNUD 2003). Aspirations and expectations of future educational attainment are also positively related to SES.

Family Relationships

In spite of rapid modernization and the greater prevalence of individualistic values over recent decades, Chileans are highly positive in their assessments of the family as a social institution (PNUD 2002) and manifest a strong family orientation. Two-parent nuclear families are the most prevalent family structure, though there has been an increase in single-parent families and a decrease in extended families since the 1990s. Nuclear families account for 57% of the homes in Chile, followed by 22% of extended families, and 12% of single-parent families (Instituto Nacional de Estadísticas 2004).

Adolescents assign great importance to family relationships and expect to form families of their own in the future. For example, in a 2003 national sample of adolescents and young adults 15 to 29 years (INJUV 2004), 76% report their strongest commitment is to be with family, and 34% of them believe that developing a family is the most important accomplishment for happiness in life. Close to 90% of adolescents 15 to 18 years consider family as a central institution in society, and 72.5% report being highly committed to their families. In the same way, for 68% of adolescents marriage is part of their life plan, and an additional 15% expect to cohabitate (SERNAM 2002b). There are important socioeconomic differences in marital expectations as 80% of high-SES but only 60% of low-SES adolescents expect to marry.

The commitment of adolescents to their families is partially based on a strong feeling of family as a caring institution. Over 96% of adolescents report liking their own family, and 77% of them consider their family home as a caring and loving place (INJUV 2003).

Relationships with parents are similarly evaluated in a positive way. While both parents are positively evaluated in different areas, mothers are more highly evaluated than fathers. For example, the average rating of the overall quality of the relationship with the mother is 6.21 and 5.63 with the father (on a scale from 1 to 7, with 7 the highest rating). From the different aspects of the relationship assessed, communication with the mother receives the highest average rating (6.51) and time spent with father the lowest (5.27). Adolescents report the highest agreement with parents concerning future plans (88%), and their lowest agreement on political issues (47%). However, 58% of adolescents consider lack of time to spend with family to be a problem. The importance of the family in the life of Chilean adolescents helps to explain the results of a comparative study that found Chilean early adolescents to be more sensitive to marital discord than U.S. early adolescents (Cummings, Wilson, and Shamir 2003).

The importance attributed to family does not preclude the fact that family is perceived as a social institution that has undergone changes. This is particularly so for family roles and the hierarchical structure of relationships (PNUD 2002). In their interactions with their adolescent children, parents perceive erosion in their parental authority when

compared to the interactions they recall with their own parents (PNUD 2002).

Studies conducted in the early 1990s suggested that negative control, characterized by the use of physical, verbal, and psychological control, was the most prevalent socialization style used by parents of adolescents 16 to 19 years, followed by an inductive style (Sepúlveda, Almonte, Valenzuela, and Avendaño 1991). Inductive style, characterized by parents' sharing of power and tolerance for adolescents' self-determination, was associated with better developmental outcomes, such as lower incidence of substance use and problem behavior. Alternatively, negative use of power was associated with more problematic behaviors. In the same way, it has been reported that unsatisfying family relationships are associated with higher alcohol and drug use (Almonte, Sepúlveda, Valenzuela, and Avendaño 1990).

Similarly, Ingolsby, Schvenedelt, Supple, and Bush (2004) also found negative family practices (parental punitiveness) to be related to lower self-efficacy and academic orientation.

Friends and Peers/Youth Culture

Social bonds with peers are important relationships in the socialization of adolescents in Chile. Of adolescents 15 to 19 years, 87.8% have a group of friends they see frequently (INJUV 2004). Socioeconomic differences are observed in that high-SES youth report a higher percentage of peer group affiliation (89.8%) compared to middle- (73.6%) and low-SES (66.6%) adolescents.

Adolescents develop friendships through interactions in their neighborhood (39.7%) and schools (36.4%). Socioeconomic differences are again noted. Some high-SES adolescents (46.2%) meet their friends at school, whereas most low-SES youth meet their friends in the neighborhood. Only 25.7% of low-SES adolescents meet their friends at school, thus reflecting cultural differences in the organization of social life by social class.

Friendship networks become an important source of emotional support for young people by providing opportunities for adolescents to share their problems (28.5%), to talk about sexuality (60.3%), interpersonal issues (55.8%), and by providing instrumental help to solve everyday issues (28.5%) (INJUV 2003). Seventy percent of adolescents 15 to 18 years confide their personal problems to friends, and over 80% seek help from a friend when facing an important problem in life. Overall, friends appear to have a more prominent role in the lives of female, high-SES, and urban youth (INJUV 2003).

Adolescents 15 to 18 years hang out with their friends at home (78.3%), at school (52.8%), and to a lesser extent in street corners (36.4%) and public squares or parks (33.2%). Only 27.7% report using public spaces to meet their friends (INJUV 2003), and this group is predominantly low-SES—a finding that reflects the different organization of social life in affluent and poor communities (INJUV 2000).

Adolescent affiliation in youth groups is low. Twenty-one percent of 15- to 18-year-olds are involved in sports, 20% in religious groups, 16.8% in virtual groups, 16.4% in cultural groups, and 14.8% in hobby groups. Involvement in other youth activities such as volunteering, Scouts, or student councils does not elicit adolescents' interest. Spending time with friends in social gatherings and parties are the most frequent activities that adolescents engage in during weekends.

Greater access to postsecondary education in middle- and high-SES youth provides new opportunities for adolescents to extend and strengthen friendships. Almost 80% of emerging adults (19 to 24 years) have a group of close friends, and friends are their best confidants and help providers. Friendship networks consolidate in long-term bonds as they also influence mating, career opportunities, and business, thus enhancing the social capital of youth development. Alternatively, the neighborhood-based social networks of low-SES youth do not necessarily extend to other contexts of social influence (INJUV 1999). Because of stronger socialization into family issues, low-SES female adolescents are more bound to their neighborhood network, but this social network decreases as they get older (INJUV 2004).

Peer influences have not been a focus of research in Chile. Most accounts rely on small case studies or anecdotal observations of peer culture. The emergence of urban tribes (*flaites,* or Chilean rappers, goths, sharps, darks, punkies, thrashers, and hip-hopers among others) (Ahumada 2000) and gangs, suggests that youth form distinct subcultures in Chile. These groups differentiate from adults in their lifestyles, slang, dress, hairstyle, and music preferences. The formation of these crowds has been related to adolescents and young adults' need affiliation and their efforts to cope with the anomie of living in a individualistic society.

Love and Sexuality

Romantic relationships are an important aspect of adolescents' social relationships in Chile. In 2001, 47.8% percent of adolescents 15 to 19 years were involved in romantic relationships. Of them, 43.7% reported going steady (INJUV 2001). Subsequent figures for adolescents 15 to 18 years (INJUV 2003) indicated that 23% were going steady, 10.5% were seeing someone, and 2.2% were cohabitating (INJUV 2004). Commitment towards marriage was rare and represented only 1.1% of adolescents.

Adolescents provided very positive appraisals of the quality of their romantic relationships. On a scale ranging from 1 to 7, how to use money (6.83), love and affect (6.82), and satisfaction with sexual life (6.69) were ranked as the most positive aspects of the relationship. Fidelity (6.28) and shared goals and life prospects (6.23) received the lowest scores (INJUV 2004), although still positive.

As for their marital status, the majority (99.4%) of adolescents 15 to 18 years are single. Only 0.3% in 2003 (INJUV 2003) were married. Former surveys (INJUV 1997, 2001) reported higher percentages of marriage in adolescents (1.4% in 1997 and 2.1% in 2000). Similarly, the percentage of adolescent cohabitation decreased from 3.3% in 1997 to 1.5% in 2000 (INJUV 2001). Only 5.4% of adolescents 15 to 18 years have children (on average, one child) (INJUV 2003), thus indicating that marriage and childbearing are transitions expected in the mid-twenties (59.8% have children by that time, with an average of 1.55 child per family).

Findings from a national survey indicate that the majority (66.9%) of Chilean adolescents 15 to 18 years are not sexually active (INJUV 2004). The study indicates that 33.1% of adolescents 15 to 18 years (INJUV 2004) have initiated their sexual life; only 13.7 % of adolescents have had sexual relationships before age 15.

Gender differences are observed in the age of first intercourse. Within the group 15 to 29 years, 76.9% of males and 69.8% females have initiated their sexual life (INJUV 2004). Additionally, the percentage of males that initiates sexual activity before fifteen (20.8%) is much higher than that of females (6.2%) (INJUV 2001), a finding related to different role expectations for each gender.

Among adolescents 15 to 18 years old who are sexually active, their first sexual relationship is reported at age 15.21 years (INJUV 2003). For the larger group 15 to 29 years the average is 16.8 years; however males start at 16.2 whereas females begin at 17.6 (INJUV 2004). Approximately 13% of adolescents 15 to 18 years report having sexual intercourse several times a week, and 19% at least once a week. At the same time, 37.1% report not having sexual relations in the last six months (INJUV 2004). Sexual activity happens in couples. For the sexually active (59%), boyfriends and girlfriends are the most frequent partners. In addition 22.6% of youth report having sex with former romantic partners, and 10.3% with an occasional acquaintance (INJUV 2004). In brief, most of adolescents' sexual activity involves stable partners.

The most frequent motivation for engaging in sexual activity that adolescents 15 to 19 years describe are to be in love (39.9%) and that both partners desire it (38.3%) (INJUV 2004). Only 14.5% state the reason as marriage or engagement, or cohabitation (7.4%). More females (45.6%) consider love to be the leading motivation for sexual activity (INJUV 2004).

Fernández, Bustos, González, Palma, Villagrán, and Muñoz (2000) found that adolescents lack appropriate knowledge about sexuality. In adolescents' views, parents and teachers should be the main providers of sexual information starting at age 10 to 15 years.

A national policy to promote responsible sexual behavior was advanced in 2005 as a joint effort of the Secretaries of Education and Health, the National Office on Women's Issues, and the National Institute of Youth. Its aim is to foster active reflection that builds on the competencies and rights of youth, families, and communities to make decisions regarding sexual matters.

Health Risk Behavior

Changes in Chilean society have brought about many of the social problems associated with modernization. Chilean adolescents present a high prevalence of behaviors that pose risks to their health, such as alcohol and drug use, antisocial behavior, and risky sexual behavior. A high prevalence of psychological problems has also been reported.

Several studies report that smoking is one of the most prevalent health risk behaviors in Chilean adolescents. For example, Valdivia, Simonetti, Cumsille et al. (2004) report a 47% lifetime prevalence of smoking in a high school population (14 to 18 years old). Prevalence rates were higher for females than males (52% versus 42%), and for low-SES compared to middle- and high-SES (51%, 44%, and 47%, respectively).

Furthermore, young Chilean adolescents 13 to 15 years rank highest in tobacco consumption in the international sample of the Global Youth Tobacco Survey (2003). Consistent with Valdivia et al. (2004), the Global Youth Tobacco Survey (2003) reports higher prevalence rates for girls (44% in Santiago) than boys (31% in Santiago). Interestingly, Chile is one of the few countries in this international sample in which prevalence rates of smoking are higher for girls than for boys.

Prevalence rates for other substances, both legal and illegal, are also high, and have increased in the last decade. For example, lifetime prevalence of alcohol use for adolescents during the last year of elementary school and through high school (14 to 19 years old) has been estimated in 2003 at 78.7%, up from 73.2% in 1999. In the same year, last-year and last-month prevalence rates were estimated at 61.2% (down from 65.1% in 1999) and 39.2% (similar to the 39.1% from 1999) respectively (CONACE 2000, 2003).

No significant gender differences are observed for alcohol use, but demographic differences have been reported. Specifically, differences in prevalence of alcohol use have been reported according to type of school. Overall, private paid schools present higher prevalence of alcohol use than both private subsidized (a type of private school subsidized with public funds) and public schools. Because school type is usually a proxy for SES in Chile, these results can reflect socioeconomic differences in consumption. On the other hand, a study of lifestyles conducted by the Chilean Secretary of Health showed that around 20% of adolescent males and 9% of females ages 15 to 19 could be considered problem drinkers according to their self-reported alcohol use (MINSAL 2001).

Illegal substances also show high prevalence rates. In 2003, lifetime prevalence of illegal drugs such as marijuana, crack, or cocaine was estimated at 22%, with a higher prevalence in adolescent males (25%) than in females (20%) (CONACE 2003). By far the most prevalent illegal drug used is marijuana (22%) followed by cocaine (6%) and crack (5%). Differences in illegal drugs use by school type are small and opposite to what is reported for alcohol use (around 22% lifetime prevalence of marijuana use for public and private subsidized schools and 20% for private schools). Consistent with what has been reported in the prevention literature, parental knowledge and monitoring are positively associated with lower prevalence of substance use (CONACE 2003).

Teenage pregnancy has been reported at 6% for the age range 15 to 17 years, and 22% for women 18 to 20 years old. About 16% of children born and registered in 2002 were born to mothers 19 years old or younger (MINSAL 2002). Nevertheless, the comparison of the 1992 and 2002 census data indicate a decrease in the percentage of children born to mothers 15 to 19 years old in the preceding year before each census (SERNAM 2002). It has also been reported (Ramírez and Cumsille 1997) that in Santiago teenage pregnancy in low-SES adolescents is almost five times higher than in high-SES adolescents.

Studies have shown that the general urban population in Chile present a high prevalence of psychological symptoms (Vicente, Rioseco, Saldivia et al. 2002). Adolescents are no exception. Epidemiological reports (MINSAL 2004) report a 14% prevalence of affective disorders in the population 15 to 24 years of age. Similarly, a study of a normative high school population (Cumsille and Martínez 1996) reported high levels of depressive symptoms, with female adolescents scoring higher than male adolescents.

The mortality rate for adolescents 10 to 19 years in 2003 was 0.32 per 1,000, for the whole population (MINSAL, n.d.). This rate was significantly higher for boys (0.45) than girls (0.19). It is also interesting to note that the mortality rate decreased from around 0.50 in 1990 (MINSAL 2001).

Education

Studying is the main activity of adolescents in Chile. Enrollment in secondary education increased by 12.3% from 1990 to 2003, reaching 92.6% for the population 14 to 17 years (MIDEPLAN 2003). Eighty-four percent of adolescents 15 to 18 years and 33% of emerging adults 19 to 24 years are enrolled in school (INJUV 2004).

Substantive efforts and resources have been invested during the last decade in order to increase the quality of education in Chile. Findings from a national survey (MIDEPLAN 2003) indicate that the educational level of adolescents and emerging adults 15 to 24 years was raised from 10.2 years in 1990 to 11.2 years in 2004. Further, gains in education are most significant for youth from less privileged socioeconomic groups. On average youth from very low-SES (the 10% most poor homes) attain 1.5 years of education above that of their parents, and 2.5 years of education above that of their grandparents. Educational gains are also higher in rural youth. This group on average has attained 1.6 years of education above that of their parents and 2.8 years of education above that of their grandparents (MIDEPLAN 2003).

Compulsory education is divided into two main cycles that comprise eight years of elementary and four years of high school education. Overall dropout rates during secondary education are 8.5%. School dropout is highest in ninth grade (11.3%) and lowest in eleventh grade (6%) (MINEDUC 2004). The majority (52.5%) of adolescents 15 to 18 years old attend scientific-humanistic education, and 35.4% attend technical school.

The Chilean educational system is highly segregated by SES and has a mixed administrative system. In 2002, 48% of the high school population attended public schools, 37% attended private subsidized schools, and 9% attended private schools.

About a third of youth who graduate from high school continue to higher education either at a college institution (23%) or a professional or technical school (11%,) but these figures vary greatly for rural and urban youth (INJUV 2004). Overall, for youth 18 to 24 years access to postsecondary education increased from 25.69% in 2000 to 33.2% in 2005, as reflected by freshmen enrollment in college institutions (MINEDUC 2005).

Access to postsecondary education varies greatly by SES. Almost 50% of high-SES youth enter college compared to 18.4% of middle- and only 5.3% of low-SES youth (INJUV 2003). Low-SES youth are selected into technical or vocational school.

Chilean adolescents have not performed well in international tests of educational attainment. For example, in the 1999 Trends in International Mathematics and Science Study (TIMMS) 14-year-old Chileans performed below the international average and ranked 35 out of 38 countries (MINEDUC 2000).

Chilean youth's assessment of the quality of the educational process that takes place in their schools are fairly positive. However, opportunities for recreation and socializing during their school hours are seen as deficient. On a scale ranging 1 to 7, 78.2% adolescents 15 to 18 years believe their teachers' technical competence is fairly high (6.3), and 68.6% adolescents think their teachers' commitment and dedication is also high (6.12). Similarly, adolescents provide positive assessments of the extent to which their schools provide a good preparation for postsecondary studies (6.02), teach values (6.17), and guide them toward a personal life project (6.12).

Work

Working is not a universal experience for Chilean adolescents. A national survey of 7,189 adolescents and emerging adults (15 to 29 years) found that 37.3% were working, and 35% were studying and not working (INJUV 2003). Within this age group, only 14.5% started working in their adolescent years. The transition to work signals a marker of emergent adulthood in Chile. As access to education and youth expectations for educational attainment have increased, the percentage of youth that works decreased only from 33.6% in 1994 to 31.2% in 2003, and the percentage of youth that combines work and school increased from 3.7% in 1994 to 6.1% in 2003.

On average, Chilean youth 15 to 29 years hold their first job at 16.7 years. Males start working earlier (16.3 years) than females (17.2 years) (INJUV 2004). Within the adolescent group, the average age for the first job is 14.5 years (INJUV 2004). Among those not looking for a job, 55.2% report being unable to balance work and studies, 21.5% report no need to work, and 8.5% report no interest in working (INJUV 2003). Socioeconomic differences are observed in that low-SES youth hold jobs at earlier ages (mean 16.2 years) than their high-SES counterparts (mean 17.9) (INJUV 2004).

The majority of adolescents and young adults 15 to 29 years who are working are employees (79.3%). Only 18.3% work independently, and no differences between urban and rural youth are observed. Youth identify economic reasons as their motivation to work, foremost to support their own family (34.6%), to pay for personal expenses (22.9%), and to contribute to their family of origin (16.8%) (INJUV 2004). Eighteen percent of rural adolescents and young adults 15 to 29 years are living on their own and are economically independent (INJUV 2004).

A different motivational pattern appears in adolescents 15 to 18 years old. They are working to pay for personal expenses (45.0%), and to contribute to their family of origin (19.0%). Only 5.4% are working to support their own families (INJUV 2004).

Socioeconomic differences are observed in the status of youth work. Twenty-four percent of low-SES youth are working with no legal contract compared to 11.3% of their high-SES counterparts. This difference may be due to lower educational levels in low-SES youth. In terms of working hours, 69.4% of adolescents and young adults 15 to 29 years who are working (predominantly male), do so on a full-time basis. Only 11.9% work by the hour, and 9.8% under other time modalities.

Historically, youth unemployment in Chile is double that of adults (Fernández 2004). Despite steady economic growth in the last 20 years, unemployment rose from 8.7% in 1994 to 15.5% in 2003 for the group 15 to 29 years (INJUV 2003). The magnitude of youth unemployment and its related consequences for the country's future development is a matter of concern in Chile.

Unemployment rates are higher for the adolescent group 15 to 19 years and have risen from 20.2% in 1996 to 32.5% in 2002. These figures reflect structural features of the labor market (Tokman 2004), as well as a misfit between youth expectations and aspirations regarding salaries, jobs profiles, and the market supply. Seventy-six percent of youth perceive that the labor market discriminates against them in favor of more experienced workers.

Unemployment rates increase significantly as age and years of education decrease. Further, unemployment rates increase as SES decreases (rate for youth whose family income corresponds to the lowest quintile of the distribution is 6.7 times higher than that of youth in the highest quintile). School attendance poses another challenge to finding a job.

On average women have higher unemployment rates than males. For the population 15 to 24 years of age, with ten or more years of education, unemployment in females is 24.3% compared to 20.0% in males. For groups with 13 or more years of education, these differences persist (17.8% males versus 19.8% females).

It is apparent that the nature of youth unemployment differs by socioeconomic status. Over 20% of adolescents and emerging adults 15 to 29 years have looked actively for a job and been unable to find one. Within low-SES youth, this figure is 36%. Twenty percent (mostly middle-SES) are looking for a job to pay for their education. Other cases reflect a mismatch between youth expectations (youths' determination to find a job that best fits their training, their vocational interests, or pays a good salary) and the labor market supply.

Relevant issues to be addressed in social policy are whether youth unemployment is a consequence of economic development or related to specific competencies of youth and whether the situation is affecting different youth in the same way.

Media

Access to new information and communication technologies has been growing steadily in Chile. Its effects are apparent in the processes of economic productivity as well as in the organization of social life. Thirty-four percent of adolescents 15 to 18 years use a computer daily, and 33.1% at least once a week. Similarly, 21.6% of adolescents 15 to 18 use the Internet daily and 31.6% at least once a week (INJUV 2004). Additionally, 44.5% of youth 15 to 18 years own a cellular phone.

The use of technology has expanded adolescents' social interaction to virtual contexts. Two percent of a national sample of adolescents, emerging adults, and young adults 15 to 29 years reported that navigating the Internet was their most preferred leisure activity; for 6.2% it is their second, and for 8.7% it is their third most preferred activity.

Public policies aimed at reducing the digital gap between the most and least economically advantaged youth introduced communication and information technologies in the school system. The program *Enlaces* (Links) created digital networks connecting 90% of public schools and 100% of private subsidized high schools. Similarly, the Public Library Network links 368 libraries across the country and provides free access to the Internet, training, and opportunities for students to create their own Web sites. The Youth Information System provides public spaces for free access to the Internet.

In Chile 75.5% of the elementary school population has access to a computer (MIDEPLAN 2003). Access is significantly higher among the higher income population (92.4% and 84.5% in the fifth and fourth quintiles respectively as compared to the first, 68.1%, and second quintile, 72.2%. Fifty-nine percent of poor youth and 80% of the most poor can only access a computer at school.

Approximately 45% of adolescents 15 to 18 years master basic computer skills (INJUV 2003), 29.6% have a medium level skill, and 20% are not skilled in computer use (INJUV 2003). Wide socioeconomic differences are observed in that 40% of high-SES youth have attained a medium level of skill, compared to 37.6% of middle-SES who have only mastered the basic level, and 57% of low-SES youth who are unskilled in computer use (INJUV 2003).

A study (PNUD 2003) assessed youth's access and competence in technology use by measuring their proficiency in English, computer skills, access to the Internet, and availability of cellular phones and cable TV. Only 12.2% of the group 15 to 29 years had access to and used the technologies above. Again, socioeconomic differences were observed in that 34.7% of high-SES youth were proficient in all technology use as well as in English, compared to only 1.5% in low-SES groups.

Zegers, Larrain, and Trapp (2004) examined the effects of Internet chatting on 124 young college freshman students. The average number of hours per week spent chatting was 4.4. However, 42.8% reported no involvement with chatting and 10.5% chatted more than eight hours per week. Significant gender differences were found in the extent that respondents used chatting as an active means to experiment with their personal identities. Males reported more involvement with multiple selves, masking and deceiving, and valued virtual interactions more positively than females.

Politics and Military

Military service has been mandatory for males 18 years old since 1900 (Maldonado 1993). Debate over its mandatory character was renewed with the advent of democracy in 1990, and a legislation change has been proposed to render it voluntary (Maldonado 2001). In reality only one out of five adolescents serve, with the majority of those serving coming from a low-SES. In 1980 almost 73% of those enrolled in military service had 11 years of education or less. Adolescents who do not serve are waived for medical (about a third) or educational reasons (Maldonado 2001). A small percentage (13%) is declared remiss. Given that the expected age of high-school graduation is 17 to 18 years, this figure suggests that adolescents that actually enroll in the service were either behind or had dropped out of school.

How are adolescents faring as future citizens is an issue of renewed interest in Chile. Youth apathy for the polity has been noted both as low involvement in political activities and political detachment (Manzi, González, and Haye 1999). Seventy-one percent of emerging adults 20 to 24 years were not registered to vote in 2000, as opposed to 47.6% in 1997. The percentage of adolescents 18 to 19 years who registered to vote decreased from 5% in 1988 to 1.5% in 2001.

Similarly, youth manifest low levels of trust in political parties, government representatives, and public institutions (INJUV 2000, 2004). The percentage of youth who identify with a political party has gone down from 67.7% in 1994 to 30.7% in 2000. Political parties are the institutions least trusted by youth (INJUV 2004). Only 25% of youth (INJUV 2002) participate in political and social organizations. Other surveys (INJUV 2002) find that youths are not interested in electoral politics and manifest low support for democracy (PNUD 2002).

Findings from the Chilean sample of IEA Civic Education Study (Torney-Purta, Amadeo, and Pilotti 2004) indicate that adolescents endorse an ample conception of citizenship that includes both conventional as well as real world politics. Their views of a good citizen include participating in activities that benefit the community (91%), protecting the environment (84%), promoting human rights (83%), and political demonstrations against unfair laws (75%). In addition a good citizen is a person who votes in every election (93%), respects government representatives (86%), and is informed of political issues through the press (85%). Gender differences on adolescents' understanding of civic issues and political attitudes were observed.

A higher percentage of female twelfth graders were interested in politics and were willing to participate in political activities (such as collecting money for a social cause or collecting signatures for a petition) than their male counterparts (Ministerio de Educación 2003).

In a sample of 1,900 urban adolescents, Velásquez, Martínez, and Cumsille (2004) examined gender differences in levels of social participation and found that females were more involved in prosocial and civic activities than males. In addition, social participation was positively related to self-efficacy beliefs and prosocial attitudes in the overall sample.

M. LORETO MARTÍNEZ, PATRICIO CUMSILLE, and CAROLINA THIBAUT

References and Further Reading

Ahumada, J. Tribus. 2000. Urbanas en Chile: El ir y venir de una re-construcción identitaria. http://www.identidades.uchile.cl/Artículos.

Almonte, C., G. Sepúlveda, C. Valenzuela, and A. Avendaño. 1990. Desarrollo psicosocial de adolescentes de 16 a 19 años. *Revista de Psiquiatría* 8:451–59.

Asún, D., J. Alfaro, and G. Morales. 1994. Análisis crítico de categorías y estrategias utilizadas para el estudio e intervención psicosocial con jóvenes en Chile. *Revista Chilena de Psicología* 15:5–14.

CONACE. 2000. *Estudio diagnóstico del consumo de drogas en población escolar de Chile a nivel comunal, año 1999.* Santiago, Chile: Gobierno de Chile.

CONACE. 2003. Quinto estudio nacional de drogas en población escolar de Chile, 2003, 8° básico a IV medio. http://www.conacedrogas.cl/inicio/pdf/Quinto_Estudio_ Consumo_Drogas Poblacion_Escolar_Chile2003.pdf.

Cummings, E., J. Wilson, and H. Shamir. 2003. Reactions of Chilean and U.S. children to marital discord. *International Journal of Behavioural Development* 27:437–44.

Cumsille, P. and M. L. Martínez. 1997. Síntomas de depresión en estudiantes de enseñanza media de Santiago. *Revista Chilena de Pediatría* 68:74–77.

Fernández, L., L. Bustos, L. González, D. Palma, J. Villagrán, and S. Muñoz. 2000. Creencias, actitudes y conocimientos en educación sexual. *Revista Médica de Chile* 128:574–83.

Fernández, P. 2004. Flexibilidad laboral para los jóvenes chilenos. Master thesis, Universidad de Chile.

Florenzano, R., M. Maddaleno, E. Bobadilla, and G. Alvarez, et al. 1988. *La salud del adolescente en Chile.* Santiago, Chile: Corporación de Promoción Universitaria.

Florenzano, R., P. Pino, and A. Marchandón. 1993. Conductas de riesgo en adolescentes escolares de Santiago de Chile. *Revista Médica de Chile* 121:462–69.

Global Youth Tobacco Survey. 2003. Differences in worldwide tobacco use by gender: Findings from the Global Youth Tobacco Survey. http://www.cdc.gov/tobacco/global/GYTS/pdf/globaluse.pdf.

Instituto Nacional de Estadísticas (INE). n.d. Chile: Censo de población y vivienda 2002. http://www.ine.cl/redatam/i-redatam.htm.

Instituto Nacional de Estadísticas (INE). 2004. Resultados del CENSO 1992 y 2002. Santiago, Chile: Gobierno de Chile.

Instituto Nacional de la Juventud (INJUV). 1999. Sociabilidad y Cultura Juvenil. Gobierno de Chile: Ministerio de Planificación y Cooperación.

Instituto Nacional de la Juventud (INJUV). 2002. La eventualidad de la inclusión. Jóvenes chilenos a comienzos del nuevo siglo. Tercera Encuesta Nacional de la Juventud. Gobierno de Chile: Ministerio de Planificación y Cooperación.

Instituto Nacional de la Juventud (INJUV). 2004. La integración social de los jóvenes en Chile 1994–2003. Cuarta Encuesta Nacional de la Juventud, Gobierno de Chile: Ministerio de Planificación y Cooperación.

Maldonado, C. 1993. La polémica del servicio militar obligatorio en Chile. In *Estudios Interdisciplinarios de América Latina y el Caribe, Vol. 4.* http://www.tau.ac.il/eial/IV_2/prieto.htm.

Maldonado, C. 2001. Estado de situación del servicio militar en Chile. *Security and Defense Studies Review* 1:84–92.

Manzi, J., R. González, and A. Haye. 1999. El mundo político de niños y jóvenes en Chile: Familiaridad, afectos y actitudes frente a referentes políticos. In *Exploraciones en psicología política.* L. Guzmán (ed.). Santiago, Chile: Universidad Diego Portales.

Martínez, M. L., P. Cumsille, and D. Rivera. 2004. Adolescents' future-oriented aspirations and goals: The role of family expectations and parental practices. Paper presented at the 18th Biennial Meeting of the International Society for the Study of Behavioural Development, Ghent, Belgium.

Martínez, M. L. and P. Cumsille. 1996. Bienestar psicológico de adolescentes urbanos: Su relación con niveles de competencia psicosocial, sistemas de apoyo social y calidad del tiempo libre. *Psykhé* 5:185–202.

Mattelart, A., and M. Mattelart. 1970. *Juventud chilena: Rebeldía y conformismo.* Santiago, Chile: Editorial Universitaria.

Mattelart, M. 1976. Chile: The feminine version of the coup d'etat. In *Sex and class in Latin America.* J. Nash and H. I. Safa (eds.). New York: Praeger.

Ministerio de Educación (MINEDUC). 2000. Resultados del TIMSS son un desafío para la educación chilena, Departamento de comunicaciones, 6/12/2000. http://www.mineduc.cl/noticias/secs2000/12/N200012061 1074214193.html.

Ministerio de Educación (MINEDUC). 2002. Indicadores de la Educación en Chile 2002. http://biblioteca.mineduc.cl/documento/Indicadores_para_la _Educ.pdf.

Ministerio de Educación (MINEDUC). 2003a. Educación cívica y el ejercicio de la ciudadanía. Santiago, Chile: Ministerio de Educación, Unidad de Curriculum y Evaluación.

Ministerio de Educación (MINEDUC). 2003b. Nota Técnica: Factores que explican los resultados de Chile en PISA+. http://biblioteca.mineduc.cl/documento/nota_tecnica_pisa.pdf.

Ministerio de Educación (MINEDUC). 2004. Sistema Educacional. http://www.mineduc.cl/sistema/index.htm.

Ministerio de Educación (MINEDUC). 2005. Educación Superior http://w3app.mineduc.cl/edusup/index.html.

Ministerio de Planificación y Cooperación Social (MIDEPLAN). 2003. Encuesta de Caracterización Socioeconómica Nacional (CASEN). Santiago: Gobierno de Chile.

Ministerio de Salud. n.d. Mortalidad de los adolescentes por servicio de salud y sexo, 2003. http://deis.minsal.cl/deis/ev/mortalidad_adolecente/consulta_servicio.asp (accessed November, 2005).

Ministerio de Salud (MINSAL). 2001a. Encuesta nacional de calidad de vida y salud. http://epi.minsal.cl/epi/html/sdesalud/cdevid/finalnacional.pdf.

Ministerio de Salud (MINSAL). 2001b. Mortalidad adolescente y sus componentes por servicio de salud.http://deis.minsal.cl/ev/mortalidad_adolecente/consulta_servicio.asp.

Ministerio de Salud (MINSAL). 2001c. Encuesta nacional de calidad de vida y salud. http://epi.minsal.cl/epi/html/sdesalud/cdevid/finalnacional.pdf.

Ministerio de Salud (MINSAL). 2002. Nacidos vivos inscritos según edad de la madre por servicio de salud y comuna de residencia de la madre.http://deis.minsal.cl/ev/def2002/t03_NV_ED_MAMA.htm. (2002)

Ministerio de Salud. 2003. Mortalidad de los adolescentes por servicio de salud y sexo. Retrieved Nov. 2005 from http://deis.minsal.cl/deis/ev/mortalidad_adolecente/consulta_servicio.asp

Molina, R. 1988. La Salud del adolescente en Chile. In *Sistemas de Atención para Adolescentes Embarazadas, Capítulo X*, 195–231. Editorial CPU.

Molina, R. 1991. Medicina reproductiva del adolescente. *Revista de Pediatría Universidad de Chile, Facultad de Medicina* 34:105–11.

Molina, R. 1994. Conceptos de Riesgo en adolescentes embarazadas. *Revista Chilena de Obstetricia y Ginecología Infantil y de la Adolescencia* 1:77–78.

Muzzo, S., and R. Burrows. 1986. *El adolescente chileno: Características, problemas y soluciones.* Santiago, Chile: Editorial Universitaria.

Programa de Naciones Unidas para el Desarrollo (PNUD). 2002. Desarrollo humano en Chile: Nosotros los Chilenos: Un desafío cultural.http://www.desarrollohumano.cl/indice.htm.

Programa de Naciones Unidas para el Desarrollo (PNUD). 2003. *Transformaciones culturales e identidad juvenil en Chile.* Santiago, Chile: Programa de las Naciones Unidas para el Desarrollo.

Ramírez, V., and P. Cumsille. 1997. Evaluación de la eficiencia de un programa comunitario de apoyo a la maternidad adolescente. *Revista Latinoamericana de Psicología* 29:267–86.

Saiz, J. L., and R. Gempp. 2001. Estudios empíricos sobre la identidad nacional chilena: Revisión y nueva evidencia. In *Identidades nacionales en América Latina.* J. L. Salazar (ed.). Caracas: Fondo Editorial de Humanidades y Educación, Universidad Central de Venezuela.

Schkolnik, M. 2004. ¿Por qué es tan increíblemente baja la tasa de participación de las mujeres en Chile? http://www.expansiva.cl.

Schwartz, S. H. 2004. Mapping and interpreting cultural differences around the world. In *Comparing cultures: Dimensions of culture in comparative perspective.* H. Viken, J. Soeters, and P. Ester (eds.). Leiden, Netherlands: Brill.

Sepúlveda, G., C. Almonte, C. Valenzuela, and A. Avendaño. Estilos de socialización de los padres y desarrollo psicosocial en adolescentes de 16 a 19 años. *Revista Chilena de Pediatría* 62:396–403.

Servicio Nacional de la Mujer (SERNAM). 2002a. Hombres y mujeres: Cómo ven hoy su rol en la sociedad y en la familia. Documento de trabajo N°78.http://www.sernam.cl/admin/docdescargas/centrodoc.

Servicio Nacional de la Mujer (SERNAM). 2002b. Análisis y detección de expectativas de vida y proyecto de vida en niños, niñas y adolescentes. Documento de trabajo N° 80. http://www.sernam.cl/admin/docdescargas/centrodoc.

Servicio Nacional de la Mujer (SERNAM). 2004. Mujeres chilenas. Tendencias en la última década.http://www.sernam.cl/admin/docdescargas/centrodoc.

Soto, F., I. Matute, and C. Peña. *Cultura de la imagen y hábitos alimenticios de los jóvenes.* Gobierno de Chile: Instituto Nacional de la Juventud.Tokman, V. Desempleo juvenil en el Cono Sur: Causas, consecuencias y políticas. Serie Prosur, Fundación Friedrich Ebert. Santiago.

Torney-Purta, J., J. Amadeo, and F. Pilotti. 2004. *Fortalecimiento de la democracia en las Américas a través de la educación cívica.* Washington, D.C.: Organización de los Estados Americanos.

Valdivia, G., F. Simonetti, P. Cumsille, V. Ramírez, C. G. Hidalgo, B. Palma, and J. Carrasco. 2004. Consumo de tabaco en población menor de 18 años: Estudio de prevalencia en escolares chilenos. *Revista Médica Chile* 132:171–82.

Velásquez, E., M. L. Martínez, and P. Cumsille. 2004. Expectativas de autoeficacia y actitud prosocial asociadas a participación ciudadana en jóvenes. *Psykhé* 3:85–98.

Vicente, B., P. Rioseco, S. Saldivia, R. Kohn, and S. Torres. 2002. Estudio chileno de prevalencia de patología psiquiátrica (DSM-III-R/CIDI) (ECPP). *Revista Médica de Chile* 130:526–36.

Zegers, B., M. E. Larrain, and A. Trapp. 2004. El chat: ¿Medio de comunicación o laboratorio de experimentación de la identidad? *Psykhé*, 13:53–69.

CHINA, PEOPLE'S REPUBLIC OF

Background Information

China has a total population of approximately 1.3 billion people, the largest in the world. Most of the population (58.2%) lives in rural areas. The age distribution of the population ranges from 21.5% for 0 to 14 years, 70.9% for 15 to 64 years, to 7.6% for 65 years and above (Bulletin 2005). According to a document of the All-China Youth Federation (China Youth 2005), there are approximately 200 million youth aged between 15 to 24, accounting for 15.5% of the total population. There are 56 ethnic groups in China, with the Han nationality representing about 92% of the population of the country. The largest minority nationalities are Zhuang, Man, Hui, Miao, Uygur, Yi, Tujia, Mongolian, and Tibetan, each having a population over four million. The minority populations are located mostly in provinces of Guangxi, Sichuan, Yunnan, Guizhou, Tibet, Xinjiang, Liaoning, and inner-Mongolia.

Mainland China established a socialist political system with the creation of the People's Republic 1949. Since the late twentieth century, however, China has carried out a full-scale reform toward a market economy that allows for the adoption of many aspects of capitalism. The centrally planned command economy has rapidly been transformed into a market economy, which has led to major changes in economic and social structures. As a result, the living standard in most parts of China has improved significantly. According to China state statistics (Bulletin 2005), the annual per capita income was 2,936 yuan (approximately $353 USD) for rural residents and 9,422 yuan (approximately $1,135 USD) for urban residents in 2004.

Period of Adolescence

Adolescence is generally recognized as a period ranging from 11 to 12 until 18 to 19 years, although there are no clear indications of transitions from childhood to adolescence and from adolescence to adulthood. The major event associated with the beginning of adolescence is the completion of primary school (first to sixth grades) and entry into middle school. The end of adolescence is often represented by the entrance to a college or university or the job market after the completion of middle school (twelfth grade).

There are no particular formal rites to mark puberty or transition into adulthood. Some high school students start to celebrate the transition into adulthood on their eighteenth birthday. Many of these celebrations are organized by schools.

The improvement in the living standard, including improved nutrition, control of infectious diseases, and provision of health care, has had significant impact on the physical growth and development of Chinese adolescents (Ye 1995). For example, the onset of the adolescent growth spurt, such as sudden change in height, has been advanced from 12.9 and 11.7 years in 1950s to 12.1 and 11.2 years in 1990s, for boys and for girls, respectively (Ye 1995). Moreover, the trends toward earlier maturation are consistent among adolescents in Han, Mongolian, Uygur, Tibetan, and Chinese-Korean nationalities although there is a specific pattern of growth in each region.

Whereas adolescence in many Western cultures is often characterized by heightened stress and social and emotional problems such as juvenile delinquency, pregnancy, identity crisis, conflict with parents and mental disorders (Irwin 1987; Powers, Hauser, and Kilner 1989), Chinese adolescents appear to be less troubled by these issues and experiences. This may be due, in part, to the consistent social and cultural norms, customs, and expectations in Chinese society that serve to guide young people in their decision-making and choice of goals. It is also possible that continuous monitoring and support from family members, including parents and grandparents, serve a protective function that buffers against the psycho-emotional problems.

There is an "emerging adulthood," mainly in urban areas, in which young people study or work outside but often live at home with their parents. During this period, parents may gradually become less involved in adolescents' social lives such as their relationships with friends and peers.

Adolescents are allowed to make decisions about many of their social activities and personal issues. However, parents exert certain control over such issues as career choices, family responsibilities, and dating, especially for girls. Since the 1990s, an increased number of adolescents and youth in rural areas have left their families and gone to cities to seek opportunities for economic advancement. For these young people, it is critical to learn to be independent more quickly because they need to be responsible for their own lives, and in many cases, to provide financial support to their families in rural villages.

Beliefs

Chinese society is relatively homogenous in its cultural background, with Confucian collectivism serving as a predominant ideological guideline for group and individual functioning. In addition to Confucian philosophy, Taoism, an indigenous religious belief system in Chinese culture, has significantly influenced the values and lifestyles of Chinese people, especially among people with low social and educational status. A major feature of Chinese culture is that individual behaviors are often interpreted and evaluated in a broad context, in terms of their connections and interactions with social relationships, group norms, and ecological factors. This holistic view is reflected in Taoist concern about how one lives in relation to one's natural conditions (such as climate, food, resources) and in Confucian notions about how one lives in the social environment. Achieving and maintaining harmonious family functioning and social relationships is particularly emphasized in Confucian doctrines. Consistent with the holistic perspective, the Chinese collectivistic orientation is highly attentive to the order and stability of society. According to the collectivistic principles, the interests of the individual are considered to be subordinated to those of the collective. Selfishness, including seeking individual benefits at the expense of group interests and indifference to group interests, is regarded as a cardinal evil (King and Bond 1985).

The emphasis on collective well-being and group achievement in Chinese culture is reflected in socialization goals and expectations. In Western individualistic societies, children are socialized to develop social and cognitive competencies that are required for personal adaptation and achievement. Accordingly, acquiring personal social status and maintaining positive self-perceptions and feelings are major indexes of developmental accomplishment. In contrast, the primary task of socialization in Chinese culture is to help children and adolescents learn how to control individualistic acts, develop collectivistic ideologies and cooperative

skills and behaviors, and finally become a part of the group and to make contributions to the well-being of the collective (Chen 2000).

The socialization goals have a strong impact on school education including various political, social, and academic activities in China. Students in Chinese schools are required to attend regular political–moral classes in which collectivistic principles and requirements are systematically illustrated. Students are also encouraged to participate in extensive extracurricular group activities that are organized by formal organizations such as the Young Pioneers and the Youth League. It is believed that during these activities, students can learn cooperation with each other and develop positive relationships in the peer group. Moreover, they are expected to learn behaviors that are conducive to group functioning such as obedience, conformity, and interdependence.

As indicated earlier, Chinese society has been undergoing dramatic changes toward a market economy that allows for the adoption of many aspects of capitalism such as privatization of state-owned industries. At the same time, Western individualistic values and ideologies such as liberty, individual freedom, and independence have been introduced into the country along with advanced technologies. Many schools have expanded the goals of education to include helping children develop social and behavioral qualities that are required for adaptation in the competitive society. Whereas academic achievement continues to be emphasized, children are encouraged to develop social skills such as expression of personal opinions, self-direction, and self-confidence, which have traditionally been neglected in Chinese culture. The macrolevel social and cultural changes may have exerted extensive influence on adolescent beliefs, attitudes, and value systems, resulting in the so-called Westernization or Americanization of youth and adolescents in behaviors and lifestyles, particularly in urban regions of China. The increasing acceptance of individualistic ideologies and abandoning of the traditional collectivistic values represent the main features of this trend.

Gender

Traditional Chinese families are authoritarian and hierarchical, with men generally the dominant gender (Lang 1968). The hierarchy in the family is backed by legal and moral rules, such as the "three rules of obedience" for women (an unmarried girl obeys her father, a married woman obeys her husband, and a widow obeys her son). Men are responsible for maintaining and enhancing the status and reputation of the family (Ho 1987).

In the feudal times of Chinese society, social contacts for girls from early adolescence on were limited to family members (parents, siblings, husband, and children). Some of the stereotypical gender values and ideologies may still exist in contemporary China. For example, girls are often more likely than boys to be expected to help parents with household chores. As a result, family influences on adolescent behaviors and developmental outcome appear more evident for girls than for boys (Chen, Dong, and Zhou 1997).

However, this distal account of gender conception has to be weaved into the tapestry of contemporary society. Gender-related ideologies in China have been affected by the major social, political, and economic events (Chang 1999). The first gender equality movement coincided with the early communist emphasis on the emancipation of the suppressed and exploited people. Enforced from the central government, a gender equality policy swept the nation overnight with the founding of the People's Republic. Women were regarded as among the suppressed, and the improvement of their social and political status was an important goal of the Communist cause. Such gender equality work appeared to take effect initially on the surface as shown by the fact that wives do not take husbands' surnames, but eventually have a substantial and long-term impact on women's status in the society. In most regions, for example, girls and women now have virtually the same opportunities as boys and men to receive education in elementary and high schools as well as colleges and universities. Women work outside the home in professions that have traditionally been mainly reserved for men, such as government, army, education, and science and technology (Chen and He 2004). A recent event that has mixed—perhaps largely adverse—effects on gender equality is the market-oriented economic reforms. Because the reforms focus mainly on economic development, the status of men and women is linked to their abilities to produce profits for the factory or company and bring income to the family. Where some women achieve success in economic activities, many others may have disadvantages and experience difficulties, particularly in areas that require heavy physical labor.

The gender equality issue is related to family socialization and school education. Due to the only-child policy, urban adolescents in the early twenty-first century are almost all only children. Whether having a daughter or a son, parents usually encourage their only child to do well in school and in society. In schools girls clearly outperform boys throughout middle school and even in college (Chen, Cen, Li, and He 2005). Ding and Yue (2004) called this a "strong female weak male" phenomenon. According to the report by Ding and Yue (2004), the freshmen students entering Peking University with the highest scores were mostly females (55.9% in 2000, 65.6% in 2001, 72.7% in 2002). Indeed, girls do better than boys in academic achievement as well as social and psychological areas (Chang et al. 2005; Chen, Cen, Li, and He 2005).

The Self

There has been extensive discussion about the nature of the self in different cultures (Markus and Kitayama 1991; Kitayama, Markus, Matsumoto, and Norasakkunkit 1997). It has been argued that members of individualistic societies are prone to the development of the self that is construed as independent, self-contained, and autonomous. In contrast, persons in collectivistic cultures are likely to have an interdependent or sociocentric self, because their definitions of themselves and their personal interests are connected to their group membership (Markus and Kitayama 1991).

Given the distinct features of collectivistic Chinese culture, researchers have been interested in whether Chinese adolescents differ from their Western counterparts in self-concept (Chan 1997; Stigler, Smith, and Mao 1985). It has consistently been found that Chinese adolescents have lower scores on self-perceptions of competence than their Western counterparts. In a recent cross-cultural study of self-perceptions of social and scholastic competence and general self-worth, for example, Chen, Kaspar, Zhang, Wang, and Zheng (2004) found that compared with their Canadian counterparts, Chinese adolescents had lower self-perceptions of their scholastic competence although they tended to perform better in academic areas. Chinese adolescents also had lower scores on perceived general self-worth than their Canadian counterparts. The relatively low self-perceptions and self-esteem in Chinese children may be due to the endorsement of modesty in self-evaluation, high social standards of achievement, and great pressure to improve and conform with the group in Chinese culture (Chen 2000).

What are the factors that may affect the development of self-concept in Chinese adolescents? Are self-perceptions of competence relevant to performance in Chinese culture? In a longitudinal study,

Chen, He, and Li (2004) found that perceived self-worth and school competence mutually contributed to the prediction of each other. The mutual contributions indicate that general self-attitudes may be determined in part by school competence and, at the same time, self-perceptions of self-worth may affect school performance. The results also indicated that whereas sociability and aggression predicted self-perceptions of social competence and self-worth, positive self-perceptions might be a protective factor that buffered against the development of social-behavioral problems such as peer rejection. The results suggest that for adolescents who experience social and behavioral difficulties, viewing the self in a positive manner may serve as a buffer that protects them from developing further adjustment problems. In contrast, negative self-perceptions and self-regard may make adolescents more vulnerable to maladaptive outcomes. Finally, in a study based on Hong Kong adolescents, Chang, McBride-Chang, and Stewart (2003) found that self-concept, particularly in the academic domain, was associated with life satisfaction. The findings may indicate the significance of self-concept for psycho-emotional adjustment in Chinese adolescents.

As indicated earlier, Chinese society is relatively homogenous, and there are virtually no immigrants. As a result, ethnic identity is not a salient issue in China. Cultural or ethnic identity among most adolescents is often associated with the nationalist values such as the "Chinese people being the descendants of the Dragon" or the "children and grandchildren of the common ancestors Yian and Huang." Although there are 56 ethnic minority nationalities in the country, it is largely unknown whether and how adolescents in these groups develop culturally distinct identities, due to the lack of research in this area. The extensive communications and interactions between individuals and families in minority nationalities and those in the Han nationality (Chen and He 2004) may have placed a great pressure on the maintenance of unique cultural identities among the minority adolescents.

Family Relationships

Unlike Western cultures, Chinese culture views the family, rather than the individual, as the basic social unit. Maintaining family harmony and well-being is considered a major goal in human lives. This is often achieved based on the hierarchical structure of the family (Lang 1968). The hierarchy may be reflected in the social and moral rules such

as filial piety for children. For example, according to the doctrine of filial piety (*xiao*), children must obey their parents, and parents in turn are responsible for governing or disciplining their children (Ho 1986). To facilitate the socialization process, parents are encouraged to use high-power strategies such as restrictive and controlling childrearing practices (Chao 1994; Ho 1986). Moreover, to maintain parental authority, the culture endorses parental control of their emotional and affective reactions in parent-child interactions. Filial piety is regarded as the "root of all virtues" and serves as a philosophical and moral basis for family organization (Ho 1986).

Findings from several research programs appear to support the arguments about the hierarchical nature of parent-child relationships in Chinese families. Compared with Western parents, Chinese parents are more controlling and power assertive and less responsive to their children (Chao 1994; Chen et al. 1998; Dornbusch, Ritter, Leiderman, Roberts, and Fraleigh 1987). For example, Chinese parents are highly concerned with children's behavioral control. They are less likely to use reasoning and induction and appear more authoritarian than Western parents. Chinese parents are also less likely to encourage their children to be independent and exploratory. Finally, it has been found that Chinese parents are less affectionate toward their children and more punishment-oriented than North American parents (Chen et al. 1998). Of course, like their counterparts in the West, Chinese parents are not identical. There are substantial individual differences in parental beliefs and behaviors within Chinese culture. Nevertheless, relative to parents in Western cultures, Chinese parents as a group display distinctive patterns of parenting styles and practices, which may be shaped by culturally prescribed socialization goals and expectations.

An important question about Chinese parenting is how parental affection and power assertion are associated with child behaviors. Researchers have argued that parenting styles such as parental warmth and parental authoritarianism, which are initially developed based on Western cultures (Baumrind 1971), may have limited relevance to social, cognitive, and emotional functioning in Chinese children (Chao 1994; Steinberg, Dornbusch, and Brown 1992). Inconsistent with this argument, however, recent studies have clearly demonstrated that these fundamental parenting dimensions are associated with child adjustment "outcomes" in a virtually identical fashion in Chinese and Western cultures (Chang, Schwartz, Dodge, and McBride-Chang 2003; Chang, Lansford, Schwartz, and

Farver 2004; Chen, Dong, and Zhou 1997; Chen, Rubin, and Li 1997a; Chen, Liu, and Li 2000). Specifically, it has been found that parental affection and inductive reasoning are likely to contribute to the development of social and cognitive competence and psychological well-being. In contrast, parental rejection and power assertion, which figure in the authoritarian style, are associated with behavioral problems and maladaptation (Chang et al. 2003; Chen et al. 2000; Chen, Dong, and Zhou 1997).

As indicated in the literature (Rohner 1986), parental warmth and affection may constitute a social and emotional resource that allows children to explore their social and nonsocial environments and contribute to the development of social and cognitive competence. In contrast, coercive, power assertive, and prohibitive strategies that authoritarian parents use in childrearing may lead to the child's negative emotional and behavioral reactions such as fear, frustration, and anger, which in turn are associated with adjustment problems. Thus, regardless of cross-cultural differences between Chinese and North American parents in the prevalence of warmth and control, the functional meanings of the parenting styles in Chinese culture seem similar to those typically found in the Western literature (Baumrind 1971; Maccoby and Martin 1983).

In Chinese families fathers and mothers differ, both quantitatively and qualitatively, in childcare, childrearing, and parent-child interactions. Like their Western counterparts (Parke and Buriel 1998; Russell and Russell 1987), Chinese mothers are regarded as important for providing care and affection to the child (Ho 1987). Unlike Western fathers, who often interact with their child like a playmate (Lamb 1987; Parke and Buriel 1998), however, Chinese fathers engage in little play activities with children (Ho 1987). The role of the father in the family is mainly to help children achieve in academic areas, learn societal values, and develop appropriate behaviors (Ho 1986). In a recent longitudinal study (Chen et al. 2000), it was found that maternal supportive parenting had significant contributions to the prediction of psycho-emotional adjustment such as feelings of loneliness and depression in Chinese adolescents. In contrast, paternal support was expressed as providing guidance and assistance to adolescents in learning social skills, acquiring social status, and achieving in academic areas. As a result, paternal supportive parenting significantly contributed to later social and school achievement, including social preference, peer- and teacher-assessed social competence, aggression-disruption, and academic achievement. It was also found that paternal—but not maternal—indulgence significantly predicted adolescents' adjustment difficulties. Therefore, although parental indulgence is a major concern in Chinese society, Chen et al.'s results (2000) indicate that indulgence of fathers, but not mothers, may lead to negative social, behavioral, and school outcomes. Thus, it may be more important to help fathers modify their indulgent style in childrearing.

In a study concerning parent-child conflict in Chinese families, Yau and Smetana (2003) compared samples of adolescents in Hong Kong and a city in mainland China, Shenzhen, on their disagreements with parents over daily issues. The results indicated that adolescents in both places reported conflicts on choice of activities, schoolwork, interpersonal relationships, and chores. However, the conflicts were generally few in number, moderate in frequency, and mild in intensity. The intensity of the conflicts appeared to decline with increasing age from early adolescence (11 to 12 years) to late adolescence (17 to 18 years). More adolescents in Hong Kong reported conflicts over chores and interpersonal relationships than in Shenzhen. In contrast, more adolescents reported conflicts over schoolwork in Shenzhen than in Hong Kong, indicating greater pressure on academic achievement in mainland China. According to adolescents' self-reports, most conflicts were resolved by giving in to parents. Yau and Smetana (1996, 2003) argue that although adolescent-parent conflict in different societies indicates the development of adolescent autonomy, specific cultural norms and values influence its expression.

Due to some social and economic factors (such as limited housing in the cities), large, or joint, families have decreased in number, and small nuclear families have increased in number in China. There are still many "medium-size" families in which three generations (parents of husband or wife, husband and wife, and children—usually only one child) live together. About a third of families consist of three generations (Chen and He 2003). Four or five generation families have become rare (below 0.3%), because most people get married in their middle- to late-twenties. According to a survey (Bulletin 2000), the average family size was 4.79 persons in 1985 and 3.58 persons in 1999.

The divorce rate is generally low, but it is growing (Liu 1998). Particularly among the younger generations with high educational levels, divorce is no longer regarded as shameful. The divorce rate has risen rapidly since 1980 (below 5% in 1980, 11.4% in 1995, and 13% in 1997; Ni 2000). It is higher in major cities such as Shanghai and Beijing than in the countryside. Accordingly, the number of single-parent families has increased considerably in urban areas.

Since the late 1970s, China has implemented the one-child-per-family policy. This policy has apparently been highly successful, especially in urban areas. The birth rate has declined dramatically from 33.43 per 1,000 in 1970 to 15.23 per 1,000 in 1999 (Achievement 2000). As a result, over 95% of all children in the urban areas are only children. Although the only-child policy has not been so successful in rural areas, most families do not have as many children as traditional families used to have in the past.

An important issue concerning the impact of the only-child program is how it affects parental behavior, which in turn affects children and adolescents' social and behavioral development. Many parents and educators in China are concerned about whether only children are "spoiled" in the family (Jiao, Ji, and Jing 1980; Tao and Chiu 1985). Early reports from China tended to suggest that only children may have more negative behavioral qualities and social and school problems such as impulsiveness, aggressiveness, selfishness, poor peer relationships, and high demand for immediate satisfaction (Jiao et al. 1980). Later studies, however, have indicated that as a group, only children and adolescents may not differ significantly from, or even show certain advantages over, sibling children (Chen, Rubin, and Li 1994; Tao, Qui, Zeng, Xu, and Goebert 1999). According to Falbo and Poston (1993), where differences are present, only children are taller and weigh more than sibling children, and only children have better verbal abilities. Similar findings have been reported by others (Rosenberg and Jing 1996).

The discrepancies between results in early and later studies concerning only children and adolescents may be related to changes in childrearing and childcare conditions in China. Most children in urban areas now go to public nursery centers at a very young age, because most parents work outside the home. The same early out-of-home care experiences may weaken the different parental influences on only and sibling children. Moreover, the participation in a variety of collective activities in the public settings such as schools may compensate, to some extent, for the lack of sibling interactions for only children and adolescents.

Friends and Peers/Youth Culture

In Chinese culture, friendship has often been regarded as a phenotype of sibling relationships. "Having a true friendship" is regarded as highly important by contemporary Chinese children and adolescents in their value systems (Sun, Chen, and Peterson 1990). In a recent study using the criterion of reciprocity in friendship nominations, Tse, De-Souza, and Chen (2001) found that approximately 66% of male and 79% of female adolescents in Chinese schools had mutual friendships. The number of children who have mutual friendships tends to decrease with age, which may indicate higher exclusiveness of dyadic peer relationships in development. While almost all adolescents reported having close friends in class, approximately 80% of them indicated that they had friends outside of the class or school. Length of friendship in the class typically ranges from two years to five years in Chinese adolescents (in contrast to one year to three years in Canadian adolescents). The longer period of friendship in Chinese adolescents may be due to the fact that most Chinese children stay together in the same school for many years. Interestingly, friendship outside of the school (usually with previous classmates and playmates in the neighborhood) tended to be even longer in length.

Like Western adolescents, Chinese adolescents consider companionship and intimacy the primary functions of friendship. There are clear gender differences; whereas females emphasize the functions of intimacy and mutual understanding, males place greater value on companionship and assistance. Unlike North American adolescents who perceive self-validation or enhancement of self-worth ("My friend makes me feel important and special") important in friendship, however, Chinese adolescents pay little attention to this aspect of friendship. In contrast, they tend to emphasize "instrumental" assistance and guidance ("My friends teach me how to do things that I don't know") and mutual understanding ("My friend really understands me") (Chen, Kaspar, Zhang, Wang, and Zheng 2004).

There are various formal or institutionalized groups and organizations in Chinese schools (groups in class, the Young Pioneers, science and technology interest groups, sport teams). For example, each class typically consists of four to five groups with 10 to 15 members in each group. These groups are the basic units of the school for social activities, and the groups are largely similar in structure. Every student belongs to a group, and group membership is determined by the teacher. In general, students are not allowed to change from one group to another, and they are encouraged to develop a sense of belonging and loyalty to the group. Children are required to participate in regular group activities such as meetings in which children discuss various social, academic, and other issues. Children also discuss group achievement and problems and evaluate each member's school performance on a regular basis. Finally, children may participate in intergroup activities organized at the higher level, such as the class committee and the school student association.

There are other groups in Chinese schools such as the Young Pioneers and the Youth League that consist of selected members. These groups are hierarchical in structure, from class level to school, to municipal, and even to national levels. Group leaders are responsible, under the guidance of the teacher, not only for planning and directing group activities but also for monitoring other students' behavior. Students who violate the rules of the group or organization may receive different types of penalties, such as warning and expulsion, which is recorded in the student's file and forwarded to the new school or work place in the future.

In contrast to formal or institutionalized groups, informal groups (*Xiao Tuan Ti* in Mandarin) that are formed on the voluntary basis are often viewed negatively and sometimes regarded as anticollective in China; children and adolescents are generally discouraged from participating in informal cliques or crowds. This may be related to the general cultural background in Chinese society, which emphasizes united and uniform social actions under the direct control of the authority. Nevertheless, similar to their Western counterparts (Cairns and Cairns 1994; Kinderman 1993), the majority of school-age children and adolescents in China are affiliated with a peer group (Chen, Chen, and Kaspar 2001; Chen, Chang, and He 2003; Leung 1996; Sun 1995). Peer groups comprise mostly same-sex members, with the average group size of four to six members. Peer groups differ in structure and organization such as group homogeneity (Chen et al. 2003; Leung 1996). There are considerable variations among peer groups in Chinese schools, but the variations emerge mostly on prosocial-cooperative and antisocial-destructive dimensions (Chen et al. 2001). For example, adolescents in China often describe group activities in terms of how they are in accord with adults' social standards such as maintaining interpersonal cooperation and achieving academic success (Chen, Kaspar, Zhang, Wang, and Zheng 2004).

Chinese culture values the socialization function of peer relationships in helping children learn social standards and develop socially acceptable behaviors (Chen 2000; Luo 1996). Thus, particular attention has been paid to the *nature* of friendship and the peer group, which is often judged according to whether dyadic or group activities are guided by the "right" social goals and norms (Luo 1996). "Good" friendships or groups are often characterized by mutual agreement among members on socially valued norms. Children and adolescents who have this type of relationship encourage and help each other to improve social and school performance and obtain achievement (Chen, Kaspar, Zhang, Wang, and Zheng 2004; Smart 1999; Sun 1995). In contrast, friendships and groups that function on the basis of antisocial norms may value hostile and irresponsible behaviors in social and school settings. Although these relationships may provide group members with social support and emotional closeness, the experience may have adverse influences on socialization, because interpersonal loyalty and group cohesiveness are not directed by nor do they serve the "right" collectivistic goals (Chen, Kaspar, Zhang, Wang, and Zheng 2004).

Consistently, Chen, Chang, and He (2003) have found peer groups in Chinese schools differ systematically in their academic achievement and prosocial-antisocial dimensions. The peer culture formed on the basis of group activities has significant impact on group organization and individual academic achievement and social functioning. Moreover, peer group contexts, particularly group prosocial-cooperative and antisocial-destructive orientations, affect how group members react to other socialization influences, such as parenting attempts, and thus moderate their contributions to social, cognitive, and psychological development (Chen, Chang, He, and Liu 2005). Specifically, whereas group prosocial-cooperative functioning may serve to strengthen the role of supportive and inductive parenting in helping adolescents develop social and school competence, group antisocial-destructive functioning may undermine the positive impact of supportive parenting on adolescents' social and academic achievement.

Love and Sexuality

Marriage has traditionally been arranged by parents in Chinese society. Soon after the Communists took power in China, the first State Marriage Law was made and took effect in 1951 and then was revised in 1980. According to the law, the convention of parental arrangement of marriage must be abolished. Men and women should be allowed to choose their own marriage partners. Arranged marriage is no longer accepted because it is regarded as the old fashion. Although the decision on a marriage may still involve the whole family, parents usually accept children's choices. For most people, marriage consists of a registration at the Register of Marriages and a wedding ceremony. The minimal legal age for marriage is 20 years for a woman and 22 years for a man. From the early 1970s, however, the government has been encouraging late marriage and childbearing to reduce the population pressure, and many municipal governments have established local policies that do not support marriage until the late 20s. Although people may marry before their late 20s by the law, they may be deprived of certain basic and privileged opportunities and rights, such as career promotion and child welfare, that are controlled by the local governments.

Adolescents in China have few opportunities to date and engage in premarital sexuality. This is largely due to the high control of adults on children's behaviors and the requirement of children to concentrate on academic achievement. Not long ago, adolescents who were found to date or engage in intimate activities such as kissing or hugging a member of the opposite sex in school or another public place might have received "political education" and some type of punishment. Young people often started to date and engage in serious relationships only after they had a secure job or graduated from a college. Accordingly, cohabitation, birth control, pregnancy, and sexually transmitted diseases are not major concerns for Chinese adolescents. However, it has been found that adolescent attitudes toward premarital sexuality have changed since the 1990s. Increased numbers of high school students believe that premarital sexual behaviors are acceptable and should be tolerated (Long 2003). Although there are still many restrictions on dating in high schools, dating and premarital sexuality have been more common in recent years among students in colleges and universities as the educational authorities start to recognize and accommodate students' demands for greater independence. The government and educational institutions are facing new problems such as birth control and pregnancy of students.

According to Johnston (2005), the total number of abortions in China had been over six million from 1980 to 1997. The percentages of abortions among pregnancies were approximately 30%. No information is available about abortions in youth.

The first case of AIDS in China was found in May 1985. By 2001, the Chinese Ministry of Health reported a total of 28,133 people infected by HIV. Among them 1,208 had developed AIDS and 641 died (Zhang and Ma 2002). Approximately 7.5% and 48% of the total HIV-affected were youth aged

16 to 19 years and 20 to 29 years, respectively (CUHK Faculty of Medicine).

Sex education still has not been included in the school curriculum, although some schools offer sex education classes and many teachers may discuss the topic in human biology classes. However, attitudes toward sex education are changing as sexual diseases become increasingly threatening in the country. Discussions about sex-related topics, particularly HIV/AIDS, among students are encouraged at many universities and colleges. And, more books, magazines, and videos involving sexual and reproductive knowledge are now available to adolescents.

Health Risk Behavior

Serious health risk behaviors such as illegal drug use, stealing, killing, and robberies are generally low in Chinese adolescents. Violent or delinquent behaviors in the form of large groups or gangs are also rare. In addition, since few adolescents possess cars, car accidents are still not a concern at this time. In a cross-cultural study (Chen, Greenberger, Lester, Dong, and Guo 1998), it was found that Chinese adolescents did not differ from American adolescents in most areas of misconduct such as getting into a fight and smoking cigarettes. However, whereas many American adolescents were involved in delinquent behaviors such as smoking illegal drugs, carrying weapons, and gang fighting, few Chinese adolescents engaged in these activities. According to Dai (2000), of total crimes and delinquencies in the country, the percentages committed by adolescents under 18 years had declined from 23.8% to 10.5% from 1985 to 1995. The percentages of murders, robberies, and injuries committed by adolescents from 14 to 17 years, relative to the crimes in the same category in the entire population, were .75%, 8.5%, and 2.6% in 1990; and .08%, 17.1%, and 3.2% in 1995, respectively. The corresponding percentages for adolescents from 18 to 25 years were 1.5%, 10.4%, and 4.59% in 1990; and 1.6%, 16.6%, and 6.3% in 1995, respectively. These rates were much lower than those in most Western countries (Dai 2000). The generally low frequencies of delinquency and crime in Chinese adolescents are largely due to the fact that they are prohibited with the many sociopolitical constraints imposed by Chinese society. Indeed, illegal drugs, guns, and other materials that can be used in crimes and delinquent behaviors are better controlled in China than in countries like the United States and are generally unavailable to adolescents in China.

Cigarette smoking and drinking are relatively common in Chinese adolescents, particularly male adolescents. In a recent study, Xu and Luo (2003) found that 37% of male adolescents at ages 15 to 19 years were smokers; this rate was 1% for female adolescents. About 38% of male adolescents and 9% of female adolescents were alcohol drinkers. In addition to gender, significant correlates of adolescent smoking and drinking included ethnic nationality (drinking: 58% and 46% for adolescents of Han nationality and minority nationalities respectively), education (smoking: 47% and 20%; drinking: 51% and 20%, for school students and nonstudents respectively), and rural versus urban location (smoking: 47% and 15%; drinking: 53% and 40%, for adolescents in rural and urban areas respectively).

In several large-scale studies, Fang and his colleagues (Fang, Zheng, and Lin 2000; Li, Fang, and Stanton 1996, 1999) found that about 15% to 20% of the adolescents (23% of male students and 5% of female students) reported smoking. Smoking increased with age and was associated with poor academic performance, behavioral problems, and participation in gang-related activities (Li et al. 1996, 1999). Adolescent smoking was also related to mothers' smoking behavior and attitude toward smoking. Other parenting behaviors and attitudes such as warmth, rejection, and family communication also were related to adolescent smoking (Fang et al. 2000). Similar to smoking, drinking was also far more prevalent among males than females. Beer was the most common, but the number of adolescents drinking wine and liquor increased with age. Like smoking, drinking was associated with the behavioral and family problems (Li et al. 1996).

Another salient health-related problem in Chinese adolescents is emotional disturbances such as depression. Adolescents in China, both male and female, may experience an equal or even greater number of psycho-emotional problems of an internalizing nature compared with their North American counterparts (Chen, Rubin, and Li 1995a; Cheung 1986; Crystal et al. 1994; Dong, Yang, and Ollendick 1995). Moreover, a high rate of "malicious incidents," such as suicide, in adolescents has been reported in the Chinese literature and in the media. According to Li (2003), the suicide rate in China was about 10.63 per 100,000 for adolescents (15 to 24 years of age) in 1998, which was one of the highest in the world. The rate was higher for female adolescents than male adolescents (15.96 versus 8.67 per 100,000), particularly in rural areas.

Individual psycho-emotional problems have not received as much attention from professionals and the public in Chinese culture as in Western cultures because they are directed toward the self, rather than the collective (Kleinman 1986; Potter 1988). This may be the case particularly in Chinese children and adolescents because they are expected to concentrate on their social and school performance (Ho 1986). Adolescents' emotional difficulties, such as depression, are sometimes considered and treated as medical problems or political-ideological problems in China, especially when they are associated with interpersonal problems.

The social and cultural neglect does not mean that emotional problems such as depression have no functional significance in Chinese adolescents. Findings from a series of studies conducted by Chen and his colleagues in China (Chen et al. 1995a; Chen and Li 2000) have shown that depression affects social and school adjustment. In these studies, male and female adolescents did not differ in self-reported depression. Depression was moderately stable over time ($r = .40$s from age 12 years to age 14 years), suggesting that adolescents who reported depression were likely to continue to suffer later. Moreover, early emotional distress has significant contributions to the development of social and school adjustment difficulties, including social isolation, low social status, and academic achievement. Thus, social and school performance of depressed adolescents may gradually decline with time. The findings concerning the significance of depression for social and school adjustment indicate a similar maladaptive nature of depression in Chinese and Western cultures, which is inconsistent with the argument that personal affects and emotions are irrelevant to social relationships and adjustment in Chinese culture (Potter 1988).

Multiple personal and social factors may contribute to the development of depression in Chinese adolescents. Chen, Rubin, and Li (1995b) found, for example, that peer acceptance and rejection, leadership, and academic achievement significantly predicted later depression. Depressed children were less popular and had lower social status and more academic problems than their nondepressed counterparts both contemporaneously and two years earlier. It is possible that adolescents who experience social and academic difficulties in the school often receive feedback concerning their performance. Social feedback might play a particularly important role in the development of depression in Chinese adolescents, because they are required to evaluate peers and themselves regularly and their social and academic achievement is often publicized.

Parent-children relationships, particularly maternal acceptance and rejection, are associated with later depression. Chen et al. (2000) found that whereas paternal warmth mainly predicted children's social and school adjustment, including social preference, peer- and teacher-assessed social competence, aggression-disruption and academic achievement, it had significant and unique contributions to the prediction of later emotional adjustment, including depression, after the stability effect was controlled. In Chen, Rubin, and Li's study (1997b), it was found that maternal acceptance and academic achievement interacted in the prediction of later depression. Children who had academic difficulties and were rejected by their mothers were likely to develop depression; however, children who had low academic achievement but were accepted by their mothers were not depressed at the later time. Thus, maternal acceptance seems to serve as a protective factor that buffers children who have academic difficulties from developing depressive symptoms. Another familial factor that had a similar buffering function was the quality of the marital relationship. For children from families in which there was high marital conflict, poor academic achievement was associated with later depression. However, academic difficulties were not related to later depression for children from families in which the marital relationship was harmonious.

A particular type of stress for adolescents in China is related to academic achievement. The limited opportunities in tertiary education in China together with a tradition that emphasizes social stratification through schooling creates a social context in which children and their parents engage in an indefatigable and ceaseless competition from kindergarten into high school. High schools and middle schools are streamed into academically elitist to poor schools. This "through train" system sometimes links good high schools to elitist primary schools and even kindergartens. Thus, academic competition starts when a child learns to read. The constant academic competition and the anxiety over the college entrance examination at the end of high school constitute substantial stress and distress for Chinese adolescents. In the section that follows, we will discuss adolescents' experiences in the school.

Education

China is working toward a nine-year compulsory education. By the end of 2004, the program had covered approximately 94% of school-aged children in the country. The enrollment rate was 98.95% at the elementary or primary school level and 92.7% at the middle school level (China sees 2005). Among the young and adults, the illiteracy rate had been reduced to less than 5%. The college and university entrance rate was 19%. Almost all schools from kindergarten to university are public schools in China. However, private schools have been increasing in number at all levels in recent years. For example, there were about 78,500 private schools in China by the end of 2004. Many universities have developed gifted programs for relatively younger bright students. The number of gifted programs, however, is declining due to the controversies over their effects. Researchers and educators have argued that although the gifted programs may benefit the intellectual development of students, the social environment that the programs create, such as the lack of social interactions with same-age peers, may have negative effects on the learning of social skills such as self-control and responsibility. In contrast to gifted programs, schools for special education for disabled children have been growing steadily. There were approximately 370,000 on-campus students in these schools in 2004 (China sees 2005).

Since the mid-1980s, academic achievement in Chinese children has received substantial attention from developmental and educational researchers. It has been consistently found that Chinese children outperform their counterparts in the United States and many other countries in academic areas and that the differences persist throughout the elementary and high school years (Lapointe, Mead, and Philips 1989; McKnight et al. 1987; Stevenson et al. 1990). For example, Stevenson et al. (1990) systematically compared children's performance in mathematics and reading in the United States, Japan, Taiwan, and the People's Republic of China. In these studies, random samples of children in each country were administered achievement tests in reading and mathematics. The findings were striking: Asian children outperformed their North American peers in various academic areas. Similar differences were reported later in a different study (Stevenson, Chen, and Lee 1993).

Academic excellence in Chinese children may be related to traditional values on achievement in the Chinese culture (Ho 1986). Success in school achievement is directly associated with attainment of a high level of education, which in turn leads to high social and occupational status. However, due to limited opportunities to receive a higher education in China, there is strong academic competition in elementary and high schools. As a result, children are pressured constantly by parents and teachers to perform optimally on academic work. The pressure is particularly high in the final years of junior and senior high schools, because acceptance to senior high schools and colleges and universities is based on scores in examinations. Almost all high school graduates participate in the three-day nationwide college entrance examinations in June or July each year on major subjects such as Chinese language and mathematics. Whether they have the opportunity to enter a college or a university completely depends on whether their scores from these examinations reach the standard. Given this background, it is understandable that the high pressure that students receive is a major factor that is responsible for academic achievement in Chinese children; without this pressure, students may not work so diligently or pay so much attention to guidance and assistance from teachers and parents.

The high achievement of Chinese children and adolescents may also be associated with effective strategies of classroom instruction, students' high achievement motivation, and positive family influences such as parental involvement (Stevenson 1992; Stevenson et al. 1990).

Chinese students, for example, spend most of their time in school and most of their schooltime on academic work. Most of them continue their academic work after school. High school students attend school full-time from 8:00 a.m. to 5:00 p.m. Most schools are open for additional self-learning or tutorial sessions either in the morning from 6:00 a.m. or in the evening, when students may return to school after dinner and stay until 10:00 or 11:00 p.m. It is also a common practice that to save time for study, students in graduating classes take up residence in the school for an extensive period, during which they bring blankets and sleep in the classroom at night.

There is a designated head teacher in each class who stays with the class, often for multiple years. The head teacher usually teaches a main subject such as Chinese language or mathematics. In addition, the head teacher is responsible for all the social, political, academic, and other affairs in his or her class. The head teacher keeps in close contact with students' families. The head teacher system in China allows the school and teachers to be involved extensively in children's and adolescents' activities that are organized to facilitate academic achievement (Chang 2003, 2004; Chang et al. 2004).

Researchers have found that some familial factors may be associated with overall high levels of academic achievement in China. These factors include parental beliefs about the role of effort in academic achievement and parental monitoring of children's academic work. Specifically, whereas American parents believe academic achievement is largely determined by innate abilities, Chinese parents believe that it is mainly based on diligence and effort. Compared with American parents, Chinese parents keep in closer contact with the school and pay more attention to their child's academic performance (Stevenson et al. 1990).

Academic achievement exerts a significant and pervasive impact on adolescent adjustment in many other areas, such as the acquisition of social status, peer relationships, and psychological well-being. It has been reported that academic achievement significantly contributes to later social competence and social status. In contrast, academic failure and learning problems significantly contribute to peer rejection and school-related social problems, such as lack of socially assertive skills and task orientation. Moreover, academic achievement in elementary school may predict social status and competence in high schools, although children change their school and social environment when they enter high schools (Chen, Rubin, and Li 1997b).

The association between academic difficulties and social and psychological maladaptation is unsurprising. First, some underlying cognitive deficits or problems may serve as a common cause for academic difficulties and the lack of skills in acquiring social status and maintaining positive social relationships. Second, academic achievement may have a direct impact on students' self-confidence and self-perceptions of general self-worth, which in turn affect their social and psychological functioning. Finally, given the high emphasis on academic achievement in Chinese schools, the negative reputation that adolescents receive on their academic competence during the process of public evaluations, may influence how adolescents initiate and maintain interactions and relationships with peers and how peers respond to their social behaviors.

Work

The Compulsory Education Law of the Chinese Constitution states that all children under the age of 16 must go to school and are not allowed to hold full-time jobs. Thus, the Chinese government officially forbids children under 16 from working. In rural areas, however, it is common that children and adolescents help parents on the farm after school. Moreover, in some rural areas poverty may have driven a large number of adolescents out of the classroom and into lives of labor. Since the mid-1990s, many adolescents from rural areas have gone to cities, such as Beijing, Shanghai, and some in southern China's coastal regions, to work for privately owned industrial or commercial firms (Ying and Lu 2003). Due to their lack of job skills, these adolescents usually work under poor conditions and earn low wages.

The situation is quite different in relatively wealthy cities in China. Most families do not need adolescents to work for extra income. As the "little emperor" in the family, many children and adolescents tend to be "spoiled" by their parents and grandparents. Some adolescents may even have few opportunities to do housework. One of the reasons for their low contribution to work inside and outside of the family is that given the high pressure on academic achievement, adolescents are often required to spend as much time as possible on their school assignments and in academic programs during evenings, weekends, and holidays.

According to the Survey Report on Youth Employment conducted in some major cities (Youth Unemployment 2005), the majority of the youth indicated that the ideal work units for them included government departments and state-run enterprises. About 20% of the youth would like to set up their own businesses. The unemployment rate for youth between ages 15 and 29 was 9%, higher than the 6.1% average unemployment rate of the society. Most unemployed youth have been jobless for a long period. The survey also indicated that the quality of employment for youth was relatively low; most of the youth had no guarantee for their work, long working hours, and low income (monthly salaries were 600 to 1,500 yuan for 60% of employed youth and less than 600 yuan for 30% of employed youth). More than half the employed youth received no relevant job training. The higher-than-average unemployment rate and relatively undesirable work conditions for youth are obviously related to the huge number of people in China's labor force, which creates enormous pressure on employment. Because young people lack work experiences, they are generally weaker candidates in the labor market.

Community service is advocated mainly as a part of school moral education in China. In 1993, the government initiated a program—Youth Volunteer Activities—to promote volunteer work among adolescents on a large scale. The program was continued and extended to most regions of the country, and numerous adolescents were involved in it each year. Some of the programs organized by the central or local authority tend to be compulsory. In a plan for the development of community service between 2003 and 2005 (Community Service 2005), for example, the Guangzhou Volunteers' Association proposed that public servants in the city must provide voluntary social service for at least 20 hours each year. Those who fail to provide such service may not be promoted. Government staff would be required to do volunteer work or participate in charity activities during holidays. Schools and universities would launch similar social service programs. Students who fail to participate in enough community service as required may not be allowed to graduate.

More recently other models of volunteer work and community service, some of which were introduced from Hong Kong and Western societies, emerged and became increasingly popular, particularly among high school students. The newer models may emphasize the moral or educational goals in a less explicit manner. In contrast, they encourage adolescents to participate in community service, such as helping with children, providing daycare in orphanages and local centers, and working with the mentally and physically challenged, on a voluntary basis. In some metropolitan areas such as Shanghai, Guangzhou, and Beijing, over 10% of high school students have participated in community service (Yu 2001).

Media

TV is common in both rural and urban areas in China. Adolescents spend a considerable amount of their leisure time watching TV programs. According to a survey conducted in 31 provinces (Extra-curricular activities 2003), over 80% of high school students spent most of their after-school time watching TV programs. In addition to watching TV, the survey indicated that over 60% of high school students reported listening to music, and about 30% reported reading books and magazines that were not directly related to school work.

Internet use and playing computer games are increasingly popular among adolescents in cities and towns. In Beijing, for example, over 70% of families possess a computer, and adolescents are the main users because many parents are unable to use a computer or the Internet (Computer use 2003). Indeed, the rate of high school students using the Internet or playing computer games is above 80% in Beijing. According to one survey (Li 2003), the majority of adolescents (66.8%) reported that they used the Internet mainly to obtain information. Other main uses of the Internet included chatting (52.9%), playing games (45.8%), reading news (42.4%), and receiving and sending e-mails (27.1%). Most computer games that adolescents like to play are related to violence and competition such as shooting and fighting, adventure, and car racing (Yi and Yu 2003).

Parents and educators in China are seriously concerned about adolescent use or excessive use of computers and the Internet, although adults and adolescents agree that they can be beneficial for learning if used properly (Li 2003). Many people believe that playing violent and sexual games may undermine adolescents' moral judgment and lead to the rationalization of aggressive, defiant, and other delinquent behaviors. Due to their poor self-control abilities, some adolescents may become indulged with computer games, often in public computer and Internet places, which may lead to "excessive computer use syndrome" or "Internet addiction" (Yi and Yu 2003). Addiction to computers and the Internet may not only cause symptoms of health problems, but may also have a direct adverse impact on academic performance. The results of several studies among university students in China indicate that time spent on the Internet is positively associated with social dissatisfaction and feelings of social isolation and negatively associated with interpersonal trust and self-esteem (Yi and Yu 2003). Teachers, parents, and professionals have been urging the government to set regulations to curb commercial Internet activities that target youths and adolescents. The Beijing municipal government has issued a law that prohibits people under 18 from visiting Internet cafés. However, the law is mostly ignored. It will be interesting and important to investigate how the development of high technologies and related public policies influence social-moral, behavioral, and academic functioning in Chinese adolescents.

A phenomenon that is related to media is celebrity worship or idolization among adolescents. Yue and his colleagues (Yue and Cheung 2000) conducted a series of studies over six years to compare idolization of media celebrities between mainland Chinese and Hong Kong Chinese adolescents. The findings indicate that idolizing pop stars, movie stars, and sports stars is common among Chinese young people, particularly in Hong Kong. In comparison to Hong Kong adolescents, mainland adolescents were more likely to worship luminary idols, intellectuals, and historical figures, and less likely to endorse entertainment and sports celebrities. In both places girls are more likely to idolize entertainment stars than boys.

According to Yue (2000), Hong Kong adolescents mainly pay attention to celebrities' romantic and sexual activities, whereas mainland Chinese young people tend to idolize celebrities in various fields mainly on the basis of their ideological and personality characteristics. This may be related to the commercial profit-making orientation of the entertainment industries in Hong Kong and the ideological orientation of moral education (Cheung and Yue 2003).

There are two types of celebrity worship among Chinese adolescents: person-focused and attribute-focused (Yue 2000). Whereas the former is characterized by augmenting all of the desirable attributes onto one or a few idols who become overly idealized and mystified, the latter is characterized by equalizing desirable attributes onto different idols so different idols are relatively equally appreciated. Yue and Cheung (2002) found that adolescents who are person-focused worshipers tended to have decreased self-efficacy and to become more passive in taking initiatives. The attribute-focused worshippers, on the other hand, demonstrated enhanced sense of self-efficacy and took more personal initiatives.

Xinyin Chen and Lei Chang

References and Further Reading

Achievement of the family planning program in China. 2000. *People's Daily (Oversea Edition)*. November 7.
Baumrind, D. 1971. Current patterns of parental authority. *Developmental Psychology Monograph* 4:1.
Bulletin of China's Economic and Social Development in 1999. 2000. Beijing: Xin Hua She.
Bulletin of China's Economic and Social Development in 2004. 2005. Beijing: Xin Hua She.
Cairns, R. B., and B. D. Cairns. 1994. *Lifelines and risks: Pathways of youth in our time*. Cambridge: Cambridge University Press.
Chan, D. W. 1997. Self-concept domains and global self-worth among Chinese adolescents in Hong Kong. *Personality and Individual Differences* 22:511–20.
Chang. L. 1999. Gender role egalitarian attitudes in Beijing, Hong Kong, Florida, and Michigan. *Journal of Cross-Cultural Psychology* 30:722–41.
Chang, L. 2003. Variable effects of children's aggression, social withdrawal, and prosocial leadership as functions of teacher beliefs and behaviors. *Child Development* 74:535–48.
Chang, L. 2004. The role of classrooms in contextualizing the relations of children's social behaviors to peer acceptance. *Developmental Psychology* 40:691–702.
Chang, L., J. E. Lansford, D. Schwartz, and J. M. Farver. 2004. Marital quality, maternal depressed affect, harsh parenting, and child externalizing in Hong Kong Chinese families. *International Journal of Behavioral Development* 28:311–18.

Chang, L., L. Li, K. K. Li, H. Lui, B. Guo, Y. Wang, and K.Y. Fung. 2005. Peer acceptance and self-perceptions of verbal and behavioral aggression and social withdrawal. *International Journal of Behavioral Development* 29:48–57.

Chang, L., C. McBride-Chang, S. Stewart, and E. Au. 2003. Life satisfaction, self-concept, and family relations in Chinese adolescents and children. *International Journal of Behavioral Development* 27:182–90.

Chang, L., D. Schwartz, K. A. Dodge, and C. McBride-Chang. 2003. Harsh parenting in relation to child emotion regulation and aggression. *Journal of Family Psychology* 17:598–606.

Chao, R. K. 1994. Beyond parental control and authoritarian parenting style: Understanding Chinese parenting through the cultural notion of training. *Child Development* 65:1111–19.

Chen, C., E. Greenberger, Y. Lester, Q. Dong, and M. S. Guo. 1998. A cross-cultural study of family and peer correlates of adolescent misconduct. *Developmental Psychology* :770–81.

Chen, X. 2000. Social and emotional development in Chinese children and adolescents: A contextual cross-cultural perspective. In *Advances in psychology research. Vol. 1.* F. Columbus (ed.). pp. 229–51. Huntington, N.Y.: Nova Science Publishers.

Chen, X., G. Cen, D. Li, and Y. He. 2005. Social functioning and adjustment in Chinese children: The imprint of historical time. *Child Development* 76:182–95.

Chen, X., L. Chang, and Y. He. 2003. The peer group as a context: Mediating and moderating effects on the relations between academic achievement and social functioning in Chinese children. *Child Development* 74:710–27.

Chen, X., L. Chang, Y. He, and H. Liu. 2005. The peer group as a context: Moderating effects on relations between maternal parenting and social and school adjustment in Chinese children. *Child Development* 76:417–34.

Chen, X., H. Chen, and V. Kaspar. 2001. Group social functioning and individual socio-emotional and school adjustment in Chinese children. *Merrill-Palmer Quarterly*:264–99.

Chen, X., Q. Dong, and H. Zhou. 1997. Authoritative and authoritarian parenting practices and social and school adjustment. *International Journal of Behavioral Development* 20:855–73.

Chen, X., P. Hastings, K. H. Rubin, H. Chen, G. Cen, and S. L. Stewart. 1998. Childrearing attitudes and behavioral inhibition in Chinese and Canadian toddlers: A cross-cultural study. *Developmental Psychology* 34:677–86.

Chen, X., and H. He. 2004. The family in mainland China: Structure, organization, and significance for child development. In *Families in global perspective.* J. L. Roopnarine and U. P. Gielen (eds.). pp. 51–62. Boston: Allyn and Bacon.

Chen, X., Y. He, D. Li, and B. Li. 2004. Self-perceptions of social competence and self-worth in Chinese children: Relations with social and school performance. *Social Development* 13:570–89.

Chen, X., V. Kaspar, Y. Zhang, L. Wang, and S. Zheng. 2004. Peer relationships among Chinese and North American boys: A cross-cultural perspective. In *Adolescent boys in context.* N. Way and J. Chu (eds.). pp. 197–218. New York: New York University Press.

Chen, X., and B. Li. 2000. Depressed mood in Chinese children: Developmental significance for social and school adjustment. *International Journal of Behavioral Development* 24:472–79.

Chen, X., M. Liu, and D. Li. 2000. Parental warmth, control and indulgence and their relations to adjustment in Chinese children: A longitudinal study. *Journal of Family Psychology* 14:401–19.

Chen, X., K. H. Rubin, and B. Li. 1994. Only children and sibling children in urban China: A re-examination. *International Journal of Behavioral Development* 17:413–21.

Chen, X., K. H. Rubin, and B. Li. 1995a. Social and school adjustment of shy and aggressive children in China. *Development and Psychopathology* 7:337–49.

Chen, X., K. H. Rubin, and B. Li. 1995b. Depressed mood in Chinese children: Relations with school performance and family environment. *Journal of Consulting and Clinical Psychology* 63:938–47.

Chen, X., K. H. Rubin, and B. Li. 1997a. Maternal acceptance and social and school adjustment in Chinese children: A four-year longitudinal study. *Merrill-Palmer Quarterly* 43:663–81.

Chen, X., K. H. Rubin, and B. Li. 1997b. Relation between academic achievement and social adjustment: Evidence from Chinese children. *Developmental Psychology* 33:518–25.

Cheung, C. K., and X. D. Yue. 2003. Identity achievement and idol worship among teenagers' in Hong Kong, *International Journal of Youth and Adolescence* 11:1–26.

Cheung, F. M. C. 1986. Psychopathology among Chinese people. In *The psychology of the Chinese people.* M. H. Bond (ed.). pp. 171–211. New York: Oxford University Press.

China sees progress in six aspects of education. 2005. *China Education and Research Network: Education in China, News and Events.* March 3.

China youth policy and youth work. 2005. All-China Youth Federation Documents. http://www.acyf.org.cn/e_doc/policy/02.htm.

Computer use in elementary and high school students. 2003. *China Youth Study* 7:92–93.

Crystal, D. S., C. Chen, A. J. Fuligni, C. C. Hsu, H. J. Ko, S. Kitamura, and S. Kimura. 1994. Psychological maladjustment and academic achievement: A cross-cultural study of Japanese, Chinese, and American high school students. *Child Development* 65:738–53.

Dai, Y. 2000. Delinquency and crime among Chinese adolescents. *Journal of Shandong Public Security College* 52:13–15.

Ding, G. and L. Yue. 2004. Educational equality in the campus environment: Investigation and consideration of the male students' inferior positions. In *China's education: Research and review.* Vol. 6. G. Ding (ed.). Beijing: Education and Science Press.

Dong, Q., B. Yang, and T. H. Ollendick. 1994. Fears in Chinese children and adolescents and their relations to anxiety and depression. *Journal of Child Psychology and Psychiatry* 35:351–63.

Dornbusch, S., P. Ritter, R. Leiderman, D. Roberts, and M. Fraleigh. 1987. The relation of parenting style to adolescent school performance. *Child Development* 58:1244–57.

Extra-curricular activities among elementary and high school students. 2003. *China Youth Study* 12:89–90.

Falbo, T., and D. L. Poston. 1993. The academic, personality, and physical outcomes of only children in China. *Child Development* 64:18–35.

Fang, X., Y. Zheng, and D. Lin. 2000. Relationships between family factors and smoking behavior of junior middle school students. *Acta Psychologica Sinica* 32:244–50.

Ho, D. Y. F. 1986. Chinese pattern of socialization: A critical review. In *The psychology of the Chinese people.* M. H. Bond (ed.). pp. 1–37. New York: Oxford University Press.

Ho, D. Y. F. 1987. Fatherhood in Chinese culture. In *The father's role: Cross-cultural perspectives.* M. E. Lamb (ed.). pp. 227–45. Hillsdale, N. J.: Erlbaum.

Irwin, C. E. 1987. *Adolescent social behavior and health.* San Francisco: Jossey-Bass.

Jiao, S., G. Ji, and Q. Jing, and C. C. Ching. 1986. Comparative study of behavioural qualities of only children and sibling children. *Child Development* 57:357–61.

Johnston, W. R. 2005. *Abortion statistics and other data.* http://www.johnstonsarchive.net/policy/abortion/.

Kinderman, T. A. 1993. Natural peer groups as contexts for individual development: The case of children's motivation in school. *Developmental Psychology* 29:970–77.

King, A. Y. C., and M. H. Bond. 1985. The Confucian paradigm of man: A sociological view. In *Chinese culture and mental health.* W. S. Tseng and D. Y. H. Wu (eds.). pp. 29–45. Orlando, Fla.: Harcourt Brace Jovanovich Academic Press.

Kitayama, S., H. R. Markus, H. Matsumoto, V. Norasakkunkit. 1997. Individual and collective processes in the construction of the self: Self-enhancement in the United States and self-criticism in Japan. *Journal of Personality and Social Psychology* 72:1245–67.

Kleinman, A. 1986. *Social origins in distress and disease.* New Haven: Yale University Press.

Lamb, M. E. 1987. *The father's role: Cross-cultural perspective.* Hillsdale, N.J.: Erlbaum.

Lang, O. 1968. *Chinese family and society.* New Haven: Yale University Press.

Lapointe, A. E., N. A. Mead, and G. W. Philips. 1989. *A world of differences.* Princeton, N. J.: Educational Testing Service.

Leung, M. C. 1996. Social networks and self enhancement in Chinese children: A comparison of self reports and peer reports of group membership. *Social Development* 5:147–57.

Li, A. 2003. The public media and the development of adolescents: A report of the current status on adolescent contact with the media. *Journal of Shanxi Youth Management College* 16:5–19.

Li, J. 2002. The importance of research on adolescent suicide in China. *China Youth Study* 22:46–50.

Li, X., X. Fang, and B. Stanton. 1996. Cigarette smoking among Chinese adolescents and its association with demographic characteristics, social activities, and problem behaviors. *Substance Use and Misuse* 31:545–63.

Li, X., X. Fang, and B. Stanton. 1999. Cigarette smoking among schoolboys in Beijing, China. *Journal of Adolescence* 22:621–25.

Liu, D. 1998. *Changes of Chinese marriage and family.* Beijing: China Social Sciences publisher.

Long, R. 2003. Teenager's premarital sexual behavior: Its current situation and countermeasures. *Journal of Guangxi Youth Leaders College* 13:15–17.

Luo, G. 1996. *Chinese traditional social and moral ideas and rules.* Beijing, China: University of Chinese People Press.

Maccoby, E. E., and C. N. Martin. 1983. Socialization in the context of the family: Parent-child interaction. In *Handbook of child psychology*, vol 4, *Socialization, personality and social development.* E. M. Hetherington (ed.). pp. 1–102. New York: Wiley.

Markus, H. R., and S. Kitayama. 1991. Culture and the self: Implications for cognition, emotion, and motivation. *Psychological Review* 98:224–53.

McKnight, C. C., F. J. Crosswhite, J. A. Dossey, E. Kifer, J. O. Swafford, K. J. Travers, and T. J. Cooney. 1987. *The underachieving curriculum: Assessing U.S. school mathematics from an international perspective.* Champaign, Ill.: Stipes.

Ni, S. 2000. How should we revise the Marriage Law? *People's Daily (Oversea Edition)*, November 3.

Parke, R. D., and R. Buriel. 1998. Socialization in the family: Ethnic and ecological perspectives. In *Handbook of child psychology*, vol 3, *Social, emotional, and personality development.* N. Eisenberg (ed.). pp. 463–552. New York: Wiley.

Potter, S. H. 1988. The cultural construction of emotion in rural Chinese social life. *Ethos* 16:181–208.

Powers, S. I., S. T. Hauser, and L. A. Kiner. 1989. Adolescent mental health. *American Psychologist* 44:200–8.

Rohner, R. P. 1986. *The warmth dimension: Foundation of parental acceptance-rejection theory.* Newbury Park, Calif.: Sage.

Rosenberg, B. G., and Q. Jing. 1996. A revolution in family life: The political and social structural impact of China's one child policy. *Journal of Social Issues* 52:51–69.

Russell, A., and G. Russell. 1996. Positive parenting and boys' and girls' misbehaviour during a home observation. *International Journal of Behavioral Development* 19:291–308.

Shenzhen Daily. 2003. Community service plan for civil servants. 2005. October 20. http://www.china.org.cn/english/China/77875.htm.

Smart, A. 1999. Expressions of interest: Friendship and *guanxi* in Chinese societies. In *The anthropology of friendship.* S. Bell and S. Coleman (eds.). pp. 119–36. Oxford, U.K.: Berg.

Steinberg, L., S. Dornbusch, and B.B. Brown. 1992. Ethnic differences in adolescent achievement: An ecological perspective. *American Psychologists* 47:723–29.

Stevenson, H. W. 1992. Learning from Asian schools. *Scientific American* 12:70–76.

Stevenson, H. W., C. Chen, and S. Lee. 1993. Mathematics achievement of Chinese, Japanese, and American children: Ten years later. *Science* 259:53–58.

Stevenson, H. W., S. Lee, C. Chen, J. W. Stigler, C. Hsu, and S. Kitamura. 1990. Contexts of achievement. *Monographs of the Society for Research in Child Development* 55:serial no. 221.

Stigler, J. W., S. Smith, and L. W. Mao. 1985. The self-perception of children by Chinese children. *Child Development* 56:1259–70.

Sun, S. L. 1995. *The development of social networks among Chinese children in Taiwan.* Unpublished PhD diss., University of North Carolina at Chapel Hill.

Sun, Y., X. Chen, and C. Peterson. 1989. A survey on value systems of contemporary Chinese adolescents. *Youth Study* 1:58–61.

Tao, G., J. Qiu, B. Li, W. Zeng, J. Xu, and D. Goebert. 1999. A longitudinal study of psychological development of only and non-only children and families: A 10-year follow-up study in Nanjing. *Chinese Mental Health Journal* 13:210–12.

Tao, K., and J. Chiu. 1985. The one-child-per-family policy: A psychological perspective. In *Chinese culture and mental health*. W. Tseng and D. Y. H. Wu (eds.). pp. 153–65. Orlando, Fla.: Harcourt Brace Jovanovich Academic Press.

Tse, H., A. DeSouza, and X. Chen. 2001. Friendship and social and psychological adjustment in four cultures. Paper presented at the biennial conference of the Society for Research in Child Development (SRCD), Minneapolis, Minnesota.

Xu, J., and M. Luo. 2003. A study of adolescent cigarette smoking and alcohol drinking. *China Youth Study* 5:60–63.

Yau, J., and J. Smetana. 1996. Adolescent-parent conflict among Chinese adolescents in Hong Kong. *Child Development* 67:1262–75.

Yau, J., and J. Smetana. 2003. Adolescent-parent conflict in Hong Kong and Shenzhen: A comparison of youth in two cultural contexts. *International Journal of Behavioral Development* 27:201–11.

Ye, G. J. 1995. The nutrient intakes of Chinese children and adolescents and their impact on growth and development. *Asia Pacific Journal of Clinical Nutrition* 4 (supplement 1):13–18.

Yi, X., and G. Yu. 2003. A review on adolescent internet addiction. *China Youth Study* 12:60–63.

Ying, M., and Y. Lu. 2003. A perspective on the phenomenon of the child labor in our country. *Labor and Protection* 6:50–53.

Youth unemployment rate remains high. 2005. *Voice of China*. May 25. http://www.chinanews.cn/news/2004/2005-05-25/4900.shtml.

Yu, B. 2001. Volunteer service and adolescent education. *Youth Studies* 5:22–24.

Yue, X. D. 2000. Selection and admiration of four kinds of idols and models among young people: A comparative study among high school students in Hong Kong, Nanjing, Changsha and Nantong. *Journal of Youth Studies* 6:152–67.

Yue, X. D. and K. C. Cheung. 2000. Selection of favorite idols and models among Chinese young people: A comparative study in Hong Kong and Nanjing. *International Journal of Behavioral Development* 24:91–98.

Yue, X. D., and K. C. Cheung. 2002. Worshiping "star idols" and "luminary idols": Reflections of 1998–2001 studies in Hong Kong and mainland China. *Journal of Youth Studies* 10:133–45.

Zhang, K. L., and S. J. Ma. 2002. Epidemiology of HIV in China. *British Medical Journal* 324:803–4.

COSTA RICA

See **CENTRAL AMERICA: COSTA RICA, EL SALVADOR, NICARAGUA**

CROATIA

Background Information

The Republic of Croatia, one of the youngest European countries, by virtue of its geographical location belongs to the middle European and Mediterranean countries. It occupies 87,661 square kilometers (56,594 square kilometers land area and 31,067 square kilometers territorial sea). According to the 2001 population census, Croatia had 4,437,460 inhabitants: 17.1% were children aged 0 to 14 years, 67.2% belonged to the working-age population aged 15 to 64 and 15.7% were aged 65 and over (Central Bureau of Statistics 2004).

Croatia is a medium-populated European country with 85 inhabitants per square kilometer. The central areas and the capital of Zagreb are the most densely populated. In its ethnic composition, more than 80% of the population is of Croatian nationality; the rest are members of other autochthonous national minorities: Serbs, Czechs, Slovaks, Italians, Hungarians, Jews, Germans, Austrians, Ukrainians, Russians, and others, who are all Croatian citizens. In democratic Croatia, efforts are being made to enable minorities to keep their ethnic characteristics and to further cherish their historical and cultural heritage.

After World War II, Croatia had been a part of Communist Yugoslavia, a socialist federation of six republics. In 1991, Croatia proclaimed independence from Yugoslavia and became a modern and internationally acknowledged state with a multiparty system based on a new constitution, which were the necessary prerequisites for a democratic society. Croatia's separation from Yugoslavia led to the war of independence (called the Homeland War). This further aggravated the economic situation, which had undergone great changes in the late 1980s, related to a recession caused by a lack of sustainability in the socialist system and the beginning of transitional processes. The new market economy was seriously jeopardized by the war, but the liberation of the occupied territories in Croatia and the peaceful reintegration of the Croatian Danube area under UN supervision in 1998 have stimulated recovery.

The most important tasks that can ensure positive outcomes in Croatia's economic and social sphere in the twenty-first century are to intensify the orientation of the Croatian economy towards increasing its overall competitiveness and openness, and to strengthen political and social safety, macroeconomic stability, and economic growth.

Period of Adolescence

According to 2001 census data (Central Bureau of Statistics 2004), Croatian youth is composed of 268,584 early-adolescents 10 to 14 years, 298,606 middle-adolescents 15 to 19 years, 305,631 late-adolescents 20 to 24, and 294,497 young people aged 25 to 29 (referred to as adolescents in Croatia). The overall number of youth aged 10 to 29 makes up 26.3% of the total Croatian population. A trend seen at the turn of the millennium indicates a falling birthrate: the 1995 birthrate of 11.2 per 1,000 inhabitants decreased to 9.1 in 2004 and to 9.6 per 1,000 in 2005, indicating a decline in the population of young people as well as an aging Croatian population. In 2004, the natural growth rate (a difference between the number of live born children and the number of dead persons) was negative at 2.1 (Central Bureau of Statistics 2005).

In compliance with the Convention on the Rights of the Child adopted by Croatia's constitutional law, a "child" is a person under the age of 18, except when regulated otherwise by special country laws (Babić and Bauer 1999). According to Croatian law, adolescents under the age of 18 (until they reach the "age of majority") are referred to as "children" and enjoy all the protection, rights, and benefits of the constitution. However, in youth-related issues and documents, organizations such as the United Nations, European Union, and Croatian institutions use the definition of youth that refers to persons aged 15 to 24, which encompasses the period of middle and late adolescence. In Croatia as well as in other European countries, the period of youth frequently lasts until the age of thirty. Therefore, the Croatian National Program of Action for Youth is targeted at young people between 15 and 29 (Dulčić and Bouillet 2003). Owing to specific socioeconomic factors, this approach is reasonable. The majority of Croatian adolescents are forced to live with their parents as they are unable to live independently, which for some is convenient but for most is a frustrating situation. The reasons are primarily growing awareness of the importance of a formal university education and its duration and in particular the unemployment problem.

The 1990s was a very difficult period for Croatian youth due to the war situation and the impoverished economy; education, health, and living standards fell significantly to a level below adolescent entitlements. At the turn of the century, Croatian adolescents were a heterogeneous population group composed of parent-dependent high school and university students (mainly from elite, higher- and middle-income families); the parent-dependent unemployed, frequently up to the age of 30; and workers who live independently, participate in society, and are committed to the roles of adulthood, sometimes from the early age of 20 usually because of economic reasons.

Physically, the beginning of adolescence in Croatian children starts at about the age of 11 with the onset of puberty-characteristic changes. However, the end of adolescence and attainment of adulthood is more difficult to pinpoint in Croatian youth, as it varies from the mid-twenties to the age of thirty. Croatian adolescents appear to be polarized between two different concepts: the youth-centric concept tending to extend dependence on parents and remain young as long as possible, and the adult-centric concept aimed at disengaging them from the family and become socially and economically independent (Ilišin 2002a).

Beliefs

Croatian society, deeply marked by the post-Communist transition, is focused toward new contemporary trends; to the market in economy, pluralistic democratic society in politics, and to the revival of old traditional values in culture.

Two basic assumptions for a social pluralist society are autonomy and freedom. In the late 1990s, Croatian adolescents aged 15 to 20, surveyed on their adolescent values and value orientation, reported the highest regard for the group of values associated with "self-realization" (love, close and friendly relationships with other people, autonomy, and freedom of personal and occupational choice). "Hedonist" values (high living standard, good income, leisure time with a lot of excitement and fun, respectful society status, successful career, social influence) were rated very poorly. Moderately rated "conventional" orientations (being with family and friends, good education, adherence to moral

and religious principles, achievement in life, contribution to society) appear as a protective factor during their socialization against a hedonist value orientation that is perceived as a risky value orientation (Franc, Šakić, and Ivičić 2002).

During the Homeland War (1992), Croatian early adolescents rated equality, inner harmony, and salvation lower than values such as wisdom, family security, self-respect, self-esteem, and freedom compared to adolescents before the war (1989). However, both groups declared world peace, happiness, family security, true friendship, and freedom as the five most important values (Raboteg-Šarić and Brajša-Žganec 1995).

The Catholic Church is very influential in Croatia, particularly in the rural areas. The majority of Croats identify themselves as Catholics. In particular, older people place more importance on their religious identity, while for young people their identity is rather secularized. Their religiousness is the result of a deeply rooted Catholic traditional pattern that prevailed despite the strong antireligious, sociopolitical climate during the Communist period of Croatia, lasting for almost half a century (1945–1991). Moreover, according to a survey carried out among secondary-school adolescents in the Croatian capital, religion is not highly rated, whereas family, material status, culture, love, friendship, health, and morality are highly appreciated (Mandarić 2000).

Religious identity in young people is mostly based on the received sacraments (baptism, Holy Communion, and confirmation) and rarely in regular church practices. Adolescents become increasingly removed from the church as they grow older. More than half of the young people go to confession once or twice a year, and only a third of Croatian adolescents regularly attend services. However, like older Croats, young people pay more attention to attending religious ceremonies on Holy Days of Obligation such as Christmas and Easter (Mandarić 2000).

Young Croats have a positive attitude toward life and its meaning, but this is more associated with the ability of every individual to employ a creative attitude toward one's own life rather than with values specified by religion. It may be concluded that younger generations express their religiousness as a part of tradition or as an indicator of their ethno-national identity and individualized faith.

Gender

In early and middle adolescence, there are generally great differences between girls and boys both in physical and mental development. Girls tend to develop earlier and are occupied with life's problems sooner. They are also more likely to view problems as more difficult.

In Croatia main gender differences arise from differences in upbringing and culturally and socially constructed roles. Boys and girls are taught to differently cope with expressing emotions. Girls are taught to express their emotions freely and openly; they pay more attention to their emotions and feelings when compared to boys who are taught to restrain from expressing their emotions.

In compliance with traditional methods of upbringing prevalent in Croatia, Croatian girls are expected to be more attentive in school, to behave decently, and to refrain from alcohol, smoking, and drug abuse (Lugomer-Armano et al. 2001). Accordingly, communication with fathers is better among boys than girls, which indicates that even in early adolescence differences may be observed in both parental treatment and expectations. Girls are more preoccupied with their future prospects, while boys are less likely to think about their future.

Gender disparities are seen in the understanding and convictions about love and sexuality, and the importance of love and previous sexual experience is almost never evaluated equally for both genders, which is mostly inherited from the traditional pattern of the past (Štulhofer et al. 2001).

As far as gender roles are concerned, the status of adolescent girls in Croatia reflects the overall status of women in society with prevailing restrictions with regard to female achievements and freedom. There is a growing awareness of girls' undeserved status in society and of their gendered inequality that increases with age. Girls are readier to invest efforts to achieve their goals, but their expectations for their successful realization are also greater.

Adolescence is a period in which intellectual development and emotional independence frequently lead to changes in the self-image of one's own body and in self-perception. It is noted that the connection between body image and self-esteem is more emphasized in girls. They are likely to evaluate their bodies differently from boys and see them as a possible way to attract attention from others, while boys see their bodies as a way to be efficient in their surroundings. Therefore, boys show significantly greater self-esteem and rate their appearance and school abilities higher than girls in early adolescence, whereas girls feel that they are given more social support from their parents and friends. Thus, parents' and teachers' support is more important for girls and their self-esteem than for boys (Brajša-Žganec et al. 2000).

For many years the social climate in Croatia, as in other European countries, contributed to the popularity of thinness and diets, which already have become an important preoccupation in adolescence. In search of the ideal body size, adolescents focus on ways to control their body weight and to achieve what are often unachievable and dangerous body sizes. Girls often overestimate their current body sizes and this is frequently an exaggeration of their true weight. They try to become thinner and some even become underweight compared to the weight standard for their age. Boys, on the contrary, view themselves as too thin and try to increase their body size and muscle mass in particular. Dieting sometimes leads to harmful side-effects that more often end in disorders such as depression and low self-esteem, rather than in the perfect body figure. Adolescent boys are less dissatisfied with their bodies compared to girls, but dissatisfaction increases with age. With respect to obesity, Croatia belongs to the countries with a low obesity rate in comparison to other Western European countries and the United States, but this rate is higher than Eastern European countries (Kuzman et al. 2004).

In regard to eating disorders among Croatian adolescents, the treatment rate of anorexia nervosa and bulimia correspond to that elsewhere in the world. This indicates that Croatian girls experience general dissatisfaction with their bodies and are likely to develop negative emotions characteristic of bulimia due to the negative influences of the media and popular world trends. Adolescent girls who manifest symptoms of bulimia often show behaviors that might be sub-risky for the occurrence of bulimia nervosa.

In general Croatian youth confirm a connection between body weight and emotional problems. Adolescents that overestimate their body sizes and suffer from eating disorders are unhappier with their bodies compared to those with normal or lower body weight (Vidović et al. 1997).

The Self

In the early twenty-first century, Croatian adolescents greatly differed from those who grew up during the 1960s and 1970s. The ways in which youth develop a sense of themselves has greatly changed. Individual development and identity formation of young Croats, which is a complex task for all adolescents, have been additionally complicated by Croatian real-life situations. A clear concept of self-identity is aggravated by several factors, such as adulthood emerging in late adolescence, education lasting longer, uncertainty about their employment prospects, the inability to move from a position of dependency on others to taking responsibility for themselves, and additional obstacles in achieving independence.

Since society does not ensure an adequate, secure context for the formation of a stable identity and an integrated sense of self, the identity of Croatian adolescents may be described as fragmentary, ambivalent, fluid, and lacking a strong sense of affiliation (Mandarić 2000).

During the late 1990s, a concept of identity shifted toward greater national affiliation. More educated young people of urban status who have liberal and social-democratic political orientations may be associated with a less strong national affiliation, cosmopolitanism, and a pro-European orientation. In comparison, young people from rural areas prefer nationally focused political programs. More developed urban settings help youth become free individuals (Baranović 2002).

In an attempt to define their own identities, Croatian adolescents aged 13 to 25 most often reported insecurities about their futures and problems related to schooling, which indicates that their need for security has not been adequately met (Lugomer-Armano et al. 2001).

Family Relationships

The average Croatian family consists of a married couple who are usually parents. Parents are usually caring and loving toward their children and are likely to invest great effort in their upbringing. Adolescents describe their relationship with their parents as good, and they report awareness of their parents' love and understanding, parental care, and good communication, which is especially important when a problem arises. In their opinion, the best way to solve any problem is to talk it over with their parents and to accept their advice (UNICEF 2001). Mothers usually show more acceptance behavior toward adolescents than fathers; mothers are more in control of their children's behavior and are more inclined to be in psychological control. Both parents are more rigorous in their behavioral and psychological control over boys than girls, whereas both parents display more acceptance behavior toward girls and younger children in comparison to older ones.

During early and middle adolescence, children usually spend a lot of time with their parents in family activities such as sports, hobbies, housecleaning, visiting family and friends, and shopping. These joint activities also extend to their leisure time and include watching TV, having family meals, and discussing daily activities and tasks.

As for sibling relations, there is great mutual attachment between them that is deeply rooted in the tradition of the Croatian people. Heritage that is passed on from generation to generation is cherished and respected. Strong intrafamily ties begin as a family is established, and as a result children are very closely connected with their brothers and sisters from early childhood. These close relationships also continue later in life, across all the stages of adolescence and into adulthood.

As most parents are employed and absent from their homes for some time during the day, siblings are frequently at home alone. This time spent alone also contributes to building strong mutual ties between siblings.

Adolescents whose parents are married estimate that they receive more social support from their parents than those from single-parent families. Girls from two-parent families also report better family cohesion (Brajša-Žganec et al. 2002).

Though family structure has no influence on children's perception of mothers' parental behavior and family atmosphere, there is a difference in the way single mothers and mothers from two-parent families evaluate family processes. Single mothers report less control over adolescents and possibly less rigorous psychological control than mothers from traditional families (Keresteš 2001).

Marriage is still highly important in Croatia as the influence of tradition is strongly felt. In the total number of marriages, divorces account for 20%, and the proportion of re-married partners, widows, or widowers is 18% (Central Bureau of Statistics 2004). The divorce rate is higher in urban compared to rural areas of Croatia, which is attributable to a more liberal lifestyle and the attitudes of urban adolescents who are less influenced by Catholic traditions, more permissive, and more tolerant.

Friends and Peers/Youth Culture

Peer relationships and the choice of friends are determined by several factors specific for Croatia. The most important factors include the system of education, a difficult economic situation, and consequent social changes. Since the majority of young adolescents grow up in families in which both parents work, schools have taken on more than an educational role. They stimulate and provide structured activities for young adolescents by engaging them in extracurricular activities. About 30% of primary school children participate in various programs that help them spend their free time in organized activities, recreation, and relaxation (Babić and Bauer 1999).

There are also a number of institutionalized programs that offer a form of nonformal education as well as create a stimulating environment for the development of peer relationships and friendships.

However, some patterns can be noted. In early adolescence there is no difference between the sexes with regard to participation in school and out-of-school activities. However, during middle adolescence, girls are more involved in reading and cultural activities during their leisure time, whereas boys more often prefer sports and recreational activities. Going to parties and visiting cafés and disco clubs are equal for both sexes. At the age of 11 to 15 years, adolescents mostly go out once or twice a week; boys go out more in the evenings than girls at age 11 (30% boys and 19% girls) and also at age 15 (41% boys and 31% girls) (Kuzman 2004).

Comparative research on how Croatian adolescents spent their leisure time in 1986 and 1999 showed the same cultural patterns: going out to cafés and disco clubs, socializing, going to parties, being lazy, and visiting concerts (Ilišin 2002b). The greatest differences were observed between the urban and rural populations and between more socially competent adolescents from higher-income families with a quality education and those from lower-income families whose interests are more traditional. In general, adolescents are more likely to spend their time having a good time in one way or another, while activities focused on the improvement of their personalities are of secondary interest (Ilišin 2002b).

Among Croatian youth, the "street corner" boys and groups of boys (škvadre) from neighborhoods representing the first-generation settlers into urban centers were the earliest subculture groups. They are characteristically male-oriented and often linked with minor criminal activities as well as aggressive behavior (štemeri). This subculture group has existed for a long time and traces can be found even today among football hooligans and skinheads. During the 1970s, the spread of rock music culture resulted in a subculture of substance users (hašomani), which was soon followed by the "preppies" associated with a higher social status. Along with these three subculture trends that can be seen even today in Croatia, the 1980s were marked by growing punk and "New Wave" identities. Music lifestyles are responsible for most subcultures that exist in Croatia, as in the rest of the world, but there

is also a trend to form a style of living based on activities other than music, as seen in "skaters" and "rollers." Subcultural identity is most often represented as an achieved identity, but also as an ascribed identity (which can be local, ethnic, or national). Football teams organized around national, ethnic, and religious identities give rise to football hooliganism as an ascribed identity, but the role of achieved dimensions cannot be completely excluded. The same can be said for the hip-hop subculture, which is predominantly a manifestation of an achieved identity in which ascribed identity characteristics play a less important role. Football hooliganism and hip-hop as subcultural lifestyles are therefore, to a certain degree, a mix between ascribed and achieved dimensions of identity in youth cultures (Perasović 2004).

Love and Sexuality

The psychosexual development of Croatian adolescents takes place within a society that is still characterized by conservative attitudes towards sexuality and gender disparities, particularly in rural areas. On the other hand, the mass media messages adolescents are exposed to at an early age have dramatically increased the availability of information of a sexual content.

The average age of menarche for Croatian girls is 12 to 13 years. Sexual activity at the age of 15 is not greatly represented (about 20% of boys and 9% of girls) compared to the rest of Europe; Croatia is among the last on the list. Among sexually active adolescents, 28% of boys and 22% of girls had their first sexual experience at the age of 13. Every fourth adolescent had unprotected sex, which involved a higher risk of probable side effects such as unwanted pregnancies and sexually transmitted diseases (Kuzman et al. 2004). These early sexual activities were mostly unplanned, between casual partners, with no established relationship or between absolute strangers, multipartner experiences, and without adequate contraceptives or any other means of protection from sexually transmitted diseases. Young people who began their sexual activity early in life are frequently regular cigarette smokers, likely to engage in binge drinking, and likely to experiment with illegal drugs.

One of the possible undesirable results of sexual activity among young adolescents is pregnancy. In 2003, out of the overall number of newborns in Croatia only five were born to girls younger than 15. Five percent were born to adolescent mothers aged 15 to 19, and 26% to those aged 20 to 24 (Central Bureau of Statistics 2004).

Early sexual activity increases the risk of sexually transmitted diseases. Since 1995, the number of registered venereal diseases such as gonorrhea and syphilis has been declining and reduced to sporadic cases. Chlamydia trachomatis is the most widely spread sexually transmitted disease in adolescents. Owing to possible consequences on prereproductive health, adolescent girls who engage in early sexual activity and who have older partners represent the most endangered population group.

In regard to risk from HIV/AIDS, at the end of 2001 the number of people with this disease was estimated at around 500. (Kuzman et al. 2002; Wong 2002). Some of the HIV-infected persons are homosexuals. In traditional Croatian society, relations between persons of the same sex are to a great degree stigmatized. Like members of any other stigmatized population, persons in same-sex relationships are confronted with no understanding and little tolerance from society. However, contacts with and cultural influences from other developed countries have brought some changes to this society in view of permissiveness and greater tolerance, mostly in urban populations. People in bigger cities are more open-minded towards homosexuality while the rural population often views it negatively. For most of the Croatian population, the main source of information about HIV/AIDS is the mass media. Adolescents have access to more and more accurate information about AIDS than the rest of the population.

Premarital sex is almost a regular practice for young people brought up on Western cultural values, but cohabitation is rare in Croatia, even in urban settings. A low standard of living and a difficult financial situation, as well as high apartment rents, make it difficult for adolescents to cohabit.

There is no permanent and adequate sex education program in the Croatian education system, but certain shifts can be seen toward providing more adequate information to young adolescents. Until some organized way of obtaining knowledge is provided, Croatian adolescents learn about sexuality primarily through youth magazines, TV, videotapes, and communication with peers. Although primary sexual socialization takes place within a family environment, many Croatian parents are reluctant to discuss sexual issues with their adolescent children. This may be due to the sensitive nature of the subject or because they are increasingly absent from home. In any case, parents often do not sufficiently fulfill their roles as primary sex educators. Abortion has been legal in Croatia since the early 1970s.

Health Risk Behavior

The distressing war situation, the post-war struggle for social and political balance and stability, as well as transitional difficulties have made young people in Croatia more susceptible to health risk behaviors since 1991. Typical health-risk behaviors include smoking, alcohol and drug use, abnormal eating patterns, bullying, and injuries in Croatia.

Drug experimentation, abuse, and addiction have become one of the most acute problems in the coastal region of the country and in Zagreb. According to a survey conducted on a representative sample of Croatian secondary-school pupils, more than 20% of adolescents have tried illegal drugs and one-fourth of them have experimented before they turned 15 (Sakoman et al. 2002).

A third of adolescents enjoy smoking cigarettes and more than 50% consume alcohol. Older secondary-school adolescents, more frequently boys than girls, use narcotics. The initial age of experimentation with drugs, binge drinking, and regular smoking is decreasing (Sakoman et al. 2002). Until the age of 15, slightly less than 20% of boys and 15% of girls had at least once experimented with marijuana. Cigarettes, marijuana, and alcohol use are often intermingled. More than one-third of adolescents reported the use of alcohol at the age of 15 (boys' starting age is lower than girls'), which is rather alarming data (Kuzman et al. 2004).

The undesirable effects of alcohol consumption in adolescents are increasingly linked with frequent traffic accidents, delinquent behavior, and criminal activities. Out of a total of 600 persons killed in road accidents a year, young drivers up to the age of 24 were responsible for 179 casualties. Moreover, alcohol consumption was a primary cause of accidents among 25% of them. Many adolescents are likely to be involved in some kind of criminal activity after they start using drugs (Kuzman et al. 2004). A link could be established between the use of heavy drugs and more serious criminal offenses. Socially deviant and antisocial behaviors in this population refer mostly to vandalism, while robbery with violence is less frequent.

Increasing attention has been paid to bullying in schools. Over 70% of boys and girls had never been subject to any form of violence in school, but every fourth boy and every fifth girl estimate that they have been exposed to violence from their peers. As could be expected, boys were more frequently the perpetrators of violence while girls were more frequently the victims of violence. The incidents of violence, committed or experienced, decline as children of both sexes get older. Children involved in violence display more psychosomatic symptoms such as headaches, stomach pains, nervousness, irritability, and depression (Kuzman et al. 2004).

One of the features of the contemporary Croatian society is trafficking. The term is used to describe a wide range of activities, from facilitated (voluntary) migration to the exploitation of prostitution, and involves mostly young women and children. Since no systematic research on trafficking has been carried out in Croatia so far, the scale of the problem is difficult to ascertain. Croatia is observed as primarily a transit country for trafficking in young women to Europe and plays a lesser role as a source and destination country. Though small in percentage in comparison to other criminal activities, trafficking of women and children should be a significant concern in Croatian society (Štulhofer et al. 2002).

In general the number of children and adolescents with symptoms of depression is on the increase in Croatia, in particular when compared to the early twentieth-century data. Girls are more likely to manifest symptoms of depression than boys (Brajša-Žganec 2005). Behavioral disorders are more explicit in adolescents who were exposed to traumatic war experiences, and their number is higher in areas of Croatia that were directly involved in war conflicts.

In regard to suicide, the incidence rate has been relatively stable over the 15-year period that covers both the war and post-war years. In the total number of suicides, most were committed by persons aged 15 to 30. Half of them were committed by hanging. It is interesting to note that in almost 80% of suicides between 1990 and 2000, victims announced their intention to commit suicide prior to their tragedy (Kozarić-Kovačić et al. 2002).

Alcohol and drug abuse is constantly increasing among young people in Croatia. The number of heroin users has remained relatively stable over the last couple of years, while a significant increase in use of synthetic drugs has been identified. Synthetic drug users are mostly young people who are insufficiently informed about their effects and the dangers of becoming addicted to heroin (Kuzman et al. 2002).

Education

Since 1991, the educational system in Croatia has improved due to significant school reforms. However, some problems still remain, such as a teaching personnel shortage and issues relating to privatization.

The educational system in Croatia includes preschool, elementary, secondary, and university education. Elementary education lasts eight years and is obligatory, as well as free of charge for all children aged 6.5 to 15. It is divided into two four-year periods: from the first to fourth grade (with one main teacher) followed by fifth to eighth grade (with different subject teachers). In principle, 98% of all children attend and complete elementary school (Dulčić and Bouillet 2003).

Upon completion of an elementary education, adolescents do not have a job qualification. They are expected to continue their education in the secondary-school system that either offers a general education (grammar schools) that anticipates further university education; a vocational education (a professional qualification that also offers the possibility of further education); or an artistic education (in music, fine arts, design, dance).

About 95% to 97% pupils continue their education beyond the elementary level, and approximately 85% to 90% of the enrolled adolescents regularly complete their selected secondary schools (Dulčić and Bouillet 2003).

Educational programs in Croatia have dealt with two distinct groups of children so far: the average and those with special needs. Special attention has been given to gifted children and more specialist efforts are being invested in development programs in line with quality, pluralistic education that would support the needs and abilities of gifted children.

Elementary education for children with special needs (children with hearing and vision impairment, motor impairments, mental retardation, autism, speech impairment, and organic behavioral disorders) is organized in the form of complete integration, partial integration, and by means of special educational programs. The same pertains to secondary-school education, but elementary schools are more easily accessible to most disabled adolescents than schools for secondary or higher education (Dulčić and Bouillet 2003). In Croatia, the illiteracy rate among persons older than ten years of age amounts to only 1.8%. According to 2001 Census data on persons over the age of 15, 21.8% of the population finished an elementary school education, 47.1% finished a secondary school education, and 11.9% completed college or university education.

Croatia has a generally well-developed system of higher education institutions, including universities, faculties, and academies of arts, polytechnics, as well as schools of professional higher education. University studies qualify students for high-level professional or artistic work and prepare them to continue their scientific work. Professional studies qualify students for high-level professional work.

In the 2000–2001 school year, about 120,000 students enrolled at Croatian universities, and on average about 33% of students graduate. In the year 2000, over 13,500 students graduated (Dulčić and Bouillet 2003). In the academic year 2003–2004, about 7.8% of the total population above 15 years were involved in higher education; there were 3,341 students per 100,000 inhabitants in Croatia (Ministry of Science, Education and Sports of the Republic of Croatia, http://www.mzos.hr).

Work

Over the past decades, Croatia has been faced with continuously increasing unemployment. Therefore, the high unemployment rate among the young population represents a great problem in turn-of-the-century Croatian society.

In Croatia the process of transition, which normally involves deep structural changes throughout the entire economy and reflects in the structure of employment, has been additionally aggravated by the impact of war. Market reforms similar to those in other Central European countries took place in Croatia in the 1990s and featured similar macroeconomic effects across the region, including Croatia. Even though the privatization process has inspired public discontent, its economic effect was less contested since it empowered Croatia to equal, in terms of GDP per capita, other Central European states such as Czech Republic, Hungary, and Slovakia, which did not have the war on their territories. However, the rate of total unemployment is still high as it remains around 13% to 19%. Thus, one of the country's top priorities is to increase employment and, in particular, to create favorable conditions for the employment of young people.

Since the mid-1980s, the proportion of unemployed young people has been decreasing, but Croatia still lacks adequate mechanisms that would ensure the gradual transition of the young from the inactive to the working segment of the population. In late 2001, according to the data of the Croatian Bureau for Employment, there were 41.6% (164,365) unemployed in the 15 to 29 age group (Dulčić and Bouillet 2003). In 2003, the overall unemployment rate decreased to 15%. However, the segment of the unemployed young population increased and in the youngest work-eligible population group, aged 15 to 24, the number of unemployed was slightly higher than 35% (Central Bureau of Statistics 2004).

In an investigation carried out on a representative sample of young Croats, 60% reported unemployment as the most important problem, and in the areas most affected by the Homeland War as many as 80% of the young were confronted with the problem of unemployment (Raboteg-Šarić and Rogić 2002). Thus, employment of the young is a priority task of both social and economic policies in Croatia. In 2002, the government activated the Program on Employment Stimulation.

An adolescent under the age of 15 cannot be employed except if the job entails light work tasks, and adolescents under the age of 18 are not permitted to do night work.

Croatian adolescents that are underage (not yet 18) cannot be employed in any job that may be injurious to the life, health, morality, and development of the adolescent. Other forbidden work includes out of the ordinary working conditions; hard, strenuous work and those involving health risks; and jobs associated with gambling, disco bars, bars and nightclubs, and the like (Sansović and Bortek-Knešaurek 1999). According to the 2001 census, 2,022 adolescents aged 15 to 17 were employed (1.1% from the total adolescent population of that age), whereas 4,623 adolescents of that age were unemployed (2.6% of the total adolescent population of that age) (Central Bureau of Statistics 2004). The number of employed adolescents depends primarily on their secondary school education. Besides, compared to the 1980s, there has been a decline in the number of family-supported adolescents and an increasing number of those who are forced to ensure their basic living needs by themselves.

Temporary work and additional support from their parents, and work on the black market provided a lot of young people aged 15 to 29 with a way to make ends meet during a period of unemployment (over 40% according to research in 1999) (Štimac Radin 2002a). Half of investigated young individuals had accepted work in the shadow economy for pocket money and to meet their personal needs. Almost 30% reported that this was their only way to survive and over 10% claimed that they had improved the family budget in this way (Štimac Radin 2002b). It should be noted that mostly urban employed as well as unemployed young men and late adolescents with a secondary school education participated in the grey economy (black market).

As for temporary paid work, about 13% of parents reported that their adolescents tried to earn money from jobs such as car washing, jobs in parking lots, administrative jobs, marketing material distribution, cleaning jobs, assisting in polls, helping in learning, and other tasks (Raboteg-Šarić and Josipović 2003).

In house chore participation, parents said that most children participate poorly but that they help more in shopping, tidying flats, and taking care of their younger brothers and sisters. According to estimates, children from one-parent families help more in washing dishes than those from two-parent families (Raboteg-Šarić and Josipović 2003).

Media

Croatia has been extremely open toward Western cultural influences, and the media plays a very significant role in the lives of Croatian adolescents. Various forms of media have become an indispensable part of every household; they are meaningful and important sources of information to the overall Croatian population. Many adolescents have learned about topics that are still taboo in Croatian society or are perceived as too sensitive to be discussed even among family members (such as sexuality and sexual deviations) through the media.

Watching TV is common among both adults and young people, although for adolescents to a lesser degree. In a 1999 survey, about 34% of adolescents reported the use of their own computer, and 57% were using one at their workplace, permanently or sporadically. About 27% of adolescents were accessing Internet only sometimes or often (Ilišin 2001). About 50% of children between 10 and 15 years do not use a computer everyday, 40% of children use it to play video games, and 20% reported using computers for school or for some other purposes (Ilišin, Marinović, Bobinec, and Radin 2001).

Young adolescents mostly use TV, the radio, teen magazines, and computers; girls are more likely to read and listen to the radio, whereas boys prefer watching television and using a computer. These gender-related differences toward preferred media type are observed in all age groups.

TV has primarily an entertaining role, though its educational function and sometimes its negative influence cannot be neglected. Adolescents from more educated parents in urban settings usually watch international programs, music clips, and documentary programs.

Politics and Military

There are three distinct issues determining the level of active participation of Croatian youth in society: distrust as seen in the social and political system toward young people, distrust of young people toward social and political institutions, and mutual distrust and insufficient cooperation between associations of young people and political institutions (Dulčić and Bouillet 2003). Croatian youth are allowed to vote when they reach the "age of adulthood," that is, at the age of 18. In Croatia young people between 18 to 29 make 22% of the total voting population, and 30% of political party members are juniors. Despite these percentages, the participation of youth in authoritative bodies, from the Croatian Parliament to local levels, is very low (from 0% to 2% in the period from 1990 to 2003). Research shows that young people see themselves as inadequately involved in the political life of the country, but at the same time their interest in politics and political events is markedly decreasing.

Dissatisfaction with the general social status of youth has triggered initiatives such as the National Program of Action for Youth. These aim at improving their status and include steps to incite the participation of youth in social processes and increase their presence in political institutions (Dulčić and Bouillet 2003).

All men over the age of 18 are obliged to serve in the army. They may choose between civil service (eight month duration) and training in the Armed Forces of the Republic of Croatia (six months). Civil service is mostly chosen by those who are not willing to accept military training due to religious, moral, or other reasons.

Unique Issues

When dealing with Croatian adolescents, it cannot be ignored that Croatia emerged as an independent state in 1991 at very high costs. This period, unique in the history of the country, was definitely a most turbulent and disruptive period for young people. For some of them, it meant exposure to traumatic events and painful experiences that have undoubtedly left deep marks on their childhood and adolescence. Many problems that are present in Croatia, such as substance abuse, juvenile delinquency, depression, and psychosocial disorders, may be attributed to war and its complex consequences.

However, there is optimism that Croatian children and young people have a great resiliency due to an awareness that Croatian society invests a lot of effort to help them. In a young democratic society that focuses on an individual approach, youth from these war-afflicted generations will be given the opportunity to become normal, satisfied, and mature persons. Placing too much emphasis on

CROATIA

war and its adolescent victims would perhaps, in the long run, only present a partial picture of Croatia.

ANDREJA BRAJŠA-ŽGANEC

References and Further Reading

Babić, V., and K. Bauer (eds.). 1999. *National programme of action for children in the Republic of Croatia*. Zagreb: Government of the Republic of Croatia.

Baranović, B. 2002. Youth of Croatia: Between national identity and European integration. In *Youth and transition in Croatia*. V. Ilišin and F. Radin (ed.). pp. 127–57. Zagreb: Institute for Social Research, Zagreb and State Institute for the Protection of Family, Maternity and Youth.

Brajša-Žganec, A. 2005. The long-term effects of war experiences on children's depression in the Republic of Croatia. *Child Abuse & Neglect* 29:31–43.

Brajša-Žganec, A., Z. Rabateg-Šarić, and R. Franc. 2000. Dimenzije samopoimanja djece u odnosu na opaženu socijalnu podršku iz različitih izvora (The dimension of children's self-conceptions in relation to perceived social support from different sources). *Društvena istraživanja* (Journal for General Social Issues) 6:897–912.

Brajša-Žganec, A., Z. Rabateg-Šarić, and R. Glavak. 2002. Gender differences in the relationship between some family characteristics and adolescent substance abuse. *Društvena istraživanja* (Journal for General Social Issues) 11:335–53.

Central Bureau of Statistics. 2003. *Statistički ljetopis Republike Hrvatske 2003 (Statistical yearbook of the Republic of Croatia 2003)*. Zagreb: Državni zavod za statistiku.

Central Bureau of Statistics. 2005. *Statistički ljetopis Republike Hrvatske 2004. (Statistical Yearbook of the Republic of Croatia 2004)*. Zagreb: Državni zavod za statistiku 2005.

Dulčić, A., and D. Bouillet. 2003. *Republic of Croatia—The National Programme of Action for Youth*. Zagreb: The State Institute for the Protection of Family, Maternity and Youth.

Franc, R., V. Šakić, and I. Ivičić. 2002. Vrednote i vrijednosne orijentacije adolescenata: Hijerarhija i povezanost sa stavovima i ponašanjima (Values and value orientations of adolescents: Hierarchy and correlation with attitudes and behaviors.) *Društvena istraživanja* (Journal for General Social Issues) 11:215–39.

Ilišin, V. 2001. Slobodno vrijeme (Free time). In *Djeca i mediji* (Children and the media). V. Ilišin (ed.). pp. 91–118. Zagreb: Institute for Social Research, Zagreb and State Institute for the Protection of Family, Maternitiy and Youth.

Ilišin, V. 2002a. Youth, adulthood and the future. In *Youth and transition in Croatia*. V. Ilišin and F. Radin (eds.) pp. 31–49. Zagreb: Institute for Social Research, Zagreb and State Institute for the Protection of Family, Maternity and Youth.

Ilišin, V. 2002b. The interests and leisure time of youth. In *Youth and transition in Croatia*. V. Ilišin and F. Radin (eds.). pp. 269–301. Zagreb: Institute for Social Research, Zagreb and State Institute for the Protection of Family, Maternity and Youth.

Ilišin, V., A. Marinović Bobinec, and F. Radin. 2001. Korištenje masovnih medija (The use of mass media). In *Djeca i mediji* (Children and the media). V. Ilišin (ed.). pp. 119–53. Zagreb: Institute for Social Research, Zagreb and State Institute for the Protection of Family, Maternity and Youth.

Kereteš, G. 2001. Roditeljsko ponašanje i obiteljska klima u obiteljima samohranih majki (Parental behavior and family atmosphere in single-mother families). *Društvena istraživanja* (Journal for General Social Issues) 10:903–25.

Kozarić-Kovačić, D., et al. 2002. Epidemiological indicators of suicides in the Republic of Croatia. *Društvena istraživanja* (Journal for General Social Issues) 11:155–70.

Kuzman, M., et al. 2002. *HIV/AIDS-related risk behaviours in especially vulnerable young people in Croatia*. Zagreb: UNICEF 2002.

Kuzman, M., I. Pejnović Franelić, and I. Pavić Šimetin. 2004. *Ponašanje u vezi sa zdravljem u djece školske dobi 2001/2002* (The health behavior in school-aged children 2001/2002). Zagreb: Croatian Institute of Public Health.

Lugomer-Armano, G., Ž. Kamenov, and D. Ljubotina (eds.). 2002. *Problemi i potrebe mladih u Hrvatskoj* (Needs and necessities of young people in Croatia.) Zagreb: Department of Psychology, Faculty of Philosophy in Zagreb.

Mandarić, V. B. 2000. *Religiozni identitet zagrebačkih adolescenata* (Religious identity of Zagreb adolescents). Zagreb: Ivo Pilar Institute for Social Sciences

Ministry of Science, Education and Sports of the Republic of Croatia, http://www.mzos.hr.

Perasović, B. 2004. The notion of youth culture in contemporary context. In *Resituating Culture*. G. Titley (ed.). pp. 177–87. Strasbourg: Council of Europe.

Rabateg-Šarić, Z., and A. Brajša-Žganec. 1995. Sustav terminalnih vrednota adolescenata prije rata i u ratu (System of terminal values of adolescents before and during the war). *Psychologia Croatica* 1-2:17–26.

Rabateg-Šarić, Z., and V. Josipović. 2003. Obitelj, rad i skrb o djeci (Family, work and child care.) In *Jednoroditeljske obitelji: osobni doživljaj i stavovi okoline* (One-parent families: personal experience and attitudes of others). Z. Rabateg-Šarić, N. Pećnik, and V. Josipović (eds.). Zagreb: State Institute for the Protection of Family, Maternity and Youth.

Rabateg-Šarić, Z., and I. Rogić. 2002. *Daleki život bliski rub: kvaliteta života i životni planovi mladih na područjima posebne državne skrbi* (Living on the edge: The quality of life and life plans of young people who live in the areas of special state concern). Zagreb: Institute for Social Research, Zagreb and State Institute for the Protection of Family, Maternity and Youth.

Sakoman, S., Z. Rabateg-Šarić, and M. Kuzman. 2002. Raširenost zlouporabe sredstava ovisnosti meu hrvatskim srednjoškolcima (The incidence of substance abuse among Croatian high school students). *Društvena istraživanja* (Journal for General Social Issues) 11:311–35.

Sansović, K., and Š. Bortek-Knešaurek. 1999. *Djeca u Republici Hrvatskoj* (Children in the Republic of Croatia). Zagreb: The Republic of Croatia—State Institute for the Protection of Family, Maternity and Youth.

Štimac Radin, H. 2002a. Risk of unemployment. In *Youth and transition in Croatia*. V. Ilišin and F. Radin (eds.). pp. 233–56. Zagreb: Institute for Social Research, Zagreb and State Institute for the Protection of Family, Maternity and Youth.

Štimac Radin, H. 2002b. Work on the black market. In *Youth and transition in Croatia*. V. Ilišin and F. Radin (eds.). pp. 259–67. Zagreb: Institute for Social Research,

Zagreb and State Institute for the Protection of Family, Maternity and Youth.

Štulhofer, A., et al. 2001. Croatia. In *International encyclopedia of sexuality*. R. Francoeur and R. Noonan (eds.). vol. 4. New York: Continuum.

Štulhofer, A., Z. Raboteg-Šarić, and L. Marinović. 2002. *Trafficking in women and children for sexual exploitation*. Zagreb: Center for Transition and Civil Society Research and International Organization for Migration.

UNICEF. 2001. *Young voices. Opinion survey of children and young people of Croatia*. Zagreb.

Vidović, V., et al. 1997. Eating behaviour, weight status and depressive feelings in female adolescents. *Collegium Antropologicum* 21:277–83.

Wong, E. 2002. *Rapid assessment and response on HIV/AIDS among especially vulnerable young people in South Eastern Europe*. Belgrade: UNICEF Area Office for the Balkans.

CZECH REPUBLIC

Background Information

The Czech Republic is located in the Central European region. The Czech language belongs to the family of Slavic languages, however the Czech culture and lifestyle is deeply rooted in Western European culture.

The Czech Republic was founded in January 1993 as a result of the peaceful split of the former Czechoslovakia into two independent states (the Czech Republic and Slovakia). Czechoslovakia (established in October 1918) was an industrial and democratic European country until 1939. After World War II Czechoslovakia became a Communist country dependent upon the Soviet Union.

However, this situation changed at the end of the 1980s, as democratic tendencies swelled in Central and Eastern Europe. Czech students initiated the so-called Velvet Revolution in November 1989. This event initiated a new era of political pluralism and democracy in Czech society.

The total population of the Czech Republic is about 10.3 million people. Adolescents (referred to here as the grouping of 10- to 25-year-olds) make up 21% of the total population.

The Czech Republic is an ethnically homogeneous country. The majority of adolescents are Czechs (94% of the total population); Slovaks represent the largest minority (2%). There are other ethnic groups, but these minorities include less than 1% of the total population (Germans, Poles, Romas, Ukrainians). However, an increase in the number of immigrants, especially young people from Eastern Europe and Asia, is expected in the first decades of the new millennium.

The Czech Republic joined the European Union (EU) in May 2004.

Period of Adolescence

As in other industrialized European countries, adolescence in Czech society has been recognized as a separate life stage since the 1850s. The recognition of this period was closely related to the establishment of a compulsory school system. It brought not only new institutions but also a new understanding of the rights and duties of young people, their cognitive competence and emotional nature, their values, and the normative steps of their transition to adulthood (Chisholm and Hurrelman 1995).

The beginning of the period of adolescence is usually related to pubertal changes. In Czech adolescents, these changes have wide variation in both timing and tempo. The acceleration of physical growth (an increase in height and weight) appears usually at age 7 or 8 in girls and 9 or 10 years in boys. The mean age of menarche for Czech girls is comparable to Western European countries (Coleman and Hendry 1999) and occurs before the age of 13. Boys mature a few months later on the average, and it is more difficult to assess the mean age of their maturation.

As in other advanced Euro-American countries, the adolescent period tends to be extended and the transition criteria into adulthood is rather vague. However, if adolescence is conceptualized as a gradual progress through specific stages on the path from childhood into adulthood, there are several important milestones marking this path.

Among the important milestones and rites of passage of the transition process are the following:

1. Age 15: this is the end of obligatory school education. It enables the adolescent to be employed with certain limitations related to the work of youth. This age is also when sexual contact and intercourse with another person becomes legal.
2. Age 18: this is the age of adulthood and full legal responsibility. Young people at this age have the right to vote, get married, obtain a driver's license, be fully employed with no limitations, and buy and consume alcoholic beverages.

It is important to note that full legal responsibility is not necessarily identical to one's subjective feeling of being an adult. Many young people connect their adulthood with economic independence from their parents and living separately from them. On the other hand, particularly amongst university and college students, there is a tendency to rely on financial support from parents.

In the Czech Republic the developmental stage defined by J. Arnett (2000) can be identified as a period of "emerging adulthood" (with a focus on ages 18 to 25). One of the characteristics of this period is a postponement of some of the goals and roles traditionally connected with adulthood. The time of study and career preparation has lengthened, the value of leisure time is enhanced, and the range of options of how to spend life as an adult is widened. The most striking changes can be seen upon entering married life and becoming a parent. Since the early 1990s, the mean age at marriage as well as the mean age of parents at first birth has risen significantly (for more details, see section on Love and Sexuality below).

Beliefs

Historically, the Czech Republic is one of a number of countries sharing a European Christian cultural heritage. The forty-year period of the Communist regime left indisputable traces in the social milieu of the country. The official ideology between 1948 and 1990 was based on an atheistic worldview and on the Marxist notion of collectivism. However, this form of collectivism was anonymous, disregarding the interests of individual people.

The political, social, and cultural changes at the beginning of the 1990s signified for many people important changes in their personal lives and destinies. More personal freedom brought a greater emphasis on the personal responsibility and value of the individual. Trends towards individualism gained in force and led to the gradual initiation of class differentiation and stratification.

The post-totalitarian generation of Czech adolescents at the beginning of the 1990s perceived social changes extremely positively, since those changes represented personal opportunities and challenges (getting a good education, the possibility to travel and live abroad, and political and ideological freedom). On the other hand, the more recent generation of adolescents is apt to view the same conditions as ordinary attributes of everyday life. Recent data reveal that Czech youth at the turn of the twenty-first century are more similar to their Western European peers than they are to the former post-totalitarian Czech generation (Macek 2003). These Czech youth experience personal freedom, but at the same time have more uncertainty and unpredictability in regard to their future. They also must take more responsibility for themselves. The value of education, money, success, social prestige, emancipation, free time, and entertainment has grown considerably.

The sense of community, which emphasizes the subordination of personal goals to group goals, does not prevail among young Czechs. On the other hand, there is a moderate growth of interest in public life, activities concerning the protection of the environment, solidarity or empathy with people in difficult life situations, and an increasing participation in volunteer and nonprofit activities.

According to their declared beliefs and values, most Czech adolescents are very liberal and tolerant (regarding drugs, abortion, and sexual freedom) and a large majority hold no religious beliefs at all. According to Czech Statistical Office data from 2002, only about 19% of contemporary adolescents consider themselves religious. The majority of these are Christian (83% Roman Catholic, 4% Protestant). Other denominations are rare. About 10% of adolescents declare themselves to be believers with no particular denomination. In regard to younger groups (15 to 19) compared to older (20 to 24) adolescents, there is no evident difference in the participation in religious activities. It is nevertheless important to note that the spiritual life and system of values of contemporary Czech adolescents has been undergoing a process of differentiation. There are a growing number of subcultures and religious and interest groups that differ substantially from the above mentioned trends. It should be noted that very often adolescents do not seek abstract ideas and values but rather choose a particular reference group and an authority they can trust (Sak 2000).

Gender

During the Communist regime Czech society underwent a specific process concerning gender roles that somewhat differed from that of Western European countries. The image of the "socially realistic" woman represented a typical example of the Czech woman (or those from other East European countries). According to this ideal she was politically involved, had her own income, and was a perfect housewife. This ideal corresponded to the image of the emancipated woman, who in Czech society was somewhat influenced by the paternalism of the Communist regime and the ideals for which Western feminists had fought.

However, only at the beginning of the 1990s did the notion of gender become an important subject for discussion by those in the social sciences in the Czech Republic. Both Western and Czech theoreticians of gender have come to the conclusion that it is vital to take into account cultural and social diversity, and that it is not advisable to uncritically apply all Western lessons to the Czech cultural and social milieu.

Changes connected with the definition of gender roles have been associated with the Czech Republic joining the EU. Among those the EU requires and is mostly concerned with are the application of equal job opportunities for both sexes, programs for the encouragement of the appointment of women to top management posts, greater participation of men in the family sphere, and the promotion of new models of professional careers based on family friendly work policies.

Findings that outline the contemporary reality were disclosed in a study that focused on the conceptions of masculinity and femininity and the perception of gender role stereotypes among Czech adolescents. The results show that young Czechs (aged 17 to 21) embody, to a great extent, both masculine and feminine characteristics and tend to blur gender differences and thus approximate the androgynous type of personality. However, boys generally manifested typical masculine characteristics (ambitiousness, self-assertion, interest in sex) rather than feminine ones, and similarly, girls proved to be more feminine. The situation was similar to the evaluation of the concepts of an ideal man and woman. Unlike boys, adolescent girls in the given sample perceived as desirable a higher degree of masculinity in an ideal woman and a higher degree of femininity in an ideal man (Wyrobková 2002).

As Western European cultural trends and ideals filtered into the Czech milieu at the beginning of the 1990s, the significance of the body—and body image—has been undergoing a gradual change. The Czech Republic has been experiencing an enormous expansion of the diet industry; body care facilities are also widespread. The ideal body type is becoming increasingly thin and is strongly supported by the mass media's propaganda of slimness being equal to success. Unhealthy media images and the pressure to be successful inevitably affect the values and lifestyle of Czech adolescents and influence their attitudes towards food and eating habits.

Data from a survey conducted with young people showed that men in the sample reflected more strongly the traditional views of masculinity and femininity than young women. Men struggled for a firm, adequately muscled body without excessive fat, and often wished to be taller. The women's concept of a female ideal ranged from tenderness to emphasizing muscles, but by no means did all women sampled view the image presented by the media (the extremely slim and tall model look) as their ideal. Nevertheless, the majority of them stressed the importance of a firm, slim body and had an aversion to being fat (Brimová 2004). Body image and related matters have become issues in connection with the almost epidemic increase in eating disorders among Czech adolescent girls and young women.

Research results show that up to 6% of Czech adolescent girls and young women suffer from eating disorders, and a third of this population is underweight. Specialists' estimates are even higher— they talk about 10% of adolescent girls experiencing chronic problems with anorexia or bulimia (Možný 2002). Most of them go undiagnosed until their illness causes secondary health problems. Another study reports that 77% of girls and 35% of boys are dissatisfied with their body, although this discontent has a different meaning for each sex. About a half of the boys wanted to gain weight and strengthen their bodies, whereas girls expressed a desire to become slimmer. Adolescent girls' attitudes towards food and their bodies were abnormal in 7% of respondents in the sample. Unfortunately, prevention and awareness programs addressing eating disorders, which must also include teacher education, are still in the early stage.

The Self

To Czech adolescents, personal identity and awareness of their own self-worth relates to their need to gain social prestige and peer respect, as well as a need for acceptance and trust of parents and other influential people, and for a concrete sense of their future as grounded in certain rules and values.

Compared to previous generations, the self-system of contemporary adolescents appears to be more autonomous. The influence and importance of adult authorities (parents, teachers, and others) upon self-definition has decreased, and there is a more realistic attitude toward their future. It is interesting to note that contemporary Czech adolescent girls presented higher self-esteem than the former generation of girls, and now there is no difference in relation to self-esteem between boys and girls (Macek 2003).

Undoubtedly, apart from individual personal and interpersonal influences, the identity formation and self-definition processes are also shaped by historical and cultural contexts. The theme of identity and self-reflection of the Czech people gained specific prominence throughout the 1990s, during the period of major political, economic, and cultural changes.

As there is an overall low mobility among the Czech population and most adolescents have spent their lives in one place, regional identity is important. At the same time, in connection with the admittance of the Czech Republic to the European Union, the issue of Europeanism has been accentuated. It is obvious that European identity is not compared to national identity by the majority of young people, but is more likely to be the opposite: those who think highly of their Czech identity also proclaim their Europeanism.

National identity and pride have their historic roots; however, research among the young generation (the age group of 15 to 30) has proven that the success of popular and universally known personalities—above all of Czech sports athletes and some celebrities—form part of the cultural sphere and are equally important in the formation of national pride (Sak and Saková 2004).

Overall democratization of the Czech society has led to the reinforcement of individual freedom and dignity, the right to express individual opinions, and respect for the opinions and attitudes of others. The drawback of the democratization process is that there is a high degree of uncertainty in the sphere of values, standards, and unwritten rules of conduct among people. A view has developed that people can only find the basis for any moral decision in themselves (Baumeister 1997), or in some cases in a moral discourse of negotiation with others in general and specific situations. This also helps us explain an increasing emphasis on the immediate and intensive consumption of pleasure in Czech adolescents and their tendency to reject long-term commitments in various spheres of life.

Family Relationships

A traditional model of parent and adolescent relationships that takes parental authority for granted still prevails. A spectrum of educational styles and practices has been widening due to the liberalization of society and due to stress on the development of the individual. Parents' personal experiences and the values connected to their own childhood values and education all play a significant role in the style in which they choose to bring up their children. Parents with less education and those who grew up in the country usually favor a traditional division of roles in the family (the woman is primarily responsible for the household and the rearing of children, and the man is the breadwinner). Parents with a higher degree of education who live in the city prefer an equal division of roles, including in rearing their children.

The interaction between children and parents at the beginning and end of this period differs remarkably in Czech culture. An apparent asymmetry of the relationships between child and parent can be observed during the early adolescent stage. On the one hand, the adolescent wants to have his or her way at all costs, on the other, the parents are often unable to refrain from their demands.

The matter-of-fact nature of the conflicts is often banal. An overwhelming majority of adolescents still live with their parents at this period of their lives (apart from the time spent at school [six hours a day on average], at after-school activities, and with peers [about 0 to 2 hours a day on the average]). Quite naturally, the arguments pivot around household chores, pocket money, school duties, and free time.

It is essential to differentiate the character, dynamics, and purpose of these conflicts from the adolescents' general attitude to their parents. Several surveys have demonstrated that the majority of adolescents get on well with their parents; nevertheless, they admit to having arguments and conflicts with them (Macek 2003).

Girls in particular bear the brunt of parental restrictions in early adolescence. Unlike boys, they are given a greater responsibility for household chores. Also, parents exert more control over them; the parents' message is "be careful nothing bad happens to you." The change of status from child to young adult brings more advantages than disadvantages for boys. If parents exert any pressure on boys, it is usually about their behavior and their need to be more determined and assertive with their peers (in other words, the parents' message in this case is "show what you can do").

There is still an asymmetry in the relationship of child and parent that continues throughout mid-adolescence; however, interaction between the two is more open and constructive than it was before. There is an intense drive for adolescents to establish their right to freedom, whereas for the parents it is still immensely difficult to give up control of their child. The fact that most adolescents between the years of 15 to 18 study at secondary schools reinforce this need. Only a minority spend their weekdays in dormitories; most commute home daily. As a result, parents are in daily contact with their children, even if it is limited to evening hours.

The atmosphere of the family and the style of communication between parents and children play a vital role in the period of "negotiations of own autonomy." Our research proves that sex differences and gender characteristics play their role as well. Girls are more sensitive to negative impulses and feelings. If they experience arguments, conflicts, and lack of interest from their parents and are distrusted by them, or if they are aware that their parents act as authority figures only, they tend to underestimate themselves. Unlike boys, they feel more responsibility for the family dynamic and perceive themselves as participants in the conflict. If, on the other hand, they grow up in a family in which members show understanding and respect for one other, their self-esteem grows accordingly.

In comparison to girls, boys seem to be more resistant to any negative atmosphere in the family, while at the same time tending to be more sensitive to positive moments in family life. Understanding and emotional support stimulates both their self-esteem and an awareness of their own achievements and successes.

A parent's control of their child's behavior rapidly decreases in late adolescence. The age of 18 represents a crucial landmark in the child-parent relationship. At this age adolescents reach adulthood in the Czech Republic and so gain all the elementary rights and responsibilities of an adult citizen. However, a surviving economical dependency of adolescents on their parents complicates the reaching of mutual acceptance and an equal, symmetrical relationship, especially for university students.

More than half of Czech adolescents have only one sibling. The quality of the brother or sister relationship is rather complicated to evaluate. Rivalry is as equally typical as cooperation. The first (rivalry), is usual for siblings where the age difference is two to three years; the latter (cooperation) can be observed with those whose age difference is minimal.

The divorce rate in the Czech Republic has been steady during the past decades—more than one third of all marriages end in divorce. Not surprisingly, about one sixth of adolescents experience their parents' divorce. In most cases it is the court's practice to give the mother custody of the child. Most adolescents who have experienced divorce describe it as a difficult time, but they don't perceive it as a stigmatizing event that negatively influences their personal development. Surveys suggest that adolescents whose parents divorce are more skeptical about their own marriage or their ability to have lasting relationships than those adolescents whose parents stay together. On the other hand, unlike their peers who do not have this experience, they are able to view divorce as less destructive and their expectations for relationships as more realistic. They are often able to establish distance between their own relationship and that of their parents' (Plaňava 1999).

Friends and Peers/Youth Culture

It is difficult to determine how much time Czech adolescents spend with their peers compared to time spent with their family or by themselves. The average time devoted to particular activities daily, inferred from the results of a survey aimed at teenagers aged 14 to 16, are thus: commuting to school, one hour; time spent at school, six hours; homework, one hour; time spent with friends, one hour; sports, .5 hour; reading, .25 hour; watching TV and listening to music, two hours; dating, 20 minutes (girls spend more time dating than boys); working at the computer, .5 hour (boys devote more time to this activity than girls); helping with housework, .5 hour (for more detail see Macek 2003). Other activities, such as earning money, are rarely mentioned.

According to research that focused on adolescents aged 15 to 23, the most frequent use of their free time was spent watching TV and listening to music, chatting with friends, reading magazines, relaxing, dating, going to pubs and cafés, playing computer games, and traveling (Sak and Saková 2004).

From the age of 10 to 18, the time spent at school and in the classroom forms the basic peer environment for Czech adolescents. Various types of interaction and relationships are established here: comradeship, deeper friendships, and their first intimate relationships. Moreover, the school organizes numerous after-school activities (such as sports, music, acting, and excursions).

Leisure centers also organize similar activities for children and young adolescents. The Scouts Union constitutes the widest membership amongst those official organizations that recruit children and adolescents. Its task is to encourage the mental, spiritual, social, and physical development of its members. The organization Pioneer holds similar ideals. The overwhelming majority of sports clubs have youth teams. In contrast to these, church organizations for teens do not have a large membership. Groups with ecological interests organize programs such as the Rainbow or the Brontosaurus and have quite high memberships.

Peer cliques have the same importance in early adolescence as do structured and organized peer activities. They are mainly formed by boys who share common interests and activities (sports activities, game playing, and trips to the country). Girl cliques are less frequent; girls, more often than boys, prefer to have close relationships only with one or a few female friends. Peer environment plays an important part in early adolescence—not only as a concrete, real social environment, but also as a referential framework for self-evaluation. Our research shows that conceptions of ideal adolescent characteristics and behavior are similar in Czech boys and girls: a sense of humor is important, as are verbal skills, the confidence that is reflected when he or she excels in something (such as sports, musical activities, school), the ability to control his or her own emotions, friendliness, honesty, and self-confidence (Macek 2003).

There are no obvious class or social barriers to the bonds between adolescents' peers and friends. However, ethnic and racial barriers are more likely to determine the initiation of new relationships. Despite the fact that Czech society has made some progress in this respect, it still remains somewhat xenophobic. Trust, or the lack of it, is unfortunately not based on following certain rules but upon shared experiences. Often when Czechs confront unfamiliar people or things ("the other"), they are a priori distrustful and rejecting. The basis of the mainstream perception of "the other" relies on a dependence on the opinion of another kind of authority. Some Czechs amongst the older generation look down on such ethnic minorities as the Roma community or immigrants from Eastern Europe and Asia, and their opinion certainly has a negative influence on potential peer friendships or relationships among adolescents of different backgrounds.

The mainstream Czech adolescent culture—however it differentiates from the adult lifestyle—has been increasingly tolerated in the Czech Republic and does not stand in direct opposition to the adult world. Czech adolescents are influenced by globalization and other mainstream trends which are typical for the lifestyle of adolescents in the cultural milieu of Euro-America. As in other countries, manufacturers in the Czech Republic also target this particular age group (in fashion, music, and the sports industry). As it is, they incorporate the most up-to-date trends, such as hairstyles, clothing, as well as other aspects of fashion such as tattoos, piercing, and so on. Some attributes of this adolescent lifestyle and culture (fashion and music) are also attractive to adults.

It is indisputable that Czech adolescent culture is also divided into many subcultures that are not only in opposition to the surrounding cultural milieu, but to each other as well. The subcultures are characterized by their unique outer attributes (slang, clothing, hairstyle) but also by their behavior and values.

Some subcultures originated spontaneously and are uniquely typical to the Czech Republic alone, for instance "tramping." This is a movement with more than 80 years of tradition and resembles a scout movement. Paradoxically enough, the movement is not inspired by Czech history but by romantic stories from the times of colonizing the Wild West in North America. The community of tramps includes many small informal groups (the so-called tramping settlements), which elect a leader they call a sheriff and which have a camping place of their own. The groups are in mutual contact and visit each other's camping sites on the weekends. While doing this, they wear contemporary costumes (of hunters and cowboys), have their specific rituals, make their own food together, and sing romantic songs sitting around campfires. They treasure values such as love for nature, freedom, equality, and unselfish friendship.

It is essential to note that most of the subcultures share traits with those established in the Anglo-Saxon world. Very often their origination is inspired by a particular musical style and is demonstrated by participation at live performances, concerts, and such gatherings as techno parties, house parties, folk or rock festivals, clubs where different types of music can be heard (hip-hop can alternate with drum'n'bass, funk, or jazz). Attitudes towards music and communication about it works as a quick prognosticator that defines peer attitudes, opinions, and values (in other words, "tell me what you listen to and I'll know who you are").

Sports club fans or groups centered around playing fantasy games also constitute an important element in the Czech subculture, as do groups with extreme political orientations, such as the skinheads and anarchists.

To be a member of a particular subculture is, for Czech adolescents, as similar in meaning as it is for their Western European counterparts: it means to be visible within the local peer group, to belong somewhere, to have their own identity, and to relate to a particular opinion (Coleman and Hendry 1999).

Love and Sexuality

Czech society can be characterized as being very liberal in respect to attitudes towards love and sexuality. Traditionally, tolerance towards premarital sex has always been quite high (50.3% men and 69.4% women consider premarital sex admissible if practiced within a lasting relationship). There is a similar attitude towards unfaithfulness in partner relationships (unconditionally rejected by 31% of Czech women and 25% of men). Only about 5% of the population is strictly against the use of contraception, and only 4% vehemently oppose abortions (Weiss and Zvěřina 2001).

Therefore, it is not surprising to state that parents are usually not very restrictive with their adolescent children in regard to their romantic relationships. Parents quite commonly tolerate their children's first dating at the age 14 to 15 (more often girls than boys). Expressions of semi-intimate behavior (holding hands, kissing) are also common and tolerated in public and in secondary schools.

However, it is usually not the parents who provide effective sex education; there is a strong reliance on the schools to take on the role of sex educator. School sex education targets boys and girls aged 11 to 14. However, the time devoted to dealing with sexual issues is quite limited (about four lessons for 11- to 12-year-olds and up to 15 lessons for 13- to 14-year-olds per school year) and in addition, teachers often fail to address important topics such as homosexuality. Many schools still do not provide effective sex education; and the media, particularly teenage magazines, take over the crucial source for information concerning sexual matters.

The legal age limit for having sexual intercourse in the Czech Republic is 15 years of age. This applies equally to both heterosexual and homosexual behavior. Data regarding the sexual maturity and the initiation of sexual life for Czech adolescents does not differ much from that of youth in Western European countries. National research shows that 5% of Czech boys and girls experience their first sexual encounter at the age of 14 (under the legal age), as do one-quarter of 15-year-olds and almost half of 16-year-olds. The rate for 17-year-old teenagers having their first sexual encounter is 64% and the figures grow to 75% of 18-year-old respondents. One third of boys and 12% of girls have their first sexual experience with a casual partner. A gradual decrease in age for a first sexual encounter, recorded during the 1990s, has stopped and remains steady as most Czech youths of both sexes become sexually active at the age of 17 to 18. Once sexually active, one-quarter of the group aged 15 to 18 reported having had one sexual partner, whereas 17% had had three partners, 13% had had sex with four partners, and 4% stated eight to ten sexual partners. The number of sexual partners increases with age, and this trend applies similarly to both girls and boys. Thus, we may conclude that sexual activity is quite common in Czech teens and increases with age.

Concerning the use of birth control, over 50% of adolescents do not use any kind of contraception, nor do they practice safe sex during their first sexual encounter. Condoms are not very popular among Czech teenagers (Weiss and Zvěřina 2001). On the other hand, the number of teenagers who use the birth control pill is steadily rising. This trend is closely connected to the substantial decrease in abortions during the last decade. Overall, we can say that Czech adolescents are more promiscuous and less responsible compared to their Western European counterparts (Weiss, Urbánek, and Procházka 1996).

Czech society has undergone significant changes in the family and in associated reproductive and sexual behavior during the 1990s. The new trends are particularly evident if viewed in comparison to data collected in 1989 and 2000, which showed that the marriage rate had decreased by half. First marriages are often postponed until the late twenties (the mean age of brides was 26.4 in 2000 compared to 21.8 in 1989, and for grooms it has risen from 24.6 to 28.8). The mean age of the birth of the first child has also risen demonstrably, almost 50% of children are born to mothers over 27 years of age.

At the same time, the number of children born out of wedlock increased dramatically (one in every fifth child). Overall, fertility has declined and childless couples are on the rise. The Czech Republic joins the countries with the lowest birth rate in Europe (1.14 children per woman in 2002). For the younger generations, the significance of marriage as a formal institution is declining. Unmarried partnerships and couples opting for a childless life are on the increase and represent a discernible trend, especially for people with university degrees (Možný 2002).

Choosing a single lifestyle represents another new phenomenon in Czech society and has become a distinct alternative to traditional partner relationships. Choosing to be single is the choice of an emerging group and illustrates the change in family and reproductive behavior (Tomášek 2003).

Czech society is also quite tolerant of homosexuality. According to data from a public opinion poll, tolerance of homosexuality has grown from 29% in 1995 to 48% in 1999 (Havlík 2002). There still exists a certain fear of "coming out" among gay and lesbian youth, but most decide to disclose their sexuality quite early on after recognizing they are gay or lesbian. Among the first people they share this new knowledge with are usually their close heterosexual friends, but their parents are among the last to be told, if at all. Teenagers questioning their sexual orientation mainly seek information on the Internet (from specialized Web sites and chat rooms) where they usually find their first information. Another option is to attend support groups for teenage gays and lesbians; however, there are only a few such groups, and they are run by gay and lesbian NGOs and operate exclusively within big cities.

Health Risk Behavior

Social problems became more visible in connection with the democratization of Czech society. State and institutional control over citizens' lives decreased, whereas the individual had to become more responsible for his or her own life. Not only did negative social phenomena become more visible, but their frequency and quantity also increased. This trend has also affected Czech adolescents.

Alcohol consumption in the Czech Republic is the highest in Europe due to the fact that Czech society is exceptionally liberal in this respect. Although serving alcohol to those under 18 years of age is illegal, reality shows that the legal age restriction does not constitute any hindrance to alcohol consumption. The majority of adolescents have their first experience with alcohol between the age of 9 to 11. Although most of those questioned admit that this can lead to obnoxious behavior and to the danger of excessive drinking, they still perceive alcohol as a natural part of their social life. Adolescents' underage alcohol consumption is a phenomenon that in itself is not harshly condemned. Among 15- to 18-year-olds, more than 50% occasionally drink alcohol, and fewer than 5% abstain completely. After coming of age at 18, nearly everyone is familiar with alcohol; among the 19- to 23-year-olds nearly 13% of them become regular drinkers (at least once a week) and 78% drink alcohol occasionally (for detail see Macek 2003; Sak and Saková 2004).

Smoking represents another major health risk. The majority of adolescents experience their first cigarette by the age of 15. According to data collected in 2000, about 13% of adolescents aged 15 to 18 smoke; the figures rise to 27% among the 19- to 23-year-olds (Sak and Saková 2004), and according to more recent surveys the rates are even higher (Miovský 2002). Unlike some Western European countries, the number of adolescent smokers in the Czech Republic is not decreasing.

The use of soft drugs, especially of cannabis, is similarly motivated. In the past decade consumption has increased a great deal, whereas recently this trend has begun to decrease. For most adolescents we can speak of experimentation, not addiction. By the age of 18, about a third of adolescents have experimented with soft drugs and about 16% admit repeated usage. As with smoking and

consumption of alcohol, the first use of soft drugs (cannabis, Ecstasy) is regarded by adolescents as a social event and as a peer standard (Miovský 2002; Macek 2003).

Concerning hard drugs, Pervitin, a notorious Czech specialty, is the most common drug abused in the Czech Republic. Homemade and concocted from available medications, it is a substance whose effects are similar to heroin, which it resembles in frequency of use. It is difficult to determine the overall number of drug abusers in the adolescent population; estimates refer to 1% of adolescents.

Hazardous sexual behavior represents another factor among the existing health risks. Compared to their peers in Western European countries, Czech adolescents are more promiscuous and less responsible.

According to surveys, only a tiny section of sexually active adolescents—10%—use condoms regularly; 27% of the entire sample of boys declared that they used condoms sometimes. Although in the long-term perspective the situation has improved and the number of adolescents who realize the risks involved is increasing (Weiss and Zvěřina 2001), the vast majority of them do not acknowledge the threat of sexually transmitted diseases, especially HIV/AIDS. Most Czech adolescents have no direct experience with HIV-positive people, so they may feel that the probability of their own contraction of this disease is little.

Disorders of identity and depression (loss of reason for living, feelings of inferiority, loss of prospects for the future) have become increasingly frequent in recent years, although this is by no means a mass phenomenon. This may be due to the fact that contemporary society values a person according to his or her output and also emphasizes personal responsibility, decision-making, and self-control.

On the other hand, the number of suicides has considerably decreased. Among youths aged 20 to 24 years, for the sample of a population of 100,000, there were 11 suicides, while in the age group of 15 to 19 years this number was ever lower.

If we focus on risks in the social behavior of adolescents, criminality is clearly the most serious. Trends in the growth of juvenile delinquency are relative to those in the whole society. In the Czech Republic there was a considerable rise of criminality during the 1990s, though it has been steadily decreasing in the last few years. In 90% of cases, it is males who commit crimes. From statistics taken from solved crimes it becomes clear that 6% of children up to 15 years of age participate in crimes, whereas fewer than 8% of adolescents aged 15 to 18 are involved. The percentage of offenders aged 18 to 25, however, is considerably higher. Property crimes constitute about a third of adolescent crimes; thefts are the most frequent crimes in this respect (money, alcohol, cigarettes, bicycles, and cars stolen or broken into). These kinds of crimes are seldom committed individually; in most cases adolescent gangs, sometimes controlled by adults, are responsible for them. There is a rise in crimes committed under the influence of alcohol or other drugs or crimes associated with the production and distribution of drugs. Juvenile prostitution, the pornography trade, and violent crimes with racist and xenophobic motivations, though quite rare during the Communist regime, have been gaining prominence.

The causes for adolescent criminality are similar to those in other European countries; they result from the weakening of family bonds, increasing unemployment of the younger generation, and the diminishing of state control over this group.

New forms of adolescent behavior, whose aim is not to break the law or cause damage to another person, remain on the edge of the law or even go far beyond it. The aim of such behavior is to experience a rush—something extraordinary—or to accomplish an extraordinary achievement that leads to such a feeling. Apart from taking part in harmless activities, such as adrenaline-producing sports, adolescents participate in those which go far beyond the legal norms. Just to mention a few: car races in normal traffic operations, graffiti-writing, riding on tram-car poles, crossing the track before an approaching train, climbing high-voltage posts and cutting-off the electricity (called "darkening"), and riding a bicycle while holding onto a car.

Education

The system of education in the Czech Republic has changed considerably since 1990. Schools ceased to be controlled by the state and became more autonomous. Apart from the state schools, private and church schools have also been introduced and represent about one-fifth of all secondary schools, which resulted in the provision of a wider educational spectrum. Thanks to the increasingly lower number of adolescents in the upcoming generations, two trends have recently become apparent: on the one hand, there is an increase in schools that are not particularly appealing to students and who try to recruit new students with little success (due to their low quality or lack of prestige and success in

teaching specialized subjects); on the other hand, there are prestigious schools that are unable to accept all the applicants who apply.

Since 1774 school attendance has been compulsory in the Czech Republic. Children usually start attending school at the age of 6 and complete their primary education when they are 15. Consequently, all Czech adolescents are completely literate and attain a comprehensive level of elementary education, except for those who are seriously physically handicapped. All schools are coeducational, and girls and boys have equal access to education.

Secondary schools prepare students either for future professions or for further studies. There are three major types of secondary schools in the Czech Republic: comprehensive secondary schools (ISCED 3A), secondary technical schools (ISCED 3A, B), and secondary vocational and apprentice schools (ISCED 3B).

In the Czech Republic, the term "gymnasium" is used for a comprehensive secondary school. On average about 50% of applicants succeed in entrance exams, although acceptance might be lower for the most prestigious schools. At present they constitute about 20% of the total number of secondary schools in the Czech Republic. Their aim is to prepare students for further academic education. Three subtypes of gymnasium exist in the Czech Republic according to the length of study, which is either four years (from age 15 to 19), six years (from 13 to 19), or eight years (from age 11 to 19). All students take the final *maturita* (graduation) exam at the age of 19. After passing the exam the student obtains a General Certificate of Secondary Education (GCSE), which entitles her or him to go to university.

Specialized secondary technical schools provide students with a four-year vocational education that concludes with a final graduation exam (*maturita*). This type of school accounts for 38% of all secondary schools; about one-quarter are private. They prepare students for technical and other specialized practical activities, as well as for college and university. About 40% of the syllabus is comprised of general subjects, and 60% are specific vocational subjects. A list of vocational school types follows:

1. Technical secondary schools teaching engineering, chemistry, mechanical engineering, agriculture, construction.
2. Business academies where future accountants, personal assistants, secretaries, and others are educated.
3. Teaching schools where future kindergarten teachers are educated.

4. Nursing schools.
5. Schools specializing in arts, crafts, and design.
6. Specialized secondary schools that are conservatories for music, dramatic arts, and dancing.

As with grammar schools, there is a difference in quality between the concrete vocational and the specialized schools, and applicants do not always succeed in getting accepted by the school they desire.

Secondary vocational schools (ISCED 3B), one-sixth of which are private, account for about 41% of all secondary schools. They offer two- or three-year apprenticeship courses concluded by a final exam, after which the apprenticeship certificate is granted. Practical training comprises about one-half of teaching time and aims at the acquisition of manual skills in a trade. The number of specializations amounts to 280. Four-year courses are also provided by secondary vocational schools, which conclude with a final exam. These courses are for training highly skilled manual workers. Graduates of the three-year courses are offered the opportunity to take the follow-up study concluded by the graduation exam.

Long-term statistics show that the number of students from vocational schools has been steadily decreasing, while the number of grammar school students and technical secondary school students has been on the increase. From the total number of 15-year-old adolescents who in 2003 applied for secondary schools, 39% started their studies at apprenticeship schools, 40% at technical schools, and 19% at the four-year curriculum grammar schools. About 8% of adolescents had already been attending grammar schools (*gymnasium*), which have a six- or eight-year curriculum (Statistical Yearbook 2003).

State policy is also oriented toward children and youth with special educational needs (Conception of the State Youth Policy 1999). A fairly efficient network of special schools, classes, and other facilities has been established for children and youth with mental or physical handicaps, with impairment of hearing, vision, and/or speech, as well as for those with developmental and behavioral disorders. Nevertheless, the desire is to fully integrate these children into mainstream education, which is a process that has only recently been introduced. In the past, handicapped children tended to be secluded from the rest of society, so their integration into ordinary life was more difficult.

Integration of Roma children and youth into Czech society is still not very successful, although

the situation has improved considerably in the recent years. An inadequately high number of Roma children are still perceived as being mentally disabled and are placed in special schools. However, even though disadvantaged socially, these children and adolescents have no mental handicaps.

As far as talented children and adolescents are concerned, attention to their needs has slightly improved (especially in mathematics and language classes that have been established for children talented in these academic areas).

According to Education Statistics and Indicators of OECD, the Czech Republic ranks among those countries with the highest standards in secondary education. Czech secondary students (aged 15 years) have been traditionally good at mathematics, science, and reading literacy. Languages, on the other hand, still seem to be a weak point both for Czech students and teachers (Možný 2002; Education at a Glance 2003).

Work

The transition from school to work represents a significant transitory stage and is often perceived as the transition from adolescence to adulthood. Compared to the OECD countries, the age of transition from school to an economically active life is younger in the Czech Republic (the average age is slightly below the age of 20). Despite this fact, the range in age during which young people start working has been widening. The number of people who combine their studies with work has also recently increased (Education at a Glance 2003).

Operative laws in the Czech Republic prevent employers from exploiting adolescents as cheap labor or from abusing them sexually. The minimum working age for young Czechs is 15 years old. In addition, legal protection guarantees that the employer must not give adolescents any overtime work or any night work. Adolescents under the age of 18 may not be employed in work that is dangerous or damages their health.

In early adolescence, work is often limited to household chores. According to daily activity surveys of 14- to 16-year-olds, they spend about a half an hour a day working in activities such as cleaning the house and shopping. (Macek 2003).

According to 2003 data, nearly 90% of 15- to 19-year-olds are students, 6% work, 4% are unemployed, and less than 1% are on parental leave (Statistical Yearbook 2003). At first glance, this fact contrasts with other data stating that about one-third of the total number of unemployed in the

Czech Republic are adolescents aged 15 to 20 (Možný 2002).

We must understand this phenomenon in connection with the fact that after leaving school, many adolescents seize the opportunity to collect unemployment benefits, which are provided by the government during the first six months of unemployment. After this period, most of them start working.

Only a very small number of adolescents work part-time during the academic year. However, they often hold jobs during the summer holidays.

The situation changes for 20- to 24-year-olds. In 2003, 56% of this age group worked, 25% were students, 4% were on parental leave, and 8% were unemployed. Data pertaining to men and women does not differ much. Also, the level of education determines the unemployment rate. From the total number of unemployed it could be inferred that 71% have an elementary education or apprenticeship certificates, 25% have a secondary education, and 4% are college or university graduates (Statistical Yearbook 2003).

Although exact figures are not known, it has become evident that in recent years the number of university students who work part-time during their studies has increased.

As wages are concerned, employees aged 20 to 24 usually receive two-thirds of an average adult salary in the Czech Republic. Again, there are remarkable differences according to the level of education. Whether they are highly educated or not, most people in this age group are not satisfied with the overall amount of their income. Compared with the incomes of the older generations, they do not see their "income handicap" as something unfair, but rather as being insufficient in relation to high expenses and especially compared to the high cost of living (Kuchařová 1998; Eurobarometr ČR 2002).

People aged 20 to 24 still clearly depend economically to a great extent on their primary family. About half of this age group still lives with their parents. This dependence is not only of an economic character; the young also use or take advantage of their parents' social milieu, including their social network and informal influence (Macek and Rabušic 1994). From the 2003 survey it could be inferred that more than half of the respondents relied on the help of their parents and friends when looking for a job.

Other results of this survey reflect that adolescents' transition from school to work is usually smooth. About 42% had no difficulty in finding a job, and more than a quarter of respondents were able to find one even while they were still studying (Burda et al. 2003).

Comparative research revealed some differences between the attitudes of Czech and European youth (according to a comparison of Czech youth with those from other European Union countries based on a 2002 survey). Young Czechs see language skills, communication skills, and good qualifications as the most important prerequisites for finding a good job. In contrast to this, young people in the rest of Europe stress the importance of a good comprehensive education and the ability to use new information technologies (Eurobarometr ČR 2002). Such results correspond with an earlier evaluation of secondary education in the Czech Republic (a high level of general knowledge and a lower level of knowledge of foreign languages).

Despite the positive evaluation of the transition from school to work by adolescents themselves, problems pertaining to the availability and demands of the market and the number of graduates of individual trades and professions has to be mentioned. The youngest and those with the least amount of education—the elementary- and apprentice-educated sections of the young population—are still trained to become manual laborers and have little ability to meet the needs of the labor market. Graduates of secondary schools specializing in training managers, accountants, and the like also have problems in finding adequate jobs. This trend was already reflected in the labor market of 1999, when the number of unsuccessful applicants recruited from apprenticeship training centers increased by 50% to 60% (Conception of the State Youth Policy 1999), and this dilemma to a certain extent still remains. The situation is critical in the textile and clothing industry, agriculture, and the building industry (Burda et al. 2003).

The academic and labor opportunities for young people are likely to increase now that the Czech Republic has joined the European Union. It is difficult to assess the situation yet, however it is evident that people are interested in working and studying in the EU countries. In 2001, more than 60% of adolescents aged 19 to 23 showed an interest in availing themselves of this opportunity (Sak and Saková 2004).

Media

Mass media and information technologies strongly determine Czech lifestyles, including that of adolescents. TV is the most influential and most widespread influence. Apart from the Czech public service broadcasting and private stations, there are many other foreign channels (mainly European and American) available due to satellite and cable transmission.

Czech adolescents spend on average a little less than two hours a day watching TV, even though the rates are higher at the weekends. It could be inferred from long-term comparisons that the generation of adolescents in the early twenty-first century do not watch TV more than the generation of the early 1990s (Macek 2003). Recent surveys indicate that adolescents as an audience cannot be perceived as a homogeneous group. Fifteen- to eighteen-year-olds are the most ardent consumers of commercial programs, including teenage series (mainly American, action movies, soap operas, quiz shows). Despite the fact that these programs are not valued much, audience participation is amongst the highest (Sak and Saková 2004). The age group of 19- to 23-year-olds is more differentiated. Education, profession, and interests play a far greater role here than with the previous age group (the higher the education is, the lower the rates of audience participation are). As a whole this age group is less interested in commercial programs. The lifestyle and habits of the adolescent's primary family still play a chief role in relation to TV consumption.

According to the 2002 survey, 86% of adolescents own a radio, and 2% never listen to any kind of radio broadcast. Compared with TV, the influence of radio is far less significant and is difficult to determine since listening is often tied to other activities. Musical and interactive programs aimed at adolescents (dating programs, competitions, leaving messages for friends) are clearly the most popular.

More than three-quarters of young people aged 15 to 30 years own a CD player, while a slightly lower number still use cassette players. About 90% of respondents own a mobile phone or at least have one at their disposal. About one-third own a computer; about three-quarters of respondents state that they have one at their disposal (at home, at work, at Internet cafés). Seventy-two percent of respondents report having access to the Internet (Sak and Saková 2004). Time spent browsing the Web increases according to the level of education. Adolescents aged 15 to 17 feel the greatest need to exploit the anonymity of online chatting (compared to other age groups of younger adolescents or young adults; Šmahel 2003).

Young adolescents spend on average half an hour a day playing computer games (however, with immense differences between boys and girls; boys spend much more time playing, one to two hours is the usual session time; Vaculík 2002; Macek 2003).

The influence of mass media, information technologies, and the virtual environment is steadily increasing, while attendance at movie theaters and interest in reading are declining. Attendance dropped dramatically during the past decade and has only evened out with the introduction of multiplexes.

Politics and Military

Political participation was not easy for the generation of Czech adolescents living in the previous few decades. During the Communist era political participation was explicitly associated with support of the Communist regime. In the second half of the 1990s the situation changed dramatically. Czech people became increasingly dissatisfied with the imperfect rule of law, the functioning of the political system, and representative and executive state institutions. Economic conditions deteriorated, unemployment rose rapidly, and much corruption was exposed. The interest of young people in homeland affairs and their active participation dropped markedly; people ceased to be interested, especially in local politics. Compared with the previous period, young people became more skeptical. In a 1995 survey data displayed that Czech adolescents' optimism was not commensurate to the rest of post-Communist Europe; at the end of the decade trends were reversed (Macek and Marková 2004).

By no means do these findings show that young people succumbed to nihilism or despair. Their attitude to the current political situation is quite realistic and corresponds to the overall atmosphere in Czech society. As a 2002 survey shows, the overwhelming majority of young people aged 15 to 26 are content with the fact that they live in the Czech Republic. On the whole, distrust and skepticism still prevails on both a local and national level. In international comparisons, young Czechs' assessment of institutions does not differ markedly from the opinions of their counterparts in some Western European countries, such as France or Great Britain (Macek and Marková 2004). On the other hand, unlike their Western European peers, young Czechs are more trusting of mass media than their counterparts in other parts of Europe.

During the years 1997–2002 Czech youth became more trustful of the repressive state apparatus, such as the army and the police (Youth 2002). As far as the army was concerned, this attitude was undoubtedly related to the Czech Republic joining NATO in 1999 and to the fact that the army gradually became more professional. After more than 80 years, the draft for all men aged 19 was abolished in 2004.

Young people over 18 have the right to vote for legislative and representative delegates, ranging from local municipal councils to members of parliament. Citizens over the age of 21 can run for a post in any representative body. On the whole, it could be said that young people are not very interested in politics. Lack of freedom during the Communist regime left significant memories; it is thus believed that changes are only important at the highest level of state administration, and people are suspicious of local politics (Možný 2002). Surveys show that voters up to the age of 25 prefer parties that are on the middle-right of the political spectrum.

The low interest that young people have in community and volunteer activities corresponds to these beliefs. A somewhat higher number of volunteers work in sports clubs and organizations, but less in cultural spheres. Young people also devote their time to ecological and volunteer activities oriented to handicapped and destitute people.

Unique Issues

The use of information technologies such as the Internet and mobile phones in particular cannot be seen as an issue unique to Czech adolescents. If, nevertheless, we are looking to identify something specific, something for which there was not space enough in the previous chapters, it is exactly this issue.

According to current data, there are about nine million mobile phones in the Czech Republic; the population of the country is ten million. Although we do not have accurate statistics concerning the adolescent population, according to a realistic estimate about 90% of young people aged 10 to 25 own a mobile phone or have one at their disposal. Those who do not have one are not part of the norm, which, for instance, twenty years ago was represented by owning a pair of jeans, or ten years ago by owning a tape-recorder. Ten years ago, however, almost no young people owned a mobile phone.

For Czech adolescents, a mobile phone, especially for those aged 14 to 20, is a highly personal object that is often worn like a piece of clothing. It can be adopted to the individual "look" or "expression" by changing the ring tone, the interface, the color of the shield, or by adding logos and/or stickers. As we have observed, teenagers use mobile phones in an almost semi-disposable way, as if they were a piece of clothing or a fashion accessory. Some of them even perceive it as an indispensable part of themselves (Hulme and Peters 2001).

Text messaging (SMS) represents the main use of mobile phones by Czech youth, who are the most active users of this form of communication in the world. The reasons may be mainly financial, but SMS communication has other advantages as well. It is not the mere transmission of information. Unlike phone calls, SMS is only interactive in an indirect way and like e-mail it gives a greater sense of autonomy in communication with other teenagers. At the same time, adolescents do not use SMS texts merely as a means of interaction with each other, but also as a way to communicate with the mass media. This can be mainly observed in various polls, quizzes, or shows where they vote for their favorite singer and other items.

The fact that SMS can be used both in free time and during classes represents another great advantage. Sometimes teenagers can surreptitiously write messages under their desks. We cannot dismiss the fact that the types of messages can range from simple social interaction to the exchanging of answers to exams.

Although no empirical data have been gathered yet, it does not seem that mobile phone communication decreases face-to-face communication. It helps parents to monitor their children better, and adolescents can solve acute problems more promptly. It should be assumed, however, that the usage of mobile phones disturbs both the quality and the quantity of interpersonal relations. Communication via mobiles dislocates natural physical and psychical barriers by its chronic presence (at school, with family, with friends, in intimate relationships). An unexpected call or a message diverts the concentration at the immediate situation and often weakens the individual's experience of the concrete moment.

PETR MACEK and EVA POLÁŠKOVÁ

References and Further Reading

Arnett, J. J. 2000. Emerging adulthood. *American Psychologist* 55:469–80.
Baumeister, R. F. 1997. The self and society: Changes, problems, and opportunities. In *Self and identity*. R. D. Ashmore and L. Jussim (eds.). New York: Oxford University Press.
Brimová, E. 2004. Ideál krásy: Štíhlí a svalnatí. *Psychologie Dnes* 10:14–16.
Burda, V., J. Festová, H. Úlovcová, and J. Vojtěch. 2003. *Přístup mladých lidí ke vzdělávání a jejich profesní uplatnění*. Praha: Národní ústav odborného vzdělávání.

Chisholm, L., and K. Hurrelman. 1995. Adolescence in modern Europe. Pluralized transition patterns and their implications for personal and social risks. *Journal of Adolescence* 18:129–58.

Coleman, J. C., and L. B. Hendry. 1999. *The nature of adolescence*. London: Routledge.

Conception of the State Youth Policy in the Czech Republic until the Year 2002. 1999. Prague: Ministry of Education, Youth and Sport of Czech Republic.

Education et Glance: OECD Indicators—2003 Edition. http://www.oecd.org.

Eurobarometr ČR 2002. 2002. Praha: Institut dětí a mládeže MŠMT ČR. http://www.idm-msmt.cz/prilohy/cz_vyz/eurobar.doc.

Havlík, K. 2002. Czech Republic. In *Mind the gap: Gay and lesbian youth on the border of EU accession*. M. Lobnik and K. Vanhemelryck (eds.). Ljubljana: IGLYO 2002.

Hulme, M., and S. Peters. 2001. Me, my phone and I: The role of the mobile phone. Paper presented at the workshop Mobile Communications: Understanding Users, Adoption and Design, University of Colorado, Boulder.

Kuchařová, V. 1998. K současné socioekonomické situaci mladých lidí u nás a v západní. Evropě. *Demografie* 40:226–71.

Macek, P. 2003. *Adolescence*. Praha: Portál.

Macek, P, and I. Marková I. Trust and distrust in old and new democracies. In *Trust and democratic transition in post-Communist Europe*. I. Marková (ed.). Oxford: Oxford University Press.

Macek, P., and L. Rabuic. 1994. Czechoslovakia. In *International Handbook of Adolescence*. K. Hurrelman (ed.). Westport, Conn.: Greenwood Press.

Miovský, M. 2002. NEAD 2000. Přehled vybraných výsledků komparativní studie. PhD diss., Universita Palackého, Olomouc.

Mládež Č. R. 2002. Zpráva z polytematického výzkumu. 2002. Praha: Institut dětí a mládeže MŠMT ČR, 2002. http://www.idm-msmt.cz/czech/cz_vyz/czvyz.html.

Možný, I. 2002. Česká společnost. Nejdůležitěji fakta o kvalitě naeho života. Praha: Portál.

Plaňava, I. 1999. Manželství a rodiny: Struktura, dynamika, komunikace. Brno: Doplněk.

Sak, P. 2004. *Proměny české mládeže*. Praha: Petrklíč.

Sak, P., and K. Saková. 2004. *Mládež na křižovatce*. Praha: Svoboda Servis.

Šmahel, D. 2003. Adolescenti a internet: identita, vztahy, komunikace. PhD diss., Masarykova Universita, Brno.

Statistical Yearbook of the Czech Republic 2003. 2003. Prague: Czech Statistical Office.http://www.czso.cz/eng/edicniplan.nsf/p/10n1-03.

Tomášek, M. 2004. Singles v české republice—o aktuálně probíhajícím výzkumu. *Gender, rovné příležitosti,výzkum* 4::5–7.

Vaculík, M. 2002. Hraní počítačových her jako specifický fenomén období adolescence. In *Utváření a vývoj osobnosti*. Vladimír Smékal and Petr Macek (eds.). Brno: Barrister & Principal.

Weiss, P., and J. Zvěřina. 2001. *Sexuální chování v ČR—situace a trendy*. Praha: Portál.

Weiss, P., V. Urbánek, and I. Procházka. 1996. Koitální debut. *Československá psychologie* 40:138–45.

Wyrobková, A. Feminita a maskulinita v představách studentek a studentů—rodové rozdíly v percepci rodových stereotypů a v hodnotové orientaci. Diploma thesis, Masarykova Universita, Brno.

D

DEMOCRATIC REPUBLIC OF THE CONGO

Background Information

The Democratic Republic of the Congo (DRC), a former Belgian colony, is situated in the center of Africa. Its capital city is Kinshasa, and it is bordered by the following countries: Central African Republic and Sudan in the North; Uganda, Rwanda, Burundi, and Tanzania in the East; Zambia and Angola in the South; and Congo in the West (Brazzaville, capital city). Since the delineation of African borders by the International Conference of Berlin in 1885, the DRC has successively been the independent state of Congo, a Belgian colony (1908), and the Democratic Republic of the Congo (since the independence gained on June 30, 1960), with Joseph Kasa-Vubu for president and Patrice Lumumba for prime minister. The River Congo, with its numerous tributaries, runs through the entire country, from its source in the south to the west where it flows into the Atlantic Ocean. The great equatorial forest, which provides wood for exportation, is found in the central basin.

The Democratic Republic of the Congo is the third largest African country, after Niger and Sudan. It is four times larger than France and 84 times larger than Belgium. The country is rich with mineral resources (gold, diamonds, cobalt, copper, zinc, and oil), water resources, flora, and fauna. In fact, some animals are unique to the DRC, such as the okapi, the bonobo, and the giraffe. Activities include agriculture, cattle ranching, fishing, and brewing. There are mining and textile industries, which require the participation of the international community to invest in their development. Each province has resources that need to be tapped. It is worth noting that the dam of Inga, one of the largest in the world, already provides electricity to three African countries: the Republic of the Congo, Zambia, and Egypt.

About 450 ethnic groups live peacefully in the country. Problems stemming from land or forest use for food crops are amicably solved by the tribal chiefs, who may at times have recourse to mediators or other chiefs familiar with the ownership rights pertaining to the disputed lands and their rightful claimants. If they cannot end such conflicts, then the state may intervene and refer to the records established by the colonial administration. This process works well across the country, except in Kivu where immigrants from Rwanda have had problems with the local population since they broke this principle of peaceful coexistence. This has not happened in other provinces, where immigrants from neighboring countries agree with this principle and live in peace and harmony with the Congolese. If requested, nationality can be obtained according to the laws of the DRC.

Tribal wars are not part of the Congolese culture, although they were revived between 1998 and 2004 by the Rwandans, who used machetes and guns as weapons. Many adolescent boys and girls died during these events that took place in the eastern part of the country.

At the beginning of the twenty-first century, DRC's population was estimated at over 57 million, more than half being young people. The Department of Demographics from the College of Economics at the University of Kinshasa projected that the population would reach 61,758,000 inhabitants in 2005, including 35,997,000 young people under the age of 19 (58.45%). This age group includes 18,071,000 boys, with 7,224,000 of them between the ages of 10 and 19, and 17,926,000 girls, 7,174,000 of them between the ages of 10 and 19.

During the war of aggression, more than four million Congolese were killed, including many adolescents. This led the International Court of Justice of the Hague to rule in favor of the DRC in 2005, and condemn Uganda and Rwanda.

In 1965, a military coup led President Joseph Mobutu to become head of state. He renamed the country Republic of Zaire in 1971 and remained in power until May 17, 1997, when Mzee Laurent Désiré Kabila ousted him. Kabila, who was assassinated on January 16, 2001, was the first president of the DRC to have graduated from college. In the early twenty-first century, the country is ruled by Joseph Kabila, the youngest president in the world, who started to rule at age 30 in 2001. In 2003, he agreed to run the country with four vice-presidents from the parties that emerged after the war. This 1+4 formula is a convention that was decided by the warring Congolese and ratified by the global and inclusive agreement signed in Sun City, South Africa. They agreed to rule together during the Transition until free democratic elections. The first democratic elections took place before 1964.

The Democratic Republic of the Congo, a peaceful cradle rocked by the war in the east, has the capacity to advance its underprivileged people and to share its resources with the rest of world with dignity and equity, and in compliance with economic market laws. In this way, young people will get to know each other and build a better world.

Period of Adolescence

In the Democratic Republic of the Congo, adolescence is generally considered to take place between the ages of 12 and 17. It is acknowledged as a life phase, especially in cities and school environments. In the DRC, however, one must distinguish between two ways of life, traditional and modern.

In the traditional way of life, adolescence is not considered a life stage. From age 5 or 6, a child starts to copy adult activities. The little girl is initiated by accompanying her mother to the fields and to the river to do laundry and wash dishes. She carries a small bunch of firewood on her head as she returns from the forest with her mother.

The boy follows and observes his father when he hunts, fishes, and sets traps for game. By age 12, girls gradually separate themselves from their parents as they practice what they have observed and lived under their mothers' supervision. They go fishing and bring back fish as well as bunches of firewood and pitchers of water to serve the whole family. They start preparing food at home to help their mothers, who discreetly direct them. When a girl has her first periods at about age 13, the mother prepares her for her woman's role by advising her about maternity, child rearing, and how to care for a husband. Such advice is intensified when the girl turns 17. The markers that indicate that the girl has moved into adulthood are menstruation and the ability to cook and serve food for the entire family or for a large number of people. For boys, the markers are the ejaculation of sperm and the building of their own houses in order to leave the parental home. Young people are thus trained for their future roles as fathers and mothers.

In rural areas, some girls marry at age 15, 16, or even 14 if they are considered to have reached physical maturity. In 1987, President Mobutu's Central Committee for the Popular Movement of the Revolution (MPR) tried to lower the constitutional, political, and judicial age of majority down to 14 for girls, but the majority of the population opposed the idea. Therefore the young adult's age remains set at 18. However, Congolese girls from urban centers or large cities such as Kinshasa may be sexually active earlier as a result of family and city poverty.

Education, as offered in the modern way of life, has led to the differentiation of stages between childhood, adolescence, and adulthood. This is amplified by the training in psychology and pedagogy as well as by higher education. Adolescence and its signs are therefore identified and studied by the adults.

Beliefs

Religious faiths in the DRC include ancestral beliefs, various sects, and beliefs taught by four religions that came to the DRC during colonial times: Catholicism, Protestantism, Kimbanguism, and Islam.

Today, the major religious groups are: Christian churches (Catholic and Protestant denominations); awakening churches; Jehovah's Witnesses; Kimbanguist church; Islam; The Way International (research, communion, and biblical teachings centers), whose headquarters are in Knoxville, Ohio, in the United States; the Unification Church; and national churches including the Black Church of Africa.

There is no state religion. DRC is an independent, democratic, free, and secular state. Cultural and religious traditions or beliefs are taught by the different churches and in parochial schools. The state, however, requires moral lessons in all schools in courses about "civic and moral education or citizenship education." Parochial schools are allowed to include religious classes without having to dismiss children who do not share the beliefs they teach.

Overall, the Congolese are believers in God. Monotheists since antiquity, they believe in a Force, a Power, a Creator of all things, and then in their ancestors who live and act in the invisible world. Modern beliefs have taught them about God, his Son Jesus Christ, and Satan.

Today, all age groups pray in the various churches, but the majority of people attending church consists of adults and women. A good number of adolescent boys and girls as well as young adults attend prayer and meditation groups, which operate mostly in academia. Young people's infatuation with prayer and trust in God was strengthened by their spontaneous revolt on June 3, 2004, against the successive raids on the DRC by neighboring countries and the ensuing laxity and indifference from the international community and the UN mission in Congo (MONUC), which was then accused of complicity with the aggressors. It is also worth noting that solid teachings are provided so that a confirmation ceremony can be held, but it is not comparable to a bar mitzvah.

Individualism exists, but so does outrageous selfishness, as seen in the wealthy and high-ranking politicians. However, these traits are counteracted by many local, regional, national, or international associations. In fact, Congolese are more community oriented than they are individualists. For example, in many areas of the DRC, young people organize self-defense teams with the help of people who know martial arts and they sometimes arrest hooligans who disturb the peace of the night. The police also come to help the residents, but they are often late due to the lack of efficient logistical means.

Gender

Specific preparation for adulthood follows either the traditional or the modern way of life. Traditionally, gendered preparation to adult work begins in childhood and continues through adolescence. Upon reaching adulthood, the male youth becomes autonomous, marries, and is responsible for his life, which includes building a home (an essential act for a young adult man), feeding himself and his family, and earning money.

In the modern way of life, on the other hand, such preparation is done mostly at school. There is elementary, secondary, and professional education. This is when pupils are taught to read, write, and do math, and when they learn about culture (customs, habits, attitudes, sciences, technology, beliefs, and religions). In the first and second year of secondary school, students between the ages of 12 and 15 are oriented toward specific fields of study. This orientation gives them the skills for the specific profession they will enter when they leave school at 18.

Often, after finishing their education, young people do not know which career path to choose. They thus have to continue studying because higher education offers clearer and more definite professional training. After school, only sections such as technology, pedagogy, business, cutting and sawing, beautician, nursing, mechanics, agriculture, and veterinary science (to name but a few) offer training that lead directly to job opportunities. Literary and scientific studies do not lead directly to work and generally require pursuing higher degrees. In DRC, as elsewhere, there are no jobs reserved uniquely for men. For example, Congolese women, or at least a few, work as technical engineers (they have their own association) or mechanics. They can also serve in the army and the police, which are ordinarily men's jobs because of the physical strength they require.

The excision of the clitoris is not practiced in Congo/Kinshasa. The surgical elongation of the clitoris to make it resemble a penis, which is practiced on the girls of some tribes, does not give them the virility to hold men's jobs. It is done mostly for libidinal reasons, to heighten sensitivity or the sensations that lead to intercourse. It is a means to remedy frigidity. This practice is not very current in the country, however, since some plant roots and leaves can be eaten to stimulate a man's virility and sexual power while different ones can enhance female sexual performance. This has no influence on the physical changes of the body that are needed to adapt it to adult work based on gender.

The Self

Before the colonization of African countries, Rwandans, a pastoral people, had good relations with the land chiefs of Kivu, an agricultural people, and brought their cows to pasture there. They lived peacefully and used to return to their homes in Rwanda.

Emigrants to the Democratic Republic of the Congo were officially let in as early as 1908, when the country became a Belgian colony. This phenomenon was particularly important in the east of the country. The colonizers led Rwandans to Kivu in the DRC because of the famine that had struck their country. They were called the "transplanted," and they held alien cards. Other Rwandans from the Hutu tribe as well as Burundians worked in the mines of Katanga or Shaba. They lived in workers' camps, while the nationals had homes in the indigenous city and white people lived in the city.

Up until 1960, when the country obtained its international sovereignty, the three social groups were thus identified and lived separately. They met only in the workplace. Nevertheless, both groups of Blacks shared similar characteristics. Children lived within the same logic and could intermarry. At the end of each year, the "transplanted" workers went to spend their time off in their home countries, in accordance with their contract terms. They were allowed to come back with their spouses. Means of transportation were provided by the employers.

There were also two categories of schools for these different groups: schools for Belgian children and schools for Black children, which also accepted other foreigners. From time to time, Congolese adolescents fought with or insulted the children of the "transplanted" because of their origins; this wounded the "transplanted" to the bottom of their hearts and they felt diminished and humiliated.

In 1959–1960, at the beginning of the First Republic of Rwanda led by president Grégoire Kayibanda from the Hutu tribe, many refugees from the Tutsi tribe left for the Congo and, in lesser proportions, for other countries, especially Uganda and Burundi.

In 1960, during the independence, Belgians fled, leaving empty posts. The Congolese took over exclusively the jobs in the public administration, leaving some to Black western Africans who brought their technical knowledge to the industries while the nationals were being trained—the western African countries were well trained and prepared by the French and English in preparation for their national independence.

Following the independence of Congo/Kinshasa, the racial divide decreased throughout the country. Congolese children from the elite families could attend school with white children. Later, during the first Democratic Republic of the Congo of 1960–1965, all forms of racism were fought, especially in school and with the help of UNESCO. Since the colonial time, Belgians have respected the cultural identity of each ethnic group. Thus, every Sunday afternoon and on the days of great celebrations, folk dances were presented by diverse ethnic groups throughout the capital city and even in the cities across the country. Such popular rejoicing brought psychological rest.

After the death of president Juvénal Habiyarimana in 1994, however, the Tutsi refugees who had stayed for 30 years in Congo (since 1960), returned to Rwanda since they had regained power. About 80% of the Hutus fled from Rwanda to Congo, carrying their weapons and with the help of operation "Turquoise."

In 1997, the Rwando-Congolese infiltration by the Movement for the Liberation of Congo (AFDL) was in fact an alliance with two objectives: Rwando-Rwandan war of the Tutsis against the Hutus who had fled to the DRC, and Congolese war by Laurent Désiré Kabila against president Joseph Mobutu.

Between 1998 and 2004, the war of aggression by the eastern neighboring countries—Uganda, Rwanda, and Burundi—was fought in Kivu for unacknowledged reasons. It should be noted that the groups of native adolescents always prevailed over the groups of attackers. Adolescents created courageous and fearsome self-defense teams called "Mayi-Mayi" to rescue their province from the attackers' savagery, because nationality cannot be gained with weapons.

It is also worth noting that the first people of the DRC were the Pygmies who live in the equatorial forest. This people had long been despised because they had not been in contact with modern technology or the civilization of the other Congolese or Bantu ethnic groups. Nowadays, their children go to college. The successive governments have fought against the rejection of this population, since all are Congolese.

In some tribes of the Democratic Republic of the Congo, adolescents are encouraged to hold on to the ways of the warrior, to self-defense, and to principles of life up to the theft, if possible, of objects needed to survive. In other tribes, they are taught about "article 15," which expresses the need to find a way to manage in order to solve one's problems, face obstacles, and find solutions with courage and determination, without relying too much on others. In fact, this slogan is thrown in some circles of friends: "Article 15?" eliciting the response "Make do!"

With regards to the idea of the self, adolescent boys and girls get along very well because of their altruistic nature. Generally, the Congolese, and especially the adolescents, are proud of their identity. They are open to other ethnic groups, but are aggressive and react violently when someone wants to crush them and not recognize the value of their personalities. This was seen during the spontaneous rebellion of youths and students all around the country on June 3, 2004, against the UN MONUC mission to Congo, which did nothing during the attack of Bukavu. This event has helped MONUC to correct and intensify its actions for the benefit of the population.

Family Relationships

The familial system is extensive in the Democratic Republic of the Congo. Adolescents' and children's relationships generally extend beyond the nuclear family made up by the father, the mother, and the children. They include cousins, uncles, aunts, and close friends of the father, mother, and their children. Such relationships are intense, notwithstanding those between street neighbors. Adolescent boys and girls spend three-quarters of the daytime in company of other young people and away from the family to which they noisily return only to eat and sleep. They rule over the younger children, and their older brothers and sisters or parents must at times intervene to keep peace and harmony in the family. Conflicts between parents and adolescents can arise from two main sources: coming home late and food or domestic work. Adolescents like to showcase their right to freedom, oftentimes forgetting their duties and chores. They cannot stand their parents' reprimands about them returning home late in the evening or at night. As for food, they eat like gluttons, except for some girls who wish to keep their figures and who also sometimes

abuse cosmetics. Music and the choice of television and movies that are not recommendable also trigger conflicts. Parental advice about education and young people's behaviors seem obsolete and harmful to the young people, who want to lead their lives as they see fit. Churches and schools help parents by providing young people with moral principles of behavior. As for the freedom to choose a mate or a fiancée, some immigrant and native families would prefer their children to retain their ethnic identity, but young people fight to break this myth and practice. Intermarriage also exists between children of the elite or the wealthy. Relationships within the global society being numerous, marriage between its members can be done without too many problems. The divorce rate is not high compared to that of marriage, nor is the polygamy rate, which is not banned by the state, but is forbidden by the church and biblical law. However, poverty, war, and rape have disorganized many family groups and increased the number of street children, called *chègues*, a group of abandoned children who will almost make up a new social class if no further efforts are made to stem the causes of this scourge.

Friends and Peers/Youth Culture

During their teenage years, young people like to be in groups or in pairs to keep their secrets. Most of their time and activities are spent with friends, away from the family home. Their main activities depend on the groups they belong to, and which can include:

- Sports (soccer, tennis, volley, martial arts, marble games, checkers, etc.)
- Music (orchestral singing, songs for religious worship, choirs)
- Meetings of political parties in their respective headquarters
- Homework or study groups, especially over the weekend
- Meetings of youth associations (Scouts; Catholic, Protestant, Kimbanguist, or Islamic youth groups, etc.)
- Prayer groups

A few idle adolescents wander about. They loiter in bars, in the street, or around bus shelters. They watch people walk by and practice stealing. Others meet in hidden places or in the forest to smoke hemp or take drugs.

In rural areas and in villages, pairs of adolescents have remunerated or survival activities. They go fishing or hunting in small groups, or go dig for minerals. In these environments, adolescents cause less damage and show little deviant or negative attitudes because adolescence is lived as a life stage linked to adulthood. During this time, social life activities are practiced, almost as if it were an internship. Hooliganism is not tolerated in this traditional environment. Respect for the individual and for the common good is held by all.

In urban areas, young people follow the customs of modern life, but there are no specific cultural traits or articles of clothing. Western behavior and fashion (Americanization) affect mostly urban youths. Across the country, blue jeans and pants have become popular with young girls and adult women. Unlike young girls who are influenced by other cultures, however, adult women retain their national cultural identity in their dress (pareos) and hairdos (braids). Young girls experience a cultural mimesis. For example, imported hair pieces are now popular with city girls.

Love and Sexuality

Adolescents live among themselves during the day and learn about sexuality on their own. Their only contact with their parents takes place in the family home. They are initiated to their future roles as mothers and fathers when they get engaged and are about to be married, around age 18 to 21, a time when parents give them advice. They also learn a lot during the preparations for the wedding ceremony, which are led by priests, reverends, godfathers, and married friends. To remedy potential educational lacks, elementary and secondary schools also offer classes on "life education" or "sexual education." Further, the media remind parents not to find it taboo nor to be ashamed of discussing sexuality with their children. Such information helps young people to behave responsibly.

Since ancient times, marriage has been endowed with great dignity by the inhabitants of the DRC. Procreation is important. It is generally believed that men and women were created to be biologically different so they can complete each other. In traditional environments and in some tribes, living together before getting married was allowed. Adolescent boys and girls coming of age, or having an adult body, lived together, experimenting with life as a couple until the marriage was made official. This was the initiation and concrete preparation to married life. Two criteria determined the age of the young adults: for girls it was the beginning of menstruation and the ability to cook for the entire family; for boys it was involuntary ejaculation and the ability to build his hut, or home. In this environment, sterility was treated, but such cases were rare. Births were controlled and a new birth would occur after two or four years using natural methods. Aside from their meals, women ate special leaves or fruits during pregnancy until they gave birth without any complications.

Modern environments, as elsewhere, have seen the emergence of a worship of sexuality. Pornographic films and photographs shown in public places have led adolescents to a dissolute and deviant sex life. Sexually transmitted diseases, including HIV/AIDS, have killed many young people. Many parents considered it taboo to discuss sex with their children. Consequently, girls suffered early and unwanted pregnancies, and some even lost their lives. Nowadays, educational campaigns in schools and from the Ministry of Public Health keep young people informed about sexuality, sexually transmissible diseases, birth control, and unwanted and wanted pregnancies. Parental advice on sexuality is supplemented by churches, health NGOs, and prayer groups. Also, in July 2005, the pharmaceutical company Pharmakina obtained the right to produce medication against HIV/AIDS in Bukavu, DRC. As a result, mortality rates decreased and sanitary progress is obvious.

With regards to adolescent sexual behaviors, homosexuality and pedophilia are introduced in cities by such factors as the media and movies. The main cause of behaviors such as prostitution is the poverty that has been amplified by the wars. Congolese tend to see homosexuality as a sexual deviance contrary to their culture and nature, which ties into the divine law of copulation between male and female.

Health Risk Behavior

In rural areas and in villages, tobacco and drug crops were already grown during colonial times. Selling and using drugs and alcohol were prohibited, especially in big cities, and led to jail sentences. After the independence, and with the cultural transfers brought on by wars and poverty, people have been enticed to take drugs and drink alcohol, in spite of governmental prevention campaigns.

Juvenile delinquency is the result of many factors, including:

- Poverty. Young people who lack healthy activities fall into taking drugs and drinking alcohol. Not all are prey to such excesses since churches, prayer groups, and the media often call upon them to correct such behaviors.

- Wars. Children and adolescents of both sexes served in the army (children soldiers) and were drugged.
- Imitation. They mimic the behaviors of young people from other Western countries as seen in the media and movies.
- Risk taking. A taste for adventure, for spiritual escapism, for challenging moral taboos without feeling any guilt leads young people to drugs and alcohol. Ultimately, some might belong to gangs of robbers, criminals, and rapists.
- Happiness. For example, when the results for the state exam are published across the country, those who passed show their jubilation by crowding bars and drinking at times to excess and coming home late. Some ride in speeding cars, bare-chested and hanging half-way out of the car windows, a beer bottle in hand. This has led to fatal car crashes, which is why the Minister of Education has banned such practices, with the assistance of the media and the police.

Education

Most young people attend school and enjoy studying. The oldest universities that welcome those who finish secondary school are the University of Kinshasa (the first university, built in 1954), the University of Lubumbashi (founded in 1956), and the University of Kisangani (1967). There are many elementary schools, secondary schools, universities, official institutes for higher education, as well as technical, medical, agricultural, commerce, management, customs, sawing, and fine arts public and official schools. For example, in 1987/1988, before the wars in the east, reliable statistics recorded 10,810 elementary schools in Congo/Kinshasa, 2,847 regular secondary schools (majors in education, literature, sciences) and 1,387 other secondary schools (technical and professional training), three public universities and 13 private ones, one college institute of agronomy in Yangambi, 18 technical institutes and 49 private ones, 15 public educational institutes and four private ones, three colleges and one theological institute. Overall, there were 107 higher education institutions, including 70 from the private sector. Today, private schools supplement the national school system, which cannot admit all the students due to logistical and budgetary constraints.

School attendance is high in DRC. Following are some sample schooling rates.

1. Elementary school:
   1959–1960: 71.5% (time of the independence)
   1962–1963: 95.8% (first Republic)
   1969–1970: 100%
   1978: 94.1%
   1992–1993: 72.3% (drop is the result of governmental disengagement caused by political troubles)
2. Secondary school:
   1959–1960: 3%
   1962–1963: 4.1%
   1969–1970: 8.7%
3. Higher education and college:
   1962–1963: 0.1%
   1969–1970: 0.3%

As an example, in 2001, the University of Kinshasa had 24,321 enrolled students, including 15,000 new students coming from secondary schools. There were 18.428 male students (75.77%) and 5,893 female students (24.23%).

Reliable statistics gathered before the wars, which hindered the proper working of schools, especially in the east of the country, show the following evolution:

1. 1962–1963: 60,020 students were enrolled in secondary schools out of which 49,152 (81.8%) had finished the orientation cycle (the first two years of secondary school).
2. 1966–1967: 138,260 students were enrolled in secondary schools; with 90,500 (65.4%) enrolled in the first two years.
3. 1967–1968: 151,850 students, including 95,300 (62.7%) adolescents.

In the DRC, education is democratic and available to all, no matter their religion or gender. Curricula are adapted to the national realities. The four national languages (Lingala, Kikongo, Swahili, and Tshiluba) are part of the elementary and secondary school syllabi. Foreign languages, including French and English, are taught in school, and French is the official language and the language of teaching in the country. Today, computer services such as "Cybernet" houses that train young people can be found especially in large cities and in schools.

Disabled adolescents have special schools and centers at their disposal, but there is no school for gifted students. Every year, the government and a few organizations offer scholarships to go study in the country or abroad to the students who finish secondary school with the highest scores on the state exam.

Work

In the traditional way of life, adolescents directly contribute to the survival of the family. Boys hunt and fish for their parents while girls help their mothers with cooking and field work. Still, they lack the manufactured products that come from urban centers.

Many parents who live in urban centers lost their jobs because of the degrading economic conditions that followed the political troubles of 1990–1992, which led to pillaging. Further, the latest wars have destroyed the economic fabric of the country, especially in the northeast. Many children thus lacked the financial support needed to attend school. Parents who worked as civil servants and teachers no longer earned enough money, and the government ignored the education sector between 1990–1997. Parents then had to pay bonuses to the teachers aside from the tuition required by the state.

Young people between the ages of 12 and 17 who drop out of school have to find jobs to contribute to the family budget and buy food. They shine shoes or sell peanuts or fruits at the market or as peddlers. Some girls sell food or braid hair, but sometimes have to prostitute themselves to add to the family earnings. As a result, some children have become "street kids," living and sleeping away from the family home. A few adolescents get organized and manage to work in small jobs after school or in the morning if they need the time to study in the evening. Such arrangements allow them to pay tuition and contribute to the family budget.

Moreover, other kinds of job training have emerged with inherent risks of exploitation, such as becoming a dancer with one of the traveling orchestras. In the country, training centers have been created for young girls and unwed mothers (e.g., seamstresses, beauticians, hotel workers). Likewise, there are vocational training centers for boys (mechanics, carpenters, etc.). Young people are very dynamic and resourceful. For example, they surprise the adults on New Year's Eve by decorating the streets themselves, without having recourse to the help or advice of the adults.

Media

Congolese adolescents love music, movies, plays, magazines, games, and Web surfing, especially in Kinshasa and in other cities where it is more readily available than in the country. In villages, young people cannot watch television for lack of electricity. Still, one set powered by a car battery can often be found in villages.

Battery-operated radios, cell phones, and phonic devices are used all over the country. They are used on an economic basis in the rural world since calls and messages are not free. In cities, phone booths can be found everywhere. In Kinshasa, young people line up in Internet cafés to go on the Internet and send messages, get in touch with the outside world, play games, and enjoy the many possibilities offered by the Web, including pornography. Access to these establishments depends on the money they have. Some of these houses or centers provide computer training.

Television is seen as a necessary tool to show the world to adolescents, yet parents are often disgusted by the pornographic movies that show obscene scenes to children any time of the day instead of being broadcasted at a time suitable for adult movies. It is difficult to control adolescent curiosity. Parents would like to see recreational programming that would be educational and scientific. Every day, three-quarters of the Congolese activities shown on the national and private channels also show commercials promoting all sorts of things, including alcohol, music, obscene dancing by female artists who work with profane orchestras, and foreign films which influence young people. Depending on the message they choose to transmit, the media can have either an educational or a negative power.

It is important to guide the positive behavior of the adolescent boy or girl. Good advice and warnings on television or on the radio about an event or some behavior are often heeded. Young people do listen to television and radio.

Politics and Military

In the Democratic Republic of the Congo, the political and judicial majority is set at 18. Boys and girls of that age can vote. They can make their own decisions about their lives, get married, and enjoy the many aspects of personal or communitarian growth.

This is also the age when they can enlist in the army, enter religious life, the ministry, and many other trades.

During the last wars, many adolescent boys and girls were seen among the soldiers. Called the "Kadogos," they were probably lured by characteristics of their age, such as a taste for adventure, audacity, altruism, courage, and aggressiveness. They were often placed in the first line to dissuade the enemy before the adult soldiers would come into play. These teens were made to take arms; that is what they revealed once they were demobilized.

Only adults go to war. Some young Congolese, however, enjoy paramilitary services such as the Scouts or the Red Cross missions during peace time. They also enjoy voluntary work and are guided by altruism. They can be seen weeding out the streets during the communal work in the village or helping to prepare a school festival or group celebration.

AGAPIT MANZANZA MUSULA NTOTILA

References and Further Reading

Assemblée Législative. *Constitution de la Transition de la République Démocratique du Congo* (*Transition Constitution of the Democratic Republic of the Congo.*) Kinshasa: Adoptée le 4 avril 2003.

Atlas du Congo, de l'Afrique et du monde. 1998. (*Atlas of the Congo, Africa, and the World*). Kinshasa: Afrique Edition, pp. 6–13.

Ekwa, M. 1965. *Le Congo et l'Education.* 1965. (*Congo and Education*). Léopoldville (Kinshasa): BEC.

Erny, P. 1968. *L'enfant dans la pensée traditionnelle de l'Afrique Noire* (*The child in the traditional thought of Black Africa*). Paris: Le livre africain.

Lamal, F. *Basuku et Bayaka des Districts Kwango et Kwilu au Congo* (*Basuku and Bayaka from the Kwango and Kwilu Districts in Congo*). Bruxelles: Musée Royal de l'Afrique Centrale-Tervuren, Belgique.

Le Thanh Khoi. 1971. *L'enseignement en Afrique tropicale* (*Education in tropical Africa*). Paris: IDES, PUF.

L'industrie de l'enseignement (*The industry of education*). 1967. Paris: Minuit.

Louis Segond. 1910. *La Sainte Bible* (*The Holy Bible*).

Lumeka-Lua-Yansenga et al. 1978. *L'auto-perception des enseignants au Zaïre, Contribution à la socio-psychologie dans les pays en développement* (*Self-Image of Teachers in Zaire, Contribution to the socio-psychology of developing countries*). Kinshasa: ECA.

Mabika Kalanda. 1967. La remise en question, base de la décolonization mentale (*Questioning, the basis of mental decolonization*). *Etudes congolaises*, 14.

Mankondo Idrissa. 2002. Vision du partenariat éducatif par les parents de Kinshasa. In *Revue de psychologie et des sciences de l'Education*, Vol. III, numéro 1–3, Université de Kinshasa: FPSE (Vision of the Educational Partnership by Kinshasa Parents).

Manzanza, A. 1970. *Education scolaire en milieu rural au Kwilu, Relation entre l'éducation traditionnelle et scolaire, séminaire de pédagogie* (*Schooling in rural areas of Kwily, relations between school and traditional Education; pedagogy conference*). Licence académique 1969–1970, Fribourg/Suisse: Université, Faculté de Philosophie et Lettres, Chaire de Pédagogie.

Manzanza, A-A. 2005. Développement du métier d'enseignant: frein au progrès de la culture (cas de l'Afrique subsaharienne francophone) (Development of the teaching profession: Hindrance to the progress of culture—example of the sub-Saharan French-speaking Africa). In *Xème Congrès international de l'ARIC,*

Recherche interculturelle: partage de savoirs et partage de cultures, ALGER: Palais des Nations, 02-06 mai 2005, Résumé des communications, p. 128.

Manzanza Musula, N. 2005. *Impact de la crise de l'enseignement sur les adolescents en République Démocratique du Congo, cas de la ville de Kinshasa* (*Impact of the education crisis on adolescents in Democratic Republic of the Congo; the city of Kinshasa.*). Kinshasa: BASE-IPED.

Manzanza Musula, N. 1983. *Orientation à l'enseignement supérieur et universitaire selon les filières suivies aux humanités* (*Orientation to higher and college education depending on the chosen humanities channels*). Kinshasa: ICP/Limete, C.U.O, FPSE (UNIKIN).

Manzanza Musula, N., 2005. *Sociologie de développement intégré et intégral, Problèmatique et stratégie, Manuel de sociologie de développement* (*Sociology of integrated and integral development, Problems and strategy; Handbook of sociology of development*). Kinshasa: P.U.C.

Manzanza Musula, N. 1996. La formation scolaire et le métier d'enseignant en détresse dans les pays en développement, le cas des pays africains: Zaïre (Schooling and teaching in distress in developing countries; African countries: Zaire) (République Démocratique du Congo). In *45ᵉ session de la Conférence internationale de l'Unesco.* Genève: Unesco. (Table ronde, section française).

Manzanza Musula, N. 1993. Contribution de l'enfant africain de 6 à 17 ans au développement socio-économique et culturel de son pays: le cas du Zaïre (République Démocratique de Congo) (Contribution of the African child between the ages of 6 and 7 to the socio-economic and cultural development of his country: Zaire). In *Séminaire sur l'enfant africain: Premières journées internationales de réflexions psychologiques et pédagogiques sur le devenir de l'enfant africain,* organisée, du 20–22 mai 1993, Kinshasa: BASE, FPSE (Université de Kinshasa). (article exposé le 21/2/1993) inédit.

Manzanza Musula, N. *Dévalorization du métier d'enseignant et dégradation de la formation académique et scolaire en République Démocratique du Congo (Recherche des causes profondes, philosophiques et politiques, appliquée à l'Université de Kinshasa)* (*Devaluation of the teaching profession and degradation of Academic and School training in Democratic Republic of the Congo—Research on the philosophical and political roots, applied to the University of Kinshasa*). Mémoire de D.E.S, Kinshasa: Université de Kinshasa, FPSE.

Manzanza Musula, N. *La déperdition scolaire au début du cycle d'orientation des garçons au Zaïre (School waste at the beginning of the orientation cycle for boys in Zaire).* Mémoire de Licence, Fribourg/Suisse: Université, Faculté de Lettres, Chaire de pédagogie.

Ministère de l'Education nationale. 1963. *Programme national de l'enseignement primaire.* (*Elementary School National Curriculum*). Kinshasa: EDNAT [Elementary School National Curriculum].

Ministère de l'Education nationale. 1986. *Recueil des directives et instructions officielles* (*Compilation of the official directives and instructions*). Kinshasa: CEREDIP, EDIDEPS.

Ministère de l'Education nationale. 1996. *Les Etats généraux de l'Education, projet du nouveau système éducatif, grandes lignes d'action* (*General states of education, project of the new educational system and its plan of action*). Kinshasa: Palais du peuple.

Ministère de l'Industrie. 2001. *Commerce et PMEA, Condensé des Conjonctures économiques, années 1991–1997* (*Commerce and small businesses, summary of economic circumstances during the years 1991–1997*). Kinshasa: CEPI.

Mungala, A. 1969–1970. *Croyance chez les Basuku/ Apport de la culture bantu à l'universel* (*Basuku beliefs/ contribution of the Bantu culture to the universal*). Travail de sociologie. Paris: Institut Catholique de Paris.

Ngub'usim, Mpey-Nka, R. 2000. Gestion et financement des universités congolaises: Expériences de sauvetage et partenariat à l'Université de Kinshasa (Management and Financing of Congolese Universities: "Rescuing" Experiences and Partnership at the University of Kinshasa). In *Congo-Afrique, 40ème année*, n° 345, Kinshasa.

Nicola, H. 1963. *Le KWILU*. Bruxelles: CEMUBAC.

R. D. C. 1968. *Rapport sur le mouvement éducatif (du congo) en 1967/68, présenté à la 31ème Conférence internationale de l'Instruction publique à Genève (1 au 10 juillet 1968)* (*Report on the education movement (in Congo) in 1967/68 presented at the 31st International Conference of Public Education in Geneva*). Genève: BIE.

R. D. C. 1970. *Annuaire de la République Démocratique du Congo* (*Directory for the Democratic Republic of the Congo*). Kinshasa: SADIAPIC- Congo.

UNICEF. 1999. Education à la paix (Peace Education). In *Unicef*, n° 13, Kinshasa: Unicef.

UNICEF. 2000. Education de base pour tous en République Démocratique du Congo (Basic education for all in Democratic Republic of the Congo). In *Journal Unicef*. Kinshasa: Unicef.

Université de Kinshasa. 1971. *Apprentissage, revue de psychologie et de pédagogie* (Training, Journal of Psychology and Pedagogy), 3, 30 avril, 1971.

Université de Kinshasa. 2005. *Projections de la population de la République Démocratique du Congo 2000–2005 en milliers* (*Population forecast for the Democratic Republic of the Congo in thousands, 2000–2005*). Kinshasa: UNIKIN, Faculté des Sciences économiques, Département de Démographie.

DENMARK

Background Information

Denmark is a small Scandinavian country. The mainland is referred to as *Jylland*, and besides this there are 406 islands. The total area is 43,098 square kilometers. There are 5,389,000 inhabitants in Denmark. Denmark also consists of Greenland and the Faeroe Islands; the inhabitants of those places vote in Danish elections, but they also have local parliaments. There are 56,600 people living in Greenland and 48,000 in the Faeroe Islands (www.Danmark.dk).

The age distribution in Denmark shows the following age pattern: 1 million people between 0 and 17 years, 3 million between 18 and 60 years, and 1 million over 60 years of age. The birth rate is decreasing and the population is getting older. In 2003 the mean age of the population was 39.4 years compared to 1980, when it was two years lower (Statistisk Årbog 2003).

Traditionally the Danish population (aside from that of Greenland) is quite homogeneous. In recent years, however, there has been an increase in the number of immigrants. In the new millennium, approximately 8% of the population consists of first- and second-generation immigrants from both European and non-European countries. Most non-European immigrants come from Turkey, Iraq, Pakistan, and Palestine. The groups with "other ethnic background than Danish" are often concentrated in the big cities and also they have more children then the "ethnic Danes" (Danmarks Statestik 2003). It is difficult to adequately categorize the recently arrived groups of young people who have roots in countries with cultures quite different from the Danish culture. The appropriate designation may be "young people with another ethnic background than Danish." For practical reasons, the term "ethnic youth" is used here in contrast to "Danish youth."

Denmark is often seen as on its way to becoming a multicultural society. Denmark, like many other European societies, is increasingly marked by tensions between Western culture and traditional Muslim cultural and social practices.

This situation creates changes in the lives of Denmark's youth. The process of social integration of the newly arrived youth groups is seen as important but is not easy. Educational practices that reflect the changing needs of society are still developing. Changes in religious practices are also noted. Denmark has a Protestant state religion. Most Danes are members of the church, but are not actively religious. Religion is a private aspect of life. The newly arrived ethnic groups often have not only another religion, but also they are much more active in their religious behavior, and their religions guide everyday behavior. This situation creates a sharpening of ethnic self-understanding among both Danish youth and ethnic youth, but also the development of a more nationalistic and religious engagement and attitude among both groups. Different religious and cultural practices therefore also lay the groundwork for religious and cultural conflicts.

In the nineteenth century, Denmark developed a strong national self-understanding, which also influenced the development of a democratic constitution in 1849. This constitution gave males from all social classes in the Danish society the right to vote. From 1915, women also were given the right to vote.

The new democratic society and the democratic development of Danish society in the twentieth century were influenced by the ideology of equality. A strong social democratic party, an organized working class, and a social democratic government resulted in a rather harmonious and stable society and, starting in the 1930s, the development of the Danish society as one of the Scandinavian democratic welfare societies (Esping-Andersen 1990; Walther et al. 2002).

This political development has had a long-term influence on youth development. The democratic constitution called for voters who were politically competent, and this made education and schooling a broad political issue. In 1902, Denmark instituted its first law creating public schools open to all children. In this way educational practice was both established as a basic component of social equality, and as a key aspect of the construction of youth as a special educational lifestyle (Mørch 2003). Of course, children and youth were still differentiated according to social class. Private schools for the wealthy and special religious and ideological groups did exist. But they had to follow the same official curriculum as the public schools.

After World War II, educational institutions in Denmark engaged a more active policy for ending the privileges of social inheritance. The aim of this policy was not only to give equal opportunities, but also to offer real equal opportunities for all young people regardless of social background. This policy, called "equality through education" and beginning in the 1970s, supported the pro-welfare support logic of Danish society.

Period of Adolescence

The theme of young people's opportunities and behavior in Denmark needs a broader theoretical background to illustrate both the general aspects of modern youth and the specificity of Danish youth life.

Much research points to the fact that youth is a historical and social construct (Gillis 1981; Mørch 1985; Stafseng 1996). Youth developed as an objective and subjective reality in modern bourgeois society at the end of the eighteenth century. The main objective of youth was the development of individualization (Gillis 1981; Mørch 1985; Aries 1973; Stafseng 1996). The individualization process had become the most important social process in the modern society. It produced skills and qualifications for business and industrial life and political competencies for the new status of being in power in the democratic society. The learning process was located in the developing educational system.

The recognition of distinct youth behavior and the "strange psychology of young people," which especially became visible in educational contexts, created an understanding of young people as in possession of a special nature, a biologically based "puberty" or "adolescence" (Hall 1904). Young people's behavior was considered, like that of children and women, as immature and more "natural" than culturally developed male behavior. Adolescents, therefore, had a particular need for education and adult guidance (Andersen 1986).

The new democratic constitutions set up all over the Western world in the nineteenth and twentieth century made it necessary to develop individualization and to broaden the educational possibilities to nearly all parts of the population. Therefore, nearly everywhere in the European modern societies youth was constructed as an objective reality in educational curricula. In the countryside or traditional farming societies with a low degree of schooling, young people were either understood as children or adults—maybe young or less-competent adults. Their developmental challenge was not individualization but contextual qualification and learning to adapt to the traditional society.

Girls developed an adolescent identity differently. They were more involved in domestic matters and took up education later than boys. Individualization demands took their own forms among girls.

The broad organization of biography was also influenced by family developments. In the newly influential bourgeoisie in the eighteenth and nineteenth century family life became important. The bourgeois family house demonstrated power and influence, and family life with wife and children also confirmed the new social position of the bourgeoisie. Family life became a social value or capital. To have a family and a family life showed that the bourgeoisie was just as valuable as the aristocracy, with their old families or kinship relations. Also the family life and family values differentiated the bourgeoisie from the poor people, who hardly could uphold a family life. The family became "the nobility of the bourgeoisie" (Andersen 1986). Within this family construction children developed a distinct form of life and psychology. They were protected from the perceived dangers of the world and cared for by mothers and nannies. They developed a special "childishness," which in many ways made them unfit for adult life. School and youth life changed children into adults, and often mothers and schoolteachers disagreed about the children's right way into adulthood (Aries 1973).

It is possible to combine these historical perspectives on youth development in a general analytical youth theory model (Mørch 2003): The drawing in Figure 1 has two dimensions. On the one hand, youth is a social construction, which reflects the issue of social integration by focusing on the individualization process and the relation between

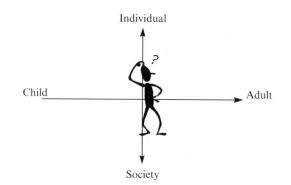

Figure 1.   Individualization in biography.

society and the individual. On the other hand, youth is also presented as a biographical and biological process, a time of psychological development during which children become adults. These dimensions both point to challenges that face the individual: to become integrated as an individual and to use and develop a personal biography. Therefore, we might present the following general theory of youth: Youth is about the social integrative challenge of individualization in biography.

The analytic value of the perspective of "integration in biography" becomes clear when we cast a short glimpse at the development in the two dimensions. Most (late) modernization literature focuses on the demands of individualization in late modernity (Beck 1992; Beck and Beck-Gernsheim 2002). Among these books, Giddens' *Modernity and Self Identity* (Giddens 1992) has become especially popular. Giddens presents a picture of how demands to individuals have changed from traditional to late modern society. In Gidddens' analysis, the individual today has to develop self-identity, reflexivity, self-assurance, knowledge, basic trust in the world and oneself, and participation. These modern requirements of individualization show that young people today not only need to learn, but they also need to develop a modern personality. Therefore these requirements are important in the process of constructing oneself as an inhabitant of modernity. Just as young people who have high self-esteem with only a low degree of knowledge will have little success in education and in the labor market, so also do knowledgeable young people with low self-esteem experience problems. Therefore, Giddens' list points to single items as aspects of a general late-modern structure.

Danish society is a knowledge-based society, and therefore education and learning are highly prioritized. At the same time, however, individual social competencies are important to manage many types of risks and uncertainties. In this way Denmark is a late modern society deeply engaged in the development of modern competencies in young people.

If we look at Bauman's perspective of consumerism, another aspect becomes visible (Baumann 1998, 2001). Young people live in a world that is governed by the logic of consumerism. Adolescents are increasingly "consumers of modernity"; therefore, youth life is expensive and increasingly integrated with commercial development. The media and computers have become the tools of youth life.

Construction of the individual in biography also is constantly in flux. If we go back in history we can see that the construction of youth in the

Youth Life as Contextually Organized Development

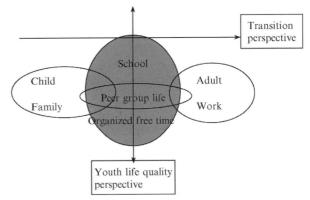

Figure 2. Youth life as a social construction.

bourgeoisie took place institutionally. Children and young people became educated or "developed" in different social contexts by answering the demands of these contexts and by adhering to the demands of those contexts. From the start of the twentieth century, school was supplemented in the development of individualization by social arrangements such as youth clubs and organized sports. From roughly the 1950s, the peer group or youth culture developed as a social reference for young people, often influenced by music and media. The most general picture of youth trajectories and individualization can be drawn as a youth life defined by quality and transition (see Figure 2).

What we might experience today among Danish youth is a change of the youth trajectory. Youth life is prolonged. In Denmark it starts early and ends late in life. We may talk about a new period of "emergent adulthood" or maybe a "disappearance of childhood and adulthood" (Arnett 2004; Postman 1982; Côté 2000). Youth life (and looking like an adolescent) has become so popular, that children want to become adolescents very early. They are supported in this not only by the media and advertisers' interests, but also by parents and other adults, who impart adolescence to children via their dress and lifestyle. At one point in earlier history, children were dressed as adults (Aries 1973). Today, they are dressed as adolescents.

Youthful lifestyles, appearances, and sexual behaviors have become the popular goal for all. The general structure of the modern trajectory could be seen as an indirect youth life trajectory. Youth life does not lead directly to adult life. It means that adulthood is more or less disappearing from young people's perspectives (Figure 3).

Instead of specific stages of life, maybe we are confronted in the modern Western world by new

Youth Life and Indirectedness

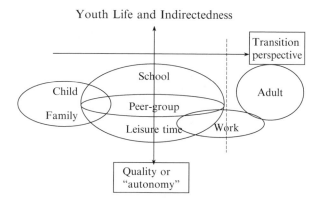

Figure 3.   The disappearance of adulthood.

Fragmented Contextualization

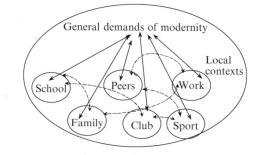

Figure 4.   Fragmented contextualization.

circumstances of fragmented contextualization. We live in a world in which more contexts are functioning as a network producing different aspects of development (Mørch 1999). Individuals have to choose between different contexts and contextual demands. They must arrange and combine the different contexts in their own life. They also must develop an individual or personal trajectory (Figure 4).

Today, therefore, social integration no longer points to one major trajectory or normal trajectory between childhood and adult life. Many more routes or pathways may exist and become trajectories inside and between different or fragmented social contexts. This means that the real trajectory challenge in Danish late modernity falls back upon the individual. Individuals more or less form their own trajectories and in this way contextualize aspects of development in their youth life by combining societal conditions and individual interests. So, therefore, in our fragmented society, the first trajectory challenge for young people is not merely to participate, but to find out what they should participate in and for what reason. Young people need to be knowledgeable. This makes educational engagement the basic challenge to young people. But at the same time it becomes nearly impossible to find out if the individual trajectory is successful or not. Nobody—and especially adults and parents—is able to find the difference between success and failure.

To understand this challenge for Danish youth it is important to include a broader view of young people's lives, pathways, and trajectories. Late modern youth life calls for a better understanding of individual activities and individual trajectories and how they create and contribute to individual development. Logic and sense do not objectively exist in formal transition trajectories—individuals have to develop them themselves. Individuals have

a new responsibility for making their own trajectory, and this calls for a better understanding of how to cope with conditions, how to become empowered to make choices inside youth and societal life. Therefore, the second trajectory challenge of youth seems to be "the construction of sense and competence" for maneuvering in a more open world. Young people should learn to "cope" or they should develop forms of "expedient" life management (Mørch and Stalder 2003).

But even in a "fragmented contextualization" situation as in the Danish society, some contexts may be "reserved" for specific age groups. It is still possible for outsiders to observe youth and for young people to see themselves as youth. Youth still exist as an objective and subjective social category. However, other identifying traits, such as ethnicity and level of education achieved, play a role in development.

This new situation creates both great opportunities and difficulties for young people. If they engage themselves in and learn from noneducational contexts of modern youth life and reject the "irrelevance" of formal education, they may gain new competence, but they may also lose their connection to jobs and the future. Individual trajectories may become too "private." The problem of a "choice trajectory" is that people may make the wrong choices.

Today the demands for young people in Denmark are not to become adults but to engage in their own developmental process. But when youth life becomes autonomous, the relation between youth and society becomes undetermined both to young people and policy planners. The question becomes which guidelines would guarantee adult life successes?

The challenge of modern fragmented and "indirect" youth life with its autonomous challenge seems to be to construct individual skills for the job market or "transversal" competence—the kind of competence that may be used in working life too. But the youth situation is so indirect that it is difficult to see connections, and an individual planning perspective can become blurred. Therefore, when developing a useful trajectory, "sensemaking" becomes important and demands both guidance and counselling in many situations.

The difficult question for many Danish young people is to find out which activities and competencies are important in youth life for their future employment careers. And one of the individual answers to this "non-planable situation" might be to get the most education. In the Danish educational system, for example, more and more young people choose to go on to grammar schools, even if their educational orientations are not academic.

Our broad and common youth and media culture, which involves all young people, at the same time has a hidden agenda, however, which not all young people are aware of. At the same time as youth life should be fun, a competition for the future exists underneath the shared youth culture. This problem is especially serious in educational curricula, where many young people are not aware of the serious consequences of bad academic performance until they experience the barriers to further education and jobs raised by underachievement. Youth and educational life in themselves differentiate young people according to future life perspectives. Educational life creates leading and misleading trajectories, but it is difficult to see which are leading somewhere and which are not.

Therefore, the great challenge in modern Danish fragmented contextual youth life seems to be able to maneuver between the different contexts and demands and engage in the "right" contexts, and to develop one's own trajectory. Giddens' concept of structuration tells about the challenge. It is important both to learn to use structures and to make new structures all the time. To young people in Denmark the overall demand seems not only to be to develop structures but also to develop competencies for their own lives, both as competencies for social life in a broad sense, but also as a sort of employability for being able to grasp work opportunities (Mørch and Stalder 2003).

Summing up this description of youth and Danish youth development, the following is clear. Youth and adolescence developed from the start of the nineteenth century in the upper and middle classes among boys and from around the start of the twentieth century also in the working class. For girls the situation has been a little different. In the end of the nineteenth century, upper-class and some middle-class girls were included in education and in individualization. But the process was rather slow. Only after World War II were girls from all social classes given the same conditions as boys for individualization in the educational system. However, today more girls then boys are in higher education.

Youth or adolescence today is starting very early and is lasting very long. But at the same time "youth" or "adolescence" is a multidimensional phenomenon. Children become youth or adolescents in some dimensions very early—and the dimensions may change. They experience a high degree of personal freedom, they may engage in sexual activity early, and they are asked to choose their own educational engagement. On the other hand, the parents may decide their economical situation and possibilities. Also, the challenge of becoming an adult is quite unclear. If we look at the traditional dimensions of having a job (own economy), leaving the family home, and becoming married, the picture is very varied. Fifty percent of young people have left home by the age of 20. Many young people still live a single life in their thirties and are still in education. Others marry or cohabit very early while still being students. We may talk about a quite new construct in late modern society, a time of "emergent adulthood," as some sort of category, which can be extended rather long (Arnett, 2004). Maybe young people in the end become adults or maybe they never do. Adulthood may be disappearing as a clear concept, and especially as a developmental goal. Maybe adulthood exists as an objective social category while it at the same time disappears as a subjective understanding. This situation of young adults as being caught in an emergent adulthood contradiction seems to follow the general pattern of late modern knowledge society development. Especially young people in higher education will belong to this category.

If we look at marriage the situation also is changing. Seventy-eight percent of couples living together are married, but among young people marriage is declining. In 1970, 88% of all women at 30 years of age were married, but today only 47% are married at the same age. In the same period, the average age of marriage has been going up. For women the average age at first marriage has risen from 22.8 to 30.3, and for men from 25.1 to 32.8. The average age at which women have their first child has also increased, from 22.5 to 27.5. (Danmarks Statestik 2003).

The changes in recent decades therefore are quite extensive. The changes in youth life and the psychological construction of adolescence follow the development of society, and especially the development of education and individualization. Therefore, globalization also influences development, given its impact on the relation between global and local changes. This creates new opportunities for young people and their individualization processes; however, the increased presence of global culture also increasingly influences local Danish life. This is especially apparent in the rise of immigration in Denmark from non-European countries. Globalization affects adolescence and adolescent development by changing people's minds and self-understanding. However, it may also lead to the development of racism and strong ethnic identities.

Puberty in a biological sense, marked by changes in hormones and the start of menstruation, may occur slightly earlier than in previous generations based on changes in nutrition. Behavior associated with the adolescent stage is changing as well. The important issue is in which "theory" is used to understand youth behavior. If youth is understood or defined as puberty, it means that the social construction of youth is not present, and that youth social behaviors as complex answers to modernity's challenges of individualization are not understood.

If we look at sexual behavior, it seems obvious that youth behavior is dependent on biology, but formed by social factors. The changes in the sexual behavior of modern Danish youth seem to follow from the autonomy and freedom of modern youth life. First sexual experiences (intercourse) may happen earlier than before, from the age of 11 or 12 for girls, but the general figures seem now to be quite steady. At the age of 16 more than half of both girls and boys have had intercourse. Girls have earlier and more sexual experience than boys. At the age of 19, 89% of girls and 78% of boys have had intercourse (Bay 1996).

In Danish society there are no special rites of passage related to puberty. Confirmation, a religious rite performed in the church, still takes place at the age of 14. The rhetoric of confirmation focuses on the fact that the individual being confirmed is now an adult, but this has little to no significance in society at large, as a 14-year-old is not considered an adult. At the most, confirmation signals a move from childhood to youth.

Young people enjoy a high degree of freedom in Denmark. Families and schools are often not authoritarian but are very democratic in their approach. Many Danish families have become "a friendly family" (Mørch and Andersen 2005), which means that parents in many situations see themselves more or less as peers of their children. They want to support and give advice to the children, but they

do not necessarily want to act as authority figures. Among newly arrived ethnic immigrant groups, another pattern exists. The parents in these families may grant a high degree of freedom to the boys, but hold the girls under very tight control. This control generally becomes especially strict upon puberty.

The Danish family response to sexual activity among youngsters seems contradictory. On the one hand, parents may want to give freedom to their children, but on the other hand, they want to control their behavior, especially that of girls. This seems to follow the general attitude toward youth. As already mentioned, to become an adolescent, and stay young, is a primary goal. Youth is the most important time in one's life, according to the messages one receives from society, and because youth has become the most valuable time in modern life, youth development is supported. Adolescent social relations are seen as important for the quality of youth life, and therefore parents are very concerned about the friends and social relations of their children. Thus the concern may not be about the sexual relations themselves, but about the peers with whom the adolescent chooses to spend time.

Beliefs

Danish young people live in a society that is highly individualized. However, the individualization perspective seems to have changed in recent years. In late modern societies such as Denmark, individualization is not necessarily increasing, but it is changing. Therefore we may discern at least two different modes of individualization. In the last 200 years, socialization agencies such as families and school systems have been engaged in the making of the individual, first as a development among the bourgeoisie and then extended to all young people. We may call this socialization perspective "modus 1." The result of this modus 1 socialization was the growing attention to individual identity and subjectivity as it was experienced in the 1960s and 1970s.

In contemporary Danish society individuals are seen as actors, and as such, they are understood as individuals before they engage in education and social life. Therefore, socialization is more about supporting the social competencies of the individual. We may talk about the development of a new socialization practice, which we may call "modus 2." The new challenge is not to create individuals (modus 1) or blindly to support the individual, but to influence individuals in the making of society

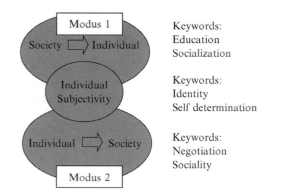

Keywords:
Education
Socialization

Keywords:
Identity
Self determination

Keywords:
Negotiation
Sociality

Figure 5. From modern to late modern individualization.

and new forms of social integration (Andersen and Mørch 2005).

The described change may be illustrated very simply (Figure 5). In Denmark, both modes of individualization exist, but modus 2 challenges modus 1. Young people are not only the result of socialization in education; they have become partners in the structuring of modern life (negotiation). Youth life is not only a transition to adult society, but also attempts to meet the demands of living in more modern social contexts. Therefore individual learning and individual competence have become crucial for making people agents or constructors of society. They have to become "subjects" in society. What is experienced, however, is the difficulties in creating social responsibility in modernity. All people—and maybe especially young people—see the world from their own perspective, as worlds-of-their-own, and often it looks as if individualization has a tendency to create a very private perspective, a "What's in it for me" thinking (Ziehe 2001) or "this is my decision" argument.

In Danish society individualization is a very strong issue. Democratization and participation is learned in all social institutions from kindergarten to universities. For the immigrant part of the population this change from modus 1 to modus 2 is of course challenging. It challenges traditional ideas of both collectivism and the place of the family and religion.

The change from modus 1 to modus 2 is most important for religious beliefs and values. In Denmark there is a broad Protestant religion. The church is a state church and most people are members of the church but only come there for special occasions such as christening, confirmation, and marriage. Christianity is not taught in schools, but is presented together with other religions. Young people who are taking part in the Christian ceremony of confirmation will have lessons in

Christianity. Seventy-seven percent of all young people in Denmark are confirmed, but only 43% of young people in the main city of Copenhagen (Bay 1996).

The general religious pattern follows the modus 1 socialization logic. Therefore, the church today finds itself in a crisis and young people are not very much engaged in religious activities. The modus 2 socialization practice seems to have brought crisis to the religious model. However, a new interest in religion has developed among Danish young people. Young people themselves engage in religious questions. Late modern freedom asks for structure and solutions, so many young people are looking for help or advice to find out what is good and bad in life. Danish society is experiencing a reengagement in religious questions, but not in participating in state church activities.

There seem to be more reasons for this development. First, young people now have become subjects of their own lives (modus 2). They have to find their way by themselves, and religion is an offer for making sense in individual life. On the other hand, strong social forces influence this subject position. The immigration challenges and terrorist activities have made religion an important issue in media and the public debate, which has created a reengagement in "national religion." Danish TV programs about religious issues have mostly exploded in recent years. A second very special influence in youth life may cause this engagement: the *Star Wars* films and other adventure films have drawn a picture of the world as divided between good and evil forces. "The force" seems to solve all problems. In the youth world religion is not seen as "God," but more like a force, which may come and save everybody.

Gender

The gender issue is most debated in Denmark. As international reports tell, Danish gender equality is among the highest in the world. This situation, however, makes it possible to see if whatever gender differences exist, still exist. This logic also followed the Danish women's movement in the 1970s: the political development of equal opportunities in education created an awareness of what did not change according to gender (Andersen 1987).

The questions of gender differences are complex. The general picture today is one of girls and women performing better throughout the educational system than boys and men. Especially during the last ten years, this development has been significant.

237

Some work areas have traditionally been and still remain occupied by men, but often these work areas consist of skilled or semi-skilled jobs. With further education, women are taking over, a shift that is central in a society where educational career becomes more and more important.

Formal equality between the sexes does exist, but in practice there are many differences in everyday life of children and young people. Girls are more often expected to be responsible, and this influences their school life. They do better in school than boys. In terms of having an education, expectations for boys and girls are mostly the same. Of course, some differences exist according to which specific education.

In the year 2000, 29% of Danish women completed a medium-length education (nurses, school-teachers, social workers, etc.) compared to 14% of the men. In 1980, the relation was 19% versus 11.5%. The growth in women's education has especially occurred in the education of teachers, pedagogues, and nurses, as the largest groups. But a growing proportion of women also complete longer academic education (medical doctors, lawyers, psychologists, etc.). In 1980, 5% of women and 6.5% of men completed an academic education. In 1998, 13% of women and 11.5% of men completed an academic education. So, women have overtaken men in regard to higher or academic education (Ministry of Education, 2000).

The choice of academic or higher education is more a result of interests than of gender. Fifty-five percent of university students are girls. Girls are especially overrepresented in the academic fields of medicine, psychology, and law. This development is also influenced by rules of admission at universities, in which good grades play a key role. Generally, because girls do better in school they are freer to choose the fields of study they wish.

In other aspects of life gender differences are more traditional. In family life there are still different expectations for boys and girls, and in many other arenas a gendered activity structure exists. This is especially focused in discussions of career development, mostly in private firms, where gender differences still seem to influence individual opportunities.

In the Danish consumer society, where media and commercial influence is rather strong, gendered lifestyles are very much a social construction. Advertising campaigns focused on beauty, appearance, health, and weight combine private commercial interests and official interests. Young people therefore live under strong influences but also under strong contradictory expectations. As consumers

they are made heavier by eating at McDonald's and drinking Coca-Cola, but they are told by fashion magazines that they should look slim. These contradictory expectations are mostly focused at girls and women. Anorexia therefore is a challenge for young girls. One percent of young girls suffer from anorexia and up to 20% experience eating disorder problems sometime in their youth (netpsych.dk 05).

The Self

Both family life and school life have supported young people in the development of independence and their own opinions. In this respect, modern young people in Denmark are extremely focused on themselves and see the world mostly from their own perspective. This is a very important development in a world where people are themselves agents and responsible for the "structuration" of everyday life. Self-confidence is a most needed quality in late modern life, and it becomes a problem if young people do not develop this self-confidence. They may lose their grip on everyday life and give up the competition of education. This especially follows youngsters from noneducated social backgrounds. They may become individual losers, or "relatively deindividualized," according to modern individual development demands (Mørch 1991).

On the other hand, this self-confidence can also become a problem. Young people may lose life perspectives if they only look for "what is in it for me," and also they may lose awareness of other people's interests and rights. The combination of high self-confidence and a strong peer group life may create problems with the development of social responsibility and also differentiation between young people.

Immigrant ethnic youth are in a different situation. Though the greatest part of young immigrant youth do very well in school, many experience problems and bad results (Indvandrere 2001). This situation leads to opposition to the Danish society as being unfair and racist. Many problems with immigrant youth groups follow this logic. The young people experience themselves as in opposition to the Danish society and find a strong anti-Danish identity in the ethnic in-group. As in other European societies, this may create new religious fundamentalism among young people (Mørch 2002).

Young people spend a lot of time in school, but activities with friends or peers also are very common. They spend their time with friends. In Danish society this friendship often includes both boy and girl friends. Maybe due to the equal developmental and educational life and opportunities in Denmark, youth life is not so sharply divided according to gender as in many other European societies.

Youth life also includes private moments. Young people, especially girls, still read books and listen to music. They also—and maybe mostly the boys— are playing computer games or are surfing the Internet (Aagre 2002).

Family Relationships

Family life is very important in Denmark. However, family life is very susceptible to individual lives and interests. For young people, family relations are increasingly moving away from being based on a state of dependence to functioning as an open supportive network.

To analyze Danish upbringing or socialization practices we may draw a picture of three different socialization styles. The first, traditional socialization style, is marked by parents who regulate individual activities by different forms of social control. The second, normative style, is where parents try to teach children and young people how they should behave. Here they try to develop normative codex and attitudes in their children. The third, a peer and network related style, is where parents only support individual decisions and leave it to the children or young people to make their own decisions, often as part of a peer relational group life (Stølan and Mørch 2004).

These styles are both geographically and social distributed. However, they also are constantly changing, both according to individual development from children to youth and according to societal changes. Therefore, the dynamics of upbringing in Denmark could be seen as divided in two broad practices that try to combine the different styles. The first is the traditional and normative family socialization practice. Here a mixture of methods is used to teach the children the right way of behaving. Both lower social groups and traditional families, including the immigrant families, use this model in everyday life. The family model in this situation is not very democratic, and children and young persons are often not recognized as equal persons. As a result, they often revolt against family life. The second style is the mixture of normative and peer-related family practice. Here the parents try to mix normative values and individual rights. In this way parents try to support a democratic family life, as the parents are able to become friends and supporters to their children. This family life often creates a comfortable but

perhaps not responsible family relation, but seems more and more common in the late modern socialization practice (modus 2).

The ordinary Danish family consists of parents and children and often includes a good relationship with grandparents, including weekly or monthly visits. Many families are single-parent families or mixed families, where the parents have new spouses and also bring children together. It is not usual for the modern Danish family to include more generations, but the new immigrant families often include both more generations and more family relatives.

Family life in Denmark is often very harmonious (Mørch 1991; Stolan and Mørch 2004). Of course conflicts develop about children's and young people's obligation to work in the family and their freedom to live a late night youth life. Conflicts are, however, most serious in the traditional family while the normative peer family seems more relaxed and more able to negotiate solutions. Therefore, immigrant children and young people experience conflicts. They experience a traditional and normative family practice but also a pressure from the Danish society to live "modern" lives. The contrasts to traditional family life create both problems in the families and an opposition between young people's family and youth life behavior.

Family size is small in Denmark, with the exception of the new immigrant families. Most Danish young people live with none, one, or maybe two siblings. However, because of divorce and remarriage, some children have more siblings, even though there has been a decrease in the total number of children from 1981 to 2000. Some children have three, four, or more siblings because they have more half-siblings through their parents' new relationships. In 1981 11% of the children had half-siblings; in 2000 this had increased to 24% (Statistisk tiårsoversigt 2000; Christensen and Ottesen 2002).

Relations to siblings are very equal, which means that young people are not responsible for taking care of younger siblings. In immigrant families this is often different; in them, gender differences make boys responsible for controlling the girls' behavior and girls responsible for taking care of younger siblings.

The way Danish people frame a family has changed during the last 30 to 40 years. Marriage is still the common organizing form, and 78% of all couples living together are married. But the share is decreasing, especially among young people. In 1970, 88% of all women at 30 years old were married, but this was the situation for only 49% of 30-year-old women in 2001.

The last 30 to 40 years are characterized by a considerable increase in the number of cohabiting couples and divorces. Around 18% of the marriages from 1950 were dissolved after 25 years, and 37% of the marriages from 1975. The marriages from 1990 so far show a lower divorce frequency than marriages from 1985 (Statistisk Aarbog 2001). In the 1960s fewer than 1% of couples living together were cohabitants, and the rest were married. In the 1970s about 10% were cohabitants, and in 1999 it was 28%. Cohabitation is most frequent among young people, but marriage is the most frequent way of living together when people become more than 30 years old (Danmarks, Statestik 2002). There are no statistics concerning dissolves of cohabitation, but different studies indicate that cohabitations are more vulnerable to dissolves than marriages, and particularly if there are no common children in the relationship.

The rate of children born outside marriage has increased considerably—in Denmark as in the other Scandinavian countries. In the beginning of the 1960s fewer than 10% of all children were born outside marriage, but this is the situation for 45% of the children born in 1998. This development reflects that an increasing number of partners are cohabitants when the child is born, and is not caused by an increase in the number of single mothers. Five percent of the children are born to single mothers, and this rate has been more or less stable for many years (Christensen and Ottesen 2002). The question about marriage or cohabitation is determined by life phase and age, and there is a clear tendency that couples get married later on.

In general, the developments in Danish childhood and family life over the last twenty years are characterized by two trends: a blurred family structure, and the survival of the nuclear family.

In general the nuclear family still is the most common frame for a child's childhood, but this is the situation for fewer children in 2000 than it was in 1981. The figures show a change from a traditional nuclear family to a more blurred/diffuse family structure. More children experience a break of the nuclear family, there are more children who live with their single mothers, and there is an increase in the number of children who live with their mother and her new partner. Twenty-one percent of the children in 2000 were living with their mother or their mother and her new partner, up from 14% in 1981.

Nearly 40% of all 17-year-olds have experienced a break in their families, and 25% of all 17-year-olds have experienced at least two shifts/breaks in their families. Fourteen percent have experienced at least three shifts, and 8% at least four shifts. But a shift/break doesn't necessarily mean that new persons are moving in/out, it might also be one of the parents who is moving out/in several times.

The nuclear family is still the most common family form. In 1981, 82% of all children were living together with both their parents, and so did 75% of all children in 2000. The older the children get, the fewer of them are living together with both parents. Still, 60% of all 17-years-olds are living together with both their parents. In 1981, 78% of children (below 18 years) had parents who were married; in 2000, this is true for 63% of the children. In 1981, 4% of the parents were cohabitants, and in 2000 the figure is 12% (Statistisk Tiårsoversigt 2000).

Friends and Peers/Youth Culture

Peer relations are the most important relations for young people. Though they use most of their time in school and with family, peers are the most important reference group for both girls and boys. Peer relations help young people learn to cope with the challenges of youth life and also to gain independence. Mostly, there are no serious conflicts between peers and families. They are both social networks that young people may use to manage challenges, and research shows that young people are open to advice from both family and peers (Stølan and Mørch 2004).

Young people see their friends primarily on Friday and Saturday evenings (23% are home with family, and 77% are with friends). On ordinary weekdays, 33% of adolescents are at home, 33% are with friends, and 33% are in clubs, organizations, or in the public space in their free time (Aagre 2002).

Danish adolescents mix freely with other adolescents of the opposite gender and different ethnicities. Youth have an open relationship according to gender and ethnic differences—they have a common youth life. However, ethnic relations show the same pattern as social class relations. Though adolescent life seems to unify all young people, some differences do exist. Young people mostly have friends in their everyday networks at school, youth clubs, and sports. In this way social class and ethnic groups divide young people.

Trends and tastes in music, clothing, and lifestyles both unify and divide young people, but the place in educational life is the main cause of different forms of youth life. Often these differentiations follow social class and ethnic lines.

In a general perspective, it seems as if Danish youth cultures follow late modern lines. They are highly influenced by media, music, and consumerism. At the same time, young people's own engagement as it is developed in education is influencing the way they use different opportunities. Therefore, Danish youth culture is mostly like other modernistic youth cultures, but at the same time it is colored by the special Danish freedom and democratic societal influence.

Youth organizations are under attack in Denmark. Traditionally, many different youth organizations existed, including political youth organizations, sports leagues, and scouting groups. However, the strong individualization and the media-influenced youth life have caused a decrease in organized youth activities. Today sports clubs are the strongest organizations. However, instead of engagement in political party youth work many young people engage in global policy issues. Most youth organizations are run by adults or young adults, and in this way they may give some pictures of a modern youth life engagement to younger youth groups.

Love and Sexuality

Most adults and young people in Denmark have a very relaxed understanding of young people's sexual activity. Young people can have girlfriends or boyfriends from a relatively young age, and generally parents allow them to be together, as they prefer. Parents do not interfere in dating behavior. Girls and boys mostly have the same freedom, but girls may experience more restrictions from their parents.

Young people take sex education classes in school, and often they are offered free contraceptives. Girls under the age of 15 have to have parental acceptance in order to receive birth control pills. From the age of 15, they can receive contraceptive pills without parental permission. Since 1973 Denmark has had free abortion available.

Parents of course are concerned, but mostly they try to advise and not forbid sexual activity. The parents' concern is maybe not so much about sex behavior as about its social arrangements. Young people from a very early age stay out at night in discos and bars and may have casual sexual partners who do not belong to their everyday and equal-age network.

In immigrant families the picture is different. Boys are mostly allowed the same freedom as Danish boys, but girls, as soon as they reach puberty, are often barred from casual contact with boys, and are forbidden from having any sexual relations before marriage.

As already mentioned, youth sexual experiences (intercourse) may happen earlier than before, from the age of 11 to 12 for girls, but the general figure seems now to be quite steady. By the age of 16 more than half of both girls and boys have had intercourse. Girls have earlier and more sexual experience than boys. By the age of 19, 89% of the girls and 78% of the boys have had intercourse (Bay 1996). This also suggests that sexual experiences are developed before marriage or cohabitation.

To have children at an early age is not popular in Denmark. The age at which women have their first child is increasing to 27 or 28, mostly because of educational life prolongation and gender equality, and early pregnancies are not welcomed.

The abortion rate is high, but maybe because of the open access to contraceptives—and the emergency contraception pill—the abortion rate is going down. In 1975, 2.4% of women of reproductive age had had an abortion (Politiken 13.05.05). Today the number is 1.4%. However, the abortion rate among adolescents is not decreasing. The abortion quotient (number of abortions per 1,000 women in the age group) is between 10 and 40, depending on whether the women live in the countryside or a main city.

The open understanding of sexual activity also makes sexual orientation a private issue. There is little to no stigma attached to homosexuality.

Health Risk Behavior

Youth life in Denmark is very closely related to educational life. Therefore youth problems relate to the educational track of the young person. Most crime is never discovered, and especially youth crime is often not reported. Only one-fifth of all crime is discovered, and shoplifting, stealing, and burglary are not seriously punished. Crime in many ways seems to be a youth problem. It increases among the 15 to 20 age group, and decreases in older age groups. Every year 2 to 3% of young men receive a sentence for crime. However, youth crime is often not serious crime. In 70% of the cases young people receive only fines as punishment (stealing, shoplifting, traffic fines). Crime committed and reported among youth is often centered on violent activity, and especially among older adolescents violent crime is increasing (Justitsministeriet, 2001).

There have been some changes in the overall crime pattern. Even though more boys take part in criminal activity than girls, today more girls are involved in criminal behavior than before. Crime and many other social problems follow both social class position and ethnic social background. Immigrant adolescents suffer higher rates of unemployed parents, are more likely to live in high-risk communities, and are less likely to do well in school. In general, crime statistics on the crime frequency rate among 15- to 19-years-old show that first- and second-generation immigrant youth are at least twice as likely to engage in criminal behavior (Kyvsgaard 2001; Danmarks Statestik 2003).

Youth life in many other ways is dangerous. Young people smoke and drink frequently, although the figures are very much debated. Some reports tell that smoking is decreasing greatly in Denmark; however, the number of cigarettes sold remains stable, and may even be growing. Statistics show that approximately 30% of young people smoke, and more then 49% of these smoke more then 15 cigarettes every day. Smoking behavior is dependent on the age of the adolescents and their educational situation. Up to 70% of young people in special short-term educational programs smoke, compared to approximately 20% attending a traditional high school (Jensen et al. 2004).

The same picture seems to exist of drinking and use of drugs. Adolescents' educational status is the crucial indicator for drinking and drug use. Seventy percent of young people between the ages of 15 and 24 report drinking during the previous weekend. More then 50% between the ages of 15 and 18 state that they have been drunk one or more times in the last two weeks (Politiken 2005). It is difficult to locate precise statistics regarding use of drugs and hashish. Hash is legal to use, but not to deal in Denmark. Statistics show that more then 50% of young people have tried to smoke hash, but only a few use it regularly (Bay 1996).

Young people in Denmark have to be 18 to have a driving license. Young people are often involved in car accidents, both because of being inexperienced but especially because of drunk driving. Young people between the ages of 18 and 20 have a seven times higher risk of accidents then their parents. Young men, especially, are at risk of involvement in car accidents.

Adolescents younger than 15 are not allowed to buy alcohol and cigarettes, and they have to be 18 to drink in restaurants and discos. In court they are not treated as adults before 18, and if they are younger than 15 they cannot be punished, but will be given special social help and support.

Suicide among youth is not as frequent as among adults. The suicide rate has declined over the last years. More men than women commit suicide.

In the 15- to 25-year-old age group, approximately 20 men and 10 women per 100,000 commit suicide, and in the 15- to 19-year-old age group, 4 out of 100,000 commit suicide. The figures of attempted suicide are much higher (Danmarks Statestik 2003).

In a general perspective, it seems that youth problems follow their success or failure in being able to take part in youth life and educational life. Young people experience their life as quite "comfortable" and are generally quite satisfied with their lives (Mørch 1991).

The greatest risks for young people seem to come from dropping out of education. Ethnic youth are especially vulnerable in this respect. If they are performing badly in school they experience problems and often develop an antagonism toward Danish society. This, combined with a strong peer relational dependency, makes this category of ethnic youth a problem both to themselves and to the rest of society.

The high expectancy for young people themselves to develop life perspectives and responsibility also makes youth life a personal challenge. Young people who are not able to cope with this challenge—often because of family problems and problems in educational life—may develop antisocial behavior, which makes ordinary social integration a challenge with big troubles to overcome. This situation creates both individual psychological problems and social problems for young people.

Education

Education level in Denmark is rather high. Education has become a double transition strategy: to become an adult and to change social class position (Jensen 2004). All children have nine years of primary school, and 80% are expected to have a secondary education. Among these, 45% will have a vocational education and 35% will have a higher (academic) education. Today women and men are on equal terms in education. However, some gender differences are developing: women are more represented in university education and men in technical education.

Danish educational systems support "modern" individual and social competence more than traditional knowledge reproduction. Maybe, therefore, Danish youth are not doing as well in international comparisons of education systems as should be expected.

The Danish educational system does not have special programs for gifted students. Mostly competition exists inside the general educational system, and access to higher and university education is restricted and therefore creates competition for education to popular professions. The Danish school system has many different programs and school forms to support young people who are not able to use the ordinary educational systems, including special education for less clever youngsters and special schools for young people who are not motivated to follow ordinary education. Many special programs exist to ensure that all young people in the end will have a fair level of education and a vocational education (Undervisningsministeriet 2002).

Ethnic youth (immigrants and second-generation foreign ethnic youth) are not yet doing as well as Danish youth in education. However, there are huge differences depending on national background, and second-generation youth are doing much better then first-generation youth. The general picture is that ethnic youth are 10% behind Danish youth in secondary education: the figures for not being in secondary education are Danish youth, 27.5%; immigrant youth, 55.5%; and second-generation youth, 35.1% (Indvandrere og Efterkommere 2001).

Work

The main occupation for young people in Denmark is education. Most young people get pocket money from their parents, and when they become 18 they will have state educational support as students. However, youth life in Denmark is commercialized and very expensive. Therefore, many young people have a part-time job to earn extra money for personal use. At the age of 12, 18% have a part-time job, and in gymnasium (age 17 to 19) 66% have a part-time job. The weekly hours are increasing from five to seven (Bay 1996). Jobs are mostly in service sectors and in shops. Only in very few situations are children and young people expected to

pay some of the expenses for living at home. Youth work is regulated in Denmark. There are minimum levels of payment according to age and also rules to protect young people from dangers and accidents.

The educational system is planned for helping young people mostly to have more education, but there are some educational activities and schools that are working together with private firms to form an apprenticeship model for practical education to labor markets.

The youth unemployment in Denmark is very low. If we look at the teenage young people it is hardly possible to talk about youth unemployment, because young people are in educational contexts. If they have left school and are without jobs, they are given more education or they will have a program made especially for them to be included in the labor market. Youth at the age of 18 to 19, however, have an unemployment rate around 4%.

Media

Young people in Denmark are very accustomed to media. They live in a computer and media world. Most young people have access to computers at home and in school, and the media are especially focusing young people both in special TV programs and in the selection of music.

It is hard to determine the number of hours spent listening to music, watching TV, and playing computer games, because these activities are mostly taking place all the time that youth are not doing anything else such as school and sport activities. Media use investigations point out that young people spend a lot of time in the media world. Fifteen- to 18-year-olds are watching TV 2.5 to 3 hours every day (Drotner and Poulsen 1997) and besides this they are using time on computers. If we ask what the youngsters are doing at home, they point to these figures in Table 1:

Table 1.

	Homework	Reading	House work	Music	Data	Physical activity	TV	Appearance	Relaxation	Hobbies
Boys	16	7	5	59	33	12	44	4	33	33
Girls	26	17	3	76	18	8	36	37	20	18
Total	20	12	4	67	25	10	40	20	27	25

Source: Aagre 2002.

Politics and Military

Danish society is a constitutional democracy. Young people may vote from age 18. About 80% of young people vote at the election, which is a little less than for the general population. Most political parties have a youth organization, but only 3 to 4% of young people are members or have been members of political parties. Fewer then 1% of young people between 15 and 29 are members of a political youth organization. The youth organizations have experienced the same decline as other organizations. Just after World War II, approximately 25% of all Danes were members of a political party. Today fewer than 10% are members. Figures also show that young people today do not become more politically active when they get older. Their arguments are: politics is boring and without consequences, and older people decide in the end anyhow (Udviklingscenter, 1995).

The Danish population does not engage in organized free-time activities as much as before. It seems as if individual interest and engagement in political and also other citizen activities are going down. There have been some projects trying to engage young people in local politics, called experimental Youth Municipalities, but rather few "expert-youngsters" took part. This political passiveness maybe is an aspect of a welfare society in which group or class interests are weakening. The Danish civic society has become more like a consumer society. People engage in work and consume, and more and more aspects of society are becoming consumer-organized. The Danish political system illustrates this development. When the Danish political parties were formed at the end of the nineteenth century they represented different groups or classes in society, such as farmers, workers, schoolteachers, and businessmen. The political parties formulated the policies for the different group interests for the debates and fights in the parliament. Today political parties do not represent specific parts of the population. They represent themselves and are formed around values and ideologies. Therefore all voters are potential voters for the parties. This makes politics a fight for values and voters, and the tools for this competition are advertising campaigns. Politicians have advisers who "construct" their way of behaving and also style the political parties as competing firms selling the same goods in a closed market. "Branding" seems to be the best example of this development.

In this situation political engagement changes. Many people, and especially young people, do not engage in party politics. Instead they may engage in local policies in schools and in more global questions and in more visionary associations like NGOs, Attack, and Greenpeace.

Denmark still has an obligatory military service for men, but only a small part of young men are actually becoming soldiers. Among the number qualified for service, approximately 10% will actually become soldiers. The Danish military is mostly taking part in peace interventions. This has caused a change in the structure of military service away from obligatory service and to professional jobs.

SVEN MØRCH

References and Further Reading

Aagre, et al. (eds.). 2002. *Nordiska Tonårsrum*. Lund Studentlitteratur.

Andersen, H. 1986. *Kvindeværd* (*Women's worth*). Copenhagen: Rubikon.

Anderson, M. 1980. *Approaches to the history of the Western family 1500–1914*. London: Sage.

Ariès, P. 1973. *Centuries of childhood*. New York: Random House.

Arnett, J. J. 2004. *Emergent adulthood. The winding road from the late teens through the twenties*. New York: Oxford University Press.

Bauman, Z. 1998. *Work, consumerism and the new poor*. Philadelphia: Open University Press.

Bauman, Z. 2001. *The individualized society*. Cambridge: Polity Press.

Bay, J. 1996. *Unges levevilkår*. København: Dansk Ungdoms Fællesråd.

Beck, U. 1992. *Risk society: Towards a new modernity*. London: Sage.

Beck, U., and Beck-Gernshein. 2002. *Individualisation*. London: Sage.

Center for Ungdomsforskning. Unge i tal. www.Cefu.dk.

Christensen, E., and M. H. Ottesen. 2002. *Børn og familier*. Socialforskningsinstituttet.

Côté, J. 2000. *Arrested adulthood. The changing nature of maturity and identity*. New York: New York University Press.

Drotner, K., and K. Klitgaard Poulsen (eds.). 1997. *Tankestreger. Nye medier, andre unge*. København: Borgen.

Esping-Andersen, G. 1990. *Three worlds of welfare capitalism*. Cambridge: Polity Press.

Facts and Figures. 2000. Copenhagen: Ministry of Education.

Frønes, I. 1994. *Den norske barndommen*. Oslo: Cappelen.

Giddens, A. 1984. *The construction of society*. Cambridge: Polity Press.

Giddens, A. 1997. *Modernity and self identity*. Cambridge: Polity Press.

Gillis, J. 1981. *Youth and history*. New York: Academic Press.

Hall, S. G. 1904. *Adolescence. Its psychology and its relation to physiology, anthropology, sociology, sex, crime, religion and education*. Vols. I–II. New York: D. Appleton.

Indvandere og efterkommere i uddannalsessystemet. 2001. Copenhagen: Ministry of Education.

Jensen, T. T., et al. 2004. *Yo Yo—Youth transitions*. Department of Psychology. University of Copenhagen.

Justitsministeriet. 2001. *Rapport om ungdomskriminalitet*. København: Rigspolitiets trykkeri.

Kyvsgaard, B. 2001. Kriminalitet, retshåndhævelse og etniske minoriteter. *Juristen*, November, Copenhagen: DJØF.

Mørch, S. 1985. *At forske i ungdom* (*Studying youth*). Copenhagen: Rubikon.

Mørch, S. 1991. *Dansk eller russisk undomsliv*. Købehavn: Institut for Psykologi.

Mørch, S. 1999. Informal learning and social contexts. In *Lifelong learning in Europe: Differences and divisions*. A. Walther and B. Stauber (eds.). Tübingen: Neuling.

Mørch, S. 2002. Social identitet og integration hos etniske unge. *Psyke og Logos*, vol 1. Copenhagen.

Mørch, S. 2003. Youth and education. In *Young*. 11(1): 49–73. London: Sage.

Mørch, S., and H. Andersen. 2005. Youth and the family: Individualization and the changing youth life. In *A new youth? Young people, generations and family life*. C. Leccardi and E. Ruspini (eds.). Aldershot: Ashgate.

Mørch, S., and B. Stalder. 2003. Competence and employability. In *Trajectories and politics*. A. Walther (ed.). Cambridge: Policy Press.

Netpsyk.dk. 2005.

Politiken. 13.05.05.

Postman, N. 1982. *The disappearance of childhood*. London: Comet.

Powell, B. 1903. *Scouting for boys*. London.

Stafseng, O. 1996. *Den historiske konstruktion av moderne ungdom* (*The historic construction of modern youth*). Oslo: Cappelan.

Statistisk Årbog. 2002, 2003. Copenhagen: Danmarks Statestik.

Statistisk Tiårsoversigt 2000. 2000. Copenhagen: Danmarks Statestik.

Stølan. L. O., and S. Mørch. 2004. *Youth transitions and family support*. Copenhagen: Department of Psychology.

Tal der taler. 2002. Undervisningsministeriet.

Udviklingscenter. 1995.

Walther, A., et al. (eds.). 2002. *Misleading trajectories. Integration policies in Europe?* An Egris Publication. Opladen: Leske and Budrich. www.danmark.dk.

Ziehe, T. 2001. De personlige livsverdeners dominans (The dominance of personal life worlds). *Uddannelse 10*, Undervisningsministeriet.

E

ECUADOR

Background Information

At the close of the twentieth century, Ecuador experienced an economic crisis unmatched by any in its long history. Debt and deficit difficulties, depreciating currency rates, reduced oil prices, and natural disasters such as *El Niño* reduced the country's gross domestic product by over 10% (Dulitzky 2003). Ecuador's substantial youth population has struggled to flourish at the outset of the twenty-first century, and their assortment of successes and setbacks will likely define what it means to be an adolescent in Ecuador for many years.

Located on the northwestern Pacific coast of South America, Ecuador is a developing nation that has operated as a republic since 1830, under which system all individuals aged 18 and over are required to vote in federal elections (CIA 2005). The Republic of Ecuador has been consistently distinguished by its political instability. Although politicians are elected to four-year terms, leadership has changed on average every 1.75 years. These changes have been largely due to consistent struggles among regions of Ecuador between the two leading Conservative and Liberal political parties, combined with the major role in national politics upheld by the armed forces (Hanratty 1989).

The origins of modern-day Ecuador can be traced back to the conquest of many South American countries by Spanish military forces in the sixteenth century. The nation was ruled as a Spanish colony until the early nineteenth century, when the Spanish monarchy was conquered by France, and rebellion against French rule in Ecuador began (Hanratty 1989). Ecuador marks as its Independence Day August 10, 1809, at which time its capital city, Quito, signed an agreement to self-govern (Hanratty 1989). The nation of Ecuador gained independence from Spain on May 24, 1822 (CIA 2005).

The people of Ecuador are primarily young, with a median age of 23.3 years, and youth account for a substantial proportion of the total population of 13,363,593 (CIA 2005). In 2003, 38.9% of the total population of Ecuador were under age 18 (UNICEF 2004), and in 1997, the proportion of the population aged 10 to 14 was 11.4%—approximately 1.4 million people (Wilkie, Aleman, and Ortega 2001). The majority ethnic group residing in Ecuador are referred to as *mestizo* (mixed racial origin), representing 65% of the population, whose heritage is a combination of *blanco* (white) and indigenous races. Other groups include indigenous people (25%), Black people of non-Hispanic descent (3%), and various minorities including Spanish (7%) (CIA 2005). Ecuador's citizens are stratified by social class, a distinction that has increased over time, with the majority of the population designated to a low socioeconomic status (Hinrichsen 2005). Estimates indicate that between 45% (CIA 2005) and 70% (de Lucas 2005) of the population of Ecuador live below the poverty line.

Period of Adolescence

Across Latin America, adolescence has been recognized as a distinct stage of life since the 1960s, due in part to increased life expectancies in the region and to a decreased fertility rate, suggesting the existence of a transitional state between childhood and adulthood that had not been apparent during the first half of the twentieth century and earlier (Welti 2002). Indeed, average life expectancy in Ecuador rose from 58.8 years in 1975 to 70 years in 2000 (Bortman 2003), and has increased to 76.2 years in 2005 (CIA 2005). Fertility rates have also decreased from 6.7 children per woman between 1960–1965 to 4.7 children between 1980–1985 (Wilkie et al. 2001), to 2.7 children per woman in 2005 (CIA 2005). The average age of menarche (first period) in Ecuadorian adolescent girls occurs around age 12 to 13. One study determined that among pregnant women aged 20 to 30, the average age of menarche had been 12.8 years, with 68% of the sample reporting menarche approximately between ages 11 and 15 (Chedraui, Hidalgo, Chavez, and San Miguel 2004). However, adolescence may not be a period of transition experienced by all Ecuadorians, as many children and youth enter the workforce full-time during their teen years, marry early, and start families. Nonetheless, the government of Ecuador's *Ministerio de Bienestar Social* (Ministry of Social Welfare) legally distinguishes childhood (birth to age 12) from adolescence (ages 12 to 18, inclusive).

A partial acknowledgment of emerging adulthood is suggested by the existence of initiatives to facilitate quality of life improvements for disadvantaged youth aged 18 to 29. The Ministry of Social Welfare reports disproportionate disadvantages experienced by youth in this age bracket as a result of national economic crises. Furthermore, Latin American youth in general tend to live at home with their parents longer than in previous generations, in part because of the difficulty in finding appropriate full-time employment (Welti 2002). However, other indicators of emerging adulthood as described by Arnett (2000) suggest that such a

period may not truly exist among Ecuadorian youth. For example, the mean age of marriage among women in Ecuador is relatively early, at 22 years (Ingoldsby, Schvaneveldt, and Uribe 2003; UNFPA 2005; Wilkie et al. 2001), and 25 years among men (UNFPA 2005). Ecuadorian women typically give birth to their first children around age 21.5 years (Eggleston 2000). However, the mean age of marriage has increased from age 19.5 since 1987 (Schvaneveldt and Ingoldsby 2003), suggesting that emerging adulthood may be on the horizon as Ecuador continues to develop and display similarities to developed Western nations.

Beliefs

Relatively little has been studied with respect to systems of belief in Ecuador and even less is known about the transmission of beliefs during adolescence. Specific rites of passage may not be practiced in contemporary Ecuadorian society, and the wide variety of indigenous groups in Ecuador (Collins 2004) suggests a preclusion of specific rituals or religious activities common to the indigenous population. In general, however, it is acknowledged that Ecuador is a primarily collectivist society that historically places emphasis on the importance of the family unit (Hanratty 1989).

Catholicism is predominant in Ecuador, with 95% of its citizens subscribing to this religion (CIA 2005). In 1994, the government of Ecuador created *Ley Religiosa* (the Religious Education Act), requiring Catholic religious instruction in all public primary and secondary schools (Roos and van Renterghem 1997). However, degree of devotion to or involvement in Catholicism may be extremely variable, and in terms of mate selection, Ecuadorian Catholic youth and adults are generally unconcerned about choosing partners on the basis of partners' active involvement in Catholicism. It appears that the most important factor among Catholic partners is that they simply belong to the same religion (Ingoldsby et al. 2003).

Gender

Men's and women's roles in Ecuador are polarized in terms of behavioral expectations. Boys are typically raised to become aggressive, "macho" men (IBRD 2000; Welti 2002), whereas girls are expected to display passivity and not to question authority (IBRD 2000). These role expectations for girls are engendered such that they pervade adolescent girls' views of a beauty standard. Indeed, Casanova (2004) determined that adolescent girls see characteristics such as respectfulness, politeness, and modesty as inherent in a model of Ecuadorian beauty.

Traditional roles dominate Ecuadorian men's and women's vocational choices. Women tend to choose humanities-related courses of study that lead to lower-paying, caretaking professions such as teaching and nursing, while men's choices tend to be technical. Although nearly equal proportions of men and women are enrolled in vocational training programs in Ecuador (43% female), programs such as construction, mechanics, and electronics are dominated by men while programs in administration and textile manufacturing are dominated by women (IBRD 2000).

Gender role expectations are promoted throughout childhood and adolescence in the school context. Textbooks used in Ecuadorian schools have been shown to deliver stereotyped messages about men's and women's roles: girls and women are portrayed in caretaking roles (teaching, mothering), while men are noticeably absent from these images. Boys and men, conversely, are portrayed in productive, scientific, and intellectual roles (IBRD 2000). Indeed, these stereotypes have been strengthened by teachers' differential expectations and treatment of boys and girls in school. For example, when boys and girls experience academic difficulties, teachers tend to attribute boys' failure to rebelliousness and behavioral acting-out, whereas girls' failure is attributed to low intelligence and lack of ability (IBRD 2000).

Virtually no research exists documenting body image issues and ideals among adolescents in Latin America (Casanova 2004). However, available research shows that adolescent girls in Ecuador agree on a standard of beauty for women that includes typically Caucasian features such as long, straight hair; tall, thin but curvaceous and shapely bodies; and light-colored skin and eyes. Additionally, non-White (especially Black) features are marked as undesirable and unattractive (Casanova 2004). Despite the existence of such unattainable beauty standards, Ecuadorian adolescent girls do not appear to measure their own worth in comparison to the ideal. Indeed, 65% of girls report being satisfied with their bodies and appearance (Casanova 2004).

The Self

In Ecuador, adolescents' sense of cultural identity can be extremely blurred. As the majority of its citizens are of mixed racial heritage, cultural self-identification by Ecuadorian adolescents is extremely variable. No formal system of racial classification exists in Ecuador, and adolescents use different strategies to place themselves in a racial category. For example, among non-indigenous adolescents, Casanova (2004) found that some adolescent girls describe their race by the color of their skin (cinnamon-colored, wheat-colored, etc.), some simply assign themselves to the dominant *mestizo* cultural group, and still others choose between *blanco* (white) and mestizo based on their social class; that is, higher-class girls of mixed racial origin are more likely to identify themselves as White rather than mestizo.

With respect to the cultural identities of indigenous people, Ecuador has a long history of racism against and control over these citizens (Beck and Mijeski 2000). During the mid- to late-twentieth century, a stated goal of Ecuadorian politicians and members of elite society was to modernize the nation by a process known as *blanqueamiento* (whitening), the gradual erasure of the non-White heritages of its citizens (Beck and Mijeski 2000; Halpern and Twine 2000).

Historically, indigenous Ecuadorians are an ethnically diverse group, and at the beginning of the twenty-first century, fully 25% of the population of Ecuador are indigenous (CIA 2005). Distinctions between ethnic groups have been blurred after centuries of control by European rulers, reducing their heritage of many languages to one spoken by most indigenous people, *Quechua* (CIA 2005; Collins 2004). Some insight into the development of modern indigenous cultural identity is derived from the findings from a study of indigenous students at a small college in Ecuador's Bolívar province: results indicate that indigenous citizens who have grown up in the urban centers of Ecuador—locations dominated by White and *mestizo* culture—develop a sense of cultural identity that is rooted in a rejection of *mestizo* society and its values (Beck and Mijeski 2000).

Given the lack of cultural and ethnic record keeping that has characterized Ecuador to date, it is unknown how families and social/cultural groups transmit a sense of self that is rooted in cultural heritage to their children, nor how that sense of identity develops in adolescence. Further research is needed to shed light on this issue in Ecuador.

Family Relationships

Ecuadorian family structures vary, but the majority of families consist of a two-parent structure. However, increased rates of divorce and separation have led to an increased prevalence of single-parent families (Guijarro et al. 1999). Data from 1990–1995 indicate that the Ecuadorian divorce rate is 6.1 per 10,000 people, or approximately one divorce for every 10 marriages (PAHO 1998). Families are predominantly patriarchal, and the acknowledged "head" of the household is male in over three-quarters of families at all socioeconomic statuses. Similarly, the principal earner in the household is male in more than 70% of all families (IBRD 2000).

Typical parenting practices in Ecuador have not been systematically documented, although it is considered common for mothers to use physical discipline with their children (IBRD 2000). Adolescent–parent and family conflicts in Ecuador remain undocumented, and the typical characteristics of adolescents' relationships with members of their families are unknown.

The degree to which any given family will recognize extended members of the family depends on their economic and social stability. Wealthy families mark their status and power by the size of their families. In contrast, lower-income families tend to be more selective about which members of the extended family to acknowledge, for practical and financial purposes (Hanratty 1989). Economic difficulties across Latin America in the late twentieth century have contributed in part to the practice of household sharing among three generations: it has become common for children and adolescents to live together with their parents and grandparents before moving out (Welti 2002). In addition, and possibly due in part to the collectivistic nature of many Latin American societies, adolescents tend not to gain autonomy or independence until they have been separated from the family by marriage (Welti 2002), which occurs for the average Ecuadorian at around age 22 (Ingoldsby et al. 2003).

Friends and Peers/Youth Culture

Research on Ecuadorian peer groups and their interactions has not yet been conducted. Indirect research evidence indicates that peer interactions among adolescent girls in Ecuador tend toward mutual support rather than competition, as is frequently observed among North American girls (Casanova 2004). Such interactions may arise from the collectivistic nature of Ecuadorian society that differentiates it from individualistic North American societies. More broadly known is that Latin American adolescent peer groups tend to form within the school and neighborhood contexts, and their primary activities include playing sports and drinking alcohol (Welti 2002). In

Ecuador, the most popular sports are soccer and volleyball (Roos and van Renterghem 1997), although the degree to which youth culture revolves around these sports is undocumented.

Youth organizations in Ecuador that are focused on sexual health education have received media attention and international support. A youth-led network known as *Ponte Once* operates in Ecuador's province of Manabi, and youth groups supported by this network are engaged in activities such as visiting schools and colleges to discuss sexual health issues, performing skits, and collaborating to produce a radio program known as "Breaking the Silence," devoted to adolescent sexual and reproductive health (Hinrichsen 2005). Other well-known youth organizations include the *Federación de Estudiantes Universitarios del Ecuador* (Federation of University Students of Ecuador, FEUE), established in 1944, and a related organization of high school students, the *Federación de Estudiantes Secundarios del Ecuador* (Federation of High School Students of Ecuador, FESE), which operate under largely political agendas aimed at the improvement of secondary and post-secondary education for Ecuadorian students, the promotion of student rights, and the involvement of students in governmental change (FESE; Hanratty 1989).

Other facets of youth in Ecuador have yet to be documented, including fashion, style, body modification, use of slang within adolescent dialogues, and the local to international influences on these trends. Further research is needed to provide a complete picture of adolescent peer groups and youth culture in Ecuador.

Love and Sexuality

Ecuadorian adolescents are legally permitted to marry starting at age 12 (girls) and age 14 (boys), and approximately 31% of adolescent girls and 12.5% of adolescent boys aged 15 to 19 were married in Ecuador in 1996 (Wilkie et al. 2001). Data collected in 1987 indicate that Ecuadorian youth on average first initiate intercourse at age 18.8 years (Schvaneveldt and Ingoldsby 2003). Park, Sneed, Morisky, Alvear, and Hearst (2002) found that 43% of adolescents aged 14 to 19 reported being sexually active, 40% of whom had at least four different partners in their lifetime. Relatively few sexually active adolescents reported consistent use of condoms (22%). Indeed, half reported never using condoms during sexual intercourse. Despite adolescents' generally good knowledge of the risk factors involved in HIV transmission, fewer than 20% believe they are at risk for contracting HIV (Park et al. 2002). Indeed, rates of sexually transmitted infections have increased sharply among adolescents aged 14 to 19 in Ecuador (UNAIDS 2004). However, general prevalence rates of HIV/AIDS in Ecuador are low or comparable to developed nations such as Canada and the United States. In 2003, the percentage of adults aged 15 to 49 living with HIV/AIDS in Ecuador was 0.3%. Prevalence in the United States for the same year was twice that rate, at 0.6%. Though its prevalence rate is low overall, Ecuador has experienced a 224% increase in its HIV infection rate between the late twentieth and early twenty-first century (Hinrichsen 2005), and it is estimated that 21,000 Ecuadorians lived with HIV/AIDS in 2005 (CIA 2005).

Pregnancy rates among adolescent girls have increased, and approximately 20% of all girls have been pregnant at least once by age 19 (Hinrichsen 2005). Among Ecuadorian women aged 15 to 24, incidence of pregnancy is inversely related to level of education: 60% of uneducated women in this age group have been pregnant, versus 29% of university-educated women (Schutt-Aine and Maddaleno 2003). However, this disparity may likely be due to the different values and priorities held by women who choose or are able to obtain post-secondary education compared to those who do not.

Typically, men in Ecuador initiate sexual activity earlier than women: on average, adolescent males' first sexual experience occurs at age 15 (IBRD 2000). Ecuadorian adolescent males are at particular risk of contracting HIV and other sexually transmitted infections (STIs) given this early age of sexual initiation, because relatively few boys use condoms at first intercourse (17% of urban adolescent males), and 30% of boys' first partners are prostitutes (IBRD 2000). Among men, homosexuality is viewed negatively across Latin America, with little variation between countries. Homosexuality is socially unacceptable and adolescent males are viewed as requiring psychiatric care for homosexual behavior (Welti 2002). Homosexual behavior among Ecuadorian girls and attitudes toward such behavior have not been documented.

The *Ministerio de Educación y Cultura* (Ministry of Education and Culture, MEC) in Ecuador has established guidelines for the provision of sexual health education in schools. In all cases, teachers must be trained to provide sexual health instruction, and curricula must be developed in cooperation and partnership with students' families and the community (MEC 1998). The effectiveness of these regulations and the degree to which they are employed in schools across Ecuador is unknown, but a unique venture sponsored by the United Nations Population Fund (UNFPA) through 2004 brought comprehensive sexual health education to small communities and approximately 140,000 adolescents in Ecuador. The youth-led project, Improving the Reproductive and Sexual Health of Adolescents, has contributed to the reduction and in some cases elimination of teenage pregnancies and sexually transmitted infections among Ecuadorian youth (Hinrichsen 2005). The UNFPA has worked with the Ministry of Education and Culture to set up a nationwide program of sexuality education in middle and secondary schools, and to improve access to sexual health information and services (Hinrichsen 2005).

Health Risk Behavior

Among adolescents aged 14 to 19 in poor areas of Ecuador's capital city, Quito, 45.4% report drinking alcohol (60.6% of males and 28.5% of females), and 13.3% report using illegal substances (IBRD 2000). Access to drugs and alcohol in Ecuador among adolescents is not difficult, particularly because there exists no minimum age restriction for the purchase of alcohol, and illegal drugs are reportedly easy to obtain (IBRD 2000). With respect to cigarette use, among urban and rural Ecuadorian adolescents aged 9 to 15, 8.6% reported smoking occasionally to at least once per week, and 24.5% had tried cigarette smoking in the past. More than half of all adolescents who had at least tried smoking did so between the ages of 10 and 12 (Padgett, Selwyn, and Kelder 1998).

Adolescents in Ecuador are also involved in gang activities, and as of 2004, estimates indicate that approximately 70,000 adolescents are involved with gangs, most of whom have access to and make use of firearms (Curbelo 2004). Details regarding the extent to which adolescents in gangs or otherwise are engaged in criminal activities are not available.

Specific information regarding mental health in Ecuador and among its youth is generally unavailable. However, suicide rates have been compiled and indicate that in 1990, males and females of all ages commited suicide at rates of 5.7 and 3.0 per 100,000 people, respectively (Schmidtke et al. 1999).

Education

During the twentieth century, Ecuador made steady progress in improving the literacy and education rates of its citizens. The average Ecuadorian born in 1933 obtained only four years of education and was illiterate, but among those born forty years later, the average level of schooling obtained increased to nine years (Rojas 2003). Ecuador's formal education system includes ten years of schooling, the last three of which are first-stage, second-level (middle school) years for students aged 12 to 15. Students may choose to attend second-stage, second-level school (specialized secondary education) for an additional three years, and go on to a technical school or university thereafter. In addition, the Ecuadorian education system formally incorporates alternative and special education programs for students with exceptional needs (Rojas 2003).

In the early twenty-first century, literacy rates among youth in Ecuador aged 15 to 24 are high (above 96% for males and females) (UNESCO 2003). However, among all Ecuadorian adolescents who are eligible to attend secondary school based on their age, fewer than 60% actually attend (UNICEF 2004).

Discrepancies exist across social classes within the Ecuadorian education system. For example, the poorest 20% of residents in rural areas obtain fewer than four years of formal education, while the wealthiest 20% of urban residents obtain more than 12 (Rojas 2003). The distinction between urban and rural levels of education may be partially explained by the different values, lifestyles, and priorities assumed by rural indigenous people compared to non-indigenous rural and urban Ecuadorians. For example, in 1974, the proportion of students entering the second stage of second-level schooling (which occurs approximately at age 15) was 11.2% among urban students and only 1.1% among rural students (Wilkie et al. 2001). However, the government of Ecuador requires that all students attend school for at least ten years, from ages 5 to 15 (Wilkie et al. 2001). Clearly, compliance with this requirement does not occur among many sectors of the population. Indeed, although the proportion of students enrolled in school at age 12 is 91%, this figure decreases to 76% at age 13, 68% at age 14, and 62% at age 15 (Rojas 2003).

Educational discrepancies between poor and wealthy sectors of Ecuador may be partially explained by the cost of sending children to school, which can include tuition fees, uniform purchases, transportation, school supplies, and textbooks. The requirement of financial support from the community for the operation of schools in poor communities caused many families to pay fees almost equivalent to those paid by wealthier families to private schools (Rojas 2003). Among adolescents aged 11 to 15 in 1998, the primary reason given by 34% for not attending school was the cost. Sixteen percent claimed not to attend school because of the need to work, and a further 10% did not attend because of a lack of access to school (Rojas 2003). For those students who do attend school, the quality of education they receive may not be adequate. Students' achievement in areas of language and mathematics is deficient, and Ecuador ranks the lowest among 19 Latin American countries in quality of education (Rojas 2003). Reasons given for poor quality of education include insufficient training of teaching staff, failure to invest in teaching materials due to economic crises near the end of the twentieth century, and inconsistent attendance due to students' involvement in work.

Work

Employment and unemployment among adolescents are by nature two conflicting issues. Youth may not attend school out of necessity to provide for themselves and their families financially, yet unemployment among youth impacts many adolescents' ability to obtain experience and training needed for higher-paying, secure adult employment.

Latin American youth aged 15 to 24 are unemployed at twice the rate of adults and tend to be employed in lower-paying jobs that require fewer skills and offer limited or no benefits (Maddaleno 1998; Welti 2002). In Ecuador, the unemployment rate for youth aged 15 to 24 was 14.8% between 2000 and 2005, reflecting only a slight increase from a rate of 13.5% for 1990–1995 (Hinrichsen 2005). However, the unemployment rate for the total adult population sits at 11% (CIA 2005), and among Ecuadorian men, the largest proportion of unemployed individuals (48%) are in the 15 to 24 age range (IRBD 2000).

Among Ecuadorian children and adolescents who are engaged in the workforce, many attend school and work simultaneously. According to data collected in 1998, 34.1% of adolescents aged 15 to 17 only attended school and did not work, 27% of adolescents attended school and worked, while 32.5% worked and did not attend school (López-Acevedo 2002). Some differences exist among urban and rural adolescents; for example, half of all rural adolescents work and do not attend school while only 18% of urban adolescents do so. Similarly, nearly half of all urban adolescents solely attended school while the same was true for only 16.9% of rural adolescents (López-Acevedo 2002).

As of late 2004, Ecuadorian legislation could not prevent the legal management of brothels, such that minors could obtain employment in the sex trade (BBC 2004). Although sexual exploitation of youth is illegal in Ecuador, protections do not extend to adolescents aged 14 to 18. The Ecuadorian government proposed changes to legislation in late 2004 that would offer complete protection of minors from sexual exploitation and that would increase penalties for such crimes (BBC 2004). Further investigation in Ecuador is needed to shed light on exploitative work such as the sex trade and slavery, as such data are currently unavailable.

Media

Adolescents' use of and exposure to media in Ecuador have not been documented. What is known are the types of media available and in use across the nation. For example, some adolescents in Ecuador may have access to the Internet, and in 2003 there were 569,700 Internet users (approximately 4% of the total population) and there are also more than two million cellular phone users in Ecuador (CIA 2005).

Given Ecuador's restricted economy, much of its television programming is imported from the United States. On the Ecuadorian television network, *Ecuavisa*, programming based in the United States accounts for nearly 40% of the total programming hours, while programs created in Ecuador only account for 22% (Davis 1997).

Politics and Military

Ecuadorian adolescents are prohibited from formally participating in military activities until they are 20 years old. Men aged 20 and over are required to submit to at least 12 months of military service (CIA 2005).

Adolescents' involvement in Ecuadorian politics can be observed through two well-known student groups: the *Federación de Estudiantes Universitarios del Ecuador* (Federation of University Students of Ecuador, FEUE) and the *Federación de Estudiantes Secundarios del Ecuador* (Federation of High School Students of Ecuador, FESE), both of whose agendas center around political and governmental protest. Across Latin America adolescents have lost considerable interest in belonging to nationwide organizations and tend to prefer to involve themselves at the community level (Welti 2002).

Supporting and promoting the rights of indigenous people in Latin American nations has become an issue of contemporary interest. Student

organizations at the university level in capital cities including Quito, Ecuador's capital, have rallied around this cause (Welti 2002). No research has been conducted to describe Ecuadorian adolescents' patterns of political participation, although if they follow the trends observed across Latin America, it is likely that Ecuadorian youth are making the transition from a period of political disillusionment to one of active involvement at the outset of the twenty-first century.

ANDREA DALTON

References and Further Reading

Arnett, J. J. 2000. Emerging adulthood: A theory of development from the late teens through the twenties. *American Psychologist* 55:469–80.

BBC (British Broadcasting Corporation). 2004. Ecuadorian government to present bill to combat child sex trade. *BBC Monitoring Americas.* August 15.

Beck, S. H., and K. J. Mijeski. 2000. Indigenous self-identity in Ecuador and the rejection of mestizaje. *Latin American Research Review* 35:119–37.

Bortman, M. 2003. Health. In *Ecuador: An economic and social agenda in the new millenium.* V. Fretes-Cibils, M. M. Giugale, and J. R. López-Cálix (eds.). Washington, D.C.: The World Bank.

Casanova, E. M. 2004. No ugly women: Concepts of race and beauty among adolescent women in Ecuador. *Gender and Society* 18:287–308.

Chedraui, P. A., L. A. Hidalgo, M. J. Chavez, et al. 2004. Determinant factors in Ecuador related to pregnancy among adolescents aged 15 or less. *Journal of Perinatal Medicine* 32:337–41.

CIA (Central Intelligence Agency). 2005. The world factbook. http://www.cia.gov/cia/publications/factbook/geos/ec.html.

Collins, J. 2004. Linking movement and electoral politics: Ecuador's indigenous movement and the rise of Pachakutik. In *Politics in the Andes: Identity, conflict, reform.* J. M. Burt and P. Mauceri (eds.). Pittsburgh, PA: University of Pittsburgh Press.

Curbelo, N. 2004. Cultural expressions as change agents in violent youth gangs. Paper presented at the dialogue on Promoting Coexistence and Security in the Information Society, Barcelona.

Davis, L. L. 1997. Prime time in Ecuador: National, regional television outdraws U.S. programming. *Journal of American Culture* 20:9–18.

de Lucas, J. A. 2005. Ecuador's working kids sometimes forsaken when child labor banned. *EFE News Service,* January 5.

Dulitzky, D. 2003. The social assistance system. In *Ecuador: An economic and social agenda in the new millenium.* V. Fretes-Cibils, M. M. Giugale, and J. R. López-Cálix (eds.). Washington, D.C.: The World Bank.

Eggleston, E. 2000. Unintended pregnancy and women's use of prenatal care in Ecuador. *Social Science and Medicine* 51:1011–18.

FESE (Federación de Estudiantes Secundarios del Ecuador). Federación de Estudiantes Secundarios del Ecuador. http://www.geocities.com/feseec.

Guijarro, S., J. Naranjo, M. Padilla, et al. 1999. Family risk factors associated with adolescent pregnancy: Study of a group of adolescent girls and their families in Ecuador. *Journal of Adolescent Health* 25:166–72.

Halpern, A., and F. W. Twine. 2000. Antiracist activism in Ecuador: Black-Indian community alliances. *Race and Class* 42:19–31.

Hanratty, D. M. 1989. A country study: Ecuador. http://lcweb2.loc.gov/frd/cs/ectoc.html.

Hinrichsen, D. 2005. Country in focus: Ecuador. http://www.unfpa.org/countryfocus/ecuador/index.htm.

IBRD (International Bank for Reconstruction and Development). 2000. *Ecuador gender review: Issues and recommendations*. World Bank Country Studies. Washington, D.C.: The World Bank.

Ingoldsby, B., P. Schvaneveldt, and C. Uribe. 2003. Perceptions of acceptable mate attributes in Ecuador. *Journal of Comparative Family Studies* 34:171–85.

López-Acevedo, G. 2002. *School attendance and child labor in Ecuador*. Policy Research Working Paper. Washington, D.C: The World Bank.

Maddaleno, M. 1998. *Plan of action for health and development of adolescents and youth in the Americas, 1998–2001*. Washington, D.C.: PAHO.

Ministerio de Educación y Cultura. 1998. Ley Sobre Educacion de la Sexualidad y el Amor. http://www.mec.gov.ec.

Padgett, D. I., B. J. Selwyn, and S. H. Kelder. 1998. Ecuadorian adolescents and cigarette smoking: A cross-sectional survey. *Pan-American Journal of Public Health* 4:87–93.

PAHO (Pan American Health Organization). 1998. *Health in the Americas*. Washington, D.C.: PAHO.

Park, I. U., C. D. Sneed, D. E. Morisky, et al. 2002. Correlates of HIV risk among Ecuadorian adolescents. *AIDS Education and Prevention* 14:73–83.

Rojas, C. 2003. Education. In *Ecuador: An economic and social agenda in the new millenium*. V. Fretes-Cibils, M. M. Giugale, and J. R. López-Cálix (eds.). Washington, D.C.: The World Bank.

Roos, W., and O. van Renterghem. 1997. *Ecuador: A guide to the people, politics, and culture*. New York: Interlink Books.

Schmidtke, A., B. Weinacker, and A. Apter 1999. Suicide rates in the world: Update. *Archives of Suicide Research* 5:81–89.

Schutt-Aine, J., and M. Maddaleno. 2003. *Sexual health and development of adolescents and youth in the Americas: Program and policy implications*. Washington, D.C.: PAHO.

Schvaneveldt, P. I., and B. Ingoldsby. 2003. An exchange theory perspective on couple formation preferences and practices in Ecuador. *Marriage and Family Review* 35:219–38.

UNAIDS (United Nations Programme on HIV/AIDS). 2004. *2004 Report on the global AIDS epidemic: 4th global report*. Geneva: UNAIDS.

UNESCO (United Nations Educational, Scientific and Cultural Organization). 2003. Country Profile: Ecuador. http://www.uis.unesco.org/countryprofiles/html/EN/countryProfile_en.aspx?code=2180.htm.

UNFPA (United Nations Population Fund). 2005. Ecuador: Overview. http://www.unfpa.org/profile/ecuador.cfm.

UNICEF (United Nations Children's Fund). 2004. *The state of the world's children 2005: Childhood under threat*. New York: UNICEF.

Welti, C. 2002. Adolescents in Latin America. In *The world's youth: Adolescence in eight regions of the globe*. B. B. Brown, R. W. Larson, and T. S. Saraswathi (eds.). New York: Cambridge University Press.

Wilkie, J. W., E. Aleman, and J. G. Ortega (eds.). 2001. *Statistical abstract of Latin America*. Los Angeles, Calif.: UCLA Latin American Center.

EGYPT

Background Information

Egypt is a country occupying the northwestern corner of Africa. Strategically situated at the crossroads between Europe and the Orient and between northern Africa and Southeast Asia, Egypt occupies 995,450 square kilometers and is bounded on the north by the Mediterranean Sea, on the east by the Red Sea, on the south by Sudan, and on the west by Libya.

From the dawn of history, human habitation has hinged on the Egyptian people's ability to harness the River Nile, which annually flooded its banks, depositing a fertile alluvium of silt brought down from lakes Victoria and Albert and from the mountains of Ethiopia. The creation of a system of basin irrigation to capture the silt and store the floodwaters, and of efficient devices to raise water from the channels and basins to the fields, was a prerequisite for the evolution of Egyptian agriculture between six and three millennia before the birth of Jesus Christ.

Egypt, which has pharaonic ancestors and Arab fathers, had an estimated population of 71,897,547 million in 2004 (*Al-Ahram*, February 16, 2005), among them 49.9% females and 51.1% males; 37.7% were less than 15 years of age; 32% were aged between 10 and 24 years; 30% were aged between 15 and 24 years; 56.5% were aged between 15 and 60 years; and 5.8% were aged 60 years and older. Statistics also pointed to an annual increase of 1.98% and a mortality rate of 19.6 per thousand. Egypt's population forms 23.5% of the entire population of the Arab countries, while population in nine other Arab countries represents only 4.2% of the total Arab population. At the same time, the individual income in Egypt reached only about 3% of the income in the United Arab Emirates. Life expectancy for Egyptians has improved during the last 15 years from 60 and 63 for males and females, respectively, to 68.4 and 72.8 years for males and females, respectively. Moreover, statistics show that the overall fertility, which was estimated in 1990 at 36.3 per 1.000, declined to 26.4 per 1.000 in 2004. The percentage of those using birth control facilities has increased from 24.2% in 1992 to 58% in 2005 (*Al-Ahram*, July 24, 2005).

Religion plays a major role in Egypt today, and approximately 90% of the population are Sunni Muslims. There are several religious minorities, the largest of which is the indigenous Christian Coptic population. In 1990, estimates of the Coptic population ranged from 3 million to 7 million (or 5% to 11% of the population). In 1990, Ciaccio and El-Shakry (1993) estimated the Egyptian Christian population at 5 million (or 8% of the total population), including approximately 350,000 followers of the Greek Orthodox Church, 175,000 Catholics, and 200,000 Protestants. In addition, an estimated 1,000 Jews remained in Egypt as of 1990. The Jewish population represents a fragment of the community of 80,000 Jews who lived in Egypt before 1948.

Broad religious tolerance has been a hallmark of traditional Egyptian culture, and the Egyptian Constitution of 1971 guarantees freedom of religion, although tensions along religious lines have risen sharply since the 1970s. The centrality of religion in defining Egypt has deep historical roots. From the time of the pharaohs (demigods in the eyes of their subjects), religion has played a central role in the life of the inhabitants of the Nile Valley. The priests of ancient Egypt, who presided over cults that defined each province, made up a central part of the ruling class. Though religion among the Egyptians took different forms through a succession of foreign conquerors, it always remained a key element of the political culture.

Ascendant Islam found fertile soil in Egypt. The Arab conquest in the seventh century gave the inherited religious bond a distinctive Islamic form. Islam ruled out any version of the old pharaonic claim of the ruler as a "descendant of the gods" and the notion of a closed caste of priests. Instead, the new faith impelled Muslims as a collective body to express their faith by founding a community of believers or *ummah*. The central moral precepts of Islam, expressed in the Koran and the traditions of the Prophet, have provided guidance for personal salvation, the moral basis for a good society on earth, and the central building block of this society.

The common language in Egypt is Arabic; however, English, French, German, Italian, and Spanish (in that order) are also known and spoken in many places, especially in the capital city, Cairo, and in the second largest Egyptian city, Alexandria. Egypt's culture incorporates a trend of open acceptance toward other cultures.

Egypt is the world's oldest continuous nation, with a recorded past of over six thousand years. Often invaded, conquered, and occupied by foreign armies, Egypt has never lost its identity. The Egyptians of today, although they have changed their language once and their religion twice, descend mainly from the Egyptians who built the Giza pyramids and the Temple of Karnak, who served Alexander the Great and his heirs, who submitted to Augustus Caesar and grew much of the grain that fed the Roman Empire, who started Christian monasticism and the veneration of the Virgin Mary, and who advanced and sustained Muslim learning in what is now the longest-functioning university in the world, Al-Azhar University in Cairo (established in 969) (Gold Schmidt 1994).

On July 23, 1952, a group of army officers (called Free Officers) seized control of the barracks and the government, deposed the king, drove out the old-style politicians, established a republican system (in June 1953), and ended the British occupation (in 1956). Thus, a new Egypt emerged, freed from foreign control (Ahmed 2005a).

Period of Adolescence

As in other Arab/Islamic countries, there is no clear-cut definition for adolescence, neither the age of its start nor the age at which adolescence as a distinct period ends. Adolescence in Egypt is characterized by physiological and psychological changes. No ceremonies or rites are used to mark its beginning or end. Legally, age distribution is structured in three major groups: 0–14 years, 15–60 years, and 60 years and older.

As in the other Arab/Islamic countries, the concept of adolescence in Egypt is rooted in Islamic traditions, and the legal point of view. According to these traditions, individuals are deemed to be responsible for their actions when they reach puberty. At this stage, Muslims are asked to fulfill all pillars of the faith. These pillars include the obligation to pray five times a day and keep the fast at Ramadan. He or she can marry at this point. Legally, individuals are considered responsible for their actions after the age of 21. Prior to that age, individuals are considered juvenile.

The psychosocial dimensions of adolescence in Egypt are not fully appreciated. One reason is that adolescence is viewed as pertaining to the realm of family, and thus varies according to cultural orientation, gender, religion, and socio-cultural status. Adolescents' rebellion and autonomy, typically observed in Europe and the United States, are not core features in Egyptian society. Very few male adolescents, and even fewer female ones, leave the family household to study, work, and live on their own before marriage.

An emerging adulthood period is not quite clear, and it is not similar to what is observed in Western societies. Children are staying with their families until they get married. It is not familiar or common to find any unmarried young man living away from his own family. Traditionally, male children are responsible for their families, and they are staying to support their families even after their marriage.

According to Egyptian law, Muslim males and females can marry at age 18 and 16, respectively. Marriage marks the end of the adolescence period for both sexes. Adolescents and youth who have the opportunity to go to university have more freedom than do their less-educated counterparts, especially females who have to stay at home and become partially responsible for household affairs. Male and female adolescents remain dependent on parents until their marriage.

Beliefs

The Egyptian lifestyle is characterized by values such as loyalty to the family and respect and obedience for elders, especially parents, grandparents, uncles, and aunts. Adolescents have to find and follow the ways that can enable them to improve and to support their family's socioeconomic status. In the past, the family's status in shaping individuals' behavior and decisions such as marriage was crucial. In the early twenty-first century, the individual's accomplishments, and educational and career level, have become more important.

Religious practices among adolescents and youth have become more visible since the last decades of the twentieth century. The numbers of youngsters, mostly males, who pray at mosque, are markedly increased, especially on major religious holy days. Examples of religious activities carried out by adolescents are: participation in group prayer on Fridays, Tarawieh prayer in Ramadan (an extra night group prayer), celebrating the Prophet's birthday, and wearing Islamic dress (especially in females). Politically speaking, more young people have adopted the slogan of Muslim Brothers, "Islam is the key."

The general cultural trend in Egypt is collectivistic, although adolescents' orientation is increasingly individualistic, especially as regards goal achievement, as a result of increasing access to the West, and globalization. There are no religious courts in Egypt. Legally, all Egyptians are equal regardless of their religious background; however, this background has to be considered in matters of personal status, such as marriage, divorce, and inheritance. Adoption is not allowed for Muslims.

Since the 1970s, a gradual increase in the number of Muslims, including male and female adolescents, who practice their religion has been observed. Similarly, the number of practitioners of Christianity has dramatically increased. Membership in religious organizations in Egypt during the same period of time has increased, especially among the poor and young, who consider religion as an identity and, at times, fanaticism as an escape from despair and lack of social, economic, and/or political opportunity.

Gender

Any discussion of gender roles in Egypt must be placed firmly within the Islamic context, as Islam constitutes the fundamental organizational background of Egyptian society. Egypt's citizens are predominantly Sunni Muslims; only 8% are Christians (Ciaccio and El-Shakry 1993). Islam is, therefore, the most significant rationale behind the delineation of men's and women's roles. The ideology derived from Islam directly impacts the roles and statuses attributed to women.

Briefly, the conceptual base of Islam consists of the following: the Koran (the holy book revealed to the Prophet Muhammad), the Sunna (sayings and traditions of the Prophet), and Shari'a law. Islam emphasizes the complementary nature of the sexes and dictates their roles accordingly. Women are placed under male guardianship to ensure the safeguarding of morality. Marriage is considered a contract between a man and a woman, and a woman must give her consent (through her father/brother/uncle, if she is less than 18 years old) for a marriage to occur. Divorce is a prerogative of men. Females are entitled to inheritance rights and the ownership of property, but they inherit one-half the portion that men inherit. These rules are being challenged daily by women, while religious leaders also argue over these dictates. Real change, however, has been slow in coming. Like many of their counterparts in other parts of the world, parents in Egypt prefer sons. It is said that a man with a son is immortal, whereas a girl is brought up to contribute to someone else's family tree. Young women typically leave their family to join their husband's

family at marriage, whereas young men, especially in the rural areas, stay at home and bring their new wife into their family. There are many compelling economic reasons why parents prefer a boy. At least 70% of Egypt is rural. Here sons are indispensable as a built-in workforce. Unlike girls, boys do not have to be supervised very closely, since their sexual behavior cannot dishonor the family or compromise their chance for marriage.

Women's chief role is still that of mother and/or wife. The Koran specifies the nature of the relationship between husband and wife: "Men are the protectors and maintainers of women, because God has given the one more {strength} than the other, and they support them from their means."

Muslim women's duty is to show obedience and respect for their husbands. It is therefore within this general framework that men's and women's roles are shaped. Gender ideologies, however, are far too complex to be attributed solely to religion, and in Egypt social and cultural conditions, influenced by Islamic belief and tradition, contribute to the demarcation of gender roles.

Egyptian society, like other Arab/Islamic societies, has been considered for a long time as patriarchal (Ahmed 1991, 2003, 2005a, and 2005b; Ciaccio and El-Shakry 1993; Sanders 1986). Like other Arab and Islamic societies, and more specifically agricultural ones, male births are preferred, which is indicative of the ascribed cultural values of males over females and perpetuates gender inequality. For example, girls are subject to increased restrictions of mobility and more participation in household chores as their age increases. Puberty for boys, however, expands male mobility outside the home and community. Although there are such restrictions for girls and freedom for boys, no significant gender difference is found between males and females in access to basic education in Egypt.

The early twenty-first century has witnessed an increased trend of wearing Islamic dress, especially among female adolescents and youth. More women, mostly younger ones, are wearing *hijab* (traditional head-covering garment) or modest Muslim dress with head, arms, and legs covered (*neqab*). As in several other Arab/Islamic countries, the majority of university Muslim female students in Egypt are wearing *hijab*, and to a lesser extent the *neqab*.

Adolescents are visibly concerned with physical attractiveness and become more concerned with clothing and style, especially in their late teens. Almost all boys are involved in sports activities, especially soccer, while very few girls are interested in sports.

Although household chores fall to the female, the increasing number of educated girls leads males to share in this responsibility. As a result, sharing in household responsibilities has become common among young couples in Egypt. Women in Egypt have taken an active role in education and in the economy along with their role as wife/mother.

The Self

Although loyalty to the family is prevalent in Egypt, recent years have witnessed an increase in individualistic trends among adolescents and youth, accompanied with an emergence of resentment of parental or societal authorities.

Several studies have focused on identity formation among Egyptians, and especially among adolescents and youth. One example is the study conducted by Morsy (2002) by using samples of male and female university students aged 21–24 years, and in which was found an identity crisis prevailing among students (20%). A positive correlation between identity crisis and depression was found. Female students suffered from depression in significantly higher numbers.

Several Egyptian studies have focused on the image of authority among adolescents (Safwat and El-Dousseky 1993). In one of these studies, secondary school students showed higher rebellious tendencies than their intermediate school counterparts. Secondary school female students, compared with their male peers, showed higher rebellious tendencies against fathers' (and not mothers') authority. No such sex difference was found among intermediate school students. Against expectations, a positive correlation between rebellion against parental authority and high socioeconomic status was found. In a similar Egyptian study but using male and female university students aged between 19 and 23 years from rural and urban areas, humanistic and social sciences college students, female, and rural students were more extreme in submissiveness to authority than the students from applied colleges, males, and urban area students. While rebellious tendencies were higher among applied colleges' students, no difference has been found between junior and senior students in their attitudes toward authority.

Egyptian studies on mutiny and mass violent events which took place in 1988 in Egypt (Safwat and El-Dousseky 1993) revealed a positive correlation between socioeconomic deprivation and awareness, with this deprivation among adolescents and youth in Egypt being the essential factor that has led to these mass violent events. This result

has repeatedly appeared in several Egyptian later studies (Maghawery 2002).

In an early study (cited in Safwat and El-Dousseky 1993) on social marginality, male adolescents were higher on extremeness (extreme violent/aggressive behavior or responses) compared with their adult peers, but no difference was found between female adolescents and female adults. In the same vein, another study reported higher levels of aggression among rural children, compared with urban ones.

Egyptians were known for a long time for their interest in Arab concerns and problems. At present, Egyptians, and adolescents and youth in particular, have become less concerned in foreigner issues, and have become more concerned with local events and problems such as economic hardships, unemployment, and local political issues.

Family Relationships

Family in Egypt is the essential source of socialization and Egyptians are widely known as family oriented (Ahmed 2005a). Marriage has special importance to Egyptians. They consider marriage as the most important event in their lives. Egyptians assume marriage is the main method to protect youth from any sacred relationships; moreover, marriage reinforces society's bonds. Marriage is a religious institution, and we can find many parts in the Koran, as well as prophetic instruction, that encourage marriage. There is no doubt that marriage customs indicate the society's culture, behavioral patterns, thoughts, and feelings. The number of families in Egypt reached 16 million in 2004, with 4.7 persons as the average family's size (*Al-Ahram*, February 16, 2005). Statistics (Abdel-Aety et al. 2000) reveal that urban, well-educated, younger women (under 40) tend to have fewer children (two to four), than rural, uneducated or less educated, and older women (40 and older), who have an average of five to eight. It seems that women's employment opportunities affect their fertility: fertility tends to be lower for better-educated women, working women with high incomes, and women in larger cities. Studies summarized by Ahmed (2005a) show that fertility tends to be higher in rural areas because of the characteristics of agricultural labor, which require and encourage large families; couples who work in the fields may wish for children, especially sons, to lessen their work load.

The large size of the Egyptian family (4.7 persons in average) has led, along with social and economic hardships, to several psychosocial problems. Several studies have focused on this issue (Salem 1990, cited in Abdel-Moety 2004). Salem's 1990 study employed 144 boys and girls aged between 10 and 13 years, and showed that a large number of siblings increases the aggressive behavior in the child, due to the increased demands in the family and the shorter time parents can spend with their children.

A divorced mother is entitled to custody rights in which she can keep her children with her until age 10 for boys and age 12 for girls. In 2005, Egypt's People's Assembly raised the age of custody to allow the divorced mother to keep her children until age 15, and until age of 21 upon children's request and the father's/husband's readiness to pay the custody's costs.

In the past, and still in some rural Egyptian areas, families tended to be extended. As a result of social, economic, and cultural changes, families, especially in urban areas, have become more nuclear. This shift has had dramatic consequences such as the lack of affection provided by grandparents, uncles, aunts, and other relatives, and the lack of security and affiliation (Ahmed 2005a). Siblings in Egyptian families are often close, with control of male children over female ones, especially in the rural areas. It was also noticed that marriages among relatives (cousin's daughter or son) have decreased over the last few decades. Due to the increase of education and knowledge, young generations became more aware about the dangerous consequences of marriage between relatives.

Like their counterparts in the third world countries, Egyptian families are facing several hardships and difficulties, which negatively affect the families' roles and duties. Among these difficulties are economic hardships and the changing role of the contemporary Egyptian family. Among the possible reasons is the emigration of about 2 million Egyptians to other Arab countries, and especially to the oil-producing Gulf Arab countries. Lesser numbers of Egyptians have emigrated to the West and especially the United States, Canada, Australia, the United Kingdom, France, Austria, and Italy (Ahmed 2003). This emigration, which took many forms and shapes, led to the overall improvement in the socioeconomic status of the emigrants and their families, and at the same caused a huge number of social, economic, and cultural problems and created a new situation in Egypt, such as the changing of the value system in the Egyptian society, the gradual decline of the family impact on their children, the absence of fathers/husbands and its negative impacts on the children's well-being, and the gradual increase of the number of women/wives who are responsible for their own families due to the absence or immigration or inability of

fathers/husbands, which was recently estimated as 28% of the total number of Egyptian families (*Al-Ahram*, August 1, 2005). Over the last three decades, Egyptians began to move out, especially to Gulf Arab oil-producing states, where they are seeking better conditions and trying to improve their lives. As a result, fathers/husbands must leave their families temporarily or permanently, in the interest of reducing expenses in the countries that receive the Egyptians, or as a result of rules and laws in these countries, which sometimes do not allow immigrants to bring their families with them, or do not welcome this sort of reunion.

Several Egyptian studies have investigated the impacts of father's/husband's immigration on the family and especially on children (Ahmed 2003, 2005a). Results of these studies showed: (1) wives of the migrant fathers/husbands became even more responsible simultaneously for caring for the children and for doing the household chores, which added extra burdens on their shoulders, and (2) negative changes have occurred in children's value systems and the structure of the family. Studies (Abdalla 1992; Abou-Elala 1994; Abou-Khair 1998) have shown that children of absent fathers are more likely to become aggressive and delinquent. It was also found that a father's/husband's absence negatively affects the psychosocial adjustment of both his wife and children. A positive relationship between children's perceived father figure and their self-esteem has been found. When fathers are absent, their influence on their children weakens dramatically. Having these negative impacts of father's/husband's immigration in mind, researchers concluded that Egyptian families are facing the following challenges: (1) the family is no longer the only source for socialization. Many other institutions in the society (e.g., school, sports clubs, social and cultural associations), are sharing the same duty, but they do not work consistently in the same direction with the family. As a result, family now has a defensive role and has to rebuild or correct ideas and behaviors acquired by children and adolescents through these institutions, instead of being able to build upon the right ideas and behaviors. (2) Most families are suffering from a lack of parenthood skills that enable them to raise their children in a healthy and positive way. Due to the dramatic decrease of the father's impact, raising children in current Egyptian families has become a mother's increasingly difficult duty. (3) Socialization in Egyptian families has to change from teaching children facts or knowledge to teaching them, instead, methods and ways of solving societal problems. Unfortunately, this new way of looking at socialization is unlikely to find widespread acceptance in the near future. (4) Contemporary Egyptian families are suffering from a severe imbalance between their incomes and their expenditures. Statistics show that Egyptian families devoted 56% of their incomes to food, 10% to housing, 9% to clothes, 7% to children's education, and only 4% to medical care. Such imbalance can negatively affect the role of family in the socialization process (Ahmed 2005a).

Recent statistics issued by the Central Authority for Statistics and Mobilization (CASM) in Egypt (*Al-Qabas*, August 4, 2005) showed that the number of marriages increased from 491,000 in 2003 to 519,000 in 2004, and the number of divorce cases decreased from 70,000 in 2002 to 60,000 in 2004. Scholars have showed concern for the high rate of divorce in Egypt, especially in the first five years of marriage and in particular in the first year of marriage, which reach about 40% of the marriage cases, and in which the couples were mostly young (*Al-Ahram*, March 4, 2005). Reasons for divorce are: man's/husband's decision, wife's request, financial reasons, and parents' interference. The CASM statistics indicated also that the number of men who are married to more than one wife decreased markedly during the last five decades and became less than one per thousand. In the same vein, the number of unmarried people, and especially girls, has increased dramatically during the last three decades and reached about 9 million, the majority of them well-educated females. It was argued that economic hardships, higher education, increased marriage costs, and media are the main reasons for the decrease in rates of marriage among Egyptians.

In order to help solve family conflicts and to reduce the divorce rates among Egyptians, special "family's courts" have been established. In these courts, psychologists and social workers were assigned to help couples to solve their conflicts before issuing a decision by a specialized judge.

In a study conducted by the Faculty of Medicine, Ain Shams University in Cairo (*Al-Ahram*, August 30, 2005), it was reported that children of divorced, separated, maladjusted, or addicted parents, were found to be higher in stuttering than children of normal and healthy families.

As in other places of the world, marital exchange in Egypt is based on gender roles. Men traditionally offer status, economic resources, and protection, while women are valued for their nurturance, childbearing ability, homemaking skills, and physical attractiveness. Recent changes in women's economic status (such as their increased participation in work and social life) give women, especially young ones, more bargaining power, while the decline in the value of bearing and raising children, housekeeping, and the greater availability of female sexual partners give men more bargaining power (Ahmed 2005a). Egyptian studies on mate selection in male and female university students (summarized by Ahmed 2005a) found that female respondents preferred for their future husband to have: respect for his wife, religious commitment, the ability to satisfy his wife's needs as a woman, and seriousness in his manner. Males preferred the following characteristics in their future wives: obedience, helpfulness, religious commitment, loyalty to her husband, and a nonauthoritative attitude.

Statistics (Ahmed 2005a) show that there are 3.5 million unmarried Egyptian women aged 30 years and older, a great many of whom are well educated. This situation has created great social concern, and some researchers are calling for a return to traditional matchmakers. The average marriage age is higher in urban areas than in the rural areas: 25 to 35 years for men and 20 to 30 years for women in urban areas, and 20 to 25 years for men and 16 to 18 years for women in the rural areas. Reasons for the higher marriage age among urban men and women, compared to their rural counterparts, include the following: urban men need first to finish their education and look for suitable work. Only then do most of them begin to think about forming their own family, which requires them to secure a suitable place (house) for marriage and the furniture and, moreover, the expenses for marriage requirements (*Shabka* and *Mahr*, or gift and dowry) and the marriage party. At present, young men—particularly in urban areas—need from 5 to 10 years after their graduation before they can meet these responsibilities. Urban girls, in turn, prefer to finish their education and then wait until the right person comes along. He, in turn, should be able to provide his future wife with good *Shabka* and *Mahr*, a suitable apartment or house, have a solid profession, and enjoy a good income. In the rural areas, where marriage expenses are much less, the parents of both the groom and bride usually provide their children with as much as possible so they can marry.

During the last three decades, and as a result of several social and economic hardships, official marriages and public weddings have become a major problem for young men and women. Consequently, they have declined in frequency and instead, secret marriages (consensual marriages—written or oral contracts between a man and a woman witnessed by two male adults and not registered officially) are often seen as a solution. However, a secret marriage has many negative aspects and consequences—legally, socially, and for the family itself (Ahmed 2005a). Among these negative aspects are: there is no social or official recognition available for this kind of marriage, the children are illegal, and secret marriages often create conflict between the couple (and especially girls) and their parents. A report (*Al-Ahram*, December 10, 2004) has estimated secret marriage cases as 3 million; 17.2% of these cases were university students, and 80% were between couples aged between 17 and 25 years. The report also indicated that 59% of young Egyptians believe that secret marriage is legal.

Friends and Peers/Youth Culture

Adolescents in Egypt, especially in urban areas, have less free time, as they are involved mostly in school activities. As a result, adolescents' friendship and aspiration have been negatively influenced. However, peers seem to have great influence on adolescents' behavior. According to Ibrahim and Soliman (2002), peers play a crucial role in reinforcing independency orientation and leadership behavior in Egyptian adolescents. M. S. Ahmed (2004) studied values, motives, and attitudes toward belonging to the peer groups in 330 general and technical secondary schools among Egyptian male students aged 15 to 16 years. Results showed that adolescents' peer groups were more interested in sports and the creation and revelation of secrets, while cultural activities have received less attention. Moral, patriotism/patriotic, ecological, and religious values were the most important values in adolescents' peer groups and were strongly related to the peer groups' activities. No significant correlation was found between students' academic achievement and their belonging to peer groups.

Love and Sexuality

Premarital sexuality is not socially, legally, or religiously accepted among Egyptians. Virginity is absolutely required for the bride who marries for the first time. Dating is neither welcomed nor accepted (Ahmed 2005a). However, young Egyptians, especially urban ones, often date secretly.

The maintenance of female chastity for preservation of the family, especially male honor, has acquired high cultural value in Egypt and other Middle Eastern societies. This has led to stringent controls on women's behavior and conduct. In Egypt, these have ranged from complete sexual segregation to female circumcision. Whereas Islam requires modesty and chastity for both sexes (Koran, Sura 24: 30), the women seem to bear the onus of the constraining cultural concept of "honor." Some authors have argued that underlying Islam and the Muslim tradition is an anxiety about female sexuality. Women's sexuality is perceived as being (hyper) active and in need of supervision because of its potential for creating *fitna* (*fitna* in Arabic means chaos and, alternatively, a beautiful woman, the implication being that women, through their seductiveness and beauty, have the potential capacity to create disorder and destruction in the community). Among the controls imposed upon women's sexuality in Egypt today is the insistence upon premarital virginity and circumcision.

Premarital virginity is considered a sine qua non for women in Egypt. This, coupled with the view that marriage is the most appropriate option for women, leads to an inordinate emphasis on the demonstration of virginity at the time of marriage. Thus, the concept of honor of a female and her entire family is contingent upon an intact hymen. Based on this concept of honor, displaying the bloody sheet after the wedding night (by the groom) or on its eve (by the groom and an expert midwife or female relative) was very common in rural areas; however, this tradition is rarely practiced anymore. This code of morality absolutely applies to women of all social classes. A sexual experience in the male's life is a source of pride, but in the life of women it is a source of shame.

The extent to which female chastity is valued is demonstrated also by the practice of female circumcision. Female circumcision still exists in Egyptian society despite governmental decrees and the efforts of civic society organization. According to some conservative figures, 75% of Egyptian women are circumcised. This figure may be as high as 98% among lower rural classes. Parental education appears to be an influential factor in determining whether a female child will be circumcised or not (Ahmed 1991; Ciaccio and El-Shakry 1993).

Circumcision can be divided into four categories. In first-degree circumcision, only the tip of the clitoris and a portion of the labia minora are removed. In second-degree circumcision, the labia minora and part of the clitoris are removed, and in third-degree circumcision, the entire labia minora and clitoris are removed. In fourth-degree or "pharaoh" circumcision, the labia minora, labia majora, and the clitoris are removed. In Egypt, the most commonly performed circumcisions are first- and second-degree. Girls between birth and the age of 11 are usually circumcised by midwives or, much less frequently, by trained doctors and nurses. The effects of female circumcision are numerous. In terms of immediate effects, it is not uncommon for the girls to suffer from shock, hemorrhaging, infection, inflammation, urinary disturbance, and severe pain, often due to the unhygienic nature of the procedure (Ahmed 1991; Ciaccio and El-Shakry 1993).

Despite the deleterious effects of circumcision, it continues to exist. It is perhaps the clearest example of the perpetuation of customs and traditions in Egypt in spite of governmental and religious sanctions. The primary manifest intent in circumcision is the preservation of female premarital virginity and chastity during marriage. Circumcision is believed to protect women from "losing their honor" by quelling their assumed incipient sexual desires. Many parents also fear that an uncircumcised daughter will be unable to marry. Other reasons for circumcision sometimes cited are cleanliness, the belief that the clitoris fertilizes a woman, and the erroneous belief that Islam requires it. Women are not expected to derive pleasure from sex; in fact, they are often physically prohibited from doing so. They are socialized to believe that their sexuality is something to be ashamed of and hidden. Indeed, this view is reinforced constantly throughout the childhood of females and is epitomized by circumcision (Ahmed 1991; Ciaccio and El-Shakry 1993).

Health Risk Behavior

Since the last decades of the twentieth century, a dramatic increase in psychological disorders among the Egyptian population has been witnessed, most likely due to the gradual increase of social and economic hardships with their negative consequences. Some sources (*Al-Ahram*, January 29, 2005) reported the following percentages: depression, 20%; high blood pressure, 20%; and psychological disturbances, 10%. As for adolescents and youth, several studies (cited in Ahmed and Khalil 2004) have shown that 54% of Egyptian male adolescents suffer psychological disturbances; male adolescents outnumber their female peers in psychosis, and secondary school students have higher levels of anxiety compared with their university counterparts. In a study seeking the prevalence of psychological disorders among adolescents in Egypt (Ahmed and Khalil 2004), 3,605 intermediate and secondary school male and female students aged between 11 and 19 years were asked to respond to some MMPI subscales: the Personal Friends Check List, Neuroticism, Scale for Depression, and State-Trait Anxiety Inventory. Results showed the following: (1) Male students, compared with their female counterparts, were significantly higher on general and positive flexibility, while female students were significantly higher than their male peers on schizophrenia, paranoia, anxiety state, depression, general and positive extremeness, and neuroticism. (2) Intermediate students (aged between 11 and 14 years) were significantly higher than secondary school students (aged between 15 and 19 years) on paranoia, psychopathic deviation, depression, and general and positive extremeness, while secondary school students were significantly higher on schizophrenia, anxiety state, indifference, negative extremeness, and neuroticism. (3) Results showed also that while age has influenced schizophrenia, psychopathic deviation, anxiety state, positive flexibility, and general and negative extremeness, gender influenced schizophrenia, paranoia, anxiety, depression, general positive and negative extremeness, general and positive flexibility, and neuroticism. Moreover, it was reported that educational level has influenced paranoia, psychopathic deviation, depression, general positive and negative extremeness, positive flexibility, and neuroticism. An interaction between gender and educational level was found to influence other variables.

While mental illness may not differ reliably in urban and rural areas, drug addiction is much more common in urban than in rural areas. Recent statistics (*Al-Gomhuria*, May 20, 2005) estimated drug addiction among children and adolescents (with age less than 15 years) as 10% of the total of children. Another study (*Al-Ahram*, May 20, 2005) showed an increase in psychological disturbances such as depression, emotional disorders, aggressive tendencies, and sleep disorders among 18- to 30-year-old individuals. Obviously, this can be accounted for by the overly loud and stressful conditions in the cities. Some other explanations include: greater availability of drugs and liquor, and better treatment of drug addicts and hence more reporting of these addictions.

An acute societal problem in Egypt is cigarette smoking. Statistics (*Al-Qabas*, March 17, 2005) show that the number of smokers in Egypt has increased during the past 25 years and became 18 million, 52% of them aged between 12 and 30 years. It was also reported that while Egyptians spend 30.4% of their income on cigarettes, they devote only 1.1% of this income to cultural issues.

The suicide rate has increased dramatically in the early twenty-first century. Three thousand cases of suicide were registered in 2003. They were mostly from urban areas, 25% of them were females, and 40% were less than 25 years old (*Al-Ahram*, January 29, 2005).

Traffic accidents in Egypt constitute a serious common concern. The number of these accidents has increased dramatically over the last 20 years as a result of increasing the number of cars and the population as well. In 2004, the number of death casualties and wounded resulting from traffic accidents reached 19,000 dead and 29,000 wounded, the majority of which were aged between 25 and 40 years (*Rose el-Youssef*, August 7–13. 2004).

Concerning the physical health of Egyptian adolescents, a study (*Al-Ahram*, September 29, 2005) found that 13% of intermediate and secondary school students aged between 12 and 18 years were suffering from high blood pressure, and 45% of them have been diagnosed as overweight.

Egypt considered the period 1989–1999 as the Egyptian Child Decade; however, street children in Egypt still form a societal problem. Statistics (*Al-Ahram*, May 13, 2005; Morsy 2001) estimate the number of street children in Cairo alone as 100,000 boys and girls, with a mean age of 13 years (25% of them aged less than 13 years, 66% aged between 13 and 16 years, and 10% aged 17 years or more). The reasons for this phenomenon are: broken homes by separation, divorce, or the death of one or both of the parents; family's lower socioeconomic status; parents' unemployment; children's abuse by parents or one of them; and child's failure in school. In a study using 8- to 17-year-old street boys and girls (Ghanem 2003), boys and girls displayed disturbances in self-concept; higher levels of neuroticism, extroversion, and lying; and higher rebellious and aggressive trends toward authority. Most of the related studies have found a link between the phenomenon of street children and the increasing amount of violent/aggressive, deviant, and criminal behavior. Unfortunately, as was noticed by local experts, the ways used in treating such phenomenon were not sufficient.

Education

In Egypt education is compulsory between the ages 6 and 14 years; however, more males than females begin and continue their primary education. Although the percentage of females enrolled at all levels of the educational cycle has increased consistently since 1952, their enrollment still lags behind that of males (Ciaccio and El-Shakry 1993). Nevertheless, Egypt has achieved reasonable progress in the field of education. In 1990, the rate of children at school age (6 years) who enrolled in primary school was 96% for boys and 89% for girls (Abdel-Atey et al. 2000). That the education of girls was increased over the last few decades can be seen in the number of enrolled girls, especially in primary schools: girls accounted for 36% of all enrolled pupils in 1960, 44% in 1990, and 47% in 2000. As for other educational levels, recent statistics show that girls make up 49% of all students in secondary schools and 46% in the 15 governmental (state) universities, nine private universities, and a huge number of technical colleges and institutes. Ninety-six percent and 93% of all girls are enrolled in primary and secondary education, respectively, compared with 100% and 98% of boys (UNICEF 2005). Only 81% of boys and 80% of girls finished primary school successfully. In the secondary schools, 38% of girls and 62% of boys are enrolled. The total number of Egyptian students in all education levels reached 18.5 million in 2004–2005, among them 3.5 million in university and college education, "or 91.8% of the population in this age category" (*Al-Ahram*, October 12, 2005). Other statistics show that the number for female enrollment in higher education has markedly improved in recent years. Female students formed 51.7% of the total number of the university students' body in the academic year 2004–2005 (*Al-Ahram*, April 29, 2005), and constituted half of the fresh students enrolled in the faculties of medicine in the academic year 2004–2005 (*Al-Gomhuria*, May 19, 2005).

There are two kinds of education in Egypt: governmental and private. The private education includes Arabic schools (where the language of instruction is Arabic, and English is introduced as a foreign language) and language schools where nearly all subjects are instructed in English and to a lesser extent in French or German. The number of private schools has increased markedly during the last few decades. In 1997, the number of governmental schools in Egypt reached 15,028, with about 7 million male and female students with a class capacity of 44.8 students; the number of Arab and language private schools reached 1,130, with 533,403 male and female students enrolled with a class capacity of 38.6 students (Beshour 2004). Coeducation existed only in the kindergarten level, some governmental primary schools, in private schools—especially language private schools—and in all governmental and private Egyptian universities except Al-Azhar University. Other kinds of education available for Egyptian male and female adolescents include: technical secondary schools, secondary schools for gifted (talented) students, sports secondary schools, and military intermediate and secondary schools.

One severe common problem in Egypt today is private lessons. Students in all educational levels tend to get help in study by hiring private teachers in order to compete, especially in the secondary school level. A survey conducted in Egypt (*Al-Ahram*, September 11, 2005) showed that 69% of Egyptian pre-college students receive private lessons; 41% of the parents help their children to study and to complete their homework. It was also found that Egyptian families spent about 15 billion Egyptian pounds for private lessons, which negatively affected the rate of development in Egypt during the last two decades.

Due to the higher rate of unemployment in Egypt (11% of the total labor force, 78% of them university and secondary school graduates), an increasing number of male and female adolescents tend more and more to seek possible ways to ensure future work. In this context, 12,000 male and female adolescents aged between 14 and 18 years who successfully finished their intermediate education joined training centers—the Vocational Training and Productivity Authority, and the Ministry of Industry (established in 1956)—which cover the whole country, in order to be trained and qualified as specialized technicians (*Al-Gomhuria*, August 26, 2005). In 2005, the first group of female technicians graduated.

In the rural areas in Egypt illiteracy was estimated in 1986 as 61% (45% for males, and 76% for females). Statistics from 2004 (*Al-Ahram*, February 16, 2005) showed the illiteracy rate had decreased to 26.8% of the total number of population older than 10 years, with higher rates in rural areas, and especially among rural females. However, international sources estimated illiteracy in Egypt as 40%.

Work

The number of people in the labor force in Egypt reached 22 million, 22% of them female. The rate of unemployment in Egypt was estimated in 2004 as 10.57% (or 2,238,000 million) of the total adult labor force, 78% of the unemployed are university and secondary school graduates, and about two-thirds of them were females (*Al-Ahram*, February 16, 2005). Several psychological and sociological studies have concluded a strong positive correlation between unemployment and violence, especially among the young unemployed (Maghawery 2002).

In order to qualify the rural girls, the International Population Council, in collaboration with the National Council for Childhood and Motherhood in Egypt, developed a special program to train and qualify 5,000 rural girls aged between 13 and 14 years who dropped out from their education. The aim is to provide them with the required skills that could enable them to find work easily, and to help to avoid the early marriage.

Usually, male and female adolescents in rural areas help their families in agricultural work and household affairs, especially during school vacations. In poorer rural families, while male adolescents either help their family by working in the field or seeking part-time work after the school day, female adolescents are usually involved in helping their mothers in household chores.

Egypt is among the countries that have seen, especially during the last three or four decades, an increasing number of working children and adolescents. In 1993, it was estimated that about 7% (or one million) of all Egyptian children aged between 6 and 12 years, went to work (Morsy 2001). More recent reports (*Al-Ahram*, February 6, 2005) showed that more than one million children and adolescents participated in the work market in Egypt, 35% of them aged between 15 and 24 years. Several studies have been conducted during the last 10 years that focused on the social and psychological impact of children's and adolescents' work. Mahmoud (1997) compared working and nonworking children aged 10 to 16 years and found that working children experienced less satisfaction and exhibited poorer psychological adjustment. Mahmoud's results are in line with the results of an earlier study on children's work by El-Deba (1993), in which it was reported that working children and adolescents, compared with nonworking peers, were higher on maladjustment, anxiety, depression, and aggressive behavior.

Media

Egyptian children, adolescents, and youth have access to several local TV channels with a wide variety of programs, series, and movies in Arabic and/or English. Satellite is widely used, especially by well-to-do families. A study was conducted by Al-Kurdy (2002) using a sample of children and adolescents aged between 9 and 15 years, which found that 95% of respondents watch TV programs for five to six hours daily with an increase in watching time coinciding with the increase in age. Boys tend more to watch action and violent programs and movies, while girls tend more to watch comic and social programs. While boys tend more to identify themselves with Western TV series or movie stars, girls are more likely to identify themselves with the local stars. Parents encourage their children, especially male—directly or indirectly—to watch TV programs instead of going out. Parents believe that watching TV programs at home is a safe way for children to spend their free time. On the other hand, the high rate of TV watching and the increased time spent in watching have led to negative consequences among the adolescents and youth. Among these consequences are low academic achievement, weakness in concentration, lack of the proper and healthy interaction with family members and friends, and a decrease in reading rate.

In a study conducted by L. Abu-Laghed and entitled "Dramas of Nationhood: The Politics of Television in Egypt" (*Al-Ahram*, October 7, 2005), it was indicated that although Egyptian Television, since its establishment in the early 1960s, has tried to reinforce the feelings of nationhood among the Egyptians, the message/mission has been overwhelmingly changed due to the changes in social, economic, cultural, and political circumstances which occurred gradually in Egypt since the late 1970s. The message/mission became more and more about entertainment.

In a survey conducted by the General Authority for Developing Technology Industry in Egypt (*Al-Ahram*, August 25, 2005), it was reported that more than one million family homes are connected with the Internet. The number of Internet users was estimated at 2.5 million, 24% of them are less than 18 years old. It was also estimated that another half million children and adolescents use the Internet in their schools. The survey reported that entertainment and chatting with friends constitute 28% and 18%, respectively, of time spent in using the Internet. The survey concluded that in most cases there is no control of children's and adolescents' Internet use, which could lead to serious problems. Several studies have been conducted in Egypt on the use of the Internet, especially among adolescents and youth. In one of these studies (Abdel-Salam 1998), results showed a wide diversity in Internet use among Egyptian adolescents and youth, such as getting scientific information (61%), art (40.8%), sports (26.2%), political and economic information (18.8%), women and child issues, and commerce (14% for each). The majority of subjects (73%) reported that they use the Internet at home, 14% in the work office, and 7% in an Internet café. Another study (Taie 2000) explored

use of the Internet by adolescents and youth in five Arab countries (Egypt, Saudi Arabia, the UAE, Kuwait, and Bahrain) and showed that 72% of the subjects use the Internet regularly. The average time spent per week was as follows: 2 hours in Egypt, 3 hours in the UAE, 4 hours in both Kuwait and Bahrain, and 6 hours in Saudi Arabia. Results also showed that males tend to use the Internet more extensively than their female counterparts. Finally, results indicated that subjects tend to use the Internet more intensively at night time compared with the day time. In another Egyptian study (Rabie 2003) on Internet addiction or pathological Internet use or compulsive Internet disorder among 18- to 21-year-old male and female students, it was found that Internet addiction is more common among males than females, more common among students who live with their parents and who possess a computer at home than in the case of students whose parents are dead and the students who do not possess a computer at home. The principal motive for addicted students was acquiring general information.

Since the mid-1990s, a large number of Internet cafés have appeared in Egypt, especially in larger cities such as Cairo and Alexandria, which are attended by young males and females. These cafés provide Internet facilities, allowing for the sending of e-mail and browsing the Internet.

Arabic and Western music is widely known and liked among Egyptian male and female adolescents. Young Egyptians, especially in urban areas and in well-to-do families, show more interest in listening to Western music (mostly American/English and French). In addition, a gradually increasing interest in listening to Oriental (classical Arabic) music is observable among young people.

Politics and Military

In general, Egyptian adolescents and youth do not tend to participate in political activities. In Egypt, all people, male or female, have to register their name in voting records as they reach 18 years of age. By law also, they should participate in the election processes for the presidency and parliament members. At the age of 30, each Egyptian male/female has the right to be nominated for parliament membership election, and at the age of 40 for the presidency. Although no obstruction concerning the females' participation in political life could be found, it is a fact that women's participation in political life is very weak, and as a result, the number of elected female representatives in the Egyptian People's Assembly (2000–2005) reached only 11 (or 2%) among 454 representatives. Moussa (2001) investigated the relationship between political participation and some psychological variables in a sample of male and female university students in Egypt, aged between 20 and 26 years. Results showed that females were lower than their male counterparts in political participation. Also, higher political participation males and females, compared with their lower political participation peers, were found to be higher on aggression, assertiveness, social responsibility, dominancy, internal locus of control, ego strength, and ambiguity tolerance, but lower on dogmatism.

In practice, adolescents and youth do not share efficiently in political life in Egypt. A recent study (*Akhabar el-Yom*, April 9, 2005) showed that 52% of the total number of Egyptian adolescents and youth are not registered in the election's records as possible voters, 57% of the registered adolescents and youth do not practice their right and duty in the voting process when required; 71% of adolescents and youth have no election card, so they are not able to practice their right and duty. The study also showed that 88% of Egyptian adolescents and youth do not belong (affiliate) to any of the existing legal parties, and 74% of Egyptian adolescents and youth do not have enough information about the legally existing political parties in Egypt. The study concluded that developing special programs for ensuring effective participation by adolescents and youth in the political life in Egypt is a must. In this vein, a study conducted by the Public Opinion Unit of Ain Shams University in Cairo on 1,017 educated women aged between 20 and 50 years (*Al-Ahram*, April 29, 2005), showed that 44% of the subjects have no time to follow politics or the programs of political parties in Egypt; 43% believed that dealing with politics will cause them trouble; and 33% reported that a woman has to concentrate on her household only.

Some studies on political socialization among Egyptian youth (*Al-Ahram*, January 17, 2005) found that 95% of the subjects are not familiar with the Egyptian political parties, 90% have no awareness of globalization; 88% do not belong to political parties; 57% do not participate in elections; 51% are not registered in voting lists; and only 8% consider political participation as a patriotic duty.

Egyptian adolescents and youth became strongly influenced by new ideas, especially in urban areas, due to globalization and the openness policy since the mid-1970s. Political and religious parties and movements make the most of adolescents' and youth's readiness to adopt new ideas. These parties and movements have already attracted a huge number of adolescents and youth. An example is the increased number of young Egyptians who took part in the political demonstrations in Egypt during the 2005 presidency and parliamentary elections. Interestingly enough, in Egypt's first ever multicandidate presidential elections in September 2005, many male and female adolescents and youth expressed their opinions and became involved, for the first time in the modern history of Egypt, in the political process. This participation of adolescents and youth took many forms, including joining the political parties and participating actively in political demonstrations organized by the government's supporters or by antigovernment such as the *Kefiah* (Enough) Movement in Cairo and other cities. Moreover, some children and adolescents whose fathers have been jailed for political reasons formed a small movement under the title "*Kefiah* Children."

Unique Issues

One of new phenomena facing Egyptian adolescents and youth is the increased number of males and females who are reported absent from their homes. Some studies (Farag 2003) indicate that among adolescents and youth leaving their homes, a great number of males and females escaped from home due to several reasons, among them broken homes, divorce of parents, abuse or maltreatment by parents or relatives, influence of peers, insufficient education, and economic hardships.

The Egyptian Scout Organization is the first and the oldest Arab organization, and was established more than 70 years ago. Later, similar organizations have been founded in Kuwait, Jordan, Tunis, Oman, UAE, Palestine, Yemen, Sudan, Libya, and Morocco, which formed—together with Egypt—the Arab Scout Organization (ASO). In July 2005, the ASO held the sixth Arab Forum for Youth Awareness, aimed at increasing awareness among youth about the dangers of smoking, addiction, traffic accidents, violence, and sexually transmitted diseases, in addition to other dangers that youth are facing, today noting that the local scout organization aims at giving advice to youth through their fellow youth of similar age groups (*Kuwait Today*, July 27, 2005).

The first SOS Village was established in Cairo in 1977. Another two villages have been founded in Alexandria and Tanta (Nile Delta). They accept homeless psychologically and physically healthy children between the ages of 2 and 6 years. SOS villages provide children with psychological and medical care, and children can join the general education system until 18 years of age.

Egypt has more than 15,000 nongovernmental societies and associations that offer services to different sectors of the population, among them children, adolescents, and the aged, and cover a variety of activities.

Personal observations, newspapers articles, and other published materials indicate an increasingly strong trend to use special language among adolescents and youth. Peer influence, the desire for independence, and as a sign for rebellious behavior against the authority of others such as parents, teachers, could be reasons for such a trend.

RAMADAN A. AHMED

References and Further Reading

Abdalla, J. G. 1992. Hostility as a function of father absence. *Psychological Studies, Egypt* 2(2):351–69.

Abdel-Atey, E., M. Bayyumi, M. Hassan, et al. 2000. *Family sociology*. Alexandria: Dar el-Maarefa al-Gamaiaa (in Arabic).

Abdel-Moety, H. M. 2004. *Family climate (atmosphere) and children personality*. Cairo: Dar al-Qahara (in Arabic).

Abdel-Salam, N. 1998. Patterns and motives of Egyptians to use internet: A pilot study. *Proceedings of the 4th Scientific Conference of the Faculty of Media, Cairo University, Egypt "Media and Youth Issues"* (pp. 85–119), May 25–27, 1998 (in Arabic).

Abou-Elala, M. A. M. 1994. *Father absence and its relation to the psychological adjustment of their mothers (wives) and children at the age of adolescence*. Unpublished M.A. thesis, Institute for Higher Studies on Childhood, Ain Shams University, Egypt (in Arabic).

Abou-el-Kheir, M. M. S. 1998. Perceived father figure and self-esteem among college students. *Psychological Studies, Egypt* 8(2–3):419–52 (in Arabic).

Ahmed, M. S. 2004. Adolescents' attitudes and motives towards belonging to the peer groups and their relationship to psychological values, activities, and academic achievement: An empirical study on general and technical secondary education students. *Egyptian Journal of Psychological Studies* 14(14):297–357 (in Arabic).

Ahmed, R. A. 1991. Women in Egypt and the Sudan. In *Women in cross-cultural perspective*. L. L. Adler (ed.). pp. 106–32. New York: Praeger.

Ahmed, R. A. 2003. Egyptian migrations. In *Migration: Immigration and emigration in international perspective*. L. L. Adler and U. P. Gielen (eds.). pp. 311–327. Westport, Conn.: Praeger.

Ahmed, R. A. 2005a. Egyptian families. In *Families in global perspective*. J. L. Roopnarine and U. P. Gielen (eds.). pp. 151–68. Boston: Allyn and Bacon.

Ahmed, R. A. 2005b. Manifestations of violence in Arab schools and procedures to reducing it. In *Violence in schools: Cross-national and Cross-cultural perspectives*. F. L. Denmark (ed.). pp. 207–36. New York: Springer.

Ahmed, R. A. and E. A. Khalil, (2004). Common psychological disorders in male and female students of intermediate and secondary school students in Menoufia Governorate, Egypt. *Egyptian Journal of Psychological Studies* (Egypt), 14(43), 1–54 (in Arabic).

Akhabar el-Youm. An Egyptian weekly newspaper. 2005. Sat., April 9 (in Arabic).

Al-Ahram. An Egyptian daily newspaper. 2004. Fri., December. 10 (in Arabic).

Al-Ahram. An Egyptian daily newspaper. 2005. Mon., January 17; Sat., January 29; Thurs., February 3; Sun., February 6; Wed., February 16; Sat., March 4; Fri., April 29; Fri., May 13; Fri., May 20; Sun., July 24; Mon., August 1; Thurs., August 25; Thurs., August 30; Thurs., September 2; Sun., September 11; Thurs., September 29; Fri., October 7; Mon., October 12 (in Arabic).

Al-Gomhuria. An Egyptian daily newspaper. 2005. Thurs., May 19; Fri., May 20; Fri., August 26 (in Arabic).

Al-Kurdy, M. 2002. TV channels and satellite and forming the attitudes towards violence in children. *Proceedings of the 4th Annual Conference on "Social and Criminological Dimensions of Violence in the Egyptian Society"* (vol. 1, pp. 173–212), April 20–24, 2005. Cairo: The NCSCR (in Arabic).

Al-Qabas. A Kuwaiti daily newspaper. 2005. Thurs., March 17; Thurs., August 4 (in Arabic).

Beshour, M. 2004. The Arab children education. *Journal on Arab Children* (Kuwait) 5(20):52–72 (in Arabic).

Ciaccio, N. V., and O. S. El-Shakry. 1993. Egypt. In *International handbook on gender roles*. L. L. Adler (ed.). pp. 46–58. Westport, Conn.: Greenwood.

El-Deba, N. R. S. 1993. *Children's work and its relation to psychological adjustment: A field study on a sample of working children*. Unpublished M.A. thesis, Institute for Higher Studies on Childhood, Ain Shams University, Egypt (in Arabic).

Farag, T. S. M. 2003. Female adolescents' leaving out (escape) the family: A psychological view. In *Social and communicative skills: Psychological research studies*. T. S. M. Farag (ed.). pp. 295–348. Cairo: Dar Ghareeb (in Arabic).

Ghanem, M. H. 2003. Self concept of street children and its relation to personality traits and their perception of authority figures. *Arabic Studies in Psychology* 2 (4):181–238 (in Arabic).

Ibrahim, F. F., and A. S. Soliman. 2002. The role of peers in reinforcing independency orientation and leadership behavior in adolescents. In *Studies on the psychology of development: Childhood and adolescence*. F. F. Ibrahim and A. S. Soliman. Vol. 1, pp. 219–85. Cairo: Zahraa el-Shark Bookshop (in Arabic).

Kuwait Today. 2005. Wed., July 27.

Maghawery, M. 2002. Unemployment and violence: An analytical study of the relationship between unemployment and stealing from an economic perspective. *Proceedings of the 4th Annual Conference on "Social and Criminological Dimensions of Violence in the Egyptian Society"* (vol. 2, pp. 812–58), April 20–24, 2005. Cairo: The NCSCR (in Arabic).

Mahmoud, M. 1997. *A study on the relationship between job satisfaction and psychological adjustment among working children*. Unpublished M.A. thesis, Institute for Higher Studies on Childhood, Ain Shams University, Egypt (in Arabic).

Morsy, A. M. M. 2001. *Street children phenomena: The concept, preference, responsible variables, risks, and efforts: A cross-cultural vision*. Cairo: el-Nahada al-Mesria Bookshop (in Arabic).

EGYPT

Morsy, A. M. M. 2002. *Identity crisis in adolescence and the need for psychological counseling.* Cairo: el-Nahada al-Mesria Bookshop (in Arabic).

Moussa, R. A. A. 2001. *Political participation: Political participation and its relation with some psychological variables in a sample of male and female university students.* Cairo: Dar el-Fikr al-Arabi (in Arabic).

Rabie, H. B. 2003. Internet addiction on the basis of some variables. *Psychological Studies (Egypt)* 13(4):555–80 (in Arabic).

Rose el-Youssef. An Egyptian weekly magazine. 2004. August 7–13 (in Arabic).

Safwat, A., and M. I. El-Dousseky. 1993. Contributions of Egyptian psychology research in study prejudice. *Psychological Studies (Egypt)* 3(4):429–77 (in Arabic).

Sanders, J. L. 1986. Egyptian and American university students' attitudes toward parents and family. *Journal of Social Psychology* 126(40):459–63.

Taie, S. A. 2000. Using Internet in the Arab world: A field study on sample of Arab youth. *The Egyptian Journal for Public Opinion Research* 4:33–68 (in Arabic).

UNICEF. 2005. *The status of children in the world.* Cairo, Egypt: Al-Ahram Press (in Arabic).

EL SALVADOR

See **CENTRAL AMERICA: COSTA RICA, EL SALVADOR, NICARAGUA**

ERITREA

Background Information

Eritrea is a small country located in the Horn of Africa, bordering the Red Sea, Djibouti, Ethiopia, and Sudan. Eritrea as its stands today was created via colonization by Italy in 1890, followed by its status as a British protectorate in 1941 and subsequent federation with Ethiopia by the United Nations in 1952. Between 1961 and 1991 Eritrea waged a long armed struggle for independence. Eritrea formally joined the UN as an independent state in 1993 after a popular referendum.

Eritrea's population structure is typical of a developing society coming out of conflict, which is characterized by fewer people in old age and a growing number of adolescents and children. The adult population is smaller compared to the population of dependent children and adolescents. There is a larger female adult population than male as a result of the long history of war and migration which disproportionately affected the male population.

Eritrea has nine officially recognized ethno-linguistic groups, each displaying distinct linguistic and cultural features. They are the Tigrinya, Tigre, Saho, Afar, Kunama, Nara, Bilen, Rashaida, and Hidareb. The population is divided between Christians and Moslems. The majority of Christians are of the orthodox or Coptic faith, which stretches back to the fourth century. There are also dispersed communities of Catholic and Protestant denominations, and a growing number of recent Pentecostal and evangelical religious movements. The varied ethnic and religious communities also inhabit different geographic regions and are involved in numerous economic activities such as farming, irrigation agriculture, nomadic and agro-pastoralism, and fishing.

Period of Adolescence

In the Eritrean context, when speaking of adolescence as a separate period in one's life course, we need to make a distinction between adolescence from a cultural perspective that is specific to each ethno-linguistic group, and a national perspective that is urban in nature. Different ethno-cultural communities have a variety of indigenous conceptions of adolescence and adulthood. Similar to other African societies, adolescence is viewed as a transitional stage out of childhood, poised for an adulthood that lies ahead. As such, it is characterized with marked social and ritual expectations and ceremonies. In traditional practice, rites of passage serve as a process whereby adolescents enter adulthood.

The ritual ceremony differs across ethnic groups, but in most cases it tends to focus more on male adolescents. For example, among the Nara ethnic group, when boys and girls reach the age of 14, a ceremony is held to celebrate their manhood and womanhood respectively. After this ritual, the youngsters are considered full adults capable of consulting with elders and taking their own initiatives. On the other hand, in the Bilen cultural group, boys until 16 years old are considered young persons or children. At the age of 16, adolescent males participate in rituals that ascertain their rights and duties of manhood. If a boy reaches 16 but does not celebrate the rites of passage, he will never be involved in society's most valued events. This transformation process is called in Bilen *Mshmqal* or *Mwtaq* and the one who is transferred to adulthood is called *Mendelay*. Similarly, among the Saho ethnic group, when a boy reaches 16 years of age, families are obliged to celebrate the process of transformation to being a man. Before he is 16 years old, the young man has to cut his hair differently from those who have been through the ceremony—that is, cut hair only on the sides, *Alibabe*.

However, at the national level, adolescence does not appear to be an exclusively marked social stage. Entry into adulthood generally occurs at 18 years of age, as exemplified by graduation from high school and joining the national service, which is required of all young citizens upon coming of age. The English word "adolescence" is used in family planning, demographic, and other policy discourses, but there seems not to be a unique local term and stage in the national language that distinguishes adolescence from young adulthood. Rather, the ages 15 to 35 are usually considered as those encompassing a broad category termed "youth." The only national organization for adolescent and young adults, the National Union of Eritrean Youth and Students (NUEYS), considers those between the ages of 15 and 35 its potential members. Secondary school completion and the immediate national service required are the turning points in terms of independence of adolescents and status of adulthood. However, it is difficult to regard the stage of adolescence as a separate developmental and societal stage with distinct roles and expectations at a national level.

Beliefs

The Eritrean belief system that determines adolescent values is based in religious and secular orientations. The secular one is associated with the collective nationalist political culture that has grown over the years of struggle for liberation of the country and still is central in the socialization of adolescents. This puts more emphasis on collective social values such as sacrifice, patriotism, and national service. This requires adolescents and young adults to care more for national values than their own individual goals. However, as Eritrea ages as an independent state and demands from adolescents and young adults also grow, young people are faced with the difficulty of reconciling the collectivist ethos of nationalism and planning for their individual future prospects. Thus, the nationalistic tradition is at a crossroads, as it is less appealing to young people, especially those from towns and cities.

However, adolescents are not just recipients of national values. Families and immediate communities play a significant role in socializing adolescents to norms and values of these communities. Family connections play a large role in everyday lives of people, and extended families are still important in decisions that affect adolescents, such as the choosing of a marriage partner. Among rural Christians, for example, the church is the center of every village. In rural areas, adolescents are socialized to contribute to the well-being of the community, participate in communal labor, and defend the community's values.

In terms of religious belief systems, both the historical religions of Islam and Christianity as well as the fast growing evangelical and Pentecostal groups share the same conservative and collectivist social orientation. Although there are no studies that show the frequency of church or mosque visitation, young adults tend to be infrequent visitors compared to adults and old people. However, there is a growing adolescent membership in the new religious movements of the Pentecostal or other reformers who come out of the traditional Orthodox and Catholic churches. Adolescence is the prime time when many join churches and cults. Sometimes, adolescent believers of such faith tend to be overly conservative in their social lives and get in trouble with family members and the dominant churches. Outsiders are less knowledgeable of the differences among many religious groups in terms of beliefs and denominations, and instead make judgments based more on how these young followers behave in public, usually characterized by using many references to God in greetings, a very loyal demeanor, an ascetic lifestyle, and a strong group orientation. Some ethnographic examples have argued that social and family problems make some adolescents more likely to be members of new churches as they provide them with a sense of purpose and a community of peers. Although there are no accurate figures about the distribution of the new churches, most members tend to be adolescents and young adults.

Gender

Gender roles and expectations have been transformed in Eritrea as a result of the long armed struggle for national liberation. During the war for independence, 30% of the Eritrean liberation army was composed of women, who served in fighting units, supporting service, and leadership positions. This has transformed Eritrean gender relations and expectations; the nationalist tradition, however, sometimes conflicts with traditional gender role expectations. For example, the national military service requires both men and women to take military training and serve in the national army. While this is taken as an affirmation of the equality and empowerment of women by some, it is regarded as a rejection of traditional ways of life by others. Many rural communities, mostly of the Islamic faith, have vehemently rejected sending their daughters for military training, and in many instances urban women have hastened marriage and childbearing to avoid recruitment into national service. Prolonged stays in the military and stories of abuse of young females by military officers have contributed to the negative view of female youth serving in the national military.

Masculine and feminine stereotyping still exists in almost every ethnic culture. Men in most cases are encouraged to be strong, aggressive, fearless, and assertive. They are expected to be analytical and curious to ask questions and even to challenge authority. Women, however, are expected to be soft, emotional, timid, shy, intuitive, and well behaved. Females are not supposed to ask questions or challenge assumption. Family socialization still transfers such gender expectation of masculine and feminine patterns. Moreover, social expectations of marriage put a lot of pressure on female adolescents to start becoming aware of their beauty. Ideals of beauty and image in Eritrea are influenced by Western style, urban trends, and rural traditions that are specific to cultural groups. Beauty is based on different criteria some of which are skin complexion, teeth, height, hairstyle, and physical fitness. Traditionally, adolescents of different cultural communities use body tattoos on the forehead, arms, legs, and gums as signs of beauty and social status. Among the Christian Tigrinya ethnic group of highland Eritrea, a cross-shaped tattoo on the forehead was traditionally a common beauty marker for female adolescents, although it is considered increasingly unattractive due to the influence of modernity and the trend toward urbanization.

Among the Saho, dress style and body decoration are used as markers of life course transitions such as marriage and puberty. The way Saho females wear their jewelry differs with age and social context; for instance, it is forbidden for married women to wear jewelry in the same style unmarried girls do. Body decorations vary based on marital status (single, married, or widowed). Unmarried women decorate their bodies with copper jewelry, and married women wear gold or silver jewelry. Generally, the ideally beautiful female is expected to be of medium height, with long hair, and of average weight. However, there is a slight difference across ethnic groups. Today, there is more focus on ways of dressing and presenting oneself than on natural endowments as urban adolescents, both male and female, are typical consumers of popular culture and fashion. Thus, beauty is measured on the basis of fashion dress, haircut, makeup, and body structure in terms of less weight and more height.

Another practice that cross-culturally affects female adolescents is circumcision. Female circumcision is still a common practice in both urban and rural areas of Eritrea, across regions, ethnic groups, and religious groups. As a matter of trend, younger females are less likely to be circumcised than older ones, but the practice is still highly prevalent. As of 2002, 78% of teenagers aged 15 to 19 were circumcised, whereas among those aged 20 to 24 the

figure is higher, at 88%. Husbands of teenage and young mothers tend to object more to the practice of circumcision than other men from older cohorts. However, such objections are not significant enough to change the overwhelming implicit acceptance of the practice. The practice still exists in spite of national and international campaigns for its elimination, given that it poses a health risk for women during pregnancy and birth. It is also considered by its opponents as a human rights violation.

The Self

Social markers that can be regarded as common nationally to all adolescents in the construction of their self are education and participation in national programs designed to integrate adolescents of different background together. High school students are involved in summer work programs every year for approximately 30 days, which takes them to different parts of the country, along with other adolescents, to participate in forestry, construction, or literacy programs. Such programs help adolescents create a sense of themselves by experiencing life away from family members, meeting people from other cultures, and learning new ways of life. For many, this experience helps them develop a sense of Eritrean-ness as well as their particular cultural heritage. For example, university students who have been to several summer work programs and then military service explain that their participation has instilled in them a sense of collective identity and nationalism as well as appreciation of their backgrounds once they meet people of different languages and cultures.

Family Relationships

The Eritrean family system is in the process of social transformation as a result of many factors. War, migration, and urbanization are changing the extended family in Eritrea. Urban Eritrean families do not resemble families in other African countries in their composition. The majority of urban families are nuclear families—that is, spouses and children—with only one-fourth of all families composed of extended families. An urban survey during Eritrea's peacetime in 1996–1997 found out that a "typical" urban household does not really exist, as many features characterize families. The urban population in Eritrea in general is characterized by out-migration of males and a high fertility rate.

Urban households also tend to have a high dependency rate. Eritrea in general, and urban areas in particular, has a high number of households that are headed by females. The surveys found out that 47% of households were female-headed. Among these female-headed households, 30% were married with absent husbands; the majority were widowed and the rest were divorced. Compared to other poor countries, there are more female-headed households in both urban and rural areas, mostly due to war and migration that affected the male population disproportionately. Therefore, a trend among families in Eritrea is the growth of female-headed households, especially in urban centers, and the subsequent feminization of poverty.

The family and extended kin remain important players in the lives of adolescents and young adults with their participation in important decisions that mark the lives of adolescents, such as marriage and mate selection. In both urban and rural areas, most adolescents until early adulthood or even later live with their families. For example, in rural Tigrinya society young newlyweds stay in the groom's family by erecting an adjacent domicile, *Gojjo*, until the next land redistribution period of the village, when they get their own land to build a house. In urban areas, it is very common for young adults to stay with their families even after getting employed and in some cases forming a family, mostly a result of the acute shortage of housing in cities. In sum, it would be difficult for adolescents and young adults to leave their parents' household before marriage while living in the same town without experiencing some social ridicule.

Females usually stay a shorter amount of time with their families than males, because females marry at earlier ages than males. In the past, females married as young as 14 years old, but this is fast changing. In some remote rural areas of Eritrea, early-age marriage is still common. Urban women tend to marry much earlier than male youth. For example, in 1997 female young adults were less likely to be dependent on their families of origin by creating their own families through marriage, while most 20- to 24-year-old males were still living in the households of their families. Although divorces are increasing in number, the magnitude is not alarmingly big. Data show that it is easier for men to remarry, while most divorced women remain single; one reason for the high number of female-headed households is that a divorced woman with children is less likely to be remarried. All these family patterns are quickly transforming the family structure and composition in Eritrea.

Friends and Peers/Youth Culture

Although there are no data or studies conducted on the amount of time spent by adolescents with their families and peer groups, it is reasonable to suggest that most adolescents both in rural and urban areas spend more time with peers than with their families. Adolescents in rural areas spend most of their time either in school and socializing with their peers, or looking after cattle outside the home and playing there with their friends. Similarly, in urban areas adolescents socialize with friends or peers, both during and after school. It is common for male adolescents to engage in self-organized soccer tournaments. In cities and towns, peer relationships are based on neighborhoods and may be more localized, but are not necessarily restricted by ethnic or religious groupings. Clearly, there is a gender differentiation, and in some cases some neighborhoods may be class delineated, although for the most part urban households are not class segregated. Usually, friendship across gender is not encouraged in most ethnic groups.

Eritrea experienced dramatic sociocultural changes due to political instability, war and displacement, and the influence of modernization. Eritrean society, however, retained a high degree of cultural survival in its traditional beliefs and life patterns in spite of rapid ecological, economic, and political changes. Adolescents and youth of Eritrea are both the actors of social transformation and the keepers of traditions. Young people were and still are instrumental in political and military mobilization for national liberation and reconstruction in Eritrea. Therefore, young citizens are viewed simultaneously as keepers of historical legacies and forces of future transformation. As such, they tend to have their own worldviews and lifestyles that are always regarded by parents as well as leaders as deviations from tradition and culture. For example, there is an urban youth style of language that is differentiated from the adult population by its constant invention and corruption of words and phrases that borrow from foreign languages and create new ones. The urban youth culture is constantly changing with the outside influences of global cultural forces. This creates a generational gap both at the family and national level, as adolescents are caught between their cultural and historical heritages and trying to change and rebel against these heritages. This is evident in the constant attempt of socializing youth to the history and values of the national liberation movement by political leaders as well as the interference of family in the decisions on dating and mate selection by adolescents.

Love and Sexuality

Like most things in Eritrea, norms and practices about love and sexuality are changing. These changes, however, are accompanied by gender and urban–rural differences that continue to exist. In almost all cultural communities in Eritrea, marriages used to be arranged and took place at a fairly early age. Eritrean societies are going through rapid transformation now, with dating becoming common before marriage in most towns and cities and the age at marriage increasing. However, dating is much more socially acceptable in young adulthood than it is in the teenage years. It is quite common for people of different age groups to be in the same peer circle, and thus dating may usually be between older male adolescents or young adults and younger females.

Adolescent cohabitation is very rare in Eritrea. A national survey found that only 2.5% of female youth between the ages of 15 and 24 are cohabiting. The figure is even lower for male youth of the same age group who have a cohabitation rate of less than 1%. By comparison, urban cohabitation is much more prevalent, as a result of the dating relationships that are more common in cities.

The legal age of marriage in Eritrea is 18 years, but half of Eritrean women have already married before they reach the legal age of marriage. Nevertheless, there are some demographic shifts that show that young women are delaying marriages. For example, the proportion of women who are married by the age of 15 has dropped from 21% among 30- to 34-year-olds to 9% among women aged 15 to 19 in 2002. Rural teenagers are much more likely to be married earlier than their urban counterparts. Some data indicate that premarital sex is uncommon among female adolescents. Interestingly, half of Eritrean women have their first sexual intercourse at age 18, thus making the onset of marriage and first sexual activity almost the same. Indeed, adolescents nowadays start sexual intercourse much later than their mothers did, probably because they are getting married much later. As a consequence, adolescent motherhood is decreasing in Eritrea and tends to be more common in rural areas, which also have high incidence of early marriages. In rural areas teenage childbearing is twice as high as in urban areas, although it is decreasing at a faster rate among rural adolescents than it is for urban teenagers. For example, in 1995 one of three rural teenagers had started childbearing; seven years later only one in five rural teenagers are having babies. This is a remarkable decline of more than 40%. A combination

of factors such as family planning, increase in age at marriage, and separation of spouses as a result of war are regarded as possible factors for this drop in fertility. It is not clear whether this will be a sustained decline. Another practice that is common to particular ethnic and religious groups is the practice of polygamy. Though current adolescents are more likely to be in single-wife marriages than their predecessors, 4% of teenagers and 6% of young female adults report that they are in a marriage with one or more co-wives. The practice is very prevalent in some specific geographic and cultural regions.

Health Risk Behavior

There are so many things that put adolescents at risk in terms of their physical and mental health. Data are not easily available on this subject; this section focuses on health issues that are identified as social problems and for which some data are available.

War and its effects are the biggest factors in terms of influencing adolescent physical and mental health. A high health risk among adolescents in war zones of Eritrea is landmines-associated disability and death. For example, right after independence Eritrea had an amputee ratio of .045 per 1,000 population. About 40% of those victims are believed to be children and adolescents between the ages of 0 and 15. In general, Eritreans with disabilities comprise an estimated 4.5% of the population. In addition, war has resulted in many mental health risks, such as post-trauma disorder, that for the large part remain untreated due to the inadequate counseling and mental health services in the country. There are no reliable data on adolescents' physical and mental well-being as there is no available research that specifically measures adolescents' well-being. However, simple observation and anecdotal evidence suggest that psychological problems and psychiatric illness among young adults due to war and related factors have increased dramatically since the beginning of the twenty-first century.

The commercial sex industry is one of the social problems identified in Eritrea. The Ministry of Labor and Human Welfare study of 1999 found that 5% of identified prostitutes were between the ages of 14 and 17. Prostitutes can vary, ranging from those who sell sex openly in brothels or in bars to those who seek customers by roaming the streets. There are several government programs designed to train and rehabilitate commercial sex workers. There are no documented cases of child or teen pornography, but there are some recent concerns that teenagers can easily access Internet pornography, and that is regarded as a potential social problem.

The rate of crimes committed by and against adolescents is low compared to other countries. However, there are some noticeable increases in petty crimes as evidenced in the increase of juvenile delinquency charges.

No accurate figures are available to indicate the extent of adolescent drug abuse in Eritrea. For the most part, drug use is not an issue that is regarded as a significant social problem and it is usually not considered a homegrown problem—that is, it is usually thought of as a problem of Eritrean youth who have moved back from Western countries. However, there is a noticeable problem of teenage as well as adult alcohol drinking as, for example, indicated by the growing number of car accidents. Another social problem that is typical of children and adolescents is that of neglected children and orphans and those referred to as "street children." This is one of the largest adolescent social problems that exposes young children and adolescents to many physical risks and mental abuse. The rehabilitation of such persons is one of the priority areas that government and international relief organizations target in Eritrea. There are several orphanages and foster homes and other community-oriented rehabilitation programs that work on integrating the orphans and street children back with extended families.

The prevalence of AIDS is so far regarded as relatively low when compared to other African countries. But with the delay in age at marriage and the increase in premarital dating and sex, the management of AIDS depends on safe sex practice. A survey among adolescents in 2001 found out the practice of safe sex is over 90% with a casual partner and 75% with a regular partner. However, adolescents are less likely to use condoms if they think their sexual partner can be trusted to be faithful.

Another health complication comes from female circumcision. Almost all ethnic and religious groups practice female circumcision. In the lowlands, infibulation—the most severe form, which involves the sewing or suturing of the vulva—is practiced. Although most teenagers report that they got circumcised before they were one month old, about 14% were circumcised after the age of 5—mainly in ethnic communities with ritualistic practices of rites of passage. In a majority of cases, circumcision is done by traditional practitioners and

remains a practice that exists in spite of national campaigns for its elimination. It is interesting to note that 37% of teenagers and 45% of 20- to 24-year-old females support the continuation of the practice of circumcision.

Education

Class, gender, and geographic location constitute the factors that determine access to and success in the pursuit of education. Education is unequally distributed among different segments of Eritrean society. Historically, education was restricted to priests and people linked with the church and mosques. The Italian colonial education system also restricted formal education for natives up to fourth grade, and it was only after the 1950s that modern mass education was distributed to the public. Access to elementary education has increased dramatically with the construction of new schools and aggressive investment in education since Eritrea's independence in 1991. However, gender and regional inequalities in education remain large. Education in Eritrea is officially compulsory between 7 and 13 years of age, though this is hardly enforced, for lack of resources. If we take female education as an indicator of development, 77% of female adolescents are literate, as opposed to 56% of young adult (20 to 24) females. Data show that each successive cohort is getting more education than the previous ones. However, Eritrea has one of the biggest gender gaps in education. While the overall access to education has improved substantially, female access to education has declined relative to that of men. Looking at the data between 1991 and 1998, all educational levels experienced a decline of female-to-male enrollment. In addition, girls are twice as likely as boys to repeat classes and not finish their studies. Females are underrepresented in both participation and performance compared to their male counterparts. National surveys show that marriage is the single most important reason for leaving school among women aged 15 to 24. The gender gap increases with age of students. In urban Eritrea, 84% of urban children between ages 7 and 12 were enrolled in school in 1997 and there was no difference between boys' and girls' enrollment. However, among urban teenagers aged 17 and 18, there are more boys enrolled in school (73%) than girls (56%).

In addition to gender, education is unequally distributed by class and geographic location. The likelihood of child and adolescent school enrollments increases with family income, whereas a family's level of poverty reduces adolescents' chance of school enrollment as they are more likely to drop out or repeat classes. Moreover, regions that were hard hit by war and conflict for years tend to have lower child and adolescent educational enrollment. In addition, small teacher–student ratios and big class sizes result in lower educational performance of adolescents. The average class size and teacher–student ratio differs from area to area, but on average it is 1 teacher to about 50 students. Clearly there are some improvements in access to education at all levels. The increase in the distribution of elementary and secondary education is also demonstrated in the growth of the number of adolescents of rural and farming family background getting in to institutions of higher education.

Work

Child and adolescent labor is an aspect of everyday life in rural and urban Eritrea. Most adolescents work in order to contribute to the well-being of their families. Rural adolescents are the main source of labor for agriculture and herding tasks. With the increase in rural education, adolescents are contributing less labor to their families. Adolescent and child labor is so important that parents of rural adolescents complain of the lack of labor to help in farming and herding of cattle when school attendance takes adolescents away from the family. It is not uncommon for rural adolescents also to work seasonally in nearby towns as construction workers. Nationally, the state of Eritrea requires all high school students that are 16 and above to participate every summer in unpaid work in the reconstruction and rehabilitation program of communities. Most of the young population of Eritrea is also engaged in military and reconstruction projects. These are mainly voluntary unpaid labor contributions for national cause and do not guarantee security of income or a future career.

There is a high unemployment rate among adolescents, and thus they are highly dependent on families. In 1996–1997, the urban unemployment rate among young adults, 20 to 29 years old, was estimated at 30%, and half of the teenager population was unemployed. Instead, most young people were supported by their families and still lived in their parents' households. Child and adolescent employment in urban Eritrea is more common among the wealthier families, who employ children and adolescents in family enterprises. Poor children were less likely to be employed. Six percent of children between 10 and 14 years of age were employed in the labor force, and recent data show that most teenagers are in school. About a third of

male teenagers are in school, while one quarter of them report that they are employed. Employment provides adolescents with a sense of independence. For example, a third of employed female teenagers report that they have the sole decision power on how to use their earnings.

Even among the most privileged adolescents and young adults in society, their view of their future prospects is related to their current status of independence. A case study of university students' aspirations and plans shows that those who live with their parents are more likely to think their life is predictable than those who live by themselves. In addition, female students are more likely to report a predictable future life and a plan to get married in the next ten years than are male students. This is important in the context of high unemployment and uncertainty, and females seem to be more focused on marriage than work. All in all, the perception of work and its prospects are central in adolescents' view of their future.

Media

There is no accurate information on media use among adolescents in Eritrea. There are no media outlets that are specifically designed for youth consumption as such. However, radio, TV, and the growing local movie production and Internet services have offered adolescents some media choices. So far, are there very few radio and TV stations, but satellite television use is growing in some selected cities. Radio is the most widely used media outlet. The demographic and health survey of 2002 found out that 82% of teenagers listen to the radio at least once a week, while for newspaper reading and watching television the percentages were at 45 and 36 respectively. In urban areas, the Internet has become the best media outlet for connecting youth to the global wealth of communication. The introduction of Internet use is fairly recent and it is not yet widely distributed, although it is growing rapidly, with many Internet cafés providing adolescents with a new source of information and communication. The Internet is sometimes viewed as having a negative influence by some, who voice a concern that it offers adolescents easy access to pornography.

Mass media, for the most part, tend to focus on nationalist messages and songs, though recently some alternative radio stations that are geared toward the young population have appeared. Print media is also very restricted, as there are very few publications and newspapers. That is why radio is the single most accessible and widespread media outlet. In general, media access is very limited in Eritrea.

Politics and Military

Eritrean adolescents are participants in the political and military aspects of the country. Actually, youth in general made up the bulk of the fighting army during the 30-year liberation movement, as they do now under the national military service program. The organization of youth during armed struggle was essential for military mobilization as it was youth who translated the nationalist grievances into military action. The Eritrean national union of youth and students (NUEYS) grew out of the mobilization of youth during the independence struggle years, and it has a big membership base both inside and outside of Eritrea.

National service for all adults aged 18 to 40 and summer work programs for secondary school students were introduced in 1994. Both are mandatory for all young citizens of Eritrea. The national service program was begun on the premise that it would introduce postwar Eritrean youth to military discipline, intended to bridge the gap between the *tegadelti* (freedom fighters) and future generations, the *Warsays*. In Eritrea there are two distinct political generations: the *tegadelti* or *Yeka'alo* (the "Can Do") and the *Warsay* (the "Inheritor of the Legacy"). The *Warsay* generation is the backbone of the defense forces of Eritrea. For example, in the recent war with Ethiopia 11% of those killed were between the age of 18 and 20, while 75% of those killed were under 29 years of age. To date, most of the contribution of adolescents and young adults has been in the national defense of Eritrea. However, some segments of youth, especially university students, have challenged the national service program by protesting against some of its effects.

There is no research to determine the psychological and social impact of military service on adolescents and young adults in Eritrea. However, it is not difficult to expect huge transformations in the lives of adolescents who have joined military service at 18 and have stayed there for long periods of time. There are many noticeable behavioral changes of drinking, sexual activity, early marriages, and increases in psychiatric problems. The effects of such huge military transformation would be noticed once the drafted youth were demobilized.

In this regard, Eritrea has a potential problem of postwar transformation and rehabilitation.

BERHANE B. ARAIA

References and Further Reading

Araia, B. B. Forthcoming. Post war politics and higher education students in Eritrea. In *Youth and higher education in Africa: The cases of Cameroon, South Africa, Zimbabwe and Eritrea*. D. P. Chimanikire (ed.). Dakar: CODESRIA.

Arneberg, M. W., and J. Pedersen. 1999. Urban households and urban economy in Eritrea. http://www.fafo.no/pub/rapp/355/355.pdf.

Bila, P., P. Buyungo, B. Djagba, et al. 2002. *Eritrea 2001 KAP*. Washington, D.C.: Population Services International.

Blanc, A. K. 2004. The role of conflict in the rapid fertility decline in Eritrea and prospects for the future. *Studies in Family Planning* 35:4.

Brixiova, B., and A. Comenetz. 2001. *The gender gap in education in Eritrea in 1991–98: A missed opportunity?* IMF Working Paper.

Connell, D. 1998. Strategies of change: Women and politics in Eritrea and South Africa. *Review of African Political Economy* 76:189–206.

Elfu, M. 2000. Traditional food and household utensils, a case study of the Nara ethnic group. BA Thesis, University of Asmara, Asmara, Eritrea.

Elfu, Y. 1999. Gender and social change. BA thesis, University of Asmara, Asmara, Eritrea.

Habteselassie, E. 2000. Saho body decoration: Hina and Eilam. BA thesis, University of Asmara, Asmara, Eritrea.

Hanevik, K., and G. Kvåle. 2000. Landmine injuries in Eritrea. *BMJ* 321:1189.

Mengsteab, H. 2000. The Bilen transformation from childhood to manhood: Becoming a *Mendelay*. BA thesis, University of Asmara, Asmara, Eritrea.

Ministry of Education. 2001. *Essential education indicators*. Asmara: Eritrea.

Ministry of Labour and Human Welfare Survey. 1999. *A survey of prostitution in Eritrea*. Asmara: Eritrea.

Mobae, Y. 2000. Customary law of the Nara ethnic group in divorce. BA thesis, University of Asmara, Asmara, Eritrea.

National Statistics Office. 1997. *Eritrea demographic and health survey*. Calverton, Md.: Macro International.

National Statistics Office. 2002. *Eritrea demographic and health survey*. Calverton, Md.: Macro International.

Nsamenang, A. B. 2002. Adolescence in sub Saharan Africa: An image constructed from Africa's triple inheritance. In *The world's youth: Adolescence in eight regions of the world*. B. B. Brown, R. W. Larson, and T. S. Sarawathi (eds.). Cambridge: Cambridge University Press.

Zewde, L. 1998 The Pentecostal movement and its impact on youth: A case study in Asmara. BA thesis, University of Asmara, Asmara, Eritrea.

ETHIOPIA

Background Information

Ethiopia is located in the Horn of Africa. The country is bordered by Djibouti, Eritrea, Sudan, Kenya, and Somalia. Ethiopia's topography differs from the highest peak at mount Ras Dashen, which is 4,550 meters above sea level, down to the Afar Depression at 110 meters below sea level. The climatic condition also differs along with the topography, with temperature as high as 47 degrees Celsius in the Affar Depression and as low as 10 degrees Celsius in the highlands. The total area of the country is about 1.1 million square kilometers (CSA 2000).

Ethiopia's total population is estimated at 73,053,286 (2005). The age structure of the household population is characteristic of a society with a youthful population, which is typical of populations with high fertility levels. Individuals below the age of 15 account for 44% of the population. Those aged between 15 and 64 make up 53.4% of the population (CIA 2005; CSA 2000).

Ethiopia is inhabited by over 80 ethnic groups, with the greatest diversity in the southwest, speaking around 70 languages belonging to four major language families. The Oromos, Amharas, and Tigrians comprise the largest proportion of the country (counting 40, 25, and 14% of the population, respectively). In the political and cultural arena of the country, of all ethnic groups, the Amharas and Tigrians were the most influential (U.S. Department of State 2005; Library of Congress 2005).

Ethiopia is one of the poorest countries in the world, with a gross domestic product (GDP) of roughly $6 billion USD, a per capita annual income of about $100 USD. The most prominent sector of the country's economy is agriculture, which contributes 54% of the GDP, involves 80% of the population, and makes up about 90% of the exports (Library of Congress 2005). There is distinct wealth difference within the country based on different factors, including spatial and social. There is, for instance, a class of very wealthy people in urban areas mainly engaged in trade business (Pankhurst and Gebre 2002).

Ethiopia has maintained its independence despite the brief Italian occupation between 1936 and 1941.

The military government came into power in 1974, overthrowing Emperor Haile Silassie. The military government was deposed in 1991 by the Ethiopian People's Revolutionary Democratic Front (EPRDF). The country experienced its first seemingly multiparty election in 1995 (CIA 2005). As outlined in the 1995 constitution of the country, a parliamentary form of government and an administration based on nine ethnic-based national states prevail in the country (Library of Congress 2005).

Period of Adolescence

Considering the wide range of ethnic groups and specific cultures, it is not possible to make generalizations regarding a distinct period of adolescence applicable to all these cultures. In rural societies, the period of adolescence starts relatively earlier than it is in urban areas. Children in rural areas are expected to assume responsibilities relatively earlier. In rural settings, children are deemed to have developed a sense of awareness to differentiate between right and wrong starting the age of 5 to 7. There is also change in the way parents treat the children, especially after the age of 7, when they expect children to execute certain household chores. This period could be considered to constitute more or less the time the period of adolescence starts.

The period at which adolescents are expected to undergo further maturity in the direction of becoming adults differs also across different cultures. There is a difference among sexes since girls are expected to join the period of adulthood on average two years earlier than boys.

Different cultural and traditional beliefs and practices result in the period of childhood as well as adolescence being cut short for many, following the expectation to assume and execute adult roles. As a case in point, it is not uncommon for adolescents to get married before they reach the age of 10. This is especially true in rural settings where, despite these acts being proscribed by law, the society is very much loyal to its age-old cultural norms. Conversely, in urban settings there is a growing recognition of adolescence as a distinct period in its own right because of the waning influence of traditional cultural values in this part of the country.

Except in some ethnic groups, there is no formal ceremony in which society approves the transition from childhood to adolescence or from adolescence to adulthood. The transition from one stage to another is a series of informal processes through which the person accepts increased responsibilities and societal values and norms proper to his or her sex. Begetting a child, and more importantly marriage, marks the transition to adult status. Menstruation is an important defining moment that signals the girls' transition from childhood to puberty (Levine 1972).

The patterns of adolescence in urban areas differ from those in rural areas. Rural adolescents (particularly those who do not attend school) are subject to strict control of their parents while a permissive approach prevails in urban areas. The intergenerational relationship in rural areas tends to emphasize continuity and connection. The expansion of urbanization, modern education, labor markets, and the mass media have ineluctably changed institutions that organize and give meaning to individual relations and processes in urban areas.

Beliefs

Religion plays a significant role in the lives of Ethiopians. Most people explain both minor events in life and significant events such as disasters (famine, HIV/AIDS, despotic rulers) with reference to God. There is a widespread conception that things—be it HIV/AIDS or famine—happen for a reason and are expressions of God's will. The most prominent religions in the country are Orthodox Christianity and Islam, adherents of each make up 40 to 45% of the population. Protestants comprise about 10% of the population. Other religions with smaller proportions of followers include Roman Catholics, Eastern Rite Catholics, Jehovah's Witnesses, Ethiopian Jews (Felasha), and traditional beliefs (Library of Congress 2005).

The advent of Orthodox Christianity in Ethiopia is attributed to the Axumite period from the Byzantine world, around 340 A.D. Islam, on the other hand, began a few centuries later after being introduced by merchants from Arabia (Library of Congress 2005).

Individuals are oriented and initiated to observe certain religious practices, starting from childhood. Most of the orientation takes place in the religious places such as churches or mosques. Parents often take their children to these religious places to this effect. As the children grow into adolescence, they start practicing the religion on their own, although with an implicit observation/supervision by parents, who try to make sure the adolescent does not go "astray" or become alien to the rules and regulations of a given religion.

Lately, especially in urban areas and among the educated, it is not uncommon to find adults or parents who claim to belong to one of the religions, but do not actively observe the religious prescriptions. The same tendency is also observed among children of such parents.

Therefore, adolescents often take up the religion of their parents. However, conversion is not uncommon, especially to Protestantism, which was introduced very recently compared to the other two religions, and seems appealing to the youth. During conversion, though, an individual is likely to face fracture of relationships with other family members and relatives, who often break relationships or put pressure on the person to return. The pressure will be even stronger if the converts happen to be adolescents, because of their dependent status in the family.

Although there are no statistics, it appears that Protestantism is gaining ground on the other religions, largely because of its appeal to the youth. The Muslims and Orthodox Christians are reluctant to use modern musical instruments for their hymns while the Protestants are keen to adopt their hymns to all kinds of styles using all kinds of instruments.

Collectivism has been the predominant perception across the country in all ethnic groups, especially among the vast proportion of the rural dwellers, who still live by traditional norms and values. In urban areas, away from one's roots and with the declining presence of the extended families and kin, people tend to adopt individualism.

Overall, it seems that religion and religiosity is reviving in the country after having been relegated to the background during the 17 years of the Marxist regime, and there is a strengthening commitment to fundamental religious identities among Christian and Muslim adolescents and young people these days.

Gender

With the vast majority of the population living in rural areas and often adhering to traditional ways of life, there is widespread inequality and discrimination in favor of men. Thus, women's contributions are less recognized and they are marginalized in different spectrums of socioeconomic life. This is the case despite the immense contribution of women to the household economy. Generally, the participation of women is confined to the informal sector and their accomplishments are little acknowledged. Most Ethiopian women spend about eight to 16 hours every day engaged in varied tasks.

The subordinate status of women is something that is reinforced through socialization, where the differential treatment of the sexes is observed consciously and unconsciously. The attitude of the majority of parents toward their female and male children is different as well, and is discriminatory against female children. As a case in point, across different parts of the country assertiveness is acceptable among boys, but it is frowned upon among girls. Girls are encouraged rather to be shy. They are also expected to mature on average two years earlier than boys. Female children also should start giving hand to parents with challenging tasks about two years earlier than their male counterparts. Educationally, boys are considered more astute than girls (CYO and Italian Cooperation 1995).

A range of bodily images that are specific to females or males are prompted or condoned in different cultures. The most pervasive of these practices is female genital mutilation (FGM). It is practiced for cultural and hygienic reasons. Such interrelated factors that serve as a justification and reinforce the practice include the need to alter the behavior of the girl child in terms of suppressing sexual urges, and the high importance placed on maintaining virginity until marriage (Alasebu 1985, in Almaz 1997).

The period during which FGM takes place differs among different ethnic groups and cultures. In the southeastern part of the country among members of the Adere and the Oromo ethnic groups, the girl is circumcised between the ages of 4 and puberty. Among ethnic groups from the northern part of the country, circumcision takes place on the eighth day after birth (Missailidis and Gebre-Medhin 2000).

Another gender-specific bodily image popular among the Suri culture is the insertion of a circular plate made of wood or clay in the girl's lip. The practice is an expression of the girl's prettiness. The bigger the size of the plate, the more pretty the girl is considered. The plate brings to girls a sense of achievement, and the practice is sustained over time by the high regard community members have toward the act, and the subsequent exclusion nonconformity entails (Almaz 1997).

Other common gender-specific differentiations toward adolescents include the practice of letting boys be free to come and go from home any time with or without parental permission. Women's presence in public space is often sexualized and, except for schooling, church, work, and other valid reasons, adolescent girls are restricted from going out of the home and occupying public space. As in many other societies, girls tend to be closely supervised and are prevented from spending time with boys/men as there is a high premium placed on the virginity of girls at the time of marriage. Particularly in the era of HIV/AIDS, parents are uncertain about how to handle the situation and how to approach the issue of the sexual behavior of their children, and strict control is inevitable (Tadele 2005).

A double sexual standard has always been in place in Ethiopia and can be attributed to the prevailing inferior social, political, and economic status of women and the imbalance of power in interpersonal relations. In most cases, premarital sex for boys is considered an ordinary course of nature, whereas girls are told that virginity is a prize to be kept for their future husbands. Household chores are the exclusive domain of women, and men are not expected to do domestic/kitchen work.

The Self

Ethiopia is known for peaceful ethnic coexistence. Since the Ethiopian People's Revolutionary Democratic Front (EPRDF) assumed power, Ethiopia has been a federal republic composed of a number of seemingly self-governing regions mainly based on ethnicity. There is strengthening commitment and identity to one's own ethnic group. As a result, minor and major ethnic conflicts have been observed in different parts of the country.

In Ethiopian society parents and children are normally not vocal about expressing their affection toward one another. It is not also common for parents to express their affection through hugging or kissing. There are, though, occasions when parents become very outspoken when they think the child deserves/requires a special praise or admonition. If ever appreciation is to be expressed, it is not done so one-on-one, but to a third party (Heinonen 1996).

An authoritarian parenting style is the most pervasive type. Children are supposed to unquestioningly live up to the expectations of their parents. Children are socialized to appreciate the need for giving due respect to parents in particular and other adults in general through constant appraisal, which is followed by physical punishment,

ETHIOPIA

reprimand, and advice. The expression of respect toward others is considered vital to ensure the child's place in the society (Heinonen 1996).

In rural communities, members of the extended family and neighbors in the village play a certain role in the rearing of the child. The role of these groups in urban areas, however, is minimal (Heinonen 1996).

Conditions at home are not conducive to spending time alone; because of poverty, many adolescents live in a single-room house along with their parents and siblings, and thus they do not have the space for private or intimate aspects of their lives. This may be different in affluent urban families where adolescents occupy their own private space within the house.

Personal and other psychosexual identity of children usually (if not always) emanates from parents of the same sex and peers. In rural areas in particular, children follow the examples of their parents and attach themselves to the same profession and other psychosocial identity of parents.

Family Relationships

There are differences in child rearing practices among different ethnic groups and across different socioeconomic classes (Heinonen 1996). Despite differences in expression, the widespread pattern of child rearing in Ethiopia is authoritarian. In the past two decades, there has been evidence of a gradual transition, especially among educated families or those living in urban areas, into a child-centered but authoritative type of child rearing (Seleshi and Sentayehu 1998).

Until children become old enough to be considered to be able to tell between right and wrong, which is assumed to occur when they are aged between 5 and 7 years, mothers are entirely responsible for their upkeep and disciplining. It is after the children get past this age that they assume roles to execute more household chores. At this stage fathers also take up the responsibility of disciplining children when they get involved in wrongdoing (Heinonen 1996).

The childhood period in Ethiopia is characterized by little communication between children and parents in the family. There is a general belief that children are subordinate to adults, and hence the former should express unconditional respect to the latter. Failure to live in accordance with these social norms might entail disciplinary measures (Seleshi and Sentayehu 1998). Fear is also incited by parents as a way of getting children to live up to the expectations of the former.

The recent massive socioeconomic changes in Ethiopian society have created a gap between young people and their parents. Despite social and economic circumstances that have changed earlier patterns of relationships between parents and children, parents usually refer back to the way they were brought up, and do not seem willing to consider the wide generation gap between themselves and their children in terms of behavior, attitudes, and values. Parents seem to have failed to understand that the world of adolescents today is very different from that of their generation, with many new influences on behavior, including mass communication, the Internet, TV, and radio. Thus, the main causes of disagreement between children and parents include children's reluctance to live by the words of their parents (rebelliousness in terms of reluctance to execute tasks assigned by parents, children's excessive indulgence in play, disputes with siblings, parents' inability to provide food for children despite the children's request) (CYAO and Italian Cooperation 1995). Other behaviors considered appropriate for children and adolescents include not being vocal, not delving into adults' discussion, and not being confrontational with parents. Likewise, parents are not supposed to respond to seemingly "personal questions," or concede mistakes to children (Habtamu 1979, cited in Seleshi and Sentayehu 1998). Looking into siblings' relationships, dispute with siblings is one of the main causes for parent–child disputes (CYAO and Italian Cooperation 1995).

Traditionally, whenever parents feel that their children have wronged one way or another, the most popular measures taken on such children include insulting/cursing, advising, and slashing (CYAO and Italian Cooperation 1995).

Friends and Peers/Youth Culture

In rural societies, the period of childhood is brief and children are expected to assume different tasks early in their lives. More often than not, they have little playing time. Conversely, in urban settings, devoid of options to wile away their spare time, adolescents and youth take up video houses, which are ubiquitous, to watch Hollywood movies and popular American music. Such video houses, which are illegal, are found in the capital as well as in towns in the regions. The Ethiopian Television (ETV) also shows movies and music from America. There is a trend of identifying with the African American artists in music and film. Adolescents wearing T-shirts having pictures of rap and R and B musicians such as 50 Cent or Eminem is a common scene in the capital and other towns. There has been a growing acceptance of clothes made locally or using traditional fibers in the aftermath of local producers adopting modern designs.

Football is the most popular sport in the country. Male adolescents are also very much into soccer, and the Premiership (the English Football League) is the most popular weekend pastime for many in the capital and towns.

Ethiopia is characterized by stable and tolerant relationships among adherents of different religions. Friendship is, hence, not dictated by one's religious allegiance. It is common for a peer group to be composed of individuals from different religions. Cross-sex fraternal friendship, however, tends to be restricted, though it is not completely forbidden.

Clubs of various types are often set up in schools. Some of the common forms of clubs include anti-HIV/AIDS clubs, children's rights clubs, and girls clubs. Such clubs are often established with the support and initiation of government and NGOs. In a period of only three years, about 3,000 anti-HIV/AIDS youth clubs were set up by HAPCO (HIV/AIDS Prevention and Control Organization) (YDIE 2004). Other kinds of clubs include music, drama, literature, and sports clubs.

Love and Sexuality

Public dating is more common and tolerated in urban areas, and it is common for nonmarried couples to be seen in public. In rural areas, a different form of dating prevails, whereby adolescents meet and share intimate moments clandestinely. It is not acceptable for nonmarried couples to engage in public dating, and sexual intercourse before marriage is strongly prohibited, as a huge value is placed on virginity of the girl until marriage.

There is a growing tolerance toward cohabitation. Due to the popularity of this arrangement, the Family Law introduced in 2000 recognizes and provides better legal status to such a relationship. There are different ways of finalizing a wedding in the country, based on culture/ethnic group or religion. The Civil Code of 1960 declares that legal marriage can take three forms: customary, religious, and civil. Qurban marriage (among Ethiopian Orthodox Christians, where the couple get united in the church by taking holy communion), civil contract marriage (semanya), temporary paid labor marriage (demoz/gered), k'ot'assir (marriage preceded by provision of labor), marriage by abduction, and other forms co-exist under the umbrella of the three recognized types of marriages, though

some types of marriage are more or less common among certain ethnic or religious groups. Customary marriage is widely practiced in rural areas, whereby the union is concluded in the presence of local elders without involving the municipality. Religious marriages are considered sacred, as they enjoy the blessing of either the church or mosque. For instance, once couples get married through qurban, terminating the marriage/divorce is only accepted in certain cases, such as the death of a partner or infidelity.

The other most pervasive form of marriage is through contract referred to as be-semania. This marital union is finalized in the presence of witnesses from both sides, in most cases (if not always) at a municipality. This type of marriage can be annulled easily. Despite being illegal, abduction is another way of concluding marriage in certain cultures. Every day, an average of eight girls are estimated to be abducted with the intention of marriage (FHI 2003; YDIE 2004).

The most common form of marital arrangement, particularly among Christians, is monogamous. Polygamy, though, is commonplace among Muslims and in the southern part of the country. In rural societies, the marriage arrangement is made by parents or clans without the knowledge and consent of the bride.

A study conducted on over 1,000 high school students across Ethiopia identified 15 years to be the average age for sexual initiation. Of the one-third of the students who have had sex, a staggering two-thirds of them did not use any protection during intercourse (Adamu, Mulatu, and Haile 2003). The national Demographic Health Survey in 2000 also found that 27% of males and 57.9% of females aged 15 to 24 were married. The proportion of females married before they reach the age of 15 was higher than that of males (27.8% and 1.4%, respectively) (DHS 2000 in YDIE 2004).

Reproductive health and rights remain a serious issue, with high rates of maternal and infant mortality combined with cultural restrictions on contraception, the HIV/AIDS epidemic, and harmful traditional practices. Little participation of men in family planning efforts is the other difficult challenge. According to the Demographic Health Survey (2000), 40% of married women between the ages of 15 and 24 were said to have no access for family planning.

In Ethiopia, homosexuality is so strongly disapproved of that it is virtually impossible to talk about it or come across the topic being discussed. Homosexuality is not only perceived as a sin or as deviant behavior, but also as a crime. If ever, the

ETHIOPIA

practice takes place in clandestine circumstances, since it is proscribed by law and entails prison sentences ranging between 3 months and 5 years. Though not common, some recent studies highlight that homosexuality seems an emerging sexual orientation in the country, particularly among street children (see Tadele 2005).

Health Risk Behavior

Socioeconomic stagnation, poor governance, and war, intensified by recurrent drought and famine, severely affect adolescents and young people and rob them of any vision of a bright future. Many young people end up as street vendors or simply hang around in the town. This indicates that they are under great economic stress, the precursor of helplessness, occasional depression, self-hatred, and involvement in activities that are commonly known as deviant behaviors (the sale of sexual labor [girls], drugs (*chat*), alcohol, theft, rape, and the like). These days, many adolescents and youngsters are willing to risk their lives in order to get out of Ethiopia. There are reports indicating that suicide rates are increasing among young people who succumb to the overwhelming frustration that results from joblessness and failure in educational achievement.

Presently, HIV/AIDS poses the major problem for adolescents and youth in Ethiopia. Prevalence of the virus among males between the age of 15 to 24 ranges between 6% and 9%. The prevalence rate is even higher among females within the same age group (10% to 13%). The highest occurrence of STDs is also prevalent among this age group, which implies little use of protection (Attawell 2004). The difference in the prevalence rate among the sexes is accounted to early sexual initiation of girls with older men.

Involvement in crime is the other challenge facing adolescents. In some cases, young people organize themselves into different gangs and draw into a wave of clashes with each other. During 2000–2001, about 143,169 young offenders were reported. The involvement of youth in crime was attributed, among other things, to economic deprivation and lack of support (MYCS 2004). The other major challenge facing adolescents and youth is related to unemployment. A study on beggary in Addis Ababa found that about 60% of the beggars in the city were below the age of 30 (MYCS 2004). For many adolescents and young people street activities such as begging, petty theft, prostitution, and involvement in other deviant and criminal activities have increasingly become the only

alternatives for survival, or just part of their daily routine.

Problems of a sexual nature are also widespread and affect a significant proportion of adolescents, particularly females. The major of these problems include prostitution, abduction, early marriage, and sexual harassment. School girls, especially those who have to travel long distance between home and school, are exposed to various forms of sexual abuse and exploitation including rape, abduction, and physical abuse. These girls are pushed to quit school. Some live in rented houses in the inner city, away from their families, for fear of being abducted or raped on their way to and from school. What is more, girl students experience various violations on the street, which are committed against them with sexual motives, including name calling, snatching property such as exercise books, threatening, stalking, and persistent requests/advances for sexual favors/relationships. It seems that lack of opportunities encumbered by hopelessness and an inability to fulfill customary economic roles and obligations to win the hearts of women has led young men to harass girls and commit other sexual violence to boost their masculinity and self-esteem.

A 1992 study on sex workers in 124 towns found that of the 44,707 sex workers, over half (58.4%) of them were between the ages of 15 and 24. Widespread poverty, rural–urban exodus, early marriage, HIV/AIDS and sexually transmitted diseases, and limited educational and job opportunities exposed adolescents to commercial sexual exploitation (U.S. Department of State 2005).

Pregnancy at an early age often lead to obstetric fistulae and permanent incontinence. According to the Demographic and Health Survey (CSA 2000), 16% of women aged 15 to 19 were already mothers or were pregnant with their first child. The proportion of teenagers in rural areas who had started childbearing was twice the rate of those residing in urban areas.

Treatment for obstetric fistulae and permanent incontinence is available at only one hospital in Addis Ababa, which conducts more than 1,000 fistula operations every year. It is estimated that for every successful operation performed, ten other young women need the treatment. This condition results in the girls being unable to control their urine and/or feces, resulting in the isolation and abandonment of the girls by friends and families.

FGM is a pervasive problem facing young girls. A national baseline survey in 2003 stated that about 90% of women undergo one of four forms of FGM: circumcision, clitoridectomy, excision, and infibulation. Over half of the circumcisions take place before the girl reaches her first birthday. The majority of girls underwent some form of FGM. Clitoridectomy takes place on the eighth day after birth, and involves an excision of the labia. Infibulation, which is another form of FGM, is considered to be the most severe and risky of all the types. It takes place between the age of 8 and the onset of puberty. There is also widespread support for female circumcision among Ethiopian women. When asked whether the practice should continue, 60% of all women stated that they supported circumcision (U.S. Department of State 2005).

Education

Primary school attendance was 74.4% for male primary-school-age children and 59.1% for female primary-school-age children. With the exception of Addis Ababa, the participation of girls is generally lower than for boys (U.S. Department of State 2005).

Despite being exempted from tuition fees, families find it challenging to cover the expenses for uniforms and other "hidden costs" of the so-called free education. The majority of Ethiopians have little or no education, with females being much less educated than males. Sixty-two percent of males and 77% of females have no education, and 27% of males and 17% of females have only some primary education (CSA 2000).

For those between the ages of 15 and 24, 44.9% of males and 65% of females were illiterate. Literacy levels vary widely among regions, from a high of 68% among women in Addis Ababa to a low of 9% of women in the Somali region. Literacy among men ranges from a high of 87% in Addis Ababa to a low of 16% in the Somali region (CSA 2000). By 2001, school enrollment had increased by 12.5% for primary, 13.6% for secondary, and 5% for higher education (MoE 2002 in YDIE 2004, draft). In urban areas, 46% of urban adolescents 15 to 19 years old are enrolled in secondary schools while only 2% of rural adolescents in the same age group are enrolled (DHS 2000).

The overcrowded schools accommodated, on average, more than 60 students per class. Two and sometimes three students (mixed or same sex) sit on logs jammed up close to each other and share one table. In most cases, the buildings of public and government schools are dilapidated, the desks, chairs, and blackboards are worn out. The level of qualification of the teachers is far from satisfactory. Some of the high school teachers do not even have an undergraduate degree from a university,

and there are no trained teachers for some subjects. As a result, there are cases in which geography teachers teach history or vice versa to fill the gap. Aware of the dwindling remuneration and the ebbing of social respect for teachers, most young people who have succeeded in entering colleges and universities all over the country do not want to be teachers, and those who are forced to do so by involuntary placement do not want to continue in this profession. The upshot is that many teachers leave the profession when they find other employment opportunities with NGOs and government organizations.

Before 2001, students used to attend high school up to grade 12, and those who scored very competitive marks would enter colleges and universities. The new educational policy dictates that students may only attend high school up to tenth grade and then enter the preparatory program. What is more disturbing is that the new education policy dictates that the old first-year undergraduate courses should be covered in high schools in preparatory programs, and that college/university study should start with what used to be the second-year course.

Most of the schools have very large compounds. Although enrollment in primary education is compulsory in Ethiopia, there is a mismatch between the number of adolescents and the number of schools available, especially in rural areas. Because of the scarcity of teachers and the shortage of classrooms and other essential facilities, students attend classes in two or three shifts and have plenty of free time on their hands. About 43% of primary and 70% of secondary schools were functioning in two shifts in 2003. In a society where other recreational facilities are scarce, a shift system presented ample time for school pupils to indulge in chewing *chat* and visit pornographic video houses. Education in Ethiopia is almost the only means of upward mobility for many young people.

There are not special programs for the specially gifted. Fairly recently, the ETV presented a special program for those with hearing impairment.

Work

Owing much to the widespread abject family poverty, adolescents have to contribute to the household economy to either support their families or sustain themselves. This engagement by adolescent members of the family is imperative, considering the complete absence of a social security system in the country.

In rural areas, adolescents are expected to be involved in farming, bringing water, and gathering firewood, and executing other household chores. In urban settings, vast proportions of adolescents are engaged in various income generating activities such as petty trade, daily laboring, domestic service, shoe shining, and street peddling. In some provincial towns like Dessie, about 32% of the school-age population in the town are illiterate and about 34% of the children between the ages of 5 and 9 do not attend primary school, for reasons that include lack of adequate income, shortage of schools, and lack of parental interest to send them to school. It seems that instead of going to school, many children in Dessie, and apparently in the country as a whole, seem to be engaged in various street-life activities such as shoe shining, washing cars, portering, and street vending such as selling local roasted grain, lottery tickets, newspapers, and the like (see Tadele 2005).

Unemployment and underemployment are rampant in both rural and urban settings. With agriculture being the major sector of the economy, education does not guarantee employment. According to the result of the 1994 Census Report, the unemployment rate in Addis Ababa, particularly among young people, was very high. Out of a total of 312,743 economically active people of the city, 52% of those in the age group of 15 to 19 years and 55% of those 20 to 24 years old were unemployed. The total unemployment for all age groups in 1994 was 35%.

Another common practice across the country, particularly in urban areas like Addis Ababa, is the migration of young girls to the Gulf countries, including Lebanon, Saudi Arabia, Bahrain, and the United Arab Emirates, to work as domestic servants. Around 30,000 women are said to work in Beirut. Most of these girls were trafficked and had problems returning to Ethiopia through legal procedures. Most of them live under appalling working conditions, and there are reports of physical and sexual abuse by employers. A case in point is a 20-year-old Ethiopian girl who was on death row in Bahrain. She was sentenced to death for allegedly murdering her Filipino employer out of desperation and was judged to be of unsound mind. The death sentence was commuted to life imprisonment in response to pressure from the Ethiopian and international communities. Millions of young people also languish in refugee camps in neighboring countries (Sudan, Kenya, Djibouti), hoping to emigrate to the West.

Another source of employment for adolescent girls is commercial sex work, which is pervasive in urban and semi-urban cities in Ethiopia. The vulnerability of adolescents to commercial sex work is further reinforced by the increasing demand for young sex workers due to the belief that because of their young age, the girls will be less experienced and less prone to HIV. The 1994 Population and Housing Census conservatively reported that among the economically non-active people in Addis Ababa, 3,346 were prostitutes. Of this total, 35% were below the age of 25. There were a few as young as 10 to 14 years of age. The same census report indicated that, out of the total economically non-active population in the country, 45,945 were prostitutes, mostly below the age of 25.

Media

Radio and TV, which are the most prominent mass media in the country, are controlled by the state. A recent clamp down on publishers, editors, and reporters of private newspapers following violence related to the May 2005 national election has left people with virtually no alternative source of information. Private groups and individuals can buy spots for programs and commercials on the state-run Ethiopian Radio and Ethiopian Television. People's access to the media (newspaper, radio, and TV) is generally low. A staggering proportion of men and women had no access at all to the media (73% and 86%, respectively). Among those aged 15 to 24, 83.1% of women and 70.5% of men have no media access (CSA 2000).

The media are dominantly indigenous, as local issues constitute much of the air time coverage. The potential of media in terms of influencing adolescents is very much recognized. Fairly recently, in urban settings, there has been a public outcry to crack down on illegal video houses, as they are thought to contribute to loss of moral restraint, and involvement in drug and risky sexual behavior among adolescents. Due to their relative accessibility—mainly cost-wise—these video houses are frequented by adolescents who cannot afford to go to cinemas. The public perceives that such pornographic films "eroded" the culture and traditions of the society and expose youths to HIV/AIDS and related problems These days, the common public discourse in Ethiopia is that young people are perceived as a spoiled or morally corrupted generation, rough and bold. They are perceived to be disrespectful of their culture, and more attracted to the Western culture they see on videos and in cinemas.

Much of the media coverage is targeted toward adults. There are weekly programs broadcasted for a few hours both on radio and TV aiming to target adolescents. However, there is an inclination to rely on imported media whenever targeting or trying to attract adolescents to certain media programs. This is particularly apparent among the print media that focus on football leagues in Europe, Hollywood movies, and hip-hop music.

Politics and Military

The youth were very active in the country's politics about 30 years ago just before the Derg regime came to power, which culminated in the 1974 revolution that led to the overthrow of the emperor. The Derg regime used excessive measures to quell the youth from opposing its administration. There had been gross torture and killings of several thousand youth, especially in the government measure referred as the Red Terror. The persecution also resulted in the exodus of adolescents to neighboring countries.

The legacy of that period forced the general public and the youth in particular to shun anything that is considered political. This has continued throughout the Derg regime and much of the EPRDF reign. Lately, there has been resurgence in youth participation in politics prior to and after the May 2005 election. There has been a huge turnout of youth on voting day, and during political demonstrations for and against the government. Most of those who perished and were detained in different parts of the country during the June and November 2005 election-related unrest and violence were youth and adolescents.

Unemployment is a very serious problem, with a significant proportion of the active urban population in Ethiopia unemployed, and hence the youth comprise the vast proportion of the military. Forcibly or with their own consent, many young people found themselves deployed in the civil war that lasted almost two decades during the Marxist regime, and in the two-year border war with Eritrea under the current regime. These wars have claimed the lives of many young people.

Unique Issues

When we talk about adolescents, the situation of those adolescents living on the street in Ethiopia deserves special attention since some of the entries in this article, such as Family Relationships, do not apply to them.

According to NGOs operating to address the issue of street children, there are between 500,000 and 700,000 of such children in Ethiopia. Addis Ababa, which is the country's capital, has the largest proportion of the street children population. According to UNICEF, there are approximately 150,000 children working and living on the streets, devoid of any care and support. Female street children are estimated to constitute one-fourth of the total street children population.

The majority of these children live in conditions of severe deprivation, suffering from inadequate nutrition, exacerbated by exposure to adverse weather and physical abuse while on the streets, which imperils their physical, mental, and social development.

They do not have the social, economic, and cultural capital to negotiate in an increasingly competitive life successfully. Their needs are not addressed adequately either by the government or civil society and they are left to fend for themselves at an early age. In their own society, they seem to have been marginalized as "strangers." They do not have an opportunity to hear from parents and other adults that they are loved, valued, and are important as individuals. They have internalized feelings of neglect and worthlessness, and their lives are characterized by low self-esteem and frequent exposure to substance abuse, poverty, and violence. Too many of them believe that neither the present nor the future offers any promise. Drugs are often used as a way of self-medication to soothe their anger or frustration.

With respect to love and sexuality among street children, although the motives in play are vague, female adolescents on the street, who comprise only a fourth of the street population, often have boyfriends either as a coping strategy to fend off abuse by other male street children or as an expression of a romantic relationship. There is competition for girls among street boys, and it is often older and aggressive boys who seem to have "wives." It is not uncommon for female street adolescents to be forced to embrace commercial sex work as a survival strategy.

Another unique issue is the border conflict between Ethiopia and Eritrea, which has strong negative implications on the welfare of adolescents. This border conflict resulted in massive rural–urban migration and displacement, forcing many adolescents to become street children in many urban areas. The conflict between the two countries escalated into full-scale war between May 1998 and June 2000. Different factors are believed to have incited the dispute. The major explanation has to do with currency and trade issues. Prior to the introduction of Nakfa, the Eritrean currency, Eritrea used to use the Birr, the Ethiopian currency. This was in accordance to an agreement reached by the two parties just immediately after the fall of the Dergue in 1991. This agreement allowed the application of a common currency until such time that Eritrea issued its own (Addis 1998).

Although there was no clarity about what would happen after an Eritrean currency was established, the expectation on the part of the Eritrean government was that the Eritrean new currency would function at a parity level with Ethiopia. This, however, did not happen, and with the introduction of the Eritrean Nakfa, the Ethiopian government declared a nonconvertibility of the two currencies and decided to conduct trade with Eritrea in hard currency. This was debilitating to Eritrea's young economy and it has been suggested that this was the real reason behind the border claim and subsequent war, namely that Eritrea had thought that they would bring Ethiopia to a negotiation position by a threat of force.

Following the independence of Eritrea in 1993, the borders between the two countries had not been demarcated, and numerous adjacent areas were contested, including Badme, Tsorona-Zalambessa, and Bure. The war broke out on May 6, 1998, with the entrance of a small number of Eritrean soldiers in Badme, who then clashed with Ethiopian soldiers. The conflict resulted in large-scale displacement, expulsion/deportation, and the death of hundreds of thousands of people from both countries. The exact number of casualties of the Ethio-Eritrean war is not known. The governments of both countries have been bent on playing down the casualties on their side while overstating the loss on the other side.

The two countries agreed to a comprehensive peace agreement and binding arbitration of their disputes under the Algiers Agreement. A 25-kilometer-wide Temporary Security Zone was established within Eritrea, patrolled by United Nations peacekeeping forces (the United Nations Mission in Eritrea and Ethiopia, or UNMEE). The Boundary commission, established under this agreement, allocating some territories among the two countries, gave Badme to Eritrea. Ethiopia rejected the decision initially but expressed its acceptance of the verdict "in principle."

Since the early 2000s, tension has increased and there are allegations that governments of both countries are using this growing tension to distract and suppress internal instability. There is a growing confrontation between the two countries and with international community that it is feared will escalate into war.

GETNET TADELE and WOLDEKIDAN KIFLE

References and Further Reading

Adamu R., M. Mulatu, and S. Haile. 2003. Patterns and correlates of sexual initiation, sexual risk behaviors, and condom use among secondary school students in Ethiopia. http://www.ncbi.nlm.nih.gov/entrez/query.fcgi?cmd=Retrieveanddb=pubmedanddopt=Abstractandlist_uids=15227975anditool=iconabstrandquery_hl=3.

BBC. 2005. Country profile: Ethiopia. http://news.bbc.co.uk/1/hi/world/africa/country_profiles/1072164.stm.

Berhan, A. 1998. *Eritrea: A problem child of Ethiopia (causes, consequences and strategic implications of the conflict)*. Marran Books.

CIA. 2005. The world fact box: Ethiopia. http://www.cia.gov/cia/publications/factbook/geos/et.html.

CSA. 2000. *Ethiopia demographic and health survey*. Addis Ababa: CSA.

CYO (Children and Youth Affairs Organization) and Italian Cooperation. 1995. *Research report on child abuse and neglecting selected parts of Ethiopia*. Addis Ababa: CYO and Italian Cooperation.

Eshete, A. 1997. Issues of gender and sexuality in the context of cross-cultural dynamics of Ethiopia—Challenging traditional pervasives. In *Ethiopia in broader perspective: Volume III, papers of the XIIIth international conference of Ethiopian studies*. K. Fukul, E. Kurimoto, and S. M. Kyoto (eds.). Shokado Book Sellers.

FHI/USAID. 2004. Assessment of youth reproductive health programs in Ethiopia. http://www.fhi.org/NR/rdonlyres/e33j4bit2pqtycz3w5yfjh5xfwuzwh6jkg5s-qygmxjue65264jrn4grcltfrqafkdm6rqadv5ngwdl/Ethiopia-AssessRpt.pdf.

Library of Congress – Federal Research Division. 2005. Country profile: Ethiopia. http://lcweb2.loc.gov/frd/cs/profiles/Ethiopia.pdf.

Lvova, E. 1997. Forms of marriage and the status of women in Ethiopia. In *Ethiopia in broader perspective: Volume III, papers of the XIIIth international conference of Ethiopian studies*. K. Fukul, E. Kurimoto, and S. M. Kyoto (eds.). Shokado Book Sellers.

Ministry of Foreign Affairs. 2005. About Ethiopia. http://www.mfa.gov.et/Facts_About_Ethiopia/Facts.php.

Mssailidis, K., and M. Gebremedhin. 2000. Female genital mutilation in eastern Ethiopia. http://www.ncbi.nlm.nih.gov/entrez/query.fcgi?cmd=Retrieveanddb=pubmedanddopt=Abstractandlist_uids=10963253anditool=iconabstrandquery_hl=2.

Muleta, M. 2004. Socio-demographic profile and obstetric experience of fistula patients managed at the Addis Ababa Fistula Hospital. http://www.ncbi.nlm.nih.gov/entrez/query.fcgi?cmd=Retrieveanddb=pubmedanddopt=Abstractandlist_uids=15884272anditool=iconabstrandquery_hl=3.

MYSC (Ministry of Youth Sport and Culture). 2004. *National youth policy (2004)*. Addis Ababa: MYSC.

MYSC Women's Affairs Department. 2004. *Gender mainstreaming guideline in the youth sport and culture sectors*. Addis Ababa: MYSC.

Negash, T. K. *Brothers at war: Making sense of the Eritrean-Ethiopian war* (Eastern African Series). Tronvoll: Ohio University.

Pankhurst, A., and A. Gebre. 2002. Country paper: The current understanding of poverty and wellbeing in Ethiopia. Addis Ababa University Paper to the Inaugural Workshop of the ESRC Research Group on Wellbeing in Developing Countries, Jan. 13th–17th 2003,

Bath, 22nd December 2002. http://www.wed-ethiopia. org/members/Ethiopia_country_paper.pdf.

Seleshi, Z., and T. Sentayehu. 1998. *Parenting styles differences among selected ethnic groups in Ethiopia*. Addis Ababa.

The Synergy Project and USAID. 2004. Going to scale in Ethiopia: Mobilizing youth participation in the national HIV/AIDS program: A lessons learned case study. http://www.synergyaids.com/documents/GoingToScale-InEthiopia.pdf.

Tadele, G. 2005. *Bleak prospects: Young men, sexuality and HIV/AIDS in an Ethiopian town*. African Studies Centre: Leiden.

Tadesse, E., and S. Nigussie. 2000. Adolescent pregnancies in Addis Ababa.http://www.ncbi.nlm.nih.gov/entrez/ query.fcgi?cmd=Retrieveanddb=pubmedanddopt=Abstractandlist_uids=12862068anditool=iconabstrand-query_hl=3.

Terefe, H. 1997. Gender and cross-cultural dynamics in Ethiopia with particular reference to property rights, and the role and social status of women. In *Ethiopia in broader perspective: Volume III, papers of the XIIIth international conference of Ethiopian studies*. K. Fukul, E. Kurimoto, and S. M. Kyoto (eds.). Shokado Book Sellers.

UN. 2005. Ethiopia-Eritrea stalemate could spark renewed war. *Voice of America*, 31 March.

UNICEF. 2004. *The state of the world's children 2005—Childhood under threat*. New York: UNICEF.

U.S. Department of State: Bureau of Democracy, Human Rights, and Labor. 2005. Ethiopia: Country reports on human rights practices: 2004. http://www.state.gov/g/drl/ rls/hrrpt/2004/41603.htm.

Wheeler, A. G. J., and H. Grosskurth. 2004. Adolescent reproductive health and awareness of HIV among rural high school students, North Western Ethiopia. http:// www.ncbi.nlm.nih.gov/entrez/query.fcgi?cmd=Retrie-veanddb=pubmedanddopt=Abstractandlist_uid-s=14660144anditool=iconabstrandquery_hl=3.

F

FINLAND

Background Information

The first crusade to Finland by the Swedes took place in 1155, and the country subsequently became part of the Swedish realm. It was handed over to Russia by Sweden in 1809, and became a partly autonomous grand duchy under the Russian emperor. Finland declared independence on December 6, 1917, and its present constitution was adopted in 1919 when it became a republic. It joined the United Nations in 1955 and became a member of the European Union in 1995.

Lying in the northern reaches of Europe bordering Norway, Sweden, and Russia, Finland's total area is 338,000 square kilometers, of which 10% is water and 69% forest. It stretches 1,160 kilometers from north to south, and 540 kilometers from west to east. Its land border with Russia (1,269 kilometers) forms the eastern border of the European Union. The population of Finland is 5.2 million (17 inhabitants per square kilometer), of which 85.6% is Lutheran and about 1% is Orthodox. Most of the people live in towns or urban areas, and 33% live in rural areas. The principal cities are Helsinki (560,000), Espoo (221,000), Tampere (199,000), Vantaa (182,000), Turku (174,000), and Oulu (124,000). About one million people live in the Helsinki metropolitan area. Finland has a Sami (Lapp) population of 6,500 and, according to the 1999 census, the following numbers of 0- to 18-year-olds: 5,000 Russians, 3,000 Estonians, 2,000 Somalis, 1,000 Iraqis, and 1,000 Swedes (Kartovaara and Sauli 2000), and the numbers of Russians and Estonians have increased in recent years. The population comprises 18% 0- to 14-year-olds, 67% 15- to 64-year-olds, and 15% over 65 years of age.

Finland has two official languages, Finnish and Swedish. Finnish, a Finno-Ugric language, is spoken by 92.1 % and Swedish by 5.6 % of the population. The head of state is the president of the Republic, elected for a six-year term by direct popular vote. The country's GDP per capita was around 26,800 euros in 2002, and the currency unit is the euro. There are three almost equally important exports sectors in the Finnish economy: electro-technical goods, metal and engineering products, and forest-industry products. Finland's forests are its most crucial raw-material resource, although the engineering and high-technology industries, led by Nokia, have long been the leading branches of manufacturing. The service industries account for over 60% of the GDP. Economic growth recently has been among the fastest in the world, and Finland belongs to the group of the richest industrialized societies in terms of GDP. Taxation levels are high: the tax rate was 46% of GDP in 2002, among the highest in the world. The proportion of women in the waged labor force is high, 70%, as is the general employment rate (Statistics Finland 2004).

Period of Adolescence

Adolescent puberty begins between 8 and 13 years of age in girls and one or two years later in boys and the transition takes about four years. Menstruation starts at the age of 10 in 3% of the female population, at 11 in 16%, 12 in 34%, 13 in 29%, 14 in 10%, and 15 in 8%. The first spermarche occurs at the age of 10 in 7% of boys, at 11 in 14%, 12 in 25%, 13 in 27%, 14 in 15%, and 15 in 12% (Stakes 2002).

An important rite of passage for adolescents has been confirmation at the age of 15, although more recent rites of passage include getting one's driver's license, and entering college and university. It has become fashionable to have a large, lavish wedding, before which friends of the bride and bridegroom often organize separate so-called *polttari* (equivalent to hen and stag parties). According to early traditions, women performed magic to bring good luck and fertility to the couple and to keep out bad spirits in the ritualism of the bridal sauna. Some of this is reflected in the *polttari* tradition, such as making noise, and wearing fancy dress. The wedding ceremony is usually held in church and is followed by a reception. In the mid-twentieth century it became more common for couples to live together before getting married.

Under Finnish law, everyone aged 18 and above has the right to vote and to be a candidate in elections, the right to get married, the right to buy tobacco, a limited right to buy alcoholic beverages (full rights to buy alcohol start two years later), and the right to get a driver's license. An 18-year-old is no longer considered a child according to the child-protection law, and men become liable for military service. The right to receive monthly child allowance ends at the age of 17, which is when young people have the right to receive unemployment allowance. In order to motivate them to continue at school instead of registering as unemployed, there are some limitations on getting the allowance for those under the age of 25. Responsibility under criminal law starts at the age of 15, which is also the age at which the right to sign labor contracts is granted.

The duration of adolescence is increasing due to the longer period of time spent in educational institutions, and the corresponding delay in the entrance to the labor force, and thus the prospect of becoming financially independent. Moreover, independent family life begins rather late, which means that social adulthood is increasingly delayed for many young people. Half of all girls have moved away from their parents' home by the age of 20, and the boys a couple of years later, partly due to their liability for military service. The high level of social security promotes independence at an early age: society provides financial support for all 20-year-olds who have left home regardless of their parents' financial situation and for university students as soon as they start studying. Young working Finns are entitled to a housing subsidy if their income does not cover their living costs. Students also receive a housing subsidy, which covers 66% of reasonable rental costs, and they are also given a small monthly study subsidy. Tuition is free and students only need to buy study materials.

Since young people make their educational and professional choices quite late, they are nearing 30 when they finish their education, begin their working life, have their first child, and become financially independent (Nurmi and Salmela-Aro 2002). Adolescents expect to leave the parental home at the age of 20, finish education at the age of 22, start work at the age of 23, get married at the age of 27, and have their first child at the age of 28 (Salmela-Aro and Nurmi 2004). Moreover, most of their goals for the future do not extend beyond the age of 30, when they no longer set them (Nurmi 1992, 2001; Nurmi, Poole, and Kalakoski 1994; Salmela-Aro 2001; see also Gordon and Lahelma 2002). All in all, it could be said that there is a long period of emerging adulthood in Finland, from at least age 18 to 29.

Beliefs

Finland is a religiously homogeneous country: 85.3% of all Finns belong to the Evangelical Lutheran Church, 1.1% to the Orthodox Church, and 1% to other religious communities; 12.6% do not belong to any religious group. Being a member of the church and using its services as rites of passage at the significant points of one's life are part of Finnish culture. Most children are baptized into the church, and over 90% of 15-year-olds are confirmed in the Lutheran Church (Statistics Finland 2000). The church also has a role in day care and the confessional religious education in schools. Most young people undergo training in confirmation camps, which is set at 80 hours. Those who choose not to may join the

Prometheus program, which organizes politically nonaligned coming-of-age camps that have no religious leanings, and are intended for 14- and 15-year-olds.

Although more than 90% of Finnish children are baptized as members of the Evangelical Lutheran Church, most young people are not interested in religion. One-fifth of 16- to 19-year-old adolescents in the Helsinki metropolitan area believe in God (as conceived by the Finnish church), although among their peers in the countryside in the central western area, the proportion of believers is 50% (Helve 2002).

Changes in the Finnish way of life have been accompanied by privatization and internationalization, which can be seen on both individual and community levels. Religion has lost its meaning in terms of people's value structures and worldviews (Helve 2002). The spheres of politics, economics, and technology have their own values and morals, and a deep adherence to religious morals has weakened. According to a longitudinal study of value changes among young people, Finns fall into five different groups with regard to their values: humanists–egalitarians; traditionalists–conservatives; environmentalists–greens; cynics and the politically passive; and internationalists–globalists (see Helve and Wallace 2001). Post-materialist values are especially prevalent among humanists supporting gender and racial equality and among international globalists, who are cosmopolitan in their worldviews. The greens also express post-materialist ideas in criticizing the raising of material standards of living, and in being willing to lower their own standards in order to eliminate nuclear power. The economic recession in Finland during the 1990s changed attitudes and values among young people. The deteriorating economic situation was reflected in their more rigid attitudes to refugees and development aid, for instance (Helve 2002).

Young Finns rate health, the family, home, close friends, and work as the most important aspects of their lives. Adolescents put more value on job content than salary. In general, those living in rural areas emphasize family values more than those living in urban areas (Helve 1996). Nine people out of ten in the 15 to 19 age group were found to value quality of life over material wealth (Youth Barometer 1999). Individualism, along with an inherited Protestant work ethic, are among the core values held by 15-year-olds from Helsinki, although traditional themes such as gender roles and employment are also represented (Karvonen 2001).

Gender

Finland was the European forerunner in giving women the right to vote in 1906. The fundamental parliamentary reforms at that time gave all adult men and women not only universal and equal suffrage, but also the full right to stand for elective office. This was unprecedented. Yet, studies on values and attitudes among young people have shown that even in Finland girls/young women and boys/young men have different attitudes and values toward life and society (Helve 2001; Karvonen 2001). Education has had some effect on these attitudes: those who stress gender equality in working life the most, for example, are girls who have been to senior high school. They want a female employer, and in their opinion it is equally important for a woman to go to work as for a man. They generally believe that both men and women need to earn money and take care of the home and the family. With respect to gender differences, girls value humanism and equality more than boys, who value technology and economic welfare more. Moreover, girls' personal goals are often related to social issues, while boys are oriented toward future work and financial issues (Salmela-Aro 2001). Girls are not as aware of party politics as boys, and are more global in their attitudes. They are more willing to increase aid to developing countries and to accept refugees, and they are also more critical than boys with respect to the capacity of science and technology to solve the problems of our era. Most, but not all, express humanist values. The space within which Finnish girls can move has expanded. Girls' perceptions of the world seem to be more varied and open than those of boys (Helve 1993, 2001, 2002).

Young Finns seem to have been affected by the changes in their role expectations. Females face greater uncertainties, and it is more common for them than for males to find themselves in situations in which their expectations conflict with their subsequent experiences. The rise in expectations associated with extended educational experiences can have an effect on the psychological well-being of girls and young women, whose lifestyles and behaviors have also changed in recent decades. Sexual experimentation among girls, with all of the health risks it entails, is also linked to the process of psychological maturation. Both bodybuilding and violence have been considered to be signs of masculinity. Although studies have shown that women, too, are quite capable of violent and criminal action (see Campell 1993) and girls also feature in the bodybuilding culture, these two elements are not similarly practiced by girls and boys. For example, there are some groups of skinheads who claim to admire the traditional patriarchal model of the man as head of the family. Gangs are bonded by violent acts and by the objectification of the "other," such as Finnish Somali refugees, as the enemy (Hilden 2001).

Today's Finnish fathers take a more active role in taking part in and overseeing their family's everyday activities than their own fathers did. Fathers are entitled to a total of three weeks of paternity leave, which they—at least to some extent—actually take, and which is not deducted from maternity leave. The full period of maternity leave is about 11 months, of which actual maternity leave is three months and the rest is termed parental leave: the parents can choose whether they want the mother or the father to care for the child at home. The spouse who typically takes unpaid care leave after maternity leave is still the mother, although some fathers, too, use this right. One reason for this is the pay differential that favors men over women (men and women are employed in different sectors). For many families it is the financial income that matters, but of course attitudes and traditions also affect the choices parents make. Parental allowance is about 60% of the salary.

In 1999 women comprised 52% of the total workforce of 2.5 million, and their average earnings were 81% of the average male earnings. Average life expectancy for females is 81 years and for males 74 years. In the parliamentary elections of 2003, women won 76 of the 200 seats.

The Self

Self-identity among Finnish adolescents has become more mobile, multiple, personal, self-reflective, and subject to change. Young people have so many different, sometimes conflicting, roles that it is difficult for them to know who they are. Identity, and the issue of identity, is becoming increasingly problematic. As the sociologist Anthony Giddens argued in his analysis of self-identity (1991), individuals of today are constantly confronted by change and uncertainty. According to Ulrich Beck (1991), this is a condition of what he calls the "risk society." For example, the Finnish adolescents of today experienced in their childhood in the 1990s the economic crisis that affected the country. They have learned to be strategic in their approach to the future. They have developed the necessary skills to envision various possible outcomes of their actions.

They may believe that they have some autonomy in making their life choices, but these often come about as results of occurrences over which they have no control, such as parental divorce, unemployment and changes in their family finances or structure.

The actions of adolescents need to be understood in relation to their everyday life in terms of practices and habits shared by many young people. The family, peers, and also the media have a strong impact on the construction of the identity. For example, for young girls it is fashionable to be thin, and slimness is associated with success and sexual attractiveness. According to an extensive study of Finnish students (Stakes 2002), 81% of 15-year-old girls would like to change some aspect of their physical appearance. Concern about weight permeates the lives of many young women. Eating disorders as a modern phenomenon are linked to the desire to establish a distinct self-identity, and could be understood as pathology of reflexive self-control.

Finnish adolescents use new technologies extensively. Computers and mobile phones also have an effect on identity formation. For example, one function of mobile phones for young people is in maintaining identity with their group, which suggests the notion of status. Mobile phone ownership is a style and fashion statement.

The Council of Europe carried out a review of Finnish cultural policy in 1994, and found that Finland had a particularly strong cultural identity. This has been seen also in Finnish youth culture in the so-called Suomi-rock of the late 1970s and early 1980s ("Suomi" being the name of the country and the language in Finnish), which reflects searching for its own cultural roots (see more about Finnish youth culture below). Cultural identity is clearly at the core of Finnish adolescents' identity. Youth culture gives adolescents a collective identity, and its products play an important role in the socialization process. Young Finns also share cultural norms and attitudes.

Family Relationships

There are about 1.4 million families in Finland. Among those with children the average number of offspring is 1.8; in 1960 it was 2.27. A typical Finnish family thus has two children. The proportion of young people living with two parents is 73.7%, with a single parent 14.6%, in a step-family 11.0%, and 0.7% have other arrangements (Statistics of Finland 2004). Among 11- to 15-year-olds, 25% have no siblings, 54% have one sibling, 14%

have two siblings, and 6% have three or more. Finnish couples marry relatively late in life, women at 29 on average and men at 31. Before marrying, the couple has usually lived together for several years and may even have children together. Common-law marriages are on the rise, and children are increasingly included in the family unit. The number of children per family is slightly up in recent years, but so is the number of childless women. The majority of young people leaving home first live on their own in student hostels or rented apartments, although a significant number move in with a companion at this early stage. A growing number of children are born out of wedlock, currently more than one-third. In 2000, fewer than half of the women giving birth to their first child were married, while 64% and 73% of second and third children respectively were born to mothers who were married. Today, about every tenth child is born to a woman who does not live in a stable relationship. The majority of single parents are female, only one in ten being male (Statistics Finland 2004). For a western European country, the birth rate in Finland is high, and among the highest in the EU countries. The family's livelihood is secured by long periods of paid maternity leave. In addition, one of the parents has the right to take unpaid leave from work to look after the child at home until he or she reaches the age of three. The government pays the family a small subsidy during this period.

Finland has the highest divorce rate among EU member nations. The marriage act that came into force in 1988 made the dissolution of a marriage accessible and simple, and as a consequence the number of divorces rose to a completely new level. The increase was almost 150%. It was generally believed that the number would return to something like its previous level after the backlog of "repressed" divorces had been cleared. This did not happen, and Finland still ranks high on divorce in Europe. The statistics indicate that almost half of all marriages will end in divorce, unless the present trend changes. Of marriages contracted in the mid-1970s, one third of them have been dissolved. Those contracted later seem to end in divorce even more frequently.

From the child's point of view the family picture is more traditional. The families of common-law couples and single parents are smaller than those of married couples and 70% of Finnish children under the age of 18 live in the latter type of family. The proportion of all families with children living in a second family has remained more or less stable and stands at 7%. Once a family has broken up, the

threshold for establishing a new one is relatively high. Finnish women are brought up to earn their own living, in addition to which the level of social security is sufficiently high for a single mother not to need a man to support her. Since 2002, two persons of the same gender have been able to register their relationship in Finland (Statistics Finland 2004).

The family as a primary social environment plays a decisive role in the individual's development of communication skills, attitudes, and behavioral patterns. Recent research highlights the influence of parenting styles, family communication, and parent–child relations on life skills, psychosocial adjustment, mental health, and health behavior. The variables related to positive relationships with parents are high self-esteem, low depression, low risk-taking, greater involvement in school, and better school performance.

In terms of communication with parents, the majority of Finnish young people report communicating easily with their mothers about things that upset them (HBSC 2004; HBSC refers to The Health Behaviour in School-aged Children Study, conducted by the WHO in 35 countries and regions in the WHO European region and North America, among 11-, 13-, and 15-year-olds). Across the ages from 11 to 15, almost all young people, both girls and boys, have said they find it easy to communicate with their mothers, while the boys in these age groups and young girls feel almost as much at ease communicating with their fathers about upsetting topics. Compared to other countries, the responses in Finland suggested a high level of ease in child–father communication, and the country ranks high on talking with both mothers and fathers (HBSC survey 2001/2002, 2004).

Young people consider family relationships to be of high importance in terms of support and feedback. The time spent with the family and in discussion with parents seems to increase the well-being of young people. Finnish adolescents see their parents as providing basic nurturing and support, as well as guidance: approximately half of those in secondary school felt they were able to discuss their lives with their parents (HBSC 2004). However, 10% felt that they could never discuss issues with their parents. Most young people (80%) feel that they receive support on school matters from their parents often or quite often, although Finnish parents are not very involved in their children's schools and school activities. In the HBSC survey (HBSC 2004; King, Wold, Tudor-Smith, and Harel 1996) the item "My parents are willing to come to school to talk to teachers" was used as an indicator of parental involvement in their child's school: Finland ranked among the lowest countries in Europe on this indicator. However, the proportions of young Finns who felt that their parents' expectations were too high were among the lowest in the large HBSC survey.

Moreover, a study by Metsäpelto and Pulkkinen (2004) on Finnish parenting styles found that mothers and fathers differed in their approaches: authoritative parenting was more typical among mothers, used by 28% of them and by only 5% of fathers. In addition, 21% of fathers and 11% of mothers practiced emotionally available parenting, and 22% and 9% respectively used emotionally distant parenting. More fathers (36%) and only 7% of mothers used authoritarian parenting (Metsäpelto and Pulkkinen 2004). Young people expect their parents to be there for them (Rönkä and Kinnunen 2002), and Finnish young people recall their best moments as being with their parents, free of time pressures. Nuclear families live together, while grandparents, uncles, aunts, and cousins are seldom seen and there are usually no "quasi-kin." When young people begin the third decade of their life, the role of the family dramatically decreases: 60% of 20- to 24-year-olds no longer live with their parents (Nuora 2000).

Friends and Peers/Youth Culture

The role of the family decreases in adolescence and the importance of friends and peers increases, as young people orient themselves toward peer groups. Studies of peer relationships suggest that having friends, and in particular supportive friends, is associated with a good self-image, a sense of belonging, a positive outlook, and success in future relationships. Young people in Finland prefer to spend their free time with their friends (77%), rather than alone (6%), with their parents (2%), or with some other people (Helve 2002).

Finnish young people ranked below the median in numbers of close friends in a representative HBSC study conducted in 35 countries (HBSC 2004). Girls usually have fewer friends but more close friends than boys, who prefer groups. About 75% of Finnish young people felt that they found new friends easily; of the boys about 80% had two or more close friends, and of the girls about 75%. However, in a large representative study among Finnish adolescents, about 6% of the girls and 15% of the boys mentioned having no friends (Stakes 2002). In the same study, 13% of boys and 5% of girls at secondary school said they had no close friends, while 44% of boys and 47% of girls

mentioned having many friends. The respective percentages of boys and girls with a steady girl/boyfriend were 12% and 16% among the eighth graders and 16% and 25% among the ninth graders. In senior high school, 22% of the boys and 38% of the girls had a steady girl/boyfriend (Stakes 2002).

According to an extensive study on young people in 35 countries, Finns spend less than the median amount of time with friends after school (HBSC 2004). Nevertheless, Finnish adolescents (especially boys) spend time with friends after school several days a week. More than 50% of the 11-year-old boys sampled spent time with friends after school four or five days a week. In turn, it is very common for Finnish young people in all age groups to spend five to seven evenings a week with friends outside of the home: almost half of the boys did so, and about 40% of girls. The percentages of girls and boys respectively spending time with friends after school four or more days a week were 30% and 36% among the 11-year-olds, 26% and 35% among the 13-year-olds, and 26% and 37% among the 15-year-olds. In addition, 41% and 34% of the 15-year-old boys and girls respectively communicate with their friends by phone, e-mail, or text messages (HBSC 2004). It appears to be very easy for Finnish students to talk to friends of the same gender.

Fighting is very rare among young people in Finland compared to those in other countries, and the country is in the lowest quartile in this respect (HBSC 2004). Only 7% of the 11-year-old girls sampled were involved in physical fighting at least once in the previous 12 months, and 2% three or more times (HBSC 2004). This suggests that fighting and the attendant victimization are rare.

Youth culture in Finland, as it is understood in the twenty-first century, developed in the 1950s and 1960s, due to the arrival and growth of pop and rock music, and was thus based largely on Anglo-American influences. More popular songs were being sung in Finnish in the 1970s, but music was still created and presented within the framework of the Anglo-American pop/rock genre. The birth of so-called Suomi-rock (Finnish-rock) in the late 1970s and early 1980s reflected an increased interest in Finnish cultural roots. Twenty years into Finnish rock history foreign and domestic national influences came together in a unique way to form a decidedly Finnish style of pop music, a rock culture testifying to its own national identity.

The latest transformations have also had an enormous impact on the Finnish culture and its role in the world. Since the early 1990s, the most prevalent force of cultural change in Finland has been economic, not political, symbolized by the globally renowned Nokia (and the business of mobile phones). It is not easy to describe the influence Nokia has on the culture of adolescents in Finland, ranging from consumption habits to views about the role of the state and society. This technological phenomenon reproduces identity and social status, and influences and develops the character of cultural communications. It has had an effect on how young people participate in or resist adult culture, and on how they develop their own subcultures in relation to identity formation and "coming-of-age" processes. Mobile phones in general, and sending text messages in particular, have indeed revolutionized the state of communications among young Finns. Peer influence, the need to belong to or to be in the "in group," and the notion of identity—being fashionable and "in vogue"—drive their decisions and motivations to have mobile phones, ownership of which is almost total: 95% of those aged 15 and over own one. The usage rate is highest in Finland among 15- to 24-year-olds in the countries of the European Union (Young Europeans 2001).

Love and Sexuality

As in other developed countries, Finnish adolescents now mature, both physically and mentally, earlier than before. Because of increased economic well-being, they adopt more mature attitudes at a fairly young age, when they also build their sexual identity through a multinational youth culture. According to a study by Kontula and Haavio-Mannila (1994), by age 13 young people are showing considerably more serious interest in the opposite sex. The data, collected in 1992, revealed that over half of the boys of this age and one-third of the girls had read sex magazines and seen sex videos, and more than half of both boys and girls had kissed. Many had experienced caressing over clothing. Almost half of the 13-year-olds interviewed were ready to accept sexual intercourse in their peers' relationships, and about as many had already had a dating relationship with the opposite sex. They tended to go out socially in groups of young people, which included the dating partner.

According to the HBSC (2004) study, sexual intercourse has been experienced by about 5% of 13-year-olds, and the incidence increases with age, to 23% of boys and 33% of girls aged 15. By this age, adolescents usually accept sexual intercourse among their peers on the grounds of love, and an important condition for starting a sexual relationship is thus that two people are in love. According to a study by Kontula and Haavio-Mannila (1994), the importance of love in legitimating sexual

relationships among young people is somewhat greater among farmers and the upper-middle class than among other social groups. This applies to both young people and their parents. The emphasis on love is closely connected with the demand for faithfulness. Young Finns of 15 are among the sexually most experienced in Europe, particularly among European girls.

Marriage is no longer considered a prerequisite for having an active sex life in Finland; the quality of the relationship is considered more important than its religious or civil form. Sexual relations are accepted in steady dating relationships and most couples live together before marriage; premarital cohabitation is experienced by at least two-thirds of emerging adults (Nurmi and Siurala 1994). A significant number of cohabiting people do not get married even after years of living together as a couple. It is also widely accepted that single people are sexually active. Dating has replaced marriage as an institution, with sexual intimacy almost universally accepted during dating, as it was earlier accepted only within marriage. As a consequence, very few young people marry their first sexual partners (Kontula and Haavio-Mannila 1994).

Sexual health is a substantial part of an adolescent's general, social, and personal well-being, the key concerns revolving around pregnancy and sexually transmitted infections. According to a study on the use of oral contraceptives by adolescents in Finland between 1981 and 1991 (Vikat, Rimpelä, Rimpelä and Kosunen 2002), use increased steadily: the usage among 14-, 16-, and 18-year-olds was 2%, 18%, and 41% respectively in 1991, compared with 0.2%, 7%, and 22% respectively in 1981. Most users had a steady partner (80% of 16-year-olds and 85% of 18-year-olds). By 1989, rates of abortion had fallen from 1.2% to 0.93% in 16-year-olds and from 2.5% to 1.92% in 18-year-olds. Gonorrhea infection decreased and HIV infection remained rare. Instituted policies for active chlamydia screening started in the early 1990s, and reporting is at a high level. The incidence of *Chlamydia trachomatis* infection has been increasing since 1995: during the six-year study period, laboratory surveillance data documented the highest increase in the youngest age group (10- to 19-year-olds). One reason for the increase in infection rates is that the use of condoms among Finnish young people is the second lowest in Europe: two out of five 15-year-old Finnish girls had not used a condom the last time they had had intercourse. On the other hand, 27% of 15-year-old Finnish boys had not used a condom, which is slightly better than the corresponding figure for girls. Adolescents seem not to be afraid of sexually transmitted diseases (WHO 2004).

Since the early 1970s, Finland has required that comprehensive health education be provided in all schools. There was an immediate effect when such education and related services were introduced in 1973 in that national teenage pregnancy, abortion, and STD rates dropped dramatically, and steadily declined thereafter. Finland's success was a direct result of its strong commitment to comprehensive sex education and the availability of free, confidential reproductive-health services for teens. It is quite telling that the rates rose again in the late 1990s when the economic crisis brought major funding cuts in adolescent health services, and sex education was no longer mandatory. Fortunately, the disturbing trends of the late 1990s sparked a renewed commitment to the needs of young people. In 2002, the government made emergency contraception available over the counter and most schools resumed health, including sexual-health, education. Starting in 2005, comprehensive sex education was once again required in all Finnish schools (Cacciatore 2004).

According to a study by Lehtonen (1995) the heterosexual gender system is reproduced in the Finnish school system. His research shows that the school system fails to support young people to identify themselves as lesbian, gay, or bisexual, because homosexuality and bisexuality are passed over in silence or otherwise marginalized.

Health Risk Behavior

Finnish adolescents are very satisfied with their lives: Finland was ranked second among 35 countries by 15-year-olds, and third by 11- and 13-year-olds, in terms of overall life satisfaction (HBSC 2004). Over 90% of the adolescents sampled scored above the mean on a life-satisfaction scale, and 91.4% reported feeling happy with their lives. Girls were typically happier than boys, and younger adolescents happier than older ones. Finnish young people were among the least likely in the European countries to experience loneliness. In all age groups less than 15% felt lonely, the highest figure being among 11-year-old girls, and the lowest among 15-year-old boys. They also experienced feelings of helplessness least often, although their level of confidence was very low: only 7% of 13-year-old girls always felt confident (HBSC 2004).

Finnish young people are healthier than the average in Europe (HBSC 2004). About two-thirds of them felt healthy, and only a little less than 10%

had severe health problems, which is very positive compared to other European countries. Only 12% of 15-year-old boys and 16% of girls appraised their health as poor, while one-third of the boys and one-fifth of the girls appraised it as very good. More girls (23%) than boys (16%) reported having average or poor health. Allergies, backache, difficulties with sleep, headaches, and psychosocial problems are the most common health problems, and girls suffer from them twice as often as boys. At least two symptoms were reported by 37% of the girls and 18% of the boys. Finnish young people seem to suffer from headaches quite often: the respective figures among girls and boys suffering once a week or more often were 35% and 23% among 11-year-olds, 41% and 26% among 13-year-olds, and 44% and 22% among 15-year-olds. A follow-up study found higher levels of health complaints among girls maturing earlier (HBSC 2004; WHO 2004).

Young people experience psychological problems twice as often as children, and about as often as adults. About every fourth adolescent reports some psychological problems, the most common being depression and anxiety. Depression rates of 15% to 17% have been reported (Aalto-Setälä 2002). Finnish young people were among those more likely to report being depressed once a week or more often, with almost 40% of the girls sampled experiencing such feelings. It is twice as common for girls to suffer from depression as for boys (Aalto-Setälä 2002). Girls suffer from more internalized conditions (depression, psychosomatic symptoms), while boys display more externalized problem behaviors (problem drinking, bullying, drug taking, and criminal activity). Among university students the prevalence of stress was found to be 25%, and every fifth respondent reported suffering from psychological problems (Kuttu and Huttunen 2001).

It is typical for Finnish young people to feel tired four or more times a week in the morning when they wake up and need to go to school. However, it is very uncommon for Finnish adolescents to take medicine or pills to help them to get sleep, and only 1% of girls and boys reported doing so (HBSC 2004). Moreover, only one-third of those who were found to have some kind of psychological problem had been in contact with the mental health services, and boys, in particular, use these services very seldom (HBSC 2004).

Being overweight is common among young Finns, affecting 17% of boys and 9% of girls, while 2% of adolescent girls suffer from severe anorexia and 4% to 15% from some kind of eating disorder (HBSC 2004). Eating disorders such as anorexia nervosa and bulimia nervosa are more common among young girls than among young boys. An ethnographic study on the cultural formulation of anorexic behavior shows how anorexia relates to a continuum of "healthy eating" and links it to the subject's mode of life management in modern Finland (Puuronen 2004; also see Helve 1999). Girls in particular are dissatisfied with their body weight, although they engage little in dieting and weight-control behavior. Eating a healthy breakfast is somewhat less common among adolescent girls than boys. Moreover, Finnish adolescents very seldom eat fruit and vegetables: among 15-year-old boys only 13% reported eating fruit and 14% vegetables every day (HBSC 2004), but they seldom have soft drinks or eat sweets. Among European youth, Finns smoke more than the average (HBSC 2004), 15-year-olds ranking fourth (HBSC 2004; WHO 2004); 22% of boys and 23% of girls smoke daily. In recent years smoking has increased among girls, and it is now as common in both sexes. About one-third of parents do not know that their children smoke (HBSC 2004).

Weekly drinking rates in Finland among 11-year-olds are among the lowest in Europe, and less than 17% of 15-year-olds drink weekly (HBSC 2004). Alcohol had never been used by 52% of eighth graders, 35% of ninth graders, and 21% of those at senior high school, and problem drinking was reported in 6% of boys and 3% of girls. Young Finns are slightly more tolerant toward alcoholics than other European young people (Helve 2002; Young Europeans 2001). There are only minor gender differences in regular drinking among Finnish youth, who start drinking relatively late. However, Finland has a high rate of reported drunkenness: among 15-year-olds, 56% of girls and 53% of boys reported having been drunk two or more times, and drunkenness has a rather early onset. Drinking could be considered a Nordic cultural tradition. Alcohol use among 18-year-old boys was reported as follows: 2% daily, 17% twice a week, 21% once a week, 25% twice a month, 10% once a month, 7% once in two months, 6% three times a year, 3% once a year, and 9% did not use it at all. The use of cannabis was also found to be rare, only 7% of 15-year-olds having tried it during the previous year. The proportions of boys and girls respectively who had never used it were 92% and 93% in the eighth grade, 85% and 88% in the ninth grade, and 79% and 81% at senior high school. Those who did use drugs received them from their friends at house parties.

The main health-related problems among Finnish young people are thus the high rate of smoking, the low consumption of healthy food, and the rare use of condoms. Moreover, obesity is more frequent than the average in Europe (HBSC 2004; WHO 2004), and Finnish adolescents are physically active each day for one hour or less, which is also less than the average in Europe (HBSC 2004).

Education

All children in Finland receive nine years of compulsory basic comprehensive-school education between the ages of 7 and 16, and most go to preschool for a year at the age of 6. Comprehensive school begins with six years at the primary level, and continues for three years at the junior-high-school level. One of the general aims of basic education is to encourage pupils to become well-adjusted and ethically responsible members of society. Comprehensive school places special emphasis on teaching the facts and skills that will be useful later in life. There is a separate school system for Swedish-speakers in Finland.

Basic education is free of charge, which means that the tuition, schoolbooks, and other materials are all free. School pupils are also given one hot meal a day. The law also states that basic education must be provided near home, and the arrangement and costs of school journeys longer than five kilometers are the responsibility of the municipality. In Finland, 99.7% of the age group complete compulsory schooling, which means that Finland has one of the lowest dropout rates in the world.

Education is voluntary beyond the age of 16, and takes the form of either a three-to-four-year program at senior high school or two to five years at a vocational school, which are also free of charge. After comprehensive school 55% enter the senior high school and 37% enter the vocational school. Moreover, 2% enter the tenth grade, which is a special class for those who want to improve their comprehensive school grades, and 6% do not start any education (Statistics Finland 2002). Young people who finish senior high school have the option of going on to any form of higher education. More than half of the pupils at comprehensive school go on to senior high school by taking the matriculation exam, which is a nationwide final assessment. Students need to make the first decision concerning their future schooling that has career implications at the age of 15 when they finish ninth grade. On what basis do they choose their future study field? According to one study, the influencing factors include their own interest (70%), family (5%), place of residence (4%), friends (4%), teachers (1%), economic situation (3%), school (5%), and chance (5%) (Helve 2002).

Those who choose initial vocational education have a wealth of different training options and subjects to choose from, both in educational institutions and in the form of apprenticeship training. It takes three years to obtain the initial vocational qualification, which also qualifies the student for further studies in higher education.

The Finnish higher education system consists of two sectors: universities and polytechnics. The polytechnics are more practically oriented, training professionals for expert and development posts. There are 29 polytechnics in Finland, which are developed as part of the national and international higher education community, with special emphasis on their expertise in working life and its development. There are altogether 20 universities in Finland: ten multifaculty universities, three universities of technology, three schools of economics and business administration, and four art academies. Geographically, the higher education network covers the whole country.

In 2000, there were about 150,000 degree students at Finnish universities, of whom 53% were women. It has become more and more common in recent years for females to complete secondary-level education. Students at universities may take a lower (bachelor's) or higher (master's) academic degree. It generally takes three years to obtain a lower degree, and about two to three years more to obtain a master's, after which students may go on to study for a licentiate and doctoral degree. The universities choose their students themselves through entrance examination, and there are enough places to accommodate about one-third of each age class.

In 1999, 84% of 25- to 29-year-olds had at least full secondary-level education (The social situation in the European Union 2001). Nearly 60% of the population has completed post-primary education. Twenty-seven percent of the population has a university or college degree or equivalent qualification (Statistics Finland 2002). It has been the government's aim to ensure that increasing numbers of people move on to higher education, the biggest sectors being technology, arts and humanities, and the natural sciences.

Finnish young people have a high rate of literacy: in the year 2001 the reading ability of 15-year-olds was the best in the OECD (HBSC 2004; PISA 2001). Girls did even better than boys, and also did well in mathematics and the natural sciences. Differences in these abilities were small. Finnish youngsters did especially well in the acquisition of information and in interpreting what they read, sharing third place with Ireland, behind Canada and the U.K., in terms of reflecting on and evaluating information, and drawing on their existing knowledge. Finland was the only country that was placed in the top five in all of the three disciplines that were assessed. Students in Finland continue to be among the world's best in reading literacy, while their contemporaries in Japan, Hong Kong-China, and Korea lead in mathematics and science (the so-called PISA study, Program for International Student Assessment, involved 41 countries, including 200 schools and 6,000 students from Finland). In the latest PISA study (December 2004) Finnish 15-year-olds were the first in mathematics as well.

Finland has the second smallest proportion of young people with no school-leaving certificate at the lower-secondary level, and practically all adolescents are literate. Those suffering from learning disabilities are entitled to special teaching under the law. The need for special education programs for low-ability students is also recognized. Such programs and any necessary extra training are given in the normal schools or at special schools. There are no special programs for those who are gifted, but there are special institutions that have been given a special mandate from the state to emphasize particular subjects in their curriculum. They also have the right to set special criteria for student enrollment. These schools can give the most gifted students the opportunity to gain a more in-depth knowledge in their chosen subjects than they would get in other upper-secondary schools.

Even though Finnish students do well at school, they do not consider themselves very good (in academic achievement) compared with those from other countries (HBSC 1996, 2004). The proportions of girls and boys respectively who credited themselves with good or very good school achievement were as follows: 50% and 53% at the age of 11, 45% and 42% at age 13, and 46% and 39% at the age of 15 (HBSC 2004). Moreover, a high proportion of young people do not enjoy school: at the age of 11, 55% of girls and 37% of boys agreed that school was a nice place to be, but at the age of 13 the figures were 55% and 33% respectively, and at the age of 15, 44% and 33% (HBSC 2004). Moreover, Finnish adolescents spend very little time doing homework on weekdays or weekends. Among the European countries, school seems to be least popular in Finland: among 11-year-olds, only 13% of girls and 8% of boys reported liking it very much (HBSC, 2004; WHO, 2004). Moreover, among 15-year-olds 10% suffer from school-related burnout (Salmela-Aro and Nurmi 2004).

Teachers are not valued very highly by the school pupils. For example, the numbers agreeing with the statement "My teacher shows an interest in me as a person" were very low—only 14% among 13-year-olds. The proportion of girls and boys respectively who agreed that their teachers encouraged them to express their own views in class were 43% and 41% among 11-year-olds, 39% and 31% among 13-year-olds, and 32% and 30% at the age of 15 (HBSC 2004). All these numbers are quite low: Finland with its quite formal educational systems and didactic teaching tends to rank lowest on this item among the European countries.

School is the main place where young people socialize, and being excluded from the peer group in this environment—even occasionally—is distressing for them. Compared with their European counterparts, young Finns are quite unlikely to feel excluded by their peers at school: the proportion of girls and boys respectively who agreed that their classmates were kind and helpful were 65% and 58% at the age of 11, 61% and 50% at the age of 13, and 67% and 65% at the age of 15 (HBSC 2004). This was among the highest in the 35 countries surveyed. A certain amount of bullying was reported: the respective proportions of girls and boys who had been bullied at least once during the previous school term were 47% and 57% of 11-year-olds, 41% and 62% of 13-year-olds, and 29% and 37% of 15-year-olds. The incidence of bullying others was rare in Finland, and school bullying decreased when young people moved to secondary school: 2.3% of boys and fewer than 1% of girls in secondary school reported being the target of mobbing on a weekly basis. Similarly, low numbers of respondents reported having been bullied at least once in the previous couple of months: only 13% of 15-year-old girls, for example (Stakes 2002).

All in all, in terms of education Finland differs negatively from other European countries in three respects. First, young people have very little opportunity to take part in decision making at school, so they feel a low sense of involvement. Second, parents are not involved in the school, and third, school is not highly liked by students.

English-language skills are widespread among Finnish youth: 92% say they are able to converse in English, and only 6% confess to being unable to use any language other than their mother tongue. Finnish young people also travel a lot: 80% reported having visited some other country during the previous two years (Eurostat 1997). More Finns are also studying abroad: in 1999, an unprecedented 6,600 university students studied abroad in the context of exchange programs.

Work

Finnish adolescents are not expected to make a financial contribution at home, do not usually participate in volunteer work or community activities, and do not tend to have part-time or full-time jobs (Statistics Finland 2004). Moreover, 13% to 15% of lower-level secondary-school eighth and ninth graders have a paid job, and about half have some experience of paid work at some point during their comprehensive school period (Kouvonen 2001). There were no gender differences in this respect in 1998, but working has been somewhat more common among girls since then.

About 80% of those who had worked had had only one job. There was great variation in the type of work, the most often mentioned being the distribution of advertisements, cleaning, babysitting, and hobby-related paid work. Very few Finnish adolescents (15- to 16-year-olds) work in the service and retail sectors, and their jobs are often informal, irregular, and temporary. They often find work through personal contacts: acquaintances, friends and family members, particularly parents, are influential in this respect. The jobs seldom require specific skills, and the first ones, at least, are gender-biased: girls typically work as babysitters while boys deliver papers.

Most adolescents have moderate working hours (one to ten hours per week), but about 16% of those with jobs work more than ten hours per week, the mean being seven hours. In Finland it is illegal for adolescents in compulsory education to work more than 12 hours per school week. Working boys tend to work for significantly more hours weekly (boys 10 hours, girls 6 hours). No notable differences in employment rates have been found according to parental socioeconomic status, but working is more common in cities than in rural areas. It has been shown in a nationally representative sample of 15- and 16-year-olds that working more than 20 hours a week is associated with being two to three times more likely to commit a variety of problem behavior, including vandalism, driving while intoxicated, and beating up someone. There is a significant association between intensive (more than 10 hours per week) part-time working and an increased likelihood of delinquency, heavy drinking, and drug use. Intensive work and "adult-like" jobs do not keep adolescents off the streets or out of trouble. Part-time work cannot therefore be used as a strategy for preventing deviant behavior (Kouvonen 2001; Kouvonen and Kivivuori 2001).

During the 1990s recession, real GDP dropped about 14% from 1990 to 1993, exports almost collapsed, the domestic market was stagnant, and there were suddenly half a million people unemployed. The unemployment rate rose from 3% in 1990 to 20% at the end of 1993. It was 9.8% in 2000, and higher among young people (21.4% for 15- to 24-year-olds). The rate among emerging adults is at least twice as high as for adults, and has increased, particularly among males: in 2002 for those under 20 years it was 30.7%, for 20- to 24-year-olds it was 15.9%, and for 25- to 29-year-olds 9.8%. It is also higher among those with a lower education. Temporary employment is common; 45% of 21- to 24-year-olds have temporary jobs (Nuora 2001). The transition from school to work is eased with the help of school counselors and employment offices with psychologists.

Over 30% of young people think they might study or work abroad temporarily, 25% are ready to move permanently, and only 10% would not even think about moving (Helve 2002). Girls are more open to the idea of moving abroad than boys. Finns have mainly moved to Sweden, Norway, and Germany.

Finnish women are well educated and going to work is the rule rather than the exception. Family finances are built on two pay packets even when the children are small. It is not only their high level of education and striving for equality, but also the state of the Finnish housing market that drives women to work, and Finnish mothers usually work full-time rather than part-time.

All in all, about two-thirds of 15- to 29-year-olds were working in normal (45%), temporary, or summer jobs (15%) in 2004, most commonly in service occupations. They had found their jobs through their social contacts (30%), their efforts (25%), their education (20%), previous work experience (15%), or personality (10%). The most important priorities were the salary (25%), interesting work (15%), a good work climate (10%), freedom (10%), and enjoyment (7%) (Youth and Work Barometer 2004). Being a medical doctor was the most popular dream job among young people, and being a teacher was in second position (Helve 2002).

Women placed more importance than men on a good working climate, while men valued freedom more than women. One-third of those working felt pressed for time every day at work. In addition, it seems that polarization is a danger: some are able to influence their working conditions and the content of their work while others cannot (Youth and Work in Finland 2004). Finnish young people are not eager to have their own company: only 11% planned to set up their own enterprise.

Media

Television arrived in Finnish homes in the 1960s, and by the end of the 1970s most homes had a color TV. Four out of ten children have a TV in their own room and three of every four children watch TV daily. In 2003, 15- to 24-year-olds watched an average of one hour 46 minutes of television per day, and less than 20% of adolescents watched it for more than four hours a day on weekdays, and about 40% on weekends. The time spent in front of the television screen decreased by about 5% in the first half of 2004, over the same period in 2003. The decline is mainly due to the fact that adolescents have started to reject television and to spend more and more time on the Internet.

A lot of public money was given to schools in the late 1990s for investing in information technology. As many families with children were purchasing home computers at the same time, Finnish school-children's opportunities to use modern information and communications technology increased quite rapidly. Those at senior high school were already searching the Internet almost routinely for information to help with their schoolwork.

Every fourth child in the 8- to 10-year-old age group owns a mobile telephone, and 70% of them use it regularly, primarily for playing games and secondarily for calling people. Sending and receiving text messages has become an essential function of mobile phones, and young people, especially women, send a large number of messages.

The third most common piece of information technology equipment in Finnish homes (after television and mobile telephone) is the computer. Eight in ten (83%) children have a PC at home (Kartovaara and Sauli 2000). Boys use computers more than girls, who read more books than boys. Music, television, movies, magazines, and the Internet are part of the daily environment for young people in Finland. The Internet has not brought drastic changes in their newspaper reading practices, and online newspapers play quite a small part in their everyday media exposure. The Internet has increased the number of newspapers young people read rather than bringing about sudden or great changes in their reading practices. The popularity of online afternoon papers in particular indicates that youngsters search for something extra on the Net.

According to statistics on households with Internet connections (Euro Flash 2002), 54% of Finnish households are connected via high-speed networks. According to the Euro barometer of 2001, around 62% of 15- to 24-year-olds in Finland had been online in the past week (Kangas and Kuurre 2003). Net surfing, text messaging, and role-playing games have increased the amount of reading and writing done by young people, although as a consequence book reading has also decreased.

Politics and Military

In March 2000, Tarja Halonen of the Social Democratic Party was elected president of Finland. After the election, young people were asked about the issues they thought had influenced their voting decision. They emphasized the personal characteristics of the candidates: tenacity of purpose, media skills, and experience of international politics were of most importance. They did not consider the election to be about gender or ideology (Nurmela and Pehkonen 2000).

In the past decade the young have often been described as socially passive because a fairly large number of them have not been interested in voting at elections or in being actively involved in different kinds of organizations and trade unions. Only 55.9% of the electorate voted in the local elections in October 2000, and only 35.6% of eligible 19- to 24-year-olds in Helsinki—12% fewer than in the 1996 elections. The reasons for the decline could include the marginalization of young people, and also their well-being. The economic recession influenced their thinking: some of them felt excluded, but others who had a good living standard may have thought that politics had nothing to do with it. Many consider the political parties old-fashioned. Over 150 different youth forums and other organizations for young people have recently been founded in Finland, most of which operate outside party politics.

The Finnish study showed that girls cared less about politics than boys. The critical stance taken by many girls heralds the birth of a new type of political culture, and their attitudes are more global than those of boys. Despite their critical attitude toward political parties, 55% of young people said that they were very or fairly interested in social issues. However, belief in the effect of politics on society increased after 1995 (Helve 2002). About one in four (26%) of 16- to 19-year-olds was of the opinion that none of the political parties addressed issues young people considered important, and 43% had no opinion about any of the political parties (Helve 2002).

Every male Finnish citizen who turns 18 must do some form of military or civilian service. The military forces comprise regulars (including conscripts), the reserve, and the auxiliary reserve. The duration of military service is 180, 270, or 362 days, and over 80% of men choose this option, usually signing up at the age of 19 or 20. Separate acts have been passed covering nonmilitary service (Ministry of Education 1999). There is also voluntary military service for women.

The conscript's allowance includes a basic allowance and possibly housing and a special allowance, and is also payable to those opting for alternative service and to the dependants of women doing voluntary armed service.

Unique Issues

There are certain aspects of adolescents' lives in Finland that are unique to the country. First, Finland is a country of equality with only minor differences between girls and boys in terms of how they live. Second, education can take a long time and tuition is free. Comprehensive schooling lasts until adolescents are 15 or 16 years old, and consequently, the choice of and training for a profession takes place quite late. Many young people are approaching 30 when they finish their education. Third, starting a family also occurs quite late, often in the thirties. Moreover, it is typical to cohabit for several years before marriage. All in all, there is a long period of emerging adulthood in Finland, but young people become independent of their parents quite early.

Between 2005 and 2010, large numbers of people, including the baby boomer generation, will retire. The number of people aged 65 and older will increase in coming decades. This aging of the population will be accompanied by a decline in the proportion of Finnish families with children. The post-war generations are reaching the age when their children have moved away from home, and families with children will soon be in the minority. There are two significant trends in how the birth rate is developing: an increasing number of Finnish women will remain childless while the number of children per family will grow slightly. Of the women who are nearing the end of their childbearing age, 15% are childless, and figures indicate that over 20% of today's young women will remain so.

The most problematic aspect of young people's lives in Finland today is the transfer from school to employment. Two questions of major political relevance arise in this respect: Are there enough rewarding training places to go around and subsequent jobs that gives satisfaction and provide opportunities for self-fulfilment? How do young people begin to build a relationship with society, especially the society of paid work? Youth unemployment rates have decreased lately, and it is fair to assume that there are suitable training places and jobs for the majority. The motivation for work is apparently particularly strong.

KATARIINA SALMELA-ARO and HELENA HELVE

References and Further Reading

Aalto-Setälä, T. 2002. *Depressive disorders among young people*. University of Helsinki: Hakapaino.

Beck, U. 1992. *Risk society. Towards a new modernity*. London: Sage Publications.

Cacciatore, R. 2004. *Kids need information to deal with sexuality*. http://seattlepi.nwsource.com/opinion/177787_sexed15.html (14.08.2004).

Campell, A. 1993. *Out of control: Men, women and aggression*. London: Pandora.

Giddens, A. 1991. *Modernity and self-identity. Self and society in late-modern age*. Cambridge: Polity Press.

Gordon, T., and E. Lahelma. 2002. Becoming adult: Possibilities and limitations—Dreams and fears. *Young* 10:2–18.

HBSC survey 1996. King, A., B. Wold, C. Tudor-Smith, and Y. Harel. 1996. *The health of youth: A cross-national survey*. Publications, European Series No. 69. www.hbsc.org/publications/reports.html.

HBSC survey. 2004. Young people's health in context. Health behaviour in school-aged children (HBSC) study. International report from the 2001/2002 survey.

Helve, H. 1993. *The world view of young people: A longitudinal study of Finnish youth living in a suburb of metropolitan Helsinki*. Helsinki: Annales Academiae Scientarium Fennicae, ser. B, Tom. 267.

Helve, H. 1996. Values, world views and gender differences among young people. In *Youth and life management. Research Perspective*. H. Helve and J. Bynner (eds.). pp. 171–87. Helsinki: University Press.

Helve, H. 1999. What happened to "young humanists," "individualists," and "traditionalists"? A comparative study of changing value-worlds of young people in the framework of post modernity. In *Youth in everyday life contexts. Psykologian tutkimuksia—Psychological reports Nr. 20*. V. Puuronen (ed.). pp. 48–66. University of Joensuu.

Helve, H. 2001. Reflexivity and changes in attitudes and value structures. In *Youth, citizenship and empowerment*. H. Helve and C. Wallace (eds.). pp. 201–18. Great Britain: Ashgate.

Helve, H. 2002. *Arvot, muutos ja nuoret (Values, change and adolescents)*. Helsinki: Helsinki University Press.

Helve, H., and C. Wallace (eds.). 2001. *Youth, citizenship and empowerment*. Great Britain: Ashgate.

Hilden, T. 2001. Skinheads: Masculinity and violent action. In *Youth, citizenship and empowerment*. H. Helve and C. Wallace (eds.). pp. 139–47. Great Britain: Ashgate.

Hiltunen-Back, E., O. Haikala, H. Kautiainen, et al. 2003. Nationwide increase of Chlamydia trachomatis infection in Finland: Highest rise among adolescent women and men. *Sexually Transmitted Diseases* 30:737–41.

Kangas, S., and T. Kuure. 2003. Teknologisoituva nuoruus tilastoina (Technologizing youth in statistics). In *Teknologisoituva nuoruus. Nuorten elinolot–vuosikirja (Technologizing youth: A yearbook of young people's living conditions in Finland)*. S. Kangas and T. Kuure (eds.). Helsinki: Finnish Youth Research Network publication no. 33.

Kartovaara L., and H. Sauli. 2000. *Suomalainen lapsi. Tilastokeskus. Väestö 7*. Helsinki.

Karvonen, S. 2001. Young people's values and their relationship with lifestyles. In *Youth, citizenship and empowerment*. H. Helve and C. Wallace (eds.). pp. 219–34. Great Britain: Ashgate.

Kontula, O., M. Rimpela, and A. Ojanlatva. 1992. Sexual knowledge, attitudes, fears, and behaviors of adolescents in Finland (the KISS Study). *Health Education Research*, 7:69–77.

Kontula, O., and E. Havio-Mannila. 1994. Sexual behavior changes in Finland during the last 20 years. *Nordisk Sexiologi* 12:196–214.

Kosunen, E., and M. Rimpela. 1996. Improving adolescent sexual health in Finland. *Choices, Sexual Health and Family Planning in Europe* 25:18–21.

Kouvonen, A. 2001. Part-time work and delinquency among Finnish adolescents. *Young* 9:30–49.

Kouvonen, A., and J. Kivivuori. 2001. Part-time jobs, delinquency and victimization among Finnish adolescents. *Journal of Scandinavian Studies in Criminology and Crime Prevention* 2:191–212.

Kuttu, K., and T. Huttunen. 2001. *Korkeakouluopiskelijoiden terveystutkimus 2003 (University students' health)*. Sosiaali-ja terveysturvan katsauksia 45. Helsinki: Kela.

Lehtonen, J. 1995. Young Finns in heterosexual school. *The Finnish Journal of Youth Research Nuorisotutkimus* 13 (4):9.

Metsäpelto, R., and L. Pulkkinen. 2004. Vanhempien kasvatustyylit ja psykososiaalinen toimintakyky (Parenting styles). *Psykologia* 39:212–221.

Nuora. 2000. Nuorisobarometri. www.mindedu.fi/nuora.

Nuora. 2001. Nuorisobarometri. www.mindedu.fi/nuora.

Nurmela, S., and J. Pehkonen. 2000. *Presidentin vaalit ja nuoret 2000. Raportti 18-30-vuotiaiden osallistumisesta vuoden 2000 presidentinvaaleihin*. NUORA:n julkaisuja nro 16. Helsinki: Opetusministeriö. Nuorisoasiain neuvottelukunta.

Nurmi, J.-E. 1991. How do adolescents see their future? A review of the development of future orientation and planning. *Developmental Review* 11:1–59.

Nurmi, J.-E. 2001. *Navigating through adolescence. European perspectives*. London: Routledge.

Nurmi, J.-E., and K. Salmela-Aro. 2002. Goal construction, reconstruction and depressive symptomatology in a life span context: The transition from school to work. *Journal of Personality* 385–420.

Nurmi, J.-E., M. Poole, and V. Kalakoski. 1994. Age differences in adolescent future-oriented goals, concerns and related temporal extension in different sociocultural contexts. *Journal of Youth and Adolescence* 23:471–87.

Nurmi, J.-E., K. Salmela-Aro, and P. Koivisto. 2002. Goal importance, and related agency-beliefs and emotions during the transition from vocational school to work:

Antecedents and consequences. *Journal of Vocational Behavior* 60:241–61.

Nurmi, J.-E., and L. Siurala. 1994. Adolescents in Finland—Growing up in the first train to welfare society. In *International handbook of adolescence*. K. Hurrelmann (ed.). Greenwood Publishing Group.

Puuronen, A. 2004. *Rasvan tyttäret. Etnografinen tutkimus anorektisen kokemustiedon kulttuurisesta jäsentymisestä* (*Daughters of fat: An ethnographic study of the cultural formulation of anorectic behavior*). Helsinki: Nuorisotutkimusverkosto, Nuorisotutkimusseura, Julkaisuja 42.

Rönkä, A., and U. Kinnunen. 2002. *Perhe ja vanhemmuus* (*Family and parenting*). PS-kustannus: Keuruu.

Salmela-Aro, K. 2001. Personal goals during a transition to adulthood. In *Navigation through adolescence*. J.-E. Nurmi (ed.). pp. 59–84. New York: RoutledgeFalmer.

Salmela-Aro, K., and J.-E. Nurmi. 1997a. Goal contents, well-being and life context during transition to university—A longitudinal study. *International Journal of Behavioral Development* 20:471–91.

Salmela-Aro, K., and J.-E. Nurmi. 1997b. Personal project appraisals, academic achievement and related satisfaction—Longitudinal study. *European Journal of Psychology and Education* 12:77–88.

Salmela-Aro, K., and J.-E. Nurmi. 2004. Adolescents' future orientation. University of Helsinki: Unpublished data.

Stakes. 2002. *Terveystutkimus 2002*. www.stakes.fi/kouluterveys/taulukot/2002.

Statistics Finland. 2000. Suomen tilastollinen vuosikirja. Helsinki: Tilastokeskus.

Statistics Finland. 2004. Suomen tilastollinen vuosikirja. Helsinki: Tilastokeskus.

Suomalainen lapsi. 2000. (The Finnish Child). Helsinki: Tilastokeskus

Vikat, A., A. Rimpelä, M. Rimpelä, and E. Kosunen. 2002. Sociodemographic differences in the occurrence of teenage pregnancies in Finland in 1987–1998: A follow-up study. *Journal of Epidemiology and Community Health* 56:659–68.

Vitikka, E. (ed.) 2004. Koulu, sukupuoli, oppimistulokset. Opetushallitus.

WHO. 2004. www.euro.who.int/eprise/main/who/InformationSources/Publications.

Young Europeans in 2001. Results of a European opinion poll. http://europa.eu.int/comm/public_opinion/archives/eb/ebs_151_summ_en.pdf.

Youth Barometer in Finland. 1999. Nuora.

Youth and Work in Finland. 2004. Helsinki: Institute of Occupational Health.

FRANCE

Background Information

With 60 million inhabitants, France is an established, prosperous, urbanized, powerful, officially monolingual, and secular country. France is a democracy in which individual civic rights are respected. In 2004, the country ranked sixteenth on the Human Development Index, which is provided by the United Nations Development Programme in order to reflect the level of development for all in terms of education, access to health services, and equality. Economically, it is one of the wealthiest nations in Europe, with comprehensive policies on education, health, family support, and the distribution of wealth. Geographically, France provides a good diversity of temperate weather and a variety of landscapes.

French demography is characterized by low rates of birth and long life expectancies with a very small positive migration balance. However in comparison to other EU countries, France has the highest levels of both life expectancy (74.9 for men and 82.3 for women, in 1999) and birth rate (1.89 children per woman). Population counts are 25% under 20 years of age (9% between 11 and 19 years of age) and 20% above 60 years. People live mostly in towns (74%). The mean population density is 108 inhabitants per square kilometer, but with a huge diversity across regions from a peak of 912 inhabitants per square kilometer in the Paris area to some almost uninhabited areas such as in Limousin (42 inhabitants per square kilometer).

France has experienced several waves of migration since the early period of its history and has been the subject of multiple invasions. A strong tradition of conquering territories between the sixteenth and nineteenth centuries, and a liberal policy regarding immigration during the twentieth century are two other sources of the diversity of its modern population. It is estimated that 17% of the general population is either a first-, second-, or third-generation immigrant. Six regional languages have a large number of speakers and one can count as many as 75 different languages. Mainly Catholic, France also has the largest Jewish and Islamic populations in the European Union.

Period of Adolescence

The period of adolescence is recognized as beginning upon entrance into junior high school (age 12) and ending at the legal majority age of 18. Sociological and demographic enquiries almost ignore the adolescent period under 15 years of age, while the media and marketing forces regard adolescents as potential consumers, with a stake in the fact that, once acquired, consuming and banking behaviors resist change (Bruno 2000).

In the nineteenth century, the term "adolescence" was narrowly applied to boys, especially those of the bourgeoisie. Other adolescents (boys of modest conditions and girls) were not considered as a special population because either parents exerted a strict control on them (in the case of girls), or they were already contributing to the workforce (in the case of peasants or the working class) (Thiercé 1999). It is only since 1890 that the concept of "adolescence" was extended progressively to all without consideration of social class.

The first psychological study on adolescents was conducted by Mendousse in 1907 for boys (1910 for girls). However, Debesse's influential work on identity and on the balance between conformism and anti-conformism (1936, 1937, 1942) is considered as the foundation of the field. Translated in several languages, his monograph of 1942 is still reedited.

At the economic and societal levels, the 1960s and early 1970s present three significant turning points: first, the economic boom and the prolongation of the mandatory school age until 16 years of age in 1959; second, the university student uprising of May 1968, joined by the majority of high school youth and a large segment of the French society with claims for more freedom and fewer social conventions; and later, in 1974 and 1975, reforms and laws for modernization such as easy access to contraception, the authorization of abortion, democratization of studies, and the lowering of the majority age. These evolutions discharged adolescents from the constraints of early entrance into the labor market, from hierarchical relationships, and from extended dependency on parents. During this period, radio stations and magazines especially devoted to the adolescent subculture emerged. The movement for a growing consideration of adolescence has not waned since. The main rites of passage such as first communion (religious custom), the *certificat d'étude primaire* (examination at the end of primary school), and military duty gradually fell away. The *bizutage*, a tradition to rag new students or recruits—which happened in post-secondary academic institutions with important selection and a strong social identity such as medical and engineering schools—has progressively disappeared. Outlawed in 1999 because of the humiliation and cruelty of some practices, it persists in a few engineering high schools.

Given the transformation of society and the new economic demands since the 1960s and 1970s, individuals enter into full adulthood later. For example, the French live with their parents until, on average, the age of 22 for men and 20.5 for women, with variations according to a conjunction of factors such as the living area (Parisian area versus other regions), the availability of an allowance, the socioeconomic level of the parents, and the status of the family (intact versus divorced) (Villeneuve-Gokalp 2000).

Two main factors explain the later commitment to adult roles: the extension of school attendance, which is longer in France and in Belgium than in other European countries, and the difficulties of gaining employment (Galland 2004). "Emerging adulthood" affects almost all, whatever the origin or social class, but two subtypes are observed. The first one concerns those who have ended their studies and live with their parents, awaiting a favorable professional situation (50% without diploma live with parents at least 6 years after the end of school, and 25% more than 10 years). The second concerns post-secondary students who, by contrast, leave their parents' home earlier but are financially dependent on them.

Legislators have taken into consideration the desire for increasing autonomy and the need for protection of adolescents and emerging adults until 25 years of age. Table 1 illustrates the progressive rights and duties in numerous domains.

Beliefs

The European values study indicates that French values stand between northern and southern

Table 1. The Adolescent and the Legal Domain: Progressive Steps

Age	Rights and Duties of the Adolescent
10	Consent to change of name and adoption
	Possibilities for the justice to pronounce educational sanctions
12	Opening of a youth bank account with parental authorization
13	Inscription in a national court register
	Work on parents' farm under their control
	Possibilities of penal sentence with extenuating circumstances of minority
14	Authorization for light work during school holidays
15	Sexual majority, right for marriage with parental consent for girls
	Beginning of apprenticeship only with a certificate of the achievement of the first cycle of secondary studies
	Individual passport
16	End of mandatory schooling
	Possibility to ask for the convocation of the board of guardian as well as for family emancipation
	Opening and management of a personal bank account
	Entry into the job market under some conditions
	Custody on remand until four months in case of offence and one year for crime
17.5	Enrollment in army
18	Civil and penal majority
	Driving license (car, motorcycle, heavy goods vehicle)
	Right for marriage for boys, right to sign a PACS ("Pacte civil de Solidarité", i.e. Civil pact of solidarity)
	Right to vote, eligible to a local mandate
20	Right for buying alcoholic beverages
	Age limit for payment to parents of family allowance
23	Eligible to national and European mandate
25	Closing of youth banking account
26	Right for income support (RMI, *minimum welfare payment*)

European ways of thinking (Bréchon 2000). Being a Latin and mainly Catholic region (in terms of cultural history), France conceives the links between the state and the individual in a hierarchical model. The large international study conducted by Hofstede (1980) observed the hierarchical nature of the French system and the prevailing authoritarianism but at the same time indicated the French values of individualism, autonomy of the individual, and, an equal balance between "masculine" (assertiveness) and "feminine" (nurturing) values. Twenty years later, the European values study revealed an evolution toward more individualism but unaccompanied by rejection of social links or by an idealization of anarchy or libertarianism (Bréchon 2000). People want to master their life and choose their ethical norms. They no longer accept imposed societal rules. There is a broad consensus for work values accompanied, nonetheless, with a wish for a balance between private and professional life. However, beyond their private lives, for which they do not accept societal control, many French people, including young people, seek collective rules and social order.

Since 1905, there has been a strict separation of church and state in France. Religion is considered a matter of private rights. The freedom of faith is guaranteed as an individual right. The main religions are part of the school curriculum as cultural heritage (faith, values, arts, customs, etc.). The religious communities collaborate with high schools and are allowed to organize teaching of religion. The main Christian, Jewish, and Muslim holy days are respected or accommodated. However, compared to other European countries, religious values are less endorsed. Some declare to have no religion or faith, but some others claim to be heathen, agnostic or laic, in other words, to have an axiological anchorage: 40.7% of people between 15 and 24 years of age (27% for all adults) declare to have no faith while 9.4% (13% for all adults) declare to have a regular practice, both indices having increased slightly in the last five years (Bréchon 2000). Among adolescents, religious beliefs are less important than gender and school identity. Muslim second-generation adolescents are the exception: about 13% claim to be religious as part of a "Who I am" test against 0% for the other groups, a fact that has to be understood as a protest or quest for group identity for this belittled religion just recently legally organized, and not as an increasing religious practice (Tribalat 1995).

Gender

The laws structuring the equality of sexes are relatively recent. Women obtained the right to vote only in 1944, and it was only in 1965 that married women became able to open a bank account without a husband's authorization and manage their own financial situation. School has been mandatory for boys and girls since 1882, but in separate establishments. Co-education became mandatory for all public schools in 1975. After this date, higher education institutions became, one after the other, accessible to both sexes. For professions such as firefighting or policing, there is a policy for attracting women. Some laws have become favorable to women, for example, advantages for retirement, or work restriction in order to protect the family; they reflect the pro-birth French policy. Unfortunately, because the European Union considers these laws as unequal for men, they tend to disappear without any strong policy to protect family life or for incitation of paternal involvement in child rearing at the daily practical level.

In spite of the law of equality and the excellent world ranking, inequalities persist in the practices and representation of differential competencies according to gender. Unequal differential treatment is noticeable for professional choices (more women work in services) and salaries (women's salaries are equivalent to 60% of men's salaries). Inequalities are obvious in the case of promotion and for political representation, especially in elective positions (in 1997, women filled only 10% of the parliament representatives positions).

In the French academic curriculum, a selective and competitive one, math is perceived as masculine. With an equal level of competence, girls ask less often than boys for scientific tracks; they are also less encouraged by their teachers in these projects (Dumora and Lannegrand 1996). Girls are underrepresented in scientific tracks and generally in all prestigious and selective tracks, while they are on average schooled longer than boys. Several information campaigns and government texts try to convince girls to choose training where boys are currently the majority. However, girls anticipate their future gendered role, for when asked for their future life projects, almost all consider their personal life, against 40% of boys. As a result, professional projects of girls are more often a compromise between professional and family life (Duru-Bellat 1999).

Although the pressure for sex role conformity is generally strong, the hierarchical sex role is in favor of masculine behavior. The adoption of the other sex role is better admitted for girls than for boys (Mosconi 1999). Sex stereotypes shape self-concept and self-presentation of adolescents. When girls describe themselves, they give more importance to emotions and interpersonal relationships. They cultivate the sense of intimacy and interiority (Boyer 1999). Preoccupied by their bodies and sensible of the regard from others, they are more subject to diffuse somatic complaints, are often depressive, and are more nervous, while boys look for self-affirmation in sports activities with or without violence (Choquet and Ledoux 1994).

The Self

French adolescent self-esteem varies according to gender and age. Girls have a lower global, emotional, and physical self-esteem than boys, while their future self-esteem is higher than that of boys. Older adolescents (between 17 and 20 years) have a higher social self-esteem than younger adolescents (from 13 to 16 years). Nonetheless, as a whole, global and specific scores of French adolescents indicate a positive self-image, even if girls between 13 to 18 years tend to belittle themselves at the emotional and physical levels (Sordes-Ader et al. 1998).

A study on the definition of the ideal self by French adolescents between 16 to 18 years, indicates that references to external criteria such as social achievement (academic performance, appreciation from others) decrease with age, while references to self and self-realization (coherence with one's principles, openness to the world, to be oneself) increase. It seems that, among developmental tasks, adolescents first build an ideal image of themselves based on external criteria and with age, they try to accomplish it (Bariaud and Bourcet 1998). The analysis of the adolescents' words shows that identity feeling, linked to both social comparison with others and self-reflection, is grounded on past elements and progressively turned toward the future (Rodriguez-Tomé and Bariaud 1987).

Their professional projects get more precise with age. Adolescents from the lower social class choose their way earlier than adolescents from the upper social class, who pursue studies to a higher education level. The last degree of the junior high school (*troisième*, ninth grade), a turning point for school or professional orientation, is a crucial stage for identity and self-esteem. However, a study on exploration and commitment process in the school sphere shows that school remains an "outside" world, a sphere of life that they do not appropriate (Lannegrand-Willems and Bosma 2006).

The Euronet study reveals that French adolescents have a modest self-esteem compared to other Western European adolescents and, unlike adolescents in other European countries, it is not dependent on control expectancies and self-efficacy (Grob et al. 1999). This fact may be explained by a conjunction of several factors such as educational practices, French cultural style, and school pressure.

Second-generation adolescents adopt a similar pattern. The ICSEY study indicates no differences between Algerian, Portuguese, and Vietnamese second-generation adolescents and French on the Rosenberg self-esteem scale, while the more recent groups of Moroccans and Turks announce higher self-esteem. However, in each group the perceived discrimination (which is very low, around 1.7 on a scale of 5) exerts a negative effect in all groups (Berry et al. 2006). This study indicates also a similar ratio to that in countries of settlement such as Canada and Australia, of adolescents who feel both French and of their origin (around 46%), or French mainly (about 26%) but more of their origin (about 21% against 12% in Canada and the United States), and less with a diffuse identity (8% against 16% in Canada and the United States).

According to adolescents, parents are important guides for the access to autonomy, blooming, and identity construction, but they are perceived as both push and pull factors. Adolescents whose parents have a rigid parenting style lack confidence in themselves in the domain of academic performance and social relationships (De Léonardis and Lescarret 1998). And with the enhancement of self-affirmation, adolescents detach themselves from parents like in other Western countries (Claes 2003).

Self-enhancement and belittlement at school is a core issue in psychology and educational sciences, mainly because the school system, which is based on selection, qualifies any poor academic performance as a failure. Students are made to feel guilty for that. In the French collective representation, the prototypic good student is the one who performs well in scientific training (Bourcet 1997). What is taken into account is the distance between each student and the achievement standards and not individual competences. In consequence, low grades are a source of anxiety and represent one of the major causes of depression for adolescents between 12 to 18 years (Bariaud and Oliveri 1989; Rodriguez-Tomé and Bariaud 1990). Baccalaureate is another source of stress for almost all students, even those who succeed at school. The school marks determine the possibility to enter high selective schools. To have the baccalaureate or not is part of the French self-concept. Compared to German adolescents, French worry more about studies and their professional future, while Germans are more concerned with peer relationships (Schleyer-Lindenmann 1997). Nevertheless, compared to the English, French pupils seem to have higher attainment in secondary school. The French educational curriculum appears to enable low attainders to retain higher morale and commitment than occurs for their English peers (Robinson, Tayler, and Piolat 1990).

Family Relationships

Family and education are national values and state concerns (Fagnani 2002). The state has traditionally encouraged childbirth and parenting through several means and has instituted initiatives for the protection of family and children. Both men and women say they want a mean number of 2.3 children when asked to answer in a realistic way (Toulemon and Leridon 1999). Among reasons to have children, 80% of people refer to happiness, love between oneself and one's spouse, and a desire to give life. Only 30% invoke financial aspects and the cost of children as reasons for not having children. However, statistics on women in the labor market indicate their presence in the workforce at all ages without any consideration for the number of children. French women do not have to choose between motherhood and a career. This situation requires a good organization of family life, different management of the parent–child bond, an effective social network, and a stable day care system.

Compared to other Europeans, French people accept the new alternative family arrangements more, despite a higher birth rate. For the French, the ideal family is overall marked by emotional social relationships. The success of the couple is based on mutual respect, loyalty, collective discussion, and egalitarian status within the family. During the last twenty years, a shift has been observed at the level of moral values: 40% of children are born to unmarried couples, but only 17% of children live in a single-parent family, and 8% of families are reconstituted. New lifestyles appear

and a new form of conjugal union has been established by law, the PACS (*Pacte Civil de Solidarité*, i.e. civil pact of solidarity), which is a contract concluded between two consenting adults, of same or different sex, in order to organize their life together (mutual moral and financial support) with the same rights and obligations as married couples. This legal arrangement recognizes homosexual unions. Homosexual marriage and child adoption are frequently under discussion.

French family members are close and maintain good relationships (Crenner 1998, 1999). Members of the same family live in nearby areas (30 kilometers on average). Adolescents participate in this familial solidarity; they meet often with older members of their family network (parents, siblings, uncles and aunts, cousins) (INSEE 2000). Networks, the density of which varies with economic level, are composed of 27 persons on average. Meetings within these networks are confined to the first family circle, with a preference for the direct line and with a frequency higher than once a week.

Family life is correlated with life satisfaction at all generations—grandparents, parents, and adolescents (Sabatier and Lannegrand-Willems 2005). The family includes typically two (married or not) adults and two or three children. One-child families comprise 10% of families with children, and two out of ten children are from a family of four or more children (Toulemon 2003). As a result of high life expectancy, numerous children and adolescents know at least two grandparents and even one great-grandparent, who live independently for the most part (Kerjosse 2000). Family relationships, including relationships with grandparents, are important for French adolescents. French adolescents endorse the desire for children and family more than any other Western European adolescents (Nurmi et al. 1999). Compared to Italians and Belgians, French adolescents visit their grandparents less often, but have a greater degree of attachment and more significant bonds (Claes et al. 2001).

Values that parents want to transmit are mainly tolerance, respect for others, and a sense of responsibility (Bréchon 2000). Independence is ranked ninth just after obedience, which indicates that French society is neither individualist nor conformist, but is looking for a way for all to live together, with each individual assuming the appropriate amount of personal responsibility. Two other studies confirm the openness to others and the education for citizenship. Suizzo (2002) shows that young parents place importance on social diversity (to be in touch with different social classes) as well as sensorial diversity (diversity of food, for example). According to Heydt (2001), adults say they encourage education for citizenship, want their children to meet diverse people, and do not select their children's friends.

French mothers are affectively near their children and stimulating, but compared to other industrial countries they are more controlling in the learning context (school and self-care) (Norimatsu 1994; Prêteur and Louvet-Schmauss 1994). They worry about the balance between their womanhood and their mother's role. They wish to maintain a good relationship with their child but do not wish to give up their sense of an independent self. Their own autonomy is as important to them as that of their child. Mothers are concerned with regular schedules and domestic routines, especially for sleep. They value school performance, and unlike American mothers, do not consider leisure activities of their children as a subject of pride. They try to inculcate modesty, self-control, and repression of feelings more than overt manifestation of feelings (Bouissou and Tap 1998; Stranger, Fombone, and Achenbach 1994). The parental control and management persist until adolescence and family life is scheduled on a regular basis; French adolescents spend more time than other European adolescents sleeping and eating (Alsaker and Flammer 1999). During late adolescence, parent–adolescent relationships are less warm but also less conflictual than in Italy and Quebec, and parents monitor less but are less tolerant to pranks (Claes et al. 2003). According to the adolescents' view, French parents offer less choice and more constraints than German ones (Schleyer-Lindenmann 1997).

The ICSEY study indicates that both immigrant parents and second-generation adolescents are more traditional than French for the family values (hierarchy and solidarity) but the generation distance is the same. The only difference is for sex relationship rules, where the generation gap is more important for Moroccans and Turks (Berry et al. 2006). However, because adolescents compare their parents to the French standard and parents compare their adolescents to the country of origin, some families exaggerate the gap and find the parents–adolescent relationship as not easy to manage.

Research studies on how French adolescents respond to the divorce or separation of their parents are very few. Parents' separation is associated with low school achievement (Archambault 2002), and family changes have connections with adolescents' drug use but not with delinquency (Mucchielli 2000, 2002). Nevertheless, these adolescents don't have particular psychopathologies compared to adolescents with not-separated parents (Messerschmitt, Legrain, and Hamasaki 1998).

Friends and Peers/Youth Culture

Social interactions with peers take an important place in the adolescent world. Most adolescents have a social life outside their family. More than 60% of adolescents go outside their family, invite each other out and organize parties with friends. Their extracurricular activities are in close relation with their desire to meet peers—they plan to go out in groups, and choose clubs or associations in order to meet peers. Listening to music, which can be done alone, is usually an occasion for socialization with peers: musical likings are a support for group distinctiveness (Boyer 1999). Friendship is a dominant aspect of the social life of adolescents, more for boys than for girls. Like boys, very few girls announce that they have not a single friend (less than 1%). However, 23% of adolescents are apart from peers, 23% never go out with other adolescents, and 28% never go to a friend's home. In one case out of five, this social isolation is explained by parental interdiction, and in one case of two, by a lack of desire. Boys and girls from early adolescence choose different activities; girls are more attracted by home activities and boys by outside activities (Boyer 1999).

As is generally observed with Western adolescents, French value more intimacy between friends in the early adolescence, especially with same-sex friends (Mallet 1993). It is only around the age of 16 to 17 years that intimacy with the opposite sex is as high as with same-sex peers (Mallet 1997). However, the intimacy between same-sex friends is remarkably valued. Less than one adolescent of four between 15 to 19 years old reports having other-sex friends and, among those who have a love relationship, 69% of them report to be more attached to their same-sex friends than to their lover (Garcia-Werebe 1988). French adolescents spend more time leaning against, stroking, kissing, and hugging their peers than do American adolescents, who show more self-touching and more aggressive verbal and physical behavior (Field 1999). The stability of friendship with same-sex peers while the love relationships gain in intimacy enlightens the absence of concurrence between the two types of relationships, and, according to Mallet (1997), suggests that friendship between same-sex peers supports the establishment of love relationships.

The opportunity for activities such as sports or cultural activities is large and well-organized everywhere in France. Sports and cultural associations should be open to all, whatever their origins, unless there are no public subsidies. In consequence, outside the classes for language and culture and associations around mosques and churches, there are very few ethnic associations, compared to other countries. However, activities such as sports cost money and, in consequence, participation is related to the family income and the level of education of mothers.

Gatherings in public areas are the only way to socialize for adolescents and emerging adults who live in unprivileged suburban areas and cannot afford leisure activities. These gatherings are considered as a new phenomenon and a nuisance by the authorities, fearing acts of delinquency. In a process of stigmatization of suburban youth, a law voted in 2003 intended to reduce the youth meetings under stairwells and in building entrances. The term "suburbs youth" has been created to point out and to stigmatize the specific population who live in areas called "sensitive," characterized by a high rate of social housing with the result of segregation (Bordet 1998). These areas count more than 80% of their populace as working class, and more than 40% of persons under 20 years old. The unemployment rate is very high and the presence of people of a foreign origin in the population is three times higher than in other areas. The suburbs youth constitute a microsociety organized around survival and defense against social exclusion. They feel themselves dominant inside their area but rejected by society. They invest in and control some spaces of their housing area (stairwells, caves, entrances) but consider inaccessible or "foreign" all spaces outside of their living area (Bordet 1998). This microsociety is an inclusive place from which one can hardly leave; however, it protects adolescents from the risk of roaming and identity loss and offers an anchorage within a social network of relationships.

Love and Sexuality

Sexuality and love behaviors visible in France are those of a Western country. Adolescents and emerging adults choose their friends and spouses. Law recognizes implicitly the right for a sexual life from 15 years of age. Any sexual activity with an adolescent younger than 15 years is considered as a crime. Parents are progressively informed by their children of the stability of the relationship in question and of the desire to live together. The choice of the spouse is based on desire and not on social rules and obligations. Even if parents, especially those of the upper class, manage occasions of socialization and meeting (parties) for their adolescents in order to supervise social encounters, they only try to regulate the socialization, they do not impose their choice for the mate. Adolescence and emerging adulthood are tolerated and even expected periods of exploration. The beginning of sexual life is clearly independent with the beginning of couple life, and it is neither hidden nor illegitimate. Parents agree with this dissociation between love relationship and couple formation, and for 25 years a majority of French have agreed with the idea of oral contraception for girls before their majority (Galland 2004). Within this social context of mate selection, education of adolescents and even children to sexuality plays a crucial role.

Puberty begins, like in most Western countries, for boys around 11.5 to 12 years of age, with the growth of testicles. First ejaculations appear on average around 14 years old and precede about six months the presence of sperm in urine. For girls, mammary development, which is the first clinical sign, appears around 11 years. The mean age for menarche is between 12.5 and 13 years, with a large variation of more or less two years around mean.

Since the late twentieth century, the rate of sexual precocity has been generally stable, but the involvement in a lasting relationship and parenthood is delayed. The mean age for first French kiss is identical for boys and girls. Among 14-year-olds, 50% have exchanged their first kiss. The first sexual relation appears on average three and a half years later: the median age is 17 years and 3 months for boys and 17 years and 6 months for girls. It occurs in two cases of three either at parents' or partner's parents' home (Galland 2004; INSEE 2000). Involvement in a lasting relationship occurs several years later. Marriage is delayed, and a period of cohabitation precedes marriage in 70% of cases. The median couple formation age is 24.5 years old for women and 27 for men; median age for marriage was 25.7 for women and 27.8 for men in 1990, and is now 29.1 for women and 31.3 for men, and the mean age for a woman at the first birth is 27.7 years (it was 24 years in 1975) (INSEE 2003). From the first kiss to cohabitation and marriage, experimentation with different partners is usual.

Patterns of family building among immigrants are in general more or less identical to the French one, but they vary according to the length of stay of the groups. People from older immigrant groups

(Italian, Spanish, Portuguese, and Algerian) follow globally the same pattern of marriage and fertility, except that the cohabitation before marriage is less frequent among Algerian immigrants. In the two main more recent groups, Moroccans and Turks, women married earlier and men later. They also have more children, and at a younger age (INSEE 2005). The arranged marriage of minors, against which associations vigorously fight, concerns Africans and Turks but there are no reliable data to evaluate its extent.

Because of the AIDS issue, one could have expected a rapid transformation of sexual practices, but sexual behaviors of French adolescents have not basically changed. The only exception is the usage of condoms, worn today by 80% of youth during their first intercourse (Lagrange 1997; Maillochon 1999). Adolescents who say they have homosexual relations are rare (1% for girls and 2% for boys), but these numbers probably underrepresent the practice in reality.

Sexual education is organized, especially within the school system. Children and adolescents are informed at school about body transformations during adolescence, sexuality, and birth control. The curriculum is planned to give information in several stages and to adjust the information according to the cognitive and sexual development of children. There is a large number of educational books adapted to ages from three years to late adolescence. With the emergence of the AIDS epidemic, the educational goal was first centered on prevention of the disease, without any account of the positive aspect of the sexual relationships. Today, in addition to the transmission of information and knowledge, the sexual education focuses on communication and relationships (Michaud 1997). The approaches are interactively centered on expectancies and questions of adolescents on both sexual and sentimental topics. A new goal is to educate young men on sexuality in a context of relationship and not as a demonstration of strength.

Since 1974, contraceptives have been offered to adolescent girls without parental authorization for girls who are already involved in a sexual relationship against their parents' advice. Family planning centers, anonymous and free for minors, inform on contraceptive methods and provide contraceptives. They take at their charge the fee of examination and of laboratory analyses. In 2002, 63% of women between 18 and 19 years used a contraceptive (80% between 20 and 24 years), usually pills. Since 1990, these centers afford for minors, on a free and anonymous basis, testing

for and treatment of sexually transmitted diseases. The voluntary termination of pregnancy is legal since 1975 until ten weeks, and after this period the only solution is an abortion for medical reasons. To have access to abortion minors should have the authorization of at least one legal responsible adult, but in case of opposition, one can refer to a judge for children. Nonetheless, parents can not oblige an adolescent to abort. Since 1999, school nurses and social workers are allowed to give the morning-after pill (RU86) without the advice of parents.

In spite of sexual education, two kinds of problems are noticeable: adolescent pregnancies and tensions between boys and girls accompanied by violence. The number of pregnancies is important. In 1994, 3.3% of girls between 15 to 18 years old declared themselves to have been pregnant at least once in their life, and among them 12% had a child. Nonetheless, France is characterized by a very low rate of adolescent pregnancy. According to UNICEF, it is among the lowest rates in the world. Eight women in one thousand between the ages of 15 and 19 years have a child, mainly Gypsies. As a basis of comparison, the European (continental) mean rate is 25 in 1,000, the U.S. mean is 60, and the Canadian mean is 24. Concerning sexually transmitted diseases, analysis of the French situation is difficult because of the lack of epidemiological studies and of screening in this domain, outside the action of familial planning. One can presume that it is like several other countries in that the principal victims are people between 15 and 25 years old, and that the bacterial causes decreased while the viral ones (for example, HPV infections for adolescent girls) are growing.

Health Risk Behavior

The main health risk behaviors indulged in by adolescents are early consumption of psychoactive products (tobacco, alcohol, legal and illegal drugs), driving at high speeds, driving without a license, drug dealing, and crime (violence and thefts). Suicide is the second cause of death among adolescents, but is less prevalent than in the previous period. However, in spite of the acknowledgment of the specificity of this period of age, specialized centers for the needs of suffering adolescents are too few, so adolescents are often taken care of in unspecialized centers either with adults or with children. Political authorities think about the possibility of opening specialized institutions, adolescents' houses, in each French region.

The European School survey Project on Alcohol and other Drugs (ESPAD) indicates the evolution of drug consumption by French adolescents in comparison with 29 other European countries. Alcohol and tobacco usage are more important than illegal products such as drugs even though experimentation with illegal products has increased (OFDT and INSERM 2003). Compared to the European mean, French youth smoke and consume cannabis more, but drink and are drunk less often, while they have the same level of illegal drugs consumption.

Cigarette smoking is a public health problem. At 14 years old, 60% of adolescents have smoked once in their life, and 8% are regular smokers; at 18 years old there are 80% who have smoked at least once, and 40% are regular smokers. Actually, boys and girls begin to smoke at about the same age, respectively 13.4 years old and 13.6 years old (INSERM 2004). Since 1971, the smoking addiction has decreased in the general population, but between 1993 and 1999 the percentage of adolescents between the ages of 14 and 18 years who have tried to smoke increased by 20 points.

Concerning alcohol intake and drunkenness, 77% of students at 16 years have drunk alcohol for the last twelve months, 60% for the last 30 days, and 8% at least ten times during the same period. Drunkenness is rare: 46% students at 16 years have been drunk at least once in their life and 36% in the last month. On the other hand, cannabis is a problem. In 1999, France became the first European country for trying and consuming cannabis, which is really problematic because it is known that in countries where experimentation is high, the frequent use of cannabis (at least 10 times in the life) is also higher than elsewhere. At 16 years, 35% of students have used cannabis at least once in their life and 12% have consumed it at least 10 times a year; at 18 years, 50% have already tried cannabis, and 25% of girls and 40% of boys have smoked cannabis in the last month. With regard to other illegal products, 5% have tried other illegal drugs than cannabis (3% ecstasy). The experimentation is more frequent among boys than girls.

Youth delinquency is a social issue largely covered by media, over which there are many debates among politicians. Suggested answers swing from the educative approaches to the repressive ones according to the ruling political party. This issue is embedded in large social problems such as insertion in the labor market, school leaving without any qualification (boys more often than girls), and the lack of future prospects for some adolescents (Coslin 1997). The number of minor delinquents increased five times since 30 years ago. Since 1994, the rate of questioning of minors by police has increased by 13% to 14% a year. Juvenile delinquency changed qualitatively: deviant behaviors changed toward an increase of acts against property (three-quarters of offenses) such as shoplifting, theft from a vehicle, car or motorcar thefts, and acts of vandalism (Coslin 1999). These misconduct behaviors are related to gender. In the whole, they involve more boys than girls: there is one girl for 8 or 10 boys. Motor vehicle thefts and thefts from vehicles are the acts of boys (respectively 97% and 94%), and most often in small groups. Shoplifting is more frequent among girls: one-third of it is committed by girls. The increase of school violence and incivilities within the school institution are the acts of boys (Coslin 1997).

Suicide in adolescence among 15- to 24-year-olds is the second highest cause of decease (15% of deaths) after road accidents (30% of deaths); among 25- to 34-year-olds it is the most frequent cause of death. However, adolescents between 15 and 19 years seldom commit suicide—data concern more emerging adults above the age 20. In 1997, the suicide rate of boys aged from 15 to 24 years was 13.4% and of girls 4.3%. For all the French population it is 28.4% for men and 10.1% for women. The suicide rate increases with age in a rising line from infancy until old age. In comparison with 17 European countries, the French suicide rate is around the mean for boys and girls. There is, however, an unequal distribution in the French territory with an overrepresentation in rural areas (Brittany, Normandy, and Centre) and in all really disadvantageous situations such as school dropouts and very low sociocultural levels (Pommereau 2001).

An INSERM survey from 1993 indicates different rates of suicidal ideation according to age (junior high school compared to high school) and gender. At the lycée level, 23% of boys and 35% of girls declare to have thought about suicide during the last 12 months and among them, respectively 8% and 13% often thought about it. Among junior high school students, 12% among boys and 22% among girls thought about suicide, and respectively 7% and 9% often thought about it. Two studies in 1978 and in 2000 (INSEE), indicate a fairly stable rate of suicidal ideation. Concerning suicidal attempts, the rate is also higher for females than for males. Among people younger than 25 years, there is one death for 22 suicide attempts among boys and one death for 160 suicide attempts among girls (Mallet 2004).

Education

Free schooling is a right (and duty) for every child from 6 to 16 years living in the French territory, even for illegal immigrant children. Since Jules Ferry's law in 1882, school that is mandatory, free, and nonconfessional has been seen as a "republican" instrument to educate peasants, the working class, and immigrants, and as a means of integration. The first article of the Jules Ferry law mentions "civic instruction" as the most important subject to be taught. School is highly valued by politicians because it is seen as the principal means to ensure the equal opportunity of chance for all, including girls and poor people (peasants and unskilled workers).

Public school is considered as good, and 70% of children attend public school, with little disparity between regions. The French state is very active in the school system and is concerned with children's education. The local initiatives are rather feeble. School programs, schedules, teachers' training, and enrollment are a matter of state decision. The teacher's role is to provide children the appropriate knowledge and all the necessary abilities for their intellectual formation. The most common attitude of teachers is conformity. They expect autonomy, which is conceived as the ability to do one's own work, to obey directives, and to anticipate what to do in new learning situations. Having genuine affective relationships with teachers is not a shared value or priority.

The typical school day lasts six hours on four and a half days a week. There is a rest day in the middle of the week where different leisure activities are offered and where children can attend catechism class. Nonetheless, the number of school days a year as compared to other countries is small (177 school days a year). Besides the two-month summer vacation and the two weeks for Christmas break, there are three other school breaks, one in each term.

The French school system is globally divided in four independent levels of institutions. The first, the preschool, is part of the educational system, and 98.5% of 3-year-olds attend school at least half a day. The second level is the primary school with five grades. The third is the "college" (first level of secondary school) with basically four grades. The program is the same for everybody, with no speciality for the two first levels (sixth and seventh grades), and the only possible diversification is the choice of the second language. At the level "4ième" (eighth grade), some different paths are possible. The vocational training can begin at the level "5ième" (seventh grade), but exceptionally. At the fourth level, "lycée," with three grades, a real diversification is possible. Students can enter vocational training which ends with a professional diploma and opens the door for a job. They can also choose a general formation either with theoretical and intellectual subjects or with an introduction to the active life and courses more oriented toward practical topics. The last year of lycée, called "terminale," ends with a national examination, "baccalauréat." This highly valued diploma is considered as the first university one, and as such it gives the right to enter the university and many professional schools. In 1984, the government planned that 80% of youth should obtain the baccalaureate with the argument that a modern and competitive society needs people with a high-level qualification and good flexibility. In fact, in 2000, the proportion of "bacheliers" is 62% (33% in the general program, 18% in technological, and 11% in professional).

Overall, with the school policies from the preschool to the end of the secondary level, France is a country where the population stays longer in the school systems (in 2000, schooling expectation is 16.5 years), and the ratio of part-time studies is especially low compared to other European countries. Table 2 indicates the proportion of the emerging adults involved within an academic system.

The level of the highest diploma follows an ascending line. Within the last twenty years, the ratio of adolescents leaving school without any diploma has been divided by two (in 1997, it was 13% of all students) and the ratio of diplomas in higher education increased more than twice (in 1997, it was around 40%). This transformation, however, masks the disparity in access to higher education. Only 22% of lower-class adolescents get a diploma at the level of higher education (against 72% of upper-class adolescents), and, among them, about 31% obtain the lowest diploma.

Table 2. Occupations of the French Emerging Adults

Age	At School or Post-Secondary Studies	Working	Unemployment	Not Active
18–19	84%	11%	4%	2%
20–21	66%	23%	8%	2%
22–23	39%	48%	10%	3%
24–25	18%	65%	12%	5%

Comparison within the European Union indicates a very similar distribution of youth in the diverse school levels according to their socioeconomic background. Among the 15 European countries, 11% of students in the higher education system come from the lower class (12% in France). It is also noticeable that the ratio of girls in higher education increased a little more than twice in the EU and in France, and women are henceforth more numerous than men in higher education (INSEE 2000).

In a survey with 12,000 participants in 1993, a large majority admitted being absent at least one day over the last 12 months, half of students admitted being late, and one-third admitted skipping classes (Choquet and Hassler 1997). However, such behaviors are frequent only for a small minority. About 7% of students in "lycée" are considered as absenteeist. Criteria for absenteeism are the combination of two among the three following behaviors: skipping of classes often, being late often, and being absent for a full day often. The habit of being late and absent increases regularly with age (2% at 13 years skip classes often, and 13% at 19 years old). It is frequent among students who have repeated grades (a usual practice with the aim to reduce academic failure).

The answer of authorities to absenteeism is adapted to each individual case according to the student's personal, social, and familial situation, but an inquiry shows a large disparity of tolerance among the different regions and institutions (Ministère de l'éducation nationale 2002). At the national level, the rate of junior high school students declared to authorities as absenteeist was 2% to 2.5% in 2001/2002. In this way, among the 82,000 recorded reports, 70% were followed by a warning to the parents from the School Inspectorate. About 20% of reports were followed by a transmission of information to the Family Allowance Department but with a large variation according to the French Departments. Justice is called for the heaviest cases (5%). Absenteeism before 16 years of age almost always indicates that the student will drop out soon or later, before the adolescent obtains any diploma or qualification necessary for a good insertion in the labor market. These early leavings can be evaluated by national annual statistics of school leaving without any qualification (8%), without diploma (about 100,000), or only with the *brevet* (the lowest diploma, 160,000 youth a year). Between 1970 and 1980, these kinds of academic failures decreased significantly, but since then the rate has been fairly stable.

Work

Adolescents are not encouraged to work, although they cost to the family about 450 € a month and more in case of some specific out-of-school activities. There is no offer for paid jobs, even for small amounts, with very few exceptions such as babysitting from the age of 14 years for girls in the evening in known families. The rate of adolescents younger than 18 years old among the salaried employees is estimated to be 0.65%. Business and car repairing receive the highest rate (2.82%), followed by agricultural and food industry, hotel business, and construction. Apprentices (211,000 contracts in 2002) are the main group among adolescents under 18 years old who work.

For more than 150 years, children's and adolescents' work has been progressively controlled. The first law, in 1841, prohibited work by children younger than 8 years old in companies with more than 20 employees. In 1926, a list of specific works was prohibited for children, and in 1933 the minimum age was fixed to 14 years. Today, work by youth under 14 years old is strictly controlled and is possible for youth between 16 and 18 years old, but under numerous conditions. The new labor regulations in 2001 set the minimum age at 16 years (15 years for apprentices) with a period of 7 hours a day and 35 hours a week. Night work is prohibited from 8 p.m. to 6 a.m. (with very few controlled exceptions). Periods of rest are structured by law: each four-and-a-half hours of work has to be followed by a rest of 30 minutes, each work day by a rest of 14 hours, and each week has to include a rest of 24 hours.

The emerging adults are the main target for employment policies because of the problems they face to find and keep a job. In 2001, the participation of emerging adults in the labor market concerned 29% between 15 and 24 years (compared to 40% on average in the European Union). The rate of unemployment of young people between 15 and 29 years has reached almost 20% for many years, that is to say, twice the rate of the general population. The level of unemployment is higher for visible minorities with two immigrant parents. This data ranks France above the European Union mean (with 15 countries). Among all the youth without the baccalaureate, more than half (more girls than boys) ask for help from special centers created to combat unemployment. Out of the measures, one finds contracts of block-release training which allows vocational training in business and adapted academic teaching. Under 18 years of age, adolescents have the possibility to sign an apprenticeship contract which is specially organized for those who do not obtain a diploma or who desire a qualified training ended by a better recognized diploma. They can also choose a more open contract whose goal is to help the young to elaborate a career project (and to enter in a process of better qualification) or to master the job-search process through several approaches. To get an occupation in which they have some interest is the main worry of French adolescents, and they are more attracted by the activity in itself than by fame or money (Nurmi et al. 1999).

In spite of the absence of incitements to work, adolescents and children do have at their disposal pocket money. Parents meet the needs of their children as long as they do not work and do not earn enough money to live; 40% of parents provide help to their children older than 18 years living outside the family home, and they do it always for students, who get 73% of their income from parental help. Emerging adults who own personal capital or income receive less help than others. Concerning pocket money, 80% of adolescents (12 to 18 years), without distinction of sex, receive a mean annual amount of 780 €. This amount, nonetheless, hides the huge disparity based on family income and familial values and practices. Banks organize these practices and make offers to parents, when their children reach the age of 12 years, with special accounts providing both a good interest rate and restricted withdrawals. Amounts given by parents are punctual and/or regular allowance. Most of the time, parents and adolescents make an agreement to fix the amount, assess the adolescents' needs, and decide which expenses are the responsibility of the adolescent. These amounts are never for the purpose of studies or of public transportation, with the only exception of transportation for leisure activities. Family strategies for help are in line with both altruism (centered on children's needs) and exchange models (in return for children's efforts): 18% of families give money as reward for academic efforts (72 € in mean) and 19% in return for household work (45 € in mean). However, only 5% of parents use the model of exchange alone (Barnet-Verzat and Wolff 2001).

All together, participation of adolescents in households is lower than in other European countries even when families value familial solidarity and family investment. This fact can be explained by less free time outside the academic workload (Alsaker and Flammer 1999). Participation in the household is seldom instituted as an exchange to obtain money pocket. Moreover, French parents and teachers consider that household participation

subtracts time from academic work, which is confirmed by French studies but is the opposite of what is observed in U.S. studies (Ferrand, Imbert and Marry 1996; Fuligni 2001).

Media

The adolescent cultural world is a tangible heterogeneous reality, including rap culture, tags and graffiti, piercing and tattooing, but also adolescents who read Le Monde, avoid TV in order to devote their time seriously to culture or sports, as well as some girls who, in an identity quest, attempt to wear the Islamic scarf even at school where it was hardly tolerated and recently forbidden (Bruno 2000). This world is clearly distinct from that of their elders and younger persons with their own styles, books, magazines, TV channels that address themselves specifically to adolescents, the numerous radio networks that have a real influence on their lifestyles and preferences, and the availability of mobile phones with the messaging (SMS) practice and its unconventional spelling usage. The diversity among adolescents, which is structured around two differentiating factors, is seriously considered by marketing agencies that organize and sustain it through their large offers, serving this way the double need of adolescents of identification with a group and distinctiveness from others.

The first differentiating factor is the divide between early (11- to 14-year-olds) and late adolescence (15- to 18-year-olds). At these ages, likings, capacity for autonomy, and thinking are considerably different. The second factor is the cultural diversity of young people. Although the democratization of school, mass media, and all the new technologies have reduced these differences, three components introduce variations: the economic capital that allows the purchase of a CD, clothes, and other consumer products; the cultural capital that shapes the likings and aesthetic values and familiarity with reading, and which counterbalances the influence of media; and the social relational capital of the environment of adolescents.

All French adolescents have access to media, either through the radio—they all own one, usually in their bedroom—or through TV (95% of households own a TV and 70% a video player). They all have a telephone at home, with very few exceptions explained by marginalization or extreme poverty. Most adolescents have access to a computer; 93% of them have used one mainly at school, and 83% have practiced on the Internet. However, only 40% of families own one, and only 21% are connected to the Internet. This creates an important gap between those who have access to this resource and those who do not. Mobile phone use is comparatively more democratic: 40% of 12- to 13-year-olds own one, and 77% of 16- to 17-year-olds. Parents justify their purchase mainly by the facility of remaining in contact at all times, particularly when they are working and their children are not at school. The use of mobile phones and the Internet is embedded in multiple networks of rather positive sociability (friends, family, associations, etc.). Surveys indicate that, in spite of parents' initial fears, the adolescent use of the Internet is above all used for socialization purposes with friends, often involving games, even if the risk of delinquent behavior can not be completely avoided.

All in all, French adolescents have access to culture. Only 20% of French adolescents have not participated, during the past twelve months, in any cultural activity (book reading, movie viewing, museum visiting, etc.) (Tavan 2003). Almost 35% of people older than 15 years read a journal or newsmagazine on a daily base, but 64% read at least one weekly magazine (the TV program is the preferred one). The press explicitly addressing adolescents offers an increasing diversity of magazines and the number of readers is growing. However, because of the school schedule, with long hours six days a week and heavy academic workload, French adolescents have less free time during an ordinary day than other European adolescents. As a result, because their time for TV or Internet use is considerably reduced compared to other Western European countries and North America, they have less experience with the Internet and they spend a smaller proportion of their free time in TV watching and Internet activities than adolescents in other countries (Alsaker and Flammer 1999).

Politics and Military

Being one of the oldest democracies and very proud of it, France holds strong political and philosophical values. The foundation myth is the belief that equality between individuals will truly be realized when society abolishes discrimination on the basis of social class and ethnic origin. State institutions are the warranty of individual rights to equality in general and the equality of chance. Individual rights for association, faith, and individual freedom to hold values and beliefs are fundamental and unquestionable. However, according to the Constitution, "The Republic is one and indivisible," which means that no community as a group, including women, can claim special rights. In this perspective, legally one should not identify groups or communities according to their gender, culture, ethnicity, or religion.

Although a democracy at peace, France believes nonetheless in the deterrent force of its army. France has not experienced war on her metropolitan land since World War II, and has not been involved as a belligerent aggressive state since 1962, with the end of the war in Algeria. As a consequence, in 1996, obligatory military duty disappeared and the army became professional and voluntary. The only obligation for military purposes is a six-day practicum preparing for defense. Girls and boys must register at the local townhouse for this practicum at the age of 16.

The construction of the European Union promoting economic exchanges as well as establishing peace with neighbors is highly valued by the French. It is taught in curriculum from the elementary school and all along the school years. France is, with Germany, one of the leaders in the construction of the European Union and is among the four countries that really pride themselves on being European (Eurobarometer survey 2000). In 2003, the French were less numerous than others in feeling belonging to their national group (34% compared to the European mean of 40% and the U.K. mean of 64%), but they were more numerous to endorse double belonging (58% feel both European and French). As a whole, the French endorse more the national identity than the local one either at the urban level or the regional level (Bréchon 2000). Children and adolescents endorse the national and European identity in the same proportion as adults. Compared to other Europeans, they are more open to people of other countries but value less their own country (Flanagan and Botcheva 1999).

Adolescents and emerging adults are concerned by social life but with a distance from political issues. More than 75% of adolescents are concerned with AIDS, poverty and hunger in the world, racism, and the environment but they are reluctant to situate themselves along the right-left axis (30% versus 82% of adults). Their civic participation is only occasional: only 7% are involved in a political association, but 45% of 17-year-olds have taken part in a demonstration and 30% have signed a petition. Between 18 and 25 years old, 25% of young people do not politically take a stand. They less often discuss politics with their friends than their elders (45% never did it in 1999 instead of 34% in 1981). Their participation to vote is relatively active at their majority but declines between 20 to 30 years old: at 18 to 19 years old, 25% have not participated in any election within two years, while 40% of those between 20 and 30 years old have not voted in any election, and it slowly increases after (Galland 2002). Nevertheless, concurrently an active protest participation is emerging with petitions and demonstrations, for example (Bréchon 2001).

Facing decreasing participation in elections at all levels (national, regional, or local), and the increase of more or less serious incivilities and violence in some urban areas and schools, the issue of citizenship has become a subject of concern. The objective of citizenship awareness programs is to make sure that adolescents know and understand the modern democratic structures and ways of life, that they understand the notion of social contract, and take collective responsibilities, at school for example. Curriculum is enriched with class discussion on a regular basis to initiate adolescents about the social organization of the collective life at their level of interest (TV, daily newspapers, racism, etc.). The experience of the electoral system begins in junior high school with the election for student representatives on the class committee. At the lycée level, there are members elected by students at all levels of the national school system, and committees for the high school life chaired by the school director and a student as co-president have been instituted in order to make suggestions to enhance the quality of the school daily life at large (internal rules, projects, schedules, health education, and security). Outside school, some municipalities have taken the initiative to institute youth local councils (starting in fourth grade and continuing through to adulthood) with various goals (education of youth or opportunity to listen to adolescents and their needs) (Koebel 2001). However, observed uncivil acts and behaviors cannot all be explained by a lack of social and moral understanding. Adolescents have quite the opposite representation, more normative than adults, and think that incivilities have to be punished, even if they allow themselves some liberty and breaches of accepted norms (Félonneau and Lannegrand-Willems 2004).

COLETTE SABATIER and
LYDA LANNEGRAND-WILLEMS

References and Further Reading

Alsaker, F., and A. Flammer. 1999. *The adolescence experience. European and American adolescents in the 1990s, EURONET.* Mahwah, NJ: Erlbaum.

Archambault, P. 2002. Séparation et divorce: Quelles conséquences sur la réussite scolaire des enfants? *Population et sociétés* 5:379.

Bariaud, F., and C. Bourcet. 1998. L'estime de soi à l'adolescence (Self-esteem at adolescence). In *Estime de soi: perspectives développementales (Self-esteem: Developmental perspectives)*. M. Bolognini and Y. Prêteur (eds.). pp. 125–46. Lausanne: Delachaux et Niestlé.

Bariaud, F., and L. Oliveri. 1989. Les états dépressifs dans le développement normal de l'adolescent (Depressive state in normal development of adolescent). *L'Orientation Scolaire et Professionnelle* 18(4):315–35.

Barnet-Verzat, C., and F.-C. Wolff. 2001. L'argent de poche versé aux jeunes: L'apprentissage de l'autonomie financière (Pocket money given to adolescents: Apprenticeship of financial autonomy). *Economie et statistique* 343(3):51–72.

Berry, J. W., J. S. Phinney, D. L. Sam, and P. Vedder. 2006. *Immigrant youth in cultural transition: Acculturation, identity and adaptation across national contexts.* Mahwah, NJ: Erlbaum.

Bordet, J. 1998. *Les jeunes de la cité (Youth of the city).* Paris: PUF.

Bouissou, C., and P. Tap. 1998. Parental education and the socialization of the child: Internality, valorization and self-positioning. *European Journal of Psychology of Education* 13(4):475–84.

Bourcet, C. 1997. Valorisation de soi et dévalorisation de soi en milieu scolaire: pour une approche psychopédagogique humaniste (Improved and belittled self-esteem in school context: A claim for an humanistic psycho-educative approach). *L'Orientation Scolaire et Professionnelle* 26(3):315–33.

Boyer, R. 1999. Le temps libre des collégiens et des lycéens (Free time of secondary students). In *Filles et garçons jusqu'à l'adolescence: Socialisations différentielles (Girls and boys till adolescence: Differential socialization)*. Y. Lemel and B. Roudet (eds.). pp. 249–68. Paris: L'Harmattan.

Bréchon, P. (ed.). 2000. *Les valeurs des Français. Évolutions de 1980 à 2000* (Values of French people: Evolution from 1980 to 2000). Paris: Armand Colin.

Bruno, P. 2000. *Existe-t-il une culture adolescente? (Is there an adolescents' culture?).* Paris: In Press.

Choquet, M., and C. Hassler. 1997. Absentéisme au lycée (Absenteism at "lycée"). Paris : INSERM, N° 90.

Choquet, M., and S. Ledoux. 1994. *Adolescents. Enquête nationale (Adolescents: A national survey).* Paris: Les Éditions INSERM.

Claes, M. 2003. *L'univers social des adolescents (The social world of adolescents).* Montréal: Presses Universitaires de Montréal.

Claes, M., E. Lacourse, C. Bouchard, and D. Luckow. 2001. Adolescents' relationships with members of the extended family and non-related adults in four countries: Canada, France, Belgium and Italy. *International Journal of Adolescence and Youth* 9(2–3):207–25.

Claes, M., E. Lacourse, C. Bouchard, and P. Perucchini. 2003. Parental practices in late adolescence, a comparison of three countries: Canada, France and Italy. *Journal of Adolescence* 26(4):387–99.

Commission des Affaires sociales du Sénat (2003). *L'Adolescence en crise (Adolescents in crisis).* Unpublished manuscript. Rapport d'information 242. http://www.senat.fr/rap/r02-242/r02-242.html.

Coslin, P. 1997. Les adolescents face aux violences scolaires (Adolescents faced with school violence). In *La violence* à l'école. Etat des savoirs (Violence at school). B. Charlot and J. C. Emin (eds.). Paris: Armand Colin.

Coslin, P. 1999. Déviances et délinquances à l'adolescence (Deviancies and delinquencies at adolescence). In Filles et garçons jusqu'à l'adolescence: Socialisations différentielles (Girls and boys till adolescence: Differential socialization). Y. Lemel and B. Roudet (eds.). pp. 303–19. Paris: L'Harmattan.

Crenner, E. 1998. La parenté un réseau de sociabilité actif mais concentré (Kinship, an active but condensed network for sociability). INSEE Première 600.

Crenner, E. 1999. Famille je vous aide (Family, I help you). Insee Première 631.

De Léonardis, M., and O. Lescarret. 1998. Estime de soi, pratiques éducatives familiales et investissement de la scolarité à l'adolescence (Self-esteem, family child-rearing practices and investment in schooling at adolescence). In Estime de soi: perspectives développementales (Self-esteem: Developmental perspectives). M. Bolognini and Y. Prêteur (eds.). pp. 217–34. Lausanne: Delachaux et Niestlé.

Debesse, M. 1936. La crise d'originalité juvénile (The adolescent identity crisis). Paris: Alcan.

Debesse, M. 1937. Comment étudier les adolescents, examen critique des confidences juvéniles (How to study adolescents: A critical examination of adolescent confidences). Paris: PUF.

Debesse, M. 1942. L'adolescence (Adolescence). Paris: PUF.

Dumora, B., and L. Lannegrand. 1996. Les mécanismes implicites de la décision en orientation (Implicit mechanisms in the careers decision). Les Cahiers Internationaux de Psychologie Sociale 30(2):37–57.

Duru-Bellat, M. 1999. Les choix d'orientation: Des conditionnements sociaux à l'anticipation de l'avenir (Career decision making: From social learning to future anticipation). In Filles et garçons jusqu'à l'adolescence: Socialisations différentielles (Girls and boys till adolescence: Differential socialization). Y. Lemel and B. Roudet (eds.). pp. 117–50. Paris: L'Harmattan.

Eurobarometer. 2000. Report n° 53. May 2000. European Commission. http://europa.eu.int/comm/public_opinion/archives/eb53/eb53_en.pdf.

Fagnani, J. 2002. Why do French women have more children than German women? Family policies and attitudes towards child care outside the home. Community Work and Family 5(1):103–19.

Félonneau, M., and L. Lannegrand-Willems. 2004. Incivilités scolaires et normativités adolescentes (Uncivil behavior at school and normative thinking of adolescents). L'Orientation scolaire et professionnelle 33(2):271–87.

Ferrand, M., F. Imbert, and C. Marry. 1996. L'excellence scolaire: Une affaire de famille. Le cas des normaliennes et normaliens scientifiques (Academic excellence: A family matter. The case of women and men selected in National Scientific College). CNRS/Ministère de l'Education Nationale.

Field, T. 1999. American adolescents touch each other less and are more aggressive toward their peers as compared with French adolescents. Adolescence 34(136):753–58.

Flanagan, C., and L. Botcheva. 1999. Adolescents' preferences for their homeland and other. In The adolescent experience. European and American adolescents in the 1990s. F. Alsaker, A. Flammer, and Euronet (eds.). pp. 131–45. Mahwah, N.J.: Erlbaum.

Fuligni, A. J. (ed.). 2001. Family obligation and assistance during adolescence. Contextual variations and developmental implications (Vol. 94). San Francisco: Jossey-Bass.

Galland, O. 2002. Les jeunes. (6th ed.). Paris: Editions La Découverte.

Galland, O. 2004. Sociologie de la jeunesse. (3rd ed.). Paris: Armand Colin.

Garcia-Werebe, M. J. 1988. Relations amicales et amoureuses entre adolescents français (Friendly and love relationships between French adolescents). Neuropsychiatrie de l'enfant 36:193–200.

Grob, A., A. Stetsenko, C. Sabatier, et al. 1999. A cross-national model of subjective well-being in adolescence. In The adolescent experience. European and American adolescents in the 1990s. F. Alsaker, A. Flammer, and Euronet (eds.). pp. 115–30. Mahwah, N.J.: Erlbaum.

Heydt, J. M. 2001. Education à la citoyenneté démocratique: des mots et des actes. Une enquête des ONG (Education for democratic citizenship: Words and behaviors. An NGO survey). Strasbourg: Editions du Conseil de l'Europe.

Hofstede, G. 1980. Culture's consequences. International differences in work-related values. Beverly Hills, Calif.: Sage.

INSEE. 2000. Les jeunes. Paris: Institut national de la statistique et des études économiques, collection, contours et caractères.

INSEE. 2005. Les immigrés en France. INSEE-références, édition 2005. Paris: Institut national de la statistique et des études économiques.

INSERM. 2004. Tabac. Comprendre la dépendance pour agir. Paris: Editions Inserm.

Kerjosse, R. 2000. Bilan démographique 1999. Hausse de la fécondité et recul de la mortalité (Demographic current state assessment in 1999. Up-rise of fertility and decline of mortality). INSEE première 698.

Koebel, M. 2001. A quel âge devient-on citoyen? (At which age does one become a citizen?). Enfants d'Europe 1:64–66.

Lagrange, H. 1997. Précautions: Préservatifs et recours au test (Safety behaviors: Protective measures and recourse to test). In L'entrée dans la sexualité: Le comportement des jeunes dans le contexte du sida H (First experiences of sexuality: Youth behavior in the AIDS context). Lagrange and B. Lhomond (eds.). pp. 281–316. Paris: La Découverte.

Lannegrand-Willems, L., and H. Bosma. 2006. Identity development-in-context. The school as an important context for identity development. Identity: An International Journal of Theory and Research 6(1):85–113.

Maillochon, F. 1999. Entrée dans la sexualité, sociabilité et identité sexuée (First experiences of sexuality, sociability and sexual identity). In Filles et garçons jusqu'à l'adolescence: Socialisations différentielles (Girls and boys till adolescence: Differential socialization). Y. Lemel and B. Roudet (eds.). pp. 269–302. Paris: L'Harmattan.

Mallet, P. 1993. L'intimité émotionnelle entre primes adolescents. Aspects socio-cognitifs, sociaux et conatifs (Emotional intimacy between early adolescents. Socio-cognitive, social and conative factors). L'Orientation Scolaire et Professionnelle 22(1):43–63.

Mallet, P. 1997. Se découvrir entre amis, s'affirmer parmi ses pairs. Les relations entre pairs au cours de l'adolescence (Discovering among friends, affirmation among peers in adolescence). In Regards actuels sur l'adolescence

(Present views on adolescence). H. Rodriguez-Tomé, S. Jackson, and F. Bariaud (eds.). pp. 109–146. Paris: PUF.

Mallet, P. 2004. L'idéation suicidaire à l'adolescence: quelles relations avec la perception du milieu familial et les modes de faire face? (Suicidal ideation in adolescence: Which relations with perceived family system and coping?) *L'Orientation Scolaire et Professionnelle* 33 (2):315–36.

Mendousse, P. 1907. *L'âme de l'adolescent (The soul of adolescent boys)*. Paris: Alcan.

Mendousse, P. 1910. *L'âme de l'adolescente (The soul of adolescent girls)*. Paris: Alcan.

Messerschmitt, P., D. Legrain, and Y. Hamasaki. 1998. Influence de la situation conjugale des parents sur la psychologie des adolescents (Influence of the conjugal status of parents on psychology of adolescents). *Annales de pédiatrie* 45(10):681–93.

Michaud, P. 1997. L'éducation sexuelle (Sexual education). In *La santé des adolescents: Approches, soins, prévention (Adolescents' health: Approach, care, and prevention)*. P. A. Michaud and P. Alvin (eds.). pp. 324–34. Paris: Doin éditeurs.

Ministère de l'éducation nationale. 2002. Les abandons en lycées professionnels en cours ou à la fin de l'année scolaire 1999–2000 (Drop-out in professional lycée during or at the end of school year 1999–2000). *Evaluations et statistiques* 135.

Mosconi, N. 1999. Les recherches sur la socialisation différentielle des sexes à l'école (Studies on differential socialization according to gender at school). In *Filles et garçons jusqu'à l'adolescence: Socialisations différentielles (Girls and boys till adolescence: Differential socialization)*. Y. Lemel and B. Roudet (eds.). pp. 85–116. Paris: L'Harmattan.

Mucchielli, L. 2000. La dissociation familiale favorise-t-elle la délinquance? Arguments pour une réfutation empirique (Does family dissociation increase delinquency? Arguments based on empirical facts against). *Recherches et prévisions*, (61):35–50.

Mucchielli, L. 2002. La dissociation familiale favorise t-elle la délinquance? (Does family dissociation increase delinquency?). *Medecine and Enfance* 22:581–95.

Norimatsu, H. 1994. Développement de l'autonomie de l'enfant en France et au Japon: Analyse des progrès d'enfant âgés de 1 à 3 ans (Child autonomy development in France and in Japan: Study of child progress between 1 to 3 years-old). In *Perspectives de l'interculturel (Intercultural perspectives)*. J. Blomart and B. Krewer (eds.). pp. 349–57. Paris: L'Harmattan.

Nurmi, J.-E., A. Liiceanu, and H. Liberska. 1999. Future-oriented interests. In *The adolescent experience. European and American adolescents in the 1990s*. F. Alsaker, A. Flammer and Euronet (eds.). pp. 85–98. Mahwah, N.J.: Erlbaum.

OFDT and INSERM. 2003. Premiers résultats de l'enquête ESPAD 2003 en France. Consommations de substances psychoactives des élèves de 12 à 18 ans. Évolutions entre 1993 et 2003 (First results of the ESPAD survey 2003 in France. Consumption of psychoactive products among students 12 to 18 years old. Evolution between 1993 and 2003). Dossier de Presse.

Pommereau, X. 2001. *L'adolescent suicidaire (The suicidal adolescent)*. Paris: Dunod.

Prêteur, Y., and E. Louvet-Schmauss. 1994. Education familiale et acquisition de l'écrit chez des enfants de 5 à 7 ans: Une approche comparative franco-allemande (Family education and writing acquisition of children of 5 to 7 years old: A French-German comparison). In *Le développement de l'enfant: approches comparatives (Child development: Comparative approaches)*. M. Deleau and A. Weil-Barais (eds.). pp. 244–54. Paris: Presses universitaires de France.

Robinson, W. P., C. A. Tayler, and M. Piolat. 1990. School attainment, self-esteem, and identity: France and England. *European Journal of Social Psychology* 20 (5):387–403.

Rodriguez-Tomé, H., and F. Bariaud. 1987. *Les perspectives temporelles à l'adolescence (Time perspectives at adolescence)*. Paris: PUF.

Rodriguez-Tomé, H., and F. Bariaud. 1990. Anxiety in adolescence: Sources and reactions. In *Coping and self-concept in adolescence*. H. Bosma and S. Jackson (eds.). pp. 167–86. Berlin: Springer-Verlag.

Sabatier, C., and L. Lannegrand-Willems. 2005. Transmission of family values and attachment. A three-generation French study. *Applied Psychology International Review* 54(3):378–95.

Schleyer-Lindenmann, A. 1997. *Influence du contexte culturel et familial sur les tâches de développement et l'investissement de l'espace urbain à l'adolescence. Étude sur les jeunes d'origine nationale ou étrangère à Marseille et à Francfort sur le Main (Influence of cultural and familial context on developmental task and investment of urban areas at adolescence. Study with foreign and national adolescents at Marseille and Frankfurt on Mein)*. Université de Provence Aix Marseille 1, Aix en Provence. Unpublished doctoral thesis.

Sordes-Ader, F., G. Lévêque, N. Oubrayrie, and C. Safont-Mottay. 1998. Présentation de l'échelle toulousaine d'estime de soi (Presentation of Toulousean self-esteem scale). In *Estime de soi: perspectives développementales (Self-esteem: Developmental Perspectives)*. M. Bolognini and Y. Prêteur (eds.). pp. 167–82. Lausanne: Delachaux et Niestlé.

Stranger, C., E. Fombone, and T. Achenbach. 1994. Epidemiological comparisons of American and French children: Parent reports of problems and competencies for ages 6–11. *European Child and Adolescent Psychiatry* 3 (1):16–28.

Suizzo, A. M. 2002. French parents' cultural models and childrearing beliefs. *International Journal of Behavioral Development* 26(4):297–307.

Tavan, C. 2003. Les pratiques culturelles: Le rôle des habitudes prises dans l'enfance (Cultural practices: Role of childhood habits). *INSEE première* 883.

Thiercé A. 1999. *Histoire de l'adolescence (1850–1914) (History of adolescence (1850–1914))*. Paris: Belin.

Toulemon, L. 2003. *La fécondité en France depuis 25 ans (Fecundity in France since 25 years)*. Paris: Haut Conseil de la population et de la famille.

Toulemon, L., and H. Leridon. 1999. La famille idéale: Combien d'enfants, à quel âge? (Ideal family: How many children and at which age?) *INSEE première* 652.

Tribalat, M. 1995. *Faire France. Une enquête sur les immigrés et leurs enfants (To make France. A survey on immigrants and their children)*. Paris: La Découverte.

G

GERMANY

Background Information

The Federal Republic of Germany (total area: 337,021 square kilometers; terrain: lowlands in the north, uplands in the center, Bavarian Alps in the south; climate: temperate and marine) lies in Central Europe and has borders with Austria, Belgium, the Czech Republic, Denmark, France, Luxembourg, the Netherlands, Poland, and Switzerland. After losing World War II, Germany was divided in 1945 into four zones of occupation. With the advent of the Cold War, two German states were formed: From three zones (U.S., U.K., France) the Federal Republic of Germany (FRG, West Germany) was developed on 23 May 1949, and from the earlier USSR zone, on 7 October 1949 the German Democratic Republic (GDR, East Germany) was created. With the fall of the USSR and the end of the Cold War, West and East Germany were reunified on 3 October 1990 (now a national holiday); the rights of the four victorious powers formally expired on 15 March 1991.

Germany is an affluent and technologically powerful economy (the fifth largest national economy in the world), but growth in 2001–2004 fell short of 1%. The modernization and integration of the eastern German economy continues to be a costly long-term process, with annual transfers from west to east amounting to roughly $70 billion. Germany's government type is a federal republic (capital: Berlin), with 16 states as administrative divisions. The bicameral Parliament consists of a Federal Assembly (Bundestag, elected by popular vote under a system combining direct and proportional representation; head of government, the chancellor) and a Federal Council (Bundesrat; state governments are directly represented by votes). The chief of state, the president, is elected for a five-year term by a federal convention. The legal system is a civil law system with indigenous concepts; judicial review of legislative is acts in the Federal Constitutional Court (*Bundesverfassungsgericht*); suffrage begins at 18 years of age and is universal.

Germany is an ageing society with (as of 2004) 82.5 million inhabitants. Ethnic groups include: German 91.5%, Turkish 2.4%, other: 6.1% (made up largely of Greek, Italian, Polish, Russian, Serbo-Croatian, Spanish); religions: Protestant 34%, Roman Catholic 34%, Muslim 3.7%, unaffiliated or other 28.3%; age structure: under 6 years: 5.5%, 6 to 15 years: 9.3%, 15 to 25 years: 11.6%, 25 to 45 years: 29.6%, 45 to 65 years: 26%, over 65 years: 18%. There is a very low birth rate: 8.45 births/1,000 population (Federal Statistics Office 2004).

Period of Adolescence

Adolescence is described as the life phase that marks the transition from childhood to adulthood, a time of life in which to learn and for specific preparation for adulthood. This transition is accompanied by a number of profound changes in the somatic, psychological, and psychosocial spheres, which on the one hand means the loss of the status of childhood (and consequent unease and uncertainty) and on the other requires a phase of reorganization (orientation, finding one's identity).

The formation of youth/adolescence as an independent life phase was only established from the eighteenth century in terms of the transition to a civil society through the emergence of the bourgeois family and the implementation of general compulsory schooling (in Prussia since 1717). Children and adolescents spent increasingly more time in the family of origin, and compulsory schooling and school year groups strengthened the trend toward the education of homogeneous age groups. Until the end of the nineteenth century, however, there was no independent period of adolescence in the public consciousness.

Today's conception of youth/adolescence in Germany was determined with lasting effect by the civically characterized "youth movement" founded in 1895. Following World War 1, in line with the Weimar constitution of 1919 (Art, 143), young people were given a better legal and social standing in terms of laws (on the protection of children and young people, on youth welfare, on organized youth work) and through the establishment of compulsory schooling (of 12 years' duration). The humanistic pedagogy and psychology of the time (Spranger, Bühler) also made a contribution in this respect. In the Third Reich (1933–1945), a large proportion of young people became socially integrated outside of the family affiliation in the so-called Hitler Youth, whereby the groups that emerged in the youth movement were politically received. In the period following World War II, this procedure of receiving youth for the state in East Germany (GDR) was seamlessly continued (Free German Youth). In the rebuilding and postwar period in West Germany, the youth was predominantly individualistic, but nevertheless adaptable and prepared to integrate, helped also by a commercially driven consumer society.

With the restructuring of the education system in Germany around 1960, an extension of education and training periods was implemented (index: increase in the number of high school graduates per year of birth of each school year group). In their wake, an independent youth culture developed, with a multitude of subcultures that differed strongly according to their contents and styles. Examples of this are the partly violent student movement of the 1960s, which aimed at total societal and institutional reforms, the hippy movement, beat and pop culture, the eco movement, and many others. This led to the fact that today, adolescents remain excluded from the adult world for increasingly longer—that is, in terms of (youth) culture they are relatively independent, but financially they are dependent on their parents for longer.

A temporal demarcation of the duration of the life phase of adolescence is difficult, as biological puberty is beginning increasingly earlier (11 to 14 years), but the extension of professional training means that entry onto the job market is taking place increasingly later (17 to 30 years, depending upon educational path). Investigations into life course changes of children and young people over the course of the last 100 years show that some marks of status (e.g., school entry, participation in youth culture, entering into long-term partnership/ marriage) are nowadays reached earlier than they were in 1890, while others (e.g., completion of mandatory school education, entry onto the job market) begin later (Chisholm and Hurrelmann 1995). "Adolescence" today stands for the time span between the ages of 10 and 21. "Transcendence" is used to mark the transition from childhood to early adolescence (i.e., the time point of sexual maturation between the ages of 12 and 14). In the course of the phases of education and training, "early adult age" is increasingly crystallized as a separate period, the period between the ages of 21 and 25, and this is for the majority of young people and not just for an elite. Adolescence cannot be regarded in Germany as a homogeneous social group that, as a generation, develops a lifestyle typical for that generation through shared basic experiences (such as the "skeptical generation" of the 1950s; the "critical generation' of the 1960s; the "alternative orientated youth" of the 1980s). The variety of manifestations of life forms in adolescence should be regarded as very differentiated.

Beliefs

Globalization, rapid technological progress, and changing family and work structures give rise to the fact that many things are being questioned which used to count as certain. A fundamental feeling that characterizes the beginning of the new millennium is a growing uncertainty with regard to one's own future and the fast-moving changes in society as a whole (Blossfeld et al. 2005).

The effect of the societal changes on the value system of the upcoming generation can be found for one thing in the fact that the development of a value system is understood as a continuous process that accompanies the biography, rather than as the result of a particular life phase. It can be assumed that adolescents possess cognitive, motivational, and social preconditions that enable them to orientate themselves in the cosmos of values, and to choose and reflect upon value dimensions.

Essential knowledge about the value orientation of adolescents in Germany is based on comprehensive empirical cross-sectional studies (Shell Youth Studies). Results can be compared over various measurement time points, which enable statements to be made about differences, but not about developments in the proper sense—which would be the case with longitudinal studies. The thirteenth Shell study (Youth 2000) assumes eight value dimensions that are important for adolescents, with autonomy (creativity and ability to deal with conflict), career orientation (good education/training and interesting job) and family orientation (partner, home, and children) occupying the top three rankings. Following these are humanity (tolerance/helpfulness), attractiveness (pleasant appearance and material success), authenticity (personal freedom of thought and action), self-management (discipline and ability to fit in), and modernity (participation in politics and technological progress). In part, there are differences between male and female adolescents with regard to the level of importance of these factors. Family orientation and humanity are preferred above all by female adolescents, while "modernness" appears to be more important to males (Fritsche 2000). Family and career orientation as well as self-management are primarily seen as being conveyed through the relationship with the parents. In contrast, attractiveness and authenticity seem to be attributed to influences of television consumption and orientation to peers.

In the fourteenth Shell study (Jugend 2002), Gensicke (2003) expands on previous results on value preferences of adolescents through findings from research on value change; in this process, overriding sets of values are extracted and characterized as "value types." The underlying methodology comprises 6,000 interviews and a three-wave value panel with approximately 2,500 respondents. The value instrument was developed in a complex pretest and tested for stability. The results show trends toward achievement and power as well as the need for security, while the interest in politics

and environmental commitment show a downward tendency. Dominant value orientations are characterized with the help of groupings: "Self-confident action men and women" represent a group that is on the rise in the broad social middle classes; they are ambitious and strive for influence, and personal achievement is more important for them than social commitment. "Pragmatist idealists" come mainly from the educated classes and are predominantly female (60%). This group is distinguished through a lifestyle marked by idealism, which expresses itself in social and ecological involvement. "Robust materialists" and "hesitant inconspicuous individuals" find it difficult to cope with the achievement demands at school and in the workplace. This also results in a skeptical view of one's personal future. The "inconspicuous individuals" react with resignation to personally unfavorable situations, while the "robust materialists" (mainly males) demonstrate, at least to the outside world, their strength, are ruthless, and will violate—in case of doubt, consciously—societal rules in order to reach their goals. Although an increasing number of them are social "underdogs," they still look down on social weakness and fringe groups; a small proportion tends toward political radicalism and rejects foreigners.

With regard to religious values, a clear decline or loss of importance can be ascertained. Traditional religious values are being pushed into the background and are also passed on to a lesser degree in the course of familial socialization. In the school context too, the obligatory participation in religious studies ends with confessional legal age. Under the primacy of free will, the participation in religious services and church activities in adolescence is falling. On the other hand, globalization promotes the development of a multireligious society, in which spiritual orientation crises result, and from this, needs for personal religiousness and ritual coping aids emerge. A clear answer to the question of how values are imparted cannot currently be given, first, because there is no uniform imparting of values, and second, due to the plurality of influential factors and their systematic networks.

Gender

Adolescence is an important developmental stage in terms of the confrontation with gender differentiation. In relation to bodily development, the adaptation to socially predefined gender roles can be seen as a developmental task. Essentially, there are two research perspectives in this regard: first, gender is seen as an independent person variable, and second, gender depicts a social category and is consequently seen as a social stimulus (Trautner 2002). The gender differences demonstrated in cognitive abilities, personality features, and social behavior may be modest, but gender-specific stereotypes can be found as early as preschool age. A broad knowledge of the cultural gender stereotypes is present in adolescents (male stereotype: aggressive, achievement-oriented, brave, self-confident; female stereotype: anxious, sensitive, social, family-oriented). Furthermore, they are aware that stereotypes neglect exceptions and similarities and that the role differentiation is based on social conventions. This becomes clear above all when specific individuals of male or female gender are to be characterized through given characteristics; research results in this regard verify that the person descriptions are not oriented to gender stereotypes.

In the school context, gender-specific differences are apparent above all in the area of interests and subject choice. They essentially correspond to the gender stereotypes: comparable trends are also apparent in the ideas of young people about gender-specific division of labor. Boys and girls continue to be categorized into "typical" professions, which is also expressed in gender-stereotypical preferences for certain occupational branches (technological versus relationship-oriented career choice).

The school and the family are held responsible for the passing down of gender stereotypes, in particular through the fact that in these developmental contexts interests are initiated and attitudes and value orientations are channeled. The style of upbringing that strengthens gender role-typical activities and confronts sons or daughters with expectations conforming to gender roles regarding their choice of career is seen as a central influence. Thus males are portrayed as thinking, self-confident, sporty, and offensive in relation to matters that signify courage and adventure, while women are frequently shown as anxious, caring, and doing household activities. In terms of occupational associations, males predominantly work in jobs with a high reputation, are socially active and career-oriented, while females traditionally practice jobs in the service industry, which in terms of social worth and financial income are clearly inferior to men's jobs. Studies relating to the psychology of media have been able to show that TV advertising in particular strengthens the traditional gender role stereotype, and regular TV consumption contributes to maintaining such clichés (Kasten 2003). Generally speaking, the research results can be seen as heterogeneous: on the one hand it is reported that the gender differences have clearly diminished

in the last few decades and that the occupational interests of female adolescents have changed in the direction of a male occupational orientation, but on the other hand meta-analyses suggest that the observed gender role-typical differences remain unchanged.

Research results on the dependency of body image on age and gender (Roth 1998) show between early (12 to 14 years) and mid-adolescence (15 to 16 years)—analogously to the continuing adaptation to bodily changes—an increasing security in one's own body image with a simultaneous decrease in the attitude of being able to influence bodily states. This trend can be observed in both male and female adolescents and suggests that both genders, in the course of this developmental process, integrate the newly developed body image into their self-perception. On the other hand, there are clear gender-specific differences in various dimensions of the body image. Female adolescents show greater dissatisfaction with their body image. The contrast between the socially imparted ideal of beauty and the body development in puberty has so far been seen as the dominant explanation for a multitude of measures for weight reduction. An alternative perspective is provided by the fact that apart from dissatisfaction and internalized body images, weight manipulation represents a salient possibility to exert control over one's own body, be it as compensation for the perceived loss of control through the bodily experiences of puberty or be it an expression of self-induced autonomy. The importance attached to body-related control is also testified by the currently rising number of adolescents who wish for or indeed carry out cosmetic surgery to correct their appearance or figure. The more positive picture among male adolescents in terms of the evaluation of the body image is based, among other things, on the greater correspondence between biological change and psychological effects; thus the muscle growth strengthens the rise in internal locus of control and both contribute to a perception of the body as more active and capable.

Although body image proves to be a multidimensional construct, "body awareness" stands out as a holistic phenomenon. Regarding the question of possible body image types, Roth (1998) was able to determine with the help of cluster analysis three main types for the age group of 12 to 16 years: (1) "Individuals uninterested in their body," who pay little attention to their appearance and show a lack of interest in body-related control; (2) "Individuals not integrated with their body," who have intensive feelings of body alienation and a lack of controllability; and (3) "Bodily-active, body-confident individuals," who have a high level of satisfaction with regard to their figure and physiognomy. The three clusters do not reveal any age differences, suggesting that body image types are not a product of adolescent body development. Clear gender-specific differences can be found for type 1 and type 2: the ratio of male to female adolescents is 60% to 40% for type 1 and 37% to 63% for type 2. This suggests that the body image is represented in a gender-specific manner (type 1 male and type 2 female). If one compares, however, the distribution of types within the male and female population, the dominance of the respective "gender-specific" type vanishes, meaning that it is not possible to speak in terms of a typically male or a typically female form of body experience.

The Self

The development of the self in adolescence focuses processes of perception, evaluation, and decision making on those features and actions that define self-perception and self-environment relationships. The search for orientation and meaning is seen as a central process of the developmentally conditioned changes of the consciousness. In this process, current life conditions, cultural traditions, and the profiling of competing lifestyles provide a basis for ideas, desires, and goals that are linked to the shaping of a personal lifestyle and a plan for the future (cf. Keupp et al. 2002; Kroger 2000). The arising awareness regarding a multitude of options, but also necessary decisions, constitutes a fundamental transition in the development of the self between early and late adolescence/emerging adulthood.

A significant difference within this development is expressed in the emphasis of temporary validity of the self-definition and is apparent, among other things, in the ability to differentiate between "momentary arbitrariness" and "acceptance of the temporary nature of things," if the concern is with attributions relevant to identity. As correlates of the changed cognitive abilities, first of all alternative, self-perceptions can be generated, discrepancies between real and ideal plans can be recognized, and changes in terms of planning for the future can be implemented.

Once such differentiated images are also drawn up from social and cultural systems and the individual is able to relate him- or herself to them, the integration of personal and cultural identity is possible. In an individualistic culture, dealing with one's own identity is deemed to be a relevant developmental process. In this regard, "identity formation" takes on an important status among the developmental tasks of adolescence. The development of one's own viewpoint, which encompasses self-awareness and value orientations for one's own actions, is a partial aim in this regard. While the formation of one's "own" viewpoint is still seen as an important developmental step in early adolescence, the weighting of the identity contribution increasingly changes in emphasis toward the ability to examine one's own viewpoints through new information and experience and, where necessary, to revise them.

The recognition that the "construction" of one's own person ensues within an existing "culture" and that the living space shows elements that remain constant while also being formed by processes of rapid change, is meaningful not only for the personal identity but also for the cultural identity. This can be shown by findings on the importance that adolescents attach to the physical-material environment. In the sense of "personal things," objects can impart cross-situational consistency and uniqueness, but also a social attachment or differentiation. With advancing development, the relevance of objects for identity shifts toward their symbolic function, which is suitable for bracketing together experiences gained in different contexts as a structure of meaning (Fuhrer and Josephs 1999). The fact that in late adolescence the development of identity is already understood as a context-dependent, life-accompanying process is demonstrated by concepts of change, which are contained in "subjective development" theories. In contrast to their parents' generation, adolescents in Germany experience, in addition to far-reaching economic changes, a sociocultural change that is based on the one hand on immigration and reunification, and on the other hand is marked by courses of internationalization within Europe and beyond our continent. In this regard, "globalization" and "localization" can be distinguished as two opposing trends that are relevant for parallel forms of ethnic identity formation and demand complex orientation accomplishments from adolescents—with and without experience of migration. The real *Lebenswelt* (life-world) that can be experienced offers a wealth of cultural dimensions of influence in the form of "styles" (e.g., music, language, eating habits, value preferences), the emergence and passing of which occur at such a great speed that children and youth are not only recipients, but also help to actively fashion cross-cultural "trends." As a considerable proportion of free time is spent with media and communication technologies, it can be assumed that the *Lebenswelt* imparted through the media not only shapes cultural practices, but also—at least from a partial and temporary point of view—co-determines adolescent identity.

Family Relationships

More than half of Germany's population (54%) lives in family households with children, and 41% in households with children under 18 years. Approximately three-quarters (78.4%) of these are married couples, 15% are one-parent families, and 6% consist of an unmarried cohabiting pair. Families with one child make up 51.2%, while 37% have two children, and 11.7% of families have three or more children (BMFSFJ 2003).

In contrast to the earlier traditional family form, nowadays large changes have emerged due to the changed role of women (employment, a different role of the mother), the changed family size (drop in the birth rate from 2.2 children per woman in 1930, 1.8 in 1969, and 1.4 in 2003), the family composition (see below), and the existing value pluralism in German society. Today's family is defined more ambiguously, and different family forms can be distinguished: the normal or nuclear family, in which the two persons of the older generation are the biological mother and father and only biological children of these parents are living together, continues to be the dominant family form. In addition, there is: the stepfamily, a family with a mother and stepfather or father and stepmother with children as brothers and sisters and half-brothers and sisters; the one-parent family (86% of which are mother–child families) with or without contact to the other parent; as well as various mixtures (patchwork family, parentless family, e.g., child and aunt, etc.). Extended families (i.e., multigenerational families under one roof) are nowadays a rare exception. For children and adolescents there is no choice between the so-called normal family and the dynamic new compositions if life situations change (e.g., through divorce) and reorganization is unavoidable.

Since the late twentieth century, the development of marriages in Germany has been marked by the following characteristics: a rise in the average age at marriage (in 2003, men married at 32 years, women at 29 years), an increase in the number of those remaining single (18% of men and 1% of women of the age of 40 to 44 years were still single), the growing proportion of divorcees among those getting married, and an increase in foreign and bi-national marriages. The risk of divorce has risen considerably since the mid-1960s: the divorce rate rose from 12% (1965) to 39.9% (1995) up to 55% in 2003. Approximately half of divorced marriages had one or several underage children.

Investigations show (cf. Fuhrer 2005) that over the last 30 years, a change has occurred in parents' attitudes toward goals of upbringing and values that they wish to impart to their children. Nowadays, independence and personality development of children are given greater emphasis than traditional goals such as diligence, orderliness, and obedience. In addition, generally more liberal models of dealing with children are reported. Currently, a generalization of goals of child rearing can be assumed, which in the past were typical for the middle and upper classes. It is now taken for granted that parents bear a great deal of responsibility for the development of their children and that "talent" and school achievement are not a "nature-given fate" but are rather closely related to the parents' behavior in fostering such factors. Accordingly, economic expenditures and the amount of time that parents spend with their children have risen sharply. At the same time, however, it can be established that parents frequently feel overstretched and uncertain in their child rearing behavior, and in terms of whether and how, with the upbringing of their children, they can fulfill the demand of enabling the children an optimal personality development/independence. Parallel to this, however, a new type of sub-proletarian milieu has emerged in which a multitude of problem situations are condensed (unemployment, alcoholism, housing shortage, etc.), with corresponding effects on the style of upbringing and the associated problem behavior of children. A retreat of the parents away from the authority function as well as a "hands-off" family atmosphere and only loose family ties (or lack of ties) are characteristic of these as pathogenic moments. For adolescents, this is linked with a deficit in terms of internalized norms and values and an associated increasing readiness toward violence and aggression.

The parent–child relationship in adolescence has therefore changed significantly in comparison to its traditional form. The authority of the parents is characterized less strongly than in the past, and adolescents no longer have to "push their parents away" in order to be able to go their own way. The "commando family" (normative regulation by cross-individual standards) has been replaced by the "negotiation family," in which rules are less fixed and are instead more frequently also explained and discussed (though this does not apply to the traditional Muslim immigrant families). However, today's parents have in no way discarded their function as educators. They continue to hold the responsibility of ensuring an optimal school career of their children and consequently enable them to have a professional career. Adolescents still see their parents as persons of authority with greater knowledge and experience. However, through an increasing independence from their parents, adolescents are beginning to relate the behavior of their parents more with the *role* of mother or father. With this process of constant change in the relationship to the parents, the two parties mutually influence one another. In this process of reorganization of relationships, parents remain important sources of support and persons to whom adolescents feel emotionally tied. However, this does not always occur without conflict—rather, the negotiating of everyday problems is a part of everyday life. The climate is more temperate; the times of great youth revolts are a thing of the past.

A central task of growing up consists in the separation from the family of origin and the building of an independent life. In terms of this situation, which makes a change in the relationship to the adolescent inevitable, parents can react differently. Dreher and Dreher (2002) examined the change in relationships in this separation phase and asked young adults to retrospectively characterize the interaction with their parents and the parents' emotional reaction. Three modes of separation were differentiated: (1) distancing without permission with increasing mutual alienation, (2) conflict-avoiding regulation mode with instrumental harmonization (do that which is not forbidden), and (3) distancing with permission, which is marked by growing mutual trust. In longitudinal studies in Germany and Switzerland, Fend (1998, 2000) was able to show that disagreement/conflict between parents and adolescents in itself is perfectly normal and does not necessarily have to damage the relationships in the long term. It depends on how different points of view are negotiated and how the parties are sensitive to one another. If, however, the conflict level is high and there is a great deal of argument, the regulating processes are so damaged that the separation cannot ensue in a successful manner.

In general, a deterioration of the well-being in the parental home is apparent for both genders between the ages of 12 and 16 years. The number of points of disagreement decreased clearly at 16 years, whereby the culmination was already reached for boys at the age of 13 years, and for girls only at the age of 15. For the 13-year-olds, "clothes" and "shopping" were the most frequently cited sources of conflict, while for the 16-year-olds,

the focus was on political differences of opinion and negotiating the evening curfew ("going out"). In relation to disagreement/conflicts, Fend (2000) differentiated three predominant groups of families: the first group (approximately 25%) reports increasing difficulties in the period from the seventh to the ninth grade. The parents had previously undertaken a great deal together with their children and the majority of them had high demands in terms of education. The children report an increase in differences of opinion and a deterioration of the relationship quality. However, they also show a reduction in motivation. The parents showed themselves to be lacking in flexibility, attempted to control the situation with strictness and pressure, and feared losing their authority. A second group (approximately 30%) experienced the most problems in early adolescence (seventh grade) and had already overcome them by the time they reached mid-adolescence (ninth grade). In such families, the adolescents felt increasingly freer and more accepted. The parents had adapted themselves to the growing need for independence of their children, but also worried about them less. The third group of parents unanimously and consistently referred to their children positively. They have a tolerant, less punitive parenting style and get on well with the child throughout the whole period of observation. The adolescents in these families are self-confident, have few disagreements with their parents, are motivated and feel accepted. One should, however, keep in mind that *both* sides contribute to a successful relationship in the transition to adulthood.

In a representative survey (German Shell Youth 2002), it was apparent that independently of gender, regional origin, or school forms (see the following section on education), the relationship to the parents is fairly good in nine out of ten adolescents, and improves further still with increasing age of the adolescents. In the evaluation of the upbringing by their parents, the adolescents reached an astonishingly uniform picture: 35% of the adolescents indicated that they had been raised strictly/very strictly. A majority of 54% stated that they had not been raised particularly strictly, and 10% rated the upbringing by their parents as not at all strict. There was very little difference between the genders, and in terms of regional origin and age group. On the whole, it was apparent that approximately two-thirds (64%) of adolescents categorized the upbringing by their parents as at least not particularly strong, and equally, more than two-thirds (71%) would raise their own children in the same way in which they themselves were brought up. This testifies that a majority of adolescents do not show any great distance from their parents in terms of questions of upbringing, and wish to adopt for themselves the child rearing style they experienced from their parents.

In the survey, the adolescents attached a high level of importance to the family: for instance, 70% of adolescents stated that one needs a family in order to be happy. At the same time, marriage is not taken for granted among adolescents: only 34% said yes to the question of whether one should marry if one is cohabiting with a partner, while 52% were undecided. On the other hand, two-thirds (67%) of the adolescents declare that they would like to have children themselves in the future (28% don't yet know, and only 5% state that they do not wish to have children of their own).

Friends and Peers/Youth Culture

In a representative survey, more than three out of five 14- to 27-year-olds in Germany indicated that they belonged to a peer group or "clique" (IPOS 2003). Such cliques (characterized by approximate equality in terms of age, rank, status, and state of personality development) generally consist of five to ten people. They are mostly composed of people of the same gender and a great deal of time is spent together in order to pursue a number of different activities. The East–West differences were found to be relatively large in the survey: in the old federal states, 66% indicated that they belonged to a clique, while in the new federal states this figure was 55%. Thus, the proportion in both areas is on a slight decline, which is clearer in the East. In 1999, the proportion in the West still lay at 69%, and in the East this was 63%. While little has changed in the West over the course of time (1963: 68%, 1995: 69%, 1999: 69%, 2002: 66%), in the East, the proportion of those who claimed to be in a clique nearly doubled (1993: 31%, 1995: 37%, 1999: 63%, 2002: 55%). This development could have something to do with the fact that the term "clique" was not particularly widespread in the East prior to reunification, or rather had a different connotation. The shift in meaning toward the West German understanding of the term clearly took place, then, over the course of time. With increasing age, the proportion of those who class themselves as belonging to a clique decreases continuously. For instance, in the West, 73% of 14- to 17-year-olds belong to a clique, but only 55% of 25- to 27-year-olds. In the East, this decline is even steeper; the number of those who are members of a clique drops from 68% in the youngest group surveyed to 36% of the oldest group. Among those studied,

in all age groups, there are somewhat more males than females who belong to a clique in percentage terms.

Within peer groups, the following developments can be established: 9 to 13 years, mostly same-sex groups; 13 to 14 years, mixing of these groups in favor of mixed-sex groups; older than 16 years, from larger groups, more intimate groups of two and four are formed, which slowly lead to adult pair behavior. The relationships within a clique, which are on a voluntary basis, do not necessarily have to show closeness to friendships, but members do mostly like and appreciate one another. Friendships are typically dyadic relationships with a certain stability, whereby mutual dependencies exist more clearly and are additionally linked to the following goals: striving for recognition, care, acceptance, and closeness, as well as requests of practical help. The degree of affection, intimacy, and mutual support varies over time between the friendships. In contrast to peer groups, however, the frequency and intensity of contact is substantially greater.

The peer group is a source for psychosocial well-being (recognition, protection), support (in terms of burdens and problems), and fostering development (with regard to social behavior, competencies, moral concepts). The peer relationships are, moreover, an important source of self-experience and consequently of self-definition for the adolescents. Adolescents of the same age have a different, namely more egalitarian position, and provide different feedback from different areas than the parents or other adults. This is important for the development of self-concept and identity formation, as well as for the acquisition of social skills. At the same time, though, the family retains its high level of importance for the adolescents: approximately 75% of adolescents between 12 and 25 years old still live in the family of origin; 90% of the adolescents indicate that they get on well with their parents in spite of occasional differences of opinion. The atmosphere (clarity, openness, positive feedback) within the peer group is even rated somewhat more positively in comparison to the family. The amount of time that is spent with peers corresponds roughly to that spent with the family. Peers mainly fulfill the task of organization of leisure time, while the family brings with it obligations and duties. A decisive difference also exists in terms of relationships of power and influence: with friends, the power relations are more or less equal, while the parents exert influence and control. The power differences do decrease over time, but even in young adulthood the relationship is still unequal;

in Germany, the family remains an important point of orientation for adolescents.

Thirty-six percent of all young Germans are members of a youth organization, a youth club, or the youth section of an association or other type of organization. At 38%, the proportion in the west of the Republic is higher than in the east at 30%. Among the adolescents and young adults who are members of youth organizations, there are clearly more males than females. In the west, 45% of 14- to 27-year-old males are members, and only 31% of females. In comparison to 1999, the percentage proportion of males is therefore on the decline, while the proportion of females is rising (in the west in 1999: males, 47%, and females, 28%). In the east, these figures are, today, a comparable 35% of men and 24% of women. Youth organizations and associations are most sought after by the younger groups surveyed: for instance, 48% of the 14- to 17-year-olds in western Germany indicated belonging to a youth organization while this figure was only 31% among the 25- to 27-year-olds. In the east, the same picture is apparent, with 38% in the youngest group and 23% in the oldest group. Further differences can be discerned based on occupation: 49% of school pupils in the west are part of a youth organization (east: 40%), 36% of apprentices (east: 31%), 35% of students (east: 27%), but only 31% of those in employment (east: 24%).

The broad majority of young Germans are members of sports clubs (west: 64%, east: 62%), followed in the west with a large gap by churches (12%), the fire brigade/*Technisches Hilfswerk* (relief organization) (8%), *Freizeit und Geselligkeit* (a type of youth club) (8%), music clubs (7%), and trade organizations (1%). In the east, the fire brigade/THW is at second place (9%), followed by *Freizeit und Geselligkeit* and churches (8% each), music clubs (7%), and trade organizations (4%). The distribution across the individual types of organization is therefore similar in both areas of the country. Comparatively few young people are part of self-organized citizen groups (e.g., citizen initiatives that work independently of parties, associations, etc.): 6% in East and West Germany.

Since the latter half of the twentieth century, various different dominant youth cultures, occurring one after the other, have been observable in Germany (cf. Bundeszentrale für politische Bildung 2004). At the end of the 1960s and beginning of the 1970s, hippies and rebellious students spread across Federal German society; ten years later punks and squatters caused a stir, marked by political impetus and staged generational conflict. This was followed by the techno scene (with the Love Parade), which,

however, was nonpolitical in nature and accompanied by a consumer-oriented fun ethos. The turn of the new millennium, by contrast, emerged without the development of a new or even political youth culture (at most, the extreme-right subculture has continued to exist since the 1980s). It was observable that each new youth culture was at some point taken over by commerce and strayed into the mainstream—anything authentically new has become rare, and not implicitly recognizable as such. Whereas in the past belonging to youth cultures was explained as an exception or a marginal social phenomenon, and attempts were made to attribute it to social causes or specific societal constellations, nowadays it is seen as more or less normal. Today, a differentiation of a spectrum of youth-cultural basic patterns can be discerned and a multitude of variants and mixtures have emerged. The existence of youth cultures (plural!) is today, in contrast to the past, something that is seen as perfectly normal. This has been contributed to by the fact that the time period of adolescence has increasingly extended, that the educated classes have grown, and that a loss of function of family and societal institutions has occurred, which has extended the potential of adolescents for participation in youth cultures. In addition, it is stated that modern Western societies (including Germany) no longer provide any institutionalized, formalized, or ritualized transitions from the adolescent world into the adult world. With their diverse offerings, youth cultures seem to have filled this gap. Media, fashion, consumption, and lifestyles and leisure styles play a role in this regard, as does the language of the adolescents.

However, using the language of adolescents to draw conclusions can be deceptive, as youth language is used consciously by the media. The resources that the adolescents draw from stem to an increasing degree from the media, which serves the commercialized youth group styles. Adolescents' manipulation of language has therefore nowadays less of a function of expressing protest (as was perhaps the case in the past). Rather, it is increasingly becoming part of the "fun ethos" molded by the media.

Youth cultures are subject on the one hand to a strong pressure for change on the part of globalization. On the other hand, they—or rather their bearers—attempt increasingly to have an influence themselves on globalization processes, to use them for their own will, to shape them or to push them back. They frequently occur as (1) the avant-garde of globalization processes, (2) as local alternative cultures, which ostentatiously oppose the cultural uniformity through globalization processes (to which extreme right trends also count), and (3) as progressive critics of globalization.

Even if the level of expectations of today's young people is strongly geared toward an identity shaped by work, from a contemporary historical perspective, the spheres of possibility and experience and the level of expectations have grown tremendously. Thus adolescents are in a position to, or rather are faced with the task of, planning their lives independently and choosing the right future for them from a multitude of possibilities and accompanied by a barely calculable societal development.

Love and Sexuality

Love and sexuality in adolescence cannot be considered independently of relationship quality, closeness, intimacy, emotions, expectations, and the sociocultural context. Due to secular acceleration (e.g., decline in the age at menarche), social changes (e.g., co-education, increasing distance from church and religion), and medical advances (e.g., contraceptive pill, intrauterine contraception), from the 1960s on a liberalization in sexual matters and a dramatic change of sexual morality took place in Germany; for example, the attitude toward premarital intercourse changed from nearly 80% rejection in the mid-1960s to almost 90% assent at the beginning of the 1990s (Fend 2000). Nevertheless, among young people today, sexuality is not marked by liberality and lack of restraint, but rather the management of sexuality is integrated in the emergence of social intimate relationships, for which responsibility, social ties, authenticity, need for ties, acceptance, and self-worth are objects of a reciprocal negotiation process.

In Germany, the choice of a partner, which is based strongly on attractiveness and "personal chemistry," is nowadays generally the responsibility of the young people themselves. This does not apply, however, to an unlimited extent to foreigners living in Germany (e.g., Muslim minorities), as in this case the establishment of partnerships is often a matter for the parents, and male and female adolescents are often kept separate from one another.

"Romantic ties/relationships" develop both in the course of a certain relationship and in the change of partnerships, whereby the integration of different behavioral systems (affiliation, attachment, caring, reproduction [cf. Furman and Wehner 1997]) plays a role. The time point of the first romantic relationship varies strongly from person to person and is influenced by sociocultural, family, and peer-group norms as well as psycho-biological maturity. The coming together of the sexes in Germany mostly takes place through "dates," although this does not correspond precisely to the U.S. understanding of the term "dating." In Germany, male and female adolescents can agree to meet up in groups. One does not require a particular date with only two people in order to go to nightclubs or parties. Often, however, adolescents go along in order to find somebody for a short-term or long-term (steady boyfriend/girlfriend) romantic relationship. For adolescents, it is a developmental task to build up more mature relationships that later lead to finding a partner and establishing a family. The social pressure in this respect can be very burdensome for homosexual adolescents, even though homosexuality is not subject to prosecution (since 1969). Coming closer to a same-sex partner requires not only recognizing and acknowledging one's own homosexual identity, but also letting another adolescent know about it, which is a difficult and fear-ridden step for many adolescents. Derogatory, offensive, and deprecatory comments about (homo-) sexual orientation as well as poking fun and swear words directed against homosexuals are fairly common among adolescents. However, to speak of discrimination would be misleading. Rather, surveys show that three-quarters of adolescents share the view that homosexuality is increasingly tolerated by society.

Once hormonal changes have occurred in puberty and it is possible for an adolescent to be sexually active, then in interaction with socially imparted models, a motivational readiness for sexuality results, whose implementation into action is culturally determined. In the life period from 13 to 16 years, we find the first serious entry into sexual behavior, which in Germany also follows an almost ritualized sequence: kissing, stroking, closer touching, petting (breasts, genitalia), sexual intercourse. Today, 38% of 14- to 16-year-old girls and 29% of boys in Germany are sexually experienced (BZgA 2004). However, there is a constantly large group (one-third of girls and 46% of boys) who have not yet had sexual intercourse at the age of 17 years. For 71% of boys and 81% of the girls surveyed, love is a prerequisite for the uptake of sexual intercourse (see above). The average age of the "first time" was 15.1 years for the age group of 14- to 17-year-olds in 2001 (modal value 16 years). A rapid change in the sexual behavior of adolescents in the form of an acceleration of early sexual contacts began as early as the late 1960s and early 1970s, and has remained relatively constant up to the present day: the sexual experiences of 16- to 17-year-olds in the 1990s correspond approximately to those of adolescents in 1970, although very early sexual contacts (before the age of 15) are today more frequent.

For the majority of adolescents, the first sexual intercourse is unplanned: only 33% of girls and 28% of boys knew in advance that "it" would happen. Contraceptives were used during the first intercourse by 89% of girls and 84% of boys between 14 and 17 years (of this, condom: 66%; pill: 23.5%). Only a minority had more than one up to a maximum of three sexual partners during adolescence. In the past, nearly one in five boys (19%) reported having had homosexual contacts; today this figure lies at only 2%.

Parents are taking on an increasing responsibility for sexual education in terms of the contraceptive behavior of adolescents; since 1980, advice imparted within the family has doubled. In 2001, 72% of girls and 57% of boys stated that they had been advised by their parents (preferably the mother) about contraception; the boys are recommended condoms (83%) and the girls the pill and additionally (45%) the condom. Boyfriend/girlfriend and sexual education in school (obligatory since the mid-1960s, but which extensively omits emotional education), as well as doctors, continue to play a role. However, 9% of girls and as many as 23% of boys stated that they currently had nobody with whom they could speak about sexual matters. Furthermore, as representative analyses show, many adolescents overestimate their knowledge about contraception (BZgA 2004).

An unplanned pregnancy is mostly described by female teenagers as a "catastrophe" and the decision to terminate a pregnancy means a further existential burden with frequently traumatic effects. The pregnancy rate (number of pregnancies per 1,000 women) lay at 3.9 for the under-18-year-olds (18- to 20-year-olds, 28.9%; 20- to 25-year-olds, 66%). As can be seen from data of the Federal Statistical Office (Statistisches Bundesamt 2004), in past years, percentage proportions of pregnancy terminations (based on the consultation regulation) in minors has risen in terms of the national average: for girls under 15 this has been gradual from 1996 (0.3% of the total of terminations in the Federal Republic) up to 0.5% in 2003; and for 15- to 18-year-olds the rate has increased steadily from 3.4% in 1996 to 5.4% in 2003. The following were cited as causes for the unplanned and mostly also unwanted pregnancies: acceleration of sexual maturity (today at approximately 11 to 12 years in girls) and a consequent acceleration of adolescent sexual behavior, deficits of information, and a lack of use of contraceptives.

The number of cases of illness registered according to the law for the combating of sexually transmitted diseases (all age groups) was 3,717 for Germany in the year 2000; of these, 6.6% were adolescents in the age range of 15 to under 20 years and 16.8% in the age group of 20 to under 25 years. The density (i.e., the number of registered sexually transmitted diseases per 100,000 inhabitants) was 4.5. For adolescents, this figure increased: at the age of 15 to under 20 years, the density was 5.3%, and for people of the age of 20 up to under 25 years it was 13.6 (Federal Statistical Office 2004).

In Germany, an increasingly early cultural independence of the adolescents and an increasingly late entry into economic independence and family obligations can be ascertained. While the process of separation from the family of origin and the uptake of sexual relationships takes place relatively early in the adolescent phase, the entry into the job market and starting a family have become temporally open status passages. The fact that the average age of marriage of singles (2002) was 31.8 years for men and 28.8 years for women (Federal Statistical Office 2004) shows that premarital (also sexual) cohabitation is normal and accepted. Over half of the population lives in parent–child communities, nine out of ten pairs (89%) are married couples, and only one in ten pairs (11%) were living in a nonmarried cohabitation, although from 1996 to 2002 this life form rose by 25% (rates of same-sex cohabitations remain infinitesimally low).

Health Risk Behavior

Problem, risk, and deviant behavior can only be defined depending on culture, social surroundings, gender, and age—that is, with reference to norms and expectations. Problem behavior is understood here as behavior that represents an endangerment of one's own development or that of others; risk behavior in this context means behavior that endangers the health and well-being and consequently the (personality) development of the person. For Germany, the following picture emerges (cf. BZgA 2001; Drogenbeauftragte 2004; Hurrelmann et al. 2003; Robert Koch Institut 2004):

1. The health situation of German adolescents is generally good from an international comparative perspective (35 countries, Canada, and the United States).
2. In a representative survey (BZgA 2001), 38% of 12- to 25-year-olds stated that they were frequent smokers (60% of smokers) or

occasional smokers (40% of smokers), with no considerable difference in terms of gender. Among 12- to 17-year-olds, the proportion of smokers (only legally permitted from the age of 16 years) increased from 20% in 1993 to 28% in 2001. Today, 25% of 15-year-old boys and 27% of 15-year-old girls are daily consumers of tobacco, which is high from an international perspective; 13% of boys and 10% of girls indicated smoking more than 10 cigarettes per day, and among pupils from the Hauptschule (see the following section on education) this figure even lay at 46%—at the same time, over 90% of adolescents see the health risk as very low. The age at which smoking begins has, however, sunk further: from 13.7 years (in 2001) to 11.6 years (in 2003) among the 12- to 25-year-olds. The smoking rate increases clearly from the age of 12; at 33%, it is higher among the East German adolescents (12- to 17-year-olds) than among the West German adolescents with 26%. The proportion of heavy smokers among adolescents, though, has on the whole notably decreased (1993, 34%; 2001, 19%). Furthermore, the proportion of those who have never smoked almost tripled between 1973 and 2001 (data for West Germany).

3. According to surveys, almost all adolescents (92%) have already drunk alcohol in their lives; 8% stated that they were completely teetotal. In terms of alcohol consumption, German adolescents lie in the top quarter in a comparison of countries, behind those from Britain, the Netherlands, and Denmark. In 2001, 30% of adolescents stated that they regularly drink alcohol (at least once a week), with males drinking more beer and females more wine. Of the 12- to 13-year-olds, only 1% regularly drink alcohol, and of the 14- to 15-year-olds 16%, while this has already risen to 37% for the 16- to 17-year-olds; only 6% of boys and 5% of girls were teetotal. A good half of 15- to 16-year-olds report risky drinking behavior (one alcohol-induced state of inebriation in the last year); 20% of those surveyed had been drunk six times or more (male: 27%; female: 12%), with the proportion higher in West Germany (21%) than in East Germany (13%). The age of beginning alcohol consumption lies at 13 years in Germany; the first episode of inebriation takes place at an average of 14 years. Alcohol abuse among adolescents is estimated to be approximately 10%, and alcohol dependency defined according to clinical criteria is at 6%. For the alcohol consumption of adolescents, besides the drinking habits of the parents, the easy availability of alcoholic beverages plays a role (indicated by 60% of the young people).

4. Twenty-seven percent of 12- to 25-year-olds and 33% of 13- to 15-year-olds have already tried an illegal drug. Cannabis is the most frequently consumed substance with 31%. In the year before the survey, 26% of the adolescents had tried an illegal drug at least once, with 15% in the last 30 days; 5% indicated that they had consumed cannabis more often than once a week. On the whole, there are only small gender differences.

5. In Germany, 10% to 20% (based on the definition) of all schoolchildren and adolescents are classified as overweight or obese. In a European comparison of countries, 11% of the 13- to 15-year-olds were classified as affected by obesity (United States: over a third). Independently of gender and age, from an international comparative perspective Germany has the highest rates of children and adolescents who are dissatisfied with their bodies (39%) or see themselves as too fat. On average, 34% of adolescents are on a diet at any given time or are of the opinion that they need to go on a diet. In the age group of 15 to 24-year-olds, anorexia (approx. 0.5–1%) and bulimia (approx. 3-4%) occur. In the majority (95%) of these cases, girls and young women are affected.

6. Emotional disorders are the most frequent of psychological disorders in adolescence, including social withdrawal (approximately 8.3%) as well as anxiety/depression (approximately 13.3%). In the age group of 15- to 24-year-olds, suicides are the second most frequent cause of death after accidents, with the proportion of male adolescents predominating (8:1). When comparing rates of suicide with rates of suicide attempts, this ratio reverses (boys: 1:12; girls: 1:39).

7. Conduct disorders (cruelties, arguments, lies, vandalism, school refusal) show a clear increase in adolescence (approximately 3.5% of 11- to 18-year-olds) and have a poor prognosis. School refusal is estimated at 2% to 4%. There is no clear relationship between these disorders and problematic family relationships.

8. Approximately 6% of all boys and 3% of all girls show strongly aggressive behavior. Among the 13- to 15-year-olds, Germany is one of the four countries showing the highest rates of bullying. This also applies for repeated bullying of classmates. Germany also shows high rates of bullying victims, and is among the ten countries with the highest rates for 13- to 15-year-olds. Nowadays, 30% of German children and adolescents report that they were involved in a physical fight in the last 12 months.

9. The registered crime rate (crime/delinquency) of young people (14 to 24 years) is clearly higher than that of adults (25 years and up), although among adolescents, "minor" offenses such as offences against property and wealth (shoplifting) and traffic offences are predominant. The range of offences only broadens with increasing age. Children up to the age of 14 years count as below the age of criminal responsibility in Germany. The level of crime (number of those suspected/convicted of a crime per 100,000) initially increases fairly steeply from the age of 13, reaches its peak among the adolescents (18 to under 21 years) and young adults (21 to under 25 years) (around 10,000 suspected criminals), but then decreases again relatively strongly, and gradually levels off from the age of 34. However, adolescents are less frequently convicted, their proceedings are more frequently halted than are proceedings among adults, or they only receive warnings or sanctions/parole. According to data of the Federal Statistical Office (2001), in 2001, from 100 German male adolescent suspects (14- to under 18-year-olds; 5% of the population with criminal responsibility), only 22 were convicted (female: 100:12), among older adolescents (18 to under 21 years; proportion 3.9%) the relation was 100:33 (female: 100:22); among young adults (21 to under 25 years; proportion: 5.2%), on the other hand, this was already 100:46 (female: 100:36). All the same, it is apparent that the proportion of men who, by the age of 25, have been informally (halting of proceedings) or formally (sentenced) sanctioned lies at over 50%. Young people are also over-represented among those registered on suspicion of violent crime. This entails approximately two-thirds "aggravated" battery (youth-typical constellation in terms of affray in groups of peers). There are signs

(no precise figures exist) for a broadly above-average level of crime among adolescent foreigners and immigrants, in particular in the area of violent crime, for which presumably unsolved integration problems are of particular significance. Moreover, a small group of "frequent offenders" commits a very high number of offenses: between 3% and 5% of offenders commit in the cross-section of one year over 30% of known offenses of their complete age group. It can be established that (adolescent) violent crime in Germany is not a quantitative problem but rather a qualitative one. The extent and the development of violent crime are determined above all by (aggravated/grievous) assault as well as theft; other forms, such as murder/manslaughter, sexual murder, or rape, have not increased. The highest victim rates and the strongest increases are found among young people, especially male adolescents. However, taking into account also family violence, young people are by far more often victims of violence than they are perpetrators (cf. Heinz 2003).

10. "Crime by foreigners" refers to offenses committed by so-called non-Germans (in the sense of Article 116 of the Basic Constitutional Law); in 2003, it amounted to 23.5% (compared to a total proportion of foreigners of 8.5%). The socio-structural and gender-specific composition of other ethnic groups and their demographically diverging stratification, as well as the imperfections of the crime statistics, lead to the fact that the ability to make comparisons between crimes committed by Germans and those by foreigners is limited. Persons staying in Germany without citizenship are on average younger and more frequently male. They are more likely to live in large cities, a greater number of them have lower income and educational levels, and they are more frequently unemployed. All of these factors lead to a greater risk of becoming known to the police as a suspected criminal (rates of alleged criminals/age distribution: 14 to 17 years, 9%; 18 to 20 years, 9.6%; 21 to 24 years, 15.1%). Furthermore, in the five former East German states, in particular in regions close to the borders, crime rates of foreigners are significantly higher (BKA 2004). The greater criminality of foreigners can be explained by several factors:

formation of ghettos, underprivileged social class, and language problems prevent an equal access to the educational and labor market and to social welfare benefits, making the integration of foreigners more difficult.

11. An increased level of crime has also been observable more recently among young so-called *late repatriates*, emigrants of German origin from Eastern European states (Pfeiffer et al. 2004). From 1950 to 1987, approximately 1.37 Germans from Eastern Europe came into the FRG. For these people, no particular crime problems are known and they apparently integrated largely without any problems. Between 1988 and 1992, they were followed by a second group of 1.43 million ethnic German immigrants, who on the whole still brought with them good language skills and received considerable help with their integration. Finally, from January 1, 1993, a third group of approximately 1.54 million so-called late repatriates immigrated to Germany. For this group, the integration perspectives were less favorable from the very outset (no/insufficient knowledge of German in 75% of the immigrants, cost saving measures, and very few language courses). As ethnic German immigrants automatically receive German citizenship, they do not emerge as a specific group in the crime statistics, and consequently few firm figures on them are available (exception: Bavaria and Lower Saxony since 2003). The (estimated) proportion of ethnic German immigrants in the German resident population today lies at about 3.2% to 3.8%, and in the age group of 14- to 30-year-olds at 5.5% to 6%. With increasing duration of residence, the proportion of ethnic German immigrants who commit crimes also rises: in a survey of school pupils, a rate of 3.7% emerged for ethnic German immigrants with a maximum of 2 years in Germany ("committed a crime"); for those with a duration of stay of two to four years, this rose to 7.4%. The rate increases to 19% among those who have lived in Germany for five years or more, considerably exceeding the comparable rate for native Germans, which lies at 14.5% (Pfeiffer et al. 2004). On the one hand, (a) language and identity problems, increasing integration problems and experiences of exclusion, unemployment, and ghetto formation ("parallel societies") are held responsible for this, but on the other hand also (b) abuse by the parents, and the "importing" of an orientation toward violence and drug dependency from their background of origin in the collapsed Soviet Union are thought to play a role. Police and social welfare organizations attempt to combat the problem through special youth programs. Rough estimates show that today only approximately one million persons of German descent are living in the post-Soviet states, meaning that it can be hoped that this problem might perhaps be reduced in the foreseeable future.

In view of the multitude of problems described, it is evident that a whole host of causes of a personal, family, and social nature—also in their complex collaboration—can be seen as possible reasons for this. Generally speaking, internalizing problem behavior is shown more by female adolescents, and externalizing problem behavior, which is also problematic for the environment, is shown more by males. It is also a fact that in adolescence, different problems often occur simultaneously (e.g., aggressive behavior and depression), which is known as *comorbidity*. The role of stressors during puberty and the development of dysfunctional schemata and reactions in problem situations is still an open research field. The provision of counseling, and measures for the prevention and intervention in health risk behavior of adolescents is in urgent need of extension in Germany.

Education

Besides the parental home, school is the most important social authority, which very strongly influences the everyday life and biography of adolescents. Due to the independence of the Laender in matters of education and culture, the school system in the Federal Republic of Germany is very heterogeneous and comprises a large number of different school types. Education is free and in most types of school is co-educational. Almost all elementary and secondary schools and about 95% of higher education institutions are public. The literacy rate (definition: those aged 15 and over who can read and write) in Germany is 99%. School attendance is mandatory for a minimum of nine years (or in some Laender, ten years), beginning at age 6. A student who starts vocational training as an apprentice must attend a part-time vocational school until the age of 18. The system of different types of secondary schools in

Germany requires that adolescents must decide at a relatively early age which direction to pursue for their education and occupation. Later, school transitions are possible, but difficult. In 2003 in Germany, there were a total of 9.7 million pupils attending schools providing general education, 9.8% of whom were foreigners (Federal Statistical Office 2003).

After a voluntary preschool education (age 3 to 6; Kindergarten), primary education (*Grundschule*) for all lasts four years (age 6 to 10). Secondary education is divided into two levels: junior (Level I: age 10 to 16) and senior (Level II: age 16 to 19) secondary education and starts with two years (grades five and six) of orientation courses during which students explore a variety of educational career paths open to them.

Secondary Education Level I: Upon completion of the *Grundschule*, students between the ages of 10 and 16 attend one of the following types of secondary schools: *Hauptschule, Realschule, Gymnasium, Gesamtschule*, or *Sonderschule* (the latter being for children with special educational needs). Students who complete this level of education receive an intermediate school certificate.

About one-third of students completing primary school continue in secondary general schools (*Hauptschule*). The curriculum of the *Hauptschule* stresses preparation for a vocation as well as mathematics, history, geography, German, and one foreign language. After receiving their diploma, graduates either become apprentices in shops or factories while taking compulsory part-time courses or attend some form of full-time vocational school until the age of eighteen.

Another one-third of primary school leavers attend the *Realschule*. These intermediate schools include grades five through ten for students seeking access to middle levels of civil service, industry, and business. The curriculum is the same as that of the *Hauptschule*, but students take an additional foreign language, shorthand, word-processing, and bookkeeping, and they also learn computer skills. Graduation from the *Realschule* enables students to enter a higher technical school (*Fachoberschule*), a specialized high school or grammar school (*Fachgymnasium*), or (for a few students) a *Gymnasium* for the next stage of secondary education.

The *Gymnasium* begins upon completion of the *Grundschule* or the orientation grades and includes grades five through twelve (in some Laender, thirteen). The number of students attending the *Gymnasium* has increased dramatically in recent decades; by the mid-1990s, about one-third of all primary school leavers completed a course of study at the *Gymnasium*, which gives them the right to study at university level. Up to the present day, the *Gymnasium* continues to be the primary educational route into the universities, although other routes have been created.

The *Gesamtschule* originated in the late 1960s to provide a broader range of educational opportunities for students than the traditional *Gymnasium*. The *Gesamtschule* has an all-inclusive curriculum for students aged 10 to 18 and a good deal of freedom to choose coursework. The popularity of the *Gesamtschule* has been mixed; their presence is marginal when compared with the *Gymnasium*.

Secondary Education Level II: The variety of educational programs, tracks, and opportunities available to students increases at level II. The largest single student group attends the senior level of the *Gymnasium* (*Gymnasiale Oberstufe*). This level includes the traditional academically oriented *Gymnasium*, the vocational *Gymnasium*, the occupation-specific *Fachgymnasium*, and the *Gesamtschule*. Graduation from these schools requires passing the *Abitur*, the qualifying examination for studying at university level.

Vocational Education and Training: The German education system has been praised for its ability to provide good-quality general education combined with excellent specific training for a profession. In 2002, about 65% of the country's workforce had been trained through vocational education. In the same year, 2.6 million young people (proportion of foreigners: 7.2%) were enrolled in vocational or trade schools.

Building upon the junior secondary program, (a) the *Berufsschulen* (in the dual system) are two- and three-year part-time vocational schools that prepare young people for a profession. In the 2002/03 academic year there were 1.7 million young people enrolled in these schools. About 452,300 individuals attended (b) *Berufsfachschulen*, also called intermediate technical schools (ITS). These schools usually offer full-time vocation-specific programs. Other types of schools designed to prepare students for different kinds of vocational careers are the higher technical school (HTS), (c) the *Fachoberschule*, attended by about 106,100 persons in 2002/03, and the advanced vocational school (AVS), and (d) the *Berufsaufbauschule*, attended by about 7,500 persons in the same year (Federal Statistical Office 2003). Students can choose to attend one of these three kinds of schools after graduating with an intermediate school certificate from a *Realschule* or an equivalent school.

The method of teaching used in vocational schools is called the dual system (*Duales System*) because it combines classroom study with a work-related apprenticeship system. The length of schooling/training depends on prior vocational experience and may entail one year of full-time instruction or up to three years of part-time training.

Students can earn the *Fachhochschulreife* after successfully completing vocational education and passing a qualifying entrance examination. The *Fachhochschulreife* entitles a student to enter a *Fachhochschule*, or a training college, and to continue postsecondary occupational or professional training in engineering or technical fields.

Vocational education and training is a joint government-industry program. The federal government and the Laender share the financing of vocational education in public vocational schools, with the federal government bearing a slightly higher share (58% in 2002) than the Laender.

Tertiary or Higher Education: In the 2002/03 academic year, higher education was available at 314 institutions (of these 99 universities) of higher learning, with about 1.9 million students enrolled. German university students can complete their first degree in about five years, but on average, university studies last for seven years. Advanced degrees require further study. The proportion of female students amounts to approximately 50%, which also corresponds to the proportion of women in the population.

Since the 1960s, an extension of the time spent in education and training and a broadening of qualified school-leaving qualifications has taken place. This has resulted in a shift in the distribution of pupils across the school forms: while in 1960 approximately 70% of all pupils attended the *Volksschule* of the time (school providing basic primary and secondary education) and 30% secondary schools, nowadays this relationship has reversed. Parallel to this, the importance of employment and work decreased: nowadays, young people complete vocational education approximately two years later than youths in the 1950s; equally, the average time spent in higher education has also increased. In 1990 in Germany, 99% of 16-year-olds, 40% of 21-year-olds and still 6% of 30-year-olds were in a state-registered education program (Ortleb 1991).

School and vocational education holds a central importance for parents and for the adolescents themselves (independently of nationality and gender). For the preparation for adulthood, its most important function is seen in the imparting of a good education (knowledge), in the support of personality development (values), and in fostering appropriate social behavior. For adolescents who are disadvantaged, either socially, physically, or mentally, there is a fully developed educational and vocational support in special needs schools. For academically gifted children, there are various region-specific support programs of enrichment, acceleration, and grouping. A good school education and a high social standing are tightly linked. However, school achievement is not solely dependent on talent, but also on social origin and the motivation of the parents. In turn, correlated with these factors are the economic conditions and the interest in attending a secondary school, and in part also the learning success of the adolescents.

In Germany, there are ethnic, social class, and gender-specific differences in academic performance: on average, girls have the better school-leaving qualifications and grades and fewer girls have to repeat a year or choose to drop out of school than boys. In the school year 2001/02, 28.7% of boys completed a leaving qualification from the *Hauptschule* (girls: 22.1%); from the *Realschule*: boys, 38.3%, girls 42.3%; *Abitur*: boys, 21%, girls 28.9%. The proportion of foreign adolescents attending the *Hauptschule* is, at 18.2%, considerably higher than in the other school types: *Realschule* (6.8%), *Gymnasium* (3.9%).

In a study carried out by the OECD (2001) in 32 industrialized nations (PISA, or Programs for International Student Assessment) with 265,000 15-year-old pupils, German adolescents (and consequently the whole school system in the Federal Republic) performed disastrously poorly: in reading literacy, the German youths occupied rank 20 to 22 (according to section), in mathematical literacy rank 20 to 22, and in scientific literacy rank 19 to 23. It was apparent that in no other country was social origin so decisive for school success than in Germany: background-based learning disadvantages were hardly compensated for, and those belonging to the lower classes and foreign adolescents had unequally low chances of obtaining a mid-level school-leaving qualification or *Abitur*. Presumably, the very early division of pupils (in the tenth year of life) into different school types (three-tier school system) is responsible for this, which makes a "rise" or an "upwards permeation" very difficult. For foreign children there is only insufficient early support in the Kindergarten or later in all-day schools. Germany had the widest range between good and poor pupils and an extremely large difference in quality between schools. The goal of a good school, to have as many top pupils as possible and at the same time lead the other pupils to a high-level middle way is, according to the

OECD criteria, not achieved in Germany. The "PISA shock" triggered a controversial education discussion, in the wake of which reforms were introduced, including the introduction of binding national educational standards for all schools, *Abitur* after 8 years, and more all-day schools.

In a further comparative study (OECD 2004) of 30 states, Germany was criticized for not achieving satisfactory reform efforts: Germany is said (in 2001) to spend too little money on education (5.3% of the GDP; United States: 7.3%; rank 15 in an international comparison), with the lag in the primary and secondary I area being particularly severe. Furthermore, the number of graduates of higher education is, at 19% of a year group, also comparatively low (OECD average is 32%). Positively emphasized, however, were Germany's efforts to expand all-day schools, the dual vocational-educational system, and the development of national educational reporting.

Work

In Germany, children (under 15 years) and adolescents (under 18 years) are prohibited by the Young Persons Employment Act from pursuing employment. With parental approval, however, from the age of 14 they are allowed to take on a minor job with temporal restrictions (e.g., delivering newspapers, babysitting, after-school tuition, messenger work, and gardening). Ten percent of German adolescents have a job outside of school, although only 4.7% of these work for more than 2 hours per day (Flammer, Alsaker, and Noak 1999). Their earnings are rarely expected to contribute to the domestic budget of the parents; generally speaking, the money serves to supplement their pocket money.

As school and vocational education in Germany is very differentiated, nowadays it often reaches far into adulthood. The multitude of different paths brings with it a broad variance in the ages at which adolescents enter into the world of work. In 2000, 100% of 16-year-olds, 42.6% of 21-year-old females, and 37.5% of 21-year-old males were in a state-registered training or education program (BMBF 2002). Indeed, for 29-year-olds, this figure still lay at 11.7% for women and 12.9% for men. For the majority of adolescent school-leavers in Germany, the following transitions into work are typical. Upon leaving the *Hauptschule*, the entry into employment ensues through work as laborers. In the last few years this has become increasingly rare. Upon leaving the *Hauptschule*, the school-leaver enters an apprenticeship, which includes approximately three days per week of guided work in the field and two days' vocational training college; following a three-year apprenticeship, commencement of full employment occurs. However, it is also possible at the end of the apprenticeship to enter into schools of the tertiary level (e.g., school for engineering) or to prepare for the *Meisterprüfung* (examination for master craftsman's certificate) alongside regular work. Another option is that of a school apprenticeship with work experience placements (vocational full-time school), such as commercial college or college of hotel management with extensive work experience placements and a diploma certificate, upon obtainment of which entry into the job market occurs. Another option is to obtain a university degree via full-time study, with or without work experience placements, with a relatively abrupt transition into the working world upon graduation. Many students take a gap year after completing the *Abitur*, during which they either work or travel. Many also interrupt their degree course for general educational or social experiences (volunteer social/ecological year, see below).

After secondary school, which is mostly full-time, many university students pay their own way by simultaneously carrying out part-time work and a part-time degree course. Students of second-chance education ("mature students") are also often working students, through the fact that they even take part in secondary or *Gymnasium* education in addition to employment (e.g., at evening *Gymnasium* schools).

So-called broken-off education in the secondary or tertiary area often results in unskilled labor. In order to facilitate the transition for the adolescents from school into the world of work, in Germany all school-leavers are offered individual "career advice" by the Federal Employment Agency, which consists of the following elements: preparation of job selection, clarification of abilities and interests, provision of information about careers (including offers of work experience and "taster" programs), help with career decisions, and help in the search for apprenticeships and job placements.

In addition, a so-called "voluntary social or ecological year" offers young people between the ages of 16 and 26 the opportunity, before commencing further education or training, to gain an insight into social work, care work, or ecological professions, and to try them out under the guidance of professionals. The framework conditions for this are regulated by law (12 months' full-time employment; pedagogical support; pocket money; free insurance, board, and lodgings). The number of young people graduating from this scheme in 2003 was approximately 15,000.

In Germany, the working conditions for young people are good, as high legal and job-related standards as well as social safeguarding provisions apply and are also monitored. However, cyclical fluctuations and economic stagnation influence the offer of work and apprenticeship places, which in 2003 led to a shortfall of approximately 30,000 apprenticeship places. This problem was combated through a joint effort of companies, associations, politics, and trade unions, and led in 2004 to a "national pact for training and trainee professionals," which aims to create new apprenticeships and enable all adolescents an entry into work. Germany is the fifth largest economic power in the world, but with a comparatively weak growth in the Euro zone (less than 1% in the period from 2001–2003). This, as well as structural problems of the labor market, economic European integration, and globalization have led to the fact that a relatively high unemployment rate (approximately 10% in 2003) has become a persistent problem.

However, in an international comparison, youth unemployment is rather low: the unemployment rate among 15- to 24-year-olds in 2003 was 9.5% in Germany, with more men (13.7%) being unemployed than women (8.1%). In comparison, the rate in the 25 EU countries amounted to an average of 18%. According to an analysis of all EU states, responsible for these favorable values is Germany's dual vocational training, which on average pushes down youth unemployment by 5%. The success of this state-controlled market model can be gauged from the number of people in Germany who achieve a higher degree: in 2002, 85% of 25- to 34-year-olds had at least a completed apprenticeship, *Abitur,* or advanced technical college certificate, compared to an OECD average of only 74%.

Germany currently finds itself in a process of great economic change that is strongly marked by globalization and has far-reaching consequences—particularly for adolescents and young people in Germany. This is shown by a cross-cultural study by Blossfeld and colleagues that was carried out in 14 OECD states and investigated life courses in the globalization process and the associated changes in the education, employment, and family system (Blossfeld et al. 2005).

Academics document how the period of transition from adolescence to adulthood has changed drastically in all modern societies. It is clear that growing uncertainties arising from globalization are increasingly foisted onto the younger generation. Thus young people are particularly exposed to changes on the labor market, as they have little or no work experience and are not in a position to benefit from contacts with employers. Establishing themselves in a job with long-term prospects under such conditions is becoming increasingly difficult for this age group. The consequences are higher and longer unemployment, part-time employment, precarious forms of self-employment, or temporary working conditions. Young people have to be a great deal more flexible than was the case just a few years ago, and they remain financially dependent for longer. This more uncertain situation influences, among other things, the readiness to make long-term ties, to marry, or to start a family. Frequently, this decision is put off or even abandoned completely—with corresponding negative consequences for the birth rate.

The younger generation in Germany is affected particularly strongly by this global (albeit with noticeable national differences such as the exception of Ireland) phenomenon. Adolescents and young people are the losers of this globalization, which no longer offers everyone the opportunity and possibility of earning an income. Their central characteristic is one of uncertainty, and education is decisive: anybody who is poorly equipped for the competition, and has a lower level of education, does not have a greater choice but rather a much smaller one. The negative effect of globalization can be softened by institutional "filters" such as social security and education systems, protection against dismissal, and the protective hand of trade unions. All of these things are present in Germany, but the pressure to water them down is growing.

Media

Article 5 of the German Constitution guarantees freedom of expression, freedom of the press, and the right to inform oneself from generally accessible sources. There is no censorship. The circulation of daily newspapers amounted to around 23.2 million per day in 2002; the average number of TV stations received in Germany lies at over 30 per household, supplemented by approximately 230 radio stations. Almost all households are equipped with one or several TV sets and a radio. People in Germany use the mass media extensively: they listen to more than 3.5 hours of radio per day, watch three hours of television, read the daily paper for an average of 36 minutes, and also read popular, TV, and special-interest magazines as well as weekly and monthly magazines. In total, purely in statistical terms, every German individual over the age of 14 years arrives at 8 hours and 22 minutes of media consumption per day (Auswaertiges Amt, Foreign Office 2004).

For male adolescents of the age of 12 to 25 years, "watching TV" is the most frequent (62%) free-time activity in the course of one week (female adolescents, 55%; unemployed adolescents, 72%), followed by "surfing the Internet" (34%) and computer games (33%). For female adolescents, in addition to socializing or "meeting up with people," (67%; boys: 57%), the main activities are "reading books" (32%; boys: 18%) and "shopping" (27%; boys: 5%). At the age of 12 to 14 years, TV is watched more frequently and more computer games are played, while older adolescents increasingly build up friendships and meet up with other people: East–West differences in terms of the free-time activities of adolescents are not significant (German Shell, 14. Youth Study 2002). Surfing the Internet increases constantly with age, with 75% of adolescents possessing their own computer (personal property) and 25% having their own Internet access. Internet use in the general population amounted to 53.5% in 2003 (occasional use), while among the 14- to 19-year-olds, this figure lay at 92.1%. Adolescents deal with the Internet more actively, more communicatively, and less user value-oriented than the average Internet user: Internet research, chat rooms, downloading computer games, audio data, online games, and looking at video data are all carried out more frequently than in the general population of Internet users. In terms of rates of Internet use, differences between school education are apparent: pupils from the *Hauptschule*: 69%, pupils from the *Realschule*: 80%, pupils from the *Gymnasium*: 92%, with two-thirds of the latter group having Internet access at home (Digital Opportunities Foundation, 2004).

In the framework of an amendment of the Youth Protection Act (age limit 18 years) and the Youth Media Protection (age limit 16 years), the problem of violence being glorified in the media is hotly discussed in the public realm, as well as the youth-specific "hate industry" of music groups, CDs, fanzines, and video and computer games. Prohibitive or repressive youth media protection aims, with its regulations, at two different spheres: on the one hand it limits the accessibility of media liable to corrupt the young, and on the other hand it aims, through this limitation, to reduce the market chances for these media, make their distribution more difficult, and deflect market activities to other media that are not thought to endanger young people.

Planned measures for youth media protection are to (a) provide computer games with an age designation analogous to cinema releases and videos (equal treatment of all media), (b) extend the jurisdiction of the German Federal Review Office for Youth-Endangering Publications (to "youth-endangering media" in general) so that they can work from their own initiative and also be responsible for the supervision of the Internet. The television institutions and the film and music industry will remain with voluntary self-control. However, it is difficult to prove or suggest an (ultimately causal) "endangerment" or damage of adolescents through media—general statements on the affect of depictions of violence are hardly possible on a scientifically founded basis, as the causal relation of "recipient medium" is too complex (Kunczik 1998). The examining bodies therefore decide on their verdicts concerning the limitation of access to youth-endangering media with the help of analogy conclusions based on their experiences and their inspection of other media, the valid system of values, and the constitutional rights, which requires a consideration of the freedom of the press and information (Article 5, German Constitution).

Because, for instance, the 13- to 24-year-olds had a total of approximately 62.1 billion Euros at their disposal in 2003, in the media they are a much courted target group by the advertising industry (Institut für Jugendforschung/Institute for Youth Research 2004).

Politics and Military

The fourteenth German Shell Youth Study (2002) showed that political interest and engagement of adolescents in Germany is on the decline, and the role of politics in their lifestyle is becoming increasingly less important. Politics, political parties, state, and society are not dimensions that play any significant role in the real lives of young people. Furthermore, they are perceived as complex systems with internal structures and interrelations that are generally not transparent, and adolescents do not perceive the results of such systems as being able to be influenced. Only 34% of today's adolescents between the age of 12 and 24 years describe themselves as "politically interested" (in comparison to 43% in 1999 and 57% in 1991). Age and level of education play an important role in this regard: It is older, well-educated adolescents who are interested in and lend their support to politics. Younger adolescents are, even in the course of the maturation process (still), primarily occupied with themselves. The younger the adolescents are, the lower their readiness to take part in a parliamentary election for the *Bundestag* (minimum voting age is 18 years); in total 35% said they were "definitely" ready, and a further 37% were only "probably" ready to vote. In contrast to the population as a whole, adolescents continue to categorize themselves politically as slightly left of center. Political extremism is strongly rejected.

In a representative population survey, it emerged that for the age group of 16- to 25-year-olds, the proportion of those disposed to right-wing extremism in the former East German states lies at 9%, while in West Germany this figure lies at 4% (BMBF 2002). Extreme right-wing parties have been represented since 2004 in two East German state parliaments, for the first time in Saxony (9.2%) and for the second time in Brandenburg (6.1%). In the other 14 federal states and at all *Bundestag* elections, extreme right parties fell at the 5% hurdle (e.g., at the state parliament elections in 2005 in North Rhine Westphalia: 0.9%; in Schleswig-Holstein: 1.9%). Reasons for voting for an extreme right-wing party are unanimously attributed to dissatisfaction with and protests against a reform policy in the social sphere, which demands from the population (among other things as a consequence of globalization) cutbacks and a need to economize; this protest is marked more strongly in the East than in the West due to the fact that people there are much more highly affected by unemployment and economic structural weaknesses. A look at the rises and falls of right-wing extreme parties since the 1980s gives rise to the suspicion that the election successes of far-right parties were more of a "flash in the pan" than a large-scale epidemic.

Although the overwhelming majority of adolescents see democracy as a good form of government, in East Germany 52% and in West Germany 27% of those asked are still critical with regard to democratic practice in Germany. Adolescents in East Germany in particular express through this their criticism of living standards and a lack of personal opportunities. The trust of the adolescents in political parties is low, and that in the federal government, churches, trade unions, and citizen action groups is only moderate. By contrast, party-independent state organizations (justice/police), but also human rights and environmental protection groups, are seen as particularly trustworthy.

In spite of the low level of political interest, many adolescents are socially active in their own living environment. In this regard, they orient themselves toward concrete and practical questions, which are linked for them with personal opportunities and use (own interests, leisure activities).

Although adolescents do lend their support to other people or environmental and animal protection, the popularity of citizen action initiatives, aid organizations such as Greenpeace or Amnesty International, parties, and trade unions is significantly lower than that of local organizations, educational institutions, and self-organized groups. Many adolescents also commit themselves individually to worthy causes. On the whole, female adolescents are more strongly active in ecological and in social fields, while male youths engage to an increased extent in achieving a better cohabitation, order, and security in their local area. Thirty-five percent of adolescents are regularly socially active, 41% occasionally, and 24% not at all. But here, too, the higher the educational level and the social class, the more intensive is the societal activity of the adolescents.

In 1949, when the Federal Republic of Germany was founded, it did not possess any armed forces. The East–West conflict and the threat by the Soviet Union changed the political post-war situation: in 1955, in the Germany Treaty, the Federal Republic obtained sovereignty once more, joined the Western European Union and NATO, and established its own armed forces. The former GDR also had its own armed forces (*Volksarmee* or People's Army), and upon reunification on October 3, 1990, the two armies were joined together. The German armed forces are a part of the executive authority of the federal government and are subject to civilian leadership. In times of peace, command is exercised by the defense minister, but if defense is necessary, command goes to the chancellor. The armed forces have the task of defending the Federal Republic of Germany in the case of an armed attack. In addition, in the framework of NATO or by order of the United Nations, the army can also be deployed in crises and conflicts outside of Germany. The German army is a conscript army, with a strength in 2004 of 262,771 soldiers (of these, more than 10,000 are female soldiers). Male citizens (from 18 to 45 years) are subject to general military service (9 months); since 2001, women too have been able to undergo voluntary military service, but are not obligated to do so. Those who refuse military service through conscientious objection (approximately 24% of those recorded as liable for military service) have to take part in an alternative community service (9 months, too). In the general consciousness of the adolescents, and due to the handling of obligatory service in practice, there is more or less freedom of choice between military service and alternative community service. A transition to the model of an army of volunteers no longer appears to be out of the question (Bundeswehr/German armed forces 2004).

Unique Issues

The reunification of Germany took place on October 3, 1990, through the "accession" of the GDR to the old Federal Republic; it was linked with an abrupt change and a seamless adoption of the complete West German societal system in East Germany. The question of how, against the background of the same cultural traditions, these new, different political-social relations affect the development and socialization of children and adolescents, and how such an exceptionally abrupt political, social, and ideological change makes itself felt in adolescents has been examined in many longitudinal studies.

In all, this social change has had less of a dramatic effect on the social behavior and the personality development of children and adolescents than was originally suspected (summarizing Silbereisen 2005). The results showed the following: East German adolescents continue to have a clear occupational goal earlier than their West German counterparts. They also become economically independent earlier in life and start a family earlier. This earlier independence, which in the GDR could be traced back to a better compatibility of employment and parenthood (although the adolescents had fewer choices and less freedom of decision), remained intact, even though the system conditions have changed.

In contrast to West Germany, in the former East German states there is a continuing tendency to hold the community responsible for one's own personal fate. Approximately two-thirds of people in the East, but only one-third in the former West German states see the state as responsible with regard to problems of unemployment. Unemployed parents in the West therefore react more depressively, while from the respective stance in the East a psychological shield is formed. For this reason, the consequences of unemployment have a less strong effect on children in the former Eastern states. Various studies have stressed the high importance of family support in East Germany for coping with the many burdens and life events. However, in the East it is also the case that in times of social change, families are "driven apart" and the sense of family is slipping down the scale of values of young people. The process of growing together appears to be

simpler for the younger generation than it is for its parents.

The congruence of moral concepts is apparently large between adolescents in the East and the West. Although xenophobia and a national-authoritarian position is marked somewhat more strongly in East German adolescents than in the West, the actual differences in attitude are here, too, discernible rather between the sexes and in school education: girls are generally less xenophobic than boys and those from the *Gymnasium* less so than pupils from the *Hauptschule*. The ability to see beauty in differences is a cultural achievement that still needs to be developed in the East. West German adolescents appear to be somewhat more helpful and less aggressive than those in the East, but the differences are not particularly marked. The political orientation of 14- to 18-year-old *Gymnasium* pupils in East and West Berlin indicates a marked humanistic attitude, a clear rejection of violence, and a high readiness to vote in both areas of the city. However, the view of the future of society is, in comparison to the view of one's own private future, rather pessimistic.

A survey carried out for the first time in 1990 and then at yearly intervals until 1997 among Berlin school pupils from the seventh through tenth grades in Lichtenberg (East) and Charlottenburg (West) and spread across all school forms, revealed as a notable finding the development and consolidation of mutual prejudices, even though the actual living conditions have gradually converged. Children and adolescents from the Eastern areas of the city, who initially looked up to West Berliners practically with awe, were clearly disappointed and saw the West Berliners increasingly more negatively, while their own self-evaluation became increasingly better. The readiness to really get to know the others is relatively low, and the mutual acceptance has even decreased. The social change does not seem to have a differing effect on the psychological health of adolescents; the frequency of neurotic and psychosomatic complaints hardly differs between East and West. Nonetheless, it cannot be overlooked that the proportion of adolescents who complain of anxious-depressive and psychosomatic problems is high in both East and West. The divorce rate was considerably higher in the former GDR, and single mothers were in a better financial position through the numerous childcare possibilities. Today, divorce does not have a fundamentally different effect on children in the East and the West; it is the poverty of single mothers that counts as a great source of stress in this regard.

In the course of the last decade, the objective life situation of East German adolescents has grown increasingly closer to the living conditions of West German adolescents (DIW 2002). In particular, an extensive alignment can be observed in terms of employment, although the proportion of unemployed adolescents in East Germany is somewhat higher. At the beginning of the 1990s, the East German adolescents were more frequently in employment and less frequently in the educational system than their West German contemporaries; today, the employment and educational patterns of the East German adolescents have practically converged with those of the West Germans. Discrepancies can be discerned more between German and foreign adolescents, with the latter more rarely to be found in school and vocational education.

A picture that deviates from this is shown in the evaluation of subjective living conditions. Although the majority of adolescents are satisfied with the standard of living and life in general, differences between East and West continue to be apparent in spite of a convergence. At any rate, East German adolescents are distinctly more satisfied with their lives today than they were directly after reunification. With regard to worries, differences can also be discerned. While the general economic development gives grounds for worry for many adolescents in East and West, clearly more young East Germans—due to the higher unemployment—worry about their own economic situation and their job security. On the whole, it can be stated that West and East German adolescents have drawn closer together in terms of the evaluation of their living conditions. This applies to an even greater extent for the objective conditions. However, the hope that objective and subjective differences would be quickly eliminated within a short space of time through the advance of these people who have not been so strongly molded by the GDR has not been fulfilled.

Although the political transformation is now complete, the transfer of establishments is not synonymous with social integration. Demographic changes—for instance, the huge migration of young, well-educated men from the former East German states into the West—have given rise to new problems, and also the long-term consequences of societal change for children and adolescents are not known. It can be assumed that it will take another generation still before the consequences of the political and social system transfer are fully absorbed.

EVA DREHER and HORST ZUMKLEY

References and Further Reading

Auswaertiges Amt. 2004. *Facts about Germany*. www.tatsachen-ueber-deutschland.de/1610.99.html.

BKA (Bundeskriminalamt). 2004. *Polizeiliche Kriminalstatistik — Berichtsjahr 2003*. Wiesbaden: BKA. www.bka.de.

Blossfeld, H. P., E. Klijzing, K. Kurz, and M. Mills. (eds.). 2005. *Globalization, uncertainty, and youth in society*. New York: Routledge.

BMBF (Bundesministerium für Bildung und Forschung). 2002a. *Grund- und Strukturdaten 2001/2002*. Bonn: Referat Öffentlichkeitsarbeit. www.bmbf.de; www.destatis.de

BMBF (Bundesministerium für Bildung und Forschung). 2002b. *Antidemokratische Potenziale—eine repräsentative Befragung*. Bonn: Referat für Öffentlichkeitsarbeit www.bmbf.de/pub/antidemokratische_potenziale.pdf.

BMFSFJ (Bundesministerium für Familie, Senioren, Frauen und Jugend). 2003. *Die Familie im Spiegel der amtlichen Statistik*. Bonn: Referat Öffentlichkeitsarbeit. www.bmfsfj.de; www.destatis.de.

Bundeswehr. 2004. www.bundeswehr.de/forces/hintergrund/personalstaerke.php.

Bundeszentrale für politische Bildung. 2004. *Jugendkultur*. www.bpb.de.

BZgA (Bundeszentrale für gesundheitliche Aufklärung). 2004. www.bzga.de.

Chisholm, L., and K. Hurrelmann. 1995. Adolescence in modern Europe: Pluralized transition patterns and their implications for personal and social risks. *Journal of Adolescence* 18:129–58.

Deutsche Shell (ed.). 2000. *Jugend 2000 (Vol. 1), 13. Shell Jugendstudie*. Opladen: Leske und Budrich.

Deutsche Shell (ed.). 2003. *Jugend 2002, 14. Shell Jugendstudie. Zwischen pragmatischen Idealismus und robustem Materialismus* (4. Auflage). Frankfurt: Fischer Taschenbuch Verlag.

Deutsches Institut für Wirtschaftsforschung (DIW). 2002. Ost- und Westdeutsche Jugendliche: Annäherungen bei den objektiven Lebensbedingungen stärker als bei der subjektiven Bewertung. Wochenbericht des DIW, Berlin, (42/02). www.diw.de.

Die Drogenbeauftragte der Bundesregierung. 2004. *Drogen- und Suchtbericht*.

Dreher, E., and M. Dreher. 2002. Familientabus und Ablösung. In *Klinische Entwicklungspsychologie der Familie*. B. Rollett and H. Wernek (eds.). pp. 137–57. Göttingen: Hogrefe.

Fend, H. 1998. *Eltern und Freunde. Soziale Entwicklung im Jugendalter*. Bern: Huber.

Fend, H. 2000. *Entwicklungspsychologie des Jugendalters*. Opladen: Leske und Budrich.

Flammer, A., F. Alsaker, and P. Noak. 1999. Time-use by adolescents in an international perspective. In *The adolescent experience. European and American adolescents in the 1990s*. F. Alsaker and A. Flammer (eds.). pp. 33–60. Hillsdale, N.J.: Erlbaum.

Fritsche, Y. 2000. Moderne Orientierungsmuster: Inflation am Wertehimmel. In *Jugend 2000 (Vol. 1)*. Deutsche Shell (ed.). pp. 93–157. Opladen: Leske und Budrich.

Fuhrer, U. 2005. *Lehrbuch Erziehungspsychologie*. Bern: Huber.

Fuhrer, U., and I. E. Josephs. (eds.). 1999. *Persönliche Objekte, Identität und Entwicklung*. Göttingen: Hogrefe.

Furman, W., and E. Wehner. 1997. Adolescent romatic relationships: A developmental perspective. In *Romantic relationships in adolescence: Developmental perspectives. S. Shulman and W. Collins (eds.). pp. 21–36. San Francisco: Jossey Bass.

Gensicke, T. 2003. Individualität und Sicherheit in neuer Synthese? Wertorientierungen und gesellschaftliche Aktivität. In *Jugend 2002, 14. Shell Jugendstudie. Zwischen pragmatischen Idealismus und robustem Materialismus* (4. Auflage). Deutsche Shell (ed.). pp. 139–211. Frankfurt: Fischer Taschenbuch Verlag.

Heinz, W. 2003. *Jugendkriminalität in Deutschland.* http://www.uni-konstanz.de/rtf/kik/

Hurrelmann, K., A. Klocke, U. Melzer, et al. (eds.). 2003. *WHO-Jugendgesundheitssurvey (The WHO adolescent health survey—Concept and selected results for Germany).* München: Juventa.

Institut für Jugendforschung. 2004. *Die Finanzkraft der 13- bis 24-Jährigen in der BRD 2003.* München: Institut für Jugendforschung.

IPOS (Institut für praxisorientierte Sozialforschung). 2003. *Jugendliche und junge Erwachsene in Deutschland 2002.* Mannheim. www.bmfsfj.de.

Kasten, H. 2003. *Weiblich—Männlich. Geschlechterrollen durchschauen.* München: E. Reinhardt Verlag.

Keupp, H., T. Ahbe, W. Gmür, et al. 2002. *Identitätskonstruktionen. Das Patchwork der Identität in der Spätmoderne.* Reinbek: Rowohlt.

Kroger, J. 2000. Ego identity status research in the new millennium. *International Journal for the Study of Behavioral Development* 24:145–48.

Kunczik, M. 1998. *Gewalt und Medien.* Köln: Böhlau.

OECD. 2001. *Knowledge and skills for life: First results from PISA 2000.* Paris: OECD. http://www.mpib-berlin.mpg.de/pisa.

OECD. 2004. *Education at a glance: OECD indicators 2004 edition.* Paris: OECD.

Ortleb, R. 1991. *Grund- und Strukturdaten 1991/92.* Bonn: Bundesministerium für Bildung und Wissenschaft.

Pfeiffer, C., M. Kleimann, S. Petersen, et al. 2004. *Probleme der Kriminalität von Migranten und integrationspolitische Konsequenzen—Arbeitsbericht.* Hannover: Kriminologisches Forschungsinstitut Niedersachsen. www.kfn.de.

Robert Koch Institut. 2004. *Gesundheit von Kindern und Jugendlichen.* Berlin: Mercedes-Druck.

Roth, M. 1998. *Das Körperbild im Jugendalter. Diagnostische, klinische und entwicklungspsychologische Perspektiven.* Aachen: Mainz Verlag.

Silbereisen, R. K. 2005. Social change and human development: Experiences from German unification. *International Journal of Behavioral Development* 29:2–13.

Statistisches Bundesamt. 2003. *Statistisches Jahrbuch 2003 für die Bundesrepublik Deutschland.* Wiesbaden: SFG-Servicecenter Fachverlag.

Statistisches Bundesamt. 2004. www.destatis.de/d_home.htm.

Stiftung Digitale Chancen. 2003. *Factsheet Jugendliche und Internet (November 2003).*

Stiftung Digitale Chancen. 2004. www.digitale-chance.de.

Trautner, H. M. 2002. Entwicklung der Geschlechtsidentität. In *Entwicklungspsychologie* (5. vollständig überarbeitete Auflage). R. Oerter and L. Montada (eds.). pp. 648–74. Weinheim: Beltz.

GHANA

Background Information

Ghana is one of the sub-Saharan African countries and is located in west Africa. Its neighboring countries in the east, west, and north are the Republic of Togo, Côte d'Ivoire, and Burkina Faso, respectively. The Atlantic Ocean is at its southern border. Ghana's total land area is 230,250 square kilometers (92,100 square miles) (Population Reference Bureau 2005).

Ghana lies completely in the tropics and has forest and savannah vegetation. Agricultural production has been the main economic activity in the country. According to the 2000 Population and Housing Census, approximately half (50.7%) of the population aged 15 years and over is employed in agricultural production. Cocoa and timber have been the most important agricultural export commodities of Ghana. Minerals, particularly gold, are the second most important export commodities. Other major economic activities are trading and manufacturing, which employ 15.3% and 11.5%, respectively, of the labor force (Ghana Statistical Service 2002).

In 2005, Ghana occupied the 133rd position on the Human Development Index. Its gross national income per capita in 2005 was $2,280 USD with 79% living below $2 USD per day (Population Reference Bureau 2005).

Ghana was a former British colony called the Gold Coast because of the abundance of gold in the colony. It gained independence in 1957, being the first sub-Saharan African country to gain independence from colonial rule. It became a republic in 1960. The first president of the independent state, Osagyefo Dr. Kwame Nkrumah, ruled until 1966 when his Conventional People's Party's (CPP) government was removed from power by the military junta of the National Liberation Council (NLC). Most of the political history of Ghana was characterized by instability. It was ruled by three military regimes over a period of 23 years: 1966–1969, 1972–1979, and 1981–1992. But stability seems to have developed over the past two decades as the Fourth Republic, which ushered in constitutional rule in 1992, has witnessed three rounds of parliamentary elections in 1996, 2000, and 2004.

And for the first time in its political history, there was a change of government through the ballot box at the 2000 elections when the government of the National Democratic Congress (NDC) was replaced by the New Patriotic Party (NPP).

Ghana has numerous ethnic groups. A broad classification of these in the 2000 Population and Housing Census shows the major groupings as follows: Akan (49.1%), Mole Dagbon (16.5%), Ewe (12.7%), and Ga-Dangme (8.0%) (Ghana Statistical Service 2002).

Ghana's population stood at 22 million in 2005. It is a young population with 40% below 15 years and 3% aged 65 years and over (Population Reference Bureau 2005). At the 2000 Population and Housing Census, the age group 10 to 24 years, who are considered as the youth, form almost a third (30.5%) of Ghana's population, with adolescents 10 to 19 years constituting 22%, and older youth 20 to 24 years forming 8.5% (Ghana Statistical Service 2002).

Period of Adolescence

There are significant differences between the traditional and modern conceptions, norms, values, and expectations of adolescence and the period so considered. In traditional Ghanaian society, there was more emphasis on the period of adolescence for girls than for boys. Puberty rites for boys were brief or absent in some parts of the country, especially the southern parts. But circumcision for boys is now almost universal and is usually performed during infancy. In the past, some ethnic groups circumcised boys at puberty to usher them into manhood and make them responsible citizens or eligible to go to war (Teyegaga 1985).

Menarche marked the beginning of adolescence for girls. It was then followed by the performance of puberty rites, sometimes immediately or otherwise planned for a later date as circumstances such as the physical development of the girl (particularly the breasts) and financial readiness of the family (Hevi-Yiboe 2003; Sarpong 1977) might dictate. The period involved ranged from a number of days to weeks and even years in some cases, especially for daughters of chiefs or traditional rulers.

The ultimate goals of the puberty rites were to supervise girls' entry into sexuality, marriage, and motherhood. Some of the names for the rites—*tugbeworwor* (celebration of beauty) of the Dodome Ewe (Hevi-Yiboe 2003), *bragoro* (celebration of womanhood) of the Ashanti (Sarpong 1977)—suggest the purpose of the rites. All the puberty rites, particularly the *dipo* (girls' initiation rite of the Krobo), had social and religious aspects. The puberty rites and girls' initiation rites like *dipo* have three stages, namely: separation, transition, and reincorporation. The period of adolescence, transition from childhood to adulthood, was generally short, especially when marriage soon followed the performance of the puberty rites. Generally, the puberty rites were performed for girls aged between 12 and 16 years (Sackey 2001) in most Akan and Ewe cultures. The separation and transition custom lasted up to three years in Krobo in the past, and the candidates were aged between 14 and 21 years (Teyegaga 1985). More often than not, marriage follows soon after the puberty rites are performed; and the birth of a child may happen within the first year of marriage (Sarpong 1977; Steegstra 2005). Formerly, a girl who was already pregnant or who had had sex was not allowed to be initiated and in some communities was banished (Sarpong 1977).

Female circumcision is a traditional practice in some northern communities and is believed by some to have been introduced into Ghana by migrating populations from the Sahelian countries of Burkina Faso, Mali, and Niger (Dorkenoo 1992, cited by Odoi-Agyarko 2001). It is dying out as it was criminalized in the late twentieth century. According to a survey conducted by Odoi-Agyako (2001) the average prevalence rate was about 36% in the Upper East Region where the practice was most prevalent, while the average for the whole country was between 9% and 12% in 2001.

As a result of modernization, there have been changes in both the duration and the traditional practices regarding adolescence. Generally, parents, particularly Christians, do not perform the rites for their daughters because of biblical teachings that do not approve the rites for Christians (Steegstra 2005; Teteyega 1985). The resilience of the *dipo* (girls' initiation rites of the Krobo) has been an exception. It has been explained that many Krobo have an attitude that *dipo* does not constitute an obstacle to the practice of Christianity (Steegstra 2005).

Demographically, the age of menarche has reduced from an average of 14 to 16 years to around 13 years since the late twentieth century, and some girls have their first menstruation around 10 years of age (Ghana Statistical Service 1998). At this age most girls are in primary school or have done a year or two of secondary education. For those who will enroll in a tertiary institution, an average of ten or more years will be spent in school after menarche. During this longer period of adolescence girls are expected to be in school, and some start to be sexually active.

Beliefs

Ghanaians are adherents of three major religions, as indicated by the results of the 2000 census: Christianity (68.8%), Islam (15.9%), and Traditional African Religion (8.5%). A very small minority (0.7%) belong to other religious faiths and 6.1% have no religious belief (Ghana Statistical Service 2002).

Religious beliefs are transmitted primarily through religious activities. Since the 1980s, all public basic schools (primary and junior secondary schools) have been required to teach all religions, and not Christianity alone, as was the practice in the past.

Differences between the participation of young people and adults in religious activities of the dominant religions may be negligible. However, adherents of African Traditional Religion are normally elderly people while cult activities are associated with the older youth.

Gender

There have been clear distinctions between the roles and expectations, rights and responsibilities of males and females in Ghana, particularly in the traditional setting. The part played by the concept of gender in Ghanaian society is best understood from the perspective of social structure and organization.

In traditional society, political and lineage authority is largely vested in males (fathers, husbands, brothers, uncles, and sons) in both patrilineal and matrilineal societies. However, females did play important parts as family elders and even heads. Age was also an important element in social organization. The elderly were accorded positions of respect and authority. Sons might be preferred to daughters in patrilineal societies because it was through sons that the patrilineage was continued and the responsibility for managing lineage was expected. However, in the matrilineal societies there was a more equal desire for sons and daughters, though nephews inherited property in the matrilineage.

Most studies indicate that women were subordinates, but a few show that they had more autonomy in the pre-colonial era than has been portrayed in some more recent feminist literature. A recent misguided stereotype is that men or husbands have been considered as breadwinners as they have been expected to provide sustenance for their families while women's primary roles have been childbearing, child rearing, and performing of domestic chores. As has been recognized, women do not perform reproductive activities only but engage in productive activities also, usually as unpaid family labor in employments that are relatively easy to combine with childbearing and related activities. Their contribution to food production especially has been noted. Trading has also been an important employment among women.

Since independence, women's participation in formal education and paid employment has been actively promoted. However, females have tended to enter programs that prepare them to become nurses, teachers, or office clerks—professions that enable them to perform reproductive activities quite effectively. A continuing problem remains the higher drop-out rates for girls after puberty. A Girl Child Education Unit has been established in the Ministry of Education to implement policies that promote training of girls for professions that were formerly reserved for men.

The notion of the ideal woman and adolescent girl in traditional society was one who was good at housekeeping and raising many children. In contemporary Ghana, however, the concept of the ideal adolescent—boy or girl—is one who is able to pursue formal education. This ideal prevails among both the elite and average Ghanaian society, though to a greater degree among the educated and urban residents.

The expectation of going through female puberty rites before marriage has been dying out as many Christians in the predominantly Christian community abandon the practice. But male circumcision, done usually in infancy, has been upheld, and has become quite a universal practice in Ghana. Female circumcision, which was practiced mainly in some northern communities, has been criminalized since the 1980s, though the enforcement of the law banning it has not been successfully implemented. Only small percentages of the younger generation in those communities have been circumcised, and societal views about the practice have been changing (Odoi-Agyarko 2001).

The traditional notion of beauty, which is equated to being plump, is changing as health education on health risks of being overweight and obesity as well as Western concepts of beauty are gradually being embraced in the society. Among educated adolescents especially, a beautiful girl must be a slender girl. This trend is portrayed at beauty pageants that are patronized by young girls.

The Self

Collectivism characterizes social life in traditional Ghanaian society, as family ties, personal social relations, and social obligations are defined in terms of kinship. The notion of the family in Africa refers to the wider kin group. Lineage and descent (patrilineal, matrilineal, and bilateral) are bases for the definition of kin groups, their ties, rights, and obligations and the associated collectivism.

Collectivism still exists, particularly with respect to participation in social activities, but the country now tends toward individualism, as a result of modernization, urbanization, and migration with dispersal of members of kin groups. Such social transformation promotes individualism as kinship ties are weakened. The household size of the population reflects this tendency toward individualism. In 2003, the mean household size in the country was four and 21% of all households were single-person households (Ghana Statistical Service (GSS) NMIMR, and ORG Macro 2004).

The sense of belonging to a particular ethnic group shaped personal development and cultural identity in traditional Ghanaian society. Identity was perceived within the context of development of bonds of communion with one's kin, a value of collectivism (Sarpong 1977).

At independence, the Nkrumah government began to build a national consciousness in Ghanaian society. Other governments also did. General I. K. Acheampong's (1972–1978) military regime, for example, used the slogan, "One Nation, One People, One Destiny," for this purpose.

National identity does not supersede ethnic identity in all spheres of life in Ghana today, but various kinds of associations with membership cutting across ethnic boundaries give identity to many people, including the youth. A typical example is old-student association (commonly referred to as "old-boyism"). Almost all secondary schools, until recently, were boarding institutions bringing together children from diverse ethnic and other backgrounds. Identity with a football club is also important in Ghana. Most clubs have membership from all walks of life.

Family Relationships

Parenting in Ghana has been an important responsibility for both parents as well as the immediate family. The mother is the primary care giver, but members of her kin group help to care for the child. Socialization of a child in the broader sense of the word was everybody's responsibility in traditional society.

Fostering of the institutional type (which is different from the crisis type resulting from death or divorce) was a common practice in traditional Ghanaian society. One of its purposes was to provide the best opportunity for the child when that was not provided by the biological parents. A member of the extended family might take over the upbringing of the child. Crisis fostering was also encouraged. All these were done within the contexts of societal norms and values of kinship ties and associated rights and responsibilities. There were no foster homes in Ghana until in 1949 when the first foster home, Osu Children's Home in Accra, was established. (It was run under a different name before this name was given to it, when it was moved from the former location to Osu.) Foster homes are now quite common in the country. Some children are also raised by relatives or friends of their parents. Fostering has remained an important aspect of parenting in contemporary Ghana.

The results of the 2003 GDHS, which is the most recent source of information on living arrangements of children, show that only 40.3% of children aged 10 to 17 years were living with both parents. There were another 19.5% who were living with their mothers only, though their fathers were alive, and 6.2% were living with their fathers only, though their mothers were alive (GSS, NMIMR, and ORG Macro 2004). This shows that a significant proportion of adolescents live with social rather than biological parents.

Such living arrangements of children may be indicative of divorce or death. The divorce rate was 4.3% among the population aged 12 years and over at the 2000 population census (Ghana Statistical Service 2002). But more children are also born outside marriage. Consequently, increasing numbers of children have been living with their mothers alone and female-headed households have been increasing in number. In 2003, 33.8% of all households in Ghana were female-headed households. In urban areas where sociocultural transformations are greatest, the proportion was 39.7% compared with 28.9% in rural areas. It must be noted that some of the female-headed households are results of other circumstances such as labor migration of a husband or a job transfer.

Family relationships are expected to be cordial, though intergenerational conflicts associated with fashion and issues of cultural values do exist between the older and younger generation. Respect for the elderly and persons in authority, which has been a traditional value in Ghana, is dying out. For example, student demonstrations, especially in secondary schools, have increased. The government and other stakeholders have adopted a number of policies to curtail indiscipline among the youth.

Friends and Peers/Youth Culture

Adolescents, particularly older ones (15 to 19 years) in boarding institutions, spend a lot of their time with their friends and peers during school time. Out-of-school adolescents also socialize in the community. Peer crowds are common sights at football games, sports activities, and in some entertainment centers.

There are no restrictions on friendship on account of social class or ethnic barriers, though adolescents of similar background have stronger attraction to one another. Some adolescents are also enrolled in boys' or girls' schools. Their mixing with the opposite sex is restricted during school periods. Parents normally discourage friendship between young boys and girls on grounds that it may result in sexual immorality. As children grow up, usually from 16 to 18 years they have boy/girl friendships, some of which may be for sexual relations and/or companionship (Nabila and Fayorsey 2000; Awusabo et al. 1999). But parents and the wider society show concern for such boy/girl relationships because of HIV/AIDS, as the youth have also been infected (1.3% of age group 15 to 24 years in 2003) (GSS, NMIMR, and ORG Macro 2004).

In tertiary institutions, home-town associations attract youths from the same ethnic group. But there are other clubs and associations that draw people from diverse backgrounds. The most common religious groups are Scripture Union, youth ministries in churches, and Muslim youth movements. Boy Scouts and Girl Guides are also found in most schools in both urban and rural areas. There are youth wings of political parties in tertiary institutions, and those aged 18 and over from different backgrounds are members.

Ghanaian youth have a distinctive culture that expresses itself mostly in youth fashion, music, and aspirations. Short, skin-tight outfits and short blouses that expose part of the body, even private parts like the breast, are the characteristic girls' fashion. Such fashion is generally referred to as *apuskeleke* (Sackey 2003). Boys' main fashion is known as *Otto-Pfister* (named after a German coach of the Black Stars, the Ghanaian national football team), which involves wearing very loose and long trousers below the waistline so that part of the hem sweeps the ground and gets dirty. When girls wear their skirts and trousers below the waistline, so that the navel is exposed, it is referred to as "I'm aware," indicating that the person in the attire is aware she has exposed part of her body and need not be told. As the name suggests, society or the older generation in particular frowns on this and other youth culture elements, which have generally been blamed on Westernization and Americanization of Ghanaian society. Indeed, the average Ghanaian youth aspires to emigrate to America or Europe.

Ghanaian youth enjoy the Western musical styles of jazz and rap or hip-hop. Also popular among the youth is a style of music called *hip-life* which is a fusion of rap and the Ghanaian highlife music. Local gospel music is also becoming a favorite of the youth. Piercing of ears among boys is rare and is not indigenous to Ghanaian culture. It can be found among some youth in the cities but is very rare. It is associated with immigrants, particularly those from Germany, who are nicknamed "German Burgers."

Love and Sexuality

According to the results of the 2003 GDHS, 9% and 4% of adolescent girls and boys respectively said that they had sexual intercourse by age 15; and by age 18, almost half (47.7%) of adolescent girls and a quarter (24.5%) of adolescent boys have had sexual intercourse. However, among the broader age group, 15 to 19 years, 61.0% and 80.0% of the adolescent girls and boys respectively have never had sex (GSS, Noguchi Memorial Institute for Medical Research (NMIMR), and ORG Macro 2004). Traditionally, however, Ghanaian society frowns upon dating and sexual experimentation among young children. It is not acceptable to discuss sex and sexuality in public. Sex education was given to adolescents at puberty as part of puberty rites. Parents do not normally discuss sexual matters with their children. As Sarpong (1977: 69) puts it,

> Traditionally, a boy or girl is supposed to be completely ignorant of sexual matters until he or she is physiologically and socially (that is by reason of performance of her initiation rites) mature. In some tribes a test of virginity is said to have, in the past, formed part of the ritual

of the wedding night of a newly married girl, and a failure to produce the evidence, a blood-stained white cloth, was a humiliating disaster which could lead to the breaking of the marriage contract. Juvenile immorality was severely punished, sometimes by death, or perpetual banishment.

It was therefore difficult to have sex education introduced into formal school curriculum. It has been treated as part of other courses such as Life Skills and Family Life Education in pre-university and tertiary institutions respectively.

The moral standard for boys and girls has not been quite the same, though. As Awusabo et al. (1999) put it, there is a double standard so far as sexuality of girls and boys is concerned. A virginity test is done for girls but not required of boys, and in marriage males are allowed multiple partners. Despite these gender differences in the attitude to sexuality among young people, Ghanaian society frowns on sexual promiscuity and the use of contraceptives among both boys and girls.

Ghanaian society has experienced considerable transformation regarding sexuality and marriage (see for example, Oppong 1981). An example is a kind of sexual relationship between a young girl (usually in secondary school and tertiary institutions) and an elderly married or unmarried man. The man is referred to as the *sugar-daddy* of the young girl. He provides her financial and/or material gifts in exchange for her sexual services.

At the 2000 census, 5% of adolescents aged 12 to 17 years were married while 1.4% were in consensual unions. But the average age at first marriage was 19 years (Ghana Statistical Service 2002). Apart from the longer period of adolescence that the average young Ghanaian girl and boy experiences, there has been an increasing proportion of women and men in the population who never marry. Consequently, the period of single-hood has been increasing for some young people, due mainly to their participation in formal education. At the 2003 GDHS, 86.3% and 99.0% of adolescent (15 to 19 years old) girls and boys respectively reported that they had never married. The proportions for the age group 20 to 24 years was 42.1% and 75.8% of young adult women and men respectively who had never married (GSS, NMIMR, and ORG Macro 2004). Considering that a large proportion of both categories are employed, it can be concluded that more young people and young adults are living independent lives outside marriage even if not outside their natal home.

Birth control has not been popular in Ghanaian society. In 2005, only 19% of married women aged

15 to 49 years were using any modern contraceptive method (Population Reference Bureau 2005). Contraceptive usage rates are lower among the youth, though a significant proportion of them are sexually active. The 2003 GDHS results show that only 6.4% and 10% of girls and boys respectively, aged 15 to 19 years were currently using modern contraceptives. Meanwhile, 24.5% of both boys and girls have their first sexual intercourse by 18 years (GSS, NMIMR, and ORG Macro 2004). Consequently, young girls seek abortions from quack doctors to get rid of unwanted pregnancies (Kom and Yeboah 2003; Nabila and Fayorsey 2000). The 2003 GDHS data on self-reporting of sexually transmitted infections (STIs) showed that 2.2% of adolescents aged 15 to 19 years self-reported an STI.

The adolescent pregnancy rate varies among subgroups of the population. The results of the 2003 GDHS showed that 24.8% of all adolescent girls aged 15 to 19 years had begun childbearing. But the rate ranged from 3.0% among those who attain secondary education to 26.0% among those who have no education. By residential background, the percentage of urban teenagers who had begun childbearing was 7.2% compared with 21.8% of those in rural areas (Ghana Statistical Service, NMIMR, and ORG Macro 2004).

Homosexuality is generally disapproved of in Ghanaian society. However, it is believed to be increasing due to the influences of globalization and tourism.

It is because of such demographic changes of the period of adolescence, sociocultural transformations, and the spread of HIV that the government adopted the Ghana Adolescent Reproductive Health Policy in October 2000 to meet challenges facing and improve the general well-being of adolescents. Having considered the available data and other information on adolescence, the policy targets adolescents and young adults—that is youth between the ages of 10 and 24 years old for the purposes of the policy (National Population Council 2000).

Health Risk Behavior

Tobacco use is a major health risk behavior among adolescents in Ghana. Statistics on tobacco and other substance abuse among the youth in Ghana is limited and the main sources are surveys. The findings of the Ghana Youth Tobacco Survey (GYTS) conducted in 2000 that covered 1,917 JSS students showed that 19.5% of them were currently using a tobacco product and another 14.3% had tried smoking cigarettes. The Ghana Education Service prohibits use of tobacco products in all schools. A draft bill on tobacco control is also in parliament. There is already a ban on tobacco use in public places including cinema halls, restaurants, and public offices (Wellington 2004).

Drug (including tobacco) and alcohol use among adolescents is found mainly among those in secondary schools and tertiary institutions where many young people are forced by peer pressure to use these substances. The effects of these include depression and other psychiatric disorders. The majority of male psychiatric hospital inmates are reported to be drug users.

One of the most common crimes among the youth is vandalism during demonstrations in secondary schools and tertiary institutions. Such behavior reflects the level of indiscipline in Ghanaian society. Often, school authorities suspend or dismiss students for such crimes. Road accidents are common in Ghana and have been a source of concern for government and the whole society. It is now a major cause of death in the population but probably not among the youth since most of them do not have access to vehicles. However, young people are among the main victims of pedestrian accidents in which pedestrians are knocked down or killed by vehicles.

Adolescent sexuality and associated risks of contracting STDs and HIV/AIDS and adolescent pregnancy are the main sources of adolescents' health risk. The findings of the 2003 GDHS, for example show that 72.1% and 97.9% of adolescent girls and boys respectively aged 15 to 19 years said they had engaged in higher-risk sex within the last 12 months before the survey. Higher-risk sex is sex with a nonmarital partner or noncohabiting partner. Again, among that age group, 1.5% of the girls and 2.4% of the boys said they had two or more partners during the same period (GSS, NMIMR, and ORG Macro 2004). The concerns for these sexual behaviors are some of the major reasons for the adoption of the Ghana Adolescent Reproductive Health Policy in 2000. Again, this concern and response are related to the spread of HIV/AIDS, which has been a great challenge to sub-Saharan African countries.

Certain categories of adolescents have peculiar problems apart from the general ones discussed here. There are a significant number of adolescents who do not go to school at all or are school dropouts. Some of these are also engaged in premarital sex and sex trade as a means of survival in some cases. Street living characterizes the lives of some of these children, who sleep in open spaces such as in front of shops. Some sell on the streets and return

GHANA

home. Others are also employed and work under conditions that adversely affect their development. The circumstances that brought about their conditions include poverty, irresponsible parenting, and a host of others. The concern for these children has yet to result in the implementation of appropriate policies that can meet their needs.

Education

Between the ages of 12 and 15, young people spend a lot of time in school. They have extracurricular activities such as sports, hobbies, and club activities. Boy Scouts and Girl Guides are popular clubs in both rural and urban communities. Football (soccer), a national game, is also a favorite of the youth.

With the introduction of formal education parents have had to face the opportunity cost of sending their children to school. Depending on parents' aspirations for their children and economic circumstances, some children go to school and others do not.

Gender expectations also influence the differences in school attendance between boys and girls. Traditionally, boys are expected to become family heads and breadwinners while girls engage in reproductive activities (childbearing and child rearing) and perform domestic chores, though they also engage in some productive activities. Thus gender gaps in education have been explained by sex or gender roles that society assigns the sexes. Where poverty prevents parents from sending all children to school, the boy is more likely to be sent than the girl. Girls may also be withdrawn to help their mothers to care for their younger siblings and perform domestic chores. Some adolescent girls may be withdrawn and given into marriage or may drop out of school because of pregnancy. Thus cultural attitudes encourage girls to be socialized to become wives and mothers instead of being determined in their school attendance.

Against this background, various governments of Ghana provided universal education, usually tuition-free at the primary level for both boys and girls. The first post-independence government, for example, implemented an education program that made it possible for school dropouts, especially adolescent mothers, to go back to school. A Free Compulsory Universal Basic Education (FCUBE) policy, introduced in 1992, requires all children of school-going age up to the ninth grade (JSS 3) to be in school. Until the 1980s, the duration of secondary education was seven years, and these years were all spent in boarding institutions. Currently, the first three years are spent in day institutions and another three years in boarding institutions, the number of years in the boarding school having been reduced. This deboardinization policy aims at reducing the cost of secondary education and making it more accessible to all children.

The enrollment and literacy rates among young people show that many are not in school and a significant number are illiterate. At the Ghana 2000 Ghana Population and Housing Census, more than half (54.3%) of females, compared with a little over a third of males (37.1%), aged 15 years and over were illiterate in English. Data on current school attendance from the Ghana 2000 Ghana Population and Housing Census showed that only 24.8% of boys and girls were in secondary school (JSS and SSS). Gender gaps in attainment of secondary school education (adolescence ages) have been decreasing. The gross enrollment rate for JSS in 2002/2003 (as reported by the Ministry of Education) was 67.3% and 59.3% respectively for boys and girls (National Population Council 2005). The difference between the percentage of boys (25.4%) and girls (23.9%) in both JSS and SSS at the 2000 census was also not great. The gap is not wide in post-secondary and tertiary institutions, where 8.1% of males and 6.2% of females are enrolled. This shows that the promotion of girl-child education has been quite successful in Ghana (Ghana Statistical Service 2002).

There are very few educational institutions for the physically challenged, such as schools for the blind and the deaf. There also are very few group homes for the mentally retarded.

Work

Depending on the financial situation or occupation of the family, a young person may spend more time participating in wage employment or contributing to family labor on the farm or other family enterprise, than attending school. Some, especially girls, perform domestic chores. Children have been sources of labor for family farms and other family enterprises such as trading. Children, particularly girls, also performed domestic chores and helped to fetch water and firewood, which were some of the most time-consuming domestic activities. Children's contribution to the family has been so important that a large family size was prestigious in Ghanaian traditional society, as in other African societies.

As children traditionally engaged in all kinds of work for their families, they continue to do so to different degrees. Depending on the socioeconomic background and aspirations of their parents, they may be involved in domestic work only or provide labor for family business as well and go to school at the same time or stay away from school. Some, however, may not enroll in school at all because their parents cannot afford their school fees or for other reasons, including distance to school, lack of parental interest in sending children to school, and childbearing in the case of adolescent girls.

The United Nations Development Programme 2004 Human Development Index Report shows that 12% of Ghana's children aged 10 to 14 years are employed in the labor force. Most children work on farms, sell on streets, or work as house-helps (domestic servants) when they are not in school. In the northern parts of the country, boys tend cattle. Along the coast and the Volta Lake, children are engaged in the fishing industry. Child trafficking in the communities along the lake has been reported where children are sold or pawned to fishermen who need labor in their fishing enterprise. Child trafficking is reported in other parts of the country too.

Street life has been a common phenomenon in large towns in Ghana over the past few decades. The capital (Accra) and the second largest town (Kumasi) have the majority of street children. Most children who live on the street work too and most of them do not attend school.

The findings of a nationwide Ghana Child Labour Survey (GCLS) conducted in 2001 that covered 17,034 children in households and 2,314 street children provides one of the most current sources of information on work and other areas of the lives of children. The targeted age group was 5 to 17 years. The results of the GCLS showed that major sources of income for Ghanaian households are self-employment from agricultural activities (49.1%) and self-employment in non-agricultural activities (28.0%). Only 14.0% of family income is derived from regular wage employment. Accordingly, Ghanaian children engage mainly in unpaid family agricultural production and non-agricultural activities, particularly trading. The survey results indicate that the major economic activities in which the 17,034 children interviewed in the households were engaged were agriculture, fishing, and forestry (57.0%) and sales (20.7%). The only exception was in the Greater Accra Region (which contains the national capital, Accra) where sales work dominated. Almost all (97.7%) the children were also involved in housekeeping activities.

Among the children interviewed in the households, 22.2% reported that their work adversely affected their studies. Vast differences existed among the various regions, however, with respect to the effect of economic activity on studies. While the great majority of children in the southern parts of the country (for example, 91.4% in the eastern region, 86.6% in the Brong Ahafo, and 79.5% in the Greater Accra region) said they could work and study without difficulty, most children in the deprived northern parts of the country (95.0% in the Upper West and 68.1% in the Upper East regions) reported that their work affected their schooling (Ghana Statistical Service 2003). School attendance was generally lower among street children; almost half (45.7%) had never attended school, compared to less than a fifth (17.6%) of those in households. The highest educational level attained by a large proportion (34.5%) of the street children is the primary level. While 64.4% of the children in the households were functionally literate in English or a Ghanaian language, about 71.0% of the street children could neither read nor write. The findings of the survey further indicated that children in the age group 10 to 14 years were more likely to combine schooling with economic activity. This corroborates findings of other studies, which show that school dropout rate increases from about the fourth grade (between ages nine and eleven) when children (both boys and girls) are able to contribute to family labor. At puberty, which is now between the ages of 12 and 14 years, the girls' dropout rate rises as a result of pregnancy too. While 71% of those between 10 and 14 years combined schooling and economic activity, smaller percentages did so among those aged 5 to 9 years (64.3%) and 15 to 17 years (53.0%), as the survey results showed (Ghana Statistical Service 2003).

The working conditions of the children were not always good, according to the findings of the GCLS. The most reported injuries associated with domestic work are cuts and wounds that were not serious and did not require medical treatment.

Sexual exploitation has been reported among street girls who, as a result of their vulnerability, are sexually abused or give in to sexual demands on the street. As a result of their financial hardship and dependence on males, they exchange sex for sleeping space and other material needs and are sometimes raped by older and stronger street boys or others (Adomako Ampofo et al. 2004).

Media

The modern media culture is not indigenous to Ghanaian society, but in the early twenty-first century, radio and TV reach almost every part of

Ghana as well as many dailies, weeklies, and journals. Programs on the radio and TV are both indigenous and imported.

According to the 2003 GDHS, 73% and 84% of adolescent girls and boys respectively aged 15 to 19 years listen to the radio at least once a week. A lesser proportion of the girls and boys (55% of each) watch TV at least once a week. These rates are not significantly different from those of the entire adult population (GSS, NMIMR, and ORG Macro 2004).

Though data are not available, a far smaller proportion of adolescents is likely to have access to computer games, the Internet, and movies, since these are not available to most students, let alone the high proportion that are not in school.

A number of media programs target young people. The *Junior Graphic*, which is published for the youth, has good information on various issues. But some negative media programs also target adolescents, and lack of parental monitoring and selectivity in broadcast items result in the exposure of adolescents to pornographic sites and advertisements on the TV and Internet especially. There is a general feeling among the adult Ghanaian population that Western lifestyles portrayed in the media—TV in particular—have a negative influence on Ghanaian traditional culture and the youth. The general tendency of the youth to show disrespect and strive for individualism is blamed on the influence of European and American culture.

Politics and Military

In Ghana, the age at which citizens can vote is 18 years. The qualifying age for parliament is 21 years. Thus some youth in secondary school and the tertiary institutions exercise their franchise and have the right to engage in political activities. The youth generally support governments (civilian and military) from time to time but shift their loyalty as and when necessary. Student political demonstrations have been an area of concern for Ghanaian society as past experience shows that they are sometimes manipulated by politicians to stage demonstrations against governments and political institutions. Youth political agitation is usually about issues of mismanagement of state resources and allegations of corruption among government officials, and for that purpose attract support from the general public and the opposition in parliament.

The youth have played increasing roles in both local and national politics since the lifting of a ban on political activities in May 1992. The political parties, recognizing the contribution of the youth, have mobilized them by establishing youth wings, which have become important structures of political parties in Ghana. The youth wing activities in tertiary institutions of the two leading parties, the NPP and the NDC, are respectively known as Tertiary Institutions Network (TEIN) and Tertiary Education and Student Confederacy (TESCON). The youth serve as foot soldiers and vehicles through which political party messages are passed on to the electorate, especially those in remote areas (Asante 2005). The youth are also the majority of militant groupings that fight for their rights, especially in urban areas and in ethnic conflict zones (Kamete 2005). The student front in politics has therefore been transformed considerably as wings of different political parties now exist in tertiary institutions and students join whichever they like, depending on their political leanings.

Youth involvement in compulsory military training has not been experienced in Ghana. A voluntary military training for National Service Personnel was introduced during the early years of the Rawlings military regime (1979–1992), but it was not well patronized and was therefore short-lived. There is a paramilitary school club called Cadets, which usually marches at school events. It started in the 1980s and is now in many JSSs, SSSs, and tertiary institutions. It has been considered as a legacy of the Rawlings regime.

Youth volunteer work usually takes the form of clean-up activities that are part of school, alumni association, church, and community programs. Individual volunteer work is not as common among the youth as such group-based voluntary activities.

DELALI BADASU

References and Further Reading

Adomako Ampofo, A., O. Alhassan, F. Ankrah, et al. 2004. Children and sexual exploitation: Report of an Accra study for UNICEF, Ghana. Institute of African Studies, University of Ghana.

Asante, R. (Forthcoming). The youth and politics in Ghana: Reflections on the 2004 general elections. In *Institutional and democratic development in Ghana: 2004 general elections*. K. Boafa-Arthur.

Awusabo-Asare, K., A. M. Abane, J. K. Anarfi, et al. 1999. "All die be eie": Obstacles to change in the face of HIV infection in Ghana. *Health Transition Review* (1999):125–31.

Brempong, O. 1997. Religious background of Ghanaian society: A general survey. *Institute of African Studies Research Review*, New Series 13(1 and 2):59–73.

Ghana Aids Commission. 2004. *National HIV/AIDS and STI policy*. Accra: Ghana Aids Commission.

Ghana Statistical Service. 2002. *2000 population and housing census: Summary report of final results*. Accra: Ghana Statistical Service.

Ghana Statistical Service. 2003. *Ghana child labour survey*. Accra: Ghana Statistical Service.

Ghana Statistical Service, Noguchi Memorial Institute for Medical Research, and ORC Macro. 2004. *Ghana demographic and health survey*. Accra: Ghana Statistical Service.

Hevi-Yiboe, L. 2003. Family resources and reproduction and reproductive health of girls: A focus on money and *Tugbeworwor*: Puberty rites among the Dodome Ewe. *Institute of African Studies Research Review*, New Series 19(1):79–90.

Kamete, A. Y. 2005. Youth in African cities. *News from the Nordic African Institute*. No. 3, October.

Nabila, J. S., and C. Fayorsey. 2000. *Adolescent fertility and reproductive health in Ghana* (Rev. Ed.). Accra: Population Impact Project (PIP/GHANA).

National Population Council. 2000. *Adolescent reproductive health policy*. Accra: National Population Council.

National Population Council. 2005. *Population of Ghana: Demographic and socio-economic indicators by district*. Fact Sheet No. III. Accra: National Population Council.

Odoi-Agyarko. 2002. *Lifelong pain of being a female in our land Ghana: An advocacy booklet on female genital mutilation*. Tema, Ghana: Ronna Publishers.

Oppong, C. 1981 *Middle class African marriage*. London: George Allen and Unwin.

Population Impact Project (PIP/Ghana). 2000. *Adolescent fertility and reproductive health in Ghana* (Rev. Ed., 2000). Accra: PIP/Ghana.

Population Impact Project (PIP/Ghana). 2005. *Socio-demographic profile of young people in the greater Accra region (2000)*. Accra: PIP/Ghana.

Population Reference Bureau. 2005. *World population data sheet*. Washington D.C.: Population Reference Bureau.

Sackey, B. 1985. The significance of beads in the rites of passage among some southern Ghanaian people. *Institute of African Studies Research Review*, New Series 1(2):180–91.

Sackey, B. 2001. Cultural responses to the management of HIV/AIDS: The repackaging of puberty rites. *Institute of African Studies Research Review*, New Series 17(2):63–72.

Sarpong, P. 1977. *Girls' nubility rites in Ashanti*. Tema: Ghana Publishing Corporation.

Steegstra, M. 2005. *Dipo and the politics of culture in Ghana*. Accra: Woeli Publishing Services.

Tawiah, E. 2002. Adolescent fertility and reproductive health in four sub-Saharan African countries. *African Population Studies* 17(2):81–98.

Teyegaga, B. D. 1985. *Dipo Custom and the Christian faith*. Accra: J'Piter Printing Press.

van Gennep, A. 1960. *The rites of passage*. Translation by M. B. Vizadom and G. L. Caffe. London: Routledge and Kegan Paul.

Wellington, E. K. 2004. *Tobacco control profile for Ghana*. Accra: Ghana Health Service.

GREECE

Background Information

Adolescence in Greece, as in most Western societies, extends well beyond puberty until about 20 years of age. Prolonged education to meet the demands of modern technology and of economic and societal changes is a major factor that contributes to this phenomenon. Globalization, on the other hand, has increased the homogenization of this group of population across the developed countries, leading to common patterns of behavior despite cultural, ethnic, racial, or religious differences.

Greece, located at the southernmost tip of the Balkan Peninsula, has land borders with Albania, the former Yugoslavian Republic of Macedonia, and Bulgaria to the north, and Turkey to the east. It has an extended coastline and hundreds of islands, mainly in the Aegean Sea. Greece is a presidential parliamentary republic and joined the European Union in 1981 and the European Union's Economic and Monetary Union (EMU) in 2001. It is also a member of the major world organizations, such as the United Nations and the Organization for Economic Co-operation and Development. The country is 80% mountainous, which led to increased urbanization, particularly after the 1950s. Of the population, 27.5% is living today in the greater region of Athens, the country's capital. The 2001 (NSSG 2001a; NSSG 2003) census recorded a population of 10,934,097 residents, with 15.2% aged 0 to 14 years, 14.3% 15 to 24 years, 53.8% 25 to 64 years, and 16.7% 65 years and over. Of them, 93% are of Greek nationality, the rest being economic migrants and refugees, mainly from Albania (4%) and the former Soviet Union (0.7%). Almost 98% of the population follows the Greek Orthodox Church; there is a Muslim religious minority in the northeastern part of Greece (about 1.3% of the population: 50% of Turkish origin, 35% Pomaks, and 15% Roma). Another 0.7% follows several other religions.

Greece's well-developed and influential ancient history and civilization goes back to about 5,000 years B.C. Ancient Greek civilization contributed greatly to art, philosophy, and the sciences, as well as in politics with the concept of democracy. Historical landmarks are the Minoan and the Mycenean civilizations, the colonization period, the classical age, the age of Macedonian supremacy with Alexander the Great and, finally, the Byzantine era that integrated the Christian religion with the Hellenic spirit of intellectual openness and philosophical inquiry. The Ottoman Empire occupied Greece in the fifteenth century for nearly 400 years; the nation gained its independence in the nineteenth century.

During the twentieth century, Greece participated in the Balkan wars and in the two World Wars. After the end of World War II, Greece suffered a four-year civil war between the communists and the nationalists, with the prevailing of the latter. As a result, Greece joined NATO and followed Western countries in their economic development. From 1967 to 1974 a military dictatorship was established in the country. In 1973 the university students revolted against the dictatorship. This led to recognition and acceptance of the political power of young people and to adolescents' involvement with politics and political parties.

Period of Adolescence

Puberty in Greece starts at about 12–13 years of age for girls and 1 or 2 years later for boys (Paraskevopoulos 1991). Adolescence, from the legal point of view, ends at the age of 18 years when adolescents obtain their voting rights. Before the 1983 legislation the age limit was 21 years.

The period of adolescence, in terms of delayed commitment to adult roles, has been remarkably lengthened in the last three decades (cf. Mourikes, Naoumes, and Papapetrou 2002). Continuation of schooling in upper secondary and for most students in tertiary education is the rule for the contemporary Greek society (IARD 2001), mainly because Greek society has always valued education and considered it a means for social mobility. This development has engendered a delay in both labor market entrance and marriage/birth of first child. Other social changes during the last decades, such as urbanization, nuclear and postnuclear forms of families, and high rates of unemployment among young people—25.6% of people aged 15 to 24 years were unemployed in 2002 (CERP 2003)—also delay commitment to adult roles until about the age of 30. The mean age of women at first marriage, for example, has increased from 23.7 years in 1970 to 25.9 years in 1998. Mothers' age of first child's birth has also increased from 23.3 years in 1980 to 28.6 years in 1998. In addition, the percentage of married men and women aged 20 to 24 years has dramatically decreased from 46.7% in 1970 to 11.3% in 2001 for women and from 12.8% to 3.2% for men. The percentage of married people aged 25 to 29 years is also low: only 37.9% of this age group is married (NSSG 2001b). However, in sharp contrast with the countries of northern Europe, the United Kingdom, and France, these changes are not compensated for by cohabiting and family forming outside marriage (IARD 2001). Indicatively, the percentage of cohabitation among 20- to 24-year-olds was only about 2% according to the 2001 census in Greece (NSSG 2001a). On the other hand, the proportion of single Greek women (25%) and men (40%) aged 20 to 24 years with more than one partner during the last year was found to be among the highest in western and southern Europe in the 1990s, according to relevant surveys (Bajos, Guillaume, and Kontula 2003).

So, on the basis of the aforementioned social changes, young people in Greece have to rely on their families as the basic support structure and to be financially dependent upon their parents (IARD 2001). Also, cultural norms regarding family closeness and mutual support are dictating parents' duties and children's expectations from them. Finally, the relatively conservative nature of family formation in Greece, in terms of forming independent households and having children after marriage, also affects the duration of the length of the period young people spend in their families (IARD 2001; Mourikes et al. 2002).

On the other hand, about 90% of young Greeks of both genders who follow university studies have the opportunity to distance themselves from the family home and become independent from parents' supervision (Dikaiou and Haritos-Fatouros 2000). Therefore, it seems that a new stage of life for most young people exists in contemporary Greece—that is, a period of an emerging adulthood that follows adolescence. This period, in social terms, involves the individuals who are no longer completely dependent on their families of origin but who have yet to establish a family of their own. It involves the ages from 19 to 29 years, and its duration is among the longest compared to the same period of life in the other European countries (IARD 2001).

Beliefs

Greek society has traditionally been collectivist (Georgas 1989). In the last five decades, due to significant urbanization and economic development as well as increased communication and use of mass media, the collectivist values progressively lessened, particularly in big cities, in favor of individualism. Still, there are aspects of Greek life and values that remain traditional. Thus, family remains the most important social value among people 15 to 29 years old. Love, friendship, and commitment to one's own country and religion are also highly valued (GSY and V-PRC 2000). There is also significant trust in the country's educational mechanisms, the army, and the church as state institutions that secure socioeconomic, physical, and psychological welfare (GSY and V-PRC 2000).

The same surveys show that young people value work and education, personal independence, and leisure activities. The latter two more individualistic values figure among the first ten of a list of predominant social values, side by side with the more collectivist ones (GSY and V-PRC 2000; IARD 2001). This pattern of values in adolescence can be explained in terms of the different sources through which values are transmitted. The Greek family, despite its changes, remains the strongest mediator of traditional values. The country's educational system also works in the same direction. School textbooks and educational expectations implicitly or explicitly transmit the traditional values of love of one's country, family, and religion along with those of work, education, and gender roles (Deliyanni-Kouimtzi and Ziogou 1995).

The church is a very significant institution in Greece which also mediates the transmission of traditional values. All major events of a person's life, such as birth, christening, marriage, and death, as well as commemoration of important historical events of the nation are linked with the church. The clergy also participates in feasts and everyday life, especially in small communities. Therefore, children are familiar with religious values and practices. Furthermore, there is a school subject on religion in primary and secondary education, mandatory prayer every day at school, and occasional school attendance of church ceremonies on important religious events.

Despite the above facts, it seems that adolescents' participation in religious activities, such as church-going, prayer, and Holy Communion, is more limited than their abstract trust in God or in the church. It is also more limited than the religious life of their mothers. For example, a study by

Tsagas (2000) found that 69.2% of teenagers who responded to the question of how often they were going to church, reported "never" (6.4%) and "rarely—only during the great celebrations of the Orthodoxy" (62.8%). The percentage of mothers reporting similarly low church-going was 53.6% (4.2% never, 49.4% rarely). According to another study (GSY and V-PRC 2000), the respective percentage of young people of 15 to 29 years of age was estimated at 73.8% (7% never, 66.8% rarely). With regard to cults, there is sporadic evidence that various sects of New Age and satanism are present among Greek adolescents (Zabelis 1996).

Mass media, tourism, and communication with other countries also contribute to awareness of other lifestyles and values as regards everyday life. Thus, TV and other mass media are powerful sources for the development of adolescents' interests and other consuming and individualistic values. Finally, language, music, and storytelling are indirect means of value transmission, particularly as regards love of the country and national pride.

Gender

In the early twenty-first century, Greek society is in a transitional phase as regards gender roles. This is evident in the existing family practices as well as in the expectations regarding adolescents' education, career, and family prospects. Thus, on the one hand, there is egalitarian and equitable treatment of both genders in the formal educational system and, on the other hand, stereotypes about gender roles in society. As concerns youngsters, according to a specific indicator drawn from a 1997 Eurobarometer, Greek youth, in general, do not consider gender equality to be of high significance (IARD 2001).

Specifically, with respect to education, parents and society in general clearly favor and support higher education studies for both genders. Education is provided in mixed-gender schools and classes and there is demand for similar skills and knowledge across subjects for girls and boys.

However, there also exist stereotypes about gender-specific school subjects and achievements that influence adolescents' career decisions. Thus, girls represent about 10% of the total number of university students in math and science and 80% to 85% in arts and letters. However, girls represent 30% to 40% of the total number of students in programs in architecture and medicine, despite the fact that math and science are prerequisites for entering these schools.

In general, sexism is manifested in the different ways in which adolescent boys and girls view their future as regards career and family. When Greek girls come to formulate occupational aspirations, they fluctuate between highly qualified but traditionally "female" professions, such as teaching or nursing/medicine, and those suitable for women (e.g., with fixed work hours), such as office work, services, and fashion. Their reasons for these choices emphasize criteria such as service, caring, social contact, but also personal integration. Boys, on the other hand, more frequently select occupations involved with sports, jobs requiring a specific technical skill, military services, and highly qualified professions (such as pilot, doctor, or engineer). Their reasons for these choices center on criteria such as high salary, security, adventure, and love of machines (Deliyanni-Kouimtzi and Ziogou 1995). Young girls also tend to consider unemployment as a more important barrier to a possible future career than young boys do. In fact, this is a realistic picture for young women in Greece: women's unemployment, in general, is about ten points higher than that of men. Specifically, 37.7% of the female labor force aged 15 to 24 years, and 24.9% of those aged 25 to 29 years are unemployed (cf. Mourikes et al. 2002).

Thus, despite the educational expectations for a similar professional career for both genders, there is still differentiation in the expectations for family roles. It is interesting that, despite boys' and young men's very positive attitudes toward their participation in housework and in the bringing up of children, the actual male participation in these tasks, in contemporary Greece, is dramatically lower than the actual participation of females (cf. Mourikes et al. 2002).

Motherhood is considered a primary role for females and financial support for the family is primarily a male duty. As a consequence, girls are expected to marry at an earlier age—about 25 years of age—than boys, without necessarily having found a job. Boys, on the other hand, are expected to marry at about the age of 30, and only after they have secured a steady job. This is an important ideology, which is transmitted through the parents' own practices at home (division of labor), through the differential assignment of home duties to boys and girls (Deliyanni-Kouimtzi, Maziridou, and Kiosseoglou 2003), and even through school texts (Deliyanni-Kouimtzi and Ziogou 1995).

The basic physical ideals that exist for male adolescents are reflected in the dominant ideology in Greek society that identifies masculinity with "biologically determined strong physical power." International fashion and ads also stress this aspect of masculinity. As a consequence, both male and female adolescents consider male adolescent violence and defiance justifiable, and gender relations are formed as relations of power of one gender over the other (Deliyanni-Kouimtzi, Sakka, and Koureta 1999).

In so far as girls are concerned, the basic physical ideals in Greece are similar to those of Western culture, which considers the ideal of thinness as essential to female beauty. In accordance with this, recent surveys have found that about 25% of the female students aged 16 to 18 years in two large Greek towns are showing symptoms of eating disorders (cf. Tsiantis 2003). In addition, female adolescents seem to manifest more depressive symptoms and report higher levels of psychosomatic symptoms than males (Petrogiannes 2001).

The Self

The fact that Greek adolescents have adopted the mixed, conservative, but also clear and strong system of values mentioned in the preceding section is helping them to develop and integrate their identity through the formation of a consistent ideology. On the other hand, despite the fact that Greek adolescents are satisfied, to a large extent, with the kind of life they are living today, they also express concerns about the future and the insecurity that comes with it, namely, unemployment, drug addiction, and AIDS (GSY and V-PRC 2000). This may interfere with the process of identity integration as regards adolescents' capability for self-projection into the future (cf. Tsiantis 1998). Concerning indigenous young Greeks' identity formation in connection with the recent influx of immigrants, it seems that Greek youths are emphasizing their "Greekness," mainly as a protective factor in fighting unemployment (Dikaiou and Haritos-Fatouros 2000).

Nevertheless, Greek youngsters' "uneasiness" with people from other countries or of other races is low and comparable to that of most of the other European countries. For example, 32.6% of Greek 15- to 24-year-olds were found to agree with the statement "there is a large number of foreigners in my country," compared to a proportion of 41% of the same age-group in Belgium, 39.6% in Germany, 36.2% in Italy, and 27.3% in France (IARD 2001). As for the main reasons for such an "uneasiness," Greek youngsters 15 to 29 years old were found to agree that foreigners come to Greece to find jobs and in this way they contribute to young people's unemployment (92.5%), and that foreigners constitute one of the causes for the increase of criminality (87.7%). Females and younger people (15- to 19-year-olds) appeared to support these arguments more than males and older people (20- to 24-year-olds and 25- to 29-year-olds) (Teperoglou et al. 1999). However, 54.5% of Greek youngsters aged 15 to 24 years reported that they did not feel uneasiness with any group of people in comparison with the respective proportions (45% to 50%) of the same age-group in most of the other European countries (IARD 2001). Yet, the "uneasiness" is quite high in the case of homosexuals or marginal groups (IARD 2001; Teperoglou et al. 1999) and this is similar to what is found in other Mediterranean countries (IARD 2001). Indicatively, Greek young people aged 15 to 29 years seem to prefer to accept foreigners from developed countries (85.1%) rather than drug addicts (35%), Albanians (36.1%), Gypsies (38.9%), people infected with AIDS (40%), and homosexuals (45.2%) (Teperoglou et al. 1999). However, these attitudes may act as protective factors of youngsters' identity in their effort to meet the society's conservative values.

However, identity formation among young immigrants is often based on rejection of their former cultural identity and total adoption of that of the host country (Psalti and Deliyanni-Kouimtzi 2001). It should be pointed out that large-scale immigration in Greece, as a host country, is a recent phenomenon, mainly occurring only since the 1990s. It is rather early to judge safely if this trend in immigrant adolescents' acculturation is due to the exceptional conditions of their coming into the host country. As for cultural minorities, it should be noted that illiteracy, as a result of a process of rejection, mistrust, and suspicion between Gypsies (or Rom) and the rest of Greeks, has been a critical dimension of young Gypsies' sociocultural identity (Dikaiou 1999). Language and religion, on the other hand, are the basic dimensions of the identity of the Muslim minority.

There is little empirical data about what adolescents in Greece do during the time they spend alone. Besides the need for self-reflection and satisfaction of spiritual needs, private use of media, especially TV, recorded music, and computer games, are the most common activities. Reading also takes some of the limited time Greek adolescents have to spend alone, because homework and extracurricular courses take a lot of their time during the week and even during the weekend (GSY and V-PRC 2000).

Family Relationships

The Greek family has always been a powerful institution characterized by strong bonds between its members. This is still true today. However, as the traditional extended family is gradually giving way to nuclear family units, the relations between parents and children are rapidly changing. Thus, there is greater psychological and social independence of adolescents and more conversational dialogues between parents and their young children about family problems (cf. Mourikes et al. 2002). These two changes are probably the most indicative expressions of a deeper transformation in parenting styles and practices in contemporary Greece; parents shift from a more authoritarian and restrictive to a more permissive and warm parental style, mainly in the case of the father (cf. Mourikes et al. 2002). On the other hand, the "child-centering" phenomenon in the Greek family is indicative of a protective and interventionist child rearing style (cf. Mourikes et al. 2002). It regards not only the parents' but also the closest relatives' strong emotional and material support of the child from childhood to young adulthood and beyond. This phenomenon explains to a large extent why parental family is the major support system during emerging adulthood in Greece, in contrast to what happens in other countries—that is, in the United Kingdom, the Netherlands, France, and Germany there are efficient labor market systems and/or state provisions (IARD 2001).

Evidently, this parenting style alleviates financial problems but also causes conflicts with adolescents' need for independence and privacy. The main sources of conflict between adolescents and their parents are the following (Teperoglou et al. 1999): (a) use of free time—entertainment, frequency and duration of the time spent out of home; (b) participation in housework; (c) spending of money; and (d) watching of TV programs. With respect to parental gender, pastime activities and housework are the most common causes of conflicts with the mother. The use of motorcycle and car, but most of all, the watching of TV programs are the most usual causes of conflict with the father. Smoking and alcohol use also generate conflicts with both of the parents, although not so often. In any case, Greek adolescents do not report very serious conflicts with their parents. On the contrary, the great majority of them see the relations with their parents as satisfying (85.5% as regards the father and almost 90% as regards the mother); they also seek to talk with parents over issues related to studies, school, employment, and personal life (Teperoglou et al. 1999).

In the case of immigrant families, adaptation to the new country, Greece, is usually connected with negative effects on the relations between adolescents and their parents. This is because parents usually work for many hours, face financial and adaptation problems themselves, and therefore, are less available to meet the emotional and other needs of their children. Of course, parental conflicts, often due to unemployment, personal, and social difficulties as well as parents' separation/divorce, is a serious problem that affects parent–child relationship for all adolescents, immigrants or not. A different source of problems is found in Muslim, Pomak, and Rom families. These families have many children and represent extended patriarchal units with hierarchically defined roles for their members. Conflicts in this case are caused by the strict traditional values (Dikaiou et al. 1996).

Contrary to the above minority groups, adolescents in contemporary Greek nuclear families typically live as only children or with only one sibling. They have no major obligation toward their siblings beyond voluntary help. As for the relation with other close relatives, although grandparents do not typically live in the same household, they usually live nearby—that is, in a nearby apartment or in the same neighborhood or district. This occurs even in big cities such as Athens (cf. Tsiantis 1998). The nuclear families, in their majority, meet or communicate by telephone with grandparents on a daily or weekly basis. Adolescents report that they often receive financial help from their grandparents and that they strongly believe that the family ought to take care of its older members when necessary. Similar, yet not so strong, relations exist with uncles, aunts, and cousins (cf. Tsiantis 1998).

As regards rates of divorce, Greece has the second lowest divorce rate among EU member states (the lowest belongs to Italy) (Hatzichristou 1999). However, there is a steady increase in the frequency of divorces—similar to that in the other countries—caused, partly, by Greek women's new and much stronger socioeconomic position. Indicatively, the number of divorces was 2,804 in 1961 (3.95% of the 70,914 marriages that took place in 1961) but was raised to 10,995 in 1995 (17.2% of the 63,987 marriages that took place in 1995). Divorce "by mutual consent" is reported as the most frequent reason for separation, and the usual children's age in which parents get divorced is adolescence or young adulthood. Although there is no official data, recent research suggests that single-parent families constitute about 5% of the total number of families with children under 18 years of age. This percentage is the lowest in the EU. The majority of these are single-mother families. Remarriage after divorce is possible; however, it is more common among divorced men than among women (Hatzichristou 1999; Mourikes et al. 2002). As for adolescents' marriage and fertility rates, in the age range of 15- to 19-year-olds there was a significant decrease during the period of 1990–1997. The fertility rate also decreased from 15.6% in 1990 to 9.5% in 1997 (IARD 2001). Marriage at young ages is most usual in cultural minorities—that is, Muslim and Rom.

As reported by teachers, students—especially male teenagers—from families with divorced parents often face difficulties both in lessons and in their social behavior. Such students seem to have lower school performance, more negative emotions, and to be more immature than their classmates. In addition, teachers reported more problems in children whose parents had found new mates (Livaditis et al. 2002). These findings, however, may be attributed to a general social prejudice against divorce and parents' personal life after separation.

Friends and Peers/Youth Culture

Friendship is a value youth in almost all member states of the EU share (IARD 2001). Friends are exceptionally important for Greek youngsters (second to the family). Friends are confidants and models of identification as well as vehicles for social identity and social relations among peers. The great majority of young Greeks have close friends from both genders. Younger adolescents usually meet with their friends every day, but in the course of time the frequency of meetings decreases and, during emerging adulthood, is limited to one meeting a week. There are also gender differences related to the frequency of contact; boys, in general, meet their friends more often than girls. Close friends come from school and from neighborhood. Young Greeks select their friends based on characteristics such as "good character," "honesty," "warmth," and also "common interests." Socioeconomic status, money, or friends' politico-ideological stance is hardly mentioned as a basis of friendship (Teperoglou et al. 1999). In general, adolescents, as they proceed from secondary to tertiary education, spend all the more time with their peers and less with their family or alone (Nikitaras and Ntoumanis 2003).

Another dimension, in which Greece and Mediterranean member states of the EU display the same profile, is the low level of youth participation in associations and organizations. In the age of 15- to 24-year-olds only 35.6% participate in any kind of organization. The percentage is distributed as follows: 2.4% are members of religious organizations, 1.5% of trade unions or political parties, 2.9% of youth organizations, and 15.5% of sports associations (IARD 2001). A significant reason why membership in associations and organizations is small in Greece is that this spirit is not so strongly embedded in the welfare system and in the institutional structure of the Greek society (IARD 2001).

The type of association or organization the adolescents join differs depending on their age. Young adolescents are participating in organizations with sports and cultural activities, the Boy Scouts, and church associations. In later adolescence they also join the youth organizations of major political parties. This trend was particularly strong after the fall of the dictatorship in 1974 and the restoration of democracy; however, nowadays this trend is declining. There is a growing preference for ecological associations and NGOs, although the percentage of participation is still quite low. It should be noted that all these types of organizations are not explicitly youth-oriented, and even if they are, their leaders are adults. This fact may be another reason for the low membership in associations in Greece nowadays (GSY and V-PRC 2000).

A particular phenomenon related to peer groups is "peer crowds." They are formed on the basis of common interest in a specific type of music or sports. Peer crowds are present in music festivals or open air performances of pop musicians or music groups. Peer crowds are also present in football (soccer) or basketball games as well as in political rallies. Within these peer crowds we can distinguish groups of fans, who in the case of football teams in big Greek cities, act with stereotyped, aggressive, and sometimes criminal behavior before, during, and after the game of their team (Myrizakes 1997). Similar groups can be identified in the case of rock music fans; they usually come from less-developed or working-class areas of Athens and of other big cities of the country. They call themselves "metal" and they adopt a distinct lifestyle marked by clothing, hairstyle, and behavior. Tattooing and piercing that characterized this group of youngsters in the past are now fashionable for all adolescents.

On the other hand, there is the "upper- and middle-class" youth subculture—that is, the "Dance Music Culture (DMC)," which in general is identified as an expressive, multicultural, post-materialism movement against the conservatism and materialism of "Yppidom." As for their

GREECE

self-presentation, these youngsters blend neo-hippy, ethnic, and cosmopolitan trends, which are often very expensive as regards money (Astrinakes and Stylianoudes 1996). Contrary to the previous two subcultures, however, this group follows the educational system and is identified with an intellectual elite that adopts more humanistic values.

More generally, the distinct character of the prevalent youth culture in Greece as compared to that of adults is the internationally promoted fashion for this age group and the casual clothes. Only members of subculture groups adopt extreme dress and hairstyle such as those characteristic of punks or heavy-metal music fans. However, even these subculture groups follow the international fashion that is pertinent to their groups (e.g., clothes, accessories, and hairstyle adopted by similar groups in other countries). Finally, teenage slang in contemporary Greek society is another dimension of culture differences between adolescents and adults (GSY and V-PRC 2000).

It can be concluded then that the youth culture in Greece is infiltrated by the Western lifestyle, and even by globalization. However, these influences are incorporated into the previously existing social structures and lifestyles, shaping a mixed and specific to Greece youth culture (Astrinakes and Stylianoudes 1996).

Love and Sexuality

Due to the aforementioned changes in the Greek society and especially in family relations, adolescents of today are allowed to date to a larger extent than they did in the past. There is no research data regarding the mean age of first dating. It usually takes place before the age of first sexual intercourse. Sexual intercourse for Greek girls is usually within the context of a steady relationship and starts after the age of 16, according to some surveys, or about the age of 18 according to others (Bajos et al. 2003; Creatsas et al. 1995). Creatsas (2003), for example, found that 32% of girls at the age of 17 and 36% of girls at the age of 18 reported having sexual intercourse. Boys start their sexual life earlier than girls do, but even for them the mean age at first intercourse has risen (Bajos et al. 2003; Creatsas et al. 1995). These findings suggest a major change in the previous strong double standard in favor of young men as concerns the age of first sexual intercourse. Another significant finding is that 20% of adolescents who dropped out from school, as compared to those who graduated, started their sexual life earlier than their peers did. This finding—similar to what was found in Finland

and Great Britain—suggests that adolescents who pursue university studies have a lifestyle in which dating and sex is not a priority, at least during secondary education. On the other hand, adolescents who leave school in an early stage in their life seem to be in a position to take independent, possibly irresponsible, decisions much earlier and free from parental and school control (Bajos et al. 2003).

In conclusion, it seems clear that in contemporary Greece youngsters are free to date. It is also common for young Greeks to have sex at around the end of adolescence or the beginning of emerging adulthood. Adolescent sexual activity seems to be unrelated to marriage, which usually takes place after the age of 25 years. Additionally, in adolescence (15 to 19 years of age) the percentage of cohabitation is low (about 0.4%), just as it happens with the same age group in western Europe (Bajos et al. 2003; NSSG 2001a).

Concerning adolescent pregnancy, abortion, and parenthood in Greece, there is also insufficient data. Abortion is not legal except for medical reasons. Therefore, it is difficult to estimate the number of illegal abortions that take place in private clinics and practice. However, decreases in the adolescent pregnancy rate and constancy of abortions were reported (Bajos et al. 2003; Creatsas et al. 1995). The birth rate was 2% for women aged 15 to 19 years in 1990 and 1.1% in 1999. As regards parenthood, it is worth noting that the percentage of unwanted pregnancies of Greek females was practically 100% (16 to 19 age group) and 50% (20 to 24 age group), according to a survey on planned and unplanned pregnancies in France, Greece, Italy, Norway, and Switzerland (Bajos et al. 2003). The same percentages were found in all the other countries except Italy. Furthermore, the 2001 census in Greece recorded a proportion of parenthood less than 1% as regards boys and girls 15 to 19 years old (NSSG 2001a). All these transformations mainly reflect the changing attitudes of young people toward family and sexuality, higher educational aspirations of young women, but also limited use of modern medical contraceptive methods, which are widely used in other European countries. It is obvious that condom use, which is the strongest contraceptive method in adolescence, and withdrawal are not always effective (Bajos et al. 2003; Merakou et al. 2002).

Introduction of sexual education into the Greek school curriculum has been a controversial issue for years and there is still no final decision on this matter. For the time being, family planning information is being given by the Greek Family

360

Planning Association, the Center for Control of Infectious Diseases of the Ministry of Health, the Orthodox Church, and the Ministry of National Education and Religious Affairs with a series of programs regarding health education (Creatsas 2003).

Birth control with the use of contraceptive methods in adolescence is limited. It is usually based on condom use, which is also advertised for AIDS prevention. Greek adolescents have a defective knowledge of contraception in general. Consistently unsafe sex practices have been reported by 28% to 40% of emerging adults. Only 5.2% of couples in which the woman is 20 to 24 years of age prefer the use of the "pill" (Kordoutis, Loumakou, and Sarafidou 2000).

With respect to sexually transmitted diseases among adolescents in Greece, Creatsas (2003) found that the most common diseases are the viral ones and especially condylomata acuminata, genital herpes, and vaginitis (yeast and trichomoniasis). As for AIDS, recent surveys show that, after 15 years of prevention activities among young people, the number of HIV infections among teenagers 13 to 19 years old in Greece has significantly decreased (13 infections in 1990 and only one in 2001). Additionally, Greek adolescents have a satisfactory level of AIDS-related knowledge and have adopted relatively safe sex behavior. However, boys, younger adolescents, students with both excellent and low school records, and highly religious adolescents seem to need more intense information (Merakou et al. 2002).

Parents in Greece are aware of sexual activity among adolescents, although they do not encourage it. Beliefs of the past, as regards girls' virginity until they get married, are hardly present any more. In fact, it has been found in a survey (Ioannidi-Kapolou 2000) that two-thirds of parents were aware that their adolescent children had already started sexual activity. Most of these parents had this information from their children, while 14.3% of the parents stated they had found out about this activity from their children's friends or from their behavior. A significant percentage of parents (54.4%) claimed also that their children used a contraceptive method. Still, children reported that they seldom talked to their parents about their sexual activities.

However, such discussions are very important. Intrafamily communication has been associated with accurate knowledge of sexual issues. In particular, it has been found that parents often talk with their sons about sexually transmitted diseases, condom use, and gender relations, while they avoid

topics such as masturbation, abortion, and orgasm. With their daughters, parents appear to discuss the same issues plus the issue of abortion, but they avoid discussing homosexuality (Ioannidi-Kapolou 2000). Thus, homosexuality is still a taboo both for parents and for youngsters (IARD 2001). There is no available research data on the rate of homosexuality among adolescents. Late adolescence and beyond is the period when adolescents realize their sexual preferences and make decisions about their sexual life. It is then that they face the problem of how to announce it to their parents.

Health Risk Behavior

Health risk behavior can be identified in various activities. Greece is among the European countries with very high adolescent mortality rates as concerns traffic accidents, but with low incidence of suicide and alcohol abuse. Motor traffic rates (per 100,000) for males 15 to 24 years old in 1995 was 54.2, whereas for females it was 9.9. The respective suicide rates were 4.4 for males and 0.8 for females (IARD 2001).

Regular tobacco smoking—that is, 11 or more cigarettes per day—among adolescents (13 to 18 years of age) is also quite substantial: it increased in 1998 (20.8%), after having fallen from 22% in 1984 to 14.6% in 1993. Furthermore, there are no significant gender differences in this age group since 21.8% of boys and 19.7% of girls reported regular tobacco smoking. Percentage of regular tobacco smoking increases dramatically in the age group of 25 to 35 years, particularly among males. According to a survey by the Research University Institute of Mental Health (EPIPSY 1998), 60% of males and 38% of females report regular tobacco smoking. According to another study, only a small percentage (2.6%) of young adolescents—that is, before the age of 15—reports smoking daily. This percentage significantly increases in the age group of 17- to 18-year-olds (Mourikes et al. 2002).

On the other hand, frequent alcohol consumption in adolescence in Greece is lower than the rates reported in other European countries. As regards mean age of first drinking, children in Greece start with occasional social drinking at about 12 years of age. This usually happens with the family in social occasions and during dinner. According to a survey (EPIPSY 1998) among adolescents of 13 to 18 years of age, 62% reported occasional alcohol drinking (less than ten times during the last month) and 15.9% reported frequent alcohol consumption (ten times and more during the last month). These percentages rise to 80% to 90% for occasional and 35.6% for frequent alcohol consumption in the group of emerging adults (19 to 24 years old), respectively (cf. EPIPSY 1998; Mourikes et al. 2002). It should be noted that alcohol consumption by adolescents aged less than 17 years who are unaccompanied by an adult in public bars or cafeterias is prohibited by law.

The drinks adolescents consume are mainly low in alcohol. There is no significant alcohol problem among adolescents, although the new lifestyle with strong alcohol drinks that are consumed by adolescents independently of dinner has started to create problems. There are no significant gender differences in alcohol consumption, but young people from urban areas drink more frequently than those from rural ones (cf. Mourikes et al. 2002).

A sharp increase in adolescents' illicit drug use has been observed in the last years. In 1993 about 6% of students (13 to 18 years old) had an experience with illicit substances during their lifetime. In 1998 this percentage increased to 13.7%; as regards boys aged 17 to 18 years, the percentage was 29.3% (EPIPSY 1998). According to reports of the National Documentation and Information Center for Drugs and Drug-Addiction (cf. Mourikes et al. 2002), cannabis is the most widespread drug. In recent years there has been a decline in the use of heroine and a respective increase in the use of cocaine. This fact, along with the methadone programs enacted by the state, have reduced the number of deaths from heroine use in young adults. Also, since the 1980s there are "dry" programs for detoxication in major cities of the country, which take the form of therapeutic communities. Such programs are supported by the state and have been extended to adolescents with substance abuse problems. However, during the last decade, a significant increase in use of "ecstasy"-type drugs is recorded, especially among younger ages.

Cannabis use starts for most users at the age of 16, whereas main substance use (usually heroine) starts at around 19 years of age. Constantly increasing rates of deaths were recorded in the 1980s to 1990s, most of which happened at emerging adulthood (21 to 30 years old) in the main cities of the country. Psychosocial factors related to increased substance use by Greek youngsters are low self-esteem, family members using tobacco and alcohol, positive attitudes toward cannabis use, and systematic smoking and use of drugs by close friends (Madianos et al. 1995).

Concerning adolescents' psychopathological risk behavior, Greece is known to have one of the lowest rates of both completed and attempted adolescent suicides, along with the other Mediterranean countries and in contrast to the Nordic ones (IARD 2001). Recent studies indicate that there were more girls than boys attempting suicide. Self-destructive behavior was related to depressive mood but was mainly due to social and personal problems (Ierodiakonou, Iacovides, and Ierodiakonou-Benou 1998). With regard to depression, a nationwide study on adolescent depressive symptomatology showed about 13% of boys and 29% of girls were showing such symptoms. These percentages were progressively increasing from younger ages (12- to 13-year-olds) to the age of 16 to 17, in which the greater prevalence of depressive cases were recorded. Female gender and urban population were related to more frequent and more severe depressive symptoms, respectively (cf. Tsiantis 1998).

Another domain of risk behavior is crime. According to police reports, there are various offenses committed by Greek adolescents, but very low levels of participation in organized gangs. The main adolescent offenses are theft, physical violence, and damage of property (Georgoulas 2000). A significant number of these offenses are committed by immigrant youth who enter the country at emerging adulthood, do not speak the Greek language, and get involved in semi-legal or illegal activities of their fellow countrymen or Greek criminals. Prostitution of young girls coming illegally from countries of the former Soviet Union is the usual offense of young females. Adolescent offenders (below the age of 18 years) in Greece are in custody, because their imprisonment is not allowed by law (Kourakes 2004; Livaditis et al. 2000). Psychosocial problems such as broken families or dysfunctional patterns of family, poverty, poor school performance and a general disliking of school, high rates of affective disorders, and family history of mental health problems are more prevalent in young offenders as compared to the rest of the youngsters (Papageorgiou and Vostanis 2000).

Overall, motor accidents constitute the major problem as regards Greek adolescents' health risk behavior. Indeed, automobile fatalities constitute the most frequent cause of death in adolescence and drowning is the second. The objective reasons for these accidents are the problematic road network and insufficient swimming or driving training. Other main reasons are the following: carelessness, competitive driving, lack of compliance to law (e.g., driving a car under the age of 18, that is, without driving license), families of low education and income, and/or substance use (Tsoumakas 2001).

Education

The educational system in Greece is organized in three levels: six years of compulsory primary school, six years of secondary education—the first three years being compulsory—and tertiary education in universities or technological institutes.

Secondary education is organized in two levels: lower secondary education (junior high school)—called *Gymnasio*—which lasts three years and is compulsory, and upper secondary education (senior high school), called *Lykeio*. The second level comprises two main types of schools: comprehensive senior high school (*Eniaio Lykeio*) and the technical vocational educational schools (TEE). Admission to *Gymnasio* is automatic on completion of primary school. Its curriculum is planned by the Pedagogical Institute and approved by the Ministry of National Education and Religious Affairs. Compulsory subjects at junior high school are religion, Greek, ancient Greek literature, mathematics, science, history, geography, civic studies, two foreign languages, physical education, information technology, vocational guidance, and home economics. Assessment is continuous and is based on oral and written tests, assignments, and end of year examinations. Students who successfully complete *Gymnasio* receive a school-leaving certificate (*Apolytirio Gymnasiou*) that grants access to upper secondary education (Eurydice 2004; MINERA 2003).

The duration of studies in *Eniaio Lykeio* is three years while in the TEE the duration is two years (Level A) or three years (Level B) depending on the program of studies. Under specific conditions TEE graduates have access to technological institutes of tertiary education. TEE students have also practice periods at places of work (e.g., business, industry). Students' transfer from one type of school to the other is possible. Students regularly take oral and written tests and end of year examinations. Promotion to the next class depends on performance. Students who successfully complete *Eniaio Lykeio* receive a school-leaving certificate (*Apolytirio Lykeiou*). Successful students at TEE receive a school-leaving certificate (*Apolytirio* TEE) or a vocational diploma.

Besides these two basic types of schools, there are also musical, ecclesiastical, and physical education junior and senior high schools (Eurydice 2004; MINERA 2003). There are no special courses for gifted, but there are schools (state or private) for physically or mentally handicapped/disabled students. Finally, a limited number of evening schools of secondary education exist in the main cities for students who work. These schools offer the same curriculum as their morning counterparts but with a smaller number of courses per day. For this reason, studies last one more year than in ordinary secondary education. Immigrant children and adolescents who enter or entered the country in their early years of life or in primary school age are integrated into the mainstream education. However, youth who enter Greece later, in adolescence, and do not have a good grasp of the Greek language can study in multicultural secondary education schools.

Tertiary education comprises universities and technological institutions. To enter tertiary education the Greek youngsters take centralized annual examinations at a national level just after the end of the final school year. Because the examinations are highly competitive, the greatest majority of students goes to private tutorial schools (*frontistiria*) or has tutors for private lessons at home. These lessons may last from two to four hours daily and may start as early as students enter upper secondary education.

A specific characteristic of the Greek educational system is that music and foreign languages, until a few years ago, did not receive much attention in public schools. To cover this need, there are state, municipal, and private conservatories for those who wish to study music. The schools of foreign language are private, and at the end of the studies students usually take exams held by educational agencies of the countries whose language they have been taught. A limited number of students in secondary education also take International Baccalaureate courses that give access to higher education in Europe and the United States. Greek students who want to study in the United States or England take exams on English language proficiency with TOEFL and GRE or the British O-level exams. Also, Greek students participate in international or European achievement contests individually or through agencies such as the Greek Mathematical Society.

As mentioned in the previous sections, education forms a central part of Greek youth identity. Indeed, the relationship between adolescence and being a student is so strong that when the convergence of the two situations is missing it is usually presumed to be a problem. This is particularly so in the case of a subgroup of Gypsies (Rom), who do not live in one place permanently and their children cannot attend school regularly. These children quit school early, even from primary school. Quitting school can also occur for other reasons, and not only for Rom children. Such reasons are, for example, a need for work in disadvantaged areas, low socioeconomic and educational level of the family, family problems, adolescents' problems with the law, and others.

The 2001 census in Greece showed that 99.4% of adolescents aged 13 to 19 years are literate and 49.6% of youngsters 15 to 24 years old attend upper secondary and tertiary educational institutions (NSSG 2001a). In detail, from the 13- to 19-year-olds group, 89.3% are secondary education students (compulsory lower secondary school: 62.3%, upper secondary: 26%, and post-secondary: 1%). This percentage is higher than the 72% reported by OECD in 1998 (see IARD 2001). Similar increase has occurred in the case of 20- to 29-year-olds: 16.5% of them study in higher education (tertiary education) and 9.9% study at post-secondary technical/vocational educational institutions (NSSG 2001a), as compared to 12% in the early 1990s (IARD 2001). In general, of the students who finish upper secondary education (18 to 21 years of age) about 60% of them are in the tertiary education institutions. An additional number of them move to universities of other countries (MINERA 2003).

Indeed, a significant number (about 30,000) of Greek youth aged 20 to 29 years follow university studies, either undergraduate or graduate, in other countries, especially in member states of the EU, in the United States, and in the Balkans. This is due to the fact that tertiary education in Greece is selective. Only 50% to 60% of the youngsters interested are accepted in tertiary education and often in fields that are not their first priority. Therefore, some of the graduates of upper secondary education either do not take the national examinations at all and move to other countries, or they do so after failing at entering in a tertiary education school of their choice. Families of low income prefer universities or other institutions in neighboring Balkan countries because they can not support expensive undergraduate studies in countries such as the United States or member states of the EU. Graduate studies are mainly pursued in countries well known for the quality of their educational system and in fields of high demand, such as medicine and informatics.

As regards gender differences, 62.5% of male and 62% of female adolescents aged 13 to 19 years are lower secondary education students, 24.5% of boys and 27.6% of girls of the same age group attend upper secondary schools, and 0.9% of males and 1.3% of females study at post-secondary educational institutions. In the 20 to 29 age group, 14.6% of males and 18.7% of females are tertiary education students, and 7.5% of young men and 12.5% of young women attend post-secondary educational institutions. Overall, it is clear that, with the exception of compulsory lower secondary education, girls are over-represented in terms of participation in secondary and tertiary schools compared to boys of the same age (NSSG 2001a).

The quantitative and qualitative over-representation of girls in education has been recorded since a few years ago and has been attributed to socioeconomic changes and gender equality awareness in the Greek society combined with female studiousness. However, female students at Greek universities still comprise only 10% to 15% of students in the faculties of sciences and there are also significant inequalities in access to tertiary education from children of low socioeconomic and educational level families (Dikaiou and Haritos-Fatouros 2000).

Positive discrimination—that is, free access to tertiary education—exists for Muslim minority youth and for a number of severely disabled youth. However, representation of these groups in higher education is still very low. Finally, primary and secondary education in Greece is mainly provided in public (state) schools. However, there are also private schools. Both kinds of schools have exactly the same curriculum, which is determined by the Ministry of Education. On the other hand, tertiary education is provided only by state institutions. There exist private post-secondary education schools, called centers of liberal studies (*Kentra Eleftheron Spoudon*), that offer courses or even degrees in collaboration with higher education institutions from the United States or European countries. The Greek state does not recognize these degrees, although they are acceptable in the private sector of the economy.

Work

Greek families, in the main, support their children until emerging adulthood. Very limited work for adolescents is provided to the family or out of it in middle and upper social classes. It is often, however, a necessity for working class or rural families. It is indicative that, according to the 2001 census in Greece, 60.8% of youngsters 15 to 24 years old were economically inactive (mainly students) and only 26.5% were employed. Of this percentage, the majority of young workers were employed in the services' sector, shop and market sales (26.2%). Another 19.5% were in crafts, 13.2% were clerks, and 12.6% were working at other occupations. There were also small proportions (less than 10%)

of technicians and associated occupations, skilled agricultural and fishery workers, plant and machine operators, and assemblers. A very small proportion (less than 5%) were professionals, senior officials, or managers (NSSG 2001a).

With regard to work conditions for adolescents, the majority of youngsters who leave school at 15 years of age or earlier are manual workers or apprentice technicians. This finding is based on nationwide surveys of the Greek Pedagogical Institute and in more recent ones of the University of Piraeus and of the Manpower for Employment Organization (1999). Young adolescents often work at part-time jobs, with minimum wages, often without social security, and in unhealthy work conditions. The majority of young workers are adolescents who leave school and Muslim minors (cf. Mourikes et al. 2002). There is also a specific category of adolescent workers at the tourist labor market in Greek islands, mainly in the services sector.

Regarding forced labor or slavery, the major problem in contemporary Greece is trafficking of migrant women for forced prostitution. Usually, it involves young women 20 to 30 years old from the Balkans and the countries of the former Soviet Union who are unemployed and with serious financial problems. In addition, most of them do not speak Greek. According to recent estimates, in Greece this problem involved 35,666 young women during the 1993–1999 period (cf. Mourikes et al. 2002).

As regards programs and institutions that assist adolescents in making the transition from school to work, we already mentioned the vocational schools of secondary education, namely the technical vocational educational schools (TEE) and also the vocational training institutes (IEK). They provide knowledge and skills for specific professions. During the last year of junior high school (Gymnasio) students follow a course on vocational guidance. There are also specialized secondary education teachers who work as counselors at vocational guidance centers of secondary education. They offer individual and group counseling on issues related to further education, vocations, and market needs.

The Greek Manpower Employment Organization (OAED), a state institution, provides vocational guidance and vocational training. Vocational training aims at preparing prospective workers to meet market needs. In this way it facilitates a smooth transition from vocational training to entering the workforce. OAED provides vocational training in two forms: (a) "initial training" that includes technical-vocational centers and vocational training institutes, and (b) programs of continuing vocational training that involve unemployed people and young people who quit school. An extensive net of 57 vocational training centers throughout the country serve the training needs of unskilled adolescents, adults, and immigrants. OAED also takes action in the promotion of employment through job placement of unemployed people or through vocational guidance. Besides OAED, private vocational training centers (KEK) also provide training to adolescents and young people.

Unemployment in Greece is currently a serious problem, particularly for older adolescents and emerging adults. Indeed, young people's unemployment rate reached 25.6% in 2002. It is more than double the unemployment rate of the total labor force, which was 10.2% in 2002 (CEPR 2003). It should be also noted that in Greece, post-secondary education students who have not worked for at least 6 months are not officially counted as unemployed. Furthermore, in order to be entitled to state unemployment allowances one has to have worked for at least six months.

Families, their adolescent children, and the Greek government respond to this unemployment problem mainly through investment in education. However, this investment has not always paid off. According to recent estimates, the lengthening of schooling from compulsory to post-secondary education increased the probability of unemployment for young people with more years of education. In addition, the probability of unemployment for university graduates in contemporary Greece is not much lower than that for secondary education graduates, in sharp contrast to other European countries that have also strongly invested in education, such as Finland (CEPR 2003). Thus, it is obvious that Greece must try for further improvement of the quality of schooling and, mainly, for stronger linking between education/training and the labor market, in order to fight effectively the major problem of youth unemployment.

Media

Mass media in Greece constitute a very significant source of information and influence. The majority of teenage boys watch TV for over two hours per day, and they prefer to watch the programs broadcast at night or else action films, athletic games/sports news, and talk shows. However, as they grow older, young males change their preferences for entertainment (e.g., meeting friends outside of home) and decrease the time they spend watching

TV. The majority of teenage girls spend less time than boys do watching TV programs. Teenage girls also prefer programs aired in the morning and afternoon or programs with informational content and romantic/social serials. They also watch romantic and action movies. As they grow, young women increase the time spent watching TV.

Radio is the mass media par excellence for Greek youngsters. About 60% of young people listen to radio programs daily, but almost all of these programs are music. Other means of listening to music—used to a lesser degree—are tapes and CDs (Teperoglou et al. 1999). The music that most of the adolescents listen to is mainly pop and rock music in Greek or English language. Traditional Greek music of urban origin gets a priority in young people's preferences, usually after 18 years of age, when they start going out to taverns with their friends. Also, traditional Greek folk songs and dances are more known to youths in the provincial parts of the country. Only young people who study music are well acquainted with classical music (GSY and V-PRC 2000).

Young people go to the movies regularly and to a lesser extent to the theater. Theater attendance is more usual among young people over the age of 18 years and depends on the area of residence, e.g., Athens or other cities, and on age and gender. On the other hand, young people constitute the main readership of magazines in Greece. These magazines are usually focused on music, sports, computers, and cars. However, more boys than girls read newspapers (Teperoglou et al. 1999).

Finally, just as in the rest of the world, young Greeks (and particularly young males) are also the main users of the Internet. This is particularly true for emerging adulthhod (18 years and over), high educational status (e.g., tertiary education), and males. Computer games are more popular among younger adolescents (GSY and V-PRC 2000; Papathanasopoulos and Armenakes 2003).

Mass media in Greece are in the main indigenous and cover all aspects of interests and life; there is truly a plurality of them. However, almost all of the movies, many popular kinds of music, most computer games, the content of adolescent magazines, even the language that the Internet users prefer to use, all are imported mainly from the United States (Papathanasopoulos and Armenakes 2003).

Young Greeks recognize the informational (particularly males) and the recreational (particularly females) character of the media (Teperoglou et al. 1999). However, they are also influenced by TV. Watching TV has been associated with unhealthy food choices (Yannakoulia et al. 2004) or with projection of sexist and violent role models (Kakana, Kamarianos, and Metallidou 2002). Internet use may also become risky as regards access to illegal pornographic material (Papathanasopoulos and Armenakes 2003).

In any case, children and adolescents are targets of the media or the advertisers to a high degree (e.g., "big brother" type games on TV). For this reason, there are laws and regulations based on codes of ethics in Greece and the EU aiming at the protection of youngsters. Examples of such laws and regulations are the following: "Advertisements should not exploit the lack of experience of young people"; and "TV advertisements should not include minors (under 18 years of age) involved in precarious and unsafe conditions without a reason." There are also regulations by the Ministry of Press and Media regarding times during which transmission of programs of violent or indecent content is not allowed. Also, all of the serials and films broadcast in times in which children may watch TV along with adults bear a symbol indicating if the program is appropriate for children or young adolescents and whether parental consent is required or not. However, there are no specific regulations for advertising in the press or on the Internet (EDEE 2002).

Politics and Military

Greek adolescents obtain the right to vote at the age of 18. However, the extent to which they get actively involved in politics is an issue of major debate, particularly as regards participation in the activities of the established political parties and leftist ideology. Thus, although adolescents are aware of the major national and international issues related to economy, globalization, terrorism, and conflicts in the world, only a small percentage of them participate in activities organized by political parties and a very small percentage in those by activists. In fact, 69.6% of youngsters have a personal opinion as regards political issues and 47.2% feel they have well-formulated knowledge about significant political problems of the country (GSY and V-PRC 2000; Teperoglou et al. 1999).

Specifically, with respect to adolescents' active involvement in politics, two nationwide surveys in 1997 and 1999 (GSY and V-PRC 2000) found that political participation and the significance of self-placement on the left–right political spectrum has lost ground nowadays. In 1997, only 1.5% of 15- to 24-year-olds belonged to trade unions or political parties (IARD 2001). On the basis of the use of a series of scales concerning the dimension "collectivism–individualism," it has been found that there is no political ideological cohesion; instead there is a blending of political attitudes of different ideological origin in over 70% of Greek youth. In detail, individual freedom, social equality, democracy, ecology, business, and modernization have been recorded as the more acceptable politico-economic values. With regard to coping with social problems, collective action seemed to be the dominant concept in youth's sociopolitical conscience: 53.6% of the Greek youngsters, as shown in the 1999 survey of the General Secretariat of Youth (GSY and V-PRC 2000).

Regarding the dilemma "society emphasizing social equality or society stressing individual freedom and creativity," 41.5% of the Greek youngsters sided with the first kind of society, 41.3% sided with a mixed society model, and only 16.3% reported believing in a society based solely on economic liberalism. Concerning four critical issues related to economy and governing, participants in the 1997 and 1999 survey (GSY and V-PRC 2000; IARD 2001) seem to adopt more the position of a "left state" ideology (e.g., "The state is responsible for finding a job for anyone who needs it"). On the other hand, they are becoming more and more conservative with regard to critical social problems (e.g., "Outlaws must be punished with more severity"): from 66% in 1997 to 74.2% in 1999 (GSY and V-PRC 2000; IARD 2001).

As for modes of social protest, the politically active Greek youth participate every year in marching for the commemoration of the students' revolt in 1973 against the dictatorship. November 17 has been established as a youth day by the state. Greek youth also participate in rallies of political parties during periods of elections, use posters and graffiti on the walls, and endorse strikes. Groups of young people of leftist ideology also participate in rallies against WTO, the EU or G7 summits. These groups are often connected to similar groups in Europe or other countries. Adolescents of an anarchist ideology initiate more extreme action such as occupying a building (sit in) or violence in rallies.

In general, there is a significant proportion of Greek adolescents who are skeptical about politicians and politics. About 28% of Greek youth, according to the 1999 survey, do not wish to vote in any kind of polls or elections. Additionally, the majority of youth lean negatively toward a possible change from a voting age of 18 to a voting age of 16, with adolescents 15 to 16 years old being the only marginal exception (GSY and V-PRC 2000). On the other hand, the Youth Parliament that was established by the Greek Parliament as a new institution a few years ago enjoys the trust of 80% of adolescents.

Military service in Greece is compulsory for males and voluntary for females. The service lasts from one to 1.5 years. Exceptions are issued only for handicapped or severely ill young persons. If they are students, they have the right to do military service after finishing their studies. Adolescents over the age of 17 also have the right to do voluntary military service for five years with payment.

As for volunteer work, even though the actual participation in voluntary organizations is still very limited among the Greek youth (about 3%), there is significant availability (72.6%) in terms of reported willingness for participation in these kinds of organizations and work, if someone asks for help (GSY and V-PRC 2000; IARD 2001). An indicative example is the great number of volunteers in the 2004 Athens Olympic Games, which surpassed all previous organizations.

Unique Issues

Summing up what has been presented about adolescence in Greece, it is obvious that Greek youth is integrating, on the one hand, values, attitudes, and lifestyles that are traditional to Greece and to the rest of the Mediterranean countries and, on the other hand, role models of Western/American origin. At this point, the European dimension of adolescents' identity as well as European citizenship is in the making; closer links, communication with, and awareness of the characteristics of the rest of the European countries and their culture is a challenge. The unemployment of Greek youth is also a critical problem.

Yet, Greek society faces another challenge as well: the acute demographic problem. It is indicative that the index of population aging—that is, the ratio of aging population (greater than 65 years old) to children's (0 to 14 years old) population, in percentage—is and will continue, increasing from 24.7% in 1951 to 104.4% in 1998 and to 113% in 2005 according to Eurostat estimates. This means that the number of older adults is higher than the number of children due to the low birth rate, on the one hand, and high life expectancy for the elderly, on the other. In addition, as regards the replacement of manpower, in 1991 for every 10 persons who retired from work there were only 12 new ones entering the workforce. If this problem is not faced, the consequences for today and tomorrow's youth may be significant as regards their economic status and quality of life.

ANASTASIA EFKLIDES and DESPINA MORAITOU

References and Further Reading

Astrinakes, A., and L. Stylianoudes. (eds.). 1996. *Heavy metal, rockabilly, fans. Youth cultures and sub-cultures in western Attica.* Athens: Ellinika Grammata. (In Greek).

Bajos, N., A. Guillaume, and O. Kontula. 2003. *Reproductive health behavior of young Europeans (Vol. 1).* Strasbourg, France: Council of Europe Publishing.

Center for Planning and Economic Research (CEPR). 2003. Education and employment. *Economic Developments* 4:27–35. (In Greek).

Creatsas, G. 2003. *Sexual education and gender relations.* Athens: Ellinika Grammata. (In Greek).

Creatsas, G., M. Vekemans, J. Horejsi, et al. 1995. Adolescence sexuality in Europe—A multicentric study. *Adolescent and Pediatric Gynecology* 8(2):59–63.

Deliyanni-Kouimtzi, K., E. Maziridou, and G. Kiosseoglou. 2003. Parents' expectations for the future of their children: Constructing gender identities in the family context. In *Scientific annals of the School of Psychology of Aristotle University of Thessaloniki (Vol. 5).* A. Efklides, A. Stogiannidou, and E. Avthi (eds.). pp. 189–213. Thessaloniki, Greece: Art of Text. (In Greek).

Deliyanni-Kouimtzi, K., D. Sakka, and C. Koureta. 1999. "Man has it inside him...": Studying adolescents' attitudes concerning violence and aggression. In *Scientific annals of the School of Psychology of Aristotle University of Thessaloniki (Vol. 3).* A. Efklides, A. Stogiannidou, and E. Avthi (eds.). pp. 219–49. Thessaloniki, Greece: Art of Text. (In Greek).

Deliyanni-Kouimtzi, K., and R. Ziogou. 1995. Gendered youth transitions in Northern Greece: Between tradition and modernity through education. In *Growing up in Europe.* L. Chisholm, P. Buchner, H-H. Kruger, and M. du Bois-Reymond (eds.). pp. 209–19. Berlin: Walter de Gruyter.

Dikaiou, M. 1999. Minority groups: Action and intervention in contemporary Greek society. *Psychology: The Journal of the Hellenic Psychological Society* 6(2):247–53. (In Greek).

Dikaiou, M., J. Gibson-Cline, P. de Weerdt, et al. 1996. Minority populations. In *Adolescence: From crisis to coping. A thirteen nation study.* J. Gibson-Cline (ed.). pp. 247–78. Oxford, U.K.: Butterworth-Heinnemann.

Dikaiou, M., and M. Haritos-Fatouros. 2000. Greece. University and technical institute students in Thessaloniki. In *Youth and coping in twelve nations.* J. Gibson-Cline (ed.). pp. 114–28. London: Routledge.

Eurydice. 2004. *The information network on education in Europe.* Retrieved from the website: http://www.eurydice.org.

General Secretariat for the Youth (GSY) and Institute V-PRC (V-PRC). 2000. *Young people nowadays. Values, attitudes, and views of the Greek youth (1997–1999).* Athens: Papazises. (In Greek).

Georgas, J. 1989. Changing family values in Greece: From collectivist to individualist. *Journal of Cross-Cultural Psychology* 20:357–71.

Georgoulas, S. 2000. *Young offenders in Greece.* Athens: Ellinika Grammata. (In Greek).

Hatzichristou, C. 1999. *Parents' separation, divorce, and children.* Athens: Ellinika Grammata. (In Greek).

Hellenic Association of Advertising Communications Agencies (EDEE). 2002. *Legislative framework.* Retrieved from the website: http://www.edee.gr/law.html.

Ierodiakonou, C., A. Iacovides, and I. Ierodiakonou-Benou. 1998. Changing patterns of attempted suicide in Greece: Clinicoepidemiological and psychodynamic data. *Psychopathology* 31(6):281–92.

Ioannidi-Kapolou, E. 2000. Attitudes of Greek parents towards sexual education. International Planned Parenthood Federation (IPPF). Retrieved from the website: http://www.ippf.org/regions/europe/choices/v28n1/greek.htm.

Istituto di Ricerca S.c.r.l. (IARD) 2001. *Study on the state of young people and youth policy in Europe: Final reports (Vol. 1). Research carried out for the European Commission D.G. for Education and Culture.* Milano, Italy: IARD.

Kakana, D., J. Kamarianos, and P. Metallidou. 2002. Gender and vocational guiding. The role of media in two genders' vocational choices. *Mentor* 6:18–28. (In Greek).

Kordoutis, P., M. Loumakou, and J. Sarafidou. 2000. Heterosexual relationship characteristics, condom use and safe sex practices. *AIDS Care* 12(6):767–82.

Kourakes, N. 2004. *Young offenders and the Greek law: A class of "weak" between protection and repression.* Paper presented at Conference in honor of Prof. I. Manoledakes, Thessaloniki, Greece. (In Greek).

Livaditis, M., M. Fotiadou, F. Kouloubardou, et al. 2000. Greek adolescents in custody: Psychological morbidity, family characteristics and minority groups. *Journal of Forensic Psychiatry* 11(3):597–607.

Livaditis, M., K. Zaphiriadis, A. Fourkioti, et al. 2002. Parental loss and problem behavior in Greek adolescents: Student and teacher perspectives. *International Review of Psychiatry* 14(1):60–65.

Madianos, M., D. Gefou-Madianou, and C. Stefanis. 1995. Factors affecting illicit and licit drug use among adolescents and young adults in Greece. *International Journal of the Addictions* 29(12):1581–99.

Merakou, K., C. Costopoulos, J. Markopoulou, et al. 2002. Knowledge, attitudes and behavior after 15 years of HIV/AIDS prevention in schools. *European Journal of Public Health* 12(2):90–93.

Ministry of National Education and Religious Affairs (MINERA). 2003. *Our education has changed outlook.* Athens: Author. (In Greek).

Mourikes, A., M. Naoumes, and G. Papapetrou. (eds.). 2002. *The social portrait of Greece 2001.* Athens: National Center for Social Research. (In Greek).

Myrizakes, G. 1997. *Free time for young people: Leisure and sporting activities.* Athens: National Center for Social Research. (In Greek).

National Statistical Service of Greece (NSSG). 2001a. *Tables (3, 6, 10, 11, 13, 38) to Eurostat.* Athens: Author.

National Statistical Service of Greece (NSSG). 2001b. *Athena 2001: Results of 2001 census.* Athens: Author.

National Statistical Service of Greece (NSSG). 2003. *Greece with numbers.* Athens: Author.

Nikitaras, N., and N. Ntoumanis. 2003. Criteria of personal, boys' and girls' popularity as ranked by Greek adolescents. *Perceptual and Motor Skills* 97(1):281–88.

Papageorgiou, V., and P. Vostanis. 2000. Psychosocial characteristics of Greek young offenders. *Journal of Forensic Psychiatry* 11(2):390–400.

Papathanasopoulos, S., and Armenakes, A. 2003. *Internet and university students in Athens.* Retrieved from the website: http://www.media.uoa.gr/main/gr/research_gr/internet_gr.html.

Paraskevopoulos, I. N. 1991. *Developmental psychology: Vol. 4. Mental life from conception to adulthood.* Athens: Ellinika Grammata. (In Greek).

Petrogiannes, K. 2001. Stressful events and coping strategies in a sample of university students. *Child and Adolescent: Mental Health and Psychopathology* 4(1):37–58. (In Greek).

Psalti, A., and K. Deliyanni-Kouimtzi. 2001. Education of children from the former Soviet Union and Albany in Greece, according to the ecological–cultural approach. In *Scientific Annals of Philosophical School. Department of Psychology (Vol. 4)*. K. Delyianni-Kouimtzi and A. Psalti (eds.). pp. 287–315. Thessaloniki, Greece: Art of Text. (In Greek).

Research University Institute of Mental Health (EPIPSY). 1998. *Data for addictive substances.* Retrieved from the website: http://www.epipsy.gr/prolipsi/el/contents.asp.

Teperoglou, A., D. Balourdos, G. Myrizakes, et al. 1999. *The identity, particular characteristics and needs of young people in the Perfecture of Thessaloniki.* Athens: National Center for Social Research. (In Greek).

Tsagas, J. 2000. *Child and adolescent in ecclesiastical community.* Athens: Author. (In Greek).

Tsiantis, I. (ed.). 1998. *Adolescence* (vol. 2, issue 1). Athens: Kastaniotes. (In Greek).

Tsiantis, I. (ed.). 2003. *Adolescence* (vol. 2, issue 2). Athens: Kastaniotes. (In Greek).

Tsoumakas, K. 2001. Accidents in childhood and adolescence. *Paediatrics* 64:261–67. (In Greek).

Yannakoulia, M., D. Karayiannis, M. Terzidou, et al. 2004. Nutrition-related habits of Greek adolescents. *European Journal of Clinical Nutrition* 58(4):580–86.

Zabelis, G. 1996. *Satanism and youth.* Athens: Photodotes. (In Greek).

GUATEMALA

Background Information

Guatemala is the largest and most populous of the Central American countries. Its population is among the youngest, fastest growing, poorest, least educated, and most heavily indigenous in the Latin American region. Forty percent of inhabitants are under 15 years of age, one-quarter are between 10 and 19, and one-third are between 10 and 24 (UN 2003). The population growth rate is 2.8%, total fertility rate is 4.4 births per woman, and infant mortality rate is 39 per thousand live births (PRB 2005). A third of the adult population cannot read. Over 40% are indigenous (mostly Mayan) and live mainly in isolated rural areas, with access to few basic services. The other half of the population is of mixed Spanish descent, known as Ladinos. Guatemala's poverty rate is high and distribution of income is unequal: 38% of non-indigenous and 74% of indigenous people live below the national poverty line (World Bank 2005). The agricultural sector accounts for about one-fourth of GDP, two-thirds of exports, and half of the labor force. Topographical features of the Western Highlands region—heavy seasonal rainfall combined with steep mountain slopes—render the area highly susceptible to mudslides. Guatemala's political system is a constitutional democratic republic (CIA 2005).

The Mayan civilization flourished in the Guatemalan region during the first millennium. After almost three centuries as a Spanish colony, Guatemala won its independence in 1821. During the second half of the twentieth century, it experienced a variety of military and civilian governments as well as a 36-year guerrilla war. In 1996, the government signed a peace agreement formally ending the conflict, which left more than 100,000 people dead and created one million refugees to neighboring countries, primarily Mexico (Doyle 2003). Since the civil war ended, the development process in Guatemala has been uneven, and as socioeconomic indicators demonstrate, there is still much progress to be made in order for Guatemala's entire population to experience stability, growth, and integration.

Period of Adolescence

A fundamental question in cross-cultural adolescent research is whether all cultures view adolescence as a unique life period (Chen and Farruggia 2002). Many believe that industrialization in the late nineteenth century brought about adolescence as a distinct period of the life cycle (Aries 1962; Cobb 1997). Schlegel and Barry's (1991) study of 170 nonindustrialized societies concluded, however, that nearly all have the concept of adolescence. In most, the commencement of this life stage is marked by initiation ceremonies, or rites of passage, that are publicly acknowledged (Delaney 1995) and the premise of which is to recognize future adult roles (e.g., productivity or fertility).

Formal initiation ceremonies among Guatemalan adolescents are not widely documented. Across the board, in fact, lifestyle information about adolescents in Guatemala is sparse. Most studies of Guatemalan adolescents' well-being focus on children or women of childbearing age, with few studies examining the years in between. Among the few existing studies of adolescents, many do not recognize the great diversity of circumstances by ethnicity, gender, rural/urban residence, or socioeconomic status.

One initiation ceremony celebrated in the Ladino (non-indigenous) culture of Guatemala is the *quinceañera*, a lavish public celebration of a girl's fifteenth birthday. In the past, this ceremony marked a young woman's entry into sexual maturity and readiness for marriage. In modern times, it marks a girl's transition to assuming additional family and social responsibilities and to begin dating. The celebration is also intended to reaffirm religious faith, good morals, and the virtues of traditional family values (Davalos 2003). Although this rite of passage appears to be widely practiced, there are few academic studies describing its significance and meaning in Guatemala.

With modernization, school enrollment and grade level are used increasingly as markers of adolescent life stages in this and other societies. Using nationally representative data to examine age, gender, and ethnic differences in school

enrollment, educational attainment, and marriage in Guatemala, Hallman, Peracca et al. (2004) find that Mayan girls start school later and drop out earlier than their male Mayan and female non-Mayan counterparts. Enrollment among Mayan boys also decreases with age, but their dropout rates are more gradual. By household poverty level, the differences among 15- to 19-year-old Mayan females are extremely large: 34% of the non-poor attend school, compared with 19% of the poor, and only 9% of the extremely poor. By age 18, 40% of indigenous girls are married versus only 20% of non-indigenous girls. In a cross-country study of in-school Central American adolescents that included Guatemala, Chen et al. (2004) found that many from families of modest socioeconomic status are more likely to spend time in "adult-role activities" (e.g., working for pay, caring for children, and cooking meals). These family responsibilities reduce time available for interacting with peers or other recreational activities. Among young people from poor families, these adult role activities mark a period of emerging adulthood; among Ladina girls the *quinceañera* also marks such an emergence. Chen and Farruggia (2002) also note that the existence of adolescence as a unique period may vary within culture, often by gender and social class.

Beliefs

Traditional Mayan culture in Guatemala is organized largely around local communities. *Municipios*, comprising a *cabecera* (municipal capital) and surrounding *aldeas* (hamlets), continue to be the focal point for rituals, beliefs, and social relations. Such local centrism helped a large proportion of Mayans maintain their distinct cultural identity and dress despite exploitation and domination by Spanish culture (Grandin 1997). Communal life of the *cabecera* centered around a hierarchy of offices held by elders that were simultaneously civil and religious in nature. Among elders were *costumbristas*, individuals who defended customs and beliefs regulating social and economic practices such as uses of communal property, land inheritance, and life-cycle rituals (Britnall 1979).

While the Catholic Church had for centuries advocated the abolition of pre-Christian beliefs and rituals, which centered around religious authority of *cofradias* (religious brotherhoods) and Mayan priests, no concerted effort was undertaken to establish Catholic hegemony until the creation in 1948 of Acción Católica (Catholic Action, or AC) (Grandin 1997). AC was created as a vehicle for anticommunist propaganda that emerged from the ruling elite's fear of the reformist tendencies of President Jacobo Arbenz; its influence was strengthened by the Catholic Church's antipathy to progressive social change at the time. At the local level, AC activists used anticommunist scares to challenge the legitimacy of traditional cultural elders. The movement's reach in local communities was amplified following the U.S.-sponsored overthrow of the Arbenz government in 1954, at which time many Mayan leaders were incarcerated or murdered. In the ensuing 15 years, the AC undertook most social and economic development activities in Mayan communities, thus increasing its power and influence at the local level. Currently 50 to 60% of Guatemala's population identify themselves as Catholic (U.S. Dept. of State 2004).

In the 1960s, missionaries from the United States began to export Evangelical Protestantism; their goal was not only to convert Guatemalans, but to also stamp out communism (Rose and Brouwer 1990). The percentage of evangelical believers in Guatemala is estimated to have increased from 3% in 1960 (Zapata 1982) to 40% today (REW 2005). The success of these churches is credited in large part to aggressive use of the mass media. Many large Evangelical and Pentecostal churches now own their own TV and radio stations, which broadcast religious programming to the most remote regions of Latin America, and often in indigenous languages and dialects (REW 2005).

The cross-country study of young people in Central America by Chen and colleagues (2004) found that controlling for other factors, males were 13% less likely than females to participate in religious activities (measured by an index consisting of praying, reading the Bible, attending church functions, religious revivals, crusades, or retreats). This is consistent with several existing theories proposed to explain male–female differences in religious experiences (e.g., gender role socialization, personality theory, and gender orientation theory). The same study found that adolescents who attend private school and those with better-educated fathers are more likely to socialize with friends and less likely to participate in "religious" and "gender socialization" activities.

A qualitative study of rural Mayan youth and their parents in Guatemala by Colom, Ruiz, et al. (2004) found that fear of adolescent pregnancy was mentioned frequently by parents as a principal reason for keeping girls over the age of 12 years out

of school and limiting their physical mobility. The risk of daughters developing a "bad reputation" was frequently mentioned by parents as a reason to limit girls' interaction with peers and link it more closely to church-based groups.

Gender

Traditional gender roles in Guatemala begin to shape men and women from early in adolescence, with a differential impact on adolescents' level of education, familial responsibilities, and reproductive roles within the Guatemalan family based on sex. Because Guatemalans, especially women, tend to start families in mid-adolescence or early adulthood (i.e., between 15 and 24 years of age), gender roles that apply to married adult men and women often also apply to their younger counterparts.

While boys are encouraged to pursue education, adolescent girls' role as future homemakers and mothers is valued more highly in Guatemala than is their formal education. Research has shown that while many younger girls (pre-puberty) are enrolled in school, dropout rates increase around the period of puberty (Hallman et al. 2004), as adolescent females are expected to take on their more gender-specific roles as wives and mothers. This trend is especially true among Mayan girls, where women's social status is often considerably lower than that of males, and girls' opportunities are limited by society as a means of maintaining control over their lives and activities (Smith et al. 2004). Among girls aged 15 to 19 at the national level, only 2% of those married are enrolled in school, compared with 27% of their nonmarried counterparts (Hallman et al. 2004). Research has shown that, due to fears of physical assault or unwanted pregnancy, Guatemalan girls, and most often Mayan girls, are restricted to very few activities or excursions outside the home.

Early marriage, especially among indigenous females, may also be one of the only ways for young women to liberate themselves from the often-restrictive living environments of their parents' homes. Young women may decide to marry earlier than they would otherwise as a means of leaving their parents' home (Colom et al. 2004). Unfortunately, due to the low social status of women in Guatemalan and especially in Mayan communities, young women may exchange the restrictive family environment for an abusive marital situation (Catino et al. 2005). Violence against women has been identified as among the most significant obstacles to women gaining equality with men in Guatemalan society (Buvinic, Morrison, and Shifter 1999).

While young Guatemalan males are more highly encouraged to attend school than are females, males also shoulder certain responsibilities that may prevent them from completing their formal education. Adolescent boys may be required to secure paid employment as a means of contributing to the family income. This employment is often in the area of agriculture or the sale of handicrafts or other products (Colom et al. 2004).

Guatemalan girls may also need to secure employment outside the home to support their families, in addition to fulfilling their domestic duties inside the home. Guatemalan women most often seek jobs in agriculture or commerce, or work in factories known as *maquiladoras,* or migrate to cities to work as domestic servants (Colom et al. 2004). Women working outside the home became essential in Guatemala during the civil war as a result of the murder of thousands of men who fell victim to state violence (Garrard-Burnett 2000). Major barriers to Guatemalan women of any age entering the workforce include the time and financial costs of obtaining care for children during the mother's work schedule. A study of mothers residing in the slums of Guatemala City showed that women with very young children are less likely to work, and if they do work, their hours of work and earnings are decreased by high fees and travel time for childcare (Hallman et al. 2005). Research has shown that when women do work, they are more likely to spend their earnings on family expenses than are men (UNFPA 2005; Quisumbing 2003).

The Guatemalan civil war had an upsetting impact on the lives of both men and women, but women faced a number of especially devastating effects. During the 1980s, the counterinsurgency groups used sexual violence, including torture and rape, as a strategy of war. In one study of violence against women during the war, it was found that following a woman's capture and rape, she was often made to cook and clean for the soldiers who abused her. Women were also faced with the reality of becoming widows as their husbands were killed in combat or during violent episodes. Losing a husband often meant losing economic resources, as well as losing the status they had enjoyed relative to their husbands. Widowed women often faced increased legal difficulties in claiming their rightful ownership to land in the patrilineal Guatemalan legal system (Garrard-Burnett 2000).

The Self

As in most of Latin America, the family is the center of adolescent life. Most young people feel a sense of obligation and commitment to their family, which provides a certain "group identity" and sense of personal belonging and security. A physical manifestation of the importance of family is the fact that young people tend to live at home with their parents until they marry, which can be very early (aged 14 years) in some rural communities or relatively late (aged 30 years or over) in more urban areas. At the time of marriage, the couple may also move into the natal home of the husband, though this is more common in rural communities and indigenous cultures. This heavy emphasis on the family in Guatemala also results in few adolescents cultivating a sense of themselves as individuals, autonomous of their family, as distinct from many Anglo cultures.

It is important to note the vast differences in Guatemala between the Ladino and Mayan populations. Though ethnic diversity is just one layer of difference among Guatemalan adolescents, it is a very important one, and of the little information that exists on adolescents in Guatemala, there is somewhat more available on Mayan than on Ladino youth. For example, a qualitative study conducted in several rural communities in Guatemala demonstrates the discrepancies and contradictions between what rural, indigenous adolescents expect for their futures and the day-to-day opportunities and constraints they face in achieving these dreams (Colom et al. 2004). Many girls appear more limited than boys in their ability to articulate a vision for themselves beyond the patterns they have seen replicated across generations of women in their families: a life characterized by early marriage, early and frequent childbearing, and chronic poverty. Young Mayan women continue to have very low expectations of what they might achieve in life and face significantly greater challenges than men and non-indigenous women in achieving even modest life goals (Colom et al. 2004).

Girls' inability to formulate or express personal goals and aspirations is undoubtedly linked to gender roles that reinforce inequity between girls and boys and women and men. From the time they are very young, girls are taught that they are less valuable than boys, and as a consequence, they tend to have low self-esteem and a negative self-image (Colom et al. 2004). In both Mayan and Ladino communities, girls and women tend to be subordinated by the authority of their fathers and husbands and the social control of their families. Mayan men make most household decisions, including how many children a couple will have, how the household income will be spent, and whether or not women leave the house (Hughes 2004).

Likewise, women are not afforded equal power in family and community decision making. Rather, they are taught to feel incapable of social and political participation, and those who do manage to become active voices for social change are often accused by men of being "prostitutes" or "inappropriate" as a social pressure mechanism to keep them from entering the sociopolitical realm (Hughes 2004). A related barrier to the self-expression and social participation of rural girls and women is physical distance between communities and language. Girls often drop out of school early and are not encouraged to learn Spanish, and are thus cut off from mainstream information and participation.

Ethnic identity is very strong and inculcates traditional attitudes and values. In many rural Mayan communities, girls and women continue to wear traditional dress, while boys and men use more Western attire. In general, girls have very limited freedom of movement and many of the young women interviewed in the qualitative study by Colom and colleagues (2004) identified this as a major limitation to acquiring formal education, employment, choosing a spouse, and participating in community activities. Puberty is a key transition to "life closing" and increased social isolation for girls and "life opening" for boys, meaning that while boys' freedom expands, that of girls contracts. In general, girls who want to pursue goals that require physical autonomy face challenges in a society that believes that women's mobility should be limited. Parents who are supportive of their daughters' educational and career aspirations must also deal with pressure that comes from neighbors and peers who do not believe that this type of behavior is appropriate for adolescent girls (Colom et al. 2004).

Despite their limited mobility, adolescent girls work very hard both in paid and unpaid labor, leaving them limited free or leisure time. A review of the limited literature indicates significant differences in the way boys and girls spend their work time, regardless of age. Boys are more likely to work for pay or for their family's economic gain, and girls are more likely to perform noneconomic household work or domestic chores. The total amount of time devoted to all work activities rises with age for both boys and girls. Girls spend longer hours than boys on all work activities combined, leaving boys more time for leisure activities (Ritchie, Lloyd, and Grant 2004).

Family Relationships

There is a paucity of published data on aspects related to parenting in Guatemala. Overall, families tend to be large (although they are getting smaller as fertility rates drop in some population segments), and there are many examples of the extended family sharing the same residence. A couple of studies have identified patterns of poor communication between parents and children in Guatemala, especially around taboo or difficult subjects, such as sexuality and male/female relationships (Colom et al. 2004; Bocaletti 2003).

Home life in Guatemala tends to reflect the violence-plagued history of the country. Heavy drinking and physical abuse are commonplace and part of a cycle of social pathology nourished by decades of violence and insecurity (Katel 2003). Domestic violence in its physical, psychological, and sexual manifestations often extends to children, and is treated as the norm both by society and by the judicial system in Guatemala (Smith et al. 2004). While reliable data are only recently becoming available, it is evident that family violence is widespread and perhaps increasing in Guatemala with growing rates of alcohol abuse, poverty, and unemployment among men (Hughes 2004). Violence within families is a major reason why thousands of children and youth end up living on the street, or spending most of their time there, a social phenomenon that carries high risk for adolescents (Katel 2003).

Early marriage is prevalent in Guatemala, especially in indigenous communities. In a qualitative study conducted among indigenous adolescents aged 15 to 19, both sexes indicated a desire to marry and have a family. Their perceived ideal, however, is to marry later than they actually do because they said they would be "more prepared." Young people also stated that it should be up to the couple to decide when and whom to marry. While many adolescents initially agreed that it was the couple's decision, other interviewees admitted that parents still influence who and how their children marry (Colom et al. 2004). Marriages continue to be arranged in some indigenous communities, whereas Ladinos tend to follow a more Western model based on self-made decisions based on romantic love (Hughes 2004).

Rates of family dissolution are high in Guatemala and the 36-year conflict split up thousands of families and scarred thousands more. By the time the Peace Accords were signed, an estimated 200,000 young people had been orphaned (Katel 2003). With few possibilities for improving their futures at home, hundreds of thousands of Guatemalans leave the country in search of a better life.

In growing numbers, Guatemalans are migrating to Mexico or the United States, maintaining their families and improving their communities with the money they send home (Katel 2003). This stream of migrants includes thousands of children and adolescents each year. Migration is placing enormous strains on already stressed families, especially on the women and children left behind. Fear of permanent abandonment by husbands is pervasive. Young people often respond to the stress by doing poorly in school or dropping out. In some cases, dropping out is a reaction to receiving money from abroad (Katel 2003).

Foreign adoption is another issue facing poor families. In a demographically young country, children bear much of the burden of poverty, and some residents view foreign adoption as a chance at a decent life for poor infants. Enforcement of child welfare laws and of the Conventions on the Rights of the Child and Intercountry Adoptions is weak. Adoption in Guatemala is frequently characterized as a business, and one that operates virtually unregulated. Babies are reported to be bought and stolen to satisfy the international demand (Katel 2003).

Between women widowed by war, women left behind because of migration, and women abandoned or divorced, an estimated 20% of Guatemalan households are headed by women. Increases in urbanization and decreases in multigenerational households are also contributing to this social phenomenon (Hallman et al. 2005). Fifty-one percent of female-headed households in Guatemala are rural, and of these, 56% are headed by widows (Hughes 2004). An unknown number of young people are living in female-headed households (Katel 2003). Protective and family support services only exist in rudimentary form in Guatemala and are vastly underfunded. Hence, single women face tremendous challenges in trying to support their children and adolescents, and conditions are often very difficult.

In urban areas, working mothers are more likely to be indigenous, single, separated, divorced, or widowed (Hallman et al. 2005). Household labor burdens also fall heavily on adolescent girls when mothers are required to work. In households with working mothers, adolescent females frequently act as substitute child caregivers (Hallman et al. 2005).

Friends and Peers/Youth Culture

Lloyd and colleagues' comprehensive review of research and policy on adolescence in the developing world (NRC/IOM 2005) notes the lack of

multidimensional research on the lives of adolescents. There is very limited research that examines the context of adolescents' self-defined identity, attitudes, behaviors, or the interrelationships among various domains (Ritchie, Lloyd, and Grant 2004). There is very little research on youth culture in Guatemala.

Guatemalan parents, at least in rural areas, tend to be protective, especially of girls. Parents fear adolescents falling under "bad influence" of peers or getting caught up in "the wrong crowd" (Colom et al. 2004). Nonfamilial friendships often are regarded suspiciously by parents, particularly where their daughters are concerned. Peer networks and friendships are limited for girls in rural communities. For example, young women who reported not being involved in church groups and not enrolled in school, also reported having few friends (Colom et al. 2004).

There are few youth-serving organizations in Guatemala, and those that exist tend to work in urban areas and serve middle-class boys. Recreational activities available to Guatemalan adolescents tend to revolve around sports for boys and church and community celebrations for boys and girls. The number of community activities open and available to boys tends to increase with age, while the opposite is true for girls. Girls and young women tend to have access only to church or other religious-oriented activities, and their opportunities for nonformal education/training/skill building are highly restricted (Colom et al. 2004).

As mentioned earlier, the situation varies considerably by gender: as boys get older, their autonomy and freedom to pursue friendships and other personal interests tends to increase, whereas the opposite is true for girls. In addition to cultural and social pressure, early marriage in Guatemala may also be seen by girls as one of the few existing and acceptable opportunities to become independent from their families.

Love and Sexuality

Patterns regarding love and sexuality in Guatemala vary significantly based on regional differences and on gender. In general, among Guatemalan women aged 15 to 19, almost 74% are single, 13% live with a partner but are not married, and 10.5% are married (DHS 1998/1999). For Guatemalan women aged 20 to 24, 30.5% remain single, 32% are married, and 31% live with their partners (DHS 1998/1999). The average age of marriage is 23.8 for men and 21.3 for

women (UNFPA 2005). The mean age at first intercourse among men and women ranges from 15 to 17 (Hidalgo 2002). Sexual activity among adolescents is not discussed openly in Guatemalan culture; especially in regards to girls, who are concerned with defending their chastity, sexual activity is seen as something to be kept a secret (Morgan 2000).

Almost 70% of 15- to 19-year-old and 84% of 20- to 24-year-old Guatemalan women know of at least one modern contraceptive method (DHS 1998/1999). Modern methods include hormonal products such as oral contraceptives, injections, hormonal rings, patches, and hormonal intrauterine devices; standard copper intrauterine devices; and barrier methods, such as condoms, cervical caps, and diaphragms. Traditional methods include abstinence, fertility awareness techniques (in which intercourse is avoided during a woman's fertile period) and pre-ejaculatory withdrawal. Almost 23% of women 15 to 19 and nearly 30% of those 20 to 24 have heard messages about contraception through TV or radio (DHS 1998/1999).

Despite knowledge about contraceptive methods, very few—only 4%—Guatemalan women between the ages of 15 and 19 actually use any contraceptive method, and even fewer (3.3%) use a modern method. Slightly more (over 13%) 20- to 24-year-old Guatemalan women use a modern method of family planning. Among the younger group, hormonal injections are the most commonly used, with 1.8% of 15- to 19-year-old women using that method. Oral contraceptive pills are more popular among the 20- to 24-year-olds, with use among 5.6% of this group, followed by the hormonal injection at 3.1% use (DHS 1998/1999).

As previously mentioned, young motherhood is a significant part of Guatemalan culture, especially in more traditional communities and rural areas. However, in larger cities, adolescent pregnancy is often unplanned and unwanted. The age-specific fertility rate per 1,000 women 15 to 19 years of age is 85 in urban areas and 133 in rural areas (UNFPA 2005). In urban areas, 33.5% of women 15 to 19 years old have already had at least one child; in rural areas, 42.4% of women the same age have already had one child (UNFPA 2005). Pregnant adolescents may carry the unplanned pregnancy to term and raise the child as single mothers or with the support of their families—frequently without the involvement of the father—or they may seek to terminate the pregnancy illegally, putting themselves at risk for unsafe treatment and dangerous health outcomes (DHS 1998/1999). Due to its

illegal status, it is difficult to identify specific abortion rates in Guatemala.

The overall estimated prevalence of HIV/AIDS among Guatemalan youth 15 to 24 years old is 0.9%; by gender, the prevalence is 0.6% to 1.1% for women and 0.6% to 1.2% for men. Estimates report that as of 2002, there were 5,700 orphans in Guatemala due to HIV/AIDS (UNAIDS 2002). There is generally more awareness and knowledge of HIV prevention methods (i.e., condom use, abstinence) among youth in urban sites than among those in rural, primarily Mayan locales. Despite awareness of prevention methods, youth 16 to 20 years of age have low condom use; boys in this age group report more condom use with commercial sex workers than they do with their regular sex partners, due to the association between sex workers and disease risk (UNAIDS 2002; Morgan 2000). Adolescent girls are less likely to use condoms with regular partners for fear of appearing as if they are sexually active with more than one person or that they are having "premeditated" or premarital sex, which is generally considered socially inappropriate (Morgan 2000).

Health Risk Behavior

The main sources of adolescents' health-related problems in Guatemala are violence, poor sanitation, sexual health risks, and lack of medical attention during pregnancy and childbirth. The overall life expectancy in Guatemala is 66 years of age, slightly higher (69 years) for women and slightly lower (63 years) for men (UNFPA 2005). According to the most recent data from Guatemala's National Statistical Institute, gunshot wounds are the leading cause of death among youth aged 15 to 19, followed by pneumonia, influenza, and intestinal infections (PAHO 2002). UNICEF reports that child homicide can be attributed to gang violence, violence from security forces, or drive-by shootings, the last of which is most common in the killing of children living on the street (UNICEF 2005). Similar to teen gang members in other countries, Guatemalan teens join gangs to gain a sense of community and increased self-esteem, or because they are coerced into doing so (UNICEF 2005). By October of 2002, there had been 408 shootings of children and youth during that year, a 27% increase from 2001 totals (UNICEF 2005).

Poor sanitation and water treatment services are responsible for the gastrointestinal and respiratory illnesses that plague the Guatemalan population, young and old alike. The water issues in Guatemala are not due to lack of water—on the contrary, the country has sufficient water sources, but the sources are not well maintained and most are contaminated with human or chemical waste. Water treatment issues in Guatemala are especially challenging because they are associated with larger infrastructural issues such as lack of land, housing, and transportation, especially in Guatemala's large rural population. Sanitation infrastructure and sewage treatment are the first steps to resolving the water contamination issues (Barrientos and Fernandez 1998). While efforts have been made to improve water sanitation, rural populations, and therefore predominantly indigenous populations living in rural areas, are those most at risk for water-borne gastrointestinal and respiratory infections.

Guatemalan teens also face multiple sexual health risks. As of June 2004, 7,054 cases of AIDS had been reported in Guatemala, 380 of which were among children 14 years old and under. Risk for HIV transmission is reported to be highest among men who have sex with men and men who have sex with commercial sex workers. Although the government promotes condoms through discount pricing and media strategies, condom use remains low, especially among the young population. A recent survey showed that only 5.2% of women 15 to 24 years old used condoms in their first sexual relationship (USAID 2004). Educated youth in Guatemala are generally aware of risk factors associated with HIV, however, most do not see themselves as at risk for contracting the disease. The cultural norm that prevents teens from discussing their sexuality more openly—especially girls—makes it challenging to convey the risk factors to this population (Morgan 2000). Estimates report that in 2000, Guatemala spent $11.9 million in HIV/AIDS related services, 60% of which was dedicated to treatment and 15% of which was used for prevention (USAID 2004).

Last but not least, Guatemala's maternal mortality is one of the most devastating causes of death nationwide. The maternal mortality ratio in Guatemala is 240 per 100,000, one of the highest in all of Latin America. Less than half (41%) of all deliveries in Guatemala are attended by a skilled professional, which means that half the time a woman gives birth in Guatemala, she is putting her life in jeopardy. Attendance by a skilled professional varies greatly by place of residence or education level: while 66% of all births in urban areas were attended by a skilled professional, only 30% of those in rural areas were attended. Similarly, while 89% of births of those at the highest educational level were attended by a skilled professional, only 21% of those at the lowest educational level were attended (UNFPA 2005).

Education

In the last decade, the Guatemalan government has made efforts to increase funding for, access to, and the quality of its education system. Examples of these strides include the federal government's program to increase educational opportunities in rural areas beginning in 1992 (Rojas et al. 2005), and a $15.36 million loan from the Inter-American Development Bank in 1997 to improve pre-primary and primary education nationwide (Drosdoff 1997). In 2001, Guatemala was investing 2% of its GDP in education, with the goal of increasing education funding—including government and private sources—to 5.3% in 2008 and 7% in 2020 (Duggins 2001). Policies to improve education—including expanding educational programs in indigenous languages and in rural areas and improving gender equity—were a part of the Peace Accords signed in 1996 (Drosdoff 1997).

The net enrollment and attendance of Guatemalan primary school-aged children between 1996 and 2003 was 78% (UNICEF 2005). In general, young Guatemalan women are less likely than their male counterparts to be enrolled in school, especially at older ages: among 15- to 19-year-olds, only 20% of Mayan girls are enrolled, compared with 41% of Ladina girls and 37% of Mayan boys (Hallman et al. 2004). Thirteen percent of 15- to 24-year-old men are illiterate, as are nearly twice as many (24%) women of the same age (UNESCO 2002). Among the Mayan population, less than 40% of girls are enrolled in school at age 14, and by age 16 their enrollment decreases to 19%. For Mayan boys aged 14 and 16 years, school enrollment is 60% and 41%, respectively. Among 16-year-old Ladina girls and boys, school enrollment is 45% and 46%, respectively (Hallman et al. 2004).

One barrier to girls' enrollment in school is the pressure placed on them to marry and begin childbearing during their adolescence, with an increased rate of motherhood among those with the least education. For example, among young women aged 15 to 19 with no or only primary school education, 62.6% have already had at least one child, while only 23.1% of those with the highest level of education have already begun childbearing (UNFPA 2005). Another barrier to education among the Mayan population in general is the lack of schools in the rural areas where most indigenous Guatemalans live (Rojas et al. 2005). To address this gap, the Guatemalan program called PRONADE (Program for Educational Development) in 1992 began a program to increase the number of schools in rural areas. The federal government provides funding for teachers' salaries and administrative training at PRONADE schools. The goal of PRONADE schools is to provide education for at least 70% of primary school-aged children in all of Guatemala's 22 departments; currently PRONADE schools are located in 21 of the 22 departments throughout the country, and, as of 2003, an average of 87% of 7- to 14-year-olds nationwide were enrolled in school (Rojas et al. 2005).

Work

High levels of poverty force many young people in Guatemala into the labor force at an early age to contribute to family income. Young people from marginalized subgroups, such as those in rural areas and of indigenous origin, are the most likely to seek work (USDOL, 2005). Most minors work at household chores, in subsistence agriculture, in family-run enterprises, and elsewhere in the informal economy (ILO 2004).

Guatemalan law sets 14 as the minimum age for employment. However, these rules are flexible and permission to work at younger ages may be granted, for example, in cases where extreme poverty justifies involvement in labor; in practice, however, permission is seldom even sought (ILO, UNICEF, World Bank 2003). It is common for children in Guatemala to combine school and work from an early age and many are unable to perform well in school or continue attending school because of the need to work, either at home or for pay. A national population-based survey in 2000 (ENCOVI) revealed that among 10- to 14-year-olds, only 47% were attending school and not in the labor force, 24% combined school and work, 14% were in the labor force but not attending school, and 15% were neither in school nor in the labor force (most likely engaged in unpaid household and domestic work). While nearly 40% of Guatemala's 10- to 14-year-old population is in the labor force, this figure increases to more than 50% for those aged 15 to 17 years. Among 15- to 17-year-olds, males are the most likely to work (70% of them). Adolescents of lower-income families are especially prone to school leaving in order to work, and with age, more adolescents are forced to leave school in order to join the country's labor force. By 17 years of age, fewer than one-fourth of adolescents dedicate their time solely to school-related activities (ILO, UNICEF, World Bank 2003).

Agriculture continues to dominate Guatemala's economy and, not surprisingly, more than half of adolescents involved in paid employment work in

agriculture and farm activities. Work in manufacturing and trade activities accounts for approximately 30% of adolescent jobs. A common option for young women has been to work in paid domestic labor in private households. Frequently, young, rural, indigenous women migrate from rural villages to work in middle-class and wealthy homes in urban areas.

Growing industries, such as *maquilas* (industries that assemble garments from imported materials and ship them to foreign destinations with favorable tax schemes), employ many young women who seek alternatives to domestic or agricultural work. Although no figures are available, it is estimated that a large number of adolescent girls work in these types of jobs (ILO, UNICEF, World Bank 2003). Unfavorable conditions are believed to predominate among adolescents working in *maquilas* and they are usually paid less than adults and are commonly forced to work longer hours.

Media

There is minimal information available on the use of media by Guatemalan youth or the general population. Anecdotal evidence shows that radio is a widespread and popular medium to promote health issues among adolescent listeners, especially in underserved rural areas, where many programs are broadcast in Mayan languages. According to national surveys, almost 23% of women aged 15 to 19 years and nearly 30% of those aged 20 to 24 years have heard messages about contraception through television or radio (DHS 1998/1999). In 2005, the U.S.-based organization Population Communications International (PCI) conducted a series of workshops to train Central and South American community leaders to design and produce radio-based entertainment education programs to promote public health and human rights messages. Many of these participants were from Guatemala and plan to use their training to develop programs for adolescent-age listeners (PCI 2005). In 2003, Teenwire.com, a subsidiary of the Planned Parenthood Federation of America, interviewed a group of Guatemalan teens who produce a radio show called *Sexo Tips* in the Peten region. The program is produced by teens for teens, and addresses issues related to teen sexuality and health. The show is sponsored by a Guatemalan partner organization of Planned Parenthood Federation of America-International known as *Tan Ux'il* (Ourian 2003). The Asociación Pro-Bienestar de la Familia (APROFAM), an International Planned Parenthood affiliate, ran a telephone

hotline from 1980–1996 to field questions and provide referrals for their health services. According to their reports, the hotline staff fielded 40 to 100 calls per day, or 7,000 per year. Based on the success of the general hotline, in 1999 APROFAM established a youth-oriented hotline that fielded 954 calls during its first 18 months, primarily coming from Guatemala City (PATH 2005).

Politics and Military

The Peace Accords signed after the end of the Guatemalan civil war included revised legislation on military service. The age for both compulsory and volunteer military service is 18; men under 18 and all women are protected from compulsory service and from being recruited for armed combat. Article 42 of the Civil Service Law established that youth between 18 and 24 were required to either serve in the armed forces or carry out a social service project. While those under 18 and women of all ages are protected from serving in the military, 16- and 17-year-olds are allowed to complete their civil service duty before they turn 18 if they choose to complete a social service project. Only men between 18 and 30 are allowed to serve in the military, and the period of service is 30 months (The Coalition to Stop the Use of Child Soldiers 2004).

Youth interested in pursuing a military career from a young age may enroll at the Adolfo V. Hall Institutes, a military training school that has prepared reserve officers and career servicemen since 1955. To enroll at the Hall Institutes, students must be between 11 and 14 years old (The Coalition to Stop the Use of Child Soldiers 2004). Political organizing among adolescents during the civil war, especially among indigenous youth exiled in Mexico, included training in human rights and conflict resolution (Rosseau et al. 2001).

The voting age in Guatemala is 18 years. Inforpress (2005) reports that fewer than half of Guatemalans who receive their legal identification cards when they turn 18 years of age bother to register for voting. A 2001 United Nations Verification Mission in Guatemala (MINUGUA) found that only 69% of women of voting age were registered to vote, and of these, only 33% actually voted (USDS 2003).

Unique Issues

Guatemalan youth, and specifically indigenous youth, face several unique issues that pose challenges to their health outcomes. One is the "triple burden" of age, gender, and ethnicity faced by

young Mayan girls. First and foremost, Mayan Guatemalans, especially females, tend to be poor, with few technical skills or educational opportunities to break the cycle of chronic poverty passed down through the generations (Catino et al. 2005). Second, education is not a priority for Mayan girls. While three-quarters of 10-year-old Mayan girls are enrolled in school, this number drops to only 19% by age 16 (Hallman et al. 2005). The focus for adolescent girls is placed on marriage and child-bearing, and research has shown that childbearing at this early age puts girls at risk for poor pregnancy and childbirth outcomes (UNFPA 2005). The virtue of being female gives Mayan girls few opportunities to break out of the cultural mold of being mothers and homemakers, and subsequently, the highest level of school dropout rates occur around age 13, when girls begin puberty. While nearly one-third (27%) of older Mayan adolescent girls 15 to 19 are married, only 2% of these remain in school (Hallman et al. 2004). Lastly, the traditional Mayan culture subordinates the value of women below that of men, which is responsible for increased rates of domestic violence and patriarchal tendencies in this community (Smith et al. 2004).

Another major issue affecting Guatemalan youth is that of "returned" Guatemalan citizens. Due to the "scorched earth policy" employed to purge military insurgents in rural areas during the civil war, many civilian indigenous Guatemalans fled the country for refuge in Mexico during the conflict. Calculations of the total number of refugees estimate that as many as 150,000 Guatemalans had fled to Mexico by 1984 (however, due to lack of registration with the Mexican government among many refugees, the exact total is unknown). In the late 1980s, many of the Guatemalan refugees in Mexico returned to Guatemala, earning them the name *retornados*, or returnees. This experience—both the fleeing and the eventual return to Guatemala—had a measurable impact on Guatemalan youth. One of the reasons cited by returnees for their return to Guatemala was a fear that living in Mexico would cause their children to lose their traditional Guatemalan values. Returned youth interviewed in a 2001 study acknowledged that the decision to return to Guatemala was most often their parents' decision and, even if they also wanted to return home, they did not feel they had a choice in the matter. In discussing their returns to Guatemala before the end of the civil war, young *retornados* express a fear of returning to a land of unresolved conflict and the political and economic ramifications of living in a war-torn country. Especially those *retornados* who spent longer periods of their lives in Mexico also express a struggle with a sense of identity divided between Mexico and Guatemala (Rosseau et al. 2001).

INGRID DRIES-DAFFNER, KELLY HALLMAN, JENNIFER CATINO, and KARLA BERDICHEVSKY

Ms. Kate Venet at the Population Council is thanked for her assistance in preparing the final manuscript.

References and Further Reading

Barrientos, C., and V. Fernandez. 1998. Case study, Guatemala: Water, population, and sanitation in the Mayan Biosphere Reserve of Guatemala. American Association for the Advancement of Science.

Bocaletti, E. 2003. *Informe final. Investigación cualitativa: La salud reproductiva en adolescentes del area Ixil (Final report: Qualitative investigation: Reproductive health in adolescents of the area Ixil). Proyecto Maya de Salud Reproductiva.* Guatemala City: Save the Children, Latin American and Carribean Regional Office.

Buvinic M., A. R. Morrison, and M. Shifter. 1999. Violence in the Americas: A framework for action. In *Too close to home: Domestic violence in the Americas.* A. R. Morrison, M. Buvinic, and M. L. Biehl (eds.). Washington, D.C.: Inter-American Development Bank.

Catino, J., K. Hallman, and M. Ruiz. 2005. Building skills to enhance life opportunities for Mayan girls. Transitions to Adulthood. Brief 5, Population Council. http://www.popcouncil.org/.

Central Intelligence Agency. 2005. *The World Fact Book: Guatemala.* http://www.cia.gov/cia/publications/factbook/geos/gt.html.

Chen, C., and S. Farruggia. 2002. Culture and adolescent development. In *Online readings in psychology and culture* (http://www.ac.wwu.edu/~culture/index-cc.htm). W. J. Lonner, D. L. Dinnel, S. A. Hayes, and D. N. Sattler (eds.). Bellingham, Wash.: Center for Cross-Cultural Research, Western Washington University, Bellingham.

Chuan-Yu, C., C. M. Dormitzer, J. Bejarano, et al. 2004. The adolescent behavioral repertoire: Its latent structure in the PACARDO region of Latin America. *Behavioral Medicine* http://www.findarticles.com/p/articles/mi_m0GDQ/is_3_30/ai_n13557280.

Coalition to Stop the Use of Child Soldiers. 2004. Child soldiers global report: Guatemala. Coalition to Stop the Use of Child Soldiers. www.child-soldiers.org.

Colom, A., M. Ruiz, J. Catino, et al. 2004. Voices of vulnerable and underserved adolescents in Guatemala. A summary of the qualitative study: Understanding the lives of indigenous young people in Guatemala. Guatemala City: Population Council. http://www.popcouncil.org/.

Davalos, K. M. 2003. La quinceañera: Making gender and ethnic identities. In *Perspectives on Las Américas: A reader in culture, history, and representation.* M. C. Gutmann (ed.). Malden, Mass.: Blackwell.

DHS. 1998/1999. *Demographic and health survey—Guatemala.* Demographic and Health Surveys.

Doyle, K. 2003. Mexico's southern front: Guatemala and the search for security. Washington, D.C.: National Security Archive Electronic Briefing Books, The National

Security Archive, George Washington University. http://www.gwu.edu/~nsarchiv/NSAEBB/NSAEBB100/.

Drosdoff, D. 1997. IDB approves $15.36 million for basic education in Guatemala. Washington, D.C.: Inter-American Development Bank.

Duggins, C. 2001. Financing of education in Guatemala. International Development Research Center (Canada).

ENCOVI. 2000. *Encuesta nacional de condiciones de vida (National survey on living conditions).* http://www.segeplan.gob.gt/ine/content/encovi.htm.

Garrard-Burnett, V. 2000. Aftermath: Women and gender issues in postconflict Guatemala. Washington, D.C.: United States Agency for International Development.

Hallman K., A. Quisumbing, M. T. Ruel, et al. 2005. Mothers' work and child care: Findings from the urban slums of Guatemala City. *Economic Development and Cultural Change* 53(4):855–86.

Hallman, K., S. Peracca, J. Catino, et al. 2004. *Causas de los bajos logros educacionales y transición temprana a la vida adulta en Guatemala (Causes of low educational attainment and early transition to adulthood in Guatemala).* Guatemala City: Population Council. http://www.popcouncil.org/.

Hidalgo, E. 2002. Encuesta cacional de salud materno-infantil. Guatemala: Instituto Nacional de Estadistica.

Hughes, J. 2004. Gender, equity and indigenous women's health in the Americas. Washington, D.C.: Gender and Health Unit. Pan-American Health Organization.

Inforpress. 2005. Guatemala: Election authority's 2005 budget increases as voter registration drops. http://www.inforpressca.com/CAR/homes/h3235.php.

ILO, UNICEF, World Bank. 2003. Understanding children's work in Guatemala. http://www.ucw-project.org/pdf/publications/report_guatemala.pdf.

International Labour Office. 2004. Summary: Analysis of child labour in Central America and the Dominican Republic. http://www.ilo.org/iloroot/docstore/ipec/prod/eng/2004_cam_sintesis_en.pdf.

Katel P. 2003. *Children abandoned: Guatemala's young people and their search for a future.* Baltimore, Md.: International Social Service, United States Branch.

Morgan, P. 2000. Let's talk about sex: Exploring adolescent sexual behavior among Guatemalans in the age of AIDS. American Public Health Association Annual Meeting.

National Research Council/Institute of Medicine. 2005. *Growing up global: Changing transitions to adulthood in developing countries.* Cynthia Lloyd (ed.). Washington, DC: National Academies Press.

Ourian, S. 2003. Sex talk live! www.teenwire.com, Planned Parenthood Federation of America.

PAHO. 2002. *Core health data selected indicators.* Washington, D.C.: Pan-American Health Organization.

PATH. 2005. *Information and communication technologies: Program examples.* PATH/Reproductive Health Outlook.

PCI. 2005. *Entertainment-education and social marketing trainings.* New York City: Population Communications International.

Population Reference Bureau. 2005. *2005 world population data sheet.* http://www.prb.org/pdf05/05WorldDataSheet_Eng.pdf.

Quisumbing, A. R. (ed.). 2003. *Household decisions, gender and development: A synthesis of recent research.* Baltimore, Md.: Distributed for International Food Policy Research Institute by Johns Hopkins University Press.

Ritchie, A., C. Lloyd, and M. Grant. 2004. *Gender differences in time use among adolescents in developing countries: Implications of rising school enrollment rates.* Policy Research Division Working Paper. New York: Population Council. http://www.popcouncil.org/.

Rojas, C., A. Valerio, et al. 2005. *Decentralizing education in Guatemala: School management by local communities.* The World Bank.

Rosseau, C., M. Morales, et al. 2001. Going home: Giving voice to memory strategies of young Mayan refugees who returned to Guatemala as a community. *Culture, Medicine and Psychiatry* 25:135–68.

Schlegel, A., and H. Barry. 1991. *Adolescence: An anthropological inquiry.* New York: Free Press.

Smith, M., M. Ruiz, et al. 2004. *Entendiendo y respondiendo a la violencia domestica en comunidades indigenas de Guatemala (Understanding and responding to domestic violence in Guatemala's indigenous communities).* Guatemala City: Population Council. http://www.popcouncil.org/.

UNAIDS. 2002. *Follow-up to the Declaration of Commitment on HIV/AIDS: Country report, Guatemala.* Geneva: Joint United Nations Programme on HIV/AIDS.

UNESCO. 2002. *Estimates and projections of adult illiteracy for population aged 15 years and above, by country and by gender, 1970–2015.* Montreal: United Nations Educational, Scientific and Cultural Organization, Institute for Statistics. http://www.uis.unesco.org/en/stats/statistics/literacy2000.htm.

UNFPA. 2005a. *Recognizing and promoting women's key economic roles.* United Nations Population Fund.

UNFPA. 2005b. *Guatemala overview.* United Nations Population Fund.

UNICEF. 2005. *The official summary of the state of the world's children. At-a-Glance: Guatemala.* Geneva: United Nations Children's Fund.

United Nations. 2003. *World population prospects, the 2002 revision, volume II: Sex and age distribution of populations.* New York: United Nations.

USAID. 2004. *Country profile, HIV/AIDS: Guatemala.* Washington, D.C.: United States Agency for International Development.

USDOL. 2005. *Guatemala.* Washington, D.C.: United States Department of Labor, Bureau of International Labor Affairs, International Child Labor Program. http://www.dol.gov/ilab/media/reports/iclp/sweat/guatemala.htm#18.

USDS. 2003. *Country reports on human rights practices, 2002.* Washington, D.C.: United States Department of State, Bureau of Democracy, Human Rights, and Labor.

USDS. 2004. *International religious freedom report.* Washington, D.C.: United States Department of State, Bureau of Democracy, Human Rights, and Labor.

World Bank. 2005. *Indigenous peoples, poverty and human development in Latin America: 1994–2004.* Washington, D.C.: World Bank.

GUINEA

Background Information

Guinea, a former French colony, is situated in sub-Saharan Africa. Its surface area is 247,857 square kilometers. Guinea is bordered by the Atlantic Ocean, Côte d'Ivoire, Guinea Bissau, Senegal, Mali, Sierra-Leone, and Liberia. It is divided into four rather distinct natural areas.

In 1958, Guinea became an independent secular republic. Guinea has had a complex political evolution since 1958, resulting in general upheaval and economic decay. Subregional fratricidal wars threaten the stability of the country. The choice of economic liberalism by the army (which assumed power through a military coup in 1984) has contributed to the continuing deterioration of the economy.

Guinea is among the poorest countries in the world. Of its nearly nine million inhabitants (2004 estimate), 40% live below the poverty line. Guinea's population is primarily young and rural: 53% of the population is under the age of 18, and only 30% of the entire population inhabits urban areas. Conakry, the capital, has a population of approximately two million people.

Approximately 70% of the population works in rural areas. One of the main industries is mining (bauxite, diamonds, and gold). French is the official administrative language. Islam is the primary religion, followed by approximately 88% of the population. To a lesser degree, Christianity and animism are practiced on the coast and in the south.

Guinea hosts more than 20 ethnic groups. The most populous are the Peulh, the Maninka, the Soussou, and those living in the forest region (Colle 1997).

Period of Adolescence

Adolescence is not recognized in the traditional culture of Guinea. When it is recognized, it is done so as a short period of time, from the ages of 14 to 16 for girls, and the ages of 17 to 23 for boys. In general, age is less of a factor in determining one's roles and duties than is gender. Upon the end of childhood, the young male or female generally leaves his or her parental home to set up his or her own home. This can occur as early as pubescence (Arcin 1907). Young adolescents are distinguished from children by the fact that they are responsible for themselves and are preparing for their own future. Adolescents differ from adults in that they have fewer resources upon which to rely. In the rural areas especially, the young become autonomous at an early age. Girls marry early, to avoid the pitfall of an out-of-wedlock pregnancy.

In the animist Kpèlè traditional society, male youths undergo an initiation rite considered very important by its adherents. The youths suffer ordeals in the "sacred wood." Male and female circumcision are also important transitional rites. Circumcision generally occurs at an early age. More than 52% of Guinean women are circumcised before the age of 10. Increasingly, however, there is resistance to the practice. Seventy-five percent of women aged 20 to 24 do not think female circumcision is necessary. Initiation rituals in general are becoming less frequent, as a result of more advanced schooling and increased urbanization.

Young university graduates who are unemployed and single, as well as some students, can be considered as representing the stage known as "emerging adulthood." However, this is a recent phenomenon, and applies only to the educated, upper classes of society.

Beliefs

A strong sense of solidarity with others remains persistent in Guinea. This attitude is particularly shared with one's ethnic group, one's family, one's neighbors, one's schoolmates, and one's co-workers.

Female children are introduced to the Koran at an early age, usually around age 5 or 6. An adult teaches a group of children together, usually gathering on a veranda, or around a wood-fire in the compound. This forms the basis of most female children's entire education. Children who attend formal schools are said to acquire an "extra soul" in the process. Even in rural areas, boys generally attend school. Boys' education culminates in the translation of the Koran into the student's indigenous language.

In areas where animist religious traditions are adhered to, ceremonies are organized to honor ancestors who hold symbolically great powers. The youth must learn to respect this cult of ancestors. These rites are at times employed to ward off the actions of those perceived to be wrongdoers or sorcerers. In these societies, young people regularly wear talisman amulets at their hips.

Gender

Girls and boys may live in the same compound, but they are generally separated between the ages of 8 and 12. The sexual division of tasks in Guinea is derived from the dominant patriarchal system. Boys are trained to play their future role of head of family and girls learn what is necessary to be a good wife and mother. The tasks that fall to boys generally require great physical exertion, or involve some degree of risk. Girls assist with household chores.

Boys generally marry later than girls. Approximately 55% of males between the ages of 20 and 24 are unmarried. In the same age range, only 15% of females are unmarried. Marriage becomes official when a dowry (usually cash) is accepted by the husband-to-be's parents and relatives. When they marry, girls move to the home of their husband, where they are responsible for all household chores. Polygamy is present in Guinea; 54% of women live in polygamous unions.

A young man's upbringing is judged by the way he carries himself, and the games he likes to play. Boys are encouraged to show off their physical strength and skills. The Maninka people favor girls who are light in complexion, slender, and long-necked. In the forest region and on the littoral, a slightly heavy girl with thick legs and a big waist is considered highly attractive. Everywhere, girls have their ears pierced with holes from which hang various gold or silver rings.

The Self

The means by which a young man shapes his individual identity depends to a large degree on whether he lives in a rural area or an urban center. In a rural village, the young man who has been initiated into adulthood via circumcision feels himself to be superior to the younger boys, whom he may mock. He is indoctrinated with collectivistic values, emphasizing clan solidarity, elder's rights, and family honor. In urban areas, speaking one's mother tongue is a means of establishing an ethnic and cultural identity.

In terms of informal everyday acts and cultural manifestations (such as the act of name-giving, funerals, or celebrations), differences between rural youth and urban youth are obvious. Rural youth see the family name as the primary means of identification, while urban youths place more emphasis on their ethnic background, and the values assumed to be concomitant with that ethnicity. Virtually excluded from the public space, girls do not have much opportunity to claim a status linked to the family or the ethnic group specifically.

In general, community life and the impulse toward collectivism is so strong as to outweigh most individualist tendencies. For example, if an adolescent chooses to spend his or her free time alone, he or she will probably be reprimanded by his elders.

Family Relationships

The family is the basic unit of Guinean society. Family members are the first educators of the child. They are concerned about seeing their child represent the proud and responsible authentic family. This strong social expectation is supported by the extended family (aunts, uncles, grandparents) in terms of love and multiple duties for the child. The father's role becomes more obvious by the end of early childhood (6 to 8 years old) in favor of the boy. However, monetary economy and growing poverty creates cracks in the extended family (Guinée 2000).

Upon reaching puberty, the girl is subject to more attention from the extended family. However, she becomes especially important to her mother. The girl is forbidden from engaging in premarital sex. Young men are allowed much more freedom, and are encouraged to socialize and work outside the home.

Problems faced by youngsters in disunited families are not well documented. The more recent study indicates a total of about 420,000 orphans, of whom 150,000 are over 18. One hundred thousand youngsters (5%) are in a situation of extreme vulnerability. The phenomenon among poor rural families of leaving a child in somebody's care involves placing the child with richer families.

In urban settings, the head of the family may be unemployed, and thus unable to provide enough resources to meet the needs of all the family members. In such situations, family bonds may be greatly strained, making relations between parents and their adolescent child difficult and tense.

Friends and Peers/Youth Culture

In Guinea, friendly relationships between young people develop easily. Young people, mainly those who are 24 or older, gather together in formal associations that receive financial backing from philanthropic investors, or NGOs. In 2004 there were 420 licensed youth associations, of which 70% were based in Conakry (Dioubate and Lachaud 1992).

The importance of physical and sports education is acknowledged by civil authorities, but there is a near-total absence of private sport centers, and fewer than 500 physical education teachers and/or coaches in the entire country. The pronounced insufficiency of sports equipment, playgrounds, and proper adult authority explains the invasion of young people into roads and public places, transforming those places into football (soccer) grounds. These games are exclusively populated by boys. Girls are discouraged from congregating in the streets or appearing in public. These games are considered to be masculine in nature.

Most cultural bodies (80%) such as libraries and museums are located in urban centers, the vast majority in Conakry alone. Therefore, such cultural organizations are available to urban adolescents for their use.

The adolescent interest in music is pronounced. Many young people try to record cassettes, which are very well liked. In rural areas, folklore dance groups give the youth dating opportunities. Hip-hop music is increasingly popular.

In urban areas, social inequality and class differences are pronounced. Youths from the upper class generally attend expensive private secondary schools, and go on to attend higher education. Practices of skin depigmentation (bleaching), homosexuality, ear and navel piercing, and tattooing are initiated by this sub-elite. These girls' and boys' clothing constitutes in itself a source of conflict with other young people, who envy them their fashionable clothes.

The effects of globalization are apparent. A survey of a high school in Conakry found that 80% of young people had joined gangs in emulation of information gleaned from Western sources, and 95.5% of nicknames loved by the youth are names of artists and sports figures established abroad.

Love and Sexuality

One generally marries very early in Guinea. Couples speak little about family planning (85% of women aged 45 to 49 have never discussed it with their partner). The rate of contraceptive availability and use, estimated at 3%, is still very low. A recent survey indicates that only 28% of girls know a contraceptive method, compared with 55% of men. Twelve percent of girls know where to find a contraceptive means and 6% of women in urban centers use a contraceptive method. Generally, there is little familiarity with or use of birth control.

In rural areas, having children is encouraged after marriage. However, a well-educated girl should manage not to "dishonor her parents" by having a baby out of wedlock. The shortage of family planning services offered is in line with the insufficiency of sexual education programs (only 17% of girls know about condoms, for example).

A recent survey indicates that 83% of boys aged 20 to 24 have sexual partners who are single. The multiplicity of sexual partners is a quite common practice in young teenagers. However, it is less pronounced in girls than in young boys.

Although illegal, prostitution is spreading. The average age of prostitute girls is 25. The youngest are around 14 and 16. Prostitution is above all practiced by girls and occasionally by students.

Homosexuality is visible in Guinea. There are little to no data available on the existence or prevalence of homosexuality in Guinea.

Sex remains taboo between parents and children. The law prohibits abortion. Health services, when they are not geographically distant, are financially inaccessible. All these factors together create and develop many health traumas, especially for girls and female adolescents. The rape and abuse of girls and young women is a serious problem.

Health Risk Behavior

The strong demographic growth (birth rate is 41 per 1,000) and general poverty in Guinea ensure a difficult existence for young people. The departure of young husbands seeking better economic opportunities or more freedom leads to the presence of numerous abandoned women in their twenties and thirties, in villages with many fewer men remaining.

Guinea has a low rate (35%) of children benefiting from a birth certificate. The illiteracy affecting most of the population makes it difficult to date and to classify births.

The greatest threat to the sexual health of teenagers is sexually transmittable diseases (STDs), especially HIV/AIDS. Fewer than one woman out of every two knows the name of one STD. AIDS strikes harder those who are more sexually active (15 to 49 years old). Malaria and tuberculosis remain threats as well.

About 40% (about 700,000) of children do not attend school or have dropped out of school as a consequence of poverty and a poor educational system.

It is not easy to categorize adolescents. However, there are roughly four types of youth and children who need special protection measures. The first are street children, who steal and prostitute themselves. As victims of the disintegration of families and of rural exodus, they are exposed to all type of diseases. Many of them end up in prison. The second are young workers. The majority of disadvantaged children live in rural areas, where the opportunity to see their situation improve is rare. Traditional farming can be tiring and demoralizing. Although suffering from a basic lack of education or training, rural working adolescents sometimes act as the heads of families while still single; that is, they must care for younger brothers and sisters and their old parents who remain in the village. They work hard without any social protection. Among disadvantaged youth there are also orphans, as well as young refugees and other volunteers involved in armed conflicts (Guinée 2000).

Young disadvantaged persons suffer from poor health and are often forced into risky situations. The most exposed to danger, numbering more than 3,000, are those who are employed in mines and quarries, where they execute painful and dangerous work. As they are less qualified than adults, they face risks of abuse and exploitation (including sexual abuse and exploitation).

Alcoholism is increasing among youth in Guinea. Almost all drug users are young: 90% of drug addicts are under the age of 35. This drug consumption leads to a rise in crime.

Violence among youth has been systematically tracked down in school and university milieu. It is composed of rudeness, eccentric clothes, fights, and destruction of goods organized by "clans." It is imperative for civil authorities to fight the extreme poverty in Guinea and to reinforce youngsters' hope for a better life. Young peasants every day leave the backward subsistence agricultural sector, though they are aware of the modern economy's difficulties. The country needs realistic educational reforms to address disadvantaged children problems (Colle 1997).

Education

At the tribal level, the common bond of kinship that binds members together encourages a certain solidarity, which is a source of strength for youngsters during difficult economic times (Ameillon 1964).

The Guinean educational system is a network of family and non-family-sponsored activities situated at two levels: formal and informal education. In the formal sector, Guinea devoted much effort to the development of its education system. Secondary education is completed by the student in seven years. From 700 junior high and high school students in 1958 the number increased to about 150,000 students within 40 years. But this improvement has profited girls less (girls constituted 23% of students in 1990/91 and 25.91% in 1996/97). The representation of girls is still weaker, particularly in the study of the sciences. Public technical and vocational training institutions enroll fewer girls than do junior and high schools (i.e., 17% of students in 1998). At the university level girls are even less present, composing less than 6% of students (Copans 1998).

Primary education generally benefits from more focus than secondary education. However, everybody agrees that the quality of secondary and technical education will be more relevant for the future of the youth. Children go to junior secondary school at a key developmental stage in life, when they enter adolescence (aged 12 to 14). By the time adolescents complete their education, they will be 21 to 23 years of age.

Although adolescents will acquire knowledge and skills needed to make future life decisions, the extremely large number of students in classes, often numbering from 80 up to 120, hinders learning and leads to disruption in class. Concerning the flux of students in the system, one notices a high repetition rate (more than 25%) and of dropouts (19.7% in junior secondary school, 25.5% in high school in 2005). The insufficient number of teaching staff and school textbooks, and the total absence of laboratories are among the main causes of these malfunctions.

Special education is mainly for physically disabled persons. It is less developed than the general education system, although a school for the deaf and an institute for the blind both exist. There is no approach in principle that distinguishes gifted students from others. However, in terms of granting access to study in foreign universities, the government gives priority to the highest-scoring students who have successfully passed their baccalaureate exams. The success rates of Guinean students attending foreign universities are above average.

The overall illiteracy rate is high, although it dropped from 72% in 1990 to 67% in 1995. The number of illiterate women is higher than that of men (80%).

Work

Traditional modes of apprenticeship are still a primary method of education in Guinea; in 1996, 110,000 apprentices were identified as actively working. Only 22.3% of active apprentices are girls. Apprentices work in the areas of agriculture, cattle-breeding, blacksmithing, and traditional crafts such as pottery. Girls learn farming methods, and are also responsible for food preparation. Men focus on producing crops that are traded for income, such as coffee, cashew nuts, and potatoes.

In urban areas, unemployment is a concern. In 2003, 40% of the population lived below the poverty line (CIA World Factbook). However, new opportunities are arising for enterprising young people. Some adolescents and young adults sell extra food their families do not eat, to bring in additional income. Others travel to neighboring countries to sell manufactured goods (mainly made in Asia) or to work in mines and on plantations (Dioubate and Lachaud 1992).

In urban areas, many young people spend most of their time in school. However, in rural areas and smaller towns, adolescents are compelled to help their families produce food. Those that do attend school may assist their teachers working in the fields on weekends. Young people are open to innovative or nontraditional ways of earning an income. Therefore, they learn quickly how to repair a watch or to serve as a guide to rich people who go to markets to do their shopping. Adolescents may learn to cut hair or polish shoes. Such jobs are preferable to those that more desperate young people may turn to, such as prostitution.

Media

As of 2001, there were six low-power TV stations available in Guinea. There are also three active AM radio stations, and one FM radio station (CIA World Factbook). Several programs target mainly the young people with programs relating to civics, scientific documentaries, general knowledge, spare-time activities, and community life. But these programs are rarely interactive. Opportunities for listeners to express their feelings about these programs are few. Young people often prefer to listen to foreign radio stations.

In general, the private newspaper industry addresses itself first to the solvent adult community. Adolescents find little that is addressed to them in the newspapers.

Telephone service is generally poor to fair. In 2003, there were 26,200 telephone landlines in use and 111,500 mobile phones in use (CIA World Factbook).

Internet access only became available in 1997. There are approximately 40,000 Internet subscribers in the country (2003 estimate), almost all of whom live in Conakry where the data-processing industry is concentrated. The young academics are very active applicants of these new technologies.

Adolescents go to the cinema assiduously. They appreciate Western and Hindu films mainly. Piracy methods allow one to watch films at home, including music videos and pornography. Religious leaders express dismay over the exposure of young people to what they perceive to be damaging media forms.

Politics and Military

Youth and women played a key role in sustaining the vitality of political parties within the framework of the integrated multiparty system. However, the prolonged presence of more than 500,000 refugees from Liberia, Sierra-Leone, and Côte d'Ivoire presented a stark contrast to the supposedly honored respect given to human rights.

Various modes of introduction into political activity are aimed at young people. Junior deputies are students who are democratically elected by their schoolmates to attend parliamentary sessions for two years. All people have the right to vote at age 18.

As a member of the Economic Community Of West African States (ECOWAS) Guinea sent military units as part of an ECOWAS-sponsored action to interpose between belligerents during civil wars in Sierra Leone, Liberia, and Guinea Bissau. Good salaries paid by the UN forces to such soldiers attracted more young "volunteers."

The civil war between Liberia and Sierra Leone affected Guinea directly in 2000 and 2001, when Guinea and Liberia each accused the other of supporting dissidents, and Liberia-backed Guinean dissidents and rebels from Sierra Leone attacked Guinea, resulting in over 1,000 Guinean deaths and the displacement of more than 100,000 Guineans. When Guinea was attacked, approximately 9,000 "young volunteers" supported the overtaxed national army. Young people displaced by the aggression against Guinea who did not join the army often became a threat to civil stability. Many of them joined various militia groups. To fight insecurity, the government involved young people in the fight against neighboring countries and internal

militias. "Communal brigades" were thus created. Town mayors recruited unemployed youths between the ages of 17 and 24 to join these brigades.

DIRUS DIALÉ DORE

References and Further Reading

Ameillon, B. 1964. *La Guinée: Bilan d'une indépendance.* Paris: Maspero.

Arcin, A. 1907. *La Guinée française, race, religion, coutumes, commerce.* Paris: Challamel.

Barry, A., et al. Enquête nationale sur la prévalence du VIH/SIDA en Guinée.

Boudon, J. 1994. *Sauvegarde des compétences structurelles et ajustement structurel: Le cas de la Guinée.* Genève: Étude de politique, N° 12 BIT.

CIA World Factbook. http://www.cia.gov/cia/publications/factbook/geos/gv.html.

Colle, C. (ed.). 1997. *La Guinée à l'aube du 3ème millénaire.* Conakry: Chantal colle conseil.

Copans, J. 1998. *La longue marche de la modernité africaine: Savoirs, intellectuels, démocratie.* Paris: Karthala.

Devet, M. 1997. *La Guinée.* Paris: Karthala.

Dioubate, Y., and J-P. Lachaud. 1992. *Pauvreté et marché du travail à Conakry.* Genève, DP/49: Institut International d'Etudes Sociales (IIED).

Ellis, S. 1999. *The mask of anarchy. The destruction of Liberia and the religious dimension of an African civil war.* New York: New York University Press.

Facteurs de blocage à l'utilisation du préservatif par les jeunes de 15 à 24 ans. 2005. Conakry: Mars.

Guinée, Enquête Démographique et de Santé (EDS). 2000. *Ministère du plan et de la coopération.* Conakry.

Mogenet, L. 1999. *Guide de la Guinée imprimerie.* Mission catholique: Conakry.

Smith Négrologie, S. 2003. *Calman levy.*

H

HONDURAS

Background Information

Honduras is one of the five Central American countries. It has an area of 112,492 square kilometers and a population of 6.5 million. The population's annual growth rate is 2.7% per year. Of the total population, 46% live in urban areas, with a high level of population concentrated in the cities of Tegucigalpa and San Pedro Sula. Approximately 5.2 million of its inhabitants live in poverty (Informe Sobre Desarrollo Humano, Honduras 2003).

For the last several decades, Honduras has been primarily an agro-forestry economy, being one of the biggest wood export countries, but the absence of rain and the high levels of deforestation have affected both activities.

Since 1980, the country has been governed by a democratically elected president and a congress composed of 128 representatives and a supreme justice court.

Six ethnic minority groups, including the mestizo population (which is the prevalent ethnic group), exist in Honduras: Chortis, Lencas, Misquitos, Tawahcas, and Xicaques.

The majority of the population is Roman Catholic, with a growing number attending Protestant churches. Protestant churches are increasingly drawing people away from the Catholic Church.

In 1998, Honduras was affected by Hurricane Mitch, which destroyed almost all the country's infrastructure, including schools, paved roads, bridges—all of which are contributing factors to the increasing poverty.

Since the 1980s, Honduras has intended to promote structural changes to overcome the situation described above by eliminating the weakness of the educational system, upgrading the literacy level, enhancing the health conditions, and improving the economic conditions of the majority of the Honduran population.

Period of Adolescence

In 2000, the estimated adolescent population was 155 million, including youth between the ages of 10 and 24. Youth between the ages of 10 and 19 represent 20% of the total population in urban areas. Honduras is a country where more than half of its population is under 15 years of age. It is expected to increase at a progressive increment of 4% per year, representing a great challenge for the

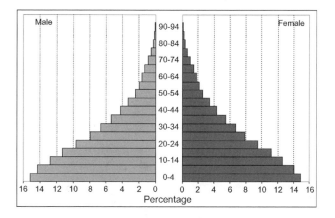

Figure 1. Honduras population structure by sex and age Honduras, 2000.
Source: World Health Organization. Pan-American Health Organization, 2002.

Table 1. Honduran Adolescent Population

Girls, boys, and adolescents	2,315,886
Girls, boys, and adolescent workers	356,241
Male	73.6%
Female	26.4%
From 5–9 years	5.3%
From 10–14 years	42.7%
From 15–17 years	52.0%
Urban residents	30.8%
Rural residents	69.2%
Total	100.0%

Source: 2002 Child Labor Survey. Statistical information and follow up program. International Program for Child Labour Eradication.

government to create social infrastructures such as schools, hospitals, and community services. The high birthrate and the migration from rural to urban areas are considered the biggest problems in Tegucigalpa and San Pedro Sula. Honduran adolescents as a group have been invisible primarily due to a lack interest among the authorities; a lack of statistical information and representative data reflects adolescents' profile and situation. Through the end of the twentieth century, the government (through the Health Ministry) considered adolescents a priority in the definition of policies, creating the unit known as Integral Attention to Adolescents (PAIA) in 1987.

It is vital for society to give adolescents a different identification, as it is a stage where early developmental conflicts are revived. It is also a key stage for identity consolidation.

Honduran adolescents, as in all societies, enter adolescence individually, and it is perceived as a time of crisis, as the child's body transforms into an adult body. Adolescence is a period of change, individuation, and identity consolidation.

The majority of the information regarding Honduran adolescents presents three main stages: early adolescence (10 to 13 years of age), middle adolescence (14 to 16 years of age), and late adolescence (17 to 19 years of age); however, the Honduras Legislation has defined the ages between 13 to 25 years of age for this stage. This ambiguity creates difficulties when applying the laws regarding the age group between 20 and 25, since sometimes they can be regarded as adults and at other times as adolescents.

The basic characteristics of early adolescence are disregard for parental authority; increased interest in one's sexuality, physical appearance, and relationships with friends; and a lack of plans for the future coupled with a focus on the present. It is also evident that many youngsters at this early stage may already become independent. During the second stage of adolescence, confrontations with parents and other authority figures continue, acceptance of one's physical appearance gradually occurs, close friendships with the other sex develop, a sense of power and invulnerability develops, and a quest for one's own identity and self-image begins. During this stage sexual activity and cohabiting may begin. The late stage of adolescence is characterized by a clear self-identity not influenced by the opinions of parents and friends, as well as a developed interest in close and lasting heterosexual relations. A sense of independence is more obvious, and the late adolescent is able to start working, which allows the development of economic independence. Each year 125,000 youths reach the category of adolescence. They represent 1.5 million of the total population of Honduras, of which 46% live in urban areas, 110,000 are the head of a family, and 47% are economically active (Ejecución de Menores en Honduras 2001).

Parents are responsible for financially supporting their children. Adolescents can either begin working very early, or they can stay at home until they married, or they can conclude their higher education.

Beliefs

In general the country tends toward collectivism, with high levels of idealism regarding religion and political parties (as well as the national soccer team). The principles of democracy, equality, freedom, and participation are strongly advertised, but in reality they are conditioned by the socioeconomic

situation. A history of strong Catholic beliefs and rural traditions centered on the extended family and community relations explains the tendency toward collectivism. However, traditional practices are disappearing in the big cities and peripheral areas, where many families from small towns have moved. There the sense of belonging to a community is almost nonexistent, thereby promoting a sense of loneliness among adolescents. Consequently, they join groups such as gangs that are socially unacceptable.

Churches also play an important role in the adolescent's life; they see churches as centers of hope when the economic and social situation is unbearable.

Values are taught by extended family relations, grandparents, and close relatives, who play an important role in cases where parents have emigrated either from the home town or from the country to get a job. Also, school is considered a means for values-teaching. All churches work hard to integrate youngsters into religious activities, with Protestant churches exerting a strong influence in rural areas.

The Catholic Church has organized different types of groups for all ages: marriage encounter groups, charismatic groups, catechumens groups, and gospel celebrators among others. Protestant churches also have special groups.

Baptism, confirmation, confession, first communion, marriages, and Sunday mass all are very strong among families and are translated to adolescents through an extended family network (grandparents, parents, uncles, and so on). Nonetheless, actually many Protestant churches are emerging in the country, and adolescents are the main target through youth groups.

Baptism is done at a very early age; parents and godparents make a promise to commit the baby to the Catholic Church. If both parents are absent or dead, the godparents have the obligation to raise and care for the child. Confirmation and first communion is done during childhood or adolescence, and they represent a big step in following the Catholic principles.

Marriage is also considered a significant celebration; the rite is followed by groups at all socioeconomic levels. It begins with the preparation of the couple to be married, which consists of several conferences with the priest and family counselors to give them an overview of the responsibilities of marriage. The marriage rite is one of the most celebrated rites of Catholic Church. A special mass is part of the rite, and again godparents are beside the future couple—most of the time these are best friends or close relatives. After the religious ceremony, a party is organized to drink and eat special food cooked by relatives.

Gender

Honduras, like many other Latin societies, has generally been marked by male dominance over women. At a very early age, girls generally recognize that they are expected to perform different roles than men and vice versa. The unequal distribution of family responsibilities among adolescents, differing reproductive abilities, and the lack of domestic service support contributes to inequity for women. Girls are expected to serve their male brothers, to have little or no opinion regarding politics and sports, to primarily stay at home, and to help with household activities such as cooking, laundry, and childcare. In so doing, it is believed that they are learning what they need to know to be good wives and mothers.

Although more men enter elementary school, the percentage of women completing secondary education is higher (63%). This is probably because many young males are forced to abandon school at an early age to enter the world of work and become the head of the family. Women are more likely than ever before to attend school and get a job. The level of education for women has increased, including higher education. Increasing numbers of adolescents attend school and earn degrees or advanced training. There is a significant difference in school attendance for boys and girls. In poor rural families with low educational levels, the number of girls studying is higher than boys, due to the fact that at a very early age boys begin to work outside the home, while girls work within the home, allowing them to attend school either in the morning or in the afternoon. When the family educational level is higher in both areas (rural and urban) the level of attendance is almost equal; therefore it is clear that higher levels of education have an impact on equity for girls and boys.

There is evidence that the family's opinion of education, as well as the mother's educational level, affects gender equity. Educated women are more likely to become teachers, nurses, and secretaries, and a few women with advance degrees hold high positions either in government or the private sector. Examples include the president of the Supreme Court, who is a woman, as well as a few congresswomen. Nonetheless, inequity persists; two out of three women are unpaid housewives. They have to struggle to obtain higher working positions.

In middle- and high-socioeconomic-level families, working conditions are related to educational levels, and both males and females look forward to obtaining a university degree. In many cases they become independent entrepreneurs as owners of small businesses such as beauty parlors, restaurants, gyms, and florist shops, which helps create more equality between the genders.

Historically, certain jobs and careers have been considered appropriate only for men and others only for women: only men were construction workers, electricians, or gardeners, while only women were nursery workers, teachers, social workers, beauticians, cooks, and maids.

At lower socioeconomic levels, both males and females are forced to abandon school and enter the labor market at an early age. Uneducated females are most likely to get jobs as housemaids, babysitters, and or in a sweatshop. Uneducated males are most likely to enter the fields of construction, farming, auto drivers. When these possibilities are not available, uneducated men and women may become street merchants, offering different products from food to auto parts.

Female adolescents increasingly work. This is a response to poor economic conditions; it also represents a qualitative behavior change as female adolescents move away from an image as a secondary labor force, and the income obtained through their work is increasingly important in terms of the overall family income. However, preconceptions regarding women's traditional roles, as well as language barriers, family responsibilities, and limited training and experience affect the acceptance of female adolescents in certain careers. This then affects young women's overall job opportunities, training opportunities, and salary options. Nevertheless, there is a strong movement among women to gain equality not only at work but in the home as well.

There is a tendency among middle- and upper-socioeconomic-level adolescents to emulate American cultural patterns, and for that reason female adolescents want to be skinny, to diet, and to regularly work out at gyms. Males also are very much inclined to follow American trends in clothing, diets, and especially exercise for muscle development. In all socioeconomic levels there is a strong motivation to look American. Girls dye their hair blonde, while boys emulate punk styles in hair and clothing. Rap music and hip-hop culture are also popular.

In relationships, male adolescent infidelity is common, and females are expected to overlook it and even to accept it as a normal male characteristic.

For females, infidelity is seen as a sign of prostitution and can be socially punishing, with not only the male partner but also the parents doing the punishing. This cultural pattern is maintained even in adult relationships.

Women are expected to become mothers before they reach their thirties, and it is considered a tragedy when a woman is not able to establish a solid relationship in which she can become a mother. Women are expected to be full-time mothers regardless of their job responsibilities outside the home. Professional women often have to leave their careers permanently, regardless of success, since mothering becomes the number one priority.

Because of the pervasive influence of the Catholic Church, abortion is frowned upon. Abortion is seen as a crime and in many cases adolescents are denied medical services in emergencies resulting from abortions. Thus, many young girls who become pregnant must become young mothers. In some cases the girl's parents adopt the child, assuming total responsibility for childrearing. Responsibility for a child conceived during adolescence generally falls to the female, who becomes a single parent at a young age.

Men are expected to be heads of their families. They are in charge, and they are the primary authority figure. As women are increasingly contributing to the overall family income through jobs, men have begun to help their wives with childcare activities such as diaper changing and feeding, that were traditionally seen as women's duties.

The Self

Honduran adolescents are shy around strangers, generally introverted, and greet non-family members with varying degrees of skepticism and distrust. They have difficulty initiating and maintaining a conversation in topics other than the national soccer team and the main news stories.

Habitat and place of origin plays a key role in the shaping of the Honduran adolescent identity. Sixty-two percent of the total population identifies more with the place they live than with their religious group, ethnic group, or social class. The place of birth creates emotional links and certain forms of closeness to their family, neighbors, and traditions that influence personality formation (Informe de Desarrollo Humano, Honduras 2003).

Among the relevant diversity of characteristics that are considered as defining Hondurans are the following: pacifist, good natured, humble, and introverted (Informe de Desarrollo Humano, Honduras 2003).

Because of the strong influence of North American culture, Honduran adolescents struggle with the need to conform; they wear imported clothes, eat imported food, and listen to imported music, disregarding native food, folk music, and lifestyles. Considering this struggle, adolescents are more inclined to the use of drugs, alcohol, and other substances that few years ago were not available in Honduras.

Because males are traditionally identified as providers for the family, to obtain a job and bring economic support to the family is an important factor for establishing male identity during adolescence, particularly in low-socioeconomic-level families.

Females are identified with household chores, raising children, and caring for the male partner. Honduran adolescents have difficulties in having a positive self-image, due probably to early work in marginal employment, early desertion from school, early sexual activity, and traumatic life experiences, including harm to the self-esteem, threats to masculinity, and hopelessness. There has been found in adolescents an inability to cope with frustration, impulsivity, and a crescendo sentiment of abandon by family and society (Krauskopf 2002).

Adolescents' invisibility is clear in Honduras, particularly in rural areas where they are ignored not only in the country's legal definition of agricultural development and by not acknowledging that children and adolescents play an important role in the agricultural field, but also in cultural aspects of the community, as when adolescents' opinions and proposals are not considered, but their labor is fundamental for family survival. In other words, children's work is invisible and unaccounted for.

Limitation of participation favors migration to big cities, which are not prepared to receive more people. This process facilitates the anomie and disorganized social behavior patterns that produce a sensation of confusion and failure.

Adolescents' visibility emerges easily in regard to negative aspects: early pregnancy, drugs, and violence. Relevance is given to those who have problems and must be helped with delinquency, use of drugs, and sexuality (Krauskopf 2002).

The vast majority of Hondurans could be characterized as mestizos (a mixed biological ancestry from Spanish and native cultures), who follow a wide variety of indigenous and Spanish customs, constituting the Hispano-American patterns of culture.

Black communities have a defined self-image and a cultural identity, with a particular language, music, and food. They are identified as the Garifuna's culture.

The U.S. influence in Honduran society has fundamentally affected the self-image of adolescents. Cable TV, fast-food franchising, music, clothing, hairstyles, and drug use are some examples of the strongest influences, because with a lack of a strong native role model they are more likely to imitate imported cultural tendencies.

Adolescents in Honduran culture are more likely to be in groups than alone, and this need for belonging has made the antisocial groups (*maras*) grow stronger.

In addition to physical conditions (appearance), educational factors (school achievement), emotional situations (conflict with parents and peers), the rapid rhythm of innovations (more information, exposure to commercial audiovisual images, and acceleration of cultural interactions), adolescents will require new cognitive, emotional, and social abilities to confront difficulties. A significant number of adolescents will have difficulty in developing a positive self-image.

Honduras' wave of immigration is not a problem; rather the problem is the rising number of adolescents who cross the Mexican border to fulfill the "American dream." Honduran authorities estimate that between 100,000 and 150,000 Hondurans travel illegally to the United States, paying "coyotes" a large amount of money (between $2,500 and $4,000). The majority of them are youths and small children, carried on their mothers' arms (Palencia 2005). The Migration National Forum in Honduras has estimated that approximately 600,000 Hondurans live in the United States illegally. The migration of Hondurans to the United States is a consequence of poverty, the lack of opportunities in Honduras, and the expectations they have about a better quality of life, considering economic aspects as the main factor of improvement. This situation has reached an important dimension in Honduras' population; although it has a positive impact in economic aspects, it has produced family disintegration. Roughly $500 million USD are sent annually by the immigrants to their families in Honduras, and it is considered that this money surpasses the amount generated by the Honduran economy from the export of bananas, wood shrimps, coffee, and tourism (Puerta 2002).

The U.S. government has granted to Honduran immigrants an opportunity to obtain a temporary permit through the Temporal Protection Program (TPS), becoming a window of legalization for Hondurans in the United States. Some 85,000 are protected under the temporal protection status

(TPS), which was given to immigrants that arrived in the United States before December 1998.

Nonetheless, according to information from the Government and Justice Ministry, from 1996 to 2003 around 41,019 Hondurans were deported from the United States (Flores and Antonio 2003).

Family Relationships

Honduras' birthrate has decreased in recent years. In 1987, the number of children per family was 5.6; in 1995 it was 4.9, and in 2000 it decreased to 4.4 children per family.

In 2001, a census showed that in Honduras there are 1,211,307 heads of homes, of which 907,609 are men and 303,698 are women. In 1988, 21.7% of homes were headed by women and in 2001 this number increased to 25.1%. This tendency is more evident in urban homes. More than 40% of female heads of families live in Tegucigalpa and San Pedro Sula. In rural areas the percentage is lower, at 19.3% (Flores and Antonio 2003).

Discussions among parents and children are common in adolescence, since through confrontation youngsters learn to define their own identity. However, not all discussions are favorable to the positive development of adolescents. In Honduras adolescents suffer the constant criticism and mock from parents regarding their inclinations to music, clothing, and for disruptive behavior at home, fights with brothers and sisters; this can be highly damaging for the definition of the adolescent's identity. The situation tends to worsen when parents and adolescents do not have open and friendly communication over topics such as drugs, alcohol, and sex, among others. These situations are more damaging in low-education-level families, due to strong traditions and illiteracy among the parents, who find it difficult to understand new social trends and to give support to their children.

Because parents' and adolescents' relations tend to be tense, adolescents lack a guide to help them recognize what is expected from them and a model figure with whom to reflect and get support. Adolescents receive messages that their needs and feelings are not important, and to attract others' attention they are inclined toward risk behaviors.

Family relationships are also influenced by socioeconomic conditions, gender, and type of residence—rural or urban. In high-socioeconomic-level families it is more probable that education, recreation, acceptance, and the ability to reconsider options figure in adolescents' lives. Introduction by the family too early to roles for which adolescents are not ready forces them to postpone developmental tasks and makes adolescence a conflictive period.

Adolescent pregnancy is common; 23.2% of adolescents have had a child before reaching 20 years of age (Encuesta Nacional de Salud 2002). In many cases the girl remains at her parent's home, and parents or grandparents raise the child, becoming an extended family in which everybody plays an important role.

As expressed by adolescents, family is considered one of the most important and reliable source of information. However, they also considered that neither school, mass media, nor the family helps them in solving satisfactorily their need for health and sexual information.

In a great number of Honduran families—regardless of the socioeconomic level—both parents have to work; in low-socioeconomic levels they work for economic factors, and in high-socioeconomic-levels they work for social status factors. Therefore, children are left in the first case either with grandparents, older siblings, aunts, or other close relatives; in the latter they are left with maids. In both cases parents have few opportunities to have quality time with their children and to have a strong influence on them.

The immigration to the United States has created a huge problem in Honduras. Parents have left their families to work in the United States, and although this results in low-socioeconomic-level families having better living conditions (because these parents send financial support back to the family), socially and psychologically problems arise due to the lack of support and appropriate role models for adolescents, creating the conditions for the development of delinquent conduct.

Friends and Peers/Youth Culture

The majority of Honduran adolescents survive under extreme poverty and unhealthy conditions. They initiate working from an early age when they should be playing, studying, and enjoying recreational opportunities. Most adolescents prefer to be around friends than with family. Peer crowds are fundamentally related to their participation as spectators in the national sport: football. Some go dancing and drinking on weekends.

Because of a strong social-class separation, adolescents most frequently get together with those who are similar; for instance, those who attend private secondary or higher educational institutions meet in particular places that are considered privileged areas. Meanwhile, those from public institutions and from poor barrios do not have

the financial conditions to do that. The *parques* (parks) have been replaced by the big malls and shopping centers where young people meet to walk, eat, and buy.

This situation has created a polarized society in which a few have access to all the commodities available, and for the vast majority they are denied, promoting conditions for social inconformity.

The government, through the Culture and Sport Ministry, has intended to create conditions to promote culture and sports activities in Honduran communities, creating the Houses of Culture and Community Sport centers. Despite the efforts made, there are still a great number of communities where children and adolescents do not have recreational opportunities and therefore are inclined to alcohol drinking and other psychotropic drugs.

Youth organizations are mainly religious groups (Catholic and Protestant), boy and girl scouts groups, and secondary school student organizations. It has been found that more than 70% of adolescents do not belong to any organization, and only 3% mention belonging to a cultural organization (Adolescents Opinion Survey 2000).

Adolescents' belonging to a group gives them a reference for their own life: to develop an acceptable identity, reach their goals, receive guidance, norms, and values. The group favors the appropriation of sex roles, transition from family dependence toward autonomy, opportunities and widening experiences, and social participation.

There has been over the years a strong influence of American music among adolescents, even to those who do not know the language. Listening to this type of music is considered an important aspect for an adolescent's popularity. Dress and hairstyle are very distinctive and copy North American youth styles. Ear piercing has been a tradition for women and is done at a very early age. Due to external influences it has become common for men too. Specific cults are not a common activity among regular adolescent groups, but existing gangs practice some types of occult behavior that is considered satanic. Tattooing, certain nonverbal behaviors, and criminal activities are among the rites these groups partake in as part of their roles among the groups. These groups have emerged as a result of lack of educational, recreational, and work opportunities. These groups give adolescents a sense of belonging, love, and power, which they lack in their own families. They are connected to crimes, drugs, and general violent behavior. The Honduran government has implemented a special law against them called the Anti-maras Law, which punishes those who participate in such groups with 20-year prison sentences and a $50,000 fine. Honduras, El Salvador, and Guatemala have in the *maras* a major security problem to the degree that in 2004 during the 26th Meeting of the Central American System of Integration, officials signed an agreement with Mexico and the United States to establish a task force against this problem (Adital).

The Inter-American Human Right Commission (IHRC) has asked to visit Honduras, El Salvador, and Guatemala to verify the application and effectiveness of the Anti-*maras* Law, since many humanitarian organizations have denounced it as arbitrary, antidemocratic, and in violation of human rights.

Love and Sexuality

In Honduras dating has been part of the traditional rituals of society. When the relation becomes formal, boys visit girls with the permission of the parents (mainly from the father) and from that point both are committed to fidelity and are seen by parents as in a premarriage relationship. During this period parents do not give consent for sexual relations, nonetheless it is known that they occur anyway.

An epidemiology and family health survey conducted in 1996 revealed that 10.5% of adolescents had had sexual activity before reaching 15 years of age, and 46.5% had it before reaching 18 years. It also revealed that more than 75% of the male adolescents had sexual activity before reaching 18 years of age, and 23% had their first pregnancy at 20 years of age (Programa de Atención Integral a la Adolescencia, Secretaria de Salud de Honduras 2001).

It is estimated that one of every five abortions is in the adolescent age group. The vulnerability of this age group is seen in the statistics of sexually transmitted diseases and HIV. The high prevalence of AIDS (12,736 cases) affects mostly those between 20 and 39 years of age.

In Honduras, as in many other Latin American countries, adolescent sexuality is still a difficult topic to discuss. There is a tendency to accept gender-based double standards, by which females and males accept and justify double sexual standards and constraints imposed on the sexual behavior of females. Young males, for example, are widely perceived to need premarital sexual experience and a variety of partners; females are not so perceived. The need to conform to this double standard may force females to fear disclosure of their own sexual activity and consequently inhibit

sexual active adolescents to seek contraception and other reproductive health services. This double standard also prevents pregnant adolescents from getting support from family and a safe resolution of pregnancy.

Sexual negotiation among female adolescents is also a double-standard-related problem; females feel that they cannot negotiate timing of sexual activity or the use of contraceptives or condoms due to their fear of being called "bad quality girls" with no morals or "Christian values."

Cohabitation is most common in rural areas due to the early participation of youngsters in the world of work. In urban middle-class families and in high-class families, sexual activity among adolescents is very common but is kept secret and they (boys and girls) live in their own homes.

Homosexuality is seen as a perversion; the topic is not discussed openly, and for families with gay or lesbian children it is a disgrace and a punishment. Due to strong Catholic influences both gays and lesbians live a "closeted life." The government has recognized the right of homosexuals to have a legal organization represent them, and the legal status has been granted. Despite this fact, a new law is going to be approved by which homosexuals will be denied the right to marry and adopt Honduran children.

Early sexual initiation and childbearing are associated with poor nutrition, poor or nonexistent prenatal care, premature delivery, complicated childbirth, low birth weight babies, a higher proportion of babies born with additional complications, poorer infant outcomes, and the probability of less adequate parenting.

Health Risk Behavior

Youth in Honduras live under many factors related to insecurity, few educational opportunities, and few job opportunities. Honduras' adolescence statistics have shown a strong correlation with violence. It affects differently women and men. Frequently, women are the victims and men the aggressors. Women are mostly affected by domestic violence; men are affected in the streets and in cases relating to alcohol, drugs, and gangs. Sexual violence is high among Honduran adolescents. In 1998, 53% of sexual aggressions occurred in adolescents 13 to 18 years of age (Diagnostico Situacional en Honduras 2000).

Epidemiologic information is scarce. Statistical information is not treated separately for age groups or for gender. Adolescent health development is threatened by many problems, including the consequences of premature or unprotected sexual activity; abuse of alcohol and tobacco; accidents; violence, including suicide; malnutrition; and certain infections, including tuberculosis. These problems not only have common origins, but they are interrelated in terms of cause and effect.

The information available regarding mortality is not representative of the actual situation. The mortality rate among adolescents is low if compared with other age groups. According to the Pan-American Health Organization, the main causes of death in those between 10 and 14 years are accidents, violence, and infections, whereas in the group between 15 to 19 years of age, the causes are accidents, homicides, suicides, and pregnancy complications (OPS 1998).

Adolescent health statistics are linked with violence. The first cause of mortality is related to homicides, suicides, car accidents, poisoning, and traumatism, making a total of 23%. Diverse infections (17%), HIV (16%), and pregnancy-associated causes (9%) are also considered important causes in adolescent death. In 1997, it was reported that at the Honduran Medical School approximately 30% of the medical attention requested for pregnancy was given to adolescents (Rodriguez and Javier 2001).

Child sexual abuse affects mostly girls, although boys are victims too. Due to the cultural norms around masculinity, many cases are not reported. According to forensic medicine information, sexual aggression in Honduras and other Central American countries affects mostly children and adolescents between the ages of 10 and 19 years of age. From 59% to 69% of rapes and between 43% and 93% of sexual abuse occur in women younger than 20 years. The gender ratios of aggression is three to four women for every man (Molina Cartes 1998).

HIV/AIDS and other sexually transmitted infections and unintended pregnancy are among the most pressing sexual and reproductive health issues that youth in Honduras face. Honduras reports an HIV-prevalence rate among the general population of between 1% and 3%. Studies conducted by the Health Ministry (ENESF 1996) reveal that 45% of the 18-year-old girls have had sexual relations; half of those who are sexually active had their first child at that age. The total fertility rate in Honduras (4.4%) is among the highest in Latin America, with 12% to 14% attributable to births among adolescents. This combination of high HIV prevalence and early sexual initiation (as evidenced by early first childbearing) increases the risk of HIV transmission. Gender disparities and the societal notions

of male and female identities also fuel sexual risk-taking behavior and young women's and men's vulnerability to STI/HIV and unwanted pregnancy. Thus, dual protection can reduce one's vulnerability to those unintended consequences.

Other adolescent social and health problems are related to pregnancy, mental health problems, juvenile delinquency, car accidents, use of drugs, nutritional problems, tuberculosis, growth alteration, and dental problems. A significant group are subject to physical and sexual abuse. The opportunities for recreations and sports are very limited, and for this reason the possibilities for getting in contact with drugs, alcohol, and gangs are high.

Drugs used by adolescents are mainly alcohol (one of every three youths), tobacco, marijuana, inhalants, and cocaine. The main factors promoting these conditions, as identified by adolescents, are family disintegration, sex work, and alcoholic parents (Ejecución de menores en Honduras, Comisionado Nacional de los Derechos Humanos 2001). The use of drugs is linked to similar problems and adolescents stated that drugs help them to "forget problems" and avoid "feeling hungry." Violence is the main mortality risk factor in adolescents. Several investigations conducted by the Health Ministry have revealed that youths initiate alcohol drinking between the ages of 10 and 16 years and that in 78% of homes where adolescents live, alcohol and tobacco are the substances consumed the most.

A study conducted by the Honduras Institute for the Prevention of Alcoholism, Drug Addiction, and Dependence on Pharmaceuticals revealed that 43% of secondary school students had used alcohol, 17% tobacco, 17% amphetamines, 2% marijuana, 1.5% inhalants, 1% cocaine, and the rest (18.5%) had used none of them (IHADFA 1998).

The environment of extreme poverty prevailing in the majority of Honduran homes has an impact on adolescents' exposure to severe risk experiences and few opportunities to access protective resources. The conflicting family relations are accompanied by abandonment, physical abuse, expulsion from home, alcoholism, absence of parental figure, and belonging to peer groups oriented toward antisocial conduct, violence, and addiction to drugs. No less important are not having a job, not assisting with school, low self-esteem, and absence of a plan for the future.

Adolescents in Honduras, mainly the poor, have no real free time. The absence of real educational and work options does not allow them to organize their time. When they become members of gangs, the initiation rites demand total dedication to compromises. Delinquent acts and recreation are not differentiated.

All these mentioned conditions contribute to a visual of adolescence as a period of risk and disorder; therefore, parents, authorities, and the community are now considering the development of special programs that will contribute to a better understanding of this stage on the adult side and a better adjustment of adolescents to new situations.

Education

The adolescent population register in the Hondurans school system represents 63% of the total population between the ages of 5 and 19; this indicates that 37% of children and adolescents have no access to education (Salud y Desarrollo de Adolescentes y Jovenes 2000).

In Honduras, out of every 100 adolescents that finish elementary education only 41% enter secondary education, and from those who finish secondary education only 14.3% continue to higher education. To a large degree, the future economic development of Honduras depends on having increasing proportions of the population who are reasonably well-educated, healthy, and economically productive. There is also an important interaction between economic opportunity and the readiness of today's youth to take advantage of it. Without the realistic hope of getting ahead economically, there is little incentive for youth to invest in education or protect themselves from some of the less healthy habits they may acquire during adolescence. But without the expectation that there will be a qualified workforce to fill newly created jobs, potential investors may be reluctant to make the necessary commitments to economic development. To the extent that the country's youth of today and tomorrow are not prepared for that future, hopes for the country's economic future become increasingly dim.

Education in Honduras is limited in quantity and quality; adolescents are confronted with the problems of insufficient and inequitable academic offerings, insufficient schools and teachers, all conditions influenced by financial factors.

Regarding education aspects measured through the literacy rate, an important improvement is shown: illiteracy rates diminished from 31.3% to 20% from 1990 to 2001. The number of study years has improved also; from 4.3 to 6.2 (in 1994 it was 4.2 years). The percentage of children attending preschool is 35.2%, whereas the elementary school rate is 75.9%, and the high school rate 22.7%. Higher education rates are 14% of the

total population that completes secondary education. Of every 100 students that complete elementary school, 41 enter secondary education.

Access to technology and information from the globalized world is not equal in rural zones, urban, and marginal urban zones. This fact means that they do not have the opportunity to receive the impact of multicultural influences in the formation of their identities.

Of all adolescents registered in secondary education, 2.5% drop out, and 10.3% fail and must repeat grades. The opportunities for professional training are very limited and when available are performed at INFOP (National Professional Training Institute).

Gifted adolescents in general do not attend special schools, and they lose the opportunity to excel in specific areas.

Disabled children and adolescents either attend special private schools or are integrated into the regular school setting, but their opportunities to be incorporated into society are very limited. IHNFA (Insituto Hondureño de la Niñez y la familia) considers that in Honduras there exists around 225,000 children and adolescents with some kind of disability, with 80% of them living in rural areas in extreme poverty. The main causes are malnutrition, diseases, and birth traumas. It is also recognized that the lack of education, information, and absence of preventive actions are a major cause of disabilities among the young population.

In Honduras there are two specific laws for the protection of disabled persons: Habitation and Rehabilitation Law and the Disabled Employment Law.

Work

Adolescent working conditions in Honduras are a consequence of the existing economic conditions, including the inequity in the distribution of the national income. Poverty in Honduras is a structural problem and is the main factor that limits social and economic rights for wide sectors of the population, including adolescents. Child labor is considered a consequence of the limited economic conditions, and to overcome it, it will be necessary to have a strong, modern, and competitive economy. Because of the marginality in which the majority of adolescents live, they are forced to work.

In 2002, 20% of the richest homes received 61.1% of the income, whereas the poorest 20% received 1.9%. Many youngsters are forced to abandon school to contribute to the family income. This situation diminishes the possibilities for a better future and quality life. The economically active adolescent population increased in 1999 to 41.9%; this is equivalent to 142,170 adolescents working, 43.8% of whom are male and 40.9% of whom work in rural areas (Salud y Desarrollo de los Adolescentes y Jovenes 2002).

In 2002, the INE (Statistical National Institute) conducted an investigation in which it was found that 367,405 girls and boys between the ages of 5 and 17 were working or looking for a job. From this group, 73.6% were male and 26.4% were girls. The situation is mostly considered a rural problem: 69.2% live in rural areas and the rest in urban areas.

Adolescents' work possibilities are sporadic, require low qualifications, and provide low salary. Work search time and absence of guarantees are sources of frustration, self-esteem distortion, and weakened social participation for adolescents.

Ten out of every 1,000 homes are headed by adolescents, eight are male and two are women. Most of them work under subemployment conditions with no access to social security and with high health risk conditions. For the majority of children who are working, it means having to leave the school. They work on cane sugar, flower, and tobacco plantations, in domestic work, garbage collection, construction, transportation, and warehouses. Most of males work in agriculture and cattle activities; women work in sweatshops and in domestic activities. Domestic labor is considered the worst type of child work because of low salaries, lack of opportunities for study, lack of social and family contact, verbal, physical, and sexual abuse. The main reasons for adolescents to get a job, as expressed by parents, are to collaborate with the family expenses, to promote responsibility, to separate them from vices, and to "become an honest person" (la Encuesta del Trabajo Infantil en Honduras, San Jose Costa Rica 2003).

One of the major problems relating to working conditions in Honduras is domestic work. It is considered an exploitation labor, linked to problems of gender, socioeconomic class, and age in the context of poverty. The working conditions of domestic labor in third-party homes are characterized by long periods of work; low salaries; social and family alienation; verbal, physical, and sexual abuse; and lack of opportunities for study and recreation.

Girls that in their own homes are dedicated to household chores do not receive any remuneration and are also deprived of study and recreation opportunities.

The described situation applies to low-socio-economic-level adolescents. A low-middle-socio-economic-class family's adolescents are dedicated to studying and entering the world of work after secondary school, or continuing university studies as part-time students. High-socioeconomic-level youngsters are dedicated to fulfilling a university degree and living with the support of their parents until they are married or get a job.

However, Honduras has made efforts to improve the conditions of children and adolescents. In 1996, the Code for Children and Adolescents (Gaceta Nacional 1996) was approved. This code established general conditions on the topic of youngster protections against economic exploitation and abuse and in favor of education and health, among others. One of the regulations is the obligation of the state to formulate policies, elaborate, and execute programs to abolish child labor and give support to those families whose girls and boys live in risky conditions.

Media

The use of media by adolescents is also directly related to the utility and benefits they consider the media will give to them (information, entertainment, communication with others).

Daily relation with media is directly related to the family's socioeconomic level, with some differences in availability, accessibility, and equipment. In general, mass media are part of an adolescent's daily life, with TV and radio exhibiting primacy over other communication media. It is considered that adolescents spend between four to six hours daily with media.

A new report from the World Health Organization regarding the role of the media in promoting adolescents' health, reveals that adolescents in Latin America believe in the health news reports they hear.

An investigation was conducted with adolescents between 12 and 19 years of age from 11 countries in Latin America. Through focal groups from medium socioeconomic levels, the survey explored experiences and opinions in relation to old communication (radio and TV) and the new (videogames, cellular phones, and the Internet). Regarding media access in general, it is revealed to have a high presence in the everyday life of adolescents, especially TV. It also demonstrates that newspapers are not the major source of information.

Youngsters mention that health information is given by parents, teachers, and the media. They

Table 2. Activities in which Adolescents Used Free Time

Activity	Percentage
Listen to music	13%
Play	13%
Practice a sport	11%
Watch TV	9%
Rest	8%
Stay with the family at home	7%
Study	11%
Nothing	9.5%

Source: UNICEF 1997.

also recognize difficulties in sharing information with parents on sex topics.

Adolescents are bombarded with contradictory messages from the media. On one side they are attracted by media advertisements to alcohol and tobacco, and on the other side they receive prevention messages.

A significant number of radio stations play only American music, and this aspect has influence over adolescents' tendency to imitate and reproduce American lifestyles.

Cable TV and ample access to the Internet through "coffee nets" have allowed adolescents to be updated on new trends in music, dress, culture, and computer games. Media is fundamentally imported, cable TV programs are mostly U.S. programming. It is considered both negative and positive, because of the exposure to fair and bad information.

There is no control over types of programming, and it is up to adolescents to choose programming. Adolescents are targeted by media advertisements, fundamentally for alcohol, food, clothes, electronic devices, and sports marketing.

Listening to the radio (music) and TV in Honduras appear as the principal media elements in which adolescents use their free time. TV is one of the most important factors of cultural homogenization. It offers models that are not realistic, promoting distortions and confusions.

Media also influence society opinions over adolescent behavior; they stigmatize youngsters that are involved in violent behavior. In extreme cases where these adolescents are killed by paramilitary groups or by other adolescents, they called them *mareros*. As mentioned above, the *maras* are organized groups with a particular purpose, mainly to commit crimes; they identify themselves by special tattoos and a certain code of conduct.

Politics and Military

The interest for politics in adolescents is not clear; there are no juvenile political organizations, and girls and boys very often live their lives in violent and uncertain scenarios, where social and family relations are far from democratic. Disbelief for state institutions is common among adolescents, and they show very little interest in political participation. Nonetheless, there is a growing interest in the government's responsibility toward meeting adolescents' needs.

During 1997, several countries including Honduras conducted opinion surveys regarding rights and aspirations. This has allowed countries to put adolescents' needs in the center of society discussions.

Every year the Honduran Parliament celebrates the Children's Congress to hear their needs and concerns. It is mainly role-playing for the children, thus it does not have any impact on the decision-making process.

In 1999, the JPD was organized (Jóvenes por la democracia de Centro América y el Caribe). It is a juvenile organization with the purpose of giving support to the economic, social, and political democratization of Honduras. The organization is considered a mechanism capable of articulating youth efforts to create a more democratic and equitable country. As a group, Honduran adolescents have not been able to articulate an alternate proposal for the improvement of general conditions in the country.

In 2000, the Adolescent National Forum was created as a permanent proposal initiative to promote youth participation in all areas of Honduras' development. A document called "Frame for Adolescents' Public Policy Initiatives" was a result of a national consultation. It was rendered to the government, but up to 2005 the participation of adolescents was still incipient. The legal voting age is 18, and in general adolescents are very important in election processes, since they represent a significant population group.

Honduran youngsters claim the need to open real participation processes. A sense of frustration seems to exist regarding participation options. Regarding the types of groups to which they belong by preference is: sports, community, and religious.

Military service was compulsory and was for a long time one of the most violent experiences for adolescents. In the name of Homeland security, the Honduras Army had abused and overridden all individual rights. At the end of the 1980s, a movement was organized to demilitarize society.

A process of citizen participation began, and by 1993 a group of Hondurans organized the Popular, Civic and Christian Movement for the Derogation of the Forced Military Service, because the military was characterized by violence, authoritarianism, exclusion, and the violation of the fundamental rights (RDS 1999). This organization worked to mobilize the Honduran population to oppose compulsory military service. It created a coordination committee with the participation of the Mennonite Church, and the Women for Peace Honduran Committee "Visitación Padilla" (Coleccion Forjando Culturas 2005). The coalition promoted citizen participation and the right to free expression.

In May 1994, the Honduran National Congress modified article 275 of the 1982 Constitution. This article stated that all healthy men between the ages of 18 and 30 are subject to compulsory military service. The amendment established volunteer military service during peace (Honduras Legislation 2001).

This event was seen by adolescents and parents as a sign of freedom and independence, although actually it is considered by some political groups as a failure, the main reason being because of the increase of delinquent activities among adolescents. Actually, military service is done by volunteer males and females from low socioeconomic levels.

Volunteer work is not common, nonetheless as part of their training in secondary education and in higher education, students are requested to complete social work in poor communities in the areas of health, education, housing, and others. The government approved a decree by which all seniors from secondary education should participate in literacy processes in poor rural and urban communities for youngsters and adults who cannot read and write.

Unique Issues

Actually, violence and citizen insecurity is an important topic on the government's agenda of all Central American countries. The increase of insecurity in Honduras has a real base from the increase of delinquent activities and the participation of adolescents in it. Adults perceived adolescents, particularly those from the lower socioeconomic class, as a menace to the security of the rest of Honduras' society.

The gangs, or *maras,* have become a major problem for Honduras society. It is known that more than 36,000 adolescents belong to gangs, and they have connections with similar groups in the United States and elsewhere in Central America.

The *maras* are a relatively new urban phenomenon in Honduras. They are defined as organized groups of youngsters that appear and proliferate in a context of urban poverty, alienation, social inconformity, and lack of opportunities. They play a major role as substitute social structures, which give social identity, belonging, and security to its members. There are two gang organizations in Honduras, the *Mara Salvatrucha* and the *Mara M18*. They identify themselves by certain tattoos, which are considered a sign of identity. The national police have developed a hostile attitude toward anybody who has tattoos, and many youngsters have been accused of being *Mareros* for the only reason of showing a tattoo.

Statistics proportioned by the Government Criminal Investigation Unit (DGIC) report that in Honduras 500 gangs exist with 31,164 members; 23,097 are male and 7,257 are female. Most of them are in Tegucigalpa and San Pedro Sula, and they are localized in marginal areas of the cities. Recreation opportunities in these geographical areas are very limited, and most of the young are forced to participate in the *mara* that are organized in their own neighborhoods. Many of these groups lack social acceptance, which then promotes a retaliation behavior, and they become violent against the environment and the people who marginalized them. These groups are a consequence of social segregation, the need for identity affirmation, and the ability to acquire power over a hostile environment. In these groups, territoriality and criminality play an important role.

Sexual exploitation of children, although difficult to measure because it occurs clandestinely, is considered a major problem. Geographically, the problem is biggest in Tegucigalpa, San Pedro Sula, Ceiba, and Puerto Cortes.

Street children are the result of a series of circumstances: family relations problems, abandonment, expulsion from home, unsatisfied basic needs, economic migration, and family disintegration.

For all these problems the country has organized strategic programs such as the Program for Intervention and Social Protection, which includes solidarity mothers, solidarity families, and protection homes, to contribute to the re-education and social re-insertion of adolescents. The solidarity families and solidarity mothers are members from communities that become surrogate mothers for children at risk and assume, with the support of local organizations, the responsibility for raising and nurturing them as their own children.

The use of drugs such as additives and ethylic alcohol by street children is one of the more devastating problems in Honduras. It has become a spiral problem that never ends; these children's mothers were also street children, have no homes, and are not competent to raise children.

The Pan-American Health Organization (PAHO) is working in Honduras to develop a new conceptual framework focusing on human development and health promotion within the context of family and community, and for social, political, and economic development (Organizacion Pnamerican de la Salud, Honduras 2002).

Traditionally, adolescent social programs have focused on youngsters who already show undesirable behaviors, for example school desertion, drug abuse, and delinquency. All programs are oriented toward secondary prevention and have already demonstrated that their impact is very low since they focus on the individual and not on the family and community context in which the behavior occurs. Therefore, in Honduras it is urgent to promote a more integrated approach toward adolescent problems.

IRIS ERAZO

References and Further Reading

Adolescent Opinion Survey. 2000. Culture and Sports Ministry, Honduras, Las Maras en Honduras. http://www.adital.org.br/site/noticias/11317.asp?lang=ES&cod=11317.

Ávila, M. O., L. Y. Sagastume, and J. F. Izaguirre. 2001. Ejecución de menores en Honduras. Comisionado Nacional de los Derechos Humanos. Programa de las Nacional de las Naciones Unidas para el Desarrollo. http//rds.org.hn/marlin-avila/inv1.pdf.

Bombarolo, F. 2000. Derechos y políticas sociales dirigidas a población joven en América Latina y el Caribe. Buenos Aires. http://www.chasque.net/frontpage/comision/Publicaciones/librillo2.pdf.

Código de la Niñez y la Adolescencia. 1996. Gaceta Nacional: Congreso nacional de la Republica, Decreto No 73-96. Republica de Honduras.

Colección Forjando Culturas. Fundación Arias y el Movimiento de Mujeres por la Paz "Visitación Padilla." Derogación del Servicio Militar Obligatorio http://www.arias.or.cr/documentos/incidencia/caso/caso8.htm.

Correia, M., and V. Pena. 2002. Panorama de Genero en América Central. Región de América Latina y el Caribe. Banco Mundial.

Diagnóstico Situacional en Honduras. 2000. Programa de Atención Integral a la Adolescencia (PAIA). Salud y Desarrollo de adolescentes y jóvenes.

Ejecución de Menores en Honduras. 2001. Comisionado Nacional de los Derechos Humanos (CONADEH). Programa de las Naciones Unidas para el Desarrollo (PNUD).

Encuesta Nacional de Educación y Salud Familiar. 1996. Organización Panamericana de la Salud. Ministerio de Salud Pública, Honduras.

Encuesta Nacional de Epidemiología y Salud Familiar. 2002. Encuesta Nacional de Salud Masculina. Informe Final. Honduras.

Encuesta Sobre el Uso de Drogas en las Escuelas Normales de Honduras. 1998. Instituto Hondureño para la prevención del Alcoholismo, la Drogadicción y la Fármaco dependencia, Honduras.

Experiencias de Participación Ciudadana. Red de Desarrollo Sostenible, Honduras 1994–1999.

Flores, F., and M. Antonio. 2003. Estado de la Población de Honduras. Instituto de Investigaciones Sociales y Económicas. Universidad Nacional Autónoma de Honduras.

Honduras Legislation. 2001. Constitución de la Republica de Honduras. Iglesia hace presión contra ley Antimaras. Organización Adital http://www.adital.org.br/site/noticias/11317.asp?lang=ESandcod=11317.

Informe Nacional de Honduras. www.children-strategies.org/Spanish%20creports/Informe%20de%20pais%20Honduras.pdf.

Informe Nacional sobre los Resultados de la Encuesta del Trabajo Infantil en Honduras. 2003. San Jose, Costa Rica: Oficina Internacional del Trabajo. www.oit.or.cr and http://www.ipec.oit.or.cr.

Informe sobre Desarrollo Humano, Honduras 2003: La Cultura medio y Fin del desarrollo. 2003. San Jose, Costa Rica: UNDP.

Informe sobre el Uso de los Medios de Comunicación. 2004. Organización Panamericana de la Salud. Agencia de Información Fray Tito para América Latina (ADITAL). http://www.adital.org.br/site/noticia.asp?cod=10943andlang=ES.

Instituto Nacional de Estadísticas (INE). 2002. Encuesta Permanente de Hogares de Propósitos Múltiples, Mayo.

Jóvenes Formación y Empleo. Cinterfor, Centro Interamericano para la Investigación y Documentación sobre Formación Profesional. Organización Internacional del Trabajo. http://www.cinterfor.org.uy/public/spanish/region/ampro/cinterfor/temas/youth/doc/.

Krauskopf, D. 2002. Juventud en Riesgo. Seminario Permanente sobre Violencia. Programa de las Naciones Unidas para el desarrollo, Agosto.

Masculinidad Ligada a la Salud Sexual y Reproductiva de Adolescentes Varones de Honduras. Programa de Atención Integral a la Adolescencia, Secretaria de Salud de Honduras www.bvshn/bva/fulltext/salud_sexual.pdf.

Memoria 2004. Centro de Derechos de la Mujer. www.derechosdelamujer.org/html/PUBLICACIONES/MEMORIA%202004.pdf.

Molina, C. R. 1998. Epidemiología del abuso sexual Simposio. XII Congreso Mundial de Ginecología Pediátrica y del Adolescente.

Organización Panamericana de la Salud. Tegucigalpa, Honduras. http://www.paho-who.hn/publidoc.htm.

Organización Panamericana de la Salud. 2004. Análisis de la Situación. http://www.paho-who.hn/honduras2004.pdf.

Organización Panamericana de la Salud. Promoviendo la Salud en las Américas. Perfiles de País. Honduras. http://www.paho.org/spanish/dd/ais/be_v24n1-Honduras.htm.

Organización Panamericana de la Salud Oficina Sanitaria Panamericana. 1998. Proyecto de desarrollo y salud integral de adolescentes y jóvenes en América Latina y el Caribe 1997–2000. Oficina Regional de la Organización Mundial de la Salud. www.adolec.org/pdf/proyecto.pdf.

Palencia, G. 2005. Periódico Raíces. Hondureños buscan sueño americano huyendo de la pobreza. http://www.raices.com.sv/Poder/detalles.asp?NewsID=386.

Programa de Encuesta de Hogares. 2001. Instituto Nacional de Estadísticas (INE), Honduras.

Puerta, R. 2002. La remesa de los emigrantes: un factor decisivo para impulsar políticas de desarrollo social en Honduras. VII Congreso Internacional del CLAD sobre la Reforma del Estado y de la Administración Pública, Lisboa, Portugal.

Red de Documentación El servicio Militar en Honduras http://www.redoc.org/concodoc/honduras.html.

Resultados de los niños en Español y matemáticas. 2000. Unidad de Medición de la Calidad de la Educación (UMCE), Honduras.

Rodríguez, J. 2001. Masculinidad ligada a salud sexual y reproductiva de adolescentes varones de Honduras. Secretaria de Salud.

UNFPA. 2002. El Estado de la población mundial. http://www.unfpa.org/swp/2003/espanol/ch1/.

UNFPA. 2006. Fondo de población de las naciones unidas. Subprograma de Salud Reproductiva. Programa de Cooperación.

UNFPA. 2002. Programa Interagencial de Fomento al Desarrollo de Adolescentes y Jóvenes de Honduras.

HUNGARY

Background Information

Hungary is located in Central Europe, neighboring Austria, Croatia, Romania, Slovakia, Slovenia, Ukraine, Serbia, and Montenegro. Two-thirds of its territory is flatlands, below 200 meters of elevation. Ninety percent of its water resources come from outside the country, the two main rivers being the Danube and the Tisza. The largest lake of Central Europe, the Balaton, can also be found here. Hungary is a middle-sized country within Europe; 10.1 million people (2.2% of the population of the European Union) live on 93,030 square kilometers. The population of Hungary has been decreasing dramatically since the 1980s, and this decrease is the second largest after Latvia among the EU countries. The density of population is on average 110 people per square kilometer. Sixty-two percent of the population live in towns and almost one-third of town-dwellers live in the capital, Budapest. Budapest has more than two million inhabitants. Hungary is a relatively homogeneous society, according to the last census; 96% of the population are Hungarian, the largest minorities in Hungary being Gypsies, Slovaks, Romanians, Germans, and Serbs. The 2001 census indicated that the Roma population is 1.9% of the whole population, but the real number of Gypsies is estimated to be much higher—in 1999 between 437,000 and 482,000, almost 5% of the population (Council of Europe 1999).

Similarly to other countries in the East-Central European region, Hungary experienced dramatic changes in its political and socioeconomic system from being a socialist country with a centrally planned economy into becoming a democratic political system with market economy. The first political election that marked this change was held in 1989. In the early twenty-first century, Hungarian adolescents were already a generation that was born after or at least had started schooling in the new democratic system, thus they are the product of a post-socialist political and economical context.

In terms of economic development, the differences are striking between various regions, creating a very different developmental context for young people. There is a sharp distinction between Budapest and the western part compared to the northeastern part of the country. Transnational companies invested mainly in the western part, while the eastern part was basically avoided by them. This resulted in a gap between a dynamically developing, internationally competitive region that provides the main proportion of the export of the country, and another region that is far behind both in technological development and in economic competitiveness.

After a considerable decline, since 1997 the Hungarian economy has been growing, with the growth rate being significantly higher than the EU average. Still, the per capita GDP is only about half of the EU average (Lannert and Halász 2003). Hungary has been a member of the European Union since 2004.

Period of Adolescence

Adolescence exists as a recognized life stage in Hungary. But this was not always the case. Hungarian adolescence is a relatively recent discovery and invention, although young people had an important role in rebuilding the country and establishing the new system after World War II and also in the 1956 revolution against the Communist regime and the Soviet presence (Csapó 1994). The Hungarian Communist Youth Association was established in 1957 as a restoration of the Soviet type *Comsomol* (Communist Youth Organization) and its members—recognized as youth—were between the ages of 14 and 26.

Adolescents, however, were first identified as a distinct age group with a specific culture only from the mid-1960s when a tentative opening to the West began. This generation distanced itself from the official state ideology and emphasized the values and attributes of the Western youth of that time, such as nonconformity (Csapó 1994).

The first identity card as an official document is given to young people at the age of 14, and the coming-of-age is 18 years. At that age young people become fully responsible legally for their acts, they can vote in elections and decide about any event in their life without the permission of their parents.

Puberty that marks the beginning of adolescence starts as an average at 9.5 years among girls and approximately two years later, at the age of 11.38, among boys. Boys also finish their sexual maturation later, at the age of 15.46. On average girls have their first period at the age 12.7 (Zimmerman 2005).

Statistical sources present data on adolescents in three age groups: 10- to 14-year-olds, termed young adolescents; 15- to 19-year-olds, termed teens; and 20- to 24-year-olds, termed young adults. The number of adolescents and young adults is decreasing in Hungarian society. In 2004, the number of those between the ages of 15 and 29 was 50,000 less than in 2000, the biggest decrease taking place in the 20 to 24 age group (Central Statistical Office, KSH 2004). According to the 2003 census, the proportion of adolescents and young adults in the society were between 6.4% and 8.3% in the three age groups. Parallel to this, the proportion of elderly compared to the active group has increased (those above 65 are 15.1% of the population in 2005); therefore, these trends bear the characteristics of a gradually aging society.

Recent sociological studies of youth in Hungary show that the period of youth has lengthened. Young people spend longer and longer times in educational institutions. Data from the 1980s and 1990s demonstrated that in the case of those who after finishing vocational school or secondary school started to work, this data closely coincided with getting married and having their first child within the first two years of their marriage as an average. By the end of the 1990s this had changed. Young people continue their studies, take their first job later, get married later, and have their first child later. The lengthened youth period produced new forms of living, such as the so-called *szingli* (single), that create a new cultural situation and a new consumption style. Because in Hungary, moving out from parents typically coincides with getting married, young people live longer in their parents' home. This lifestyle also extends the period of adolescence.

The whole society and also the government recognizes that young people from the age 14 to 29 are a group in the society with distinctive characteristics and features. Therefore, a comprehensive research project has been set up by the Ministry of Youth, Family, Social Welfare and Equal Opportunities and the Office of the Prime Minister. The first such study took place in 2000 (Youth 2000), and it is repeated each four years. It is aimed at documenting the speed and nature of changes among young people in Hungary in connection with the rapid societal changes taking place in the country. It is conducted with a representative sample of 8,000 young people between the ages of 15 and 29. In this entry we will rely on the data of these representative studies extensively (Youth 2000, 2004).

Beliefs

Hungarian adolescents growing up in one of the so-called transitional societies of Central and Eastern Europe have had different experiences from those of their counterparts in the European countries that have not gone through major structural changes during the last 60 years. There are two reasons for such differences. Partly, they are being brought up in a society that had, for many decades, very different guiding principles from those of the traditional, capitalist market economies and democracies of Western Europe. Their parents and teachers were educated and employed in a society that propagated a Communist-Socialist ideology and in an economy that was mostly state controlled. This difference, in the broader societal system and within the microsystem of the school and family, might be expected to lead to different norms, values, and other cultural products in the two groups of adolescents. Secondly, in the post-Communist/Socialist countries young people are growing up in a period of abrupt social change (Pinquart and Silbereisen 2004; Fülöp 2005a).

Van Hoorn et al. (2000) describe those young people who grow up in societies undergoing structural change as the "omega-alpha generation," because they are the last children of the old system and the first adults of the new. These young people are in fact in a double limbo, or in a double transition (Roberts et al. 2000). Their developmental transition from adolescence to young adulthood has had to face, in parallel, both the grave politico-institutional and social changes of the transitional societies and their own transition from child to adult. They are leaving childhood without established adult roles, yet at the same time the society into which they will be integrated is also in transition. The result is that conditions surrounding young people in the "limbo countries" are not easily predictable.

One of the core aspects of adolescents' evolving sense of self is the setting of goals for the future. One basic motivation for human behavior is the need for security. People want to know what the future will be like in order to resolve uncertainty, and planning and committing to goals reduces uncertainty and anxiety with the sense of being able to

control the future (Trommsdorff 1994). However, according to studies with Hungarian young people, those who had a well-structured plan for the future had—on contrary to the expectations—a higher level of anxiety (Vári-Szilágyi and Solymosi 1999). This can be explained by the characteristics of the society. If somebody plans well-ahead in an environment that is rapidly and sometimes unpredictably changing, then there is a high probability that his or her plans cannot come true, so there is a cause for worry. Short-term thinking is an adaptive reaction to a rapidly changing environment, in a situation where careful planning ahead would lead to frustration and not real control over the course of life (Fülöp 2005a).

Because there had been four decades of ideological emphasis on the collective as opposed to the individual in Hungary, we could expect that young people and their teachers should be more collectivistic and less individualistic in their attitudes than their counterparts in Western Europe. But longitudinal research suggests that they have managed to catch up with individualism very fast. Fülöp et al. (2002) compared Hungarian and English teachers' ideas on citizenship and the good citizen. English teachers place much more emphasis on the need to educate pupils to be responsible members of society and they spoke a great deal about the importance of cooperating and behaving in a way that will benefit the community, while Hungarian teachers stressed the importance of individual rights and did not consider the community so important. Self-interest has eclipsed public interest in the goals of young people too. Young people have retreated from politics and civic concerns, commitment to the welfare of the broader community has declined, and materialist aspirations have increased. Hungarian adolescents do not perceive their local society as cohesive and caring, and they like to be engaged in individual activities and can be characterized by lack of interest in communities (Macek et al. 1998; Youth 2004). They have a more misanthropic view of their fellow students when compared to their American or Australian counterparts. They feel that most students only care for their friends and only look out for themselves, rather than helping others (Flanagan et al. 2003).

The excessive individualism of these young people and their focus on self-interest rather than on public or community good can be attributed either to the extreme speed of the acculturation process, to the former political system having failed to sufficiently instill the principles of the collective, or to a rebound effect. In the socialist system, collectivism was the main ideological expectation and people conformed with this to various extents. After the political changes, collective goals and the public interest were denigrated and private interests became much more important than public interests (Fülöp 2005a).

Among 20-year-olds Csukonyi et al. (1999) found that there were equal numbers of individualists and collectivists, and there were also those young people who either showed both individualism and collectivism at a high level or refrained from both. This result might also refer to the transitional state of individualism and collectivism in Hungary, as it was impossible to find a simple unidimensional picture of these cultural dimensions among Hungarian young people.

Individualism and self-interest are accompanied by money-orientation. In a free market economy the relative income equalities of the socialist system turned into huge inequalities. Money, which had been ideologically unacceptable as a motivator for human behavior, now became the key force in most areas of life, seemingly gaining priority over other values. Saris and Ferligoj (1995) found that social contacts were more closely related to general life satisfaction than finances in Western Europe, while the reverse is the case in most of the East and Central European countries, including Hungary, where satisfaction with one's financial situation is much more important than satisfaction with social contacts.

Hungarian adolescents considered money as the main goal of competition in their society compared to their English peers, for whom competition in sports, for good jobs and in education were the leading areas of competition (Fülöp 2002). One explanation of this phenomenon is that attitudes towards money are inversely related to comparative gross domestic product (GDP), but positively related to economic striving and resulting growth. Furnham et al. (1994) argues that once economic wealth has been secured, being money-oriented becomes less prevalent: when enough money is available, then striving for more is less important.

Orientations towards money and striving to be rich can be a logical consequence of the previous emphasis on the principle of equality and of the new opportunities opened by the capitalist economy (Fülöp 2005a). Those who are affluent are also better buffered against the negative consequences of an unpredictably changing social and economical environment (Noack et al. 1995).

Competition has a long history in the Western capitalist democracies, but it was ideologically banned during the socialist system and has become the central guiding principle of the society and

economy after the political changes in Hungary. Fülöp (2002) compared English and Hungarian teenagers' (16- to 17-year-olds) perceptions of the role of competition in their society. While in general both Hungarian and English respondents saw competition as playing an important role in their society, there were qualitative and quantitative differences in their views. For instance, while large groups of English and Hungarians had neutral attitudes towards competition, they expressed this in slightly different ways. The Hungarian neutral answers showed an acceptance of the inevitable: "Hungary *must* compete in order to . . ." or "We *must* compete for . . ."; competition was seen as unavoidable rather than naturally present. The English students in the neutral group took competition for granted, not as an outside constraint, but as an inherent, self-evident characteristic of a capitalist society. Those Hungarians who were not neutral were largely negative towards competition, and they had a considerably more structured picture about the disadvantages of it. The most frequently described negative consequences were immorality, interpersonal conflict and aggression, and the development of money-oriented people. According to adolescents, Hungarians want to win at any cost (particularly in the material sense) and by any means (aggressive or immoral). In contrast to this, the English had a less critical attitude towards competition.

When Fülöp and Berkics (2003) compared English and Hungarian adolescents' reactions to winning and losing, they found that Hungarian young people tended to be happy and enthusiastic about winning but with a tendency to hide this feeling from others, and were mostly deactivated, sad, and depressed about losing and were less able to cope with this than their English counterparts. The English respondents took winning as a natural outcome of competition and confidently attributed it to being "the best" or being "better than others." They were also more activated by losing (being disappointed but "standing up" to it) than were the Hungarians, so fewer of them expressed explicitly negative views about losing. This reflects the different societal context for winners and losers in Hungary and in England.

Given the fact that Hungarian adolescents are self-interested, individualistic, and money-oriented, it is interesting to see how they relate to spiritual values and religion. If we take into consideration that religion was not supported by the socialist system of Hungary, and the parents of the early twenty-first-century Hungarian adolescents grew up in an ideological-political system that discouraged religious affiliation, and during the early years of socialism people who took charge of their religious beliefs faced social disadvantages, it is striking that according to the Youth 2004 study the majority of the 15- to 29-year-olds (58%) consider themselves religious. Religious traditions are important to them; however, most of them do not consider regular attendance of religious services a necessary requirement of being committed to a religious community. Only 35% of 15- to 29-year-olds said that they are not religious at all. Adolescent girls consider themselves religious, pray, and attend religious services more frequently than boys (Pikó and Fitzpatrick 2004). Among those who categorize themselves as belonging to a certain religion, 69% are Roman Catholics, 20% are Calvinist, the remaining 11% stands for Lutherans, Greek Catholics, Jews, and Muslims. The proportion of those who consider religious belief a very important or important value in life shows a considerable growth between 2000 and 2004 (from 24% to 35%).

Gender

Gender role expectations show a mixture of traditional and modern values among the Hungarian youth. Feminism has never gained ground in the Hungarian society. The explanation lies in the history of the last fifty years. After the Communist takeover, the socioeconomic structure in Hungary was based on a dual-earning family, and this was supported by an ideology claiming that women are equal to men to the extent of being a miner, a construction worker, or a tractor driver. Therefore, during the socialist system the majority of women were full-time employees, but this did not change the gendered division of domestic responsibilities. It was women who had to do the house chores when the workday was done. Women were assumed to have equality but in reality they bore the burden of having to maintain the home while working full time. Women continued to be socialized into conservative gender roles while supposedly enjoying gender equality. From the 1980s, young husbands gradually started to take a more active part in the household by doing more childcare, cooking, and cleaning, but still these are the major responsibilities of women within the family in Hungary.

Conservative gender roles were reinforced after the political changes partly as a rebound effect of the previous ideal of the working woman, partly because after the political changes, an unprecedented number of Hungarian women became unemployed; that is, full-time housewives. The presence

of traditional expectations towards women's and men's family roles is reflected in the different reactions of the family to the father's and the mother's unemployment. While father's unemployment in the household usually plays a negative role in the general health and well-being of the family, a non-employed woman becoming a full-time housewife actually may have a positive effect on children's psychosocial health (Piko et al. 2001).

Values and attitudes towards men and women are in harmony with this. Among Hungarian young men and women, unlike among their U.S. counterparts, only hostile sexism is perceived as a clear case of prejudice, and benevolent sexism (that is, women needing men's protection or only men willing to take risks) that helps to maintain the disadvantaged status of women is perceived positive and good for women (Nguyen Luu et al. 2003–2004).

In a study of Hungarian university students' representation of the ideal man and the ideal woman, it was found that the ideal man is considered to be independent, self-confident, strong, cool, autonomous, successful, and competitive, while the ideal woman is rather shy, gentle, dependent, and sexy. In the case of the ideal man, young women and men do not have significant differences in their views, but there is a difference in the case of the ideal woman. Young women consider the ideal woman to be more independent, more self-confident, stronger, more competitive, and more successful than young men. This clearly shows that the notion of the ideal woman is changing in the case of young women, while young men still hold a more traditional feminine stereotype (Fülöp and Berkics 2005).

While gradually more and more women get into prestigious and powerful jobs, girls are still expected to be less competitive than boys; competitiveness is considered to be a masculine trait. This gender-role expectation may make it harder for girls to feel comfortable if they act competitively. In a study with 20- to 22-year-old university students it was found that compared to their Canadian and Japanese counterparts, Hungarian young women are those who say the most frequently that women compete in a manipulative, hidden, and also emotional way. Male competition is considered to be more open, more aggressive, fairer, and less emotional. The areas of competition attributed to males and females show a mixture of traditional and modern gender role expectations. The most prevalent area of competition for women is considered to be looks, competition for partners, intellectual achievement, money, and work. In case of men the list starts with career and work, followed by money, partners, physical strength, and power (Fülöp 2005b).

The most important area of women's competition is considered to be looks, according to young females. This has several severe consequences. The cultural ideals of dieting and slimness that predominate modern societies have fully influenced Hungarian adolescent girls too. A WHO cross-national study (Health Behaviour in School-Aged Children [HBSC]) covering almost 162,000 young people in 35 countries carried out in 2001 and 2002 among 11- to 15-year-olds indicated that the older Hungarian girls get, the fatter they consider themselves and the more dissatisfied they are with themselves. This tendency starts already with the 11-year-old girls. One-third of them consider themselves fat, while this is only one-tenth among the same age boys. Among all participating countries, the proportion of 11-, 13-, and 15-year-old girls being on a diet is the highest in Hungary. Opposite to this, obesity is more common among adolescent boys; however, it is less common in both genders than weight control (Mulvihill et al. 2004 [HBSC]). Eating disorders like anorexia nervosa and bulimia nervosa (clinical and subclinical forms), are both more widespread among adolescent girls than boys, and the prevalence of them is equivalent with the Western European frequency, approximately 3% in the case of girls (Szmuska et al. 2001).

Intellectual achievement and academics are also considered to be important competitive areas for young women. The gender ratio has reversed in higher education since 1995, since more girls are now enrolled in higher education than boys. Therefore, the number of highly educated women is growing rapidly in Hungary. This is due to attitudinal and performance differences. Girls are more likely than boys to report that they are happy with school, and they have better grades (Pikó and Fitzpatrick 2004). There is a significant difference in the average performance in reading literacy to the benefit of girls in Hungary. Boys show a minor advantage over girls in mathematical literacy, while there is virtually no difference in the field of sciences (Lannert and Halász, 2003).

Physical strength and fitness is a field of competition and a source of self-esteem more for adolescent boys than girls. Boys spend more time with sports and participating in sports clubs than girls (Pikó and Fitzpatrick 2004; HBSC 2004). There is a gender inequality in terms of health perception too. More girls rate their health as fair or poor; they have higher rates of health complaints and at the same time lower rates of life satisfaction. This

difference between boys and girls increases with age. One possible explanation of this phenomenon is related to gender role expectations and socialization. Girls are more willing to acknowledge health problems, while boys tend to underreport them because "boys do not cry and do not complain" (Torsheim et al. 2004), and also because being sick is not part of the "strong man" ideal.

Traditional gender role expectations are present in parents' socialization too. The greater degree of independence that parents afford to their sons compared to their daughters is reflected in the fact that 15-year-old boys meet with their friends after school and in the evening more frequently than girls (Settertobulte and de Matos 2004 [HBSC]).

The Self

Identity formation of Hungarian adolescents is influenced not only by their upbringing in their family and their participation in the school system, but it is also a result of a more and more globalized lifestyle due to the opening up of the country and excessive travelings. Although in a comparative study between 16- and 18-year-old Hungarian and French teenagers, fewer Hungarians had already visited one or more foreign countries (88% and 69% respectively). The Hungarian proportion shows the tremendous social and political changes in a country where their parents' generation, less than fifteen years ago, had only very limited travel opportunities (Fülöp and Roland-Levy 2004).

Also, role models and social/commercial influences are considered to have a particularly strong impact on the construction of identities. Consumerism and the influx of Western consumer preferences have been present since the late 1960s among Hungarian young people, but the political changes speeded this up, and by the end of the 1990s a consumer culture had become dominant among youth. Therefore, they are surprisingly similar to their Western European peers (Gábor and Balog 1999). This is also the result of the modern media-dominated information society that provides Hungarian adolescents with data that functions as building-blocks of identity. Common frames of references have evolved thanks to television, films, and the music industry (Thorensen 2005). Commercial as well as cultural symbols are transported to Hungary, just like to all other corners of the globe, to a degree never experienced in former decades. A wide variety of products now fill the shelves in Hungarian shops. Adolescents are tempted by choices their parents could hardly dream of. Food, clothing, entertainment, and technology from around the globe are accessible and close at hand. This diffusion of goods and symbols greatly influences identity formation.

For example, among Hungarians 16 to 18 years old the examples of the ideal man are American or English actors and sportsmen like Bruce Willis, George Clooney, David Beckham, Ben Affleck, Brad Pitt, or Leonardo di Caprio. The ideal woman is also an internationally known actress or a singer like Jennifer Lopez, Angelina Jolie, Britney Spears, or Julia Roberts. Youth culture is globalized (Fülöp and Berkics 2005).

While most Hungarian adolescents have a balanced relationship with the adult world and they do not consider intergenerational conflict a necessary phase of establishing an independent self, there exists an emerging phenomenon called "youth centrism"—a strong youth identity combined with conflict with the adult world. For this group of young people, independence and freedom are the main values. Their opposition might be increased by the institutions like school that can hardly tolerate their being different and their search for identity. The early independence of these adolescents is often intertwined with identity crisis; therefore, it is not uncommon among them to turn to drugs as a potential tension relief. Drug use might also symbolize for these young people the "youth lifestyle" and the experience of freedom (Gábor and Balog 1999).

House, techno, rave, and disco were found to be the most popular music trends among young people, creating a techno-house subculture (Gábor and Balog 1999; Mészáros 2003). The main spaces of this subculture are the discos with the disc jockey as a key figure, the parties and the clubs. Parties are so-called Temporary Autonomous Zones where the PLUR ideology prevails (Peace, Love, Unity, and Respect), a pacifist—and tolerant—liberal ideology. Everybody is accepted. The party culture is intertwined with typical disco drugs like hallucinogens (LSD) and stimulants (Ecstasy or amphetamine). There also exists a specific party slang: "grizzlies" are huge, sometimes aggressive party goers, "pussycats" are pretty girls dressed in a sexy way, and "pocemon" are young adolescent party-goers. The core group consists of 20- to 25-year-old young adults, but the number of adolescents among them is growing (Mészáros 2003).

Other characteristic subgroups are the skinheads, the Satanists, the punks, Hare Krishna believers, and others. They are only very small, but due to their outlook they make up a visible proportion of young people in Hungary.

Family Relationships

The average family size in Hungary was 2.96 in 2001, meaning that the most common is a one-child family. Young adolescents face growing problems if their parents divorce or separate. In 2001, 16% of the families were one-parent families and in the majority of them (87%) the mother was the caretaker of the child (Bukodi et al. 2004).

While individualism and being autonomous in one's life goals are prevalent among Hungarian young people, closer family ties and relationships are basically unaffected by the transformations. The relationships of adolescents in Hungary towards their family can be characterized along a different dimension than individualism versus collectivism: separateness versus relatedness (Kagitcibashi 2005). In Van Hoorn et al.'s (2000) study, the majority of Hungarian adolescents viewed themselves as members of a close and well-functioning family. In contrast to adolescents in Western European countries, they did not view this stage in their lives as a time when intergenerational conflict might be expected. This was true even among those who talked about disagreements and arguments with their parents. The development of a psychosocial identity appeared to be a quiet process, unremarked by family and friends as being "critical." Sixty-two percent of 15- to 19-year-olds agree with those principles according to which their parents live, and they have become generally less critical towards their parents in the last four years. In accordance with this, the proportion of those who completely refuse their parents' values and lifestyles decreased from 13% to 11% (Youth 2000, 2004).

Another study, by Flanagan et al. (1998), shows the different ways in which teenagers conceptualize their position in the family. In many societies adolescents are expected to do chores at home, but in Western Europe these jobs are more likely to be linked to payment, and giving an allowance or pocket money is considered the norm. In Hungarian families the adolescent is generally not conceptualized as an autonomous and independent individual "employee" who gets payments for work, but as a family member who carries out domestic tasks for the welfare of the family group for free.

The family has an important role in helping to solve personal problems too. Mothers are seen to be a more accessible source of social support. After the best friend, Hungarian adolescents discuss their most intimate problems with their mother (Pedersen et al. 2004), with their siblings, and finally with their father. The result that 19-year-olds, regardless of their gender, share their complaints with their mothers way more often than with their fathers shows that the mother has a more intimate relationship with her adolescent child than the father (Sefcsik 2003).

Young people typically live in the parental home until they get married or establish a permanent partnership. The age of moving out from the parents is growing. Young adults do not connect finishing their studies or getting a job with leaving the family home. According to the Youth 2004 study 72% of 15- to 29-year-olds live at home with their family. Only 20% of them have their own home.

These findings suggest that we are witnessing an interesting cultural phenomenon. In Western Europe individualism is associated with a growing separateness and independence from parents, while this link is less obvious in Hungary. Young people in Hungary are individualists outside the family, but they have more interdependence and relatedness within the family.

Friends and Peers/Youth Culture

Friendship is a very important part of Hungarian adolescents' lives. Adolescents discuss their intimate problems primarily with their best friend. More than 90% of the Hungarian 15-year-olds reported to have at least three friends in the HBSC study, the highest proportion among the participating countries (Settertobulte and de Matos 2004). The majority of them find their friends in the school (Lannert and Halász 2004). Adolescent boys and girls have a different concept about friendship. Boys are more willing to report girls as friends (10%) than girls report boys as friends (1%) (Settertobulte and de Matos 2004 [HBSC]).

On an average weekday, almost half of 15- to 29-year-olds have one to three hours free time, and one quarter of them even four to six hours. The older a young person is, the less free time he or she has. Young people living in Budapest and the cities have less free time than those who live in the countryside. One third of the 15- to 19-year-olds have the whole weekend as free.

Although Hungarian young people mostly spend their free time at home watching television, friends have an important role in free time activities. During weekdays one-third and on weekends almost half of the 15- to 19-year-olds hang around with friends (Youth 2004). Since 1995, many big shopping malls have been built in all major cities and Budapest. These shopping malls offer very different activities for young people: multiplex

cinemas, cafés, games, bowling, fast food restaurants. To spend a whole day in a "plaza" with these different activities—or just with hanging around—became a popular activity for adolescents living in the capital or bigger cities. Young people living in the big cities are also frequent consumers of culture like movies, theater, concerts, museums, exhibitions, and libraries, but this is not the case with those who live in the countryside; they prefer to go to discos and privately organized parties as there is a huge gap between these two groups in terms of the availability of cultural products.

According to the Youth 2004 study, 41% of the 15- to 19-year-olds had been in a library within the last one month of the investigation, 40% in a movie or a multiplex, 28% in a bookshop, 28% in a video and DVD shop, 15% in a museum, and 10% in the theater. It was also found that 86% of the 15- to 19-year-olds never go to the opera, 76% of them never go to a classical music concert, 47% of them never borrow a video or a DVD, and 34% of them never go to a bookshop. Besides sites of the consumption of the elite culture there are other sites that are used by young people; for instance, for discussions there are places like pubs, cafés and jazz clubs, but only 10% of the respondents reported attending these places regularly—at least once a month.

If friends cannot meet personally, nowadays they have other means to replace it. The uses of electronic communications media have been common, particularly since the boom of mobile phone use. A quarter of Hungarian 15-year-olds reported communicating with friends via telephone, e-mail, or text messages every day (Settertobulte and de Matos 2004).

Organized peer activity and spending time in groups decreased a lot after the political changes. Although the so-called Pioneer Movement and the Communist Youth Organization had less and less ideological content in the 1970s and 1980s and they were primarily responsible for different kinds of organized peer activity (like summer camps), they understandably did not survive the transition. When the socialist system was over there was nothing to replace them. In some schools the scout movement of the pre-World War era was revived, but it has not spread out in the country. The government tries now to support programs that are offered to young people as a communal activity without an ideological content.

In the last ten years there has been a gigantic and very popular program in Budapest for young people, the so called *Sziget* (Island) Festival that is organized each August for a week on an island in the River Danube. Young people, if they want to, can live on the island for a week and there are many concerts with famous Hungarian and international celebrities. There are also lots of cultural activities, public lectures, and the possibility for ethnic and religious minorities to present themselves. In 2005, the Island Festival had altogether 385,000 visitors, mostly adolescents and young adults who listened to and watched more than 170 performers from abroad, representing 50 countries around the world. There was reggae from Jamaica, electro-Afro pop from Guinea, Swedish garage rock, teenage punk from the United States, the premiere of an Australian opera, and so on. In the 62 different program sites there were 200 different programs per day. In addition to foreign performers, also some 450 Hungarian bands and disc jockeys were entertaining the audience. Moreover, 120 different organizations, including NGOs and institutions were represented on the "Civil Island" with diverse programs. The Island Festival is one of the major and hugely popular meeting points of Hungarian adolescents each year.

There is another yearly summer program, the so-called Valley of Arts. Although it is not aimed specifically at young people, still it has become a popular get-together place for those who have an interest in elite culture. The Valley of Arts is the most extensive pan-cultural festival in Hungary and has been organized consecutively in the past 15 years. It takes place in a picturesque valley above Lake Balaton and is hosted by six settlements. In ten days, 800 productions, 3,500 artists, the residents, the squares, the courts, the sheds and the fields of the valley wait for the travelers. Theater and dance; classical, religious, jazz, and world music concerts; folk music and dance; craftsman productions; literary events; film screenings; more than 50 exhibitions; a National Potter Summit; handicrafts sales; and a musical camp make the program of the Valley exciting.

The Island Festival and the Valley of Arts are programs mainly attended by more-educated, middle-class young people who are students of academic high schools or study in colleges and universities, and also those from the capital, Budapest. These programs are rather expensive, so they are not available for those who live among poor circumstances. Still, almost one-third of all the 8,000 respondents in the Youth 2004 study participated in the last three years in the Island Festival and 12% in the Valley of Arts.

Cyber-communication establishes the possibility for new kinds of networking among young people. Who Is Who (WIW) is an online sociometric

network that was founded by two young professionals in 2002. Since the political changes in 1989, there has not been such a large-scale civil movement among the young generation of Hungarians. New members are invited based on personal acquaintances with an already existing member of the community. Every member presents him or herself and indicates who else he or she knows from the network. If the contact is confirmed then there is an established link between those members. This way every participant can see his or her own sociometric status, individualized network, or personal community. This online community has gained more than 100,000 registered members during its three-year existence. Almost half of the members log in to the system at least once a week. Most of the members are from Budapest and the major cities and are mainly secondary school, college and university students, or young professionals (Hain 2005).

Love and Sexuality

Romantic love is the second most important value for young Hungarians following having a secure family. It is considered a necessary requirement of intimate relationships, however, more in the case of girls than boys (Youth 2004).

Love and sexuality are closely related to each other in young people's ideals; however, in practice a sexual relationship does not always reflect love. More than half of the 15 to 19 age group has an active sexual life. The average age for the first sexual encounter is 17 years, but boys start to be sexually active somewhat earlier than girls, and about one-third of the sexually active adolescents had their first sexual encounter before the age of 14. If they have a permanent sexual partner then their sexual life is rather active, especially if we take into consideration that typically they do not cohabit. Twelve percent report to have sexual intercourse every day, 60% several times per week, and 20% once a week. Sexual relationships among young people are mainly monogamous in character (Youth 2004).

The majority of those with an active sexual life use contraceptives. The most frequent methods are birth control pills and condoms. In the 15 to 19 age-group 64% use condoms and 33% birth control pills. This shows that boys are more likely to use contraceptives then girls. Six percent of adolescents do not use any prevention. This proportion changes in the next age group. Among the 20- to 24-year-olds, a lower percentage of the couples (47%) use condoms, a bigger percentage (55%) use birth

control pills, and 4% does not apply any prevention. The result of not using any prevention is that in 1,000 pregnancies that ended with a live birth, there were 21 teenage pregnancies (between ages 15 to 19) in 2002. The teenage abortion rate is high. Among 1,000 abortions there were 20 that were carried out on teenagers in 2002. This number was even bigger (34) among the 20- to 24-year-olds in spite of the fact that in this age group there are fewer young people who do not use any contraceptives.

Until 1966, homosexuality was a criminal act in Hungary. It was only in 2004 that all discriminatory legislations were abolished and the "equal opportunity act" was established. We do not have reliable data on the number of gays and lesbians in the Hungarian society (3% to 5% of the population according to the president of the "Back-up Society for Homosexuals" in 2004) and especially no data about its prevalence among adolescents and young adults. Homosexuals are mainly considered to be outsiders, a minority group that is mostly invisible. There are no distinct locations of a "gay district" in Budapest or in the major cities. There is no fully developed gay community and the gay scene is mainly underground. Since 1996, each summer there has been a Gay Pride Day and a parade in Budapest with approximately 1,500 to 3,500 participants representing all age groups.

The incidence rate of AIDS is lower than the EU average in Hungary, and the number of newly registered cases has been approximately the same each year since 1993. The largest transmission groups are homosexuals and bisexuals (70%). Almost 90% of the registered cases are men. In 2005, among the newly identified patients around 8% were 13- to 19-year-olds and 35% were 20- to 29-year-olds (National Epidemiological Centre 2005).

Early marriages and young motherhood were long typical of family patterns in Hungary. Today, though, these are things of the past. The willingness of young people to get married has significantly diminished since about 1990. The rate of marriage dropped by more than 40% between 1990 and 2002. In 2004, for the first time there were more non-married persons in the population above 15 than married persons (Hungary 2004). If this practice is indicative of future attitudes, more than half of today's young people will live their lives outside the bond of marriage.

In 2004, most of the marriages took place between 25- and 29-year-old women and 30- to 34-year-old men (Central Statistical Office, KSH 2004). The average age of getting married is increasing rapidly,

partly because young people study longer, partly because there are many who do not get married but cohabit for an extended period of time. By 2005, 46% of women aged between 20 and 24 lived in relationships of cohabitation, as opposed to a mere 2% at the beginning of the 1970s (Bukodi et al. 2004).

In the early 1990s, the modal age of women marrying for the first time was 21 years; that is, this was the age which saw the highest rate of first marriage. In 2004, the corresponding age was 27, and single women in their early 30s were more likely to get married than women of 20 or 21 years of age (average age: 29.3). The average age of getting married among men also has increased from 24 to 32.3 by 2004. This means that by the age of 25 to 29, 43% of the women are married while only 28% of the males are (Hungarian Central Statistical Office, KSH 2004).

Those young people who live in Budapest are less willing to get married and rather remain single or cohabit, while in smaller cities and villages the number of marriages is higher, showing a difference in modern and traditional values between the capital and the countryside. Socioeconomic background also counts. The higher the SES, the higher the probability is of being single or cohabiting.

Stability of marriage is typically measured by the divorce rate. The trend shows that of every 100 marriages, 42 will end in divorce if the divorce trends of 2002 continue. In 1995, this rate was around 30, thus the increase has been significant (Bukodi et al. 2004). As we noted previously, the birthrate has been decreasing since 1980. The average birthrate was 1.28 in 2004, compared to 1.92 in 1980 (Hungarian Central Statistical Office, KSH 2004). The number of women giving birth before age 25 has been also decreasing, while the number of those who have their first child in their late twenties or between the ages of 30 and 39 has been increasing. The number of children born out of wedlock has been also growing rapidly: it was 12% in 1989 and reached its peak in the history of the statistics of the country—34%—in 2003. With this percentage Hungary is in the middle among the European Union countries (the average in the EU being 30% in 2003).

In the Youth 2004 study 20% of the 15- to 29-year-olds had one child, and another 20% had more children. Eleven percent of them were single parents and 25% were not married to their partner. Among those who still have no children, 9% do not plan to have children at all, and the others would like at least one child. The desire to have a child is generally not very high.

Health Risk Behavior

For both sexes, life expectancy in Hungary was about two years less than the EU average in 1970. By 1998, this gap had widened to six years for women and eight years for men (WHO 2000). Since then, life expectancy has slowly increased in Hungary, but it is still significantly lower than the European average: in the case of women it is 77 years and for men only 68 years (Hungary 2004).

Hungarian adolescents' health conditions and mortality and morbidity statistics are, however, good (Susánszky and Szántó 2002). Still, in some respects the health of youth is deteriorating. The prevalence of allergic diseases is growing rapidly. The leading illnesses are the musculoskeletal diseases that are related to a sedentary lifestyle and lack of exercise. The proportion of posture problems is 10% among the secondary school students. Vision problems are the next most frequent ones, followed by endocrine-digestive diseases.

Perception of subjective health is good in this age group. Three-quarters of young people perceive their health as excellent; an additional 20% considers it good and only 5% says that their health is poor. The objective situation corresponds with this; only 2% of the 15- to 29-year-olds suffer chronic illness, are handicapped, or have severe psychological difficulties. An additional 8% have minor health problems (Youth 2004).

Most adolescents are free of serious physical illness, yet they experience and report a growing number of psychosomatic and psychological distress symptomatologies (Susánszky and Szántó 2002). Sleep disorders, backache, and headache are the most frequent symptoms among Hungarian adolescents (Piko et al. 1997). Stress-related somatic diseases like ulcers doubled among the adolescents in the last decade (Jánosi 2002). Psychosomatic and distress symptoms are characteristic more to girls than boys (Piko et al. 1997).

In the Youth 2000 study, approximately every seventh respondent belonged to the "high level of somatic symptoms" category (14%). Adolescents who evaluated their socioeconomic situation higher report better psychological well-being, lower levels of psychosomatic symptomatology, and more positive assessment of their own health. Both fathers' and mothers' education levels are positively related to adolescents' self-perceived health (Piko et al. 2001). Exceptions are those adolescents whose mothers work as entrepreneurs: they had higher than average somatic symptom formations. The lowest risk proved to be growing up in a two-parent family; every other formation had a higher risk

in terms of psychosomatic diseases. Among adopted children and among those who were brought up in orphanages, double the average occurrence was found. Among all examined factors, alcoholism in the family proved to be the most important predictor of psychosomatic symptoms in adolescence.

In Hungary one of the most socially accepted, health-damaging behaviors is tobacco use, mainly cigarette smoking. Prevalence of daily smokers is 38% among adult males, but it is also high among females: almost every fourth adult woman is a daily smoker (23%). Compared to the European average (and to most countries of this region) these percentages are extremely high. This extensive tobacco use has considerable and serious health outcomes. In Hungary, 140,000 people die in each year and 28,000 of them die because of diseases caused by tobacco use. Lung cancer in the age group of 0 to 64 is the highest in the WHO European Region (WHO 2000). Thus, smoking has a crucial role in the decrease of the Hungarian population. As all studies show that the parental model has a major effect on the offsprings' tobacco use, the prevalence of smoking in the adult population has an enormous significance. Only one-fourth of children of non-smoking parents smoke, while this is around 50% among the children of parents who are smokers (Youth 2004).

Unfortunately but not unexpectedly, there has been an increasing trend in tobacco use among young people in the last decade. More than two-thirds of 13- to 16-year-olds have already experimented with smoking, and one-third of them have remained smokers. In addition to this, adolescents start smoking at a younger and younger age. Among those who have already tried smoking, almost 20% said that they did this before the age of ten. By 2003, Hungary was tenth in tobacco usage among adolescents among 35 countries in the ESPAD (European School Survey Project on Alcohol and Other Drugs 2003) study that was carried out among 2,500 ninth- and tenth-grade vocational training school and secondary school students (the target population being the 16-year-olds) in Budapest. The permissive environment also supports this. Although it is prohibited by law to sell cigarettes to those under the age of 18, 76% of those young people who regularly smoke said that they have no difficulty buying cigarettes in shops (Németh 2003).

Tobacco use has a close connection with educational level. Almost three times more young people with a vocational education smoke than university students (45% and 16% respectively). Unemployed young people and those with a lower socioeconomic background also smoke significantly more than the employed and those with a higher SES. In all age groups, males smoke more than female (Youth 2004).

Alcohol is a regular feature in the lives of many Hungarian adolescents; however, alcohol consumption in public places is illegal under the age of 18. Among causes of mortality, chronic liver disease and cirrhosis due to excessive consumption of alcohol are three times higher in Hungary than the EU average (WHO 2000). This is imperative because if alcohol dependence is present in the family it is more probable that young people drink alcohol weekly themselves. The Youth 2004 study nevertheless shows a favorable tendency, as the number of those who consume alcohol has decreased from 59% to 41% among 15- to 29-year-olds compared to the Youth 2000 study.

The level of education does not really count in the case of alcohol consumption. Young people with university degrees consume as much alcohol as those with a vocational education. However, unemployed young people consume more alcohol. There is also a significant difference between males and females. Among the 15-year-olds there are more boys who drink weekly or who have been drunk twice or more in their life (Schmidt and Gabhainn 2004 [HBSC]). There are also more binge drinkers among them (more than five drinks in a prescribed period of time, Pikó and Fitzpatrick 2004). Their first exposure to alcohol was at an earlier age too. One-quarter of the 15-year-old boys drinks beer weekly, while this number is 12% in the case of girls (Schmidt and Gabhainn 2004 [HBSC]). By the time they are 17 years old, 70% of boys have been already drunk several times in their life and drink regularly with their friends (Youth 2004). Wine and beer are the most popular among boys, and spirits and wine among girls. In Hungary among adults there is a more spirit-oriented drinking culture, but spirit intake in contrast to the adult population in the 15-year-olds is relatively low (Schmidt and Gabhainn 2004 [HBSC]). Hungarian adolescents as a group are mainly wine drinkers. Regular alcohol consumption is associated with heavy smoking in almost every case.

Drug consumption habits have changed dramatically since the 1990s. Adolescent narcomania was a recognized problem already around 1975. Because of relative isolation, currency exchange problems, and the narrow market, Hungary was not a target of international drug trafficking at that time. As hard drugs were hardly available, the use of inhalants and later the combination of alcohol,

tranquilizers, and sleeping pills were the most common. The political changes in 1989 opened the borders of Hungary not only for travels and cultural exchange but also for illegal drugs. The latest survey was carried out with 16-year-olds by Paksi and Elekes in 2003 as a part of the ESPAD study. Their results show that approximately 40% of this age group has already tried some kind of illegal drugs. Almost half of them did this more than ten times and a quarter of them more than forty times. The most frequently tried drugs are marijuana (illicit in Hungary) and hashish. Very frequently used drugs are the so-called "disco drugs" (amphetamine, ecstasy). About 5% use LSD. The use of inhalants is less common in Hungary than the average of all ESPAD countries (5% versus 10%). The proportion of students who have ever used tranquilizers or sedatives without a doctor's prescription is above average (10% compared to 6%), and the tendency is the same for alcohol together with pills (11% and 7% respectively).

The first trial with a drug is typically at the age of 14 to 15, but every sixth drug user had the first encounter before the age of 14. Curiosity is the most frequent motivation (60%), followed by the desire "to feel good" (26%) and "to forget" (16%). There are significantly more boys who tried drugs than girls, but girls more often use sedatives and sleeping pills and alcohol together.

Since 2000, illegal drug consumption shows a mostly linear increase by an average of 1.5% per year, which is slower than between 1995 and 1999. The rate of illegal drug use in the capital and the national average were getting closer in 2003; still it was at least 30% higher in Budapest. In terms of proneness to drug abuse, it was found that there was no relationship between depression, negative self-concept, and drug use. But there has been a relationship between sensation-seeking and marijuana consumption. The higher SES of the family together with a higher-level education of the young person itself meant higher probability of drug use (ESPAD 2003).

Substance use (the consumption of alcohol, drugs, and smoking) sharply increases from the age of 15 to approximately 18 to 19 years and then reaches its peak and basically stagnates until the age 29. The use of drugs is the most frequent among the 20- to 24-year-olds. Religiosity (in case of marijuana use), being a member of a school club, being happy with school, and getting higher grades seem to be significant protective factors in Hungarian adolescents' substance use (Pikó and Fitzpatrick 2004).

A favorable tendency is that the popularity of sports is increasing among 15- to 29-year-olds.

According to the Youth 2004 study, 41% of 15- to 29-year-olds do sports regularly in their spare time. There is a significant gender difference, because boys participate in sport activities more frequently than girls (48% and 34% respectively), and young people living in Budapest also do more sports than those living in the countryside. In spite of the increase, in the HBSC study Hungarian adolescents were only the thirty-first among the 35 countries in terms of involvement in sport activities.

Among men, the most popular sports have been traditionally football (37%), bicycling (14%), jogging (7%), working out (6%), and body building (6%). Among young women, aerobics is the most popular (15%), followed by bicycling (14%), jogging (13%), working out (11%), and swimming (6%). Those who do not do sports mainly explain this with a lack of time (52%); others say that they do not like sports (19%), or they do not consider it important (8%), or they do not have enough energy (7%) (Youth 2004).

Hungary used to have one of the highest suicide rates in the world, but parallel with the political changes and presumably due to the more adequate therapeutic (for example widespread usage of antidepressants) and preventive strategies (National Programme for Suicide Prevention), Hungary currently stands in fifth place—following the countries of the former Soviet Union—of suicide statistics. Since 1980, there has been a 30% decrease in the overall suicide rate (from 45 per 100,000 in 1980 to 28 per 100,000 inhabitants in 2002). While in the 7 to 14 age-group the proportion of completed suicides has not changed, among the 15- to 24-year-olds there has been a 30% decrease as well (in 2002 total 10.5 per 100,000: males, 17.1 per 100,000; females, 3.6 per 100,000) (WHO 2004; Figure 1).

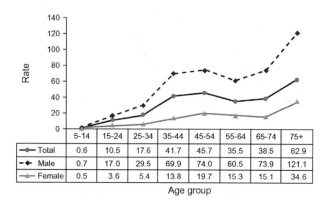

	5-14	15-24	25-34	35-44	45-54	55-64	65-74	75+
Total	0.6	10.5	17.6	41.7	45.7	35.5	38.5	62.9
Male	0.7	17.0	29.5	69.9	74.0	60.5	73.9	121.1
Female	0.5	3.6	5.4	13.8	19.7	15.3	15.1	34.6

Figure 1. Suicide rates (per 100,000), by gender and age, Hungary, 2002.
Source: WHO 2004.

Nevertheless, it is peculiar that in spite of the 30% decrease of completed suicides in the last two decades the number of suicide attempts—particularly in the adolescent population—shows a growing tendency. The "Child and Adolescent Self Harm in Europe" (CASE) study investigated the factors associated with attempted suicidal acts in ten European countries, like the United Kingdom, Denmark, Belgium, Germany, Ireland, Italy, the Netherlands, Norway, and Austria. It had a special focus on suicidal thoughts, ideation, deliberate self-harm, suicide attempts, and other self-destructive behavior (drug, alcohol, eating disorders) as well as psychopathological symptoms (anxiety, depression, impulsivity, aggression) and it also investigated how coping strategies, life events, family background, or social maintenance influenced possibilities of prevention. In the Hungarian part of the study, conducted by psychiatrists Sándor Fekete and Péter Osváth, 4,400 adolescents between the ages of 15 and 16 participated. They found that 7.8% of the adolescents (males, 4.6%; females, 11.6%) reported a former suicide attempt, and 1.6% of the boys and 3.6% of the girls reported about more than one suicide attempt. Suicidal thoughts were reported in one-quarter of the pupils, and almost 10% had suicidal thoughts in the previous months (Fekete and Osváth 2005).

According to the statistical analysis, the group of self-harmers greatly differed from the nonsuicidal one. Negative life events (former traumatic events or actual stress situations) were found to be more frequent in suicidal adolescents, and these pupils were more likely to use alcohol, drugs, or nicotine than their nonsuicidal peers. Students of the suicidal group were more likely to live without parents (brought up by relatives) and they were more often the subjects of sexual abuse. Suicide attempters usually had higher scores in the scales of measuring anxiety, depression, and impulsivity, while their self-esteem was significantly lower. In their conflicts they were more inclined to use inadequate solutions (self-blame, hostility, alcohol), and they were generally more ready to use less-effective coping strategies.

Comparing the results to other European countries, Fekete and Osváth found that there was a remarkable similarity in patterns across countries, despite some noteworthy differences. Corresponding to the average in Europe, a relatively low suicide attempt rate was found among adolescents in Hungary, while there was a high rate of suicidal ideation. Among those who already had a reported suicide attempt, the Hungarian adolescents had higher anxiety, depression, and impulsivity and lower self-esteem scores in both genders.

In terms of the role of family models in suicide acts, Fekete and Osváth found that the proportion of emotionally close models of suicide (family members) was the highest among the young suicidal people as opposed to the middle-aged and old ones.

Society may also affect young people's likelihood of committing or attempting suicide through the attitudes it inculcates toward it. In a cross-cultural study comparing mass media reports on suicide in four countries—the United States, Japan, Germany, and Hungary—Fekete and Osváth (2005) found that the most positive, accepting attitude toward suicide could be observed in the Hungarian media. Negative evaluations of suicide, its criminalization, and psychiatrization were much more frequent in the U.S. and German material, while positive, sometimes heroizing valuation (suicide as a tragedy) was found more often in the Hungarian one. Showing the negative consequences of suicide (suffering) was of a significantly higher rate in the American as well as the German material, which decreased the possibility of imitation-identification.

The frequency and level of depression among adolescents also contributes to suicidal ideas and acts. In 1998, among all those children and adolescents (3 to 18 years old) who visited five selected child and adolescent outpatient clinics in Hungary, every third met the diagnostic criteria of DSM-IV for depression (Sarungi et al. 1998). A representative study with more than 4,000 12- to 18-year-olds applying the Child Depression Inventory (Rózsa et al. 1999) found that in accordance with the international results, total scores on the CDI increased by age in both sexes, and girls attained higher mean scores than their male counterparts. In another representative study of 14- to 24-year-olds, 26% of females had depressive symptoms and 2.3% suffered severe depression (Kopp et al. 1999). In a more recent study, among 15-year-old girls 30% were in a depressive state, while among boys this was 18% (Aszmann 2003).

Around 90% of adolescent crimes in Hungary are committed by males (Jánosi 2002). The number of crimes committed by adolescents between the age of 14 and 17 has been decreasing from 1997, but from 2003 to 2004 there was an increase of 18%. The most common crimes committed by adolescents are property crimes (shoplifting, theft, and robbery). The number of drug-related crimes committed by underage young people has been increasing too. Among the crime victims, the number of adolescents shows a considerable increase around

20% yearly from 2000 to 2004 (Jánosi 2002; Hungary 2004). The most common crimes committed against adolescents are property crimes and rape.

Education

The literacy rate among the adult population (aged 15 or older) is 96% in Hungary. Compulsory schooling lasted from 6 to 16 years of age for many decades, but in 1996 the end of the compulsory schooling was extended to the age of 18 for those who began schooling in 1998–1999. The system of Hungarian school education has been under review for many years. The structure of the eight-grade general school and the consecutive three or four years of secondary education established in most socialist countries of Europe after 1945 started to come under scrutiny after 1990, when autonomy of the local and the institutional levels increased and the educational monopoly of the state was abolished. The 1993 Public Education Act already reflected the changing school structure. As a consequence, the definitions of primary schooling and secondary schooling were modified and the formerly firm division between general and vocational secondary education disappeared (Forgács and Lannert 2001).

The primary education of the early 2000s can be followed by the general secondary school offering an academic track with general university preparatory functions, the four-year-long vocational secondary school that offers a school-leaving exam that in principle makes it possible to continue studies in higher education, and the three-year vocational training school that prepares students for trades.

Forty-three percent of the students in secondary education complete compulsory schooling and go on to a vocational training school, 34% attend general secondary schools and 23% study in vocational schools (Youth 2004). The level of schooling is strongly dependent on the parental background. Those students whose parents have a low level of education are more likely to get into vocational training schools (Youth 2004). These schools enjoy a poor reputation amongst the general population in that they are judged to have low academic standards; and indeed, they have to cope with a proportion of students who remain functionally illiterate, despite having completed compulsory schooling.

At the turn of the twenty-first century, three different combinations of the elementary and academic track secondary education exist parallel in the Hungarian educational system: four-grade primary school with eight-grade general secondary school, six-grade primary school with six-grade general secondary school, eight-grade lower and upper primary and four-grade general secondary school. All three prepare students mainly for higher education, but they typically represent three different academic levels. Pupils who apply to the secondary school when they are fourth graders are typically high achievers, and they have to pass a very challenging and competitive entrance exam before they can start their studies in the eight-grade general secondary school. Those who are in the six-plus-six system are the second wave in academic terms, and those who stay in the lower and upper primary for eight years and continue to the four-grade secondary school are typically the lowest in terms of their academic achievement, however, they still aim towards higher education. In the 2004–2005 school year, 16% of the general secondary school students studied in the four-plus-eight system, 18% in the six-plus-six, and 66% in the traditional eight-plus-four primary and secondary school structure (Hungary 2004).

Most schools are public in Hungary. Three-quarters of the students study in public schools, 16% in religious or church schools, and only 5% in private secondary schools (Hungary 2004).

The qualification level of the Hungarian population has been constantly improving in the past decades. While in 1995 between 10% to 15% of each age cohort in Hungary did not complete the eight-year compulsory education (Tóth 1995), in 2004 97% of the 14- to 17-year-olds were in public education and the number of 18-year-olds participating in education was exactly the same as the EU-25 average, 76% (Hungary 2004).

The number of those who study in universities has also grown rapidly. In 1990–1991, only 5.5% of all 18- to 22-year-olds studied in universities; by 2005 this was more than 24%. Among those who aimed for higher education, 58% were accepted in 2004 (Hungary 2004). The most popular studies are economics, law, computer sciences, and psychology. The proportion of female students is 54%.

The socioeconomic background of students influences significantly the educational chances of young people in Hungary. The higher number of students having the possibility to continue their studies in universities does not mean a heightened opportunity for those young people whose parents have lower than a secondary education and for those from the countryside (Youth 2004). Hungary belongs to a group of countries (Belgium, Germany, Slovak Republic, and Turkey) defined by the PISA

(Programme for International Student Assessment) survey as one in which student performances are influenced above the international mean by the socioeconomic status of the student family and the presence of classical cultural assets (Lannert and Halász 2003). This means that those students who attend the general secondary schools have a more highly educated parental background and they achieve in many parts of PISA 2003 tests and subtests much better than the OECD average. However, those who attend vocational secondary schools and vocational training schools have a less-educated parental background and also much worse results in the international comparison. The offspring of low-status families have a higher than average probability of belonging to the "at risk group," with poorer chances of labor market success due to low competencies (Róbert 2004). On the contrary, those who are educated in the best secondary schools in Hungary get an exceptionally good, internationally highly competitive education. For instance, on the International Physics Olympiad in 2002 the Hungarian team was fifth among 67 nations; the same year on the International Chemistry Olympics they were the twelfth among 57 nations, and also the twelfth among 48 nations in mathematics. (Actually, in 2005 a Hungarian student—and a student from Taiwan—was the absolute winner of the International Physics Olympiad with the second best total scores in the last decade.)

The PISA 2000 and 2003 results drew attention to other shortcomings of the Hungarian education system too. Fifteen-year-old Hungarian students scored significantly below the average on exercises testing their reading and text comprehension ability, and nearly half of them failed to reach the level of reading comprehension necessary to successfully enter the labor market. On the other hand, according to the IEA studies (TIMSS 1995, TIMSS-R 1999) the performance of Hungarian eighth-graders was not only above the international average, but even improved between 1995 and 1999. Therefore, the lower than the average 2000 and 2003 PISA results, producing scores significantly below the international average, came as a surprise. Also, the biggest achievement difference among schools in terms of mathematic performance has been found in Hungary and Turkey, more than double the OECD average. Experts believe that the main reasons for the poor performance levels of Hungarian students may be attributed to the differences between the content and the practice of Hungarian education and the approach of the PISA assessment. Education in Hungary is still too academic: mainly theoretical, quite far from real life problems. The recent findings show that Hungarian students are not—or not effectively—trained for using their academic knowledge for problem solving in everyday situations. Actually, more than 40% of Hungarian students agree that school has done little to prepare them for life (OECD average: 32%).

The classroom management displays dominance of frontal teaching. Cooperative learning and new methods such as project work are scarcely used. The school environment is competitive and performance-oriented. Students therefore prefer to study on their own or competitively, and they do not prefer cooperative learning (Lannert and Halász 2003). Students clearly like more those lessons where there is competition, and they consider themselves more curious, energetic, active, and attentive during these lessons. While they are slightly more stressed, they also learn faster compared to noncompetitive lessons. The latter they characterize by a relaxed atmosphere but also with boredom and exhaustion (Fülöp 2005c).

Of all the countries surveyed, the 15-year-old students of Hungary spend the second longest period of time on completing their homework and are second only to Greek students in this respect (Lannert and Halász 2003). According to the HBSC study, a Hungarian secondary school student spends one hour and 45 minutes as an average on studying on a weekday and more than three hours during the weekend. Still, only every third respondent feels pressured by schoolwork (Samdal et al. 2004). Twenty-nine percent of the 15-year-olds like to go to school (Samdal et al. 2004), 35% do not like it at all (Lannert and Halász 2003), and also only 35% of them are satisfied with their achievement. The proportion of young people who like school a lot and also who report performing well or very well at school declines with age (Samdal et al. 2005).

Since Hungary ratified the Act LXIII of 1992 on the Data Protection Act, schools are prohibited to register pupils as Roma and this hinders gathering relevant statistical information on the real number of Romany students. The last national representative survey including real educational statistics on the Roma was conducted in 1993. Since there has been a significant shift in the school population as well as changes in the education system, researchers can reckon only trends concerning the participation of Romany children in different levels of schools. Despite the fact that we may conclude that the number of Romany children studying and finishing primary school has considerably

increased, as has their participation in secondary schools, the number of Roma students leaving secondary education institutions with a final exam is still very low (Kurucz 2004). The low performance and the high dropout rate of the Romany adolescents are due to a set of interweaving factors: the impact of deprived settlement, lack of school facilities, a hidden curriculum in schools, a discriminative attitude and negative expectations from teachers, low qualification of parents, lack of motivation to learn, diminished self-esteem, a tense situation between family and school, and other factors (Havas et al. 2002; Kende 2005). In 2003, it was estimated that 78% of Romany children finish a maximum eight grades, 18% of them study in vocational training schools, and only 3.4% of them have a final school-leaving exam from either a vocational training school or a general secondary school. The number of Romany young people studying in higher education is only about 1% (Kemény et al. 2004).

In the curricular content of mainstream education there is hardly any material on the language, history, and culture of national minorities, ethnic groups, and immigrants. The majority of immigrants come from neighboring countries and are mostly of Hungarian nationality and are Hungarian-speaking and have similar historical, cultural, and religious backgrounds to that of the host population. Their children do not face special educational difficulties in the Hungarian schools. However, children of non-Hungarian-speaking immigrants face serious linguistic and cultural challenges. Following the political transition, the number of permanent and legally settled foreigners (such as the Chinese, Vietnamese) increased significantly in Hungary, yet the majority of schools accessible to immigrant children only offered Hungarian language education. In schools maintained by local governments, the Hungarian language is taught only as a mother tongue, which is an inefficient solution for immigrants. They are often forced to repeat a school grade due to language difficulties, thus attend classes grades below their age level (Lannert and Halász 2003). This is far from an ideal context for the socialization of self-confident adolescents with a positive self-image among those young people who are not Hungarian in origin.

Work

In the changing economy of the Hungarian transitional society, the structure of employment underwent significant changes. The proportion of workforce among the major sectors of economy has changed in harmony with the international trends. Hungary has already moved to the pattern of postindustrial economies, meaning that employment in the agricultural sector has decreased significantly (now less then 6%) while the number of those employed in the service sector increased, with services being the most important sector of economy (60%) (Lannert and Halász 2003).

Right after the political changes the economy went through a long-lasting crisis; by the end of the 1990s the GDP dropped by 20% and one-and-a-half million workplaces disappeared, which resulted in mass unemployment. Unemployment in itself and in this proportion was unexpected for the society as it had been an unknown phenomenon during the state socialism that guaranteed full employment. The society was not prepared mentally and institutionally to deal with these changes. Nowadays Hungarian young people have to find their jobs in a post-socialist society that is shifting from a dependence culture to an enterprise culture (Crawford and Foster 2001), and from a security society to an opportunity society (Flanagan et al. 2003). Such a shift entails replacing the basic existential stability, available for all in the socialist countries, with opportunities for the individual citizen. This process is a transition from constraint to choice, from uniformity to pluralism. In brief, the new social order provides more autonomy, but less security: there is more to gain, but also more to lose. Individual responsibility and agency is emphasized in finding a place in the job market.

The unemployment rate has been decreasing sharply since around 2000, and it was 5.9% in 2004. In the 15- to 24-year-old group it reached its peak in 1993 when it was 33% and has been also decreasing dramatically to 15.5% by 2004. The 2004 rate is somewhat lower that the EU average (18.6% in 2004) (Hungary 2004). Among the economically inactive and the unemployed youth, approximately 30% have only a primary school education, while this is 10% among the economically active (Youth 2004). This means that young people who have a low educational level have a much greater chance to become inactive and unemployed than those with at least a vocational level education, and their realistic prospects are dead-end jobs, often in the black economy. However, the unemployment rate of those with a fresh university degree has been growing too, and it was 6.7% in 2004 (Hungary 2004). A high proportion of the respondents of the Youth Study 2004 expressed fears related to losing their job: 44% among the blue-collar workers and 33% among those with a

university degree. There is also a big regional divide in terms of the probability of becoming unemployed in the country. It is the lowest in the capital (only 6% of the 15 to 19 age-group and 31% of the 20 to 24 age-group has experienced unemployment) and the highest in Northern Hungary (11% of the 15 to 19 age-group and 49% of the 20- to 24-year-olds have experienced unemployment). While unemployment affects unskilled youngsters the most, there is a large demand for trained personnel in services and business. Foreign language knowledge, computer literacy, and business administration skills are highly appreciated in the job market (Laki 2002).

Roma young people have severe difficulties in finding a job. Their highly marginalized position in the labor market is a consequence of their marginalization and exclusion from education: very high proportions of young Roma do not complete compulsory schooling, and they are therefore hopelessly disadvantaged when it comes to finding jobs. Their families are generally unable to cushion their difficult transition to paid work, since they too are the poorest section of Hungarian society.

The timing and mode of the transition from the world of school into the world of work depend primarily on the type of education the young person participates in. The number of active workers among the 15- to 24-year-olds is decreasing (at the moment 23.6%) due to the later entry to the job market as a result of the longer studies and also as a consequence of the growing difficulties of finding a job among those who start their career (Hungary 2004). The school-to-work transition is not smooth. It is uncommon among adolescents who are still studying in the secondary education to take a part-time job either during the school year or during the summer vacation, especially because there are not many work opportunities. It changes somewhat by the university years. About 10% of those students who are in higher education combine their studies with work (Youth 2004). Therefore, most of the young people do not have employment experiences before they appear in the job market looking for work.

In the 15 to 29 age-group, 39% are fully employed and an additional 5% both work and study full-time. The others are either full-time students (40%), or unemployed (7%), or economically inactive (10%). The percentage of blue-collar workers among those who work has been decreasing from 66% in 2000 to 58% in 2004 (Youth 2004). Approximately 30% of the working young people are very satisfied with their income, while exactly an equal 30% of them are not satisfied at all. Thirty-eight percent of the

actively working young people have to commute between their home and their workplace (Youth 2004).

The majority of young people (40%) find a job by the recommendation of friends and acquaintances. The second most common way to find a job is by the help of parents or relatives. In 2003, only 4% got a job via an employment center and 1% via the Internet (Central Statistical Office, KSH 2003).

Young people who are about to enter the job market of the newly established capitalist market economy are divided in their ideas. They are partly pro-reform, rejecting socialism and preferring capitalism and the market economy; on the other hand, they believe that socialism gave many important and valuable securities that they would like to have back (Fülöp 2005a). University students and young professionals (economists, agricultural engineers, and architects) were found to be in a kind of "ideological limbo." They agreed that the most important features of a well-functioning society were free economic competition, market-led economic processes, and significant income differentials; but they also wished for full employment and that the state should care for the weak. This combines capitalist and socialist principles: young adults would like the advantages of capitalism—consumer choice and productivity of the market—without losing the security of jobs and social services provided by socialism (Vári-Szilágyi and Solymosi 1999).

Under the Communist-Socialist system, all members of society received social support, regardless of their level of contribution to the society. Individual rewards did not depend on individual effort ("from each according to ability, to each according to need"). In practice, advancement had less to do with hard work and dedication than it did to political connections, and was based on subjective—and often political—assessments. Part of the transformation to the market economy was aimed at eliminating this disjunction between individual effort and economic reward.

In theory, competitive market economies and political pluralism should offer the optimal motivation to develop individual capacities and abilities, and this should differentiate people solely on the basis of their achievements. This should mean acceptance that there will be winners and losers and of the principle "let the better win: this is how we will progress." However, if there is a perception that competition is unfair, and the income gap does not necessarily reflect hard work, merit, or talent, but sometimes is the consequence of private

connections, corruption, and illegal ways of getting resources, then there will be negative attitudes towards winners, the successful, and the wealthy (Fülöp and Berkics 2003).

When Hungarian and French adolescents were compared in terms of their views on competition in the market economy, the majority of the French 16- to 18-year-olds agreed that competition in economic activity or in other aspects of life rewards the persistent and hardworking, while this was the minority opinion among the Hungarian adolescents (69%, compared to 29% for the Hungarians). The French also agreed more with the statement that entrepreneurs work hard to achieve success. In contrast, more Hungarians agreed that competition rewards the strong but not the weak. French teenagers showed a belief in meritocracy, while Hungarians took a more social-Darwinist view (Fülöp, Roland-Levy and Berkics 2004).

In another study carried out in 2001, a group of 16- to 18-year-old Hungarians was examined. It was found that at the end of their year studying in a special economic education program (Junior Achievement Program), secondary school students had one of three distinctively different, coherent views about business and people dealing with business. Besides a positive view of business life (including such statements as "businesspeople are the driving force of the economic development"), there was a negative view too. The negative concept sees businesspeople as getting rich at the expense of others, exploiting those that work for them, and being immoral. According to this view, in business there is no humanity; only achievement counts, no one can be trusted, only money is important, and the market economy is only beneficial for a narrow group of society. This combination of ideas resembles the socialist ideology that emphasized equality and condemned wealth because it is derived from the exploitation of the majority. The third concept revealed a realistic but rather cynical view of business life; that is, connections are the most important element in being successful, and the majority of entrepreneurs are believed to have established close connections with political leaders (Fülöp and Berkics 2003). In spite of these disillusioned views on the world of work and business life, going into business is a popular career choice for young people in Hungary.

Media

Time spent watching TV was about 85 minutes per day in 1986 among adolescents, but in 2004 it was already 138 minutes on a weekday and 240 minutes on a weekend day among the 15- to 19-year-olds, the commercial TV channels and MTV being the most popular (Youth 2004).

The proportion of Hungarian households having a computer in 2004 was 32% and Internet availability was 14% (World Internet Project—TÁRKI 2004). However, the Youth 2004 study shows that in those households where there are adolescents the proportion is somewhat higher; it is 57% and 24% respectively. The number of the households with adolescents owning a computer has been growing rapidly and almost doubled as the Youth 2000 study showed that only 29% owned a computer at that time. There are significant regional differences in the country. Adolescents living in the more developed western and central parts of Hungary have a bigger chance to have access to computer and the Internet at home, and 71% of those living in the capital Budapest live in households owning a computer. The highest availability of computers is among the 15- to 19-year-old age group. Boys typically spend more time in front of the computer playing computer games than girls.

In terms of Internet usage the numbers are higher: 77% of the 15- to 19-year-olds use the Internet either at home, in the school, or elsewhere (Youth 2004). There are more boys among them. Internet availability also increased rapidly from 2000 to 2004. In 2000, only 9% of the young people had access to the Internet at home (Youth 2000).

The Internet can serve several purposes. Among those who have Internet access, 51% use it for electronic communication (e-mail, chatting) at least once per week. Seventeen percent use the Internet daily to get news and information about the world and 47% of them do this at least once a week. As an information source for work and study, 51% use the Internet. Forty-two percent download music, games, and films, and 10% use it for online shopping or for bank transactions (Youth 2004).

In the beginning of the 1990s, the use of mobile phones started to spread out. However, one obstacle was a cultural one. There was a widespread belief that mobile phones are the status symbols of those who were the so-called "new rich" of the Hungarian society after the political changes. The "new rich" were looked down upon because they wanted to show off and demonstrate their financial status by these phones, therefore mobile phones got a nickname: the "dumb phone" (a phone for those who are stupid). This view has gradually changed with the growing number of mobile phone owners in the society. Young people between 14 and 20 who attend the Island Festival (who are mostly from Budapest and from a higher

Table 1. Percentage of Adolescents Aged 14 to 20 Who Owned Various Devices between 1999 and 2004

	1999	2000	2001	2002	2003	2004
Mobile phone	17.8	41.8	73.5	90.0	95.2	97.0
CD-player	54.6	63.8	68.8	79.4	82.7	90.2
Desktop Computer	43.0	47.7	53.1	65.3	69.3	77.8
Own apartment	13.6	19.5	20.2	22.5	22.1	23.5
Valuable sports gear	30.0	19.9	18.8	19.6	19.3	28.4
Own car	11.0	12.9	15.7	19.2	17.2	17.3
Motorbike	13.1	10.8	11.1	12.2	9.0	11.6

Source: Czeizer and Gábor 2005.

SES background) are more into cyber-culture and own much more valuable objects than the representative sample of young people in the Youth Studies. Ninety-seven percent of them have a mobile phone. (Higher Education Research Institute 1999–2004; Czeizer and Gábor 2005). See Table 1.

More than 75% of the respondents stated that they could not imagine their life without a mobile phone. In the last decade text messages (SMS) became more popular than conversations over the phone or personal face-to-face meetings. The majority of adolescents use text messages to set up dates and to flirt. One-third of the boys and one-fourth of the girls do not see any objection against breaking a love affair via a text message. More traditional activities like reading are less and less popular among adolescents. The average number of books read per year beyond the school textbooks is 8.7 (Youth 2004). Girls own more books at home than boys (105 and 78 respectively). Time spent with reading has been constantly decreasing (from 39 minutes per day in 1986 to 13 minutes per day among 15- to 19-year-old boys and 17 minutes among the same age girls in 1999) (Central Statistical Office, KSH 2000). Only 12% of young people read the daily papers regularly, but magazines and yellow pages are more popular, especially among girls.

Politics and Military

Hungary is a parliamentary democracy with a multi-party government system. After the socialist era, the first freely elected government was set up in 1990. The main parties are the Hungarian Socialist Party (MSZP) and the Hungarian Civic Alliance (FIDESZ). Hungary is a republic. The head of the state is the President of the Republic, who is elected by the parliament. Real executive power is exercised by the Prime Minister.

Young people have the right to vote and participate in the political elections from the age of 18. Studies on political socialization carried out in the last fifteen years, however, constantly showed a very low level of interest towards political activity. In spite of this, between the two rounds of the 2002 general elections many teenagers made a surprising exception of this pattern. The application of new communications and information technology mostly utilized by young people suddenly became important. Grassroots e-mail and text message campaigns were started and used to activate people to join political rallies. Cell phone users sent around four to five million text messages daily, an approximately 20% increase over average nonelection periods, and most of them were sent by adolescents and young adults (Hain and Nguyen Luu 2003). There were a growing number of young people present at the election rallies too. While this behavior was directly observable during the elections of 2002, the answers of the Youth 2004 survey did not verify a higher interest in politics. On a five-point Likert-type scale it was 2.19. University students had the highest average: 2.9, but 63% of the respondents reported not to be interested in politics at all. Only 39% of the respondents would go and vote if a political election happened now, and 13% definitely would not participate. Another dimension of political activity is participation in different civil organizations. There is a kind of passivity in this respect too. Only 15% of the respondents are members of any social, political, religious, charity, or cultural organizations.

The low level of political interest is accompanied by a high level of distrust towards democratic institutions. On a scale from −40 to +40, the lowest average belongs to the political parties currently in the government (−33.4); the opposition parties have the second lowest average (−25.7); followed by the parliament and the government as a whole. The highest level of trust was indicated towards the army (+5.2), the police (+11.1), and the justice system (courts, +19.4), institutions that might be considered to strengthen the feeling of safety among youth (Youth 2004).

While young people have a negative view of the democratic institutions of the society, Flanagan et al. (1998) found that Hungarian adolescents perceive their school climate as democratic as American and Swedish young people do, whereas Czech, Bulgarian, and Russian adolescents report perceiving their schools as significantly less democratic. This might relate to Hungary having had relatively the greatest degree of political freedom among the post-socialist countries in the pre-1980 period.

The perception of the political changes is rather negative among the young people. This means that according to 55% of respondents of the Youth 2004 study, the standard of living of the majority of the society has been decreasing since the political changes. Fifty percent have the opinion that the economy of the country has also deteriorated, and in addition to this 34% think that his or her own family's situation has also deteriorated. In all three dimensions only about one-quarter of the respondents experienced improvement.

This perception, however, changes with the level of education. Twenty-six percent of the university students think that their family has been a winner of the political changes, but this is only 8% among those who have only primary schooling. In fact, 42% of them consider his or her own family the loser of the changes. The youngest age group (15 to 19 years old) with a highly educated family background and living in Budapest has the most positive opinion about the political changes.

In terms of parental influence on political views, there seems to be a high level of correspondence between parents and children. Forty-three percent of the respondents say that they have the same political standpoint as their parents, and only 10% have a completely opposite opinion. Those between the age of 15 and 19, female respondents, and respondents whose father has a university degree had the most similar political attitudes as their parents.

After the collapse of the socialist regime, a rise of prejudice against ethnic groups such as Romas, Jews, and immigrants was experienced in Hungary. The first examination measuring anti-Semitic attitudes was carried out in 1993 (Kovács 1999). This study measured the strength of anti-Semitic prejudice among university and college students ("the possible members of the country's future elite"). It demonstrated that about 8% of Hungarian college and university students were extreme anti-Semites, 18% were anti-Semites, 32% accepted some anti-Semitic stereotypes, and 42% were not anti-Semites. The Youth 2000 study had striking results related to racism and ethnic prejudice. Only 32% of young people in Budapest would accept a Jewish person in the family and 21% of them would not wish to live in the same country with them. In the case of the northern region of Hungary, the region that lags behind the most, 41% of the respondents would not wish to share the country with Jews. Anti-Gypsy attitudes are much more prevalent than other ethnic prejudices, and the Roma are the least accepted out-group. Besides old people, adolescents have the most negative attitude towards them. Fifty-five percent of the 15- to 19-year-olds would not wish to live in the same country with Roma people. Those young people living in urban areas are less nationalist and racist than those living in the rural areas (Youth 2000). Religiosity among adolescents is accompanied by more tolerant views and attitudes towards the Roma, but it is just the opposite in the case of anti-Semitism: those who are more religious are more likely to accept anti-Semitic views (Enyedi and Erõs 1999).

Hungary became a member of NATO in 1994. Military service starts at the age of 18. The compulsory draft was abolished in 2004. Serving in the army has not been popular among young men. While it was still compulsory, many young men tried to avoid it by finding different kinds of health reasons. Mainly those who had a lower education served full-time in the army or chose it as a potential career path.

MÁRTA FÜLÖP

References and Further Reading

Aszmann, A. (ed). 2003. *Iskoláskorú gyerekek egészségmagatartása (Health behavior of school-age children)*. Budapest: Országos Gyermekegészésgügyi Intézet.

Back-up Society for Homosexuals *(Háttér Társaság a Melegekért)*. http://www.hatter.hu/.

Bauer, B., and A. Szabó. 2005. *Ifjúság 2004. Gyorsjelentés (Youth 2004)*. Budapest: Nemzeti Ifjúságkutató Intézet.

Bukodi, E., I. Harcsa, and Gy. Vukovich. 2004. Hungarian Society Reflected in Indicators. In *Social Report 2004*. T. Kolosi, I. Gy. Tóth, and Gy. Vukovich (eds.). pp. 17–46. Budapest: TÁRKI Social Research Centre.

Council of Europe. 1999. Recent Demographic Developments in Europe. Strasbourg: Council of Europe Publishing.

Crawford, K., and R. Foster. 2001. Education for citizenship in Romania and the U.K.: A comparison. *Children's Social and Economic Education*. 4:170–83.

Csapó, B. 1994. Hungary. In *International handbook of adolescence*. K. Hurrelman (ed.). pp. 170–90. Westport, Conn.: Greenwood Press.

Csukonyi, Cs., H. Sallay, and Á. Münich. 1999. Individualizmus és kollektivizmus: csoportkülönbségek egyetemisták körében *(Individualism and collectivism: Group differences among university students)*. *Alkalmazott Pszichológia*. 1:19–31.

Czeizer, Z., and K. Gábor. 2005. *Az ifjúsági korszakváltás és az új kommunikációs státusz kapcsolatának vizsgálata (Study of the relationship between youth culture and communicational status)*. pp. 22–33. Szabadpart.

Enyedi, Zs., and F. Erõs (eds.) 1999. *Authoritarianism and prejudice. Central European perspectives*. Budapest: Osiris.

ESPAD. 2003. European school survey project of alcohol and other drugs. http://www.espad.org/key_hungary.html.

Fekete, S., and P. Osvath. 2005. *Suicide studies—From genetics to psychiatry and culture*. Pécs: University of Pécs.

Flanagan, C. A., J. M. Bowes, B. Jonsson, B. Csapo, and E. Sheblanova. 1998. Ties that bind: Correlates of adolescents' civic commitments in seven countries. *Journal of Social Issues*. 54:1–9.

Flanagan, C. A., B. Campbell, L. Botcheva, J. Bowes, B. Csapo, P. Macek, and E. Sheblanova. 2003. Social class and adolescents' beliefs about justice in different social orders. *Journal of Social Issues* 59:711–32.

Forgács, A., and J. Lanner, eds. 2001. *Education in Hungary 2000*. Budapest: National Institute of Public Education.

Fülöp, M. 2002. Competition in Hungary and Britain perceived by adolescents. *Applied Psychology in Hungary* 33–55.

Fülöp, M. 2005a. The development of social, economical, political identity among adolescents in the post-socialist countries of Europe. In *Growing up in Europe today: Developing identities among adolescents*. M. Fülöp and A. Ross (eds.). pp. 11–39. Stoke-on-Trent: Trentham Books.

Fülöp, M. 2005b. The role of gender in competition viewed by Canadian, Hungarian and Japanese young adults. Paper presented on the VIIth Regional Congress of the International Association of Cross Cultural Psychology, San Sebastian.

Fülöp, M. 2005c. A versengés hatása a tanórai motivációra (The effect of competition on motivation to learn). Paper presented at the National Conference on Education, Budapest.

Fülöp, M., and M. Berkics. 2002. Economic education and attitudes towards enterprise, business and competition among adolescents in Hungary. In *Young people's understanding of economic issues in Europe*. M. Hutchings, M. Fülöp, and A. M. Van Den Dries (eds.). pp. 129–53. Stoke-on-Trent: Trentham Books.

Fülöp, M., and M. Berkics. 2003. Socialisation for coping with competition, winning and losing in two societies: Hungary and the U.K. In *A Europe of many cultures*. A. Ross (ed.). pp. 263–73. London: CICE Publications.

Fülöp, M., and M. Berkics. 2005. University students' representation of the ideal woman and ideal man. Unpublished manuscript.

Fülöp, M., I. Davies, M. Berkics, M. Hutchings, and A. Ross. 2002. Ki a jó állampolgár Magyarországon és Nagy-Britanniában? *(Who is a good citizen in Britain and Hungary?)* In *Identitás és pedagógia (Identity and education)*. Á. Gocsál (ed.). pp. 11–23. Pécs: Pécsi Tanoda Alapítvány.

Fülöp, M., C. Roland-Levy, and M. Berkics. 2004. Economic competition perceived by French and Hungarian adolescents. In *The experience of citizenship*. A. Ross (ed.). pp. 325–31. London: Metropolitan University.

Furnham, A., B. D. Kirkcaldy, and R. Lynn. 1994. National attitude to competitiveness, money, and work among young people: First, second, and third world differences. *Human Relations* 47:119–32.

Gábor, K., and I. Balog. 1999. The impact of consumer culture on Eastern and Central European youth. *Education* 2:311–26.

Hain, F. 2005. A WIW: egy online közösség elsõ két éve két kutatás eredményeinek tükrében (WIW: An online community in the light of a two-years-long research). Paper presented at the Hungarian Sunbelt Network Analysis Conference, Budapest.

Hain, F., and L. A. Nguyen Luu. 2003. Grassroots e-mail and SMS political campaign—an unusual political action of the young generation in the 2002 Hungarian elections. Paper presented at the Annual Conference of the Royal Geographical Society and Institute of British Geographers, London.

Havas, G., I. Kemény, and I. Liskó. 2002. *Cigány gyerekek az általános iskolában (Romany children in the comprehensive school)*. Budapest: Oktatáskutató Intézet and Új Mandátum Kiadó.

Jánosi, Gy. 2002. J/1861. jelentés a gyermekek és az ifjúság helyzetéről, életkörülményeik alakulásáról és az ezzel összefüggésben a 2001. évben megtett kormányzati intézkedésekről. A Magyar Köztársaság Kormánya (Report on the circumstances of youth and governmental guidelines in connection with it in 2001). http://www.parlament.hu/irom37/1861/1861.html.

Kagitcibasi, C. 2005. Modernization does not mean Westernization: Emergence of a different pattern. In *Culture and human development: The importance of cross-cultural research to the social sciences*. W. Friedlmeier, P. Chakkarath, and B. Schwarz (eds.). pp. 255–72. Hove, U.K.: Psychology Press.

Kemény, I., B. Jánky, and G. Lengyel. 2004. *A magyarországi cigányság 1971-2003 (Romany people in Hungary 1971–2003)*. Budapest: Gondolat.

Kende, A. 2005. Értelmiségiként leszek roma és romaként leszek értelmiségi. Vizsgálat roma egyetemisták életútjáról (I am an intellectual and a Romany person and I am a Romany person and an intellectual. A study about the life course of Romany university students). In *Kisebbségek kisebbsége*. M. Neményi and J. Szalai (eds.). pp. 376–408. Budapest: Új Mandátum kiadó.

Kopp, M., Cs. Csoboth, and Gy. Purebl. 1999. Fiatal nők egészségi állapota (The health status of young females). http://www.tarki.hu/adatbank-h/nok/szerepvalt/Kopp99.html.

Kovács, A. 1999. *Antisemitic prejudice in contemporary Hungary*. Jerusalem: The Vidal Sassoon International Center for the Study of Antisemitism at the Hebrew University of Jerusalem.

Kurucz, E. 2004. Black and white trapped in integration. www.policy.hu/Kurucz/polpap.pdf.

Laki, L. 2002. Munkaerõ-piaci helyzet, gazdasági aktivitás, foglalkoztatottak, földbirtoklás és vállakozás (Conditions in the job market, economic activity, employees, landowners and enterprise). In *Ifjúság 2000 (Youth 2000) Tanulmányok I*. A. Szabó, B. Bauer, and L. Laki (eds.). pp. 61–115. Budapest: Nemzeti Ifjúságkutató Intézet.

Lannert, J., and G. Halász. 2003. *Education in Hungary in 2003*. Budapest: National Institute of Public Education (OKI).

Macek, P., C. Flanagan, L. Gallay, L. Kostron, L. Botcheva, and B. Csapó. 1998. Postcommunist societies in

times of transition: Perceptions of change among adolescents in Central and Eastern Europe. *Journal of Social Issues.* 54: 547–56.

Magyar Statisztikai Évkönyv (Hungarian Statistical Yearbook). Budapest: Központi Statisztikai Hivatal (Central Statistical Office—KSH).

Magyarország 2004 (Hungary 2004). 2004. Budapest: Központi Statisztikai Hivatal (Central Statistical Office—KSH).

Mészáros, Gy. 2003. Techo-house szubkultúra és iskolai nevelés (Techno-house subculture and education in school). *Iskolakultúra* 9:3–63.

Mulvihill, C., Á. Németh, and C. Vereechen. 2004. Body image, weight control and body weight. In *Young people's health in context. Health behaviour in school-aged children (HBSC) study: International report from 2001/2002 survey.* C. Currie et al. (eds.). pp. 120–29. Copenhagen: WHO Policy Series: Health Policy for Children and Adolescents.

National Epidemiological Centre. 2005. AIDS Statistics (Országos Epidemiológiai Központ). http://www.oek.hu/oek.web?nid=334&pid=1.

Németh, Á. 2003. Global youth tobacco survey. Hungary national report. National Center of Health Promotion and Development. http://www.cdc.gov/tobacco/global/gyts/reports/hungary01.htm.

Nguyen Luu, L. A., M. Kovács, and I. H. Frieze. Values and ambivalence towards men and women. *Applied Psychology in Hungary* 5–6: 5–21.

Noack, P., M. Hofer, B. Kracke, and E. Klein-Allerman. Adolescents and their parents facing social change: Families in East and West Germany after unification. In *Psychological Responses to Social Change.* P. Noack, M. Hofer, and J. Youniss (eds.). pp. 129–48. Berlin: deGruyter.

OECD. 2004. Learning for tomorrow's world: First results from PISA 2003. http://www.pisa.oecd.org/pages/0,2987,en_32252351_32235731_1_1_1_1_1,00.html.

Paksi, B., and Zs. Elekes. 2003. A középiskolások drogfogyasztása 2003-ban Budapesten (Drug use among secondary school students in Budapest, 2003. Report and Tendencies). *Addiktológia* 3–4:275–305.

Pedersen, M., C. M. Rodriguez, and R. Smith. 2004. Family. In *Young people's health in context. Health behaviour in school-aged children (HBSC) study: International report from 2001/2002 survey.* C. Currie et al. (eds.). pp. 26–30. Copenhagen: WHO Policy Series: Health Policy for Children and Adolescents.

Pikó B., and K. M. Fitzpatrick. 2001. Does class matter? SES and psychosocial health among Hungarian adolescents. *Social Science & Medicine* 53:817–30.

Pikó, B., K. Barabás, and K. Boda. 1997. The frequency of common psychosomatic symptoms and its influence on self-perceived health in a Hungarian student population. *European Journal of Public Health* 7:243–47.

Pikó, B. F., and K. M. Fitzpatrick. 2004. Substance use, religiosity, and other protective factors among Hungarian adolescents. *Addictive Behaviour* 29:1095–1107.

Pinquart, M., and R. K. Silbereisen. 2004. Human development in times of social change: Theoretical considerations and research needs. *International Journal of Behavioral Development* 28:289–98.

Róbert, P. Educational performance and social background in international comparison. In *Social Report 2004.*

T. Kolosi, I. Gy. Tóth, and Gy. Vukovich (eds.). pp. 186–97. Budapest: TÁRKI Social Research Centre.

Roberts, K., S. C. Clark, C. Fagan, J. Tholen. 2000. *Surviving post-communism. Young people in the former Soviet Union.* Northampton: Edward Elgar Publishing.

Rózsa, S., Á. Vetró, A. V. Komlósi, J. Gádoros, N. Kõ, N. Csorba, and J. Csorba. 1999. Gyermek és serdülõkori depresszió kérdõíves mérésének lehetõsége a klinikai és normatív mintán szerzett tapasztalatok alapján (Measuring child and adolescent depression with questionnaire on a clinical and a normative sample). *Pszichológia* 19:459–82.

Samdal, O., W. Dür, and J. Freeman. 2004. School. In *Young people's health in context. Health behaviour in school-aged children (HBSC) study: International report from 2001/2002 survey.* C. Currie et al. (eds.). pp. 42–52. Copenhagen: WHO Policy Series: Health Policy for Children and Adolescents.

Saris, W. E., and A. Ferligoj. 1995. Life satisfaction and domain satisfaction in 10 European countries: Correlation at the individual level. In *A comparative study of satisfaction with life in Europe.* W. E. Saris, R. Veenhoven, A. C. Scherpenzeel, and B. Bunting (eds.). pp. 275–81. Budapest: Eötvös University Press.

Sarungi, E., E. Kaczwinszky, A. Vetró, J. Csorba, and S. és Rózsa. 1998. A gyermek—és serdülőkori depresszió előfordulási gyakorisága és mérésének lehetőségei gyermekpszichiátriai betegeknél (Frequency and measurement of child and adolescent depression). Paper presented at the IV National Conference of the Hungarian Psychiatry Society, Budapest.

Schmid, H., and S. N. Gabhainn. 2004. Alcohol use. In *Young people's health in context. Health behaviour in school-aged children (HBSC) study: International report from 2001/2002 survey.* C. Currie et al. (eds.). pp. 78–83. Copenhagen: WHO Policy Series: Health Policy for Children and Adolescents.

Sefcsik, T. 2003. A panaszkodás természetrajza (The nature of complaining). Master's thesis, Szeged University.

Settertobulte, W., and M. G. de Matos. 2004. Peers. In *Young people's health in context. Health behaviour in school-aged children (HBSC) study: International report from 2001/2002 survey.* C. Currie et al. (eds.). pp. 34–42. Copenhagen: WHO Policy Series: Health Policy for Children and Adolescents.

Susánszky, É. and Zs. Szántó. 2002. Az egészségi állapot szempontjából veszélyeztetett fiatalok demográfiai és társadalmi jellemzői (Demographic and social characteristics of youth at health risk). In *Ifjúság 2000 (Youth 2000).* A. Szabó, B. Bauer, and L. Laki (eds.). pp. 154–65. Budapest: Nemzeti Ifjúságkutató Intézet.

Szabó, A., B. Bauer, and L. Laki, eds. 2002. *Ifjúság 2000 (Youth 2000)* Tanulmányok I. Budapest: Nemzeti Ifjúságkutató Intézet.

Szumska I., F. Túry, Á. Hajnal, Cs. Csoboth, Gy. Purebl, and J. Réthelyi. 2001. Evészavarok prevalenciája fiatal nők hazai reprezentatív mintájában. (The prevalence of eating disorders among a representative sample of young females). *Psychiatria Hungarica* 16:374–83.

Thoresen, V. W. 2005. The development of consumer identity in adolescents in Europe. In *Growing up in Europe today: Developing identities among adolescents.* M. Fülöp and A. Ross (eds.). pp. 153–64. Stoke-on-Trent: Trentham Books.

Torsheim, T., R. Valimaa, and M. Danielson. 2004. Health and well-being. In *Young people's health in context. Health behaviour in school-aged children (HBSC) study: International report from 2001/2002 survey.* C. Currie et al. (eds.). pp. 55–63. Copenhagen: WHO Policy Series: Health Policy for Children and Adolescents.

Tóth, O. 1995. Political-moral attitudes amongst young people in post-communist Hungary. In *Growing up in Europe: Contemporary Horizon.* L. Chisholm (ed.). pp. 189–94. Berlin: Walter de Gruyter.

Trommsdorff, G. Future time perspective and control orientation: Social conditions and consequences. In *Psychology of Future Orientation.* Z. Zaleski (ed.). pp. 39–62. Lublin: Towarzystvo Naukowe KUI.

Van Hoorn, J. L., Á. Komlósi, E. Suchar, and D. A. Samelson. 2000. *Adolescent development and rapid social change.* Albany: State University of New York Press.

Vári-Szilágyi, I., and Zs. Solymosi. 1999. *A siker lélektana (The psychology of success).* Budapest: Hatodik Síp Alapítvány. Új Mandátum Könyvkiadó.

WHO Health Report. 2000. Highlights on Health in Hungary. http://www.who.dk/eprise/main/WHO/CountryInformation/HFAExtracts?Country=HUN&Ctry Name=Hungary&language=English.

World Internet Project—TÁRKI. 2004. http://www.tarki.hu/research/wip/.

Zimmerman, J. 2005. A pubertáskori növekedés és a nemi érés kapcsolata (The relationship between growth and sexual maturation). Paper presented at the Országos Tudományos Diákköri Konferencia, Budapest. http://biol-otdk2005.pte.hu/11abs_human.html.

I

ICELAND

Background Information

Iceland is an island in the North Atlantic Ocean, with a total land area of 103,000 square kilometers (about 40,000 square miles). It sits directly on the fault line between the tectonic plates of the Eastern and Western hemispheres. With its mountains and deep fjords, glaciers and volcanoes, Iceland is often called the country of ice and fire.

Starting in 874, Iceland was settled by Norsemen and Celts. The settlers felt the need for general laws and rules, and in 930 established a parliament based on democratic principles. The historic treasure of the Icelandic culture is the sagas, written between 1180 and 1300 A.D. Icelanders are known for their passion for literature and poetry and Iceland publishes more books and magazines per capita than any other nation (Bureau of European and Eurasian Affairs 2004).

In 2004, the population was around 294,000 people, of whom over 60% lived in the metropolitan area of Reykjavik, the capital. That year, 23% of the population were under age 15, with 7.1% between 15 and 19, 7.7% between 20 and 24, and 12% age 65 and older (Statistics Iceland 2005).

The population has always been very ethnically homogeneous, but toward the end of the twentieth century the number of immigrants increased rapidly. In 1995, 1.8% of the population were immigrants, rising to 3.6% in 2004, with 37 languages spoken in the country, including Icelandic, the national language. Migration is from various countries: by 2004 about 15% of those who had immigrated came from the other Nordic countries (890 from Denmark, 306 from Sweden, 293 from Norway); 55% were from other European countries—mostly Poland (1,903), but also from the former Yugoslavia (670), Germany (540), Lithuania (423), Britain (341), and Italy (229). A further 19% came from Asia (647 from the Philippines, 490 from Thailand), 8% from America (515 from the United States), and 3% from Africa. In 2003, of the population aged 15 to 19, 2.2% were immigrants, along with 1.4% of those between 20 and 24, 4.7% of those between 25 and 64, and 0.9% of those 65 and older (Statistics Iceland 2005).

Iceland is a republic, a parliamentary democracy with a president. The president is elected to a four-year term by popular vote, as are the 63 members of Parliament. The majority of the population (86% in 2002) belongs to the state church, the Evangelical Lutheran Church. Another 5% belong to other Lutheran churches, 1.7% to the Catholic

425

Church, and 7% to about 20 other religious congregations (Statistics Iceland 2005).

Since the end of World War II, which coincided with full independence from the Danish crown in 1944, Iceland has been undergoing rapid and radical social, economic, and political changes, moving from a traditional agricultural community to a modern industrial society. Around 1900 it was one of the poorest countries in Europe, but by the 1960s it had already become one of the world's ten wealthiest nations per capita (Olafsson 2003). The country frequently ranks among the world's top five nations in terms of such quality-of-life markers as rates of infant mortality (in 2002, 2.2 out of 1000), life expectancy (78 years for men and 82 for women), literacy rate (99.9%), and life satisfaction, as well as low unemployment rates (2% to 3% in 1998–2002) (Statistics Iceland 2005).

Period of Adolescence

In the early 1900s Icelanders made a sharp distinction between childhood and adulthood. A century later, they recognize a clearly defined life stage of adolescence.

By about the middle of the twentieth century, adolescents had gradually become a special group, particularly in the more urban areas. Up to then, starting at age 14 with confirmation, most young people worked to help provide sustenance for the family, whether in farming, fishing, or other work on the labor market.

As several of Iceland's employment sectors grew—for example the fishing industry—the population density increased. Many people moved from farms to seaside villages and towns, particularly to Reykjavik. With this change in residence the circumstances of children and adolescents changed radically. In these new and growing villages and towns, they spent more time in school, compared with children and adolescents on farms, though they still had considerable work responsibilities. Over time, as adolescents spent more time in school (more years of schooling, more months per year, more hours each day) and participated less in making a living, people saw adolescence as being a special period.

Gradually a new adolescent lifestyle emerged. Until around 1960, most adolescents dressed like their parents, but then they began to dress differently. Before Icelandic TV started broadcasting in the middle 1960s, sailors imported movies, and some people who lived near the U.S. army base could hear and watch American radio and TV. This provided young people with information about what was going on in the Western world. They started listening to rock music, which was the first music to appeal to them in particular, and began dressing and dancing like their role models in the movies. They changed their hairstyles, behavior, and use of language. Gradually, adolescents and young people started to create their own lifestyle, hanging out together around kiosks or in their bedrooms at home. The first real adolescent culture in Iceland had arisen (Gudmundsson 1990).

It has been argued that in the 1950s and 1960s Icelandic adolescents were in many ways more autonomous and thus more receptive to an independent adolescent culture than were their peers elsewhere in Western Europe. The radical economic and sociological changes during the century may have played a large role. World War II and the arrival of the British and later the U.S. army brought much employment, for example in construction and services. Young people, including adolescents, now had an opportunity to earn considerable amounts of money, which earlier had been unusual. These new employment opportunities gave them much freedom. They could decide what they wanted to do, where to live, and how to spend their money. They now had ways to "live high": to have more time for leisure with friends and peers, look for excitement, buy more things, learn foreign languages, travel abroad, and have a freer sexual life (Gudmundsson 1990).

The transitional period of adolescence has also lengthened, for several reasons: adolescents now attend school longer, start working later, and are more engaged in their peer worlds and in urban life. After completing their required schooling at age 15, well over 90% of adolescents continue their studies (Statistics Iceland 2005).

Little research is available on the age at which children reach puberty, but between 1983 and 1987, on average, girls had their first period at age 13.26 (Thorsson et al. 2000). A clearly defined life stage of adolescence has gradually emerged. Now, in the early twenty-first century, it is more distinct than ever before, to adolescents themselves, and to parents, professionals, and politicians, all of whom have gradually begun paying special attention to this period.

Parents have the duty to take financial care of their children until they are 18. At that age, young people acquire special civic rights, which can be considered a turning point in the move from adolescence into adulthood. For example, they can then decide by themselves how they want to spend their money and where they want to live; they can

marry without parental permission and can vote in elections. In this light we can conclude that in Iceland adolescence lasts until age 18. However, we can also talk about a period of "emerging adulthood," as a large proportion of young people enjoy their parents' financial support at least until their early twenties while they continue their studies in upper secondary school (ages 16 to 20). Those who have the opportunity to study in their home towns usually stay with their parents. Also, most young people who must move away from home to continue their education receive financial support from their parents.

When this period of emerging adulthood ends depends on several milestones: the young people start working and earning their own money to support themselves, move out, start cohabitation or marriage, and even begin a family. Over 40% of young couples, however, are estimated to start cohabiting in the homes of their parents (Juliusdottir 2001).

Beliefs

Given its historical roots, the Icelandic nation shares political, social, and economic values, as well as educational and cultural values, with the other Nordic countries: Norway, Sweden, Finland, and Denmark. The democratic values of freedom, equality, and brotherhood are strongly emphasized. These countries are considered to have a relatively good balance between their emphases on individualism and collectivism. The autonomy of the individual is considered essential as well as the solidarity of the society's members; this is reflected, for example, in the social welfare system. In the name of equality, health services are almost free of charge, along with education at all school levels.

As in many Western countries, some people in Iceland are concerned that the values of the youth are changing toward more individualism. At this point, however, little data is available to support such a hypothesis.

Interestingly, Olafsson (2003) suggests that by nature Icelanders might have more individualistic values than people in the other Nordic countries because, historically, the Icelandic people were settlers. His studies of values indicate that Icelanders seem to be "strong individualists" (p. 8), and have a very strong work ethic. For example, they stress individual achievement, emphasize self-help and independence, work long hours, and have a high rate of employment. In this sense, Olafsson claims, Icelandic and American values are similar. He

argues that both nations are so-called new societies that "share some common broad cultural characteristics because of the comparable experiences of the settlers" who paved the way for the formation of these societies (p. 7). Contrary to American values, however, Olafsson claims that Icelanders strongly emphasize equality, more in line with the Scandinavian tradition: equality of status, of the sexes, and of opportunities for work, education, and health service.

When Icelandic people are asked what is most important to them, the majority mention family and health, and when they are asked what is most important to them for living a happy life, the majority mention "strong bonds of family and friendship." Also, the virtues of honesty and trust are important to them, as well as being industrious, positive, and frank (Proppe 2000).

Icelanders report being very religious; 85% report they believe in God. However, a small percentage attends church—one of the lowest in any Western society—and most who do are members of the older generation (Petursson and Jonsson 1994). Historically, in addition to instruction in the home, Christian values have been transmitted to children and adolescents in the schools as a special subject. At age 14, the church provides adolescents with religious education before their confirmation. Some adolescents (1.8% in 2003) choose civic confirmation and at age 14 receive a values education within a related association. Similarly, adolescents who adhere to religions other than Christianity receive their religious education from their family and within special religious associations. As more people with various religious beliefs immigrate to Iceland, teachers are challenged to change the traditional teaching of Christianity at school.

Gender

Iceland's legacy of the sagas describes women as being strong, having their own opinions, and taking a stand. Men are described as brave, rough, and poetic. These cultural values, among others, have been transmitted across many generations. For example, the strength and independence of Icelandic women were reflected in the Icelandic culture century after century, and communicated to girls and young women. When women marry, most keep their father's name; this is considered to indicate a certain independence from the husband. When fishing was the main source of income, being a sailor's wife meant great responsibility. She had to take care not only of the children but also of the

household, both indoors and out; this experience is believed to have encouraged their independence.

In spite of these cultural messages, Icelandic women have long had to fight to have the same rights as men. In 1915 they gained the right to vote. Seven years later the first woman was elected to Parliament. From 1908 to 1926 and again from 1982 to 1996, women developed their own separate candidate lists for both municipal and national elections. In 1980, Icelandic women experienced a milestone in their struggle for public trust, respect, and power: the nation was the world's first to select a woman, Mrs. Vigdis Finnbogadottir, as its president.

Other gender-specific cultural values and social norms have been transmitted to both girls and boys. In earlier times, as Icelanders struggled to survive, facing difficult socioeconomic conditions and the often unkind forces of nature, men were responsible for being the external providers for the family and women for taking care of the inner household. These role expectations are still evident among young men and women. Accordingly, even though girls and young women have many strong role models to follow in the society, women still have a way to go in getting prestigious and powerful posts, and in many occupations men still earn more than women for the same type of work (see overview in Einarsdottir 2003). Also, even though men have gradually started taking a more active part in the household in doing more childcare, cooking, and cleaning, these are still the major responsibilities of women within the family.

The role of nature and nurture in girls' and boys' thinking and activities is, however, open to debate in Iceland as elsewhere. Gender role expectations appear from early on in girls' and boys' activities. In general, girls are often expected to behave according to a certain female image by being more quiet, passive, and caring than the boys. Similarly, boys may behave according to a certain male image by choosing tasks that require activity, and by being loud, pushy, and forward.

Icelandic adolescents, both girls and boys, are quite fashionable. They dress well and tend to follow the images they see in various media (Internet, TV, magazines). Beauty competitions are relatively common; internationally, Icelandic women have succeeded in such competitions and as models. In a small society this high level of publicity quickly focuses much attention on appearance, leaving some adolescents feeling insecure about their looks. The majority of those who have eating disorders are women aged 15 to 24. In a cohort of 21-year-olds in Reykjavik, 1.1% reported having

had such disorders (Adalbjarnardottir 2004). This would confirm other studies estimating that 1% to 2% of young people develop eating disorders (Gotesdam and Agras 1995).

Also, in spite of the messages Icelandic girls receive about being strong and autonomous, at age 14 they have lower self-esteem than boys; this difference, however, is no longer significant when they reach age 21. The girls' self-esteem becomes more positive across these seven years while the boys' self-esteem appears to stay about the same during that period (Adalbjarnardottir and Gardarsdottir 2004).

In general, Icelandic society is concerned about gender role expectations. The educational policy has been to encourage schools to pay special attention to supporting and enhancing girls' self-confidence and self-efficacy so that they can have the same opportunities as boys to show their competence and be empowered (Ministry of Education 1990). Also, teachers are expected to pay special attention to boys within the school system because they seem not to do as well as girls; for example, they earn lower grades and have more behavioral problems (OECD 2003).

In the spirit of working toward equality between men and women, specific efforts have been made to encourage girls to choose traditionally male-dominated subjects, such as engineering, for their careers. Similarly, boys have been encouraged to choose careers that have been female-dominated, such as teaching and social work. Gradually, more women are going into the male fields, for example choosing to study natural sciences and medicine (Statistics Iceland 2005) and to play soccer, which has become popular among girls. It may be relatively easier for girls to move into fields that have been male-dominated than for boys to go into fields that have been female-dominated. The question is whether that stems from gender role expectations.

The Self

The self-identity of young people in Iceland changed greatly along with the economic and social shift from subsistence farming to industrialized society, providing them with opportunities to acquire a lengthier education and a variety of work experience. This change led to more possibilities for self-exploration in connection with love, work, and worldview and gave young people more opportunities to explore their individual capabilities and educational and work options. At the same time, it can be said that young people now need a longer

period "to find themselves," to realize who they are and what they wish to stand for in this world. In a way, young people are wrestling with many types of identity. Arnett (2001) has suggested that today young people around the world acquire a bicultural identity: both an international or global identity and a local one.

With regard to the global identity, young people in Iceland communicate extensively with others around the world. They travel widely (sometimes explained by their Viking blood!), use the Internet, and absorb international youth culture through TV and other media. Young people around the world want to eat hamburgers, be just like a certain pop star, and wear t-shirts, Nike shoes, and baseball caps (see Arnett 2001). Icelandic adolescents are no exception. At the same time, they may struggle with their identity in their local community: the identity they acquire in their daily relations with their families and immediate environment. They form this identity with regard to the values and traditions dominant there. Considering some adolescents' attitudes and lifestyle (e.g., consumption, sex, substance use, clothing), tensions can naturally arise between the values of the local community and the youth culture in the wider community.

Because the wave of immigration to Iceland is quite recent, little is known about the personal, cultural, and ethnic identity formation of immigrant adolescents. Professionals who work with these adolescents report, however, that they see the potential for identity crisis. Some who immigrated before adolescence report conflicts with their parents during adolescence because of conflicting cultural values. They face the challenge of adhering to the values of their original country along with those of Iceland. For example, many experience less parental discipline in Iceland, where adolescents can stay out later and date at younger ages.

One of the hardest challenges immigrant children and adolescents face in developing an identity in their new culture, however, may be learning the Icelandic language. Because of this, those who immigrate during adolescence tend to be isolated—a difficult experience at a time when friendship in the peer group is particularly important for self-identity.

Certainly, some adolescents do not develop a positive self-identity, due to complicated and interactive physical, sociological (e.g., circumstances at home), educational (e.g., academic achievement), psychosocial (e.g., relationships with peers), and/or ethnic factors. Others seem to thrive: they are active and vibrant, exploring and taking initiative.

Family Relationships

During the twentieth century radical societal changes occurred in the Icelandic family structure. Three-generation households are less common than before, and each family has fewer children. Around 1960 each Icelandic woman had four live births; around 1970 each had three, and on average between 1996 and 2000 the figure was 2.06. In 2002, the figure fell below 2.0 for the first time; it was 1.99 in 2003 (Statistics Iceland 2005).

Matrimonial norms have changed along with the rising educational level; people marry later and have children later than they did in the early twentieth century. In 1961–1965 the mean age of brides was 24.4 years and of grooms 27.4 years, which rose to 32.8 and 35.4 respectively in 2002 (Statistics Iceland 2005). Unlike the situation between 1961 and 1970, it is now exceptional for people to marry before age 20. The rate of marriage is relatively low, with 5.6 residents per 1,000 marrying in 2002 compared to 8 to 9 around 1950. About 34% of the population is married, and many young people cohabit before they marry. Of those who got married in 2002, 89% had lived together for some time, half of them more than five years. A lower fertility rate goes hand in hand with a higher mean age of mothers, indicating a trend toward delaying motherhood. In 1970, the mean age at first child's birth was 21.3, but in 2003 it was 26 (Statistics Iceland 2005). The society has long acknowledged and approved childbearing outside marriage.

The divorce rate rose gradually during the twentieth century, from 10% in the early 1960s to 40% in 1975, and has been steady since, with 1.9 divorces per 1,000 residents (Statistics Iceland 2005). Because divorce and remarriage have become more common, many children and adolescents live either with a single parent or in a stepfamily.

Both men and women participate actively in the labor market. Given their increased education, autonomy, and equality, more women work outside the home and for longer hours than in earlier times. Between 1960 and 1985 the proportion of women working outside the home more than quadrupled. In 2004 73% of Icelandic women aged 16 to 24 worked in the labor market along with 85% of those aged 25 to 54. On average in the age group 25 to 54, women had a work week of 37.3 hours in 2004 and men averaged 49.4 hours; 37% of women worked part-time, along with 10% of men (Statistics Iceland 2005).

Parents in Iceland are very active in educating themselves. Along with working long hours, they

have active social lives, and value a comfortable lifestyle (Juliusdottir 2001). These facts, combined with the sociological changes outlined above, mean that parents and their children spend less time together than in the past. Children may experience insecurity because adults now expect more of their own lifestyles and want a high standard of living, or because of other problems within the family, such as the financial stress involved in meeting such demands, divorce, and health-related problems (e.g., alcoholism).

Although no valid research has been conducted on the most common parenting practices in Iceland, we can speculate about some trends based on a three-year study that followed the same cohort of 1,300 Reykjavik adolescents from age 14 in 1994 to age 17 (Adalbjarnardottir 2004). At ages 14, 15, and 17 they responded to the same questions about their parents' styles with regard to behavioral control, involvement, and granting of autonomy. Table 1 shows examples of their responses to specific questions; for example, on behavioral control they were asked how late they could stay out on a typical Friday or Saturday night.

We notice that relatively many adolescents aged 14 and 15 are allowed to stay out very late on weekends. For example, only 18% of the 15-year-olds had to be home before 1 a.m., and very few 17-year-olds (only 2%) reported they had to be home before 2 a.m. Also, relatively many (e.g., one of four at age 14) report that their parents trust them to decide this question by themselves. In comparison with their peers in Europe, Icelandic adolescents are known for having relatively more autonomy from early on with regard to where, with whom, and how often they spend time, which often

Table 1. How Late Icelandic Teenagers Can Stay Out on Weekends

	Age 14	Age 15	Age 17
Not allowed to go out	1	1	0
Before 12 am.	17	8	0
12 to 1 am.	18	9	0
1 to 2 am.	21	14	2
2 to 3 am.	13	18	5
After 3 am.	3	13	7
My parents don't care when I come home	1	1	1
My parents trust me to decide myself when I come home	26	36	85
	100%	100%	100%

Note: Figures are percentages.
Source: Adalbjarnardottir 2004.

affords them the opportunity to stay out late at night. This may be because Iceland is a rather safe society with a relatively low crime rate (Gunnlaugsson 1998) and bright summer nights.

With increased substance abuse, however, society has become more concerned about adolescents staying out late. Since the above study was conducted, both professional committees and parents' associations have collaborated more actively on various issues related to the welfare of adolescents. For example, in Reykjavik and its metropolitan area they focus on encouraging parents and their children to maintain society's rules about when children and adolescents should be home at night and they encourage parents to stay informed about where their children are and with whom.

In the longitudinal Reykjavik Adolescent Study mentioned above, the responses to a question related to involvement—"How often do your parents spend time just talking with you?"—showed little change by age. The majority of the adolescents reported that their parents spent time talking with them almost daily (40%) or a few times a week (30%); a minority (7%) reported that they never spent time talking together. Also, 80% to 90% felt they could count on their parents if they had a problem. Similarly, with regard to a question about granting autonomy, a majority (80% to 90%) reported that their parents encouraged them to think independently (Adalbjarnardottir 2004).

Typical conflicts between parents and their adolescents concern lifestyle issues: how they spend their money, dress, and take care of their room; how much they take part in household activities, how loudly they play their music, how often they go out with friends, and how late they come home at night.

Increased knowledge about children's general growth and ways of upbringing can leave parents facing a tension between maintaining old values and accepting new ones. Accordingly, many may feel insecure about how to best bring up and take care of their children. Professional guidelines for parents have proliferated. Also, parents' associations, in which parents support each other in their important role, have become stronger and more effective.

In the early twenty-first century, family ties are strong in Iceland. Family members build their relationships by sticking together, helping each other out, and making direct contributions. For example, parents and other family members provide the younger generation with financial support, housing, and childcare, in addition to personal support (Juliusdottir 2001).

Friends and Peers/Youth Culture

As a result of longer schooling hours, longer work hours for parents, and adolescents' own summertime work in the labor market (not with their parents as in earlier times), adolescents increasingly spend more time with their friends and peers than with their parents.

Adolescent girls and boys of different social classes and ethnic groups study and play together at the same schools, as nearly all schools are public. In this sense the society is very open; gender, social class, and ethnicity present few barriers to friendship. In fact, many Icelanders establish lifetime friendships during childhood and adolescence.

At the same time, however, adolescents group themselves depending on their values and competencies. For example, some academically bright adolescents may become friends, as might those with athletic gifts or those who are interested and talented in music. Immigrant adolescents may tend to form their own groups in response to shared challenges such as the new environment and the language barrier in learning Icelandic. Also, Icelandic adolescents may show some prejudices toward immigrant adolescents, making friendship more difficult. In 1999, however, in a study on 33 European countries, findings indicated that Icelanders (at 3%) and Swedes were the least opposed to having people of other ethnic groups as their neighbors. Moreover, the younger generation in Iceland (i.e., those under 30) were less opposed than the older generations (Jonsson 2003), an attitude that might lower the barriers to friendships across ethnic groups.

Several youth organizations base their work on the premise that it is educational for youth to participate in various social activities. Many sports associations focus on providing young people with an opportunity to play soccer, handball, basketball, table tennis, and so forth. Chess, swimming, and skiing are also popular. Young people also sing in choruses, dance (ballet, ballroom), take part in drama, and are active in the social life associated with these activities. Other youth organizations involve scouts associations, rescue teams, bands, religious associations (mainly Christian), and political associations. Both girls and boys are active in these groups (Thorlindsson et al. 2000).

Music plays a significant role in the world of young Icelanders. For decades they have formed bands (mostly of young men but also of young women) that play in public. Some Icelandic pop singers and bands have had great international success.

Other Western countries exert a strong influence on the lifestyle of Icelandic adolescents, who follow the newest fashion with regard to hairstyles, clothing, and music. Thus we see some signs of a distinct youth culture in Iceland, one distinguished from adult culture by dress, hairstyle, tattooing/piercing, music, and slang. In discussing a generation gap, however, it should be noted that the parents and even the grandparents of Iceland's current adolescents belong to a generation that experienced tremendous changes in their culture in the 1950s, 1960s, and 1970s and may, in fact, have experienced Iceland's largest generation gap up to the present (see section on Period of Adolescence).

Love and Sexuality

Dating is relatively easy among Icelandic adolescents, given their considerable freedom to choose both their companions and their activities. Young people select their partners; parents do not arrange marriages.

Sexual experience before marriage is quite common. For both boys and girls the mean age at first experience of intercourse dropped during the second part of the twentieth century. For those born in the late 1970s, this age was just over 15 for both males and females, compared to about 18 for those born around 1940 (Jonsdottir 1994).

Young women get pregnant and have children at a higher rate in Iceland than in the other Nordic countries. For example in 2002, of all live births in Iceland 4.6% were among girls 15 to 19 years old, compared to 1.4% in Denmark (Nordic Statistical Yearbook 2002). Fewer Icelandic adolescents are having children, however, a trend that has been traced to the provision of mandatory sex education, effective contraception, and abortion services. In the age group 15 to 19, of all live births the rate was 14% in 1980 compared to 3.9% in 2003 (Statistics Iceland 2005).

When an Icelandic adolescent girl becomes pregnant, traditionally the attitudes of both family and society have been to encourage her to have the baby rather than an abortion. Gradually, however, this attitude has been changing. At the end of the twentieth century about half of all adolescent pregnancies ended in an abortion (Bender, Geirsson, and Kosunen 2003).

By law, sexual and reproductive health services must be available from a variety of community health centers and hospitals in connection with services like antenatal care and family counseling. Access to contraception is relatively easy for

adolescents. Sex education is mandatory; however, the teachers and the schools determine how much time and attention it is given in the schedule. Many teachers still find it difficult to discuss these issues. Moreover, even though many parents educate their children about sex, the topic still seems to be a sensitive one in the home (see Bender et al. 2001).

Sexually transmitted diseases are most common among young people aged 15 to 29 who are not in steady relationships. Toward the end of the twentieth century around 15% of those aged 16 to 19 had had one or more sexually transmitted diseases, the most common one being chlamydia (see overview by Bender et al. 2001).

Within Icelandic society, a public and official dialogue about homosexuality developed considerably during the 1990s. This has helped the general public better understand the situation of homosexual people and diminished the prejudices toward them. For example, in 1981, 20% of the Icelandic population did not want gay people as neighbors, compared to 8% in 1999. Similarly, in 1981, 48% felt homosexuality could never be justified but that percentage fell to 12% in 1999. Moreover, among people in 36 European countries plus the United States, only Sweden and Holland had more tolerant views than Iceland on the question of justifying homosexuality (see overview in Hardarson 2003). Further, a survey conducted in 2004 found that almost 90% of the Icelandic population wanted homosexual people to have the right to marry, and around 70% felt they should be allowed to marry in a church (IMG Gallup 2004).

Most adolescents who realize they are homosexual do not find it easy to explain that fact to those who are closest to them: parents, family, and friends. Most take a long time to do so—months and even years. Most Icelandic parents who learn that their child is homosexual react by standing fully behind him or her to offer support. The family bond is of great importance in the Icelandic society, and sincere support for every family member is generally considered a moral duty. Where Icelandic families formerly greeted the lesbian or gay member of the family with a massive silence (the best support one could then imagine!), a relaxed openness now seems more typical. Spokespersons for the lesbian and gay movement attribute this rapid change of values, mainly since 1995, to the fact that lesbians and gay men enjoy progressive laws—including the right to a registered partnership that gives them the same status as married people—and supportive media, as well as effective educational work led by the gay movement (Kristinsson 2003).

All this is of tremendous help to gay teenagers during the coming-out process, in which they manifest their sexual orientation. In spite of some confusion and the worries common to parents facing the fact that their child is homosexual, most of them see it as their moral duty to educate themselves and seek solid information about the issue; some even seek professional counseling. The annual gay pride festivities in Reykjavik attract around 40,000 people—more than one-fourth of the population of the city and its surrounding areas, mainly families and friends of lesbians and gay men. This fact makes the Icelandic gay liberation day almost unique in the world, and it is frequently described as a "family feast" (Kristinsson 2003).

Health Risk Behavior

Three cross-national studies, each including roughly 30 European countries plus the United States, on substance use by 15-year-olds, found that the rate of cigarette smoking in the previous 30 days has been steadily dropping in Iceland since 1995: from 32% in 1995, to 28% in 1999, to 20% in 2003. This trend was exceptional within the study; only Ireland had the same trend, but it has a higher percentage of smokers. In 1995 Iceland rated number 11 out of 25 countries; in 1999 only 3 countries out of 30 had lower rates, and in 2003 only one country (Turkey) out of 36 had a lower rate.

In 1995 Iceland was also seventh lowest in the percentage of those who had tried any alcoholic beverage 40 or more times (boys 14%, girls 13%); in 1999 it had the third lowest percentage (boys 15%, girls 14%), and in 2003 the fifth lowest (boys 16%, girls 12%). No country had lower rates for the use of any alcoholic beverage ten or more times during the last 30 days (1% for both boys and girls each year). Studies have found, however, that when Icelandic adolescents do drink—whether beer or spirits—they tended to drink more heavily each time compared to their peers in most other European countries, with the exception of wine. With regard to consumption of 101 centiliters or more of beer on the last drinking occasion, Iceland rated fifth among 21 countries in 1995 (19%), fifth among 29 countries in 1999 (26%), and sixth among 32 countries in 2003 (24%). The pattern has been changing, however, with regard to the consumption of 11 centiliters or more of spirits on the last drinking occasion; Iceland rated second among 21 countries in 1995 (32%), seventh among 29 countries in 1999 (23%), and fourteenth among 32 countries in 2003 (15%) (Hibell et al. 1995; 1999; 2003). Thus while Icelandic adolescents are

consuming relatively fewer spirits at each drinking occasion, they still drink relatively more beer at each drinking occasion.

The adolescents were also asked about specific potential drinking-related problems, classified as problems with relationships, sex, and delinquency. For Iceland, a special concern arose in the 1999 study: Icelandic girls reported one of the highest rates of sex that they regretted the next day, along with girls in Denmark, Sweden, and the United Kingdom, all at 11% to 13%. Only girls in Greenland, at 24%, had a higher rate (Hibell et al. 1999).

A longitudinal study on adolescent substance use in Reykjavik followed the same 1,300 adolescents—from age 14 in 1994 through the ages of 15, 17, and 21—and found a steady increase in substance use (tobacco, alcohol, hashish, amphetamines) up to around age 18. Figure 1 illustrates these findings. The age period 14 to 18 is clearly a special risk period in this regard. The only exception is the use of cocaine. Also, at 21, almost half reported having had unprotected sex under the influence of drugs and one-third reported regretted sex (Adalbjarnardottir et al. 2003).

It should be noted that this age cohort—15-year-olds in 1995—is the same as in the 1995 cross-national study that showed relatively high substance use compared with the same age cohort in 1999 and 2003. The decline in 15-year-olds' use of tobacco and alcohol between 1995 and 2003 can be attributed to a governmental and local policy of prevention work in this area, nationwide. As outlined in the section on Family Relationships, both professional committees and parents' associations have collaborated more actively on various issues related to the welfare of adolescents.

Depression occurs among Icelandic adolescents at proportions similar to those in the other Nordic countries. Around 20% of young people are estimated to experience some form of a depressed mood (Hannesdottir 2002). Of those who committed suicide in the years 1988 to 2001, 18% were between age 15 and 25. The suicide rate among young men has been high in Iceland. In the years 1951 to 1995, on average, 19 men and 2 women per 100,000 residents in the 15 to 24 age group committed suicide. For men this rate is higher than in other Western countries but for women it is lower (Bjarnason, Asgeirsdottir, and Sigfusdottir 2002).

Gang activities are relatively rare in Iceland. However, with increased drug use, violence seems to have increased. Now it is more common for a person or a group to attack a person for no apparent reason. Also, robbery of houses and offices has increased, mostly by people who are looking for valuable items such as computers that they can sell to buy drugs (Reykjavik Police 2002).

Young people are involved in several categories of illegal activities. Among those accused of drunk driving, for example, 17% were 20 or younger. Car accidents were most common among those aged 17 to 20. Of those accused of violence, mostly minor physical violence, 31% were 20 or younger; 18-year-olds were the most common offenders. Of those accused of sexual harassment (97% men), 18% were 20 or younger (Reykjavik Police 2002).

Adolescents' problems stem from various and interrelated social, economic, psychological, and

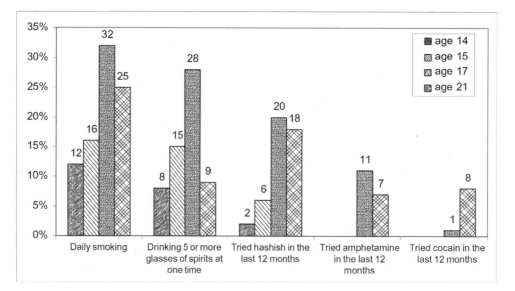

Figure 1.   Substance use: percent of the cohort in Reykjavik at ages 14, 15, 17, and 21.
Source: Adalbjarnardottir et al. 2003.

educational factors. Adolescents face various challenges that can create problems. As outlined earlier, Icelandic society changed very rapidly during the twentieth century, placing much pressure on the family: fewer generations now live in the same household, leaving the older generation less available to help take care of children on a daily basis. Now, both parents are more likely to be employed and divorce is more common than before. Spending less time with adults, watching their parents divorce, and living in complicated patterns of stepfamilies may not best serve the needs of those adolescents who are vulnerable. Also, adolescents may not experience enough security at home because their parents expect a more varied lifestyle and a higher standard of living (adult social life, sports, trips). Problems with finance and health can also influence adolescents' well-being. In addition to genetic and health-related issues (e.g., adolescent depression, addictions), some adolescents simply may not feel comfortable at school. They may be low academic achievers and even drop out of school: a risk factor for their welfare.

A key question is how the society—both the state and the private sector—supports the family in taking care of its children. Iceland provides less official support for families than do the other Nordic countries. For example, in 1995 and 2000 Iceland contributed 2.4% and 2.3%, respectively, of GNP on benefits and services for families and children, compared with 4.0% and 3.6%, respectively, in Sweden (Nordic Statistical Yearbook 1995, 2000). Some firms have started to implement a plan called "the golden balance"—harmony between family life and work through flexibility in work hours that allows parents to stay home more often with their children. Most firms, however, still have a long way to go in this regard. Moreover, in 2000 a new act on maternity/paternity leave and parental leave was accepted in Parliament. It states that parents have each an independent right to maternity/paternity leave up to three months when they have a baby. They have a joint right to three additional months, to be used entirely by one parent or divided between them (Act on Maternity/Paternity Leave and Parental Leave 2000).

Education

All children and young people, regardless of their gender, place of residence, religion, ethnic affiliation, and social and economic circumstances, have equal rights to education in both compulsory school (primary and lower secondary, ages 6 to 15) and upper secondary school (ages 16 to 20).

Iceland's Ministry of Education provides the overall framework for the nation's educational system by setting policy and developing legislation. The National Curriculum Guidelines set out the basic objectives and content for preschool, compulsory, and upper secondary school, as well as directing educational assessment and supervision. On the other hand, the municipality is responsible for implementing educational policies and running the schools (OECD 2003).

By law, the major responsibility of the educational system is to provide students with a good general education and strengthen their general life skills, in order to prepare them to live and work in a democratic society. Education aims to promote students' physical, cognitive, social, moral, and emotional growth in a constantly changing world. This includes educating students about human rights, respect, tolerance, and democratic values.

The ten years of required schooling are free of charge for all students, as are the four years of upper secondary school, except for a registration fee and the cost of books. In the very few private primary and secondary schools, students pay a small enrollment fee; the state provides housing and pays staff members' salaries. No tuition is charged and only a registration fee is charged at state-run Icelandic institutions of higher education such as the University of Iceland, and the Iceland University of Education. Some new colleges and universities that define themselves as private charge some tuition fee. Whether young people pursue their higher education in Iceland or abroad, a state-sponsored Students' Loan Fund provides them with relatively reasonable loans.

Young people who have completed their compulsory education have the right to pursue four years of full-time upper secondary education. In 2004 well over 90% took advantage of this opportunity (Statistics Iceland 2004). Students can choose between grammar schools, comprehensive schools, industrial-vocational schools, and specialized vocational schools. Grammar schools and comprehensive schools offer four-year academic courses—in natural sciences, social sciences, and foreign languages—leading to matriculation, the university entrance examination. The comprehensive schools also offer theoretical and practical training (as do the industrial-vocational schools), as well as programs providing vocational and artistic education. Industrial-vocational schools offer theoretical and practical programs of study in the trades. Finally, specialized vocational schools offer preparation for specialized employment.

Dropout rates for the first year of upper secondary school have been high. In 2002–2003 the rate was 12% for 16-year-old students, with more boys dropping out than girls (Statistics Iceland 2005). Some of them, however, are only taking a break from their studies for one or two years. In 1999, of those who were then age 24, a full 36% had not completed upper secondary school (Jonasson and Blondal 2002). It should be noted, however, that many stop studying for a while and return later, even after several years, a trend that has been increasing in recent decades (Statistics Iceland 2005). In Iceland, completing upper secondary school or the equivalent is considered the minimum requirement for success in the labor market.

Since the 1960s Iceland has seen a gradual increase in the number of young people who continue their studies at the university level. In 1980 10% of those aged 20 to 29 studied at the university level, but 27% did so in 2003 (Statistics Iceland 2005). Accordingly, the nation's educational level is relatively high; in 2000, one person out of three aged 30 to 34 had a university degree, as did one out of five aged 25 to 64. Moreover, the rates of men and women aged 20 to 29 studying at a university level have gradually turned around. In 1980 60% of the students were men and 40% women, but in 2003 41% were men and 59% women (Statistics Iceland 2005).

Although Iceland has made considerable progress toward equality between the sexes, young people make highly gender-segregated choices about their education. Among university students in 2003, women were 84% of the students in education and 83% of those in health studies, but only 24% of those in technology and engineering. Also noteworthy is the fact that a full quarter of Icelandic students enrolled in higher education go abroad to study (Statistics Iceland 2005).

The literacy rate is 99.9% for people aged 15 and older (OECD 2003). In 2000 the OECD conducted a Programme for International Student Assessment (PISA) to explore the academic achievement of 15-year-olds in reading, mathematics, and science in over 40 countries all over the world. In both reading and mathematics the Icelandic students scored above the average grades for their peers in other countries (in mathematics, significantly above); they scored just below the average grades in science but non-significantly. Icelandic girls scored higher in reading than the boys, but there were no gender differences in mathematics and science. Moreover, in the OECD 2003 PISA report, which focuses on academic achievement in mathematics, unlike students in all other countries in the study 15-year-old girls in Iceland scored higher on average in mathematics than did the boys (www.pisa.oecd.org). This result has received special attention from both educators and the media (e.g. *Time Magazine* 2005).

In comparison with many other countries, only a very small and non-significant difference was found in the Icelandic students' grades as a function of school, local municipality, part of the country, or school's economic status. This reflects the homogeneity of Icelandic schools and confirms earlier statements that the students have easy access to education.

Minority language students face particular linguistic and cultural challenges in education. In response to the increasing immigration to Iceland, special programs at so-called "reception departments" have been founded in several primary and lower secondary schools to welcome and support immigrant students. They focus mainly on teaching Icelandic. In 2000, one of these schools was designated as a "mother-school"; it emphasizes intercultural education using a whole-school approach and aims to guide other schools in this area. The high dropout rate among immigrant students at the upper secondary level is also a concern. In response, increasing numbers of secondary schools have started running bilingual programs for immigrant students.

At all school levels, students with mental or physical disabilities have the right to a learning environment suited to their needs. They enjoy special state subsidies. In compulsory school most of them are integrated into the mainstream. They are in regular classes and have special teachers and other professional staff to support them during both class lessons and special individual lessons. A few specialized schools provide for some who are mentally disabled. Mentally and physically disabled people also have access to educational opportunities after they complete their required schooling, and can enroll in different programs, such as upper secondary school, according to their interests. Physically disabled students are also provided with support according to their disabilities. For example, deaf students have access to sign language interpreters and blind and motor handicapped students are provided with appropriate educational and physical aids.

Like all students, gifted students can attend various programs outside school that are run by various associations both within and outside the state and the municipal educational system. Many upper secondary schools offer special courses that allow gifted students to move through the program more

quickly. Also, one school has been founded to meet the needs of any students who want to move more quickly through the programs leading to the matriculation exam.

Work

The Icelandic society considers it a very important learning experience for young people to take an active part in the labor market and learn about various occupations. Accordingly, it has been viewed as a "must" for each adolescent to take on a summer job.

As Iceland's employment sectors changed across the twentieth century with increased mechanization allowing fewer seasonal jobs, adolescents aged 13 to 15 had more difficulty finding summer jobs. Adults became concerned about unemployment among adolescents, who they thought might wander around the streets, risk getting into trouble, and not get used to work. The first "work-school" started in a fishing village in 1937. Reykjavik's first such school started in 1948, and around that time they were founded in other towns around the country (Gardarsdottir 1997).

Ever since, the ideology behind the work-school has been to provide young people with work education, emphasizing general work principles and work skills, such as being punctual, careful, attentive, self-disciplined, and responsible. The most common tasks at the work-schools are grounds work: gardening, planting trees, making paths, and so forth.

Many adolescents try to find work through family ties or friends, but in a typical summer around half of those aged 13 to 15 work at the work-school; another 20% take care of children, and 10% work in the fish or food industry or agriculture. During the winter many also work along with attending school. For example, during the school year 1997–1998, 25% of adolescents aged 13 to 17 worked during the school week and 29% worked during weekends. Their most common types of term-time work were caring for children (22%, largely girls), delivering newspapers (17%, largely boys), assisting in a shop or supermarket (10%), house cleaning (9%), and working in the fish or food industry (7%) (Rafnsdottir 1999).

By age 18 young people have more possibilities for various kinds of jobs in the labor market. The principal employment sectors in 2004 were: fishing and fishing processing (14%), industry (20%), and services (66%) (Statistics Iceland 2005).

In a survey, people under 20 were asked why they worked during the school year, allowing them to give more than one reason. For 65% the goal was more pocket money, but 35% said they needed to make a living, 30% wanted to buy something specific, and 20% were interested in the job (Sigurdsson 1990). Not surprisingly, their answers depended on family circumstances. More of those from the countryside who were attending school away from home said they were working to make a living. Also, while "making a living" was the response for more children of workers, sailors, and farmers, "pocket money" was the response for more children of clerks, specialists, and employers. In general, families support their adolescents by providing housing and food, but many adolescents pay for their own clothing and entertainment. In general, few adolescents seem to be working to support their families.

Unemployment has been relatively low in Iceland; from 1998 to 2002 the unemployment rate for both men and women varied from 2% to 3%. In general, however, the unemployment rate has been highest among those 16 to 24; it was 4% to 6% between 1998 and 2001 and in 2002 rose to 7%, with women at 4% and men at 10%; the 2004 figure was similar at 6.9% (Statistics Iceland 2005).

The government's reaction to young people's unemployment is to find ways to provide them with occupations. The Ministry of Social Affairs and the Institute for Work Affairs make special efforts to counteract both youth unemployment and long-term unemployment by surveying the situation and proposing solutions. For example, they have created jobs in areas of relatively high unemployment (Ministry of Social Affairs 2003). Such efforts are essential to adolescents and young people as they move into adulthood; they need social networks—which are a form of social capital—that include both people (family, friends) and institutions (educational, employment, health care, social security) (see Larson, Brown, and Mortimer 2003).

Media

In a study on the media use of 1,200 adolescents (aged 10 to 15, from both Reykjavik and several small towns), 72% of the youths aged 14 and 15 said they read magazines, more girls than boys. They were also asked how often they listened to music, watched TV, and played computer games. Figure 2 shows the usage of those who replied with either "very often" or "often." We notice that they often engage in these activities on their own. Moreover, compared to girls, more boys played computer games either alone or with friends. A low percentage—under 3%—of the adolescents

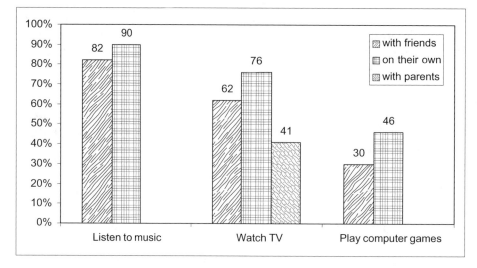

Figure 2. Percentages of adolescents aged 14 and 15 in 2003 who very often and often (combined) listen to music, watch TV

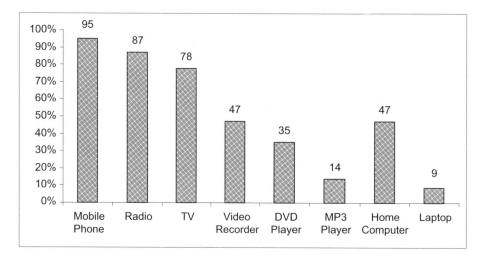

Figure 3. Percentage of adolescents aged 14 and 15 who owned various devices in 2003.
Source: Broddason 2004.

reported they never or almost never listened to music or watched TV. On the other hand, 21% said they never or almost never played computer games alone, and 25% said they never played computer games with their friends. Nearly all (96%) reported they used computers at home, and almost half (44%) had their own Internet connection. A full 60% reported using the Internet at least once a day (more boys than girls), and only 2.5% said they never used it (Broddason 2004).

Reflecting Icelandic adolescents' frequent use of media and easy access to it, in 2003 relatively many of them owned various electronic devices that must influence their lifestyle. For example, on the question of having a TV in their bedroom,

75% of the 14-year-olds reported having one, as did 80% of the 15-year-olds. Figure 3 illustrates their ownership of various devices.

Adolescent ownership of these devices increased considerably between 1997 and 2003. For example, in 1997, 46% of those aged 10 to 15 reported owning a TV, compared to 66% in 2003. During this period, the proportion who owned a home computer rose from 24% to 36%, and the proportion who owned a cell phone rose from 3% to 79% (Broddason 2004).

Icelandic adolescents are exposed to many imported TV programs, mostly from the other Nordic countries, Great Britain, and the United States. However, some popular programs are

produced locally. In general, adults appreciate the educational value of adolescents' easy access to various types of national and international media—as viewers, readers, listeners, and Internet surfers. Simultaneously, however, they are concerned about the violence and sex the media promote and their influence on youth. In addition, the media show adolescents aspects of the global lifestyle that may not always be healthy for them.

Politics and Military

Traditionally, a high percentage of Icelanders vote in each election. The voting age is 18. In the 2003 parliamentary election 87% of eligible people voted, with the estimation of over 80% of people aged 18 to 25 (Hardarson 2004).

Studies of young people's interest in politics have found a range of involvement. Figure 4 presents the findings of one such study conducted in 2003.

As illustrated in Figure 4, 61% of people aged 18 to 25 reported they had high, much, or some interest in politics (compared to 72% of all eligible voters). Surveys in 1995 and 1999 found similar results (57% and 53% of people aged 18 to 25, compared to 68% and 67% of all eligible voters). In 2003, 37% of the young people reported they supported a specific political party, with 12% of them being members, and 18% had been active within a party during a campaign (e.g., attending meetings, volunteering). Also, 16% reported having participated in public protests over the last five years and 18% had worked for a cause with people who hold similar opinions. Reflecting the personal contacts that Icelandic people at any age can have with their politicians, a full 16% of the young people surveyed had contacted a politician (Hardarson 2004), indicating their belief that they can have a voice on political issues.

The question is whether these rates reflect much interest and activity of young people in political affairs. The answer must depend on what each country considers a sign of "satisfactory" interest. A glance at Web sites—including those of political youth organizations within each party and of nonparty groups such as feminist organizations—reveals a very lively debate among Icelandic young people on political issues. It is a real melting pot of ideas, and they focus critically and thoughtfully on various sides of questions.

On the question of how democracy works in Iceland, in the 2003 survey three out of four people aged 18 to 25 reported that they were very or rather pleased with it. When asked to take a position on the proposition that "Democracy is not without its faults but is the best political form available," 95% agreed, with 59% agreeing totally (Hardarson 2004).

Icelandic people are increasingly discussing democracy: how important it is and how it can be preserved and fostered. Secondary schools, youth organizations, and the state's spokesperson for children have run projects like "Youths Assemble." This aims to give youths an opportunity to meet and critically discuss various important current issues, such as substance use, pornography, violence, prejudice, and environmental issues, along with various organizational issues that concern them in their daily life. Sometimes they then make suggestions to the mayors, receiving publicity that is also stimulating for them. It is difficult to estimate how widespread such discussion is among

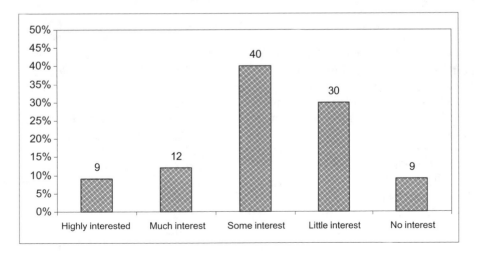

Figure 4. Political interest among people aged 18 to 25 in 2003.
Source: Hardarson 2004.

young people, but such steps toward youth democracy are essential.

As Iceland has no military, young people do not participate in any military activities. Only few community service projects involve adolescents.

Unique Issues

The proportion of adolescents in Iceland should remain relatively stable for the next few decades. In 2003, people aged 15 to 24 made up about 15% of the population. This percentage is expected to decline to 13% in 2020, and stay the same in 2030 and 2040 (Statistics Iceland 2005).

In general, young people in Iceland are vibrant, healthy, and well educated, as well as optimistic and energetic. They have rich opportunities to flourish in education, arts, music, and sports. Living in a small society where each individual counts, it is relatively easy for each person to cultivate his or her special competencies. At the same time, in the twenty-first century, adolescents and young people in Iceland face several challenging decisions that may affect them—and the wider society—for decades to come, including the following.

Health: Obesity is expected to increase, as will related diseases such as diabetes. In particular, illegal drug use is increasing and seems difficult to control despite various intervention programs and the country's geographical isolation as an island. And young people will likely continue to face mental health problems such as depression, suicide, and eating disorders.

Lifestyle: Given the high standard of living in a materialistic and consumer-driven culture, adolescents and young people face social, financial, and psychological pressure to meet the standards set by their local and global peer groups.

Family: With increased education and both men and women working outside the home, young people must find and maintain harmony between family life and work.

Education: Richer opportunities, along with lengthier education and deeper skill development create the challenge of choice between interesting areas of study and career. They also face changing job markets.

Work: Adolescents and young people face the highest unemployment rate of the population. The available occupations constantly require more educated people, and even Icelandic firms are beginning to produce goods in

countries where employees are paid less. Faced with this increased global interdependency, low academic achievers are most likely to suffer. Also, girls and women still experience occupational segregation and wage discrimination.

Self: Iceland's increasingly multicultural society, in combination with globalization, may challenge young people more than ever to strengthen their self-identity and agency: to know what they want to stand for and act on it. Their diverse interpersonal relationships and social worlds challenge their social competence and skills in communicating, collaborating, and solving conflicts. And as they face the rising expectations for their education, work skills, and lifestyle, their other challenge will be to strengthen their resilience.

Citizenship awareness: Like other Icelanders, young people face the political challenge of working toward harmony between individualism and collectivism—that is, how can they find balance between the democratic values of freedom on one hand and brotherhood on the other, with equality as the base? In particular, they face the political question of how to preserve the welfare system, as reflected in equal rights to education and health service. As increasing numbers of Icelanders enjoy longer state-financed education, and as the state also pays for improved health care, this is a crucial issue for the future.

From both a local and global perspective, another major challenge is to cultivate values of mutual respect, trust, and tolerance—independent of gender, sexuality, mental and physical ability, religion, and ethnic group. Two related and crucial challenges are working toward peace around the world and preserving nature. These are two very special resources that young people in Iceland, in collaboration with young people around the world, are challenged to contribute to the world.

Sigrún Adalbjarnardottir

References and Further Reading

Act on Maternity/Paternity Leave and Parental Leave, No. 95/2000. Retrieved March 15, 2005 from the Web site of the Ministry of Social Affairs: http://eng.felagsmalara-duneyti.is/legislation/.

Adalbjarnardottir, S. 2004. Ahættuhegðun ungs folks (Adolescent risk-taking behavior). Unpublished study,

University of Iceland: Faculty of Social Sciences, Department of Education.

Adalbjarnardottir, S., and K. L. Gardarsdottir. 2004. Depurd ungs folks og uppeldisadferdir foreldra: Langtimarannsokn (Depressed mood in adolescents and parenting style: Longitudinal research). *Sálfræðiritið (The Journal of Psychology)* 9:151–66.

Adalbjarnardottir, S., A. G. Dofradottir, Th. Thorolfsson, and K. L. Gardarsdottir. 2003. *Vímuefnaneysla og vidhorf. Ungu folki i Reykjavík fylgt eftir fra 14-22 ars aldurs (Substance use and attitudes: Young people in Reykjavik followed from age 14 to 22)*. Reykjavik: University Press.

Arnett, J. J. 2001. *Adolescence and emerging adulthood: A cultural approach*. New Jersey: Prentice Hall.

Bender, S. S., R. T. Geirsson, and E. Kosunen. 2003. Trends in teenage fertility, abortion and pregnancy rates in Iceland compared to other Nordic countries 1976–1999. *Acta Obstetricia et Gynecologica Scandinavica* 82:38–47.

Bender, S. S., S. Juliusdottir, Th. Kristinsson, and G. Jonsdottir. 2001. Iceland. In *The International Encyclopedia of Sexuality, Vol 4*. R. T. Francoeur (ed.). London: The Continuum International Publishing Group.

Bjarnason, Th., B. B. Asgeirsdottir, and I. D. Sigfusdottir. 2002. *Sjalfsvig og sjalfsvigstilraunir medal islenskra ungmenna (Suicides and suicide attempts among Icelandic youth)*. Reykjavik: Directorate of Health.

Broddason, Th. 2004. Youth and media in Iceland. Unpublished study, University of Iceland: Faculty of Social Sciences, Department of Sociology.

Bureau of European and Eurasian Affairs. 2004. Background note: Iceland. http://www.state.gov/r/pa/ei/bgn/3396.htm.

Einarsdottir, T. 2003. Iceland. In *The Greenwood encyclopedia of women's issues worldwide: Europe*. L. Walter (ed.). London: Greenwood Press.

Gardarsdottir, O. 1997. Working children in urban Iceland 1930–1990. In *Industrious children: Work and childhood in the Nordic countries 1850–1990*. N. de Coninck-Smith, B. Sandin, and E. Schrumpf (eds.). Odense: University Press Odense.

Gotesdam, K. G., and W. S. Agras. 1995. General population-based epidemiological survey of eating disorders in Norway. *International Journal of Eating Disorders* 18:119–26.

Gudbjornsdottir, G. 1994. Sjalfsmyndir og kynferdi (Identities and sexuality). In *Flettur: Rit Rannsoknastofu i kvennafraedum (Laces: The publication of The Center for Women's and Gender Studies)*. R. Richter and Th. Sigurdardottir (eds.). Reykjavik: University Press.

Gudmundsson, G. 1990. *Rokksaga Islands. Fra Sigga Johnnie til Sykurmolanna (Iceland's rock and Roll history. From Sigga Johnnie to the Sugar Cubes)*. Reykjavik: Forlagið.

Gunnlaugsson, H. 1998. Icelandic sociology and the social production of criminological knowledge. In *From a doll's house to the welfare state: Reflections on Nordic sociology*. M. Bertilsson and G. Therborn (eds.). Copenhagen: International Sociological Association.

Hannesdottir, H. 2002. Studies on child and adolescent mental health in Iceland. Ph.D. dissertation, University of Turku, Finland.

Hardarson, O.Th. 2003. *Samkynhneigð og breytingar a gildismati almennings a Vesturlondum (Homosexuality and changes of values among the public in Western countries)*. Paper prepared for the meeting of the Organization of Icelandic Lesbian and Gay Men, Reykjavik.

Hardarson, O. Th. 2004. Parties and voters in Iceland. Unpublished study, University of Iceland: Faculty of Social Sciences, Department of Political Science.

Hibell, B., B. Anderson, Th. Bjarnason, et al. 1995. *The 1995 ESPAD report: Alcohol and other drug use among students in 26 European countries*. Stockholm: The Swedish Council for Information on Alcohol and Other Drugs, CAN.

Hibell, B., B. Anderson, S. Ahlstrom, et al. 1999. *The 1999 ESPAD report: Alcohol and other drug use among students in 30 European countries*. Stockholm: The Swedish Council for Information on Alcohol and Other Drugs.

Hibell, B., B. Anderson, Th. Bjarnason, et al. 2003. *The 2003 ESPAD report: Alcohol and other drug use among students in 35 European countries*. Stockholm: The Swedish Council for Information on Alcohol and Other Drugs.

IMG Gallup. 2004. Gifting samkynhneigðra (Homosexual marriage). http://www.gallup.is/index.jsp.

Jonasson, J. T., and K. S. Blondal. 2002. *Ungt fólk og framhaldsskólinn. Rannsókn á námsgengi og afstöðu '75 árgangsins til nams (Youth and the upper secondary school: Research on the academic achievement and attitudes toward study of those born in 1975)*. Reykjavik: The Social Science Research Institute and the Iceland University Press.

Jonsdottir, J. L. 1994. *Konnun a kynhegdun og thekkingu a alnaemi (A survey of sexual behavior and knowledge about AIDS)*. Reykjavik: The Directorate of Public Health.

Jonsson, F. H. 2003. Afstada Islendinga til utlendinga (Icelanders' attitudes toward immigrants). In *Rannsoknir i Felagsvisindum, IV (Research in Social Sciences, Vol. 4)*. F. H. Jonsson (ed.). Reykjavik: The University of Iceland Press.

Juliusdottir, S. 2001. *Fjolskyldur við aldahvorf (Families at the turn of the century)*. Reykjavik: The University of Iceland Press.

Kristinsson, Th. 2003. Sendu mer Eyjolf minn aftur! Samkynhneigðum unglingum til ihugunar!" (Give me my Eyjolf back! To homosexual adolescents to reflect on). In *Samkynhneigdir og fjolskyldulif (Homosexuality and family life)*. R. Traustadottir and Th. Kristinsson (eds.). Reykjavik: The University of Iceland Press.

Larson, R. W., B. B. Brown, and J. T. Mortimer (eds.). 2003. *Adolescents' preparation for the future: Perils and promise. A report of the Study Group on Adolescence in the Twenty-First Century*. Oxford: Blackwell.

Ministry of Education. 1990. *Jöfn staða kynja i skólum (Equality among girls and boys at school)*. Reykjavik: Ministry of Education.

Ministry of Social Affairs: Director of Labour. 2003. Unemployment among young people in Iceland. http://www.vinnumalastofnun.is/news.asp?ID=873andtype=oneandnews_id=624.

Nordic Statistical Yearbook. 1995, 2002. Copenhagen: Nordic Council of Ministers.

OECD (Organization for Economic Co-operation and Development). 2000. Literacy skills for the world of tomorrow: Further results from PISA 2000. http://www.uis.unesco.org/TEMPLATE/pdf/pisa/exec_sum_eng.pdf.

OECD (Organization for Economic Co-Operation and Development). 2003a. Preliminary Results from PISA 2003. http://www.pisa.oecd.org.

OECD (Organization for Economic Co-operation and Development). 2003b. The Dakar Objectives and the Nordic approach. http://www.unesco.no/utdanning/efa.nordiskrapport.html.

Olafsson, S. 2003. Contemporary Icelanders: Scandinavian or American? *Scandinavian Review* 91:6–14.

Peturson, P., and F. H. Jonsson. 1994. Religion and family values: Attitudes of modern Icelanders in a comparative perspective. In *Scandinavian values: Religion and morality in the Nordic Countries*. Th. Petterson and O. Riis (eds.). Uppsala: University of Uppsala.

Proppe, J. 2000. Dyggdirnar og Islendingar (Virtues and Icelanders). *Timarit Mals og Menningar (Journal of Language and Culture)* 61:6–17.

Rafnsdottir, G. L. 1999. *Barn- och ungdomsarbete i Norden (Youths' occupations in the Nordic countries)*. Copenhagen: Nord.

Reykjavik Police. 2002. The annual report of the Reykavik Police. http://www.police.is.

Sigurdsson, K. 1990. Vinna framhaldsskolanema med nami (Upper secondary school students' occupations). Report for the Ministry of Education. Reykjavik: University of Iceland, Social Science Research Institute.

Statistics Iceland. 2005. http://www.hagstofa.is/template41.asp?PageID=251.

Thorlindsson, Th., K. Olafsson, V. Halldorsson, and I. D. Sigfusdottir. 2000. *Félagsstarf og frístundir unglinga (Youths' social activities and leisure times)*. Reykjavik: Aeskan.

Thorsson, A. V., A. Dagbjartsson, G. I. Palsson, and V. H. Arnorsson. 2000. Kyntroski islenskra stulkna (Puberty in Icelandic girls). *Læknabladid (The Icelandic Medical Journal)* 86:649–53.

Time Magazine. Retrieved March 5, 2005 from the Web site: http://www.time.com/time/covers/1101050307/sciceland.html.

INDIA

Background Information

The Indian subcontinent is currently a region of tremendous geopolitical significance. Together, Indians and Chinese make up 43% of the world's population and therefore hold an important potential influence over world affairs in terms of human resources. Historically known for exotic spices and rich textiles, India is now recognized as one of the largest consumer societies in the world. Much of this is possible because of the massive population of the subcontinent, which despite the rather poor developmental profile, has made an improvement in the Human Development Index from .595 to .602 with a ranking of 127 out of the total of 177 countries (UNDP 2005). This slow progress coexists with the fact that in absolute numbers, Indians form one of the largest pools of technically qualified personnel anywhere in the world. This paradox is the reality of India, where diversity in every sphere of life is more the norm than the exception. There are a total of 1,652 languages spoken in the country (Ramanujam 1994/1991), many of them already in the process of dying out. In terms of religious diversity, India remains home to several religions where the populations of groups in absolute numbers often outnumber total populations of countries. For instance, outside of Indonesia, India has the largest number of Muslims in any single country. The heterodoxy of religious and social life in India is a feature that has often been camouflaged by external evaluations of the country as highly religious (Sen 2005). "India's proverbial diversity applies in particular to literacy and education. On the one end of the scale, remaining uneducated is almost unthinkable for a Tamil Brahmin, or Bengali Kayastha, or Goan Christian. At the other end, literacy rates in 1981 were as low as 2.2 per cent among the Musahars of Bihar and 2.5 per cent among the Kalbelias of Rajasthan" (Drèze 2003, p. 974).

Historically, India has attracted travelers and invaders from different parts of the world, many of whom stayed on to make India their home. Impressions of these are seen even today in archaeological sites as well as modern day expressions. India became independent from British rule in 1947, through a long struggle led by leaders like Gandhi and Nehru. Today, despite significant poverty, illiteracy, and many other difficulties, natural and man-made, India has become an important contender in the global market. Achievements in trade, commerce, and technology have been nothing short of remarkable (Central Statistical Organisation 2003).

India's estimated demographic features are briefly summarized here. The total population is 1,080,264,388. The age structure is as follows: 0 to 14 years: 31.2% (male 173,634,432/female 163,932,475); 15 to 64 years: 63.9% (male 356,932,082/female 333,283,590); 65 years and over: 4.9% (male 26,542,025/female 25,939,784). The median age is 24.66 years (male: 24.64 years, female: 24.67 years). The population growth rate is 1.4%. The death rate is 8.28 deaths per 1,000 population. The sex ratio is: at birth: 1.05 male/female; under 15 years: 1.06 male/female; 15 to 64 years: 1.07 male/female; 65 years and over: 1.02 male/female; total population: 1.06 male/female. The total birth rate is 2.78 children born per woman (CIA 2005).

In sum, the demographic statistics on India show us a clear picture of certain features that will impinge upon our discussion of adolescence. In terms of proportion, adolescents form 21% of our population (UNFPA 2000). According to the 2001 census, 54% of the Indian population is younger than 25 years of age (555 million), while a massive 45% is younger than 19 years of age.

Within this group at the macro level, several important difficulties persist in terms of gender relations, employment, education, and health. Except among the urban, educated middle- and upper-class families, the two-child norm has still to find acceptance, leading to a discernible but slow decline in population growth in the future. Better health and life expectancy in comparison with earlier years will lead to increased numbers of older people, making an important transformation in the age-related issues of importance.

Period of Adolescence

In Indian thought and writing, the idea of adolescence per se is rather ambiguous. On the one hand we have texts suggesting that the interpersonal

distance away from adults is not experienced in India, where young people spend more time with rather than away from their family (Verma and Larson 1999). There is a correspondence of interests, activities, and presence of children of all ages in most social settings. On the other hand, in the Hindu view, the idea of *kishore awastha* places the child (particularly the male child) away from the family for a period of learning, dedication, and service. *Kishore awastha*, the phase of being the equivalent of an adolescent, appears within the following sequence: *balavastha* (childhood), *kishore awashtha* (adolescence), *yuvawastha* (youth), *prodawastha* (middle age), and *vridhawastha* (old age). These can be said to be based on the functional sequence of the *ashramas* from childhood through *brahmacharya* (apprenticeship) to *grihastha* (householder), and old age.

Contemporary positions on childhood are different for different domains of activity. Legally a person is not an adult (and therefore a child or a juvenile) until 18 years of age. Men can marry at 21 years whereas women can legally marry at 18 years. However, the legal, social, cultural, and conventional markers in contemporary India are without consensus. According to a report of the UNFPA (2000), at the macro level, Indians have a basic "resistance to the idea of adolescence," attributing this phenomenon to a delay in the onset of puberty due to malnutrition, and prevalence of early marriages. This is further supplemented by the fact that the distance between the different generations is not so wide, although, the report says, the patterns are changing, particularly for urban, educated youth.

The intergenerational continuity that is suggested in such an approach to developmental changes is also encountered in other research. While investigating interpersonal disagreements between adolescents and their parents in middle-class urban families, Kapadia and Miller (2005) found that there was very little disagreement and a favorable attitude toward compromise between the two generations in the resolution of hypothetical issues related to marriage. The basic understanding between both parties is that parents have the best interest of their offspring in mind. This belief leads to the fundamental acceptance of the intentions behind parents' actions. For the Indian urban adolescent, however, the distance between childhood and adulthood has begun to extend. The discourse of adolescence and its problems has begun to find attention. Age at marriage, women's employment, changes in family structure, and media influences are all beginning to exert

consistent impact on the Indian social scene. However, it is still to be seen whether these changes represent all types of urban settlements or mostly the major cities. Largely, one could say that modernity and change of outlook has affected some areas more than others. The first ones to become affected are women's employment, fertility rates, and educational status. Co-residence, family arrangements, residential patterns, and independent living for youth are still guided by tradition in most Indian homes. Of course, there are pockets of Indian elite society that live like their counterparts anywhere else in the world, but that is only a small minority.

Legal provisions for children and youth in India cover a whole range of issues. Among the critical issues facing the state is the fact that children grow up in very difficult circumstances due to poverty, destitution, disease, and disability. Many of our poor live on the streets of urban areas and the livelihood, health care, nourishment, and education of these children is hard to meet. Many live and earn on the streets from a young age. Unfortunately, India's vast expanse and large numbers interfere with the appropriate delivery of programs, whether these are government run or voluntary. This makes the children and youth from poor clusters a very vulnerable group. Having passed the test of physical survival, poor youth face hunger, malnutrition, illiteracy, disability, destitution, prostitution, and crime on the street and in the neighborhood. Sexual health and AIDS control has become an increasingly important area to be addressed among these clusters.

For a juvenile (who is no longer a child between 14 and 19 according to the law), legislation has had separate coverage since the Juvenile Justice Act of 1986. Up till then, young people of this age were also covered under the Children's Act of 1960. The Juvenile Justice Act differentiates between the neglected adolescent (through Juvenile Welfare Boards) and the one who is prone to criminal acts (through Juvenile Courts). The welfare boards deal with children on the streets, or those who are found to be exploited by employers or guardians. Mostly children are likely to be kept in an observation home. The second arm of the Act deals particularly with children who indulge in criminal acts, who are to be treated differently from adult criminals. A juvenile may not be handcuffed, arrested, or imprisoned. After a hearing, appropriate action is suggested for the care and rehabilitation of the child. Despite careful provision under the law, young offenders and youth on the street often find themselves in confrontation with the law, and largely

unprotected. The family is supposed to be the protective cocoon (as mentioned earlier), but in the absence of the family, or in situations where the family members themselves turn exploiters, the adolescents may find themselves in a desperate situation. Legal provisions for the care of the young person on the run are inadequate. In 1996, reports were received about the plan to make better provisions for protection of young people through a National Perspective Plan for Youth Development (1996–2000), to cover areas such as substance abuse, sexual health, disability and gender justice (D. Sharma 2003). One remarkable truth about policy and planning for youth in India is the deep chasm between intention and practice.

The following is a summary of legal provisions for children and adolescents.

- Criminal Law (Indian Penal Code)—Child under 7 years is not responsible for offences. The age of responsibility for a criminal act is raised to 12 years if the child is found not to have attained the ability to understand the consequence of the act.
- The age of sexual consent for girls is 16 years
- The Juvenile Justice Act, 1960 (amended 1986)—A juvenile is a child who has not reached the age of 16 years in the case of a boy or 18 years in the case of a girl.
- Child Marriage Restraint Act, 1978—*Child* means a person, if a male, who has not completed 21 years of age and if a female, has not completed 18 years of age.
- Factories Act, 1948—A child below 14 years of age is not allowed to work in any factory. An adolescent between 15 and 18 years can be employed in a factory only if the adolescent obtains a certificate of fitness from an authorized medical doctor.
- Article 45 of the Constitution—States shall endeavor to achieve, within 10 years of commencement of this Constitution, for free and compulsory education for all children till the age of 14 years.
- The Child Labour (Prohibition and Regulation) Act, 1986—*Child* means someone who has not completed 14 years of age.
- The Immoral Traffic (Prevention Act), 1956 (Amended in 1986)—The amended Act provides enhanced penalties for offences involving children and minors. It continues to prohibit prostitution in a commercialized form without rendering prostitution per se as an offense. (Source: UNFPA. 2000. Adolescents in India: A profile. UNFPA: New Delhi. p. 45)

Research on adolescence in India is a recent area of interest (Pandey 2001) and only lately have researchers begun to view adolescents as not just "older than children," therefore more information is now available about the personal, social, and personality characteristics of adolescents, treating them either as dependent or independent variables (e.g. Patil, Gaonkar, and Katarki 1994; Arora, Sinha, and Khanna 1996).

All societies do not adhere to a common chronological age definition of the stage of adolescence (Brown, Larson, and Saraswathi 2002). Indian researchers have provided different age spans at different points in the last decade or so, starting from 13 to 19 or 11 to 19 years and enlarging the range with time (N. Sharma 1996; N. Sharma and B. Sharma 1999). The present coverage is from 10 to 19 years (Bezbaruah and Janeja 2000; Verma and Saraswathi 2002).

It has been observed in both Indian and Western literature (e.g., N. Sharma 1996; Larson 2002) that adolescence, as generally depicted in psychological discourse, is "marked by a discontinuity between childhood and adulthood" (Saraswathi 1999, p. 214). Undeniably, human development subsumes that in the life cycle the individual will enter puberty, which is a precursor to adult appearance and also adult roles. This physiological stage of the growth spurt is experienced universally between ages 10 and 19. Regarding female sexual development, some studies display a general trend found in other parts of the world with a reduction in the age at menarche for girls. The significant feature of this change is that the difference is higher for Indian girls (lowering by 6 months per decade) than it is for Western populations (3–4 months per decade), perhaps on account of the improvements in nutritional and health status; in consonance with data from other sources, around 68% of girls achieved menarche between 12 and 14 years of age (Bagga and Kulkarni 2000). Changes in patterns have also been reported in delay of age at marriage and better nutritional status, although some amount of anemia and lower outcomes of growth spurt have been reported among young girls (n = 2,500) in lower socioeconomic families (Saibaba et al. 2002). Some evidence for late menarche has been reported among specific populations, either on account of lower nutritional intake, specifically protein intake (Bagga and Kulkarni 2000; Padmavati, Poosha, and Busi 1984), or higher sporting activity (Sidhu and Grewal 1980). Typically, among both boys and girls, the growth spurt tends to occur more slowly and over a longer period of time than among populations of developed countries (Elizabeth 2001).

For this age group, there are several recent programs that have been implemented in the ninth five-year plan (1997–2002). In addition to marking the age of adolescence as a special phase of life in the National Youth Policy (2000), there are specific provisions for education, fertility, health, AIDS prevention, nutrition, women's empowerment, sports, and gainful employment (Planning Commission 2001). Additionally, future planning of the Commission highlights the importance of this stage of life for learning, appropriate guidance, and enrichment in the areas of health, nutrition, work, life-skills for out-of-school adolescents, vocational guidance, sports, and adventure. Special concerns for girls and boys have been listed (Planning Commission 2001).

Beliefs

Regarding the issue of individualism versus collectivism, it can be proposed that the Indian sense of self is highly committed to family values (Roland 1988) and displays a combination of agency/autonomy and interpersonal relatedness (Kagitcibasi 2002) that has been encountered in other modernizing populations. There is a strong commitment to family values (Chaudhary and Kaura 2001) but children, adolescents, and youth are also actively encouraged by the family to have a simultaneous and situation-related autonomy and competitiveness with the outside world. This is all to be accomplished along with a sense of lifelong loyalty to selected social groups and individuals. Socialization practices are deeply embedded in social relations, as is displayed in the rich and complex kin terminology (Chaudhary 2004). Children grow up among others and are often cared for by other people within the family rather than exclusively by their mothers or parents (Kurtz 1992; Trawick 2003). This develops an early sense of "belongingness" that lasts a lifetime, making the identity of the Indian adolescent deeply connected with the social relationships within which he or she is growing up.

Although the Indian social world is characterized by multiple religions with their particular practices, there are many similarities with regard to the socialization of children. As a matter of fact, there may be more regional, ecological, and socioeconomic differences than religious ones, since communities have taken over many of the local practices over the years.

Within Hindu thought, rather than prescribing a uniform moral code of conduct, the belief system prescribes that the notion of right and wrong, the very foundation of morality (*dharma*) is linked to the situation in the time-space-person dynamics (it is important to note here that although Hindu is a religious category, the expression is used here as a social label rather than a religious one; a label that includes multiple ideologies, including skepticism and atheism) (Sen 2005). The notion of the essential but indiscernible (under ordinary circumstances) selfhood is, developmentally speaking, highly individualistic in nature. The fundamental purpose of an individual soul is to gain gradual but effective separation from all worldly experiences, whether they are material, personal, or social. It may be speculated that this construction is contingent upon, linked with, or at least a reaction to the expectation of the intense immersion in social life as a growing person (Trawick 2003). Participation in religious activity is difficult to estimate, although it would not be wrong to say that children and adolescents form an integrated part of the collective religious activity at the time of festivals, rituals, and family and community functions. There is no segregation of children, except perhaps for occasions like death ceremonies and last rites. During festivals, particularly among the community celebrations of *Dussehra* among Gujarati Hindus in central India or *Durga Pooja* among Bengali Hindus in the east, young men and women take to the streets to actively participate in the community song and dance festivities. Similar festivities have also been observed during Christmas time in the former Portuguese colony of Goa, where a substantial number of Christians live. Among children and adolescents, therefore, we find an active participation in community living along with families in celebrations, festivals, and religious and other occasions.

Gender

As in other parts of the world, gender relationships in India remain largely problematic. Although gender discrimination is more a problem in the underprivileged sections of Indian society, these are features that impact the demographic profile of the country as a whole. It is also pertinent to mention here that for the middle and upper classes, education and career for women are often as important as for men. Increasingly, young men (even among the urban and rural poor) are seeking out partners who are educated, arguing that an educated woman is an asset to the family (World Bank 2004). There is no denying that the outcomes of modernization, education, and economic progress have significantly reached the lives of a large

majority, but India still struggles with population figures that require mention.

The female child in a poor family is at a demographic disadvantage even before she is born. The national and state statistics reveal a reversed male-female ratio (Bose 2001), a clear indicator of disadvantage despite the biological stability of the female. Of the total 1,017 million Indians in the 2001 census count, 51.7% are males and 48.3% are females (CSO 2003). This pattern has been observed as far back as 1881, in a count during the colonial times with an increasing deficit per 100 females, from 103 in 1901 to 108 in 1991 (Visaria and Visaria 2003). The analysis of the deficit rate shows that it has been higher than the growth of population would suggest (Visaria 1999). Interesting patterns also show the deficit to be lower in tribal areas, where women enjoy higher status than their rural and urban counterparts. This lag carries on through childhood into adolescence with lower access to food, schooling, health care, and other resources. Many analysts argue that such a ratio can indicate sex-selection before birth; however, it could also be as a result of systematic underreporting of female births and higher female mortality (Visaria and Visaria 2003).

For literacy rates, for instance, the focus on compulsory and free education for all until the age of 14 years corresponds to eight years of schooling. For the country as a whole, we find that in 1991 this (eight years of schooling) was completed for 30% of boys and only 16% of girls (Drèze 2003, p. 977). In higher education, on the other hand, we find that since 1951, when only 10% of girls were being enrolled in education beyond high school, that figure has risen to 39.9% in 2000–2001 (Selected Educational Statistics 2000–2001).

Gender relations have been paradoxical to say the least, where there is an easy acceptance of women as political leaders, yet the woman in the home continues to face subjugation in many families. Gender equality is a major concern for India. Social activists have reported a disadvantage to the girl from the day she is born, even being expressed in the form of female foeticide or infanticide (Visaria and Visaria 2003). The expectation for fertility and domestic work place tremendous pressures on young women, especially (although not exclusively) among the poor (Chaudhary and Mehta 2004). Among the urban middle class, however, increasing attention to gender issues has led to positive responses toward gender equity, and girls enjoy equal status (Datar 1995; Saraswathi and Pai 1997). As a matter of fact, girls are known to share a greater bond with adult females of the house than boys share with the adult males, indicating a greater degree of intimacy and shared time (Schlegel 2003).

India's traditional ethos clearly separated the sexes and promoted sex-specific roles and relationships, and school remains one of the important institutions that can challenge such a stance (Kumar 1986). Gender is a serious issue at the macro level. Through an analysis of demographic information, it was estimated that a total of 13 million girls were in the category of "missing girls"—those who could be seen as having been affected by discriminatory practices against the female child in India. An increase in the mortality rates of girls between 15 and 19 is actually attributed to the early marriage of teenagers, resulting in higher episodes of pregnancy and maternal mortality at this age. In India, 50% of girls between 15 and 19 are already married (UNFPA 2000), although one finds a gradual rise in the age at marriage in recent years: from 13.1 years in 1901 to 15.6 years in 1951 (Agarwala 1962, p. 238), then rising to 16.1 years in 1961 and 19.6 years in 1991, with slightly higher ages for urban areas (21.3 years) in comparison to rural areas (19.0 years). There are also significant differences in the gender statistics according to state—Kerala (23.9 years) and Goa (27.0 years) to as low as 17.6 years and 17.9 years in Rajasthan and Bihar—indicating serious differences in the social status of women in different regions of India (Visaria and Visaria 2003). With reference to age-related fertility rates, we find that the level of fertility among married women has also come down, leading to a significant slowing down of population growth due to voluntary adoption of contraception (Visaria and Visaria 2003).

Regarding government provisions for adolescents and youth, some programs are worth mentioning here. First, the ninth Five Year Plan of the government outlines the thrust toward nutritional supplementation, schemes for adolescent girls, and assessing health needs of children and youth. The National Youth Policy (2000) views youth as a vital resource for the country's future and gives them an important place in planning for their own future in each of the areas of employment, education, nutrition, and health. Additionally, the National Plan of Action on Children (1992) and the SAARC Decade of the Girl Child placed special emphasis on the needs and requirements of adolescent girls and young women in India. The National Population Policy (2000), Health Policy (1999), Nutritional Policy (1983), National AIDS Policy (2000), and National Education Policy (1986/1992) all placed emphasis on adolescents, with special attention to

the adolescent girl. Regarding the education policy, an important dimension is the specific effort at providing nonformal and need-based vocational programs.

Gender as a variable has been of significance in the study of socialization of children in the predominantly patriarchal communities in India, in every domain of research. For the study of adolescence, it is of particular importance. Discrimination against the female child is quite well documented in psychological, sociological, and developmental research (e.g., Girl Child in India, 1995), especially among poor communities. However, most such research draws a generic profile of a girl victimized by her status and circumstances. A longitudinal study of the developmental journey of the girl child from childhood to adolescence and later is largely missing. With all the obvious and subtle forms of discrimination, what forms the core of the adolescent girl's identity, and what gives her the resilience to negotiate the vicissitudes she is surrounded with, is little known in psychological literature. The urban educated female, on the other hand, has a higher access to education, marries later, and also participates more in the workforce. It is also relevant to state here that the data related to women's participation are more prone to errors of enumeration due to their relative distance from public spaces (Visaria and Visaria 2003), implying that population estimates may indeed be lower, and more women may be participating in work than is reported in demographic literature.

In a countrywide study of 13,200 girls in the age range 7 to 18 years and their mothers drawn from 14 states of India (Anandalakshmy 1994) the findings revealed a complex web of familial-social-cultural factors in the girl's context that determine the course of her life. The social class, level of economic development of the village/district she lived in, parental education levels, her birth order, the number and sex of siblings, and her family's caste influenced her status within the family and in the community. When several factors were aggregated, being able to go to school and remaining there seemed to be crucial in governing her chances for development. On the whole, 61% of girls were attending school. Others had either dropped out or had never been to school. A somewhat higher economic level of the family, a better developed village/district, not being from the lowest caste, literacy of parents, being the firstborn, and having fewer siblings, were positively related to a somewhat reasonable place of the girl in the family. Theoretically speaking, these correlations signify that the identity of the Indian adolescent girl is constructed socially, by a variety of proximal and distal factors. Her niche thus prescribed is integral to her sense of self and would constitute an important element in the psychological enquiry into her personality development.

Probing the identity of the adolescent girl among 150 adolescent girls in the age range 16 to 19 years, N. Sharma (1996) found that gender identity was the primary feature of the female adolescent's sense of self. Influenced by the ecological setting, socioeconomic status, level of traditionality, and formal education (all of which have interactive effects), the girl's identity was strongly bound to the sex role rather than being diffused. Although formal education generated certain questioning about self-worth and future aspirations, it did not seem to overwhelm her sense of identification with her gender role. The emphasis on her role as a future homemaker is never lowered, even at the highest level of education.

It is therefore possible to assess that gender is an influential feature of Indian social and personal life and an important determinant of the circumstances that will be encountered through the course of life. Obviously, there is an interaction with situational factors like economic status, region, community, educational level, and others.

The Self

The understanding of the person-community interface, where a person is believed to be integrally linked with the context, company, and circumstances, is an important feature of Indian social life. As discussed in the preceding section, gender is a strong feature of an Indian person's sense of self. Additionally, social status is also determined by age and relative position in the network of relationships within the group, family, or community. Together, age and gender become the key features for determining the life chances within the constraints of the social situation.

A specific cultural setting will evoke particular images of the self that necessarily deviate from those in other locations. In some places, the idea of an independent "self" or a separate identity is not easily communicated in the native vocabulary and may even evoke laughter or incredulity (Chaudhary and Sriram 2001; Kitayama and Markus 1994). The interdependence with the context and others in the environment is now accepted as an important point of departure from the Western sense of self. In India, children are largely believed to be "self-objects," and with this belief socialization is seen as an opportunity for self-expression

(Misra, Srivastava, and Gupta 1999, p. 195) and parents often find it uncomfortable to detach themselves from the lives and loves of their children. It is "connectivity" and not "separation" that characterizes group relations and self-orientations (Seymour 1999). Traditional Indian childcare is conceived of as needing the unique contributions of both parents, where the mother is visualized as providing physical and emotional comfort and the father as the moral and intellectual guide. Krishnan (1998) is of the view that children are believed to require specific themes in care at different ages. The child under 5 should receive affection, which is followed by discipline for the next ten years. At 16, the child is believed to be like a friend and should be treated as such by the family, with respect for girls and regard for male children as responsible for the family line. The daughter is regarded as an essential but temporary member of her natal family, although evidence has pointed toward a greater intimacy between daughters and mothers subsequent to their marriage (N. Sharma 1996).

Similarly, the great deal of interdependence that can be found within the Indian family can be described, at the individual level, as a collective feeling. To make matters more complex, there are likely to be intra-individual differences as well, depending upon the situation or domain of activity. For instance, it is not unusual for a person to be quite competitive and individualistic in the workplace while carrying a high interdependence at home, without much conflict of interests. Indian urban parents socialize for and carry expectations for a kind of dual manifestation of interpersonal distance, sometimes leading to stress among adolescents and youth in India (Kaura and Chaudhary 2003) and elsewhere (Bosma and Gerlsma 2003). It is not unusual for older siblings to be expected to "take care of" younger ones (Mascolo and Bhatia 2002), and also for brothers to be protective of their sisters. The early network of relationships "predisposes children to develop not simply some kind of a homogenous group self, but rather a socially embedded, relational self that includes affective identifications and representations of multiple caregivers" (D. Sharma 2003, p. 39).

Within the physical limits of this life-world, the sense of self among Indians is believed to be constantly changing, evolving partly because the context is given primacy. Bodies are considered to be relatively "porous," "permeable," and predicated upon the different life circumstances and relationships (Menon 2003, pp. 431, 433). The transformations possible will be determined by the social and biological state of being woman or man, pregnant or young, and so on. This open and heterogeneous nature of the Indian personality has received some attention, sometimes even being discussed as resulting in people who are better referred to as "divisible" in their very nature (Marriott 1976, p. 111). The existence of human beings is essentially linked to society, and social processes are believed to have the same organic quality as bodies (Menon 2003; Trawick 2003).

Regarding psychological adjustment of adolescents in contemporary society, Singhal and Rao (2004, p. 204) found that in their research on a large group of adolescents (n = 25,796) as many as 38% of adolescents were found to have "problematic psychological concerns." The young women were more concerned with issues of looks and nervousness, and were indecisive and misunderstood; whereas boys reported feeling more shy, frequently being rejected by peers, being uncomfortable in the company of girls, and troubled by feelings of anger. Interestingly, more problematic issues were displayed in the responses of private school children in comparison with those from government schools. It is important to remember that this difference may also be related to a higher level of comfort and acceptance of having psychological difficulties among the more affluent families. From this research, we can discern that although family relationships are critical to young people, difficulties with the individual self are present especially among urban, school-going adolescents. Not much work has been done on the identity of rural youth.

Family Relationships

Relationships within the family form an integral part of the self of the Indian person. This also holds true for the relationships with siblings (Roland 1988; Sriram, Chaudhary, and Ralhan 2002), and there was some evidence of phenomena like compensation (not being like an undesirable sibling) or competitiveness (not being as good as a positively evaluated sibling) processes that were deeply guided by parents and others in the family (Kaura and Chaudhary 2003). Older siblings were also found to experience isolation when there was a greater sibling distance (Singh 1998), thereby suggesting the sensitivity of factors like birth order, age, and gender of sibling among other family variables.

There are several accounts of the family being at the center of adolescent lives, a feature not unusual in a society where relationships are based on interdependence and dependence. According to Larson,

Verma, and Dworkin (2003), if one has not grown up within such a social climate, it is difficult to understand the close relationship between adolescents and parents because one does not experience the culture. In a detailed cross-cultural study of 100 Indian middle-class adolescents, both girls and boys, at the mean age of 13.2 years, were compared with 220 middle-class European and American youth. Indian adolescents were found to spend much more time with families than their American counterparts and to feel positive in doing so most of the time. Very few of them reported any signs of conflict with their parents and there was no attempt at breaking away. When together, Indian families were invariably at home and involved in routine activities such as watching TV, talking, or doing homework (for school). In conclusion, "this greater degree of family interaction, especially given that it is experienced positively, is developmentally beneficial" for the growing person (p. 282). S. Verma and Sharma (2003) examined the adolescents' use of free time and found gender differences in free-time activities regarding content, duration, frequency, and quality. Leisure for girls was primarily home-based, such as watching TV, reading, cooking, and embroidery, while boys reported more outside activities such as playing sports, going to movies, and hanging out with friends. Since this study has been reported in the context of leisure-time use reports from other countries including Japan, Korea, the United States, and European nations, the cultural differences observed are significant. The authors concluded that in urban areas technology has had a mediating role in replacing traditional leisure-time activities among youth with a more Westernized pattern, although family time and community activities seem to enjoy an important place in these as well.

For the first time in psychological discourse Kakar (1981) invoked the Hindu view of life to remind the academic community that for the majority of Indians, the first formal stage in the *Ashrama* scheme of the life cycle is *brahmacharya* (apprenticeship), and it includes the period of adolescence, wherein competence and fidelity are essential virtues to be acquired. Reaffirming the notion of continuity rather than the lack of it, Saraswathi (1999) has argued that the absence of the notion of adolescence in any society would be linked to greater continuity between childhood and adulthood and in the similarity in life events across the life span. She also believes that "adolescence as a life stage is both gendered and class based" (p. 222). Girls and boys are involved by their

parents in gender-specific household and livelihood chores and their lives are quite comfortably enmeshed with the lives of the adults in the family.

Contextualizing Indian data in a cross-cultural scenario, Saraswathi compares findings from Indian studies with anthropological investigation by Schlegel and Barry (1991) to adolescence in 186 preindustrial societies. She observes that continuity in transition from childhood to adulthood is clearer in the lower social class than in the upper social class. Yet, during this period of continuity, there is a brief transitional stage before marriage when the girl is trained in assuming greater responsibility for tasks at home so that she becomes a competent member of another family after marriage.

With reference to males, the picture is somewhat ambiguous (Saraswathi 1999). While lower-class boys are expected to "earn before they learn," those from the higher social class are expected to perform well academically. In all cases, conformity to family norms is deemed essential, which according to the author, leaves little scope for the emergence of a distinct adolescent culture. The only exceptions are among affluent youngsters, where association with the peer group, permission for alternative lifestyles, and exposure to global television images brings about intergenerational conflicts and some discontinuity in the child-adult continuum.

On the whole, the single most significant leitmotif that characterizes Indian adolescents is their constant pull toward the family ethos that encourages them to place individual needs secondary to family needs, and subjugate their decisions to those made by the family to "maintain cohesiveness." However, it is essential to understand that earlier interpretations of Indian collectivity are rather misplaced since there was no realization of the deep openness to debate (Sen 2005) and negotiability (Kapadia and Miller 2005) in relationships and perspectives. The dominant misunderstanding has been that Indian society is deeply hierarchical and authority bound, always subordinating the self to the group; this position is a misconstruction (Miller 2002).

Research has shown that family-related issues are critical to the adjustment and well-being of an adolescent. There are strong linkages between family dynamics and adolescent health and well-being (Sartor and Youniss 2002). While expressing their concerns about parents, as many as 34% of adolescents reported having negative feelings toward their families, while 24% were concerned about family issues (Singhal and Rao 2004). This research also highlights that these school-going adolescents, both boys and girls, expressed that their feelings of

inadequacy, self-confidence, and disinterest in activities were indeed related to parental attitudes. This, the authors report, is an important concern for parents of today.

Friends and Peers/Youth Culture

Adolescence is developmentally an age at which young people increasingly seek the company of their age mates. However, with reference to Indian adolescents, although the above statement may be true, time spent with the family is still significant. Further, adolescents retain a great deal of regard for compromise rather than conflict, particularly within the family. This was found to be particularly true for urban middle-class adolescents (Kapadia and Miller 2005). The prevalence and continued importance of the large family network, both in reality and ideology (Uberoi 2003), allows for peer interactions within the family that become an important social feature. However, there is evidence to support the increasing evidence of what may be termed as "peer culture" among middle- and upper-class urban youth (Verma and Saraswathi 2002) as affluence, mobility, and consumption become common. The extent to which these features will actually impact the primacy of the family as a socialization agent, is yet to be discerned (Schlegel 2003).

Another feature of Indian society is the early age of marriage for a majority of young men and women. Thus, peer contact gets significantly truncated due to the fact that many youth are already married at this age. It is also true that peer contact for boys remains much higher than for girls, primarily due to the greater mobility that boys are allowed, although this feature is applicable to all societies. Girls spend more time interacting with adult women all over the world in comparison with the amount of time that boys spend with adult males (Schlegel 2003). In this regard, acceptance by peers and social standing were found to be far more critical for boys than for girls (Singhal and Rao 2004, p. 10).

In contrast to the West, self-reliance and engagement with age-mates is not perceived to be a critical expectation from adolescents (Saraswathi and Ganapathy 2002), and individual autonomy is encountered only in older adults (Mines 1988). In the process of making decisions, as well, Indian adolescents continue to look to the family rather than to peers for choices of import like career and family (Ramu 1988; Uplaonkar 1995). Although there is not much written about peer influence and the young adolescent, one study finds that Indian

adolescents spend a majority of time with their family rather than with friends; but whatever time is spent with friends is evaluated as very positive in terms of emotional affect (Larson, Verma, and Dworkin 2003).

Love and Sexuality

Since the idea of adolescence is Western in its origin, the nature of adolescent sexuality is also largely based on the behavior of unmarried sexually active adolescents (Bruce 2003), most adolescents in the West being unmarried. This position stands challenged in most developing nations, and issues of fertility replace those of sexuality, making it essential to address policy and programs related to delay of age at marriage. In one estimate, as many as 55% of girls under 19 are already married (Singhal and Rao 2004, p. 17), whether or not they have had the formal departure to the husband's home. The sexual behavior of sexually mature individuals is a matter of grave concern for the community in India, particularly the rural and tribal regions. Delay of marriage beyond puberty is considered a risk in many communities, placing several pressures on parents to get daughters married early. Even if departure to the husband's home may be delayed until some years later, marriages are usually fixed and solemnized before or soon after puberty. Attending school has significantly delayed age of marriage, as per the census records. However, there is no denying that once maturity is reached, parents in a majority of Indian homes display latent or overt signs of eagerness for the daughter to find a home outside of her natal one. The unmarried daughter/sister is seen as a threat to the dynamics of a community, especially a rural community, a fact that is repeatedly displayed in cultural content like myth, folktales, and film (Kurtz 1992). Parents feel forced to marry off their daughters at a young age due to fears of sexual exploitation, reproductive health (Bruce 2003), and greater choice in finding a spouse.

Marriage under the age of 18 is argued to be an abuse of human rights (Bruce 2003) and it is essential for developing nations to work systematically to ensure that there are opportunities for providing education, employment, training, or whatever action it will take to reduce the panic that parents of young women (particularly the poor) face before a daughter's marriage. Of course action has to be initiated from all sides, not just the state. Community level organizations, educational institutions, health workers, and others need to work actively toward the delay in age of marriage of young

people in India. As has been demonstrated in China, the enforcement of the policy of "later, longer, and lesser" with reference to age at marriage, the gap between children, and fewer children respectively, has been very effective. This has now been transformed into the one-child norm, at least in the urban centers, and has significantly slowed down the population growth of the nation, a problem with which India is still grappling.

Regarding the popular trend of arranged marriages in India in contrast with love marriages, it is difficult to make estimations of the exact figures for several reasons (Mathur n.d.). First, there are very few examples of "pure" forms of either marriage—young people who may find romantic love often choose to work through the known system of introductions through parents to keep respect for the system. In arranged marriages as well, more freedom is given to young couples to make choices of whom they would like to marry by encouraging some interaction before finalizing matters. Traditionally, there has always been a precedence of family over individual with reference to marriage choices. Appropriateness and social characteristics were always more important than romantic love. Love was believed to start after and before a marriage (Mathur n.d.). It remains true for many rural communities that early marriages of men and women are encouraged to prevent young people from making their own choices regarding a spouse. Among urban, educated populations, however, the delay in marriage and the increased contact between young people that is typical of an urban environment have led to an increase in the frequency and tolerance of marriages of choice.

A more recent trend has been the introduction of several Web sites that display captions like "Arrange your own love marriage," "Meet your match online," etc. Although no accurate data is available, there is much evidence of young people and families increasingly using Internet encounters through Web sites for both arranged and dating choices, but with marriage as the objective. Living with a heterosexual partner without being married is still restricted to a small section of the upper-class elite society. Similarly, homosexuality is only now becoming a matter of public opinion. Despite the fact that ancient Indian art, architecture, and literature demonstrate a great variety in sexual expressions of men and women, over the years this variety seems to have become suppressed for the common person. Many social practices have also responded to the peculiar history of the Indian subcontinent, including frequent invasions and fluctuating ideologies. Examples of these influences can be seen in every sphere of life.

There is no doubt that being married and having children is the ideal outcome of an individual's youth. Parents believe that they have not fulfilled their duty if their child has not been married and not had any children. The pressure for getting and staying married and also having children has clear manifestations in the fertility figures and lower divorce rates for India among all religious and ethnic communities. These patterns are slowly changing and only time will tell whether the vibrancy of familial relationships, marriage, and childhood is able to sustain the pressures of modernity (Trawick 2003). Although primarily understood as a system that is dominated by family, arranged marriages and vows exchanged between partners at the time of the ceremony display a somewhat different flavor. In a Hindu marriage ceremony, the following vows are exchanged during the seven steps that a couple takes around the sacred fire (Badrinath 2003, p. 136):

"With these seven steps, become my friend.
I seek your friendship. May we never deviate
From this friendship.
May we walk together.
May we resolve together.
May we love each other and enhance each other.
May our vows be congruent and our desires shared"

Like all other issues in India, love and sexuality remain a complex matter. On the one hand there are instances of polygamous marriages in some communities, child marriages in others, matriarchy and matrilineal practices in yet others. But patriarchy and monogamy with prevalent intolerance for premarital sexuality and homosexuality remain the order of the day. In a recent controversy over public comments, a southern Indian actress faced threats of imprisonment for liberal remarks about premarital sex. Each day, the newspapers covered the voices on both sides of the argument (*The Times of India* November 19, 2005). From this and other public debates one can argue that certainly these remain contentious issues that will raise passions in Indian society, despite the increased tolerance in urban areas.

Changing trends in sexuality outside of marriage have become a matter of concern, especially on account of the health risks involved. HIV/AIDS has become a serious matter and educational institutions are increasingly recognizing the need for early introduction of sex education. Public radio and TV have always been important sources of awareness for the public, ever since they

popularized the family planning and small family norm in the early 1970s. More recently, through the efforts of the National Aids Campaign (National Aids Control Organization NACO), online campaigns (http://www.nacoonline.org/), radio programs, and TV announcements have taken on more aggressive nationwide campaigning for sexual health safety and awareness.

Health Risk Behavior

With reference to survival, the improvement of the health statistics in all aspects of the population in India can also be seen among adolescents. For 10- to 14-year-olds, mortality rates reduced from 1.7 in 1980 to 1.3 and 1.4 in 1995 in males and females respectively. For 15- to 19-year-olds, figures went from 2.9 in 1980 to 2.0 for females and 2.0 to 1.7 for males (CSO 1998). Figures for youth from the lower economic groups in urban areas are substantially higher than others (Diniz 2003).

The period of adolescence and the habits picked up therein, have a lifelong impact on the future health of an individual. The most important areas of concern are reproductive and sexual health, accidental and intentional violence, substance abuse, mental health, and nutritional problems (WHO 2001). Due to the significance of adolescent health for later life, the economic investment in youth has been justified to improve productivity, avert future health expenditure, as well as lead to well-being of the adolescents themselves. The incidence of HIV/AIDS has brought the discussion of sexual conduct into the open. Some research highlights the increase in sexual activity among adolescents, especially males. One important detail about the Indian population that would have an impact on sexual conduct is the fact that a high percentage of adolescents, particularly women, are already married by this age, thereby making them functionally monogamous.

Regarding concerns about health, in the study of 25,796 adolescents from government and private schools mentioned earlier (Singhal and Rao 2004) it was found that around 30% of children emerged as having health concerns, with girls emerging as marginally more concerned with health than boys (31.16% versus 29.56%). Although this study was done only on school-going adolescents, there was a fair representation of family income groups (under 1,500.00 to 30,000.00 and above per month). Health concerns included appearance, frequent aches and pains, inability to eat regularly, frequent illnesses, and weakness. There were no noticeable income-level differences in the problems identified by the respondents. Interestingly, regarding appearance, boys outnumbered girls by 7 to 1 in assessing themselves as weaker than similar others (p. 164). Thus, although reproductive health remains a critical issue during adolescence, other concerns linked with nutrition, body image, and peer pressure are important concerns of adolescents in India.

Education

Education has been highlighted as the critical factor in the improvement of the Human Development Index (HDI) status of the country and the recommendation is for increased efforts in the universalization of educational facilities to improve status and reduce the gender gap in the country (UNDP 2005). The educational system in postcolonial India is a collaborative reconstruction of missionary efforts, the British rule, and the increasing importance given to indigenous ideologies, strongly supported by eminent Indian educationists like Tagore, Gandhi, Dayan, and Sarawsathi and others (Srivastava 2003). This reconstruction has had several important impacts on the way schooling is understood today. Some of the features can be easily discerned, like the struggle with the domination of the English language and the rather difficult state of the vernacular. Several important indigenous movements like the *Arya Samaj*, which attempted to return education to the glorious past of the Vedic period, have made significant contributions to the cause of education at all levels, especially education for girls.

India has made regular progress in education over the last several decades; however, access, enrollment, retention, and quality of schooling are matters of serious concern that prevent many children (more girls than boys) from entering or sustaining school education (CSO 1998, p. 44). Despite legislation and planning, access to schools remains elusive for many communities. Nevertheless, the motivation for and the belief in schooling as a solution for individual and family progress are encountered even among the poorest of the poor. Significant efforts of the state to provide special institutional support for excellence in school through the *Navodaya Vidyalayas* (Srivastava 2003)—special policies for school enrollment and retention, and mid-day meal programs to encourage children to come and stay in school—have had some impact, but at a national level much more needs to be done to realize the goal of universalization of education of all children and adolescents, especially of primary education (as the commitment of the state articulates). Repeated situational

evaluations have suggested that no longer can the blame be placed on parents for not sending children to school; it is far more significantly a result of poor distribution of schooling facilities, especially at the primary level of schooling. If one compares educational achievement between India and China, these "are not only much lower in India than in China, they are also much less equitably distributed" (Drèze and Loh 1995, p. 2,870).

Regarding national government expenditure in education, we find a concerted effort at an increase in budgetary allocations at the state level.

From Table 1, one can see the tremendous jump that has taken place between the number of educational institutions that adolescents can enter for higher education. Although these are still a long way away from providing occupational, technical, and professional training for all interested youth, it has led to a substantial jump in the gross number of youth with higher education. A total of 27.6 million children were estimated to be enrolled at the high school level (16.9 million boys and 10.7 million girls). Girls' enrollment has been steadily increasing over the years, and an estimated 36.9% of girls enter college level educational institutions.

In Table 2 we can see the outcome of the changing scenario of the educational status of youth in India. Increasing numbers of adolescents are attending and successfully completing school. Although boys still outnumber girls, there is a tremendous improvement in the literacy rates for young women. This brings us to the trend toward the emergence of a very large population of technically qualified youth in India. Increasingly, this potential availability of technically qualified youth is gaining international attention, and India is accessing more jobs for its youth today than ever before. Much of this employment is linked to improved communication links and access to computer technology, but behind this is the fact of educational and training facilities for youth in India.

According to one estimate (Singhal and Rao 2004, p. 15), only 59% of boys and 38% of girls between 10 and 24 years of age are enrolled in school. We find therefore, that a substantial number of adolescents are outside of school. For families from middle and upper classes, education-related issues are top priority. While discussing family time, parents declare that much of the scheduling of family time is negotiated around children's academic commitments (Verma, Sharma, and Larson 2002). Despite national and state level action and personal motivation, schooling remains elusive for the very poor. In most instances, reasons that keep children out of school are linked with responsibilities for work in the home (especially so for the firstborn child, male or female), like care of younger children while the parents are out to work, lack of accessibility to school, frequent migration of families for work, harsh attitudes of teachers, and the absence of positive role models within the community (Chaudhary and Sharma 2005).

According to a World Bank study (2004), those children who do reach school despite all odds do so for factors including the following: they are later-born children (so an older child can take on household responsibility), a member of the family is keen to send them to school, school is accessible, there is encouragement from teachers, and the children are male. In this study of poor communities in three different states of India, it was clear that getting to

Table 1. Growth of Recognized Educational Institutions between 1950–1951 to 2000–2001

Years	High School	Colleges General	Colleges Professional	Universities
1950–1951	7,416	370	208	27
1990–1991	79,796	4,862	886	184
2000–2001	126,047	7,929	2,223	254

Source: Selected Educational Statistics 2000–2001.

Table 2. Percentages of Literate Adolescents by Age and Sex

Age Group	1961		1991	
	Males	Females	Males	Females
10 – 14 years	54.4	28.4	77.0	68.8
15 – 19 years	52.0	23.8	75.3	65.8

Source: CSO 1998.

school and staying there is a task that is filled with hurdles for children and adolescents—hurdles of physical distance, gender, nutritional disadvantage, economic hardship, teacher attitudes, occupational responsibility, and household responsibilities. Education thus remains largely problematic, and with the absence of serious commitment from the state to provide schools in every neighborhood; to train teachers for commitment and positive attitudes toward poor communities; and to provide infrastructure like classrooms, toilets, and books, a large section of children of all ages (mostly girls) remain outside of school—keen to enroll but unable to do so. For those upper- and middle-class children who do reach school and are potential members of the technically trained force of the subcontinent, the major challenge is to face the deepening crisis of competing against large numbers of peers in education, training, and the job market. Academics remained the largest factor contributing to stress among urban adolescents (Kaura 2004). Interestingly, it was not fear of failure or difficulty to learn but the high expectation of families that were the most stressful for the adolescents in this study. Identifying the key factors in the adolescent–parent interface, Kaura (2004) found that when there were large gaps between what parents believed, what they did, and what they expected, the children were faced with difficulties and insecurity. On the other hand, when there was a reasonable correspondence between ethos, experience, and expectation, the adolescents felt most comfortable.

In a study of around 26,000 school-going children (in and around Delhi) from different economic backgrounds attending both government and private schools, it was found that academics posed the most serious problem among 41% of children, both boys and girls. School tasks at this stage were found to be uniformly difficult across gender, social class, and type of school. Boys more frequently complained about "not liking" studies, and both sexes complained about classroom experiences, inability to comprehend, and examination fear. These concerns were irrespective of the type of school attended (Singhal and Rao 2004, p. 203).

Thus, getting to school and remaining there remains a serious problem for a vast majority of Indian children and adolescents. This reality coexists with the tremendous success of professional higher education, thus making educational accomplishment depend largely on the social context (Drèze, 2003, p. 989). Neither side of the extreme can adequately explain the other, and this remains a feature of the inequality and diversity of the Indian scenario and makes a critical call for the reduction of the educational gaps that persist both at the state and community levels. Some of the persistent reasons for the low participation have been identified as the lack of parental motivation, economic deprivation, and poor school quality (Drèze 2003).

Work

Modern society sets children apart and outside of the work force and production of value (Nieuwenhuys 2003). As discussed earlier, this is a symptom of the value system of modernity, having grave consequences on the ways in which childhood and adolescence are described and understood. While reading the data on adolescent work participation and employment, it is important to reflect on some of these issues that we have begun to take for granted as members of modern society. However, these issues remain contentious, if not paradoxical. In a recent document of the International Labour Organisation (ILO), for instance, we read that: "We have no problem with the little girl who helps her mother with the housework or cooking, or the boy or girl who does unpaid work in a small family business....The same is true of those odd jobs that children may occasionally take on to earn a little pocket money to buy something they really want" (ILO 1993, p. 22). In many instances, such assistance to family can be quite exploitative of children (Nieuwenhuys 2003). It remains, therefore, very difficult to take a uniform stance on children's contribution to work that becomes largely defined by chronological age.

The law in India prohibits the employment of young children under the age of 14 through the Child Labour (Prohibition and Regulation) Act of 1986. However, due to economic difficulty, children of all ages find themselves in jobs, either with family or outside the family. According to the 1991 census, out of a total of 200 million children between 5 and 14 years of age, around 11.28 million are in jobs. Other estimates are even higher (UNFPA 2000, p. 21). The visibility of children at work is higher for boys, making accurate estimations very difficult. The participation of older adolescents (15 to 19 years), particularly boys, was as high as 50% of the population, according to one estimate (Singhal and Rao 2004, p. 18). Unemployment among youth is another problem that is facing India (Visaria 1999), primarily due to lack of training, high population growth, increase in

education (which has led to the phenomenon of educated youth who do not want to work in traditional occupations), slow economic progress, and poor quality of education.

According to the fiftieth round of the National Sample Survey (NSS), the work participation of adolescents between 15 and 19 years was fairly high, with more males (54.7%) than females (30.7%) participating. It is also important to note that estimates of employment among children and youth are very difficult to ascertain, especially for situations like domestic, construction, and agricultural labor (Planning Commission 2001; UNFPA 2000). Also, it must be remembered that there are more adolescents in the educational system than before, so employment rates will also reflect this accordingly.

Media

The media show clear preferences for the urban Westernized youth. Images of fashion models, Bollywood actresses and actors with light eyes, and svelte images of scantily clad women adorn glossies and dailies in the Indian market. Rural youth are not a popular topic with the media; they are treated merely as consumers to be targeted for some advertisement or other, either to be turned into a smart woman or a confident man, but certainly not to be accepted as they are. In this sense, the Indian media are far more Westernized than the general population.

India has always been very open to technological advancement. This was a policy pursued by the leaders soon after the British left India in 1947. This choice allowed a periodic surge in technology. People all over the country use technology with ease and for innovative functions, sometimes even defying the initial purpose for which a machine may have been meant. One example that comes to mind is the use of the manual washing machine to churn butter from curds in rural India (Chowdhury 1994). The most recent advance has been in the mobile phone industry, and the Indian market is reeling from demands for unprecedented sales. Just over a total of 63 million mobile phone users and 500,000 Internet users have been identified in the subcontinent (Bhatnagar 2005). This unprecedented expansion in the communication sector is bound to impact the lives of young people in significant ways. It remains to be seen how these changes will become absorbed into the existing social and personal lives of Indian families in general and adolescents in particular.

Politics and Military

The Indian constitution provides a democratic framework within which the term "secular" is understood somewhat different from the way it is understood in the West. "Secular" in India means the freedom to follow one's own religion and tolerance toward other religions. The government does not fund or follow any particular religion. This policy has been a part of Indian ideology for centuries, as a result of which India is one of the most religiously diverse countries of the world. Whereas political policy presents democracy and equality as important principles, Indian social and family life is rife with hierarchy and stratification. In social life, caste, class, and family are important divides. Within the family, age and gender form important distributive principles (Mandelbaum 1970).

Regarding political activity and youth, a common lament is the lack of motivation for political participation and voting among youth (Raedler 1999), for which the country faces a grave need in order to benefit from the energy and enthusiasm that is lacking (Solomon 2003). Young voters reported being more concerned about their careers than about political parties, as they believed politics to be riddled with corruption (Raedler 1999; Solomon 2003), something they would rather stay away from.

Diversity is also found in other features, both cultural (languages, food, costume) and natural (seasonal, geographical). The four main regions of north, south, east, and west include people who actually look different from each other. Governance of such a vast state is quite problematic, and the subcontinent is bound together more by the idea of India than by any homogeneity.

Militarily, India is an advanced country. The armed forces have always been an attractive career, especially for young men. The association has also been linked with the colonial period when the British deliberately encouraged people from the warrior castes in the north (particularly Punjab and Haryana), through positive associations with their masculinity and a career in the army, to serve as soldiers in the British Army (Chowdhury 1994). The trick worked, and the states of Punjab and Haryana still carry a great deal of enthusiasm toward a career in the army and provide the armed forces. The armed forces of the Army, Navy, and Air Force in India carry an image and function way beyond the idea of war, although that thought is invariably present, and defense of the country is always in the background as a noble idea. The armed forces also provide administrative, social,

and emergency assistance to the government. Cantonments built during the British Raj are organized "havens" adjunct to the rather chaotic, organic townships typical of the Indian countryside. Being in the army does not carry the stigma that it does in other parts of the world, and it offers a lucrative career for young men and also young women now. The local belief is that a person becomes more disciplined after a few years in the army.

The National Cadet Corps (NCC) Act was passed by Parliament in India in 1948 with the objective of instilling discipline and unity among youth to enhance their participation in the nation, the armed forces, and community living. With these objectives, the NCC has recruitment centers all over the country and encourages the enrollment of young men and women. There are a total of 1,023,000 cadets enrolled in the NCC in the country as per the latest records (Keshavan n.d.). The cadets are trained for social, community, and military activity in regularly held camps all over the country. Cadets are selected through the educational institutions in which they are studying. They can volunteer to join the NCC, after which they are trained and given uniforms and ranks. The NCC forms one of the largest collection of organized youth activity in India and is also an important training ground for youth interested in joining the armed forces.

Unique Issues

From the preceding discussion on adolescence in India, several critical issues have come to the surface. Although there is traditional acceptance of a transition from childhood to adolescence, the basic function of that age has been to focus on learning and preparation for adult roles. The increasing distance between adult responsibility and childhood abandon has led to a progressive need to discuss issues of youth as uniquely important. It is essential, however, to understand that the adolescent in India faces a situation that is quite different from his or her Western counterpart. Some of the ways in which the situation is different are:

- People will continue to live with their families until marriage or departure for work or school. Living separately is not a common practice.
- Parents continue to be concerned with the everyday lives of youth (and even adult children) for the rest of their lives. This concern often translates into advice, assistance, or interference.

- The belief in lifelong commitment to the family makes the network of social relationships very enduring and family cohesion is highly valued.
- There is a great value for compromise rather than conflict in all relationships.
- Young adolescents in India spend much more time with their families than do their counterparts in other parts of the world.
- Adolescents truly believe that their parents have their (the young persons') best interests in mind.
- The social unit of the peer group, fraternity, or any other collectivity is almost always subordinate to the family.
- The family remains an ideal group even among the homeless, abandoned, and street-based children.
- The heterodoxy of Indian community living leads to several significant variations according to region, religion, caste, income, or language.
- There is no doubt that modern influences have led to a greater negotiability in life choices and individual preferences of young people.

These features of family life in India make the experience of adolescence quite distinctive from adolescence in other parts of the world. Therefore, any discussion of intergenerational dynamics in India must account for these features of social reality in India. Policy, planning, and action related to adolescence have to work within the framework of these patterns of social life in general, and family life in particular.

NANDITA CHAUDHARY and NEERJA SHARMA

References and Further Reading

Agarwala, S. N. 1062. *Age at marriage in India.* New Delhi: Kitab Mahal.

Anandalakshmy, S. (ed.). 1994. *The girl child and the family: An action research study.* New Delhi: Department of Women and Child Development, Ministry of Human Resource Development, Govt. of India.

Arora, M., P. Sinha, and P. Khanna. 1996. A study of relationships between crowded residence in a group of adolescents and their mental health in living conditions. *Indian Journal of Psychological Issues* 4(1):25–31.

Badrinath, C. 2003. The householder, grhastha in the Mahabharata. In *Family and gender: Changing values in Germany and India.* M. Pernau, I. Ahmad, and H. Reifeld (eds.). pp. 113–39. New Delhi: Sage.

Bagga, A., and S. Kulkarni. 2000. Age at menarche and secular trend in Maharashtrian Indian girls. *Acta Biologica Szedegiensis* 44(1–4):53–58.

Bezbaruah, S., and M. K. Janeja. 2000. *Adolescents in India: A profile.* New Delhi: United Nations Population Fund.

Bhatnagar, S. September 8, 2005. India's mobile base surges to 63 million in August. Reuters, India. Accessed on September 12, 2005. http://in.today.reuters.com/news/NewsArticle.aspx?type=technologyNews&storyID=2005-09-08T180604Z_01_NOOTR_RTRJONC_0_India-215462-2.xml.

Bose, A. 2001. *Population of India: 2001 census results and methodology*. Delhi: B. R. Publishing House.

Bosma, H., and C. Gerlsma. 2003. From early attachment relations to the adolescent and adult organisation of the self. In *Handbook of developmental psychology*. J. Valsiner and K. J. Connolly (eds.). pp. 450–90. London: Sage.

Brown, B. B., R. W. Larson, and T. S. Saraswathi (eds.). 2002. *The world's youth: Adolescence in eight regions of the globe*. U.K.: Cambridge University Press.

Bruce, J. 2003. Married adolescent girls: Human rights, health, and developmental needs of a neglected majority. *Economic and Political Weekly* XXXVIII(41):4378–80.

Central Statistical Organisation (CSO). 1998. *Youth in India*. Government of India, New Delhi: CSO.

Central Statistical Organisation (CSO). 2005. India in figures (2003). Government of India. Accessed on 11 September, 2005. http://mospi.nic.in/mospi_cso_rept_pubn.htm.

Chaudhary, N. 2004. *Listening to culture*. New Delhi: Sage.

Chaudhary, N., and I. Kaura. 2001. Approaching privacy and selfhood through narratives. *Psychological Studies* 46(3):132–40.

Chaudhary, N., and N. Sharma. 2005. From home to school. *Seminar* 546:14–20.

Chaudhary, N., and S. Sriram. 2001. Dialogues of the self. *Culture and Psychology* 7(3):379–93.

Chaudhary, S., and B. Mehta. 2004. Adolescents and gender equality: A pedagogic concern. *Perspectives in Education* 20(1):28–49.

Chowdhury, P. 1994. *The veiled women: Shifting gender equations in rural Haryana*. New Delhi: Oxford University Press.

CIA. 2005. The world factbook. http://www.cia.gov/cia/publications/factbook/index.html. Accessed on July 1st 2005.

Datar, C. 1995. Democratising the family. *Indian Journal of Social Work* LV(1):211–24.

Diniz, M. 2005. Premarital sex among youth today. March 3, 2005. http://in.rediff.com/getahead/2005/mar/23youth.htm. Accessed on January 14, 2006.

Drèze, J. 2003. Patterns of literacy and their social context. In *The Oxford India companion to sociology and social anthropology*, Vol. 2. V. Das (ed.). pp. 974–97.

Drèze, J., and J. Loh. 1995. Literacy in India and China. *Economic and Political Weekly* 30(45):2868–78.

Elizabeth, K. E. 2001. A novel growth assessment chart for adolescents. *Indian Paediatrics* 38:1061–64.

Girl Child in India (special issue). 1995. *The Journal of Social Change* 25(2–3):3–254.

International Labour Organisation (ILO). 1993. *World of work*. Geneva: ILO.

Kagitcibasi, C. 2002. Autonomy, embeddedness and adaptability in immigration contexts: A commentary. *Human Development* 20:1–6.

Kakar, S. 1981. *The inner world* (2nd ed.). Delhi: Oxford University Press.

Kapadia, S., and J. G. Miller. 2005. Parent-adolescent relationships in the context of interpersonal disagreements:

View from a collectivist culture. *Psychology and Developing Societies* 17(1):33–50.

Kaura, I. 2004. Stress and family environment: Adolescents' perception and experiences. Unpublished doctoral dissertation of the Department of Child Development, University of Delhi.

Kaura, I., and N. Chaudhary. 2003. Continuity and change: Narratives of conflict from the lives of Indian adolescents. Paper presented at the conference of the International Association for Cross-cultural Psychology, Budapest, Hungary, 2003, July.

Keshavan, S. P. 2005. National Cadet Corps. The official Web site of the NCC (n.d.). Accessed on September 12, 2005. http://www.bharat-rakshak.com/LAND-FORCES/NCC/.

Kitayama, S., and H. R. Markus. 1994. Culture and self: How cultures influence the way we view ourselves. In *People: Psychology from a cultural perspective*. D. Matsumoto (ed.). pp. 17–37. Pacific Grove, Calif.: Brooks/Cole.

Krishnan, L. 1998. Child rearing: The Indian perspective. In *Child Development: The Indian perspective*. A. K. Srivastava (ed.). pp. 25–55. New Delhi: National Council for Educational Research and Training (NCERT).

Kumar, K. 1986. Growing up male. *Seminar* 318:21–23.

Kurtz, S. N. 2003. *All the mothers are one: Hindu India and the cultural reshaping of psychoanalysis*. New York: Columbia University Press.

Larson, R. 2002. Globalisation, societal change and new technologies: What they mean for the future of adolescence. In *Adolescents' preparation for the future: Perils and promise*. R. Larson, B. Brown, and J. Mortimer (eds.). pp. 1–30. Ann Arbor, Mich: The Society for Research on Adolescence.

Larson, R., S. Verma, and J. Dworkin. 2003. Adolescence without family disengagement: The daily family lives of Indian middle class teenagers. In *Cross-cultural perspectives in human development*. T. S. Saraswathi (ed.). pp. 258–86. New Delhi: Sage.

Mandelbaum, D. G. 1970. *Society in India. Volume 1: Continuity and change*. Berkeley, Los Angeles, London: University of California Press.

Marriot, A. M. 1976. Hindu transactions: Diversity without dualism. In *Transaction and meaning: Directions in the anthropology of exchange and symbolic behaviour*. B. C. Kapforer (ed.). pp. 109–42. Philadelphia: Institute for the Study of Human Issues.

Mascolo, M. F., and S. Bhatia. 2002. Culture, self and social relations. *Psychology and Developing Studies* 14(1):55–91.

Mathur, I. 2006. First comes marriage, then comes love. http://www.geocities.com/Wellesley/3321/win4a.htm. Accessed on January 14, 2006.

Menon, U. 2003. Morality and context: A study of Hindu understandings. In *Handbook of developmental psychology*. J. Valsiner and K. J. Connolly (eds.). pp. 431–49. London: Sage.

Miller, J. G. 2002. Bringing culture to basic psychological theory: Beyond individualism and collectivism. *Psychological Bulletin* 128(1):97–109.

Mines, M. 1988. Conceptualising the person: Hierarchical society and individual autonomy in India. *American Anthropologist* 90:568–79.

Ministry of Human Resource Development (MHRD). 2000. *National youth policy*. New Delhi: Dept. of Youth and Social Affairs, MHRD, Govt. of India.

Misra, G., A. K. Srivastava, and S. Gupta. 1999. The cultural construction of childhood in India: Some observations. *Indian Psychological Abstracts and Reviews* 6 (2):191–218.

Nieuwenhuys, O. 2003. The paradox of child labour and anthropology. In *The Oxford India companion to sociology and social anthropology*, Vol. 2. V. Das (ed.). pp. 936–38. New Delhi: Oxford University Press.

Padmavati V., D. V. R. Poosha, B. R. Busi. 1984. A note on the age at menarche and its relationship to diet, economic class, sib ship size, and birth order in 300 Andhra girls. *Man in India* 2(64):175–80.

Pandey, J. 2001. *Psychology in India revisited* (Vols. 1 & 2). New Delhi: Sage.

Patil, M. V., V. Gaonkar, and P. A. Katarki. 1994. Sex-role perception of adolescents as influenced by self concept and achievement motivation. *Psychological Studies* 39 (1):37–39.

Planning Commission. 2001. Report of the working group on adolescents for the tenth Five Year Plan (2002–2007). Planning Commission, Government of India.

Raedler, J. 1999. India's dissatisfied youth stays away from polling booths. Accessed from CNN.com on September 12, 2005. http://edition.cnn.com/SPECIALS/1999/india. elections /stories/young.voters/.

Ramanujam, A. K. 1994/1991. *Folk tales from India*. New Delhi: Penguin.

Ramu, G. N. 1988. *Family structure and fertility*. New Delhi: Sage.

Roland, A. 1988. *In search of self in India and Japan: Towards a cross-cultural psychology*. Princeton, N.J.: Princeton University Press.

Saibaba, A., M. Mohan Ram, G. V. Ramana Rao, et al. 2002. Nutritional status of adolescent girls of urban slums and the impact of IEC on their nutritional knowledge and practices. *Indian Journal of Community Medicine* XXVII(4):151–57.

Saraswathi, T. S. 1999. Adult-child continuity in India: Is adolescence a myth or an emerging reality? In *Culture, socialization and human development*. T. S. Saraswathi (ed.). pp. 213–32. New Delhi: Sage.

Saraswathi, T. S., and Ganapathy, H. 2002. Indian parents' ethnotheories as reflections of the Hindu scheme of child and human development. In *Between culture and biology: Perspectives on ontogenetic development*. H. Keller, Y. P. Poortinga, and A. Schlomerich (eds.). pp. 79–88. Cambridge, U.K.: Cambridge University Press.

Saraswathi, T. S., and S. Pai. 1997. Socialisation in the Indian context. In *Asian perspectives on psychology*. H. S. R. Kao and D. Sinha (eds.). pp. 74–92. New Delhi: Sage.

Sartor, C. E., and J. Youniss. 2002. The relationship between positive paternal involvement and identity achievement during adolescence. *Adolescence* 37:221–34.

Schlegel, A. 2003. Modernisation and changes in adolescent social life. In *Cross-cultural perspectives in human development: Theory research and applications*. T. S. Saraswathi (ed.). pp. 236–57. New Delhi: Sage.

Schlegel, A., and H. Barry. 1991. *Adolescence: An anthropological inquiry*. New York: Free Press.

Selected Educational Statistics. 2000–2001. Retrieved 11 September, 2005. http://www.azimpremjifoundation. org/downloads/edustats_03.pdf.

Sen, A. 2005. *The argumentative Indian: Writings on Indian history, culture and identity*. London: Penguin.

Seymour, S. 1999. Cooperation and competition: Some issues and problems in cross-cultural analysis. In *Handbook of cross-cultural human development*. R. H. Munroe, R. L. Munroe, and B. B. Whiting (eds.). pp. 717–38. New York: Garland Press.

Sharma, D. 2003. Introduction. In *Childhood, family and socio-cultural change in India: Reinterpreting the inner world*. D. Sharma (ed.). pp. 1–12. New Delhi: Oxford.

Sharma, N. 1996. *Identity of the adolescent girl*. New Delhi: Discovery.

Sharma, N. 1999, 2003. *Understanding adolescence*. New Delhi: National Book Trust.

Sharma, N., and B. Sharma. 1999. Children in difficult circumstances: Familial correlates of advantage while at risk. In *Culture, socialisation and human development*. T. S. Saraswathi (ed.). pp. 298–448. New Delhi: Sage.

Sidhu, L. S., and R. Grewal. 1980. Age of menarche in various categories of Indian sportswomen. *British Journal of Sports Medicine* 14(4):199–203.

Singh, A. P. 1998. Sibling distance and feeling of isolation. *Perspectives in Psychological Research* 21 (1 and 2):69–73.

Singhal, S., and U. N. B. Rao. 2004. *Adolescent concerns through own eyes*. New Delhi: Kanishka Publishers.

Solomon, P. 2003. Youth of India's lack of interest in politics. November 2003. Accessed on September 12, 2005. http://www.prashantsolomon.com/views-youthandpolitics.htm.

Sriram, S., N. Chaudhary, and P. Ralhan. 2002. The family and self in dialogue. Paper presented at the Conference of The Dialogical Self, Ghent, Belgium, October 2002.

Srivastava, S. 2003. Schooling, culture and modernity. In *The Oxford India companion to sociology and social anthropology*. Vol. 2. V. Das (ed.). pp. 998–1031. New Delhi: Oxford University Press.

The Times of India. 2005. Pre-marital sex: Papa preaches for Sania. November 25, 2005, p. 6.

The World Bank. 2004. Snakes and ladders: Factors influencing successful primary school completion for children in poverty contexts. Discussion paper series, report no. 6, South Asia Human Development Sector, New Delhi: The World Bank.

Trawick, M. 2003. The person behind the family. In *The Oxford companion to sociology and social anthropology*. V. Das (ed.). pp. 1158–78. New Delhi: Oxford University Press.

Uberoi, P. 2003. The family in India: Beyond the nuclear versus joint debate. In *The Oxford India companion to sociology and social anthropology*. V. Das (ed.). pp. 1061–1103. New Delhi: Oxford University Press.

UNDP. 2005. The Human Development Report, 2005. New York: UNDP.

UNFPA. 2000. *Adolescents in India: A profile*. New Delhi: UNFPA.

Uploaonkar, A. T. 1995. The emerging rural youth: A study of their changing values towards marriage. *Indian Journal of Social Work* 56(4):415–23.

Verma, S., and R. Larson. 1999. Are adolescents more emotional? A study of the daily emotions of middle class Indian adolescents. *Psychology and Developing Societies* 11(2):179–94.

Verma, S., and D. Sharma. 2003. Cultural continuity amid social change: Adolescents' use of free time in India. In *Examining adolescent leisure time across cultures*.

S. Verma and R. Larson (eds.). pp. 37–41. San Francisco: Jossey-Boss.

Verma, S., and T. S. Saraswathi. 2002. Adolescence in India: Street children or Silicon Valley millionaires. In *The world's youth: Adolescence in eight regions of the globe*. B. B. Brown, R. W. Larson, and T. S. Saraswathi (eds.). pp. 105–40. U.K.: Cambridge University Press.

Verma, S., D. Sharma, and R. Larson. 2002. School stress in India: Effects on time and daily emotions. *International Journal of Behavioural Development* 26(6):506–8.

Visaria, L. 1999. Deficit of women in India: Magnitude, trends, regional variations and determinants. In *From independence towards freedom: Indian women since 1947*. B. Ray and A. Basu (eds.). pp. 8 –99. New Delhi: Oxford University Press.

Visaria, P., and L. Visaria. 2003. India's populations: Its growth and key characteristics. In *The Oxford India companion to sociology and social anthropology*, Vol. 1. V. Das (ed.). pp. 184–218. New Delhi: Oxford University Press.

World Health Organization (WHO). 2001. *Child and adolescent health and development*. Report on the inter-country meeting. Bali, Indonesia, 9–14 March, 2001. New Delhi: WHO.

INDONESIA

Background Information

The Republic of Indonesia (capital: Jakarta) came into existence on August 17, 1945, when Indonesia declared its independence two days after Japan, which had occupied Indonesia for almost three and a half years, surrendered to the Allies. Indonesia is an archipelago with 17,000 islands, and some of the largest islands are Sumatra, Java, Kalimantan, Sulawesi, Papua, Bali, and Maluku. The most populated island is Java.

There are about 300 distinct indigenous ethnic groups, with more than 500 local languages and dialects spoken. A national language, Bahasa Indonesia, functions as a unifying language. With so many ethnic groups and languages and dialects, Indonesia has adopted the credo "Bhineka Tunggal Ika" or "Unity in Diversity," and the national philosophy is "Pancasila" or the five principles, (1) belief in God, (2) humanity, (3) unity of Indonesia, (4) deliberation and cooperation, and (5) social justice.

With a population of more than 200 million, the majority (87% to 88%) of them Muslim, Indonesia is the largest Muslim country in the world. The rest of the population is Christian (Protestant and Catholic), Buddhist, Hindu, and other.

About 20% of the population is between 15 and 24 years of age; in real numbers, that comes to more than 40 million. If the 12- to 14-year-olds are included, the percentage reaches 23.9% (United Nations 2001, in Brown, Larson, and Saraswathi 2002).

At present the political system is a democracy, with direct election for the president (in 2004), members of parliament, and governors of the provinces in 2005. In terms of the economy, Indonesia has an open-market policy.

Period of Adolescence

Taking the definition of adolescence from WHO, the Indonesian Ministry of Health considers unmarried people between the ages of 10 and 19 as adolescents (2002–2003 Indonesia Young Adult Reproductive Health Survey or IYARHS). Although the concept of adolescence is a popular one in Indonesia, as yet different laws implemented here rarely mention the adolescent. For example, the 1979 Laws on the Child's Welfare stated that "a child is any person who is under 21 and not married." The 1974 Laws on Marriage stipulated that "a child under 21 years old has to get permission from his/her parents to get married; males can get married at 19 years, and females at 16; a child is under the authority of the parents until 18 years old, or has been married." Indonesian laws have included a part of the period usually known as adolescence under the umbrella of childhood.

There are rites of passage for different life events in different ethnic groups. These include birth rituals among the Batak Toba ethnic group and the fisherman community in Madura; rituals for mothers at the seventh month of pregnancy; the Javanese ritual that takes place the first time a baby steps onto the ground; and numerous wedding and death rituals. However, according to Koentjaraningrat (1985) in Indonesia, there is no rite of passage marking adolescence. In the Biak-Numfor (in Papua) culture, young males of 15 to 16 years of age carried out the rites called k'bor. The meaning of k'bor is "to stab or cut the tip of something"—in this case, the tip of the male genital (Mansoben 1994). K'bor is a ritual to affirm the change in someone's status from an ordinary member into a formal member in his society. This tradition became extinct when the Christian religion came to Biak-Numfor at the beginning of the twentieth century.

A kind of rite of passage that is known in Indonesia is sunatan. Sunatan, or circumcision for young boys, is regarded as a puberty rite, in which the boys' entrance into adulthood is being proclaimed. The sunatan ritual is an important religious (Islam) practice. The Islamic law obligates sunatan for boys and girls before they reach adulthood, which is the time when one is required to do sholat (praying five times a day). Parents usually teach their children to do sholat and fasting at Ramadhan (perhaps for a few hours or half a day) at a younger age; however, when they reach akil baliq or puberty, then sholat and fasting at Ramadhan become obligations.

In the more traditional societies, circumcision is done when boys reach puberty (Putranti, Faturochman, Darwin, and Purwatiningsih 2003). The more modern and educated families, however, opt to circumcise their sons when they are younger or even when they are still babies, and the circumcision is conducted by medical doctors. *Sunatan* for girls in Indonesia is usually carried out when the baby is just born, performed by the midwife who helps with the delivery or the pediatrician in the hospital.

Adolescents become young adults when they finish school or university and enter the world of work. Young adults usually still live at home with their parents, but they enjoy more freedom due to their financial independence. In the eyes of the law, after the age of 21 one is no longer a child; thus, one acquires the rights that are bestowed to adults, such as the right to marry. However, parents will probably not consider the young adult as having reached full adulthood until he or she marries and begins a family. Arnett (2004) calls this transitional period from adolescence into full adulthood "emerging adulthood," and this period is more common among the urban middle-class young people who further their study beyond the university's undergraduate level, to meet the demands of the job market.

Beliefs

Islam came to Indonesia centuries ago through Muslim traders. It spread throughout the archipelago and became the dominant religion. Hindu and Buddhist kingdoms used to exist in Java, but with the arrival of Islam the Hindu kingdom was forced to the island of Bali. The strong Hindu influence in Bali is expressed in the religious rituals and cultural manifestations that are an integral part of people's lives. Ramayana and Mahabharata are two famous Hindu epics still popular in Java. For more than 300 years the European influence (especially Dutch) was also present in Indonesia. A kind of Islamic syncretism developed in some parts of the island of Java.

As the most populated island and the center for government, trade, and education, Javanese culture has a great influence on the nation overall. For the Javanese, cooperation and social attitudes are highly valued characteristics. Togetherness is a desirable way of life, as expressed by the Javanese saying *"mangan ora mangan, asal kumpul,"* which translates as "eating or not eating, as long as we are together." Deliberation and cooperation have been adopted by the country as the way to solve problems or conflicts, as shown by the idiom *"musyawarah dan mupakat"* (literal meaning: deliberation and cooperation to reach an agreement).

Hofstede (1980 in Berry, Poortinga, Segall, and Dasen 1992) classified most developing countries as displaying "dependent collectivism." Indonesia is a developing country, and as was said previously, cooperation is a way of life. Thus, it is safe to conclude that Indonesia tends to be more collectivist than individualist. Like any other cultural value, collectivism is socially transmitted from the older generation to the younger ones. The collectivist tradition is still prominent in the rural areas, and in small towns where kinship and neighborhood relationships are still close. However, life in the large cities has changed the character of human relationships. The fast pace and hectic lifestyle in cities leave people with little time for social interaction. Collectivism, in the sense of encouraging cooperation, has faded, and exists in major urban centers as little more than a symbol of the ideal value of togetherness.

Religious teaching is a part of the school and university curricula. Although no hard data are available to support this statement, observation of people's religious activities seems to demonstrate high participation. A study conducted by *Gatra* magazine in cooperation with the Political Science Laboratory and the Faculty of Social and Political Science of the University of Indonesia found that 95% of the 800 respondents, aged 15 and 22, believed that "religion is the guide to develop good moral and character."

Occasionally religious denominations arise that can be considered cults. It is difficult to observe the presence or influence of cults, as they usually operate covertly. The government, especially the Ministry of Religious Affairs and the Office of the Attorney General (Sarwono 2001), tries to monitor and control cults and their influence by issuing edicts for those systems or organizations considered to be contrary to the legal religions. Previously, cults were usually treated as illegal organizations.

Gender

The 1945 Constitution of Indonesia states that males and females have equal rights and obligations to support the country's development (Setiaji, in http://www.pikiran-rakyat.com/cetak/0902/27/0802.htm). Slightly over 50% of the Indonesian population is female, and their participation in the labor force is between 38% and 41% of the total labor force in Indonesia (http://www.bina-desa.or.id/jender1.htm). The number of female

workers in North Sumatra has increased since the year 2000, exceeding the male workers, but their welfare is still an overlooked issue. For example, the law states that female workers are not obliged to work on the first and second days of their menstrual period, yet this right is not always fulfilled by the employers. Available data seem to show that a large gap still exists between the male and female population. For similar work, female workers often are paid less than their male counterparts.

Discrimination based on gender can often be seen early in a child's life. In her study of Balinese school children, Parker (1997) discovered that school-age girls are expected to help with housework in their out-of-school time, thus they have to stay at home. Meanwhile, the boys are free to spend their time away from home, playing or socializing with friends. This gender role expectation is not only typical for Bali, but is also found in other subcultures in Indonesia.

Male and female children are socialized to gender role expectations in the two villages studied by Tjitarsa (1995, in Saifuddin and Hidayana 1999). Boys aged 11 to 12 years begin to assist their fathers in catching fish or working in the fisherman's boats, while girls help their mothers at home or work as babysitters or clothes-washers in other homes.

In a discussion on gender bias in primary education in December 2003, some participants (Sinaga, Missiyah, and Hermawaty) argued that the low quality of education for females is due to various factors such as access, participation, mastery, and value. Access and participation in education for females are lower than for males, as shown by the higher rate of female's illiteracy, which is 20% compared to 9% for males. Compared to males, years of school attendance for females are also shorter. Parents also usually put more value on education for boys than for girls, as the traditional role for males is as the breadwinner and as homemakers for females.

Gender stereotyping is observed in the choice of education by adolescent males and females: 99% of the students in the Teachers Education School (senior high school level) are female, while the students at the Senior Technological School (also senior high school level) are 99.5% male. More females work as kindergarten and primary school teachers, and more junior and senior high school teachers are males. One researcher (Salim 1998) found that only 19.5% of her 13- to 16-year-old female subjects wished to attend the Senior Technological School.

Although no data can be found at present, the stereotype of the female role as the nurturer is also observed in the field of psychology. More female than male students enter the faculty of psychology in Indonesia, as for example shown by the ratio of female and male students (3 to 1) at the Faculty of Psychology, University of Indonesia.

Senior high school students, aged between 16 and 18 years, in five cities expressed their different views and opinions about gender-related issues in the discussion titled "Menyosialisasikan isu gender lewat film" or "Socializing gender issues through films," held in the British Film Festival, organized by the British Embassy (http://www.media-indonesia.com/berita.asp?id=60405). The article did not mention what exactly the content of the film was, or the gender of the participants (assumed to be mixed), but it reported that the values expressed by the participants from different cities were also different. For example, the participants from Yogyakarta stated that females have to obey their husbands, and accept whatever happens to or is given to them (*nerimo*, in the Javanese language). These participants also considered society's reactions and restrictions as very important. The participants' view can be categorized as traditional.

With globalization, the physical ideals of young people are also influenced by the physical ideals of celebrities they see in the media, especially on TV (cable, MTV, etc.). Girls want to have bodies like famous singers or actresses (i.e., tall, thin, and slender). The phrase to describe the physical ideals for young girls is "*kutilang*," an abbreviation from *ku*rus (thin), *ti*nggi (tall), and *lang*sing (slender). The same phenomenon is also observed with male youth, but it is not as extreme as among girls. Data about the number of young people suffering from eating disorders are not available.

A small study conducted by Handayani (2005) with obese adolescent subjects (male and female) shows that although the subjects are overweight, they seem to have a positive body image because they think their obesity is caused by heredity.

The Self

The many subcultures existing in Indonesia have had an impact on the cultural and personal identity of the adolescents living in those subcultures. The family, or more specifically parents, are still an important socialization agent for the Indonesian children. In subcultures where tradition plays a major role, parents socialize their children according to the customs and beliefs practiced in their communities.

Javanese children reared in a small traditional town in Central Java will develop a personal and

ethnic identity that is distinctly Javanese, and stronger than that of Javanese children brought up in the metropolitan Jakarta. In her study of street children in Yogyakarta, Beazley (2003) emphasized the role of socialization in a subculture of street children in developing their collective identity. Beazley found that within the marginal urban niches where they live and earn money, the street boys construct their individual identity in interaction with the subculture's collective identity. The street boys created a doctrine for themselves that "it is great in the street," and "street life is better than conventional life." Over a long period, the street boys establish a new identity.

Except for communities living in remote areas, a large proportion of young people in Indonesia have been exposed to the changing way of life, from the traditional to the more modern. Advanced technological information has opened up the world for adolescents. Globalization seems to be unavoidable, and affects tastes in clothing, music, food, and so forth. For young people living in the large cities, globalization and trends have shaped their social and collective identity. They dress in the same way as any other adolescents: t-shirts, jeans, and sneakers. Mobile phones seem to be the order of the day for adolescents.

Family Relationships

In a country populated by diverse ethnic groups, the parenting practices in Indonesia also reflect diversity. People continue to rely on tradition, while at the same time they try to adapt to modern developments. The extended family, which traditionally was the custom for family living, is now becoming rare. For the younger generation, especially those living in the cities, the nuclear family has become more predominant (Santa Maria, in Brown, Larson, and Saraswathi 2002). However, many families have a housemaid, who after a long period of working, becomes more like a family member. Sometimes the housemaid has an especially close relationship with the child/adolescent in the family.

For the Javanese, the heredity of both parents is important. The family is usually headed by a father who is usually authoritarian, and who in many cases acts as an emotionally distant figure who has to be respected (Mulder 1999). However, family life is centered on mothers. Home is the mother's territory, while affairs in the outside world are the father's domain.

One study conducted by Joewono (2002) with mothers who work professionally shows that more than half of the mothers display an authoritarian parenting style toward their children aged 8 to 10 years. On the other hand, Purwadi (2003) found that his subjects (middle adolescents from urban and rural areas) perceived their parents' parenting style as "enabling," more popularly known as democratic.

A cross-cultural study by Hoffman (1987, in Hadis 1993) found that the most desired value by urban and rural Javanese and Sundanese parents was obedience from their children. In her study, Hadis (1993) also discovered that traditional parents wanted children who were obedient, honest, and diligent. More modern parents, however, generally preferred children who were independent, unspoiled, responsible, and had a sense of freedom. Parents were categorized as traditional or modern by their belief system. The traditional parents were usually females, living in rural and urban slum areas, with low educational and socioeconomic levels. This group perceived mothers as the person solely responsible for the upbringing of children. The modern parents consisted of males living in urban areas who had high education and worked as professionals. They believed that fathers had to play a role and help mothers in raising children. Although this different perception on how to raise children seems to reflect gender bias, it is possible that different educational level is the reason behind this perception.

Past generations of immigrants to Indonesia have been integrated into the main culture. Problems between adolescents and their parents usually center on the adolescents' need to have more attention from parents. A lack of communication because of limited time makes it difficult for adolescents to have discussions with their parents. Adolescents perceive their fathers as "headstrong," and mothers as more often angry. Parents are often seen as discriminatory—that is, they favor certain children and not the others (in Remaja dan Permasalahannya 1998).

In 2002, 52,000 couples sought consultation from the Badan Penasehat Pembina Pelestarian Perkawinan (Marriage Counseling Bureau, a government-sponsored organization) in the five municipalities in Jakarta. Only 40% to 50% could save their marriages; the rest were divorced. The rate of divorce seems to be increasing (in www.glouanet.org/berita). Data on rates of remarriage cannot be obtained.

Friends and Peers/Youth Culture

A strong emotional attachment between friends is revealed in a study by Arswendo and colleagues (1985), who found that more than 80% of their subjects (210 senior high school students) have been involved in fights because they wanted to show their solidarity with and support of their friends.

Young people who are still at school or university spend about 6 to 8 hours of their time each day in classes. For some, after-school activities will take up more of their time. Time is usually spent with family in the late afternoon or evening, if there are no other activities (like homework) the young people have to do.

With Saturdays free for some schools, the adolescents can spend their day in the shopping malls and other entertainment centers. A survey conducted by *Gatra* magazine concluded that Indonesia adolescents spend most of their time on *hura-hura* (i.e., leisure and pleasure) instead of doing more positive activities. Cliques are established according to mutual interests. The Indonesian youth like music. Musical shows, whether they showcase underground music, heavy metal music, *dangdut* (a typical music popular in Indonesia), or another genre, are usually packed with young people.

According to Pickles (2000), "close-knit communities of young people sharing an interest in underground music have emerged throughout Indonesia, and punk is the most theatrical youth culture in Indonesia." The way these youth dress and style their hair proclaims their unique identity. Pickles (2000) also stated that "punk and other underground music may have originated in the West, but Indonesia's youth have indigenized these cultures and give them new meanings." Western influence is very strong in Indonesia. Traditional music has lost much of its appeal for adolescents. With the development of information technology (TV, cable TV, CDs, etc.), Indonesia became like a borderless country: whatever is in fashion abroad will soon be in the market in Indonesia.

In his study, Tjitarsa (in Saifuddin and Hidayana 1999) found that adolescents in Medan–North Sumatra tend to group together based on their socioeconomic status, but especially on ethnic background. However, the adolescents in the town of Banjarmasin in South Kalimantan are homogeneous in terms of culture. Thus, restrictions on friendships due to ethnicity seem to exist in Medan, but not in Banjarmasin.

Adolescents in Indonesia are generally apolitical. Youth organizations usually focus on sports, music, or religious or social activities.

Love and Sexuality

Attitudes toward sex and adolescents' sexual behaviors have undergone remarkable changes in recent years. Formerly, sex was regarded as a taboo topic and censorship was applied to the media. In the large cities, adolescents enjoy more freedom in their personal conduct, and dating is more common than in rural areas.

According to Indonesian marriage law, girls can get married at 16 and boys at 19 years of age. Teenage girls' marriage usually occurs in areas where there is extensive poverty, or due to out-of-wedlock pregnancy. It seems that young people are becoming more permissive and relaxed in their sexual behavior, and premarital sexual intercourse is reported to occur more frequently (Kumala 2003). If out-of-wedlock pregnancy occurs, the couple are either forced to get married or the girl seeks an illegal abortion, as abortion is prohibited by law. Cohabitation is regarded as an unacceptable and sinful behavior by society in general, and as the adolescents usually still live at home with their parents, it is not commonly practiced.

Not all schools provide sex education. Some schools, usually private ones, provide sex education in the sixth grade of primary or junior high school. In the 2002–2003 IYARHS, about 50% of young people aged 15 to 24 mentioned that information about reproductive health was given at junior high school. Condoms are sold openly in drugstores, but young people's awareness of birth control is still limited. Only about half of the respondents in the 2002–2003 IYARHS had clear knowledge about the risk of pregnancy. Teenagers' unwanted pregnancies are usually caused by unplanned sexual intercourse and limited knowledge of human reproductive mechanisms. For social and religious reasons, providing contraceptive service to unmarried adolescents is difficult in most Southeast Asian countries, including Indonesia (Brown, Larson, and Saraswathi 2002).

In the 2002–2003 IYARHS, about 87% of the respondents had heard about HIV/AIDS. Syphilis is another sexually transmitted disease with which the respondents were familiar. Education level attained and where they lived seemed to influence the respondents' knowledge of sexually transmitted disease. It is difficult to obtain data about sexually

transmitted diseases among the adolescents, but with more permissive attitudes toward sexual relationships, it is assumed that the figure will increase.

Only recently did homosexuality become an open topic for discussion; however no figures can be found as to the number of teenagers who are homosexuals. Homosexual communities do exist in larger cities in Indonesia, albeit covertly, but open homosexuality is still unacceptable.

There are many different ethnic groups in Indonesia. They differ in their openness and acceptance of open sexuality and sexual expression. However, with the geography of Indonesia at the intersection of Asia and Australia, and its policy of an open market, all kinds of cultural influences penetrate the daily lives of adolescents. Pornographic films, comics, magazines, and so on are sold on the street, cheaply. Therefore, even in areas that are known for their strict religious beliefs, parents are not always able to control their adolescents' sexuality.

Health Risk Behavior

In August 2003, articles in the local daily newspapers shocked readers, and later on, the community in general. A boy, a sixth-grader in a primary school in a small town in Java, tried to kill himself because he could not pay for the extracurricular activity in his school. The amount he had to pay was Rp. 2,500, at that time the equivalent of around 30 U.S. cents. He was already in a coma when his parents rushed him to the hospital. Although this boy survived the ordeal, the effect of the traumatic event will be with him for life as he suffered brain damage and mental retardation.

After this appalling incident, more articles about suicide (or attempted suicide) carried out by young people appeared in daily newspapers. The reasons were almost always similar: young people felt ashamed because their parents did not have the money to pay the school fees, final exam fees, or graduation ceremony fees. The family's poverty was usually cited as the major reason for the young person's (attempted) suicide.

Drug addiction has become a social disease. Indonesia has become not only a transit country for narcotics, but also a producer country. A National Narcotics Bureau has been established to handle the problems and crimes created by narcotics, but it seems that narcotic uses have even spread to wider community groups. Many raids have been conducted by the police, some with the expected results, although some have not yielded the hoped-for results.

The majority of the population is Moslem, and in general Islam forbids alcohol. However, in some areas of Indonesia local traditions make it possible to produce traditional alcoholic drinks. Moreover, modern alcoholic brews such as wine, whiskey, and vodka are sold legally in supermarkets or other establishments, or illegally in the little shops or *warung* that dot the cities.

With the abundance of cafés, discotheques, pubs, and other entertainment venues, young affluent people are introduced to alcohol widely and repeatedly. Meanwhile, the less privileged consume cheap drinks that contain a dangerously high content of alcohol (illegally produced in home industries, or a mixture of different alcoholic drinks). Sometimes people die as a result of consuming these drinks.

In large cities such as Jakarta, motorcycle and car racing, usually at night, seems to be quite common. Motorcycle racing—popularly known in the lingua franca of young people as *treak-trekan*—usually involves several motorcycles. This kind of racing is illegal. Sometimes collisions between the racers and ordinary motorcyclists occur, with fatal consequences. During the fasting month of Ramadan, after the final meal and before dawn, young people come together on the streets, which are still very quiet, and race their motorcycles. Spectators often gather to boost the racers' spirit and enthusiasm.

Many factors have been mentioned as the source of adolescents' problems. The family's economic status is assumed to play an important role in driving young people from home to the street or to suicide. The economic crisis that started in the mid-1990s has reduced the income and spending power of most families. Increased tuition fees (even at the state schools) and expensive schoolbooks have forced many young people to drop out of school. With no other substitute or alternative activities, it is not difficult for them to get involved in drug use and dealing.

Population density is another factor: there is no place to play at home due to the small and crowded housing environment. Open space such as gardens, lakes, or playing grounds for sports activities has disappeared from the cities, replaced with malls and other entertainment centers. The pressure and stressful living conditions in large cities, with inadequate public transportation, has added to the hardship for some disadvantaged youth.

Education

School in Indonesia can usually be categorized as state- or government-funded schools, and private schools. Secondary schools are divided into junior

and senior high school. Besides the general secondary school, there is also secondary vocational school, offering more specialized subjects such as agriculture and technology.

Children usually enter primary school between the age of 5 and 7, and finish senior high school at around 18. For economic reasons, or due to the unavailability of kindergarten, not all children attend preschool. Compulsory education was implemented by the government decades ago, but in reality a number of children have to drop out of primary or junior high school due to economic hardship. The tsunami that hit the Aceh region in 2004 wreaked havoc upon people's lives. As a result of the tsunami's devastation, children have to be educated in makeshift schools, and a large number of high school students failed final exams due to their disrupted daily lives.

The adult literacy rate in 2000 was 87.9%. The net primary school enrollment or attendance for 1996–2003 is 87% (from http://www.Unicef.org/infobycountry/indonesia_statistics.html). Gross enrollment for the secondary and tertiary level was 56% and 11% in 1997 (Santa Maria 2002).

Data from the BPS Statistics Indonesia show a wide gap in the attainment of educational level, literacy, and political participation in Parliament and the People's Assembly for males and females. When parents experience economic hardship, it is often the girls who are forced to leave school.

Benchmarking for secondary schools has not been officially conducted; the international test of achievement is therefore not usually taken by school children or adolescents in Indonesia.

A special education program for gifted children was started in 1983 as a pilot project of the Department of Education and Culture in some primary, junior high, and senior high schools. An enrichment program was provided for children and adolescents identified by psychologists and teachers as gifted. This pilot project lasted for three years; the project was then cancelled due to a lack of funding. A few years later, the gifted education program surfaced again, and at present, most schools that offer gifted education usually adopt the acceleration program. In general, education for gifted adolescents is conducted in schools where non-gifted adolescents also study (usually in a different class).

Educational programs for disabled adolescents are also available, in the forms of inclusive education or special schools for various disabilities. Special schools for mentally retarded adolescents existed long before gifted education started.

Work

As in other Asian countries, the number of adolescents and young adults is growing rapidly. It is estimated that in 2000, about 21% of Indonesia's total population was young people between 15 to 24 years of age. The increasing number of young people increases the problem of work and employment availability.

The economic crisis that hit Indonesia in 1997 severely affected the country's economy and the livelihood of the Indonesian people. After a few years of hardship, the economy seemed to have improved. However, rising oil prices and mismanagement of resources led to an economic downturn in the new millennium. Open unemployment (i.e., openly jobless people, or people who in the whole week do not work at all) in 2004 reached 9.5 million, while disguised unemployment (i.e., people who are technically unemployed but survived on odd jobs done for family members, friends, or associates) (Ikhsan, in Indonesia outlook 2005–Economic) had risen to 43 million. Thousands of workers in various sectors of industry were laid off. This has grave consequences on family life and welfare, and children's education. According to the Baseline Survey of Young Adult Reproductive Welfare in Indonesia (Demographic Institute 1999), young people with a low educational level living in urban areas were especially hard hit by the economic crisis. This finding has been supported by data from the capital, Jakarta.

About three out of ten members of the workforce aged between 15 and 24 are jobless. This youth group constitutes two-thirds of the unemployed (Ikhsan in Indonesia outlook 2005–Economic). The rate of unemployment for university-educated young people is only 4.86%.

Poverty has pushed many adolescents to work; more than 2.56 millions adolescents aged 10 to 17 years work in various sectors. More young people in the rural areas have to work than their counterparts in the urban areas, and more males than females work. As the majority of them live in the rural areas, they primarily work on farms.

In its effort to protect young people from work that is harmful and hazardous, the government has stated in the Labor Laws the five sectors of work that are forbidden for them. The government has also established a National Action Committee for the Prevention and Monitoring of Child Labor. However, some young people are still found working in hazardous places.

In large cities, many young people work on the street, selling magazines, newspapers, candy,

drinks, and cigarettes. Some of them will ply the trains and buses, playing guitar and singing for money. Young females from the rural areas come to the cities to work as housemaids. According to data from the 2001 Population Survey—Statistics Indonesia (in *Kompas* daily, 24 April 2005), 26.7% of 570,059 house helpers registered in Indonesia are adolescent females. They usually live with the family they work for, with lodgings and food provided.

Apprenticeships are the traditional way of educating young people. However, this old tradition is probably more common in rural areas in the agricultural sector. More formal training programs are offered by various institutions or vocational schools.

Media

Television arrived in Indonesia in the early 1960s. Urban respondents in the 2002–2003 IYARHS watch more TV (92.4%) than the rural subjects (79.1%). The male and female urban and rural subjects in the IYARH Survey also enjoy listening to the radio.

The Internet can be accessed easily and cheaply in "Internet shops." In one survey, 80% of the 200 senior high school students had been familiar with the Internet since they were in junior high school (Using Internet as a source for students' learning 2003). The city-bred adolescents like to play computer games.

To a large extent, media in Indonesia are imported, with a strong Western flavor. Complaints have been directed to media, especially magazines and TV, for their vulgar and graphic presentation of violent acts and sexual exploitation.

Advertisements in newspapers, magazines, and TV have targeted children and adolescents as potential consumers (konsumerisme & gaya hidup remaja, in http://www.freewebs.com/kolektifbunga/konsumerisme.htm). The advertisers use teenaged models to make the advertised products appear closer to the "created needs" of the adolescents. A finding from a study conducted by Dewi and Suyasa (2003) is that positive attitudes toward a product's advertisement on television is significantly correlated with adolescents' consumptive behavior.

Politics and Military

Indonesian adolescents tend to be cynical toward politics, political parties, and the democratic process (National Democratic Institute for International Affairs 2002).

Adolescents' participation in political activity is usually limited to voting in general elections.

In 2004 Indonesia held direct elections for the presidency and also for the members of Parliament and regional representatives. The election committee had encouraged a more "rational and educated" campaign, but sadly this kind of campaign was not too popular. The open forum type of campaign, with music and singers, attracted more people, including adolescents.

Military activities seem to be considered as adults' business. Compulsory service for young people does not exist in Indonesia, and armed combat is also an unfamiliar phenomenon. Paramilitary organizations are not known; however, there are some youth organizations that like to simulate the military in the way they dress. What proportion of the youth organizations' members are young people under 18 is unknown.

At the level of the smaller community, young people organize themselves in a group called Karang Taruna Youth Centers. One of the activities of Karang Taruna is to "mobilize media to encourage involvement of youth in development" (in Brown, Larson, and Saraswathi 2002, p. 202). Occasional voluntary or community work by adolescents does exist in Indonesia.

Unique Issues

One of the TV channels in Jakarta broadcast that when people in Indonesia were celebrating the sixtieth anniversary of the country's independence, some groups of high school students fought on the streets of a town in Java. Street fighting on the streets is usually known as *tawuran*.

Tawuran between junior and more often senior high school students, mostly males, seems to be a common phenomenon of urban life in Indonesia. In Jakarta, for example, the Metropolitan Police Department noted that from year to year the amount of street fighting has increased steadily, and the number of people who were killed has also increased. *Tawuran* usually occurs between students from different schools that have a long history of hostility.

Casual observation of *tawuran* seems to show that it is seasonal (i.e., occurring more often at certain time than at another time). An Indonesian sociologist, Wirutomo (in Tambunan 2001) has even said that *tawuran* is now functioning as a means of relief from the boredom of the daily

routine. *Tawuran* seems to occur more often after mid-semester examinations, or after the results of exams have been announced. It seems that *tawuran* offers adolescents a means to reduce post-exam stress.

It has been said that high school students who fight on the streets come from vocational schools and from low economic background. However, it is not easy to identify one single factor as the main cause for street fighting. It is true that a large proportion of the students involved in street fighting are from vocational schools (considered to be inferior to the general high schools). Social, economic, and psychological factors such as the density of the residential areas, lack of open space for sports and recreational activities, bad public transportation system, and low motivation for academic achievement are intertwined, making it difficult to recognize one single factor as the motivation to fight.

Another interesting phenomenon to be observed is the appearance of Chinese youth in the political arena and entertainment world. Formerly, due to discrimination and other limiting factors, Chinese people focused their activities in trade and business. However, with the fall of the New Order, the political and social climate became more open for anyone who wants to be involved in politics, the economy, the human rights movement, entertainment, and so forth. Young Chinese have stepped forward and become involved in a world that previously seemed to be taboo for them: politics and entertainment. With the mushrooming of political parties, people are free to choose the party that suits their ideology, and at present some Chinese sit in the House of Representatives.

The world of entertainment is becoming the new main focus for young people; it promises glamour, fame, and wealth. Contests similar to "American Idol" or "Academia Fantasy" are very popular, and thousands of adolescents try their luck at these competitions. They know that if they succeed, then instant fame, recognition, and wealth will be theirs.

HERA LESTARI MIKARSA

References and Further Reading

Arnett, J. J. 2004. *Emerging adulthood: The winding road from late teens through the twenties*. Oxford: Oxford University Press.

Arswendo Atmowiloto, et al. 1985. Hasil angket: Jangan Kaget. In *Hai*, 26 November–2 December 1985.

Beazley, H. 2003. The construction and protection of individual and collective identities by street children and youth in Indonesia. *Children, Youth and Environments* 13(1).

Berry, J. W., Y. H. Poortinga, M. H. Segall, and P. R. Dasen. 1992. *Cross-cultural psychology*. Cambridge: Cambridge University Press.

Brown, B. B., R. W. Larson, and T. S. Saraswathi. 2002. *The world's youth: Adolescence in eight regions of the globe*. Cambridge: Cambridge University Press.

Dewi, F. I. R., and P. T. Y. S. Suyasa. Sikap terhadap tayangan iklan shampoo di televise dan perilaku konsumtif pada remaja. Studi pada 177 siswa SMU Tirta Marta BPK Penabur, Jakarta. Retrieved from http://www.psikologi-untar.com/psikologi/skripsi/tampil.php?id+211.

Hadis, F. A. 1993. Gagasan orang tua dan perkembangan anak. Unpublished doctoral dissertation. Faculty of Psychology, University of Indonesia.

Handayani, P. 2005. Gambaran citra tubuh dan penerimaan diri pada remaja akhir yang mengalami obesitas karena factor keturunan. Unpublished undergraduate skripsi. Faculty of Psychology, University of Indonesia.

http://www.binadesa.or.id/jender1.httm.

http://www.freewebs.com/kolektifbunga/konsumerisme.htm.

http://www.media-indonesia.com/berita.asp?id=60405.

http://www.unicef.org/infobycontry/indonesia_statistics.html.

Ikhsan, M. 2006. A flexible market will solve manpower issues. Indonesia outlook 2005—Economic. Jan 06, 2006. The Jakarta Post.com.

Joewono, E. B. 2002. Parenting pada ibu yang bekerja sebagai professional dengan anak usia 8 – 10 tahun. Unpublished master thesis, Faculty of Psychology, University of Indonesia.

Koentjaraningrat. 1985. *Ritus peralihan di Indonesia*. Jakarta: PT Dian Rakyat. *Kompas* (daily newspaper). 24 April 2005.

Kumala, M. L. 2003. Proses pengambilan keputusan remaja akhir untuk melakukan hubungan sexual pranikah. Unpublished magister thesis. Faculty of Psychology, University of Indonesia.

Mansoben. 1994. Ritus K'bor dalam masyarakat Biak-Numfor di Teluk Cenderawasih. In *Irian jaya: Membangun masyarakat majemuk*. D. K. K. Koentjaraningrat. Jakarta: Penerbit Jambatan.

Mengapa bunuh diri sering terjadi? Kompas daily newspaper. In http://www.Kompas.com/kesehatan/news/0406/16/114850.htm.

Mulder, N. (1999). Agama, hidup sehari-hari dan perubahan budaya. Jakarta: PT Gramedia Pustaka Utama (original title: Inside Southeast Asia Thai, Javanese and Filipino, interpretations of everyday life).

National Democratic Institute for International Affairs. 2002. Report on Penyelenggaraan Parlemen Remaja Indonesia (Indonesia Young People's Parliament). A Pilot Project by Indonesia Child Welfare Foundation, and Directorate of Primary and Secondary Education, Ministry of National Education-Indonesia.

Parker, L. 1997. Engendering school children in Bali. *Journal of the Royal Anthropological Institute* 3(3):497.

Pickles, J. 2000. Punks for peace. In *Inside Indonesia*, Oct–Dec 2000. Retrieved from http://www.insideindonesia.org/edit64/punk1.htm.

Potret Kawula Muda (Main Report). In *Gatra* 2/IV, 29 November 1997.

Purwadi. 2003. Hubungan gaya pengasuhan orang tua dengan eksplorasi dan komitmen remaja tengah dalam domain pekerjaan. In the Proceedings of the 3rd National Seminar of the Indonesian Association of Developmental Psychology. Yogyakarta.

Putranti, B. D., D. Faturochman, Muhadjir, and S. Purwatiningsih. 2003. *Male and female genital cutting, among Javanese and Madurese. Yogyakarta.* Indonesia: Center for Population and Policy Studies, Gadjah Mada University.

Remaja dan Permasalahannya. 1998. An explorative study on adolescents' psychosocial development and perception towards the eight functions of family. The Office of State Minister for Demography.

Saifuddin, A. F., and I. M. Hidayana. 1999. *Seksualitas Remaja.* (1st ed.) Jakarta: Pustaka Sinar Harapan.

Salim, W. D. 1998. Aspirasi remaja putri untuk melanjutkan pendidikan ke sekolah menengah kejuruan (STM). Unpublished undergraduate thesis. University of Indonesia.

Sarwono, S. W. 2001. *Psikologi Remaja.* Jakarta: PT RajaGrafindo Persada.

Santa Maria, M. 2002. Youth in Southeast Asia: Living within the continuity of tradition and the turbulence of change. In *The world's youth: Adolescence in eight regions of the globe.* Brown, Larson, and Saraswathi. Cambridge: Cambridge University Press.

Setiaji, K. In http://www.pikiran-rakyat.com/cetak/0902/27/0802.htm.

Sinaga, B. D., R., Missiyah, and R. Hermawaty. (resource persons). 2003. Bias gender di pendidikan dasar: Kondisi dan solusi jangka pendek & menengah. Diskusi pendidikan, December 2003. In http://www.cbe.or.id/comments.php?id-70 0 10 C.

Tambunan, R. 2001. Perkelahian pelajar. Retrieved from http://www.e-psikologi .com/remaja/161001.htm 16 October 2001.

2001 Population Survey—BPS Statistics Indonesia. 2005. In *Kompas,* 24 April 2005.

2002–2003 Indonesia Young Adult Reproductive Health Survey. BPS-Statistics Indonesia, funded by United States Agency for International Development, through ORC Macro.

Using Internet as a source for students' learning. 2003. Seminar conducted by Yayasan Kesejahteraan Anak Indonesia (Indonesia Child Welfare Foundation), June 19, 2003.www.glouanet.org/berita.

IRAN

Background Information

Iran is a Middle Eastern country that until 1935 was referred to in the West as Persia. Iran was a monarchy until 1979, when the shah was overthrown in a popular uprising that was headed by Ayatollah Khomeini. Soon after, Iran was established as an Islamic republic. In 1980 Iran was attacked by neighboring Iraq, and the Iran–Iraq War continued until 1988.

Iran is a constitutional Islamic republic. The nation's political system has several connected governing bodies, some of which are democratically elected and some of which operate by co-opting people based on their religious expertise. The struggle persists between reformists and conservatives over the future of the country through electoral politics. The Iranian presidential election of 2005 led to the victory of conservative candidate Mahmoud Ahmadinezhad, succeeding previous reformist president Muhammad Khatami.

The population of Iran is 68 million, and the area in square kilometers is 1,648,000, giving it a population density of 41 persons per square kilometers. Iran is highly urbanized, with 66% of the population living in urban areas. About 35% of Iran's population is younger than 15 years old, and 37% of the population is between 15 and 29 years.

Ethnically, Iran is quite diverse. The majority of Iran's people are ethnic Persians (51%). Other ethnic groups are: Azeris (24%), Gilaki and Mazandarani (8%), Kurds (7%), Arabs (3%), Lurs (2%), Baloch (2%), and other (3%) (Stalker 2004). Persian (Farsi) is the official language, however, one-quarter of the people use Turkic languages. The religion is predominantly Muslim; 89% belong to the Shia branch of Islam, the official state religion, and 9% belong to the Sunni branch, which predominates in most Muslim countries.

Much of Iran contains a central plateau ringed by mountains. More than half the territory is barren wasteland, most of which is salt desert and uninhabited.

The economy is a mixture of central planning, state ownership of oil and other large enterprises, village agriculture, and small-scale private trading.

Iran is the world's second largest oil producer and holds 10% of the world's proven oil reserves. It also has the world's second largest reserves of natural gas. Unemployment is about 25%. Many professional people are on such low salaries that they need to take on two or three extra jobs (Stalker 2004).

Period of Adolescence

The term "adolescence" may be applied to the emotional and behavioral states supposedly associated with becoming an adult. It is the phase in the life cycle before the physical changes associated with puberty are socially recognized, or the transition in status from childhood to adulthood (Dictionary of Sociology 1998).

Traditionally, the teen years in Iran, as in other Muslim countries, are seen as a period of apprenticeship and companionship for parent and child. This is the period when parents are expected to advise their adolescents.

In Muslim tradition maturity is defined in two ways: the onset of spiritual awakening and the attainment of intellectual maturity. A girl of 9 and a boy of 15 are judged to have reached the onset of spiritual awakening. The rituals, obligations, and duties of Islam become incumbent on them, such as daily prayer and abstaining from food during periods of prescribed fasting. The attainment of intellectual maturity is determined by a person's ability to live and function independently, which may occur at any age. Once a person is considered intellectually mature, that person is considered to be an adult. This is usually decided on an ad hoc basis (Hedayat and Pirzadeh 2001).

Modest dress is incumbent on all Muslims on reaching the onset of spiritual awakening. Boys and girls are expected to wear clothing that does not reveal the curves of the bosom, hips, or behind. All females past puberty have to observe *hijab* (veiling) by covering their hair and neck, and wearing a loose long coat, trousers, and socks to cover their feet (Culture of Iran 2001–2005).

The tradition and Iran's legal code permits parents to marry off girls at the age of 9 and boys at

the age of 14. In 2002 Iranian authorities approved a law requiring parents to obtain court permission for marriages of girls under the age of 13 and of boys younger than 15. Adolescent marriages are permissible; the practice has long been considered the norm in the countryside and in smaller towns where traditional values rule. Parents often arrange marriages for their children long before the children themselves are old enough to give their informed consent (Recknage and Gorgin 2003). However, adolescent marriages are less common in urban areas because of the emphasis on higher education for girls. Surveys carried out by the National Youth Organization suggest the average marriage age has gone up from 25 to 26.85 years for men and from 18.4 to 23.7 years for women during 1966 to 2002 (Iran Daily 2005).

Legal adulthood has little practical meaning in Iran. Children are always the responsibility of the father, regardless of their age. During the war with Iraq all males over the age of 12, except the only sons of widows, were conscripted to active combat. If a man dies, his brother automatically takes on the financial burden and social responsibilities of the widow and children. Culture and custom compels him in this (Drew 1997–2001).

It is possible to observe some signs of "emerging adulthood" in urban areas. According to research, 27% of youths from Tehran are leading a single life. They are willing to pay high prices for housing and have a lifestyle based around being single, and this is considered by Iranian sociologists as a new phenomenon and an inevitable result of globalization. Dr. Taghi Azad Armaki, sociologist and head of the Social Sciences Department of Tehran University, stated that a new style of social living has been shaped in Tehran, and one of its dimensions is the married life without its traditional forms and norms. According to Dr. Azad Armaki, this lifestyle can be dangerous, but it also creates changes and transformations in lifestyles in Tehran. This group of youths has attained a new form of modern life which focuses on personal freedom, taking responsibility, giving importance to one's self, and sometimes running away from social responsibilities (Shahriari 2004).

Beliefs

Traditionally the country tends toward collectivism. In Iran, being a member of a family and of a close group of friends and in-group is very important to people. Family traditionally comes before the individual, and the young are brought up and expected to understand and respect such a notion.

It is not unusual to forgo due diligence, or equal employment opportunity, and to favor a family member or close friend in recruiting or in allocating rewards and promotions. Research results show that Iranians ranked conformist and sociocentric values highly and displayed a high tendency toward collectivism and a weak commitment to individualism (Amirshaki 2002).

The Constitution of Iran declares that the religion of Iran is Islam and the doctrine followed is that of Ja'fari (Twelver) Shi'ism. According to the Constitution, all laws and regulations must be consistent with Shari'a (Islamic law). The overwhelming majority of Iranians (89% of the total population) are Muslims who adhere to Shia Islam.

The Constitution also states that other Islamic denominations are to be accorded full respect. Sunni Muslims constitute approximately 9% of the Iranian population. A majority of Kurds, virtually all Baluchis and Turkomans, and a minority of Arabs are Sunnis, as are small communities of Persians in southern Iran and Khorasan.

Religious minorities (Baha'i, Christian, Jewish, Zoroastrian) constitute about 2% of the total population. Iran's Christians include Armenians, Assyrians, and a small number of Roman Catholic, Anglican, and Protestant Iranians converted by missionaries in the nineteenth and twentieth centuries. Zoroastrians, Jews, and Christians are recognized as religious minorities, guaranteeing their right to religious practice in personal affairs and religious education. The Baha'i faith is defined by the government as a misguided Islamic sect with a political orientation that is antagonistic to the Iranian revolution (Religious Freedom Report 2003).

Religious minorities, by law and practice, are barred from being elected to a representative body (except to the seats in the Majlis, the legislative body reserved for minorities, as provided for in the Constitution) and from holding senior government or military positions. They are also barred from serving in the judiciary and security services and from becoming public school principals.

All public school students, including non-Muslims, must study Islam. University applicants are required to pass an examination in Islamic theology. All non-Muslim females must follow Islamic dress code. Non-Muslims receive lower awards than Muslims in injury and death lawsuits and incur heavier punishments (Religious Freedom Report 2003).

There are signs that traditional religious values are currently changing, as globalization and exposure to Western culture have presented this traditionally Islamic country with alternative ideologies.

An opinion poll conducted in Tehran and Qom has shown that the majority of the people (68.2% in Tehran and 62% in Qom) believe that religious beliefs have weakened compared to their status in the past. The majority (59.5% in Tehran and 51.5% in Qom) also believe that the influence of religion in the personal lives of youth has been diminishing. Respondents also referred to the factors that were said to be weakening religious beliefs. The most important factors were cultural invasion in the form of video and satellite films, economic inflation, and failure to understand the needs of the youth. Research conducted by the Islamic Propagation Organization has revealed that 36.2% of the youth in Tehran have never attended mosques and 45.7% have gone to mosque when they have had an opportunity. This study shows that only 2.6% of the youth have been constant attendants at mosques and 15.5% have often attended mosques (Nouri-nia 2000).

Gender

Traditionally Iranian culture has been patriarchal, with the father or the husband as the head of the family. A son is subordinate to his father, uncles, and grandfathers until the age when his own children are marriageable. His major arena of power is the control of his wife and children. As a father, uncle, and father-in-law, a man's power of veto in family decisions increases with age. Traditionally, the male head of the family makes most major domestic and financial decisions, quite often with consultation with other male relatives but not with female members of the household. Modern Iranians involve wives and grown-up children in such decision making. However, this might not be the case with traditional classes, and bank accounts and major assets might be only accessible by the husband/father or other males (Culture of Iran 2001–2005; Drew 1997–2001).

As in most patriarchal cultures, earning a living is seen as mostly appropriate for men, while child rearing and domestic work has been as a rule the responsibility of women. Nevertheless, it is possible to observe some changes in the understanding of woman's role in society. In 1998, 52% of the students entering universities were female, and the worsening economic situation has forced millions of women to enter the workforce.

It is important to stress that Iran's revolution in 1979 reverted the country from a legal system based on that of Switzerland to Islamic law, under which females are not considered legally or mentally the equal of males (Drew 1997–2001). The testimony of a woman is worth half that of a man in court. A married woman must obtain the written consent of her husband before traveling outside the country. All women, no matter their age, must have the permission of their father or a living male relative in order to marry (Religious Freedom Report, 2003). Single women can go abroad for higher education using government subsidies as long as they have written permission from their fathers. Nevertheless, women are active in professional capacities and as elected representatives, appointed government officials, and judges, making Iran one of the most progressive Muslim countries with respect to women's rights (Oxford Dictionary of Islam, 2003).

An important part of the female role, in the capacity of mother, aunt, or grandmother, is to participate in the continual supervision of younger females, preserving their virginity. Virginity is a major issue with many Iranian families, and premarital sex is prohibited for most girls, while with many families there are no taboos with respect to boys dating and having sex. Once the marriage occurs, the mother-in-law takes over from the bride's mother the responsibilities of supervising her new daughter-in-law, ensuring her fidelity as a wife. As a wife, a woman is subordinate to her husband and his older kin, particularly his parents and older sisters.

By puberty, all Muslim Iranian boys must be circumcised if they are to participate fully in religious activities. It is preferable for the circumcision to be performed on or after the seventh day of life, but it is not a problem if it is performed sooner. Earlier it was performed when the boys were between 5 and 7 years old. Till the nineteenth century there was a party with elaborate meals, musicians, dancers, and street performers. The local barber carried out the actual surgery. A sharp knife was used to cut the foreskin and the area was covered by fresh ash. The circumcised child would wear a long white skirt or a long colored cloth. The parties were very elaborate for the rich and were the most conspicuous after the wedding celebrations. There are no parties for the circumcision any more. The surgery usually is performed at the hospital by professional medical staff only and mainly at the time of birth (Culture of Iran 2001–2005).

Women are not free to choose what they wear in public. They need to observe the Islamic dress code. Women are subject to harassment by authorities if their dress or behavior is considered inappropriate and they may be sentenced to flogging, imprisonment, or imposed monetary penalties for such violations. There are penalties for failure to

observe Islamic dress codes at work (Religious Freedom Report 2003). However, enforcement of the dress code has been relaxed: for example, dark colors are recommended and makeup is discouraged, but many women in large cities use makeup, wear loose and colorful head scarves, and show some of their hair beneath their scarves. Modern Iranians are very liberal with respect to their daughters' fashion styles and are not concerned about body parts being exposed. However, traditional Iranians are concerned about such issues and expect their daughters to dress and act modestly (Culture of Iran 2001–2005). Education appeared to have a stronger effect than age on people's attitudes toward the veil in Iran. Only 15% of those who have a university education considered it very important for women to wear the veil versus 46% of those who were not educated; 69% of the Iranians agreed that being religious was a very important trait for a woman (Moaddel and Azadarmaki 2002).

Segregation of sexes is one of the fundamental principles in Islam. The sexes are separated by adolescence. Young single males join male kin for most social activities. Young single females stay with the women in the family. Islamic law prohibits women from interacting openly with unmarried men or men not related to them. Women must ride in a reserved section on public buses and enter public buildings, universities, and airports through separate entrances. Many stores have sex-segregated service lines, often with a curtain separating the two. Schools, too, are segregated to the point that girls' schools employ only female personnel at any level. Places of worship are divided into men's and women's quarters with separate entrances. Many celebrations and funerals in private houses send males and females into separate rooms. Women are barred from many places, such as some cinemas, restaurants, and tea houses (Drew 1997–2001). However, in large cities it is possible to find ladies' sport clubs and even ladies-only coffee shops (Beiglarkhani 2004).

The Self

Following Islamic religious traditions is considered a major constituent of national identity in Iran. People (adult population) are more likely to describe themselves as Muslims, above all, than as Iranians: 61% of the respondents said that they are Muslims above all, while 34% said they are Iranians above all (Moaddel and Azadarmaki 2002).

Research showed that 60% of Iranian adolescent school student girls residing in Tehran were interested in performing religious rites while only 10% of Iranian adolescent girls residing in the United States were interested in such matters (Sayf 1994). Another study conducted on Tehran's university students and youth showed that in response to a question about cultural identity, around 53% of the subjects said they experienced a feeling of nihilism and lack of identity. Eighteen percent did not respond to this question. In reply to another question about the tendency of the youth and the young generation toward religion, more than 81% believed that the two groups have a lower inclination toward religion. In response to a question about the ideals and wishes of the youth and the students, 61% said they wished to become rich, while 30% hoped they could continue their university education at higher levels. Faced with another question on the mode of dressing and restrained relations, 88% of the subjects said they favored wearing fashionable clothes and having unbridled relations (The Political Inclinations of the Youth and the Students 1995). It seems that Iranian youth tend to explore the values and lifestyles that are in contradiction with traditional values of society, and they tend to be less religious and more individualistic.

Family Relationships

Iranian society places a great deal of importance on the family. According to Nassehi-Behnam (1985), the traditional Muslim family traced its ancestry through the father, tended toward marriage between cousins, favored polygyny, and was male dominated.

Children are raised to be dependent on other family members and to remain so throughout their lives. They are taught to contribute their labor to the family as part of their duty. The process of autonomy and separation is not to as great degree as it is in Western societies, placing greater value on connectedness than in Anglo-American society (Hedayat and Pirzadeh 2001). Research showed that 66% of Iranian adolescent girls residing in Tehran stated that their fathers had a kind attitude and behavior toward them while 6% of the girls believed they had aggressive fathers (Sayf 1994).

Family members are expected to spend lots of time with each other, and socializing with relatives is a very important part of Iranian life. There is a strong emotional component in father–daughter and brother–sister relationships. Research showed that 94% of Iranian adolescent girls stated that their leisure times were spent with family members (Sayf 1994).

Although both parents have a responsibility to raise children, the mother's role is considered more important in early childhood. The father is responsible for education, marriage, and all financial costs related to child rearing, whereas the mother may contribute financially if she is able and wishes to (Hedayat and Pirzadeh 2001).

At a suitable age, determined by the parents and other older kin, a husband or wife will be selected for a daughter or son by the mother. She will investigate the health, wealth, and character of the proposed spouse and bring about the agreement of the person's parents that the marriage will take place. She will also ensure the compliance of her son or daughter. The father will negotiate with the proposed spouse's male kin with regard to all financial aspects of the marriage (Drew 1997–2001). Arranging suitable marriages is one aspect of family relations that still involves parental supervision and involvement. The matter is complicated by the high costs of elaborate weddings and dowry, which means the couple will have to rely on parental financial support in most cases. This in turn increases their dependency on parents and increases parental control. Despite the fact that many modern and educated Iranians have stopped interfering in their children's affairs and their choice of spouse, many still follow the traditional patterns (Culture of Iran 2001–2005).

Polygyny is permissible in Iran as long as such marriages are in accordance with Shia religious law. However, only 1% of married men in Iran have multiple wives, and most of them are outside of urban areas (Tertilt 2004). Monogamy has long been established as the norm for both urban and rural households (Drew 1997–2001).

Under Islamic law and traditional practice, divorce in Iran has been easier for men to obtain than for women. Men could exercise the right of repudiation of wives according to the guidelines of Islamic law. Since 1989 divorce registration requires the permission of the Special Civil court. Men are required by law to provide a sound argument to the court, which the court can reject if it does not comply with *Sharia* (Islamic law) (Gheytanchi 2001). Women were permitted to leave their husbands on narrowly defined grounds, such as insanity or impotence. Beginning in the mid-1960s, the royal government attempted to broaden the grounds upon which women could seek divorce through the Family Protection Law. This legislation was one of the first laws abrogated after the revolution. In 1985, however, legislation was passed permitting women to initiate divorce proceedings in certain limited circumstances (The

Family 1987). Remarriage is possible, but for women this usually means becoming the wife of a man with custody of children from previous marriage.

Marriage in Iran has had a growth of 8.4%, but at the same time divorce has grown by 6.51%. In the first 9 months of the year 2003, from each 5.25 marriages in Tehran and from each 9.24 marriages in Iran there was one case of divorce. Research that studied 2,100 cases of divorce revealed that the lowest rate of divorce, from 4% to 6%, is among female teachers and most cases of divorce are among housewives by 60% (Shahriari 2004). Factors effective in the emergence of divorce are addiction, poverty, and unemployment (Afruzmanesh 2002). Most divorce requests are made by women because of the spouse's addiction and abandonment of alimony (67% of cases), financial burden of divorce for men, lack of or insufficient mutual understanding, distress, and constriction (Paak 2002).

Friends and Peers/Youth Culture

One of the important developmental tasks of early and middle adolescence is achieving mature relationships with peers (Newman and Newman 1975). According to the findings of the study, mingling with their classmates was very limited for the girls residing in the south of Tehran, who are usually from poor families. They were not allowed to go to the houses of their schoolmates nor invite them home unless they were relatives or neighbors. If there was any opportunity to go out, they had to be accompanied by their elder brother or a family member, unless they went out without the knowledge of their parents, particularly the father and the brothers. Many girls, even including those who have reached the age of 20, mentioned the library as the only public venue to which they were permitted to go alone. For this reason, most girls met their friends in the library. Girls spent far more time at home than boys. Boys faced fewer restrictions in mingling with their friends. They were more actively involved in sports, the most popular of which was football. Another favorite sport was wrestling. Based on the survey, it was gathered that association between members of the opposite sex consisted of short encounters in parks, which only brought about superficial acquaintance (Ebrahimi 1998).

However, more young Iranians are risking jail for wearing makeup, slow dancing at parties, or holding hands with members of the opposite sex (Basmenji 2005). Young people have become more daring since president Mohammad Khatami was

elected in 1997. Mixed dancing to pop music is forbidden in Islamic Iran, but it happens underground. It is also common for Iranian girls and boys to dance together and even drink alcohol at parties in private homes, even though the feared moral police have been known to arrive and arrest everyone in sight, and beat them before their sentencing (Davis 1999). Morteza Mir-Baqeri, head of the National Youth Organization, states that there is a sharp difference between the culture institutionalized in the regime and the culture the youth want (Mamarian 2002).

The first meeting of Iran's youth NGOs in 2003 called for measures to prepare grounds for the active participation of the youth in social and policy-making affairs of the country. The youth NGOs of Iran called for establishment of a "National Youth Parliament" and creation of the appropriate atmosphere for activities of the NGOs run by girls (Iran's Youth NGOs Call for Establishment of the "National Youth Parliament" 2003).

Love and Sexuality

Islam prohibits premarital and extramarital sex. Sex between two adults married to others is condemned as the most serious of sins under Islamic law. Adultery and fornication incur the penalty of stoning to death. However, in 2002 the government suspended this practice.

Premarital sex is forbidden and abstinence is expected of both boys and girls until marriage. In practical terms, premarital sex and dating are forbidden only for girls. However, 74% of Iranian adolescent girls residing in Tehran stated that they had no friends of the opposite sex and 4% stated that they had very close and intimate relationships with friends of the opposite sex (Sayf 1994).

Courtship takes place in a supervised setting. All marriages are arranged; the older generation controls meetings between those seeking to marry each other. Marriage often follows betrothal by a matter of days. Often a contract is signed in the presence of a mullah, making the couple legally married and all financial agreements legally binding. The wedding celebration for the families is held off for up to a year. In some families, especially in Tehran, the couple is allowed to go out together between the official signing of the marriage contract and the wedding celebration. Sometimes the groom's family and sometimes the bride's family will prohibit such contact because during negotiations proof of virginity has been spelled out as a prerequisite to the finalization of property transfers. Mild public displays of action are tolerated between urban middle-class couples during the prewedding period (Drew 1997–2001).

Birth control is permissible in Islam for married couples. The two criteria for contraception use are that it does not cause permanent damage to the (male or female) reproductive organs and that it prevents fertilization. Condoms, diaphragms, spermicidal creams, intrauterine devices, Norplant (Population Council, New York, NY), tubal ligations, and vasectomies are all permissible. Abortion, defined as the willful evacuation of an embryo, is considered equivalent to murder and is not ordinarily permitted (Hedayat and Pirzadeh 2001).

Shia Islam, unlike Sunni Islam, recognizes a special form of temporary marriage called *muta* or *sigheh*. In this form of marriage the man and woman sign a contract agreeing to live together as husband and wife for a specified time, which can be as brief as several hours or as long as 99 years. The man agrees to pay a certain amount of money for the duration of the contract. Resulting offspring are legitimate, with a claim to the father's support and a right to his name on the birth certificate. Any man, single or married, can have as many temporary marriages as he wishes and the woman, once the contract is terminated, cannot enter into another contract for three months to make sure she is not pregnant. Temporary marriages were common during the times when long religious pilgrimages were undertaken. Under the monarchy, the government refused to grant any legal recognition to temporary marriages in an effort to discourage the practice. Since the revolution, temporary marriages have again become acceptable (The Family 1987; Drew 1997–2001). The issue of temporary marriage evokes a lot of debate in Iranian society. The country's ruling clerics, including former president Ali Akbar Hashemi Rafsanjani, have suggested that young Iranians adopt the temporary marriage as a temporary substitute for establishing families. This idea was widely criticized in Iranian women's magazines and other publications. The main concern among women was that this might jeopardize the security and sanctity of the family (Gorgin and Recknagel 2000). Temporary marriage is mainly practiced by widowed or divorced women. When teenagers run away, this is often their only means of making money. In the majority of cases, women resort to temporary marriage under the pressure of debts and financial stress. Most of those seeking temporary marriage are in their thirties (*Iran Daily* 2004).

Homosexuality is condemned by Islam and overt homosexuality is not possible because of strong societal pressures (Drew 1997–2001).

Health Risk Behavior

The recreational use of all intoxicating or mind-altering substances is forbidden in Islam. This includes alcohol, stimulants, and hallucinogens; mild stimulants such as caffeine are permitted. There is still some debate about cigarettes, with most scholars saying that it is forbidden based on the concept of not using what is harmful to the body (Hedayat and Pirzadeh 2001). However, simultaneous with the victory of the Islamic revolution in Iran, cultivation of opium was transferred from the Golden Triangle of Laos, Burma, and Thailand to the Golden Crescent, covering Afghanistan, Baluchestan of Pakistan, and Baluchestan of Iran, thus turning the region into the main center of the international drug trade and transit to Europe (The Silk Road or Drug Transit Route 2000). Narcotic drugs are one of the most important problems faced by Iran. Half of the seven million people arrested since the victory of the Islamic revolution were related to narcotic drugs. It takes only 20 to 30 minutes for an addict to procure narcotic drugs in Iran. It is estimated that there are two million drug addicts in the country (Akbari 2004).

Research that assessed the rate of substance use among Iranian secondary school boys aged 12 to 14 years showed that 22.3% reported usage of a substance one or more times during their lives: tobacco 17.5%, alcohol 6.8%, opium 0.6%, hasish 0.2%, and heroin 0.4%. Results also showed that 8.3% of the students were currently substance dependent: 6.2% were tobacco dependent and 2.8% were alcohol dependent. Some were using more than one substance. Tobacco and alcohol were found to be the most prevalent form of substance use. Seeking pleasure, modeling, and release of tension were the most common reasons for initial substance use. The most common reasons reported for current use were seeking pleasure, habit, and release of tension (Jamshid, Mohammadjavad, and Maryam 2004).

Statistics indicate that inmates under the age of 19 account for 1.06% of prisoners. In the 15 to 19 age group, one out of 2.228 are kept in special centers for youngsters. Boys constitute 92% of the delinquents and the girls account for 8%. Robbery constitutes 47.4% of the offenses committed by male delinquents; drug-related offences constitute 21.6%, pestering 16.66%, raping 7.1%, and anti-convenience offenses 1.82% of the offenses carried out by male delinquents. Prostitution is a common offense committed by female delinquents, who are mostly runaway girls. Drug-related offenses, pestering, robbery and anti-convenience offenses are the next most significant offenses committed by female delinquents. Female and male delinquents commit 20% of drug offenses. Two-thirds of delinquents abandon school education while they are at primary school or high school (Zarezadeh and Moulavi-Ganjeh 2002). It is important to notice that the age of penal responsibility in Iran is 9 years for girls and 15 years for boys, which means that adolescents can face adult punishments—for example, they can be sentenced to death. This is partly consistent with Islamic law (according to Islamic law a girl of 9 and a boy of 15 are judged to have reached the onset of spiritual awakening), obviously in contradiction with the Convention on the Rights of the Child.

Runaway girls in Iran are becoming an important social problem. According to the State Welfare Organization, the number of runaway girls jumped by 15% in 2003. Research showed that 51.66% of them are dropouts, 72% have left their homes because of joblessness; 95% of the fathers and 92% of the mothers of the runaway girls are still alive. Research also showed that 66.67% of runaway girls pass the nights with their boyfriends or other single men. Some of them eloped with their boyfriends because their fathers were against their dating and had beaten them. Research indicated that 42.5% runaway girls like to have a boyfriend. Many runaway girls do not dare to return home for fear of bad behavior from their families. The main motivation for the runaways was their family pressure. The problems usually stem from poverty and joblessness (Runaway Girls Flourishing 2004, p. 660).

Education

The youth literacy rate (ages 15 to 24) for both sexes is 95%. The net enrollment ratio is above 97% and is almost equal among girls and boys. However, while the overall enrollment rate for boys is 98%, it varies significantly between provinces. For girls, the range is between 99% in Tehran and 84% in Sistan and Baluchestan. The enormous gains in the educational status of the Iranian population can be attributed to massive government investment in public education (on average 45% of the government's social affairs budget since 1989) (At a Glance: Iran [Islamic Republic of] 2005).

Primary education is compulsory and lasts for five years, leading to the Certificate of Completed Primary Education. Secondary education covers three years of lower secondary school (guidance school, which is compulsory), upper secondary

school, and a one-year pre-university program. Secondary education comprises three branches: theoretical, technical-vocational and skill-knowledge. The required total number of credits leading to the high school diploma is 96. The one-year pre-university program prepares students to enter university and higher education institutions. To enter this course, students should pass the appropriate exam. After successfully passing the one-year period, they are granted the Pre-University Certificate and can sit for the National Entrance Exam of universities and higher education institutions. Qualified students entering the technical-vocational branch can continue studies leading to the Post-Diploma degree (technician) or sit for the Pre-University Examination. Those who wish to acquire skills before completing secondary education can enter the skill-knowledge branch and obtain a first or second Skill Certificate or sit for the Pre-University Examination as well (Iran-Education System 2001).

The statistics of schools, students, and teachers in the education system point to the existence of discrimination between men, women, boys, and girls in studying and teaching in the educational system in Iran. For example, the number of boys' exemplary schools is twice that of girls' schools. Out of 540 technical arts schools, 509 are for boys and only 31 for girls. Out of 73 agricultural institutes at the national level, none is for girls (Fatemi 1998).

A survey on educational advancement of Iranian primary and upper secondary school students conducted by the International Evaluation Association (IEA) in mathematics and sciences courses indicated that the average performance of Iranian students is lower than that of students in other countries. Their learning level in such activities as collecting and demonstrating data, analysis of findings, design of experiments, solving problems, and employment of necessary means to solve problems is low, and they are weak in giving answers to written questions and describing scientific processes. The findings of this study also showed that the educational level of teachers in Iran is lower than that of teachers in other countries. Density of students in classrooms is high in Iran, and the educational period in one academic year is lower than that in other countries. The overall literacy level in society is low and there are few books and other cultural and educational means available to each family. Education is offered in the forms of description and lectures, and use of new teaching and educational methods has no place in classrooms (Evaluation of Educational Progress in Iran 1998).

Since 1998 the number of females admitted to universities has exceeded the number of males. The statistics taken in 2000 show the rate of females admitted to universities at 59.92% compared to the male, which stands at 40.08%. (In 2001 girls were again ahead of boys.) The mixing of girls and boys in universities has been controversial and a subject of commotion (some branches of the Islamic Free University introduced separate classes for men and women) (Seradjeh 2003). The university of Qom medical school for women is an ideal example of an Islamic institution since it trains female doctors and all their teachers and patients are women (Gheytanchi 2001).

Based on a report issued by the International Monetary Fund in 1999, out of 61 countries, Iran experienced the highest rate of brain drain (educated people who left Iran during that year) (Brain Drain the Full Story 2004).

Work

In 1958 the Labor Law was approved which prohibited labor for children younger than 12 years of age in Iran except in family workshops. The law led to many protests. In 1990 the minimum age for employment of children was raised to 15 years.

Traditionally, the Iranian community has not seriously combated child labor because Iran has a background of employing persons below the lawful age. Family members had always worked together, and the family income both among farmers and other professions was earned by family members. Such employment helped children to help their fathers with their jobs and generated income and prevented the waste of manpower and spread of vagrancy; for these reasons, employment of children below 12 had always been practiced in Iran. Also, many families are poor and there are children who earn bread for their families. Usually problems in their lives and school lead children to believe that they cannot learn in the school and must work (Labor Law and Child Rights in Iran 1999).

Analysis of employment of persons ranging from 10 to 19 years of age in Iran during the years 1956–1996 showed that adolescent employment has remarkably dropped. Such a change for children below 15 has happened even more rapidly. The proportion of this group of teenagers who were employed in 1956 was 6.5 times greater than the number employed in 1996. The majority of children are generally employed in nonofficial and family professions. The proportion of female child and adolescent employment compared to adult women

is above the employment of boys compared to men. Carpet weaving is one of the main fields that attracts adolescent girls' employment, because they have smaller hands, which help them to make smaller knots and render the carpet more delicate. The most important factor that influences changes in the volume of employment of children in various regions in Iran is the volume of adult employment. Naturally, with the increase of adult employment the need for child employment evaporates. Also, unofficial and family duties create more jobs for children (Abdi 2000).

A survey of the job inclination of youth in the rural areas showed that only 31.2% of young peasant farmers had continued their father's occupation. Reasons cited for not following the father's footsteps in the job arena included the lack of possibilities to go ahead with the job (32.5%), meager income derived (31.44%), lack of interest in the father's work (25.4%), and the absence of the required skills to engage in the same occupation as the parent (10.7%) (Rezvani 1995).

Unemployment is an important concern of the society. It is especially high (at 34%) among the 15- to 24-year-olds who officially constitute 25% of the labor force. Among these job seekers more than 10% are classified as college graduates, and 30% are high school diploma holders. Unemployment is highest among women of all ages. Only 15% of female university graduates are able to find suitable work (Amuzegar 2004, p. 486).

Media

Research showed that Tehran's teenagers watch TV for three hours per day. Video is also popular; 60% of teenagers in Tehran use video, watching about four video films per week. Nearly all products of Hollywood are illegally recorded in the country of origin within two or three months of their first release and are smuggled into Iran for reproduction and distribution. Around 35% of the teenage population has access to satellite TV (despite its being banned by the state), and watches two or three TV programs aired by satellite every day. Invasion of the products of Western culture in the form of video and satellite films is regarded as creating cultural contradiction which influences the sexual and social behavior of the teenaged population and diminishes religious beliefs (Niya 1998; Nouri-nia 2000).

Around 5% of Tehran's teenagers have access to computers. Most teenagers use computers for entertainment, playing games, or learning sciences.

The government is trying to centralize all access to the Internet through the Ministry of Posts and Telecommunications, which is struggling to screen the rapidly increasing number of sites on the World Wide Web, and block access to objectionable sites (Drew 1997–2001). The number of regular Internet users increased by 1.820% between 2000 and 2004. The total number of users is over 7% (Lobe 2004). Internet cafés are very popular with young people, students, and intellectuals, especially in the capital. By 2001, Tehran alone boasted 1,500 Internet cafés. Most Internet users (75%) are between the ages of 21 and 32, and 14% use the Internet 38 hours or more per week (Slavin 2005).

Tehran's university students and youth responding to a question about music declared that they favored Western music (50%) and Iranian revolutionary songs and music (15%). In response to another question on the extent of interest in Western music, 31% said they favored classical music, 14% pop music, 24% jazz, and 21% electronic music (The Political Inclinations of the Youth and the Students 1995, p. 328).

Politics and Military

The minimum voting age in Iran is 15. Iran's youth is a pivotal voice in politics, because about 70% of the population is under age 25. They were the most influential force in the 1997 upset victory of President Khatami, a reformer candidate.

Students were active during the Islamic revolution. The Office for Strengthening Unity (DTV), Iran's largest student organization with branches on 50 campuses, emerged after a 1979 meeting of Islamic student associations and first gained fame by leading the 1979 takeover of the U.S. Embassy. This organization turned from Islamic radicalism to a pro-democracy agenda (Wright 2004). In June 2003, thousands of students took to the streets of Tehran, the capital, and at least six other cities. The demonstrations echoed others, in 1999 and 2002, centered in Iran's universities. Students were disappointed with the government of President Khatami, whose reform efforts in parliament were blocked by the council of conservative mullahs (Iran: Facing a Demographic Revolution 2005). DTV was urging people not to vote in the June 17, 2005, presidential election in the hope that this would be interpreted as a vote against the system.

Research findings showed that around 27% of Tehran's university students and youth indicated pessimism toward politics, while 41% expressed indifference, and less than 32% voiced optimism

toward politics. The research findings further showed that 35% of the subjects followed news on the day's political events, while 65% did not do so. The responses provided to another question on reading dailies showed that less than 32% of the subjects regularly followed up the political news and read the dailies (The Political Inclinations of the Youth and the Students 1995, p. 276).

Unique Issues

Suicide is not permissible in Islam. Nevertheless, analysis of completed and attempted suicide in Ilam province (western Iran) (1995–2002) showed that the annual completed suicide rate was 10.0 and 26.4 per 100,000 men and women. The attempted suicide rates were 41.8 and 64.5 per 100,000 men and women. About 74% of the suicides occurred between the ages of 10 and 29 years. Suicide and attempted suicide rates were highest among 20- to 29-year-olds and decreased with increasing age. Self-immolation was the most common method of suicide, while drug overdose was the predominant method of suicide attempt. Females were about three times more likely to commit suicide, and they were about 50% more likely to attempt suicide (Janghorbani and Sharifirad 2005). Contrary to Western countries where single old men form the majority who commit suicide, in Iran the majority rests with young married women. Research on women who have taken their lives shows that they have suffered from degradation in the family, male domination and arrogance, premature married age, clan arbitrary marriages, difference of age between the couple, and lack of children. Unequal opportunity for the two sexes, the traditional male dominating codes in the community, and lesser respect for women has placed women in an unequal and unfair scale in Iran (Askari 1998, p. 207).

JOLANTA SONDAITE

References and Further Reading

A Dictionary of Sociology. 1998. G. Marshall (ed.). Oxford University Press. http://www.oxfordreference.com/views/ENTRY.html?subview=Main&entry=t88.e32.
Abdi, A. 2000. An analysis of child labor in Iran. *Andisheye Jameah* pp. 27–30. http://www.netiran.com/?fn=artd(942).
Afruzmanesh, M. 2002. Triangle of unemployment, poverty and addiction the main cause of divorce; An interview with Mr. Nemati. *Hambastegi* 579:7. http://www.netiran.com/?fn=artd(695).
Akbari, A. 2004. Narcotic drugs are distributed easier than sugar. *Vaghaye Ettefaquien* p. 6. http://www.netiran.com/?fn=artd(1775).

Amuzegar, J. 2004. Iran's unemployment crisis. http://www.mees.com/postedarticles/oped/a47u41d01.htm.
Armirshaki, A. A. J. 2002. The Iranian manager: Work values and orientations. *Journal of Business Ethics* 40:133–43.
Askari, S. 1998. Women, main victims of suicide in Iran. *Farhang-Tose* pp. 37–42. http://www.netiran.com/?fn=artd(985).
At a glance: Iran. 2005. http://www.unicef.org/infobycountry/iran.html.
Basmenji, K. 2005. *Tehran blues: Youth culture in Iran*. London: Saqi Books.
Beiglarkhani, S. 2004. Ladies only coffee shop opens. *Hamshahri* 3395:18. http://www.netiran.com/?fn=artd(1446).
Brain drain the full story. 2004. *Iran International* 28:32–35. http://www.netiran.com/?fn=463.
CIA World Factbook. 2003. http://www.cia.gov/cia/publications/factbook/geos/ir.html.
Culture of Iran. 2001–2005. http://www.cultureofiran.com.
Davis, J. M. 1999. Iranian teens just wanna have their fun. http://www.iran-e-sabz.org/news/youth.htm.
Drew, P. E. 1997–2001. Iran. In *The international encyclopedia of sexuality*. R. T. Francoeur (ed.). http://www2.hu-berlin.de/sexology/ies/iran/iran.html.
Ebrahimi, M. 1998. The cultural and social development of the youth in the south of Tehran. *Goftegoo* 19:39–53. http://www.netiran.com/php/artp.php?id=969.
Evaluation of education progress in Iran. 1998. *Goftegoo* 19:88–93. http://www.netiran.com/?fn=artd(973).
Fatemi, P. 1998. Eradication of discrimination in education. *Farhang-e Tose'e* pp. 64–67. http://www.netiran.com/?fn=artd(983).
Gheytanchi, E. Chronology of events regarding women in Iran since the revolution of 1979. http://www.wluml.org/english/pubs/rtf/dossiers/dossier23-24/D23-24-07-iran-chron.rtf.
Gorgin, A., and C. Recknagel. 2000. Iran: Temporary marriages fuel debate. http://www.fww.org/famnews/09182000.htm.
Hedayat, K. M., and R. Pirzadeh. 2001. Issues in Islamic biomedical ethics: A primer for the pediatrician, *Pediatrics* 108:965–71.
Iran. 2003. http://earthtrends.wri.org/pdf_library/country_profiles/Pop_cou_364.pdf.
Iran Daily. 2004. www.iran-daily.com/1383/2134/html/panorama.
Iran Daily. 2005. www.iran-daily.com/1383/2181/html/panorama.
Iran-Education System. 2001. http://www.lmu.edu/globaled/wwcu/background/ir.rtf.
Iran: Facing a demographic revolution. 2005. http://www.cbc.ca/news/background/iran.
Iran's youth NGOs call for establishment of the "National Youth Parliament." 2003. http://www.payvand.com/news/youth.html.
Jamshid, A., A. Mohammadjavad, and A. Maryam. 2004. Substance use disorders in a sample of Iranian secondary school students. *Social Indicators Research* 65:355–60.
Janghorbani, M., and G. Sharifirad. 2005. Completed and attempted suicide in Ilam, Iran (1995–2002): Incidence and associated factors. *Archives of Iranian Medicine* 8:119–26.
Labor law and child rights in Iran. 1999. *Andisheye Jameah* 7:3–21. http://www.netiran.com/?fn=artd(947).

Lobe, J. 2004. Rights groups condemn Iran's Internet crackdown. www.eurasianet.org/departments/civilsociety/articles/eav111604.shml.

Moaddel, M., and T. Azadarmaki. 2002. The worldviews of Islamic publics: The cases of Egypt, Iran, and Jordan. http://www.Worldvauessurvey.org/upload/5_Iran. Pdf.

Memarian, O. 2002. State entities gasping for the youth affairs; An interview with Morteza Mir-Baqeri. *Bonyan* 1:8. http://www.netiran.com/?fn=artd(744).

Nassehi-Behnam, V. 1985. Change and the Iranian family. *Current Anthropology* 26:557–62.

Newman, B. M., and P. R. Newman. 1975. *Development through life. A psychosocial approach.* Homewood: Dorsey Press.

Niya, O. H. 1998. Transnational visual media and their impacts. *Naqd-e Cinema* 14:63–71. http://www.netiran.com/?fn=artd(1015).

Nouri-nia, H. 2000. The press and people's religious beliefs. *Mosharekat* 44:7. http://www.netiran.com/php/artp.php?id=933.

Oxford Dictionary of Islam. L. Esposito (ed.). Oxford University Press. http://www.oxfordreference.com/views/ENTRY.html?subview=Main&entry=t125.e1064.

Paak, A. 2002. 80% of divorce requests are made by women; An interview with Hassan Hamidian. *Entekhab* 805. http://www.netiran.com/?fn=artd(764).

Recknage, C., and A. Gorgin. 2003. Human right activists win partial victory in battle against child marriage. www.parstimes.com/women/child_marriage.html.

Religious Freedom Report. 2003. http://atheism.about.com/library/irf/irf03/blirf_iran.htm.

Rezvani, N. S. 1995. A survey of the Joc inclinations of youth in the rural areas. *Jihad* 173:32–37. http://www.netiran.com/php/artp.php?id=2365.

Runaway girls flourishing. 2004. *Hamvatan* 33:13. http://www.netiran.com/?fn=artd(1696).

Sayf, S. 1994. A comparison between problems of Iranian adolescent girls residing in Iran and the United States.

Farzaneh 1:169–74. http://www.netiran.com/php/artp.php?id=1937.

Seradjeh, B. 2003. Gender separation in Iran. http://freethoughts.org/000212.php.

Shahriari, M. 2004. 27% of Tehran youth live a single's life. *Sqarq* 189:27. http://www.netiran.com/php/artp.php?id=1338.

Slavin, B. 2005. Internet boom alters political process in Iran. http://www.usatoday.com/news/world/2005-06-12-iran-election-internetx.htm.

Stalker, P. 2004. *A-Z of countries of the world.* Oxford University Press. http://www.oxfordreference.com/views/ENTRY.html?subview=Main&entry=t42.e98.

Tertilt, M. 2004. Polygyny, fertility, and savings. http://www.econ.yale.edu/seminars/trade/tdw04-05/tertilt110804.pdf.

The Family. 1987. http://reference.allrefer.com/country-guide-study/iran/iran65.html.

The New Oxford American Dictionary. 2005. E. McKean (ed.). Oxford University Press. http://www.oxfordreference.com/views/ENTRY.html?subview=Main&entry=t183.e39789.

The political inclinations of the youth and the students. 1995. *Asr-e-Ma* 2:5. http://www.netiran.com/php/artp.php?id=1852.

The Silk Road or Drug Transit Route. *Cheshmandaz-e Iran*, Biweekly Magazine. 3 (2000): 43–48. http://www.netiran.com/php/artp.php?id=936

This year again girls are ahead of boys. 2001. *Peyk-e Sanjesh* 6:25. http://www.netiran.com/php/artp.php?id=.

Wright, R. 2004. In Iran, students urge citizens not to vote. http://www.washingtonpost.com/wp-dyn/articles/A61117-2004Nov18.html.

Zarezadeh, S., and S. Moulavi-Ganjeh. 2002. Statistical review of teenage juvenile delinquents. *Abrar* 1:46–47. http://www.netiran.com/php/artp.php?id=686.

IRELAND

Background Information

The Republic of Ireland, as it is politically constituted in the early twenty-first century, has its origins in the Anglo-Irish Treaty of 1921, which conferred a high degree of political autonomy from Britain on 26 of the country's 32 counties. It was not, however, until 1948 that this new state left the British Commonwealth and declared itself a republic. The Irish Constitution was enacted in 1937 but has since been modified through a number of referenda. According to Article 8 of the Constitution, Irish is the first, and English the second, official language of Ireland.

The population in Ireland in the last national census was 3.9 million, one million of whom live in Dublin. Sixty percent of the population lives in urban areas. The number of children aged 0 to 19 was 1,130,016 and the number of young people aged 20 to 24 was 328,334. The birth rate declined at the end of the twentieth century but has risen again and is still rising, albeit slowly, and currently stands at 15.7 per 1,000 (2004). Until the recent past, Ireland was a country of emigration. However, data from the 2002 census indicate that 6% of the population living in Ireland is non-Irish. Approximately 24,000 people belong to the Travelling community, an indigenous group of nomadic or quasi-nomadic people. Sixty-three percent of Travellers are under 25 years of age, compared with 37% of the general population.

Since the mid-1990s, Ireland has experienced a period of unprecedented economic growth which has transformed the country from a society with high unemployment, low demand for labor, and high emigration to what is now know, both colloquially and internationally, as the "Celtic Tiger" economy. Although many citizens have benefited from the country's new wealth, socioeconomic inequality remains a persistent characteristic of Irish life. Ireland ranks third highest in terms of the level of "human poverty" in the 18 OECD (Organisation for Economic and Co-operative Development) countries, with one in seven children living in "consistent poverty."

Period of Adolescence

Adolescence does exist as a recognized life stage in Ireland and there is, generally and in the media, much discussion about adolescents, teenagers, and "young people." Typically, adolescence is seen to coincide with the teenage years, but there has been some recognition that, for many children, puberty commences earlier than 13 and that childhood is becoming abbreviated. This perception is partly fueled by the behavior and appearance of 10-, 11-, and 12-year-olds, rather than the actual onset of puberty.

Adult status is defined in different ways. The voting age is 18, and 18 is also the legal age for buying and consuming alcohol. Despite the significance of these markers, the twenty-first birthday is seen as a major rite of passage. The average age at marriage has been increasing in recent years and, in 2002, was 32.5 for men and 30.4 for women. Many more young people are cohabiting before marriage. The average age of a woman at maternity in 2004 was 30.7 years, which is higher than the EU average. In 2002, 517,000 children were living with cohabiting parents and 31.4 % of births in 2003 took place outside marriage.

Although the term "emerging adulthood" is not used outside academia, the phenomenon is certainly evident and recognized. As more young people enter third level education and postpone marriage and other commitments, parents are faced with supporting their children far beyond the age of 18. Even when working, young people in their twenties often continue to live with their parents. Children growing up in poverty, on the other hand, are more likely to leave school early to enter the world of work.

Beliefs

The predominant religion in Ireland is Christian, with the majority of the country (over 90%) being members of the Roman Catholic faith. The practice of religion has declined markedly in recent years, especially among the young. Among 18- to 26-year-olds attendance at religious services has declined

from 75% attending services once a week or more in 1981 to 48% attending at that rate in 1999. Ireland is fast becoming a more secular society, although the practice of religion remains higher than in many other northern European states. Most of the remaining minority belong to Protestant denominations (e.g., Church of Ireland, Methodist, and Presbyterian) but, as immigration increases, there is a growing number of Muslims and other people of non-Christian faiths.

Ireland can be seen as in transition from a communitarian to an individualistic culture, but there remains a strong commitment to social and communal goals (Cassidy 2002). Irish data from the European Values Study (Breen 2002) give a picture of young people rejecting traditional authorities (such as the Church) and espousing more liberal, secular values. There is some concern that young people are adrift in terms of their values, having rejected traditional sources of moral values without finding a new moral code.

A recent study reported that Irish people were generally more optimistic and more satisfied with life than their European counterparts (Alber et al. 2005). The economy and quality of employment are valued very highly and Irish people also place high value on their family ties. They are more likely than others to say they would turn to family members rather than friends if in trouble.

Gender

Until recently, traditional gender roles were strongly maintained in Ireland, with boys expected to be more assertive and stoic and girls more nurturing and emotionally labile. Boys and girls were socialized to occupy adult roles conforming to the traditional pattern of men being breadwinners and distant authoritarian fathers and women being stay-at-home housewives and mothers. A number of factors have combined to undermine these traditional stereotypes. Education for girls has led to their having aspirations beyond marriage and motherhood, and contraception—which was banned by the Roman Catholic Church—is now widely used and as a result childbearing can be postponed and family size reduced. Young women are thus more enabled to pursue education and a career. Starting in primary school, girls are more successful in academic terms than boys, thus putting paid to notions of female intellectual inferiority. Nearly 45% of all girls leaving secondary school progress to further study compared to only 34% of boys (Economic and Social Research Institute, 1998). More than half of university students are women and, in some universities, women make up 60% of the student population. Nonetheless, ideological notions of "traditional" family remain strong and women continue to be seen first and foremost as mothers and wives. Teenage girls' responsibility for domestic chores far outweighs that of boys, and this division of labor appears to be strongly influenced by traditional gender expectations (Leonard 2004).

In Ireland, boys' average academic attainment is lower than that of girls at junior and leaving certificate levels (Hannan et al. 1994), and there is increasing concern about adolescent boys and men falling behind. However, while there have been attempts to explain class differences in attainment, the problem of male underachievement is poorly understood (Mac an Ghaill et al. 2004). Boys are also more likely to drop out of school and figure more in antisocial and criminal activities. Nonetheless, it is important to note that girls still tend to be less confident about their abilities and are underrepresented in many occupations. When employed, females earn less on average than their male peers and appear far less often in the ranks of senior management.

Some discussion in the media and academic circles has centered on "the crisis in masculinity" for young Irish males, particularly working-class males, as they move from a predictable, stable, traditional masculine role to a more fluid, less gender-stereotyped role. The number of young women choosing to have children out of wedlock and to rear them alone is seen also as threatening to the self-esteem and emotional stability of young men.

The Self

There is much written on Irish identity and what it means to be Irish but this literature is typically produced by writers and historians rather than social scientists. To a considerable extent, literary and historical interest in identity reflects Ireland's prior status as a small postcolonial country dominated by a more powerful neighbor. However, young people in the early twenty-first century seem less obsessed by Ireland's past and more confident in what it means to be Irish. Today, Irish identity is probably more tied up with prosperity, artistic and music success, and the common perception that Ireland is a "happening place" where it is good to be young. The proportion of 18- to 24-year-olds who said that they were "very proud" of their national identity in 1988 was 55%, but by 1997 it had risen to 72% and remained at that level when assessed again in 2003 (Fahey, Hayes, and Sinnott 2005).

In the past, teenagers and young people would have had a clear shared identity as Irish marked by homogeneity of experience and outlook. This was, for the most part, narrowly defined in terms of belonging to the Catholic faith, being born in Ireland, and speaking (or learning to speak) Irish and tended to exclude individuals who did not fit that profile. With exposure to global culture and increasing immigration, Ireland is now much more heterogeneous and young people can discover or construct new versions of what it means to be Irish. To incoming young people, Irish youth are seen to be friendly but "cliquish" and not very open to strangers from different cultures, suggesting perhaps that they are still more comfortable with the established homogeneity. Immigrant children and adolescents experience intolerance, and many immigrants attribute racism to the lack of knowledge that Irish people have of other cultures (Immigrant Council of Ireland 2004).

There has not been much research to date on the experience of minority adolescents. A survey published in 2000 focused on the experience of racism and psychological distress in a sample of minority (Afro-Caribbean, South Asian, Oriental, Arabic, and mixed race) adolescents and adults. Seventy-two members of this sample were aged between 12 and 18, and these young people reported many incidents of racism and a higher level of psychological distress (as measured by the General Health Questionnaire) than the general population (Casey and O'Connell 2000).

Family Relationships

The family is accorded pride of place in the Constitution, which states that, "The State recognises the Family as the natural primary and fundamental unit group of Society, and as a moral institution possessing inalienable and imprescriptible rights, antecedent and superior to all positive law" (Article 41.1.1). Some commentators feel the family has been "idealized" in Ireland, and that only recently have some of the more negative aspects of traditional Irish family life—such as unacceptable levels of physical and sexual abuse of children—come to light. The view that children are the property and responsibility of parents means that there is very little state support for parents. For example, state investment in preschool care and education is very low by European Union standards.

There has been very little work conducted on family relationships in Ireland, but this is one area that the forthcoming National Longitudinal Study of Children in Ireland will address.

Small-scale studies indicate that in contemporary Irish child rearing there is evidence of elements of both traditional authoritarian parenting and modern democratic or permissive parenting styles (Greene 1994a). For example, parents often use corporal punishment with their young children (Greene 1994b). In the same study, 80% of the children were classed as securely attached to their mothers, a high rate in international terms. Fathers are becoming more involved in parenting but attitudes remain generally conservative, with parenting seen to be the primary responsibility of women (McKeown et al. 1998). There are institutional barriers to greater paternal involvement such as lack of extended paternal leave.

The structure of Irish families has changed substantially in recent years with more families headed by single parents (mostly mothers) and more blended families. Two manifestations of the recent rapid social change are the increasing numbers of women choosing to rear children alone and the increase in rates of marital breakdown and separation, which results in children and young people having to cope with the impact of parental separation or divorce. Divorce was illegal in Ireland until 1997 when it was introduced after a second national referendum. The number of divorces granted in 2004 was 3,305 and there were 1,216 judicial separations (Central Statistics Office 2005). This rate of divorce is low compared to other developed economies and reflects an enduring adherence to Roman Catholic views on marriage and to other traditional values. A qualitative study published in 2002 on children's experience of parental separation (Hogan et al. 2002) suggested that children and young people whose parents had separated had more opportunity in Ireland to maintain connections with their nonresident parent (typically their father) and also with their grandparents. This indicates that grandparents are still important to young people growing up in Ireland. In the past, Ireland was noted among anthropologists for its "stem" families, with several generations living under one roof. Although this is far less common today, it seems that family connections nonetheless remain very strong.

Friends and Peers/Youth Culture

The pace of change in Ireland's economic and social landscape over the past 20 years has undoubtedly brought about significant change in adolescent lifestyles. The move away from religion is a key factor shaping the belief system of young Irish people, as is their exposure to global influences and consumer culture. Although there is not a strong tradition of research on youth culture in Ireland, a discrete youth culture clearly exists and is distinguishable from adult culture in terms of dress, hairstyle, and musical taste.

Dillon's (1984) study of youth culture in Ireland, based on a survey of 14- to 16-year-olds, revealed a high degree of orientation to peers both inside and outside of school. Participation in sporting activities with friends, going to discos, and "hanging around" were preferred free-time activities and the vast majority of the young people surveyed did not smoke cigarettes or cannabis, or drink alcohol on a regular basis. The latter finding contrasts sharply with more recent evidence pointing to high levels of alcohol (and drug) consumption among school-going youth. This quite dramatic shift in adolescent drinking and drug use and, in particular, the growing trend toward "binge" drinking among the young has been linked to the growth in the value youth culture attaches to consumer goods (Mayock 2004).

Adolescents are an important sector of the consumer market in Ireland and it appears that consumption plays a far more important role in the lives of adolescents than previously. The growth of both mobile phone and Internet usage across all sectors of the population has been phenomenal and a large majority of Irish teenagers and young people own mobile (cell) phones and own or have home-based access to the Internet. Teenagers' preoccupation with commodities—from clothing to music to technology—is clearly observable on the high streets of towns and cities throughout the country.

There is no nationally representative study of teenagers' and young people's use of free time. Fitzgerald et al.'s (1995) quantitative study of the leisure needs of adolescent school-goers living in a disadvantaged urban area found that young men preferred sports and watching TV and videos, while the young women enjoyed going to youth discos and talking to friends. Research suggests that teenagers from low-income families engage more in unstructured leisure activities—watching TV, listening to music, and "hanging around" with friends—that have no cost attached and that far fewer participate in organized activities (Daly and Leonard 2002). Adolescent participation in sporting activities outside school is relatively high in Ireland and many second-level students, particularly boys and those in the early years of the second-level cycle, are regular participants in sporting activities (Fahey et al. 2005). The Gaelic Athletic Association (GAA), an Irish amateur sporting organization, attracts large numbers of young people as club members throughout the country. It appears, however, that boys and girls behave differently and feel differently when it comes to sports and that boys spend more time at sports and they enjoy it more than girls (Fahey et al. 2005).

Love and Sexuality

There is a dearth of Irish research on adolescent sexual behavior, a situation that undoubtedly reflects Ireland's historical conservatism in relation to sex and sexuality (Inglis 1998). While the absence of research on adolescent sexuality at the national level precludes a complete picture of Irish teenage sexuality, a number of regional and area-specific studies provide valuable information on levels of teenage sexual activity and they also tell us a great deal about young people's attitudes toward and beliefs about sex and sexual relationships. Available research suggests that up to one-third of 16-year-old school-going adolescents may be sexually active, with adolescent boys more likely than girls to state that they have had first sexual intercourse (MacHale and Newell 1997; Dunne et al. 1997). This figure may be higher for specific or "high risk" groups such as early school leavers (Mayock and Byrne 2004). These studies have also documented relatively high levels of sexual risk-taking and noncompliance with safe sex practices among adolescents, particularly on the occasion of first sex. The factors associated with inconsistent use of condoms and nonconformity to safe sex practices are complex and include embarrassment about purchasing condoms (Dunne et al. 1997; Mayock and Byrne 2004) and alcohol use and intoxication (MacHale and Newell 1997). There is also evidence that social factors influence conformity to safe sex practices. For example, constructs of masculinity and femininity have a profound impact on sexual attitudes and behavior and on the social meanings young men and women attach to sex and contraception (Hyde and Howlett 2004). Of significance in this regard is that many young women perceive carrying condoms as a risk because it implies that they are interested in or prepared for sex (Hyde and Howlett 2004; Mayock and Byrne 2004). There is great diversity in the range and quality of young people's sexual knowledge and in the perceived value they attach to available knowledge sources, including peers, home, school, and the media. It appears, however, that a large number rely on their peers for information on sex and sexuality.

There is also evidence that young people's knowledge about sexually transmitted infections is inadequate and that many perceive themselves to be invulnerable to HIV/AIDS, which they associate primarily with drug users and gay men. Although injecting drug users and men who have sex with men are recognized risk categories for HIV infection, many young people are clearly unaware of the risks of heterosexual transmission. Of a total of 356 newly diagnosed cases of HIV infection in 2004, 178 were heterosexually acquired. The mean age of HIV diagnosis was 28.8 years in females and 33.7 years in males. HIV infection was diagnosed in fifteen 10- to 19-year-olds in 2004 (Health Protection Surveillance Centre 2005).

Almost all published research on adolescent sexuality has focused on heterosexual sexuality. There are very few studies of the life experiences of lesbian, gay, and bisexual individuals (Gay HIV Strategies/NEXUS 2000). This is despite strong evidence that gay men and lesbian women of all ages suffer harassment, discrimination, and prejudice in a variety of settings, including schools (Norman 2004). One study of educational equality climates within twelve second-level schools in different counties throughout Ireland found that students were not generally accustomed to addressing the subject of sexual orientation and that there was very limited awareness among students about sexual difference (Lodge and Lynch 2003).

Relationships and Sexuality Education (RSE) was not introduced into Irish schools until 1995 and only modest progress has been made with the implementation and delivery of this program in schools nationwide (Morgan 2000a). Gay and lesbian youth are largely invisible in the guidelines and resources for relationships and sexuality education and this silence undoubtedly reflects the discomfort with sexual issues that has characterized Irish society over a lengthy period.

Health Risk Behavior

Irish adolescents are among the most regular users of alcohol and illegal drugs in Europe. Over half of Ireland's adolescents begin experimenting with alcohol before the age of 12 and, by the time young people reach the age of 15 or 16 years, half of the girls and two-thirds of the boys are current drinkers (Hibell et al. 2000). The results of two consecutive ESPAD (European School Survey Project on Alcohol and Other Drugs) studies (Hibell et al. 2000) indicate high rates of heavy episodic drinking among both boys and girls up to the age of 16 years.

Drug consumption among Irish youth increased steadily throughout the 1990s and Ireland currently has one of the most drug-experienced youth populations in the European Union (Hibell et al. 2000). Since the 1980s opiate epidemic, drug problems have been associated primarily with young males living in urban areas characterized by socioeconomic disadvantage. Although young people who live in poverty continue to be particularly susceptible to heavy or problematic patterns of drug consumption (Mayock 2002, 2005), it is increasingly recognized that, irrespective of social class or gender, adolescents of all ages are susceptible to illicit drug experimentation and use. In recent years, there has been much public debate and concern about substance use among adolescents and about alcohol consumption and "binge" drinking, in particular.

Research on psychological problems in Irish school-going adolescents has been carried out with varying results across a number of studies. Lawlor and James (2000) found that 21.3% of 16-year-olds attending second-level schools in one regional district (the North Eastern Health Board) reported problems that place them in the clinical range of total problem score on the Youth Self Report, with 23% of girls compared with 19% of boys reporting problems in the clinical range. There is also evidence that psychological problems persist in both adolescent males and females from mid- through to late adolescence (James et al. 2004). Research also indicates that being a victim of bullying is significantly associated with depression and suicidal ideation among 12- to 15-year-old pupils attending secondary school (Mills et al. 2004). Suicide rates among Irish adolescents have risen markedly in the past ten years, particularly among Irish males and to a lesser degree among adolescent females. Rates of suicide in 15- to 24-year-old Irish males per 100,000 have increased from 5.79 in 1980, to 14.52 in 1990, and 25.93 in the year 2000 (Central Statistics Office 2003). Suicide is now the leading cause of death in Irish males in this age range, having surpassed road traffic accidents (Lynch et al. 2004).

Ireland has a low level of recorded crime when examined in an international context and overall trends suggest that recorded crime involving juveniles has remained steadily low over the last decade (Walsh 2005). Crime prevention initiatives in Ireland have involved increased investment in projects to tackle disadvantage and social exclusion among children and young people. However, the virtual absence of research means that baseline information is rarely available about the suitability and appropriateness of planned criminal justice interventions (Seymour 2006).

Education

A system of state-funded denominational schooling dominates in Ireland and the majority of adolescents attend Roman Catholic schools. Education in Ireland is compulsory until the age of 16 years. Available figures suggest that 98% of males and 100% of females at age 15 were enrolled in educational institutions in the 2003/4 school year (Central Statistics Office 2005). While this figure was similar at age 16, the figures for 17-year-old males and females dropped to 79% and 92%, respectively.

Single-sex schooling remains relatively commonplace, particularly at the second level, where 39% of second-level students are in single-sex schools. At second level, the curriculum centers around formal accreditation through state examinations, with the Junior Certificate taken at the end of the first three years and the Leaving Certificate after an additional two or three years. During the 1990s a more differentiated Leaving Certificate curriculum was developed and extended to include the Leaving Certificate Applied and Vocational programs. Irish is a compulsory subject in both primary and second-level schools but there are circumstances in which exemption is granted to students (e.g., if s/he has a learning disability or has not lived and been educated in Ireland prior to age 11). The average period spent in the Irish education system is 16.7 years (OECD 2005). Ireland spends almost €6,000 per year on students on average in the education system, which is significantly below the OECD average.

A number of special schools cater for pupils between 5 and 18 years old, and special classes for students with special educational needs are provided in some post-primary schools. These classes usually cater for the learning needs of students with a mild or moderate level of learning disability. The Department of Education and Science provides extra resources for schools in designated areas of disadvantage and also provides extra teaching hours for students who are members of the traveling community. The Centre for Talented Youth in Ireland, located in Dublin City University, provides programs for gifted children and adolescents between the ages of 8 and 16 years and also provides support for parents and teachers.

A dramatic increase in participation at secondary school has been evident in Ireland since the early 1980s. Between 1980 and 1998, the proportion of students taking the Leaving Certificate examination increased from 60% to 82% (National Economic and Social Forum (NESF) 2002). However, despite this increase, participation continues to be strongly influenced by socioeconomic background and is far higher among those adolescents from professional backgrounds than among those from unskilled manual backgrounds. Early school leaving has been identified as among the most serious social and economic problems facing certain sectors of Irish adolescents and is strongly associated with social class (NESF 2002).

In the 2003 PISA International Assessment of Mathematics, Reading Literacy, Science and Problem Solving among 15-year-olds, Ireland was ranked sixth out of 29 countries participating on reading literacy, thirteenth on science, seventeenth on overall mathematics and eighteenth on cross-curricular problem solving. Male students outperformed females in mathematics, while females outperformed males in reading. The distribution of achievement was narrower in Ireland than in most OECD countries, indicating greater equity in student outcomes in Ireland, while still achieving comparatively good scores among lower achievers (Cosgrove et al. 2003). Ireland has one of the highest rates of upper secondary graduation among OECD countries, with over 90% of students graduating (OECD 2005).

Work

A considerable number of Irish young people have a paid job while at school and schools and teachers have expressed concerns over the effects of employment on students' school participation and attainment.

In a study carried out in 16 Dublin schools, Morgan (2000b) found that three-quarters of Junior Certificate, fifth year, and Leaving Certificate (age 15 to 18 years) students held a part-time job. A more recent study designed to assess the prevalence, nature, and impact of part-time employment among school students found that over 60% of Leaving Certificate students had a regular part-time job (McCoy and Smyth 2004). Boys were found to work longer hours than girls, with 23% of male, compared to 12% of female students working more than 20 hours weekly. This study also found that school-going adolescents work to finance short-term consumption (entertainment, clothing, and music) rather than because of financial difficulty and indicated that, on average, working students achieved lower grades than students not in paid employment. Students who did not engage in part-time employment while at school were found to be motivated by a concern about grades and examination performance. The Protection of Young Persons (Employment) Act (1996) imposes certain limitations on the employment of young people. Under the terms of the Act, a student must be at least 15 years of age to be employed during the school term. The Act also stipulates that, before employing a young person, an employer must see evidence of age, and before employing under-16s must get written permission of a parent. However, concern has been expressed regarding the enforcement of this legislation and there is a general belief that legislation in this area is more often breached than observed by employers (McCoy and Smyth 2004).

Media

Children's and young people's exposure to the electronic media has increased dramatically since the arrival of Irish TV in 1963. Such exposure has brought about change in adolescents' knowledge of, and familiarity with, the wider world and with the adult world in all its manifestations. For example, it is estimated that over half of general audience programs broadcast on Irish TV contain sexual references, although the vast majority of this material would be considered "cursory" or "mild" (MacKeogh 2004). Over the years, concern has been expressed about the negative impact of media messages on children and young people. For example, it is claimed that teenagers are strongly influenced by alcohol advertising and that they associate many alcoholic products with pleasure, fun, and with cool and sophisticated places and people (Dring and Hope 2001). This study also produced evidence that adolescents believed particular beverages and brands to have sexual currency. Apart from potentially influencing young people's views and perspectives on a whole range of issues, the Irish media play a prominent role in shaping public discourse on adolescence and have contributed strongly to Ireland's ongoing conversation with itself about the state of "its youth" (Devlin 2003). There are many examples of bouts of media coverage of adolescent hedonism, including drinking and drunkenness, drug use, and risky or "inappropriate" sexual behavior. Media coverage has also played a part in creating a misplaced fear of juvenile crime (Walsh 2005).

Politics and Military

The political situation in Ireland is very stable and is still dominated by parties that emerged during the Civil War, most of which are moderate in their political ideologies. In the 2002 general election 42% of 18- to 19-year-olds exercised their right to vote, and this figure was half the voting rate of those over the age of 55 years. There is considerable concern about the political apathy of young people and their lack of participation in politics, both in terms of voting rates and membership of political parties. A relatively small number of young people have a passionate commitment to "green" or human rights issues or to paramilitary republican activities, but they are in a minority and are not representative of youth in Ireland.

There is no compulsory military service in Ireland. Joining the armed forces is voluntary and the size of the military is small, in any case, by international standards. Most of its activities are related to peacekeeping and, with the positive recent developments in relation to Northern Ireland, the Irish army now uses less of its resources on border duties.

Unique Issues

Knowledge about the status of young people in Ireland is patchy but will be greatly strengthened when the findings of the National Longitudinal Study of Children in Ireland, due to commence in 2006, come on stream. The study, which will be conducted by a team led by the Economic and Social Research Institute and Trinity College Dublin, is government-funded and will follow two cohorts, one of 10,000 9-month-olds and one of 8,000 9-year-olds. This study should help in addressing issues presently under-researched, such as the specific experience of adolescents growing up in rural areas.

Young people in Ireland are living in a country that is experiencing a period of unprecedented affluence and economic growth. Unlike previous generations, they are not facing the threat of having to emigrate in order to make a living. At the same time, Ireland has become more cosmopolitan and Irish young people travel abroad frequently and have taken on the values and aspirations typical of their counterparts in the affluent minority economies. They are generally well-educated and can be optimistic about their employment prospects. The growth in the number of young immigrants and children born in Ireland to emigrants has transformed and will continue to transform what was until recently a very homogenous society. Ireland now faces the challenge of successfully integrating these children and young people who have different ethnic, religious, and cultural commitments. Irish young people who grow up in poverty have an unequal chance of thriving and succeeding in modern Ireland. They disproportionately occupy the ranks of the homeless, the unemployed, drug addicted, and the imprisoned.

SHEILA GREENE and PAULA MAYOCK

References and Further Reading

Alber, J., J. Delhey, W. Keck, and R. Nauenberg. 2005. *Quality of life in Europe: First European quality of life survey 2003*. Luxembourg: European Foundation for the Improvement of Living and Working Conditions.

Breen, M. 2002. Different from their elders and betters: Age cohort differences in the Irish data of the European Values Study (EVS) 1999. In *Measuring Ireland: Discerning values and beliefs*. E. G. Cassidy (ed.). Dublin: Veritas Publications.

Casey, S., and M. O'Connell. 2000. Pain and prejudice: Assessing the experience of racism in Ireland. In *Cultivating pluralism: Psychological, social and cultural perspectives on a changing Ireland*. M. Maclachlan and M. O'Connell (eds.). Dublin: Oak Tree Press.

Cassidy, E. G. 2002. Modernity and religion in Ireland 1980–2000. In *Measuring Ireland: Discerning values and beliefs*. E. G. Cassidy (ed.). Dublin: Veritas Publications.

Central Statistics Office. 2003. Rates of suicide in Ireland. http://www.cso.ie.

Central Statistics Office. 2005. *Statistical yearbook of Ireland 2005*. Dublin: Central Statistics Office.

Cosgrove, J., G. Shiel, N. Sonfroniu, et al. 2003. *Education for life: The achievements of 15-year-olds in the second cycle of PISA (summary report)*. Dublin: Educational Research Centre.

Daly, M., and M. Leonard. 2002. *Against all odds: Family life on a low income in Ireland*. Dublin: Combat Poverty Agency.

Devlin, M. 2003. A bit of the "other": Media representations of young people's sexuality. *Irish Journal of Sociology* 12(2):86–106.

Dillon, M. 1984. Youth culture in Ireland. *The Economic and Social Review* 15(3):153–72.

Dring, C., and A. Hope. 2001. *The impact of alcohol advertising on teenagers in Ireland*. Dublin: Department of Health and Children.

Dunne, M., D. Seery, E. O'Mahoney, and M. Grogan. 1997. *What on earth are they doing?* Cork: Cork AIDS Alliance.

Economic and Social Research Institute. 1998. *Annual school leavers survey*. Dublin: Economic and Social Research Institute.

Fahey, T., L. Delaney, and B. Gannon. 2005. *School children and sport in Ireland*. Dublin: Economic and Social Research Institute.

Fahey, T., B. Hayes, and R. Sinnott. 2005. *Conflict and consensus: A study of values and attitudes in the Republic of Ireland and Northern Ireland*. Dublin: IPA.

Fitzgerald, M., A. P. Joseph, M. Hayes, and M. O'Regan. 1995. Leisure activities of adolescent children. *Journal of Adolescence* 18:349–58.

Gay/HIV Strategies and NEXUS. 2000. *Education: Lesbian and gay students*. Dublin: Gay HIV Strategies.

Greene, S. 1994a. Growing up Irish: Development in context. *Irish Journal of Psychology* 15(2 & 3):354–71.

Greene, S. 1994b. Why do parents smack their children? *Journal of Child-Centred Practice* 1:27–38.

Hannan, D. F., E. Smyth, J. McCullagh, et al. 1994. *Co-educational gender equality*. Dublin: Oak Tree Press.

Health Protection Surveillance Centre. 2005. *Newly diagnosed HIV infections in Ireland: Quarter 3 and 4 2004 & 2004 annual summary*. Dublin: Health Protection Surveillance Centre.

Hibell, B., B. Andersson, S. Ahlstrom, et al. 2000. *The 1999 ESPAD report: Alcohol and other drug use among students in 30 European countries*. Stockholm: Council of Europe, Pompidou Group.

Hogan, D., A. Halpenny, and S. Greene. 2002. *Children's experience of parental separation*. Dublin: Children's Research Centre.

Hyde, A., and E. Howlett. 2004. *Understanding teenage sexuality in Ireland*. Dublin: Crisis Pregnancy Agency.

Immigrant Council of Ireland. 2004. *Voices of immigrants: The challenges of inclusion*. Dublin: Immigrant Council of Ireland.

Inglis, T. 1998. *Lessons in Irish sexuality*. Dublin: University College Dublin Press.

James, D., M. Lawlor, and N. Sofroniou. 2004. Persistence of psychological problems in adolescents: A one year follow up study. *Irish Journal of Psychological Medicine* 21(1):11–17.

Lawlor, M., and D. James. 2000. Prevalence of psychological problems in Irish school going adolescents. *Irish Journal of Psychological Medicine* 17(4):117–22.

Leonard, M. 2004. Teenage girls and housework in Irish society. *Irish Journal of Sociology* 13(1):73–87.

Lodge, A., and K. Lynch. 2003. Young people's equality concerns: The invisibility of diversity. In *Encouraging voices: Respecting the insights of young people who have been marginalised*. M. Shevlin and R. Rose (eds.). Dublin: National Disability Authority.

Lynch, F., C. Mills, I. Daly, and C. Fitzpatrick. 2004. Challenging times: A study to detect Irish adolescents at risk of psychiatric disorders and suicidal ideation. *Journal of Adolescence* 27:300–441.

Mac an Ghaill, M., J. Hanafin, and P. F. Conway. 2004. *Gender politics and exploring masculinities in Irish education: Teachers, materials and the media*. Dublin: National Council for Curriculum and Assessment.

MacHale, E., and J. Newell. 1997. Sexual behaviour and sex education in Irish school-going teenagers. *International Journal of STD & AIDS* (8):196–200.

MacKeogh, C. 2004. *Teenagers and the media: A media analysis of sexual content on television*. Dublin: Crisis Pregnancy Agency.

Mayock, P. 2002. Drug pathways, transitions and decisions: The experiences of young people in an inner-city Dublin community. *Contemporary Drug Problems* 29 (1):117–56.

Mayock, P. 2004. Binge drinking and the consumption of pleasure. In *Binge drinking and youth culture: Alternative perspective*. M. MacLachlan and C. Smyth (eds.). Dublin: Liffey Press.

Mayock, P. 2005. "Scripting" risk: Young people and the construction of drug journeys. *Drugs: Education, Prevention and Policy* 12(5):249–368.

Mayock, P., and T. Byrne. 2004. *A study of sexual health issues, attitudes and behaviours: The views of early school leavers*. Dublin: Crisis Pregnancy Agency.

McCoy, S., and E. Smyth. 2004. *At work in school: Part-time employment among second level students.* Dublin: The Liffey Press.

McKeown, K., H. Ferguson, and D. Rooney. 1998. *Changing fathers? Fatherhood and family life in modern Ireland.* Cork: Collins Press.

Mills, C., S. Guerin, F. Lynch, et al. 2004. The relationship between bullying, depression and suicidal thoughts/behaviour in Irish adolescents. *Irish Journal of Psychological Medicine* 21(4):112–16.

Morgan, M. 2000a. *Relationships and sexuality education: An evaluation and review of implementation.* Dublin: Stationery Office.

Morgan, M. 2000b. *School and part-time work in Dublin—The facts.* Dublin: Dublin Employment Pact. Policy Paper No. 4.

National Economic and Social Forum. 2002. *Early school leavers.* Dublin: National Economic and Social Forum.

Norman, J. 2004. *A survey of teachers on homophobic bullying in Irish second-level schools.* Dublin: School of Education Studies, Dublin City University.

Organization for Economic and Co-operative Development. 2005. *Education at a glance 2005 executive summary.* Organization for Economic and Co-operative Development.

Seymour, M. 2006. Transition and reform: Juvenile justice in the Republic of Ireland. In *International handbook of juvenile justice.* J. Junger-Tas and S. Becker (eds.). Springer Publications.

Walsh, D. 2005. *Juvenile justice.* Dublin: Thompson Round Hall and Dept of Justice, Equality and Law Reform.

ISRAEL

Background Information

Israel was established as a state in 1948, following a 1947 UN resolution to establish a Jewish state in parts of Palestine. At that time, the local population consisted of 640,000 Jews and 1,300,000 Arabs (Kimmerling 2001). However, the war that broke out following the UN resolution and the establishment of the State of Israel, as well as the massive immigration of Jews to Israel, led to drastic demographic changes.

By the end of 2005, the Israeli population consisted of 5,238,000 Jews, 1,340,000 Arabs and Druzes, and 292,000 non-Jewish new immigrants (Israel Central Statistical Bureau 2005), inhabiting an area of 22,145 square kilometers (not including the West Bank area). Among the non-Jewish population, 63% are Muslims, 9% are Christians, 8% are Druze, and 20% are of unclassified religion. Until August 2005, about 4% of the Jewish population lived in the West Bank (*Jehuda VeShomron*) and the Gaza Strip, reduced to 3% following the Israeli disengagement from the Gaza Strip. The Jewish population is older than the Arab population: 33% and 51% of the Jewish and Arab population, respectively, are children and adolescents under age 20, and 25% and 41% of the Jewish and Arab population, respectively, are children and adolescents under age 14 (Israel Central Statistical Bureau 2004).

Geographically, Israel is part of the Middle East. Politically, economically, educationally, and culturally it is in line with modern, Western, industrial countries. The establishment of Israel as a democratic Jewish-nation state, the Declaration of Independence promising full social and political equality to all its citizens, and the Israeli "Law of Return" granting citizenship to almost every Jew created many inner tensions. Thus, Arabs and Druzes have been citizens participating in the democratic life but have not had equal access to educational and economic resources. Consequently, in 2002 the median level of education for the Jewish population was 12.6 years and for the non-Jewish populations (Arabs, Druzes, and others of unspecified religion) was 11.2 years (Israel Central Statistical Bureau 2003). Whereas among Jewish adults (25 to 54 age group) the median years of education of men and women is similar, with older women (45 to 54) having only slightly fewer years of education than men (12.5 and 13.0 for women and men, respectively), among the non-Jewish adults, women are considerably less educated than men. For the 35 to 44 age group, the median years of education is 10.6 and 11.3 and for the 45 to 54 age group the median is 8.1 and 10.3, for women and men respectively (Israel Central Statistical Bureau 2004). Of the total Jewish and Arab workforce, 10% and 11% respectively have been unemployed. Unemployment goes down with years of education so that 17% of the labor force with 0 to 4 years of education and 6% of the 16+ years of education have been unemployed (Israel Central Statistical Bureau 2004).

Period of Adolescence

Adolescence is a marked developmental period in all sections of the Israeli population. Legally, its end is marked by the minimal age of marriage: 17 for girls and 18 for boys. While the biological indicator of puberty is individual, entrance into junior high school at age 13 (seventh grade) may be regarded as a collective marker of the beginning of adolescence.

The trend of an extended adolescence and the emergence of the new developmental period referred to as emerging adulthood (Arnett 2000) that characterizes the Western world has also been prevalent in Israel. One clear indicator is mean age of marriage: for Jewish women and men it rose from 22 and 25 respectively in 1970 to 25 and 27 in 2002. For Muslim, Christian, and Druze women it rose from 20, 22, and 19 respectively in 1970 to 22, 24, and 22 respectively in 2002. For Muslim, Christian, and Druze men it rose from 24, 28, and 23, respectively in 1970 to 26, 29, and 26, respectively in 2002 (Israel Central Statistical Bureau 2004).

Military service, compulsory for Jewish girls and boys (with several exceptions reported in the Politics and Military section) and for Druze boys, creates a special developmental setting in which at the age period of 18 to 21, individuals have opportunities for assuming high personal responsibility within a hierarchical military framework. Adolescents not participating in military service (i.e., Jewish religious girls and Orthodox boys, Arab adolescents, and Druze girls) may continue their education by studying either at one of Israel's universities, colleges, or teachers' colleges or (for Orthodox boys) pursuing religious studies (*Yeshiva*).

Altogether, adolescence has been considered an important developmental period in Israel and especially in the Jewish Israeli ethos. Two conditions have led to it: the history of Israeli Jewish society as founded by young adults (who immigrated to Palestine at the end of the nineteenth century and the first half of the twentieth century), and Israel's condition as a society at war depending on its young generation for defense.

The first condition is illustrated by the role high school students (the *Herzelia gymnasium*) played in the early years of the twentieth century in determining Hebrew (rather than German) as the language of school learning and teaching (Seginer 1999). The second condition is illustrated by the relatively young age of army high-ranking officers. However, as entrance to adulthood has been gradually delayed in recent decades, economic, political, and military advancement is slower and army soldiers (age 18 to 21) are often referred to as "children."

Beliefs

Israel is a multiethnic, multicultural society. As such, it is not possible to describe it as guided by a single value orientation. Instead, some sectors of Israeli society endorse collectivistic orientations and some hold more individualistic orientations. This division overlaps with ethnicity and religious beliefs. Ethnic minorities in Israel, and particularly the Arabs and the Druzes, tend to endorse more collectivistic value orientations than do Jewish Israelis (Seginer and Vermulst 2002). However, within Israeli Jewish society, orthodox Jews endorse more collectivistic value orientations than do traditional and nonreligious Jewish Israelis.

Research on political attitudes of parents and their adolescent children (Ichilov 1985) indicates that in Israel, as in other Western settings, values and beliefs are mainly transmitted within the family (Grusec 2002). However, the nature of Israel as a multiethnic, multicultural nation has led the school system to take upon itself the responsibility for maintaining national solidarity (Dror 2004). Thus, the present minister of education has instructed all schools to place the Israeli flag in each classroom.

Regardless of religious practicing, Israeli Jews celebrate the Bar Mitzvah of their sons (at age 13) and the Bat Mitzvah of their daughters (at age 12). In the majority of families, including families who do not practice religion in everyday life, the Bar Mitzvah celebration also involves a symbolic religious ceremony that takes place in the synagogue and for which the boy prepares himself for several months. Nevertheless, for nonreligious adolescents and their families, the Bar Mitzvah celebration is a family rather than a religious event, and its tone is that of a grand birthday party.

Given that puberty starts earlier for girls than for boys, girls celebrate the Bat Mitzvah one year earlier, at age 12. As for boys, the meaning of the Bat Mitzvah for nonreligious and religious girls is considerably different: for religious girls, the Bat Mitzvah marks the beginning of the obligation to follow religious rules (*mitzvoth*), whereas for the nonreligious it is mainly a large-scale birthday party and a big family celebration. A religious Bat Mitzvah ceremony, comparable to that of Bar Mitzvah boys, can be practiced only in Reformist synagogues where women participate in religious ceremonies.

In the seventh grade—the grade in which the majority of children reach their thirteenth birthday—students (girls and boys) work on a family history project devoted to studying and recording their family roots. The children are instructed to trace back the biographical story of their grandparents, underscoring events that have not only family but also national meaning, such as the Holocaust and the survival of the Jewish people and their immigration to Israel. In many schools this assignment is considered a Bar Mitzvah project.

Among the Muslim Arabs and Bedouin tribes in the northern and southern parts of the country no such ceremonies take place. Among Christian Arabs, Catholics hold the Confirmation ceremony.

Gender

Israel's Declaration of Independence, announced on May 15, 1948, guarantees "...full social and political equality of all its citizens, without distinction of race, creed or sex...." Thus, legally, Israeli women of all ethnic groups enjoy equal rights and equal opportunities for education, career, and political participation. In practice, the extent to which legal rights for equality are materialized are both ethnicity and domain specific. Overall, Jewish women are more emancipated and experience greater equality of the sexes than do Arab, Druze, and Bedouin women. However, given that all matters of marriage and divorce are governed by religious rather than by civil law, women often suffer greater inequality in these than in other everyday matters.

Data about gender role expectations draw on girls' responses as well as on objective statistics such as percentage of girls completing high school education and attending higher education programs, and female representation in the world of work and politics. Considering occupations, three issues are particularly relevant: percentage of women holding a paid job, their distribution across different occupations and careers considered "feminine" and "masculine," and their participation in management positions. Considering politics, the relevant issues are the extent to which women are represented in local and state government.

Examination of gender role expectations of Israeli Jewish and Arab girls and boys (Seginer, Karayani, and Mar'i 1990) showed that Jewish adolescents were less conservative than Arab adolescents and girls were less conservative than boys. Research carried out in Jewish schools showed that both teachers (Ben Tsvi-Mayer, Hertz-Lazarovitz, and Safir 1989) and children (Safir, Hertz-Lazarovitz, and Ben Tzvi-Mayer 1992) judged boys more than girls as better students in general, and particularly in mathematics. Teachers (Ben Tsvi-Mayer et al. 1989) judged girls as gaining higher academic achievement than boys in Hebrew, as well as in social skills. Overall, gender stereotypes are shared by teachers and students, and schools may play a role in the transmission of gender stereotypes.

Census data (Israel Central Statistical Bureau 2004) show that among Israeli Palestinian women aged 15 and over, 8% have 16 or more years of education. By comparison, among Israeli Palestinian men aged 15 and over, 10% have 16 or more years of education. Gender differences are more pronounced when the median years of education of adult groups is compared. Specifically, for the group aged 35 to 44 the median for women is 10.6 and for men 11.3, and for the group aged 45 to 54 it is 8.1 and 10.3 years of education. Regarding paid jobs, 23% of Arab women hold part- or full-time paid jobs. Moreover, employment goes up with years of education, so that 10% of the women with 0 to 8 years of education and 66% of the women with 16 or more years of education are holding paid jobs.

Among Israeli Jewish adults, 18% of the women and 19% of the men have 16 or more years of education. The median years of education for women and men in the groups aged 34 to 44 and 45 to 54 is 13. Paid jobs are held by 55% of the women and 60% of the men 15 years old and older. Among women and men with 0 to 8 years of education 14% and 32%, and among women and men with 16 or more years of education, 79% and 76%, respectively, hold paid jobs.

However, poverty, early marriage, childbearing, and growing up in ultra-orthodox families lower girls' chances of entering higher education and pursuing a career. Regarding ultra-orthodox girls, in recent years a growing number of girls have continued education beyond high school in teachers' colleges or other occupational training programs. While this training prepares them for a job they may have to take to increase the family income, it also serves to postpone age of marriage and childbearing.

Arab high school girls—particularly those growing up in traditional Muslim families—are in a quandary. Although believing "education is a weapon in women's hands" (Seginer and Mahajna 2003) and aspiring to university education, the prospects that their families will allow them to travel to the city and enroll in an Israeli university are slim. Instead, they stay home and commute to a Muslim or Jewish teachers' college in their area. The alternative is that they become engaged to get married while still at high school and get married as soon as the law permits it (age 17 for girls).

Globalization of the mass media has led to the rapid transmission of information and values in general and for youth in particular. Consequently, a body image based on the notion that "slim is beautiful" has been adopted by Israeli girls, except for the ultra-orthodox Jewish and traditional Muslim girls. Surveys conducted in 1994 and 1998 (Harel et al. 2002) showed that the number of girls describing themselves as overweight has been 40% and stayed stable over the years. However, a recent survey of the eating habits of Israeli adolescents in the 11 to 15 age group (Harel, Molcho, and Tilinger 2004) showed that although the majority (70%) of Israeli youths think they look good, 24% of the 11-year-old girls and 36% of the 15-year-old girls think they are overweight. This may be related to the finding that 27% of the girls and 12% of the boys of the 11 to 15 age group who participated in the Harel et al. (2004) survey are dieting, but only 14% of them did it under professional supervision. Moreover, although among the 13-year-old age group 10% of the girls and 15% of the boys and 7% of the girls and 14% of the boys among the 15-year-old age group suffer from being overweight, 27% of the girls engage in weight-losing diets (Harel et al. 2004).

Several studies (Lubin, Chetrit, and Modan 1995; Stein, Luria, Tarrasch, Yoeli, Glick, Elizur, and Weizman 1999; Stein, Meged, Bar-Hanin, Blank, Elizur, and Weizman 1997) examined the eating disorders of Israeli Jewish girls. These studies show that eating disorders vary by age and time of assessment and rose considerably from the early to late 1990s. Thus, a study conducted in the early 1990s among women soldiers (18 to 20 years old) showed that the overall frequency of eating disorders ranged from 0.2% anorexics and 0.5% bulimics to 2.4% suffering from a "partial eating disorder syndrome" (Scheinberg, Bleich, and Kolovsky 1992). A study conducted among 12- to 18-year-olds reported 0.5% of the girls as suffering from eating disorders (Mitrany et al. 1995). However, in two studies of high school girls (Stein et al. 1997) and of young Israeli women soldiers (Stein et al. 1999) that assessed partial eating disorders, the numbers were much higher. Specifically, 21% suffered from partial anorexia nervosa and 11% from partial bulimia nervosa. These findings may explain the great concern in Israel with eating disorders, which are treated by about 20 eating disorders clinics and centers (Latzer, in press).

The Self

Israel, as noted previously, is a multiethnic, multicultural society. Hence, issues of personal and cultural identity should be analyzed in their sociocultural context. Among the Israeli Jewish population, the main cultural groups are: the secular Israeli-born, the national-religious (modern orthodox), the ultra-orthodox, immigrants from former Soviet Union countries, and immigrants from Ethiopia. Among the non-Jewish population, the main groups are Muslim and Christian Arabs, Druzes, and Bedouins. For reasons of access and researchers' interests, data on issues pertinent to personal and cultural identity are inconsistent, and cultural identity has been studied especially among the non-Jewish and Jewish new immigrants.

Data on personal identity draws on studies of the self-concept of young (Seginer and Somech 1991) and middle (Seginer and Flum 1987) adolescents and their self-esteem (e.g., Kurman 2003; Seginer, Vermulst, and Shoyer 2004) and studies of adolescents' future orientation (e.g., Seginer et al. 2004) describing adolescents' anticipated self. These findings suggest that when responding to multiple self-image scales such as the SIQYA (Petersen, Schulenberg, Abramowitz, Offer, and Jarco 1984) and the OSIQ (Offer, Ostrov, and Howard 1982), young and middle adolescents describe themselves

favorably. Specifically, on a scale of 1 to 5, the self-image scores of young adolescents range from 4.3 to 4.8 (Seginer and Somech 2001). The self-image of young and middle adolescents (Seginer and Flum 1987) was computed as standard scores; compared to an American norm group, Israeli Jewish adolescents scored higher on all the psychological (e.g., impulse control), family, and coping (e.g., superior adjustment) self scales and lower on the sexual self and two of the three social self scales (morals and vocational-educational goals). Moreover, young adolescents' self-image is more positive than the image teachers and educational counselors hold of them (Seginer and Somech 1991).

Analysis of self indicators of new immigrants from the former Soviet Union and of veteran Israeli adolescents (Ullman and Tatar 1999, 2001) showed that while the multiple changes new immigrant adolescents experience did not affect their global self-esteem, adolescents who recently immigrated (less than five years since immigration) were more engaged in self exploration, as a precondition for forging an Israeli identity and developing a sense of integration and belongingness.

Future orientation data show that middle adolescents construct their prospective life space in terms of core life domains common to adolescents across different cultural settings and setting-specific domains (Seginer 2005). The core domains pertain to higher education, career, marriage and family, and self concerns ("to be happy") and the setting-specific domains are military service for Jewish adolescents and Druze boys, and significant others and the collective for Arab and Druze adolescents.

These data show that despite political and cultural differences, the constructed future space of Jewish, Arab, and Druze adolescents is partly similar (Seginer 2001). Specifically, about 25% of the future life space of adolescents of all three political-cultural groups relates to work and career and about 20% to self concerns. They differ in the extent to which three life domains are represented in their future life space: higher education (16%, 26%, and 16% for Jewish, Arab, and Druze adolescents, respectively), collective issues (1%, 6%, and 1% for Jewish, Arab, and Druze adolescents, respectively), and military service, which is relevant only to Jewish adolescents (15%) and Druze boys (12%). The constructed future life space of former–Soviet Union immigrants (Toren-Kaplan 1995) differed from that of their Israeli-born classmates, particularly in one life domain: military service, which was less salient for the former–Soviet Union immigrants than for the Israeli-born adolescents.

The hegemonic Israeli society in place since the pre-state era has traditionally consisted mainly of East European Jews and their descendents, and the expectation for new immigrants has been to be "absorbed" into this society and adopt its values and norms (Eisenstadt 1952; Kimmerling 2001). Thus, research on new immigrants in general and on recent new immigrants from the former Soviet Union and Ethiopia in particular has been mainly concerned with acculturation patterns. These studies showed that, despite cultural differences, adolescents who immigrated from both the former Soviet Union and Ethiopia were more inclined to balance their established cultural identity and their new Israeli identity than to reject one at the expense of the other (Orr, Mana, and Mana 2003). Several studies (e.g., Mirsky and Prawer 1992; Toren-Kaplan 1995) of adolescents who immigrated from the former Soviet Union during the 1990s showed that only a minority (8% to 27%) considered themselves Israelis, whereas the majority considered themselves either Jews or Russians. Toward the end of their high school education—when Israeli youths start their military service—30% of the former Soviet Union adolescent immigrants did not want to serve in the army (in comparison to 10% of veteran adolescents) (Tatar et al. 1994).

During some of the time adolescents spend alone they use electronic media, either passively by watching TV or listening to the radio or actively by using the Internet and entering chat sites (Lemish and Liebes 1999). These data are presented in the section on media use.

Family Relationships

The majority of Israeli children—86% of the Jewish children and 94% of Arab and Druze children and youth (age 0 to 24)—grow up in two-parent biological families (Israel Central Statistical Bureau 2004). While in recent years the rate of divorce in Israeli families has risen (e.g., from 5% in 1961 to 15% in 2001) (Israel Central Bureau of Statistics 2004), overall it is still lower than in many Western countries. This rise has been related to world divorce trends and to the massive immigration from the former Soviet Union countries during the 1990s, which included a relatively large number of single-parent families. In 1992, 13% of families with children (Habib et al. 1998) and in 1995 20% of families with children that immigrated from former Soviet Union countries were single-parent families; by comparison, in 1995 the rate of single-parent families in the rest of the Jewish population was one-third of it (Horowitz 1995). This immigration also differed from other Israeli groups in having more three-generation households than among the veteran Jewish population in Israel.

As in other Western countries (e.g., Larson, Richards, Moneta, and Holmbeck 1986), as children grow up and enter adolescence relatively more of their time is spent with unrelated peers than with family members. However, this pattern is somewhat different for Arab and Druze adolescents, for in their culture there is more overlap between family and peer relationships, so that one's social circle consists mainly of kin (Seginer 1992). However, spending more time with peers does not affect the sense of closeness Jewish adolescents feel with their parents.

Several studies conducted in the last two decades indicate that Israeli Jewish adolescents experience warm relationships with their parents. Specifically, in a survey of a random-systematic sample of 13- to 18-year-old Israeli Jewish adolescents (Sherer, Karnieli-Miller, Eizikovitz, and Fishman 2001), two-thirds of the respondents felt close to their parents, thought their parents readily listened to their problems, and got along well with them.

This pattern was also found in an earlier study (Seginer and Flum 1987) of Israeli Jewish adolescents (aged 14 to 18) where the majority (75%) described themselves as having good relationships with their parents, and over half of them took part in family decision making, felt their parents were proud of them, accepted parents' authority, and would like their future families to be similar to their own families. Overall, the family relationships score of the Israeli Jewish adolescents was higher than that of the American adolescents' norm group.

More recent data (Seginer 2000) comparing adolescent–parent relationships among Israeli Jewish and Arab adolescents (eleventh graders) showed that Jewish adolescents describe both their mothers and fathers as more emotionally accepting and as providing greater emotional support than do Arab adolescents, and Arab girls describe their mothers and fathers as more accepting than do Arab boys.

Much of the recent research on adolescent–parent relationships focused on the effect of positive parenting—as perceived by adolescents and/or as reported by parents—on Jewish adolescents' functioning. Several studies (Mayseless, Scharf, and Sholt 2003; Scharf and Mayseless 2001; Seginer 1998; Seginer et al. 2004) conceptualized positive parenting in terms of acceptance and independence granting (Epstein 1983) whereas others (Ben-Zur 2003; Shulman and Ben Artzi 2003) employed indices of emotional closeness between adolescents and parents.

Overall, these studies showed the facilitating weight of positive parenting on such indicators of psychological functioning as life satisfaction (Ben-Zur 2003), coping and adaptation of adolescent boys (age 18) to military service (Mayseless, Scharf, and Sholt 2003), relationships with close friends (Scharf and Mayseless 2001), sibling relationships (Seginer 1998), adult status (pertaining to self-governance, consolidated outlook of life, and practical independence), ego identity (Shulman and Ben Artzi 2003), and the construction of future orientation about education (Seginer 2005), career, and family (Seginer et al. 2004).

Affectionate parenting—similar in definition to positive parenting—also has been related to the extent to which Jewish adolescents (aged 16 to 18) accurately perceived both mothers' and fathers' values (Knafo and Schwartz 2003). However, studies examining the effect of adolescent–parent relationships on adolescents' outlook on life (Ben-Zur 2003; Shulman and Ben Artzi 2003) showed that only the adolescent–father relationship reached a significant effect.

Whereas much of this research was conducted as a single time point design, at least one study (Aviezer, Sagi, Resnick, and Gini 2002) demonstrated the long-term effects of parenting on adolescent outcomes. This study examined the effect of infancy attachment to mother on the school adaptation of kibbutz-raised early adolescents (12-year-olds), demonstrating that infant attachment to mother (but not to father) had a direct net effect on young adolescents' emotional maturity and scholastic skills beyond concurrent effects of representation of relationships (indicated by Separation Anxiety Test), self-esteem, and changes in caregiving arrangements (age of transition from communal to home sleeping arrangements).

The effect of parenting on the psychological functioning of Arab and Druze adolescents has been less often studied. However, recent studies employing an Arabic version of the Mother-Father scale (Epstein 1983) showed the positive effect of positive parenting on psychological empowerment (Mahajna 2005), optimism (Suleiman 2000), future orientation about career (Margieh 2005), higher education and family (Mahajna 2005; Margieh 2005; Seginer and Mahajna 2003, 2004), and sibling relationships (Huseissi 1999; Tanus 1999). Thus, altogether, the effect of positive parenting—indexed by such indicators as emotional acceptance and independence granting—on the growth and development of Israeli Jewish, Arab, and Druze adolescents is similar to that reported in research conducted in other Western countries.

Adolescent–sibling relationships have been studied in the Jewish, Arab, and Druze communities. All studies (Huseissi 1999; Seginer 1992, 1998; Tanus 1999) showed that, when asked to relate to the one sibling they considered closest to them, eleventh graders of all three ethnic groups describe relationships with this sibling as consisting of high warmth (indicated by such indices as friendship, intimacy, and admiration) and low negative relationships (indicated by such indices as rivalry, jealousy, and antagonism).

However, the meaning of sibling relationships among the three ethnic groups may differ. This is particularly reflected in the role of the older sister, considered in the Arab but not in the Jewish families as the "mother deputy" (Seginer 1992) whose responsibilities change with siblings' age. Whereas at a younger age her responsibilities are mainly in helping her mother with household chores and care of her younger siblings, as the family grows older and the younger sisters (but never any of the brothers) share with her household chores, the responsibilities of the older sister shift to the interpersonal realm.

This is reflected mainly in two responsibilities assumed by older sisters. One is counseling her younger sisters about issues ranging from school matters to relationships with boys that their mother—leading a more traditional life—is unfamiliar with. The second is acting as a mediator between the young adolescent girl and her mother, who in turn will negotiate the issue in question (e.g., participating in a school trip) with the father, as the family head.

Friends and Peers/Youth Culture

Two recent surveys (Harel, Ellenbogen-Frankovits, Molcho, Abu-Asba, and Habib 2002; Sherer et al. 2001) examined peer relationships, focusing on the frequency of spending time with peers after school and on attitudes toward friends. Their findings show that of the Jewish respondents, 87% strongly agreed and only 2% disagreed with the statement "it is important for me to spend time with friends" (Sherer et al. 2001). The majority (75% to 80%) of these respondents also reported having close friends for many years who were willing to listen to their problems (66% endorsed the "strongly agree" category).

Moreover, as adolescents move from young (age 13 to 14) to middle adolescence (age 17 to 18) they feel closer to their friends, get along with them, and feel friends willingly listen to their problems. In a similar vein, less than 10% reported having only one or no friends (Harel et al. 2002). Separate analyses for Arabs and Jews showed that more Arab than Jewish adolescents (25% and 6%, respectively) reported having only one or no friends. The difference is particularly noticed among boys (29% and 6% for Arab and Jewish adolescents, respectively). However, the larger number of siblings and greater proximity to extended family (see the family relationships section) may explain this difference.

Friendship patterns notwithstanding, time spent with friends is similar for Jewish and Arab adolescents. Specifically, 41% of the Jewish adolescents and 38% of the Arab adolescents spend four or five afternoons each week with their friends and 19% of both Jewish and Arab adolescents spend five or more evenings per week with friends. Gender differences in number of evenings spent with friends were found only among Arab adolescents: fewer girls (14%) than boys (25%) spend five or more evenings with friends (Harel et al. 2002).

One correlate of peer relationships is Internet use. A recent study (Mesch 2001) indicated that in a multivariate analysis controlling for demographic characteristics as well as several leisure time activities (e.g., reading books, participating in parties), peer relationships and prosocial attitudes were negatively related to Internet use among a representative sample of 13- to 18-year-old Jewish adolescents. Unfortunately, data for Arab adolescents and for such groups as new immigrants from the former Soviet Union and Ethiopia are not available.

A basic assumption of peer relationships research has been that these relationships occur within ethnically homogeneous groups. Given that to date the majority of countries are multicultural, a recent study (Pitner, Asor, Benbenisty, Haj-Yahia, and Zeira 2003) on ingroup and outgroup peer retribution in the Israeli context where Jewish adolescents are the majority and Arab adolescents are the minority is an important development in peer relationships research.

Findings of this study showed the asymmetry between the stereotypes Jewish and Arab adolescents hold about the other group: 88% of the Jewish adolescents and 50% of the Arab adolescents believed adolescents from the outgroup (Arabs in the case of Jews and Jews in the case of Arabs) were more violent than adolescents from the ingroup. Regardless of ethnicity, more girls than boys believed Arab adolescents were more violent than Jewish adolescents. Although the majority of respondents (75% and 76% of the Jewish and Arab adolescents, respectively) condemned violent retribution, Jewish and Arab adolescents differed in the number of violent retribution justifications. For reasons related to cultural orientations or to their status as an ethnic minority, Arab adolescents endorsed more social conventional ("their families do not care") and personal ("they are self-centered and primitive") but not moral ("they hate others for no reason") justifications.

Historically, in the pre-state era and the early years of the State of Israel known as the Golden Period of intensive nation building, youth movements played an important role in the social life and personal, political, and ideological socialization of Jewish adolescents, and balanced individual and collective goals. Consequently, youth movements contributed their share to the nation building and social development of the Israeli Jewish society (Kahane 1997). Ideology varied from centrist (Scouts) to moderate socialist (the Working and Studying Youth), leftist socialists (Young Guards), and national religious (Bnei Akiva), but regardless of ideology all Israeli youth movements were characterized by an informal structure (Kahane 1997).

After the establishment of the State of Israel and the gradual value shift from collectivistic to individualistic orientations, youth movements lost their meaning as the center of peer activities particularly serving as a transitional setting, as well as their role as agents of ideological-political socialization and consequently their public image (Kahane 1997). The exception has been the national religious Bnei Akiva youth movement, that "...has moved in the direction of parochialism, slowly assuming the form of religious sect... [Thus] members of the movement tend to express their religious commitment in extra-institutional activities, such as settlement in disputed territories" (Kahane 1997, p. 94).

As indicated by rate of participation, youth movements attract young rather than middle adolescents. Specifically, 26% of Jewish and 23% of Arab ninth graders but only 15% of the Jewish and 18% of the Arab eleventh graders belong to a youth movement (Harel et al. 2002). Moreover, youth movements appeal more to Jewish girls than boys and more to Arab boys than girls. The age-related decline in youth movement participation suggests change in the nature of youth movement activities.

Over the years, youth movements have retained the form of their activities: members convene twice a week (on a weekday and on Saturday) for a structured afternoon or early evening activity and for more extended activities such as hiking trips or camp activities during school holidays. Altogether, members of Israeli youth movements engage in seven major activities: hiking trips and excursions, camping, political activities, cultural activities, sports, intellectual discussions, and games (Kahane 1997). However, the underlying messages conveyed by these activities vary with the ideological coloring of each youth movement, age of members, and time. For middle adolescents, youth movement membership also offers an opportunity for personal growth and development provided by acting as youth leaders for groups of younger adolescents.

Love and Sexuality

With the exception of one large-scale study (Antonovsky 1980), research on sexual behavior among Israeli youths has been limited to only a few small-scale studies (Harel et al. 2002). Antonovsky's study was large both in terms of number of participants and range of the research questions. The stratified random sample consisted of 5,410 Israeli Jewish girls and boys aged 14 to 15 (younger group) and 16 to 17 (older group). These adolescents attended academic, vocational, agricultural (boarding schools), and apprenticeship secular schools. The research questions related to adolescents' sexuality attitudes and behavior as well as the effect of family, peer, and school settings on them. Although these data were collected over 30 years ago, they show stability over time.

Specifically, the Antonovsky study reported that considerably more older boys than older girls (41% and 16%, respectively) were engaged in sexual relations. A survey conducted 20 years later among secular Jewish adolescents attending the tenth grade (age 16) showed a similar trend: more boys than girls (44% and 11%, respectively) reported they had engaged in sexual relations at least once (Harel et al. 2002). On average, boys started having sexual relations one year before girls (age 14 and 15, respectively).

Pregnancy was reported by 0.6% of the girls, and responsibility for the impregnation of a girl was reported by 4.6% of the boys (Harel et al. 2002). Medical approval for termination of pregnancy for out-of-wedlock pregnancy reasons was given to 1,431 women 19 years old or younger and to 3,343 women 24 years old or younger (1 and 2 out of 100,000, respectively) (Israel Central Statistical Bureau 2003). These figures are an underestimation of pregnancy termination in general and for adolescent girls in particular since they do not include pregnancy termination in private clinics. Condom use was reported by the majority of sexually active boys and girls (83% and 76%, respectively); however, 3% of them contracted sexually transmitted diseases. Although the figures regarding sexual relationships were stable over a period of 30 years, issues like pregnancy, condom use, and sexually transmitted diseases included in the Harel et al. survey were not touched upon by the Antonovsky study.

The prevalence of romantic relationships increases with age. In one study (Shulman and Scharf 2000) of 168 14-, 16-, and 19-year-old Israeli Jewish adolescents, the number of those reported to be currently involved in romantic relationships rose from 15% to 45% to 51%, respectively. Girls of all age groups were involved in romantic relationships for a longer duration and with greater emotional intensity. Moreover, for adolescents engaged in romantic relationships, affect intensity was related to affect intensity with same-sex friends but not with parents.

Although legal, homosexuality is still not socially acceptable in Israel and homosexual and lesbian individuals may suffer discrimination and harassment. According to data published by the Israeli Homosexual, Lesbian, Bisexual and Transgender Association, of the 3,000 individuals asking for help via the Association stress line, 40% were under 22 years of age (Yachad 2002). The Israeli Gay Youth organization is currently operating 15 branches, offering gay youths both help and a place for social activities. The organization is supported by voluntary and professional organizations as well as by the Ministry of Education, and its activities are led by psychologists, social workers, and professionals in the arts (e.g., theater and creative writing) (Israeli Gay Youth 2004). It is important to note, however, that both the adult and the youth organizations serve mainly the Jewish population. At present, no parallel activities and organizations exist in the Arab and Druze sectors.

Health Risk Behavior

According to the 1998 survey (Harel et al. 2002), close to 70% of Jewish adolescents and 80% of Arab adolescents did not drink at all in the 30 days before responding to the questionnaire. Among both Jewish and the Arab adolescents more boys than girls drink at least once a month (37% of the Jewish boys and 22% of the Jewish girls and 31% of the Arab boys and 10% of the Arab girls). The rate of drinking grows higher with age, so that by tenth grade 39% of the Jewish adolescents (49% of the boys and 28% of the girls) and 18% of the Arab adolescents (31% of the boys and 9% of the girls) drink at least once a month.

While for Jewish adolescents pubs are the main source of alcohol, for Arab and Druze adolescents it is the home. Jewish and Druze adolescents obtain alcohol by themselves whereas Muslims get it from same-age friends and Christians from their parents (Weiss 1995). Adolescents studying in vocational schools start drinking earlier than adolescents attending academic high schools (age of drinking initiation 12.8 and 13.4, respectively) and have less knowledge regarding the potential harmful effects of alcohol drinking than have academic school students (Brook and Tepper 2002).

Incidents of getting drunk were reported by fewer Arab (12%) than Jewish (20%) adolescents. The difference between Jewish and Arab adolescents was more due to differences between Jewish (16%) and Arab (4%) girls than boys (24% and 20% for Jewish and Arab boys, respectively). As further noted by Harel et al. (2002), although Israel is ranked last among 29 western countries (e.g., U.K., United States, Canada, Germany, Poland, Russia) in problem drinking, and in the four years between 1994 and 1998 the rate of moderate drinking remained stable, problem drinking among Jewish adolescents rose from 7% to 11% for binge drinking and from 13% to 20% for getting drunk at least once. The rise was greater for boys than for girls, though both sexes reported higher rates of problem drinking in 1998 than in 1994. Changes in alcohol use among Arab adolescents could not be reported because the 1994 survey included only Jewish adolescents. Jewish adolescents listed three reasons for drinking: it prompts a sense of belonging, makes one feel like an adult, and helps one forget daily anxieties and conflicts (Brook and Tepper 2002).

Three surveys conducted in 1992, 1995, and 1998 (Bar-Hamburger 2003) among 12- to 18-year-old adolescents, pointed to two important findings: (1) the number of drug users among adolescents attending school ranges between less than 1% to 12% and is growing: in the period between 1992 and 1998 drug use has increased. (2) Drug consumption varies more by the kind of psychoactive material than by immigration status (i.e., Israeli-born versus old-comers and newly arriving immigrants). To illustrate, in the 1995 survey of 12- to 18-year-old junior and senior high school students, users formed 3.4% of Israeli-born, 2.6% of immigrants arriving until 1985, and 2.7% of immigrants arriving after 1986. More recent estimates (Israeli Knesset 2003) indicate that 10% of Israeli adolescents (age 12 to 18) use drugs, 5% use hard drugs, the age of drug use initiation has been gradually going down, and the number of girls using

drugs is gradually going up so that girls form about 25% of drug users and about 50% of marijuana users.

In a telephone survey conducted in 1995 among Israeli adolescents, 72% of the Israeli-born (n = 922), 71% of the new immigrants arriving until 1988 (n = 38), and 60% of the new immigrants arriving in 1989 and later (n = 63) replied they would refuse using drugs if offered. Among school dropouts, the number of drug users in 1998 was higher, particularly among new immigrants. T illustrate, cannabis has been used by 23% of Israeli-born school dropouts, and 42% and 37% of the new immigrant dropouts arriving to Israel in the time periods of 1988–1992 and 1993–1998, respectively. Hard drugs (e.g., cocaine, heroine, LSD) were used by 12% of Israeli-born school dropouts and by 21% and 9% of the new immigrant adolescents arriving in Israel in the time periods of 1988–1992 and 1993–1998, respectively (Bar-Hamburger 2000).

Recent data on the smoking habits and attitudes of Israeli adolescents were collected as part of the third international survey on social welfare, health, and risk-taking behaviors in international perspective (HBSC) and presented in a report about the smoking habits of Israeli adolescents (Israeli Minister of Health Report on Smoking 2003). This report shows that the average age of cigarette smoking initiation is 13 and that by the time Israeli adolescents reach tenth grade, 12% of the Jewish boys and 8% of the Arab boys smoke at least one cigarette per day. While in comparison to 1998, Jewish and Arab adolescent boys smoke less, Jewish girls smoke more. Knowledge and attitudes about smoking were as follows: 16% of Israeli adolescents did not know that nicotine is habit forming. Whereas 80% of Israeli adolescents agreed smoking at school should be banned, only half of those smoking admitted they were willing to stop smoking.

Age of smoking initiation is considered an important health risk indicator. A recent cross-sectional national survey among adult smokers (Baron-Epel and Haviv-Messika 2004) showed that age of smoking initiation has been going down in recent years so that younger cohorts reported starting at an earlier age. However, Jewish women (56%, compared to 47% among men) and Arab women (90%) and men (60%) start smoking at age 18 or older. Early smoking initiation is associated with several factors, among them legislation (as the tax has gone up and advertisement has been limited cigarettes became less available to adolescents), family factors (one or both parents smoke, family neglect) and demographic factors (more adolescent immigrants from the former Soviet Union than Israeli-born Jews start smoking at an early age).

Recent reports about the prevalence of Nargila (hookah) smoking as a social pastime among Israeli Jewish adolescents (48% and 37% of the Jewish tenth-grade boys and girls, respectively, and 33% and 5% of the Arab tenth-grade boys and girls reported Nargila smoking with friends) and the general public unawareness of its health hazards led the authors of the Israeli Minister of Health Report on Smoking (2003) to devote a large section of the chapter on adolescents' smoking to Nargila smoking. The report indicates that 40% of Jewish sixth, eighth and tenth graders smoked Nargila at least once and that in the eighth- and tenth-grade age groups, the number of Jewish adolescents who experienced Nargila smoking was higher than that among Arab adolescents (57% and 38% of the Jewish and Arab students, respectively).

Data for tenth graders show that Arab boys close the gap between them and Jewish adolescents found for younger ages (62% and 64% of the Arab and Jewish tenth-grade boys, respectively). However, among girls the difference grows larger, as 51% of the Jewish girls and 25% of the Arab girls reported smoking Nargila at least once. The number of regular Nargila smokers is much lower, ranging from about 20% (20% for Jewish boys and 22% for Arab boys) to about 10% (9% and 10% of the Jewish and Arab girls) of once-a-week smokers to less than 10% of the adolescents smoking at least once a day (5% and 8% of the Jewish and Arab eighth-grade boys and 2% and 3% of the Jewish and Arab eighth-grade girls).

Parents' objection to Nargila smoking is relatively low: only 35% to 40% of Nargila smokers reported that their parents disapproved of their Nargila smoking. Moreover, in the Arab section 11% of the young adolescents (sixth graders) smoked Nargila with their parents. However, the hazardous effects of Nargila smoking must be understood in light of the high association between Nargila and cigarette smoking. Specifically, 97% of the adolescents *not* smoking Nargila also do not smoke cigarettes and 85% of those *not* smoking cigarettes also do not smoke Nargila (Israel Minister of Health Report on Smoking 2003).

Israeli police official information (2004) shows that in the two age groups of 17 to 18 and 19 to 29, the percentage of drivers involved in car accidents is higher than their percentage in the drivers' population. Thus, although 2.7% of the total population are 17 to 18 years old, 4.1% of this age group were involved in car accidents. In a similar vein,

14.9% of the total population are 19 to 29 years old, but they were involved in 20.8% of the car accidents. Moreover, for both age groups, involvement in car accidents is caused more by self (as drivers) than by others: of the total number of drivers involved in car accidents, 36.5% are from the 17 to 18 age group and 24% from the 19 to 29 age group.

Official statistics report that the number of committed suicides among children and adolescents up to the age of 17 went up from 9 in 1990 to 15 in 1997 and 14 in 1999 (Israel Central Statistical Bureau 2003). Among the 15 to 24 age group, 53 and 74 youths committed suicide in the years 1996 and 1997, respectively. The rise in the number of committed suicides among this age group reflects a similar trend in the Israeli population at large: the number of persons committing suicide went up from 306 in 1996 to 379 in 1997. In terms of the total number of youths in the 15 to 24 age group, the ratio was 8.6 and 12.6 for 100,000 boys in 1996 and 1997 respectively, and 1.8 for 100,000 girls in both 1996 and 1997 respectively (Israel Central Statistical Bureau 1999). Overall, during the time period of 1998 to 2000, the average number of suicides in the Israeli population was 350. Of them 22% were adolescents (15 to 24 years of age); of the adolescents who committed suicide, 85% were boys (Israel Central Statistical Bureau 2001). Thus, the larger number of committed suicides among men than among women reported in world statistics holds true for Israeli adolescents as well.

The number of suicide attempts is much larger. In the 1997 to 2000 period, the number of emergency room referrals due to suicide attempts was between 3,500 and 4,000 per year. Of the total number of suicide attempts, 35% were committed by individuals aged 15 to 25, 70% of whom were girls. In the 10 to 19 age group, 75% of the suicide attempts were committed by girls and in the 20 to 24 age group, 61% were committed by girls. A follow-up study of adolescents who attempted suicide (Farbstein et al. 2002) found marked differences between the adjustment of girls and boys to military service. Specifically, girls who attempted suicide had slightly more problems than the controls, whereas boys who attempted suicide did very poorly in their military service.

In sum, these data point to three tendencies. One is that in all age groups, including adolescence, suicide is committed by more men than women, but more women than men attempt it. The second is that with age the number of suicide attempts among girls goes down and that of boys goes up.

ISRAEL

The third tendency pertains to the ratio of suicide and suicide attempts of adolescents, which has been higher than their share (18%) in the population (Israel Central Statistical Bureau 2001).

The HBSC (Health Behaviors in School-Aged Children) surveys of Israeli adolescents for 1994 and 1998 (Harel et al. 2002) included a set of items regarding the prevalence of physical and emotional symptoms. Physical symptoms pertained to headache, stomachache, backache, and dizziness. Emotional symptoms pertained to anger, nervousness, or bad mood. Responses indicated that overall, Arab adolescents reported a higher rate of symptoms than did Jewish adolescents.

Thus, 51% of Arab adolescents and 37% of Jewish adolescents reported having physical symptoms at least once a week or more often and 34% of the Arab adolescents and 14% of Jewish adolescents experienced emotional symptoms almost daily. Only 9% of Arab adolescents but 32% of Jewish adolescents reported they feel tired on the way to school at least four times a week. However, twice as many Arab (35%) as Jewish adolescents (17%) find it difficult to fall asleep at night (Harel et al. 2002). Harel et al. (2002) suggested that the markedly higher rate of feeling tired among Jewish than Arab adolescents was related to attitudes toward school, which have been more positive among Arab than among Jewish adolescents (see section on education).

Education

In 2002, the majority of the population aged 15 and over had some education. However, the median level of education for the Jewish population was 12.6 and for the non-Jewish populations (Arabs, Druzes, and others of unspecified religion) it was 11.2 (Israel Central Statistical Bureau 2003). Among the Jewish 15-year-old and above group, 3.3% of the women and 1.5% of the men never attended school. Among the Arab 15-year-old and above group the numbers and the difference between women and men are higher: 9.9% of the women and 2.4% of the men never attended school. Viewing schooling in historical perspective, in 1961 12.5% of the Jewish and 49.2% of the Arab of 15 years old and above groups had never attended school. In the Jewish population, 28.3% of the women and 26.2% of the men and in the Arab population 9.5% of the women and 12.6% of the men had higher education (Israel Central Statistical Bureau 2004).

As noted above, the majority (about 70%) of secondary school students attend 6-3-3 schools and a minority attends 8-4 schools. However, current discussions about school reform have also brought to the fore a call for replacing the 6-3-3 with 8-4 or 6-6 programs. Each Jewish school is under the supervision of one of three systems: state, state-religious, and ultra-orthodox. Eighty-one percent of the junior high school and 66% of the senior high school students attend state schools, 19% and 17% of the junior and senior high school students respectively attend the state-religious schools, and less than 1% and 18% of the junior and senior high school students attend the ultra-orthodox schools. The majority of the ultra-orthodox children attend 8-4 schools.

Within each sector (supervision) a student may attend one of three tracks: general-academic, vocational, or agricultural. As indicated below, the general-academic track attracts the majority of students and has the highest rate of students who at the end of twelfth grade meet university entrance requirements. The Arab high school education has only two tracks: general-academic and vocational.

Data for 2003 show that 519,568 Jewish adolescents and 132,361 Arab adolescents attended sixth to twelfth grades. In both the Jewish and the Arab sectors, the majority of sixth to ninth graders attended junior high schools (73% and 71% of the Jewish and Arab students, respectively) whereas the others attended 1-8 elementary schools. Of the total number of twelfth graders, 60% of Jewish students and 67% of Arab students attended academic programs, whereas the others attended vocational schools (Israel Central Statistical Bureau 2004).

University admission requires that students meet two criteria: holding a complete matriculation certificate (awarded to high school graduates who pass external state examinations held by the Ministry of Education) and achieving a minimum score on the psychometric examination. However, each criterion has an alternative: students who did not complete their high school education or the requirements for matriculation certificate may attend a university preparatory program for 1 to 2 years. The 2004 data show that among the Jewish twelfth graders, 58% of the students attending the general-academic track (n = 50,357), 37% of those attending the vocational track (n = 25,661), and 33% of those attending agricultural schools (n = 1,021) met university entrance requirements.

Among Arab twelfth graders the rate of those meeting university entrance requirements was lower: 35% of the students attending the general-academic track (n = 9,613) and only 23% of those attending the vocational track (n = 4,449). This has been reflected also in their representation in higher education. In 2003 the total number of undergraduates was 76,581 (1.5% of the total adult population of 15 years or older and 7% of the 20 to 29 age group). Of them, 81% were Jewish and 19% were Arab. The total number of MA students was close to 35,000; 57% were women, 95% were Jewish, and 5% were Arab. The total number of PhD students was 8,000; of them 53% were women, 95% were Jewish, and 3% were Arab (Israel Central Statistical Bureau 2004).

The difference in number of students in the Jewish and Arab educational tracks reflects the total number of Jews and Arabs as well as the larger dropout rate in the Arab than in the Jewish education. Specifically, in the 2001/2002 academic year, the percentage of Jewish school dropouts grew from 1.6% after seventh grade to 6.7% after eleventh grade, whereas the percentage of Arab school dropouts grew from 2.2% after seventh grade to 13.5% after ninth grade (end of compulsory education), and 10.2% and 8.8% after the tenth and eleventh grades, respectively (Israel Central Statistical Bureau 2004).

According to an HBSC (Health Behaviors in School-Aged Children) Israeli survey (Harel et al. 2002), Israeli Jewish sixth to tenth graders like their school less than do Israeli Arab sixth to tenth graders. Specifically, only 18% of the Jewish students and 44% of the Arab students reported they liked school very much. Girls liked school better than boys (22% and 15% of the Jewish girls and boys and 55% and 33% of the Arab girls and boys endorsed the "I like school very much" response option), and among Arab adolescents younger adolescents liked school better than older adolescents.

Among Jewish adolescents the most dissatisfied group is eighth graders (only 14% like school very much) whereas sixth, seventh, ninth, and tenth graders are somewhat more satisfied (18% to 20% like school very much). Similar findings were reported in another survey of 13- to 18-year-old Jewish adolescents (Sherer et al. 2002). Adolescents' reports about their satisfaction with teacher–student relationships showed a similar picture: only 10% were highly satisfied with teacher–student relationships but 27% were highly satisfied with the school's academic level and 50% were highly satisfied with relationships with their classmates. However, findings of the HBSC survey (Harel et al. 2002) showed that regardless of how much they liked school, the majority of students in both the Jewish and the Arab educational systems feel a sense of belongingness to their school (66% of the Jewish and 67% of the Arab adolescents participating in the survey). The sense of belonging of the girls is higher than that of the boys (72% and 60% of the Jewish girls and boys and 77% and 57% of the Arab girls and boys).

School climate pertains to three aspects: school regulations, and relationships with teachers and peers. The overall picture regarding the three aspects is positive, and more so among Arab students than among Jewish students. To illustrate, 50% of Jewish and 58% of Arab students agree that school is a pleasant place and 46% and 64% of the Jewish and Arab students, respectively, regard the school's rules and regulations as fair. Regarding teachers' attitudes and behavior, 67% of Jewish and 68% of Arab students felt they would receive help from their teachers when necessary, and 54% and 69% of the Jewish and Arab students, respectively, felt teachers were interested in them as human beings. Both surveys assessed students' satisfaction with teachers' fairness. Overall, over half of the high school students think their teachers' behavior is fair (Harel et al. 2002) or quite fair (Sherer et al. 2002).

Regarding peer relationships, 58% of Jewish and 75% of Arab students described their classmates as courteous and willing to help, and 79% of Jewish and 73% of Arab students felt their peers accepted them "as they are." However, whereas 82% of Jewish students feel physically secure at school, among the Arab students only 63% feel so. The difference is larger for tenth graders: 86% of the Jewish and 59% of the Arab students feel physically secure at school. Finally, while the Jewish students' sense of security goes up with age, among the Arab students it goes down with age, so that tenth graders feel least secure (Harel et al. 2002).

Special education is defined by Israeli law as teaching and systematic treatment provided to special needs children (ages 3 to 21) with physical, cognitive, emotional, or behavioral disabilities. The objective of special education is to advance and develop the abilities and skills of special needs children to support their integration in society and the world of work. The original special education law was amended in 2003, emphasizing the mainstreaming of special education students. The mainstreaming of special needs children includes remedial teaching by special education specialists and services adapted to the children's special needs. In reality, however, not all special needs children are provided with the teaching, treatment, and services adapted to their special needs (Israel Ministry of Education 2004a). In 2004, close to 19,000 special education children attended regular schools and 17,000 attended special education schools; of them, about 40% (n = 7,016) were junior and high school students. Overall, adolescents (14 to 21 years old) with special needs attend 857 classrooms, whose average size is nine students (Israel Ministry of Education 2004b; Tal 2005).

Gifted students attend one of three educational programs: special classrooms (17%), weekly enrichment day (41%), and after-school programs conducted by higher education institutions (42%). High school students are encouraged to take university classes; however, in practice university courses are offered only by the Open University in the Tel Aviv and Beer Sheba areas. Special classes for the gifted have been operating in junior and senior high schools (one in each municipality) in the three main cities (Jerusalem, Tel Aviv, Haifa) and in smaller towns in the Greater Tel Aviv area (Ramat Gan, Holon, Herzelia, Petach Tikva) as well as in one southern (Ashdod) and one northern town (Ma'alot). The weekly enrichment day operates in 34 Jewish education centers, 14 Arab education centers, and 4 Druze education centers (Israel Ministry of Education 2004).

In recent years Israel participated in several international achievement studies. The earliest was the TIMSS 1995 for mathematics and science. Israeli Jewish eighth graders ranked twenty-first out of 41 countries in mathematics (with average achievement score of 522; Singapore ranked first with an average achievement score of 643) and twenty-third in science out of 41 countries (average achievement score 524; Singapore ranked first with an average achievement score of 607). In the TIMSS 1999 for mathematics, Israeli eighth graders ranked twenty-eighth out of 38 and below the international average on all subjects (e.g., fractions and number concepts, algebra, geometry). The 1999 study further showed that Israel was one of the few countries with gender-related differences (girls had lower grades than boys) and ethnicity-related differences (non-Jewish students had a lower achievement than Jewish students) (Zozovsky 2000).

Work

The 1953 law on adolescent work maintains that the minimum age for work is 15 for a regular job and 14 for summer jobs (Israel Ministry of Industry, Commerce and Employment 2004). The law also states that adolescents' work should not exceed 8 hours per day and 40 weekly hours. Adolescents who have reached 16 may work more than 8 hours per day provided they do not exceed 40 weekly hours. Adolescents should not be employed on their religious free day (i.e., Friday for Muslims, Saturday for Jews, and Sunday for Christians), and each of them is entitled to an annual 18-day vacation.

Despite the clarity of the law, information on adolescents' work is scarce. Particularly missing are the number, work conditions, and wages of working underage adolescents (below 15). Overall, of the 15 to 17 age group 9% are listed as participating of the civilian labor force. Among men the number is higher than among women (11% and 7% respectively). Official data further show that among the 15 to 17 age group, 18% of the men participating in the labor force but none of the women have only elementary school education (5 to 8 years of schooling). The 15- to 17-year-old women participating in the labor force have 9 to 12 years of education (Israel Central Bureau of Statistics 2004). This may indicate that among the 15- to 17-year-olds participating in the workforce, more men than women are school dropouts.

The small number of under-18-year-old adolescents in the labor force reflects the Ministry of Education efforts to encourage high school attendance. Specifically, although compulsory education applies to kindergarten to tenth grade, education from kindergarten to twelfth grade is free of charge. Low achievement high school students from economically underprivileged and new immigrant families are encouraged to pursue college-bound programs by participating in special enrichment programs subsidized by the Ministry of Education (Seginer, Dan, and Naor-Ram 1994, 1995; Seginer, Dan, Naor-Ram, Schlesinger, and Somech 1996). These efforts as well as the unemployment rate in the adult labor force (close to 11% of the labor force in 2002) all led to the low number of adolescents in the labor force.

Media

A recent survey of TV viewing among a representative sample of 1,000 Israeli Jewish youths aged 12 to 17 showed that 64% of the youths had a TV set in their room (Midgam 2004). During weekdays, adolescents watch TV more than adults do (for 3.5 and 2.9 daily hours, respectively). Assessing adolescents' attitudes toward TV watching, the survey shows that 80% of the adolescents regard TV as entertainment, 41% regard it as news channel, 31% think TV should provide its audience with general knowledge, and 25% believe it should communicate educational messages.

Over half of the adolescents (57%) watch TV alone, 20% with their parents, and 17% with friends. One-fifth (22%) of them watch TV until midnight and one-fifth (21%) until 2:30 a.m. (Midgam 2004). In an older sample consisting of ninth to twelfth graders (Cohen and Weimann 2000), adolescents reported watching TV for 3.9 hours per day and an average of 6 daily hours during school vacations.

Analysis of favored genres (Cohen and Weimann 2000) showed that on average, the most frequently watched genres have been movies (M = 3.88 daily hours, SD = 0.973), comedies (M = 3.60, SD = 1.28), MTV (M = 3.30, SD = 1.37), horror and mystery series (M = 3.30, SD = 1.26), and news (M = 3.17, SD = 1.03). The majority of the programs in each of these genres, except for the news, are imported. Although the majority are imported from the United States and U.K., one of the most popular series for adolescents in recent years—the "Rebels"—was imported from Argentina.

According to the Midgam (2004) survey, the majority of adolescents believe TV programs have an influence on adolescents like them (65%) and on younger children (74%), and fewer (44%) believe in the influence of advertisement on adolescents. Focusing on the positive and negative influence of TV and advertisement, fewer adolescents (23%) believe in the positive influence of TV than in the positive influence of advertisement (34%); a third of the respondents (34%) had heard of the bad influence of TV and only 6% had heard of its positive influence on children and adolescents' behavior. Consequently, about two-thirds (67%) of the adolescents believe TV programs should be controlled and three-quarters (74%) believe advertisement should be controlled. Moreover, more 12- to 14-year-old adolescents (61%) than 15- to 17-year-olds (50%) believe it is more important to control TV programs than advertisement.

A study carried out as part of a multicultural project (Lemish and Liebes 1999) showed that Israeli adolescents watched TV less than adolescents in Western European countries (e.g., Denmark, France, Germany, U.K.), with the exception of Switzerland. However, data on time spent on TV watching varies by data source. Thus, while the Cohen and Weimann (2000) ninth to twelfth graders spend 3.4 hours per day during weekdays and the Midgam (2004) 12- to 17-year-olds spend 3.9 hours, according to Lemish and Liebes, among those watching TV, young adolescents (age 12 to 13) watch 129 minutes per day and middle adolescents (age 15 to 16) watch 99 minutes per day. By comparison, Danish young and middle adolescents watch 158 and 168 minutes per day, respectively,

and British young and middle adolescents watch 164 and 171 minutes per day, respectively.

Israeli Jewish adolescents who use the computer use it slightly more than adolescents from European countries, with the exception of Dutch computer users who use it more (48 and 41 minutes per day for Israeli young and middle adolescents and 50 and 74 minutes per day for Dutch young and middle adolescents). In a similar vein, Israeli adolescents who use the Internet use it more than adolescents from European countries, with the exception of Dutch Internet users (30 and 32 minutes per day for Israeli young and middle adolescents and 49 and 42 minutes per day for Dutch young and middle adolescents). Israeli adolescents use the telephone considerably more than adolescents from other European countries (43 and 73 minutes per day by young and middle adolescents, respectively, and 21 and 25 minutes per day for Finnish adolescents) (Lemish and Liebes 1999). The rate of computer users decreases for the older adolescents age groups: 45% for the 18- to 21-year-olds and 41% for the 22- to 24-year-olds. Thus, it is plausible that schools prompt computer usage; it is also possible that at least for some adolescents computers are available only at school.

Polling of the reading habits of 14- to 24-year-old Israelis (The Israel Central Bureau of Statistics 1999) shows that 80% to 85% read a daily paper at least once a week, 52% to 58% read at least one book in the last month, and 58% of the 14 to 17 age group used a computer during the last week.

Politics and Military

Adolescents' political involvement has two major aspects. One is related to the endorsement of political parties' views and their ensuing behavior and the other pertains to Jewish–Palestinian relationships. The views of political parties are most clearly expressed in general elections. Although the voting age in Israel is 18 and the majority of Israeli youths are not commonly involved in politics, during the election period political issues become more salient, leading larger numbers of adolescents to be politically interested and active in informal political debates and endorsement of political parties and their campaigns. Some of these activities take place in high schools, supported by the school educational staff. Particularly known are trial elections in several high schools whose voting patterns resemble the official election results, and thus unofficially are considered as their predictors.

Exceptions to Israeli youth's low interest in politics have been two groups holding extreme political attitudes: Arab students identifying with the communist party and Jewish national religious Bnei Akiva youths identifying with messianic parochialism, which has led some of them to active resistance and violent behavior in disputed territories settlements (Kahane 1997).

A small group of ultra-orthodox youths holding extreme messianic nationalistic attitudes operates in the West Bank and—until the evacuation of the Jewish settlements—in Gaza Strip settlements. The informal name of this group is the Hills Youth (*Noar Hagvaot*). The group consists of unemployed *yeshiva* dropouts who direct their violent behavior toward the Palestinian inhabitants and toward the Israeli security forces engaged in the evacuation of illegal Jewish posts in the West Bank. Prior to the August 2005 disengagement many of them moved to the Gaza Strip Jewish settlements, training themselves to resist by force the anticipated evacuation of the Jewish settlements (Harel and Hasson 2005).

The second aspect, pertaining to Jewish–Palestinian relationships and peace education, has mainly focused on the dialog between Israeli-Jewish and Palestinian encounter groups (Maoz 2004; Maoz and Ellis 2001; Salomon 2004). Despite the difficulties inherent in changing the nature of the relationships between two conflicting groups (Bar-Tal 2004), adolescents participating in peace education intervention programs showed more positive views of peace, greater sensitivity to the other side's perspective, and higher willingness for contact with the other side than control groups.

The Israeli law of mandatory military service requires Jewish boys and girls and Druze boys to serve in the army. However, whereas boys serve for three years, girls serve for only two years. Moreover, women declaring a religious background and orthodox men enrolled in religious studies (*Yeshiva*) are granted exemption from military service. These exemptions have been intended to protect orthodox youth from unsupervised interaction with the nonobservant Israeli society, deemed particularly important for girls who attend all-girls schools and are not expected to socially interact with nonfamily men.

Altogether, 23% of the Jewish men and 40% of the Jewish women are exempted from military service. Among women, the main reason for exemption is religious background; among men, 10% are exempted for religious studies reasons and 13% for medical and mental health, low intellectual ability, and criminal record reasons (Schtrasler 2005). In response to public protest against granting orthodox men exemption from military service, in recent years a growing number of them, especially those not studying in the *Yeshiva*, have been conscripted.

While the age of entering military service has been 18, or upon high school graduation, youths accepted to selected university programs (particularly in science, engineering, and professional programs such as law and medicine) participate in a special program (similar to the American ROTC) by which completion of their course of academic studies precedes their active military service.

Several surveys of the motivation of potential conscripts to serve in the Israeli army (e.g., Gal 1986; Ezrahi and Gal 1995) showed that the majority are highly motivated to serve in the army and view it as fulfilling a personal duty. As noted by Gal, military service has become "...an integral phase in the life of any Israeli youth" (1986, p. 59) and should be understood in terms of the cultural heritage of voluntary participation in self-defense organizations since the beginning of Jewish immigration to Palestine at the turn of the twentieth century (Seginer 1999). Until recently, dissidence has been limited to a relatively small number of reservists who opposed military action during the Lebanon war and the first Intifada (Linn 1996) as well as the al Aksa Intifada (started in October 2000), and an even smaller number of mandatory service soldiers who refused service for conscientious objection reasons.

However, in light of the Israeli government decision to disengage from the Gaza Strip and part of the West Bank and the strong opposition of the Jewish settlers to being evacuated and resettled, dissidence as of the winter of 2005 was associated with nationalistic right-wing political attitudes. Although the political views of the leftist and the nationalistic soldiers represent two extremes, underlying their dissidence are moral convictions (against Israeli occupation in the West Bank and Gaza Strip in the case of the leftists, and against handing back parts of the Promised Land and particularly the disengagement from the Gaza Strip in the case of the Orthodox rightists), described by Helman (1993) as the dissidents' sense of duty and continued contribution to the moral stance of the Israeli society.

Developmental studies of the military recruits focused on two issues: the effect of military service on the recruits' sense of personal growth and the interdependence between adolescent–parent relationships and adjustment to military service. Both lines of research showed the positive effect of military service. Specifically, military service has a positive effect on a sense of personal growth (Lieblich and Perlow 1988) and particularly on the development of future orientation (Seginer and Ablin 2005), a growing sense of such attributes as independence, self-confidence, social sensitivity, and ability for intimate relationships (Dar and Kimhi 2001), as well as improved adolescent–parent relationships (Mayseless and Hai 1998). Moreover, a sense of parental autonomy granting had a positive effect on adjustment to military service (Mayseless and Hai 1998; Mayseless, Scharf, and Scholt 2003).

Unique Issues

This section is devoted to new immigrant adolescents, particularly focusing on new immigrants from the former Soviet Union and Ethiopia who immigrated to Israel during the 1990s. The immigration of former Soviet Union Jews was much larger and the background of the immigrants much more diversified. The number of former Soviet Union children and adolescents immigrating to Israel during the 1989 to 1995 period was 151,517. They came from small families (57% of them were only children) and their chances of growing up in single-parent families (20%) were three times as high as that of children growing up in veteran Jewish families. About 6,000 of them immigrated without their parents and were placed in Youth Alia boarding schools and kibbutz schools (Horowitz 1998).

Several criteria were used for assessing the adjustment of new immigrant adolescents to Israel. Two criteria pertain to academic achievement relative to (1) adolescents immigrating from the Soviet Union during the 1970s and (2) Israeli-born adolescents. The two other major criteria were the extent to which the new immigrants defined themselves as Israelis and their motivation for military service (Horowitz 1998). According to both criteria, new immigrant adolescents fell behind.

Underlying the lower academic achievement of the former Soviet Union new immigrants were several conditions related to the social change brought by the 1980s *glastnost* and *perestroika* and the rise of alienated youth culture rejecting such adult values as academic achievement, as well as the unawareness of the Israeli educational system of the significance of these social changes for the 1990s new immigrants. Consequently, fewer of them (78% versus 97% of the nonimmigrant Jewish students) took the Ministry of Education matriculation examinations, and even fewer (14% of the 1992 cohort) obtained the matriculation certificate (Horowitz 1998) awarded to high school graduates who pass external state examinations held by the Ministry of Education.

The extent to which adolescent new immigrants forge an Israeli identity varies by study and relates to such factors as immigrating with their families and taking part in the decision to immigrate to Israel (Mirsky 1994; Rapoport and Lomsky-Feder 2000), experiencing low psychological distress, developing social relationships outside the new immigrant community, and mastering the Hebrew language (Mirsky 1994).

Identifying three patterns of adjustment, Eisikovitz (1995) showed the interdependence between academic achievement and Israeli identity so that students with high academic achievement in mathematics and science developed a more balanced identity than students with academic interest and achievement in the humanities and students of moderate academic achievement. However, integration and separation acculturation attitudes were unrelated to the academic adjustment of former Soviet Union sojourner adolescents in Israel (Eshel and Rosenthal-Sokolov 2000).

Attitudes toward military service and actual experience while in military service underline the differences between veteran Israelis and former Soviet Union new immigrants (Eisikovitz 2005). These differences are reflected in less positive attitudes of new immigrants than of veteran Israelis toward military service, lack of prior knowledge about the army even though high schools offer a program of preparation for military service (Israelashvili and Taubman 1997), and lack of parental involvement in military service. Thus, former Soviet Union immigrants enter the army less motivated (see also Toren-Kaplan 1995), less prepared, and lacking family support.

In light of this situation, it is no wonder that the majority of soldiers (especially boys) do not feel a sense of growth and development during military service and sever interpersonal relationships with veteran Israelis soon after completing military service. It is important to note that new immigrant girls enter the army with more positive attitudes and experience their military service as a period of personal growth. However, they too reported they did not keep social relationships with veteran Israelis (Eisikovitz, in press). Thus, while traditionally the Israeli army has been viewed as a social integration setting, it has not been serving this purpose for new immigrants from the former Soviet Union.

Although immigration of Ethiopian Jews started in the 1970s and still continues, the majority of Ethiopian Jews arrived to Israel in one of two immigration waves known as the Moses Operation (*Mivzah Moshe*) in 1984–1985 and the Salomon

Operation (*Mivzah Shlomo*) in 1991. The majority of the Ethiopian adolescents (85% to 90%), altogether over 10,000 girls and boys, were educated in Youth Alia boarding schools (Amir 1997). It is important to note that the majority of Ethiopian Jews resided in remote rural areas and therefore were detached from Orthodox Jewry and unaffected by the modernity brought by the Italian occupation prior to WWII and the reform of the Marxist revolution in the 1970s (Adler, Toker, Manor, Feuerstein, and Feldman 1997).

The majority of Ethiopian Jews (90%) were illiterate. Among the adolescents admitted to the Youth Alia schools, 22% were one to two years below the achievement level of their age group in Youth Alia. The rest were further behind (three to four years below their age group achievement or unable to take the tests). The educational gap, cultural differences, and dark complexion led to the phenomena of school dropout, alienation from the Israeli society, and identification with Black culture (Sawicki 1994), and lower motivation to serve in the army, interpreted as an expression of the disillusionment of Ethiopian-born army graduates who encountered difficulties finding jobs.

Nevertheless, within a ten-year period, the percentage of students completing high school education rose from 1.5% in 1985 to 16% in 1995 (Adler et al. 1997). Given that military service is considered an important marker of adjustment to Israeli society, Ethiopian youths have been known for their overall high motivation and good adjustment to military service, and the number of officers among them rose from 5 in 1991 to 15 in 1994 and 30 in 1996 (Adler et al. 1997). In a similar vein, in the early 1990s 3% of the 22- to 35-year-old Ethiopian new immigrants were university students (Lifshitz and Noam 1994).

RACHEL SEGINER and SHIRLI SHOYER

References and Further Reading

Adler, H., D. Toker, Y. Manor, et al. 1997. Absorption of Ethiopian youth in Youth Alia, 1985–1995. In *One root many branches: The story of the absorption of young immigrants from Ethiopia in Youth Alia.* E. Amir, A. Zehavi, and R. Pragayi (eds.). pp. 255–303. Jerusalem: The Magnes Press.

Amir, E. 1997. Introduction. In *One root many branches: The story of the absorption of young immigrants from Ethiopia in Youth Alia.* E. Amir, A. Zehavi, and R. Pragayi (eds.). p. 8. Jerusalem: The Magnes Press.

Antonovsky, H. F. 1980. *Adolescent sexuality: A study of attitudes and behavior.* Lexington, Mass.: Lexington Books.

Arnett, J. J. 2000. Emerging adulthood: A theory of development from the late teens through the twenties. *American Psychologist* 55:469–80.

Aviezer, O., A. Sagi, G. Resnick, and M. Gini. 2002. School competence in young adolescence: Links to early attachment relationships beyond concurrent self-perceived competence and representations of relationships. *International Journal of Behavioral Development* 26:397–409.

Bar-Hamburger, R. 2000. *Drug use among new immigrants in the State of Israel.* Jerusalem: The Anti-Drug Authority.

Bar-Tal, D. 2004. Nature, rationale, and effectiveness of education for co-existence. *Journal of Social Issues* 60:253–71.

Baron-Epel, O., and A. Haviv-Messika. 2004. Factors associated with age of smoking initiation in adult populations from different ethnic backgrounds. *European Journal of Public Health* 14:301–5.

Bendes-Yakov, O., and Y. Friedman. 2000. *NALEH: Youth immigrating to Israel without their parents.* Jerusalem: The Henrieta Szold Institute.

Ben Tzvi-Mayer, S., R. Hertz-Lazarovitz, and M. Safir. 1989. Teachers' selection of boys and girls as prominent pupils. *Sex Roles* 21:231–46.

Ben-Zur, H. 2003. Happy adolescents: The link between subjective well-being, internal resources, and parental factors. *Journal of Youth and Adolescence* 32:67–79.

Brook, U., and A. Tepper. 2002. Consumption, knowledge and attitudes of high school pupils towards alcohol and alcoholism: The Israeli experience. *Patient Education and Counseling* 47:115–19.

Cohen, J., and G. Weimann. 2000. Cultivation revisited: Some genres have some effects on some viewers. *Communication Reports* 13:99–114.

Dar, Y., and S. Kimhi. 2001. Military service and self-perceived maturation among Israeli youths. *Journal of Youth and Adolescence* 30:427–48.

Dror, Y. 2004. The educational system as an agent of Jewish patriotism in the State of Israel: From "pioneering Zionism" to "balanced Israeliness." In *Patriotism: Homeland love.* A. Ben-Amos and D. Bar-Tal (eds.). pp. 137–73. Tel Aviv: Hakibutz Hameuchad (Hebrew).

Eisenstadt, S. N. 1952. *The process of absorption of new immigrants in Israel.* London: Tavistock Publication.

Eisikovitz, R. 1995. "I'll tell you what school should do for us": How immigrant youth from FSU view their high school experience in Israel. *Youth and Society* 27:230–55.

Eisikovitz, R. 2005. Intercultural learning among Russian recruits in the Israeli army. *Armed Forces and Society* 32:1–15.

Epstein, S. 1983. *The mother-father-peer scale.* Unpublished manuscript. Amherst, Mass: University of Massachusetts.

Eshel, Y., and M. Rosenthal-Sokolov. 2000. Acculturation attitudes and sociocultural adjustment of sojourner youth in Israel. *The Journal of Social Psychology* 140:677–91.

Ezrahi, Y., and R. Gal. 1995. *World views and attitudes of high school students toward social, security and peace issues.* Zichron Ya'akov, Israel: The Carmel Institute for Social Studies.

Farbstein, I., A. Dycian, D. Gothelf, et al. 2002. A follow-up study of adolescent attempted suicide in Israel. *Journal of American Academy of Child and Adolescent Psychiatry* 41:1342–49.

Gal, R. 1986. *A portrait of the Israeli soldier*. New York: Greenwood Press.

Grusec, J. E. 2002. Parenting socialization and children's acquisition of values. In *Handbook of parenting: Vol. 5: Practical issues in parenting* (2nd ed.). M. H. Bornstein (ed.). pp. 143–67.

Habib, J. 1998. Groups at risk among the new immigrants. In *Profile of an immigration wave: The absorption process of immigrants from the former Soviet Union, 1990–1995*. M. Sicron and E. Leshem (eds.). pp. 409–41. Jerusalem: The Magnes Press. (Hebrew, with English Abstract).

Harel, A., and N. Hason. January 2, 2005. *The Hills' Youths moved to Gaza and began training to undo the disengagement*. *Haaretz* Newspaper (Hebrew & English).

Harel, Y., S. Ellenbogen-Frankovitz, M. Molcho, et al. 2002. *Health behaviors in school-aged children (HBSC): A World Health Organization cross-national study*. Jerusalem: The Center for Children and Youth JDC-Brookdale Institute and Ramat Gan: Department of Sociology and Anthropology, Bar Ilan University.

Harel, Y., M. Molcho, and A. Tilinger. 2004. *Youth in Israel: Health, psychological and social well-being and patterns of risk taking behavior*. Ramat Gan: Bar Ilan University. (Hebrew).

Helman, S. 1993. Conscientious objection to military service as an attempt to redefine the contents of citizenship. Unpublished doctoral dissertation, Hebrew University of Jerusalem.

Horowitz, T. 1998. Immigrant children and adolescents in the educational system. In *Profile of an immigration wave: The absorption process of immigrants from the former Soviet Union, 1990–1995*. M. Sicron and E. Leshem (eds.). pp. 368–408. Jerusalem: The Magnes Press. (Hebrew, with English Abstract).

Ichilov, O. 1985. Family politicization and adolescents' citizenship orientation, *Political Psychology* 9:431–44.

Israel Central Statistical Bureau. 2004a. *Israel statistical yearbook*. Jerusalem: Central Bureau of Statistics.

Israel Central Statistical Bureau. 2004b. *Pupils in grades VII-XII: Staying on vs. dropping out, 2001/2*. Jerusalem: Central Bureau of Statistics.

Israel Gay Youth. 2004. *About Israeli gay youth*. http://www.igy.org.il/content/about/ (Hebrew).

Israel Knesset Research and Information Center. 2003. *Drug use among Israeli youths*. Jerusalem: Israeli Knesset (Parliament).

Israel Ministry of Education. 2004a. *Gifted students programs*. http://www.education.gov.il/gifted/misgarot.htm (Hebrew)

Israel Ministry of Education. 2004b. *The law of special education*. http://cms.education.gov.il/EducationCMS/Units/Special/hukimUnehalim/HokHinuchMeyuchad (Hebrew).

Israel Ministry of Education. 2004c. *Number of classrooms and students in special education programs 2004*. http://cms.education.gov.il/EducationCMS/Units/Special/HaagafBepeula/NetuneyKitot/ (Hebrew).

Israelashvili, M., and O. Taubman. 1997. Adolescents' preparation for military enlistment in Israel: A preliminary evaluation. *Megamot* 38:408–420. (Hebrew).

Kahane, R. 1997. *The origins of postmodern youth: Informal youth movements in a comparative perspective*. Berlin: Walter de Gruyter.

Keniston, K. 1970. Youth as a stage of life. *American Scholar* 39:631–54.

Knafo, A., and S. H. Schwartz. 2003. Parenting and adolescents' accuracy in perceiving parental values. *Child Development* 74:595–611.

Kurman, J. 2003. The role of perceived specificity level of failure events in self-enhancement and in constructive self-criticism. *Personality and Social Psychology Bulletin* 29:285–94.

Larson, R. W., M. H. Richards, G. Moneta, and G. Holmbeck. 1996. Changes in adolescents' daily interactions with their families from ages 10 to 18: Disengagement and transformation. *Developmental Psychology* 32:744–54.

Latzer, Y. In press. Disordered eating behaviors and attitudes in diverse groups in Israel. In *Eating disorders in the Mediterranean area: An exploration in transcultural psychology*. M. R. Giovanni (ed.). Huntington, N.Y.: Nova Science Publisher.

Latzer, Y., and I. Gilat. 2000. Calls to the Israeli hotline from individuals who suffer from eating disorders: An epidemiological study. *Eating Disorders: The Journal of Treatment and Prevention* 8:31–42.

Lemish, D., and T. Liebes. 1999. *Children and youth in the changing media environment in Israel*. Jerusalem: The Hebrew University, School of Education, the NCJW Research Institute for Innovation in Education. (Hebrew).

Levinson, D. J. 1978. *The seasons of a man's life*. New York: Ballentine Books.

Lieblich, A., and M. Perlow. 1988. Transition to adulthood during military service. *The Jerusalem Quarterly* 47 (Summer):40–78.

Lifshitz, C., and G. Noam. 1994. *A survey of young Ethiopian immigrants: Interim report*. Jerusalem: JDC-Brookdale Institute.

Linn, R. 1996. When the individual soldier says "no" to war: A look at selective refusal during the Intifada. *Journal of Peace Research* 33:421–31.

Mahajna, S. 2005. Future orientation: Its nature and meaning for adolescent females growing up in different Israeli Arab sectors. Unpublished PhD dissertation, University of Haifa, Israel.

Maoz, I. 2004. Coexistence in the eye of the beholder: Evaluating intergroup encounter interventions between Jews and Arabs in Israel. *Journal of Social Issues* 60:437–52.

Maoz, I., and D. Ellis. 2001. Going to ground: Argument in Israeli-Jewish and Palestinian encounter groups. *Research on Language and Social Interaction* 34:399–419.

Margieh, I. 2005. Future orientation in social context: The case of Israeli Palestinian high school students. Unpublished master's thesis, University of Haifa, Haifa, Israel.

Mayseless, O., and I. Hai. 1998. Leaving home transition in Israel: Changes in parent-adolescent relationships and adolescents' adaptation to military service. *International Journal of Behavioral Development* 22:589–609.

Mayseless, O., M. Scharf, and M. Sholt. 2003. From authoritative parenting to an authoritarian context: Exploring the person-environment fit. *Journal of Research on Adolescence* 427–56.

Mesch, G. S. 2001. Social relationships and Internet use among adolescents in Israel. *Social Science Quarterly* 82:329–39.

Midgam. 2004. *Adolescent attitudes about channels 2 and 10 advertisement and programs*. Tel Aviv, Israel: Midgam Yeutz Umechkar. (Hebrew).

Mirsky, J. November 21, 1994. *Adjustment patterns of new immigrant university students*. Paper presented in the Identity and Transition Culture conference. Jerusalem: The Hebrew University.

Mirsky, J., and L. Prawer. 1992. *To immigrate as an adolescent: Immigrant youth from the former Soviet Union to Israel*. Jerusalem: ELKA and the Van Leer Institute.

Mitrany, E., F. Lubin, A. Chetrit, and B. Modan. 1995. Eating disorders among Jewish female adolescents in Israel: A 5-year study. *Journal of Adolescent Health* 6:454–57.

Offer, D., E. Ostrov, and K. I. Howard. 1982. *The Offer self-image questionnaire for adolescents: A manual* (3rd ed.). Chicago: Michael Reese Hospital.

Orr, E., A. Mana, and Y. Mana. 2003. Immigrant identity of Israeli adolescents from Ethiopia and the former USSR: Culture specific principles of organization. *European Journal of Social Psychology* 33:71–92.

Petersen, A. C., J. E. Schulenberg, R. H. Abramowitz, et al. 1984. A self-image questionnaire for young adolescents (SIQYA): Reliability and validity studied. *Journal of Youth and Adolescence* 13:93–111.

Rapoport, T., and E. Lomsky-Feder. 2002. "Intelligentsia" as an ethnic habitus: The inculcation and restructuring of intelligentsia among Russian Jews. *British Journal of Sociology of Education* 23:233–48.

Safir, M., R. Hertz-Lazarovitz, S. Ben Tzvi-Mayer, and H. Kupermintz. 1992. Prominence of girls and boys in the classroom: Schoolchildren's perceptions. *Sex Roles* 27:439–53.

Salomon, G. 2004. Does peace education make a difference in the context of an intractable conflict? *Peace and Conflict: Journal of Peace Psychology* 10:257–74.

Sawicki, T. 1994. Dancing to an African beat. *Jerusalem Report* 53:22–24.

Scharf, M., and O. Mayseless. 2001. The capacity for romantic intimacy: Exploring the contribution of best friend and marital and parental relationships. *Journal of Adolescence* 24:379–99.

Scheinberg, Z., A. Bleich, and M. Kolovsky. 1992. Prevalence of eating disorders among female Israel Defense Force recruits. *Harefuah* 123:73–78 (Hebrew).

Seginer, R. 1992. Sibling relationships in early adolescence: A study of Israeli Arab sisters. *Journal of Early Adolescence* 12:96–110.

Seginer, R. 1999. Beyond the call of duty: The service of Israeli youth in military and civic contexts. In *Roots of civic identity: International perspectives on community service and activism in youth*. M. Yates and J. Youniss (eds.). pp. 205–24. New York: Cambridge University Press.

Seginer, R. July 2000. Adolescent-sibling relationships in the context of adolescent-parents relationships: Congruence is not enough. In *Family congruence and adolescent well-being*. R. Seginer, A. Vermulst, and J. Gerris (conveners). Symposium conducted at the 16th biennial meeting of the International Society of Behavioral Development, Beijing, China.

Seginer, R. 2001. Young people chart their path into adulthood: The future orientation of Israeli Druze, Arab and Jewish adolescents. Special Issue: The child in Israel (Eds., C. Greenbaum and I. Levin), *Megamot* 41:97–112. (Hebrew).

Seginer, R. 2005. Adolescent future orientation: Intergenerational transmission and intertwining tactics in culture and family settings. In *Culture and human development: The importance of cross-cultural research to the social sciences*. W. Friedelmeier, P. Chakkarath, and B. Schwarz (eds.). pp. 231–51. Hove, U.K.: Psychology Press

Seginer, R., and E. Ablin. 2005. Can military service enhance the future orientation of emerging adults? A short-term longitudinal analysis. Unpublished manuscript. Haifa, Israel: University of Haifa.

Seginer, R., O. Dan, and A. Naor-Ram. 1994. *Do schools need consultants? Screening candidates for the Mabar special project for advancing low S.E.S senior high school students*. First interim report to the Israeli Ministry of Education and Culture. (Hebrew).

Seginer, R., O. Dan, and A. Naor-Ram. 1995. *Expert intervention programs in classes of the Mabar special educational project for advancing low S.E.S senior high school students*. Second interim report to the Israeli Ministry of Education and Culture. (Hebrew).

Seginer, R., O. Dan, A. Naor-Ram, et al. 1996. *The operation of Mabar special educational project in high schools: From screening to teaching, learning, and plans for the future*. Final report to the Israeli Ministry of Education and Culture. (Hebrew).

Seginer, R., and H. Flum. 1987. Israeli adolescents' self image profile. *Journal of Youth and Adolescence* 16:455–72.

Seginer, R., M. Karayanni, and M. Mar'i. 1990. Adolescents' attitudes towards women's roles: A comparison between Israeli Jews and Arabs. *Psychology of Women Quarterly* 14:119–33.

Seginer, R., and S. Mahajna. 2003. "Education is a weapon in women's hands": How Israeli Arab girls construe their future. *Journal for Sociology of Education and Socialization Zeitschrift für Soziologie der Erziehung und Sozialisation* 23:200–14.

Seginer, R., and S. Mahajna. 2004. How the future orientation of traditional Israeli Palestinian girls links beliefs about women's roles and academic achievement. *Psychology of Women Quarterly* 28:122–35.

Seginer, R., and A. Somech. 2001. In the eyes of the beholder: How adolescents, teachers and school counselors construct adolescent images. *Social Psychology of Education* 4:139–57.

Seginer, R., and A. Vermulst. 2002. Family environment, educational aspirations, and academic achievement in two cultural settings. *Journal of Cross-cultural Psychology* 33:540–58.

Seginer, R., A. Vermulst, and S. Shoyer. 2004. The indirect link between perceived parenting and adolescent future orientation: A multi-step model. *International Journal of Behavioral Development* 28:365–78.

Sherer, M., O. Karnieli-Miller, Z. Eizikovitz, and G. Fishman. 2000. *Attitudes of Israeli Jewish adolescents 2000*. Haifa, Israel: The Minerva Center for Youth Studies, University of Haifa. (Hebrew).

Shulman, S., and E. Ben Artzi. 2003. Age related differences in the transition from adolescence to adulthood and links with family relationships. *Journal of Adult Development* 10:217–26.

Stein, D., O. Luria, R. Tarrasch, et al. 1999. Partial eating disorders in newly drafted Israeli servicewomen. *Archives of Women's Mental Health* 2:107–16.

Stein, D., S. Meged, T. Bar-Hanin, et al. 1997. Partial eating disorders in a community sample of female adolescents.

Journal of the American Academy of Child and Adolescent Psychiatry 36:1116–23.

Stransler, N. January 6, 2005. How lovely is "civilian service." *Haaretz* newspaper (Hebrew and English).

Suleiman, M. A. 2001. Parental style and Arab adolescents' future orientation. Unpublished master's thesis, University of Haifa, Haifa, Israel. (Hebrew).

Tal, D. 2005. *Special needs adolescents and curricula developed for them*. Jerusalem: Israeli Ministry of Education.

Toren-Kaplan, N. 1995. Adolescent future orientation in the context of immigration and absorption: The case of former-USSR immigrants to Israel. Unpublished master's thesis, University of Haifa, Haifa, Israel. (Hebrew).

Ullman, C., and M. Tatar. 2001. Psychological adjustment among Israeli adolescent immigrants: A report on life satisfaction, self-concept, and self-esteem. *Journal of Youth and Adolescence* 30:449–63.

Ullman, H., and M. Tatar. 1999. *Self definition, self esteem, and life satisfaction among veteran Israeli and former Soviet Union new immigrant adolescents*. Jerusalem: The Hebrew University, School of Education, the NCJW Research Institute for Innovation in Education. (Hebrew).

Weiss, S. 1995. How do Israeli adolescents of four religions obtain alcoholic beverages and where? *Journal of Child and Adolescent Substance Abuse* 4:79–87.

Yachad. 2002. *The condition of homosexuals and lesbians in Israel*. Yachad.snunit.k12.il/upload/homo5/homosexualityIsrael.html. (Hebrew).

Zozovsky, R. 2000. *The international study in mathematics and science TIMSS 1999*. Jerusalem: Office of the Chief Scientist, Israel Ministry of Education.

ITALY

Background Information

Geographically, Italy is a peninsula in the center of the Mediterranean Sea. It is made of many different kinds of territories: coasts, islands, plains, and even high mountains. Both the climate and the economic activities, particularly agriculture, vary according to the regions. The number of inhabitants is around 58 million (ISTAT 2004; all the statistics reported come from ISTAT, National Institute of Statistics, if no other reference is indicated) making Italy one of the most densely populated countries in Europe. The inhabitants are not distributed evenly; nearly two-thirds live in urban zones. There are significant differences among the various regions; the main industries of the country are concentrated in the north, while the south accounts for the lower range of income. Despite the post–World War II economic boom, which made Italy one of the ten most industrialized countries in the world, the unemployment rate remains high (about 10%) and it varies from zone to zone: ranging from 5% for some parts of the north to 22% for the south. Emigration has always been a reality since the end of the nineteenth century; after World War II and up to the end of the 1960s there was an important internal immigration from the agrarian south to the industrialized north. Today Italy is a country of immigration, especially from Eastern Europe and the Mediterranean basin. Immigrants are estimated to be 2,500,000, plus around 10% illegal immigrants (Caritas 2003).

Italy has been a unified nation since 1861; since 1946 it has been a parliamentary democratic republic. Italy is part of the European Union and adheres to the Euro.

Period of Adolescence

As in other postindustrial European societies, adolescence is socially recognized as a period of social suspension and preparation for the entrance into adulthood. The extension of such a period for all adolescents, and not only for those of a higher social class, took place in the decades immediately after the 1950s, and this was in relation to the minimum school leaving age being raised, and to the growing industrialization and increased welfare of society.

The first signs of physical maturation are visible in girls between 9.4 years and 12.4 years, and for boys between 10.8 and 13.6 years. Menarche begins between 10.6 and 13.6 years, the average age being 12.3 years (Centro Studi Auxologici 2004). From a legal point of view, the coming of age is 18, but this does not correspond to an emotional and economic independence and to the assuming of adult responsibilities. In Italy there is a long period of emerging adulthood, longer than in other European countries. Economic and social differences existing amongst various Italian regions and social classes, related to the continuation of studies and the beginning of working life, are also reflected in the duration of adolescence and in the period of emerging adulthood. In some groups, emerging adulthood is accompanied by unemployment, under-employment, and temporary work, while on the contrary in other minority groups it leads to a longer education in regards to preparation for a more advanced career.

Nevertheless, there is a common tendency, which emerged at the end of the 1980s, to continue living longer in the parental home. Nearly 73% of young people between 18 and 30 live with their family; the percentage is higher for boys, even when they work, and it is found to be higher in the south and in the islands. Therefore, there is a generation for whom entering adulthood does not necessarily mean leaving the family—a family in which there are relationships based primarily on compromise and negotiation, and not on conflict (Scabini, Lanz, and Marta 1999; Scabini et al. 2006). At the root of this phenomenon are various interacting causes: unemployment, difficulty in finding a stable and adequately paid job, a lack of homes available for rent and a lack of specific social policies. Psychologists have highlighted the prevalence of an enlarged and multigenerational family, but its future development and positive outcome raises a lot of doubts. In this, in fact, a lot of adults show difficulty in regulating a generational distance in regards to the children, and in promoting a reciprocal autonomy; while young people can't manage to define with sufficient clarity their own life project (Caprara and Fonzi 2000).

On a social level, representation of adolescents, especially regarding teenagers, is quite negative, and does not correspond to reality; mass media greatly emphasize negative events (for example, suicides and acts of aggression) in spite of statistical evidence to the contrary. There are not any recognized rites of passage that specify the transition from adolescence to adulthood; it is thought that some adolescent risk behavior can subjectively have the role of visibly marking this passage (Bonino et al. 2005).

Beliefs

As with the majority of other European Union countries, Italy has a set of prevalently individualistic and not collective values. However, some studies group the south of Italy in a particular collective area, more common to other countries of southern Europe, that privileges the family as a group. In Italian society, family still carries great importance also for adolescents, and adolescents tend to live with their families for a long time. For the future, family is a significant goal that most adolescents aspire to, and that is immediately followed by a rewarding job.

The dominant religion in the country is Catholicism and nearly 86% of children are baptized; the number of confirmed adolescents is lower, and both percentages have decreased in recent years. Even if the majority of adolescents and their families choose to attend religious lessons at school, some of them (around 12%) abandon it during the year. Adolescents attend church more than adults but the number of those who go at least once a week decreases strongly as they get older: it goes from nearly 65% when they are under 13 years old to nearly 25% when they are between 18 and 19. At the same time, the number of adolescents who never go to church increases: at 18 to 19 this is around 15% and it tends to increase in the following years. The majority of adolescents do not follow moral Catholic indications regarding premarital sexual relations and the use of marijuana.

As in other Western countries, the values that are offered to adolescents vary a lot depending on the family and their living context. At a more general level, communication media mainly promote consumer-led values that privilege appearances and possession of some status symbols, such as mobile telephones, that are actually very diffused amongst adolescents. One can in fact affirm that adolescents live in a society where points of reference for values are very different—often contradictory and opposite. This multitude of possibilities of offers leaves space for a lot of individual choices but it can also create difficulty in choosing.

Research has shown that adolescents mostly place themselves as conservative toward traditional values: they privilege family, school, work, and health. A minority of around 10% place themselves in a position of opposition and defiance toward the dominant values, but without proposing a precise alternative (Sgritta 2000). Adolescents are significantly involved with voluntary work, especially in local organizations, in different fields (health, education, environment, church, etc.). The percentages of involvement are estimated for emerging adults to be between 8% and 14%, but they vary a lot depending on the various fields. Their participation in political groups is much lower.

Psychologists consider adolescents' involvement and activity in voluntary work a significant experience for the development of responsibilities and social participation in the transition process toward adulthood in a society like the Italian one, characterized by a late entrance into adulthood and a prolonged dependence on the family (Marta, Rossi, and Boccacin 1998; Marta and Pozzi 2006).

Gender

Even with the differences among the various regions and social classes, Italian society presents a particularly complex and contradictory situation regarding women's role in society. Basically, girls are offered two roles: the traditional role of motherhood, offered to girls from childhood, or a career outside the home. The fact that this latter possibility is seriously considered by girls and by their families is shown by the high level of attendance in secondary school, where there are more females than males, and also at university, and by their commitment in school, which leads to results generally superior to those of males. In concrete reality, not only are the two roles difficult to integrate, but they are both also difficult to obtain. Fulfilment in a family and maternal role is first of all postponed, because of the generalized condition of prolonged emerging adulthood. The average maternal age for a firstborn, varying greatly according to the region, ranges from 28.6 to 32 years old. Furthermore, the average number of children is very low: Italy has got the lowest birth rate in Western Europe at 1.2 children per woman. This phenomenon is the object of great discussion.

According to some social scientists it is strongly tied to the lack of adequate policies supporting motherhood and family: for this reason it is particularly difficult for women to reconcile the role of mother with that of the worker.

Outside the family, a good education and good academic results achieved by girls in secondary school and during university do not lead to an adequate and easy insertion into a job. The rate of unemployment for women, although differing a lot according to the various Italian regions, is always higher than the rate of unemployment for men, and in some cases is nearly double; furthermore, the kind of jobs women receive is often of an inferior level and for lower pay, compared to the school qualifications obtained. It is generally jobs in education, health, and personal care that continue to be more available to them.

To this it must be added that, as happens in many other Western countries, the media offer girls a strong and sexually active female role, based primarily on physical appearance. In this situation the body becomes an object of attention, and adolescents mostly manifest dissatisfaction toward their physical appearance, which is considered inadequate compared to the unobtainable models of thinness, beauty, and physical perfection offered by the media. For this reason, the body becomes the main target of discomfort for a lot of adolescents. Girls are significantly more prone to eating disorders than boys (Bonino, Cattelino, and Ciairano in press). Disturbed diet (comfort eating, diets, elimination behavior) is a mainly female phenomenon that shows itself in the first period of adolescence but tends to last even in the passage to emerging adulthood. This is accompanied by an excess of attention to one's body and to one's physical image: girls are unhappier with their appearance and their weight and mostly judge themselves as too fat even when they are completely within the normal weight range. More generally, girls set themselves higher targets of realization at a social and academic level; their levels of self-esteem and self-efficacy are lower than those of males of the same age, despite good school results.

For boys, the conflict of roles is not centered as much around family and work as around the model of masculinity: on one side is the role of the strong aggressive male, sure of himself and powerful, while on the other side there are ever-increasing requests of a greater emotional involvement toward the partner and children. In this situation males mostly carry out, especially during the first stages of adolescence, behaviors that could lead to "externalizing," deviance, dangerous behavior, sexually promiscuous behavior, and dangerous driving (Bonino, Cattelino, and Ciairano in press). These behaviors are thought to have the function of expressing, in a visible and exaggerated way, a strong masculinity in a condition of psychological uncertainty.

Males show, even after their twenties, a stronger tendency to stay in their original nuclear family, even when they work: the majority of males between 25 and 29 still live with the family. This tendency has been growing during the last 30 years for both genders.

The Self

As in other Western societies, the development of personal identity in Italian adolescents cannot be described in absolute terms (Bosma and Kunnen 2001). The construction of identity does not occur in a single way: the construction of the different components of identity is a long and differentiated process, depending on the different life areas. This means that the exploration and the commitments in significant life areas are diverse, they can happen at different times, with a different level of criticism, and with different solutions. As a result of this, in adolescence one can find a development of identities that have been defined as "imperfect" (Palmonari 1997).

In recent years this process has shown a tendency of increasing and lengthening itself toward emerging adulthood, and according to some, also into adult age, because of the difficulties met by a growing number of people in structuring a steady and coherent identity, in a context socially definable as postmodern.

The development of identity is strongly tied to the opportunities offered by family, school, groups, and geographic economic context of belonging. The development of identity is also tied to regional belonging, even if this does not constitute a prevalent aspect. We note regarding this that the different regional dialects, even if in a simplified and "Italianized" form, continue to be used by Italian families and young people. It is thought that the diffused involvement in numerous risk behaviors carries out relevant functions for the development of identity (Jessor, Donovan, and Costa 1991; Jessor, 1998; Silbereisen, Eyferth, and Rudinger 1986), especially for those Italian adolescents who have minor personal and family contextual resources, in the school and community of origin. These behaviors are different according to gender and type of school attended (Bonino, Cattelino, and Ciairano in press).

The number of immigrant adolescents is estimated at around 330,000 (plus the illegal ones who are mostly dedicated to illegal activities) and varies depending on the different Italian regions. This number is destined to grow rapidly in the coming years; already today more than 6% of children in elementary schools in northern regions are immigrants (MIUR 2004). Immigrant adolescents attend mostly vocational secondary schools, where they include more girls than boys; their number decreases from the first year (3.24%) to the last year (0.89%); the percentage of success is lower than for Italian students (around minus 13%) (MIUR 2004).

In their free time girls spend more time alone than boys do (nearly 25% of free time versus 17%); the percentages are less than those that measure time spent with friends or in groups, but more than those that measure time spent with parents or siblings. The time spent on their own is mostly taken up by activities such as reading, hobbies, and going to libraries; only the girls mostly stay on their own without doing anything, and such a condition is accompanied by feelings of loneliness and boredom.

Family Relationships

Family in Italy plays a central role in social organization and in individual life for adolescents, who find in their family a valid source of support and see the building of a future family of their own as a main value for their own fulfilment.

During the last century, family structure has undergone important transformations and, especially in urban centers, there has been a change from an extended family, characterized by the presence of more generations (grandparents, parents, uncles, children, nieces, and nephews) to a more limited family nucleus made up of the parents and one or two children. The main family types, apart from 25% single people, are about 20% childless couples, 44% couples with children, 8% families made of a single parent with children, and 3% other. This data will undergo further variations in the coming years in relation to two main factors: the ever-increasing average age, so that the proportion of over-65-year-olds continues to increase; and the migratory flux. Adolescents generally live with both parents, and nearly two-thirds have at least one brother or sister. The presence of grandparents inside the family nucleus is from 10% to 16%, depending on the district, with a greater proportion of grandmothers. Finally, extended "almost-kin" families, made by persons not biologically related to the adolescent, represent a marginal phenomenon statistically not relevant.

Family relationships between adolescents and parents are mostly characterized by an open attitude to dialogue, confrontation, and support (Marta 1997). The prominent educational style is the authoritative one, characterized by high levels of control and support. Starting from 16 to 17 years of age, the authoritative style tends to become for both genders a supportive one, characterized by lower levels of supervision and control and higher levels of support (Cattelino, Calandri, and Bonino 2001). Relationships between mother and daughter are generally characterized by greater closeness, but also by greater conflict. Fathers seem to have greater difficulties, compared to some years ago, in placing themselves as a go-between for family and society, acting out a role of mediation with the social world. Thus, in most cases mothers have to take on this role also to avoid or reduce as much as possible the break between family and society.

The good quality of relationships represents a resource, helping adolescents to face, with minor anxiety, some roles of development, in particular those tied to school and working experiences; but it also contributes to rendering the break more difficult, creating obstacles for the acquisition processes of emotional independence. Thus national research speaks of "a long family for adolescents" and defines Italy as "the country of mummy's boys" (Scabini 1995).

Though conflict is present in families with adolescent children, in most cases it is neither heated nor frequent, and concentrates mostly on exterior aspects (such as hairstyles and clothes styles) or on behavioral autonomy (hours, friends, proper behavior). However, especially in some southern areas, there seems to be a greater conflict and interference from parents toward daughters. Both from the children's and the parents' side, the style of the conflict is mainly oriented toward compromise. So we are not talking about conflicts that create a fracture between generations, but of conflicts that tend to create new balances and consolidate deep existing ties (Honess et al. 1997). Therefore, the conflict doesn't seem to have a use in favoring a break, but instead in building a new balance inside the family. It must in fact be highlighted that more than 70% of emerging adults between 18 and 30 continue to live with their families.

Italian families who have lived the experience of internal immigration have also experienced a bigger conflict, because of the considerable changes that have taken place. But we are now almost at the third generation and the phenomenon is quite contained. Concerning the present immigration from other countries, episodes are starting to occur that show a presence of conflict within these foreign families, especially in those coming from cultures very different from the Italian one. At the moment there are no data about this phenomenon.

The tendency for a low birth rate has led to a reduction in the presence of siblings and a full third of adolescents are an only child, while the rest mostly have only one brother or sister. The relationship between siblings is very different and strictly connected to the difference of age and gender. When the siblings are more or less of equal age (only a couple of years of difference) they carry out an important role model; an older brother represents a particularly important model for a younger sister. The presence of siblings of different gender makes the execution of family rules more difficult: in fact, in Italy males generally have greater freedom outside the domestic walls and they have to tolerate fewer rules concerning participation in housework. So when there are adolescents of different genders there is the possibility of numerous conflicts both among siblings and parents. Siblings in general, apart from being a model, are a source of support and confrontation. Such a role grows in importance in situations of separation or divorce of the parents or when a loss of one of the parents occurs.

The number of separations and divorces is in constant increase (separations were 15.8% in 1995 and 22.4% in 2000; divorces were 8% in 1995 and 11.5% in 2000), and these generally have a negative impact on the feelings of well-being of adolescent children. Italian law tends to give custody of children under 18 years old to the mother (over 90% of the cases) and often the relationships with the father are relegated to some weekends and half of the summer holidays. Formally rebuilt families are around 5% of the couples (this percentage is lower for women); most parents look after the children on their own or look for support from their family of origin, in particular from their own parents. The consequence is that extended enlarged families including more generations—not necessarily living together—take care of the children.

Friends and Peers/Youth Culture

During adolescence, friends and peers become very important for Italian boys and girls, as in other Western countries. In fact, constructing new social relationships constitutes one of the developmental tasks of adolescence. The amount of time spent with friends, with the family, and alone is almost the same (more than eight hours per week), although time with peers increases during adolescence and is greater for boys: girls spend more time at home alone. Nevertheless, in Italy the family still has a relevant influence (Scabini, Lanz, and Marta 1999). In fact, adolescents perceive strong parental support, feel close to parents, and often refer to parents for important life decisions. Adolescents also are likely to select friends whose opinions on important issues in life are quite similar to the opinions of their parents.

During a normal school week adolescents usually spend more time at home (studying, reading, and listening to music) than outside of it (e.g., in pubs and discos) and they are more likely to have dinner at home with the family than to eat out with friends. Meeting friends, going out and sharing meals with them (a pizzeria is more likely than a fast-food restaurant) is more frequent during the weekend and especially on Saturday evenings. Nevertheless, time spent outside the home varies greatly based on gender, age, and place of residence. Family rules about the time to come back home at night and the people the adolescent is allowed to spend time with are more strict for girls, even older ones, especially in small towns and in the south. However, staying at home with friends (watching TV programs or videos, playing with the computer, and also eating with friends' parents) is common and generally approved of by the parents. Throughout Italy, sharing meals is part of the normal process of maintaining friendships and building new ones, during adolescence and beyond.

Adolescent peer groups fulfill several positive functions for the development of identity of Italian adolescents (Kirchler, Palmonari, and Pombeni 1993). For instance, they offer the opportunity to experiment with new social roles and behaviors (both healthy and risky ones) and to share feelings and problems. Peer crowds are usually formed on the basis of common interests in sports, music, school, or sharing other types of activities. Generally, there are great similarities between the behaviors of the adolescents and those of their friends. However, among Italian adolescents the type of high school also is important (Buzzi, Cavalli, and de Lillo 2002): the lyceum students are more likely to select friends among their classmates and to have groups that are more homogeneous for age, value placed on academic achievement, and parental level of education. In fact, in Italy the parental level of education, which is generally lower than in Northern European countries (only 10% of the population between 25 and 64 years old has a university degree), is strongly related to their children's academic achievement and type of educational path.

Generally speaking, adolescents are more involved in sports groups (around 30%) than in other types of organizations. Belonging to a sports group is more common for boys and in the north or center of Italy. Nevertheless, belonging to a sports group does not imply exercising regularly, since watching sports matches or using the sports group as a recreational place is also widespread. Sports groups are followed in importance by church groups, including scout groups, which are more attended at younger ages and by girls, and by volunteer and political groups, which are more attended by older adolescents and emerging adults. The Italian church group has some peculiarities, such as the fact that not only very religious people belong to it and that recreational activities are also offered. In many small towns it is often one of the few social outlets for adolescents. In addition, the church group has been shown to fulfill a protective role against involvement in risk behaviors, as it offers the opportunity to participate in organized and long-term planned activities (Bonino, Cattelino, and Ciairano in press).

The tendency to move from more person-centered needs (such as those expressed by participating in sports) to more socially oriented values (such as participating in volunteer work or political activities) is characteristic of the transition from adolescence to emerging adulthood. However, while adolescent involvement in volunteer work is rapidly increasing in Italy, only a small percentage belong to political groups (around 5%) and generally they have extreme (left- or right-wing) political views. Nevertheless, interest in major issues such as peace, equality, and pollution has increased in the last few years, especially among older adolescents and emerging adults, though it is not related to a particular group. Other types of organizations of emerging adults are more local than those described above, such as the cohort of youths born in the same year who carry out their military service together, which is common in the small towns of the northern regions, or musical groups.

A distinct youth culture exists to the same extent as in other Western countries. This culture is influenced by both Americanization and globalization and is marked off from adult culture by dress, music, piercing, and—less frequently—tattoos. Italian adolescents, especially girls, attribute great value to the freedom to choose their clothes, and generally parents are likely to accept their choices.

The clothes and hairstyles worn by adolescents and emerging adults vary in relation to the type of music they listen to (more or less commercial, such as disco and pop, rap, and metal), the value attributed to physical appearance (in terms of clothes as well as body image), involvement or disengagement from community activities, ways of spending free time with peers (going to shopping centers to shop and walk around or going to public libraries and the cinema). However, clothes and hairstyles change very rapidly, making it impossible to distinguish stable, specific groups. Furthermore, what is peculiar of Italian adolescents is the widespread use of mobile telephones and cars (sometimes even before the legal age), which are among the highest in Europe.

Love and Sexuality

In Italy, as well as in all of Western society, the ability to construct interpersonal relationships with the other gender, based on both love and sex and characterized by parity and reciprocal respect, is widely acknowledged as one of the features of adulthood. This acknowledgement results from a change in the general attitude toward sexuality, which nowadays is more accepted than in the past, even before or outside marriage, though not homogeneously for boys and girls. Learning to be involved in dating, romantic, and sexual relationships may be considered one of the main adolescent developmental tasks (Zani 1993; Ciairano et al. 2006).

Italian adolescents are increasingly engaged in love and sex (Buzzi 1998): at older ages, having a boyfriend/girlfriend becomes more common (from about 30% at 15 years to 60% at 19 years), and engaging in sex increases (from less than 10% at 15 years, to 50% at 19 years and 80% after 23 years). Some differences exist, especially based on the type of school. Lyceum students are less engaged in sex than other students. Marriage before 20 years old is very rare (around 2%), and even at 29 years old only 30% are married. The percentage of cohabitation is low (around 5% of couples) and leaving home usually occurs with marriage.

Birth control is commonly used. The most widely used contraceptive methods are condoms (around 75%), the pill, and withdrawal (about 20% each, although use of the pill increases after 20 years). The majority of adolescents always use some contraceptive method and a low percentage (less than 10%) never use contraceptives (Buzzi 1998). In fact, the incidence of teen pregnancy is one of the lowest in Europe (around 5% of total birth and abortion rates). Only 1% of women have a child before they are 20 years old, around 11% before 24 years, and 30% between 25 and 29 years.

Not using contraception is more likely to be related to a low ability to insist on its use within an emotionally overloaded situation than to a lack of information (Buzzi 1998). Also, adolescents who frequently change partners are less likely to use contraception than those who can share this responsibility with a steady partner. About one-third of the adolescents do not always use safe prevention methods: 10% of adolescents who have sex have been infected with sexually transmitted diseases (STDs) other than AIDS.

The self-reported age at which boys and girls start having sex differs and is younger for boys. Boys and girls also differ in the way they choose to start (much more frequently within a steady relationship for girls, while boys are as likely to start with a close friend, a person they know just a little, a chance meeting, or a steady relationship) and for the sexual patterns they adopt (girls are more likely to adopt a high faithfulness pattern and boys a low faithfulness pattern). Pornography and sexual harassment toward peers are both higher among boys.

Attitudes toward sex are still different for boys and girls. In continuity with the traditional model, the image of male sexuality is strong and aggressive. Boys who have already had sex are likely to be more appreciated than the others in the peer group. Attitudes toward female sexuality are more ambivalent. Nowadays willingness to have sex is normally expected of girls, but a negative attitude toward women who have sex with a series of partners is still common, especially among men.

In general, attitudes toward sex are rapidly becoming more liberal and a matter of individual choice, which is different from the past (Buzzi, Cavalli, and de Lillo 2002). Nevertheless, there are varying degrees of approval for gender, age, and level of education. Older adolescents and emerging adults, girls, and better-educated people are more likely to approve. Parental attitude toward adolescent sex is in line with the general attitude. Generally speaking, mothers talk more than fathers of sex with their children, especially daughters. More precisely, mothers talk with their daughters in terms of postponement and contraception. Boys are less likely to talk of sex with their parents and more with friends.

In Italy, contraception and abortion became legal only during the 1980s. Minors are required to have the consensus of parents or a sentence by a juvenile judge in order to have an abortion. The rate of minors' abortion is less than 3% of all abortions. After the coming of age, this rate increases, and at 19 years old is more than 5%.

Sex education in the school and social policies for safe sex were uncommon until the 1990s, when AIDS started to become a problem of worldwide relevance. The first campaigns against AIDS and the other STDs were managed by a number of different public and private organizations, and only later was an institutional policy organized. This policy was more focused on limiting the damages than on a positive and psychological approach, such as the enjoyment of sex and gaining a greater confidence with one's own body. The programs of sexual education are often still very limited in duration; most of them are simply confined to one or two lessons by medical experts coming to the classroom, or addressed to the whole student population of a school during a general meeting. Also, the contents are often limited to the physical aspects of risk. Only since the late 1990s have more general programs, based on the improvement of life skills, been introduced; they concern the cognitive, social, and emotional resources that may promote a better adjustment to daily life situations including sex (namely communication, problem solving, and controlling positive and negative emotions).

Homosexuality is present in low percentages of male and female adolescents (from 1% to 6%). The attitude toward homosexuality is also becoming more liberal among Italian adolescents, though attitudes vary greatly based on cultural and educational contexts. The number of adolescents and emerging adults who approve of homosexuality for other people is much higher than the number of those who consider it possible for themselves (Buzzi 1998).

Health Risk Behavior

In Italy, as in other European countries, adolescence is a crucial period for experimentation with most behaviors that put people at risk for health and well-being (Currie et al. 2004). Furthermore, a lot of these behaviors diminish over time, some already after the ages of 16 to 17 (e.g., marijuana use) some after the age of 24 (e.g., deviance), while others stabilize themselves in time (e.g., risky driving).

Among legal drugs the most common are alcohol and tobacco, and among illegal drugs the most used is marijuana (Bonino, Cattelino, and Ciarano in press). In Italy the consumption of alcohol, particularly wine, is deeply rooted in the national economy and culture. The consequence is that most youngsters between 15 and 34 occasionally drink wine. It is generally a moderate consumption and abuse is quite rare. The early initiation generally happens in the family, and for this reason it is associated with a moderate consumption and tied to the participation in special occasions. On the contrary, the initiation during adolescence, which is less common, happens mostly in a friendly context, which also favors less control and a greater consumption. Beer is the most common alcoholic substance among young people. Even in this case, consumption is usually occasional, generally tied to going out at the weekend. Habitual beer drinkers and those who drink more than half a liter a day only represent a low percentage.

European statistics underline that in recent years in the countries of the south of Europe (in particular Italy) there has been a gradual decrease in the overall consumption of alcohol and in the problems associated with this. Such a decrease mainly leads back to a reduction in the consumption of wine and a parallel increase in the consumption of nonalcoholic drinks and of beer, characterized by a lower alcoholic percentage. However, an increase in the consumption of spirits has also been noted. So it seems that even in Italy "the Mediterranean" style, characterized by mainly drinking wine during meals or on special occasions, may be in the process of being replaced by a "Northern" style, which is characterized by a high consumption of beer and the consumption of spirits (Ciairano 2004).

Cigarette smoking among adolescents aged between 14 and 24 varies from 20% to 25%, depending on the gender, the age, the place of residence, and the social cultural context. The near totality of smokers are habitual smokers, and among this group nearly 22% are heavy smokers (20 or more cigarettes a day). Males smoke more and are generally more prone to a heavy and habitual consumption. Furthermore, young people who live in metropolitan and central areas smoke more. Most young people start smoking between the ages of 14 and 18. A premature start (before 14) represents a low percentage, with girls making up a larger proportion. Parents' and other family members' smoking behavior strongly conditions adolescents' behavior. In particular, the mother's behavior seems to greatly influence the adolescent's behavior. Moreover, smokers are more numerous among young people whose parents have a lower school qualification.

The most-used drug is marijuana: its use ranges from 12% to 30% depending on the gender, age range, type of school attended, and the place of residence. Marijuana is a drug that in Italy is defined and perceived as "soft" and not dangerous. After marijuana, the most hallucinogenic drug used is ecstasy, which has a much lower consumption. Even less used are the so-called "hard" drugs, only used by about 2% of the young population. The initiation age for cannabis-derived products is between 15 and 17 years, while for heroin, cocaine, and other hard drugs it is between 18 and 25.

Juvenile delinquency is not particularly high, but there are great differences connected to gender (with a greater implication for boys), age, and geographical area. Young people between 14 and 17 reported for crimes in a year are three-quarters Italians and one-quarter foreigners. Theft is the crime mostly committed by young people, in particular underage people, but in the last ten years a decrease in theft and an increase in drug production and dealing have been registered. The phenomenon of criminal gangs is limited.

Official data do not take into consideration criminal acts that are not reported. These are mostly acts of minor seriousness with which nonserious damage is associated; the exception is rapes and attempted rapes, which often are not reported for other reasons (such as shame or family relations with the perpetrator). Young people are the category most at risk of being victims of crimes against the individual (individual properties and violent crimes).

Even if the number of deaths is progressively decreasing, road accidents remain the main cause of death among adolescents and young people between 14 and 24 years old. For the younger ones (14 to 17) accidents mainly occur with a motorcycle, while between the ages of 18 and 24, nearly half of the accidents involve young people driving a car. Road accidents that mainly involve adolescents and emerging adults happen in the night hours of the weekend, frequently while they are coming back from a disco. The causes can be mostly found in a lack of respect toward the traffic code, while the seriousness of the effects is increased by the lack of attention given to safety: in fact, crash helmets on motorbikes and seatbelts in cars are regularly used only by a very low percentage of youngsters.

Considering gender, males are significantly more involved in drug and alcohol use, deviant behavior and risky driving, while female are much more involved in eating disorders.

The number of suicides and depressions among adolescents of 15 to 24 years old is very contained. In fact, among European countries Italy has one of the lowest suicide rates (about 7.5 out of 100,000 youngsters). Furthermore, the number of suicides and attempted suicides is slightly but continually decreasing. There are some differences in gender: suicide is most common among boys, especially underage ones (under 18) and attempted suicide is more common among girls. In both cases, the motivations are mainly of an emotional kind. Summarizing, the two most problematic behaviors seem to be cigarette smoking and dangerous driving.

Education

The level of literacy in Italy varies greatly depending on the geographical area and on the age of people: nearly a third of the whole population over 6 has a very low level of education (no title of study or primary school certificate), but such a percentage decreases to 5% for the age range of 25 to 34. Taking into consideration only this group, the majority of emerging adults have a secondary school certificate. The minimum school leaving age was one of the lowest in Europe; in 2000 it was raised from 14 to 16 years and in 2005 to 18 years. Even when the legal leaving age was 14, about 85% of young people continued their studies, with big differences connected to the geographic area: for example, the percentage increased to over 90% in the northwest and decreased in certain regions, especially in the south of the country. The rate of dropping out of school is different according to the geographic area and to the cultural level of the parents.

Adolescents with a regular school path enter secondary school at 14 years; this lasts five years, and at the end of this they take an exam equal to A-levels. There are different paths for secondary school with diverse specializations. Generally, they can be divided into lyceums (classical, scientific, linguistic, psycho-pedagogic, artistic schools), technical institutes (for accountants, surveyors, industrial technicians), and professional institutes (with different specializations ranging from artisan or secretarial and tourism to social care). The lyceums offer a wider general culture education, giving more space to Italian and foreign literature, history, and philosophy; the technical and professional institutes mostly teach practical subjects and give a preparation that aims for a faster insertion into the workforce. Access to the different types of school is free and generally the choice is influenced by the previous scholastic career of the adolescent, the level of education of the parents, and their expectations about the educational outcome of their child. The consequence is that the more gifted and motivated students generally enroll in a lyceum while the students who previously encountered

some problems in their studies and who think that they do not want to continue with a university path tend to choose a technical institute. Students whose career has been particularly troubled, and have had one or more failures of the scholastic year, generally enroll in a professional institute. Some of these pupils tend to reach the legal school-leaving age and then abandon school at 16 without any qualifications.

Even the social representations of the different kinds of secondary school are very different; generally the representation of lyceums and of the students who attend these schools is more positive compared with the representation of professional and technical institutes and the students who attend them. In the different institutes classes are mixed in gender, even if some specializations are chosen mainly by boys and some mainly by girls. Most students attend public school (around 98%) even if there are private schools, mostly tied to the Catholic Church. Some of these offer adolescents the possibility to attend colleges with canteen services after school, and sometimes offer boarding facilities on working days.

School experience varies greatly depending on the gender and type of school attended: girls generally commit themselves more to their studies and obtain better results. School is lived as a more rewarding and useful experience for the present by lyceum students, while students of the technical institutes—and especially students of the professional institutes—more frequently experience lack of success; they live the school experience as scarcely satisfactory and useful, and the subjects studied appear to be too difficult. Furthermore, they have a lower sense of school self-efficacy and a greater intention to leave the school.

At the end of the school path, regardless of the kind of school attended, all the students have access to a university path, and generally around 70% of young people continue to study after their A-levels. A lot of differences have been noted regarding university specialization connected to gender: boys are more numerous in the scientific and engineering degree group, while girls mostly choose a literary, linguistic, psychological, or education degree group. No differences emerge for the medical, biological, law, economic, and architectural degree group. The high percentage of enrollment to university degrees is due to the fact that alternatives to the traditional forms of higher qualifications are limited and professional advanced training is not very developed. It must also be underlined that levels of irregular careers and dropping out before obtaining a university degree are high. Undergraduates who obtain the best results are the ones coming from a lyceum (55% manage to get a degree), while the biggest problems are met by young people coming from professional and technical institutes (with success rates respectively of 23% and 31%). Girls commit themselves more and have a greater success compared with boys also at university. In Italy 17 out of 100 emerging adults have an honors degree (four or five years) while 1 out of 100 have a university diploma (two or three years). Official statistics place Italy amongst the first Western countries for the achievement of honors degrees and among the last ones for university diplomas. In fact, most university courses were of an honors kind up to 2001, when the academic system changed with the introduction of a greater number of three-year degree courses. University reform and revision are still underway.

High school provides differentiated programs for disabled adolescents—individualized educational programs (PEI). Furthermore, for young people with physical or sensory disabilities or with slight cognitive developments, classes have fewer students and there is the presence, at least for some hours a week, of a support teacher. Adolescents with severe handicaps are mostly placed in educational structures alternative to school, funded by public territorial structures (regional, provincial, or town council). On the contrary, there are no specific programs for gifted students.

Work

Three age periods may be distinguished in adolescent work. First, there is the work of adolescents younger than 15 years (or those who have not yet finished the period of compulsory education), which is not allowed by Italian law. Second, there is the work of adolescents from 15 to 19 years old, though school continues to be their main activity. Third, there is work in emerging adulthood after completion of high school or university education.

It is very difficult to estimate the extent of work by children, which is illegal. However, official statistics indicate that around 3% of children younger than 15 years work (this percentage is higher for boys and increases sharply at 14 years) and that around 1% are exploited. However, most work by children is seasonal, although intensive. The activities may be distinguished in two types. The first is more similar to adult work, such as working in a garage, a construction site, or a factory (more common for boys and more at risk of exploitation). The second consists of supporting the work of the family (more common when the parents are farmers, or own a shop, restaurant, or small business). In the second case, the work by children represents the attribution of some responsibility within a specific family culture; generally the children do not perceive their work as tiring or dangerous and they like it, sometimes even more than going to school. The link between school failure, dropping out, and work is greater for the adult-like work than for family work. Besides, competition between work and school is greater, especially when the parental level of education is low, in two opposite conditions: where the employment rate is high (such as in the northeast of the country; in this case school may not seem too important for gaining economic well-being) and where it is low (in this case work by children may be an important source of earning for the family).

The work of immigrant children is even more difficult to investigate than that of native Italian children. Two elements have to be taken into consideration: continuity with the original culture (whose representation of adolescence may be different from the Italian one) and the novelty of the new cultural context (whose moral values may be different). A third element consists of the difficulty in distinguishing between legal and illegal activities, such as when children beg for money, wash car windows, or sell something in the streets. The likelihood of being obliged to work in slavery conditions and to be sexually exploited is higher when the children are clandestine or alone. Nevertheless, the majority of immigrant children combine work and school. The original culture fulfills an important role. Two different cases have been most investigated: the case of Chinese children, who generally work with their parents in family activities, and the case of the Northern-African children, who are more likely to have come to Italy alone to work and to send money to the family in their country of origin.

Some experience with work also involves about 30% of adolescents between 15 and 19 years, who are normally attending high school. However, the large majority of this work is related more to the desire to gain some economic independence than to the need to contribute to the family economy or to the obligation to work. In fact, most of these adolescents work during the summer school holiday or on the weekend. They work in public places (such as pubs, restaurants, and shops), or do some type of apprenticeship (more or less related to their studies, though this is more likely for boys) or care-work (e.g., babysitting or helping younger children with their homework, though this is more likely for girls). In general the work by adolescents is paid "under the table"—that is, it is not registered officially and the owners do not pay taxes and health contributions to the national institutions. Adolescents generally like to work, although work may negatively influence their interest in academic achievement and performance. Moreover, the availability of money, often outside the control of the family, may offer these adolescents more chances than their peers to be involved in emerging adult-like activities, such as going to pubs and discos or buying legal and illegal substances.

The situation is different when the apprenticeship is part of a structured vocational course and is regularly and officially registered. Although there are some difficulties in organizing these courses effectively and in motivating pupils to participate, a regular apprenticeship may fulfill an important protective function for adolescents with a history of school failures who do not want to continue studying. Sometimes it may also promote a desire to return to high school.

The percentages of emerging adults who work regularly increases from 10% at 19 to 20 years to 70% at 29 years. The job market is probably more open now to emerging adults than it was a few years ago (the highest proportion of youth unemployment was registered during the 1990s), because of a more flexible job market. However, most of these jobs are precarious, temporary, and part-time. This condition of uncertainty is likely to be one of the reasons for the continuing postponement of further steps toward adulthood (e.g., independent living and marriage), which is characteristic of Italian society.

There are great differences in job opportunities in relation to gender, level of education, and region: finding a job is less likely for girls, despite their higher levels of academic achievement, for emerging adults with lower levels of education, in the south, in the islands, and in the northern zones characterized by industrial crisis. In addition, a lack of job orientation and of communication between the school and the job market is still common in Italy, despite the recent introduction of some orientation programs in schools and of private agencies for temporary work. Most emerging adults are still more likely to find some job within their family or friendship networks than in other more structured ways.

Media

As in other Western countries, TV has gained a growing importance in the life of adolescents in the last 30 years. The majority of Italian families own two or three TV sets. Research shows that adolescents under 19 watch TV for nearly 2.5 hours a day; this time varies according to the context, and is less than for elementary school children (around 4 hours). The time adolescents give to TV is nearly the same as or just more than the time given to studying, while it is more than the time given to listening to music, playing with video games, using the computer, or speaking on the phone.

It is a shared opinion that the qualitative level of Italian TV, both public and private, is generally lower than in the past and has been progressively decreasing in the last 20 years. Even if there is a code of protection for minors, there are numerous shows of violence and sex during daytime programing. The influence of TV is prevalently considered negative, not only for the exposure to violence, but also for the consumerist messages offered both by the programs and publicity. The latter is very frequent and fragments nearly all TV programs, including movies. Adolescents constitute a specific marketing target, in particular for dietary and beauty products, some foods, clothes, mobile telephones, and electronic gadgets. It is thought that TV influences women in a particularly negative way, giving extreme importance to ideals of excessive thinness and unobtainable beauty; but also in males the praising of models of a strong, confident, winning masculinity is thought to have an unfavorable influence on the development of identity.

TV in particular, and media in general, contribute in a relevant way to spread a negative image of adolescence as a period characterized by strange and dangerous behaviors; in fact, they give a lot of space to scoops and reports that show adolescents involved in crime or suicides, transferring the erroneous message that the majority of adolescents are involved in them. TV programs, just like films, are both local productions and imported, especially from the United States.

The radio audience is very high, especially among very young people. Adolescent readership of newspapers is quite low; only 20% of adolescents read them more than five times a week. On the other hand, comics and magazines especially printed for teenagers are widespread among this age group. Furthermore, the readership of books is not very high—about 55% read one to three books a year—even if there are great extremes among the different social classes and the types of schools.

The rate of adolescents having a computer available at home is more than 52%; adolescents use computer games both at home and in public places, like bars.

The wide diffusion of mobile telephones among adolescents, especially for the very young ones, has been a recent success; adolescents use them for conversations with friends and for sending a lot of short messages (called SMS).

Politics and Military

In Italy the voting age corresponds to the legal age, which is 18 years of age. From 18, people vote for the European Parliament, for one of the two Houses of the Italian Parliament (it is possible to vote for the Senate only after the age of 21 years), and for the local administrations (municipality, province, and region). Moreover, they can vote for referenda (special votes on specific subjects, which take place after being proposed by 500,000 citizens). From the foundation of the Republic in 1946, men and women have had the same voting rights.

Generally speaking, Italian adolescents do not participate much in the political life of the country, at least not through institutionalized political groups or other political organizations, from which the majority seem to be detached. Furthermore, the majority of today's adolescents have conventional social values and future plans that are quite similar to those of their parents' generation: finishing their studies, building a new family, and finding a good job. Nevertheless, the accomplishment of their plans is usually postponed compared to the past. Most youths also value peace, environmental protection, and justice, but only a minority actively participate at the demonstrations against war and globalization (e.g., anti-World Trade Organization). The participation in community life is increasing, including participation in volunteer work, but it only concerns around 10% to 15% of the youth population.

The rules concerning military service were changed in 2005, transforming it into a voluntary service. The change from a one-year period of compulsory military service for all young men aged from 18 to 26 years to a voluntary military service was made to guarantee a more qualified presence of Italians in international peacekeeping initiatives, in cooperation with other European and Western countries. Voluntary military service was possible previously but it concerned a minority of the soldiers (about the 10%).

The current voluntary military service is better paid and more flexible than the previous one: volunteers have the opportunity to choose the duration of their military service and are offered positions in public administration upon finishing. For all these reasons voluntary military service is likely to become an important source of work for youths. Voluntary military service is now open also to women, although very few women choose it (Esercito Italiano 2005).

A new voluntary national civil service was introduced in 2001. It was meant as a substitute for the civil service that had been available since the 1980s, instead of the compulsory military service, for young men refusing to serve in the army for ethical or religious reasons. This new voluntary service is open to both men and women aged from 18 to 28 years. It lasts 12 months and it involves activities in the following areas: assistance, civil protection, environment, artistic and cultural heritages, education and cultural promotion, and civil service abroad. From its initiation, the national voluntary civil service has involved an increasing number of girls. However, the phenomenon still concerns only about 1% of the female population (Ufficio Nazionale Servizio Civile 2005).

In Italy, youth paramilitary organizations are practically nonexistent. Only a small number of groups of hooligans are somewhat organized as paramilitary organizations.

Unique Issues

A characteristic trait that distinguishes Italian society from the rest of the countries of the European Union, even Mediterranean ones, is the very low birth rate, a phenomenon that has been happening since the 1960s but has worsened since the 1990s. The birth rate has decreased in the last 40 years from 2.6 to 1.2 children per woman; it is the lowest in Western Europe. This does not guarantee a generational renewal and the maintenance of the actual number of the population. Together with this low birth rate, there is a constant growth in the population of the elder generation due to increased longevity, which is one of the highest in the world: the lifespan in Italy is 77 years for men and 83 for women. Italy was the first nation where the number of people over 65 outnumbered (in 1993) the number of minors under 14. The population of minors has decreased in the last decade by about 12.5%. It is not yet clear whether immigration could change this trend.

This unbalanced number between the older generation, the adolescents, and the younger generation is creating heated debates on the future of the retirement system, on the welfare system, on the social politics for the family, and also on immigration. The phenomenon reflects on adolescence; in fact, the decrease in the number of adolescents and the parallel augmentation of the number of older people contribute to the intensification in negative and erroneous prejudice toward adolescents and young people. Furthermore, there is an augmented negative impression in adolescents and young people of having to take the responsibility in future, for a large part of the life cycle, of an enlarged older population that is no longer productive, and of having to continue to work well into old age to guarantee an adequate welfare system.

Although there are more grandparents living in the family circle in Italian society compared with the rest of Europe, there is a rise in the tendency for separation between adolescents and the elderly. Some local communities are committed to offering different activities and voluntary work that involve adolescents, youngsters, and the elderly, with the purpose of increasing contacts between the different age ranges.

As a consequence of the low birth rate, a full third of adolescents are the only child in their family, while the rest mostly only have a brother or a sister. According to some, this phenomenon has contributed to an increase in the tendency to lengthen the time adolescents live at home, or only leave the family in a partial or temporary way: ties between children and parents are tighter, rendering the break more difficult. The tendency to live longer at home is more marked in Italy than in the other European countries. The point of view from other scholars is that this preference is also influenced by another newer phenomenon, not unique to Italian society: the introduction of flexible, temporary, and precarious job styles, which lead to greater financial insecurity and generate greater preoccupation with the future.

SILVIA BONINO, ELENA CATTELINO, and
SILVIA CIAIRANO

References and Further Reading

Bonino, S., E. Cattelino, and S. Ciairano. 2005. *Adolescents and risk. Behaviors, functions and protective factors.* Berlin: Springer-Verlag.

Bosma, H., and S. Kunnen (eds). 2001. *Identity and emotion. Development through self-organization.* Cambridge: Cambridge University Press.

Bosma, H. A., S. E. Jackson, D. H. Zijsling, et al. 1996. Who has the final say? Decisions on adolescent behaviour within the family. *Journal of Adolescence* 19 (3):277–91.

Buzzi, C. 1998. *Giovani, affettività, sessualità. L'amore tra i giovani in una indagine IARD* (*Youths, affection, sexuality. Love among youths in a research of IARD*). Bologna: Il Mulino.

Buzzi, C., A. Cavalli, and A. de Lillo (eds.). 2002. *Giovani del nuovo secolo. Quinto rapporto IARD sulla condizione giovanile in Italia* (*Youths of the new century. Fifth report of IARD on the juvenile condition in Italy*). Bologna: Il Mulino.

Caprara, G. V., and A. Fonzi (eds.). 2000. *L'età sospesa* (*The suspended age*). Firenze: Giunti.

Caritas. 2003. *Immigrazione* (*Immigration*). XII Rapporto. Roma: Anterem.

Cattelino E., E. Calandri, and S. Bonino. 2001. Il contributo della struttura e del funzionamento della famiglia nella promozione del benessere di adolescenti di diverse fasce di età (The role of the family structure and the family functioning in the promotion of well-being in adolescents of different ages). *Età Evolutiva* 69:49–60.

Centro Studi Auxologici (Center for Auxological Studies). 2005. Growth and development of the baby and adolescent. http://www.auxologia.com/centroauxologico/index.html.

Ciairano, S. 2004. *Risk behaviour in adolescence: Drug-use and sexual activity in Italy and the Netherlands.* Groningen: Stichting Kinderstudies Publisher.

Ciairano, S., W. Kliewer, S. Bonino, R. Miceli, and S. Jackson. 2006. Dating, sexual activity, and well-being in Italian adolescents. *Journal of Clinical Child and Adolescent Psychology* 35:275–82.

Cicognani, E., and B. Zani. 1998. Parents' educational styles and adolescent autonomy. *European Journal of Psychology of Education* 13(4):485–502.

Currie, C., C. Roberts, A. Morgan (eds.). 2004. *Young people's health in context. Health Behaviour in School-aged Children (HBSC) study: International report from the 2001/2002 survey.* http:// www.hbsc.org/.

Esercito Italiano (Italian Army). 2005. http://www.esercito.difesa.it/.

Honess, T. M., E. A. Charman, B. Zani, et al. 1997. Conflict between parents and adolescents: Variation by family constitution. *British Journal of Developmental Psychology* 15(3):367–85.

ISTAT (National Institute of Statistics). 2004. *Rapporto annuale. La situazione del paese 2003* (*Annual report. The situation of the country 2003*). Annuario statistico italiano 2004. (*Statistical Italian Yearbook–2004. L'Italia in cifre–2004* (*Italy in figures–2004*). Roma: ISTAT. http://www.istat.it.

Jessor, R. (ed.). 1998. *New perspectives on adolescent risk behavior.* Cambridge: Cambridge University Press.

Jessor, R., J. E. Donovan, and F. M. Costa. 1991. *Beyond adolescence. Problem behavior and young adult development.* Cambridge: Cambridge University Press.

Kirchler, E., A. Palmonari, and M. L. Pombeni. 1993. Developmental tasks and adolescents' relationships with their peers and their family. In *Adolescence and its social world.* S. Jackson and H. Rodriguez-Tomé (eds.). Berlin: De Gruyter.

Marta, E. 1997. Parent-adolescent interactions and psychosocial risk in adolescents: An analysis of communication, support and gender. *Journal of Adolescence* 20:473–87.

Marta E., G. Rossi, and L. Boccacin. 1998. Youth, solidarity and civic commitment in Italy: An analysis of the personal and social characteristics of volunteers and their organizations. In *Community service and civic engagement in youth: International perspectives.* J. Youniss, M. Yates (eds.). pp. 73–96. Cambridge: Cambridge University Press.

ITALY

Marta E., and M. Pozzi. 2006. Young volunteers, family and social capital: From the care of family bonds to the care of community bonds. In *Citizenship education: Youth theory, research and practice*. M. Hofer, A. Sliwka, and M. Diedrich (eds.). Münster/ New York: Waxmann.

MIUR (Ministry for Education, University and Research). 2004. *Alunni con cittadinanza non italiana (Pupils with not Italian citizenships). Indagine sugli esiti degli alunni con cittadinanza non italiana (Survey on outcomes of pupils with not Italian citizenship)*. Roma: Servizi di consulenza. http://www.istruzione.it.

Palmonari, A. (ed.). 1997. *Psicologia dell'adolescenza (Psychology of adolescence)*. Bologna: Il Mulino.

Scabini, E. 1995. *Psicologia sociale della famiglia (Social psychology of the family)*. Torino: Bollati Boringhieri.

Scabini, E., M. Lanz, and E. Marta. 1999. Psychosocial adjustment and family relationships: A typology of Italian families with a late adolescent. *Journal of Youth and Adolescence* 28:633–44.

Scabini E., E. Marta, and M. Lanz. In press. *Transition to adulthood and family relationships: An intergenerational perspective*. London: Psychology Press.

Sgritta, G. B. 2000. Adolescenza: La transizione difficile (Adolescence: The difficult transition). In *L'età sospesa*. G. V. Caprara and A. Fonzi (eds.). Firenze: Giunti.

Silbereisen, R. K., K. Eyferth, and E. Rudinger. 1986. *Development as action in context. Problem behaviour and normal youth development*. Berlin: Springer-Verlag.

Ufficio Nazionale Servizio Civile (National Office for Civil Service). 2005. http://www.serviziocivile.it.

Zani, B. 1993. Dating and interpersonal relationships in adolescence. In *Adolescence and its social world*. S. Jackson and H. Rodriguez-Tomé (eds.). Berlin: De Gruyter.

523

J

JAPAN

Background Information

In 2004, about 126.2 million people were living on the small islands of Japan (37,800 square kilometers), which lie in the northwestern corner of the Pacific Ocean near the Eurasian continent. Of these people, nearly 2 million (1.5% of the population) were foreigners. Koreans made up the largest group at 635,000, followed by Chinese and Brazilians. Thus, modern Japan is a multiethnic country rather than a monoethnic one. The population density was 337.4 persons per square kilometer.

Contemporary Japan is highly industrialized and economically successful; its population is well-educated and aging. As Ezra Vogel wrote in his compelling book, *Japan as Number One: Lessons for America* (1979), the world has kept a vigilant watch on Japanese economic prosperity. Such economic success has enabled more than 99% of the Japanese to be literate, and has supported a high standard of health, along with the highest average life expectancy in the world (85.2 years for women, 78.3 years for men in 2004). Statistical indicators of the population structure show a decline in fertility and a concomitant increase in aging. The pyramidal distribution of the population is quickly shifting. While the percentage of people over 65 is increasing (19% in 2004), the percentage of people under 25 (26% of the population in 2004, as against 53% in 1955) is decreasing.

The "bubble" economy collapsed in the early 1990s after decades of enormous economic growth. Since then, the Japanese economy has been in a state of recession bordering on depression. The bankruptcy of major enterprises, including big banks, has made people rethink their economy-oriented values and productivity-first lifestyles. The highest unemployment rate in the nation's recorded history (4.6% in 2004) has kept demand low. In the early years of the twenty-first century, signs of recovery were reported, and Japan's GNP (the Gross National Product) accounted for 13.6% of the world's total GNP in fiscal 2003; but Japan's GNI (Gross National Income) dropped from third to fifth among major countries. The national treasury, which survives by issuing government bonds, cannot sufficiently support the economically weak segment of the population. In prosperous times, most Japanese people firmly believed that they belonged to the middle class; however, since the start of the recession, some social scientists have published evidence of accelerating societal stratification (Kariya 1995).

These changes in society have most directly influenced adolescents, as we will discuss here. In particular, adolescents cannot look forward, as did the previous generation, to a peaceful and well-ordered future life, because of the lifelong employment system that once characterized the Japanese economy has been disrupted. On a positive note, the recession has cooled the national enthusiasm for academic elitism, which attaches high value to diplomas from prestigious universities. This attitude, which verges on snobbery, had long characterized Japanese society. Instead, adolescents today have explicitly or implicitly been urged to find and choose a lifestyle that suits them as individuals.

Coming out of a feudal society through the Meiji Restoration in the middle of the nineteenth century, the Japanese rapidly and continuously developed modern socioeconomic systems. Moreover, the defeat in World War II in 1945 allowed a fresh start for contemporary Japan, namely, the transformation from a militaristic, nationalistic, and feudalistic society to a democratic one. Japan has proclaimed its peaceful antiwar attitude by renouncing war in its Constitution. However, as an inevitable consequence of the American postwar occupation, ending in 1952, Japanese independence was tied to a military and economic alliance with the United States, over the objections of left-wing parties, labor unions, and students. In accord with the Japan–United States Security Treaty of 1953, Japan has continued to provide bases for American troops, aircraft, and ships. Even today, the treaty is controversial and is often criticized in the media. In addition, because of their traumatic experiences under the militaristic and nationalistic government, Japanese citizens often express objections to any political backlashes in the direction of the prewar style of government. Moreover, because they are the victims of the atomic bombs dropped on Hiroshima and Nagasaki, the Japanese people have a particular sensitivity to nuclear power and the dangers it poses, even when it is used for generating electricity.

Period of Adolescence

It was during the Meiji Restoration, the end of the closed-door policy of the feudal government in the middle of the nineteenth century, that adolescents became visible as such within Japanese society. Through the restoration, from the 1850s to the 1880s, Japanese society rapidly and successfully achieved economic, military, and technological modernization. This drastic change attracted adolescents and inspired them to pursue their dreams and beliefs. In the succeeding decades, many youngsters fought against the feudal government and the existing imperial social system; some of them were living in rural areas and moved to the cities to actualize the possibilities they dreamed of; some others went abroad to study. These prosperous years brought with them democratic ideas and the establishment of a democratic culture, known as the Taisho Democracy, in the 1910s. The dark side of this success was the nation's development as a colonial power, which dragged young people into wars up until the end of World War II.

The defeat of Japan was traumatic economically and psychologically, especially for children and adolescents. However, the Japanese people energetically struggled through the chaos and rapidly recovered their self-confidence. For instance, when the Revised Security Treaty with the United States was ratified in 1960, hundreds of thousands of Japanese people who belonged to left-wing parties, labor unions, and student associations, as well as unaffiliated individual citizens, expressed strong objections. From then until the late 1970s, students strongly protested against existing social systems and values, particularly as embodied in colleges and universities. These students' protests contributed at least to the addressing—if not the solving of—such problems as the hierarchical, authoritarian structure of faculties, professor-centered curricula, and student-teacher relationships. However, the Japanese economic prosperity of the 1960s and 1970s, in which Japanese electric and industrial products flooded markets worldwide and companies suffered from a shortage of labor, spoiled young people and led them to be nonpolitical and conservative. Since then, adolescents have been confronted with psychological consequences that could be said to be symptomatic of an "overdeveloped" country.

In 2004, over 97% of 15- to 18-year-olds of both genders were in high school, and 74% of male and female 18-year-olds were in college, junior college, or vocational school. Only 10% of the labor force consisted of people under age 24. The unemployment rate among the younger generation was higher than that among the older generation: 13% for ages 15 to 19 and 9% for ages of 20 to 24 (the overall unemployment rate was 4.6%). An estimated two million or more young people were working as "job-hoppers," part-time workers employed on a flexible basis. In accord with Japanese customs, young people have generally lived with their parents before they married. In recent years, perhaps because of a confluence of circumstances, such as the delay of marriage and the preference for a single lifestyle, adolescents of both genders have continued to live with their parents well into their thirties and beyond. These young people are reluctant to accept conventional ways of living as adults, and they are parasitic on their parents as to food and shelter. However, on the positive side, they prefer to enjoy an unsettled but self-determined life (Sengoku 2001). Thus, we observe truly a new developmental stage among the Japanese, "emerging adulthood" as Arnett (2004) put it.

Beliefs

The individualism versus collectivism concept has been the most popular framework for comparing Eastern and Western cultures. In it, the various cultures of the world are plotted on a single continuum, where two extremes—the individualistic and the collectivistic—are at either end. It is hypothesized that on this bipolar dimension, most Western cultures are placed relatively close to the individualistic end, and Eastern cultures are placed toward the collectivistic end (Markus and Kitayama 1991). However, today most social scientists do not give unqualified support to this concept, which has been widely criticized. For instance, the dichotomy is too simplistic; there is no consistent empirical evidence that definitely supports the dichotomy, and there are not only commonalities across cultures, but also variations within each culture. In fact, a comparative study of social relationships between American and Japanese adolescents and adults indicated that only half of the hypotheses generated by the individualism versus collectivism concept were supported by empirical data (Takahashi et al. 2002). In any culture people can be expected to have dual, seemingly incompatible tendencies toward attachment and detachment, dependence and independence, harmony and autonomy.

A survey indicated that young people in their teens and twenties were not as motivated to work toward high achievement as they were to pursue happiness and close relationships with others. The survey showed that at the turn of this century young people tended to establish "loose" social relationships within the family and the workplace, and they frequently interacted with friends through mobile phones and computer devices (Nitto and Shiozaki 2001). Young people were looking for their own paths to self-actualization. In particular, they were less reluctant to change jobs and less interested in working at a big enterprise than were their counterparts in the 1980s and 1990s. Instead, some of them

preferred to "job-hop" from one non-permanent job to another.

According to a study comparing youth in Asian countries (the Philippines, Thailand, and Korea), Japanese adolescents in the early 2000s were not very religious, similar to adolescents in Europe (France, Germany, and the United Kingdom). Although they were accustomed to Buddhist ceremonies and traditions, such as the worship of their ancestors, only 3% of them marked that religion was "very important" and only 27% indicated that it was "important" (Ministry of Education 2003). Traditional religious people were shocked to learn that a cult named Aum, which killed innocent citizens by releasing sarin gas on a Tokyo subway in 1995, had attracted young people, including university graduates with majors in chemistry, technology, and medical science, who had been unsatisfied with their lives and appeared to have lost their direction.

Gender

The first wave of the feminist movement in Japan was found in the 1880s, when a few female groups protested inequalities between the genders and the unfair treatment of females in the society. In 1945, the vote was extended to females by the Occupation officials. The Japanese government declared that all women and men are equal before the law, but the reality has been quite different. In the 1970s, in the second wave of feminism a number of groups of women in different places in Japan organized to achieve women's liberation. While coping with attacks by the existing male-dominated powers, the movement gradually raised women's awareness of their situation under a system that often amounted to patriarchy. In 1976, the Women's Institute was organized in Kyoto, and from there many controversial and stubborn advocates of feminism have emerged. By 2005, discussions of and research on gender equality have begun to enter the mainstream of Japanese journalism and academic societies.

In and after the 1970s, gender equality and concepts of equity that were advanced by the feminist movement have slowly but steadily infiltrated Japanese law, social systems, the work place, school curricula and administration, academic organizations, and civic life. Laws related to women's welfare in Japan (the Law of Equal Employment Opportunity in 1986; the Child-Care Leave Law in 1991) are not sufficient enough to support people who are suffering from gender-biased ideas and treatment in society, but people have responded favorably to the Basic Law for a Gender-equal Society, enacted in 1999, which guarantees basic human rights to women. However, as in other countries, there have been various "backlashes" by politicians and scholars with conservative views.

Citizens, politicians, and scholars who are concerned with human rights keep a close watch on a variety of issues related to gender discrimination. One survey indicated that the majority of people of all generations witnessed unfair conditions for females in the family, schools, and workplace. Clearly, there are still many problems to be addressed. For example, in the family, many studies suggest that parents continue to treat females and males differently and encourage them to accept traditional gender roles.

Although the percentage of females who advance to higher education (junior college, technical college, and university) has doubled in recent decades, fewer girls than boys attend four-year universities (34% versus 48% in 2004). In school gender-biased themes, descriptions, and figures have been identified in textbooks. Numerous cases of academic harassment, including sexual, have been brought before committees or the court. Moreover, school systems in Japan are still dominated by males. For example, in 2004, 31% of the teachers in junior-high schools were females, but only 4% of school principals were female. In most academic societies the percentage of female members has been rising, but executive positions have continued to be predominantly occupied by males. In the universities, only 14% of professors on average were female.

There have often been occupational segregations by gender in Japan. Females were assigned nonprofessional jobs and worked as mere clerks for many years, while their male counterparts of similar educational background were placed on a career track with key responsibilities, promotional opportunities, and more. Mothers with young babies experienced many difficulties in continuing to work. Although the bottom was gradually rising, there was an M-shaped curve in the labor force. Only 29% of mothers who had young children (0- to 3-year-olds) worked, whereas 49% of mothers of 4- to 6-year-olds, and 63% of mothers of 7- to 9-year-olds had returned to the work place (Ito and Sugihashi 2003). In a society such as Japan, young working women who are highly educated and motivated to pursue their self-actualization as skilled professionals have been reluctant to marry because they are not very optimistic about life as a wife. Even if they have married, many have put off childbirth until after they established their own

careers. As a natural consequence, the total fertility rate is very low and falling: it was 1.29 in 2004. The male-dominated government purportedly takes the looming decrease in population seriously and has announced plans to build childcare facilities and create social networks to support young parents, but feminists have coolly pointed out that such proposals only indicate the government's misunderstanding of young women's views on current society and the future (Ogura 2003).

Thus, although unresolved gender problems abound, grass-roots feminism will not permit progress to be rolled back. The Japanese are making progress toward gender equity and equality. For instance, a survey in 2002 indicated that the majority of individuals in the younger generations objected to traditional gender roles, including the statement that "males work outside of the home and females stay home." In 1993 in junior-high schools and in 1994 in high schools, students of both genders began to study home economics. In universities, many lectures and seminars relating to gender issues have been presented, and some universities have developed special courses, graduate programs, and research centers on the topic. Moreover, some big enterprises such as Shiseido, a cosmetics company, are developing female-friendly and gender-blind employment systems. Finally, in this era of information technology, every citizen can freely access information related to gender issues. In particular, the database provided by the National Women's Educational Center (http://www.nwec.jp) and by the government (http://www.gender.go.jp) have been widely accessed.

The Self

A recent survey indicated that along with the recession in the Japanese economy, survey scores that reflect the national identity of the Japanese people, including young people, have gradually decreased. Nearly 70% of the respondents were satisfied with their present conditions regarding food, clothing, housing, amenities and social relationships, but only 31% of the young people were satisfied with the present society (Cabinet Office 2004a). Another study indicated that, as shown in Figure 1, a majority of the adolescent participants preferred to live to fulfill their own interests or hobbies (82%) and to think of themselves first (57%). They reported that they were self-confident (48%), but did not want to stand out as unique (61%). It has often been pointed out that these individualistic attitudes have become prevalent among Japanese people in general and not only among young

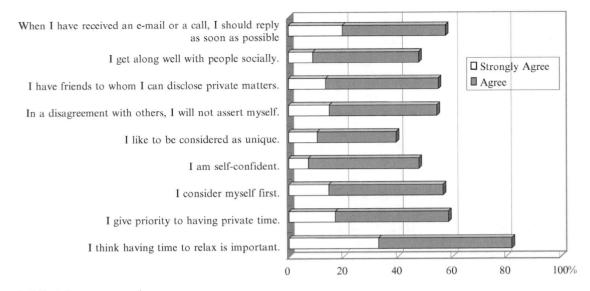

Figure 1. Lifestyle among youth.
Source: Tokyo FM 2004.

people (Tokyo FM 2004). Another survey of young people indicated that only 66% would be willing to defend their country. If Japan suffered an attack from a foreign enemy, they believed that they could and would move to a more peaceful place.

Equality and fairness toward minorities and other disadvantaged groups such as children, females, handicapped persons, elderly people, aboriginal Japanese, Japanese people who are socially isolated for one reason or another, and people from other countries—including hundreds of thousands of Korean nationals born and raised in Japan—are areas of serious consideration. For instance, it is often maintained that Japan is a mono-ethnic and culturally homogeneous country (Reischauer and Jansen 1995). However, in reality Japan includes a variety of ethnic groups: the Ainu (who are regarded as native Japanese or Japanese aborigines), non-Japanese-Japanese (Korean-, Chinese-, and Brazilian-Japanese), and Japanese-Japanese (mainstream Japanese). By the early twentieth century, the Japanese government was strongly engaged in a policy of integrating the minority Asian ethnic groups, forcing them to adopt Japanese names and the Japanese language, and the mainstream Japanese were indifferent to this officially sanctioned prejudice. From years of work to win reasonable rights for minorities and the weak, violations of human rights, privacy, and identity are no longer treated with impunity, although there are still conflicts and social stigmas in schools and the workplace. The Convention on the Rights of the Child took effect in 1994. While there are still abuses of children's human rights, including physical abuse,

and sexual/academic harassment, a greater sense of human dignity has filtered into the hearts of young people.

Family Relationships

In Japan the family has been the most basic unit of society and continues to function as such. Most children grow up in intact, two-parent families and continue to live with their parents until they themselves marry. The divorce rate is increasing, but at 2.3 per 1,000 in 2003, it—and the ratio of unwed mothers—is lower than in Western "overdeveloped" countries.

However, as in Western countries, both the social and the psychological roles of the family are changing. First, young people, especially females, are showing greater indifference to marriage and being parents than in the past. In a 2003 survey, only 16% of adolescents answered that humans should by all means marry, whereas 22% claimed that marriage was unnecessary. In addition, 48% of the participants accepted the concept of divorce (Cabinet Office 2004a). The age of marriage has been rising: in 2004 it was 28.6 for females and 30.8 for males, and the proportion of unmarried people has been increasing; among Japanese aged 25 to 29, 54% of females and 69% of males were single. The total fertility rate has also been decreasing; it was 1.29 in 2004. The average number of family members was decreasing: 2.7 in 2004, as opposed to 4.5 in 1960. A survey in 2000 indicated that 39.5% of Japanese families consisted of a parent(s) and a child(ren). Only 10% of families lived with three generations under one roof. The average number of siblings among people who were born in 1975–1979 was 2.38.

Second, the relationships between parents and adolescents have been changing from authoritative to virtually friend-like. After the loss of World War II, the traditional authority and power of parents were largely rejected as feudalistic or old-fashioned. Parents were not as self-confident in their discipline as they had been in previous generations. Some of them were very protective and preferred a laissez-faire policy. In fact, many recent studies among youngsters indicate that their parents are not strict, but affectionate and protective. Their parents report that they trust their children and allow them to be independent. At the same time, the parents report having various conflicts with their children with regard to schoolwork, TV programs, and behavior (NHK Broadcasting Culture Research Institute 2003).

Third, family members are too busy to experience many close interactions with each other. Many wives are working outside the home; if their children are adolescents, more than 70% of wives have a job, mostly for economical reasons. Husbands spend a long day at the office. After the recession set in, husbands' working conditions became so demanding that some of them died of overwork (*karo-shi*, death from overwork), and others suffered from mental disorders such as depression. In these families, 83% of the wives are forced to take care of the house, and, if they are mothers, perform childcare in addition to their paying job. Thus, wives bear heavy burdens both inside and outside the home. Because parents expect their children to graduate from college (66% for girls and 78% for boys), junior-high and high school students attend prep schools after school to train for the required entrance examinations. Surveys have often indicated that family members eat separately.

Fourth, there have been some mental problems relating to the family. There is a group of adolescents who simply stay at home for more than six months (in many cases for many years). They are specifically called *hikikomori* (withdrawer) because they hate to join in any social activities, including school and work. In 2003, about 15,000 withdrawers (77% of them were males) and/or their parents asked for support from guidance and health agencies. They stay home while their parents take care of their financial and physical needs. The reasons these young people are reluctant to be social remain poorly understood; in some cases, there is evidence for traumatic causes both inside and outside the family. The parents of the withdrawers are often criticized and accused of being the cause. Some shelter programs have helped these young people and their parents.

Violence between a parent and an adolescent is not infrequently reported. First, there are abused parents. Some adolescent offenders have violently abused their parents, especially their mothers. In some cases youngsters have killed their parents, and in others parents killed their adolescent children out of fear and desperation. One cause of abuse seems to be that the adolescent seizes upon the mother as a scapegoat for her or his failure to achieve success in school or in a job. Second, even adolescents can be victims of child abuse. Recently, a 15-year-old boy was killed because his parents deprived him of food for months. Because parental authority has traditionally been regarded as sacred and special, institutional authorities suspecting abuse have been prevented or felt inhibited from intervening in family matters. It is hoped that an amendment of the Child Abuse Prevention Law in 2004, in which the parents' rights are weakened, will be effective in rescuing children from abusive parents.

In Japan, people have long believed that a blood relationship is important for being a family, and adoption is not common. If a couple wishes to adopt a child, it will most often be from a blood relative, and usually the parents and the relatives will not tell the child that he or she was adopted. Recently, there has been some movement towards adopting "non-kin" children and telling the child and others about the adoption. Nevertheless, while mixed marriages have become more prevalent, the adoption of a child with different heritage from the parents is still not common in Japan.

In a registered marriage, civil law requires each couple to register one and the same family name. At present, 98% of the couples choose the husband's family name. Because of the inconvenience caused by changing one's family name—such as in their careers—many young women continue to use their maiden name as a nickname at school and at work. An annual national survey indicated that the proportion of citizens who agree that the civil law should be changed to allow each spouse to keep her or his family name after marriage is increasing.

Friends and Peers/Youth Culture

For adolescents, friends are their most important social figures, and they spend many hours with them. In a survey, they reported that "friendship" was the most important (62% of the participants) and an indispensable (78%) factor in their life.

They consulted with friends about their worries (59%). Ninety percent of the participants stated that they had best friends, and 31% in junior-high school and 40% in high school had friends of the opposite gender. At school, 24% to 65% of students of both genders from junior-high school to college were involved in club activities. Ninety-three percent of junior-high school and 90% of high school students reported that they enjoyed school life because they had friends at school. Similarly, undergraduate students reported that the most important aspect of their college life was the expanding and deepening relationships they had with friends (Takeuchi 2003). Now that the five-day work week and five-day school week have taken hold, the Japanese enjoy their "off" days by participating in sports and social activities, and youngsters spend much of their weekend time with friends. On holidays, 71% of students reported spending time with friends (Cabinet Office 2004a).

On the other hand, some negative aspects of peer interactions have been reported, such as severe bullying. A majority of junior-high and high school pupils reported having some experiences of being teased, and most confessed to sometimes being very irritated by their peers (NHK Broadcasting Culture Research Institute 2003).

By the 2000s, many young people could not conceive of interacting with their friends without the privacy and frequency permitted by having one's own mobile phone. The economic success of the family provides a private room and a private phone. Through phone calls and e-mails, adolescents can actively interact with their friends without parental control. In 2003, 41% of junior-high school, 89% of high school, and 98% of college students had their own phone; and 90% of high school and 98% of college students used e-mail. This consequence of affluence seems to allow youngsters to perceive themselves as living apart from the family, weakening their emotional bond with older generations (Information and Communication Policy Bureau 2003).

There are many cross-cultural studies on friends and friendships, but an important question is whether the term "friend" connotes the same thing to adolescents in every culture and whether they similarly differentiate the "best friend" from more casual friends and/or newcomers. In one study, students of both genders from junior-high school to college were individually interviewed as to their moral understanding of friendship by using a dilemma story which posited conflict between one's best friend and a newcomer (who might not be a friend in the Western sense of friend). The findings indicated that the meaning of "best friend" was similar to previous findings in Western studies (Krappmann, Oswald, and Uhlendorff 1994). The participants clearly stated how the best friends were special. However, they largely resolved the conflict through a different strategy from their Western counterparts. That is, the Japanese adolescents considered the newcomer as a friend and expressed a preference to solve the conflict by treating both the friend and the newcomer well. This research suggests that the category of "friend" for Japanese young people must be broader than that of their Western counterparts, although they articulated the same psychological meanings for various types of friends (Hirai and Takahashi 2003).

While adolescents actively interact with friends, they also love to be alone, usually playing their favorite music and movies in their own room with various types of audiovisual equipment such as a VCR, DVD player, MD player, and personal computer. As noted above and below, mobile telephones are essential to young people. Through their own telephone, they exchange e-mails and pictures, obtain information, reserve seats, and enjoy games and music.

Love and Sexuality

Opposite-gender interactions are one of the most important concerns for adolescents. Figure 2 shows the results of a study indicating who was the closest, that is, the core partner in the social relationships of junior-high school to college students. As the figure shows, the proportion of romantic-partner types, for whom the romantic partner or the closest opposite-gender friend was the most highly rated among several significant others, such as parents, siblings, friends, and teachers, increased with age (Takahashi 2004).

Both rapid biological maturation and the urbanization of society have accelerated the age of sexual activity among adolescents. Surveys have consistently reported that adolescents experience sexual activities at an increasingly younger age. One-third of high school pupils and more than half of college students reported having had sexual intercourse. Seventy-one percent of the females and 64% of the males stated that they loved their partner; the rest said they had engaged in sex out of curiosity.

Sex education from early childhood through high schools was started in the early 1990s. Students are taught not only biological information but also about the psychological nature of relationships with the opposite sex. Equality and equity between the two genders and reproductive rights should be

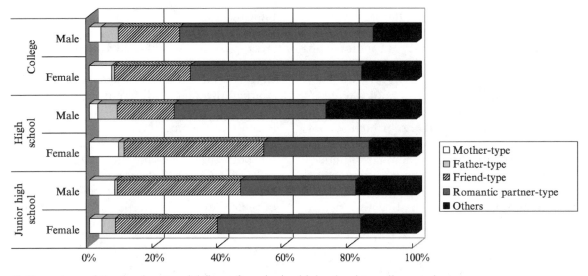

Figure 2. Percentage of the dominant social figure from junior-high school to college students.
(Note: The participants identified their social relationship type in terms of the dominant figure. The dominant figure was a figure who was rated predominantly among several significant others by each adolescent; for example, the mother-type adolescent more highly rated her/his mother than other figures.)
Source: Takahashi 2004.

main issues in sex education. However, there are implicit and explicit conflicts between innovative and conservative educators and politicians. Conservative people claim that sex education awakens and stimulates students to engage in sexual activities. Innovative educators, female lawyers, and medical doctors of obstetrics and gynecology have been heavily involved in developing the sex education curriculum for adolescents, especially for females.

A study showed that in 60% of the sexual activities, males took the initiative, whereas females did in only 2%. As a result of these male-dominated activities, 20% of the females became pregnant unexpectedly. Adolescents have not always been careful about using contraception, and the abortion rate among teenagers was reported to be increasing: 11.8 per 1,000 teenage girls had such experiences in 2001 (Japanese Association for Sex Education 2001). Another issue is that of sexual harassment. The Ministry of Education has urged the use of systems to prevent sexual harassment in the schools, and every year, some professors and teachers are forced to resign for inflicting such harassment. Sex education also includes information about the nature and prevention of HIV/AIDS and other sexually transmitted diseases. A survey indicated that students lacked sufficient knowledge and showed little interest in these infections. However, as of 2005, more than six thousand cases of HIV infections and three thousand cases of AIDS diagnosis have been reported in Japan. Furthermore, the number of HIV infections is increasing

among Japanese and foreigners living in Japan in their twenties and thirties. In 2003, 630 new cases of HIV infections were reported.

As seen above, young people are not as interested in getting married as were previous generations. In one survey, 22% of adolescents claimed that one did not need to marry at all. Fifty-four percent of females and 69% of males aged 25 to 29 years were single in Japan in 2004, and 30% of all marriages ended in divorce or desertion. The divorce rate was highest among young couples. Thus, young people did not appear to insist on upholding the traditional marriage system in which couples registered their marriage. A majority of high-schoolers had a steady opposite-gender friend, and the high-schoolers expressed frank attitudes about sexual behavior. They reported that if a couple loved one another, it was natural to have sexual relations and to live together.

Females have long been the primary victims of such sexual offenses as violence, rape, stalking, molestation, pornography, and prostitution. Although there are several laws against these deplorable and traumatic acts, protective practices that show more sensitivity toward the victim are needed. The sexual human rights movement has promoted a better understanding of homosexuality and of various disorders of gender identity. Medical operations for these disorders were legally permitted in 1998 in Japan, and in 2003 an individual was permitted to change her or his gender in the family registration information. Responding to protests against the tradition of asking the sex of an applicant, some local governments have deleted the question from their official forms.

Health Risk Behavior

Juvenile penal code offenders aged 14 to 19 who are cited by the police are governed by several laws concerning antisocial behavior. There were 17.5 violators per 1,000 among 14- to 19-year-olds in 2003; 43% of them were high school students and 26% were junior high school students. The proportion of females was 24%. The ratio of juveniles to all code offenders was 38%. Seventy-two percent of these offenders were arrested for initial delinquencies such as shoplifting, bicycle or motorbike theft, and misappropriation of lost property, which were committed for simple motives including mere curiosity. However, the findings also suggest that these initial violations often led to serious crimes. Adolescents who were neither in school nor working committed even more serious crimes, including murder. The low number of serious crimes occurring in Japan can be attributed in large part to the strict control of weapons, such as guns, swords, and knives, and the high arrest rate of offenders. For driving-related violations, such as driving without a license or speeding, half-a-million adolescents were cited. For sexually deviant acts and damages, such as prostitution and playing or working at adult amusement places, more than 4,000 adolescents were given guidance (Cabinet Office 2004a).

Over the past decade, as more serious crimes such as murder and bus-hijacking were committed by teenagers, authorities have begun to claim that the juvenile penal codes are not effective enough for either prevention or rehabilitation. However, experts on adolescent mental problems have asserted that these teenage offenders, who have mostly been brought up in a normal middle-class environment with highly educated parents and had been doing well in school, represented tension or abnormalities caused by contemporary societal pressures in Japan. In relation to this trend, a survey suggested that Japanese people felt that society was becoming unsafe.

Drug problems are not common among Japanese adolescents at present, but authorities warn of an increase in numbers. In 2003, nearly 500 juveniles (60% female) were cited for offenses involving stimulant drugs, nearly 200 adolescents (9% female) were arrested for cannabis use, and nearly 2,000 (43% female) were cited for abusing paint thinner. Thus, among the drug-related offenses of adolescents, abusing paint thinners accounted for the majority. The proportion of females abusing drugs has been increasing. For heinous drug offenses, more than 2,000 adolescents were cited, an 11% increase from the previous year (Cabinet Office 2004a).

Violent acts by students were reported by 32% and 44% of junior-high and high schools, respectively. Peer abuse (teasing and bullying among students) was also reported by 37% and 25% of public junior-high and high schools, respectively (Cabinet Office 2004a). Unlike school violence, incidents of teasing and bullying were not often apparent, and some severe cases were revealed only after the targeted students committed suicide or were killed.

In 2003, more than 1,000 cases of domestic violence perpetrated by youngsters were reported. Twenty-two thousand adolescents ran away from home. Forty-one percent of them were junior-high school students and 59% were females. An analysis of the home environments of a group of delinquent boys indicated that 40% of their families had no apparent problems, whereas 24% had no close relationships with family members, 15% had difficulties with family members, and 8% were neglected by family members (Cabinet Office 2004a).

Nearly 500 young people committed suicide in 2002. Authorities became focused on a new type of suicide, the "Net" suicide, in which some people, including teens and people in their twenties, looked for persons through the Internet who wished to die with them, who then committed suicide together by carbon monoxide poisoning. An increase in eating disorders among adolescents (95% of them are female) has been proposed to be a new disease symptomatic of an era of satiation. Some studies have indicated that eating disorders are culture-bound pathologies because the media, peers, and other influences create sociocultural pressures upon females to be slim. An analysis of female patients indicated that a strict diet for weight loss often led to such disorders (Makino 2004).

There are many kinds of support in Japan to aid the adjustment of juveniles to society through probation systems such as autonomy-support residences and consulting organizations. There were 2,200 public counseling offices for the prevention of serious problems among adolescents and their parents. In 2003, 820,000 cases were accepted by these offices.

Education

After World War II, the 6-3-3-4 system of schooling and coeducation was adopted. In addition to the 6-3-3-4 system, there are two-year colleges, five-year technical colleges, and a variety of vocational training schools. Schooling is compulsory for nine years in elementary and junior-high school for students from 6 to 15 years of age. Almost all students who have completed junior-high school are entitled to apply to a high school or a college of technology; 97% went on to such institutions in 2004. Forty-eight percent of females attended two- or four-year colleges (34% in four-year colleges/universities; 14% in two-year colleges) and 50% of males (48% and 2%, respectively). After graduation, 12% advanced to graduate programs. Less than 2% of young pupils at the ages of compulsory education were in special programs for the handicapped. The University of the Air, which has undergraduate and masters degree courses, provides a variety of educational television and radio programs. More than 12,000 students from all parts of Japan attended the University of the Air in 2004. The national expenditure for education (the ratio of the expenditure to the general annual expenditure) was 10.2% in 2004.

For a few decades, the Japanese people had regarded education as the one and only passport to a happy life. Both parents and children strongly believed that at all costs one must enter a prestigious college. How to release adolescents, parents, and teachers from focusing on the academics-oriented, grade-centered, and highly competitive schools has been the most urgent educational issue in Japan. Since the early 1990s, the Ministry of Education (now called the Ministry of Education, Culture, Sports, Science, and Technology) has been changing Japan's educational policies and has introduced a "releasing policy" in schools. The new principles and rules were proposed to give pupils and teachers more latitude. Some curricula contents were deleted, the length of the school day was decreased, and a five-day school week program was introduced into schools. However, the swing of the educational pendulum to release students, which was accompanied by the economic recession of the 1990s and a drastic decrease in the number of children, is producing new and complicated problems in education.

First, some surveys have indicated a definite stratification of society in Japan (Kariya 1995; Nitto and Shiozaki 2001). In education, studies have indicated that the higher the social class the parents belong to, the longer the children study per day. Moreover, the parents of middle-class families prefer to send their children and adolescents to private schools, which maintain the previous curricula and six-day school week program. In these private, prestigious junior-high and high schools, pupils are taught beyond the curricula that the government suggests for ordinary schools. Thus, to get into these schools children and adolescents (50% of junior-high school students) attend *juku* (prep schools) often until nine or ten o'clock at night for many years, at great expense. High school students who have failed their college entrance examinations usually study in private prep schools, *yobiko,* with their parents' financial support. Consequently, prestigious schools tend to consist of students from middle-class families. In fact, the average annual income of the parents of students at a high-ranking institution such as Tokyo University is higher than that of others. This cycle thus widens social inequality.

Second, after the releasing policy in schooling took effect, some teachers and scholars suggested there was a decline in the academic ability among students. In fact, a nationwide achievement test among high school students in 2002 and an international academic competition in 2004 produced clearly lower scores, especially in mathematics and the sciences. In addition, surveys repeatedly indicated that students in high school were losing their motivation to learn, and one-third of them reported experiencing zero learning time per day. In 2001, the Ministry of Education reluctantly admitted that the new policy was unsuccessful. Even under the releasing policy, 2.7% of all junior-high school students were not attending school and 2.3% of all high school students were dropouts in 2003. The survey indicated that most of the students left school because of difficulties in adjusting to the school climate and in studying. About 11% of college students also dropped out before graduation, because they no longer wanted to study (Ministry of Education 2004).

Third, the decrease in academic aptitude is becoming the most serious problem for colleges. Because of the decreasing number of students, the competition for entrance is becoming less severe. Without intensive preparation for the entrance examinations, most students can enter college if they do not mind which college they go to. In fact, 84% of candidates were able to enter college in 2003. It is anticipated that in several years every student who would like to enter college could be accepted at one. There were 508 two-year and 708 four-year colleges in Japan in 2004. For their survival, each college is developing attractive new programs and curricula. A variety of entrance exams have been designed to attract excellent students. The government has required 176 national and public universities to be financially self-supporting and has strongly recommended that colleges and universities evaluate the quality of the teaching and the research abilities of their staff. A survey indicated that these modifications were positively accepted by students (Takeuchi et al. 2004).

Japanese educational policy is controlled by the state. Scholars, teachers, and parents have begun to speak out against the nationalistic backlashes. In this vein, at least two controversial issues should be pointed out: the official screening of textbooks from elementary school through high school, and the displaying of the national flag and the singing of the national anthem at school ceremonies. The government's flag-and-anthem policy has grown so strict that a large segment of the population, including teachers, parents, and students, are protesting because the Japanese flag and anthem were used as symbols of a nationalistic, militaristic Japan in the imperial age.

As to the screening of textbooks, a Japanese historian, the late Professor Saburo Ienaga, and his supporters began a court fight in 1965 against what they considered to be the constitutional illegality of the system. This fight continues. In 2002, a textbook of Japanese history for high school students written by a group of nationalistic scholars was approved by the Ministry of Education. Scholars have many disputes with those authors' interpretations of Japanese history, especially concerning Japan's military affairs during World War II with Asian countries; such as Japan's domination of Korea, China, and other Asian countries, and the reasons for the conflicts and the number of victims of misdeeds.

The high percentage of school participation suggests that almost all Japanese are literate. A majority of those in their twenties are graduates of higher education, and less than 2% of young people start to work immediately after the compulsory schooling cut-off age of 16. Moreover, the international student assessment of 15-year-olds among the OECD countries grouped Japanese adolescents into the higher achievement group (Ministry of Education 2004). However, are the young Japanese really literate?

Some researchers claim that young people are not intrinsically motivated to learn. In fact, a survey indicated that only a small group of youngsters enjoyed reading books. That is, the average number of books read per month by junior-high and high school students was less than two (Mainichi Newspaper 2004). It is often pointed out that young people have been losing the ability to read and write *kanji* (Chinese characters). Another survey found that the average study time (homework) on a weekday after school among college students was one hour, less than half that of junior-high or high school students, but similar to that of elementary school children (NHK Broadcasting Culture Research Institute 2002). Moreover, studies have indicated that adolescents' understanding of societal systems and institutions is not adequate. Although living in a capitalistic society in which economic literacy is indispensable for competent citizens, they hardly understand the profit-making mechanism of a large enterprise such as a bank (Takahashi and Hatano 1999).

There are new educational programs with an international focus that foster intercultural contacts. However, the education of "returnees"—children and adolescents who have returned to Japan after spending time in foreign countries—and "newcomers" who came to Japan from Brazil and elsewhere in Latin America are controversial. In addition to having language problems and trying to catch up academically, these young people are confronted with cultural gaps between Japan and the other countries in which they have lived. Such children and adolescents encourage their Japanese classmates and teachers to accept multiplicities of values and even to change systems. Moreover, there are many Asian students who come to learn in Japanese colleges and universities. In response to the booming demand for learning Japanese, some colleges are developing new courses to teach the Japanese language to foreigners.

Work

Since most adolescents graduate from high school and 49% of them enter college, the youth workforce accounted for 1.8% (in the 15 to 19 age group) and 8.3% (in the 20 to 24 age group) of the total national workforce in 2003. A majority of the youth workers had jobs in manufacturing and in small- or medium-sized enterprises. The average normal workweek for these individuals was less than 40 hours in 2003. Eighty-eight percent of the workplaces followed the five-day work week. The number of paid holidays granted to each worker per year was 18.2 days, but workers used an average of 8.8 days (Cabinet Office 2004a).

The job-leaving rate within one year of employment was relatively high in 2004: 47% and 25% among junior-high school graduates and high school graduates, respectively. Within three years, 70% and 50% left for "personal reasons" (Cabinet Office 2004a). A survey indicated that 14% of young workers wanted to leave and 43% sometimes considered leaving because of low wages (50%), difficulties in human relationships (26%), and job satisfaction (23%) (Tokyo FM 2004). Although the government has suggested that the national unemployment rate is declining (4.6% in October 2004), the unemployment rate of youth has been relatively high: 11.9% in the 15 to 19 age group and 9.8% in the 20 to 24 age group in 2004.

As Figure 3 shows, there is clear gender discrimination in the starting salaries of new graduates and in monthly wages and promotions. A governmental statistical report indicated that the differences became greater with increasing worker age. Because these wage differences are used as the basic standard with which to estimate compensation for accidents, the inequity of the wages is one of the most serious problems in the Japanese working system.

Increasing attention is being focused on "job-hoppers," individuals who work part-time and often change their workplaces. It is estimated that there are two million job-hoppers, and one out of four college graduates begins her or his working life as a job-hopper. Some of them, the majority of whom in 2004 were females, stated that they prefer to pursue a certain way of life than a career and hope eventually to find an appropriate steady—if not permanent—job that fits their lifestyle. Thus, some young people, rejecting the values of the traditional lifelong employment system, feel free to place priority on their way of life over the demands of their vocation. While some of these individuals may be enjoying a moratorium on becoming full-fledged members of society, others no doubt suffer from the instability of being intermittently jobless and the fact that they do not possess solid enough qualifications to earn a livelihood.

Another type of lifestyle among young people has been identified: a group in their teens and twenties (estimated at a half million by the Ministry of Health, Labor, and Welfare in 2004), who were not in education, employment or training, in short, NEET. This new phenomenon has been interpreted as a manifestation of "student apathy" following the collapse of the bubble economy.

With the exception of so-called vocational schools or high schools specializing in technology, commerce, or agriculture, most school students are not intensively trained in the special knowledge and techniques required to perform jobs. After school or graduation, students attend special training schools, such as schools for foreign languages, computers, or various arts. Some other students enter graduate programs or take courses to obtain special licenses, such as those needed to work as clinical psychologists, medical technicians, and lawyers.

Media

The media in contemporary Japan are definitely characterized by the rapidly advancing electronic technology and communication engineering. Adolescents are the most active users of these devices. According to a survey, the favorite media among younger generations are the mobile phone, mobile tape recorder, CD/DVD/VCR players, game players, computers, and magazines, whereas the hours spent on newspaper reading and TV watching are shorter among young people than among the older generation. Thus, adolescents are more concerned with personal media than mass media, except for magazines. In particular, for personal communications besides talking, they exchange voice mail, text messages, e-mails, and pictures/photographs through mobile phones, mostly with age-mates and colleagues. In addition, over 90% of adolescents in 2004 were using the Internet through mobile phones and computers for exchanging e-mails, downloading and listening to music, downloading graphics, and gathering information; there were no gender differences in the percentage of users (Information and Communication Policy Bureau 2003). In 2003, it was reported that 72% of households had at least one personal computer. The compulsory

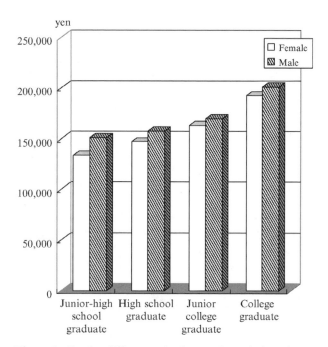

Figure 3. Gender differences in the starting salaries of new graduates of March 2003.
Source: Cabinet Office 2004a.

education in computer sciences in schools is likely to be accelerating this trend.

Of mass media, a survey indicated that adolescents enjoy TV programs, music on CDs and audiotapes, movies on DVDs and VCRs, magazines, and comic books. The most popular mass medium is TV, which youngsters watch two to three hours per day. An annual survey on reading (Mainichi Newspaper 2004) indicated that half of the adolescent participants read books (1.3 to 2.3 titles on the average) and 70% of them read magazines, but less than 20% of them had read a newspaper in the previous month. Ten to 15% of young people bought the books through an online system, mostly through mobile phones.

A survey of the youth culture showed that young people of both genders from junior-high school pupils to 25-year-olds were commonly interested in computer games, comics, music, and movies. They loved Japanese pop music and Asian (mainly Korean) movies (Tokyo FM 2003). In addition to these passive forms of entertainment, young people produce music, drama, cinema, and photography. For example, a group of female photographers in their early twenties has created a new type of photograph that daringly violates traditional techniques. The women have won prestigious awards, and the attention to their work has attracted other young people to this discipline.

There have been various discussions on the influences of media on human development. First, some sociologists (Yoshimi 2004) have pointed out that mobile phone communication has definitely changed the social relations within families. Previously, a family landline phone in the living room essentially functioned as a public phone in the household; parents often knew who their children were talking with on the phone, and others in the living-room could hear their side of the conversation. In contrast, mobile phones brought private conversation or text communication with speakers or senders who were unknown to the other family members, without any apparent need to consider an appropriate time, place, or occasion. As we mentioned above, almost all adolescents in Japan from high school students to young workers have a mobile phone, whereas 59% of all Japanese had them in 2002. Second, media content is often argued to be high in violence, human rights violations, and gender bias. Psychologists have warned that the violence pervasive in videogames subtly gives rise to aggressive behaviors among college students beyond the virtual world (Sakamoto 2005). Gender bias in advertisements has often been pointed out by citizens and feminists. Third,

it is becoming apparent that adolescents need media literacy to be wise and autonomous users. Aggressive words blurted out or hastily e-mailed have reportedly touched off conflicts between young people, especially teens, leading in extreme cases to homicide.

Politics and Military

Japanese parents must declare the birth of a child within two weeks and have it recorded in a family register. At age 20, each individual automatically obtains voting rights. A 25-year-old is qualified to run for a seat in the Lower House, but for the Upper House one must be at least 30. After violent objections against ratification of the New Security Treaty in 1960, and the intense revolutionary movement in colleges during the 1970s, young people today tend to be conservative or uncommitted voters. The voting rates among people in their twenties were recently the lowest (30% to 35%) among the Japanese, and many of these were floating voters. As we mentioned above, like their Western counterparts, Japanese 18- to 24-year-olds are more satisfied with their life outside of the job than on the job.

Defeat in World War II brought great changes to the military system, based upon Article 9 of the Constitution, through which Japan declares that she shall renounce military force forever and will not have an army, navy, or air force:

> Article 9: 1. Aspiring sincerely to an international peace based on justice and order, the Japanese people forever renounce war as a sovereign right of the nation and the threat or use of force as means of settling international disputes. 2. In order to accomplish the aim of the preceding paragraph, land, sea, and air forces, as well as other war potential, will never be maintained. The right of belligerency of the state will not be recognized.

This "peace clause" has prevented the Japanese from joining any war since 1945, including the Gulf War and Iraq War. Telephone interviews with electors in 2004 (Asahi Newspaper 2004) found that 58% of the Japanese expressed strong objections against Prime Minister Koizumi's cabinet's decision, for the reason of supporting Iraq's reconstruction, to extend the stay of Self-Defense Force troops in Iraq. The survey indicated that females (especially middle-aged women) were more negative than males. Conscientious citizens, including jurists, claimed that the decision of the Koizumi cabinet violated Article 9 and they are concerned that the cabinet is leaning toward reformation of the Constitution because of Article 9. A big survey among high school students (n = 9,000) indicated that 67% of the adolescents believed that the "peace clause" contributed as a deterrent to conflicts between nations. Forty-nine percent of the participants expressed their objection to reforming the Constitution, and only 11% of them agreed to reform Article 9 (Japan High School Teachers Union 2004).

Traditionally, social services in Japan were based on the religious precepts of Buddhism or Christianity. Even social scientists claimed that community services were offered mostly by religious persons and they often wondered how to promote citizens' active involvement in voluntary helping behaviors. To remedy defective social perceptions and raise social awareness, community services began to be encouraged in schools in 1989. In high schools, subjects such as social welfare, community service, and voluntary activity were introduced. College students must have social service experiences to obtain a teacher's license. Such attempts in the schools appear to have had some cumulative effects. The Hanshin-Awaji earthquake of 1995, in which more than 6,000 were killed, brought about a drastic change in the concept of volunteering among the Japanese people. Against expectation, just after the earthquake, many, including students and young workers, devoted themselves to voluntary activities. It was reported that 60,000 persons per day performed voluntary work, and a total of one million worked to help victims cope with the aftereffects of the earthquake. Sixty-three percent of them came from outside the city. Half the volunteers did not belong to any organization, and most of them were young people (Honma and Deguchi 1996). Voluntary activities at the Chuetsu earthquake in 2004 proved anew that Japanese people, especially adolescents, have learned to be prosocial. A survey indicated that 20% to 40% of teens and young adults had participated in volunteer activities in 2004.

Generally speaking, young people are politically conservative with no firm political allegiance. The seventh international comparative study indicated that, like their counterparts in other countries (Korea, the United States, Sweden, and Germany), about half the Japanese adolescents (18- to 24-years-old) were interested in their national politics. Similar to Koreans and Germans of the same age, a majority were unsatisfied with their country's social conditions. Nearly 70% of the young Japanese wanted to contribute to social welfare and 30% to 40% had worked as volunteers (Cabinet Office 2004b).

Unique Issues

Confronted with the recession of the Japanese economy, adolescents have been floating around, seeking direction (Takeuchi 2004). Another researcher summarized their characteristics in terms of "neo-egoists" (Sengoku 2001). As mentioned, studies have repeatedly indicated that adolescents are conservative and not very involved in social matters, instead voicing without hesitation that they think of themselves first. They are not very satisfied with their situation and disregard figures of authority such as famous universities, major enterprises, and the government, with many of them being reluctant to follow traditional customs such as lifelong employment and marriage.

However, if viewed from a different angle, one can see adolescents as preferring to make their own decisions about their lives and as being self-confident. Most of them are excellent users of sophisticated technology and through the new devices they are expanding their social networks and social resources beyond traditional borders. Although they are politically indifferent, they are active in voluntary activities and have clearly developed a sense of equality and fairness.

These new lifestyles among adolescents were brought about by Japanese economic prosperity, and the recession has released adolescents from various traditions and values and urged them to be independent. Through its youth, Japanese society is moving toward a new stage of development, that is, toward a less competitive, more mature stage after 60 years of reckless postwar rehabilitation.

KEIKO TAKAHASHI and KIYOSHI TAKEUCHI

The authors gratefully acknowledge Giyoo Hatano for his providing valuable comments on earlier drafts of this article.

References and Further Reading

Arnett, J. J. 2004. *Emerging adulthood: The winding road from late teens through the twenties.* New York: Oxford University Press.

Asahi. 2004. http://www.asahi.com.

Cabinet Office. 2004a. White paper on youth.

Cabinet Office. 2004b. The Japanese youth: The 7th international comparative study among adolescents.

Hirai, M., and K. Takahashi. 2003. Culture and the concept of friendships: How do Japanese children resolve a conflict between the best friend and a newcomer? *Japanese Journal of Psychology* 74: 327–35.

Honma, M., and M. Deguchi. 1996. *Volunteers revolution* (in Japanese). Tokyo: Toyo-Keizai-Shinpo-sha.

Information and Communication Policy Bureau. 2003. http//www.stat.go.jp/data/it.

Ito, Y., and Y. Sugihashi. 2003. *Statistical data book for gender-equal plan*. Tokyo: Gyosei.

Japan High School Teachers Union. 2004. *A survey on attitude toward the Constitution among high school students*. Teachers Union.

Japanese Association for Sex Education. 2001. *White paper on sexual activities among adolescents*. Tokyo: Syogakkan.

Kariya, T. 1995. *Mass educational society: A postwar-history of diplomatism with equal-opportunity ideology* (in Japanese). Tokyo: Cyuokoron.

Krappmann, L., H. Oswald, and H. Uhlendroff. 1994. *The emergence of intimacy in peer relationships during preadolescence*. Berlin: Max-Planck Institute for Human Development and Education.

Mainichi. 2004. *The 57th survey of reading*. Tokyo: Mainichi Kikaku Service.

Makino, Y. 2004. Eating disorders as culture-bound pathologies: The idealization of thinness among young people. PhD diss, University of the Sacred Heart.

Markus, H. R., and S. Kitayama. 1991. Culture and self: Implications for cognition, emotion, and motivation. *Psychological Review* 98:224–53.

Ministry of Education. 2003. *A reply to the Educational Committee*.

Ministry of Education. 2004. *Japanese education at a glance*.

NHK Broadcasting Culture Research Institute. 2002. *Life time survey 2000*. Tokyo: NHP Publishing.

NHK Broadcasting Culture Research Institute. 2003. *A survey of life and attitude among junior- and high-school students*. Tokyo: NHP Publishing.

Nitto, H., and J. Shiozaki. 2001. *The changing Japanese: A survey of values and lives as consumers* (in Japanese). Tokyo: Nomura Research Institute.

Ogura, C. 2003. "Conditions of marriage" (in Japanese). *Asahi*.

Reischauer, E. O., and M. B. Jansen. 1995. *The Japanese today: Change and continuity*. Enlarged ed. Cambridge, Mass.: Belknap.

Sakamoto, A. 2005. Video games and the psychological development of Japanese children. In *Advances in applied developmental psychology: Theory, practice, and research from Japan*. D. W. Shwalb, J. Nakazawa, and B. J. Shwalb (eds.). pp. 3–21. Greenwich, Conn.: Information Age Publishing.

Sengoku, T. 2001. *Neo-egoism among youth: A value of self-determinism*. Tokyo: PHP Interface.

Takahashi, K. 2004. Close relationships across the life span: Toward a theory of relationship type. In *Growing together: Personal relationships across the lifespan*. (F. R. Lang and K. L. Fingerman (eds.). pp. 130–58. Cambridge, U.K.: Cambridge University Press.

Takahashi, K., and G. Hatano. 1999. Recent trends in civic engagement among Japanese youth. In *Roots of civic identity: International perspectives on community service and activism in youth*. M. Yates and J. Youniss (eds.). pp. 225–44. Cambridge, U.K.: Cambridge University Press.

Takahashi, K., N. Ohara, T. Antonucci, and H. Akiyama. 2002. Commonalities and differences in close relationships among the Americans and the Japanese: A comparison by the Individualism/Collectivism concept. *International Journal of Behavioral Development* 26:453–65.

Takeuchi, K. (ed.). 2003. *Campus life* (in Japanese). Tokyo: Tamagawa University Press.

Takeuchi, K. 2004. A survey among junior-high and high school students. *AURA* 168:2–6.

Takeuchi, K., K. Iwata, and K. Hamajima. 2004. *A survey among twelve colleges: 1997 vs. 2003*. Paper presented at the 56th Conference of Japanese Educational Sociology.

Tokyo, F. M. 2004. An analysis of life styles among young people (radio broadcast). http://www.tfm.co.jp/wakamono/top.html.

Vogel, E. F. 1979. *Japan as number one: Lessons for America*. Cambridge, Mass.: Harvard University Press.

Yoshimi, S. 2004. *Theory of media culture: The fifteen lectures for introduction* (in Japanese). Tokyo: Yuhikaku.

JORDAN

Background Information

Jordan is located in the northwest section of the Arab Peninsula, with an area of 92,300 square kilometers. Its estimated population is about 5,480,000, of whom about 36.6% are less than 15 years of age, 60% are between 15 and 64, and about 3.4% are older than 64 years of age. There are approximately 200,000 (13%) individuals in the age range of 13 to 18 years. The great majority of the population is Arab (98%). Only 1% of the population is Circassian and 1% is Armenian. Muslims represent about 92%, and Christians about 6%, of the population. A little more than half of the population is male (52%). Also, a little less than half of the population is composed of displaced Palestinian refugees.

Britain recognized Trans-Jordan as an independent state in 1923. However, Jordan acquired its independence in May 1946. Jordan participated in the Arab-Israeli War in 1948, during which Israel conquered two-thirds of Palestine and established its state. Jordan controlled the other third, including the West Bank and East Jerusalem. In 1950, a joint Jordanian-Palestinian conference declared the West Bank of River Jordan as part of the Hashemite Kingdom of Jordan. The first parliamentary election was held in 1956 but was interrupted for a variety of internal and external reasons. In 1967, Israel launched a war against three Arab states: Jordan, Egypt, and Syria, and Israel occupied the West Bank of Jordan, thus Jordan lost half of its population, which has been ever since under Israeli occupation. In 1988, Jordan severed its ties with the West Bank of Jordan but kept religious authority over Jerusalem.

Jordan follows the constitutional monarchy as a political system. King Abdullah II is the fourth king; he has ruled Jordan since its independence. As a young monarch, he has influenced the country's attitude toward young men and women, their education, and their roles in development.

Jordan's history and development can only be properly understood in terms of the influence of the Israeli-Arab conflict and the issue of Palestine. Jordan participated in two wars and several battles with Israel for the cause of Palestine, and Jordan suffered a civil war in 1970 in which the Palestine Liberation Organization (PLO) fighters and some East Jordanian sympathizers fought against the Hashemite regime.

Following the Iraqi invasion of Kuwait in 1990 and the subsequent war, large numbers of work migrants to the Gulf States were expelled and returned to Jordan. This occasioned the third major population influx into Jordan. In 1991, Jordan, jointly with Palestinian delegates, participated in the Middle East Peace Conference in Madrid, and in 1994 Jordan signed a peace treaty with Israel.

Period of Adolescence

Adolescence per se is not an officially and legally recognized life stage in Jordan. Adolescence is not treated as a separate stage of life in the constitution, by the judiciary, or within the social context. The law in Jordan, which is partly rooted in the Islamic religion (*Shari'a*), treats individuals younger than 18 years of age as minors. Aside from within academia, "adolescence" and "youth" are used to refer to individuals between the ages of 13 or 14 and 24. Each term has a different connotation. "Adolescent" (*moraheq*) is frequently used to refer to unusual behavior, dress, or appearance. That is, when a behavior is out of context or in contradiction with normal acceptable conduct, people may justify such a behavior by describing the doer as an adolescent. "Youth" (*shab*), on the other hand, has a more positive connotation. A person may be referred to as young or a youth when a young person expends an appropriate level or energy in accepted activity.

As Jordanians are mostly Muslims, Islam expects that parents urge their children to pray (prayer in Islam is five times a day: dawn, noon, afternoon, sunset, and night) at the age of 7 and punish them at the age of 10 if they do not pray. However, not all Muslims in Jordan and outside Jordan practice this religious command. Also, Islam orders Muslims to fast during the month of Ramadan from the sunrise to sunset. Since this religious practice is once a year, many Muslim children do fast as early as the first and second grades in school. Fasting is a private religious affair and cannot be observed, hence no statistics are available as what the ratio of those who fast is, and for that matter no statistics are available about the number or ratio of families who order their children to pray. But one can say with confidence that the number of children and adolescents who pray nowadays is more than before. One explanation of this change in number is the challenge Muslims face, whether in Jordan or elsewhere. It seems that the more Western and anti-Islam propaganda attacks Islam and the more Muslims are challenged to adopt Western standards and norms and abandon their religion, the more they get closer to it. Yet, many Muslim adolescents in Jordan do adopt Western standards and norms.

Married life is considered to be one of the most important aspects of the transition to adulthood. Up until the mid-twentieth century, men and women married at a younger age than in the twenty-first century. The agricultural and tribal pattern of life required strength in the form of a large number of individuals, especially males. Therefore, families were concerned to marry their children at younger ages—at puberty—for reproduction purposes. A simple life and fewer financial demands made it easier for parents to accommodate their married children in the same house. Islam urges parents to have their children marry as soon as they can afford it. For example, pilgrimage for Muslim parents can be waived until all their children are married.

In the early twenty-first century, however, only a small portion of young men and women get married young. Only about 3% of young men got married at the age 15 to 24, compared to about 20% of women of the same age (Jordanian Youth Survey 2000). In a five-year period (1997–2001) about 69,953 girls of ages 15 to 19 years got married; however, the ratio of those marriages to the total marriages is decreasing from 36% in 1997 to 30% in 2001. As such, adolescence, though a vague period, is longer today than in the past. Although no exact statistic is available on the average age for marriage in Jordan, the average marriage age is certainly well above 25 years. In some rural and nomadic areas the average age of marriage is probably less than 25.

As in other societies, there is a period of emerging adulthood. However, this emerging period is vague and cannot be characterized as being practiced exclusively by one social class or another. It is not similar to the same period found in the West and does not entail that adolescents be independent of their parents. It is uncustomary to find an adolescent or even an adult Jordanian who is not married and lives away from his or her family. Children who are not married after adolescence stay with their parents and in most cases they are dependent on their parents. In some instances, however, emerging adults support their parents and other family members (such as brothers and sisters) if the family is in need of their support. One should distinguish between men and women when dealing with emerging adulthood. Girls get married at a younger age than boys. However, if a girl is not married, she can never be independent of her parents, whether financially, socially, or personally. The family supports the girl as long as she is not married. In rare cases, however, the girl can support the family if she has work, but this is contingent upon the economic state of the family. The occurrence of the family being dependent on the boy is rare, but it is even rarer that the family depend on the girl.

Beliefs

Jordan is subject to influences from abroad through the large share of the inhabitants that move in and out of the country in search of work. As Jordan is basically a Muslim and developing country, it can be classified as a collectivistic or semi-collectivistic country. Collectivistic vis-à-vis individualistic means that individuals are group-oriented. So, whereas the center of all social processes and activities is the individual in the case of individualistic cultures, family, tribe, or any other social unit is the focus of social process in collectivistic cultures. Also, Jordan is mainly conservative in that individuals adhere to family norms and values. Values are usually taught to children and adolescents in two ways: formal and informal. Schools and their curricula undertake the formal type of teaching values. As part of formal education, Islamic education and national education are essential parts of the school curriculum that emphasizes social and family conservative norms and values such as respect for elders, respect and care for neighbors, as well as the value of cooperation vis-à-vis competition.

Conformity to social and tribal norms and values is one characteristic of the Jordanian society. Also, conformity to religious and national values is of great concern to many families in Jordan. It is probably important to refer to one of the convictions held by many Jordanians of Palestinian origin, and that is the right of return to Palestine as it is the land of their ancestors. Extended family, regardless of ethnicity, origin, or religion works hard to secure children's conformity to its norms and values.

Adolescents in Jordan have always been influenced by new ideas and fads, especially in the city and urban areas. Political and religious parties realize the readiness of adolescents to adopt new ideas and fads. They used to attract a significant portion of adolescents in Jordan. Recently, political parties (for example, national, radical left) have lost some footage and sheen, and consequently their roles and significance have been reduced. Religious parties and groups have also been successful in attracting a significant number of adolescents. The number of children and adolescents who go to mosques in the 2000s is much greater than the number in the past.

Also, a significant portion of adolescents has adopted liberal ideas and behavior. In addition to the weakness inherent in political national and radical left parties, two other reasons have caused some adolescents to tilt toward liberal ideas. The first is education and the other is technology. Public schools have lost some of their enrollment to private schools. Since the late twentieth century, a significant number of private schools have opened in the capital, Amman, and other major cities. Many of the private schools adopt Western (American, English, or French) curricula that have influenced adolescents' thinking and behavior. The number of private schools in Jordan was about 1,981 schools in 2002, of which 628 schools were in basic education and 137 were secondary schools (Ministry of Education 2002). Some of the private schools have adopted the coeducation approach that was foreign to Jordan. It should be noted, however, that only financially able families send their children to private schools. Therefore, the culture of private schools, namely those of Western approach, has an influence on rich and financially able students, and those students may influence their peers of different classes.

Gender

Socialization and parenting practices are not the same for boys and girls in Jordan. The Jordanian family socializes and prepares its boys to shoulder financial and social responsibilities and help the parents when they are aging. The boys, namely the first, are expected to carry the name of the family. Families usually educate their boys to preserve and maintain the family norms and values and its social and economic status. Also, families count on their boys' education more than girls' education to move the family up the ladder of class. The girl, on the other hand, is socialized and prepared to be a housewife and to carry out her duties as a mother, with cooking and cleaning as major skills needed of her to carry out her responsibilities. Educated women were a tiny minority before 1985. Twenty years later, however, women's enrollment in schools and universities had markedly increased and had exceeded the number of men. Also, female labor-force participation is increasing, suggesting new roles for women in the economy and in the family.

Concerning the differential roles of men and women in the Jordanian society, some traditional customs are still practiced. One such custom is that men are counted and are responsible for the family or tribe affairs. Male members of the smaller families pay dues to the larger tribe, but females do not. The money is collected and saved in case any member of the family or tribe is involved in killing a person from outside the family, whether this killing is by accident or on purpose. The money is paid as compensation to the other family (Diyyah).

As regards circumcision, only male Muslims are circumcised, but not females and male Christians. Circumcision for Muslim males is a religious practice and it is usually done either at birth or after a short time of birth. Circumcision is a genital alteration performed by cutting the extra flesh over the head of the penis.

As far as self-image is concerned, there has been a shift in the way society, adolescents included, view the ideals of man and woman. In the past the main criteria for the woman was reproduction and next came beauty. For the man the main criterion was and still is work, but due to education, girls can have a say in their marriages and the kind and shape of man they accept as a husband. Therefore, shape and image is becoming more important nowadays than in the past. Girls in the past were forced to marry the cousin or another male of the family. Nowadays, the girl has a share in deciding whom she can marry.

Dress is an important issue in deciding standards for beauty. However, clothes worn by girls and women have changed since the 1980s. Traditional dress (*thoub*) was worn in rural areas. Western dress (skirts or pants) was worn in urban areas. In the late 1960s, the 1970s, and 1980s, skirts—even miniskirts—were clearly observed in cities. However, *hijab* was rarely noticed during those decades. In the twenty-first century, more girls and women wear *hijab* in urban and rural areas.

Women tend more often than men to describe a gap between their own self-image and that which society has of them, while men's self-image usually corresponds to that which society has of them.

Many young people say they feel bored, empty, depressed, or constrained by social norms, with few outlets for their energy, lack of opportunities to express themselves, and no adults who understand their needs, listen to them, or talk with them about their concerns.

As for eating disorders, Shuriquie (1999) indicated that it is classically perceived as a Western culture-bound syndrome associated with culture-driven factors, such as unrealistic expectations of slenderness and attractiveness, changes in the role of women, and social standards and attitudes towards obesity. He stated that no study addressing eating disorders in Jordan has been found. However, eating disorders are not uncommon in Jordan and Arab countries. Eating disorders and subsequent behavior, such as dieting, are artifacts of the openness of the country to Western modes of behavior. Quick-meal restaurants are spreading rapidly in major cities of Jordan. And as women's roles have changed from being only a housewife and a reproduction machine, many women have become obsessed with plumpness, which was the ideal for body weight and feminine beauty in the past. While fatness—whether for men or women—was considered a sign of respect (for men) and beauty (for women), nowadays, being slim and fit has been adopted from Western cultures. Consequently, being thin is highly rated and symbolizes certain cherished notions, such as social acceptance, self-discipline, self-control, sexual liberation, and assertiveness (Jordanian Youth Survey 2001).

The Self

As in other Arab societies that belong to a more or less collectivistic culture, the self in Jordan can be seen as an aspect or part of one or more in-groups or collectives. Compared to the family or tribe, the self is very small. One should sacrifice self or personal interest for the family's or tribe's interest. Personal ambition should be in harmony with group's interest. A man's family, tribe, or locale usually identifies the notable individual. For example, if one achieves a good position, whether professionally or financially, one is always referred to as the son or daughter of such and such family or village or town. He or she is from the south or north. The self to the group is like a tree to the forest. It is hard to recognize the tree without referring to its surroundings—the forest.

As indicated earlier, Jordan is a conservative country. Conservatism has emerged and developed from the social units of the family, tribe, village, and others. Each social unit or group, whether local or immigrant, strives to conserve and maintain its traditional norms and values. Immigrants from Palestine, Chechnya, or elsewhere try to make sure that affiliation and ties with origin are maintained. If changes to norms are to be made, the approval of the origin is usually sought. Due to logistic or other reasons, some norms such as weddings, funerals, or other social practices may need to be modified. In such cases, those changes have to be approved by old and notable men in the country of origin.

Family Relationships

Since Jordan has experienced a tremendous economic development during the past decades, one might expect that there will also have been substantial changes in social and cultural relations. Family structure and relationships have been subject to some changes. However, family relationships, size, and parenting practices are not the same across locality and ethnicity. Family size is one facet that may help understand parenting practices and family relationships. Until recently, the extended family had been the prevailing type in Jordan. The extended family is still prevailing in rural areas. Even as the extended family has shrunk in urban areas, the larger family or tribe still has power over individuals and nuclear families within the tribe. When a newly established family moves out of the parents' dwelling, it is psychologically and socially tied to the greater family or tribe, and it adheres to the rules of the greater family or tribe. The smaller family and its members share with the greater family its responsibilities, whether in happy or sad occasions.

Family members are strongly tied together. In disputes, adolescents play an important role in defending the family and its members. If any individual suffers harm or causes harm to individual(s) from another tribe, all family or tribe members share responsibility. That is, the liability of any wrongdoing is not confined to only the individual wrongdoer, but all family or tribe members are liable. Females are usually exempted from such liability and are exempted from revenge if it is to be carried out: females do not take revenge and are not subject to revenge from the opposite side.

As for relationships within families, Araji and Carlson (2001) observed that interactions between Arab parents and their children in Jordan indicate a greater latitude of acceptable behavior before disciplinary actions, particularly physical discipline, occurs, as compared to Western cultures. This is especially true for male children. Also, they reported that the types of abuse that the lowest percentages of Jordanian university students viewed as very serious problems were associated with child physical abuse (about 56%) and use of harsh discipline by parents (about 55%). Contrary to this view, however, Aamiry (1994) reported that 86% of university students indicated there was at least one type of abuse occurring in their families. Intimidation was the most prevalent (75%), followed by emotional abuse (40%). Physical abuse of family members was reported by 33% of the students.

Although mothers are subordinates in the family, they play significant roles in motivating children and keeping them together ("*al em betlem*" means "mother keeps the bond"). The emotional influence of the mother cannot be ignored in many functions of the family. Despite the fact that the father is the leader in the Jordanian family, the mother sometimes plays a vicarious but essential role in conveying the ideas and directives of the father to the children. The mother also plays an important role in socializing the girls of the family. The mother is the one who tells girls and often boys what the father or the family at large wants. the kind of behavior that is acceptable, and the norms and standards according to which children should adhere.

Marriage and divorce are two important aspects of family and inter-family relationships. Marriage in Jordan is considered a bond between two families rather than two individuals. Families, especially in rural areas, used to be more closely related. Divorce was less executed in the past. Families used to play a role in reducing the divorce rate. Presently, individuals are more educated and girls tolerate family decisions less than before. As such, the rate of divorce now is much more than before, especially in cities. The Department of Statistics (DOS) reported that 80% of divorce cases in 2003 occurred in three cities (Amman, Zarqa, and Irbid). The ratio of divorce to marriage is 18.5% in the country, about 21% in Amman, and about 23% in Zarqa. No statistics are available on the rates of remarriage.

Friends and Peers/Youth Culture

Verbal communication is very important for Jordanians. Talking and listening represent most of the entertainment for many Jordanians in rural areas. After a working day, relatives or neighbors get together and talk well into nighttime. Adolescents learn this practice from the adults. Adolescents spend a great deal of their time talking to their friends. This is usually done because many topics related to the adolescents are not discussed with parents. Love and sex subjects pertinent to adolescents are not discussed with parents. Only about 8.5% of male adolescents sought information about puberty and family planning from their fathers, compared to less that 1% of female adolescents. In contrast, about 15% of males (3% females) sought information about puberty from friends (National Youth Survey 2001). Therefore, adolescents resort to peers and friends to discuss such subjects. This is usually done within one gender and not across genders. Boys and girls cannot intermingle freely. If it is done it is only done in the dark. Friendship between a boy and girl is restricted, particularly for the girl. The girl symbolizes the honor and pride of the family. Girls are not allowed to build romantic friendships with boys in and outside of the family. Most romantic relationships between boys and girls are kept secret, and most of these relationships are of a Platonic type.

When it comes to career goals, adolescents in Jordan still consider friends a good source of information. About 46% of males indicated that they discussed career goals with friends compared to 48% with their fathers (29% with mother); while 35% of females discussed career goals with their fathers, 38% with friends, and 41% with their mothers (Jordanian Youth Survey 2001).

Regarding youth organizations, no systematic political, religious, or social organizations are licensed in Jordan. Two religious youth societies are exceptional: the Muslim Youth Society and the Young Men's Christian Association (YMCA). However, their memberships are very small.

In fact, adolescents, especially during the early few years, have no interest in organized politics. Also, there is no distinct and clear youth culture in Jordan. However, one can notice adolescents in some parts—mainly in the rich areas of the capital—who wear clothes and have hairstyles similar to what one may see in the West. This small segment of adolescents may have been influenced by Western youth appearance that adolescents see on the TV or in the movies or during their visits to the West. This segment of adolescents represents a small portion of adolescents in Jordan. The fads of hairstyles and dress are usually of foreign origin, and they are not indigenous. On the other hand, some adolescents have resorted to religious practices and groups to oppose extreme foreign fads.

Love and Sexuality

Biologically speaking, love and sexuality in Jordan are no different from that of any other society. However, the way love and sexuality among adolescents in Jordan are expressed and practiced is entirely different. Sex education is not part of the school curriculum, nor is it part of any informal education. Sex matters are kept out of any public discussion, whether in the family or in society at large. Whether for boys or girls, sex cannot be discussed until marriage time. Parents keep the subject away from children on the assumption that shielding the subject will keep children innocent and avoid wrong practices. It happens sometimes that a boy and a girl may date, but this kind of dating is kept very secretive. The cost of announcing such dating may be the life of the boy or the girl. If the relationship involves sex and the relationship becomes known, the boy and the girl are usually forced to marry. The law has no mention of any punishment to romantic relations between adolescents. Religion (*shari'a*), however, states punishment for those who may be involved in sex provided that four male witnesses can prove the case. The religious punishment is 80 spanks for the single male or female, and death by stoning if the male or female is married. Sometimes, though rarely, families carry out such punishment (the death penalty) if a female in the family is involved in sex. The male, if from a different family, may get his share of punishment by the female's family. If the male is from the same family or tribe, he is forced to marry the girl.

Another paradoxical issue worth noting is that the Jordanian family (mainly the father and mother) may talk and even brag about the romantic relationships of their adolescent boys, but such relationships of their girls may not even be mentioned at all, even if the relationships actually exist. Fear of shame to the family and harm to the girl by any male member of the family is usually behind hiding such information. Also, the female represents a symbol of honor to the family and it should be kept intact. Talking and bragging about boys' romantic relationships is viewed as a sign of manhood.

Since Islam does not allow premarital sex and romantic relations between a male and a female, and as families do not tolerate interaction between male and female adolescents, most marriages are arranged. This kind of marriage has changed in the past few decades, especially in urban areas. Boys and girls can nowadays meet in school, college, and university. Nevertheless, arranged marriage still prevails in many parts of Jordan, even among educated men and women.

Johns Hopkins University published a report of a survey about Jordanian youth knowledge, attitudes, and practices on health and life planning (Jordanian Youth Survey 2001). The project concludes that the Jordanian youth lack information about the notions of reproductive health and family planning. The report also interpreted that the lack of familiarity with the subjects reflects the fact that sexually transmitted diseases are rare in Jordan, as sexual promiscuity is not tolerated.

Health Risk Behavior

Most of Jordan's population is Muslim, and alcohol is religiously prohibited. Therefore, alcohol is not a serious problem for adolescents, and neither is suicide. However, with globalization and urbanization, drug use, crime rates, and gang activity are increasing. Poverty and unemployment are serious problems for adolescents, since about 60% of the unemployed persons are less than 25 years old.

Twenty-four percent of all persons above the age of 15 are daily smokers, 44% of the men and 5% of the women. Nearly 20% of men less than 19 years smoke compared to less than 1% of women. Almost 50% of the men between 20 and 24 years are smokers but less than 5% of women the same age are. Moreover, 67% of all dwellings inhabited by children less than fifteen years of age are used for regular smoking. This might indicate that passive smoking is a national health problem (Fafo 1998).

As for psychological and mental disorders, information is scarce. Many Jordanians mix psychological and mental disorders with insanity. Therefore, many Jordanians hide information about mental and psychological disorders and may express such disorders as physical disorders. The Fafo team surveyed some psychological disorders and found that anxiety and depression are somewhat more widespread among Jordanian women than among men, higher in the poorer segments of the population, higher in the refugee camps than among non-refugees, and higher in suburban and rural areas than in urban areas (Fafo 1998). As the Fafo data was self-reported one may question the validity of its results. For example, Araji and Carlson (2001) postulated that moving from the simple life in the rural areas to the complex life in the city might influence negatively the psychological life of the migrants.

However, in a study conducted in northern Jordan, Zaidan, Alwash, Al-Hussaini, and Al-Jarrah (2000) showed that proportionately more patients from the city of Irbid attended a hospital psychiatry clinic (71.5 per 100,000) compared to those from the peripheries (64.4 per 100,000), indicating that psychiatric morbidity is more common in urban than in rural areas. The easy access for city patients to the clinic could be a factor. Also, they reported that more males than females attended the clinic.

As for the kinds of psychological disorders, Zaidan et al. (2000) reported that diagnosed disorders were anxiety (23.6%), schizophrenia (20.6%), affective psychosis (18.4%), epilepsy (9%), mental retardation (6.6%), personality disorder (4%), and alcoholic and drug dependence (2%).

Also among the cited problems for adolescents in Jordan are poverty, lack of suitable work opportunities, and divorce of parents. Many of the working adolescents work without any regulations and rights that may keep them safe. Street boys, orphans, handicapped, and refugees are the most exposed to dangers due to the weak supervision and observation, absence of one or two of the parents, since many of those children come from broken families (Rodz, AlHaseen, Mehiar, and Cliff 2003). Rodz et al. (2003) indicated that children and younger adolescents, whether boys or girls, are subject to harassment and sex molestation by their employers or by the bullies in the gang. Additionally, those disadvantaged boys and girls may get into risk behaviors such as violence, abuse of narcotic substances, and dropping out of school.

As per street children, it is difficult to get an accurate picture of the magnitude of street children in Jordan, because no social census has been conducted specifically examining this group. The closest indicators available are those relating to working children, children in conflict with the law, orphans, children in poverty, abused children, or dropouts from the school system. Lower estimates may therefore range from including the 4,000 children who drop out of school every year to the 10,000 children annually passing through the juvenile justice system, up to the 390,000 children who live in poverty (depending on the poverty line chosen).

According to a UN humanitarian news and information service, the number of young offenders in Jordan is not large, in such crimes as burglaries or quarrels and disputes. Some 60% of the youngsters were of school age and had committed crimes mainly because of ignorance of the law. In 2003, there were 5,878 male and 248 female young offenders, according to government statistics. Of those, 180 boys and all of the girls were in need of protection, as they had either run away from home or had not been taken care of by their parents.

Education

Jordan has realized the seriousness of the illiteracy problem and its negative impact on all aspects of life. The 1987 Conference for Educational Development confirmed the importance of nonformal education and set a goal of reducing the overall illiteracy rate to 8% by the year 2000. Jordan has required six years of basic education since 1952. The duration of compulsory schooling was later extended to nine years in accordance with the Education Act of 1964, and to ten years in 1987. Currently, education is compulsory and available to all children aged 6 to 16. The number of schools in Jordan is about 5,048, of which 2,948 are public schools. These schools host about 1,459,141 students, of whom 47% are boys. A little over a million students (612,689 [51%] boys; 586,406 [49%] girls) are in basic education and represent about 82%, while 86,500 (6%) are in preschool.

About 173,546 (12%) are in secondary schools, of which approximately one-third sit for a general high school exam called *tawjihi.* Usually, the family with a member studying for *tawjihi* lives in emergency for the whole academic year. The time of *tawjihi*—June and July—is a stressful time for the whole country. *Tawjihi* marks a point in life that is very important: for those who pass with high marks can go to college. It is a celebration time for those who pass and it is a very sad occasion for those who do not. Names of passing students are announced in newspapers and radio. Accordingly, the event has gained importance.

Well over a million students are in public schools, while a little less than half a million (48.5%) are in private and UNRWA schools. The number of adolescents in grades seven to ten in schools is about 697,366 (http://www.moict.gov.jo and http://www.nic.gov.jo/en/index.html). The participation rate in Jordanian secondary schools is about 67%. The number of students enrolled in public and private universities in Jordan in year 2003–2004 is 166,598, of whom 83,321 (50%) are girls (http://www.nis.jo/ar/micro/edu.htm).

Young Jordanian women enjoy virtual equality with men in terms of developing their educational and cultural capabilities. About 54% of adolescent students who attend public schools are girls, but about 42% attend private schools. UNEP released statistics for year 2001–2002 showing that enrollment rates in primary schools are 91% for males (92% females), and in secondary schools 86% for males and 89% for females (http://globalis.gvu.unu.edu/indicator_detail.cfm?Country=JOandIndicatorID=125).

These statistics have strong social and economic implications. Previously, families used to invest in their boys but not in their girls. Families used to count on their boys to support them when their boys had grown up. Sending children to private schools is costly, which means that Jordanian families have changed their attitudes towards women's education and there is a growing tendency for middle- and upper-income families to send their children to private schools. Nevertheless, we should point out that this change might be more in urban areas than in rural areas since most private schools are in cities and mainly in the capital.

Illiteracy has declined in Jordan and especially among women. According to the Department of Statistics, illiteracy rates in 1996 were 9% for men, 20% for women, and 14% overall. In 2003, the rate for men dropped to 4.2% and for women to 13.4%. For the age group between 15 and 45, the rates in year 1996 are 5% for men, 9% for women, and 7% overall (http://globalis.gvu.unu.edu/indicator_detail.cfm?Country=JOandIndicatorID=91). However, this pattern of equality between men and women changes after they graduate. The economic and political participation rates for women are much lower than for men (Fafo 1998).

Furthermore, many forms of inequality remain. Functional literacy is still relatively low for adult women in rural areas, even among women in their twenties and thirties. Basic and secondary school dropout rates are significantly higher for rural and lower income children, and especially those from less-educated households. These families also have lower expectations for their children who are still in school, and there are large differences in the expectations of parents who support and do not support higher education for women (Fafo 2000).

Illiteracy rates are lower for refugees and displaced persons (14%) than for non-refugees (19%). There are also large differences by governorate, with more than 25% illiteracy in remote rural governorates such as Ma'an (28%), Mafraq (26%), Balqa (25%), and Karak (24%). The urban governorates of Amman, Zarqa, and Irbid have below-average rates.

As part of its efforts to create a more skilled labor force, Jordan has placed special emphasis on vocational education in recent years. By 2005, about 20% of all secondary school students were enrolled in the vocational stream. Low-income children, boys, and refugees have relatively high rates of vocational enrollment; rural children are underrepresented. Vocational education remains an unpopular choice among parents, although that may change now that it has become possible to continue on to higher education after taking a vocational secondary degree.

The Ministry of Education officials pointed out that in government schools, the dropout rate is less than 1% (Al Abed 2003). However, according to the U.S. Department of Labor (USDOL), dropout rates in Jordan are relatively high, particularly in rural areas after children reach the age of 13 years. The primary reasons for dropping out of school, the USDOL explained, are financial pressures, poverty, disability, poor performance, teaching styles, parental attitudes, and lack of adequate transportation. In a study conducted by the Ministry of Labor in Jordan in 2001, it was found that most of the child workers had completed at least nine years of education or more (www.dol.gov/ilab/media/reports/iclp/tda2003/jordan.htm#_ftnref2307).

Work

The unemployment rate is high among the young, with 25% of men and 48% of women in the age group 15 to 24 years. In the refugee camps, unemployment rates are 26% for men in general and nearly 40% for men below 25 years of age. For elderly people, part-time work is common, as 20% of employed men and nearly 40% of employed women above 55 years of age work part-time (Fafo 1998).

The slow economic growth of less than 3% and lack of jobs appear to be the most important reasons for unemployment. There also is some frictional unemployment among highly educated men and women due to incompatibility between the jobs offered and the person's available skills. Although low-status occupations are predominantly signs of low education, they also include some 8% of men with higher education, an indication of under-utilization of skills in the Jordanian labor market. The public sector is the largest employer in Jordan, and 20% of all employed men work in public administration. Among male Jordanian non-refugees with any education, as many as 37% work in public administration. Women predominantly work in education and health services (44% of all employed women). Among non-Jordanian workers, men work mainly in the construction sector, while women are cleaners and housemaids. Employees in the service sector are the least exposed to dangerous working environments, while construction workers most often report exposure to work related dangers. These workers seldom have access to equipment to protect themselves against accidents and exposure to hazards. Less than 15% of the employed population receives updated, job-relevant training paid by the employer. Most of these employees work in the public sector (Fafo 1998).

The working-age population is on the rise both in absolute and relative terms. Thus Jordan's characteristic of being a labor-surplus economy is likely to continue in the foreseeable future. Given that unemployment is already high, Jordan faces acute challenges in providing enough jobs for its labor force. This is particularly so because the proportion of labor force participants in the population is currently extremely low. As the country continues to modernize, labor force participation is expected to rise, mostly due to higher rates among women (Fafo 1998).

UNICEF reported that 34% of working young men and women started work before the age of 15 and some started work at the age of 6. Approximately 290,000 children in Jordan are considered working children, either part-time or full-time. The type of work these children undertake is usually in car mechanic shops, carpentry, agriculture, house-cleaning, and others. Poverty and child exploitation (molestation) due to lack of laws protecting children have been cited as main reasons for the work of children (Rosdz, AlHaseen, Mehiar, and Cliff 2003).

In 2001, the ILO estimated that less than 1% of children ages 10 to 14 years in Jordan were working. In 1997, the Department of Statistics estimated that approximately 13% of boys ages 15 to 16 years and 1.1% of girls of the same age were working. An MOL study published in 2002 stated that children are employed in automobile repair, carpentry, sales, blacksmith shops, tailoring, construction, and food services. Child vendors on the streets of Amman work selling newspapers, food, and gum. Other children provide an important source of income for their families by rummaging through trash dumpsters to find recyclable items. A 2001 study by the MOL found that working children are primarily concentrated in the cities of Amman, Zarqa, and Irbid. Another study of working children in Irbid found that children who work often grow up shorter and leaner than others in the same age group and remain smaller through adulthood. The study also found that many working children had been victims of physical, verbal, and sexual abuse in the workplace and had been exposed to hazardous chemicals and dangerous working conditions (www.dol.gov/ilab/media/reports/iclp/tda2003/jordan.htm#content).

As for kinds of work performed by men and women in Jordan, the Department of Statistics reported that in 2004 about 13.5% of working men (and 41% of working women) worked as professionals; about 5.7% of working men (8.8% of women) worked as clerks; 15.6% of working men (7.4% of working women) worked as service, shop, and market sales workers; 2.5% of working men (less than 1% of women) worked as skilled agricultural and fishery workers; about 20% of working men (6.5% of women) worked as craft and related trades workers; 14.4% of working men (1% of women) worked as plant and machinery operators and assemblers; and about 19% of working men (6.4% of women) worked in elementary occupations (www.dos.gov.jo/sdb_pop/sdb_pop_e/inde_o.htm).

Media

Most media in Jordan has been either run or directed by the government. Historically, Jordanians have only been able to view Jordan state TV and the other three or four surrounding states' TV programming, but they can listen to several radio stations broadcasting from different parts of the world, with different and maybe opposing views and ideas. With the proliferation of satellite channels, Jordanians in general and adolescent Jordanians in particular can see and listen to TV and radio from any part of the world that may express different and foreign views and ideas. Jordan is considered among the most tolerant countries of the third world.

Three in four Jordanians were found to have obtained news from a newspaper, radio, or TV station. TV is the most popular source of information, followed by radio and newspapers. More men than women follow the news. The widest gender gap is for newspaper consumption, due to higher illiteracy rates among women and their weak interest in politics. Nearly three in ten Jordanians supplement the mentioned three Jordanian information sources with non-Jordanian TV news at least once a week. Twenty percent of the adults watched non-Jordanian Arab channels; 15% watched Israeli news, while 2% followed news put on the air by Western TV stations (Fafo 1998). Modern mass media is widely distributed, and 82% of men and 72% of women had read a newspaper or received news from TV or radio. Twenty-eight percent received news from wireless sources abroad (Fafo 1998). Also, as of December 2003 about 457,000 used the Internet (7.9% penetration). This number may have increased drastically in the following two years since the telecommunications company offered access to the Internet via dial-up to all who have a telephone and a computer. No reliable statistics are yet available on the exact number and the breakdown by sex or region.

In the early twenty-first century, a significant number of adolescents have access to the Internet. Most of those who have access to the Internet reside in the capital and the other major cities. As the Internet has been introduced to many public and private schools throughout the country, students are exposed to information, ideas, and music from all sorts of cities and in different languages. The influence of the Internet can be noticed in the jargon used by many adolescents, and it will be noticed even more in the near future.

The average Internet user uses the Internet between 40 and 50 hours per month. According to information provided by the Arab Club for Media and Information Technologies, the number of Internet users in Jordan is about half-a-million people, of whom half are females. With reform of the pricing structures, the number of Jordanians with access to the Internet could be far larger. The Jordanian government has approved decisions that will systematize the activities of Internet cafés and centers. These decisions will help create encouraging conditions for investment in the information realm and allow people over 13 (previously 16 years) to enter an Internet café without family permission. The new decisions also ease the regulations concerning location and size that Internet cafés have to meet (www.hrinfo.net/en/reports/net2004/jordan.shtml).

Politics and Military

Among adolescents, particularly in early years of adolescence, participation in politics in Jordan has been limited as the voting age is 18 years. Although elections are old in Jordan, political parties and elections have been hampered by marshal (emergency) law. Marshal law was implemented after the elections of 1956 and remained in force until the election of 1993. The wars in 1967, 1970, and 1973 were used as a pretext for forcing the marshal law. After Jordan cut ties with the West Bank, Jordan organized elections regularly.

As for the military, all Jordanian male individuals are to serve in military after finishing high school or at age 18. Families with one son are exempted from such service. This service was postponed if the individual went to college. The law was frozen after Jordan signed the peace treaty with Israel. However, each male before the age 40 should check with the military to get waiving papers. The law still exists but it is not enforced.

Young people's limited political participation is due to lack of opportunities and to skepticism among youth about the efficacy of political action. About half the youth voted in previous parliamentary elections, mostly for their tribal candidates. Most Jordanians between 15 and 29 years of age rate the performance of government institutions as excellent or good.

The Fafo report (1998) on living conditions in Jordan showed that the political organization of Jordan is influenced by what may be called "traditional" groups based on kinship and locality. The Fafo study (1998) documented the role of social networks in Jordanian society, pointing out that while many of those networks are not now based in locality, they are virtual localities.

Unique Issues

Whenever young Jordanians discuss issues of importance to them, they consistently express a range of common concerns and hopes, regardless of their age, education level, location, religion, or ethnic or geographical background. Typical are the following concerns that have been identified by young men and women who participated in youth forums and focus group research in recent years:

1. A lack of sports facilities and leisure activity centers.
2. A contradiction between youth's perceptions of their own roles and identities and society's perceptions of the young's place in society, both within the family and in society as a whole.
3. Lack of communication between young men and women, which negatively affects their understanding of each other.
4. Unequal educational opportunities and discrimination, particularly in university admission.
5. Economic pressures on youth, especially on young men; a high rate of expatriate labor that appears to reduce youth's job opportunities; limited extracurricular programs that link education with employment; and a serious lack of vocational training centers, combined with society's underappreciation of vocational professions.
6. Anxiety resulting from the secondary school (*tawjihi*) exam as the decisive factor that determines a student's future, and school curricula that are not relevant to market job demands or other aspects of Jordanian life.
7. Shortage of social rehabilitation and counseling centers for young men and women.
8. Restrictions on girls' involvement in decision-making related to all aspects of their lives.
9. Limited political involvement of youth.
10. Negative peer pressures on youth, reflected in phenomena such as smoking and drug use.

Another unique issue is Jordanians' attitudes toward Western influences and interference in the Middle East. Although much of the country lives a semi-Western life, many Jordanians have negative sentiments and attitudes toward the way Americans and Europeans have handled the conflict in the Middle East, and they reject interference in Iraq. Wilson (2005) wrote in the *Guardian* that Jordanians, unlike many other Muslim countries, endorsed suicide bombings against the Western powers in Iraq, Palestine, and Afghanistan. He cited a survey conducted by the Pew Center for the People and the Press of Washington, who found that 57% of Jordanians said that suicide bombings and violence were justifiable in defense of Islam.

MAHER M. ABU HILAL

References and Further Reading

Aamiry, A. 1994. Domestic violence against women in Jordan. *Al-Raida* 11:33–39, 65–66.

Abu Hilal, Maher. 2005. Generality of self-perception models in the Arab culture: Results from ten years of research. In *The New Frontiers of Self Research*. H. Marsh, R. Craven, and D. McInerney (eds.). pp. 157–96. Greenwich, Conn.: Information Age Publishing.

Al Abed, M. 2003. Child-to-child working to end school dropouts. *Jordan Times*, March 2.

Araji, S., K. Carlson, and J. Carlson. 2001. Family violence including crimes of honor in Jordan: Correlates and perceptions of seriousness. *Violence Against Women* 7:586–621.

Fafo. 1998. The Jordan living conditions survey. http://globalis.gvu.unu.edu/indicator_detail.cfm?Country=JOandIndicatorID=91.

Jordan Department of Statistics. 1992. Household expenditure and income survey. Amman: Department of Statistics.

Jordan Department of Statistics. 1995. *Statistical yearbook 1994*. Amman: Department of Statistics.

Jordan Department of Statistics. 1997. Results of the general census of population and housing of Jordan. Amman: Department of Statistics.

Jordan Ministry of Education, Directorate of Planning. 1997. A report on educational indicators within the period 1993–1997. Amman: Ministry of Planning.

Jordanian youth survey: Knowledge, attitudes and practices on reproductive health and life planning. 2001. Johns Hopkins Center for Communication Program.

Ministry of Education. 2002. www.moe.gov/stat/stat2002/.

Rodz, K., E. AlHaseen, H. Mehiar, and J. Cliff. 2003. The national study of disadvantaged children in Jordan. A report for the World Bank. Washington, DC: World Bank.

Shuriquie, N. 1999. Eating disorders: A transcultural perspective. *Eastern Mediterranean Health Journal* 5:354–60.

Wilson, J. 2005. "Muslim world rejecting violence, says poll." *Guardian*, July 15. www.hrinfo.net/en/reports/net2004/jordan.shtml.www.dol.gov/ilab/media/reports/iclp/tda2003/jordan.htm#_ftnref2307.WWW.moe.gov./stat/stat2002/.www.nis.jo/ar/micro/edu.htm.www.dos.gov.jo/sdb_pop/sdb_pop_e/inde_o.htm.www.dol.gov/ilab/media/reports/iclp/tda2003/jordan.htm#content.

Zaidan, Z., R. Alwash, A. Al-Hussaini, and M. Al-Jarrah. 2000. Psychiatric morbidity in Northern Jordan: A ten-year review. *SQU Journal for Scientific Research: Medical Sciences*. (http://www.squ.edu.om/mj/Archive/Jan2000/Zaidan).

INDEX

INDEX

INDEX

INDEX

INDEX

INDEX

INDEX

INDEX

INDEX

INDEX

INDEX

INDEX

INDEX

INDEX

INDEX

M

INDEX

INDEX

INDEX

political instability in, 842
politics/military in, 853–854
poverty in, 845
refugees in, 854
self concept in, 844–845
unique issues in, 854
work in, 851–852
SES. *See* Socioeconomic status
Sex education
in Argentina, 8
in Armenia, 20–21
in Austria, 49
Bangladesh's lack of, 59
Belgium's lack of, 70
Belize's lack of, 81
in Botswana, 89, 94
Brunei Darussalam's lack of, 103
Bulgaria's lack of, 114
Burundi's lack of, 123
Cameroon's lack of, 134, 138
in Canada, 147
China's lack of, 186
Croatia's lack of, 200
Czech Republic's lack of, 212
in Denmark, 241
in D.R.C., 226
in Ecuador, 251
in Finland, 296
in France, 311
Ghana's lack of, 348
in Greece, 360–361
Guinea's lack of, 383
in Iceland, 431, 432
India's lack of, 451
in Indonesia, 464
in Ireland, 485
in Italy, 516
in Japan, 531–532
Jordan's lack of, 545
Kuwait's lack of, 567
Kyrgyzstan's lack of, 576–577
in Malawi, 615
in Malaysia, 625
Morocco's lack of, 650–651
Nepal's lack of, 661
in Netherlands, 673
Oman's lack of, 720
Pakistan's lack of, 735
in Paraguay, 761
in Philippines, 782
in Puerto Rico, 816
Russia's lack of, 828
in Senegal, 839
Serbia/Montenegro's lack of, 848
in Singapore, 860
in Slovenia, 871
Somalia's lack of, 883
in South Africa, 897
in Spain, 915
in Sweden, 954
in Switzerland, 972
in Tajikistan, 985
Thailand's lack of, 1002
Turkey's lack of, 1016
in Ukraine, 1031
in United States, 1068
Yemen's lack of, 1088
in Zambia, 1102
Sex segregation
in Iran, 473
in Oman, 715
in Papua New Guinea, 752
in Tanzania, 990
in U.A.E., 1039
in Yemen, 1086
Sexual abuse
in Central America, 164
in Honduras, 394
in Nepal, 661–662
in Yemen, 1089
in Zimbabwe, 1113
Sexual activity
in Argentina, 7–8, 9
in Australia, 32–33
in Austria, 49
in Bangladesh, 58
in Belgium, 69–70
in Bulgaria, 114
in Burundi, 123
in Cameroon, 133
in Canada, 145–146
in Central America, 158, 161
in Chile, 172
in China, 186
in Croatia, 199
in Denmark, 236, 241
in Ecuador, 250, 251
in El Salvador, 161
in Eritrea, 273
in Ethiopia, 281
in Finland, 295
in France, 310
in Germany, 330
in Ghana, 348
in Greece, 360
in Guatemala, 375
in Honduras, 388, 393
in Hungary, 409
in Iceland, 431
in India, 450
Iran's prohibition of premarital, 475
in Ireland, 484
in Israel, 497
in Italy, 515
in Japan, 531
in Kazakhstan, 555
Kuwait's prohibition of premarital, 567
Kyrgyzstan's prohibition of premarital, 576
in Lithuania, 597
in Malawi, 615
in Malaysia, 625
in Mexico, 636–637
in Morocco, 650
in Netherlands, 672
in Nigeria, 690–691
in Norway, 705
in Oman, 719
Pakistan's prohibition of premarital, 735
in Panama, 746
in Papua New Guinea, 754–755

INDEX

INDEX

INDEX

INDEX

INDEX

domestic/household chores in, 124, 136, 163, 215, 228, 284, 350–351, 558, 578, 840, 874, 900–901, 919, 932, 961, 1071, 1104, 1115
in D.R.C., 228
economic collapse/corruption in, 22, 228, 466
in Ecuador, 252–253
education as, 243
in Egypt, 264
in Eritrea, 275
in Ethiopia, 283–284
exploitation in, 61, 124, 137, 163, 215, 252–253, 284, 351, 396, 397, 454, 519, 548, 579, 723, 738, 786, 886, 1071–1072, 1091, 1105
in family business, 117, 136, 163, 558, 617, 673, 986, 1019
female restrictions for, 55–56
in Finland, 299–300
in France, 314–315
gender discrimination in, 536
in Germany, 337–338
in Ghana, 350–351
globalization and, 338, 723
in government, 105, 190
in Greece, 364–365
in Guatemala, 377–378
in Guinea, 385
in Honduras, 395–396
in household, 50, 84, 136, 163, 264, 315
in Hungary, 416–418
in Iceland, 436
Icelandic work-school, 436
immigration and, 519, 653, 920, 961
in India, 454–455
in Indonesia, 466–467
Institutes of Technical and Further Education on, 38
in Iran, 477–478
in Ireland, 486–487
in Israel, 502
in Italy, 519–520
in Japan, 535–536
in Jordan, 547–548
in Kazakhstan, 558–559
in Kuwait, 570
in Kyrgyzstan, 578–579
in Lebanon, 588
in Lithuania, 603
in Malawi, 617
in Malaysia, 629–630
male/female participation rates in, 61
in Mexico, 639–640
migration due to, 23, 300, 378, 749, 756, 1018
in Morocco, 653
in Nepal, 663
in Netherlands, 673–674
in Nigeria, 694–695
in Norway, 708
Occupational Health and Safety Act on, 150
occupations in, 38, 61, 84, 105, 136–137, 150, 228, 299, 314, 364–365, 436, 478, 535, 547, 548, 558, 588, 617, 629–630, 653, 663, 694–695, 737, 756, 771, 789–790, 818, 831, 852, 862, 920, 932, 960–961, 1019, 1034, 1057, 1071, 1090–1091, 1104–1105, 1115–1116
in Oman, 723
in Pakistan, 737
in Panama, 748–749
in Papua New Guinea, 756

in Paraguay, 762
in Peru, 771
in Philippines, 789–791
in Portugal, 807–808
poverty in, 23, 124, 377, 396, 466, 477, 653, 694, 737, 749, 830
prostitution/trafficking in, 284, 351, 365, 579, 663, 977, 986–987, 1006, 1082, 1091, 1105, 1116
in Puerto Rico, 818
restrictions for, 12, 73, 109, 124, 189–190, 202, 215, 243, 314, 337, 377, 454, 466, 477, 487, 502, 519, 558, 570, 603, 639, 762, 807, 874, 943, 975–976, 1005, 1018, 1034, 1072
Rosetta Plan for, 73–74
in Russia, 830–831
school/work combination in, 37, 150, 252, 377, 417, 486, 519–520, 640, 674, 694, 749, 852, 862, 1057, 1071
for secondary school students, 12
in Senegal, 840
in Serbia/Montenegro, 851–852
SES in, 175, 397, 640
in Singapore, 862–863
in Slovenia, 873–874
in Somalia, 885–886
in South Africa, 900–901
in Spain, 919–920
of street children, 351
in Sudan, 931–932
in Swaziland, 943
in Sweden, 960–961
in Switzerland, 975–977
in Tajikistan, 986–987
technical/vocational schools for, 228, 365, 536, 558, 589, 723, 737, 771, 791, 807, 976, 1057, 1082
in Thailand, 1005–1006
tourism industry in, 96, 723
transition from school to, 151, 174–175, 202, 216, 365, 417, 852, 901, 1006
in Turkey, 1018–1019
in U.A.E., 1044–1045
in U.K., 1057–1058
in Ukraine, 1034–1035
unemployment in, 22, 38, 51, 73, 105, 117, 137, 163, 175, 190, 202, 215–216, 243, 252, 264, 275, 284, 300, 314, 338, 365, 385, 416, 436, 454–455, 466, 478, 536, 547, 558, 559, 570, 579, 589, 603, 629, 663, 674, 708, 723, 737, 762, 771, 789, 807, 808, 830–831, 851, 862–863, 874, 886, 901, 920, 960, 976, 1006, 1019, 1034–1035, 1044, 1057–1058, 1072, 1082–1083, 1105
unhealthy conditions for, 62, 84, 150–151, 673, 975, 986, 1019
in United States, 1071–1072
university v., 96, 150
urban/rural participation rates in, 61
in Uruguay, 1082–1083
volunteer, 190
WTO and, 663
in Yemen, 1090–1091
in Zambia, 104–1105
in Zimbabwe, 1115–1116
World Health Organization (WHO)
on health risk behavior in Austria, 49
on HIV/AIDS in Bangladesh, 59
on Indonesia, 460
on media in Honduras, 397
World Trade Organization (WTO)
Brunei Darussalam, 106
Nepal in, 663
WTO. See World Trade Organization

INDEX